Lifespan Development

FOURTH EDITION

JEFFREY S. TURNER ** **DONALD B. HELMS**
MITCHELL COLLEGE

HARCOURT BRACE COLLEGE PUBLISHERS
Fort Worth Philadelphia San Diego New York Orlando Austin San Antonio
Toronto Montreal London Sydney Tokyo

Publisher Ted Buchholz
Acquisitions Editor Tina Oldham
Developmental Editor Tod Gross
Project Editor Catherine Townsend
Production Manager Annette Dudley Wiggins
Art & Design Supervisor Vicki McAlindon Horton
Text Designer Lurelle Cheverie
Cover Designer Brenda Chambers
Compositor TSI Graphics

Library of Congress Cataloging-in-Publication Data
Turner, Jeffrey S.
   Lifespan development / Jeffrey S. Turner, Donald B. Helms. — 4th ed.
     p. cm.
   Includes bibliographical references and indexes.
   ISBN: 0-03-032858-6
   1. Developmental psychology.   I. Helms, Donald B.   II. Title.
BF713.T87 1990   90-23698
155—dc20   CIP

Requests for permission to make copies of any part of the work should be mailed to: Permissions Department, Harcourt Brace Jovanovich, Inc., 8th Floor, Orlando, Florida 32887.

Address Editorial Correspondence to: 301 Commerce Street, Suite 3700, Fort Worth, TX 76012

Address Orders to: 6277 Sea Harbor Drive, Orlando, FL 32887 1-800-782-4479, or 1-800-433-0001 (in Florida)

Printed in the United States of America

   3 4   069   9 8 7 6 5 4

Cover: Vincent van Gogh, *First Steps,* oil, The Metropolitan Museum of Art.

WE DEDICATE THIS BOOK TO
BAXTER VENABLE
UNEQUALED EDITOR, GOOD FRIEND, AND GENTLEMAN

PREFACE

This is a textbook about the life cycle. Our objective in this book is to share with you the nature of human growth and development from the very beginnings of life to its culmination. We hope that our narrative of the life journey provides you not only with an understanding of developmental psychology but also with insights into your own lifespan.

Developmental psychology continues to be an active field of study in the 1990s; exciting research findings have emerged since the previous edition of this textbook. Developmental psychologists have added new dimensions to our understanding of research methods, genetics, prenatal development, infancy and childhood, adolescence, adulthood, and dying and death. On the part of the general public, interest in aging processes continues to grow, and all indications are that such research activity and general interest will only increase in years to come.

In light of such developments, revising *Lifespan Development* to accurately portray the field as it exists today was not an easy task. Of course, we wanted to build upon the success of earlier editions and develop a superior pedagogical tool. Ultimately, our goal was to provide readers with a comprehensive yet understandable view of contemporary developmental psychology. The text, which consists of 12 chapters, has a number of important features:

■ Readability

A concerted effort was made to keep the book readable, one of the critically acclaimed features of earlier editions. Rather than providing an encyclopedic account of developmental psychology, we try to convey the essence of this discipline in an interesting way. We have attempted to make our writing style fluid and concise and to offer readers practical translations of theoretical material.

■ Balanced Coverage of the Entire Life Cycle

Lifespan Development offers balanced coverage of the entire life cycle. Unlike many other books, this text devotes full attention to all stages of human development, including the adult years. Chapters relating to adulthood are not simply tacked on at the end of the book. Instead, they are an integral part of the main theme of this textbook—the total development of the person from conception to death. Such integrated treatment enables students to see the continuum of the life cycle, as well as to understand how early growth stages influence later life.

■ Flexible Table of Contents

The structural framework of *Lifespan Development* continues to allow readers to study human development in a chronological or topical fashion. This feature is not available in most textbooks and provides instructors with course flexibility. Each chronological stage of this book is divided into relatively small, compact units; and because of the continuity of these units, a topic such as "personality and social development" can be studied from a chronological, topical, or combined approach. Thus, "personality and social development" can be dealt with as a subject in itself (with appropriate readings from each developmental chapter) or within the chronological framework of each developmental chapter as the semester progresses. A chronological as well as topical table of contents is provided in the pages that follow.

■ Relevancy and Up-to-Date

Throughout the fourth edition of *Lifespan Development,* new material has been added and existing sections have been expanded to give readers the most up-to-date information possible. As a result, the book is soundly based in research and offers the reader the most current information available. A glance at the bibliography reveals an abundance of contemporary research citations, including over 300 post-1988 studies for the fourth edition. Of course, classic studies in the field have been retained and their relevancy explained.

■ Complete Teaching Package

A comprehensive *Study Guide* and an *Instructor's Manual* are available. The *Study Guide* contains a generous assortment of learning aids designed to assist the student in mastering text material. The *Instructor's Manual* offers a wide selection of test items for classroom use. In addition to these two ancillaries, a developmental psychology transparency package is also available. The package consists of 50 color transparencies with a resource guide of lecture notes for the instructor. The transparencies represent a unique visual dimension to any course on human development and complement the presentation of text material.

■ Pedagogical Aids

Lifespan Development contains a variety of pedagogical aids designed to promote the comprehension and retention of textual material. The generous but selective use of figures, graphs, charts, and photos calls visual attention to important points raised in each chapter. At the beginning of each chapter is an outline, which includes the major contents of the chapter. The book includes a complete bibliography and glossary. More specialized pedagogical aids include the following:

☐ What Do You Think? (Introductions)

Each chapter begins with a section designed to stimulate thinking and arouse curiosity before the chapter is read. By the time each chapter is concluded, the issues raised will have been addressed.

☐ Application Boxes

These boxes are clearly identified throughout the book and offer applied formulations to the main body of the text. They relate to the everyday lives of students and are designed to bridge the gap between theory and the real world.

☐ International Lifespan Development Boxes

These boxes are also clearly identified throughout the book and explore important cross-cultural topics in the field of human development. We believe that one of the best ways to understand human development is through a knowledge of other cultural practices and behaviors.

☐ Unit Reviews

Interspersed within each chapter are brief summaries. These are designed to crystallize the material being read, integrate the major points, and unify the major points.

☐ Chapter Reviews

Each chapter concludes with a detailed summary focusing on the major points covered. This pedagogical aid is designed to further help students recall important concepts and assist in overall rates of retention.

☐ Key Terms

Following each chapter review is a listing of key terms. Definitions of the key terms can be found in the respective chapter or in the glossary at the conclusion of the book. Glossary items are italicized throughout the text.

☐ Recommended Readings

We end each chapter with an annotated list of ten readings or more. These recommended publications represent some of the most recent and important contributions to the field of human development.

Combined, we believe that these textbook features give both students and instructors a well-rounded and comprehensive learning package. Above all, we hope that you will find the fourth edition of *Lifespan Development* enlightening and enjoyable. We are eager to share with you the excitement of studying the development of the most complex of all life forms—human beings. Welcome to the field of developmental psychology.

■ Acknowledgments

While authors bear the responsibility for the textbook's contents, many individuals contributed to its development, preparation, and ultimate publication. We extend our appreciation to those psychologists who played a role in the success of the first three editions as well as those who reviewed the manuscript and contributed to the improvement of the fourth edition:

Betty Biernat, St. Mary's Junior College
Robert E. Billingham, Indiana University
John R. Brownlee, University of Utah
Bridget Coughlin, Hocking Technical College
James R. Council, North Dakota State University
Carroll Doolin, Henderson County Junior College
Vickie Dosset, Trinity Valley Community College
Eileen Edelstein, North Shore Community College
Mary Francis Farkas, Lansing Community College
Juanita L. Garcia, University of South Florida
William Hampes, Louisiana State University at Eunice
Elior Kinarthy, Rio Hondo College
Louis A. Martone, Miami-Dade Community College
Carolyn J. Meyer, Lake-Sumter Community College
Thomas P. Moeschl, Broward Community College
Karen H. Nelson, Austin College
Rob Palkovitz, University of Delaware
Patricia Petretic-Jackson, University of South Dakota
Nicholas R. Santilli, Mt. Vernon College
Richard Sebby, Southeast Missouri State University
Ralph G. Soney, Western Piedmont Community College
Robert S. Stowe, Central Connecticut State University
William J. Struhar, Sinclair Community College
Lori L. Temple, University of Nevada, Las Vegas
Paul E. Thetford, Texas Women's University
Thomas J. Weatherly, DeKalb College

We also wish to thank the people at Holt, Rinehart and Winston who brought their expertise to this project: Tina Oldham, Acquisitions Editor; Tod Gross, Developmental Editor; Catherine Townsend, Project Editor; Annette Dudley Wiggins, Production Manager; and Vickie McAlindon Horton, Design Supervisor.

Grateful appreciation is extended to Molly Helms for typing and preparing the manuscript. We owe her special thanks for a variety of services, including always meeting our deadlines, deciphering illegible handwriting, adding suggestions along the way, and understanding the various idiosyncrasies of authors that go along with the job.

And finally, to our wives and children go our heartfelt appreciation. Writing always requires its share of personal and family sacrifices, but the patient understanding of our loved ones enabled us to devote the long hours necessary to complete this project successfully. Their empathy, support, and love were sources of continual inspiration from the beginning of our efforts to produce this book. Because of them, the fourth edition of *Lifespan Development* has become a reality.

Jeffrey S. Turner
Donald B. Helms
New London, Connecticut
June, 1990

ABOUT THE AUTHORS

Jeffrey S. Turner teaches psychology at Mitchell College. He has taught at the college level for over sixteen years, and with co-author Donald B. Helms, has written four textbooks in the area of developmental psychology. He has also authored numerous articles dealing with childhood and adolescent behavior and is in demand as a speaker on topics relating to human development. His current areas of interest include Piagetian reasoning processes, early childhood education, and adult development and aging. He is married and has three children, including twin boys.

Donald B. Helms is Chairman of the Psychology Department and heads the Early Childhood Education Program at Mitchell College in New London, Connecticut. His background includes training in counseling, psychometrics, and industrial and physiological psychology. For four years he was stationed at the School of Aerospace Medicine in San Antonio, Texas, as a neurophysiological research psychologist with the Air Force. There he was a member of a research team that participated in basic and applied investigations for the Air Force's vestibular laboratory, often under contract to NASA, and was involved in the screening process for the astronaut program. Since then he has taught a wide variety of psychology courses at several colleges. His current areas of interest are moral and cognitive development, including abstract and creative thought processes. He is married and has three children.

CONTENTS IN BRIEF

CONTENTS

Chapter Seven Middle Childhood 249

Chapter Eight Adolescence 303

Chapter Nine Young Adulthood 359

TOPICAL TABLE OF CONTENTS

Introduction to Human Development

WHAT DO YOU THINK?

- How long do you expect to live? If you haven't thought much about it, this chapter will provide you with some things to consider, including life expectancy. For example, whereas at the turn of the century, life expectancy at birth was about 49 years, today it hovers near 78 years for females and about 72 years for males. What factors account for this increase in life expectancy, and what have researchers learned about aging processes in general?

- Although developmental psychology is one of psychology's youngest subfields, our knowledge of the life cycle has grown rapidly. Today, developmental psychologists are able to explain many facets of aging processes, be it during the beginning or waning years of life. How do they set out to explore growth and development and design the research they undertake? What problems, if any, do they encounter in their quest for scientific explanations of human development?

- They call themselves the mountain people of Abkhazia and they live in the land of Caucasus, in Russia. The Abkhazians possess remarkably long lifespans, many over 100 years. What is it about these people and the lives they lead that promotes such lengthy lifespans? Are there hints that we can take to increase our prospects for living longer? There may be some answers in this remote mountain land.

INTRODUCTION

Sandra M. enjoyed limited popularity and sustained a low "B" average through her public schooling. She dated and fell in love with her boyfriend while in high school and, although tempted, they held back from having sexual intercourse. About a year after high school, Sandy and Bill were married and in the next seven years added two girls and a boy to their family. Sandy was a respected and able civic leader, but, although busy, she always refrained from taking on too many tasks so that she could spend time with her family. All who knew them were aware of how happy Sandy and Bill were. A week after Sandy's 29th birthday, she left a note on the mantel telling Bill she had to "find herself" and would never again return to him or the kids.

George G. is a happy but often lonely octogenarian. The youngest of seven children, George helped around the house as a youngster and worked in a general store when he was 12. He held similar part-time jobs until he was 15 and announced to his family (all of whom were either living at home or had homes minutes away) that he was "off to see the world." He left home with a suitcase of clothes, about $9 in his pocket, and two letters of recommendation, one from his priest and the other from the owner of the store where he had worked. George had many adventures while he traveled and had the opportunity to learn a great deal about himself and others. By the age of 26, George had settled down, married, and started his own family. All of his children are now grown and have families of their own. At the present time, George still takes special delight in recalling his exciting adventures to the other residents of the Oakdale Home for the Aged.

As a child, Marsha J. was a classic underachiever. She possessed much potential but never took full advantage of it. Although she passed in the school system each year, teachers regularly commented on her lack of both motivation and academic desire. It was not until Marsha left high school and enrolled in a college business course that things began to change. For the first time in her life, she really enjoyed the course content, so much so that she enrolled in several other classes the following semester. The next year, she went to college full time and, after completing her degree work, graduated at the top of her class. Today, Marsha is in charge of an extremely successful accounting firm with office centers in ten cities. Regarding her life accomplishments, she likes to call herself a late bloomer.

For years, David L. had been a dedicated company man. He worked hard at his job, seldom took time off, and often put in overtime. Moreover, he never complained about his work, which is why it came as a surprise one day when he announced that he was tired of his job and its repetitious routines. He left the company a few weeks later, saying that he had found a job in a totally different and more challenging line of work.

What causes people to behave the way they do? What might have influenced the behavior of Sandra M.? Why would she suddenly run away from a seemingly rewarding family life? Her friends (some of whom married right after high school and are still happily married) were unable to see any inner torment before she ran off. What motivated George G. to leave the "nest" and embark on his own to see the world? These are but some of the questions and problems that developmental psychologists seek to explore. Could any of these behaviors have been predicted? How do psychologists go about studying people's behavior? What effects do childhood experiences have on adult behavior? Investigating such issues lies at the heart of this textbook.

■ Developmental Psychology Defined

These introductory examples indicate that people do not remain constant—nor does their behavior. Throughout our lifespan, we change from year to year, month to month, and even day to day. To live is to change. *Developmental psychology*, which explores these lifelong changes, is one approach to the study of behavior. More specifically, developmental psychology is the scientific study of the growth, development, and behavioral changes of humans, from conception through old age.

The comprehensive study of the life cycle has only recently emerged as a pursuit of scientific research, particularly in comparison to the investigation of childhood and adolescence, which has been the focus of most scientific literature. A number of reasons account for this lag: First, life expectancy was relatively short in the past, so the study of the all-too-brief adult years was, apparently, of little interest to researchers. Second, it was (and to some extent, still is) assumed that adults are best understood in terms of their childhood experiences; thus, an adult was perceived as an end product

Developmental psychologists explore all stages of the life cycle.

rather than as a continuously developing person. Third, infancy, childhood, and adolescence present the researcher with obvious and observable changes—especially physical, mental, and personality differences—to study. Although such changes, in fact, occur throughout the life cycle, they are not as readily detectable later in life, with the possible exception of old age. Thus, in the past few decades, considerable time, money, and research have been directed toward the preadult stages of the life cycle. This is a paradox because many psychologists believe that adulthood represents the longest and perhaps most significant stage of the life cycle.

The rapid increase of the adult population has stimulated research interest. A glance at demographics reveals that there are more individuals in the life stage of adulthood than in any other stage. Approximately 61 percent of the population is between the ages of 18 and 64 and the median age is 30.6 years. Another 11.6 percent is 65 years and older. This latter group represents one of the fastest growing population segments in the country today (U.S. Bureau of the Census, 1989). Figure 1-1 displays the aged population as a percentage of the total U.S. population.

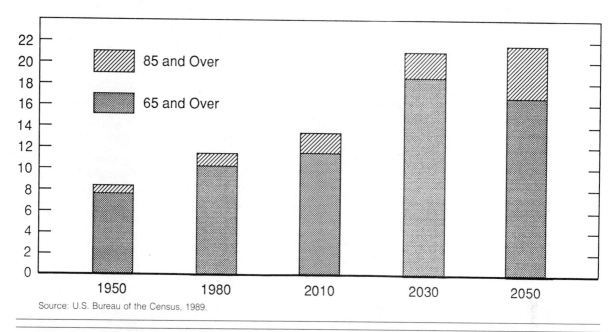

Source: U.S. Bureau of the Census, 1989.

FIGURE 1-1   Age distribution of U.S. population with projections to 2050.

Today, developmental psychologists recognize adulthood as a critical phase of the life cycle and view the later stages of life as important periods for studying a diversity of scientific issues. By studying the events of adulthood, such as occupational status, marriage, or parenthood, the life cycle is placed in a more balanced perspective. Coupled with the accumulated research on the years preceding adulthood, the aging process, consequently, may be viewed as a lifelong process.

What are the major factors that help transform a child into an adolescent and, later, into an adult? Is an adult solely the sum of past experiences, or does an adult outgrow childhood experiences and start behaving according to social factors and stimuli from adult society? These types of questions are difficult to answer, for uncovering the trends of human development is not an easy task. Indeed, psychology might be called the obstinate science, for it is most difficult to discover any *laws* of behavior. But we must begin somewhere. We must take that first step, open that first door, and peer down the corridor in the hope of finding the pathway that leads to knowledge of human behavior, for it is knowledge that allows us to reach our potentials and lead fuller, richer lives. When the study of psychology started, that door was opened, but it was dark on the other side; we did not understand behavior. But one candle was lit and then another. Maybe we have reached only the anteroom, but we have even more candles, and their brilliance illuminates further recesses—more paths for us to pursue. Today, we are still following those paths in the hope of discovering more principles of behavior so that we can learn how and why people develop and behave as they do.

To answer the questions regarding lifespan development, we must examine and investigate seemingly diverse areas: physiology, education, religion, family, home, community, culture, socioeconomic status, genetic inheritance, psychosocial history, and countless other areas. To evaluate all these variables is a massive undertaking, but also a tremendously exciting task, particularly since the discipline of developmental psychology itself is in a state of infancy: As one of psychology's newest subfields, its scientific lifespan lies ahead. Welcome to developmental psychology.

☐ Stages in Development

When does life begin? Does adolescence begin at age 13 or at puberty? When does early adulthood end and middle age begin? When does one reach old age? To investigate human development, it is helpful to have systems of age classification (see Figure 1-2). These systems, which psychologists have arranged and rearranged, are constructed primarily to help clarify and organize data. Some psychologists propose that the stages of the human life cycle may be interpreted in various ways. For instance, the same person might be classified as mature, old, or developing, depending on whether physiological, social, psychological, or anatomical criteria are being used. It should be recognized, however, that there is continuity in the life cycle of the human being. Only for scientific convenience do we identify stages of development. Life does not start or stop at the beginning or end of stages or age classification systems.

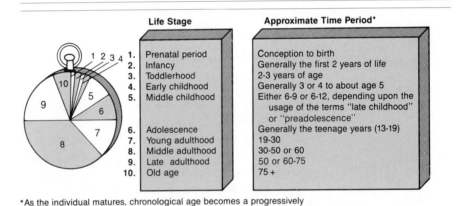

	Life Stage	Approximate Time Period*
1.	Prenatal period	Conception to birth
2.	Infancy	Generally the first 2 years of life
3.	Toddlerhood	2-3 years of age
4.	Early childhood	Generally 3 or 4 to about age 5
5.	Middle childhood	Either 6-9 or 6-12, depending upon the usage of the terms ''late childhood'' or ''preadolescence''
6.	Adolescence	Generally the teenage years (13-19)
7.	Young adulthood	19-30
8.	Middle adulthood	30-50 or 60
9.	Late adulthood	50 or 60-75
10.	Old age	75 +

*As the individual matures, chronological age becomes a progressively poorer criterion to use.

FIGURE 1-2
A timetable of human development.

☐ Aging Processes in Perspective

From the moment we are conceived, aging processes begin. Every human being, regardless of age, race, sex, or economic status, shares these common experiences, however individuals differ widely in their reactions to aging processes. Some may fear the reality of aging and deny its very existence. Others may cling to characteristics deemed youthful by society, while still others philosophically accept the inevitability of advancing age and its accompanying changes. Regardless of our reaction to aging processes, the fact remains that time continues to pass and each of us continues to grow older (McKenzie, 1980).

There are primarily three different types of aging processes: biological, psychological, and social. *Biological aging* refers to the manner in which the body functions over time. As we grow older, the body experiences changes in skeletal composition, sensory capacities, heart rate, and tissue structure, to name but a few areas. In general, the biological aging process causes the body to build toward its peak potential (anabolism) and, after about age 26, then slowly deteriorate (catabolism). Anabolism and catabolism are both aspects of the biological process we know as metabolism. In the past decade, a wave of investigations has been aimed at learning how to retard the effects of biological aging. Many researchers firmly believe that as we learn more about aging, including the nature of the body's molecular changes and the total effect of nutrition and exercise on physiology, the lifespan will markedly increase (Hayflick, 1980; Mann, 1980; Waldford, 1983; Pearson and Shaw, 1982). Others, however, such as James Fries and Lawrence Crapo (1981), maintain that vitality, rather than lifespan, will be prolonged. They believe that this will be achieved, in part, through the ability to delay the onset of serious diseases that ravage vitality.

Psychological aging is the individual's own perception of the aging process. In this regard, psychological aging can be defined as the mental reactions that accompany the experience of growing old. A comment such as "I feel as old as the hills" is an example of a psychological reaction to a bodily state or change. Interestingly, a biologically young person may feel psychologically old, and the reverse may also be true.

Social aging refers to the manner in which individuals relate aging to their own unique society. Some societies, for example, encourage youthful behavior and downplay the role of the elderly, while others regard maturity as a virtue. It has been suggested that each of us has a *social-age clock* that is a reflection of our society. Society defines expectations concerning how people should behave at given ages or phases. For example, we generally expect an older couple at a rock music concert to react differently from adolescents attending the same event. We also expect such events as marriage and child rearing to take place at certain ages. Neugarten acknowledges, though, that the concept of the age clock is slowly losing popularity because lifestyles are changing and our society is becoming age-irrelevant (Neugarten, 1980, 1968).

Other factors, particularly socioeconomic backgrounds and the type of vocation one selects, affect the social-age clock. Blue-collar workers seem to reach both middle and old age much sooner than white-collar workers. We may perceive one whose livelihood depends on intense physical labor as being old by age 30, whereas a professional person, who is hired to think, may appear to be relatively youthful at age 65. This is one illustration in which we find that chronological age is not the only criterion for developmental classification.

It is important to stress that these three main processes of aging are interwoven throughout the life cycle. No one process of aging exists alone. Thus, a 14-year-old adolescent in the throes of puberty (biological aging) may feel that mentally she is a mature woman in the full sense of the word (psychological aging), but her parents may feel that she is too young to begin dating and thus place restrictions on her social life (social aging). Another illustration is that of a 75-year-old man (biological aging) who is very pleased with his past life experiences and does not regard advancing age as an obstacle to future success (psychological aging). He fully enjoys the retirement community in which he resides because it encourages an active lifestyle and places no age restrictions on activities or entertainment (social aging). These two examples illustrate the manner in which aging exists as a multifaceted experience (see Figure 1-3).

In formulating theories concerning the aging process, some researchers have emphasized the biological or genetic factors involved in aging (Hayflick, 1980), whereas others (Geist, 1980) have chosen to stress psychological issues. Still others (McPherson, 1983), are sociological in their theories. Many researchers choose to combine bits and pieces from each approach. Even though developmental psychologists are

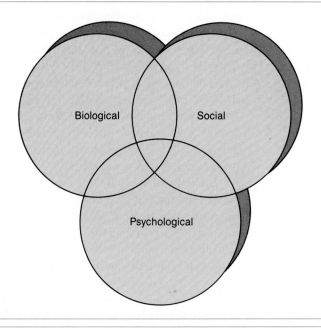

FIGURE 1-3 Aging is a multifaceted experience. Developmental psychologists maintain that the three main processes of aging are biological, social, and psychological.

aware of the major processes of aging, differences of opinion exist concerning age classification systems. Age alone is not an adequate criterion for stage classification, as one can easily observe by examining cross-cultural life expectancies: One might be considered old in one culture but not in another. For example, in Upper Volta in Africa, the average life expectancy hovers near 40 years. Indonesia's people live on the average of 50 years, whereas in the Philippines, the average life expectancy is 60 years. Sweden boasts the extreme in life expectancies, with the average individual living nearly 78 years. Cross-culturally, then, it is possible at a given age to be a young adult in one country, middle-aged in another, and elderly in yet another. Thus, it is impossible for developmental psychologists to devise a universal age classification system.

The reasons for such differences in cross-cultural life expectancy are difficult to pinpoint. The greater life expectancy in developed nations, compared to underdeveloped countries, has been attributed to such factors as improved medical care, control of infectious diseases, technological advances, better working conditions, and nutritious diets. Such illustrations of the nature of aging processes underscore the need to carefully examine both the individual and the generalizations made in age classification systems.

This discussion also implies that life expectancy at various historical periods must also be taken into consideration. More specifically, we would have difficulty in attempting to adapt present-day life expectancies to those of past eras. For example, in the United States today, the average person can expect to live about 74 years. Compare this to a life expectancy of about 25 years in Rome at A.D. 100 or 35 years in England during the 1200s! Moreover, consider the problems we face when attempting to understand the developmental period known as *childhood* as it existed in past centuries. In many cultures, right up through the medieval period, there was not one word to capture this critical developmental stage, largely because childhood, as we know it today, simply did not exist. In most cases, *infancy* was the term applied to the first six years of life. During this period, children were kept at home and attended to by their mothers to learn the folkways and mores of their culture.

Between the ages of six and nine, children, for all intents and purposes, entered *adulthood.* They either were sent directly into the workaday world or were given an apprenticeship to train for a particular vocation. Remarkably, the developmental period classified today as middle childhood was nonexistent, and most, if not all, of adolescence was omitted because the child began assuming adult responsibilities early in life (Muuss, 1989; Aries, 1962).

In past historical eras, children were often viewed as miniature adults. Note the attire and activities of these eighteenth-century children.

The aging experience, while universal, brings unique cross-cultural variations.

Furthermore, the term *youth* generally signified *the prime of one's life.* Youth, during the Middle Ages, was followed immediately by the stage referred to as *old age!* Moreover, at 20, an age when most young adults in modern society are still preparing for a career, William the Conqueror had already been victorious in the Battle of Normandy. Charlemagne had recorded numerous victories in battle before he was crowned King of the Franks at age 26. There are young adults today who make significant and sometimes truly great contributions to society, but few, if any, are capable of shaping history as these individuals did. In contemporary western societies, it is far more likely that such feats are accomplished by "older" adults.

As civilizations changed and technology progressed, the lives of humans changed also. With the advent of more complex divisions of labor, additional training and education were needed for job preparation, a factor that extended the developmental periods. As the lifespan lengthened, the periods of early, middle, and late adulthood emerged, lengthened in time, and began to assume their own unique identities within the life cycle. Compared with past centuries, our view of various life stages has changed considerably. Furthermore, it is expected that age classification systems will continue to change in years to come.

International Lifespan Development

■ GROWING OLD IN THE MOUNTAIN LAND OF ABKHAZIA

At age 95, he goes to work each day, picking apples from the top of a rickety ladder. At age 93, his wife remains home and tends to domestic chores: preparing the daily meals, attending to the children and animals, mending, cleaning, and the like. Their children, all in their 70s, lend a hand for the more physically taxing jobs, such as plowing or carrying buckets of water from nearby streams.

Discussions of longevity and the prospects for living longer in future years are incomplete without some reference to the people of Abkhazia, a mountain village tucked between the Black Sea and the High Caucasus in the Soviet Union. For years, reports have focused on the remarkable longevity of these mountain people and their active lifestyle that extends well into their twilight years. Indeed, these rural Soviets are still vigorous and performing everyday chores when many Americans are placed in nursing homes.

Abkhazia boasts five times the number of centenarians as the United States. In a recent survey, 548 residents of Abkhazia, out of a population of 520,000, were 100 years of age or older. While earlier longevity records were suspect because of poor recordkeeping and the tendency of residents to overstate their age, more sophisticated research attests to the aforementioned statistics.

What is it about Abkhazians that promotes such pronounced longevity and active lifestyles? Blood tests show that Abkhazians are not strikingly different from their geographical neighbors, but they may have a genetic resistance to disease. Their diet is wholesome but not unusual and, for the most part, they do not consume large quantities of alcohol. Cancer rates are also low among Abkhazians, probably because of their rural way of life.

Gerontologists believe that the Abkhazians' active lifestyle and the reverence for old age that exists among them contribute to the longevity phenomenon. In addition to the maintenance of their vocations, Abkhazians of advanced years participate in a council of elders. They serve a number of hospitality roles, an important element of the village culture, and are regularly sought out by the young for advice.

All of this contributes to a smooth aging transition that helps to avoid the shock of retirement. These cultural practices help to preserve the real power that elders have in both the family and village life. Such conditions create psychological comfort among the aged and may help explain why people live longer in the remote land of Caucasus (Sullivan, 1982).

■ The Science of Human Development

As stated in the beginning of this chapter, developmental psychology is generally defined as the scientific study of the growth, development, and behavioral changes of humans from conception through old age. Science has many definitions. It refers to the techniques and methods used in gathering facts or data and may also be used in reference to an organized and systematic body of knowledge. The field of developmental psychology qualifies on both counts. In this section, we take a look at a few of the many techniques developmental psychologists use to collect data.

■ Scientific Methods

When developmentalists are curious about some behavioral phenomenon, they use a *scientific method*—a system of procedures for identifying the problem, gathering data, arriving at conclusions, and checking the accuracy of their conclusions.

We often use the term scientific method as though there were only one way to do a scientific investigation. This is not the case, for there are many methodologies that can be used to search for knowledge. In this section, we take a look at the naturalistic observation, survey, experimental, and correlational methods. All of these are scientific methods and sometimes researchers use more than one method in their search for truth and understanding.

□ Observation—The Key to Knowledge

The collection of data begins when some type of observation is made, whether by somewhat unsophisticated means (watching children at play) or by very technical processes (recording brain waves on an electroencephalograph). Regardless of the techniques employed to gather data, these methods fall under the general classification of *observation*. Theories or, possibly, laws may be formulated from observations, provided, of course, that the data are supportive.

In surveying past literature, one finds that some ideas about adult behavior were developed without the support of empirical evidence. The difficulty with such theoretical preconceptions is the assumption that one's point of view is correct because it makes a sensible story. This is the primary problem of myth versus science. Even some highly developed theories of human development require more data than that which is provided. A theory may make a good narrative about how things evolved to where they are now, but if the theory contains little empirical evidence, it cannot offer a plausible basis for action.

While it is true that ideas may emerge following the observation of a solitary incident, one must recognize the danger of generalizing from a limited number of situations. Consequently, while a study of one subject may be of assistance toward studying that individual, it does not necessarily mean that other subjects will exhibit identical behavior or, if they do, that it will be for the same reasons.

Seeing the dangers in single-subject research methods (while still acknowledging their significant role in psychology), researchers have striven to test their suppositions on larger segments of the population. Many graduate schools, for example, now have working agreements with nearby hospitals that enable researchers to study newborns, with the parents' permission, within hours after birth. New techniques of study and evaluation, especially in such areas as electroencephalography (study of brain waves) and visual abilities (seeing objects, tracking moving objects, visual preferences, and so on), have been discovered and put to use.

☐ Types of Observation

Naturalistic observation is the examination of behavior under *unstructured* (natural) conditions. *Structured observation* represents a slight extension of naturalistic observation, enabling the researcher to administer simple tests. *Participant observation* involves the researcher as a participant in the interaction being studied. When this is done, the researcher's direct involvement with the subjects provides observational data. These forms of observation differ markedly from *controlled experiments,* which employ situations that require subjects to be placed in contrived and perhaps unnatural environments.

Sometimes, the results obtained from certain controlled expriments are of little value because they have a tendency to create unnatural behavior. However, it is felt by some researchers that the same could hold true for observational techniques in general. Gerald Adams and Jay Schvaneveldt (1985), for example, feel that this is especially true when researchers become obtrusive and thrust themselves onto others without invitation. The more obtrusive the observer, the greater the chance of subjects behaving in atypical or guarded ways.

The observation of children is often enhanced with the use of a one-way window.

The foregoing suggests that research designs must be carefully executed. Naturalistic and structured observations, as well as controlled experiments, can be extremely valuable in gathering significant information. However, the fact remains that the naturalistic method, at least partially, reduces the individual's awareness of being observed.

☐ Historical Antecedents of Human Observation: The Baby Biography

Historically, the earliest recorded forms of human observation were termed *baby biographies,* day by day accounts of the development of an infant or young child. One of the earliest baby biographers, Johann Pestalozzi (1740–1827), a leading educator of his day, recorded his son's activities (age two and a half) for three weeks and later published the account. Included in his many observations were comments on the role of the mother, whom he believed to be the most important educator in the child's life. Pestalozzi stated that behavioral patterns are first learned through the child's *observation and imitation* of the mother's actions.

Wilhelm T. Preyer (1841–1897), a physiologist, was interested in overall mental development. This interest was manifested in an account (later published as three separate books) of his son's development during the first four years of life, a baby biography that many psychologists consider collectively a classic. Preyer, like Pestalozzi, observed several behavioral patterns, including socialization processes, and the child's tendency to imitate others.

Charles Darwin
(1809–1882)

Charles Darwin (1809–1882) impressed many people with his interest in children, particularly in 1877, when he published a baby biography on the development of his firstborn son. The following quotation shows his observational skills:

> During the first seven days various reflex actions, namely sneezing, hiccupping, yawning, stretching, and of course sucking and screaming, were well performed by my infant. On the seventh day I touched the naked sole of his foot with a bit of paper, and he jerked it away, curling at the same time his toes, like a much older child when tickled. The perfection of these reflex movements shows that the extreme imperfection of the voluntary ones is not due to the state of the muscles or of the coordinating centres, but to that of the seat of the will. . . .

With respect to vision,—his eyes were fixed on a candle as early as the 9th day, and up to the 45th day nothing else seemed thus to fix them; but on the 49th day his attention was attracted by a bright-coloured tassel, as was shown by his eyes becoming fixed and the movements of his arms ceasing. It was surprising how slowly he acquired the power of following with his eyes an object if swinging at all rapidly; for he could not do this well when seven and a half months old.

(Kessen, W. *The Child*. New York, Wiley, 1965, pp. 118–119)

Most baby biographies were a progressive step forward from the armchair philosophies and philosophical presuppositions that had dominated the past. The resulting interest in these accounts during the eighteenth and nineteenth centuries helped, in turn, to give impetus to all subfields of developmental psychology, not just to the study of the early years of life. As more and more observations were made, simple techniques and testing devices were initiated, giving rise to a number of highly sophisticated observation and measuring devices.

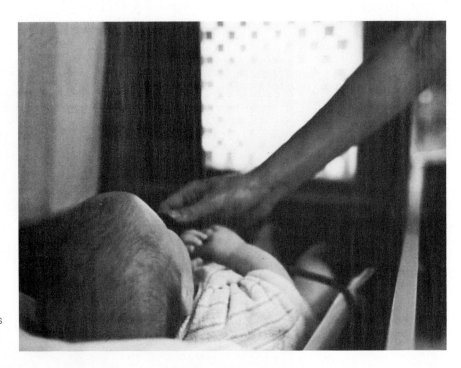

Contemporary visual apparatus is highly sophisticated compared with Darwin's early methods of observation and assessment.

☐ Techniques of Naturalistic Observation

Frequently, developmental psychologists are required to observe human behavior, especially that of children, in a number of different situations, such as during school, at play, or even in a grocery or department store. Whether observers are stationed behind one-way windows or simply attempt to keep unobtrusively out of sight, certain points regarding effective observation skills should be kept in mind. The following may serve as general guidelines for observing people of all ages, although it must be noted that observation techniques are used on children more than adults.

1. Remain out of the way as much as the setting requires. When people know that they are being watched, especially children, they sometimes change natural behavior, shy away from strangers, or suddenly start showing off.

G. Stanley Hall (1844–1924), Father of Human Development?

Born in Ashfield, Massachusetts, Granville Stanley Hall originally wanted to pursue a career in the ministry and received a B.D. degree from Union Theological Seminary. Hall developed an interest in philosophy and psychology, however, and eventually received a Ph.D. in psychology from Harvard in 1878. Hall appears to be "first" in many areas of psychology, although it should be recognized that he lived during the early infancy of this science.

While Hall is generally recognized as the father of child psychology, he was also one of the pioneers of developmental psychology. It seems apt that his early efforts in attempting to systematically analyze the lifespan should earn him the nomination for father of developmental psychology as well.

He was the first American to receive a doctorate in psychology at Harvard and, in 1879, he became the first American student of Wilhelm Wundt of Leipzig, the father of psychology, who founded the first laboratory for experimental psychology in the same year. Thus, Hall was the first American to study in the first psychological laboratory in its first year of existence. In 1883, Hall established the first psychological laboratory in the United States at Johns Hopkins University. He was the first president and the first professor of psychology at Clark University, an institution that would become famous for producing great psychologists, and he was influential in shaping the careers of such notable psychologists as Lewis Terman, Arnold Gesell, and John Dewey.

In 1891, Hall founded and initially financed the journal *Pedagogical Seminary* (since renamed the *Journal of Genetic Psychology*), which focused on studies of childhood. A considerable amount of research was being done at Clark University, where Hall and his students were developing the *questionnaire,* a technique that Hall believed would allow for a more systematic investigation of individuals and afford more opportunities to investigate larger samples of the population. In particular, he became interested in children's minds and developed a questionnaire designed to elicit knowledge from them. While it lacked

G. Stanley Hall (1844–1924)

the sophistication of modern questionnaires, it nevertheless served its purpose well. Two of Hall's better known publications are *The Contents of Children's Minds* (1883) and *The Contents of Children's Minds on Entering School* (1891). By 1915, 194 different types of questionnaires had been developed at Clark University and Hall had succeeded in enlightening the general public on matters related to child development and education.

Hall's interest in genetics and evolutionary theory led him to study not only childhood, but also adolescence and old age. Possibly his most influential work is the two-volume (about 1,300 pages) *Adolescence: Its Psychology, and Its Relations to Physiology, Anthropology, Sociology, Sex, Crime, Religion and Education* (1904). Finally, during his later years, he published *Senescence: The Last Half of Life* (1922), a considerable portion of which was based on Hall's observations of his own aging process.

2. With paper and pencil, tape recorder, or camera, record such things as the physical setting and the activities the people are engaging in (lunch period, rest period, boarding a plane, shopping, etc.).

3. After quickly scanning the scene and taking appropriate notes, focus on the activity of *one* person for at least 10 to 15 minutes. Observe play behavior, awareness of others, aggressiveness, passivity, prosocial behavior, and so on.

4. Refocus on the group at large and notice other interactions. If you are observ-

ing a class, note the teacher's behavior toward various children. Are all children treated identically? If you are observing adults in a social situation, refocus on their interaction.

5. Immediately upon finishing the observation, write a report while the various scenes are still fresh in your mind.

Other items to look for while observing people are physical appearance, speech, emotional reactions, and relationships with others (Carbonara, 1961; Irwin and Bushnell, 1980; Cartwright and Cartwright, 1984; Beaty, 1986).

Whether subjected to simple or complex methods of observation, it is important that people feel at ease so that the observation or measurement will not affect their spontaneity and natural behavior. Thus, if testing is to be effective, it must take place in a friendly, nonthreatening atmosphere. If feasible, the researcher should spend several sessions with the subject(s) (beware of allowing positive or negative emotions to interfere with scoring—i.e., an extra point because the child is "cute" or the adult has a friendly smile) to avoid any unnecessary apprehensions or other behavior that might interfere with the situation.

Rapport is especially important if accurate responses are to be elicited. It would be unwise, for example, to tell people who fear failure that they will be tested to see how well they compare with associates. Failure of the test may occur not because of limited capabilities, but because the experimenter has raised their anxiety level to a point that interferes with an otherwise natural response. This may be avoided if rapport and understanding are established initially. In other situations and with different individuals, minimal anxiety may produce a higher degree of motivation and, consequently, a higher test result. Part of the scientific method is knowledge of individual differences (Matlin, 1980).

Ethologists study animal behavior in natural settings; they represent another group of scientists that uses naturalistic observation. Some ethologists attempt to gain insights into human behavior by comparing animal behavior with human behavior. Konrad Lorenz and Niko Tinbergen, two Nobel Prize-winning ethologists, believed that humans, like many other animals, will band together to protect a territory—one of the primary reasons for human aggression. For more on ethology, see Chapter 2.

☐ The Case Study Method

The *case study* focuses upon a single person rather than a group of people. Its purpose is to accumulate developmental information. Studying a single subject over an extended time period yields a great deal of information on that one person. While this method is excellent in such areas as clinical treatment of maladjusted individuals, we can never be certain that this knowledge will help us in understanding others.

☐ The Survey Method

Surveys can be valuable in research endeavors. A *survey* is a technique for gathering information from people and usually takes the form of a questionnaire or an interview. A survey is directed toward a sample, a group of people representative of a larger population.

A requirement of questionnaires is that respondents mark their own answers. This makes questionnaires relatively inexpensive, simple, and fast to execute. Moreover, questionnaires can be administered so that respondents remain anonymous, an important advantage in encouraging complete responses, especially when what is being researched is socially sensitive. Another advantage of questionnaires is that interviewers do not need to be recruited, trained, and sent out. Questionnaires thus reduce the personnel costs that accompany the interviewing technique (B. C. Miller, 1986).

Researchers must take care in the wording of instructions as well as the actual items appearing on questionnaires. Wording must be concise so that respondents do not get frustrated or confused. Frustrated or confused respondents often give inaccurate information or, in some instances, give up completely. Surveys can supply researchers with valuable data on how people think and act, but only if this assessment device is properly designed and worded (Sax, 1989).

Interviews, on the other hand, require a face-to-face encounter. In the standard procedure, a trained interviewer asks questions and then records the responses. Although the interview technique is more expensive than questionnaires, it is generally more flexible and yields more accurate data. When used properly, the interview has the following advantages over the questionnaire:

- Interviewers can explain the purpose of the investigation, establish rapport, discuss the interview, and respond to questions at any time. Such factors tend to enhance the cooperation rate.

- A primary strength of the interview is its participation rate. Conversely, a limitation of the mailed questionnaire is its return rate.

- Interviewers can listen to the responses as well as observe the respondent. Facial expressions, mood, and body language are often valuable in fathoming the totality of information provided by the interview.

- Related to the previous point, skilled interviewers can "read" respondents. That is, a respondent's moods can be assessed and information can be sought accordingly. It is likely that the same data can be gathered in a different way at a later time in the same interview, thus enabling the interviewer to determine the truthfulness of the gathered responses and look for developmental trends.

- Face-to-face interaction can be important in building needed rapport, which, in turn, often leads to a higher level of respondent motivation. When this happens, the quality of data is likely to be superior to that gathered when respondents are participating out of pressure or obligation.

- The interview is especially valuable for collecting data that is sensitive or personal. Once trust has been established by skilled researchers, respondents tend to disclose such information.

- It is generally recognized that people enjoy talking. Employing the proper skills, interviewers can channel conversation so that a more thorough understanding of the topic can result.

(Adams & Schvaneveldt, 1985)

It is important to recognize, though, that interviews have their drawbacks. For example, while items on questionnaires are uniform and consistent, a staff of interviewers can ask the same question in different ways. Such a mixture of interviewing styles can contaminate a research design. Additionally, interviewers may not record clear and concise responses. For that matter, some interviewers may be uncertain as to which responses to record, and as we pointed out earlier, the interview technique is more expensive to operate than the questionnaire format.

Establishing rapport with subjects and creating a nonthreatening atmosphere are important research considerations.

☐ The Correlational Method

There are times when developmental scientists wish to see if a relationship exists between variables. For example, we may wish to see if there is a relationship between mothers-to-be who drink or smoke and mental retardation or low birth weight children. Obviously, we cannot expect pregnant mothers to drink or smoke excessively. Instead, we use a technique called *correlation.* Although the mathematics involved are somewhat complicated, the idea is simple: Two variables are correlated when changes in one variable are associated with changes in the other variable. Thus, we compare the intelligence of babies who are born of women who consumed alcohol during pregnancy with those children born of mothers who did not imbibe. The same technique would be used to compare birth weights of infants born to smoking and nonsmoking mothers.

☐ The Experimental Method

The *experimental method* in psychology is a series of steps by which the researcher tries to determine relationships between differing phenomena, either to discover principles underlying behavior or to find cause-and-effect relationships. The experimental method is employed in developmental psychology just as it is in other scientific fields.

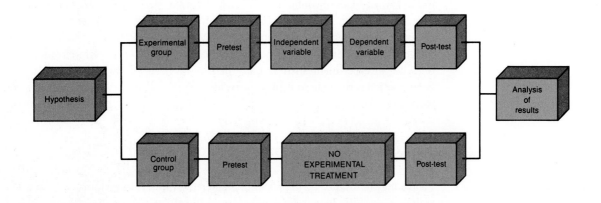

FIGURE 1-4 The experimental method.

Each experimental investigation must follow a procedure that is relevant to the phenomenon being investigated. Therefore, the scientific method used for one experiment may differ completely from the method used for an investigation of a completely different nature. For example, studying how schoolchildren relate to authoritarian teachers would involve methods totally different from those employed for investigating the behavioral reactions of the middle-aged adult to stress. However, the basic principles of experimental methods remain the same. Regardless of specific experimental differences, certain common terms, definitions, and formats are universal to those using the experimental method.

The experimental method typically begins with a *hypothesis,* an educated guess made by researchers regarding what they think the results will be. Let us suppose our hypothesis is that students will know more about the discipline of developmental psychology after a semester is over than they did before they enrolled. Before testing our hypothesis on a large group of people, say 1,000 undergraduate students, we would perform a *pilot study,* a small-scale research investigation designed to discover problems, errors, or other obstacles that might develop when the large-scale study is undertaken. Discovering procedural problems while testing 10 or 20 subjects will save much time, effort, and many headaches before we begin testing 1,000 subjects.

In some types of research, two groups of subjects are chosen to prove or disprove the hypothesis. One group is called the *experimental group,* which is subjected to special conditions and is carefully observed by the experimenter. The special treatment given to the experimental group is called the *independent variable.* Concerning our hypothesis, the experimental group would comprise students enrolled in and receiving formal instruction (the independent variable) in developmental psychology. The behavior affected by the independent variable, that is, the degree of knowledge acquired in class from the professor, is termed the *dependent variable.*

Our other group of subjects, called the *control group,* is used primarily for comparison purposes. The control group would not receive the independent variable, the formal instruction in developmental psychology, given to the experimental group.

To determine whether a hypothesis is correct, pre- and posttests are usually administered to both experimental and control groups. In our case, the pre- and posttests would seek to measure the students' knowledge of developmental psychology. Changes (if any) would appear in the experimental group, especially when contrasted with the control group.

Some research designs do not use a control group. Let us assume we want to discover what types of configurations (shapes, forms, etc.) appeal to newborn infants. In this experiment, we might hook up a pacifier to a TV set. If an infant sucks on the pacifier, the configuration remains on the TV screen; if the infant fails to suck, the image disappears. Studies have shown that infants prefer complex patterns over simple ones. In an experiment such as this, there is no need for the control group. The configuration is the independent variable, and the time spent sucking is the dependent variable (behavior).

☐ Longitudinal and Cross-Sectional Designs

People may be studied by implementing different research approaches. Two common techniques are the longitudinal and cross-sectional designs.

When using the *longitudinal design,* the analyst collects data on the same group of individuals at intervals over a considerable period of time, generally at least 10 years and sometimes even decades. Let us suppose someone wants to collect data concerning various facets of development. The researcher employing the longitudinal design might begin studying a particular group whose members are five years of age. Follow-up studies would be made at fairly regular intervals, maybe once a year until the subjects reached age 25. At each follow-up session, relevant data would be recorded and eventually analyzed. This research design would allow the analyst to see how each individual changes through middle childhood, adolescence, and young adulthood.

Researchers using the *cross-sectional design* obtain comparative data from different groups of subjects more or less simultaneously. Using this approach, the researcher would select a number of groups of subjects, aged (for example) 5, 10, 15, 20, and 25, and record the differences among the various age groups. These differences would then be recorded and analyzed.

Each design has its own advantages and disadvantages. For example, the cross-sectional approach is relatively inexpensive, easier to execute, and not overly time-consuming, but it sometimes overlooks individual changes, and it is contaminated with generational differences. The longitudinal approach probably provides a fairly accurate assessment of developmental changes within an individual, but this approach takes a long time, is generally expensive, and frequently suffers from subject attrition.

In an attempt to nullify the weaknesses of the longitudinal and cross-sectional designs, researchers have developed combinations of these two approaches. They are called *sequential designs* and include the *short-term longitudinal method* and the *cross-sectional short-term longitudinal method.* The short-term longitudinal method is a less complicated longitudinal study, requires a maximum of five years to complete, and investigates fewer behavioral phenomena. Because it is less time-consuming, subject attrition is less frequent and the original staff of investigators is less likely to abandon the project. As its name implies, the cross-sectional short-term longitudinal method combines the cross-sectional design and the short-term longitudinal method (Baltes, 1973; Schaie, 1965). If one were to study certain personality traits developmentally, let us say from ages 15 to 25, a ten-year longitudinal study would be in order. However, by doing simultaneous cross-sectional studies of two groups, one for ages 15 to 20 and the other for ages 20 to 25, the study could be completed in five years—hence the term cross-sectional short-term longitudinal study.

Table 1-1 summarizes the differences in the longitudinal and cross-sectional designs. It is obvious that each of these approaches has its own strengths and weak-

TABLE 1-1 Comparison Between Longitudinal and Cross-Sectional Designs

Factor	Longitudinal	Cross-Sectional
Method of procedure	Examines and reexamines same group repeatedly over the years	Examines several groups (from different levels of development) simultaneously over a short time period
Cost	Research is generally expensive	Research is relatively inexpensive
Time involved	Several years to several decades; frequent loss of contact with subjects	Relatively little time—months, weeks, or even days
Collection and use of data	Collection of data is as long as the experiment. Because many data are collected, much time is needed for interpretation	Quick collection with rapid interpretation of results
Personnel needed	Many people under capable researcher	Relatively few (may need only one researcher)
Major advantage	Allows many data showing individual growth and developmental changes	Large amounts of data can be gathered within a short period of time
Major disadvantages	Requires much time and finance; loss of subject by moving, death, and the like	Loses sight of individual changes; provides only a representative group of various ages, controls, and the like

nesses. Whichever design is used, the data will be as good as the measurement techniques used to obtain it and the conception behind its collection. These factors operate in any methodological design.

☐ Age and Cohort Factors

To fully comprehend the differences between the longitudinal and cross-sectional designs, one must understand such factors as age and cohorts. In either approach, *age* is always a variable. A second variable is *cohort,* a reference to those people born at approximately the same time (the same year or within a year or two of each other). Because they are born about the same time, cohorts have experienced situations and events unique to their particular age group. For example, being a 20-year-old in 1930 was different from being a 20-year-old in 1991. Thus, the age factor distinguishes people by their chronological age and the cohort factor places that age within a time frame.

With age and cohort factors in mind, let us reexamine the nature of cross-sectional and longitudinal studies. All the subjects in a longitudinal study are members of the same cohort. If a study were started in 1950 with 20-year-olds, and these subjects were tested every five years, we would be gathering information about *age changes.* In a cross-sectional design, we would be studying subjects who were, let us say, 25, 30, 35, and 40 years of age. Here, we would be gathering information about *age differences.* In a cross-sectional study, the results may be affected by age or cohort differences.

Cohort analysis is the method by which researchers explore the experiences common to a particular age group. Whenever a research design is put into operation and data are collected, one must go a step further and examine cohort differences. This is especially true in cross-sectional studies since we are dealing with subjects of varying ages at the same time. For example, suppose 20-year-olds score higher on intelligence tests than 70-year-olds. Is it because the former group is intellectually superior or because they received more schooling as they grew up? To cite another instance, let us say we discover in our data that 70-year-olds are more financially cautious than 25-year-olds. Could the stock market crash and the great depression, through which the 70-year-olds lived, be influential here? Or is it more significant that the 25-year-olds were reared in a world of charge cards, layaways, and instant credit?

When such factors as age and cohort cannot be assessed separately, the data are *confounded*. Cross-sectional designs, for the most part, are inexpensive and can be quickly executed, but they contain confounded data, in that the facts may be attributed to either age or cohort differences.

Confounded data may also be found in longitudinal studies, which have a tendency to confound a person's age with time of measurement changes. As a result, we can not accurately determine whether changes in a person are the result of developmental processes or environmental influences.

Another weakness of the longitudinal design is that of *repeated measurement*. Here, the subject is repeatedly given the same tests over a period of time. The gathered results, therefore, may not be owing to improvement, but rather to familiarity with the test itself. Scientists, then, are confronted with confounded data in many ways.

☐ Time-Lag Design

One other design worthy of noting is the **time-lag design**. This methodology is employed when researchers want to compare people of the same age but at different times. Suppose someone had studied the morals of 20-year-old college students back in 1930 and you want to compare them with today's 20-year-old college students. To do this, you would replicate the 1930 study. Since age has been held constant, it is not a variable that would confound your results, however differences related to time of measurement might be confounded with cohort differences.

☐ Research Problems

Numerous difficulties confront researchers studying human behavior. Researchers must never manipulate the subjects and their environments to a degree that will endanger their physical, mental, or emotional well-being, or that will interfere with normal developmental processes. Ethical standards, therefore, must be foremost in the researchers' minds. For example, some researchers believe that children are more vulnerable than adults to stressful situations; therefore, more care must be taken when planning a study or experiment in which children are involved. Examples of other considerations are: Is it ethical to subject individuals to situations where they are bound to fail? Is it ethical to issue to the subject misinformation to see how it affects behavior? Is it ethical to mistreat a child or an adult? Is it ethical to observe people when they are not aware they are being observed? The answer to some of these questions is obvious: *NO*. In practice, many questions of ethics are not so easily answered.

The growth and development of females throughout the life course needs more extensive exploration.

A second research problem, particularly when a study involves older adults, is that there are relatively few research instruments available to measure the various characteristics of aging processes. Those in use tend to be questionable not only in terms of validity and reliability but also in regard to distortion of actual findings. Even the observation of adults poses difficulties for the researcher, especially when adult behavior is compared to that of children or adolescents. Once they know they are being observed or questioned for a purpose, adults are not as spontaneous as and are much more suspicious than their younger counterparts. The longitudinal research technique has also been especially vulnerable to criticism. While it can be a reliable design, adults represent a highly mobile segment of the population and are unlikely to remain in the same location for repeated testing. Other problems relative to the longitudinal study are its rather expensive operating costs and its time-consuming nature—subjects may die before the study is completed.

Third, not enough research has been directed toward women and their aging experience. Past research was biased in favor of males, but today we are seeing more extensive investigations of women's development (Rosenthal, 1990; Garner and Mercer, 1989; Grau, 1989; Grambs, 1989; Mercer, Nichols, and Doyle, 1989), and it is our hope that this trend will continue. There are many topics regarding women that need to be explored, such as satisfaction over the life cycle, role adaptation, and achievement motivation. With more women in the labor force for longer periods of time, we are also in need of research examining their career lives, including retirement (Gratton and Haug, 1983).

As with women, there is limited information available on aging among racial and ethnic groups. While interest and data on blacks have been growing, there is still a void in the literature available on Spanish-speaking Americans, Puerto Ricans, Orientals, and American Indians, to name but a few groups. All old people do not have the same needs or experience the same conditions of aging. Rather, the circumstances of one's existence and background, to a large extent, shape one's ways of adapting to aging (Crandall, 1980; Manuel, 1982).

☐ Ethics

All scientists face questions of ethics, especially those whose research involves humans. Psychologists must be especially concerned with ethical standards and the American Psychological Association (APA) has studied, developed, and revised ethical guidelines over the years (1990; 1981; 1973). The guidelines state that the researchers' ultimate responsibility is to assess their research to determine if any ethical problems exist and discuss such problems with collaborators, assistants, students, and employees. In other words, a full ethical evaluation by the entire research team, as well as fellow psychologists, should be undertaken before research commences. Some other important considerations are:

> Ethical practice requires the investigator to inform the participant of all features of the research that reasonably might be expected to influence willingness to participate and to explain all other aspects of the research about which the participant inquires.

> Ethical research practice requires the investigator to respect the individual's freedom to decline to participate in research or to discontinue participation at any time.

> Ethically acceptable research begins with the establishment of a clear and fair agreement between the investigator and the research participant that clarifies the responsibilities of each. The investigator has the obligation to honor all promises and commitments included in that agreement.

> The ethical investigator protects participants from physical and mental discomfort, harm, and danger. If the risk of such consequences exists, the investigator is required to inform the participant of that fact, secure consent before proceeding, and take all possible measures to minimize distress. A research procedure may not be used if it is likely to cause serious and lasting harm to participants.

> Where research procedures may result in undesirable consequences for the participant, the investigator has the responsibility to detect and remove or correct these consequences, including, where relevant, long-term aftereffects.

Information obtained about the research participants during the course of an investigation is confidential. . . .

Because children may be more susceptible to stress, extreme care must be taken when a researcher is planning to involve them in a study. Because of this, the Division of Developmental Psychology of the APA has added additional ethical standards, including:

No matter how young the child, he/she has rights that supersede the rights of the investigator.

The investigator uses no research operations that may harm the child either physically or psychologically. Psychological harm, to be sure, is difficult to define; nevertheless, its definition remains a responsibility of the investigator.

The informed consent of parents or of those legally designated to act *in loco parentis* is obtained, preferably in writing. Informed consent requires that the parent be given accurate information . . . on the purpose and operations of the research, albeit in layman's terms. The consent of parents is not solicited by any claims of benefit to the child. Not only is the right of parents to refuse consent respected, but parents must be given the opportunity to refuse.

Teachers of courses related to children should present the ethical standards of conducting research on human beings to their students.

Developmental psychologists must adhere to ethical research practices.

CHAPTER REVIEW

Behavior, never constant, ever changing, is the subject matter of the field of developmental psychology. More precisely, developmental psychology encompasses the growth, maturation, and learning of the organism from conception to death.

Three main processes are thought to exist in aging: biological, psychological, and social. Fundamental to any classification system is the life expectancy and lifestyle of a culture or social group. What may be defined as old age in one culture may be middle age in another.

Developmental psychology is considered a science, and scientific methodology is being widely applied to the study of the developing organism. Today's methods, undoubtedly, are more precise than the single-baby biographies of the past or the mass questionnaires developed by G. Stanley Hall.

Adult psychology is the most recent division of developmental psychology. Today, its primary focus is to examine critically the biological, personal, and social forces affecting the individual during the years of adulthood.

Studying the adult population poses numerous problems. It is necessary to avoid preconceptions and to challenge societal myths in order to obtain accurate data. Other difficulties include experimenter, survival, cultural-economic bias, and the limited number of sophisticated research techniques available.

There are numerous methodological formats for accumulating data: observational methods, including naturalistic techniques; the case study; and the survey method.

The correlational method involves statistics, and the results indicate if a relationship between two variables are correlated. However, it does not prove that one variable actually is the cause of the other.

The experimental method is a systematic means by which the experimenter seeks to determine relationships between differing phenomena. It is employed either to discover principles underlying behavior or to find cause-and-effect relationships. The experimental method includes independent and dependent variables, the former referring to the stimulus, or special treatment, given the subjects and the latter referring to the behavior subjects exhibit after they have received the independent variable.

With the longitudinal design, the developmental processes of the same group of subjects are studied over a period of years. The cross-sectional design is quicker and easier to use than the longitudinal design because data can be collected from many age groups simultaneously. On the other hand, subtle changes, perceptible in the longitudinal design, are often missed in the cross-sectional approach.

Some aspects of developmental psychology pose problems that can not be concisely answered. Ethical considerations for human rights and dignity disallow experiments that, although they may provide information, may do so only by inflicting possibly irreparable damage upon the subjects (especially children).

KEY TERMS

baby biography	hypothesis
biological aging	independent variable
case study	longitudinal design
cohort	naturalistic observation
cohort analysis	participant observation
confounded data	pilot study
control group	psychological aging
controlled experiments	scientific method
correlation	sequential designs
cross-sectional design	short-term method
dependent variable	social-age clock
developmental psychology	social aging
ethological observation	structured observation
experimental group	survey
experimental method	time-lag design

RECOMMENDED READINGS

Baltes, P. B., Reese, H. W., and Nesselroade, J. R. (1977). *Life Span Developmental Psychology: Introduction to Research Methods.* Monterey, Calif.: Brooks/Cole.
An excellent introduction to research methods as applied to developmental psychology. Especially appealing are chapters dealing with the nature of theories and models, scientific methods, and cross-sectional and longitudinal designs.

Cohen, D. H., and Stern, V. (1983). *Observing and Recording the Behavior of Young Children,* 3rd ed. New York: Teachers College Press.
This paperback describes methods for observing and keeping records of children's behavior.

Finch, C. E., and Schneider, E. L. (Eds.). (1985). *Handbook of the Biology of Aging,* 2nd ed. New York: Van Nostrand Reinhold.
See Section 1 of this book for a statistical analysis of the elderly in the United States as well as evolutionary aspects of longevity.

Gold, J. A. (1984). *Principles of Psychological Research.* Homewood, Ill.: Dorsey Press.
A good examination of how research methods are used in psychology. Experimental and correlational techniques are clearly explained.

Howard, G. (1985). *Basic Research Methods in the Social Sciences.* Glenview, Ill.: Scott, Foresman.
A broadly based perspective on methodology. Howard surveys the various research methods used in the social sciences, showing the logic, strength, and weakness of each.

Irwin, D. M., and Bushnell, M. M. (1980). *Observational Strategies for Child Study.* New York: Holt.
In addition to the fundamentals of observation, this book presents interesting historical material on child study and structured lab assignments.

Keith-Spiegel, P., and Koocher, G. P. (1985). *Ethics in Psychology: Professional Standards and Cases.* New York: Random House.
This text is based on the ethics code of the American Psychological Association. The authors discuss the profession's ethical standards and how they apply to specific situations.

Lonner, W. J., and Berry, J. W. (Eds.). (1986). *Field Methods in Cross-Cultural Research.* Beverly Hills, Calif.: Sage.
Topics include fieldwork in cross-cultural psychology, sampling and surveying the targeted population, and methods of observation.

McCluskey, K. A., and Reese, H. W. (Eds.). (1984). *Life-Span Developmental Psychology: Historical and Generational Effects.* New York: Academic Press.
Topics include historical time and cohort effects, historical and contemporary perspectives on fatherhood, and grandparenthood in transition.

Rosenthal, E. (Ed.). (1990). *Women, Aging, and Ageism.* New York: Harrington Park Press.
One of the better readers focusing on female aging experiences.

Summerville, J. (1982). *The Rise and Fall of Childhood.* Beverly Hills, Calif.: Sage.
A brief overview of the history of childhood throughout the ages with a look at the child's place in the family and society.

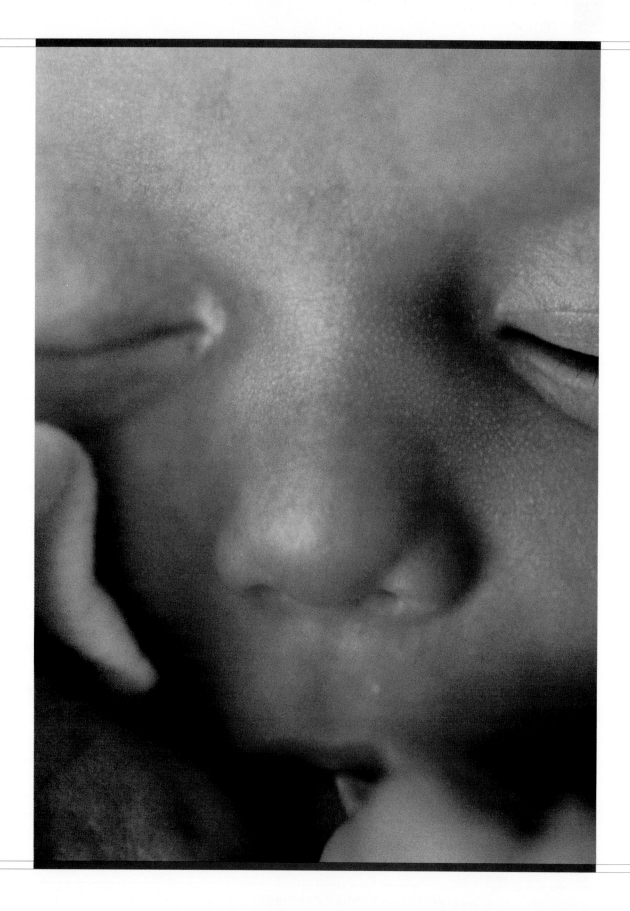

Theories of Human Development

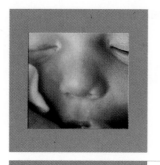

WHAT DO YOU THINK?

■ "As the twig is bent, so grows the child." Undoubtedly, you've heard that expression many times, but we'd like to give it a new twist in this chapter. As you launch into this material, consider the importance of the early years to the life cycle. Do they shape the destiny of the person? We would like you to consider other related issues, as well. For example, some researchers feel that locked within an infant's mind and body are the genetic blueprints that will dictate the course of all future growth and development. Others maintain that it is the environment that brings out a person's unique characteristics and qualities. Still others say that it is a mixture of these two forces. What do you think? This chapter will help you in your search for answers.

■ Observe any playground filled with children and you'll see a mixture of individual differences. Some children are playing actively, some competitively, and others remain on the sidelines with little apparent interest or enthusiasm. Various forms of behavioral expressions will also become obvious: Some children are emotional, some withdrawn or shy, and others aggressive. What creates such vast individual differences? What is it that determines what children will learn and how they will behave? Will early childhood behaviors such as these persist throughout the life cycle? This chapter will give you food for thought as we explore the major theories of human development.

INTRODUCTION

Development is a lifelong process. In human development, we assume that changes in behavior are not random or accidental. We believe that all behavioral change can be understood in terms of developmental principles. While we all develop in similar ways, we also develop in uniquely individual ways. We need to understand what principles are involved that produce similarity and what factors produce individuality (Baltes and Reese, 1984).

Though psychology is a young science and developmental psychology is even younger, we are discovering new facts at an amazing rate. Indeed, it is becoming difficult to organize and integrate new data with already existing data. But this is true in any science when observations and experiments are made and data are continually collected. We call collected data *facts;* a *fact* is simply a statement of an observation.

Facts are extremely important to any scientist. They have been called the building blocks of a science; however, just as a pile of bricks does not make a house, a pile of facts does not constitute a science. A pile of facts is useless without a structure. The structure that we build in human development is called a *theory*. A theory is really a perspective, one of several ways that we can view development. A developmental theory not only attempts to describe and explain changes in behavior as we age but attempts to show individual differences in these changes, for example, differences between males and females, blacks and hispanics, and so on (Baltes, Reese, and Nesselroade, 1977). In other words, a developmental theory should be able to describe and explain the course of your cognitive development in general as well as specifically (Italo-American, middle class, and female for example). A good theory will also explain why your best friend is changing but in a different way than you are.

There are a wide variety of theories, many of them no more than speculative. The better theories are generally those supported by the most research or empirical evidence. But we must note that theories, like boxers, are always contenders but often get knocked right out of the ring. Theories, like people, do not always remain constant. The most speculative, weakest theories need considerably more research to support them. They are sometimes based on preconceptions. In speaking on the inherent dangers in preconceptions, Deese (1972, pp. 84–85) warns,

> The trouble with theoretical preconceptions in developmental studies is the assumption that a point of view is correct simply because it makes a sensible story. This is the problem of myth versus science. Even some highly developed and rigorous theories of developmental psychology require more data than they explain. A given theory may make a good story about how things got to be the way they are, but if it has little empirical content, it does not provide a plausible basis for action.

Theories are constructed with whatever knowledge is available at any given time. They are never complete and thus are always open to challenge. They must be dynamic—open to change and able to accommodate new facts discovered by research scientists.

■ Three Major Influences That Affect Development

Why do we develop? Where does development originate? Why do we change? These are seemingly simple questions but they are difficult to answer because development is very complex, involving many variables. We can seldom say factor *a* causes factor *b*. For each of us, there are multiple interacting factors that produce any given behavior (Baltes, 1979). Some developmentalists believe that there are three major sets of factors that influence individual development: normative age-graded, normative history-graded, and nonnormative life events (Baltes, Cornelius, and Nesselroade, 1979). See Figure 2-1 for a model of this concept.

Normative age-graded influences are those determinants that are closely related to one's age and therefore rather predictable since they are similar for most of us. The onset of speech, walking, and puberty are obvious examples. These have a basis of biological maturation and, of course, there is interaction with the environment. Also included among age-graded factors are socialization processes, such as entering school, starting a career, or retiring from the workplace. These are sometimes referred to as developmental influences because, as mentioned previously, their occurrence correlates highly with chronological age.

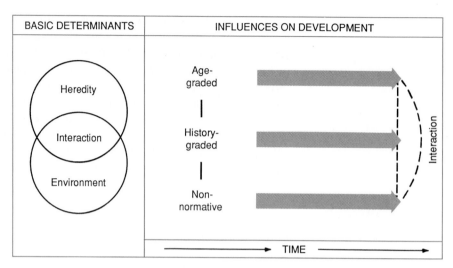

BASIC DETERMINANTS	INFLUENCES ON DEVELOPMENT

FIGURE 2-1 The interaction of three systems of influences regulates the nature of lifespan development: ontogenetic (age-graded), evolutionary (history-graded), and nonnormative. Further explanation of the figure is contained in Baltes, Cornelius, and Nesselroade (1979) and Baltes and Willis (1978). (Modified from Baltes et al., 1979)

Normative history-graded influences also have biological and environmental determinants but they involve cultural history. In Chapter 1 we referred to cohort studies and discussed how people of the same age share similar environmental influences such as living during a war or an economic depression. These are examples of an individual's history-graded influences.

Nonnormative influences on development refer to environmental and biological determinants that, while significant, are unpredictable: They do not affect everyone and they do not occur at a particular age. Nonnormative influences include unemployment, sudden wealth, a birth defect, disease, or death of a loved one.

These three sets of influences interact and appear to wax and wane at different times in an individual's life. Age-graded biological factors appear to dominate development from conception through childhood and puberty, but wane until they reemerge in old age, when they are less influential. As the role of the environment increases, the history-graded influences become more common and powerful determinants. Nonnormative influences, being less predictable, may become determinants at any given time.

■ Theoretical Issues

Before introducing the major theories of human development, we must look at some of the issues and philosophical viewpoints that underpin these theories.

☐ The Interaction of Heredity and Environment

A major problem, not only in psychology but also in education, politics, and all other forms of human endeavor, is the relative role of one's genetic or inherited endowment in respect to the relative importance of the nurturing environment. This is known among psychologists as the *nature-nurture controversy*. For example, is intellectual potential inherited? Can IQs be changed by environmental variations? Does one inherit tendencies or predispositions toward certain behavioral characteristics? These and dozens of other questions of equal difficulty have plagued scientists for years, with many camps developing in the process. Currently, psychologists who are *hereditarians* believe that most behavior is dependent on genetic endowment. The opposite group, the *environmentalists,* assert that environment is the major contributor to an individual's behavior. Unfortunately, there are few definitive answers to the issue of heredity versus environment, thus it is probably a futile debate. To most psychologists today, the critical issue is how these two forces *interact* to affect development; these people are known as *interactionists* (Plomin, 1989).

☐ Epigenetics

Hereditarians and some interactionists also subscribe to the *epigenetic principle;* the theory of epigenesis holds that genetic programming significantly influences development. Thus, those who accept the theory believe that a significant amount of human development is controlled by our inherited genetic structure, a set of blueprints or directions that all humans possess. However, we must not play down the role of experience, for epigenetics recognizes the constant interplay of genetic and environmental factors as contributors to development. This view is closely related to the discontinuous, or age-stage theory, which holds that as we reach each higher level, new characteristics emerge. Just as a house starts with the foundation and is built upward, so humans sit up before they creep, creep before they walk, and walk before they run. To give another example, in adolescence there is a specific sequence of physical development. For example, in girls, breast buds appear early, followed by pubic hair growth, vaginal development, and menarche. Freud's and Erikson's theories of personality development and Piaget's theory of cognitive development are also based on the epigenetic principle. See Chapter 3 for a more thorough discussion of genetics, heredity, and environment.

The manner in which heredity and environment shape the course of development has sparked considerable debate.

☐ Growth, Maturation, and Learning

Growth refers to an actual biological or quantitative increase in size, such as the enlargement of the body or any of its component parts by an increase in the number of cells. An infant who is 20 inches long at birth and later measures 30 inches has *grown* 10 inches. Increases in head size, heart size, arm and leg length, weight, and so on, are generally referred to as results of the growth process (as distinguished from maturation or learning).

One major difference between growth and maturation is the greater possibility of environmental effects on growth; for example, if you eat more, you may gain more weight. *Maturation,* like growth, is also most easily understood as a biological change. But, whereas growth refers to an increase in the number of cells, *maturation* refers to the development of the cells to the point that they can be fully utilized by the organism. Maturation involves genetically controlled alterations that bring the cell to a point of ripeness, or *readiness.*

To demonstrate the relationship between maturation and learning, a definition of learning is needed. *Learning* is generally defined as a relatively permanent change in behavior as the result of experience (learning does not include behavioral changes from injury, drugs, fatigue, or maturation). Learning is dependent upon maturation, for learning cannot take place until appropriate maturation has occurred. For example, the ability to learn abstract concepts cannot occur until both the growth and maturation of the cortical cells in the brain that are used for abstract thinking have reached a state of readiness; until that happens, we cannot learn certain concepts of mathematics, operate at higher levels of morality, or understand metaphors.

☐ Development and Sensitive Periods

Not only is there increasing evidence that organisms are especially sensitive to certain external stimuli, there is also evidence that some minimal sensory stimulation is needed during a specific time period if the organism is to develop normally. A *critical* (or sensitive) *period* is a specific period of time when an environmental event will have its greatest impact on the developing organism. For example, in humans there seems to

Early attachment seems to affect later behaviors, including affection.

be a *critical period* between 6 and 16 months, when the infant will attach itself to the primary caretaker. Prior to six months, babies may be handled by one and all, but it is during the critical period that attachment appears to develop. We will later see that those infants who, for one reason or another, are not left long in the care of one person may have difficulties in experiencing and expressing warm human relations.

Other sensitive periods seem to be between 18 months and 3 years (development of cognitive abilities and early socialization patterns), 3 and 6 years (learning appropriate modes of behavior), and 6 and 10 years (further development of cognitive abilities, greater socialization, and increasing maturity) (Kagan, 1966).

☐ Continuous and Discontinuous Human Development

Are changes in behavior gradual and continuous or sudden and discrete? Or, are they both? Continuous processes of change seem more evident in such phases of development as socialization and emotion because, evidence indicates, those phases are gradually learned through interaction with the environment. On the other hand, discontinuous developmental theories (frequently called *age-stage* theories) assert that certain developmental trends are based on internal biological states that allow for distinct spurts in growth and development.

Discontinuous development theory emphasizes stages of development, the assumption being that before one stage or step can occur, the person must emerge from a previous stage. According to this theory, stages of development are sequential, each stage is associated with a specific age group, and no stage is skipped. *Stages* refer to periods of characteristically distinct psychological functioning. Examples of discontinuous, age-stage theories are psychoanalytic (Freudian) and cognitive-developmental (Piagetian) theories, which presume progression through successive stages, each of which represents a transformation of the previous stage and prepares the way for the next one.

A *continuous development theory* stresses a slow, methodical change, or gradation, which is less related to age. The concept of distinct change gives way to the one-stage model of growth with its emphasis on subtle changes in the maturation process. (See Figure 2-2 for a diagrammatic comparison of continuous and discontinuous theories.)

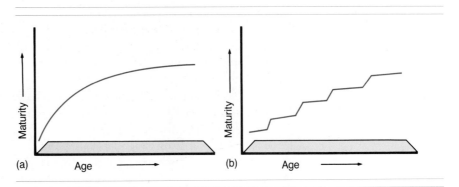

FIGURE 2-2 Graph *a* illustrates the continuous theory of development. Here we see a gradual increase in maturity during childhood and adolescence.
Graph *b* represents the *discontinuous* developmental theories (such as proposed by Freud and Piaget). Here we can see how "stages" of maturation exist at certain age levels.

☐ Active and Reactive Theories of Development

Human development theorists often view people as either active or reactive in relationship to their environment. Environmentalists, for example, believe that environmental forces shape human behavior, much as rocks, sand, water, wind, and waves shape a piece of driftwood. Driftwood exposed to a harsh and rugged environment has a splintered and jagged appearance, while driftwood softly molded and shaped over time by sands and calm oceans has a much smoother surface.

Behaviorism exemplifies a *reactive theory* because it holds that the environment is critical in the overall development of the individual. Theorists such as Skinner maintain that behavior is conditioned by forces (e.g., reinforcement) from the environment. The example of the driftwood exposed to any elements symbolizes this position.

An *active theory*, on the other hand, suggests that individuals are not passive, but capable (motive power) of actively governing and regulating their development. Imagine, for example, that our piece of driftwood has acquired a sail or motor that will allow it to escape hostile elements. Under these conditions, the organism can chart its own path in a self-directed way. The latter theory stresses one's intellectual ability to seek from the environment that which arouses one's interest. We select the environments suitable to meet our rational needs. Throughout this and future chapters, we examine these issues in greater detail.

■ Theories of Human Development

☐ Psychoanalytic Theory

The *psychoanalytic theory* was founded by Sigmund Freud. Freud, like so many others of his day, came to psychology via other routes. While practicing medicine in clinics, he became interested in neurophysiology, especially the functions of the brain. He spent considerable time seeking to understand abnormal brain functions and mental disorders, a pursuit that would eventually lead him to the field of psychology.

Although many of his views are controversial, quite a few psychologists have been influenced by at least one of his ideas on human development. He devised a theory of personality (with the underlying dynamics of the id, ego, and superego) that has applications to the behavior of both child and adult. He also proposed the theory of psychosexual stages of development, an explanation of behavior that places great importance on the development and maturation of body parts and on early life experiences. One's past, he felt, plays an important role in determining one's present behavior. Furthermore, Freud's analysis of defense mechanisms has helped to explain how defensive behavior originates.

Freud perceived human beings' essential psychological nature as based on *desire* rather than on *reason.* His focus in psychoanalysis was primarily upon human passions or emotions and only secondarily upon rational abilities or intellect. According to Freud the child is born with basic animal instincts that operate at the unconscious level of thought. These instincts, or irrational needs, require immediate gratification. Development, therefore, is partially dependent upon the transformation of the so-called animal desires into socially acceptable, rational behavior.

Freud's influence can be seen in the research of other psychologists, including that of his daughter Anna Freud, who was one of the early investigators of child's play. He also stimulated the works of a number of neo-Freudians, particularly Erik Erikson, who

Sigmund Freud.
Birthplace: *Frieberg, Moravia.*
Born: *1856.* Died: *1939.*
Education: *M.D., University of Vienna (1881).*
Important Works: *Beyond the Pleasure Principle* (1920), *The Ego and the Id* (1924), *Introductory Lectures on Psychoanalysis* (1933).

devised a theory of personality that stresses psychosocial stages of development. We look at Erikson's theory later in this chapter.

Sigmund Freud developed a theory of how neuroses develop. This theory, in conjunction with his explanation of personality, describes the developmental stages through which a child must pass prior to reaching adulthood and normal maturity. His developmental explanation, referred to as *psychosexual stages* of development, originated not from his direct study of children but from the extraction of information from adult neurotics, initially through hypnosis and later through the cathartic process termed *free association*. The only child Freud ever saw as a patient was Little Hans, and he was seen only once (the remainder of his analysis was conducted via correspondence with Hans's father). Freud's method of study raises serious questions about how much faith to place in the childhood events postulated in his theory. Patients may be unable to recollect events that took place years ago, and, even if they can, their experiences may have no correlation with the experiences of more normal children. Nonetheless, his work stands as an important hallmark in the development of personality.

FREUD'S THEORY OF PERSONALITY

Three Levels of Consciousness

One of Freud's major beliefs was that individuals are generally not aware of the underlying reasons for their behavior. He assumed that mental activity must occur at three levels of consciousness. He called the first level the *conscious.* Freud used this term to refer to what a person is thinking or experiencing at any given moment. Immediate awareness of one's surroundings are very fleeting: Our conscious thoughts flow as water in a stream, hence, this phenomenon is sometimes called our *stream of consciousness.*

The second level of consciousness is called the *preconscious* and refers to all of a person's stored knowledge and memories that are capable of being brought up to the conscious level. For example, if we ask you what your home telephone number is, you are capable of retrieving it from your preconscious even though you were probably not thinking of your telephone number as you were reading this sentence.

The third and largest level of consciousness is the *unconscious,* a vast area of irrational wishes, shameful urges, socially unacceptable sexual desires, fears, and aggressive feelings, as well as anxiety-producing thoughts that have been *repressed* (pushed down to the unconscious to be forgotten). Because these feelings are very threatening to us, we keep them locked up in the unconscious. When we dream, these feelings and urges are sometimes released, but generally in a distorted way so that we will not recognize them. However, these beliefs, urges, desires, and so forth are all motivators of behavior and influence us in some unconscious way.

Personality Components: Id, Ego, and Superego

According to Freud, the *id* is the original inherited system, the instinctive aspect of the personality triumvirate. The id contains the basic motivational drives for our physiologic needs such as food, water, sex, and warmth. All emotions are housed within the id and add a further dimension to what Freud described as "unconscious motivational forces."

The id contains the driving life force of an organism. One such dynamic force is the *libido,* which supplies *libidinal energy.* (Libido means lust or desire in Latin.) When this energy builds up, there is an increase in *tension* and unhappiness, which must be released by the organism. When the *tension level* is lowered, feelings of contentment and pleasure arise. The id also operates on the **hedonistic principle** (pleasure principle), which is, in many respects, an extension of homeostasis (the tendency of the body to maintain internal equilibrium). This hedonistic drive pushes the organism to seek that which produces a pleasurable state and to avoid that which causes any discomfiture. The id's forces, operating at the unconscious level, drive the organism toward instant gratification of its primary or biological needs. Freud also writes of a *tension level.* Without tension we have no motivation, but as a biological need arises, it increases the tension level, and the higher this level, the greater our motivation to satisfy this emerging need.

Freud believed that an infant operates solely at the id level for the first eight months of life until the ego commences its slow and gradual development. Until this time, the id is in total control of the child's behavior. Thus, when the internal tension level increases because of hunger pangs, soiled or wet diapers, gas bubbles, or other tension-producing stimuli, the infant will cry until the tension level is changed to an acceptable or pleasurable state.

The *ego* is the organism's contact with the external environment. Its purpose is to satisfy the desires or demands of the id and, later, the superego. As the ego develops, it learns to operate on the **reality principle;** that is, it learns to choose attainable goals before discharging tension or energy, which makes for a more efficient ego. However, Freud viewed the ego as a servant of the id, not as a separate or sovereign entity. According to Freud, the ego exists to further the aims of the id. Over a long time, socially acceptable behavior may prove to be more beneficial to the organism than behavior that produces instant gratification. However, until the former type of behavior is learned, infants, toddlers, or preschoolers operate at a "gimme, gimme, gimme" level, wanting everything for themselves immediately and exhibiting little tolerance for more acceptable behavior. Ego maturity is, in part, the process of restraining the id's demands until they can be met according to the mores, folkways, and values of one's culture.

The third component of the Freudian personality system is the *superego,* which appears when the child is approximately five years old. It operates on what might be called the *perfection principle.* The superego consists of the internalization of the morals taught by one's religion, society, and family. The superego is similar to the id in that it makes largely unconscious demands on the ego. However, the superego also resembles the ego by virtue of its intent to exercise control over the id's urges. The child who steals without compunction because it is allowable according to his or her principles will suffer no emotional consequences for such an act or, at best, might intellectualize the possibilities of getting caught. The child whose values say theft is improper behavior and whose superego is sufficiently developed to operate on such a principle will be bothered by the *conscience* and will most likely experience emotions such as guilt or remorse. The opposite set of emotions originates from the *ego ideal,* the portion of the superego that makes one feel good for having behaved according to one's internalized principles.

Behavior, then, can be defined as *the result of the interaction of these three personality components* and their relationship to the outer world, each one seeking to attain a form of psychological satisfaction by directly influencing behavior (see Figure 2-3). Thus, when the id signals the ego that the body is in need of fluids, the ego, evaluating reality, attempts to choose an appropriate form of behavior to satisfy the id. This would be accomplished by conforming to acceptable social behaviors (such as not drinking from a puddle) and by adhering to standards within the superego (not stealing soda water).

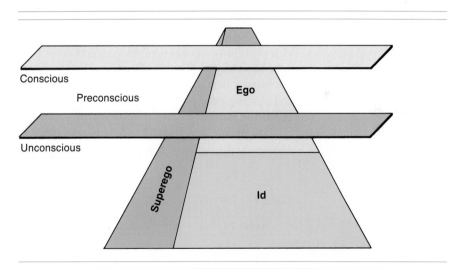

FIGURE 2-3   The relationship of the id, ego, and superego to levels of awareness.

The Ego and Defense Mechanisms

Freud believed that sex and aggression are two basic instinctive drives of the id. These drives cause no conflict in most of the animal kingdom, but in humans, they are often diametrically opposed to cultural values. The satisfaction of these basic drives leads to a struggle between the id, ego, and superego as to what behavior should be adopted. In the course of this struggle, the individual often becomes highly anxious, which produces an increase in the person's tension level. The ego must alleviate this tension;

if it can not be accomplished by consciously coping (that is, finding a satisfactory solution), unconscious ego forces take over. These protective devices are called *defense mechanisms*—the unconscious means used by the ego to reduce conflict and tension. Many people believe the explanation of ego defense mechanisms to be among Freud's major contributions to psychology.

Probably the foremost defense mechanism described by Freud is *repression*. Here, tension- or anxiety-producing thoughts and experiences are forced to the unconscious level. Mild repression, such as conveniently forgetting your dental appointment, may help lower your anxiety level for a while. However, when anxiety-producing thoughts and experiences are repressed, but continue to operate at the unconscious level, more serious behavior disorders may develop. Other defense mechanisms such as rationalization, projection, and regression are discussed in Chapter 7.

FREUD'S PSYCHOSEXUAL THEORY

Freud identified five stages of psychosexual development. During the *oral stage* (ages 0 to 1½), the mouth is the primary source of pleasure. Enjoyment is derived from being fed or from sucking on a pacifier or one's thumb. Freud maintained that either the overgratification or undergratification of this need—and of others to follow—may lead to, what he labeled, a *fixation*. A fixation is a preoccupation with one particular aspect of psychosexual development (e.g., thumb sucking) that may interfere with or manifest itself in subsequent psychosexual stages. Thus, the child fixated at the oral stage, perhaps deprived of thumb sucking, may seek to fulfill this need later in life. Such behaviors as smoking, gum chewing, or nail biting may be the individual's way of gratifying the previously deprived oral need.

During the *anal stage* (ages 1½ to 3), the anus and the buttocks become the source of sensual pleasure. Satisfaction is derived from expelling or withholding feces, but external conflicts are encountered when toilet training begins. Freud maintains that the manner in which parents conduct toilet training, particularly the use of rewards and punishments, may have consequences for the development of later personality traits.

The *phallic stage* (ages 3 to 5) is characterized by interest in the genital organs. Pleasure is derived from manipulating one's genitals and curiosity is directed toward

TABLE 2-1   Freud's Psychosexual Stages of Development

Stage	Age	Psychosexual Developments
Oral	0–1½	Pleasure such as eating, sucking, and vocalizing derived from oral cavity.
Anal	1½–3	Pleasure derived from anal area, including retention and expulsion of feces. External conflicts may result when toilet training begins.
Phallic	3–5	Pleasure derived from manipulation of genital organs. Curiosity directed toward sexuality of self and others. Emergence of Oedipus and Electra complexes for males and females, respectively.
Latency period	6–11	Tranquil period of time between stages. Refinement of self-concept and increased peer group interaction. Emergence of coping or defense mechanisms.
Genital	Adolescence	Onset of puberty and discovery of new sexual feelings. Development of heterosexual attraction. Beginning of romantic love.

the anatomical differences between the sexes. Children also have a tendency to develop romantic feelings toward parents of the opposite sex. The attraction of boys to their mothers is called the *Oedipus complex* and the romantic feelings of girls toward their fathers is labeled the *Electra complex.*

The *latency period* (ages 6 to 11) represents a rather tranquil period compared to the psychosexual turbulence of previous stages. However, there is an increased awareness of personal identity, surroundings, and the importance of social interaction. The latency period is also a time of ego refinement, for the child seeks to develop those character traits deemed socially acceptable. Coping or defense mechanisms begin to develop as children attempt to avoid failure or rejection in the face of life's growing expectations and demands.

Freud's final psychosexual period is called the *genital stage* (the adolescent years). This stage chronicles the simultaneous reemergence of the first three stages, as puberty introduces a time of biological upheaval. During this time, adolescents become interested in members of the opposite sex. Individuals may encounter their first experience with romantic love, although immature emotional interactions permeate the early phases of this stage. In time, however, people realize that they are capable of giving and receiving mature love.

ERIKSON'S PSYCHOSOCIAL THEORY

Erik H. Erikson is one of the world's foremost psychoanalytic scholars. His fascinating early life included crafting large woodcuts, especially of children, and teaching art in Vienna, where he received a Montessori teaching certificate. He also studied with Anna Freud. Finally, he combined these interests and published articles on the application of psychoanalytic theory to educational issues. He later studied children's play and child-rearing practices and observed growth and developmental processes of the ego.

Of his many books, *Childhood and Society* (1963) is probably the best known, for in it Erikson first presented and summed up his major theory. This theory converts the

Erik Homburger Erikson.
Birthplace: *Frankfurt, Germany.*
Born: *1902*
Important Works: *Childhood and Society* (1963), *Identity, Youth and Crisis* (1968), *Identity and the Life Cycle* (1980), *The Life Cycle Completed* (1982).

psychosexual theory of Freud to one of *psychosocial* stages of ego development. Erikson contends that the process of socializing the child into a given culture occurs as the person passes through eight innately determined, sequential stages he calls *psychosocial development.* Like Sigmund and Anna Freud, Erikson is concerned with ego development. However, while recognizing the individual's instinctual drives and interest in different parts of the body in a prescribed sequence, Erikson emphasizes the child's interactions with the environment. Thus, he views the ego, not the id, as the major driving force of behavior. Erikson also differs in that he studied healthy personalities (rather than neurotic people, such as Freud analyzed) to arrive at his theory.

Erikson also disagrees with Freud's emphasis on infantile sexuality. Owing to his anthropological training, Erikson perceives the child's behavior as resulting from societal influences. His comprehensive theory of development encompasses the years from infancy through old age. For Erikson, the course of development is reversible, meaning that the events of later childhood can undo—for better or worse—personality foundations built earlier in life. For Freud, basic personality structure is essentially fixed by the age of five. However, for both theorists, stages are related to ages in the sense that age leads to movement to a new stage, regardless of experience and regardless of reorganizations at previous stages.

Essential to Erikson's theory is the development of the ego and the ego's ability to deal with *a series of crises* or potential crises throughout the individual's lifespan. Each stage of life has a crisis that is related in some way to an element in society. The development of personality begins with ego strengths that commence at birth; as the years pass, ego strength is accrued, one quality at a time. Each quality undergoes rapid growth at a critical period of development.

The first of Erikson's eight psychosocial crises (see Table 2-2) is called *basic trust versus basic mistrust* (ages 0 to 1). During this stage, the nature of parental interactions with the infant is critical. If infants are recipients of proper care, love, and affection, they develop a sense of trust. If these basic needs are not met, they become suspicious, fearful, and mistrusting of their surroundings.

During *autonomy versus doubt* (ages 1 to 3), developing motor and mental abilities gives the child the opportunity to experience independence. If this growing urge to explore the world is encouraged, children grow more confident in themselves and more autonomous in general. However, if their developing independence is met with parental disapproval or discouragement, children may question their own abilities and harbor doubts about their own adequacy.

During the third stage, children experience the psychosocial crisis known as *initiative versus guilt* (ages 3 to 5). Increasingly refined developmental capacities prompt

TABLE 2-2 Erikson's Stages/Crises of Psychosocial Development

Stage/Crisis	Age	Human Relationships Involved	Desired Outcome of Crisis
Trust vs. mistrust	0–1	Parents/caretaker	Hope
Autonomy vs. doubt	1–3	Parents/caretaker	Will
Initiative vs. guilt	3–5	Family	Purpose
Industry vs. inferiority	6–11	Neighborhood/school	Competence
Identity vs. role confusion	Adolescence	Peer groups	Fidelity
Intimacy vs. isolation	Young adulthood	Friends/spouse	Love
Generativity vs. self-absorption	Middle adulthood	Family interactions/job acquaintances	Care
Integrity vs. despair	Old age	All people	Wisdom

the child to self-initiate environmental exploration and discovery. Parental reinforcement will encourage such initiative and promote purpose- and goal-directiveness. Parental restrictiveness, on the other hand, is likely to promote guilt whenever children seek to discover the world on their own.

Industry versus inferiority (ages 6 to 11) is characterized by the child's desire to manipulate objects and learn how things work. Such an industrious attitude typically leads to a sense of order, a system of rules, and an important understanding about the nature of one's surroundings. Inferiority may result, however, if adults perceive such behavior as silly, mischievous, or troublesome.

The fifth psychosocial crisis, perhaps Erikson's most famous concept, is *identity versus role confusion* (adolescence). The task is to develop an integrated sense of self, one that is personally acceptable and, it is hoped, distinct from others. Failure to nurture an accurate sense of personal identity may lead to the dilemma of role confusion. This frequently leads to feelings of inadequacy, isolation, and indecisiveness.

The task of *intimacy versus isolation* (young adulthood), stage six, is to develop close and meaningful relationships with others. Having attained a sense of personal identity in the previous stage, individuals are now able to share themselves with others on a moral, emotional, and sexual level. For many, intimacy means marriage; for others, it implies the establishment of warm and nurturant friendships (not that the former cannot encompass the latter). Those unable or unwilling to share themselves with others suffer a sense of loneliness or isolation.

Erikson's seventh stage is called *generativity versus self-absorption* (middle adulthood). The positive pole of this stage, generativity, means that adults are willing to look beyond themselves and to express concern about the future of the world in general. A caring attitude, for example, is directed toward the betterment of society and future generations. The self-absorbed person tends to be preoccupied with personal well-being and material gain.

The final stage is *integrity versus despair* (old age). Those persons nurturing a sense of integrity have typically resolved previous psychosocial crises and are able to look back at their lives with dignity, satisfaction, and personal fulfillment. The unsuccessful resolution of previous crises is likely to produce a sense of despair. For these individuals, past lives are usually viewed as a series of disappointments, failures, and misfortunes.

From this brief account of psychoanalytic theory, we can see that both Freud and Erikson are interactionists. First, they describe basic biological (heredity) drives. Both theories have an epigenetic basis; they believe that development is predetermined by genetic principles and proceeds along a discontinuous or age-stage pathway. They both recognize the importance of environment. For example, Freud states that psychosexual fixations occur when the biological needs are not met through interaction with the environment. (How does Mom or Dad toilet train the child?) Erikson expresses environmental importance when he discusses the organism's transition through a psychosocial crisis. (Does the infant receive enough care and trust from the environment?)

A CRITIQUE OF PSYCHOANALYSIS

American psychology has placed heavy emphasis on empirical evidence to support a theory. Unfortunately, psychoanalytic theory does not lend itself to such experimentation and thus is not as popular as it once was. Objective data is rarely found, therefore much support of this theory is subjective. While it is practically impossible to test and measure the unconscious forces that Freud describes, many still recognize its presence. Freud is also criticized for overemphasizing childhood sexuality and the correct way to interpret dreams.

On the positive side, his theory has influenced thinking and research in developmental psychology. For example, his concepts of identification and sex typing (discussed in more detail later in this text) have produced much research activity.

Erikson's theory has increased the credibility of psychoanalysis. By extending the psychosexual with the psychosocial and adding the cultural to the biological, as well as ego strengths and identities to ego defense systems, he has broadened the psychoanalytic framework. His ideas appear to be much more acceptable than those of many of his cohorts who also wrote in the psychoanalytic tradition.

Although Erikson's writings are interesting, he has been criticized for his loose connections of case studies and conclusions. His theory, like Freud's, is difficult to support with empirical evidence.

□ Cognitive-Developmental Theory

Our understanding of the cognitive developments in childhood has been considerably enhanced through the efforts of Swiss psychologist Jean Piaget. His theory of conceptual development is unique and one of the most comprehensive to date. Although his work was not widely recognized by the psychology community in the United States until the 1950s, Piaget has been regarded as a leading authority in the field of *cognitive-developmental theory.*

While often referred to as a child psychologist, Piaget characterized himself as a *genetic epistemologist* (genetic means beginning; epistemology is the study of knowledge). Piaget asked how knowledge develops in the human organism. To answer this question, he studied children and their mental processes. To Piaget, the term *cognition*

Jean Piaget.
Birthplace: *Neuchâtel, Switzerland.*
Born: *1896.* Died: *1980.*
Education: *Ph.D, University of Neuchâtel (1917).*
Important Works: *The Origins of Intelligence in Children* (1952), *The Language and Thought of the Child* (1952), *The Psychology of the Child* (1969).

was synonymous with intelligence, and he considered cognition to be a biological process, just as biologists consider digestion to be a biological process. We might say that Piaget studied the "biology of thinking."

Piaget was not so much interested in what kinds of knowledge we learn as he was in how the thinking brain functions to process or biologically digest the incoming information. His is an age-stage, or discontinuous, theory of development that stresses the action of the mind on the environment. He viewed humans as being self-generated and essentially rational and intellectual.

For example, Piaget had observed that different age levels yield different levels of comprehension and reasoning. A 3-year-old, for example, has rudimentary reasoning skills but can solve problems that escaped him or her at two. Similarly, a 4-year-old may be able to deal with some concepts unsolved a year before yet be unable to keep pace with the thinking of a 7-year-old. All of this led Piaget to believe that intellectual development proceeds in an orderly sequence that is characterized by specific growth stages. He postulated that these growth stages enable the child to develop certain concepts necessary for intellectual maturity. Consequently, Piaget believed conceptual development to be a building process, a series of qualitative intellectual advancements that can transport the child from a world of fantasy into a world of reality.

His explanation of this systematic process, the most important theme in all his writings, has provided fields such as psychology and education with a detailed and methodical analysis of cognitive development. In it, people, especially children, are viewed as developing organisms acquiring conceptual awareness as they pass through five orderly and progressive stages. At the base of these stages is an explanation of how people interpret and store the vast amounts of stimuli to which they are exposed. These concepts now require our examination.

ELEMENTS OF COGNITIVE ACTIVITY

The design for mental growth, as proposed by Piaget, hinges on two important principles: *organization* and *adaptation*. Both will sustain an orderly, structured development of conceptual awareness and understanding.

Organization is the ability to order and classify in the mind new experiences, termed *schemata;* it is a fundamental and innate process in all children. As the infant is exposed to new stimuli, the mind is able to construct a mental organization that is capable of categorizing and integrating these schematic elements into regular systems. Sensory stimuli—objects and events—are just two examples of schematic organization. This type of classification system constitutes the beginning of intellectual activity.

Adaptation cannot take place unless there is a schema. Successful adaptation will give the individual a meaningful understanding of the surrounding environment. Adaptation depends on the mental processes Piaget labels as *assimilation* and *accommodation.*

Assimilation is the more primitive of the two conceptual organizations. Through assimilation, the child will perceive and interpret new information in terms of existing knowledge and understanding. Put another way, children attempt to explain new phenomena by referring to their current frame of reference. Assimilation is conservative in that its primary function is to make the unfamiliar, familiar, to reduce the new to the old. A child who has been exposed only to cars, for example, may call a truck or a bus a car, simply because this is the only vehicle name that is stored in the child's existing mental organization. Along the same lines, a young child, after learning what a horse is, may see a cow and also call it a horse. In learning theory, this is called *stimulus generalization:* responding to similar stimuli as though they were the same.

Accommodation, on the other hand, is the more advanced form of adaptation. Accommodation refers to the restructuring of mental organization in order that new information may be included. Whereas the process of assimilation molds the object or event to fit within the person's existing frame of reference, accommodation changes the mental structure so that new experiences may be added. Thus, if an incident takes place that does not correspond with an existing mental framework, individuals may revise their way of thinking in order to interpret that event. The child who effectively used accommodation skills in the previous example will develop a new mental structure to categorize a truck after it is realized that trucks cannot be put in the category of cars, or that cows belong in a category separate from horses. In learning theory, this is called *stimulus discrimination,* defined as the ability to distinguish between different but similar stimuli.

The development of thinking, therefore, relies on *changes* made in the mental structure of the child. The balance between assimilation and accommodation, called *equilibration,* is the key; the ability to change old ways of thinking in order to solve new problems is the true yardstick for measuring intellectual growth.

PIAGET'S COGNITIVE-DEVELOPMENTAL STAGES

The first stage of cognitive development proposed by Piaget (Table 2-3) is labeled *sensorimotor development* (ages 0 to 2). During this early phase of development, the infant exercises rudimentary sensory and motor awareness and functions almost exclusively by means of reflexive responses. In the beginning, limited cognitive activity takes place and little distinction is made between the self and the environment. By the end of the first year, however, meaningful interactions with one's surroundings have begun. For example, by the end of this period the infant may shake or strike a crib mobile if its movement proves to be interesting; and when objects disappear from sight, the infant knows that, instead of disappearing totally "out of sight, out of mind," they remain permanent in reality.

During *preoperational thought* (ages 2 to 7), the child demonstrates an increase in language abilities, and concepts become more elaborate. Children are largely *egocentric* (self-centered) and view the world from their own perspective. Developing imagination abilities frequently promotes a type of thinking called *animism,* the tendency to give life to inanimate objects. Thus, a tree may be treated the same as a large animal or

TABLE 2-3 Piaget's Stages of Cognitive Development

Stage	Age	Significant Cognitive Developments
Sensorimotor development	0–2	Engagement in primitive reflex activity. Gradual increase in sensory and motor awareness. Little distinction made between the self and the environment, although meaningful interactions with surroundings and the establishment of object permanence characterize later phases of this stage.
Preoperational thought	2–7	Increase in language and concept development. Child is largely egocentric. Animism is prevalent in thinking. Employment of mental images to represent the world is increasingly evident by the end of this stage; increased perceptual sensitivity, although discrimination is based on obvious physical appearances. Failure to understand the law of conservation. In general, thinking is intuitive in nature and frequently impulsive.
Concrete operations	7–11	Can understand the law of conservation and reverse mental operations. Objects can be classified and ordered in a series along a dimension (such as size), and relational concepts (A is larger than B) are understood. Abstract problems remain elusive.
Formal operations	11–15	Abstract thought and scientific reasoning emerge. Problems are approached with advanced logic and reason. Individuals follow logical propositions and reason by hypothesis.

TABLE 2-4   Major Epigenetic Theories: A Summarization Through Adolescence

Freud	Erikson	Piaget
Psychosexual	Psychosocial	Cognitive-developmental
Oral Stage (0–1½) The oral zone is the first erogenous zone to reach neural maturation. Thus, the infant's primary environmental interaction is around mouth.	**Oral-Sensory Stage (0–1)** Oral and sensory maturation interact with environment. Crisis of trust vs. mistrust.	**Sensory-Motor Stage (0–2)** Maturation of sense organs and the sensory and motor areas of the brain precede cognitive functioning.
Anal Stage (1½–3) Anal zone neural maturation precedes awareness of these body functions (bowel and bladder training).	**Muscular-Anal (1–3)** Neurologic maturation precedes environmental interaction and resolution of autonomy vs. doubt crisis.	**Preoperational Stage (2–7)** Areas of the brain (e.g., hearing and speech centers) must mature prior to basic thought processes involving vocabulary, mental imagery, intuitive thought, etc.
Phallic Stage (3–5) Neural maturation surrounding sex organs brings awareness of sex identity. Curiosity about self and others.	**Locomotor-genital (3–5)** Maturation of neurons surrounding sex organs and continued neuromuscular development interact with environment when initiative vs. guilt crisis must be resolved.	
Latency Period (6–11) No major biological changes occurring. Sensory-motor development continues bringing pleasure from knowledge, skills, interpersonal relationships.	**Latency Stage (6–11)** Essentially the same as Freud's description of the latency period with addition of industry vs. inferiority crisis.	**Concrete Operations (7–11)** Continued maturation of cerebral cortex brings cognitive skills to new level. Also allows awareness of other people's viewpoints and improvements in interpersonal relations.
Genital Stage (Adolescence) Biological upheaval (hormonal and neurological) incorporates first three stages. Pleasure from heterosexual relations.	**Puberty & Adolescence** Biological maturation processes unfolding while psychological crisis of Identity vs. role confusion peaks and needs to be resolved.	**Formal Operations (11–13)** Brain maturity allows for scientific reasoning, logic, abstract thinking.

All three theories are based upon the maturation of biological systems before the person can enter a new stage of development.

a fence post might be given the characteristics of a person. By the end of this stage, the world is increasingly represented by the use of mental images.

By the time *concrete operations* (ages 7 to 11) is reached, the law of conservation (see Chapter 7) is understood. The *law of conservation* states that children cannot understand that an object can conserve its amount, weight, or mass when it is poured into a different-sized container, placed into a different position, or molded into a different shape. The ability to consider viewpoints of others, classify objects and order them in a series along a dimension (such as size), and understand relational concepts (A is larger than B) is evident. However, a significant limitation of this stage is the child's inability to solve problems of an abstract nature.

Formal operations (ages 11 to 15), sometimes called *formal thought*, is the final stage of Piaget's theory. Abstract thinking is now possible and scientific problem-solving strategies emerge. When a problem is approached, a hypothesis is drawn and the individual develops several potential solutions. Advanced logic and reason accompany formal operations. Such thinking abilities herald the relinquishment of childhood mental operations and the emergence of mature adult thought.

Piaget, like Freud, has a biological background that shows up in his explanation of cognitive development. He places heavy emphasis on genetics with his age-stage theory based on epigenesis. He is an interactionist, however, in that he accents how the environment provides the food for thought. His theory also places humans in an active (versus passive) role of learning.

A CRITIQUE OF COGNITIVE-DEVELOPMENTAL THEORY

Piaget spent his lifetime modifying and expanding his theory, which was instrumental in changing how psychologists view human development. Once exposed to Piaget's ideas, no one can view child development in quite the same way. While Freud emphasized emotional development, Piaget gave cognition the central role in development and gave developmental psychology a whole new perspective.

Piaget's theory integrates many facts, some of which might first appear unrelated. It also has stimulated a vast amount of research which has generally been supportive of his ideas (see, for example, Beilin, 1989). All this empirical evidence has made his theory more viable, especially since it addresses more areas of behavior (e.g., learning, education, and social development) than probably any other stage theory.

Much of Piaget's research was done on a very small sample of the population—sometimes only on his own three children. For this he has been criticized extensively, even though replication studies have supported his ideas on the concepts but not always on the ages when children reach a given stage (see, for example, Overton, 1989; Lapsley, 1989; Kuhn, 1988). Piaget's theory has also been criticized because he never attempted to show its applicability to everyday life. He has also been faulted for using the interviewing technique. An interviewing style is difficult to duplicate with each and every subject due to individual differences of examiner and examinee. Overall, however, Piaget's dynamic theory can readily be altered if evidence indicates changes are needed.

☐ Behaviorism

More attention has probably been paid to learning theory than to any other psychological process. Psychologists run rats through mazes, put pigeons and rats in Skinner boxes, and devise numerous experiments to measure human learning. While we have learned many facts as a result, there are still many unanswered questions about what actually constitutes learning.

Some psychologists, especially learning theorists, feel very uncomfortable with theories of behavior that propose such abstract concepts as *mental elements* (e.g., ego, conscience, and soul) or *mental functions* (e.g., assimilation, repression, and cognition). Piaget, Freud, Erikson, and others who study mental life often present a somewhat untestable theory. Learning theorists often have misgivings over such mentalistic theory and have attempted to be more objective and scientifically oriented (Bijou, 1989). Stated more bluntly, their credo is, "If you can't measure it, it doesn't exist." The first theorist to proclaim this position was John Broadus Watson, whose theory is known as *behaviorism*.

THE CONTRIBUTIONS OF JOHN B. WATSON

The school of thought known as *behaviorism* emphasizes that learning involves the interaction of the organism with the environment. Behaviorists maintain that it is through interaction with the environment that children learn various types of behaviors: how to get along with others, pass tests, or cope with a variety of everyday situations, to name a few.

Children's behavior as a product of experience (conditioning) was placed into prominence by John B. Watson. As a researcher, Watson was dissatisfied with the field of psychology because it strove to be a science, yet was filled with introspective theorizing rather than with experimental data. In his estimation, psychology as a *science* should deal only with human behavior that can be accurately measured; that which takes place inside an organism (thoughts, feelings, etc.) should be secondary.

THE INFLUENCE OF IVAN PAVLOV

In the early 1900s, Watson read the experiments of Ivan Petrovich Pavlov, a Russian Nobel Prize-winning physiologist, who had won acclaim for a series of experiments now referred to as *classical conditioning.* A specialist on the digestive system, Pavlov was initially interested in the effects of saliva on food.

Using dogs as subjects, Pavlov found that he could stimulate the salivary glands by placing food powder in the dogs' mouths. The amount of saliva was then measured. To Pavlov's surprise, however, the dogs also began to salivate at the sight of their keepers, evidently in anticipation of the food (the stimulus). Motivated to seek an explanation for such responses, Pavlov embarked on a scientific pursuit that would eventually provide the field of psychology with a series of data concerning classical conditioning.

Pavlov introduced a number of scientific terms that contrasted sharply with the vague terms that had been used in the past. He wrote that a reflex reaction was an unlearned response to a natural stimulus. For example, a dog will salivate (reflex) to food (stimulus) placed in its mouth just as an eye will blink (reflex) when a puff of air (stimulus) is directed toward it. Since a reflex is a natural, or unlearned, event Pavlov named the reflex response to a natural stimulus an unconditioned response (he preferred the term conditioning to learning) and the natural stimulus an unlearned, or unconditioned, stimulus. A neutral stimulus is one that does not elicit a response. Thus, we can diagram the relationship as follows:

Unconditioned Stimulus——→Unconditioned Response
(US) (food powder)   (UR) (salivation)

Pavlov discovered that learning, or conditioning, will take place when a neutral stimulus is paired contiguously with the US. For example, when the ringing of a bell (neutral stimulus) was paired with food powder over successive trials, it eventually led to a conditioned response, the dog salivating at the tone of the bell. The model for a typical classical conditioning experiment can be diagrammed as follows:

Before conditioning

bell ———→no response
(NS)

food———→salivation
(US)   (UR)

After conditioning

bell———→salivation
(CS)   (CR)

Conditioning has occurred when the dog responds (CR) to the previously neutral stimulus (bell).

Pavlov also stated that the CR would eventually extinguish itself if reinforcement (US) ceased to be present. (Extinction differs from forgetting, which refers to the elimination of a response due to lack of practice over a period of time).

Spontaneous recovery is an unusual phenomenon that Pavlov discovered sometimes follows extinction. Even though a response has been extinguished through lack of reinforcement, a re-presentation of the CS will suddenly elicit the conditioned response, although no reinforcement may be present.

Stimulus generalization is said to occur when the organism responds to similar stimuli just as it responded to the original stimulus. Thus, a dog will salivate to bells having tones different from those used as the original conditioned stimulus. The more nearly the new stimulus resembles the original conditioned stimulus, the stronger the response will be.

Stimulus discrimination is the ability to distinguish between two similar stimuli that have already produced stimulus generalization. Thus, a dog may be conditioned to salivate to one tone, but not to tones that are slightly higher (or lower).

After reviewing Pavlov's research, Watson hypothesized that the conditioning process might be the answer to understanding all facets of behavior, both normal and neurotic. Watson conducted a Pavlovian conditioning experiment, which led him to conclude that all behavior is the product of environmental learning.

Watson's classic experiment in the field of child psychology was conducted to illustrate how fears may be learned. Albert, an 11-month-old child, was conditioned to fear the presence of a white rat (Figure 2-4). The rat (conditioned stimulus) initially produced no fear in the infant. However, the presence of the rat was accompanied by a loud noise (unconditioned stimulus). The unconditioned stimulus produced a fearful response in Little Albert. After a number of trials in which the two stimuli were paired (CS and US), Albert reacted fearfully (conditioned response) to the sight of the rat alone. Then Albert began to generalize his fear to stimuli similar to the rat. Albert would cry and tremble at the appearance of other white fuzzy objects, such as a rabbit or a man with a white beard. This experiment helps to explain how children's fears—which often appear irrational and ill founded to adults—have a basis in fact (Watson and Rayner, 1920).

Through Watson's efforts, behaviorism began to emerge as a total environmental science. He may best be remembered for a statement that he wrote in his *Psychological*

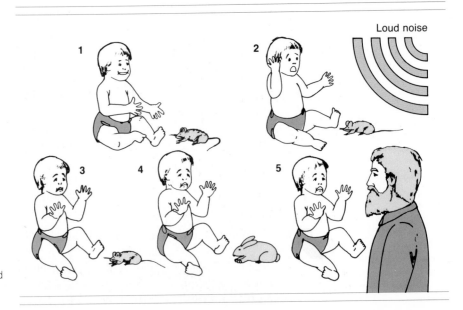

FIGURE 2-4

The generalization of fear, as displayed in Watson and Rayner's (1920) classic experiment.

Care of Infant and Child, a child-rearing book published in the late 1920s. The statement reflects the importance he placed on the environment.

> Give me a dozen healthy infants, well-formed and my own specified world to bring them up in and I'll guarantee to take any one of them at random and train him to become any type of specialist I might select—a doctor, lawyer, artist, merchant, chief, and yes, even into a beggarman and thief regardless of his talents, penchants, tendencies, abilities, vocations, and race of his ancestors. I am going beyond my facts and I admit it, but so have the advocates of the contrary and they have been doing it for many thousands of years. (Watson, 1928, p. 104)

THE CONTRIBUTIONS OF B. F. SKINNER

The behavioristic school of thought was advanced in the 1950s by B. F. Skinner, who explored reinforcement and reinforcing stimuli. Skinner devised elaborate problem boxes for his experimental animals, popularly known today as *Skinner boxes.* The boxes were designed in such a way that a reward (food pellet) would be dispensed if a lever or button was correctly manipulated by the subject. Skinner found that through trial-and-error responses, animals could indeed learn to operate the proper mechanisms in the box to receive a reward. His theory, explaining the nature of this type of learning, has come to be known by several titles, including *operant conditioning, instrumental learning,* and *Skinnerian conditioning* (Skinner, 1951, 1957, 1961).

B. F. Skinner.
Birthplace: *Susquehanna, Pennsylvania.*
Born: *1904.* Died: *1990.*
Education: *Ph.D, Harvard University (1931).*
Important Works: *Science and Human Behavior* (1953), *Verbal Behavior* (1953), *Cumulative Record* (1961).

The emphasis in operant conditioning is on *positive reinforcement,* the idea that a response followed by a reward is more likely to be repeated when the organism finds itself in a situation similar to the original one in which reinforcement occurred. Skinner reasoned that organisms are not normally under conditions that allow continuously paired stimuli from the environment. He postulated that although an organism learns to some degree through trial-and-error responses, true learning depends primarily on which behaviors are accompanied by *reinforcement.* Skinner stated that most behaviors are responses emitted by an organism when it has a choice of various responses. His view is that most responses are not associated with any stimuli; they simply occur. These instrumentally conditioned responses are called *operants* because they operate on the environment. Skinner believed the consequences of operants to be critical, since they determined the future behavior of the organism. Furthermore, Skinner's definition of learning is strictly *operational;* if the behavior cannot be measured, then no learning is assumed to have taken place. And, no assumptions can be made regarding internal cognitive states, since they are considered immeasurables.

EXPLORING THE CONCEPT OF REINFORCEMENT

While Skinner differentiates reinforcement into various types, one must remember his contention that learning is measured by overt muscular responses to a stimulus or stimulus situation. Skinner's concern was not with the growth and development of an individual nor with inherited potential; it was with types of reinforcers and their effects on behavior.

Let us examine Skinner's concept of positive and negative reinforcement. *Positive reinforcement* is a stimulus that, when presented to a subject, strengthens and increases the likelihood of a desired response. For example, a gold star attached to the homework paper of a young child may increase the probability of acceptable schoolwork in the future. In this example, the gold star is a type of stimulus that a child might seek or approach. On the other hand, there are stimuli or situations that we try to avoid or escape from, such as pain, being yelled at, or being hurt in some way. These stimuli are called *aversive* or *noxious.* *Negative reinforcement* occurs when we behave in a way that reduces or eliminates an aversive stimulus. For example, it is 10 A.M. and the teacher announces to her third-grade students that it is time for arithmetic. As the students get out their books, Johnny, who hates arithmetic, begins to misbehave. The teacher tells him to stand in the corner; Johnny is now pleased because he got out of doing math. Note that the teacher believes she is punishing Johnny but, in actuality, she has negatively reinforced his behavior, thus increasing the chance that he will misbehave again in order to avoid arithmetic.

Negative reinforcement is not the same as punishment. Punishment usually follows an unacceptable response in a desire to eliminate its future probability: scolding a child for unacceptable classroom behavior, for example. Negative reinforcement seeks to increase the probability of a desired response by removing annoying aversive—noxious—stimuli. Therefore, the Skinnerian approach defines a *reinforcer* as anything that strengthens the probability of a response. The definition of a reinforcement depends entirely on its effects on future behavior. There is no assumption of need reduction.

Primary and secondary reinforcers are two additional types of reinforcement. *Primary reinforcement* represents satisfying stimuli related to primary, unlearned drives (food and drink are primary reinforcers related to the hunger and thirst drives).

A *secondary reinforcer* is a stimulus that was previously neutral but, when paired frequently over successive trials with a primary reinforcer, gains reinforcing qualities of its own. (This is also called the conditioned stimulus in classical conditioning.) For example, if a light flashes on in a Skinner box every time the bar is pressed, the light soon acquires reinforcement properties because it is paired with the resulting reward. Eventually, the organism will press the bar simply to see the light turn on. For children, praise, approval, attention, or toys all represent secondary reinforcement.

PRACTICAL APPLICATIONS OF REINFORCEMENT

Positive reinforcement, negative reinforcement, and punishment are naturally occurring events in the lives of children and, as such, play vital roles in determining behavioral patterns. In fact, some behaviorists believe them to be the sole determiners of whether a stimulus-response (S-R) unit will become part of a child's repertoire of behavior. S-R learning refers to any solitary behavioral unit in which a stimulus is followed by one response. Most behaviors, however, are composed of a series of complex actions, or a string of S-Rs. A number of S-Rs placed in a series is called a *chain.* Chains may consist of a series of nonverbal behaviors, such as getting in a car, closing the door, fastening the seat belt, putting the key in the ignition, and placing the foot on the accelerator. Chains may also consist of verbal associations, such as reciting the Pledge of Allegiance or singing a song. Each link in a chain is learned from external cues and then placed in an appropriate position to produce the desired behavior. Chains represent a natural extension of S-R conditioning.

Shaping behavior, an outgrowth of operant conditioning, is the establishment of desirable chains by molding, or developing, a series of S-R situations into a desired behavioral pattern. A shaping technique called *successive approximations* refers to the step-by-step series of reinforcements that eventually produces a desired S-R behavior. Suppose that we wish to develop in a child a behavior never previously exhibited. Obviously, no correct, rewardable behavior is present in the child. Therefore, behaviors that are close, or *approximate,* to the desired behavior are rewarded. Each time the *general* response is emitted, it is rewarded, until it becomes frequent. Thus, shaping and successive approximations represent the dispensing of reinforcements in order to refine a response gradually and produce a chain, or behavioral pattern, similar to the one desired.

Punishment, as we learned earlier, is incorrectly and frequently used interchangeably with such terms as *discipline, negative reinforcement,* and *nonreward situations.* Punishment, or aversive conditioning, does not imply negative reinforcement; the two can be distinguished by their *effects* on behavior. As noted earlier, both positive and negative reinforcement *increase* the probability of a given response being repeated. However, it is highly questionable whether punishment can completely extinguish an organism's response. It appears more likely that punishment brings about temporary suppression of a given behavioral response. When the threat of punishment is removed, the suppressed behavior may reappear. In fact, punishment has been found to actually produce increased resistance to extinction; instead of eliminating a response, punishment may lead to its greater persistence.

As an attempt to extinguish behavior, punishment is used either by applying an unpleasant stimulus (a spanking) or by withholding a pleasant stimulus (no chocolate cake for dessert) (see Figure 2-5).

Punishment is a very significant aspect of our everyday behavior. Society punishes criminals, parents punish children, and teachers punish pupils. Yet there is a question as to how effective punishment is. Do criminals leave a penal institution rehabilitated?

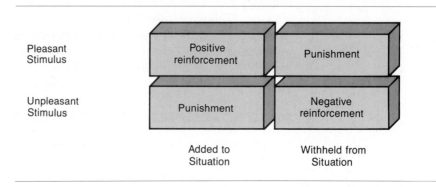

FIGURE 2-5
Model depicting
punishment and
reinforcement variables.

Does the child who is kept after school for not doing homework suddenly change and become a dedicated student? Does one sibling stop picking on another because of punishment?

Almost without exception the answer to these questions is no. Undesirable behaviors may be temporarily suppressed only to reappear hours or days later, perhaps with greater persistence and intensity. The child who behaves well in school will tend to continue to behave well, while those who have undesirable behaviors will probably maintain them in their behavioral repertoires as long as they remain in school (the stimulus situation). Usually, an improvement in behavior will be brought about by innate changes (maturation) or by the child's discovery of a satisfactory behavior to *replace* the undesirable one.

For obvious ethical reasons, little experimental research with children is available on punishment and its effects, but it is generally recognized that punishment may have deleterious effects on the organism, especially in the realm of emotional development. Upon being punished by parents, children may exhibit an increase in arousal level, generally in the form of aggression outside the home. Usually they become less aware of environmental happenings as they withdraw from the threatening situation. This response limits the child's ability to attend to and process educational and personal information. Moreover, as in the case of Watson's experiment with Little Albert, negative emotions may become generalized, extending from one situation to others.

Behaviorism is a continuous theory of development, as opposed to the age-stage or discontinous theories proposed by Freud, Erikson, and Piaget. Developmental changes do not depend on biological maturation, but on reinforcement from the environment. As such, it emphasizes the environmental, rather than hereditary position. Epigenesis has no role in this theory.

A CRITIQUE OF BEHAVIORISM

Behaviorism was the dominant theory in the United States until Piaget's theory of cognitive development added a new perspective on developmental change.

Under the early guidance of Watson and the subsequent tutelage of Skinner, behaviorism has been experimentally vigorous. Indeed, no psychological theory is supported by as much empirical evidence as behaviorism.

However, many theoreticians believe behaviorism is inadequate because it reduces behavior to simple, robotlike S-R units, which has led some to label it the "mechanical person" theory. Behaviorism has also been criticized for inadequately explaining the role of cognition.

☐ Social Learning Theory

THE CONTRIBUTIONS OF ALBERT BANDURA

The theory of *social learning* represents the fourth major viewpoint in human development. Social learning theorists maintain that most learning theories are based on structured laboratory situations, which often have few similarities to real-world learning. Much of human behavior involves the simultaneous interaction of people and multiple stimuli. Experiments involving puzzle boxes, mazes, and operant chambers may offer learning principles, but they hardly explain a child's table manners or why one child shares toys with another. In short, most laboratory experiments do not explain many aspects of social behavior.

Social learning researchers devote their time not to laboratory research but to direct observation of children's behavior in both structured and unstructured situations. Albert Bandura, one such researcher, casts serious doubts on Skinner's theories of successive approximations as a means of explaining all behavior. Bandura does not dispute that shaping can occur, but he asserts that this is only a partial explanation of behavior and that other aspects of learning are probably more important, for example, learning by imitating the cues emitted by others (Bandura, 1962, 1989).

Albert Bandura.
Birthplace: *Mundare, Canada.*
Born: *1925.*
Education: *Ph.D, University of Iowa (1952).*
Important Works:
Aggression: A Social Learning Analysis (1973), *Social Learning Theory* (1977).

Bandura states that verbal cues generally accompany other techniques of shaping and can serve as symbolic models that can be imitated. He believes that *imitation, modeling,* and ***observational learning*** account for many of a child's behavioral patterns. It has been questioned, however, whether imitation is truly a different form of learning. Some theorists (e.g., Miller and Dollard, 1941; Skinner, 1953) have maintained that reinforcement of specific imitative responses leads to a generalized tendency toward imitation. In this fashion, they believe, many behaviors can be imitated without being reinforced. According to this view, imitation is a special case of instrumental conditioning. Bandura, on the other hand, argues that imitation is a separate and distinct form of learning, requiring unique principles.

In an interesting series of studies, Bandura and associates have shown how and under what conditons observational learning occurs. In one study, 5-year-old children were brought individually into a room in which an adult *model* was playing with Tinker Toys. Suddenly, the model turned to a large inflated Bobo doll and began to assault it in novel ways. The doll was knocked over, sat on, and punched in the nose. The adult model then let the Bobo doll up, only to smash it repeatedly on the head with a wooden mallet. Finally, the doll was thrown in the air and kicked by the adult, who all the while muttered, "Sock him in the nose, hit him down, throw him in the air, kick him, pow!"

Shortly after being exposed to this situation, the children were deliberately made angry by having attractive toys withheld from them. This part of the experiment was intended to enhance the possibility of an aggressive behavioral display. A second group of children was angered in the same fashion but was not exposed to the model.

When the experimenter left the room, toys were provided for each child to play with alone. Meanwhile, a group of hidden "judges" rated the resulting behavior. It was found that the children who had observed the model's behavior became aggressive, exhibiting behavior almost identical to that displayed by the model. They too punched the doll in the nose and walloped it with a mallet and yelled "Kick him, pow!" and other phrases used by the model. This experiment emphasizes that children not only learn certain behavioral patterns through observation but also learn them *without any external reinforcement.* In another phase of this experiment, under the same experimental conditions, the children saw similar acts of aggression committed in an animated cartoon film. The results were very similar (Bandura and Walters, 1963).

Having established that learning can occur without reinforcement, Bandura designed a similar experiment to determine the exact roles of reward and punishment in influencing behavior. In this study, three groups of children viewed three different films of a model yelling at and punching the Bobo doll. However, one movie showed the model being punished for the aggressive behavior, the second film ended with the model being praised, and the third film ended with neither praise nor punishment being given to the model.

After the films were viewed, each child was left alone in a room. Children from the group seeing the model being praised for aggressive behavior were more apt to behave aggressively than either of the other groups. The least aggressive group was the one that saw the model being punished. However, in a later phase of the experiment, the children were told that they would be *rewarded* if they did everything the model had done in the film. Differences between groups immediately vanished. Thus, reinforcements administered to a model influence the performance, but not the acquisition, of initiative responses. However, Bandura's frequently contrived procedures make it difficult to determine the extent to which observational learning applies to the everyday lives of children (Bandura, 1962).

OTHER DIMENSIONS OF SOCIAL LEARNING THEORY

Although Bandura and others have criticized behaviorism, Skinner did not modify his position. This has forced some dissatisfied behaviorists to move toward the social learning theory position, and they have been joined by some cognitive psychologists who wish to study dimensions of behavior other than cognition. Thus, a revised social learning theory school of thought, or what some are calling *cognitive social learning theory,* has emerged.

This new school of thought emphasizes a number of general themes:

1. Human beings and environment continously interact. In other words, we influence our environment as much as it influences us.

2. We can learn through observation without any immediate external reinforcement.

3. Learning and acquiring knowledge must be distinguished from performance. Reinforcement may not be essential in acquiring behavior; it is important in guiding and influencing our daily behaviors.

4. Our cognitive expectations and perceptions affect what we do, and our awareness of the consequences of a given behavior influences our choice of behavior.

5. We are active processors of information, not, as behaviorists might have us believe, mechanical persons. Because of our cognitive processes, we engage in *self-regulation,* evaluating and controlling our behavior.

As these themes illustrate, cognitive social learning theory encompasses not only the original school of thought but also cognitive theory, behaviorism, and ideas from humanistic theory (Mischel, 1977, 1987).

Of the theories presented in this chapter, social learning theory is undergoing the most rapid changes. Initially it was a social-personality theory (e.g., Miller and Dollard, 1941); then came observational learning (e.g., Bandura, 1962). These two forces gradually merged and expanded to become social learning theory. Today the movement is expanding even more as theorists recognize that behaviorism and cognitive development are valid and not mutually exclusive.

Originally, then, social learning theory was interactionist and, on the nature-nurture continuum, environmentalist. As the theory continues to develop and assimilate cognitive theory, we see the inclusion of epigenesis and some accompanying age-stage factors that have more of a hereditarian viewpoint.

A CRITIQUE OF SOCIAL LEARNING THEORY

Social learning theory focuses on the interplay of internal cognitive states and social behavior, which behaviorism does not. By itself (without incorporating cognitive theory), however, it does not adequately explain cognition. The observational learning dimension of social learning theory has some empirical support but lacks the experimental data and precise definitions that support behaviorism. Yet, it is more scientific than either cognitive theory or psychoanalysis.

Social learning theory adds a significant dimension to behaviorism. First, by recognizing the role of cognition in learning and that learning can occur without reinforcement, Bandura's work has helped explain the more complex behaviors that puzzled critics of behaviorism.

Critics have said that social learning theory is no more than observational learning which, in turn, is no more than mimicking behavior. Bandura, however, believes that people can symbolically construct complex new behaviors by watching or listening to others.

☐ Ethological Theory

Ethology is the study of human and animal behavior in natural settings. Initially influenced by the writings of Charles Darwin, this school of thought seeks to understand behavior in an evolutionary context and places considerable emphasis on the role of instinct in development. Notable contributors to ethology, besides Darwin, include Konrad Lorenz and John Bowlby.

Observing an organism in its natural setting enables ethologists to learn how a species adapts to its environment. Ethologists maintain that we cannot understand why birds build nests unless we see how this behavior protects them from natural predators. Similarly, we cannot hope to understand the development of children's social groups or status hierarchies unless we observe free-play situations and appreciate how and why such socialization behavior emerges. Psychologists who restrict themselves to the laboratory study of animals and humans may miss critical aspects of behavior. Thus, ethologists engage in *naturalistic observation* (Crain, 1985).

Ethologists regard instincts as important aspects of behavior to study. Instincts have several dimensions. First, instincts are activated by a specific *external stimulus*. The rescuing behavior of a hen when her chicks are in danger is a reaction to the chicks' distress calls. Similarly, a young pheasant will rush for cover when it hears its parents' warning call, and a young jackdaw will follow its parents in the air only when they take off at a certain angle and speed. Such protective parental behaviors toward offspring, although differing in content, are not so different for the human species (Crain, 1985; Thomas, 1984).

THE CRITICAL PERIOD AND IMPRINTING

Ethologists maintain that in some species possessing instincts, there is a *critical period*, that is, a specific time in which an environmental event will have its greatest impact on the developing organism. According to Austrian zoologist Konrad Lorenz and others, strong bonds of attachment develop between the caretaker and the young during the critical period. Lorenz also suggests that imprinting is important for some species. *Imprinting* is an organism's rapid attachment to an object, usually its caretaker, and usually takes place shortly after birth. This type of behavior is readily observed among fowl, which attach themselves to and follow their mother just hours after birth.

Lorenz wanted to know if imprinting would occur if another stimulus were introduced during the critical period. To find out, he divided a number of Graylag goose eggs into two groups. One group was hatched by the mother, while the other group was placed in an incubator. After the goslings in the first group were hatched, Lorenz observed that they immediately followed the mother wherever she went. However, the goslings hatched in the incubator never saw their mother and attached themselves to the first moving object they encountered, which happened to be Lorenz. Subsequently, the goslings followed Lorenz about each day; later in life, they even preferred his company to the company of other geese (Lorenz, 1952).

Konrad Lorenz.
Birthplace: *Vienna, Austria.*
Born: *1903.*
Education: *M.D., University of Vienna (1928), Ph.D, University of Vienna (1933).*
Important Works: *King Solomon's Ring* (1952), *Evolution and Modification of Behavior* (1965), *On Aggression* (1966).

Other imprinting studies have revealed more dramatic findings. For example, mallard ducklings exposed to a wooden decoy (equipped with a concealed tape recorder emitting duck sounds) hours after birth followed it rather than their mother. Other objects, including footballs and tin cans, have been successfully implemented during the critical period.

Several factors are related to the critical period and imprinting. Of paramount importance is the fact that the critical period varies among species and imprinting can occur only during this short period. For example, the critical period for rhesus monkeys seems to span the first six months of life, while in fowl, as we observed earlier, it is much shorter.

Another important dimension of imprinting is the amount of time spent in contact with the mother object. Longer periods of contact with the object during the critical period (and the earlier in the critical period the better) are more effective than shorter periods. Furthermore, such attributes as movement, color, and size seem to capture the attention of the organism more than objects without distinguishing characteristics.

It is difficult to assess if a critical period exists in humans, and no conclusive answers have been furnished. Humans are far more complex than other species and exhibit unique attachment behaviors. The issue is also complicated because human infants do not possess the necessary locomotor skills to physically follow their caretakers.

This does not mean that the work of Lorenz and other ethologists has no application to the study of human behavior. On the contrary, we are beginning to see the relevance of animal behavior to our own behavior in such areas as the establishment of territory, the expression of aggression, and the striving for dominance.

Ethology places a heavy emphasis on the biology of behavior. Ethologists are biologists; thus, hereditary, epigenetic, and species-specific behavior are important to them. As evolutionists, they recognize that the organism's survival mechanisms are tied to the environment; ethology is therefore an interactionist theory.

A CRITIQUE OF ETHOLOGY

In the past, ethology has limited itself to describing the behavior of birds, mammals, fish, and the like; only recently has it included the behavior of humans. Therefore, as a newcomer to the field of developmental psychology, it has not yet become a strong force. As with any scientific endeavor, the description of the phenomena being studied comes before the explanation of the phenomena. Thus, one weakness is the lack of an explanation for *why* certain behaviors occur. Perhaps in time, ethology will have a greater impact on the field. Meanwhile, ethology broadens our perspective, gives us new ideas and, and, as a theory should, raises more questions about human development (Dewsbury, 1989).

As already indicated, the field of ethology has helped psychologists gain greater understanding of human attachment behavior. Such applications suggest that animal and human behavior are not as unrelated as one might initially expect.

☐ Humanistic Theory

Humanistic theory emphasizes the individual's uniqueness, personal potential, and inner drives. A person's self-concept and the maximization of human potential are paramount concerns of this school of thought. Humanistic psychology is often referred to as the *third force* in psychology because it challenges environmental learning the-

Abraham Maslow.
Birthplace: *Brooklyn, New York*.
Born: *1908*. Died: *1970*.
Education: *Ph.D, University of Wisconsin (1934)*.
Important Works: *Toward a Psychology of Being* (1968), *Motivation and Personality* (1970), *The Farther Reaches of Human Nature* (1971).

ories and psychoanalytic stances. Humanists contend that individuals are not controlled exclusively by their external environment, nor is their behavior dominated by the irrational forces of the unconscious. Rather, people are free and creative and capable of growth and self-actualization.

The Quest for Self-Actualization

At the heart of Maslow's theory is the assumption that human needs (and consequently motivations) exist in a hierarchy, from the most basic to the most advanced. The further one progresses up this motivational pyramid, the more distinctly "human" one becomes. Higher motives will develop only when the more basic ones have been satisfied.

As Figure 2-6 shows, the two basic needs are *physiological well-being* and *safety*. To fulfill these two needs, adequate rest, nourishment, and shelter must be found, and individuals must strive to achieve a sense of security. When these two needs have been satisfied, psychic energy can be directed to the need for *belongingness* and *love*. Belongingness is the need to be part of a group and experience sharing. *Esteem* is the fourth level of the hierarchic pyramid. By esteem, Maslow means that individuals must receive feedback from others (in the form of respect and assurance) in order to realize that they are worthwhile and competent. The fifth need, *self-actualization*, means fulfilling one's individual nature in all its aspects. To fulfill one's potential, all previous needs have to be met adequately. An essential component of self-actualization is freedom from cultural and self-imposed restraints.

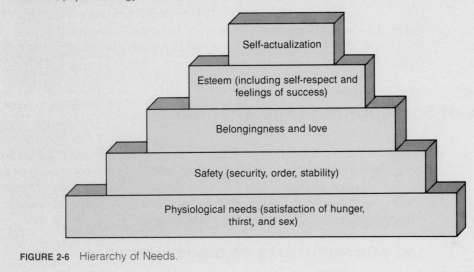

FIGURE 2-6 Hierarchy of Needs.

THE CONTRIBUTIONS OF ABRAHAM MASLOW

Like the other schools of thought we have discussed, humanistic psychology has been shaped by numerous contributors. Most notable is Abraham Maslow, who developed a theory of motivation stating that individuals are driven to attain uniqueness and the full development of their potentialities, capacities, and talents. This uniqueness and pinnacle of success is referred to by Maslow as *self-actualization*. To reach this goal, certain basic needs must first be satisfied (Maslow, 1968, 1970). Figure 2-6 portrays Maslow's *hierarchy of needs*.

The quest for self-actualization begins early in life. According to Maslow's hierarchy of needs, neither children nor adults can strive toward creativity unless fundamental needs have been met. The attainment of self-actualization also requires considerable ego strength, acceptance from peers, and self-respect. Self-actualization may not be attained until the middle years of adulthood. In the years prior to middle age, energy is frequently dissipated in diverse directions, including sexual relationships, educational advancement, career, marriage, and parenthood. The need to achieve financial stability during the young-adult years consumes considerable psychic energy. By middle age, however, many people have managed to fulfill most of these needs and can spare the energy to strive toward ego maturity.

Although Maslow's theory has focused mostly on the adult personality, its main ideas—and those of the humanistic approach in general—have recently been applied to children. More adults, especially educators, are beginning to realize the value of stressing individual uniqueness and helping individuals to utilize their potential. Carl Rogers, another humanist, stresses the notion of helping people accept their total being (C. Rogers, 1961). The application of humanistic theories to early development may help us create the best environments for nurturing intrinsic creative forces (Crain, 1985).

A Critique of Humanistic Theory

Humanists have reacted negatively to dry, "mechanical person" theories because they believe there may be dignity and richness in human life, which are not included in the other types of developmental theories. Unfortunately, humanistic theory has less empirical evidence to support it than does any other theory mentioned in this text. There simply are no methodologies that allow us to measure self-actualization, fulfillment of potential, happiness, and so forth.

■ Overview of Some Adult-Stage Theories

Most of the theories we have discussed have emphasized development through adolescence, although they suggest the continued importance of childhood developmental factors throughout adulthood. Now we outline three adult-stage theories and briefly examine their theoretical operating principles and emphases. More detailed coverage of each theory appears in appropriate units of the textbook.

THE CONTRIBUTIONS OF DANIEL LEVINSON

Daniel Levinson (1978, 1980) has investigated adult male personality growth. He studied 40 males ranging in age from 35 to 45 and representative of a variety of occupations, including company executives, novelists, biologists, and hourly wage earners. The subjects were interviewed over a period of 10 to 20 months for a total of 10 to 20 hours. Although the study was limited in subject population and experimental design, Levinson, nonetheless, uncovered interesting life trends suggestive of the changes and growth that accompany adult life. It is conceivable that women also experience the developments outlined by Levinson.

Levinson and his colleagues describe what they call a *life structure,* which refers to the underlying pattern of a person's behavior at a given time in life. There are three aspects to the life structure:

1. the person's *sociocultural world,* including ethnicity, occupation, class, status, religion, and so forth.

2. *self-aspects*—involving a complex pattern of wishes, anxieties, conflicts, and ways of resolving or controlling them; moral values; talents and skills; fantasies; and modes of feeling, thought, and action.

3. *participation in the world,* or how a person uses and is used by the world.

Life structure is revealed primarily through the choices a person makes. Levinson's research reveals that, for most people, the central components were chosen from the areas of occupation, marriage-family, ethnicity, and religion.

THE CONTRIBUTIONS OF ROGER GOULD

Roger Gould (1978, 1980) has also explored the stages of adult personality development. His research is similar to Levinson's, although Gould used a more extensive population sample. His research suggests that adulthood is not a plateau, but rather a time for the continuous unfolding of the self. Gould emphasizes the importance of striving toward adult levels of consciousness and discarding irrational childhood notions about oneself and the world in general.

THE CONTRIBUTIONS OF ROBERT HAVIGHURST

Finally, Robert Havighurst (1972, 1980) stresses the importance of mastering developmental tasks appropriate to a given life stage. He borrowed Erikson's concept of interaction of individual and society and noted that most societies appear to have a timetable for the accomplishment of various tasks. He has identified what he terms *developmental tasks,* which may originate from physical maturation, from the pressure of the surrounding society on the person, and from the desires, aspirations, and values of the emerging personality. For example, infants and young children must learn to walk and talk, to distinguish right from wrong, and so forth. Adults, too, have developmental tasks appropriate to various stages of their personal and social growth. Successfully achieving these tasks fosters success with future tasks and also leads toward happiness. Failure to complete these tasks satisfactorily can lead to unhappiness, difficulty with accomplishing future tasks, and disapproval by society. Havighurst suggests six developmental periods throughout the life cycle that require the mastery of developmental tasks. Note that they do not have to be accomplished in the order presented. These tasks are presented in each of the developmental chapters that follow.

You will be introduced to many other theories throughout this textbook, many of which encompass only one aspect of adult development. For example, we look at Eli Ginzberg's theory of vocational development; Robert Butler's theory of life review (a mental process promoted by approaching death); and Elisabeth Kübler-Ross's theory of the stages of dying.

■ Putting Theories into Perspective

These theories and others have provided numerous answers about the nature and development of human behavior. However, we must stress that these theoretical positions do not have to be examined in an either-or perspective. They are not necessarily mutually exclusive, and several may be operating at different times or under different conditions. For example, the fact that a person is at a specific stage of Piaget's cognitive development theory does not mean that principles of reinforcement are not operating at the same time, nor does it mean that one's acquisition of knowledge is not being shaped by observational learning. Thus, while each theory is an effort to explain behavior, it is not uncommon for one or all theories to be applied simultaneously.

This is the primary reason many students and professors are eclectic in their evaluations of theories. That is, they pick and choose those bits and pieces of theories they can accept and then develop their own theoretical judgments about human behavior. The primary responsiblity of a textbook is to present all aspects of a theory objectively so that such judgments can be made. We hope this chapter has given you some insight into the theoretical positions currently held by most developmental psychologists. Subsequent chapters provide more details on each major theory.

Finally, although each of the theories has broadened our horizons and uncovered new areas of exploration, we have not yet been able to answer all our questions about human development. Some issues still elude theoretical explanation. For example, a seemingly unanswerable question related to learning concerns the nature of our relationship with the environment. Psychoanalytic and behaviorist theorists view people as maintaining a passive role and being continually shaped by the environment. Others, like Jean Piaget, believe individuals are actively participating in the environment, curiously seeking out what interests them and avoiding what does not. Still others believe our relationship with the environment is a combination of these two positions. Issues such as these underscore the need for further investigation and reassessment of our facts and theories.

CHAPTER REVIEW

According to developmentalists, there are three major sets of factors that influence individual development. The first, normative age-graded influences, refers to those determinants that are predictable because they are associated with our age. Examples include the onset of walking, puberty, and marriage. The second, normative history-graded influences, refers to how cohorts share similar environmental influences such as war or economic depression. Nonnormative influences refer to factors that can occur at any time and are not predictable, such as disease, death, or unemployment.

A fundamental controversy among psychologists is the heredity versus environment (nature-nurture) issue. Adult developmentalists seek to define the relative contributions of each of these factors to overall behavior. Are biological factors (genetic predispositions and physiology) the major determinants of behavior, or do environmental factors (experiences) play the dominant role? Despite considerable research, the nature-nurture controversy is unresolved. Many adult developmentalists today emphasize the interaction that takes place between genetic and environmental forces. Epigenesis is a theory associated with the hereditarian position. It states that humans develop according to genetic programming.

Changes in behavior are thought to be either gradual and continuous (for example, socialization) or sudden and abrupt (for example, cognitive development). The former concept views people as developing from interactions and experiences with the environment. The latter considers developmental trends to be based on internal biological states (growth and maturation).

The active-reactive issue questions whether we are passively shaped by our environment and simply react to it, or whether we actively seek out the environmental stimuli we desire.

Theories are perspectives or explanations of how we develop, both as a species and as individuals. A good theory is supported by empirical evidence.

The psychoanalytic school of thought, initially proposed by Sigmund Freud and further developed by Erik Erikson, emphasizes the importance of personality development. Freud identified psychosexual stages of growth and the continuous interaction of the id, ego, and superego. These psychosexual stages include the oral stage (infancy and toddlerhood), the anal and phallic stages (early childhood), the latency period (middle childhood), and the genital stage (adolescence).

Erik Erikson, a neo-Freudian, emphasizes psychosocial stages of development and lifelong personality growth. He postulates eight stages of personality development, each characterized by a crisis that must be resolved. Erikson's theory includes the stages of trust verus mistrust and autonomy versus shame or doubt (infancy and toddlerhood), initiative versus guilt (early childhood), industry versus inferiority (school-aged childhood), identity versus role confusion (adolescence), intimacy versus isolation (young adulthood), generativity versus self-absorption (middle adulthood), and integrity versus despair (old age).

One of the leading schools of thought in contemporary developmental psychology is the cognitive-developmental approach. Swiss genetic epistemologist Jean Piaget has been most active in this area and has offered perhaps the most influential theory. He postulates that intellectual maturity is achieved through four orderly and distinct stages of development. These stages include the following: sensorimotor (ages 0 to 2), preoperational thought (ages 2 to 7), concrete operations (ages 7 to 11), and formal operations (ages 11 to 15).

Another school of thought is behaviorism, which traces its roots back to Pavlov and classical conditioning. Pavlov's early experiments on dogs excited John Broadus Watson (father of behaviorism) so much that he hoped to prove that humans could also be conditioned. His "Little Albert" experiment demonstrates his theory. More recently, behaviorism has been significantly modified and formulated by B. F. Skinner. Today behaviorism is synonymous with operant conditioning. B. F. Skinner's detailed experimentation not only kept behaviorism alive but brought it to the forefront of American psychology. Skinner's investigations clarified the nature of positive and negative reinforcement and shed some light on punishment. Skinner's theories of learning are called operant conditioning and instrumental learning.

The research of Albert Bandura and other theorists has led to the development of the social learning school of thought. This approach to developmental psychology emphasizes observational learning, imitation, and modeling. Proponents of the social learning school maintain that there is a strong likelihood that individuals will observe and copy behaviors of others.

We have discussed the ethological and humanistic schools of thought. Ethologists study animals and humans in natural settings by means of naturalistic observation. Researchers such as Konrad Lorenz and John Bowlby have sought to apply their studies of animals to human behavior. Humanists such as Abraham Maslow and Carl Rogers have emphasized individual uniqueness and strivings for self-actualization. Maslow has been particularly active in the latter area, developing a hierarchy of needs that progresses from basic motives to full actualization of potentials. Humanistic psychologists believe we must create environments that will nurture inner potentialities and creative forces.

Last, we outlined three adult-stage theories. Daniel Levinson described male personality growth, although on a limited sample. Roger Gould's theory emphasizes the need to discard irrational ideas of childhood as we strive toward adult levels of consciousness. Robert Havighurst lists developmental tasks and maintains that society has expectations that individuals strive to meet.

KEY TERMS

active theory	interactionist
accommodation	learning
adaptation	libido
age-stage theories	maturation
assimilation	modeling
behaviorism	nature-nurture controversy
chain	negative reinforcement
classical conditioning	nonnormative influences
cognitive-developmental theory	normative age-graded influences
cognitive social learning theory	normative history-graded influences
conscience	observational learning
conscious	operant conditioning
continuous development theory	operants
critical period	organization
defense mechanism	perfection principle
discontinuous development theory	positive reinforcement
ego	preconscious
ego ideal	primary reinforcer
environmentalists	psychoanalytic theory
epigenetic principle	psychosexual stages
equilibration	psychosocial stages
ethology	reactive theory
fact	reality principle
fixation	reinforcer
free association	schemata
genetic epistemology	secondary reinforcer
growth	self-actualization
hedonistic principle	shaping behavior
hereditarians	social learning theory
humanistic theory	superego
id	theory
imitation	unconscious
imprinting	

RECOMMENDED READINGS

Boakes, R. (1984). *From Darwin to Behaviorism.* New York: Cambridge University Press.
An explanation about theories of human development and how they have changed since Darwin's time.

Bornstein, M. H., and Lamb, M. E. (Eds.). (1984). *Developmental Psychology: An Advanced Textbook.* Hillsdale, N.J.: Erlbaum.
A higher-level but excellent account of a variety of theories and methods covering cognitive, perceptual, language, moral, social, and emotional development, among others. This book is for the student who enjoys exploring philosophical ideas.

Cairns, R. B., and Ornstein, P. A. (1979). Developmental psychology. In *The First Century of Experimental Psychology,* edited by E. S. Hearst, 459–512. Hillsdale, N.J.: Erlbaum.
This chapter reviews the history of developmental psychology. Very informative.

Crain, W. S. (1985). *Theories of Development: Concepts and Applications,* 2nd ed. Englewood Cliffs, N.J.: Prentice-Hall.
Crain presents the major developmental theories, extracts the critical ideas, and offers readers practical applications.

Gay, P. (1988). *Freud: A Life for Our Time.* New York: Norton.
A comprehensive and thought provoking look at the contributions of the father of psychoanalysis.

Gholson, B., and Rosenthal, T. R. (Eds.). (1984). *Applications of Cognitive-Developmental Theory.* New York: Academic Press.
Cognitive-developmental theory is applied to numerous facets of growth, including social cognition, metacognition, and mathematical reasoning.

Miller, P. H. (1989). *Theories of Developmental Psychology,* 2nd ed. San Francisco: Freeman.
Balanced coverage is given to major developmental theories (including behaviorism, ethological theory, and others), particularly the works of Piaget, Freud, and Erikson. Each theory receives an excellent analysis.

Offer, D., and Sabshin, M. (Eds.). (1985). *Normality Through the Life Cycle.* New York: Basic Books.
Articles include patterns of normal development throughout the life cycle, stages of maturity, and perspectives on normality.

Schlein, S. P. (1988). *A Way of Looking at Things: Selected Papers of Erik H. Erikson, 1930–1980.* New York: Norton.
For those wanting more insight into the life of Erikson, this book provides the vehicle.

Vasta, R. (Ed.). (1989). *Six Theories of Child Development: Revised Formulations and Current Issues.* Greenwich, Conn.: JAI Press.
One of the better overviews of developmental psychology's major theories.

Genetics, Heredity, and Environment

What Do You Think?

■ Bill and Jim are in the third grade. They are fraternal twins, yet Bill's reading level is two years ahead of his chronological age, while Jim is barely able to keep up with his classwork. How can we account for the difference in their reading abilities?

■ Through chromosomal aberrations, that is, too many or two few chromosomes or genes, normal growth and development are disrupted. For example, a male can develop such female physical characteristics as enlarged breasts, or a female may never enter puberty and consequently remain sterile for her entire life. Other genetic aberrations create webbed fingers and toes, heads with distorted shapes, and other deformed body parts. How do chromosomes and genes cause such abnormalities? Read on to discover the answers that genetic researchers have supplied.

■ Two brown-eyed parents with dark, wavy hair have three children who are spitting images of them. But their fourth child is tall and has straight, blond hair and blue eyes. How can these latter differences be explained? How can two brown-eyed parents have a blue-eyed child? Why do some children born of the same parents have such similarities, whereas others bear no resemblance to anyone in the family? We'll unravel some of the genetic mysteries about generational similarities and variations.

INTRODUCTION

Conception occurs, and nine months later Ann is born. Her physical appearance is determined primarily by genetic inheritance, which endows her with a blueprint for her biological growth and development. If her parents are Ugandans, her genetic code will contain a program for her to look, grow, and develop along the lines of other Ugandans. If they are Eskimo, Navajo, Siberian, or Swedish, for example, she would inherit a different genetic code that would express itself in different ways.

The genetic blueprint also bestows certain behavioral predispositions. Ann may have inherited a biochemical or neuromuscular makeup that will give her the potential to become an outstanding athlete, a musical virtuoso, a math whiz, a vocalist, or an intellectual. She may have inherited a tendency to be hyperactive, very passive, alcoholic, or even schizophrenic.

There is more to behavior than genetic inheritance, however. Ann was born into a family within a specific culture. She will learn which behaviors are acceptable in the family, the neighborhood, and society. She will also develop her own interests and motivations. Her environment may be restrictive or supportive, and she may have few or many opportunities to develop the skills that match her inherited aptitudes. Environment and heredity are strong forces that will help determine not only how she will behave but how long she will live. How do environment and heredity interact? What is their role in influencing behavior? This chapter will investigate and try to answer these questions.

■ The Genetics of Life

What governs the process whereby a fertilized egg develops into a fully functioning infant, complete with arms, legs, nose, eyes, ears, internal organs, and an individuality all its own? The key to this magnificent story is a special code contained in the nucleus of each cell. This code, unique to and different for every individual, is gradually being understood by scientists.

Each cell contains a set of genetic blueprints that direct the cell to multiply itself and become a fully developed organism. It is true for all animal species: Each cell contains a full set of directions locked inside its nucleus. This is what makes a mouse different from a bird, a flower different from a tree, and siblings different from each other.

Frequently, the terms *genetics* and *heredity* are used interchangeably. They are not synonymous, however, and each term should be understood if one is to venture into the field of genetics. The word ***genetic*** (genesis) refers to the origin, or beginning. When one speaks of genetics, one refers to the beginning life cell and its progressive development according to the principles of genetics. Because this cell has received developmental instructions from both parents, the organism will inherit characteris-

Genetic inheritance is responsible for a wide range of traits and predispositions.

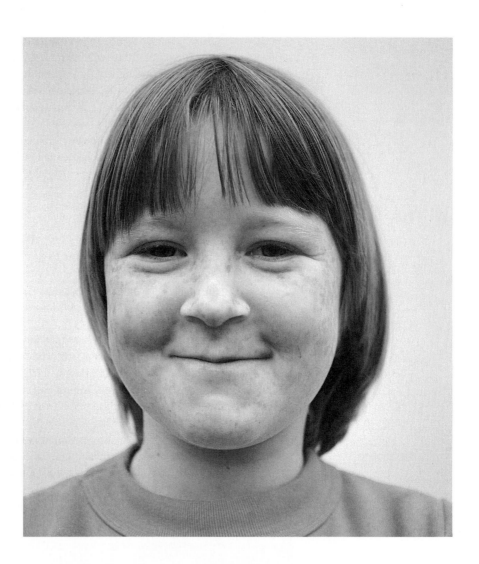

Genes control inheritable characteristics, from freckled skin to eye and hair color.

tics from both of them; this is known as heredity. *Genetics* is the scientific study of how inheritance operates.

Heredity refers to the parents' transmission of certain characteristics to their offspring. Put another way, it is the tendency of offspring to resemble their parents. When offspring, whether plant or animal, are different from their parents, these differences are referred to as *variations*. Generally, fewer variations among closely related species are expected than from more divergent or less closely related animals. For example, the children of two brown-eyed, dark-haired, and olive-skinned people or two blue-eyed blonds will look more like their parents than will the children of a father of Irish-Scottish-Norwegian background and a mother of Italian-Mexican-Eskimo genetic background. The offspring of this latter mating would have more variation.

Although genetics did not become a science until recently, trial-and-error methods of manipulating inherited characteristics of plants and animals from one generation to the next have been used for centuries. Even without a working scientific knowledge of genetics, we have, over thousands of years, developed hundreds of species to serve specific functions. For example, observing that a large bull tends to produce similar offspring, farmers bred species of cattle solely to increase the quantity of beef. Cows have been bred that can produce many gallons of milk. Others, although producing fewer gallons, yield milk high in butterfat, especially usable for butter, cream, and similar dairy products. In other instances, some species of horses have been bred for pure strength to pull plows and heavy loads, whereas others are bred primarily for their racing ability.

Dogs and dog breeding stand out in the field of heredity; the American Kennel Club currently recognizes 130 breeds of dogs in the United States. Although virtually all of today's dogs originated from either one or two common ancestors, natural selection and artificial breeding have produced well over 150 species. Dogs can be categorized into groups according to certain behavioral characteristics, enabling breeders to capitalize on inherited genetic predispositions. For example, because terriers have an inherited predisposition to dig in the ground, they are used to help rid the land of small vermin. Collies and sheepdogs have a natural herding instinct, and sporting dogs such as setters and pointers may have either unusually good sight or a good sense of smell that enables them to aid sportsmen. The resultant behavior of each breed is partially determined by inherited characteristics, but it is the environment (training) that helps develop these inborn traits. Observant trainers will note a dog's natural tendencies and train the animal accordingly. For example, it is easier to train a collie than a bulldog to herd sheep. Heredity and environment go hand in hand.

What is true of other species is also true of humans. If two pygmies mate, you get a pygmy; if two very tall, blond people mate, they will most likely have tall, blond offspring; if two schizophrenics mate, there is a strong likelihood that their children will inherit schizophrenic tendencies. That is the nature of inheritance.

Although scientists have long observed "hereditary tendencies," no meaningful explanations for the phenomena were put forward until the mid-1800s when Gregor Mendel, a monk, discovered some fundamental laws of genetics while experimenting with peas. Since that initial breakthrough, the science of genetics has been active and there have been many dramatic breakthroughs. However, before we can understand some of these genetic revelations, we must first understand cells, and cellular behavior.

■ Biochemical Genetics: Basic Concepts

Biology, genetics, and developmental psychology are, at first glance, three different and separate disciplines; yet upon inspection, they are closely related. Earlier, we mentioned that genetics is the science of heredity. More specifically, it is the science that studies chromosomes and genes and how they control a cell's activity and govern life processes. The geneticist is interested in the chemical analysis of the chromosomes. Behavior genetics attempts to understand how these chemical processes produce physical and behavioral characteristics.

Although the field of psychology is mainly interested in the processes by which genetics *affects* behavior, psychologists need not understand all of the biochemical processes that occur in the cell. They should, however, be familiar with the fundamental principles of genetic and hereditary processes.

☐ Basic Cell Structure

A *cell* is a living unit of organized material that contains a nucleus and is enclosed in a membrane. The entire living substance that constitutes a cell is known as *protoplasm,* which can be subdivided into two general types: *cytoplasm,* the protoplasm found inside the cell but outside the nucleus; and *nucleoplasm,* the protoplasm found inside the nuclear membrane. The cell also contains *ribosomes,* small particles in the cytoplasm that manufacture essential products for the cell.

The *nucleus,* located in or near the center of the cell, is the control center of the cell's activity. Inside the nucleus are *chromosomes,* thin rodlike structures that contain the directions for the cell's activity. Chromosomes occur in pairs and the number varies according to the species. Humans have 23 pairs of chromosomes per cell, or 46 chromosomes altogether (see Figure 3-1).

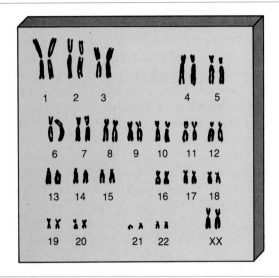

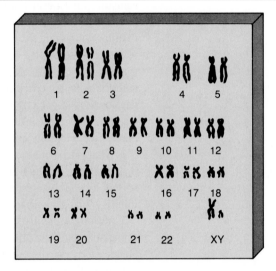

FIGURE 3-1 Human chromosomes grouped into 23 pairs, with female chromosomes on the left and male chromosomes on the right.

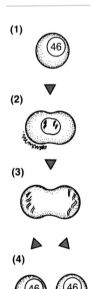

(1)

(2)

(3)

(4)

Organisms have only two types of cells: *somatic cells* and *germ cells.* The term *soma* means *body;* thus most of the approximately 1 trillion cells found in the human body, are *somatic cells.* In order for growth to take place, somatic cells undergo a process of division called *mitosis.* In mitosis, the chromosomes inside the nucleus pair up along its center; then, after duplicating themselves, they move to opposite poles. The original cell (and nucleus), called the *parent cell,* begins to pull apart and two new nuclei are formed that contain the new sets of chromosomes. Each of these new cells is called a *daughter cell.* The key fact to remember about mitosis is that the two new daughter cells are identical to the original parent cell and maintain the same number of chromosomes. Figure 3-2 illustrates the process of mitosis.

When a cell has its full quota of chromosomes, it is said to be in the *diploid state.* In humans, the parent cell always has 23 pairs of chromosomes (diploidy), and, by means of mitotic division, the cells duplicate their chromosomes so that the daughter cells will also have 23 pairs, which is the diploid, or full species number, of chromosomes—46 chromosomes.

FIGURE 3-2 Mitosis is the process whereby a parent cell divides to become two daughter cells, each containing the original number of chromosomes. The diagram illustrates (1) the body cell with the original 46 chromosomes; (2) before cell division, the chromosomes duplicate themselves; (3) the chromosomes migrate to opposite sides of the dividing cell; and (4) the two new cells each contain 46 chromosomes.

The second type of cell found in the human body is the *germ cell.* This cell undergoes division in the *gonads,* which are the reproductive organs: the ovaries in the female and testes in the male. Germ cells become the cells of reproduction, or sex cells, but must first undergo certain changes before they achieve their new state. These sex cells are called *gametes.* The male gamete is the *sperm,* which is produced from the germ cells in the testes, and the female gamete is the *ovum,* or egg, which is produced from the germ cells of the ovaries.

The cell division of germ cells is called *meiosis,* a series of divisions that transforms a germ cell from the *diploid* state to a *haploid state* (haploidy means that a cell contains only half the number of chromosomes that is natural for that species). Meiotic division, therefore, pertains to a parent germ cell splitting into two daughter cells, the same process as mitosis *except* that the chromosomes do not duplicate themselves. This leaves each daughter cell in the haploid state. Thus, meiosis in the male organism produces a sperm sex cell that contains 23 chromosomes and in the female, an ovum with 23 chromosomes. Conception occurs when the sperm fertilizes the ovum and creates a single cell in the diploid state. This enables a cell to receive its full component of chromosomes, complete with coded instructions. Figure 3-3 shows the process of meiosis.

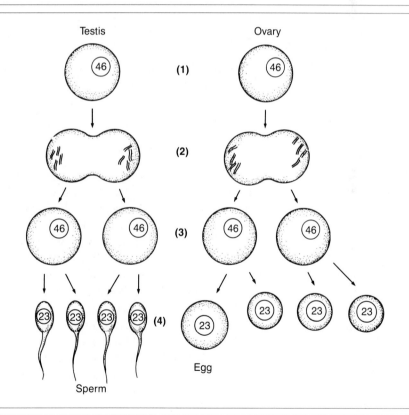

FIGURE 3-3 Meiosis is the cell division in which sperm and ova are created. Compared to mitosis, there is a reduction in chromosomes when the sex cells divide. The diagram shows (1) the sperm and egg cell, each containing 46 chromosomes; (2) each chromosome duplicates itself before cell division takes place; (3) cell division creates two new cells, each with 46 chromosomes; and (4) another cell division occurs, resulting in four new cells, each having 23 single chromosomes.

☐ Determination of Gender

If we were to line up the 46 chromosomes of the human female somatic or germ cell in two columns, each containing 23 chromosomes, we would see that all 23 are in pairs; they are identical in appearance, and they have the same function (e.g., to determine eye color). The twenty-third set of chromosomes are usually referred to as the sex chromosomes, for they determine the sex of the child (Figure 3-1). In the female's cells, the twenty-third pair ordinarily consists of two X chromosomes. However, when we look at the chromosomes in a male, we see that the first 22 are pairs, but in position 23, we can easily see that it is not a pair at all—it is a mismatch. One chromosome is shaped like an X, the other like a Y.

Throughout history, many a queen has lost her throne (or even her life) for not giving birth to a male heir. But it is not the female who determines the sex of the child, but the male. Remember that during meiosis the chromosomes in the gamete divide in half and that one-half becomes the egg. For the female, no matter which half becomes fertilized, the egg always—and only—contains an X. The male, however, can contribute a sperm cell that has either an X or a Y chromosome. If the X-carrying sperm penetrates the egg, the offspring will be a girl; if the Y does, it will be a boy (see Figure 3-4).

Recent evidence indicates that there is one gene (a small segment of a chromosome that controls or influences an inheritable characteristic), ordinarily found on the Y chromosome, that determines a person's sex. The *testis determining factor,* or *TDF,* is associated with that gene. Researchers believe that this gene launches a sequence of events that leads to male sexual development. If the gene that contains the TDF is absent, the individual will be female (Page et al., 1987).

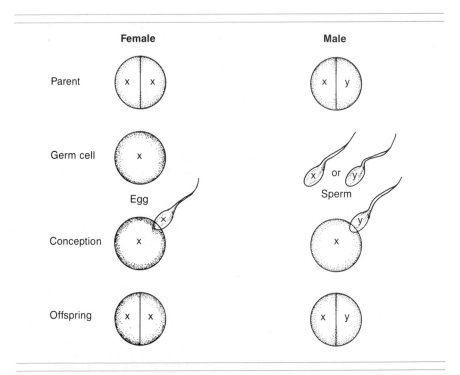

FIGURE 3-4 The mating of sex chromosomes and the resultant sex of the offspring.

☐ Sex- or X-Linked Inheritance

The chromosome in the twenty-third position not only determines the sex of one's offspring but the *sex-linked characteristics* as well. Since the X chromosome is approximately three times as large as the Y chromosome, a female has approximately three times as many genes on her twenty-third chromosome as a male does. The difference in gene numbers on the sex chromosomes is the key to understanding sex-linkage. From the 22 pairs of autosomes (any chromosome other than the sex-determining pair), an individual might inherit a recessive gene for some undesirable trait, but if inheritance has also given that individual a normal dominant gene, the undesirable trait will not be expressed. However, on the sex-determining chromosomes, there is frequently no such balancing tendency because the Y chromosome lacks corresponding genes.

The best way to illustrate the possible inheritance from parents to offspring, including sex-linked characteristics, is to utilize the Punnett square (named after an English geneticist), a diagrammatic means to compute the possible genotypes and phenotypes for any given characteristic (Figure 3-5). Since chromosomes and their component genes occur in pairs but separate during mitosis, there are two gametes left for any one sex. Although there is no way of knowing exactly which male gamete will fertilize which female gamete, one can calculate, in advance, the statistical probabilities of certain characteristics.

One of the better known sex-linked characteristics is color blindness. The retina of the eye contains cones, specialized nerve cells that respond to color stimuli. There are

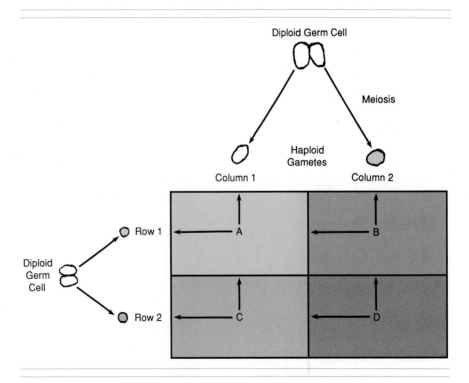

FIGURE 3-5 The columns represent the two possible female gametes; the rows, the two possible male gametes. The four squares A, B, C, and D represent every possible genotype available for that one characteristic. For example, square A represents the fertilization of the egg type represented in Column 1 by the male gamete in Row 1. Square D represents the female type of gamete 2 as fertilized by the male gamete from Row 2.

three kinds of cones, each of which is sensitive to one of three basic colors; red, green, and blue. The most common form of color blindness is the *deutan*, or green, insensitive type, where the weakness of color perception makes the color green appear to be red.

The gene for determining color vision is located on the X chromosome. If the male has this recessive, faulty gene on the X chromosome, he will be color blind because there is no corresponding gene on the Y chromosome to counteract this condition. Affected fathers will have no affected offspring unless the mother is a carrier. Since all of his sons receive Y chromosomes from him and X chromosomes from their mother, they will in no way be affected. However, all of his daughters will be carriers and the chances are that 50 percent of their male offspring will be color blind (see Figure 3-6).

Another well known sex-linked characteristic is hemophilia, or bleeders disease. This condition is caused by a recessive X-linked gene that fails to produce the plasma protein *antihemophilic globulin* (AHG), which is necessary for normal blood clotting. Persons with this disease bleed excessively from minor injuries and are more likely than

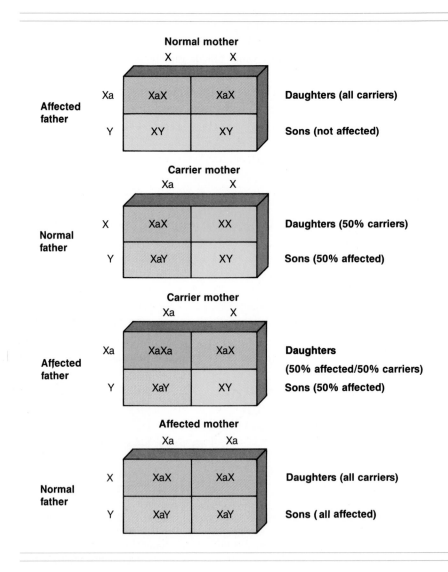

FIGURE 3-6
Transmission of sex-linked characteristics such as color blindness and hemophilia. The lowercase *a* represents the recessive characteristics.

the average person to bleed to death from serious injury. The same inheritance pattern that color blindness follows is in operation with the inheritance of hemophilia. Males with the faulty X chromosome become hemophilic because they have no alternate gene on the Y chromosome to counteract this condition (see Figure 3-6).

We have considered only sex-linked characteristics that are carried on the X chromosome, but there is evidence that there are also Y-linked sex characteristics. Unlike X-linked, the Y-linked are passed on only from father to son. For example, *Hairy pinna,* long hair growing on the ears, appears to be Y-linked. To date, there is much uncertainty as to what other Y-linked characteristics exist.

Finally, we should mention *sex-limited genes.* These genes are normally expressed in only one sex, although they are carried by both sexes. Unlike X-linked genes, sex-limited characteristics include primary sex traits (related only to the organs of reproduction) and secondary sex characteristics (differences in skeletal and muscular growth, breasts, beard, etc.). *Pattern baldness,* a trait common to males, is also considered to be sex-limited.

☐ DNA: The Blueprint of Life

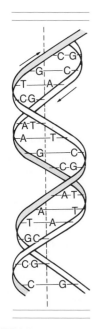

FIGURE 3-7

A section of the DNA molecule as described by Watson and Crick. Each rung on the helix is composed either of adenine (A) and thymine (T) or guanine (G) and cytosine (C). (Adapted from J. D. Watson and F. H. C. Crick, 1953)

Now let us peer inside the nucleus of a cell to discover just what the genetic code entails. Under a microscope, the chromosome looks like a thin, colored, rodlike thread. A gene is simply a very small portion of a chromosome, and it has a specific function. Chemically, the structure of a chromosome (or gene) is called *deoxyribonucleic acid,* or more simply **DNA**. The genes are the part of the DNA structure that carry hereditary instructions for the development of the organism (Watson and Crick, 1958).

The study of DNA offers researchers many puzzles. Slowly, though, we are increasing our knowledge of its role in genetic functioning. In future years, we hope to learn how DNA interacts with other cellular components to express the information it encodes (Felsenfeld, 1985).

DNA looks like a long spiral staircase or twisting ladder. It has rungs, or steps, that are attached to and supported by an external framework. This framework consists of alternating molecules of sugar and phosphate. The steps are composed of only four chemicals—adenine (A), thymine (T), guanine (G), and cytosine (C). Each step consists of two chemicals joined together (Figure 3-7). The chemical adenine will bond (link up) only with the chemical thymine, and guanine and cytosine will bond only with each other.

A *gene* is a segment of a chromosome that controls or influences inheritable characteristics. A gene comprises several hundred or even several thousand rungs of the DNA ladder. When activated, each rung will lead to the production of specific proteins or enzymes. Some genes may be several hundred steps long, others several thousand. Although it is not known exactly how many genes are on a chromosome, a frequent estimate has been 20,000, which would give human beings approximately 460,000 gene pairs. Some theories even double this number, bringing the total closer to 1 million (see box on genetic terminology).

A gene is DNA material arranged in a specific fashion so that an accompanying specific protein can be synthesized (manufactured). To make a long and complex story short and simple, this dormant genetic blueprint becomes active at an appropriate time. The activated gene duplicates itself, but with minor chemical alterations (uracil replaces thymine, for example). Instead of being DNA, it now become *ribonucleic acid,* or *RNA*. More specifically, it is called *messenger RNA* because its purpose is to carry a

Understanding Fundamental Genetic Terminology

The biological symbol for male ♂ The biological symbol for female ♀

Chromosomes and genes. A chromosome (colored body) is a thin rodlike structure found within the nuclear membrane that contains small genetic units called genes, the true units of heredity.

Dominant gene. Any gene that, when present, always expresses its hereditary characteristic. An uppercase letter is used to represent the dominant condition (e.g., B for brown eyes).

Recessive gene. A gene whose hereditary characteristics are present only when paired with another recessive gene. Its hereditary characteristics are not observable when paired with a dominant gene. It is designated by the lowercase letter that is used for the dominant gene (e.g., b for blue, gray, hazel, or green eyes—all recessive to brown).

Homozygous (sameness of genes). A condition in which both genes of a gene pair are identical for a given trait—both dominant or both recessive (e.g., BB or bb).

Allele. Any member of alternate sets in the same gene pair. The alleles for eye color might be B from the father and b from the mother.

Heterozygous (mixed or two types of genes). A condition in which each gene of a gene pair differs for a given trait—one dominant, one recessive gene (e.g., Bb).

Phenotype. The visible or easily measurable appearance of an organism. A brown-eyed person is said to have a brown phenotype for eye color, while a blue-eyed person has a phenotype for blue eyes.

Genotype. The actual genetic makeup (gene pair) of an organism. If the blue-eyed person has a bb gene pair, its genotype is blue for both genes. When an organism exhibits a dominant phenotype, we can only guess at the genotype. Is a brown-eyed person genotypically BB or Bb? He or she could be either.

genetic message (the genetic code) outside the nucleus to a ribosome, a cellular body that synthesizes protein.

To understand the process of protein synthesis, you should know that your body consists of protein from the top of your scalp to the tip of your toes. Your eye color, your bones, your heart, your spleen, and everything else is protein. It is in the ribosomes that protein is manufactured. Remarkably, ribosomes can synthesize almost a million different types of proteins by mixing together various amino acids. *Amino acids,* which exist in only 20 to 30 different varieties (no one knows for sure), are the true building blocks in life. All protein in all life originates from amino acids.

We might compare the ribosome to a pharmacist, who follows the directions on a prescription (the chemically coded message that messenger RNA delivers). The directions might read: "mix one part amino acid 2 with two parts amino acid 18, add one part amino acid 12," and so on. This combination of amino acids would produce one protein. If the genetic code was calling for heart muscle protein, many messenger RNAs would be sent to all the ribosomes in the cytoplasm. The RNAs would deliver their directions to the ribosome, which would then mix the appropriate amino acids according to the genetic instruction.

Soon the cell would be swollen with heart protein, and mitosis would take place. Now two cells would manufacture heart protein, divide, and then there would be four. In nine months' time, in a similar way for every body part, a total of approximately seven pounds of protein is produced. In this complex fashion, a single cell becomes a human infant.

For any given characteristic, an organism may receive one dominant gene from *each* parent (homozygous genotype and dominant phenotype), or one recessive gene from each parent (homozygous genotype, recessive phenotypic characteristic), or a dominant gene from one parent and a recessive from the other (heterozygous genotype, phenotype of the dominant characteristic).

☐ Genetic Individuality

To understand physical and psychological inheritance, one must understand that during the process of meiosis, chromosomes line up opposite each other and then meiotically split into daughter cells. But remember that most of the genes on one chromosome differ from the genes on the opposite chromosome. Although chromosomes line up, there is no factor requiring that they line up on the right or the left side. They may do either (Figure 3-8).

This means that the number of genetically different sex cells an individual can produce is 2^{23} or 8,388,608. In other words, the male can produce over 8 million

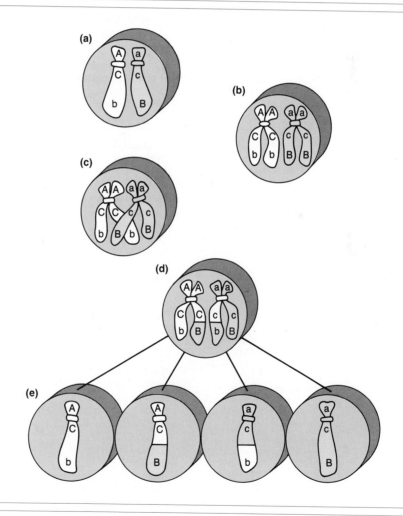

FIGURE 3-8 This diagram illustrates crossing over—the exchange of genes from one chromosome to another. (After G. E. McClearn, "The Inheritance of Behavior." In L. J. Postman [Ed.], *Psychology in the Making.* New York: Knopf, 1963, p. 163)

genetically different sperm and the female can produce the same number of different eggs. By calculating the various combinations of sperm penetrations of the egg, one finds that one man and woman together can produce approximately 64 billion genetically different offspring without ever having two that are identical (identical twins being the exception).

Among other things, this means that in organisms as genetically complex as humans, heredity represents not only the passing on of certain characteristics (Table 3-1) but also the transmission of individual differences. Consider a family in which the children have physical characteristics that are as different as night and day. Yet, there are other parents who produce offspring whose appearances are almost mirror images of each other. How is this possible? The answer is that when both parents carry homozygous genes for a certain characteristic, the children will all be homozygous for that same characteristic. If both parents have paired homozygous genes for blue eyes, black hair, and a "Roman" nose, all children will have these characteristics. Those parents who are heterozygous for various traits may have offspring without recognizable similarities. Therefore, heredity means familial similarities as well as individual differences. We shall soon see that as early as the second month after conception, some inherited physical characteristics begin to develop.

TABLE 3-1 Dominant and Recessive Characteristics

Characteristics in the left-hand column (the phenotype) dominate characteristics in the right-hand column.

	Dominant Traits	*Recessive Characteristics*
Eye coloring	Brown eyes	Gray, green, hazel, blue eyes
	Gray, green, hazel	Blue
	Blue	Albino (pink)
Vision	Farsightedness	Normal vision
	Normal vision	Nearsightedness
	Normal sight	Night vision
	Normal color vision	Color blindness*
Hair	Dark hair	Blond hair, light hair (red hair)
	Nonred hair (blond, brunette)	Red hair
	Curly hair	Straight hair
	Full head of hair	Baldness*
	Widow's peak hairline	Normal hairline
Facial features	Dimples in cheek	No dimples
	Unattached earlobes	Attached earlobes
	"Roman" nose	Straight nose
	Broad lips	Thin lips
Appendages	Extra digits	Normal number
	Fused digits	Normal
	Short digits	Normal
	Fingers lacking one joint	Normal length
	Limb dwarfing	Normal proportion
	Clubbed thumb	Normal thumb
	Double-jointedness	Normal joints
Other	Immunity to poison ivy	Susceptibility to poison ivy
	Normal coloring (pigmented skin)	Albinism
	Normal blood clotting	Hemophilia*
	Normal hearing	Congenital deafness
	Normal hearing	Deaf mutism
	Normal intelligence	Amaurotic idiocy
	Normal enzyme production	Phenylketonuria

*Sex-linked characteristics.

☐ Simple Types of Gene Action

The statement that brown eyes dominate blue eyes does not account for the various *shades* of brown and blue, as well as hazel, green, and gray eyes. It is because of such complexities that *dominant* and *recessive* are inadequate terms for the more complex features of biochemical activity. In fact, strictly speaking, both terms are partial misnomers. A dominant gene does not actually dominate a recessive gene. The terms *active* and *passive* serve much better to describe a gene's activity (sometimes referred to as *biochemically active* or *passive*).

An albino has deficient pigmentation, including translucent or milky skin, white or colorless hair, and a pink coloration within the pupils of the eyes.

The recessive, or passive, gene manufactures very few messenger RNAs and, consequently, very little protein. The dominant gene is more active, manufacturing more RNA and, consequently, more protein. To illustrate this point, let us examine eye coloring, a prime example of a gene's *activity level*. The iris (colored part) of all eyes is made up of practically the same protein (called *melanin*). The so-called color of the eyes is, in essence, an optical illusion, dependent on the amount of melanin produced. Babies, whether kittens, puppies, or humans, are usually born with blue eyes, regardless of the eventual eye color. Does this mean that the iris first produces blue melanin then brown melanin? The answer is no. It means that melanin, in small amounts, appears blue. The more active a gene is, the more melanin (pigment) will be produced and the darker the iris appears (see Figures 3-9 and 3-10).

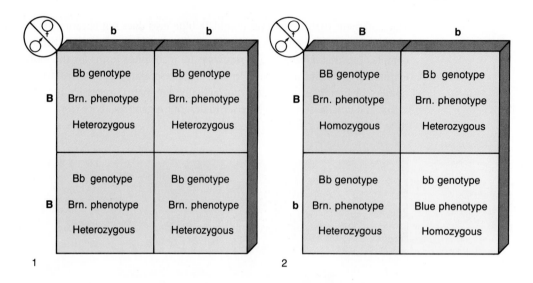

FIGURE 3-9 Punnett square. (1) All children born to this couple, regardless of how many, will have brown eyes but will be "carriers" (have recessive genes) for blue eyes. (2) Two parents with brown eyes (their phenotype) may have a heterozygous genotype—Bb. If the recessive gene is present in an egg that is fertilized by a sperm carrying the recessive gene for blueness, they can have a blue-eyed child. In theory, one-quarter of their children would have blue eyes.

No melanin at all indicates that the gene is neither biochemically active nor biochemically passive. Rather, the gene is inactive. Without the production of melanin, the eye has no coloration and appears to be pink because, without pigmentation, the small blood vessels at the rear of the iris are visible. People unable to produce any melanin are called *albinos.*

A person's eye color is an "effect." That is, blue eyes appear "bluer" under a clear blue sky or when a person wears blue clothing. Likewise, complimentary brown clothing will make brown eyes appear darker or lighter.

Hair color is determined by the same principle; very little melanin produces naturally white hair (found primarily in Scandinavian peoples); small amounts of pigment produce blonds; larger melanin deposits produce brown hair; and the largest deposits of pigment granules produce black hair. As with eye coloring, it is the same melanin but in different quantities. Hair color, like eye color, is affected by other factors, such as the thickness, dryness, or oiliness of the hair or the lightness or darkness of a room or other environmental surroundings. Red hair seems to be caused by a supplementary gene, one that appears only if no other dominant gene is present (see Figure 3-11.)

Genes, then, have *degrees of activity* whose rates may change during the course of development. It is somewhat uncommon, but not unusual, for a person's hair color to change (genetically, not artificially) throughout his or her life. For example, it is possible for a person born with platinum hair color to become blond at age 5; "strawberry blond" at age 20; red-headed at age 23; blond, again, at age 25; and so on. Scalp hair is frequently a different color from facial, pubic, or other body hairs, whose characteristics are evidently governed by separate genes.

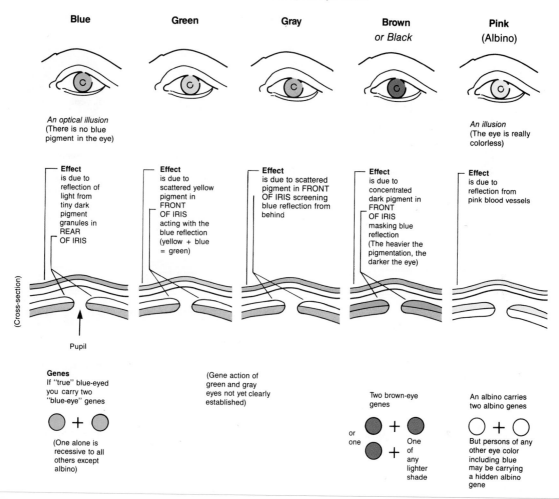

What makes your eye color?

Blue

An optical illusion
(There is no blue
pigment in the eye)

Effect
is due to
reflection of
light from
tiny dark
pigment
granules in
REAR
OF IRIS

(Cross-section)

Pupil

Genes
If "true" blue-eyed
you carry two
"blue-eye" genes

(One alone is
recessive to all
others except
albino)

Green

Effect
is due to
scattered yellow
pigment in
FRONT
OF IRIS
acting with the
blue reflection
(yellow + blue
= green)

(Gene action of
green and gray
eyes not yet clearly
established)

Gray

Effect
is due to scattered
pigment in FRONT
OF IRIS screening
blue reflection from
behind

Brown
or Black

Effect
is due to
concentrated
dark pigment in
FRONT
OF IRIS
masking blue
reflection
(The heavier the
pigmentation, the
darker the eye)

Two brown-eye
genes

or
one

One
of
any
lighter
shade

Pink
(Albino)

An illusion
(The eye is really
colorless)

Effect
is due to
reflection from
pink blood vessels

An albino carries
two albino genes

But persons of any
other eye color
including blue
may be carrying
a hidden albino
gene

FIGURE 3-10
(Adapted from Scheinfeld, 1950)

Blood typing provides another illustration of why dominant and recessive are inadequate terms that should be replaced by the terms active and passive. Although there are over 100 different chemicals in the blood, most people are familiar with only the four main blood types: A, B, AB and O. Figure 3-12 shows two homozygous blood types; the female has type A, and the male has type B. All of their offspring will be type AB, with neither A nor B dominating the other. Each child receives an active gene for the production of the chemical labeled A, as well as an active gene for the protein chemical called B. Therefore, both proteins (chemicals) are found in the bloodstream. The genetic action is mutually exclusive, not additive as in eye or hair coloration. The so-called recessive gene in blood typing is type O, a blood type that produces so little protein, it is barely measurable.

In Figure 3-13 we can see that a type A or B person knows his or her phenotype, but not genotype, whereas type AB or O knows both phenotype and genotype. Because type O is recessive (passive), one must inherit an "O" from each parent, otherwise the active gene would be dominant. Persons with phenotype A or B do not know their genotype (it could be AA or AO; BB or BO).

What makes your hair color?

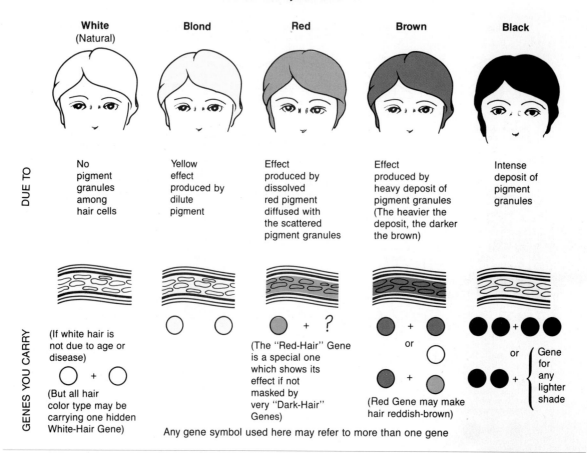

White (Natural)	Blond	Red	Brown	Black
DUE TO No pigment granules among hair cells	Yellow effect produced by dilute pigment	Effect produced by dissolved red pigment diffused with the scattered pigment granules	Effect produced by heavy deposit of pigment granules (The heavier the deposit, the darker the brown)	Intense deposit of pigment granules

GENES YOU CARRY

(If white hair is not due to age or disease)

○ + ○

(But all hair color type may be carrying one hidden White-Hair Gene)

(The "Red-Hair" Gene is a special one which shows its effect if not masked by very "Dark-Hair" Genes)

(Red Gene may make hair reddish-brown)

Gene for any lighter shade

Any gene symbol used here may refer to more than one gene

FIGURE 3-11
(Adapted from Scheinfeld, 1950)

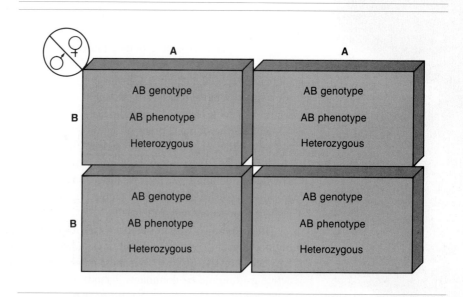

	A	A
B	AB genotype / AB phenotype / Heterozygous	AB genotype / AB phenotype / Heterozygous
B	AB genotype / AB phenotype / Heterozygous	AB genotype / AB phenotype / Heterozygous

FIGURE 3-12
All children born to this couple will have type AB blood. One gene does not dominate the other.

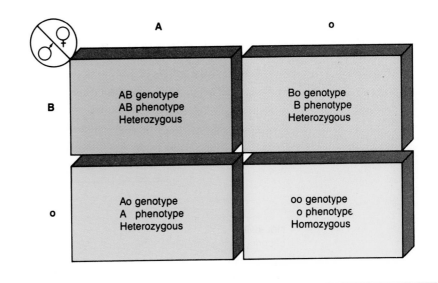

FIGURE 3-13
Blood type O, like other recessive characteristics, does not express itself unless a dominant gene is absent.

Genetic *blending action* is the last type of biochemical activity we discuss in this chapter. It refers to the process whereby a person inherits two different genes, but rather than one dominating the other or both acting independently of each other (e.g., blood type), they blend together.

The "Andalusian fowl," a chickenlike creature, provides a good example of genetic blending action. In nature, Andalusian fowls occur only in two strains—they are either black or white—and they live geographically separated; thus, all black fowl are homozygous for black and always produce black offspring; white always produce white. However, if the geographical separation is removed (e.g., in a zoo) and a white fowl mates with a black fowl, neither color dominates. Rather, the offspring is irridescent blue! Here, the proteins have blended, evidently forming another chemical reaction that causes this beautiful new color. To answer the question that students usually ask next, what happens if two irridescent blues mate?, Figures 3-14 and 3-15 help to unveil

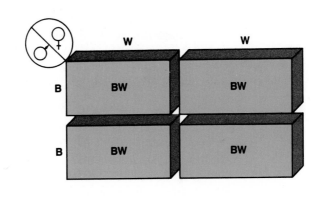

FIGURE 3-14
When an all-black Andalusian fowl mates with an all-white one, all young are BW genotype and iridescent blue phenotype.

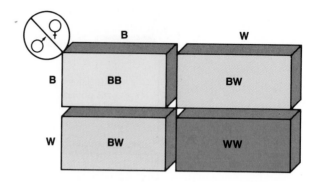

FIGURE 3-15   The mating of two iridescent Andalusian fowl results in 50 percent of their offspring being iridescent, 25 percent black, and 25 percent white.

the "mystery." As one can see, the resulting possibilities are one-fourth black, one-fourth white, and one-half irridescent blue.

We have offered relatively simple examples of physical characteristics. Behavioral traits, however, are more difficult to explain. They are more complex, therefore, more difficult to study. Thus, we know more about the inheritance of superficial traits, such as pigmentation, than we do about the inheritance of more complicated characteristics, such as intelligence.

■ Behavioral Genetics

A little boy, hugging a violin, walks out onto the stage at New York's Carnegie Hall. There is a flutter of applause from the thousands of persons filling the auditorium. The little boy tucks his violin under his chin and begins to play. The audience, skeptical, watches, listens. A tiny hand sweeps the bow back and forth, tiny fingers fly over the strings, streams of melody, now shrill, now full-throated, cascade forth. Already, in those first minutes, many mature musicians out front know that in all their years of study and work they have not been able to achieve such mastery. Soon they, and the others, quite forget that this is a little boy who is playing. As if drawn by invisible bonds, they are carried out of the hall, into the night, higher and higher. Then suddenly there is a burst of notes like a rocket's shower of golden stars . . . the music stops . . . and they are all back again in Carnegie Hall, incredulously storming with their bravos a little boy—a little boy who in a few hours may be crying because he isn't allowed to stay up and play with his toys.

(Scheinfeld, 1950, p. 234)

In his study of musical inheritance Scheinfeld noted that such situations have occurred periodically, although infrequently, through the centuries. He also pointed out that true virtuosity in playing an instrument appears extremely early in life, the average age being just 4¾ years. For those who believe environmental factors, rather than genetic, are the major influence of musical talent, Scheinfeld cites case histories. Arthur Rubinstein, for example, was brought up in a poor family in which no musical instruments were available. However, Rubinstein spontaneously created and sang his own songs. Scheinfeld also tells of a number of children exhibiting musical greatness in their second and third years of life; the more familiar names include Chopin, Mozart, Heifetz, Rachmaninoff, Ormandy, and Toscanini.

Scheinfeld's evidence suggests that truly great musical ability depends heavily on genetics. In all probability, several genes are involved in producing such virtuosos. This, however, does not eliminate the role of environment; rather, a favorable environment must exist if the talent is to be allowed full expression. Yet, the most conducive environment in the world for the development of musical ability will be of limited value if the inherited potential is not present. Consider, for example, the sheer number of children who have suffered through years of music or voice lessons, simply because their parents may have believed "practice makes perfect."

The study of the relationship between genetic variations and behavioral variations (such as that of musicality), is known as *behavioral genetics,* a fairly recent and complex field of exploration. Behavioral genetics studies behavior that is directly or indirectly under genetic control. Behavior is seldom controlled by one protein, which is the case with certain physical traits. Rather, most behavior is influenced by the multiple production of proteins (genetic traits), the individual's past interactions with the environment, current environmental factors, and the organism's current biochemical state (Plomin, 1990).

The complexities of these interacting variables makes their scientific investigation difficult. Consequently, our knowledge of human inherited behavior is extremely limited, forcing us to use such terms as *behavioral predisposition.* Such a term implies that one may have a *tendency* toward certain behavioral characteristics, given certain unspecified environmental conditions.

☐ Polygenes and Behavior

It has been implied that each gene has a definite and singular task, yet this is seldom the case. Instead, most physical and behavioral characteristics are under the direction of *polygenes,* genes that work together with additive and/or complementary effects. Obviously, the more genes that work together on a single task, the more difficult the research becomes. Polygenes increase the number of individual differences one finds in the anatomical and physiological structure of persons. In fact, no two people are biochemically identical. Therefore, they will react differently to similar biochemical environments (not only medicines but all food, which, in the final analysis, are chemical compositions). This partially explains why some people can eat or drink foods that may upset the systems of others.

To understand polygenes, one must be aware of an individual's *constitution,* a reference to the physical and mental makeup of a person. *Makeup* is a rather vague term that refers to the general biochemical state created by polygenes. When we speak of a person having a strong physical constitution, we are referring to his or her strength or health. When a person is said to have a "weak stomach," the inference is to a constitutional weakness established by polygenes. One's biochemical makeup seems to contain varying degrees of immunity or susceptibility to irritations, allergies, tuberculosis, poison ivy, diabetes, and hundreds of other biological disorders.

All diseases interact to some degree with the environment. People who are susceptible to tuberculosis, for example, may never develop it if they live in a healthy, clean-air environment. A person who is susceptible to poison ivy may seldom contract it if he or she has no contact with the plant. By the same token, a person basically immune to poison ivy may be exposed to it many times without contracting a rash. If, however, this person were to lie down in a poison ivy patch, there probably would not be enough "immunity" to keep him or her from contracting a good case of it.

Another example is *diabetes mellitus,* a condition that—the evidence suggests—begins as a constitutional tendency (possibly two or more recessive genes, i.e., biochemically inactive). These inactive genes can produce only limited amounts of insulin; therefore, when a person gains too much weight or eats too many carbohydrates, insulin production becomes insufficient, forcing the person to add insulin to the system. In this instance, environmental interaction is the amount and type (protein, carbohydrates, etc.) of food intake, the consequent body weight, and the quantity of insulin produced (a genetically determined factor).

Sickle-cell anemia, a disease of the red blood cells, is a relatively common disorder (1 in 400) among blacks of African background (Whaley and Wong, 1989). Normally, a red blood cell is shaped like a disk, but a minor genetic mutation changes the shape of the red blood cell to a hooked-shaped "sickle" (Figure 3-16). These cells die very quickly (causing anemia and, possibly, death) because of their inability to carry oxygen. Because it is a recessive trait, individuals who inherit this recessive homozygous condition may eventually die from it. Blacks may have SS (normal red blood cells), Ss (a tendency toward anemia), or ss (sickle-cell anemia). It is interesting to note that in this country, an Ss constitution can weaken a person's health, but the recessive "s" gene plays a dual role: It produces a protein (chemical) makeup that immunizes the individual from malaria. Therefore, blacks who live in Africa and have the heterozygous Ss, possess a biological advantage over those carrying homozygous SS genes!

In summary, genes and polygenes produce a biochemical state that may be referred to, currently, only as one's constitution or predisposition. Because these predispositions are heritable, it can be advantageous to a physician to know a patient's family medical history, which is why we spend a considerable amount of time in doctors' offices and hospitals listing the diseases and illnesses of our parents and other relatives. Diabetes, sickle-cell anemia, heart and kidney conditions, cataracts, and even mental disorders often are familial.

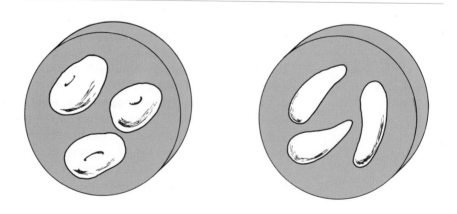

FIGURE 3-16 Erythrocytes (red blood cells) on the left are capable of carrying the "normal" amount of oxygen, while the sickle-shaped cells, on the right, are incapable of carrying sufficient oxygen. (From R. A. Goldsby, *Race and Races.* New York: Macmillan, 1971)

The following case clearly shows how a familial disorder may be diagnosed by genetic means even when symptoms might indicate conditions other than those that actually exist:

> This child had a very dry skin, sparse hair, poorly developed teeth, and a tendency to become feverish upon the slightest exertion. Hypothyroidism (undersecretion of the thyroid gland) results in such symptoms, and the child's condition was thus diagnosed and he was put on thyroid medication. But the treatment seemed to aggravate the condition, and another doctor was called in. Fortunately, this man had had training in genetics, and made a study of the child's family history. He found that one of the parents and a number of the relatives showed similar, but less severe, symptoms, and he diagnosed the condition as an inherited disease, ectodermal dysplasia. Among the symptoms of this disease is an absence of normal sweat glands. In a normal person the body is cooled through the evaporation of perspiration from the skin, but in persons without normal perspiration, the body is easily overheated. Hence, the administration of thyroxine was the worst sort of treatment, for thyroxine speeds body metabolism and increases the heat output.
>
> (Winchester, 1975, pp. 4–5)

Our discussion demonstrates that genes are not just simple units of hereditary matter; they also combine into working groups called polygenes. This complexity makes it very difficult to identify behavior that is influenced by genes. Scientists, however, are reaching a point in their research where they can see signposts pointing in the direction their scientific inquiry should follow.

☐ Intelligence and Behavior

Psychologists most often disagree among themselves about the nature and origin of mental disorders, personality traits, and, especially, intelligence. Some favor the explanations offered by the environmental camp, others adhere to the inheritability of these characteristics, and still others take a middle course.

Concerning the controversy over intelligence, the evidence indicates that people are born with differing genetic makeups, and it is also more or less obvious (depending on your outlook) that people inherit differing potentials, abilities, and intelligences.

TWIN STUDIES: METHODOLOGY In theory, the only way to determine which effects are genetic and which are environmental is to hold one of these variables constant while manipulating the other. In other words, if one could totally control the environmental conditions of persons from the moment of conception onward, any resulting difference could therefore be considered as genetic. This method, of course, is impossible. The alternative is to manipulate the environment of two persons who have an identical genetic makeup. Through the phenomenon of identical twins, this is possible.

To design an experiment that will yield practical data, three groupings of twins are required. Group 1 should consist of identical twins (genetically identical) who have been reared together, thus providing *similar* environments. Group 2 should consist of identical twins reared apart, preferably in *dissimilar* environments. Group 3 should comprise fraternal twins (genetically dissimilar) reared together and preferably of the same sex—opposite sexes have a greater variance in their environment because they tend to socialize more with members of their own sex (Smith, 1965). See Table 3-2 to see how this trigroup methodology is executed.

Studies involving identical twins enable researchers to better understand the interaction of heredity and environment.

Comparing these three studies (and their very similar results) demonstrates that identical twins reared together are much closer in intelligence than are fraternal twins reared together, both having similar environments. In other words, similar environments are not sufficient to equalize intelligence. In support of this thesis, the results also indicate that the intelligence scores of identical twins reared apart are more similar than are the scores of fraternal twins reared in the same environment. But this does not rule out varying degrees of environmental effects. It has been found (Smith, 1965) that identical twins are more likely to have mutual friendships and share experiences than are fraternal twins, possibly accounting somewhat for the higher correlation in their IQs. Because fraternal twins are more likely to share similar environments than other siblings are, there should be a closer correlation for fraternal twins than for other siblings, which indeed is the case. Environment, therefore, though evidently not the major force shaping intelligence, does have an influence.

Another method of demonstrating the degree of inheritability of intelligence is to compare children brought up with their biological parents with children reared by

TABLE 3-2 Trigroup Method of Studying Genetic versus Environmental Influences on Behavior: Examples for Intelligence

	Twin Type	Environmental Factor	Interpretation of Results
Group 1	Identical twins (genetically identical)	Reared together (similar environment)	Assuming IQs are similar, these results could be due to either genetic or environmental factors.
Group 2	Identical twins (genetically identical)	Reared apart (dissimilar environment)	If IQs are markedly different, the assumption will be that environment plays a major role. If IQs are similar, a genetic influence will be assumed.
Group 3	Fraternal twins (preferably of the same sex) (genetically different)	Reared together (similar environment)	If environment is the significant factor, correlations will be about the same as for identical twins reared together.

foster parents (Table 3-3). Theoretically, if environment were the major determining factor, children's IQs would be approximately the same as those of the other people in the household environment in which they were reared. Normally, we find the relationship between genetic parents and children to be 0.50. Therefore, the similarities in children adopted by foster parents would point to the greater importance of environment, whereas the differences would suggest the hereditary role. Some researchers have found that adopted children have IQs closer to those of their genetic parents than to those of their foster parents.

TABLE 3-3 Statistical Correlations of Intelligence among Family Relations

Relationship	Correlation
Monozygotic twins	
Reared together	.86
Reared apart	.79
Dizygotic twins	
Reared together	.60
Siblings	
Reared together	.47
Reared apart	.24
Parent/child	.40
Foster parent/child	.31
Cousins	.15

These correlations are composited from 111 different studies from all parts of the world. In general, the closer the genetic relationship of two people, the higher the correlation between their IQs. (From Bouchard, Jr. and McGere, M. 1981)

While the controversy about the major influences on intelligence continues, we can only await methodological breakthroughs to supply us with the answers to our questions. Meanwhile, we must also explore the nature of both intelligence and intellectual potential. If society (parents, educators, psychologists, etc.) can provide appropriate vehicles for the enhancement of each individual's potential, the questions now being asked regarding the nature-nurture issue may become moot.

INHERITABILITY OF BEHAVIORAL TRAITS The same general methodology for determining inheritability of intelligence can be used to discover to what degree, if any, various other behavior patterns are influenced by the laws of genetics. Behavior that is unique, different, or even bizarre is more noticeable and measureable than is so-called normal behavior. This is because distinct abnormal behavior is more readily measured by a statistical analysis than is the range of more normal behaviors.

There are studies revealing at least minimal evidence that certain basic behaviors are inherited (Tellegen, Lykken, Bouchard, Wilcox et al., 1988; Plomin, McClearn, Pederson, Nesselroade et al., 1988). However, it is a very unclear area and one where it is wise to tread lightly until experimental results offer more substantial evidence. It is speculated, however, that certain personality traits (e.g., aggressiveness, smiling responses, fear, shyness, moodiness), as well as certain psychological disorders (such as depression and schizophrenia) may be inherited (see Horowitz and Dudek, 1983; Gottesman and Shields, 1982). The activity level evident in a newborn seems to persist through at least the first few years of life, indicating again a genetic predisposition. Children assessed at 21 months of age as being inhibited or uninhibited in social situations continued to exhibit these traits at ages 5½ and, at least to a certain extent, 7½ (Kagen, Reznick, Snidman, Gibbons et al., 1988).

Certain personality traits, such as aggression, may be inherited.

Schizophrenia is one of the most common (about 2 million people in the United States) and most studied of the severe behavior disorders (Martin, 1977). It is a psychotic disorder characterized by thought disturbances and often accompanied by delusions, hallucinations, and other maladaptive behaviors. There are strong arguments to support both genetic and environmental causes of schizophrenia. The question is whether schizophrenia develops from traumatic early childhood experiences or from genetically produced chemical imbalances—or from a combination of both.

Again, studies of identical twins reared in the same environment, identical twins reared in separate environments, and fraternal twins reared in the same environment are the preferred methods for studying the genetics of schizophrenia. The compilation of studies shown in Table 3-4 shows that the statistical evidence points directly to an inheritable genetic predisposition toward acquiring schizophrenia. There are several significant studies, however, that indicate zero concordance (degree of similarity between twins) rate.

In one study, researchers discovered a significantly higher concordance for schizophrenia between members of identical twin pairs than between members of fraternal twin pairs (Gottesman and Shields, 1982). They found that of 28 pairs of identical

TABLE 3-4 Schizophrenia: Concordance in Recent Twin Studies

Investigator	Year	Country	Identical		Fraternal	
			Concordance (%)	Number of Pairs	Concordance (%)	Number of Pairs
Kringlen	1967	Norway	45	55	15	90
Fischer	1973	Denmark	56	21	26	41
Gottesman and Shields	1972	U.K.	58	22	12	33
Tienari	1971	Finland	35	17	13	20
Pollin et al.	1972	U.S.	43	95	9	125

The concordance rate is the percentage of pairs in which both twins are diagnosed as schizophrenic (see I. I. Gottesman and J. Shields, "A Critical Review of Recent Adoption, Twin, and Family Studies of Schizophrenia: Behavioral Genetics Perspectives." *Schizophrenia Bulletin*, 1976, 2, pp. 60–101)

twins, there was a 42 percent concordance for schizophrenia. Their procedure was to identify members of twin pairs from among a population of schizophrenic patients and then to determine how many of these individuals had a twin who was also schizophrenic (of all members of the twin pairs who were schizophrenic, 42 percent had a schizophrenic twin). The concordance between the members of fraternal twin pairs was only 9 percent, from a sample of 34 pairs.

An environmental argument is that although one may inherit the predisposition to schizophrenia (or any other behavioral trait), it does not necessarily follow that an individual will actually become schizophrenic (if that were the case, our correlations for identical twins would be a perfect 1.00). Organisms interact with their environment; therefore, a person who is predisposed toward schizophrenia may never develop it if he or she is in an appropriate, positive environment. As in the example of immunity or susceptibility to poison ivy, persons may be highly susceptible to schizophrenia, but if they never are in an environment capable of triggering it, they will never contract it.

It is by now evident that the influence of polygenes and an organism's genetic interaction with the environment are difficult areas to explore. Although it is true that animal research has yielded significant results, human behaviors are generally investigated with fewer controls. However, even though general personality traits and characteristics remain difficult to discern, chromosomal changes can be detected through modern techniques. Gross changes in chromosomes allow insights into the tiny world of the gene. In the next section, we discuss the more obvious and common genetic problems.

■ Genetic Aberrations and Mutations

The activity of a cell, including the chromosomes' activities, is governed by biological principles. Biological principles reveal a somewhat high frequency of errors in the chemical behavior of the genetic code. One such "error," or dysfunction, is termed *mutation,* which refers to any sudden change that occurs in the genetic material of an organism. The word *mutant,* in any of the forms, does not imply *negative* change, although one generally conjures up ideas of some horrible change or deformity. Mutations may be positive, negative, or neutral. They also signal that a change in the genetic code (sex cells) has taken place, whereby a new gene can be passed on to the next generation.

In this textbook, the causes of mutations are divided into two groups: chromosomal abnormalities and mutagenic, or teratogenic, agents. Chromosomal abnormalities are occurrences that affect either the number of genes and/or chromosomes for a given species or the arrangement of genes on a chromosome. During normal meiosis, the 23 pairs of chromosomes line up, divide, and go to their new sex cell. Suppose, however, that one pair of chromosomes does not separate but, rather, migrates to the same sex cell. In the case of a woman, one egg would now have an extra chromosome ($23 + 1 = 24$) and one egg would have lost a chromosome ($23 - 1 = 22$). If one of these eggs became fertilized, the absence or excess of 20,000 to 40,000 genes would obviously cause some change in the offspring. Chromosomal abnormalities increase as age increases (Hook, 1981).

When a chromosome is lost, the condition is called *monosomy.* Another abnormality is having an extra chromosome, called trisomy (tri = 3, somy = bodies), which can occur on any chromosome position. If, for example, there are three chromosomes on chromosome position number 21, it is referred to as trisomy 21; if three chromosomes are located in the seventeenth position, it is termed trisomy 17. Trisomy may also occur if one chromosome duplicates itself after meiosis has taken place. Some of the names of the more common and severe mutations are recognized, at least in name, by many laypersons, whereas others are less well known. The following discussion briefly describes some chromosomal abnormalities. Chromosomes are classified according to number and letters.

Down Syndrome, or Trisomy 21 *Down syndrome* (formerly called Down's syndrome), named after its discoverer, results when there is an extra chromosome on the twenty-first position. Individuals with this condition generally have an epicantric eye fold (resembling that of Asians) and round heads. They are mentally retarded and, until recently, died young because of respiratory problems, heart weaknesses, and high susceptibility to leukemia. Antibiotics have extended the lifespan of many who suffer from this disorder. Statistics show that women over age 40 are more likely to give birth to Down syndrome babies than are younger women. More specifically, young mothers have an incidence of 1 birth in 1500; by maternal age 35, 1 in 300; and by age 45, a staggering 1 birth in every 3 to 50 (Masters et al, 1985). Although numerous theories attempt to explain this phenomenon, none have done so satisfactorily.

Klinefelter's Syndrome (XXY) Males with *Klinefelter's syndrome* have two normal X chromosomes plus the Y chromosome (although they may have more than two X chromosomes—e.g., XXXXY; see Sheridan and Radlinski, 1988). They have small

A child with Down syndrome.

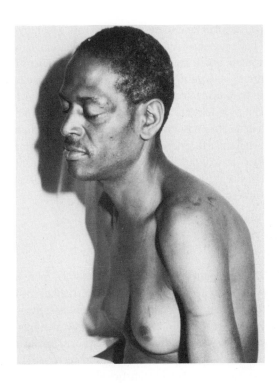

An adult male with Klinefelter's syndrome.

external male sex organs but the general body contour of a female, including enlarged breasts. Those affected are sterile and often below average in intelligence. Like trisomy 21, older women more frequently give birth to males having this condition than do younger women.

Turner's Syndrome (XO) *Turner's syndrome* is a monosomy condition (only one sex chromosome) that affects approximately 1 female of every 2,000 births (Sutton, 1980). The afflicted female may look somewhat normal at birth because clinical signs don't appear until puberty. The physical characteristics include a webbed neck, short fingers (polydactylism), and short stature. No secondary sex characteristics appear at the time of puberty and those afflicted with this syndrome are sterile. Although they are normally not mentally retarded, they often have learning problems (Kalat, 1980).

Cri-du-Chat Syndrome *Cri-du-chat syndrome* is caused by a partial loss of chromosome 5 and produces many disorders, including severe mental retardation, microcephaly (very small brain), growth retardation, low birth weight, and divergent strabismus (little eye control). In French, cri-du-chat means cry of the cat, a reference to the mutated vocal cords that only allow the afflicted youngster to make mewing sounds. These children generally die shortly after birth.

Triple X Syndrome The *triple X syndrome* affects females, many of whom are virtually physically normal except for menstrual irregularities and premature menopause. However, mild mental retardation is common. Females possessing three, four, and five Xs have also been found. Usually the more sex chromosomes, the greater the level of retardation (Rovet and Netley, 1983).

XYY Syndrome The *XYY syndrome,* sometimes called the *aggressive syndrome* or the *crime syndrome,* was popularized by the news media when cases such as Richard Speck's arose (Speck brutally killed eight nurses in Chicago in the 1970s). People carrying the XYYs (and sometimes XXYY) are generally taller than average (over 6 feet) males, have personality disorders, and below average intelligence. Sexual disturbances are common, and antisocial and, occasionally, violent behavior appear early in life. As youngsters, some tend to be unmanageable, destructive, defiant, and fearless.

We have discussed but a sample of chromosomal abnormalities in this section. Others include trisomy 17, 18 (Kupka and Miller, 1989), 22, and partial trisomy; the Philadelphia chromosome (monosomy 21, which causes leukemia in later life); E trisomy syndrome; D syndrome; and many more (Schinzel, 1984). As genetic advances take place, so will our knowledge of these and other forms of human behavior. With such knowledge, our understanding of growth and development for all stages of the life cycle will escalate.

■ Genetic Counseling

Although some genetic defects occur randomly, more often there is a pattern to their occurrence. As geneticists have learned more about the way one generation transmits a defect to another, they have been able to counsel parents about the potential risks to their unborn children. Today, there is a network of genetic counseling centers across the country. They are staffed by physicians or specially trained "genetic associates" and equipped with computerized information retrieval systems that provide immediate access to available facts and statistics about certain problems (Black and Weiss, 1989; Mack and Berman, 1988).

Most expectant parents are at a low risk for having a baby with genetic problems and need never see a genetic counselor. In many cases, an obstetrician will talk to a couple about the most common problems, referring to a genetic counselor those with a need for more expertise:

Couples whose blood tests show them both to be carriers of a genetic disorder.

Prospective parents who belong to certain racial groups who are at high risk for certain genetic disorders. For example, blacks of African background are vulnerable to sickle-cell anemia.

Prospective parents who have already borne one or more children with genetic birth defects.

Couples who know of hereditary defects in their families.

Women who have had three or more miscarriages.

Couples who are closely related, because the risk of inherited disease in the offspring is greatest when parents are related (for example, one in eight for first cousins).

Women who are over 35.

(Eisenberg et al., 1984)

STAGES OF GENETIC COUNSELING   There are three stages of the genetic counseling process (Lauersen, 1983). The first stage is assembling a complete family history, which can provide information about the genetic basis of any disorder that might be present. Once this information has been gathered, the genetic counselor often recommends special blood tests or a complete chromosome count for the wife and/or the husband.

The second stage is the genetic counselor's interpretation of the evidence. Each case is different, and any number of conclusions are possible. Establishing or excluding a genetic or chromosomal condition is often a complex undertaking, as birth defects are not always the result of genetic factors. A birth defect can be caused by a random or inherited chromosomal abnormality; it can be transmitted by a single gene from one parent or a matching gene from both parents; it can be caused by environmental factors; or it can result from what is called multifactorial inheritance—a combination of environmental and/or several genetic causes. After the counselor has assembled the available evidence, he or she will try to diagnose the disease and then calculate the chances of an occurrence or recurrence within a couple's immediate family, by consulting statistics from other, similar cases.

The final stage occurs after the genetic counselor has outlined the probable or possible risks and presents the available options to the prospective parents. Here, the couple makes its own decision. Some prospective parents with a heritable genetic disorder may choose artificial insemination or try to adopt a child rather than to risk an affected pregnancy. Others may take a calculated risk and the woman becomes pregnant, or they may choose to continue an existing pregnancy, hoping that the child will not be seriously handicapped.

GENETIC COUNSELING AND MEDICAL TECHNOLOGY Today, the risk of bearing a child with a disease incompatible with normal life has been considerably reduced by new prenatal testing methods. For example, *amniocentesis* allows the detection of chromosomal abnormalities in the fetus. The amniotic fluid is sampled by inserting a hollow needle through the mother's abdominal wall and into the amniotic sac. A syringe is then attached, and the amniotic fluid is withdrawn. This fluid contains

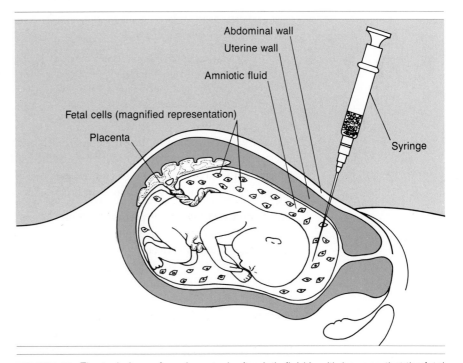

FIGURE 3-17 The technique of amniocentesis. Amniotic fluid is withdrawn so that the fetal cells can be analyzed.

discarded fetal cells, which can be observed, measured, and analyzed for size, shape, and number (see Figure 3-17).

Amniocentesis is an important medical advancement, but it does not always provide clear-cut answers. If an extra chromosome is found at chromosome 21, for example, we know that the child will inherit Down syndrome and will be mentally retarded. However, other test results offer only statistical data. Hemophilia, the inability of the blood to clot, is a good illustration. If two XXs are found, the fetus is female and will probably not have hemophilia. If the test reveals that the fetus is male, there is a 50 percent chance that he will be a hemophiliac. Which X chromosome he inherited from the mother cannot, as yet, be determined.

Another example is the Lesch-Nyhan syndrome, a severe neurologic disease that occurs in males and is characterized by mental retardation, involuntary writhing motions, and compulsive self-mutilation of the lips and fingertips by biting. In amniocentesis, the fetal cells are removed, cultured, and submitted to X-ray film. Whereas normal cells absorb the radiation, the Lesch-Nyhan cells remain free of radioactivity.

Another rare condition, found mostly among Jews of northern European origin, is Tay-Sachs disease, which causes blindness, mental retardation, and early childhood death. This disease is caused by an enzyme deficiency that can be detected in fetal amniotic cells.

In addition to these conditions, other forms of information related to prenatal life can be gathered by amniocentesis, including:

Sex of the fetus: Skin cells sloughed off by the fetus accumulate in the amniotic fluid. Under the microscope all male cells are different from all female cells.

Age of the fetus: Measuring discarded cells in the fluid also tells the maturity of the lungs, which is itself an indication of fetal age.

Metabolic disorders: Amniotic fluid reveals metabolic disorders caused by missing or defective enzymes.

Oxygen flow to the fetus: Gases dissolved in the amniotic fluid reveal the amount of oxygen that the fetus is receiving and whether it is at risk. Acidity of the amniotic fluid, often caused by an inadequate flow of oxygen, is another indication of fetal distress.

(Hotchner, 1984)

For women wishing to undergo amniocentesis, the fourteenth to the sixteenth week of pregnancy seems optimal. There are sufficient fetal cells in the amniotic sac, which itself is large enough to lessen the likelihood of the needle injuring the fetus. This also allows time for a safe abortion, if desired.

Ultrasonography Another prenatal testing apparatus that can uncover genetic defects and other disorders is ultrasonography. Briefly stated, ultrasound employs short pulses of high-frequency, low-intensity sound waves (above the normal range of hearing) to create images. Ultrasound was first used in industry to detect flaws in construction and during World War II to locate submarines below the ocean surface. As the sound waves echo off structures in the mother's body, they are converted into electrical signals and transformed into images on a display screen (Figure 3-18). A physician with specialized training evaluates the sonographic images and photographs them for further analysis.

Ultrasonography can confirm or rule out potential problems, eliminating the need for additional testing procedures that may be hazardous to the mother or fetus. It can

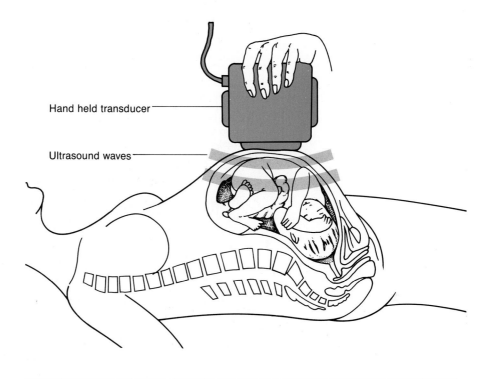

Hand held transducer

Ultrasound waves

FIGURE 3-18 An ultrasound examination with a hand-held transducer. Ultrasound waves will be transmitted to and from the mother's abdomen, creating an image of the fetus on a special monitor (not shown).

confirm a pregnancy within a few weeks of conception and is the definitive means of determining whether the mother is carrying more than one fetus. Obstetricians also use ultrasound to diagnose a miscarriage or a misplaced (ectopic) pregnancy or to detect fetal malformations, including limb abnormalities, hydrocephalus (excessive fluid in the skull), some congenital heart and kidney defects, and excessive or insufficient amniotic fluid. It is the best method for examining the placenta's size, shape, and location: Such information may be critical to pregnancies complicated by diabetes, blood incompatibility, or growth problems. If bleeding from the vagina occurs in the last trimester, ultrasound may show whether the placenta is blocking the baby's way out of the uterus (a condition called *placenta previa*) or whether the placenta is separating from the uterine wall too soon, known as *placental abruption* (Hales and Creasy, 1982).

Fetoscopy Usually performed after the sixteenth week of pregnancy, fetoscopy uses a tiny telescopelike instrument, complete with lights and lenses. It is inserted through a tiny incision in the abdomen into the amniotic sac, where it can view and photograph the fetus (Figure 3-19). At the same time, fetoscopy allows the diagnosis, through tissue and blood sampling, of several diseases that amniocentesis cannot detect. Still a relatively new procedure, its usefulness in certain high-risk pregnancies is speeding its acceptance by the obstetrical community. It is most commonly recommended when there is a family history of a blood disease, particularly when one or both parents are carriers, or of certain skin disorders (Eisenberg et al., 1984).

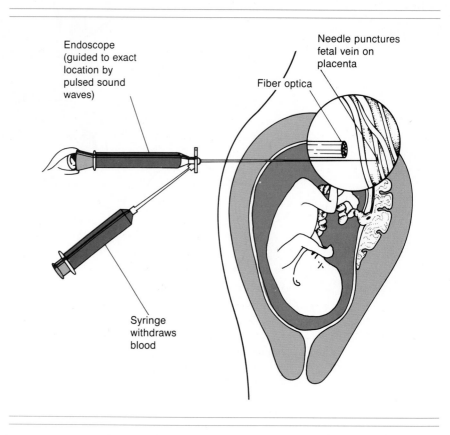

Endoscope
(guided to exact
location by
pulsed sound
waves)

Needle punctures
fetal vein on
placenta

Fiber optica

Syringe
withdraws
blood

FIGURE 3-19
The fetoscopy procedure.

CHAPTER REVIEW

Human genetics is the study of the origin of life. Geneticists study chromosomes and genes to determine what inheritable characteristics they contain. Heredity refers to what and how characteristics are transmitted from parent to offspring. Offspring can be genetically similar to their parents or exhibit genetic variation.

Within the nucleus of a cell are chromosomes that are made up of genes. The chemical makeup of a chromosome is called deoxyribonucleic acid, or DNA, sometimes referred to as the blueprint of life. Its structure is like a spiraling staircase, each step or rung consisting of two bases that bond together: adenine bonds with thymine, and cytosine bonds with guanine. A gene is made up of hundreds to thousands of these rungs having a common function such as eye or skin color. When a gene is activated, it makes a copy of itself, although some chemical changes also take place. This copy is named messenger RNA (ribonucleic acid) which carries a genetic code to the ribosomes that lie outside the nucleus. The ribosome mixes amino acids to produce protein (all body cells are made of protein).

Humans have 23 pairs of chromosomes, or a total of 46, both parents each contributing 23 chromosomes. The cell division of the body or somatic cells is termed mitosis. During mitosis, the parent cell with its diploid or full species number of chromosomes produces two daughter cells, each of which also contains the diploid number of chromosomes (46). In the sex cells (sperm and egg), the parent gamete, which has 46 chromosomes, undergoes meiosis, a type of cell division in which each new sperm or egg is given half the number of chromosomes (23). This is called a haploid state. When a sperm penetrates the egg, the fertilized egg or zygote has the full quota of chromosomes for a new life to begin.

A child's sex is determined by the chromosomes that appear in the twenty-third position. If the offspring receives an X from both parents, the child will be female (XX). If the child receives an X from the mother and a Y from the father, the child will be a boy (XY). In this chapter we also discussed how genes located in the twenty-third position transmit sex-linked characteristics.

Genes are generally considered to be dominant or recessive; that is, the dominant genes express themselves in an observable way. This is called a person's phenotype. Genotype refers to a person's actual gene makeup. Blending occurs when two proteins produced by two genes mix and create a totally different phenotype.

Behavioral genetics is the field that studies the inheritance of predispositions, such as aptitude, intelligence, behavior disorders, aggressiveness, and passivity. Because it is so difficult to separate environmental influences from genetic influences, few data have yet been collected. However, by studying identical twins reared apart (identical genetic makeup, dissimilar environments), statistics can be correlated. To date, there is fairly strong evidence that many characteristics have a high degree of inheritability. There is also evidence that environmental forces are important to the development of these behaviors.

Genetic aberrations are the inheritance of mutated genes, genes that are mutated because of terratogenic agents or the inheritance of too many or too few chromosomes. One of the more common problems is Down syndrome, a condition in which an infant receives an extra chromosome in the twenty-first position, which leads to such physical characteristics as epicanthic eye folds and almost always to mental retardation. Other genetic aberrations include Klinefelter's syndrome (XXY), a condition in which a male with an extra X chromosome has underdeveloped sex organs and enlarged breasts, and Turner's syndrome (XO), a condition in which a female missing one sex chromosome has such physical defects as short fingers and stature, no secondary sex characteristics, and therefore no functional sex organs.

We concluded this chapter with an examination of genetic counseling, what it entails, and who would benefit most from it. Also explored were the modern medical technologies used by genetic researchers and obstetricians, including amniocentesis, ultrasonography, and fetoscopy.

KEY TERMS

allele
amino acid
amniocentesis
behavioral genetics
behavioral predisposition

blending action
cell
chromosomes
cri-du-chat syndrome
cytoplasm

daughter cell	nucleus
deoxyribonucleic acid (DNA)	ovum
diploid state	parent cell
dominant gene	phenotype
Down syndrome	polygenes
fetoscopy	protoplasm
gamete	recessive gene
genes	ribonucleic acid (RNA)
genetics	ribosomes
genotype	sex-limited genes
germ cells	sex-linked characteristics
gonads	sickle-cell anemia
haploid state	somatic cells
heredity	sperm
heterozygous	testis determining factor
homozygous	triple X syndrome
Klinefelter's syndrome	trisomy 21
meiosis	Turner's syndrome
messenger RNA	ultrasonography
mitosis	variations
mutation	XYY syndrome
nucleoplasm	

RECOMMENDED READINGS

Clark, J. (1985). *The Cell.* New York: Torstar Books.
The genetics of life are covered in Chapter 4 of this understandable and lavishly illustrated text.

Fuller, J. L., and Simmel, E. C. (Eds.). (1983). *Behavior Genetics.* Hillsdale, N.J.: Erlbaum.
A good assortment of readings focusing on many different aspects of behavioral inheritance.

Loehlin, J., and Nichols, R. C. (1976). *Heredity, Environment, and Personality.* Austin: University of Texas Press.
This book presents a good review of research into genetic influences on abilities and personality, including the results of a study that investigated 850 pairs of fraternal and identical twins.

Plomin, R., Defries, J. C., and McCleam, G. E. (1990). *Behavioral Genetics,* 2nd ed. New York: Freeman.
The authors include a good discussion of twin studies and chromosomal abnormalities, among other interesting topics.

Scheinfeld, A. (1972). *Heredity in Humans,* 2nd ed. Philadelphia: Lippincott.
A wonderfully informative book about the real-life meanings of genetic inheritance.

Stebbins, L. (1982). *Darwin to DNA, Molecules to Humanity.* San Francisco: Freeman.
The focus of this book is on how genetics provide the blueprint for growth and development and shape the course of evolution.

Tsuang, M. T., and Vandermey, R. (1980). *Genes and the Mind: The Inheritance of Mental Illness*. New York: Oxford University Press.
This text explores the possible biological and genetic origins of many serious mental disorders.

Watson, J. D. (1968). *The Double Helix*. New York: New American Library.
An interesting account of the ways of scientists and scientific inquiry. Watson describes how he and Francis Crick discovered the DNA structure. Enjoyable reading.

CHAPTER FOUR

Prenatal Development

CHAPTER OUTLINE

WHAT DO YOU THINK?

■ At the moment of conception, it's a single cell containing a genetic message from the mother and father. Approximately nine months later, this microscopic fleck of tissue has been transformed into a fully developed fetus, weighing, on the average, six to seven pounds and measuring between 18 and 21 inches, head to toe. The processes and events responsible for this development are one of nature's truly astounding miracles. Join us as we examine the earliest beginnings of lifespan development.

■ In a recent Gallup Poll, one-third of the pregnant women surveyed said they quit or cut back their cigarette smoking during pregnancy. However, one-third continued to smoke the same amount during pregnancy. For these women, what effect does smoking have on the developing organism? For that matter, what about the consumption of alcohol and other drugs during pregnancy? Just how important is proper maternal nutrition? This chapter will supply answers to these questions as we explore the importance of a healthy prenatal environment.

■ Each year, about 3.5 million babies are born in the United States. Most of them will be brought into the world by traditional delivery techniques in standard hospital facilities. However, a growing number of couples are choosing alternatives to traditional childbirth practices, such as the Lamaze and Leboyer methods and home births. We'll look at these and other practices and the advantages and disadvantages of each. By the time we're done, you'll understand why the question "How do you plan to have your baby?" has become so popular today.

INTRODUCTION

The average full-term human pregnancy lasts for about 280 days and is generally referred to as being a nine-month *gestation period.* Using the more common, but less accurate, nine-month description, pregnancy can be subdivided into three equal divisions, called *trimesters.* Each trimester is three months in length (Table 4-1). Although the organism is both growing and developing throughout all phases of pregnancy, trimester division is somewhat simplified by the following classification system: The first trimester is primarily characterized by differential development of basic struc-

TABLE 4-1 The Three Trimesters of Prenatal Development

Trimester	Major Characterization
First (0–3 months)	Begins development of all internal organs, appendages, sense organs.
Second (4–6 months)	Continuation of development plus growth of organism from 3″ to 1′ in length and from 1 oz. to 1½ lbs. in weight.
Third (7–9 months)	Grows about 8″ in length, gains about 6 lbs.

tures; the second trimester is characterized by both further development and growth; and the third trimester is characterized predominantly by growth.

■ The First Trimester

☐ The First Month

After the ovum (egg) has been fertilized, the zygote (fertilized ovum) undergoes mitosis to become two cells. Ten hours later, these two cells again undergo mitosis to become four cells. This process of cell division continues for approximately two weeks, in what is called the *period of the ovum.* During this two-week time span, there is considerable biological activity as the rapidly multiplying ball of cells travels along the fallopian tube. Even though the cells keep multiplying, there is virtually no increase in mass, as there is no source of nourishment, other than that which is already stored, available to this group of free-floating cells.

On or about the fourth day, the cluster of cells reaches the uterus, at which time it drifts about for another three or four days before embedding, or nesting, itself in the spongy vesseled wall of the waiting uterus. At this time, the entire cluster of cells is no larger than the head of a pin. This process of mitosis and nesting continues for another week.

The *embryonic period* begins when the ovum becomes implanted in the uterine wall and the cells begin to exhibit marked differentiation. The organism is called an

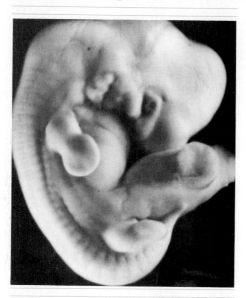

FIGURE 4-1
The embryo at one month.

Identical and Fraternal Twins

Conception usually occurs when a single sperm cell penetrates the female ovum to create a zygote. As a result, a single child is conceived. However, more than one child can be created at one time, a phenomenon known as multiple conception.

Multiple conceptions are far rarer than single ones. Approximately 30,000 sets of twins are born in the United States each year. Twins occur approximately once in every 90 births; triplets about once in 9,300 births; quadruplets once in 490,000; and quintuplets once in every 55,000,000 births. Blacks give birth to the most twins, and Asians give birth to the fewest.

These figures indicate that although the conception of twins is relatively infrequent, they are the most common of multiple births. There are two types of twins. **Identical twins** (monozygotic) result when a single fertilized egg splits after conception. Identical twins are genetically alike, including having the same physical characteristics such as sex, blood type, and eye color.

Fraternal twins (dizygotic) result when two female eggs are fertilized by two separate sperm cells. Fraternal twins are no more alike than are any two single children born to the same parents. They may or may not be of the same sex, and each possesses individual characteristics. To determine whether twins are fraternal or identical, certain tests, such as fingerprinting or blood typing, are made (the results should be the same for identical twins).

Cojoined twins (Siamese) are considered an obstetrical rarity. The ratio of Siamese to normal twin births is approximately 1 in 1,000. Siamese twins are always identical and usually female.

On the average, twins have a gestation period that is approximately 25 days shorter than normal. Almost half of all twin births are premature. When they are delivered, the first twin is usually born head first while the second is often a breech (buttocks first) delivery.

(Noble, 1980; Abbe and Gill, 1981)

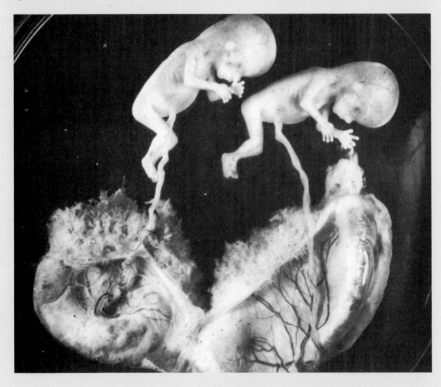

Fraternal twins develop from two separate ova and usually have separate placentas. Identical twins typically share the same placenta.

embryo from the beginning of cell specialization until the end of the second month of pregnancy (approximately two to eight weeks after fertilization).

Four weeks after conception, the embryo measures only three-sixteenths of an inch long, but this is 10,000 times the size of the zygote. The specialization of cells has

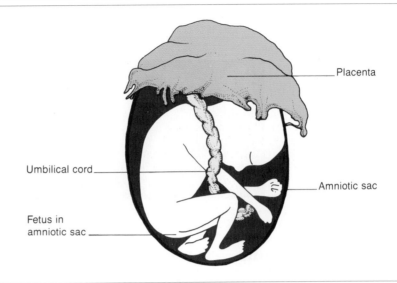

FIGURE 4-2
The intrauterine environment of the fetus.

produced an embryo that now has a short, pointed, curled-up tail and a primitive umbilical cord through which it will eventually be nourished.

We need to emphasize the importance of the developing umbilical cord, amniotic sac, and the placenta. The *amniotic sac* is a transparent membrane completely enveloping the embryo, except where the umbilical cord passes through to the placenta (Figure 4-2). The *placenta*, or afterbirth, is the membrane that allows nourishment to pass from the mother to the embryo, and waste products to be channeled from the embryo to the mother. There is no direct connection of blood vessels between the mother and the embryo. Substances are transmitted to and from the mother's and child's blood vessels *via* the placenta. Eventually the placenta will be connected to the fetus by the umbilical cord.

Contained within the sac is *amniotic fluid*, which holds the embryo or fetus in suspension and protects it not only from being jarred but also from any pressures from the mother's internal organs. The fluid also provides an even temperature for the fetus. The *fetus* is the name given to the organism from about the third prenatal month until birth. The suspension allows the fetus to move freely and also keeps the mother from being unduly jarred.

The *umbilical cord*, or body stalk, contains three blood vessels: One vein carries oxygenated blood from the placenta to the infant, and two arteries carry blood and waste products from the fetus to the placenta. Because the umbilical cord has no nerves, the baby feels no pain when the cord is severed and tied at delivery.

As the unborn's sole source of food, oxygen, and water, the placenta must grow in relation to the organism's needs. Originally microscopic in size, it becomes three or four inches in diameter by the fourth month and at birth weighs about a pound and measures eight inches in diameter.

On approximately the eighteenth day, the embryo's heart begins to appear. By three weeks the heart is functional (it undergoes muscle contractions) but not under neural control. It is beating, however, and blood pulsates through a small, enclosed bloodstream, which is separate from the mother's. A backbone encloses a spinal cord, and internal organs, such as lungs, liver, kidneys, and endocrine glands, begin to develop. The digestive system has also begun to form. Small "buds" that will eventually become arms start developing on day 24 and leg buds appear on day 28. Throughout development, the legs lag behind the arms.

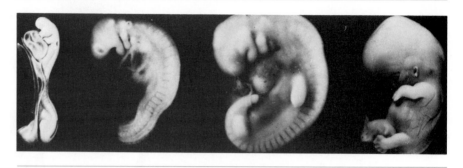

FIGURE 4-3
Four stages in the development of the human embryo: from left, at about two weeks, four weeks, six weeks, and eight weeks.

☐ The Second Month

As the embryo enters its second month (Figure 4-4), the rapid cell division and specialization that occurred during the first month continues. By the end of eight weeks, the embryo is about one inch long and weighs one-thirtieth of an ounce. Facial features and a neck are forming. The limbs are elongating, showing a distinct division of knee and elbow, although they are less than one-quarter of an inch long. More specifically, about day 31, the shoulders, arms, and hands develop; on day 33, the fingers; and on days 34 through 36, the thumb completes its development. Underneath the tissue of the arms and legs, long bones are forming and becoming padded with muscles.

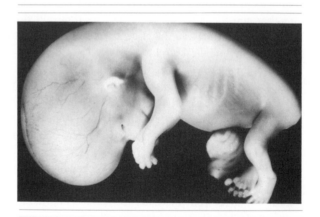

FIGURE 4-4
The embryo at two months.

In addition to these progressions, the internal organs continue to develop quite rapidly, not only in form and structure but also in functional properties. The nervous system becomes operative, the kidneys are capable of removing uric acid from the bloodstream, and the stomach is able to manufacture digestive juices. It is during these first two months that the organism is especially vulnerable to external disorders or mutagenic agents. Should the genetic code be disrupted during this most critical period of development, irreversible abnormalities of any of the organs could result.

Although the organism totals only one inch in length, it already exhibits some of its inherited genetic characteristics. For instance, the earlobes will already be attached or unattached and certain nose types will be making their appearance on day 37. These characteristics, as well as finger and toe shapes, are just a few of the genetically inherited traits that express themselves as early as the embryonic period.

☐ The Third Month

The end of the eighth week and the start of the ninth week mark the end of the embryonic period and the start of what is called the *fetal period*. During this time span, nerves and muscles mature, leading to generalized movements in response to external stimulation. The fetus will begin to turn and rotate, perhaps as early as the ninth or tenth week (although the mother will be unaware of all this activity). These movements appear to mark the beginning of what some psychologists consider to be true, albeit reflexive, behavior.

By the end of 12 weeks, the fetus can kick, curl its toes and fingers, move its thumb, and even squint in response to external stimulation. It is three inches long and weighs one ounce. Its arms, hands, fingers, legs, feet, and toes are now fully formed. Even nails are developing on its 20 digits. Tiny tooth sockets, containing the buds of future teeth, are present in the jawbone. The eyes, almost fully developed, have lids that remain fused.

By the end of the trimester, a very tiny but highly complex organism has been formed. Other developments reveal how complex the organism has become. The nerves and muscles triple in number during the third month; the heart can be heard by means of special instruments; the kidneys become operable; and sexual development has progressed to the point where the fetus's sex can be noted by a cursory examination. Meanwhile, the soft cartilaginous substance of the ribs and vertebrae are turning to bone.

■ The Second Trimester

☐ The Fourth Month

The second trimester is characterized not only by a continuation of the developmental processes but also by a rapid increase in growth as well. The fetus now approaches seven inches in length and weighs approximately four ounces (Figure 4-5). The head is

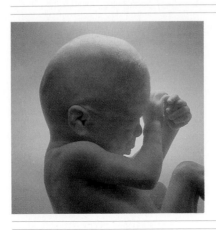

FIGURE 4-5
A 14-week-old male fetus is settling down for the latter two-thirds of prenatal life.

disproportionately large in comparison with the rest of the body. A strong heartbeat is present, along with a fairly well-developed digestive system. The eyebrows and genital organs are quite noticeable. As the fetus is now very active, there is an increase in the intake of food, oxygen, and water. The placenta has increased in size from three to four inches in diameter, allowing for a more rapid exchange of nutrients and waste products between mother and child. In appearance, the transparent fetal body is bright pink or red because it lacks pigmentation, so the red coloration is owing to the blood flowing through the circulatory vessels.

☐ The Fifth Month

By the end of 20 weeks, the fetus has grown much bigger. It now measures one foot in length and may weigh anywhere from one-half to one pound, a considerable gain from the four ounces of 16 weeks earlier. Pigment has still not been produced, so the fetus remains bright red in color. Its eyelids are still fused shut, and a fine, downy growth of hair, termed *lanugo*, appears on the entire body, and its skin is usually covered with a waxy substance called *vernix caseosa*, which protects the fetus from the effects of constant exposure to the amniotic fluid. Its internal organs are also rapidly maturing—with the exception of the lungs, which lag behind in development. The fetus's size

Cephalocaudal and Proximo-Distal Development

The nature of human growth and development is said to be cephalocaudal and proximo-distal (Figure 4-6). **Cephalocaudal development** means a head-to-tail, or downward, progression of bodily and motor skill growth. If we compare the physical rates of development of the head, trunk, and legs, we find that the head grows the fastest. The trunk is next in overall rate of growth, followed by the legs. (This is true from conception through the full attainment of growth and development in young adulthood.) During the embryonic stage, the head and upper trunk develop before the abdominal area and the arms develop before the legs. (Those motor skills involving the use of the upper body will develop before those using the lower body.) Infants are capable of lifting their heads before they can lift their trunks and can sit upright before they can walk.

Proximo-distal development refers to the physical and motor-skill growth that progresses from the center of the body outward. For example, in the embryo and fetus, the trunk develops earlier than the shoulders or arms, whereas the fingers and toes develop at a much slower rate. Also, infants, young children, and even adolescents are capable of mastering motor skills involving the central parts of the body before those requiring the use of peripheral parts. Because of this, we typically develop the use of the shoulders and arms before we can master the use of the hands and fingers.

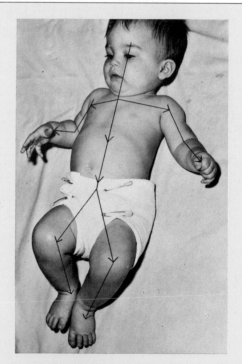

FIGURE 4-6 Development and muscular control proceeds from head to tail (cephalocaudal) and from the center to the periphery (proximo-distal).

and movement are such that the mother is now very much aware of the ripplings and flutterings inside her. Its activities now include both sleeping and waking. During the latter, it may cry, suck its thumb, hiccup, and perform head-over-heels somersaults.

☐ The Sixth Month

Just over one foot in length, the fetus has begun to accumulate subcutaneous fat and now weighs up to one and one-half pounds. Still wrinkled and red, it is a baby in miniature. The eyelids have separated, tiny eyelashes are visible, and the fingernails are extended to the ends of the fingers. The fetus can now make a fist. Ossification (the hardening of bone) has started. But there is only a slim chance of survival should the fetus be born at this time. The primary reason for death in premature infants is immaturity of the lungs.

■ The Third Trimester

The third trimester—the seventh, eighth, and ninth months of pregnancy—is marked by rapid gains in the fetus's growth and weight. The fetus grows in length by 50 percent and gains nearly six pounds in these last three months (Figure 4-7). During the last two months, the fetus gains an average of one-half pound per week. In the seventh month, the reflexes that will be seen at birth begin rapidly developing. Crying, breathing, and thumb sucking are included in the fetus's behavioral patterns. As growth increases (much of the weight gain is subcutaneous fat), movement is curtailed, owing to cramped quarters. Periods of sleep alternate with periods of activity.

Most of the fetus's organs mature enough to allow them to function outside the prenatal environment. The capacity for independent respiration, however, is dependent upon the maturation of the brain stem (medulla oblongata). Until there is appropriate neural functioning, respiration cannot occur. Thus, respiratory problems are among the main challenges in keeping the prematurely born infant alive.

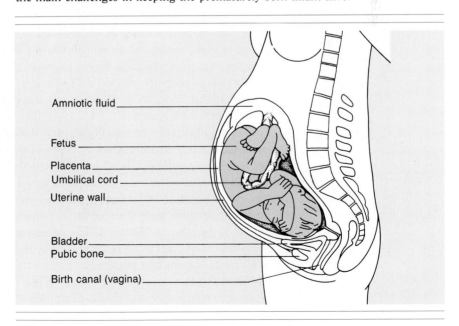

Amniotic fluid

Fetus

Placenta
Umbilical cord
Uterine wall

Bladder
Pubic bone

Birth canal (vagina)

FIGURE 4-7
A full-term fetus.

☐ Prematurity

Because it is rare that a mother can pinpoint the exact day of conception, *prematurity* cannot effectively be defined in terms of days or months of gestation. Therefore, most medical doctors define a *preemie* as an infant who weighs less than 2,500 grams (five and one-half pounds) and has developed *in utero* for less than 36 weeks. Any neonate (newborn) weighing less than this will probably have at least some difficulty surviving, for a baby this tiny will not have reached a stage of sufficient development to survive outside of its mother. Premature infants often are incapable of breathing without aid or of regulating their body temperature. They also may lack the protective subcutaneous layer of fat.

There are other important factors that possibly contribute to prematurity. Preemies are most often born to women who are nonwhite, come from poor neighborhoods, suffer from malnutrition, or are diabetic. It has also been discovered that premature infants are not always just underweight. Relationships have been established between prematurity and cerebral palsy, epilepsy, hearing difficulties, and mental retardation. Some research (i.e. Mazer, Piper, and Ramsay, 1988) indicates that premature infants perform less efficiently in locomotor and eye-hand coordination.

Besides their low birth weight and small size, premature infants typically encounter difficulties during the first few years of life. Although most infants will eventually overcome these difficulties, a developmental lag is apparent. For example, Susan Rose (1983) discovered that full-term and premature infants show differential rates of visual information processing. In her investigation 80 six- and twelve-month-old full-term and premature infants were given a shape to view for short intervals of time. Using a paired comparison technique, they were then tested for visual recognition memory. Although the older subjects showed evidence of recognition memory after less familiarization time than the younger ones had, at both ages the premature infants required considerably longer familiarization than did the full-term babies. This pattern of performance was evident at the sixth as well as the twelfth month of life. This suggests that there are persistent differences between premature and full-term infants, at least in the first year, in this important facet of cognitive functioning.

Another study, conducted by Keith Crnic (1983), suggests that prematurity may also affect later social interaction. In his investigation, he observed the psychosocial functioning of premature and full-term infants during their first year of life. In general, he found the premature infants to be less active and less responsive than full-term infants. Nor did the preemies vocalize and smile as frequently, and they showed less positive affect in their vocalizations. The pattern was apparent not only at age 4 months but also at ages 8 and 12 months.

Finally, an investigation by Judy Ungerer and Marian Sigman (1983) explored the developmental lags in premature babies for the first three years of life. The researchers assessed the play, sensorimotor, language, and general developmental skills of 20 preterm and 20 full-term infants at comparable corrected and postnatal ages in five sessions during the second and third years of life. The effects of biological maturity on play and sensorimotor skills were observed at 13.5 months, and less pervasive effects remained at 22 months. The premature infants were significantly delayed in sensorimotor, personal-social, and gross-motor abilities at 13.5 months and in language abilities at 22 months beyond that predicted by biological maturity alone. Although these deficits had mostly been overcome by 3 years of age, the preterm infants performed somewhat more poorly on visual information-processing tasks.

■ The Prenatal Environment

The organism developing under genetic direction is influenced by its external and internal environments. The external fetal environment is the amniotic fluid. The internal environment consists of not only the proteins and enzymes manufactured within the organism but also of a continuous inflow of nutrients, hormones, oxygen, chemicals, and other substances from the mother's bloodstream.

We noted earlier that there is no direct connection between the blood vessels of the mother and the child. The blood in the placental region never mixes. Rather, molecules of many substances are released by the maternal bloodstream and pass through the placenta. If small enough, these substances are assimilated by the blood vessels within the umbilical cord, thus making the placenta an area of exchange. But the placenta is not a filtration system. The environmental impact, then, is what is exchanged in the placenta. Obviously, a physically healthy mother who is eating the proper foods for both herself and the fetus (something from the dairy group, meat group, vegetable and fruit group, and cereal group) will help provide the proper environment. In addition to maintaining a well-balanced diet, the mother should be free of disease and under the care of a physician who can offer the appropriate prenatal care (Krause, 1984; Hamilton and Whitney, 1982). Table 4-2 is a daily food guide for pregnant women.

TABLE 4-2 Daily Food Guide for Pregnant Women

Food	Number of Servings		
	Nonpregnant Woman	Pregnant Woman	Lactating Woman
Protein foods			
Animal (2 oz serving)	2	2	2
Vegetable (at least one serving of legumes)	2	2	2
Milk and milk products	2	4	5
Enriched or whole-grain breads and cereals	4	4	4
Vitamin C-rich fruits and vegetables	1	1	1
Dark-green vegetables	1	1	1
Other fruits and vegetables	1	1	1

Source: Reprinted by permission from Eva May Nunnelley Hamilton and Eleanor Noss Whitney, *Nutrition: Concepts and Controversies.* 2nd ed. Copyright © 1978, 1982 by West Publishing Company. All rights reserved.

Unfortunately, it is difficult to state exactly what constitutes a good prenatal environment, for our knowledge of this area is lacking. Until recently, very little was known about the prenatal environment and what affects the developing organism, either positively or negatively. Of course, experiments are performed on pregnant animals but what is true for the rest of the animal kingdom does not always apply to people. Because ethical considerations—namely, the concern for human life—prohibit research regarding the effects of various drugs and other chemicals on humans, researchers can only accumulate data in retrospect, that is, after the fact. Should a child be born malformed, doctors will attempt to ascertain which drugs, illnesses, and so on could have affected the mother's system during the critical time period when the embryo was most susceptible. Often our knowledge of such matters consists solely of retrospective data and statistics about degrees of relationship.

Some studies indicate what constitutes a good environment. The age of the mother is one variable that must be considered. Data show that the best childbearing years are between ages 20 and 35. Before or after these years there is a greater risk of miscarriages and retardation. For example, the overall chances of giving birth to a Down syndrome child are 1 in 600. Women between the ages of 20 and 30 have 1 chance in 1,000. Women over 40, however, have 1 chance in 100 of giving birth to a child with Down syndrome. For women younger than 20, there are also increased risks, including premature births, delivery difficulties, and stillbirths. This is especially true for the growing number of mothers ages 15 and younger (Simkins, 1984).

☐ Maternal Nutrition

The developing fetus must, in the course of nine months, grow from a single cell to a highly complex structure weighing approximately seven pounds. Its ability to develop normally depends on nourishment supplied by the mother. Poor maternal nutrition may either directly affect the fetus by not meeting its nutritional needs, or indirectly affect it by increasing the mother's susceptibility to disease. Not only can malnutrition cause poor health, rickets, scurvy, physical weakness, miscarriage, and stillbirth, but it can produce mental subnormality as well. One source (Winick, 1981) estimated that a seriously malnourished fetus has as many as 20 percent fewer brain cells than the normal fetus does. However, maternal nutrition is not the only condition that influences prenatal development: Malnourished mothers frequently come from an environment of poverty, inadequate medical care, and inferior sanitation conditions.

An interesting distinction has been drawn between two types of nutritional inadequacy: qualitative hunger (malnutrition caused by deficient supplies of the vitamins necessary for normal growth) and quantitative hunger (insufficient amounts of food). Of the two, the former is more serious. Apparently, the amount of food the pregnant mother eats is not as important as what she eats (Bratic, 1982).

During pregnancy, mothers need to maintain good health and follow proper nutritional guidelines.

The most serious damage (physical and mental abnormalities) occurs during *organogenesis* (the period marking the beginning of organ development, from the third week of pregnancy through the second or third month). After the period of the ovum, the embryonic cells proliferate rapidly and are unusually sensitive to environmental changes. The developing nervous system is vulnerable for at least the first three, or possibly six, months after conception, but it is especially sensitive from days 15 to 25. The heart is particularly susceptible from the twentieth through the fortieth day.

The Rh Factor: Combating Incompatible Blood Types

Although modern medicine has found a cure, many fetuses and newborns still die because their blood is Rh positive (Rh⁺) and their mother's blood is Rh negative (Rh⁻). Rh⁺ is a genetically dominant trait; thus, the child of two Rh⁻ parents, or an Rh⁻ father and Rh⁺ mother is not affected. The **Rh factor** becomes important only when the father is Rh⁺ and the mother Rh⁻ **(A).**

Positive and negative blood types are incompatible. It is common during the birth process for fetal blood to enter the maternal bloodstream during hemorrhaging **(B).** When the child is Rh⁺, this substance, foreign to the Rh⁻ mother, is combated by the production of antibodies **(C).** During the first birth, few, if any, antibodies are present, so the Rh factor is unimportant. But when the female becomes pregnant again, these antibodies pass through the placenta and cause **erythroblastosis,** a condition in which the antibodies attack the fetal blood cells, generally causing death **(D).**

Today, Rh immune globulin can be administered to the mother after the birth of each child, thus preventing the formation of antibodies and allowing an Rh⁻ incompatible couple to produce more healthy children. The globulin should also be given to Rh⁻ women after an abortion or miscarriage. Failure to receive Rh⁻ immune globulin, for whatever reason, poses obvious risks during the next pregnancy.

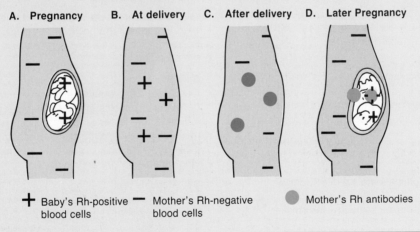

A. Pregnancy   B. At delivery   C. After delivery   D. Later Pregnancy

+ Baby's Rh-positive blood cells   **—** Mother's Rh-negative blood cells   ● Mother's Rh antibodies

FIGURE 4-8

Nicotine

Nicotine evidently affects development, but how much nicotine is needed to produce which prenatal effects is unknown. Researchers have weighed and measured newborn babies of both smokers and nonsmokers and found that the average weight of a baby born of a mother who smokes tends to be less than that of a nonsmoking woman. But, while statistical evidence supports this, it is not known how or why this phenomenon occurs. An educated guess would be that the fetus of a nonsmoker is receiving its full quota of oxygen, whereas a smoking mother, having various gases, tars, and nicotine in her system, passes along unhealthy substances through the placenta. The fetus receives these chemicals possibly at the expense of oxygen and/or of other nutrients (Hillard and Painter, 1985). Nicotine apparently has other effects. Just as adult heavy smokers experience an increase in heart rate, it has been suggested that smoking not only increases the fetal heart rate, but that it may also lead to fetal hyperactivity. In addition, heavy smokers (as opposed to nonsmokers) are more apt to give birth to premature babies, and recent evidence suggests that smoking may increase the frequency of cleft lip and cleft palate (Khoarg, Gomez-Farias, and Mulinare, 1989). Finally, women who smoke are more likely to birth infants having life threatening complications (Naeye, 1981; Fribourg, 1982). However, there is little evidence that moderate amounts of nicotine during pregnancy affect neonatal behavior (Richardson, Day, and Taylor, 1989).

Suggestions for a Healthy Pregnancy

During the course of a normal pregnancy, most women feel as well as at any other time in their lives. In fact, many feel even better while pregnant than ever before. However, even a low-risk pregnancy is put at high risk if prenatal care is absent or poor. Seeing a qualified practitioner regularly, beginning as soon as pregnancy is suspected, is vital for all expectant mothers. You should consult an obstetrician experienced with your particular condition if you are in a high-risk category. But being a good patient is just as important as having a good doctor. Be an active participant in your medical care—ask questions, report symptoms—but don't try to be your own doctor. In addition, pay attention to the following important areas:

Maintain a balanced diet A good diet gives every pregnant woman the best odds of having a successful pregnancy and a healthy baby. It may also help to prevent gestational diabetes and hypertension.

Stop smoking Quitting as early in pregnancy as possible reduces many risks to mother and baby, including prematurity and low birth weight. Stopping smoking means both partners, too. If only one partner gives it up, he or she will continue to smoke passively by inhaling the smoke exhaled by the smoker.

Abstain from alcohol Drinking very rarely or not at all will reduce the risk of birth defects, particularly of fetal alcohol syndrome, the result of high alcohol intake.

Avoid drugs So little is known about the effects of drugs on fetal development that it is best to avoid tak-ing any during pregnancy unless they are absolutely essential and prescribed by your doctor. This includes caffeine as well as over the counter drugs.

Strive for a sensible weight gain A gradual, moderate weight gain may help prevent a variety of complications, including diabetes, hypertension, varicose veins, hemorrhoids, low birth weight, or difficult delivery due to an overly large fetus.

Seek to prevent infections All infections—from common flu to urinary tract and vaginal infections to venereal diseases—should be prevented whenever possible. If contracted, however, infection should be treated promptly by a physician who knows that you are pregnant.

Stay fit It's best to begin pregnancy with a well-toned, exercised body, but it's never too late to start deriving the benefits of fitness. Regular exercise under a doctor's orders prevents constipation and improves respiration, circulation, muscle tone, and skin elasticity, all of which contribute to a more comfortable pregnancy and an easier, safer delivery.

Get adequate rest Getting enough rest during pregnancy is far more important than getting everything done, especially in high-risk pregnancies. Don't wait until your body starts pleading for relief before you slow down. If your doctor recommends that you begin your maternity leave earlier than you'd planned, take the advice.

(Adapted from Eisenberg, Murkoff, and Hathaway, 1984)

☐ Drugs

Drugs pose another problem for the embryo and fetus. Again, research findings are limited to animal studies or human observations in which, frequently, there are few controls. The specific effects of drugs vary, depending not only on which drug is involved but also on the quantity used and the time during pregnancy when it is taken. If a pregnant mother is given a sedative during labor, the pattern of electrical activity in the infant's brain will decelerate following birth. If the sedation has been excessive, permanent brain damage can result. Overloading the fetal bloodstream with sedatives may produce asphyxiation at birth. It is also known that addictive drugs, such as alcohol, heroin, and methadone, readily pass through the placenta, causing addicted mothers to give birth to babies who are also addicted (i.e., they have developed a physiological dependence on the drug). As a result, an addicted newborn must pass through all of the withdrawal symptoms (tremors, fever, convulsions, and breathing difficulties) that adults do when they "dry out."

Although most evidence indicates that addicted infants have no abnormalities, these babies are generally smaller (heroin babies seldom weigh more than 5.5 pounds) than the average newborn. The offspring of alcoholic mothers, though, develop an assortment of other complications: facial abnormalities, heart defects, abnormal limb development, and lower-than-average intelligence (Hotchner, 1984).

Exploring the Effects of Prenatal Contamination

As researchers continue to investigate the effects of drugs and other agents on the prenatal environment, we learn more about their detrimental effects. Sandra Jacobson (1984), for example, focused on the consequences of the mother's smoking, caffeine, and alcohol use during pregnancy. She interviewed mothers who smoked and consumed caffeine and alcohol and compared their newborns with those whose mothers did not engage in such activities. The results showed that smoking during pregnancy was related to smaller birth size and less irritability. Caffeine was related to shorter gestation and poorer neuromuscular development and reflex functioning. Finally, alcohol was related to greater placidity among the newborns.

In another study, Ann Streissguth (1984) concentrated on how intrauterine alcohol and nicotine exposure affects children's reaction times. In the study, 452 four-year-old children, whose mothers had smoked and consumed alcohol during pregnancy, participated in a problem-solving task designed to assess attention and reaction times. Their mothers' alcohol use during early pregnancy was significantly related to poor attention among the children, including more errors of both omission and commission. Moreover, their reaction times were longer than those of children whose mothers did not smoke or consume alcohol. The mothers' smoking was significantly related to poor attention and poor orientation to the task at hand. The results support the hypothesis that both alcohol use (even moderate use) and smoking by pregnant women are related to poorer attention in their preschool-age offspring.

Another investigation headed by the same researchers (Streissguth, Barr, and Martin, 1983) examined the effects of the mother's alcohol use during midpregnancy and neonatal habituation. The mothers' alcohol consumption was obtained by self-report during the fifth month of pregnancy, and the newborns were evaluated by means of the Brazelton Neonatal Assessment Scale. It was found that maternal alcohol consumption was significantly related to poorer habituation and increased low arousal in the newborns, even after the researchers adjusted for the following: the mothers' smoking and coffee drinking, age, nutrition during pregnancy, sex and age of the infant, and obstetric medication. Another investigation (Streissguth, Barr, Sampson et al., 1989) showed that the use of more than 1.5 ounces of alcohol per day during pregnancy was significantly related to an average IQ decrement of almost five points by the time children reached their fourth birthday.

Contamination of the fetal environment was considered by one source (Lipson, 1984) to be a type of prenatal abuse. But often, it is unintentional abuse, as women who are unaware that they are pregnant during the first two months may smoke and drink alcohol and coffee. These and other agents can easily enter the prenatal environment and affect the developing organism. The detrimental effects that we have discussed could be prevented if more women were made aware of prenatal contamination dangers. More education and publicity, though only partial answers to the problem, may help reduce this form of fetal abuse.

It has only been since the late 1950s that researchers have concentrated their efforts on understanding prenatal environment. Unfortunately, before then, drugs were administered indiscriminately to women—pregnant or not. Few seemed to realize that drugs, although having no adverse effects on adults, could have damaging effects on the unborn. Today, though, we are more aware of dangers associated with certain drugs, as researchers keep supplying us with the latest findings (see Box).

☐ Maternal Emotions

There are many old wives's tales regarding the pregnant woman's environment and how it will affect the fetus. For example, if a woman had been frightened, the child would be born with a birthmark shaped like the object that had upset the mother. Another belief was that happy mothers would give birth to happy babies and worried mothers would have unhappy children. Although there is no truth to these old superstitions, there are some closely associated biological factors that must be considered. It must be stated, however, that it is not the mother's emotions per se but the physiological changes that accompany her emotional state that may affect the behavior of her offspring (Chalmers, 1982).

Emotions (happiness, sadness, worry) do not directly influence the developing organism, but there is growing evidence that the hormones released while an organism is under great stress (anxiety) do affect the unborn. In fact, the mother's emotional state may affect both fetal and subsequent behavior. For example, willing pregnant women can be given a test to determine the degree of their anxiety. They are then classified as having high or low anxiety. The infants of these two groups of mothers are later observed and tested. By comparing the test results of the two groups, we discovered that women subjected to severe or prolonged emotional stress during pregnancy are more prone to give birth to infants who are hyperactive, have low birth weights, are irritable, and have feeding problems and digestive disturbances. Furthermore, highly anxious women appear to have more spontaneous abortions and a higher percentage of premature infants, and they spend an average of five more hours in labor. They also tend to have more complicated and abnormal deliveries (Bloomberg, 1980).

☐ Teratogenic Agents

A *teratogenic agent* is any environmental substance that causes a change in the genetic code, which in turn produces any abnormality, anomaly, or malformation. It is important to distinguish between teratogenic agents and inherited teratogens (inborn errors of metabolism—genes from one or both parents that will produce a mutant child).

Teratogenic agents affect genes and protein production in several ways. They may damage genes and make them inoperable. Some agents are also chemically capable of substituting themselves in the genetic code, bonding themselves to a gene (or genes). In this way, a mutant enzyme is produced. At other times enzymes may be blocked or totally destroyed. More technically, teratogenic agents may act by means of any of the following: *agenesis* (genes cease their protein production so development halts); *incomplete development* (the failure of genes to complete the development or growth already commenced); or *developmental excess* (overgrowth of the whole organism or any of its parts).

A teratogenic agent is especially dangerous during the development of an organ (organogenesis). For example, thalidomide, which affects those genes that control the development of the appendages, can do its damage only when the genes for arms and legs are activated. It is during this time that the gene is vulnerable, as it is in an unbonded state. The thalidomide chemicals probably permanently bond the thalidomide with the developmental gene, resulting in agenesis. German measles (rubella), on the other hand, evidently enters into the genetic developmental code, producing mutant brain protein. From this discussion it should be understood that the most dangerous time for the developing organism is the first two or three months after conception, for this is the major developmental period. However, deformations can occur at *any* time during development. Table 4-3 lists some suspected teratogenic agents.

TABLE 4-3 Possible Teratogenic Agents

Category	Causative Agent	Effect
Physical agent	Irradiation (X rays)	Malformation of any organ, the organ involved depending on organism's state of development
Infectious agent	Rubella (German measles)	Brain damage (mental retardation), sensory and cranial nerve damage (especially vision and hearing)
	Quinine (?)	Possible deafness and congenital malformations, but not totally substantiated (*Note:* quinine water lacks sufficient quinine to be included in this group)
	Cortisone	Possibly contributes to formation of cleft palate
	Paint fumes (?)	Suspected by some of causing mental retardation (pregnant women would probably have to be in unventilated paint area for a substantial length of time to be affected)
Chemical agents	Thalidomide	If taken 21 to 22 days after conception, may cause absence of external ears, cranial nerve paralysis; 24 to 27 days, agenesis of arms; 28 to 29 days, agenesis of legs
	Vitamin A	Large doses taken throughout pregnancy may cause cleft palate, eye damage, congenital abnormalities
	Vitamin D	Large doses taken throughout pregnancy may cause mental retardation
	Alcohol	New evidence indicates possibility of heavy drinkers (pregnant females) producing infants with subnormal IQs

ACQUIRED IMMUNE DEFICIENCY SYNDROME In the United States today, children under 13 years of age account for between 1 and 2 percent of all AIDS cases. By the early 1990s, 3,000 cases are expected. About 75 percent of AIDS children are infected by their mothers during pregnancy or birth. During prenatal development, the HIV virus may pass through the placenta and mix with fetal blood. Infants born by cesarean section have also been infected by the HIV virus. In rare instances, there have been cases of infants acquiring the virus through ingestion of breast milk (the HIV virus has been shown to be present in the breast milk of infected mothers). Also, the HIV virus can be contracted from contaminated blood or blood products. This has happened with hemophiliacs and children having surgery (Task Force on Pediatric AIDS, 1989).

Infants born with AIDS have certain distinguishing characteristics. Most have a small head, prominent forehead, protruding lips, flattened nose bridge and wide-set eyes. Many have a bluish tinge to the whites of the eyes. Some infants do not seem sick at birth, but most will develop symptoms within eight or nine months. Infected infants often exhibit a failure to thrive, developmental delays, and chronic diarrhea. Many experience enlargement of the lymph nodes, liver, and spleen. Many will also become susceptible to bacterial infections such as pneumonia (Task Force on Pediatric AIDS, 1989; Grossman, 1988).

The prognosis of children with AIDS is not favorable. The majority live less than three years and die from infection thriving within a hopelessly weakened immune system. In rare instances, some children may live as long as six years. Similar to adults infected with the HIV virus, there is no specific treatment or cure for children with AIDS (Hales, 1989; Seibert and Olson, 1989).

A number of controversial issues surround mothers and children infected with the HIV virus (Grossman, 1988). One of these is whether or not mothers-to-be should consider HIV antibody testing before they contemplate pregnancy. Relatedly, many feel that high-risk women who do become pregnant should be tested. Furthermore, these mothers need to be informed of the deleterious effects of pregnancy on the immunological status of the mother as well as the baby. Support services should be made available for the mother wishing to consider termination of pregnancy.

Other concerns focus on the actual delivery of an infant from an HIV-infected mother. Even though the virus cannot be spread by casual contact, the pediatrician and delivery room attendants need to be informed. Body fluid and the placenta contain the HIV virus and require that infection control precautions be taken.

Other issues become even more probing. While many HIV-infected mothers and children remain together, many do not because of maternal medical and social problems. This raises the question of who is going to care for HIV-infected children. In some respects, HIV-infected babies represent the children no one wants. Putting the youngster up for adoption isn't always the answer, either. In recent years, shelter and foster care programs have been reluctant to accept HIV-infected infants. Many communities have had to resort to some form of institutional care for these infants, an alternative which is less likely to meet their development and emotional needs than an individual foster home. Obviously, children with AIDS pose a number of delicate and serious problems, ones that will demand our attention in years to come (Grossman, 1988; Prothrow-Stith, 1989).

■ The Birth Process

☐ Stages of Labor and Delivery

The fetus's physical development is complete by the end of the third trimester of pregnancy. At this time, most fetuses move into a head-downward position for delivery. Approximately 10 percent, though, move into a breech position. This means that the buttocks will move into the cervix (lowest part of the uterus) first. It is generally recognized that a *breech delivery* is the more difficult of the two.

The birth process consists of three stages. The first is the onset of the uterus's *rhythmic contractions*. Initially, the uterine contractions are irregular, but they increase in strength and become more regular as labor progresses. The length of the first stage varies with each woman and birth. It can last anywhere from 2 to 18 hours. First labors are generally longer than successive ones. At their peak, contractions will occur about every two to three minutes and last for approximately 45 to 60 seconds. These contractions cause the cervix to open until it reaches *full dilation.* When this happens, the baby begins to move out of the uterus.

Expulsion, or *delivery of the baby,* is the second stage of labor. Uterine contractions now push the baby into the birth canal (the vagina) and out of the mother's body. This stage, on the average, lasts for approximately one hour. If the position or size of the baby is a concern, or if the mother develops physical problems, a *cesarean section* may be performed. As we will see, this means that the baby is delivered through a surgical incision made in the abdominal and uterine walls. It is estimated that about 15 percent of all births are of the cesarean variety (National Institute of Health, 1981).

The last stage of labor is the *expulsion of the placenta.* Usually within five minutes after the baby has been delivered, uterine contractions expel the placenta and the remaining portion of the umbilical cord. In some instances, the placenta is removed by the physician, as it does not easily disengage from the uterine wall. Figure 4-9 illustrates the three stages of labor.

FIGURE 4-9
The birth process consists of three stages. The first is rhythmic contractions of the uterus, a phase that enables the cervix to open. During the second stage, the uterus contracts and the body is pushed into the birth canal and out of the mother's body. The third stage is the expulsion of the placenta.

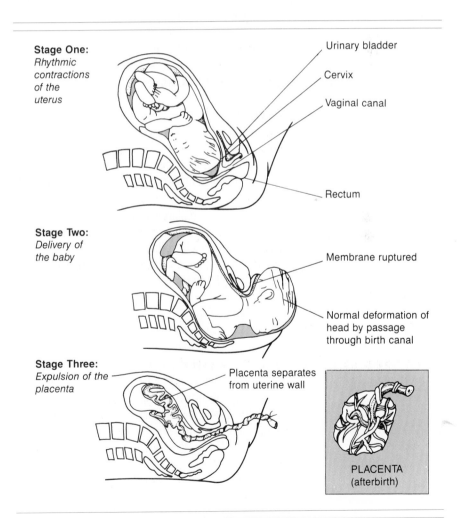

Stage One:
Rhythmic contractions of the uterus

Urinary bladder

Cervix

Vaginal canal

Rectum

Stage Two:
Delivery of the baby

Membrane ruptured

Normal deformation of head by passage through birth canal

Stage Three:
Expulsion of the placenta

Placenta separates from uterine wall

PLACENTA (afterbirth)

A nine-month journey ends, and a new chapter of the life cycle begins.

☐ Nontraditional Delivery Techniques

Although large percentages of mothers continue to deliver their babies in conventional medical and hospital settings, growing numbers are pursuing alternatives to hospital labor and delivery. Most are doing so because they object to the use of anesthesia during delivery and to other medical intrusions on the mother and the baby. Some also object to the deemphasized role of the father in the delivery of the baby.

Natural childbirth is an attempt to avoid the use of anesthesia and to allow both husband and wife to play an active role in the delivery of their baby. Expectant couples attend classes that stress special breathing exercises and relaxation responses. It is reasoned that fears during delivery cause women to tense their muscles, which delays the birth process and increases the mother's pain. Proponents of this approach feel that if women know what to expect and learn how to relax, their discomfort can be significantly reduced. Such preparation for birth was developed as early as 1940 by the English obstetrician Grantley Dick-Read.

The *Lamaze method* (named after Fernand Lamaze, a French obstetrician) is one of the most popular alternative approaches. In Lamaze classes, mothers learn the importance of *prepared childbirth*. They learn breathing techniques and muscular exercises and are taught about prenatal development and the stages of labor. The Lamaze method and others like it are a conditioned learning technique that teaches the mother to replace one set of learned responses (fear, pain) with another (concentration on relaxation and muscle control).

The *Leboyer method* emphasizes the importance of a gentle delivery and minimal trauma for the newborn. Developed by French obstetrician Frederick Leboyer, this delivery method offers a marked contrast with conventional childbirth procedures. The baby is born into a dimly lit delivery room that is kept relatively silent. Immediately after birth the infant is placed on the mother's stomach to be gently massaged, the belief being that tactile stimulation and contact soothe the baby. The infant is further soothed by receiving a warm bath. Only after this is the baby given a routine medical examination.

Leboyer suggests that such steps are transitions that minimize the trauma of birth and the abrupt departure of the infant from the womb. Leboyer's ideas have not gained universal acceptance. Critics maintain that it is dangerous to postpone the examination of the neonate after birth, especially when dim lighting may prevent the detection of vital life signs.

More couples today opt for *home births.* Such births are likely to increase, as many parents are rebelling against rising hospital costs and impersonal neonatal and post-partum care. Home births are often conducted by licensed *nurse-midwives,* trained delivery specialists who offer qualified medical care to expectant mothers. Usually the midwife has earned a bachelor's degree in nursing and a master's degree in nurse-midwifery and works on a medical team consisting of a gynecologist and an obstetrician. The nurse-midwife spends considerably more time with the mother before, during, and after the delivery and offers close, personal attention in a relaxed and comfortable setting.

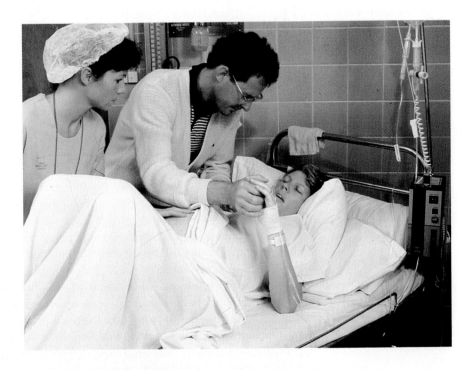

More couples today are sharing the childbirth experience.

Rooming-in and birthing room hospital facilities are also increasing in popularity. Hospitals offering *rooming-in* allow the mother to care for her newborn in her own room. The infant is usually brought to the mother's room within the first few hours after birth and remains there (rather than in the nursery) during the duration of hospitalization. A *birthing room* offers a homelike and relaxed atmosphere in the hospital delivery unit. The mother goes through labor and delivery in this room rather than being rushed to the delivery room before birth.

The advantage of and rewards from these progressive concepts are numerous, including the father's easy access, the greater attention and care directed to the newborn, and the opportunity for both husband and wife to assume more directly their new roles as parents.

■ HOME BIRTHS IN THE NETHERLANDS

At the turn of the century in the United States, all but 5 percent of babies were born at home. Because there were fewer hospitals and physicians, a midwife was typically summoned to deliver the baby. But because of infant mortality and the availability of hospitals to handle difficult deliveries, home deliveries became less common. Today, about 95 percent of all births take place in a hospital (D. Knox, 1985a).

A unique comparison to the United States lies in the Netherlands, where about 35 percent of all Dutch women give birth at home. Even though the Netherlands has a highly sophisticated health-care system, it leads the industrialized world in the proportion of women having babies at home. Midwives perform virtually all home and hospital births.

Interestingly, statistics show that the rate of infant mortality within a week of birth is higher in hospitals than at home. However, this is because virtually all problem births are detected in advance and take place in a hospital. In the Netherlands, national health insurance policies cover most deliveries and regard home births as so safe that they will not pay for a hospital birth unless it is medically advised.

The popularity of home births is in large part due to the importance of the home in Dutch social life. The small geographical size of the Netherlands and its above-average roads enable expectant couples from any location to be at a hospital within half an hour, if need be. Should delivery take place in a hospital, a "short-stay" policy adds further testimony to the importance placed on the home. Most mothers and their newborns are back in their homes within five hours after delivery.

☐ Cesarean Delivery

As we mentioned, a *cesarean delivery* means that the baby is delivered through a surgical incision made in the abdominal and uterine walls. The word cesarean is from the Latin word *caedere,* meaning "to cut." Reasons for a cesarean section include the mother's failure to progress normally through labor, disproportion between the size of the fetus and the birth canal, fetal distress, complicated breech presentation, or abnormalities in the labor process.

A cesarean delivery is not a recent surgical innovation. An early Roman law required that a baby be removed from the uterus of any woman dying in late pregnancy. This law persisted under the rule of the Caesars. Contrary to popular belief, the cesarean procedure was not named after Julius Caesar nor was he delivered this way. As far as the latter is concerned, Caesar's mother lived many years after his birth, which makes a cesarean delivery improbable because mortality rates for abdominal operations were high in antiquity.

In recent years, rates of cesarean births have sharply increased. In the 1950s, the rate was about 4 percent, whereas today the rate is over 15 percent. Without question, cesarean sections have helped to reduce infant deaths in the recent past. However, critics of the upsurge in cesarean births feel that many of the sections being done today are unnecessary and even potentially harmful. Moreover, opponents maintain that an unexpected cesarean delivery can be a negative emotional experience for the woman who hoped for a normal birth. Finally, recovery from a cesarean may make the postpartum adjustment and new baby care that much more difficult.

When a cesarean section is performed, the operation may occur before or during labor (the mother is usually admitted 24 hours before surgery). This is to ensure that the uterine contents are sterile. Once labor begins, bacteria tends to ascend from the vagina into the uterus and represents potential sources of infection.

Preparations for a cesarean section are similar to those for any other abdominal operation, except that it includes preparation for the care of the baby. However, the use of narcotic drugs prior to delivery is avoided because of their depressant effect on the baby. In the classic cesarean operation, the incision itself extends directly into the uterine wall. Once this is accomplished, the baby and the placenta are extracted. The incision is then closed with sutures. A more popular technique today is called the *low cervical transverse cesarean section.* Here, the incision is made through the tissues of the lower uterine segment and cervix. Compared to the classical cesarean operation, scar tissue from the low cervical transverse section is much less likely to rupture during later labors. This is because most of the force from a uterine contraction comes from its upper, rather than lower, segment. Thus, many women having this type of section can deliver vaginally in subsequent pregnancies.

Recognizing the Danger Signs of Pregnancy

There are a number of important danger signals during pregnancy that should be promptly reported to your practitioner. Do not hesitate to notify your specialist about any of the following symptoms. Be sure to explain how long the symptom has existed, how often it occurs, and how severe it is:

- Severe abdominal pain

- Increased, unusual thirst with reduced amounts of urine, or no urine for a day despite normal fluid intake

- Severe nausea or vomiting

- Vaginal bleeding, including any sign of bloody discharge

- Puffiness of the face, eyes, or fingers, especially if very sudden

- Persistent, severe headaches, especially in the second half of pregnancy

- Chills and fever over 100 degrees Fahrenheit not accompanied by a common cold

- Dimness or blurring of vision

- Painful urination, or burning when urinating

- Rupture of membranes (near your due date this is less significant)

- Absence of fetal movements for 24 hours from the 30th week on

(Adapted from Hotchner, 1984)

■ Neonatal Adjustments and Adaptations

Neonate is the technical name given to the newborn. As the neonate is adjusting to extrauterine life, delivery attendants are taking measures to ensure its survival. Respiration and heartbeat are the first concerns, with steps being taken to assure that respiration occurs as soon as the neonate makes its appearance. Mucus and fluids are wiped from the nose and mouth to assure normal respiration. After the delivery is completed, the neonate is held in a head-down position, which prevents mucus and other matter (amniotic fluid, blood, etc.) from entering the respiratory passage. Gauze, or a small suction bulb, is generally used to clean out this matter, especially when a newborn has more than the normal amount of liquid present in the respiratory passage.

The birth cry does not always occur simultaneously with the birth of the baby. Rather, the neonate gasps or cries shortly after the mucus has been removed and respiration commences. All that is required to stimulate crying is gentle rubbing of the neonate's back, which also promotes the drainage of liquids from the respiratory passage. The proverbial, but obsolete, slap on the buttocks not only is an unnecessary irritation but also can be dangerous to the neonate.

☐ Tests and Preventive Measures

Approximately one minute after birth and again five minutes later, a "score" is given to the neonate based on a "systems check" designed to evaluate critical life signs. The *Apgar test* is a relatively quick, simple, and safe test designed to evaluate the neonate's overall condition.

The Apgar test is based on five life signs: heart rate, respiration, muscle tone, reflex irritability, and color. A score of 0, 1, or 2 is given for each sign according to the degree of "life" present. By taking all of the vital life signs into account, the newborn can be given an Apgar score in a surprisingly short time. A total score of 7 to 10 indicates that the neonate is in generally good condition, whereas a score from 4 to 6 is considered fair. In the latter case, there will most likely be further clearing of the air passage and immediate administration of oxygen. A score of 0 to 3 indicates that the neonate is in critical condition, requiring immediate emergency procedures.

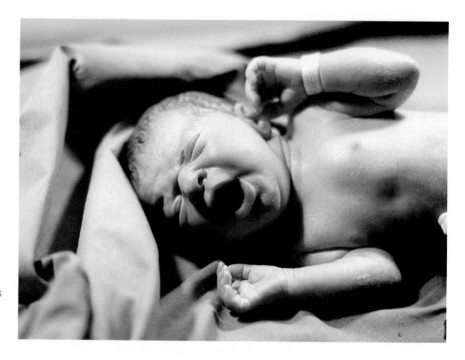

The study of the newborn is a newly emerging subfield of developmental psychology.

In addition to the Apgar test, the neonate's footprints are taken as well as a fingerprint of the mother. This is required by law and is essential for identification purposes (even in the rare event of a mixup in the hospital nursery). Weight in pounds and ounces (and in grams), head-to-heel length in inches, and the diameter of the largest part of the neonate's head and chest are recorded. The neonate's temperature is also recorded with a rectal thermometer.

There are also certain preventive measures given to the neonate. For example, an injection of vitamin K1 is given to prevent hemorrhaging. Eye drops of silver nitrate are administered to prevent contracting highly contagious gonorrhea in the eyes. The eyes are especially vulnerable if gonococci are present in the birth canal. Currently, it is a legal requirement in all states for newborns to receive this eye treatment.

Sudden Infant Death Syndrome (SIDS)

Crib death or **sudden infant death syndrome (SIDS)** is a phenomenon almost everyone has heard of, yet few laypeople know much about it. This is not so surprising, for no one, including members of the medical profession, really understands this most puzzling event.

Although crib death can occur during the neonatal period, its peak incidence is between the second and third months of age. It is actually uncommon during both the first two weeks of life and after 6 months. The following is a list of basic facts as supplied by the National Foundation for Sudden Infant Death:

- SIDS kills more than 5,000 infants every year in the United States.

- SIDS cannot be predicted, even by a physician.

- SIDS cannot be prevented; death occurs during sleep.

- The cause is not suffocation, aspiration, or regurgitation. Studies have proved that covering the faces of babies with blankets does not result in anoxemia.

- A minor illness such as a common cold may often precede death, although a completely healthy infant may die as well.

- There is no suffering; death occurs within seconds.

- SIDS is not hereditary; there is no greater chance for it to occur in one family than in another.

- SIDS is not contagious in the usual sense. Although a viral infection may be involved, it is not a "killer virus" that threatens other family members or neighbors. SIDS rarely occurs after seven months of age.

- SIDS is at least as old as the Old Testament and seems to have been at least as frequent in the eighteenth and nineteenth centuries as it is now. This demonstrates that new environmental agents, such as birth control pills, fluoride in the water supply, and smoking, do not cause SIDS.

- SIDS occurs more frequently in the winter months.

- SIDS is higher among premature births and low income families.

- SIDS often produces disabling guilt reactions in parents.

☐ Circumcision

For many neonates, *circumcision* is another adjustment to extrauterine life. Circumcision is the surgical removal of all or part of the prepuce, or foreskin, of the penis. Such a procedure thus permits exposure of the glans. About 90 percent of all babies in the United States were circumcised in the 1950s and 1960s, but this figure has dropped to about 75 percent today.

One of the major reasons for circumcision is the easier retraction of the foreskin for cleansing purposes. However, there are other reasons beyond cleanliness for circumcising a newborn. For instance, circumcision is a rite of the Jewish religion. Motivating many parents is the fact that rates of cancer of the penis seem to be lower in circumcised males, although there is conflicting evidence on this. Additionally, the incidence of cervical cancer appears to be lower in females married to circumcised males.

Opponents maintain that such surgery represents an unnecessary trauma in the life of the newborn. For that matter, circumcision may pose certain surgical risks, such as the development of penile ulcerations following the operation. With continued retraction of the foreskin and good hygiene, opponents also feel that uncircumcised males can be equally clean and comfortable.

Should the procedure be chosen, surgery is usually scheduled the day prior to discharge. This is to ensure that the neonate has become well stabilized. A variety of surgical procedures are possible, and all produce minimal bleeding. In one of the more common techniques, the prepuce is pulled back and then clamped. Excessive prepuce is then cut off, and the prepuce is sutured in place.

CHAPTER REVIEW

Gestation lasts for 280 days in the human, although it is more convenient to refer to pregnancy as lasting for nine months. It is during the first trimester that most developments occur. In these three months, the body, head, arms, legs, nerve cells, heart, and other internal organs are formed. The fourth, fifth, and sixth months are characterized by continued development and also growth. From weighing a mere ounce and being approximately three inches in length, the fetus becomes over a foot long and weighs 1.5 pounds.

In the last trimester, all of the organs, including the late-developing lungs, become functional. The fetus gains nearly six pounds in weight during the last three months and grows at least half a foot in length. After nine months, the fetus is fully developed and is called a full-term baby.

Although ethical and moral considerations prohibit prenatal research (especially on humans), there is nevertheless considerable knowledge available. The best prenatal environment is produced by a woman in her twenties who is strong and healthy, has a well-balanced diet, and doesn't smoke, drink, or take supplemental drugs.

Nicotine, alcohol, heroin, and other drugs have negative effects on the developing organism. Although the mother's emotions do not affect the fetus, evidence indicates that hormones secreted while the mother is under stress may. Teratogenic agents, such as thalidomide or rubella, produce abnormalities, anomalies, or malformations. Amniocentesis, a relatively new technique, allows medical authorities to detect chromosomal abnormalities by removing a sample of amniotic fluid and examining the fetus's genetic makeup.

Delivery of the newborn consists of three stages: rhythmic contractions of the uterus, delivery of the baby, and expulsion of the placenta. In recent years, many couples have opted for nontraditional delivery approaches, including the Lamaze and the Leboyer techniques. Also increasing in popularity are home births and birthing-room facilities in hospitals.

This chapter concluded with a discussion of neonatal adjustments and adaptations, including the tests and preventive measures administered following birth.

KEY TERMS

acquired immune deficiency
   syndrome (AIDS)
agenesis
amniotic fluid
amniotic sac

Apgar test
breech delivery
cephalocaudal development
cesarean delivery
circumcision

embryo

embryonic period

erythroblastosis

fetal period

fetus

fraternal twins

gestation period

identical twins

Lamaze method

lanugo

Leboyer method

natural childbirth

neonate

organogenesis

period of the ovum

placenta

prematurity

proximo-distal development

Rh factor

sudden infant death syndrome

teratogenic agent

trimester

umbilical cord

vernix caseosa

RECOMMENDED READINGS

Abdul-Karim, R. W. (1981). *Drugs During Pregnancy.* Philadelphia: George F. Stickley.
A good account of how drugs affect prenatal development.

Abel, E. L. (1984). *Fetal Alcohol Syndrome and Fetal Alcohol Effects.* New York: Plenum.
A thorough examination of the relation between alcohol consumption during pregnancy and the health of the newborn child.

Goldberg, S., and DiVitto, B. (1983). *Born Too Soon: Preterm Birth and Early Development.* New York: Freeman.
A well-written text that examines the research on the development of prematurely born infants during their first three years of life.

Hall, R. W. (1983). *Nine Months Reading.* New York: Bantam.
A highly readable and thorough medical guide that explores pregnancy from conception to postnatal care.

Hotchner, J. (1984). *Pregnancy and Childbirth.* New York: Avon Books.
Chapter 3 of this book focuses on fetal development, maternal nutrition, and the effects of drugs taken during pregnancy.

Lauersen, N. H. (1983). *Childbirth with Love.* New York: Berkeley Books.
Readers will find chapters on fetal development, genetic counseling, and the birth process to be especially informative.

Loader, A. (Ed.). (1980). *Pregnancy and Parenthood.* Oxford, England: Oxford University Press.
This collection of articles includes the following topics: pregnancy problems, prematurity, twins, expectant fathers, and the anatomy and physiology of labor.

Moore, K. L. (1988). *The Developing Human,* 4th ed. Philadelphia: Saunders.
An authoritative and clinically oriented textbook on the anatomic and physiological development of the human embryo.

Shapiro, H. I. (1983). *The Pregnancy Book for Today's Woman.* New York: Harper & Row.
New obstetrical technology is given full coverage in Chapter 10 of this book.

Verny, T., and Kelly, J. (1981). *The Secret Life of the Unborn Child.* New York: Simon & Schuster.
An excellent narrative of prenatal development, with special emphasis on the pregnant mother.

Infancy and Toddlerhood

WHAT DO YOU THINK?

■ In the United States, children begin walking sometime between 13 and 15 months of age. In other nations, though, this timetable varies. For example, in Uganda, Africa, walking commences at about 9 months, and in Stockholm, Sweden, it begins at approximately 12 months. What factors account for such international differences? Can genetic factors or environmental factors explain such differences? We'll try to supply the answers later in this chapter.

■ Out of the mouths of babes. Although infants present their parents with many diverse and exciting accomplishments, perhaps none overshadows the emergence of the first spoken word. This developmental milestone, which has something magical attached to it, is eagerly anticipated by parents. And rightfully so, as initial words are often designations for the mother or father—or are taken to be such by the parents. What cognitive and linguistic forces produce these early words? What stages of language precede and follow the first-word stage? We shall explore these and other issues in our discussion of language development during infancy and toddlerhood.

■ Linus of Peanuts fame never leaves home without his security blanket. Chances are that you had something similar when you were a child, although you were probably not as dramatic about it as this cartoon strip character is. You might have owned a security blanket, huggable doll, or a threadbare stuffed animal. These security objects are usually the recipients of childhood attachment behaviors: They are clung to in times of peace as well as turmoil; they are stroked and hugged; and they usually end up each night cradled in the arms of the sleeping child. What is it about soft and comforting objects that promotes a sense of security? How does such behavior relate to attachment? This chapter will give you some answers, some that may make you pause and reflect on your own childhood guardian keepers.

■ They have been called the children of the dream, the children of the Israeli kibbutz. They are separated from their parents shortly after birth and through their teenage years are reared in a collective farm settlement. Among other goals, such child-rearing practices were implemented to eliminate Israel's patriarchal family structure, social classes, and sex-role stereotyping. Have these goals been attained? What is it like to spend one's childhood and adolescence in a kibbutz? Read on to learn more about this unique style of upbringing.

■ Unit One:

Unlike the virtually helpless, generalized movement of the neonate, the infant's movement consists of a complex hierarchy of specific muscular behaviors. Control over voluntary movement is evident in numerous forms of physical expression, including walking and prehensile abilities, which develop in a sequential fashion. Although there are individual differences among infants in rates of body growth and motor achievement, growth and maturation for the most part proceed in a definite order.

This sequence of development is, to a great extent, due to the gradual maturation of cells in the brain. Even though the neonate is born with 10 to 14 billion cells in the cortex, most of these cells are immature and not yet able to function. As the cranial bones enlarge, the brain cells grow, mature, and become more chemically active. Until a cell reaches this physical and chemical level of maturity, learning cannot take place.

The foregoing is a simplified explanation of the brain's role in physical movement development. In order to comprehend its impact, we need to understand how the nervous system develops and how its primary parts function. Such an understanding will help explain many of the developments that occur over the course of the life cycle, including those changes accompanying aging processes.

■ Development of the Nervous System

The nervous system consists of two parts: the central and peripheral systems. The brain and the spinal cord constitute the *central nervous system,* while the *peripheral nervous system* is a network of neural tissue that connects the brain and spinal cord with other parts of the body. Together, the central and peripheral nervous systems connect the body into a unified system under direct control of the brain (Levinthal, 1990).

The central nervous system grows rapidly during the early years. By the first year, the brain has attained nearly 60 percent of its adult weight of approximately three pounds. Over the next five years, it will increase in weight by some 400 percent. Much of this weight gain is from the expansion of the dendrites and axons of the neurons (nerve cells) as well as the elaboration of the brain's supporting cells. As time passes, the cranial bones also enlarge to accommodate the growing brain (Kolb and Whishaw, 1988).

Brain function is a complex activity involving the interaction of its parts. Let us say at the outset, though, that the parts of the brain do not develop evenly. Rather, its parts develop at different rates and follow unique timetables. Some parts of the brain, such as the cerebral cortex, experience both rapid and slow phases of development. We will spend more time on this topic shortly.

The brain can be divided into three major parts: the forebrain, midbrain, and hindbrain (Figure 5-1). The *forebrain* is the frontal and upper part of the brain and represents the largest of the three divisions. It contains the brain center responsible for conscious thought and higher-order behavior. It is the forebrain that enables humans to surpass lower animal species in such areas as reasoning, speech, and complex patterns of muscle coordination.

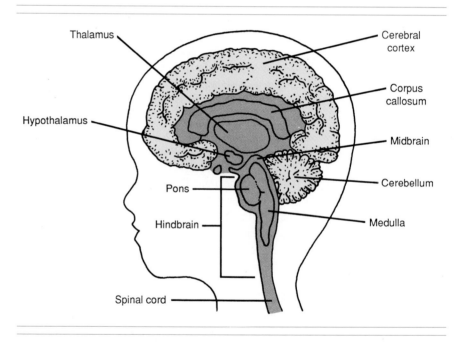

FIGURE 5-1 Major structures of the brain.

The *cerebrum* is the largest portion of the forebrain and consists of a left and a right cerebral hemisphere connected by a bundle of nerve fibers called the *corpus callosum*. It is the corpus callosum that enables one hemisphere to know what the other is doing.

While the two cerebral hemispheres look very much alike, they differ greatly in function. The left hemisphere controls movement on the right side of the body, and the right controls movement on the left. For example, if you scratch your head with your right hand, the left hemisphere of the brain is responsible for your movements. In addition, the left and right cerebral hemispheres control different functions. This type of hemispheric specialization is known as *lateralization* and emerges gradually during development. The left hemisphere is the site of language ability, systematic and logical thought (math, science, and so on), and writing, among other specializations. The right hemisphere controls primarily nonverbal functions, such as artistic or musical abilities, imagination, and the expression of emotion.

The two cerebral hemispheres are covered by the *cerebral cortex,* which is grayish and wrinkled in appearance. The cerebral cortex has a number of important functions, including memory, concentration, problem solving, and muscle coordination. It is the last part of the brain to develop, continuing its growth beyond adolescence into adulthood.

The cerebral cortex is divided into four lobes, or areas. The *occipital lobe,* located at the back of each hemisphere, enables the brain to interpret sensory information transmitted by the eyes. The *parietal lobe,* found at the top of each hemisphere, controls the sense of touch and transmits essential spatial information. The *temporal lobe,* located at the side of each hemisphere, is responsible for hearing and storage of permanent memories. The *frontal lobe,* located behind the forehead and at the front of each hemisphere, regulates the sense of smell as well as body movement and control.

Two other parts of the forebrain are the thalamus and hypothalamus. The *thalamus,* located at the base of the cerebrum, relays nerve impulses from sensory pathways to the cerebral cortex. The *hypothalamus,* located beneath the thalamus, has a variety of functions, including the regulation of hunger, thirst, sexual functions, and body temperature. The hypothalamus is also a control center for pleasure and pain.

The *midbrain* is a connecting link between the forebrain and hindbrain. The midbrain controls movements of the eye muscles and relays visual and auditory information to higher brain centers.

The *hindbrain* is the lower portion of the brain and is responsible for bodily functions necessary for survival. The *medulla oblongata* connects the brain and spinal cord and helps regulate heartbeat, respiration, digestion, and blood pressure. The *cerebellum* controls body balance and coordination. It grows rapidly during the first two years of life and attains almost full size by the fifth year. The *pons* is located above the medulla and acts as a bridge between the two lobes of the cerebellum. The *reticular activating system* runs through the hindbrain into the midbrain and part of the forebrain. It is involved in arousal, attention, and the sleep cycle.

■ Myelination and Brain Maturation

The maturity of neurons in the brain is determined by the size of the cell, the length of the dendrites and axons, and the degree of myelination. *Myelination* is the process by which the neuron develops an outside coating, called *myelin.* This coating, or sheath, insulates the nerve cell and allows for the rapid transmission of chemoelectrical messages. Before myelination, signals may be dissipated in the surrounding body fluids instead of proceeding along the neural pathway. Figure 5-2 shows the different parts of the neuron, including the myelin sheath.

We mentioned earlier that different parts of the brain develop at different times. During the first half year of life, those cells develop whose functions pertain to primary bodily movements. These cells are found in the motor (output-muscular) and the sensory-motor (input-muscular) areas of the brain, which control the development of various physical skills. Areas that mature later direct the development of various thinking processes. Figure 5-3, a diagram of an infant's brain, indicates the progression of development in the cortex.

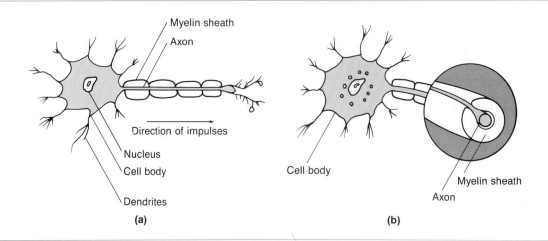

FIGURE 5-2 At left (a), a diagram of a peripheral nervous system neuron. At right (b), the manner in which the myelin sheath envelops the axon and insulates the nerve cell.

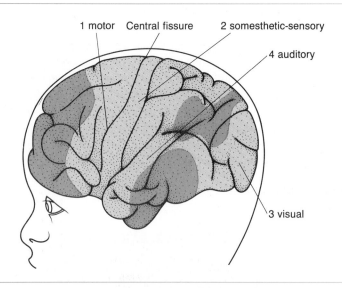

FIGURE 5-3 The cortex develops at different rates. Darker shadings indicate the areas that mature earlier, and the numbers indicate the sequence of development.

■ The Readiness Principle

A child's ability to perform a physical task depends not only on the maturation of the neurons in the brain, but also on the maturation of the muscle and skeletal systems. Such a state of maturation is known as *readiness*. Until children reach a state of readiness, they will be unable to perform a task, even with training or practice.

Consider the accomplishment of walking. A child will walk only when all systems are developed; if any of the systems are immature, the youngster will be unable to walk, despite all the coaxing in the world. In fact, too much pressure may result in frustration and anxiety. This does not mean that an enriched or stimulating environment is not beneficial; just the opposite is true. Once the organism has reached a sufficient level of maturity, environmental enrichment can increase the learning of physical skills. Moreover, after the early years of physical development, motor skills are heavily influenced by the environment.

☐ Locomotion

Locomotion is the ability to move from one location to another. The onset of locomotion occurs at about 2.5 months, the time when infants can raise their chest by means of arm support. By five months, infants can sit erect when supported.

Locomotion accelerates when infants acquire skill in using their arms and hands. This can be seen at the fifth month, the time when infants can roll over if placed on their back or stomach. Some forward mobility is evident by six months, and crawling begins by eight months. Over the next several months, crawling acquires greater coordination as the legs develop and have an opportunity to exercise.

The first step is taken sometime between 13 and 15 months. Although this marks a time when body weight can be consistently supported, infants indeed look fragile and

Greater coordination in the legs helps to perfect locomotion.

unsteady. Their legs are bowed because their weight is on the inner part of their feet, and their stomach is thrust forward, all of which gives them a rounded appearance. To maintain balance, their arms extend outward from their body.

During their early efforts, children try all types of steps imaginable. Early walking often includes staggering, lurching, sidestepping, and even stepping backward. Falling is very common during this stage, but infants always get up and continue with boundless energy.

It is important to mention that growing physical capacities blend with other developmental forces, including the cognitive prowess to master motor skills and the motivation to explore the environment, which Erik Erikson suggests is part of the toddler's quest for autonomy and initiative. Walking does present dangers, though, and parents must realize that the child is now able to explore and investigate areas that were previously inaccessible. It is a challenge to keep a constant eye on the busy explorer. Because it is common for children to reach and examine lamps, cords, bottles, and

International Lifespan Development

■ ARE SOME TODDLERS A STEP AHEAD OF OTHERS?

The first step. It's a developmental achievement that invariably earns the excitement and pride of parents, relatives, and interested onlookers. Many record the event on camera while others make sure that it's included in the baby's record book. However it's remembered, the development of walking symbolizes an important achievement in the life of the youngster: the transformation from infant to toddler.

As we've indicated, the first step is taken usually between the ages of 13 and 15 months, but this is just an average. Averages can be very misleading, and it must be emphasized that walking can begin before or after this time. Similar to all facets of growth and development, individual differences must be taken into account.

Furthermore, many of the developmental timetables established for motor skills are based on the maturity of children in Western cultures. Children from other cultures do not necessarily follow these prescribed norms.

The motor-skill development of Ugandan infants in Africa illustrates this latter point. Ugandan infants, on the average, sit without support as early as 4 months of age and walk by about 9 months. These achievements obviously come sooner than do those demonstrated by American infants. Certain prehension abilities, muscle tone, and head control are also superior in Ugandan babies, although all of these advancements over Caucasian infants are greatest during the first year and then taper off.

There are several explanations for these cross-cultural variations in motor-skill development. One explanation is that it is a genetic variation, as black American babies appear to be more advanced than are white American infants in various phases of motor development during the first year. However, this is a controversial explanation. A more widely accepted theory is that African mothers encourage early head support and other types of muscle control. The infant is often carried on the mother's back (with no means of head support) and the infant spends considerable time on the floor, which provides an environment for exploration and muscular exercise. There is also considerable social stimulation and conversation from mother to child, factors that may also enhance motor precocity.

Interestingly, the age at which walking occurs also varies among European nations. Children from Stockholm and Brussels take their first step at about 12.5 months, whereas youngsters from Zurich, London, and Paris do not do the same until about 13.5 months. Explanations here are even more difficult to formulate, although genetics, environmental stimulation, and the quality of health care have been offered. The lack of precise answers notwithstanding, this discussion shows how motor-skill timetables may vary. Moreover, it illustrates how the nature-nurture issue covered in Chapter 1 expresses itself in many ways throughout the course of development.

other potentially dangerous objects, such items should be kept out of the child's reach. Without curtailing the toddler's developing initiative, we want to safeguard the environment.

☐ Prehension

Being able to grasp objects between the fingers and opposable thumb, known as *prehension,* is a difficult area to study because the neonate is born with a grasp reflex, a subcortical response that will enable the hand to close if an object is placed in the palm. But the grasp reflex is not the same as the cortically controlled individual movements of fingers and thumbs that represent true prehension. At approximately 4 months of age, the grasp reflex subsides, and then prehension does not occur until about 5 to 6 months of age.

Prehension, like locomotion, follows a sequential pattern of development. At 20 weeks, the beginning of eye-hand coordination results in fewer misdirected attempts to reach objects. Although they have considerable difficulty in maintaining their grasp on an object, infants can direct their arm movements with greater efficiency. A study by George Butterworth and Brian Hopkins (1988) shows how infant reflexes and overall coordination become more refined during the early months. The two researchers filmed the spontaneous motor activity of newborns and analyzed arm and hand movements in slow motion. Their observations revealed that newborns move their hands to their mouths fairly regularly. It is particularly interesting that the mouth was eventually opened in anticipation of the arrival of the hand and that the movement did not require visual guidance. Research such as this shows how motor behaviors are characterized by growing levels of efficiency and refinement.

Researchers once thought that the sequence of reaching, and prehension in general, was the result of maturational processes. Today, though, there are other theories. For example, some feel that eye-hand coordination involves a cognitive mapping of visual and motor schemes. This means that infants acquire reaching and retrieval behavior by observing their hands within their visual field. One investigation discovered that when infants less than 3 months old could not see their hands as they reached for an object, it did not appear to disrupt their reaching behavior. However, in 5.5- to 6.5-month-old infants, there was a definite disruption. Although reaching and retrieving were not entirely inhibited, it was hypothesized that the behavior pattern was disrupted—not because of lack of visual feedback but because the infants' cognitive expectations of seeing their hands were not met (Lasky, 1977).

The ability to reach for (and grasp) objects continues to be refined. Between 5 and 6 months of age, the infant begins to use both hands simultaneously and becomes considerably more efficient in picking up objects. This advancement not only increases further hand-eye coordination but also gives the infant a greater variety of objects to manipulate.

Between 8 and 10 months, infants use their thumb and fingers together fairly consistently and discover many new uses for their hands and arms. For instance, infants of this age are able to support their weight on one arm while reaching for objects. They can also consistently pick up both large and small objects with a better coordinated movement. Figure 5-4 displays the development of prehension and how it compares to milestones in locomotion.

In time, the grasp reflex will subside, giving way to the developmental stages of prehension.

At this point, we will say a few things about handedness and its role in prehensile development. *Handedness* is the preference for and subsequent predominant use of one hand. Handedness shows few signs of developing during the first year. Most infants are ambidextrous and show no real preference for either hand. At approximately 19 months, though, hand preference makes its appearance, and an active and a passive hand emerge. By 2 years of age most children exhibit a definite preference, which is generally firmly established by the time they enter school. For about 95 percent of people, this preference is for the right hand (Coren, Porac, and Duncan, 1981; Michel, 1981).

It is difficult to determine what factors create handedness. It could be caused by either environmental or genetic factors, but there is not a logically sound argument for one or the other. For example, when both parents are right-handed, there is a 92 percent chance that their offspring will be right-handed. Should one parent be left-handed, there is an 80 percent chance that their offspring will be right-handed. If both parents are left-handed, the figure for right-handedness diminishes to 50 percent. Such percentages might indicate a hereditary predisposition toward handedness. However, one should also consider environmental influences. For example, left-handed parents could be left-handed models whom the child may imitate (Longstreth, 1980; Hardyck and Petrinovich, 1977; Hicks and Kinsbourne, 1976).

Right-handers have advantages not available to left-handers. Left-handers gradually discover that they must adjust to a predominantly right-handed world. For example, learning to write is one of the biggest obstacles, as the left hand often smears the letters that have just been written. Other disadvantages for the left-hander continue even after childhood. Sports equipment, games, tools, doorknobs, and even the handles on drinking fountains all are designed with the right-hander in mind.

Left-handers can overcome such hurdles, though, and they have no more adjustment difficulties throughout life than right-handers do. Research indicates that there are no noticeable differences between the two in such areas as school achievement, motivation, and intelligence. Findings such as this indicate that left-handers are perfectly capable of overcoming whatever obstacles confront them in our predominantly right-handed world (Hardyck, Petrinovich, and Goldman, 1976; McManus, Sik, Cole, Mellan et al., 1988).

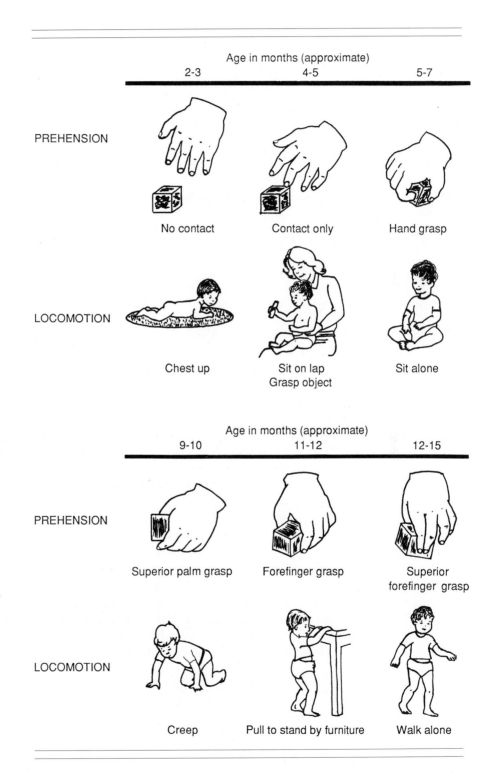

FIGURE 5-4
Milestones in motor-skill development.

PREHENSION AND THE DEVELOPMENT OF CHILDREN'S ART

One of the several observable indicators of children's developing prehensile abilities is their artwork, beginning with the scribbling stage. Manipulating an artistic instrument requires considerable fine-motor skill dexterity, and the progression of children's artwork reveals increasing refinement in this area. It is shortly after the first year that most infants become capable of making their initial attempts at *scribbling,* the first stage of artistic development. Before and even at this age, infants will attempt to eat or taste the drawing instrument rather than use it on paper. (For this reason, drawing instruments should be given to infants only under supervision.) However, once the purpose of the pencil or crayon has been demonstrated, most infants will immediately begin scribbling with delight and enthusiasm.

Scribbling: The Building Blocks of Art

Scribbles are numerous and diverse during the years of infancy and toddlerhood, offering to the sharpened eye of a skilled observer a variety of different sizes, configurations, and page placements.

In a most elaborate fashion, children's art expert Rhoda Kellogg (1970) classified the possible variations of the basic scribble. In all, she discovered 20 such fundamental markings, leading her to believe that every form of graphic art contains one or more of these variations.

As you examine this classification (Figure 5-5), trace a few of these scribbles with your hand as if you were making them yourself. Can you appreciate the range of motions required for the production of each? Are some scribbles more difficult to make than others are? If so, might this affect the appearance of certain scribbles in the overall time frame of the scribbling stage? This type of analysis illustrates the diversity of scribbles as well as the relationship between prehensile and eye-hand coordination. It also underscores the fact that scribbles form the foundation of later artistic development.

FIGURE 5-5 Kellogg's classification of 20 basic scribbles. (From R. Kellogg and S. O'Dell, *Psychology of Children's Art.* New York: CRM-Random House, 1967)

Unfortunately, scribbles are neglected by many adults, who insist that the marks are nothing more than "meaningless lines." On the contrary, scribbling is important to growing infants, not only because it enhances prehensile development and is one of their first visual accomplishments, but also because it gives them a sense of personal achievement and satisfaction.

Furthermore, scribbling becomes an activity with a purpose. Once they have made these marks, children will want to repeat the activity because of the pleasure it offers. Many find the task pleasurable, and others seem intent on varying their mark. Whatever the motivation, scribbles are a delightful creation during this early stage of development (Gardner, 1980).

At first, infants are severely hampered in their attempts to produce marks on paper, the limits caused primarily by insufficient neuromuscular development and eye-hand coordination. Fine-motor skills such as these typically lag behind large- or gross-motor skills. Frequently, children drop the pencil or crayon or do not hold it at the proper angle. At other times, they miss the paper completely. But eventually, their arm-banging actions develop into more coordinated arm and hand movements. One of the more interesting qualities of scribbles is that they follow a fairly predictable pattern of development. The scribble first is a continuous to-and-fro movement represented graphically by a zigzag of predominantly horizontal strokes; later, as circular movements of the hand become possible, "round" scribbling emerges (Dileo, 1980, 1983).

Between the ages of 16 and 20 months, children acquire considerable flexibility and fluidity. Whereas their earlier attempts were characterized by jagged and abrupt markings, there is now a freer flow of artistic expression. Toward the end of the second year, there is increased refinement in children's scribbles, as evidenced by their ability to keep their marks within the boundaries of the page. This phase of development is sometimes referred to as controlled scribbling. In addition, they may experiment with a wider range of complex scribblings, as well as vary the amount of pressure they exert on the crayon.

UNIT REVIEW

- The ability to perform motor skills depends on both neural maturation and readiness.

- Locomotion is the ability to move from location to location, and it progresses in a developmental fashion. Cross-cultural variations exist in motor-skill accomplishments.

- Prehension is grasping objects between the fingers and opposable thumb. It, too, proceeds in a developmental fashion. Handedness is the preference for, and the subsequent predominant use of, one hand.

- Prehensile development is enhanced through artwork, as it encourages fine-motor-skill dexterity and eye-hand coordination.

MENTAL DEVELOPMENT

Developmental psychologists have long been interested in the higher-order mental processes that pertain to thinking, perceiving, and understanding. Technically, this field of study is known as *cognition*. Researchers in this area study the mental facilities that process, interpret, and categorize stimulus information.

The development of logical thinking is a highly complex process. Because of children's undeveloped reasoning capacities, their interpretation of their surrounding environment is frequently illogical and unrealistic. Loose concepts and explanations are formed and oriented into their existing frame of reference. Over time, though, children develop an accurate understanding of objects, people, and events in their surroundings, and they abandon illogical ideas in favor of logic and reason.

How these cognitive developments unfold is one of the central themes of this text. Before we begin our examination, though, we want to emphasize that mental gains throughout life take place against the backdrop of social relationships. As Kenneth Kaye (1982) observed, children's mental growth depends as much on adult stimulation and universal human interaction patterns as it does on their intrinsic cognitive abilities. Symbolic representation, thought, and language cannot develop without interaction between adults and children.

With this understanding in mind, we first turn to the sensorimotor stage of cognitive development proposed by Jean Piaget. Then, we examine early concept formation, sense organ development, and, finally, language development during the first three years of life.

Jean Piaget's Sensorimotor Stage

The first period of cognitive development, known in Piagetian terms as the *sensorimotor stage,* occurs during approximately the first two years of life. This stage is so named because most of the infant's learning abilities are directed toward the coordination of simple sensorimotor skills, which include such activities as grasping objects and the basic reflexes. The concepts covered in this stage may be of particular concern to parents of newborns or anyone observing children of this age level. Six substages comprise the sensorimotor period, each of which facilitates overall mental development.

Reflex Activities (0–1 month)

During their first month, infants are limited to only primitive *reflex activities,* such as crying or sucking. This is primarily because their cerebral cortex has not yet developed. However, as the cranial bones enlarge, the brain cells develop and become more chemically active. As a result, the infants' reflexes are modified and become more efficient. For example, whereas the sucking reflex is first directed toward all objects, the infant can later discriminate between objects that can be sucked, such as a breast or a bottle, and objects that cannot.

Primary Circular Reactions (1—4 months)

Should an infant discover a pleasurable behavior pattern, the chances are that it will be repeated for its own sake. This is a *primary circular reaction.* For example, if sucking the thumb brings enjoyment, active efforts will be made to reproduce that action. Infants also begin to display signs of coordinating one action with another. This can be seen in the coordination of the hand and arm, which may permit greater coordination of thumb sucking. Infants may also try to look at whatever is grasped and reach for whatever happens to be seen. This is also a period when infants take a great deal of interest in themselves. They frequently are preoccupied with their own arms, hands, legs, feet, and the investigation of simple movements of their bodies.

Secondary Circular Reactions (4—8 months)

During the fourth to the eighth months, infants attempt to reproduce interesting events in the external environment that might have been first caused by accident. This is a *secondary circular reaction.* For example, infants may find that the sides of the crib make an interesting noise if they are struck with the foot. Along these lines, if a rattle is

Infancy and toddlerhood represent the dawning of intellectual activity.

shaken properly, it will create an interesting sound. Infants gradually become aware of the changes they can make, especially if a created event is different, amusing, or interesting. Another cognitive development during this stage is the anticipatory, or "power of association," effect. This advancement will become an important aid to understanding cause-and-effect relationships because infants learn that certain events may be associated. Piaget observed that his son Laurent, especially during feeding time, associated a cradling position with being fed. As soon as he was in this position to eat, he wanted contact only with his mother's breast. An obvious associational bond had been forged.

☐ Coordination of Secondary Schemes (8–12 months)

During previous substages, infants have trouble understanding the concept of *object permanence,* the realization that objects exist even when they cannot be seen. If any object is hidden behind a pillow, infants lacking object permanence will not search for it. An "out of sight, out of mind" principle is operating. But after 8 months, about the time that object permanence is acquired, infants will search under and behind obstructions to recover desired objects. Fairly recent experiments are challenging the limitations of an 8-month-old's memory ability and suggest that the ability to locate hidden objects is better developed than prior research suggests (see, for example, Baillargeon and Graber, 1988).

☐ Tertiary Circular Reactions (12–18 months)

Infants' heightened interest in creating changes in their environment fuels primitive reasoning skills. By the end of the first year, the beginnings of simple trial-and-error behavior emerge. Also at this time are further gains in the understanding of object permanence. More specifically, infants no longer will look for an object in the place where they first found it if they see its position being changed. This is the *tertiary circular reaction,* which fooled them in the previous substage. However, if the change is not visible, they will continue to look for it in the first location. They still lack the ability to take into account displacements outside their immediate perception.

☐ Invention of New Means Through Mental Combinations (18–24 months)

Before their second birthday, toddlers start creating mental images that enable them to devise new ways of dealing with the environment. This is the *invention of new means through mental combinations.* Now, simple problems may be "thought out" before they are undertaken and "inner experimentation" allowed in order for new mental combinations to be formed. Toddlers can now locate an unseen object, even when they have not observed it being moved, because they can infer its possible movements. Such reasoning abilities herald the beginning of true conceptual thought. At the end of the sensorimotor stage, other noteworthy advances include the acquisition and refinement of basic sensory skills and motor responses, the establishment of anticipatory reactions, and the beginnings of mental flexibility. All of these cognitive advancements form the foundation for later developmental stages.

When concepts such as object permanence are understood, the environment acquires new meaning.

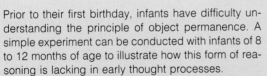

A Demonstration of Object Permanence: Out of Sight, Out of Mind?

Prior to their first birthday, infants have difficulty understanding the principle of object permanence. A simple experiment can be conducted with infants of 8 to 12 months of age to illustrate how this form of reasoning is lacking in early thought processes.

Select a small shiny object that is likely to capture the infant's attention, such as a coin, key, or ring. In plain view of the child, place the object in the palm of your left hand. Then, close both hands into a fist, making sure that the fingers of the left hand hide the object from the infant's view. (During the initial trial, open both hands for several seconds in order to ensure that the infant knows in which hand the object lies.) When given the opportunity to search for the missing object, the infant will undoubtedly seek to open your closed left hand. Repeat the process several times, each time hiding the object in the same hand.

Now, again in plain view, place the object in your right palm and, as in the initial trials, place both fists in front of the infant. Because the object is still conceived of as being in a special location, that is, in the place in which it was first hidden and found, your now empty left hand is often searched by the infant, who may ignore the right hand. Successful understanding of object permanence has yet to be developed.

DOES PIAGET'S THEORY HAVE A BIOLOGICAL BASIS? As we learned in Chapter 2, the foundation of Piaget's theory rests on the notion that individuals must pass through age-related stages. Such a progression begins with the sensorimotor stage just described, and will continue until the stage of formal operations is reached. Early stages will provide the foundation for later, sophisticated cognitive structures.

Over the years, Piaget has received credible support for his views, which have launched the research of numerous investigators. A recent vein of research has revealed that specific growth cycles of the brain parallel the stages of cognition proposed by Piaget. Such research sheds interesting light on our earlier discussion in this chapter of brain growth spurts and development as a whole.

One representative study, launched by William Hudspeth (1987), explored the EEGs of 561 children and young adults between the ages of 1 and 21. Constructing individual growth curves for each region of the brain, Hudspeth found discontinous growth rates at the four recording sites (sensory-motor, visual-spatial, visual-auditory, and frontal divisions).

For example, Hudspeth found that the sensory-motor system acquires about 21 percent of its total development in the first stage proposed by Piaget. In the second stage, the visual-spatial system attains 48 percent of adult maturity, with the next highest growth rate in the visual-auditory system, which reaches about 20 percent of adult maturity. The frontal system remains stable from ages 3 to 5, then enters a growth cycle in which it attains 16 percent of its adult status. At age 5, the other three systems enter stable periods. The total growth curve of the brain exhibits growth cycles at the ages Piaget has identified in his cognitive-developmental theory.

Hudspeth discovered that the brain's global maturity begins at the back and moves forward. The overall process is characterized by cycles of growth and stability of varying duration in each region. The brain's growth cycles are often synchronized across different areas at different ages, when various brain functions are becoming integrated.

Further support for Piaget's theory emerges from the research of Robert Thatcher and his colleagues (1987), who studied the EEGs of 577 children, from infants (the youngest were 2 months old) to young adults. Systematic evaluation revealed that specific growth spurts of the brain, again, paralleled the major stages of cognition postulated by Piaget.

Interestingly, these researchers also discovered that the right and left hemispheres of the brain matured at different times and different rates. For instance, the left hemisphere (which controls analytical operations) acquires almost 90 percent of adult size by age 5. It then tends to level off from 6 years of age to young adulthood. The right hemisphere (which helps to discern relationships and put elements into context), however, reaches 90 percent of adult size by age 9. Compared to the discontinuous development of the left hemisphere, development for the right hemisphere is much smoother. Moreover, different *regions* of the left and right hemispheres were found to develop at different times and at different rates. According to the researchers, their findings indicate that specific cortical connections are genetically programmed to unfold at relatively specific ages.

■ Concept Development

Developing cognitive skills relies considerably on the establishment and refinement of concepts. Broadly defined, a *concept* is a mental image that represents an object or event. As they become more complex, concepts connect groups of objects and events sharing common properties. Because concepts sort out and categorize daily experiences, they are regarded as underpinnings for cognition as a whole (Daehler and Bukatko, 1985; Houston, 1981; Wessells, 1982).

The refinement of concepts is slow and often difficult for children. As youngsters are saturated with new information every day, they must either establish new concepts to represent this material or relate it to existing concepts. The difficulty of this becomes apparent when one considers, for example, how the concept "ball" must be refined. Once they have learned the proper verbal designation, children must learn that balls come in many different sizes, weights, and colors. Some bounce higher than others do, and some, such as snowballs, don't bounce at all. Some are used in sports activities and can be pitched, dribbled, or rolled. Children must also learn that the word *ball* has other meanings, such as "have a ball," ballroom dancing, or "the whole ball of wax." From this one simple concept, you can see how difficult a concept refinement is. Now let us examine concept development during the early years.

☐ Shape and Size Concepts

Before children can develop accurate concepts, an object's properties must be correctly distinguished. Such properties include shape and size. The perception of shape and size begins early in life. Newborns, for example, are especially attracted to novel patterns, including depictions of the human face. When they look at faces, infants are especially attracted to contrasting areas of lightness and darkness, such as between the hairline and the eyes. As their scanning abilities become more refined, infants, by the sixth month, can also understand facial composition and recognize whether facial elements presented in drawings are scrambled or correctly arranged (Rose, 1988; Kaplan et al., 1988; Bushnell, 1982; Lasky and Klein, 1980).

Accurate shape and size concepts rely considerably on *perceptual constancy,* the tendency of objects to appear the same under different viewing conditions. Because the retinal image changes when objects are examined from different standpoints, children may become confused when attempting to gauge their actual size or shape. For instance, when youngsters understand the concept of size constancy, a figure walking away or a boat disappearing into the horizon are not perceived as being miniature versions of the actual objects. Likewise, when shape constancy is understood, the various angles of a perceived object do not distort the object's actual shape. Thus, although dinner plates on the table appear elliptical when viewed at a certain angle and distance, shape constancy enables us to perceive them as circular. Surprisingly, infants seem to recognize size and shape constancy early in life. And with age, more accurate discriminations develop (Bower, 1981; Day and McKenzie, 1981).

Perceptual constancy is important throughout the entire life cycle. As Hans Wallach (1985) noted, the world continues to shift around observers as they move through it. As objects are approached, they expand and turn with respect to one's changing position. A turn or nod of the head alters the orientation of the surroundings; eye movements shift the image of the environmental motions caused by one's activity. With perceptual constancy, however, we perceive our surroundings as stable because we have compensated for such displacements.

Over time, youngsters will properly identify shapes and forms in their surroundings. Simple shapes, such as circles and squares, are learned first and more complicated shapes, such as triangles and diamonds, are acquired later. Young children, however, cannot detect all shapes. Shapes having ambiguous or hidden dimensions are especially difficult to perceive (Abravanel, 1982).

Another feature of objects that has to be learned is size. At first, the concept of size is difficult for children to grasp. Think of the trouble toddlers have in understanding, for example, how hollow cubes of varying sizes fit into one another. Initially, children may only handle the blocks or stack them upon one another. By age 2 or 3, though, children understand that the "little" blocks can be placed inside the "big" ones. As they become acquainted with familiar objects, such as other toys or household items, children gradually add a variety of "size" words to their vocabularies (Stevens, 1981; Ebeling and Gelman, 1988).

☐ Spatial Concepts

Spatial concepts are also difficult for youngsters to grasp. Because of their inexperience as observers, youngsters often do not realize that an object can take on different spatial appearances. In this respect, a child may have difficulty telling whether a standard figure has been placed to the left or right or in front of or behind other objects. Likewise, deciding whether an object is right-side up or upside down frequently produces confusion (Bower, 1981).

Children's difficulty in understanding spatial concepts is, in part, caused by their not knowing the terminology for describing the objects' different appearances. Their egocentric view of the environment also restricts development. In time, though, youngsters learn the correct terminology and transcend such egocentrism. In so doing, they can discriminate among spatial orientations and become aware of environmental change (Wishart and Bower, 1982).

☐ Class Concepts

Mental images representing object categories are known as "class concepts". Confusion is apparent when children are presented with object-class problems. For example, suppose youngsters are given a variety of blocks of different colors and shapes (see Figure 5-6). When asked to group these objects together, children of this age would most likely categorize them by *serialization,* or *chaining.* This is the process whereby objects are grouped on a perceptual basis, in this case by color rather than shape. Although this is one kind of grouping organization, young children tend to rely on this one dimension. Older youngsters, however, are capable of classifying by shape, as well as color, if need be.

Understanding the relationship between subclasses and classes also poses problems. To illustrate, suppose that a youngster was given four red checkers and two black checkers and was asked if there were more black or more red checkers. This would not be difficult for the child. But if he or she were asked whether there were more red or more black *plastic* checkers, confusion would result. This is because parts and wholes cannot be comprehended simultaneously. This cognitive advancement, as we shall see, develops later in childhood (Winer, 1980).

Further, a recent study of the ability of preschoolers and second graders to understand classes and subclasses indicates that age, indeed, makes subjects more sensitive to differences (Gelman and O'Reilly, 1988).

Some researchers (Mervis and Mervis, 1988) believe that the best way to help children learn to classify objects is through demonstration. Children aged 9 months were followed up to 30 months of age to determine their ability to classify objects. While they could classify, efforts were characterized by earlier mentioned generaliza-

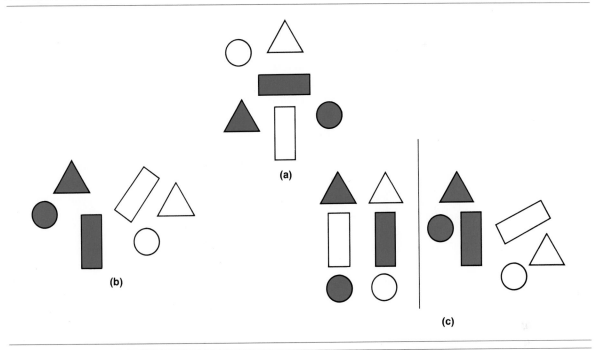

FIGURE 5-6 When asked to group blocks of different shapes and colors (a), younger children typically restrict themselves to one dimension, such as color (b). Older children, though, can group according to other dimensions, in this case, both shape and color (c).

tions, unless guided by an adult. Of three types of aids offered by adults (supplying the correct label, correction of the child's errors, and demonstration), the latter was found to be the most important factor. Studies such as this reinforce the notion that adults are instrumental in shaping the child's early conceptual learning.

☐ Time Concepts

Young children have a limited concept of time. Often, their understanding of it revolves around their daily activities, such as when dinner is served or when a parent comes home from work. Children also use, almost exclusively, the present tense when they converse. But by about age 3, they begin to understand words related to the past and the future.

■ Cognition and Memory

Mature cognition cannot exist without memory. Indeed, the ability to retain information and apply it to present and future situations is one of our most important mental abilities. It is through memory that our past influences our present and future thoughts, plans, and actions (Norman, 1982; Klatzky, 1980).

There are three types of memory: sensory, short-term, and long-term. *Sensory memory* refers to all of the sensory stimuli to which an individual is exposed. Many sensory impressions can be retained for only short periods of time (less than a second). They then decay and are replaced by new sensory impressions.

Short-term memory is more selective than immediate memory is, but this type of storage system is still quite temporary. It also is affected considerably by interruption and interference. A good example of short-term memory is finding a telephone number and remembering it just long enough to dial it.

Long-term memory can retain large amounts of information for relatively permanent amounts of time. For information to pass from short- to long-term storage, repeated rehearsal may be needed. *Coding* is also required, which is a process of compacting information so that it may be placed into appropriate long-term memory categories. At other times, some information may pass directly from the short-term to the long-term store, presumably as the result of its importance to, or impact on, the individual. Compared with short-term memory, long-term memory undergoes little or no decay.

The development of memory throughout childhood reveals several interesting trends. At first, children are capable of holding only a few words or ideas in their minds. They frequently have difficulty remembering events that happened weeks, days, or even only hours before. This problem points to the small amount of information in their long-term memory store. However, it is generally recognized that, with age, memory significantly improves. Certain factors account for this improvement. First, children are able to increase their overall memory span as they grow older. *Memory span* refers to the number of items that can be held in the short-term bank. Whereas the average 3-year-old can store only three items in his or her memory span, the typical 8- to 12-year-old can hold six (Case, Kurland, and Goldberg, 1982; Wilkinson, 1981).

Another factor leading to improved memory abilites, as well as cognition as a whole, are metacognitive abilities. *Metacognition* refers to one's awareness of how a cognitive process can be applied to a given mental task; for example, the rehearsal of events so that they can be remembered or the use of other memory strategies to prevent forgetting are metacognitive abilities. Such strategies are referred to by some as *metamemory* skills.

Metacognition has other important dimensions. Youngsters discover that paying close attention to objects and events and ignoring any distractions assists memory. So

Attention and attending skills allow infants to become more aware and alert.

too does employing more efficient information-processing and organization abilities and higher levels of motivation. Children's comprehension of these and other metacognitive processes steadily increases with age. The result is more refined and elaborate strategies for perceiving, storing, and retrieving environmental information (Flavell, 1981; Bjorklund and Hock, 1982; Miller and Weiss, 1981a, 1981b; Miller and Zalenski, 1982).

■ Sense-Organ Development

With age, sense-organ efficiency improves because of the growing physical maturation of the sense organs as well as the increasing amounts of perceptual information that can be processed. The youngster's developing awareness of objects and events in the world also assists the maturation process. All of these developments enable toddlers to make remarkably fine discriminations of sights, sounds, and other sensory stimulations.

☐ Vision

The visual system develops rapidly. By 4 months of age, infants' visual accommodation and focusing abilities are close to those of mature adults. Also developing rapidly is brightness sensitivity, which matures by approximately 3 months. The ability to see small objects with increasing clarity is evident by 7 to 9 months. In one study involving 7-month-old infants (43 full-term and 50 high-risk preterm) visual recognition memory was tested. The preterm infants showed significantly less differential attentiveness to novelty and required longer exposure times during visual familiarization (Rose, Feldman, McCarton, and Wolfson, 1988). By age 12 months, children can follow and track remote objects as efficiently as adults can. Color perception is also evident at an early age. By approximately 4 months, the visual spectrum of the primary color categories of red, yellow, and blue can be perceived (Adams, 1989; Adams, Maurer, and Davis, 1986; Bronson, 1982; Bornstein, 1981).

☐ Depth Perception

Depth perception is an important visual ability that allows a person to distinguish downward slopes, descending steps, or edges of precipices. As one can imagine, the lack of depth perception for children may retard the development of their creeping, crawling, and walking abilities. However, it is known that infants perceive depth as early as the crawling stage.

We can measure depth perception by means of a *visual cliff* apparatus. This device is a split-level table designed with a "shallow" and a "deep" end (Figure 5-7). Half the table is on a normal plane and ends abruptly, although a glass plate extends over the entire table. The other half of the visual cliff drops several feet below the "edge." (Both sides of the table are covered with a checkerboard design to show the drop.) Thus, infants are able to see the differences in depth, even though the surface is safe to crawl on.

Research has revealed that infants will not cross over to the deep end. Most crawling infants will peer through the glass, sometimes pat it, or even rest their faces on it. However, they will not venture over to the deep end. Even when mothers stood at the deep end and tried to coax their babies across, 81 percent refused to move forward.

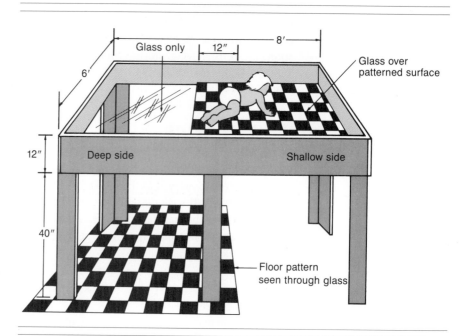

FIGURE 5-7
A typical visual cliff.

Findings such as this indicate the presence of depth perception at the crawling stage. Interestingly, depth perception is evident early in the life of not only humans, but in other land animals as well. Young chicks, rats, kittens, and goats all refuse to cross over the deep sides of a visual cliff. However, nonland animals such as turtles and ducks have a different reaction to a visual cliff. In fact, they show little, if any, hesitancy about crossing over to the deep side. It is conceivable that the deep side of the visual cliff more closely resembles their natural surroundings.

Other investigations in depth perception show that infants as young as 2 or 3 months show differences in heart rate at the shallow and deep sides of the table. More specifically, the infants' heartbeat *decreases* when they are placed on the deep side, a common reaction of humans when they pause to orient themselves to new situations. At 8 months, however, the infants' heartbeat *increases,* an emotional reaction that typically accompanies fear. It has been surmised that older infants, having had more experiences in crawling—and falling— are able to perceive the potential danger associated with the deep side (Campos et al., 1978; Campos, Bertenthal, and Caplovitz, 1982).

Finally, research has been directed at the role of emotional signaling from caregivers on infants' visual cliff behavior. Of significance was a study headed by James Sorce (1985) that examined the effect of mothers' facial expressions of emotion on the visual cliff behavior of their infants. In this study, which consisted of four parts, 108 twelve-month-old infants were observed.

In the first part of the study, 19 infants viewed a facial expression of joy, and 17 infants viewed one of fear. In the second part, 15 infants viewed interest, and 18 infants viewed anger. In the third part, 19 infants viewed sadness. In the last phase, 23 infants were used to determine whether the expressions influenced the infants' evaluation of an ambiguous situation or whether they were effective in controlling behavior merely because of their discrepancy or unexpectedness.

The researchers found that the infants watched facial expressions to clarify situations. For example, if the mother looked joyful or interested and the infants used this as a social reference, they would cross over to the deep side. On the other hand, if the mother showed fear or anger, few infants would cross. In the absence of any depth whatsoever, few infants looked at the mother, but those who did, when the mother looked fearful, hesitated but crossed nonetheless. All of this prompted the researchers to conclude that facial expressions regulate behavior most clearly in uncertain situations.

☐ Audition

The auditory system also matures rapidly as children learn the associative value of sounds. At about 16 weeks, infants are aware of the sound of a familiar voice, crying, or novel sounds and will turn their heads in the direction of the sound (see DeCasper and Fifer, 1980; Rheingold and Adams, 1980; Martin and Clark, 1982). At approximately 5 to 8 months, infants can distinguish different sound frequencies and make relatively fine auditory discriminations (Olsho, 1982).

☐ Taste and Smell

Taste and smell both are remarkably well developed at birth. Through direct contact with many tastes and odors, children can differentiate and recognize these sensory stimuli. By the early years, children seem able to detect the same pleasant and unpleasant odors that adults can. However, it must be recognized that there is a wide range of individual differences in taste and smell sensitivity (Rosenstein and Oster, 1988; Acredolo and Hake, 1982; Alberts, 1981; Ziporyn, 1982; Hubert et al., 1980). Infants as young as two hours old appear to be able to discriminate between sweet, sour, bitter, and salty tastes (Rosenstein and Oster, 1988).

☐ Touch

The sense of touch is exercised considerably during the first year as infants explore objects not only with their fingers but with their tongue and lips as well. Skin contact and warmth provide stimulation for infants. During toddlerhood, touch is one of the most pleasurable of the child's sensations. Furthermore, the sense of touch adds a great deal to cognitive awareness during these years, especially when exploration of the sensations of hardness and softness, roughness and smoothness, and warmth and cold are at their peak. Learning environments for infants and toddlers should thus provide as many experiences as possible to elevate touch sensitivity as well as the other major senses (see Reisman, 1987; Cataldo, 1984; Honig and Laly, 1981; Jones, 1980).

■ Language Development

One of developmental psychology's most fascinating areas of study is how children learn to talk. The study of this developmental area, known as *psycholinguistics,* traces how children pass from the early stages of crying and babbling to spoken words and meaningful sentences. Psycholinguistics embraces the closely related areas of mental imagery, cognitive development, symbolization, and speech.

At the outset, it should be realized that speech and language are related to, though also different from, each other. *Speech* is the concrete, physical act of forming and sequencing the sounds of oral language. *Language* is the system of grammatical rules and semantics that makes speech meaningful.

☐ Language and the Brain

The part of the brain that is most directly associated with language and its subsequent development is the left cerebral hemisphere. Rarely does damage to the right hemisphere produce any language disorders. Researchers have identified three areas in particular that serve specific biological functions. One of these parts is *Broca's area,* located adjacent to the region of the motor cortex (which controls the movements of the lips, jaw, tongue, soft palate, and vocal cords). Its function apparently is to incorporate programs to coordinate these muscles in speech. Damage to Broca's area produces *motor aphasia* and causes speech to be slow and labored. However, comprehension of language is still possible.

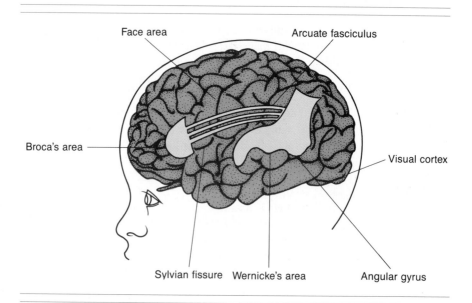

FIGURE 5-8 Areas of the brain associated with speech.

A second region, located in the temporal lobe, is referred to as *Wernicke's area.* Wernicke's area is believed to be related to the comprehension of speech. When this part of the brain is damaged, speech is fluent but has little meaningful content, and comprehension is usually lost. Such a condition is called *sensory aphasia.*

The third area, a nerve bundle that connects the Broca's and Wernicke's areas, is called the *arcuate fasciculus.* When damage occurs here, speech remains fluent but it is abnormal. Such afflicted individuals utter meaningless phrases, and although they are able to comprehend spoken or written words, they cannot repeat them. Figure 5-8 depicts the brain's language centers.

☐ Theoretical Interpretations of Language Development

Thus far, we have explained what language is and which parts of the brain control its expression. What we haven't explored is how a child learns a language. In other words, what factors account for an infant's babbling, the emergence of a child's first word, and the eventual fabrication of sentences? To answer such questions, three major theories of language development were proposed: the reinforcement, social learning, and innate approaches.

Reinforcement theory, in large part formulated by B. F. Skinner, states that language acquisition is a form of operant behavior in which children add new words to their vocabulary. New words are acquired because they fulfill the child's needs. The parents' use of positive reinforcement when their child uses the appropriate words or correct grammar may also increase his or her vocabulary (Skinner, 1957).

To date, the reinforcement theory of language acquisition has not gained much support. One of the main criticisms is that many parents usually pay more attention to whether their child's speech patterns are factually correct than to whether the grammar is correct. Consider the following: Suppose that a child sees you reading this book and asks, "That a book?" A normal and seemingly natural inclination is to respond, "Yes, it is." If you do that, though, you are responding to the truth of the proposition, not to the fact that the child's question was ungrammatical. Put another way, you paid more attention to the facts of the remark than to the (incorrect) grammar.

Social learning theorists maintain that children are able to acquire language by observing and imitating the adults in their surroundings. In this sense, parents may serve as models, not only offering remarks that the child may imitate, but also expanding on the child's utterances themselves. Imitation, thus, should play an important role in language development, especially because children want to be like adults, and fluent speech is an obvious characteristic of grown-ups. In this sense, an adult may say, "This is the baby's high chair," to be followed by the child's response of "baby high chair."

However, much like reinforcement theory, the social learning approach has fallen victim to criticism. Its critics maintain that although imitation does occur, it is not the pivotal feature of language acquisition. Even when children do imitate adult speech, they reformulate the sentence by using their own grammar. Acquiring new grammatical features through imitation, when it is exactly these new features that are omitted, hardly explains the nature of acquisition. Yet the most dramatic evidence refuting imitation as an explanation of language acquisition is the language patterns of those children who cannot speak, yet can hear normally. The case of a young boy who fit into this category and never had the opportunity to imitate adult speech is an excellent example. He did, however, learn to comprehend a language. Results such as these support the conclusion that the theory of social learning leaves many questions about language development still unanswered (Lenneberg, 1962).

Finally, we come to the innate theory, proposed by Noam Chomsky (1968, 1980). Chomsky suggested that the human brain is programmed to enable individuals to create and understand language. This system of programming is called the *language acquisition device* (LAD), which depends on mature cells in the cerebral cortex. Because the cortex is not totally functional at birth, it must mature during the first year if the child is to develop an understanding of words. This innate device allows the brain to perform cognitive operations upon the sounds received, enabling infants to produce grammar and to invent totally new sentences. Innate theory, then, views language development as a genetic phenomenon. Chomsky also asserted that sentences are gen-

The manner in which children acquire a spoken language has different theoretical possibilities.

erated by a system of rules, which enable children to listen to language and eventually fabricate sentences.

Also important to Chomsky's theory is the ability to analyze sentences, rather than just how sounds and words combine to form sentences. Sentences are analyzed by examining its two parts, the *surface structure* and the *deep structure.*

The rules of grammar dictate a sentence's surface structure. The deep structure is what a particular sentence means to the individual, or the conceptual framework of a language. Several examples should clarify the distinction between the two types. Consider the following:

The student attended the developmental psychology class.
The developmental psychology class was attended by the student.

The two surface structures are obviously different, but both sentences have the same meaning. That is, both share the same deep structure. Now, consider the following set of sentences:

They are eating apples.
They are eating apples.

Now the surface structures are identical, but the two sentences may have different deep structures. The sentence could mean that "People are in the process of eating some apples" or "The apples are the type that people like to eat." These examples show that sentences may have the same surface structures but different deep structures.

Understanding the relationship between the deep and the surface structure of a sentence is referred to as a *transformation.* Transformations include the realization that statements not only can be interpreted differently but also can be expressed in different tenses. Although our example, "The student attended the developmental psychology class," used the past tense, it could also have been expressed in other ways, such as "The student attends the developmental psychology class" or "The student will attend the developmental psychology class."

Chomsky stated that certain facets of the deep structure are innate and universal among all natural languages. But the surface structures are specific to each language. He also maintained that children may learn to make correct transformations by first forming *kernel words,* words that can be strung together to make a statement that is usually declarative. From these basic words, transformations are learned and sentences are produced.

Chomsky's theory is an important contribution to the field of psycholinguistics, and some research supports his ideas. For example, children do follow the same universal patterns of speech sounds, such as cooing and babbling, before uttering their first word. A number of researchers have also observed that the early sentences of children of different nationalities are grammatically similar. Although individual languages (surface structures) vary from country to country, the underlying deep structures are remarkably uniform. From 1.5 to 2 years, children everywhere learn their native language and use similar grammatical systems (R. Brown, 1973a, 1973b; Slobin, 1970).

The innate theory of language development also is supported by the fact that speech is possible only when youngsters have attained a certain stage of physical maturation. Language is thus seen as developing in children as a product of biological development, rather than as being initiated by external influences. In support of this, it has been found that certain phases of language development correlate consistently with specific motor-skill accomplishments (Lenneberg, 1967).

Although this theory is controversial (Harman, 1982; Rice, 1989), Chomsky's ideas have influenced contemporary researchers. Total and conclusive support for this theory remains elusive, but psycholinguists are actively investigating Chomsky's ideas.

☐ Developmental Stages of Language

Understanding the developmental stages of language requires an awareness of *phonology,* the speech sounds relevant to a language. More specifically, we need to examine the nature of phonemes, morphemes, vowels, and consonants.

A *phoneme* is a language's most fundamental element. English has more than 40 such basic sounds, and when combined, phonemes form words. A *morpheme,* on the other hand, is the smallest meaningful unit of a language. Some words contain one morpheme, and others have several. For example, the word *boys* has two morphemes: *boy* and *s.* A *vowel,* the most prominent sound in a syllable, is produced when air flows freely through the mouth cavity as it passes over the vocal cords. A *consonant* is a speech sound characterized by constriction or closure at one or more points in the breath channel. Now that we have identified these speech sounds, let us turn to the early stages of language development.

CRYING: THE INFANT'S FIRST COMMUNICATION Crying represents infants' earliest vocalizations. There are many different varieties of cries, from the whimpering to the fussy to the more piercing, colicky cry. Each type of cry usually has meaning, and parents usually learn to distinguish among the many varieties. Although crying is not a language, it represents a type of communication, as it is the means by which infants convey their basic needs. Usually variations of the cry are the only vocalizations that take place during the first six to eight weeks of life.

How do adults learn to recognize the various types of infant cries? Abraham Sagi's (1981) research underscored the importance of experience. Sagi designed an experiment that required 36 mothers and 32 nonmothers to identify infants' hunger, pain,

Crying represents an early form of communication.

and pleasure cries. The nonmothers were pregnant women, 14 experienced in child care and 18 inexperienced. Among the mothers, 17 had one infant and 29 had one infant and an older child. The mothers responded more accurately than the nonmothers did, and in comparison with both the experienced and the inexperienced nonmothers, they were more skillful in identifying the infants' cries.

COOING AND BABBLING: OUT OF THE MOUTHS OF BABES Between the second and third month, a type of vocalization called *cooing* emerges. Cooing includes such sounds as gurgling and mewing and generally indicates that the infant is pleased, happy, or even excited. Though still not considered language, cooing, like crying, is a form of communication. It follows no grammatical rules and is an innate response. Also, it is expressed after a certain degree of maturation has been attained. More specifically, cooing requires muscular movements of the tongue that were not possible at birth. Cooing is a behavior that occurs not only in normal children but also in deaf youngsters. At approximately 8 months of age, it diminishes in all children.

At about 6 months, *babbling* emerges. Whereas cooing consists of vowel sounds, babbling includes both vowels and consonants. Infants from a variety of linguistic backgrounds babble in a similar fashion. This was shown in one study (Oller and Eilers, 1982) in which Spanish- and English-learning babies were compared. Syllable and vowel production was perceived as remarkably alike. In fact, for even the most sophisticated listeners, differences in the babbling of the two groups were hard to discern (see also Roug, Landberg, and Lundberg, 1989).

Babbling is important because it allows infants the opportunity to exercise their vocal apparatus, and it enables them to hear the range of sounds that they are capable of making. Babbling is also important because it is the first vocalization that bears any real resemblance to speech. Early phases in this developmental stage are often accompanied by excitation and motor movement. Infants seem to make sounds that arouse their interest. They often lie quietly while listening to sounds; at other times they babble in response to the verbal stimulation around them. Whatever the context, babbling leads to increased control of sound.

During these early stages of development, children need the benefit of adult language stimulation. Such stimulation is regarded as critical to children's overall language development. Children need to hear speech around them in order to realize their linguistic potential (Slobin, 1982; Cazden, 1981; Moerk, 1983; Ausberger, Martin, and Creighton, 1982; Faber and Mazlish, 1980).

Adults who offer language stimulation to infants will encourage more sound production than will adults who offer no stimulation at all. For example, even though most babies will babble to some degree, reinforcement seems to affect the amount of vocalization. Furthermore, such early stimulation appears to have long-lasting linguistic and cognitive benefits (Stevens, 1981; Lewis and Coates, 1980; Masur, 1982; Barnes et al., 1983).

An interesting cross-cultural investigation (Sigman et al., 1988) illustrates the positive benefits that language stimulation has for the child. In this study, the social interactions experienced by Embu children between 15 and 30 months of age growing up in a rural Kenyan community were observed bimonthly. Children who were talked to frequently, whose vocalizations were responded to, and who engaged in sustained social interactions were rated higher on motor and mental achievement scales and showed more positive effect than children who were involved in limited forms of linguistic and social interaction.

However, we must point out that the infant's state of readiness greatly influences the effects of adult verbal stimulation. To respond to adult stimulation, infants need to gain control over the muscles of their throat, mouth, and tongue. Their brain cells also need to mature so that infants can understand the linguistic stimulation.

Variations in Parental Language Stimulation. We need to also acknowledge that the manner in which parents provide linguistic stimulation to their children has interesting variations. Indeed, parents not only employ a unique communication style but there also are sex differences in how mothers and fathers talk to their children.

The unique communication style among adults is known as *motherese* (so-called because it's observed more frequently among mothers of infants). Motherese is simple, redundant language. Research reveals that sometimes this speech style is as unique as that of youngsters. When talking with children, adults often raise the frequency of their voices and use brief sentences with concrete nouns, diminutives, and terms of endearment (Fernald and Simon, 1984; Kavanaugh and Jirkovsky, 1982; Gleitman, 1981; Kaye, 1980; Ringler, 1981).

Parental speech also contains interesting sex differences. For example, Barry McLaughlin and his associates (1983) recorded the speech of parents as they interacted with their children during free-play situations. The mothers tended to give their children linguistic support, modifying their language to the youngsters' needs. The fathers were less sensitive to their children's linguistic abilities. Instead, they put more demands on their children during the play situations and, in so doing, raised their performance levels. These findings are similar to those of other studies. In one (Bright and Stockdale, 1984), fathers were found to make more demands on their children in structured play sessions. Mothers played a less active and demanding role. Interestingly, mothers who are depressed are significantly slower to respond to the infants' vocalization and, when they do, they are less likely to utilize exaggerated intonations (Bettes, 1988).

One other study (Bellinger and Gleason, 1982) explored the differences in directives given by mothers and fathers to their children, ages 2.5 to 5 years old. The children joined separately with each parent in a construction task. It was found that fathers issued more directives than mothers did and tended to phrase them as imperatives (e.g., "Put the screw in") or as indirect "hints" (e.g., "The wheel's going to fall off") more often than mothers did. Mothers tended to rely more on relatively transparent indirect forms (e.g., "Can you put the screw in?"). There were no differences in the form of the directives addressed to girls and boys, nor were there any cross-sex effects. The authors concluded that parental modeling, rather than the differential socialization of girls and boys, was the mechanism by which children learn to request action in sex-associated ways.

THE FIRST WORD: THE HOLOPHRASE STAGE Few verbal accomplishments are more exciting to witness than the emergence of the first word, known technically as the *holophrase* stage. After cries, gurgles, cooing, and babbling, there is something magical about an infant's first word, especially as the child's initial words often are designations for the mother and father. On the average, this milestone occurs between the ages of 12 and 18 months. Although there are variations in the types of words acquired (Rice, 1989; Nelson, 1981; Peters, 1982), young children appear first to learn words that relate to food, toys, body parts, animals, and people. These early words are primarily concrete nouns and verbs. However, one must recognize that the child may not understand all words spoken. That is, some words are acquired through imitation, so the youngster may not know what they actually represent (McShane, 1980).

This one-word stage becomes surprisingly complex over time. In fact, a one-word utterance may represent a complete sentence with its own sentence structure. As an illustration, the word *toy* may mean "I want my toy," "My toy is in the corner," or "My toy makes funny sounds." Holophrases thus come to mean the designated objects as well as the roles that these objects play in the child's environment. Understanding the various meanings of one-word expressions is a difficult task for adults, who frequently have to pay close attention to voice intonations, gestures, and facial expressions in order to understand what is being said.

We might add, too, that before and during the holophrase stage, there is frequently a gap between the words to which children can mentally respond and those that they can express verbally. Typically, infants can understand words before they can speak them. Known as the receptive versus the expressive lag, this linguistic phenomenon means that even though children cannot articulate words, they can nevertheless demonstrate their understanding of them or of directions spoken by adults. Thus, an infant of 11 months may be able to follow the directive "Get the ball," yet may lack the linguistic ability to speak that same sentence or even parts of it. In time, however, the discrepancy between reception and expression lessens. Alert adults realize that a child's inability to express words does not automatically mean that he or she does not understand the situation at hand. On the contrary, children know much more than their linguistic ability allows them to express (Clark and Hecht, 1983).

THE TWO-WORD STAGE: FROM WORDS TO SIMPLE SENTENCES By approximately 18 months, children start using two-word expressions. Usually these utterances consist of single words that exist as separate entities. When spoken, there are separate intonations and pauses between the words. But eventually, they are connected and used in succession.

Sentence arrangement during toddlerhood consists of *pivot* and *open class words*. Pivot words are usually shorter and slower in developing than open class words. For instance the word *go* may be acquired and later become a pivot word used in such combinations as "Toy go," "Mommy go," or "Me go." The pivot word is usually, but not always, used as the second word in these sentences. Compared with open class words, pivot words rarely exist as single-word expressions. Open class words, conversely, consist of any of a large number of words that are not considered pivot words. Early vocabulary growth usually is of the open class variety.

Following the development of two-word expressions come telegraphic sentences. *Telegraphic sentences* are short and simple and consist mainly of nouns and verbs. They are labeled telegraphic because the sentences lack some words, as well as tense endings on verbs, plural endings on nouns, prepositions, and conjunctions. Despite such grammatical omissions, the words necessary to give the sentence meaning are included. As an illustration, suppose we wanted to put the following sentence into telegraphic form: "The soup that I'm eating is hot." The telegraphic version is "Soup hot" or "This soup is hot." Note that the telegraphic sentence resembles a telegram.

Besides the developments made in sentence structure, there are other important linguistic gains. For example, the average vocabulary of a 3-year-old hovers near 900 words. Children's knowlege of *syntax,* or knowledge of grammatical rules, and *semantics,* understanding word meanings, increases daily as they use language more and more as a vehicle to express their thoughts. By their third year, youngsters are capable of becoming effective participants in conversations, even when the conversation involves more than two people (Dunn and Shatz, 1989).

Toddlers are also adept at using a variety of word elements. For example, they are able to make plural nouns by adding an "s" and are able to put verbs in the past tense by adding "ed." Although such general rules permit inflections of regular words, irregular words pose difficulties. Consequently, the logical rules for making nouns plural and putting verbs into the past tense are indiscriminately applied to irregular words. Thus, "foots" or "feets" may be the result of incorrect pluralization, and the "ed" ending may produce such incorrect inflections as "goed" for "went" or "doed" for "did."

Although such word endings may be amusing, pause for a moment and consider the child's logic for using them. If you look beyond the obvious incorrect inflection, the child has in fact mastered an important principle of the English language. That is, to form the past tense, one must add "ed." This the child has correctly done but has been tricked by the inconsistency of the English language.

Such a mistake is called an *overregularization* and is evidence that a language is not exclusively acquired through reinforcement or imitation. Youngsters could not have learned such words as "goed" or "doed" from adults because grownups do not use such overregularizations. Rather, children fabricate these words on the basis of overgeneralizing the principles they have learned (Schacter and Strage, 1982; Platt and MacWhinney, 1983).

UNIT REVIEW

■ Cognition consists of those mental processes pertaining to thinking, perceiving, and understanding.

■ Piaget's sensorimotor stage encompasses the first two years of life and has six sub-stages.

- Key concept refinement occurs in the areas of shape and size, space, class, and time.

- Cognition is greatly enhanced by developing memory abilities. Long-term memory is the most resistant to decay. Metacognition and metamemory skills also improve memory abilities.

- Children are also more alert to their environment because of improvements in vision, audition, taste, smell, and touch. Depth perception is present early in life, usually at the crawling stage of infancy.

- The brain contains language centers. There are numerous theories regarding how children learn a language, the most popular being the innate theory. Language follows a developmental progression: crying, cooing and babbling, the holophrase stage, and telegraphic sentences.

◼ Unit Three:

PERSONALITY AND SOCIAL DEVELOPMENT

Humans are social animals, and learning to make social adjustments is one of life's most important and complex developmental challenges. This task begins early in childhood and continues throughout life. In the beginning, socialization experiences are limited, but in time, youngsters become able to participate in new and challenging situations with others. The family, peer groups, and the school—to name but a few socialization agents—each influences the child in a unique way. The child will succeed in some social experiences, and these will generate positive self-regard. But other occurrences will be anxiety producing and ego threatening for the child. How each social situation is handled as time progresses will become a vital component of the child's developing personality (Aronson, 1984; Maccoby, 1980).

Early social experiences enable children to understand themselves and their surroundings better. Indeed, their developing mental abilities fuse with early personality and social forces and enable them to realize that they are separate and unique individuals. This developing awareness of how individuals perceive themselves and others, including other people's thoughts and feelings, is known as *social cognition*. Social cognition, requiring the use of developing mental strategies to understand oneself and the general fabric of social relations, clearly shows how developmental processes blend together.

◼ Early Attachment Behavior

Socialization typically begins during the early months of life when contacts are made with the mother, the infant's primary source of food, comfort, and attention. To most infants, the mother offers an early social and emotional experience that is both satisfying and rewarding. The close interaction between the two also enables the infant to recognize the mother as someone separate and unique in an otherwise bewildering environment. This interaction usually creates *attachment* between the mother and the child, an affectionate bond that strengthens over time.

We must add that attachment is not the exclusive domain of mother and child. Children are also capable of developing different and separate bonds of attachment with their fathers or significant others. Many youngsters develop strong attachments to both parents. However, it is not uncommon for a child to have a strong attachment to the mother but not the father, or vice versa. The fact that attachment behavior can be directed toward either parent also has implications for the nurturance of trust and security: Such psychological reassurance need not always originate from the mother (Bowlby, 1980, 1988; Etaugh, 1980; Londerville and Main, 1981).

Both early and later social development appear to be affected by early attachment experiences. Contemporary lifespan psychologists feel that one's general extraversion, social independence, and emotional investments in others may be traced to the outcome of these early social experiences. To go a step further, early attachment promotes such positive behaviors as trust and security, whereas its absence can result in anxiety and inner turmoil. In this sense, infants' attachments may determine the type of social animals that they will become.

International Lifespan Development

■ EARLY SOCIALIZATION: VARIATIONS IN PARENT-CHILD INTERACTIONS

The seeds of socialization are sown when the interaction between parent and child begins. These early patterns of interaction are important, as adults can provide critical stimulation of the child's linguistic, cognitive, social, and physical capacities. Early interaction also strengthens bonds of attachment. The absence of parent-child interaction, on the other hand, retards growth in these areas.

The patterns of behavior displayed by parents as they interact with their children have received considerable research attention, not only in the United States but in other lands as well. For example, one study (Dixon, 1984) compared the manner in which African and American mothers interacted with their children during a teaching task. In the study, 36 African and American mothers were videotaped as they performed the task with their children, who ranged in age from 6 to 36 months.

It was discovered that the African mothers more often repeated instructions, pulled their children's hands, and were less verbal overall. Moreover, the African mothers repeatedly focused and modeled the task in its entirety and seldom reinforced their infants' efforts, except for a simple confirmation of success. On the other hand, the American mothers

used much praise, encouragement, and reflective speech in their efforts to shape their children's activities.

There were also differences among the infants in this study. The African infants tended to be persistent in their efforts, often interacted socially with their mothers, and did not resist the hand tugging or pulling. The American children used the toys in more diverse play activities, showed shorter attention spans with some tasks, and became frustrated by tugging or restraining activities. It was felt that both cultural groups demonstrated contingent, reciprocal, and affectively positive interactions.

Patterns of interaction were also explored in Hindu and Sikh mothers in another study (Mukerjee and Ganguli, 1984). The study had the mothers interact with their children while their behavior was observed through a one-way mirror. The two groups of mothers were matched with respect to their age, education, and family income.

Overall, it was found that the Sikh mothers were more actively involved with their children's activities and imposed greater control over their children's behavior. The Hindu mothers were less involved in and interfered less with their children's activities but appeared more nurturing. The study also indicated that individual differences were evident among the mothers. Each mother revealed a specific style of maternal behavior that was quite stable over time.

Observations of Guatemalan parents and infants in everyday situations (Lasky, 1981) revealed that the mothers were much more active than the fathers were in overall interactions. Most of the interactions initiated by the mothers appeared to consist largely of caregiving. The mothers interacted verbally with their children, increasing this with the age of their children. When there was social play, it was more likely to take place between siblings and not between parents and children.

In one other study by Michael Lamb and his associates (1982), patterns of parental behavior were investigated in both traditional and nontraditional Swedish families. This research team observed 45 couples interacting at home with their 16-month-old infants. The researchers identified 15 fathers who had been the primary caretaker for more than one month as *involved,* whereas their partners were labeled as *less involved.* Fathers who did not take advantage of the nation's parental leave program (available to both mothers and fathers) were considered *less involved,* and their partners were deemed *involved.*

The researchers found that, in general, the mothers were more likely to vocalize, display affection toward, touch, attend to, and hold their infants than the fathers were, regardless of their involvement in the caregiving. Overall, the amount of involvement in the caregiving had no significant effects on the parents' behavior. However, *in-*

Bonds of attachment are formed early in life.

volved mothers scored highest on the degree and intensity of parental interaction patterns. Findings such as this suggest that gender differences in parental behavior are much less amenable to social influence than many psychologists believe, although it has not yet been determined whether gender differences in parental style have some biological basis.

☐ Theoretical Perspectives of Attachment

How and why does attachment occur? What determines the strength of the attachment bonds? Does attachment follow a developmental progression? Answering such questions has been an active field of investigation, and from this research, four theoretical perspectives have emerged. These interpretations reflect the major schools of thought discussed in Chapter 2.

Learning theory stresses that attachment is a learned, rather than an innate, process. This viewpoint suggests that attachment is a series of stimulus-response mechanisms, much as many other childhood behaviors are. It is reasoned that the mother, or other caregiver, who is initially a neutral stimulus, acquires secondary reinforcing properties over time. Infants learn that the mother is the agent responsible for their primary reinforcers, such as tactile stimulation, milk, or warmth. Because she is continually associated with the dispensing of these primary reinforcers and with the satisfaction of the infant's basic needs, her continual physical presence becomes important to the infant.

Cognitive-developmental theory views the attachment process as a reflection of the infant's developing mental abilities. Attachment and proximity-seeking behavior ensue because the infant is cognitively aware of the perceptual differences between the mother and others in the environment. Attachment is further strengthened when the infant understands person permanence, a concept closely related to the Piagetian principle of object permanence. By age 2, infants realize that the caregiver can exist even though she may not be physically present in the same room. The child's ability to construct a mental image of the mother's distinguishing characteristics will result in more proximity-seeking behavior. In this way, cognitive and social behavior are said to be related.

The ethological interpretation proposes that an infant's social responsiveness develops largely through innate tendencies. A critical or sensitive period during the early months of life is said to make the infant especially receptive to the caregiver. During infancy, these innate systems are activated by the environment, and their expression elicits specific responses from the caregiver. Infant behaviors such as clinging and sucking promote close contact with the mother. Crying and distress capture the caregiver's attention, as do smiling and cooing. Later, infants call their mothers and follow them, further strengthening the bond between the two. Combined, these behaviors result in physical nearness and attachment to the caregiver. And as history reveals, infants who can maintain this closeness have the best hope for survival.

Finally, the psychoanalytic view, similar to the ethological approach, emphasizes instincts. Attachment is regarded as an emotional relationship shaped by the Freudian concept of instinctive psychic energy. During the child's psychosexual stages of development, this energy is directed toward the mother because she is perceived as a source of pleasure and satisfaction. As the child's primitive needs are met during the oral and anal stages, bonds of attachment strengthen, and the mother is recognized as a "love" object.

☐ Indicators of Attachment

Besides the infant's desire to maintain contact with the caregiver, there are several visible clues to the developing attachment behaviors. One of these is the infant's smiling responses. During the first month, the infant may form a *reflex smile*. This smile is primarily physiological and may be the infant's response to a number of different stimuli, including internal stimulation (a bubble of gas in the stomach), being fed, or being stroked on the cheek. Reflexive smiles are not socially oriented.

The *social smile* appears between the second or third month of life. This is true smiling as we know it and can be evoked by the appearance of a caregiver, a voice, movement, or certain noises. Many infants smile, open their eyes wide, and make cooing noises at the same time, called a "greeting response." Interestingly, the caregiver's returning the greeting response may prompt the infant to continue this behavior (Lewis and Coates, 1980; Kaye and Fogel, 1980).

The *selective social smile* occurs approximately between 5 and 6 months. Instead of smiling in an undifferentiated way, as in the social smile, the smile is now directed only to familiar social stimuli, such as the mother or other familiar caregivers. Unfamiliar faces are readily detected at this age and cause the infant's withdrawal behavior.

Another clue to developing attachment behavior is *stranger anxiety*. During the first six months of life, infants do not express distress toward unfamiliar faces. At this point, though, anxiety and wariness are apparent when strangers are introduced. The

Stranger anxiety usually produces emotional distress.

infant is evidently able to detect a noticeable difference in the stranger's face, as compared with the mental image of the caregiver's features stored in his or her developing mind. Growing levels of cognitive awareness are thus connected to stranger anxiety as well as to the development of the social smile. As one might expect, the infant's overall distress levels are reduced when the primary caregiver is present, when the stranger approaches the infant with no sudden moves, and when the stranger behaves naturally (Smith, Eaton, and Hindmarch, 1982).

Remarkably, neonates just a few days old show some signs of distinguishing their mother's face from that of a stranger. This was explored by Tiffany Field and her colleagues (1984) in a unique study. During repeated trials, neonates who showed an initial preference for their mother's face were shown her face alone as well as her face plus her voice. This was done until the neonates had reached a state of habituation. When a stranger's face was later introduced, the neonates looked longer at it, suggesting to the researchers that they had distinguished their mother's face after limited experience (see also Bushnell, Sai, and Mullin, 1989).

Another indication of attachment is *separation anxiety,* which occurs by approximately the twelfth month. Separation from the caregiver is likely to result in the infants' considerable protest and distress. However, the infants' degree of protest and distress is affected by the situation in which they are left. For example, both their familiarity with the environment and their possession of a favorite attached object tend to reduce the protest levels.

☐ Individual Variations in Attachment

Attachment does not follow a universal pattern. Rather, there are individual variations in attachment behavior. For example, the strength of the attachment bond and its quality and security may differ from child to child.

The research of Mary Ainsworth (1979) revealed the individual variations in attachment behaviors. Ainsworth proposed three types of attachment: *securely attached, anxious-resistant,* and *anxious-avoidant.* Behaviors unique to each category can be observed when infants are placed in strange and unfamiliar surroundings, such as a room they've never seen before.

When placed in such a situation, securely attached infants typically turn to their mothers for comfort when it is needed, but they also attempt to explore the environment. They also exhibit little anxiety when their mothers are away for short periods of time. Upon the mother's return, however, these infants are happy and desire close contact with her.

Anxious-resistant infants do not explore the environment when they are placed in unfamiliar situations with their mothers. They are likely to be anxious and distressed when the mother is temporarily away and are ambivalent toward her when she returns. Upon her return, infants may cling to her at one point and then push her away.

Anxious-avoidant infants are relatively unattached to their mothers and exhibit little anxiety or distress when left alone. Furthermore, they demonstrate little response when their mothers reappear. Often, many will ignore their mother when she returns.

These three types of attachments are the result of different parenting styles. The mothers of securely attached infants usually are responsive and sensitive to their infants' needs. These mothers have succeeded in fostering a sense of trust and security in their children. The mothers of anxious-resistant infants tend to be insensitive and unresponsive to their children's needs. The latter holds true for mothers of anxious-avoidant infants, although they also tend to be more rejecting, particularly when their children desire close physical contact (Smith and Pederson, 1988; Thompson, Connell, and Bridges, 1988).

There also appear to be other ramifications of these categories of attachment. Mary Durrett and her associates (1984), for instance, found that the mothers of securely attached infants perceived greater support from the father than did the mothers of anxious-resistant and anxious-avoidant infants. It is proposed that mothers who do not perceive support from their husbands may experience higher levels of stress than those who do receive support. Consequently, they may be less psychologically available to their infants.

Finally, how these categories develop over time has fallen under the scrutiny of researchers. One of the more noteworthy studies was undertaken by Byron Egeland and Ellen Farber (1984). In the experiment, data were collected from 189 mother-infant pairs during the infants' first two years of life. The data included maternal and infant characteristics, mother-infant interactions during feeding and play, life-stress events, and family living arrangements.

The researchers uncovered several unique patterns. For example, the mothers of securely attached infants were consistently more cooperative and sensitive with their infants than were the mothers of anxiously attached infants. The anxious-resistant infants tended to lag developmentally behind their counterparts and were less likely to solicit responsive caretaking. The anxious-avoidant infants, although robust, tended to have mothers who had negative feelings about motherhood, were tense and irritable, and treated their infants in a perfunctory fashion.

Interestingly, the male infants were somewhat more vulnerable to qualitative differences in caretaking. But the female infants seemed to form more secure attachments. Changes from secure to anxious attachments were characterized by initially adequate caretaking skills, but prolonged interaction with an aggressive and suspicious mother. Changes toward secure attachments reflected growth and increasing competence among young mothers.

☐ Attachment and Contact/Comfort

Researchers have long sought to find out why youngsters are drawn to soft objects that offer comfort and how this behavior relates to attachment. Such behaviors often range from clinging to the mother's clothing or to a security blanket, to cuddling stuffed animals and huggable dolls.

An impressive array of research undertaken by Harry Harlow (1958, 1962, 1971; Harlow and Zimmerman, 1959; Suomi and Harlow, 1971) has helped supply some of the answers to why such behaviors exist. Harlow's research focused on the behavior of rhesus monkeys in laboratory situations. In this study, two surrogate (substitute) mothers were built and placed in a cage; one was constructed of wire meshing and the other of the same material covered with a terry cloth wrapping. Each "mother" was equipped with a nursing bottle (the nipple of which protruded through the "chest") and a light bulb behind the body, which provided heat for the infant.

The infant monkeys were then divided into two groups; Group A could receive nourishment from the nursing bottle placed only in the wire mother, whereas Group B could receive milk from the bottle of the cloth-covered mother. The monkeys in Group A fed from the wire mother, but they gradually spent less time with her. Eventually, these monkeys took nourishment and then spent the intervening time with the more comforting cloth mother. Several infants even clung to the cloth mother while reaching over to feed from the wire mother. On the other hand, the infants in Group B spent considerable time clinging to the soft covering of their cloth mother and almost never ventured over to the other wire figure.

The cloth mother also played a central role in reducing the infant's fear and anxiety. This was apparent when a strange object (a mechanical teddy bear) was intro-

The need for comfort and security is expressed in many ways.

duced into the cage with the infant, the cloth mother, and the wire mother. The infant invariably ran to the cloth mother and clung to her for security. After its fear was reduced by this form of contact and comfort, the infant would venture short distances from the mother and eventually attempt to explore the new object.

Harlow also studied the later behavior of those monkeys not benefiting from a real mother. It was learned that the mother's absence had severely hampered the monkeys' normal development, particularly in social and emotional maturation. Whereas the monkeys reared with cloth mothers overtly showed no problems in infancy, some were retarded later in life when compared with monkeys brought up by real mothers. More specifically, the experimental monkeys became socially maladjusted, ignoring others, and frequently passing time by biting and hugging themselves. Later, some of the females in the study group proved to be poor mothers, neglecting and abusing their young. However, when placed in the company of normal monkeys, the socially isolated monkeys began to recover from the effects of their experimental environment. This was largely because the normal monkeys encouraged social interaction and play behavior and discouraged solitary behavior. More recent research supports these studies and also suggests that formerly isolated monkeys adopted by a female within a social group become less maladjusted over time (Reite, Kaemingk, and Boccia, 1989).

Harlow maintained that the maladjusted behaviors were probably caused by the real mothers' gradually curtailing the clinging activities and promoting the infants' autonomy. The contact in infancy that real mothers provide also promotes the formation and differentiation of facial and bodily postural expressions, a factor that may make later social interactions easier.

All of Harlow's research has given us more insight into the overall concept of attachment behavior. His research indicates that satisfaction of the hunger drive does not by itself promote and nurture the infant's attachment to the mother, a belief held for years by many. Rather, the attachment to the mother is encouraged by the need to establish contact with something that can offer comfort, softness, and warmth. Coupled with our previous discussion, we can add that infants need quality more than quantity in the attachment relationship. Those parents who supply attention, sensitivity, consistency, and responsiveness to their infants' needs are most likely to produce the healthiest attachment. These are the necessary ingredients needed to sustain emotional security and satisfaction in the attachment relationship.

International Lifespan Development

■ CHILDREN OF THE ISRAELI KIBBUTZ

The Israeli kibbutz is a collective settlement in which work is shared and children are reared away from their parents. This type of child-rearing practice contrasts sharply with the American style of upbringing and offers a unique cross-cultural view of attachment and maternal separation.

In the kibbutz arrangement, children are reared in group settings, from the nursery to high school. The group of children into which one is born remains the same, and as a result, close bonds of attachment usually develop. During infancy, a metapalet (a child-care worker of the kibbutz) tends to the baby's basic needs. Parents visit the infant daily, and the mother returns as often as necessary to feed the child. When the infant is weaned from the mother, the metapalet assumes full responsibility for feeding the youngster. As the children grow older, they move to other living arrangements and come into contact with other metapalets and teachers. During adolescence, teenagers are part of the "youth movement" that exposes them to the kibbutz and communal sphere. They are encouraged to make group decisions and to develop such capacities as cooperation and sensitivity toward others. At the end of adolescence, members of the kibbutz work with the adults and contribute to the economy.

Initially, it was hoped that the kibbutz arrangement would revolutionize Jewish society and remove the division of social classes. The elimination of sex-role stereotyping and the patriarchal family structure was also envisioned. However, these goals have not yet been attained (Rabin and Beit-Hallahmi, 1982).

Research does show, however, that the children of the kibbutz do not suffer from the lack of parental care and nurturing. On the contrary, the children grow up to be emotionally stable and well adjusted. This has been borne out in a number of studies, including one designed by Rachel Levy-Shiff (1983). In the experiment, the individual adaptation and competencies of preschool kibbutz children were compared with those of Israeli family-reared youngsters of the same age. Adaptation and competences were assessed by means of semistructured interviews, observations, questionnaires, and a series of problem-solving tasks (matching colored disks, working on an insoluble jigsaw puzzle, and fitting cutouts) testing aspects of performance such as systematic approach and perseverance.

The results indicated that the kibbutz children were more instrumentally independent and self-reliant in routine and daily tasks but less effective in the problem-solving tasks. They were also less responsive to and cooperative with adult strangers. However, there was no significant difference between the two groups in regard to attachment, difficulty in separation from parents, adjustment to a nonfamilial setting (nursery school), and developmental disturbances.

Children of the kibbutz may also have an edge in certain coping behaviors. Alvin Shapiro (1982), for instance, found that kibbutz-born 13-year-olds showed fewer increases in pulse rates on the day of school examinations than did Israeli urban-born subjects. Interestingly, the kibbutz-born children showed greater levels of test anxiety just before examinations than on the previous day, whereas the urban-born children expressed less anxiety, the latter suggesting the coping behavior of denial. Shapiro proposed that the more effective stress-coping strategies of the kibbutz-born children may be related to the many attachments and adaptation abilities formed during the early years in the kibbutz.

Research also reveals that kibbutzim children are better at sharing and cooperating than are nonkibbutzim youngsters. One study (Nisan, 1984) compared how kibbutzim and nonkibbutzim first and fifth graders distributed rewards between themselves and a partner who had produced either more or less than the subjects had. As anticipated, in both age levels, the kibbutz children, for whom equality was a central norm in socialization and practice, tended more than the nonkibbutz children did to distribute equally rather than equitably. The older subjects were also asked about the level of effort and merit of themselves and their partners. Their answers revealed that both the kibbutz and nonkibbutz children maintained that rewards should be distributed according to effort. However, they differed in their assessment of their partner's level of effort. The nonkibbutz children inferred the level of effort from the level of output, whereas the kibbutz youngsters tended to believe that their partner had tried as hard as they had, even if the partner had produced less.

There is evidence that does not support the claim that the kibbutz children are more altruistic than the nonkibbutz children are. One study headed by Daniel Bar-Tal (1981) explored the motives for helping, as expressed by 80 children between ages 4 and 5 and between ages 7 and 8. Half of each age group were from a kibbutz and half from a city. Half of each group were boys, half girls. The subjects were given three pictures depicting three situations in which one child had an opportunity to help. They were asked whether the child in the picture would help and, if so, what the child's motive would be for such an action. They were also asked questions regarding motives for helping behavior in general.

The researchers proposed three hypotheses: (1) the older subjects would express higher-level motives for helping than the younger subjects would; (2) the kibbutz subjects would express higher-level motives than would the city subjects; and (3) the girls would express higher-level motives than the boys would. Contrary to what was expected, however, only the first hypothesis was confirmed. No differences were found between kibbutz and city subjects or between boys and girls.

■ Emotional Development

Emotions are defined as changes in arousal levels that may either interfere with or facilitate motivated behavior. Usually emotions are accompanied by a physiological response, such as an increase in blood pressure, heart rate, or muscle tension. Furthermore, there are overt emotional behaviors, such as facial expressions or body movements, as well as an individual's cognitive interpretation of his or her emotional state (Campos and Sternberg, 1981; Pribram, 1980; Brown and Wallace, 1980).

Emotions are highly complex states, not only in children but in adults as well. Consequently, they are difficult to define and categorize. It becomes especially hard for researchers exploring infant emotions, as there is a lack of differentiated emotional responsiveness at birth. Often, broad labels are applied to the infant's emotional behavior, such as "relative calm" or "diffuse excitement."

Complicating the issue is that the infants' outward emotional expressions may not correspond to their inner state. For example, crying or weeping are behaviors that may mean, among other things, a reaction to pain, hunger, or discomfort. With time, however, it is generally acknowledged that infants' emotional behavior becomes more complex and differentiated (Bloom, Beckwith, and Capatides, 1988; Izard, 1980, 1982; Lewis and Michaelson, 1983).

Recent research attempts to evaluate infant emotions not by studying just the infant but by attempting to study the interaction between the infant and the environmental stimuli that are causing the emotion. More specifically, it has been theorized that infant behavior is goal directed (Bowlby, 1982); for example, they want to play peek-a-boo or socialize in some other way, or look at an object. If the infant changes goals while interacting with the caregiver, but the caregiver does not realize this, the interaction may become unsatisfactory to the infant, thus producing an emotional change (Tronick, 1989). For example, when mothers stare at their infants using an expressionless or "still-face," 6-month-old infants decrease smiling and gazing at their mothers and grimace more during this time (Gusella, Muir, and Tronick, 1988).

The infant, then, is part of a two-way affective communication system in which the infant's goal-directed strivings are aided by the caregiver. This has been called *other-directed regulatory behaviors* because it is an attempt by infants to have some other person satisfy their goals (Gianino and Tronick, 1988). The infant, however, is not solely dependent on the caretaker, for infants have coping behaviors such as looking away or sucking the thumb during a disturbing event. Both of these actions lower the heart rate, indicating an emotional change. These coping behaviors have been labeled *self-directed regulatory behaviors,* suggesting that their function is to control and/or change the infant's emotional state (Gianino and Tronick, 1988; Beebe and Stern, 1977). Let us now take a look at some emotions and emotional behaviors.

☐ Crying

The infant cries with vigorous and total bodily expressions, largely as a result of hunger or other internal discomfort. Crying is also triggered by fatigue and environmental tension. The parent's ability to soothe the baby and provide continuous stimulation during these emotional outbursts are also critical to the length and the intensity of the crying.

The total amount of crying is generally reduced and the bodily expressions are milder by the end of the first year. Crying becomes less frequent over time. The reasons for crying depend on the situation, such as separation from the caregiver, unfamiliar and fear-invoking situations, physical pain, or frustration when goals are blocked.

☐ Laughter and Humor

Smiling and laughter become part of a person's emotional mosaic at an early age. You will recall that smiling is usually elicited by the sound of a human voice and may eventually serve as an indicator of attachment to the caregiver. Interesting events, such as bright moving objects or the sounds of other people's voices, also produce smiling.

Simple interactions with adults may also elicit smiling and laughter. For example, the baby may smile, which prompts the mother to smile. The mother's smile may, in turn, motivate the child to smile again. In time, laughter becomes associated with other types of stimulation (e.g., tickling) or with feelings of well-being. Games, stories, and television may also develop humor at an early age. Similar to other emotions, humor becomes more fully developed as childhood progresses and cognitive skills become more mature (McGhee and Goldstein, 1983a, 1983b).

☐ Fear and Anxiety

A youngster's maturation level has much to do with early fears. As youngsters grow older, their social environment expands and exposes new areas of uncertainty and possible danger. However, what might have evoked fear in children at an early age may no longer do so as their cognitive skills develop. This suggests that the individual's emotional susceptibility to some fears increases with age. Supporting this is the fact that in early childhood, a youngster's fear of strangers decreases but that the fear of imaginary creatures increases. As with all emotional adjustments, children unquestionably need the support, guidance, and gentle understanding of adults in overcoming their fears (Schaefer and Millman, 1981).

Anxiety, a state of inner apprehension toward a subjective danger, also has its beginnings in infancy. Two good examples of this emotional reaction are stranger and separation anxiety, discussed earlier in this chapter. As infants and toddlers expand their social environments, they may encounter stressful situations. Parental demands such as weaning, eating on a schedule, and toilet training may contribute to their anxiety. Especially stressful are crisis events such as divorce, abuse, or hospitalization.

☐ Anger and Aggression

Anger and aggression often result when attempts to reach a desired goal are blocked. When such an obstacle is encountered, the child will try to remove it. This reaction can be seen most readily when the child is threatened with the loss of the mother. Anger is often expressed for the first time when such a separation occurs.

As more demands are placed on the child, angry behavior becomes fairly commonplace. Temper tantrums are especially prevalent at this time. Adjustment is particularly difficult for the infant and toddler in regard to personal care and social training. Outward-directed anger is frequently aimed at rigid demands in toilet training, dressing, eating, interruptions in desirable playtime activities, and being forced to go to bed. Frequent irritability on the part of the child may develop from other causes, including bedwetting, fatigue, or illness (Haswell, Hock, and Wenar, 1982).

Children's Temper Tantrums: Understanding the Eye of the Storm

The scene is probably familiar to parents of young children everywhere. A youngster is interrupted during a favorite playtime activity and told to go to bed. Another picks up a new, unaffordable toy in a store and is instructed to put it down. Some youngsters may respond with a *temper tantrum,* an outward-directed and emotionally laden flow of anger. Temper tantrums are expressed in many ways, from crying and screaming to head banging and kicking. Yet, no matter how they are channeled, tantrums seem to express the same message: anger and frustration in having to adjust to the rituals and demands of grown-up life.

Temper tantrums are a normal phase of childhood development, yet they represent the ultimate in negative expression. While handling temper tantrums is an individual affair, most experts agree that giving in to the child's demands only reinforces this type of be-

havior and increases the likelihood of its future reappearance. Getting angry and upset also serves as a reinforcer, since children can see that their behavior is taking its toll. Most experts suggest that ignoring the tantrum until it has extinguished itself and then talking to the child at a less emotional moment is an effective technique. In social situations, some parents may prefer to remove the child in a firm manner to another location (e.g., bedroom, car) to avoid social discomfort. Whatever course of action is chosen, adults must choose an approach that they are comfortable with and exercise *consistency.* Seeking to understand why temper tantrums develop from the child's standpoint and taking into account things such as irritability, fatigue, and adult demands on children may go a long way in dealing with this stormy stage of emotional development.

■ Socialization Through Play

Play greatly influences personality and social development. In a sense, play represents children's work, a meaningful set of activities that will help them relate in a special way to their surroundings. Few activities reveal the child's character and resources for coping with the world more than everyday play does.

A personal sense of identity is also established through play, as children realize who they are and what effects their actions may have on the people around them. In this sense, play serves important cognitive functions. Furthermore, play has individual as well as social functions. Individually, it gives children the opportunity to experience many of life's emotions and to view their position in life in relation to the rest of the world. Socially, play and games can bring children into contact with one another and make them aware of the meaning and value of rules, order, and structure (Howes, 1988; Howes, Unger, and Seidner, 1989; Fowler, 1980; Sluckin, 1981; Piers and Landau, 1980; Sutton-Smith and Roberts, 1981; Kaplan-Sanoff, 1981).

Even when toddlers are as young as 16 months, they pay attention to the behavior of others, especially slightly older children. Thirty toddlers aged 16 to 23 months were observed in family day-care homes. Each had access to both same-age and older peers. The toddlers preferred 2-year-olds to same-age peers and were more imitative and talkative when they were with the 2-year-olds than when they were with their peers (Rothstein-Fisch and Howes, 1988).

☐ Exploratory and Manipulative Play

By the third or fourth month of life, infants engage in exploratory play. At this age, with their body movements becoming better controlled and organized, infants may enthusiastically examine and observe objects of interest in their surroundings. One early object of interest is their own body; delight may be expressed, for example, in placing the fingers in the mouth, inspecting the feet, or stimulating sensitive parts. Not only does this activity represent a source of amusement and pleasure, but it also enables infants to realize that these body parts are their own. This realization, in turn, helps develop early self-concepts.

As infants gain control of their hands, they begin to engage in manipulative play. Here, they become preoccupied with the feel of different items, such as a rattle, blanket, and pillow. This type of activity represents another enjoyable learning experience and allows infants to realize that objects can vary in size, shape, color, and texture. As play becomes more skilled and sophisticated, the treatment of objects becomes more diverse and sophisticated (Greenfield and Tronick, 1980).

Interactions with the environment often lead to other types of play. In some instances, primitive games may evolve, depending on the reciprocity that an adult can offer or the environmental effect a given action can cause. For example, an infant may laugh and solicit a smile from a nearby adult. This may encourage the infant to laugh again, with the hope of receiving another response. This type of exchange, with anticipated reactions from both partners, may soon develop into a game.

Play such as this gives children the opportunity to observe the effects that their actions have on their surroundings. These games may even represent the origin of a sense of competence. Similar games continue, as when the infant pulls at a dangling toy, knocks toys against the sides of the crib to hear the noise they make, or drops them so as to watch them fall to the floor below. A fundamental understanding of cause-and-effect relationships has begun to develop. These games also reflect unique operating principles. Note that the infant not only is acting on the environment but that the environmental objects also have reinforcing properties. This combination of Piagetian and behavioristic principles is another illustration of the interaction of developmental psychology's major schools of thought.

Early play behavior is often exploratory and manipulative.

☐ Destructive Play

Another type of play taking place at this time and during the later years of childhood is *destructive play*. After building a tower in which one block is precariously balanced on another, for example, the structure may be playfully knocked down, only to be rebuilt again. Or after taking considerable time in creating a design on paper, the child may, moments later, destroy the picture by brushing wide streaks of dark paint across it.

This type of play is common and completely normal and has been given several explanations. While indulging in certain types of play, such as the aforementioned, the child is in the process of creating. Through creating, the child realizes that certain objects have component parts that somehow relate to one another. Large blocks, he or she learns, will support smaller ones, and in the art example, dark colors overshadow light colors. In order to explore the endless possibilities of play toys, the child may try to change them, either by rearranging them or knocking them down. Through this process, a further understanding of causal relationships is nurtured, a cognitive development critical to the overall refinement of mental abilities.

Another explanation is that destructive play is the child's way of exhibiting control over the environment. To be sure, the creations made are the child's, and the child can do with them whatever he or she pleases. Furthermore, destructive play may serve as a means for releasing inner tensions and hostilities, particularly on nonthreatening objects. Such behavior is discussed more fully in Chapter 6, where we learn how the developing child learns to cope with life's failures and frustrations.

■ Theories of Personality Development

☐ Sigmund Freud's Psychosexual Theory

Sigmund Freud, as we learned in Chapter 2, was the founder of the psychoanalytic school of thought. In his psychosexual theory of personality development, Freud defined the first 18 months of life as the *oral stage* of development and suggested that the mouth is the primary source of pleasure and satisfaction to the developing child. (The mouth and other sensitive body parts, such as the anus and the genitals, are referred to in Freudian terminology as *erogenous zones*.) Freud stated that the infant is "pleasure bent on sucking," and regardless of whether or not one is an advocate of Freudian theory, any individual who observes an infant sucking nipples, thumbs, fingers, or pacifiers has little doubt that much of the infant's interaction with the environment occurs through contact with the mouth.

Freud further divided the oral stage into the oral sucking and oral biting stages. Oral sucking is a stage of dependence in which the baby can only suck, whereas the oral biting stage (commencing at 18 months) is that point at which the infant can also bite the nipple. It is possible that the latter stage occurs only in children who are frustrated when gratification is not immediate. The biting stage could thus be considered a form of aggressive behavior.

If there is satisfaction during the oral stage, a foundation will be laid for the continuation of normal personality development. However, if the infant's needs are not gratified, or if they are gratified excessively, a *fixation* is said to occur. That is, oral needs may continue throughout life and greatly influence behavior. Behavioral examples of an oral fixation include thumb sucking; cigarette, cigar, and pipe smoking; and the manipulation of the lips with the fingers or other objects such as pens or pencils

FIGURE 5-9 During the Freudian stage of oral development, a fixation may occur that might have a consequence for later behavior. Shown here are different types of oral behaviors.

(Figure 5-9). Other oral personality characteristics are overeating, greediness, and nail biting. However, research has not demonstrated any relationship between these behavioral traits and either frustration or overindulgence at the oral stage.

☐ Erik Erikson's Psychosocial Theory

You will recall that, whereas Freud stressed psychosexual development, Erikson emphasized psychosocial stages of growth. The two psychosocial stages of importance during infancy and toddlerhood are *basic trust versus basic mistrust* and *autonomy versus shame and doubt.* Basic trust versus basic mistrust occurs during the first year of life. During this time, Erikson believes the infant develops physically as well as psychologically. Furthermore, the infant learns (in an unspecified way) to deal with the environment through the emergence of trustfulness or mistrust. Trust is a feeling that some aspects of the environment are dependable. Events that may lead to such a feeling include feeding, tactile stimulation (cuddling, fondling, holding), and diaper changing.

The infant's initial relationships with the environment establish a feeling of social trust or social mistrust. Because the mother provides the child with the first social relationship, her task is to create a warm environment conducive to the nurturance of positive feelings. Trust, however, entails more than just physical reassurance:

> Let it be said that the amount of trust derived from earliest infantile experience does not seem to depend on absolute quantities of food or demonstrations of love, but rather on the quality of the maternal relationship. Mothers create a sense of trust in their children by that kind of administration which in its quality combines sensitive care of the baby's individual needs and a firm sense of personal trustworthiness. . . .
>
> (Erikson, 1963, p. 249)

Erikson feels that trust forms the first building block of the infant's development: a sense of identity. Without the ego strength of trust, various behavior problems will arise:

> In psychopathology the absence of basic trust can best be studied in the infantile schizophrenic, while lifelong underlying weakness of such trust is apparent in adult personalities in whom withdrawal into schizoid and depressive states is habitual. The reestablishment of a state of trust has been found to be the basic requirement for therapy in these cases.
>
> (Erikson, 1963, p. 248)

Basic trust provides the foundation for stable personality formation.

We must understand that basic trust and basic mistrust are at opposite ends of a continuum. In fact, Erikson pointed out that the ego qualities at each stage have been misconstrued as discontinuous traits, with one being good and the other bad. For example, mistrust, like the other so-called negative qualities, is not to be avoided altogether, because life presents some very real dangers and pitfalls of which one should be apprehensive. Rather than viewing trust and mistrust as a dichotomy, Erikson sees them as a continuum along which it is desirable to be farther on the trust than on the mistrust side.

The adult who meets the baby's physical and psychological needs will produce a child who is happier and more content, thus reciprocating the parents' enjoyment. Parents who have happy, trusting babies are apt to spend more time with them, which in turn results in the establishment of even more trust by the infant. This phenomenon is termed the *benign cycle*. The *vicious cycle* occurs when the parent ignores the baby's needs. For example, rather than cooing and gurgling in trusting contentment, such an infant may be hungry or wet and express frustration and irritability. The infant whimpers, cries, and finally may scream as the hunger pangs or skin irritations increase. The screaming baby may become an irritant to the parent, who may become cross and handle the screaming infant roughly, which produces further annoyance in the infant. The vicious cycle eventually leads to an ego characterized by an uncomfortable and insecure relationship with the environment, resulting in a predominant sense of mistrust.

Basic trust, over time, assists in the development of a continuum of emotional responses, ranging from the very pleasant emotions to the very unpleasant. The more severe the basic mistrust is, however, the more limited the infant's repertoire of emotions will become. A child who is mistrustful of the environment may exhibit only the emotions of anger, fear, distress, or apathy. This child may never learn how to respond to positive emotions such as love and warmth. Whereas Freud emphasized in this first stage the quantity of oral pleasure that the infant feels, Erikson stressed the quality of care provided by the mother.

The second psychosocial stage of concern to us is autonomy versus shame and doubt. This stage occurs between the ages of 1 and 3 years. As infants become increasingly aware of their environment, they have new interactions. Their self-awareness has developed to the point that they now realize that the self is an entity separate from the environment; thus their egos can develop more strengths or weaknesses. As their perceptual skills develop and their neuromuscular skills increase with maturation, their newly found self becomes aware of its autonomy but simultaneously realizes its vast limitations. Children attempt to assert themselves during this phase and frequently come into conflict with parental standards of behavior, leaving the psychological door open to feelings of shame and doubt. It is in this way that the children's developing physical abilities (walking, exploring the environment) conflict with their social interactions (parental standards) and personality dynamics (strivings for autonomy).

At this time, toddlers desire independence and want to participate in the decisions affecting their daily lives. For example, they may assert their autonomy by not eating at mealtime, by saying "no" to an adult's request, or by making demands at inappropriate times. This type of resistance is known as *oppositional behavior,* and many researchers (and parents) can testify to its prevalence during the early years (Haswell, Hock, and Wenar, 1982; Londerville and Main, 1981; Wenar, 1982). This behavior often upsets all concerned. The child's goals of autonomy are frequently thwarted, and the parent may become angry and aggressive with the tyrant, thus producing doubt (Can I do things for myself?) and shame (Should I do things for myself?) in the child and, possibly, guilt in the parent.

This stage of psychosocial growth is all part of the socialization process, however, and strivings for autonomy are considered normal. The child's healthy autonomy will be the outcome if he or she encounters a reasonable balance between parental freedom and control. Here again, Freud's and Erikson's differences in emphasis become apparent. Whereas Freud focused on anal gratification, Erikson considered the decisive event to be the battle of wills between the parent and child.

By the second year, autonomy unfolds at higher levels (for example, a child strives for autonomy during the first year by resistance to being held), producing the conflict between independence and dependence. The child wants both, producing an ego struggle that may last months and even years until a comfortable compromise is reached. The emotions of shame and doubt may arise during this stage if the child is not allowed to develop freely. The parent who is intolerant and continually browbeats the child will raise a child who feels ashamed and doubtful and who lacks the independent spirit necessary for healthy autonomy. Jerome Kagan (1981) agrees with this and suggests that 2-year-olds need supportive guidance and understanding. Adults need to be sensitive to the toddler's desire to try out new behaviors. They must realize that toddlers need to test the validity of adult standards in order to understand what will and what will not be allowed. In the midst of such strivings, overbearing adults run the risk of crushing the child's emerging self-awareness.

CHAPTER REVIEW

■ Unit One: Physical Development

Physical development continues to grow sequentially throughout childhood, the result of the gradual development of brain cells. This unit examined how the nervous system develops, including the central and peripheral systems. The central nervous system consists of the brain and spinal cord, and the peripheral nervous system is composed of neural tissue that connects the brain and the spinal cord with other parts of the body.

Maturation, often called readiness, is based on the development of brain parts as well as the muscle and skeletal systems. Once the organism has attained a sufficient level of maturity, environmental stimulation can speed the learning of a particular physical skill. The fact that areas of the cortex mature at different rates accounts for the emergence of thinking processes and motor reactions at varying times. Maturation and readiness are greatly affected by myelination. Myelination is the process by which a neuron develops an outside coating or sheath (myelin). Myelination allows for the rapid transmission of chemoelectrical messages.

Prehension, the ability to grasp objects, also matures as the result of sequential patterns of development, particularly those involving neuromuscular control and coordinated hand and eye movements. Children's artwork illustrates their increasing neuromuscular ability. Handedness—the preference for, and subsequent predominant use of, one hand—develops at approximately 2 years of age. There appear to be both environmental and genetic forces responsible for handedness.

■ Unit Two: Mental Development

Cognition refers to thinking, perceiving, and understanding. Jean Piaget's theory of cognitive development has given us insight into how mature thinking unfolds. The sensorimotor stage is characterized by six sequential substages, which lay the foundations for later cognitive functions. Important phases of development include the mastery of fundamental sensory and motor skills, the establishment of anticipatory reactions, an understanding of object permanence, and the construction of mental images that will facilitate later problem solving.

Advancements in cognitive functioning rely heavily on the establishment and refinement of concepts. A concept is a mental image that represents an object or event. This unit examined refinements made in shape and size, spatial, class, and time concepts. We also explored the importance of memory to cognition and differentiated among the sensory, short-term, and long-term storage systems.

The study of language development is known as psycholinguistics. The brain and the vocal cords enable humans to match symbolic representations with comparable meaningful vocalizations. The left hemisphere is the part of the brain most directly associated with language and its development.

No one theory fully explains language development, although three theories have been proposed: the reinforcement, social learning, and innate theories. Of the three, the innate theory is considered the most influential among contemporary developmental psychologists.

Developmental patterns of language follow a fairly stable sequence. Following the cooing stage at approximately 2 months, the infant proceeds to the babbling stage at approximately 6 months. Imitation appears to pave the way for the first word, which is spoken, on the average, between 12 and 18 months of age. The emergence of the first word is referred to as the holophrase stage, and there is often a gap between the infant's receptive and expressive abilities. Following the emergence of the first word, vocabulary acquisition is quite rapid, and marked advancements are made in grammar during the remaining years of infancy and toddlerhood. Of particular importance in sentence development is the use of open and pivot class words, followed by telegraphic sentences.

■ Unit Three: Personality and Social Development

During the early years, personality and social growth is largely shaped by the family. From early interactions with the parents, children gain a better understanding of themselves and their social surroundings. This awareness of oneself and society is called social cognition and is an active field of investigation.

This chapter discussed attachment, the affectionate bond between the caregiver and the infant. Four theories of attachment were considered: learning, cognitive-developmental, ethological, and psychoanalytic. Possible clues to the development of attachment are the selective social smile, stranger anxiety, and separation anxiety. Three categories of attachment are the securely attached, anxious-resistant, and anxious-avoidant. These three classifications underscore the individual variations that accompany attachment behaviors. Harry Harlow's research indicated that the contact/comfort motive needs to be considered when examining the topic of attachment in general.

Emotions, described as changes in arousal levels, are difficult to measure, as researchers are not able to record an infant's feelings. This unit examined some of the more common emotional expressions during the early years, including crying, laughter and humor, fear and anxiety, and anger and aggression. It is generally recognized that with age, emotions become more complex and differentiated.

Personality and social growth is influenced by play. During these years, play is often exploratory and manipulative. Playful interactions with the environment help foster an early sense of competence. Moreover, children will be able to observe the effects that their actions have on the environment.

Freud and Erikson devised theories of personality development that cover the years of infancy and toddlerhood. Freud pointed to an oral stage of pyschosexual development, which encompasses the first two years of life. Two of Erikson's psychosocial stages also occur at this time, basic trust versus basic mistrust and autonomy versus shame and doubt.

KEY TERMS

anxiety	babbling
anxious-avoidant attached	basic trust versus mistrust
anxious-resistant attached	Broca's area
arcuate fasciculus	central nervous system
attachment	cerebellum
autonomy versus shame and doubt	cerebral cortex

cerebrum
chaining
coding
cognition
concept
consonant
cooing
corpus callosum
deep structure
depth perception
destructive play
emotion
forebrain
frontal lobe
handedness
hindbrain
holophrase
hypothalamus
invention of new means through
    mental combinations
kernel words
language
language acquisition device
lateralization
locomotion
long-term memory
medulla oblongata
metacognition
metamemory
midbrain
morpheme
motherese
myelin
myelination
object permanence
occipital lobe
open class word
oral stage

overregularization
parietal lobe
perceptual constancy
peripheral nervous system
phoneme
phonology
pivot word
pons
prehension
primary circular reactions
psycholinguistics
readiness
reflex activities
reflex smile
reticular activating system
secondary circular reactions
securely attached
selective social smile
semantics
sensorimotor stage
sensory memory
separation anxiety
serialization
short-term memory
social cognition
social smile
speech
stranger anxiety
surface structure
syntax
telegraphic sentence
temporal lobe
tertiary circular reactions
thalamus
transformation
visual cliff
vowel
Wernicke's area

RECOMMENDED READINGS

Barclay, L. K. (1985). *Infant Development.* New York: Holt.
    Barclay explores the major developmental processes of infancy in a readable and under-
    standable fashion. A good resource book.

Bowlby, J. (1988). *Secure Base: Parent-Child Attachment and Healthy Human Develop-
    ment.* New York: Basic Books.
    A noted contributor to the field sheds light on the importance of attachment and its
    influence on the course of development.

Erikson, Erik (1982). *The Life Cycle Completed: A Review.* New York: Norton.
Among a diversity of topics is an exploration of Erikson's now famous eight psychosocial crises, including the strengths and virtues emerging from each.

Gottfried, A. W. (Ed.) (1984). *Home Environment and Early Cognitive Development.* New York: Academic Press.
This reader considers the impact of the home environment on intellectual growth, as well as the implications for intervention.

Izard, E. E. (Ed.) (1982). *Measuring Emotions in Infants and Children.* Cambridge, England: Cambridge University Press.
This reader contains numerous points of view regarding the physiological, expressive, and subjective dimensions of emotion.

Kagan, J. (1981). *The Second Year: The Emergence of Self-Awareness.* Cambridge, Mass.: Harvard University Press.
Kagan thoughtfully describes the competencies that forge early levels of self-awareness.

Kail, R. (1984). *The Development of Memory in Children,* 2nd ed. New York: Freeman.
This text examines memory and its relationship to developing cognitive abilities.

Lamb, M. E., and Campos, J. J. (1982). *Development in Infancy: An Introduction.* New York: Random House.
A thorough discussion of development from the prenatal period to 36 months, including, among other topics, physical, perceptual, emotional, cognitive, and social development.

Levinthal, C. F. (1990). *Introduction to Physiological Psychology,* 3rd ed. Englewood Cliffs, N.J.: Prentice Hall.
Among other topics, Levinthal explains the brain's role in growth and development.

Lindfors, J. W. (1987). *Children's Language and Learning,* 2nd ed. Englewood Cliffs, N.J.: Prentice Hall.
A well-written book that explores the basics of linguistic and mental competency.

Smolak, L. (1986). *Infancy.* Englewood Cliffs, N.J.: Prentice-Hall.
An excellent examination of this life stage. Special attention is given to attachment, motor development, language, and other key areas of growth.

Wachs, T. D., and Gruen, G. E. (1982). *Early Experience and Human Development.* New York: Plenum.
The dynamics behind early cognitive and social development is at the heart of this book.

Early Childhood

CHAPTER OUTLINE

What Do You Think?

■ Practice makes perfect. How often children hear that expression, in regard to such activities as handwriting, movement exercises, or sports. But does practice always lead to the successful execution of all motor skills? Developmental psychologists inform us that skillful performance requires more than just practice.

■ The preschooler's thinking often reflects the elements of fantasy and make-believe: dolls and other toys have feelings, the sky has been painted blue, and the world has its own built-in sense of law and order. Preschoolers are egocentric—self-centered, often thinking that the world has been created just for them. What contributes to this, and what can adults do to facilitate cognitive growth at this time?

■ Boys will be boys, and girls will be girls. Sex-role development begins early in childhood in both subtle and direct ways. How does it take place? What accounts for sex-appropriate behavior? What impact does sex typing have on children's behavior? We'll seek answers to these and other questions in this chapter, including how traditional sex-role standards seem to be diminishing in contemporary society.

■ Home sweet home. For countless children, the family unit serves as the provider of love, care, and security. Yet for a growing number of youngsters, the household has been transformed into a nightmare, filled with violent assaults, sexual molestation, verbal insults, and even death at the hands of their parents. Episodes of domestic violence have reached such huge proportions that many researchers feel that the very foundation of the family structure is starting to crumble. For the abused, there's no place worse than home.

Unit One:

PHYSICAL DEVELOPMENT

The child's rate of physical growth begins to taper off after toddlerhood, the period when physical development is at its greatest. Yet body proportions continue to change, and motor skills continue to be refined at a relatively fast rate, enabling children to become more adept at dealing with their own needs and coping with their physical surroundings.

By the age of 5, the average child stands 43 inches tall (about 3.5 feet), which is just over double the birth length, and weighs 42.8 pounds, approximately five times the weight at birth. Differences in height between the sexes are very slight, although boys weigh more than girls and tend to have more muscle and less fatty tissue.

Also during childhood, the head and brain approach their adult size. At birth, the head measures between 12 to 14 inches in circumference; By the first year it has increased 33 percent, and at the fourth year the head has increased approximately 48 percent. And by the end of the sixth year, the head has attained almost 90 percent of its adult size.

The brain, growing in relation to cranial growth, has attained 75 percent of its adult weight by the fifth year, as the billions of nerve fibers become increasingly myelinated and the dendrites in all layers of the cortex increase in both size and number. These maturation processes will enhance the connectivity and transmission of nerve impulses, which is critical to more complicated brain functions (Malina, 1982; Schmidt, 1982). Figure 6-1 displays the growth of dendrites in the cortex.

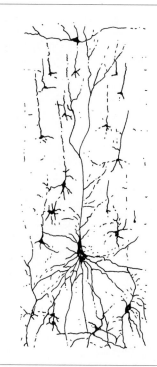 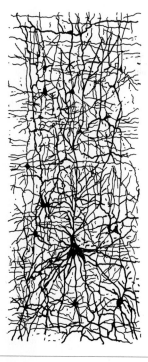

FIGURE 6-1
The growth of dendrites in the cortex. Compared to the first few months of life (left), dendrites increase in both size and number of connections (right) during the first five years.

■ Physical Changes During Early Childhood

By the time children enroll in nursery school or kindergarten, there have been noticeable physical changes in their bodies. The toddler's babylike contours, especially the round and chubby appearance, have given way to a more slender appearance. This is largely due to a growth spurt that affects height, as well as to the preschooler's participation in numerous and diverse physical activities, which affect muscular growth and body build.

Changes in postural patterns also become quite evident during the early years. And changes in body dynamics contribute to the child's physical and emotional well-being, as inefficient use of the body can lead to lack of muscle tone, a lower threshold of fatigue, and less available mechanical energy. A number of physical and psychological factors change the child's postural patterns:

Force of Gravity The force of gravity affects the body (the center being the trunk), whether sitting, standing, or running. Although the battle against the pull of gravity is more obvious for some children than others, each child must maintain equilibrium in order to produce good posture and balance. With age, body proportions change, and the center of gravity drops lower in the trunk. This makes it easier for the child to maintain equilibrium in the standing position.

Type of Body Build Posture is also affected by the child's body build. The posture of the heavier child will differ from that of the lighter or smaller one. Correct posture is also influenced by the strength of the bones, the firmness of the muscles, and the kinesthetic sense.

Course of Development The stages of the child's development are another factor to consider. The early phases of locomotion, for example, influence certain parts of the

Diverse physical activities affect the preschooler's muscular growth and body dynamics.

body, such as the neck muscles or the lumbar curve in the lower part of the back. When walking, the weight of the body falls on the inner part of the foot, resulting in the foot's sagging in the area of the ankle.

Interactions with the Environment Environmental factors, such as nutrition, rest, and activity, also are important to posture. The child now has incentives to excel in certain areas, such as sports, to be physically attractive, or to perfect certain motor skills. All of these may encourage a child to learn proper body balance and posture (Endres and Rockwell, 1985; Holt, 1982; Hendricks and Hendricks, 1983).

■ Motor-Skill Development

Motor-skill development rapidly accelerates in the physical-play world through such activities as jumping, climbing, running, and tricycle riding. Knowing what preschoolers are physically capable of undertaking and their degree of efficiency is important not only to parents but also to day-care and nursery-school teachers, people who will be structuring their physical activities. Adults need to structure children's motor-skill activities so that they will alleviate any frustration. Such frustration is usually the result of a task's being too difficult. But boredom may result if a task is too easy.

Both gross (large) and fine (small) motor skills advance during early childhood. Gross-motor skills, requiring the coordination of large body parts, include such activities as tumbling, skipping rope, or playing on a seesaw. Fine-motor skills require the coordination of small body parts, mainly the hands. Fine-motor skills include such activities as turning the pages of a book, using scissors, or fitting together a jigsaw puzzle. Learning to write, which for many begins at this time with simple exercises, also gives preschoolers the opportunity to refine their fine-motor skills (Vukelich and Golden, 1984; DeFord, 1980).

A number of factors account for the preschooler's ability to engage in more diversified motor-skill activities. Before the preschool years, muscular development was proportionate to overall body growth. Now approximately 75 percent of the child's weight gains are due to muscle development. Other developments evident at this time are increases in reaction times and refinements in eye-hand coordination, manual dexterity, and general body awareness (Wickstrom, 1983; Ridenour, 1980; Gallahue, 1982).

■ Stages of Motor-Skill Development

Similar to other spheres of growth, the coordination of motor skills follows a sequential pattern. Although individual variations are apparent within the time frame required to perfect coordination, virtually all motor skills develop in stages, including both gross- and fine-motor skills.

There are three stages of motor-skill development. In the *cognitive phase*, the child seeks to understand the motor skill and what it requires. At this point, mental awareness is critical to developing certain strategies or to remembering how similar tasks were handled in the past. The *associative phase* is characterized by trial-and-error learning, in which errors in performance are recognized and corrected in the future. In this stage, the strategy changes from the previous phase's "what to do," to "how to do it." The *autonomous phase* is the last stage, in which performance is characterized by efficient responses and fewer errors. Children appear now to respond more automatically (Schmidt, 1975, 1982).

This stage theory suggests that motor skills advance in a series of stages as do the locomotion and prehension sequences of infancy and toddlerhood (see Chapter 5). Indeed, virtually every aspect of physical development seems to follow an overall order

TABLE 6-1 Motor-Skill Development of Preschoolers

Motor Pattern	Skill Characteristics		
	3-Year-Old	*4-Year-Old*	*5-Year-Old*
Walking/ running	Run is smoother; stride more even. Cannot turn or stop quickly. Can take walking and running steps on the toes.	Run improves in form and power. Greater control stopping, starting, and turning. In general, greater mobility than at age 3.	Has adult manner of running. Can use this effectively in games. Runs 35-yard dash in less than 10 seconds.
Jumping	42% rated as jumping well. Can jump down from 8-inch elevation. Leaps off floor with both feet.	72% skilled in jumping. Jumps down from 28-inch height with feet together. Standing broad jump of 8 to 10 inches.	80% have mastered the skill of jumping. Makes running broad jump of 28 to 35 inches.
Climbing	Ascends stairway unaided, alternating feet. Ascends small ladder, alternating feet.	Descends long stairway by alternating feet, if supported. Descends small ladder, alternating feet.	Descends long stairway or large ladder, alternating feet. Further increase in overall proficiency.
Throwing	Throws without losing balance. Throws approximately 3 feet; uses two-hand throw. Body remains fixed during throw.	20% are proficient throwers. Distance of throw increases. Begins to assume adult stance in throwing.	74% are proficient throwers. Introduction of weight transfer; right-foot-step-forward throw. Assumes adult posture in throwing.
Catching	Catches large ball with arms extended forward stiffly. Makes little or no adjustment of arms to receive ball.	29% are proficient in catching. Catches large ball with arms flexed at elbows.	56% are proficient in catching. Catches small ball; uses hands more than arms.

Adapted from Corbin, C.B. *A Textbook of Motor Development*. Dubuque, Iowa: W. C. Brown Co. Publishers, 1980.

in which visible changes regularly follow one another. Thus, early efforts are often prone to mistakes, whereas later attempts are characterized by skillful execution of the required task. This latter accomplishment represents mastery of the mechanics underlying motor skills: accuracy of movement, precision, and economy of performance (Malina, 1982). Table 6-1 highlights some of the major motor-skill developments of preschoolers.

■ Rehearsal of Motor Skills

Practice makes perfect . . . or does it? We've all heard about the supposed importance of practice, be it large- or small-motor skills. In this context, practice is the continuous repetition of a motor skill so as to find the correct response. However, whether practice increases certain motor-skill efficiency is open to question. Not everyone accepts the notion that practice leads to perfection.

Whether practice is beneficial depends on the child's maturational state. You will recall that this refers to the readiness principle discussed in Chapter 5. Unless there has been sufficient neurological maturation, certain kinds of motor-skill activity are impossible, and practice will not help. Extended practice sessions or accelerated training are not necessarily linked to motor-skill performances. Rather, motor-skill efficiency is the product of maturation and experience (Williams, 1983; Schmidt, 1982).

We need to stress the role of experience in motor-skill development. The youngster who has participated in a wide variety of activities and who has explored and experimented with movement is usually able to acquire a specific motor activity at an earlier

Practice with motor skills gradually produces coordination and refinement.

age than can the child not benefiting from such experiences. Learning opportunities and adult encouragement are thus important to the development of motor skills (Ridenour, 1980; Wickstrom, 1983).

■ Motor-Skill Development and Art

While youngsters are refining their gross-motor skills, their fine-motor skills are also developing. During the preschool years, artwork greatly contributes to fine-motor-skill development. Once restricted to awkward hand movements, preschoolers are now able to use a wide variety of drawing instruments. By the end of the preschool period, children can produce recognizable pictures.

Shapes are usually formed by concentrating scribbles on one area of the paper; a circle, for example, is the result of continual circular scribbles. The ability to draw certain shapes follows a definite pattern. Because being able to draw vertical lines seems to precede the ability to draw horizontal lines, crosses, squares, triangles, and diamonds follow a sequential order. (You might want to try drawing a circle to see how much easier it is than drawing a triangle or a diamond. The latter require more precise movement and eye-hand coordination.) These first shapes and forms, even if they are primitive and distorted, are another satisfying accomplishment for children. Not only have they created something pleasing, but they also have become aware that they have done it by themselves (Francks, 1982; Dileo, 1980).

These early attempts at shapes and forms are also characterized by isolationism, the child's tendency to create them as independent markings on the paper. Shapes and forms are not combined or interrelated, and so they have no associative values. Thus, children in the early stages of this period may refer to a mixture of lines on a page as being separate and distinct from a circle that appears on the same surface.

As children move into advanced stages of shape and form development (3½ to 4 years), they become more capable of using a rhythmical stroke and are more aware of the range of movements that their hands can make. During this time, children establish associative values among shapes and forms that were lacking previously. Circles, squares, triangles, and rectangles are fused together to form numerous designs.

Between their fourth and fifth birthdays, children usually attempt to create their first pictures. Pictures do not abruptly appear but develop in a structured and orderly fashion. Early attempts are mere extensions of the shape stage; that is, children usually use a variation of one or two basic shapes to construct their early pictures. An example of this is their portrayal of the human figure, which most experts agree is the first recognizable picture to emerge. In drawing a person, children will use a large circle to represent the head and add smaller ones for the eyes, nose, mouth, and ears. Initially, longitudinal scribbles are used to represent the extension of the body, giving the human a "tadpole" appearance. Shortly afterward, however, arms and legs in the form of connected lines are added. In this way, children move from a motor exploration of marks to a symbolization of the human (Ives et al., 1981; Taylor and Bacharach, 1981).

In support of artwork's unique developmental progression, researchers recently examined the human figure drawings of 344 3- to 8-year-olds. Most subjects drew the head first and overestimated its size. Children who drew the trunk first, portrayed relatively smaller heads. When the head was drawn first, children often left too little room for the trunk, which then had to be drawn relatively too small. However, when the trunk was drawn first, subjects always left enough space for the head, and the figures were well proportioned. The investigators contend that the typical drawing with a large head is a function of lack of planning rather than the child's misconception of the human figure (Thomas and Tsalimi, 1988). When children were asked to draw a man and a dog, or a dog and a house, young children were able to draw them to approximate size (Silk and Thomas, 1988).

Prehension, Motor Development, and Children's Art

How a child grasps a crayon is an excellent clue to developing prehension abilities (see Figure 6-2). The following timetable offers a rough approximation of how this phase of prehension progresses:

One year. The crayon is enveloped in the palm in a firm and primitive fashion and is wielded with full arm-banging and brushing movements.

Two years. The crayon is picked up by putting the thumb at the left of the shaft and the fingers at the right. Most hold the butt of the crayon against the palm of the hand and extend the index finger down the shaft.

Three years. The child can imitate the adult by resting the shaft at the juncture of the thumb and the index finger; the medius extends with its tip close to the point of the crayon, and the thumb opposes the index finger higher up on the shaft.

Four years. The crayon is firmly gripped and moved by flexing and extending the fingers; it is held with the tip of the three radial digits near its point.

FIGURE 6-2

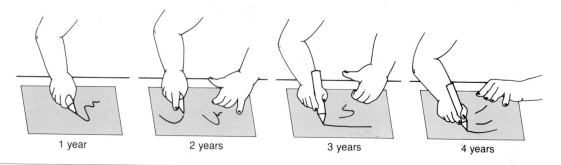

| 1 year | 2 years | 3 years | 4 years |

■ Guiding Early Motor-Skill Development

We mentioned at the outset that the years of early childhood are physically active ones. Preschoolers can now engage in playtime activities that were virtually impossible for them during infancy and toddlerhood. However, their ability to participate successfully in more demanding activities hinges not only on their overall muscular growth and coordination but also on their ability to develop a sense of self-confidence and assurance. Note the connection here between physical growth and psychological well-being, one more illustration of how developmental forces are interrelated. Adults can help nurture motor-skill development by means of the following:

Provide materials and an environment in which motor skills can be exercised. Appropriate indoor and outdoor equipment, as well as space in which to run and play, helps children develop both healthy minds and bodies. When selecting toys, adults should choose those that exercise both the small and the large muscles. Suggestions are available in Sanoff (1982), Rowe (1982), Magg and Ornstein (1981), and Riggs (1980).

Avoid comparisons. No two children develop at the same rate or exhibit the same degrees of proficiency in motor skill. Some youngsters develop rapidly, whereas others mature slowly. Likewise, some become highly skilled in an activity, and others have only little success. In this respect, comparisons accomplish little, except to produce anxious feelings about one's competencies.

Realize that success in one motor skill doesn't ensure success in another. Motor skills are usually acquired individually, each requiring special training and practice. It is wrong to assume that because one skill has developed, all others will too. Proficiency will also vary from skill to skill.

Be patient with the child. Motor skills require time and effort to develop. Although encouragement is helpful, adults should avoid pushing children past their limits. Furthermore, children should be allowed to set their own pace when developing a skill, as they know best what they are capable of doing at any given time.

UNIT REVIEW

- Youngsters are becoming more physically adept at dealing with their surroundings. Rates of physical growth are slower than in previous years, but motor skills advance rapidly.

- Changes in posture become evident, caused by the force of gravity, body build, developmental forces, and interactions with the environment.

- The three motor-skill development phases are the cognitive, associative, and autonomous.

- Both the child's maturation and environmental stimulation contribute to motor-skill efficiency.

- Children's art is an excellent vehicle for mastering fine-motor skills and many facets of expression.

Unit Two:

MENTAL DEVELOPMENT

The progression of higher-order cognitive facilities is influenced heavily by preschool children's continuing mastery of spoken language. Using words and being able to understand what they represent give their surroundings new meaning and significance. Spoken language is the essential link in communication between meaning and sound and the means by which one person's thoughts can become another's. Because of this, language and thought are closely related developmental processes and reflect the youngster's general cognitive activity (Flavell, 1985; Ault, 1983).

Cognitive advancements during early childhood enable the advancement of language acquisition. Language acquisition reflects three important cognitive functions. First, it allows youngsters to have verbal exchanges with others, thus beginning the socialization of their actions. Second, language acquisition stimulates the internaliza-

Thinking during early childhood becomes more deliberate and has a quality all its own.

tion of words, or thought. Third, language aids in the internalization of action. Now rather than being purely perceptual and motor, as it was previously, action can be represented intuitively through pictures and mental experiments (Dodd and White, 1980).

Cognitive development also enables preschoolers to think in qualitatively different ways than infants or toddlers do. Preschoolers' thinking is more advanced, expecially in regard to the refinement and elaboration of concepts. Their thinking becomes more methodical and deliberate, and they do not become discouraged as easily with cognitive challenges, so they become motivated to do the tasks at hand. Moreover, preschoolers' curiosity climbs to new heights. All of this suggests that a number of developmental forces interact and affect the course of cognition (Stipek, 1983; Gottfried, 1983; Bradbard and Endsley, 1982).

However, as we shall soon see, there are a number of cognitive limitations at this age. For example, preschoolers' mental processes are largely dominated by perceptual processes of what seems to be, rather than what logically must be. Preschoolers have not yet mastered the logical operations that influence the thinking of older youngsters.

■ Piaget's Stage of Preconceptual Thought

Jean Piaget referred to the second stage of cognitive development as *preconceptual thought.* This stage occurs between the ages of 2 and 4 and is a part of the much longer *preoperational thought* stage, which encompasses ages 2 through 7. It is an important subdivision because it focuses on the preschool years, a heightened period of cognitive activity (Case and Khanna, 1981).

Much like the sensorimotor development stage, preconceptual thought provides a foundation for later cognitive functions. When preschoolers have new experiences, they structure them in accordance with their existing mental schemes or place them into new mental categories. It is in this way that mental structures become more detailed and elaborate (Kuhn, 1981; Kamii, 1981a).

Several cognitive developments occur during the preconceptual thought stage, including the ability to engage in symbolic functioning. Other cognitive activities include the development of egocentrism, animism, artificialism, and immanent justice.

☐ Symbolic Functioning

The development of symbolic functioning is an important cognitive advancement. *Symbolic functioning* is the ability to differentiate *signifiers* (words, images) from *significates* (the objects or events to which signifiers refer). In a broad sense, symbolic functioning is an act of reference whereby a mental image is created to represent what is not present. For example, a signifier such as the word *ball* can be mentally created to represent the toy when it is not present.

Symbolic functioning thus enables children's intelligence to become more flexible and elaborate. Earlier, their cognitive activity was restricted to immediate space and the present perceptual situation. Now, however, because of symbolic functioning and developing linguistic skills, children can generate mental images of objects not present perceptually.

Children's play behavior is one of the most clear-cut examples of symbolic functioning. When mental images are created to represent objects that are not present, children can engage in make-believe play. For example, they can select an object and imagine it to be whatever they desire. Thus, a block of wood may become a car, boat, or airplane; a box may be imagined to be a fort or castle. Over time, this type of symbolic play will become more complex as pretend objects acquire various characteristics and dimensions (Nicolich, 1981; Case and Khanna, 1981).

☐ Egocentrism

Also emerging during this time is egocentrism. *Egocentrism* is a style of thinking that inhibits a person from seeing another person's point of view. In other words, it is a person's tendency to think that others see the world from the same perspective. As we shall see, egocentrism affects both social relations and problem-solving situations.

Because of their egocentrism, children may reason that everything in the world was created for them. Snow, then, as viewed by the egocentric child, is not a product of inclement weather but is something to play in; music is labeled happy because it puts them in a cheerful mood. It is also difficult for children to realize that everyone else experiences the same phenomena. Consequently, learning to share or take turns becomes a chore for many youngsters.

The manner in which preschoolers communicate with one another also reveals their egocentrism. Because of their self-orientation, each child has great difficulty "hearing" what the other is saying. Piaget called the egocentricity expressed in children's communication *collective monologue*. Because children are so involved in their own thoughts and feelings, they cannot truly listen to what others are saying, much less understand the context of the speaker's thoughts. Children talk *at* one another rather than *with* one another.

Collective monologue is similar to *parallel play,* a type of egocentricity that emerges during play sessions of two or more children. Because of children's inability to separate themselves from their own thoughts, meaningful interaction with their playmates is limited. What may appear as two children playing together may actually be two children in their own private play worlds.

Egocentrism is apparent in the make-believe world of the preschooler.

Egocentrism often interferes with reasoning skills. Because real-world concepts cannot be properly understood, children relate whatever they can to their personal experience. Their interpretation of objects and events is often based exclusively on their assimilative powers; that is, children explain phenomena by consulting their existing frames of reference. As a result, many of their conceptions are illogical, either because their own imagination and personal needs are being satisfied or because their existing knowledge and understanding are extremely limited.

But not all researchers agree on the prevalence of egocentrism at this age. For example, some researchers (Black, 1981; Grusec and Arnason, 1982; Hobson, 1980) maintain that preschoolers are capable of abandoning their egocentricity to some degree and appreciating the position and feelings of others. Furthermore, research in the field of psycholinguistics (e.g., Schmidt and Paris, 1983) suggests that when speaking, preschoolers do consider the needs of listeners. Finally, research reveals that prosocial, or helping, behavior starts to develop at this time, which shows that preschoolers can think to some extent beyond themselves (Honig, 1982b; Grusec, 1981). Research such as this indicates that egocentrism may not be the driving force in all spheres of expression.

☐ Animism

Animism is attributing life to inanimate objects. During early childhood, many youngsters insist that objects have lifelike properties like those of people. In an effort to understand and explain the nature of their surroundings, children often attribute thoughts and feelings to lifeless objects. Preschoolers, for example, may believe that boats don't appear on lakes at night because they're "asleep"; the wind "sings" if you listen carefully; and trees "cry" when their branches are broken.

Animism is often evident in children's fairy tales. Geppetto's Pinocchio, Alice's Queen of Hearts, Dorothy's Scarecrow, and Christopher Robin's toys were given human qualities and brought to life. With such character portrayals, is it possible that adults unwittingly contribute to the animism prevalent at this stage?

Sometimes, adults may fail to realize, or forget, that animistic qualities are attached to a child's toys. As a result, a doll with thoughts and feelings may be thrown into a toybox, or a favorite stone having animistic qualities may be maligned. For children, this type of adult behavior may be a personal blow to the world that they have created.

☐ Artificialism

Another misconception during the preschool years is artificialism. *Artificialism* is the belief that everything in the world, including natural objects and events, has been created by humanity. Because they reason that everything in the world is created for human use, the child assumes that humans must be responsible for all worldly creations. The sky, then, has been painted blue by someone; rain comes from giant watering cans; and mountains are built by strong people who stacked rocks together. One 4-year-old acquaintance of ours was convinced that thunder was caused by angels bowling.

The Development of Questions During Early Childhood

During the preschool years, children demonstrate growing curiosity about their environment. Such curiosity is an important part of their developing cognitive awareness. Many times, curiosity will surface in the form of questions, many of the "why" variety. "Why" questions offer insight into children's mental activity (Formanek and Gurian, 1980).

From a superficial point of view, most why questions do not require a causal explanation. This is especially true for young children, who may be asking a question merely for the sake of asking. Questions may be purely verbal and indicate pure astonishment, without calling for any answer. Some questions may be asked of no one and are merely a roundabout way of stating something without its being contradicted. Often, if their questions are not answered immediately, children will answer the questions themselves.

What is the best way to answer why questions? Adults should first try to understand the child's intent in asking them. Adults need also to select answers suitable for the child's frame of reference and keep in mind that preschoolers often assume that physical events have psychological causes, and vice versa. Thus when children ask "Why is the sky blue?" or "Why do the stars shine?" they really want to discover their purpose and not their physical explanation. Likewise, if an adult answers the question "Why do stars shine?" by saying, "Because they are like fire" many youngsters will not be satisfied because they do not yet understand the relation between heat and light. More important, though, the answer does not fit the question's intention. What children really want to hear from adults is something like "So that sailors can find their way home at night." This type of answer is suitable for their existing mental awareness. In time, children will be ready for more sophisticated explanations (Elkind, 1971, 1981).

The questions that adults direct *to* children also influence their mental growth. Close-ended questions, those requiring a simple yes or no answer, are the least likely to stimulate children intellectually or to encourage the use of representational abilities. Open-ended questions, conversely, move children beyond a simple yes or no reply and require elaboration. As Stacie Goffin and Claudia Tull (1985) put it, mental reflection can be encouraged by asking children to justify an answer, explain an outcome, or predict the consequences of an action. Open-ended questions thus encourage both cognitive and linguistic activities. Thus, whether on the receiving end of children's questions or directing their own questions to youngsters, adults can be influential in stimulating mental development (French and McClure, 1981; Bartlett, 1981).

☐ Immanent Justice

One final misconception obvious in early childhood thought patterns is a type of reasoning called immanent justice. *Immanent justice* is the notion that the world is equipped with a built-in code or system of law and order. Through this reasoning, children try to figure out how justice and order are maintained. Whenever there is a misfortune or wrongdoing, they try to explain why it happened. Many of the resulting interpretations are also sprinkled with egocentric overtones. For example, a child who stumbles and falls may reason that children are not supposed to run fast. Perhaps youngsters get burned by matches because they're not supposed to handle them. In some families, children are also taught that when misfortune strikes, it is "God's way of getting even," another variation of immanent justice.

■ Concept Development

Children's developing perceptual abilities greatly influence their concept development during the preschool years. *Perception* is the cognitive activity that allows individuals to detect and interpret relevant environmental information. Although this process varies from person to person, developing perceptual awareness generally contributes to more complex and refined levels of mental operations. For instance, a youngster's growing ability to detect differences in shape, size, or space contributes to a broader understanding of the physical world. Consequently, the objects and events in their surroundings gradually acquire greater meaning and relevance (Wellman, 1982; Siegler, 1981).

There are several factors that inhibit the accurate perception of environmental information during the preschool years. Paramount among these are limited attention and attending skills. Children need to learn how to tune into sensory information and seek useful information. Often, children do not pay attention to the aspects of a situation that attract adults. Their span of attention also needs to be lengthened. Because of their limited mental abilities, children often don't pay attention to information that they cannot discriminate. As a result, adults need to teach children what characteristics of situations are important (Jackson, Robinson, and Dale, 1977; Stevens, 1981).

As we indicated earlier, egocentrism affects many facets of mental growth. The failure to distinguish between one's own perceptions and those of others has important implications for cognitive skills.

☐ Shape and Size Concepts

Accurate shape and size discrimination during childhood results from learning experiences and is affected by a number of perceptual conditions, including distance and the relation of one object to another. Although perceptual discrimination improves during early childhood (Sera, Troyer, and Smith, 1989), the accurate perception of shape and size still remains elusive.

For instance, although children can discriminate among such shapes and sizes as big, little, or round, this does not automatically mean that they have a true perception of these categories (Coley and Gelman, 1989). That is, they may not remember the existence of these objects by means of their dimensions or characteristics unless adults force them to pay close attention to such details. The fact that distance has a dramatic

During early childhood, youngsters become more inquisitive.

effect on the preschooler's perceptions supports this latter point. Because of the child's undeveloped perceptual constancies and egocentrism, objects appear to change as they move away.

In this sense, a preschooler may think that a distant house becomes larger as it is approached or that a mountain changes its shape when it is viewed from a new location. Consider the following: A preschool acquaintance of ours watched his mother depart on an airplane. As the plane gradually disappeared from view, the youngster turned to us and asked, "Is Mommy getting as small as that plane?" All of these different viewing conditions tend to distort preschoolers' perception.

☐ Spatial Concepts

An accurate interpretation of the environment relies heavily on understanding spatial relationships. Similar to other perceptual challenges, advancements in understanding spatial relationships are limited during the preschool years. Once again, egocentrism hampers children as they try to comprehend such spatial discriminations as near, far, down. Usually, such designations are first learned as they personally relate to the child (e.g., the toy is near me).

Egocentrism creates other problems, especially in understanding relationships in such areas as direction and distance. To make these discriminations, children must learn to coordinate their self-centered points of view with other systems of reference. To appreciate how difficult this is for young children, imagine the problems that preschoolers have in discriminating left and right. Once this has been mastered, think of the difficulty in understanding left and right from another person's perspective—especially if this person is face-to-face with the child. Such difficulty in perspective occurs in many situations, particularly those that require alternative points of view (Roberts and Patterson, 1983).

In an interesting experiment, David Uttal and Henry Wellman (1989) explored young children's representations of spatial information acquired from maps. In the first part of their investigation, the researchers found that all 6- and 7-year-old children and many 4- and 5-year-olds could learn the layout of a large playhouse composed of six adjoined rooms by memorizing a map. Children who learned the map before entering the playhouse more quickly learned a route through it than children who were not exposed to the map, and older subjects performed significantly better than younger children.

In the second part of the experiment, preschoolers learned a map of a space that contained six spatially separated small rooms within one large room. Children could therefore view the entire configuration of smaller rooms as they traveled around the larger room. The preschoolers performed significantly better in the second half of the experiment than in the first half, and the majority of them performed perfectly or almost perfectly. Taken together, these findings suggest that preschoolers' map-reading abilities and spatial understandings are more advanced than many realize.

Adults can help preschoolers acquire more accurate spatial concepts. For example, they should use precise terminology when referring to spatial relationships and provide situations that allow children to see more than one spatial orientation. Mirrors, for instance, give children the opportunity to observe different viewpoints. Activities involving maps or a globe, or games requiring an analysis of spatial relations are other good learning opportunities. Adults can also encourage multiple spatial viewpoints by actively eliciting children's perceptions of their surroundings. For example, when viewing a particular situation, adults might ask, "Does it look the same for me?" or "How would that look if we moved away?" and the like. These types of activities help reduce children's egocentrism and reveal that there is more than one way to view the world.

☐ Quantity Concepts

Although preschoolers are better at discriminating quantities, they often make judgments on the basis of perception alone. Put another way, children are not yet able to discriminate quantities logically, independent of misleading perceptual cues. As we have learned, this problem is often compounded by the children's lack of appropriate terminology for discriminating such quantities as more and less or few and many. Moreover, even when children have learned the correct terminology, it is no guarantee that they have learned the related discrimination. For example, in one experiment, 3- and 4-year-old children were asked to sort the numbers 1 through 9 into a small, medium, or large category. Three-year-olds tended to name 1 as a small number and all others as large. Four-year-olds discriminated among 1, 2, 3, and 4, medium, and large numbers. These results suggest that readiness skills needed for early childhood mathematics education should include development of appropriate concepts of number magnitude (Murray and Mayer, 1988).

Some adults may unintentionally confuse preschoolers by using ambiguous terminology. Terms such as *some* and *many* are often confusing. Consider the problems that preschoolers may encounter when hearing sentences such as "Is there *much* left?" or "We need some *more* money." Such quantitative terms are general and vague and difficult for youngsters to understand.

Numbers are an important part of quantity concepts. There is usually a significant gap between preschoolers' counting abilities and their ability to understand conceptually what is being counted. Often, preschoolers use serial order but are unable to recognize figures. Furthermore, preschoolers poorly understand concepts of measure, simple addition, and fractional amounts. It is suggested that the development of number concepts hinges on children's ability to arrange a series of items according to their observable differences. This occurs by age 7, when the average child can arrange a series of sticks in order of their increasing lengths. Even when one stick has been omitted from the series, the proper place for it can be found (Kamii, 1982).

Once again, adults can do much to help preschoolers learn number concepts. Unfortunately, counting to 10, which is so often encouraged by adults, merely represents serial and rote memory rather than conceptual understanding. Instead of this, educators suggest that children be given structured learning exercises that emphasize the quantities that the numbers represent. For example, arranging groups of pencils or checkers in different patterns and having the preschooler count the items—as well as paying attention to the perceptual differences in the numbers—is one approach. Or after children have watched a "Sesame Street" episode on the number three, adults should follow up on this learning exercise. At the dinner table, one might say, "Show me three beans or three spoons." These types of exercises emphasize the qualitative aspects of numbers and not rote memory.

Money is another facet of quantity concepts. Generally, money concepts are difficult for preschoolers to understand. However, by the end of the early childhood years, youngsters usually have some understanding of what a penny, nickel, and a dime are. The names of other coins, though, are more elusive. This age is also when children realize what the value of each coin is. By age 6, children are usually capable of using money in simple mathematical transactions.

☐ Time Concepts

We mentioned earlier that young children refer almost exclusively to the present before they do the future or the past. Furthermore, preschoolers have difficulty distinguishing morning from afternoon and the days of the week. Usually, children's understanding of time is bound by the immediacy or recency of situations (Harner, 1982).

Similar to the difficulty with quantity concepts, children are frequently confused by adults' often vague time references. For example, such phrases as "We'll go in a *little* while," "Wait a *bit*," or "We'll do that *later*" are extremely vague and general. Although such references to time are common, adults can help preschoolers by not always speaking in such sweeping generalities.

When children have a rudimentary understanding of time, they relate events to certain hours of the day, such as the beginning of school or lunch periods. Their egocentrism is apparent when they distinguish routines in the day that relate directly to themselves. In most cases, children learn hours first, followed by half hours and then quarter hours. Children are usually able to name the days of the beginning and end of the week before they reach kindergarten, although the days in the middle of the week may remain elusive. Also elusive are the different representations for the same time designations, such as "It is now one thirty-five," or "It is now twenty-five minutes to two" or "We'll go on vacation in two weeks" or "We will go away the week after next." These different ways of referring to the same period require considerable thought and frequently confuse youngsters.

■ Language Development

By early childhood, youngsters have acquired the basics of the spoken language. This linguistic milestone gains significance when one considers that an 18-month-old child knows only approximately 25 words. During the next three years, however, this figure soars to over 1,800 words. In addition to this dramatic vocabulary increase of approximately 600 new words per year, preschoolers also demonstrate significant gains in semantics and grammar (Cazden, 1981; Corrigan, 1983).

Those adults having contact with children will agree that preschoolers are charming and entertaining conversationalists. Compared with infants and toddlers, preschoolers use language in a variety of different ways, including questions, dialogues, songs, and chants. Language also becomes a vehicle for experimentation, such as rhythm and cadence exercises (Schwartz, 1981).

□ Influences on Language Development

Language development is affected by numerous factors, including socioeconomic influences, intelligence levels, sex, and the presence or absence of a twin.

The familial setting in which the child is reared, particularly its socioeconomic level, is believed to influence language growth. It is maintained that lower-class parents may be unsatisfactory speech models from whom the child can learn the foundations of a spoken language. Often, lower-class parents lack the vocabulary skills necessary to provide proper language instruction. On the other hand, children from the upper socioeconomic classes tend to acquire words at a faster rate and use more complex sentence structures (Honig, 1982a).

Language differences among the social classes may also be explained by other factors. For example, lower-class parents do not often verbally stimulate their children, at least not as much as middle- and upper-class parents do. Upper-class parents tend to also emphasize proper word usage and correct grammar, many feeling that correct language reflects conscientious and proper family upbringing. In addition, many middle- and upper-class parents give more praise and affection to youngsters when they use words correctly. Middle- and upper-class homes also expose children to a greater array of educational aids. The household containing newspapers, magazines, encyclopedias, tape recorders, radios, and television offers advantages over the household that can offer the child only limited stimulation (Schacter and Strage, 1982; Honig, 1982a; Hess and Shipman, 1982).

We need to emphasize that although there are language differences among socioeconomic classes, lower-class children are not linguistically inferior. More often than not, they have their own dialect, a language style differing from that of the middle and upper classes. Although these children possess a fully structured language, they are not bidialectical. In this sense, their communication difficulties may originate from the

Socialization will stimulate developing linguistic abilities, a good illustration of the interplay between developmental forces.

dialect's vocabulary limitations, not from the child's inability to handle the communication situation. This means that linguistic differences among socioeconomic classes are differences in the rules of their languages (Schacter and Strage, 1982).

Language acquisition rates are also closely related to children's general intelligence levels. Children with above-average intelligence usually begin to talk at an early age, acquire words at a rapid pace, articulate efficiently, and use grammatically correct sentences.

A somewhat controversial factor that may cause differences in language development is the child's sex. On the average, females have been considered superior to males in overall language development. During the first year, there is little difference in the number of phonemes spoken. However, after this point many studies have shown that females are superior in overall acquisition rates. Generally, females also seem to be more articulate than males are and do better in tests of word usage, grammar, and spelling. And on the whole, this superiority in language-based skills may persist throughout life (Springer and Deutsch, 1985; Demo, 1982). However, this view has been challenged in recent years. For example, two researchers located and analyzed 165 studies that reported gender differences in verbal ability. Overall these studies support the viewpoint of female superiority, but the difference is so small it is practically insignificant (Hyde and Linn, 1988). Obviously more research is needed.

It is not unusual for children to be reared in a *bilingual* household, one in which two languages are spoken. The implications are interesting. At one time, it was maintained that attempting to learn two languages placed the youngster at a disadvantage and interfered with overall linguistic growth. Today, though, it is believed that the effects of a bilingual home may instead depend on whether adults reprimand children for using their native dialect and insist that they speak standard English. Thus, *bilingualism* is not a problem restricted to a language; rather, it may be a problem of cultural conflict.

Research also revealed that exposure to two languages and a proficiency in these two languages do not retard linguistic or cognitive development. On the contrary, bilinguals may sometimes be cognitively superior to monolinguals. This is often the case in cognitive flexibility and creative expression (Garcia, 1980; Lambert, 1981; Bialystok, 1988).

Finally, whether the child is born a singleton or a twin affects language development. Although research on this question has been limited, twins frequently have slower overall rates of language development when compared with singletons. This is particularly apparent in average lengths of responses and annual word gains. One factor contributing to the twins' lag in development may be that they grow up closely together, learning to understand each other's speech patterns at a very early age. Many twins develop what is known as *twin speech,* a type of language consisting of words known only to the two. Twins also may not have the initiative to make their verbal behavior known to others. Or twins, compared with singletons, may receive less verbal stimulation from their parents, who must divide their time between them.

☐ Semantic Development

Semantic development is significant throughout all stages of childhood. Recall that semantics is the study of how words represent objects and events. Simply stated, it is the study of word meanings.

Although understanding word meaning begins with the child's first word, semantics becomes progressively harder for children as they grow older. By early childhood, the youngster is faced with having to learn the meanings and interrelationships of over 1,800 words. Needless to say, learning so many word meanings poses a staggering challenge to their developing cognitive skills.

Certain processes underlie semantic development during the early years. It seems that youngsters first learn simple associations or words' semantical features. Objects' perceptual features are usually learned first, such as size or shape, and the objects' functional qualities. There is no clear-cut evidence regarding which (perception or function) is learned first. We do know that the overextension of word meanings is fairly common among younger children. For example, the word *moon* may mean the spherical object in the night sky or be used to refer to such objects as cucumber slices or grapefruit halves (Kay and Anglin, 1982; Dickson, 1981).

Over time, children acquire more abstract word meanings that are not directly perceptible. Rather than just defining a word on the basis of its physical appearance, older children can construct word meanings on the basis of such dimensions as subjective affect. In this way semantics progresses from a concrete to an abstract level (Tomikawa and Dodd, 1980).

The fact that concrete words are learned before abstract terms may help explain why young children have trouble understanding that certain words have both physical and psychological meanings. For example, if preschoolers were asked the meanings of the words *green* or *shady,* they would most likely offer physically oriented definitions (green is a color, and shady means protected from the sun). Older children given these words, however, would most likely supply extended meanings that embody psychological connotations. Thus, *green* could mean an emotional state (green with envy), and *shady* might imply unreliability (a shady character). Children's initial limited understanding of words may also explain why they literally interpret adult figures of speech or metaphors. For this reason, it is understandable that some preschoolers look skyward when someone remarks, "It's raining cats and dogs outside."

Certain word meanings are also more difficult to learn than others are. Especially difficult for the preschooler is mastering the correct meaning of word pairs, such as *more* and *less* (Grieve and Dow, 1981). Apparently, children learn one word of the pair first and overextend its meaning to the other word. For example, if preschoolers are asked which of two trees has more or fewer apples, they frequently will be confused. Most know the meaning of more but not of fewer. As a result, the latter word is interpreted in much the same way as the former is (based on the single concept of quantity). Preschoolers have similar difficulties with such word pairs as *before* and *after* (Trosberg, 1982), *front* and *back* (Levine and Carey, 1982), and *same* and *different* (Speer and McCoy, 1982).

☐ Syntactic Development

Children's use of syntax, the use of proper grammar, is one of the best indicators of their overall cognitive development. Proper sentence structure is a key to logic and organization of thought. It also is the guiding principle in children's efforts to understand the words that are spoken to them (Dodd and White, 1980).

Following the telegraphic sentence stage of toddlerhood, sentences have a fairly complex syntactical construction. Compound sentences, formed by joining two or more simple sentences, also begin to be formed by the preschool years. Such developments indicate that youngsters are mastering the syntax of their language.

Most children are able to understand the concept of higher-order sentences, especially the formation of word classes and the rules for combining them. Learning the proper location of words in a sentence is a remarkable feature of language development, as is the ability to form past tenses, make words plural, and create negatives. Each of these advancements means a greater awareness of linguistic rules. As they listen to others, children are able to extract the rules for putting words together. First they master simple linguistic rules and then move on to more complex ones, such as those regulating complex syntactical structures (Slobin, 1982; Cazden, 1981; Bohannon and Stanowicz, 1988).

☐ Pragmatics

Pragmatics is how language is used in a social context, including the use of a wide range of behaviors, such as gestures, facial expressions, pauses, pointing, or turn taking. Pragmatic rules exist in every language, and adults usually begin teaching them to children at a very early age. During early verbal interactions, for example, children learn to establish eye contact and pay attention to their partners when communicating (Dale, 1980; Bruner, 1980).

Compared with that of toddlers, a pragmatic quality of preschoolers' language is more diverse. Reciprocal turn taking and a greater range of expressions to convey messages now accompany preschoolers' speech. More complex styles of interaction between speaker and listener are also evident. For example, recent research suggests that preschoolers can tailor their speech, such as expanding or deleting their sentences depending on the listener's needs. They also know that when listeners move away they have to raise their voices in order to be heard. All of this indicates that in addition to their awareness of grammatical rules, preschoolers are better understanding the social implications of language use (Schmidt and Paris, 1983; Johnson et al., 1981).

Guidelines to Improve the Preschooler's Language Development

By responding to and encouraging young children's speech, adults can do a great deal to help facilitate overall language development. Grown-ups can become active stimulants when they offer novel verbal learning situations to the child by playing jingle and rhyming games, reading aloud, or expanding upon their youngster's remarks. In addition, adults should consider the following suggestions:

ESTABLISH A SATISFACTORY SPEECH MODEL

Active steps should be taken to ensure that the child is learning from a good speech model. Adults should seek to provide the best possible instruction, pay careful attention to their speed of speech, and use clear and concise statements.

ENCOURAGE VERBAL AND NONVERBAL COMMUNICATION

Children need to communicate with others, either verbally or nonverbally, such as with a smile, gesture, drawing, painting, or through musical activities. Since each, in its own right, becomes a vital part of the communication process, these media should be supported and encouraged by adults.

PROVIDE EXPERIENCES THAT WILL MAKE WORDS MEANINGFUL

In order to talk, children must have something to talk about. Asking questions, providing toys, picture books, pets, or going on field trips supplies youngsters with experiences that they can experiment with and talk about.

ENCOURAGE LISTENING AND ATTENTION SKILLS

No matter how good a speech model is, children's articulation skills will not improve unless they listen effectively. Playing such games as "What is that sound?" or "What makes a loud sound?" helps improve children's listening abilities, as does paying attention to the sound and rhythm of nursery rhymes and jingles.

ENCOURAGE SPEECH AS A SUBSTITUTE FOR ACTION

In giving directions to children, adults can help to ensure understanding by making sure that their speech patterns are appropriately at the child's level of syntax. Substituting words for action also increases children's ability at self-expression. For example, the action of a child who is attempting to physically take a playmate's toy may be substituted with words if the parent remarks, "Tell him what you want, maybe he will give it to you."

USE EXACT TERMINOLOGY AND TALK WITH CHILDREN AT THEIR LEVEL

Adults can help the child immensely by being exact in their use of words. For instance, in referring to a tricycle a child is riding in the nursery school, "Your turn on the tricycle" establishes the temporary nature of ownership, whereas a careless referral to "your tricycle" may lead to a property problem. Equally important are respecting the language that preschoolers use and seeking to converse with them at their own level. Complexity and confusion should be avoided. A child's unclear words or lack of exact terminology should be corrected without criticism, and you should take time to let children express themselves—don't rush them or answer for them.

(Landreth, 1972; Honig, 1982; Morrison, 1984)

UNIT REVIEW

■ Thought and language are related cognitive activities.

■ Piaget's stage of preconceptual thought encompasses the preschool years. It is part of the much longer preoperational thought stage, which lasts from ages 2 through 7.

■ The key cognitive developments outlined by Piaget are symbolic functioning, egocentrism, animism, artificialism, and immanent justice.

■ Shape and size, spatial, quantity, and time concepts are refined.

■ The course of language is influenced by the child's family, intelligence, sex, and whether the child is bilingual and a singleton or a twin.

■ Linguistic growth is evident in children's semantics, syntax, and pragmatics.

■ Unit Three:

PERSONALITY AND SOCIAL DEVELOPMENT

During the preschool years, children expand their social horizons and become quite independent and autonomous. Once socially restricted and dependent, preschoolers become more involved with their environment and venture into new and challenging social situations with peers and adults. Experiences in the neighborhood, school, or other socializing situations are integrated into the child's sense of being and help develop his or her personality and social awareness (Walsh, 1980; Blatchford, Battle, and Mays, 1983; Burchinal, Lee, and Ramsey, 1989).

In the company of others, youngsters become individuals in their own right, gaining insight into their own personalities. Socially, children can observe what effects their behavior has on others, a developing social-cognitive power that enables them to realize the rights and privileges of others. In addition, these social interactions help children refine their self-concepts—how individuals perceive themselves.

None of these social abilities develops independently of the others. Instead, all are intertwined and related—the result of the child's growing interaction and experiences with the environment. Personality and social dynamics also blend with those cognitive and linguistic developments previously discussed.

Developmental Tasks of Early Childhood

1. Learning sex differences and sexual modesty.

2. Forming concepts and learning language to describe social and physical reality.

3. Getting ready to read.

4. Learning to distinguish right and wrong and beginning to develop a conscience.

(Havighurst, 1972, 1980)

■ Sex-Role Development

Sex-role development is the process of socialization through which appropriate male and female behaviors are learned. Such behavior includes both personality characteristics and attitudes and beliefs. Sex-role development begins early in life, from a variety of sources.

Before examining sex-role development during early childhood, we need to clarify some important terminology. *Sexual identity* refers to the physiological differences between males and females. *Gender identity* is the psychological awareness of being either a male or a female. It is generally accepted that gender identity occurs by age 3. *Sex roles*, or gender roles, are those socially defined behaviors associated with being either male or female. Thus, in order to understand the differences between the sexes, one must take into account these physiological, psychological, and sociological processes (Jacklin, 1989; Eisenberg, 1982; Honig, 1982a; Stockard and Johnson, 1980).

■ Theories of Sex-Role Development

Different theories have been proposed to explain how sex roles develop throughout life. These interpretations reflect the major theories of developmental psychology discussed in Chapter 2.

Social learning theory examines how boys and girls imitate sex-typed behavior displayed by parents and others in their surroundings. Significantly, children are rewarded and punished for certain sex-role behaviors. For example, girls are reinforced for engaging in feminine activities and not being aggressive, while boys receive encouragement for being the aggressors and participating in more physically oriented activities.

Cognitive-developmental theory postulates that sex-role development emerges through the child's growing cognitive awareness of his/her sexual identity. Early in life, boys and girls become mentally aware of the fact that specific roles, activities, and behaviors are appropriate for their own sex. As cognitive development increases, children are better able to understand and sort out these roles and behaviors. Awareness of sexual identity leads to natural identification with the parent, the adult typifying the sexual role that the child has come to mentally recognize.

Psychoanalytic theory proposes that sex-role development is the result of close interaction and emulation of one's parents. *Identification* is the manner in which parental behaviors serve as models for the child. Proposed by Sigmund Freud, this theory emphasizes how a boy assumes his father's sex-typed behaviors because of the *Oedipus complex*. This is the boy's romantic attachment to his mother. The attributes of the father are perceived as being those which captured the love of the mother, and are thus emulated by the boy. For girls, the *Electra complex* creates a similar situation, although in this case it refers to the daughter's romantic attachment to her father and imitation of the mother's behaviors.

In addition to the Oedipus and Electra complexes, Freud offered one other perspective on identification. That is, children develop strong emotional attachment to and dependence on nurturant parents. The closeness offered by such parents leads to childhood identification and emulation.

■ Factors Influencing Sex-Role Development

Sex-role development begins early in life and originates from a variety of sources. Among the more influential sources are parents, peers, play behaviors, teachers and schools, and the media. Let us examine each of these a bit more closely and trace how children learn sex-role behaviors.

PARENTS From the very beginning, parents exert a significant influence on a child's sex-role development. Should traditional sex-role stereotypes prevail, boys and girls receive differential treatment. Females are usually taught to be affectionate, gentle, and quiet, while males are often instructed to be aggressive, independent, and active. In time, boys will be taught that being employed and providing economic support to the family will be their primary adult tasks. Females are taught to engage in domestic activities, have babies, and handle most of the responsibilities associated with child rearing. Parents succeed in teaching many sex-typed standards through their own behaviors. Mothers are usually more nurturant and emotional while fathers are traditionally more dominant, competitive, and unemotional (Plomin and Foch, 1981; Honig, 1983b; Scanzoni and Fox, 1980).

Over time, there are several important variables related to parents and the transmission of sex-role stereotypes. It appears that fathers, more so than mothers, are concerned about transmitting appropriate sex-role behaviors to their offspring. Moreover, fathers usually take active steps to discourage cross-sex behavior in their children. As far as other findings related to parents are concerned, nontraditional rather than traditional parents are likely to rear children who resist sex-role stereotyping and are more flexible in their overall view of masculinity and femininity (Langlois and Down, 1980; Zuckerman and Sayre, 1982).

PLAY BEHAVIORS Another factor promoting sex-role development during the early years is playtime activity. Very often, stereotypes abound with children's toys and play behaviors. Females are frequently given dolls or they engage in playing house, while males often indulge in aggressive games, are given masculine toys, such as guns and trucks, and avoid "sissy" play activities. Female play behavior is usually more dependent, quieter, and less exploratory. Males often become preoccupied while playing with toys that require more gross-motor activity and are more vigorous and independent. Such sex-typed play behavior for both sexes is also frequently supported and reinforced by parents (Caldera, Huston, and O'Brien, 1989; DiPietro, 1981; Fagot and Kronsberg, 1982; Muller and Goldberg, 1980).

Consistent with our earlier point, fathers in particular seem to be more vocal about the selection of sex-appropriate toys and play behaviors. Further pressure to engage in sex-typed play emerges from the peer group, an increasingly important source of social approval and reinforcement (Pitcher and Schultz, 1983; Maccoby, 1980; Langlois and Down, 1980; Lamb, Easterbrooks, and Holden, 1980).

An interesting aspect of sex-typed play is that boys seem to be more aware than girls are of sex differences; boys avoid playing with objects that might be labeled feminine or "sissy" but girls seem to be willing to engage in male-oriented activities. Although both sexes congregate in sex-typed play groups, boys seem to hold more rigid, stereotyped beliefs than girls do (DiPietro, 1981; Fagot and Kronsberg, 1982; Carter and Levy, 1988).

There is some evidence that the traditional classification of "masculine" and "feminine" forms of play may be changing. Society's attempt to promote a more unisexual definition of the sexes may reduce the gap between male and female activities. Although girls still engage in "feminine" activities, they now also enjoy types of play previously cast as "masculine," such as track and field competition, basketball, golf, and softball. Indeed, girls are now involved more in organized sports activities than ever before. Schools are enlarging their athletic programs and encouraging females to participate more actively and competitively. Furthermore, success in sports and the accompanying social prestige no longer appear to be the exclusive domain of the male (Murphy, 1983).

Sex-role stereotyping becomes very evident during early childhood.

PEERS Peers also influence the course of sex-role development. As children experience greater amounts of socialization, they usually learn more about sex-role standards and behaviors from the peer group. Often, failure to adhere to such expectations represents grounds for peer group rejection. The reinforcement of sex-appropriate behaviors from within the peer group also helps to explain the early sex-typed differences apparent in children's play (Lamb, Easterbrooks, and Holden, 1980; Harris and Satter, 1981; Reis and Wright, 1982).

It is during the preschool years that children start to prefer same-sex peer groups. Close friends share the same dimension. This will persist and even intensify throughout the years of middle childhood, although it is more pronounced in males than females (Fu and Leach, 1980; Reis and Wright, 1982). Often, same-sex play groups openly torment one another, further solidifying gender boundaries. As Evelyn Pitcher and Lynn Schultz (1983) observe, when boys taunt and tease girls, the stage is usually set for the catcalls and whistles that will appear in the future.

TEACHERS AND SCHOOLS Teachers also contribute to sex-role development. As significant others in the child's life, the behaviors and attitudes displayed by teachers are considered influential. Some may deliberately, others unwittingly, contribute to sex-role stereotypes. For example, George Morrison (1984) points out that some teachers may reinforce stereotypes taught at home or on the playground. This means that within the classroom, girls may water the plants, but not empty the wastebaskets. Also they may be rewarded only when they are passive, well behaved, and well mannered.

Boys, on the other hand, may be reinforced for being assertive and asking questions, and they are encouraged to use trucks, racing cars, and other physically oriented toys during play periods.

Teachers and schools exert other influences as time goes on. Kevin Ryan and James Cooper (1980) tell us that some teachers may perpetuate stereotypes by advising students that certain professions are appropriate for women, while others are appropriate only for men. Often, a school's curriculum may stamp a course as being masculine or feminine, such as requiring a course in home economics for females and automobile mechanics for males. Many of the nation's schools, however, have removed the sex-based exclusivity attached to such courses. Indeed, some strongly recommend that all students enroll in a mixture of such courses.

Lucille Lindberg and Rita Swedlow (1985) emphasize that teachers should downplay sex-role stereotyping. From earliest schooling to the end of formal education, children and adolescents need to receive instruction in an objective and sexually unbiased fashion. To reach such a goal, teacher behaviors need to be carefully examined and the curriculum objectively assessed.

THE MEDIA Another source of sex-role development is the media, particularly television. Television programming very often promotes sex-role stereotyping. Males are often portrayed as leaders, while females are cast as passive, submissive, and defenseless characters. Also males usually outnumber female cast members. Moreover, many programs lack a regular female character. Similar sex-typing and disproportion are evident in television commercials as well (Downs, 1981; Feldstein and Feldstein, 1982; Williams, LaRose, and Frost, 1981).

Several studies support these facts. In one research investigation of television (Stewart, 1983), a total of 551 major speaking characters in 191 programs was examined, and males clearly outnumbered females in all program types. When family themes were portrayed, most males were employed in white-collar jobs while women were typically full-time housewives. In another investigation of older persons portrayed on television (Cassata, Anderson, and Skill, 1983), males outnumbered females in professional or managerial positions by a ratio of four to one. Females accounted for 100 percent of homemaker, service, or clerical positions.

How do children in the midst of their sex-role development perceive such stereotyped portrayals? Do they understand the sex-role stereotypes seen on television? Apparently so, at least according to one investigation (Durkin, 1984). In this study, 17 children aged 4½ and 9½ years were interviewed individually and asked to discuss features of a series of highly stereotyped male and female behaviors shown on television. The children were found to display considerable knowledge of sex-role conventions and to reveal a clear ability to relate this to their accounts of the excerpts presented. Children are able to infer feelings and motives appropriately and offer plausible accounts of portrayed stereotypes by using their existent sex-role knowledge.

Finally, let's acknowledge the role that children's literature plays in the transmission of early sex-role behaviors. Similar to trends we've uncovered in this section, sex-role stereotyping is quite evident within the pages of children's books. According to Evelyn Pitcher and associates (1984), sex-role stereotyping in children's literature begins very early for youngsters. Consider some of the rhymes that await children in Mother Goose tales alone: "What are little girls made of?" "Georgie Porgie . . . kissed the girls and made them cry." "Bobbie Shaftoe's gone to sea . . . he'll come back and marry me." "Bye, baby, bunting, Daddy's gone a-hunting." Even Jill comes tumbling down the hill *after* Jack. Within the pages of children's books, girls are often portrayed as passive and domestic, while boys are more active and adventurous. Boys also outnumber the females portrayed in many stories. Stereotyping also exists when certain careers are cast as exclusively masculine or feminine.

Today, there is a growing movement to eliminate sex stereotyping in children's books, especially the male chauvinism frequently manifested in character portrayals and language. Attempts to make books nonsexist may take several forms. Women may be portrayed as more confident and independent and they may have occupations traditionally reserved for males. Removing females from the household and placing them in the world of nature, business, science fiction, or other male-dominated domains helps to remove sex stereotyping. Removing some of the stereotyping of males also helps to make books nonsexist. Instead of portraying males as cool, competent, fearless, and sometimes insensitive, more books are making an effort to show that boys can be sensitive, loving, and emotional. Some stories show that there are boys who do not fit the stereotype of the competent, "superior" male, who is in control of every situation and every emotion.

What will be the outcome of efforts to remove stereotyping from children's literature? There are indications that nonsexist literature can change children's stereotyped images of the sexes. However, because sexist attitudes are woven through the whole fabric of society, we can hardly expect that books alone will produce children who are unbiased and unstereotyped in their attitudes. Also, while nonsexist books are important, many persons feel that literary quality should not be sacrificed to meet this need. Thus, a good novel should not be attacked because it has no female characters. Few people would suggest rewriting the classics or historical fiction, or discarding them altogether. The process of eliminating stereotyping in children's literature has many facets and more research is needed to assess the impact of nonsexism on children.

■ Contemporary Influences on Sex-Role Behaviors

Combined, these factors serve to transmit sex-role behaviors to children in a mixture of subtle and direct ways. The result is that children learn to behave in sexually appropriate fashions within the framework of their society. Furthermore, these sex-typed behaviors will become more deeply rooted as time goes on (see Travis and Wade, 1984; Fu and Leach, 1980; Basow, 1980; Harris and Satter, 1981).

Sex-role reversals are becoming more evident in contemporary society.

Before leaving this topic, let us remind you that some rigid sex-role standards seem to be diminishing. In support of this, there are adults sharing roles that had been previously labeled as solely "feminine" or "masculine." Several reasons account for this turnabout. The similarity of educational experiences that many males and females receive during their early schooling, and the fact that males today engage in more "feminine" chores around the house (e.g., cleaning or doing the dishes) are contributing factors. Females are also employed outside the home more frequently, sometimes in jobs previously held down by males (and vice versa). Finally, more fathers are taking active roles in child rearing, a factor that may help to reduce traditional sex-role typing in the household. How all of this affects children is currently under the scrutiny of researchers.

Such role reversals are welcomed with open arms by those concerned with society's sex-role stereotypes. It is proposed that rigid standards of masculinity and femininity may be maladaptive to both child and adult, since they do not allow the full expression of one's personality. As Sarah Cirese (1985) sees it, sex-role stereotypes strip people of their individuality and pose awesome barriers to intimacy and genuine relationships between males and females.

To help overcome sex-role stereotyping, a concept known as *androgyny* has emerged. In addition to the previously mentioned sharing of roles and chores, this concept suggests that both male and female personality traits are beneficial and important to possess. Androgynous persons view themselves as human beings, not typecast males or females. Because of this, personality traits are not compartmentalized by sex. Both males and females are encouraged to be nurturant, assertive, sensitive, dominant, affectionate, and self-sufficient, to cite a few examples.

Research suggests that the androgynous personality has many positive character traits. Compared to persons with traditional sex-role behaviors, androgynous individuals seem more competent and demonstrate higher levels of self-esteem. In addition, androgynous persons seem to deal more effectively with their surroundings. They are also more secure with themselves, more flexible in their behavior, and less anxious (Wiggins and Holzmuller, 1981).

Without question, the concept of androgyny is controversial (see, for example, Blitchington, 1984; Baumrind, 1982). There is also evidence (Werner and LaRussa, 1985) that many sex-role behaviors and stereotypes in existence for years refuse to budge. However, proponents of androgyny maintain that the removal of sex-typed behavioral constraints would allow males and females to demonstrate the best qualities of both sexes. Children, especially, would benefit from a more tolerant acceptance of their total selves, rather than being continually told how society expects them to behave.

■ Emotional Development

Emotional reactions and expressions become highly differentiated during early childhood. This is in contrast with the rather generalized responses that characterized the early years. Several factors account for this change in emotional expression. First, their increasing cognitive awareness enables children to perceive their surroundings in new and different ways. The preschoolers' imaginations, for example, are largely responsible for the imaginary fears occurring at this age. Cognitive advancements also make youngsters more alert to situations capable of eliciting emotions and allow children to express a wider range of feeling (Ribordy et al., 1988; Denny, Denny, and Rust, 1982; Harris et al., 1981).

Additional factors influencing emotional expression during early childhood are expanding social horizons and new developmental challenges. An example of this is the transition from the home to an early childhood educational program or the pre-schooler's greater involvement with peers. Each of these experiences broadens the child's overall emotional repertoire. Clearly, emotional expression is intertwined with many developmental processes (Waggoner and Palermo, 1989; Nunner-Winkler and Sodian, 1988).

Several representative research studies provide testimony to this latter point. One (Carroll and Steward, 1984), sought to find a relationship between cognition and children's understandings of their own feelings. In this experiment, 30 four- and five-year-olds and 30 eight- and nine-year-olds were interviewed individually and given a series of Piagetian tasks and the Peabody Picture Vocabulary Test. The test is designed to measure the amount of vocabulary a child has acquired. Verbal responses to questions about feelings were interpreted according to a cognitive-developmental framework that hypothesized hierarchical levels of understanding.

It was discovered that the child's level of performance on affective and cognitive tasks correlated significantly. Older children appeared to be more likely than younger children to describe feelings as an internal, rather than a situational, experience. They also perceived their feelings from the perspective of another, understood multiple feelings, and saw themselves as capable of changing or concealing their feelings. Although age differences were pervasive, the researchers found that sex differences were not. However, there was some evidence to indicate that bright children were more aware of their feelings.

In a related study (Reichenbach and Masters, 1983), researchers wanted to know how accurately preschool and third-grade children could detect the emotional states of others. The subjects were asked to evaluate the happy, sad, or neutral emotional states of other children on the basis of expressive cues only (i.e., slides of children's facial expressions), contextual cues only (i.e., vignettes describing the stimulus of children's emotion-inducing experiences), or both expressive and contextual cues. Older children had the cognitive ability to be more accurate than younger children did only when given multiple cues. For children of both ages, contextual cues were seen to elicit greater accuracy in the recognition of emotional states than were expressive cues. When multiple cues conflicted with one another, younger children relied more on the expressive cues, whereas older children seemed to prefer the contextual ones. Interestingly, children from broken homes less accurately judged emotion in their peers, and their misjudgments were less often judgments of happiness and more often judgments of anger. In regard to the judgments of anger, it is plausible that social experiences may have affected the children's cognitive and emotional monitoring.

☐ Fear

Children's fears are a good illustration of how increased imaginative abilities affect emotional expression. Because they still cannot understand many objects and events, they often exaggerate them. An example is the nighttime ritual of many preschoolers. Some will not venture into a dark bedroom alone, and others will remain in the lit hallway while groping for the light switch on the bedroom wall. Others will inspect the closet before bedtime, hoping not to find an imaginary creature lurking inside. They know that they will not sleep peacefully until this dreadful task is done. Still others will peer quickly under their bed, hoping that the mysterious unknown will not reach out and grab them before they can jump under the covers.

Recently, 42 kindergartners were assigned to experimental and control conditions. The experimental group heard stories in which the characters coped positively with the dark, while the control group heard neutral stories, irrelevant to the fear of the dark. Results indicated that the children in the experimental group showed a significant reduction in self-reported fear of the dark—they also increased their coping statements as compared to the control group (Klingman, 1988).

Fear of imaginary creatures and the dark are two of the more common fears expressed by preschoolers. Other widely reported fears are those related to death, dangerous animals, and thoughts about physical injuries, such as drowning or fire. Such an assortment of fears clearly illustrates the youngster's emotional susceptibility.

Several trends are evident in the development of fears. For instance, females are more susceptible to fear than boys are. However, males report a greater variety of fears. Youngsters from higher socioeconomic settings have a greater number of fears, particularly those related to personal health and safety, than do youngsters from lower-class environments. The latter report more supernatural fears. Finally, television also contributes to children's fears, with its frequent attempts to scare its viewers (Beale and Baskin, 1983; Morris and Kratochwill, 1983; Moody, 1980).

Children's Fears: Stopping the Things That Go Bump in the Night

Adults who understand children realize that frightening and unhappy incidents may enter a child's life any day and create special fears. Although grown-ups cannot protect the child from all fears, nor should they, they can take certain measures when the child is afraid:

Respect Children's Fears. Respect and understanding should always be accorded to children who are afraid of an object or event. Making fun of fears or shaming the child in front of others does not help children to cope effectively with this emotion. Also, adults should never punish a child for being afraid. We point out that adults themselves take their own fears and apprehensions quite seriously.

Realize Children Will Outgrow Most Fears. Since some fears may take longer than others to overcome, adults should exhibit patience. This may take the form of patiently listening to the child and exhibiting empathy and understanding. Achievements should also be praised, no matter how small.

Allow Children to Become Accustomed to Fears Gradually. Adults should seek to build faith in children and their abilities. If heights are a feared situation, let the child get accustomed first to small elevation; if dogs are feared, getting the child acquainted first with a puppy may be a starting point. This gradual adjustment to a feared stimulus is called "desensitization." Another way to help children become accustomed to fears is through imitation, or modeling. That is, fears might be overcome by watching someone else deal with the situation.

Try to Understand Fears in Relation to the Child's Overall Personality. Attempt to observe how fears relate to the child's daily behavioral patterns. If strange sounds, sights, and sudden movements are characteristically feared, situations causing them should be avoided as much as possible, or you can help the child to gradually develop specific means of dealing with such situations.

Familiarize Yourself with the Fears That Children Experience at Different Ages. A better understanding of most fears will result if adults analyze the reasons for them and their underlying dynamics. If a fear involves a major situation, such as school, adults should take the time to analyze its origin and the circumstances that caused it. Adults should also set an example by rationally dealing with their own fears (Ilg, Ames, and Baker, 1981).

☐ Anger and Aggression

The expression of anger changes with age. Undirected, physical, angry outbursts, such as kicking and hitting, begin to decline after the second year. Temper tantrums, which started during toddlerhood, persist into the early childhood years. In addition, the use of threats and insults also increases. It can be said, then, that though the amount of anger and aggression seems to remain stable, its mode of expression changes.

There are two types of aggression. *Instrumental aggression* is directed at acquiring objects, territory, or privileges. *Hostile aggression,* on the other hand, is aimed at another person with the intention of hurting that individual. Among young children, aggression is mostly instrumental (Maccoby, 1980).

Outbursts of anger and aggression are influenced by certain factors. For example, males display more overt anger and aggressiveness. This may be because males are *expected* to be more aggressive, a finding presented in our earlier discussion of sex-role development (Maccoby and Jacklin, 1980; Ullian, 1981; McCabe and Lipscomb, 1988).

The home environment is also important to aggressive behavior. Aggressive children are often reared by aggressive parents, the latter frequently serving as models for this type of behavior. Other models for aggressiveness can be found among peers or are portrayed on television, where frequently the program's theme is "might makes right." In regard to all of the foregoing, note the developmental interaction between socialization and emotional expression (Parke and Slaby, 1983; Singer and Singer, 1980; Finkelstein, 1982).

Imitation also affects aggression, an area extensively explored by Albert Bandura in a series of research investigations. One of his studies (Bandura and Huston, 1961), you will recall, revealed that preschoolers exposed to the sight of an adult aggressively knocking down a rubber doll and then being rewarded tended to use similar types of behavior. In another study (Bandura, Ross, and Ross, 1961), the researchers sought to discover whether the sexual similarity of an aggressive adult model influenced the

Instrumental aggression is common among preschoolers.

degree of aggressiveness that children later demonstrated. After viewing the aggressive model, the children were subjected to a mildly frustrating situation and then left to play with several toys, including the doll that had been attacked earlier by the adult model. The children's resultant behavior revealed that the boys more often imitated physical aggression and identified with the actions of the same-sex models than the girls did.

Research such as this strongly suggests that modeling and reinforcement do affect children's expressions of anger and aggression. It also underscores the need for suitable adult models, not only in the home, but also on the playground and in the media. Anger and aggression may also be manipulated through the proper use of meaningful reinforcers, such as verbal approval or toys. Positive reinforcement of nonaggressive behavior often enhances the chances of that behavior being repeated. But positive reinforcement directly following aggressive behavior, such as the approval of or attention from playmates for acting tough, increases the likelihood of that behavior's persisting (Hom and Hom, 1980).

Adults can do other things to reduce childhood anger and aggression. Not giving in to children's demands if they resort to aggressive behavior is important. Firmness is also important. Grown-ups should try to comprehend why and how the child's anger originated. Observation of the events that caused the outburst is important. Lastly, youngsters should be encouraged to verbalize their feelings when the emotion of the event has subsided.

■ Family Influences on the Developing Child

The family not only transmits appropriate behaviors, values, and knowledge to children, but it also provides an emotional setting in which youngsters can feel loved and accepted. According to Hamilton McCubbin and Barbara Dahl (1985), such a setting plays a critical role in shaping the child's personality and social development. A youngster's lengthy period of dependency underscores the family's overriding influence.

Certain factors related to the child's interaction with the family are particularly important during early childhood. For example, the parents' support, guidance, understanding, trust, and security are significant. Also important are the types of discipline employed by parents and the child's relations with siblings. Overall, children's personal and social growth is greatly affected by their sense of identity and belonging to the family unit, as well as the warmth and acceptance given by others (Westlake, 1981; Bradley, Caldwell, Rock, Ramey et al., 1989; Smith, 1982).

☐ Child Discipline

One of the more frequently discussed family interaction patterns is discipline. *Discipline* is defined as the teaching of acceptable forms of conduct or behavior. The goal of discipline is to make children responsible and to make them realize that they are accountable for the consequences of their behavior.

There are several styles of parental discipline, although parents do not always fall into only one category. Rather, parents often mix approaches when dealing with their children. *Authoritarian* parents attempt to shape and control their children's behavior by enforcing a set standard of conduct. The emphasis is on obedience and the use of punitive, forceful measures to enforce proper behavior. *Authoritative* parents also attempt to direct their children's activities, but in a more rational fashion. Firm control is exerted, but verbal give-and-take is also stressed, and parents attempt to convey to the child the reasons for their discipline. *Permissive* parents are usually nonpunitive and behave in an accepting and affirmative manner toward the child. The child is consulted about policy decisions and given explanations for family rules.

It is important to realize that parents do not always fall into only one category. Rather, parents may mix their approaches in dealing with children. As far as overall effectiveness of each approach is concerned, the authoritarian and permissive styles appear to produce the least favorable results. Authoritarian parents generally allow little freedom of expression and dominate many aspects of the child's behavior. Frequently, this method of control breeds conformity and submissiveness. Among older children, it may breed rebellion. Permissive parents, on the other hand, with their limited overall sanctions on behavior, have a tendency to nurture such child behaviors as selfishness and immaturity (Baumrind, 1971, 1980; Kochanska, Kuczynski, and Radke-Yarrow, 1989).

The authoritative method of control appears to produce the most favorable home climate. This democratic relationship has a tendency to foster such childhood behaviors as independence and self-confidence. Children reared in authoritative homes also have a tendency to be more cooperative and sensitive to the needs of others (Honig, 1982b; Baumrind, 1980).

Ten Steps Toward Effective Discipline

One of the more frequently expressed concerns among parents is how to effectively discipline children. Perhaps the first step is to develop an understanding of exactly what discipline means. Discipline is the setting of limits in an effort to teach acceptable forms of conduct or behavior. The ultimate goal of discipline is to produce responsibility in children. Furthermore, children must come to realize that they are accountable for the consequences of their behavior. The following suggestions are recommended to assist adults confronted with the task of disciplining children:

1. **Realize that there are motivations for misbehavior.** Misbehavior doesn't just happen on its own. Rather, the child may be motivated in some way to engage in disruptive behavior. Some of the more common reasons for misbehavior include boredom or a desire for attention, revenge, power, and control.

2. **Act with confidence.** Adults must believe in themselves and their abilities to promote responsible behavior. They should adopt a take charge attitude and handle disciplinary situations with self-assuredness and confidence.

3. **Relate the discipline to the situation at hand.** Adults should focus on the central issue and not stray into unrelated problems. Also, it is important to tell children that it is the misbehavior being rejected, not them as individuals.

Furthermore, adults need to explain why they are upset with the misbehavior. ("You broke the vase and I'm angry because it was special to me.") This helps to teach youngsters that misbehavior has implications for others.

4. **Be consistent.** Erratic discipline confuses the youngster and seems unlikely to prevent similar problems in the future. If adults are going to discipline the child for one particular type of misbehavior, the reoccurrence of this misbehavior must also be disciplined. If there is more than one child at home, discipline should also be consistent among each of them as well.

5. **Do not make discipline a public spectacle.** Discipline can be a sensitive affair, especially among older children. Talking with children alone, rather than in front of others, reduces embarrassment and other painful emotions. Also, adults should respect children's feelings after discipline has been administered. Shame and guilt are fairly common reactions. Understanding adults do not attempt to increase the child's guilt after the situation has transpired, and they are open to whatever resolution the youngster wants to make.

6. **Avoid angry emotional outbursts.** There is no evidence that yelling, screaming, or other emotional tirades promote effective discipline.

In fact, it is conceivable that youngsters listen *less* when this sort of adult behavior occurs. Adults should avoid impulsivity and take time to carefully organize their thoughts. When this is done, speech should be deliberate and controlled, but firm. Children also seem to listen better when adults talk *with* them, not *to* them.

7. **Establish limits in a clear and precise fashion.** Children need to know what is acceptable and what is not. Spell it out so that there is no question regarding what misbehavior is or what it can encompass. Also, remember that many children, naturally, are going to test limits, which is all the more reason to be clear and consistent about behavioral expectations.

8. **Make the discipline fit the misbehavior.** Adults need to carefully examine the type and degree of disciplinary measure employed in relation to the misbehavior at hand. The discipline administered should be compatible with the nature of the misconduct and not too lenient or too extreme.

9. **Discipline should be as close in time as possible to the misbehavior.** Once adults have gathered their thoughts, discipline should be quickly administered. Children have a tendency to better remember and more clearly associate those events occurring together in time and space. Misbehavior and discipline should thus be yoked together, the latter not being put off for hours or until day's end.

10. **Follow through at an appropriate time.** Discussing the disciplinary situation during a follow-up conversation often helps to ensure that a lesson has been remembered. This does not mean dwelling on the misconduct nor accentuating the negative. Rather, it implies that both adult and child have the opportunity to reflect on the issue and the role that discipline plays in creating a more harmonious living arrangement.

☐ Birth Order and Sibling Relations

A question often directed to child psychologists is whether children's birth order in the family has any effect on subsequent behavioral development and the treatment that they will be receiving. The question is difficult to answer, especially since there is conflicting evidence concerning what behavioral characteristics are affected and the type of attention that will be directed toward children.

Although research material concerning birth order has been gathered, clear-cut answers concerning its total effects have yet to be found. It is accepted by some that firstborns enjoy a favorable position in the family. Usually, they represent the center of attraction for the parents and receive a monopoly of their time. The parents of firstborns are usually not only young and eager to romp with their children, but they also spend considerable time talking to them and sharing activities, something that tends to strengthen bonds of attachment (Dunn and Kendrick, 1982; Bank and Kahn, 1982).

Certain developmental characteristics and personality traits may be affected by birth order. For example, firstborns, more so than laterborns, seem to perform better on early motor-skill tasks. Firstborns are also generally more successful in life. They tend to be more conscientious and have higher levels of self-esteem than laterborns. As far as mental abilities are concerned, firstborns exhibit superiority in intelligence levels over siblings born later. In general, the more children in the family, the lower the IQ of each subsequent child. The higher levels of achievement attained by firstborns may be due to their experiencing greater parental expectations and pressure for success (Malina, 1982).

On the other hand, being a firstborn may not be as advantageous as it is built up to be. Parents of firstborns may be inconsistent and inexperienced in child-rearing practices. Firstborns are usually punished more severely and rewarded more generously than laterborns, thus creating an imbalance. And because the parents are eager to succeed and see clear-cut results, such as with mental abilities, the firstborn is sometimes forced to succeed and strive for approval (Adams and Phillips, 1972; Kidwell, 1981).

Relations between siblings offer a unique slant to the topic of birth order. The arrival of a second child has a tendency to create anxiety for many firstborns, especially if they are of the preschool age. Unsettled feelings may give rise to sibling rivalry, a form of competition between children of the same family for the attention of the parents. If the former only child is old enough to perceive that the newcomer will be sharing the mother, there may be a considerable amount of jealousy exhibited during the early years (Kendrick and Dunn, 1980; Dunn, 1983).

Sibling rivalry is most likely to develop if the parents exercise inconsistent discipline or if the parent is overindulgent toward a particular child. If little time has elapsed between births, older children will still receive their share of maternal attachment. If the interval is greater than three years, older children may develop other interests, which often serve to lessen their jealous feelings.

Although jealousy toward a new arrival is a completely normal emotion for the child, parents can take definite steps to help make the adjustment period smoother. Making the child aware of the baby's arrival beforehand and attempting to tell him or her of the personal significance involved (having a new brother or sister) may prove particularly helpful. Allowing children to become involved with the infant's homecoming preparations can indicate to them that they are active and important in the family's activities. Later on, the proper attitude demonstrated by the parents can help to keep sibling rivalries at a minimum. Parents should avoid showing any kind of favoritism or comparing one child with another.

It is not uncommon for sibling rivalries to persist for years, however. In fact, competition between siblings may be the norm rather than the exception. While it is recognized that the most intense sibling rivalry is between sisters, this may be due to the fact that females are more willing than men to express their rivalry openly (Bank and Kahn, 1982).

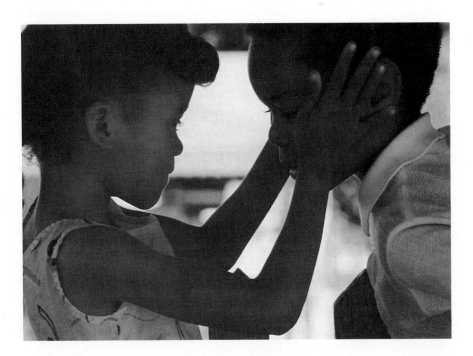

The attachment between siblings represents a special bond.

The degree and nature of sibling interaction varies greatly, not only from one set of siblings to another but within the same pair at different points in their lives. Some siblings become best friends, while others detest each other. In some instances, love and hate may exist side by side in an uneasy equilibrium (V. Adams, 1981).

Siblings appear to have the most interaction and greatest influence on one another when they are close together in age. Significant age differences alone are enough to create physical and psychological distance between siblings. If they are similar in age, siblings may experience positive patterns of interaction, such as shared activities and interests, as well as negative patterns, including intense competition and a continuous struggle for separate identities. These patterns of interaction usually intensify when siblings are of the same sex. Research also discloses that younger siblings, more often than not, try to imitate older siblings. They are far more likely to be followers of their older siblings, the latter often assuming the role of model and initiator (Bank and Kahn, 1982; Dunn and Kendrick, 1982; Dunn, 1983).

In most families, the oldest sibling is usually expected to assume some degree of responsibility for younger siblings. The fact that this expectation exists may help to explain why firstborns are generally more adult-oriented and responsible than later-borns. Interestingly, older siblings in single-parent homes often serve as attachment figures for their younger counterparts (V. Adams, 1981; Dunn, 1983).

While the study of sibling relations has not received as much past attention as have other aspects of family life, researchers today recognize its importance. As a result, many new and diverse thoughts are emerging on the topic (Lamb and Sutton-Smith, 1982). Sibling relations have come to be recognized as a unique facet of the child's life. Furthermore, the attachment between siblings often transforms itself into a special bond that endures as time goes on, even after brothers and sisters have gone their separate ways in the world.

☐ The Battered Child Syndrome

Discipline is not always handled properly, and family life is not always harmonious and stable. Indeed, many children live in domestic disharmony and a negative emotional climate. One such family problem, growing in frightening proportions in recent years, is child abuse, known more technically as the *battered child syndrome*. It is estimated that as many as 2 million children are abused annually. Broken bones, lacerations, concussions, limb dislocations, and abrasions are commonplace. So, too, are instances of sexual and emotional abuse, neglect, and abandonment.

Child abuse is most common among children 6 years of age and younger. Several reasons account for this. For one, the child, at this time, is especially susceptible to parental frustration as adults adjust to the rather tedious chores of early child care. Early economic hardships also cause tensions. Parental frustration may also develop because of the child's inability to interact with the adult in a socially meaningful manner. Finally, abuse is most prevalent under 6 years because the child is most defenseless and unable to absorb the amounts of physical violence that the older young-ster can.

What factors cause parents to abuse their children? Pressures from work, the home, financial difficulties, a history of maltreatment in the parent's background, and low levels of self-esteem are frequently cited as reasons behind violence. A recent study of transgenerational child abuse showed that mothers abused their children in much the same way that they had been abused as children, and the husbands abused their

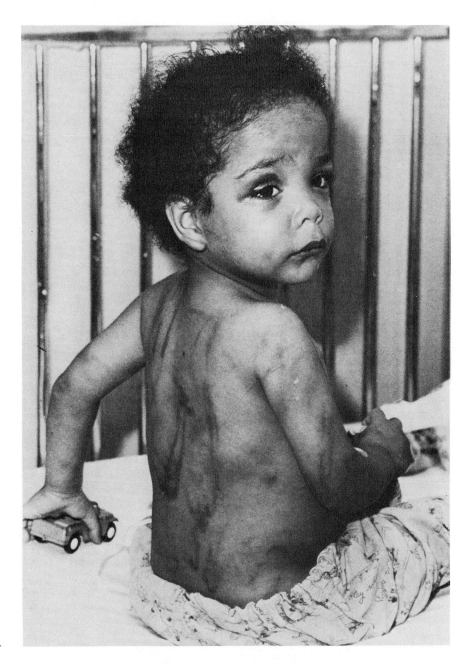

Physical injury is the most visible form of child abuse.

wives much as they had been abused when young (Ney, 1988). Many abusers are lonely, frequently depressed, and have never learned how to contain their aggression (Straus and Geller, 1988; Ulbrich and Huber, 1981; Steele, 1980; Gelles, 1980). James Garbarino (1984) adds that physical illness, untimely childbearing, and a parent's poor ability to empathize with youngsters can substantially increase the likelihood of child maltreatment. This is particularly true when social stress and social isolation characterize the family.

Many parents also abuse their children in an effort to enforce discipline. Some have an overpowering need to impress other adults with a well-behaved child. Still other child abusers identify with the youngster and consider every fault and mistake of the child to be their own. Too, there are those who perceive themselves as failures in life and feel they are attaining superiority and command by exerting such forceful dominance.

A particularly bothersome feature of child abuse is the consequence of battering in later life. Many abused children run a risk for self-destructive behaviors, school failure, and delinquency. Many abused children are insecure, foster poor self-concepts, and have low overall levels of self-confidence and self-reliance. An adult who has been abused as a child often lacks trust, has low self-esteem, poor communication skills, and has difficulty making decisions.

International Lifespan Development

■ Sweden Bans Spanking

In Sweden, parents are forbidden to spank, beat, or harm their children in any way. If parents do, they are breaking the law and can be arrested by local police. In addition, Swedish children have access to an emergency phone network, and an ombudsman has been hired by the government to protect children's rights. Such legislation and progressive change, enacted in 1979, makes Sweden the first nation to legally protect children within the home.

The antispanking law informs parents that any act which, for the purpose of punishing, causes the child physical injury or pain, is prohibited. This includes pain that is even mild and passing. It is also meant to include psychological punishment, but Swedish legal experts feel that this aspect of the law is vague and much more difficult to enforce. Actually, the punishment for spanking does not parallel any consequences for breaking the law in the United States. Social pressure and the threat of social ostracism, though, is law enforcement enough in Sweden.

Reactions to this law have produced mixed responses. Many social workers, doctors, and psychologists hail it as a tool to curb child abuse and

maltreatment. Many parents, though, are annoyed with the new legislation. Some firmly believe that spanking is a good disciplinary technique. Others report that while they would not spank their children under any circumstances, a parental right has been arbitrarily taken away.

Despite the antispanking law, child abuse is no stranger to Sweden. In fact, recent research undertaken by Richard Gelles (in press) indicates that Swedish children may be abused just as often as American children. However, the intensity of abuse may not be as great as it is for American youngsters. For example, Swedish children are less apt to receive injuries from physical assault or require hospitalization.

Other nations have also initiated programs to curb child abuse. West Germany, for example, has a government-sponsored 24-hour abuse hotline and an information center located in Hamburg. Poland employs a protective court system to separate abused or neglected children from their parents, and some Australian states provide a 24-hour reporting center and offer extensive protection to those who register complaints.

☐ Sexual Abuse and Incest

The sexual abuse of children, including incest, has received considerable attention from all factions of the media in recent years. Most experts agree that the experience of being sexually molested occurs to a shocking number of children. However, we should point out that because most victims usually do not tell anyone about what has happened, reported cases barely scratch the surface.

We can make estimates, though, of the epidemic proportions of child molestation. One source (Stark, 1984) proposes that as many as 15 million individuals in the United States have been victims of incest. We also know that the problem is far from going away. It is estimated that the reported cases of childhood sexual abuse have increased over 200 percent since 1976 (Kempe and Kempe, 1984).

In nonfamily sexual abuse, girls are molested more than boys are. A stranger is not likely to be the offender; indeed, assaults on children by strangers represent only a slight percentage of child sexual abuse cases. The perpetrator is far more likely to be someone who has developed a close relationship with the child, someone the child probably trusts, and someone he or she cares for (Nielsen, 1983; Peters, 1988).

Extrafamilial sexual abuse was the focal point of research undertaken by David Finkelhor (1985). His review of the literature uncovers the following facts:

- Estimates drawn from surveys of men in the general American population suggest that 2.5 to 5 percent of men are sexually victimized before age 13; a comparison of similar studies of girls suggests that two to three girls are victimized for every boy.

- Girls as well as boys are most commonly victimized by men.

- Sexual abuse and social class are unrelated, and blacks have no higher abuse rates than whites.

- The abuse of boys is more likely to be reported to the police than to a hospital or child protective agency.

Incest is defined as sexual intercourse or sexual relations between persons so closely related that they are forbidden by law to marry. Girls are much more likely to be victims of incest, often within the nuclear family. The father (biological, step, foster, or adoptive) is typically the leading perpetrator. Father-daughter incest typically begins when the daughter is between the ages of 6 and 11. While wide variations are reported, it is generally acknowledged that the average relationship lasts about two years (Stark, 1984).

Although extreme physical force is seldom used in sexual contacts with children, the use of mild to moderate amounts of parental force occurs frequently. In addition, extensive use is made of psychological pressures, such as verbal threats, bribes, intimidation, trickery, and outright seduction. The psychological force most often brought to bear is the natural authority of adults over children. In this sense, the existence of this powerful psychological force obviates the need for physical force (Geiser, 1982).

The victim's hesitancy and fear in reporting incest contributes to the conspiracy of silence that exists (Summit, 1988). The victim's suffering may be expressed in physical ailments, such as chronic pelvic pain, or psychological disturbances, such as depression and hysterical seizures. Typically, victims are left with a strong feeling of guilt, a trauma that often requires intensive therapy (Finkelhor, 1988; Brier and Runtz, 1988; Peters, 1988).

Similar to other disturbing life events, incest also tends to destroy the victim's perception of daily living. One study (Silver, Boon, and Stones, 1983) indicates that in the wake of such experiences, searching for the meaning of one's existence is a common adaptive process. The study examined this type of behavior in 77 adult women who had been victims of father-daughter incest as children. There was no clear-cut answer as to whether the women in this sample were able to find meaning in their victimization; more than half of the women who were actively searching for meaning (an average of 20 years after the incest had ended) reported that they could make no sense of it whatsoever. However, researchers believe that the ruminations and remembrances, which are part of the search for meaning, serve an adaptive function; they are likely to be the means by which individuals begin to gain control over and make sense of their experience.

How Parents Can Help Prevent Child Sexual Abuse

There are numerous things that parents can do to help prevent the sexual abuse of their children. The Children's Protective Society (1981) offers the following suggestions.

What to Teach Children:

1. No one has the right to touch the private parts of their body or make them feel uncomfortable. They have the right to say no.

2. To tell you if anyone asks to take, or has taken their picture.

3. Adults do not come to children for help. Adults ask adults for help.

4. To never get in a car without your permission.

5. To make you aware of any unusual discussions or strange requests.

6. To tell you when any adult asks them to keep a "secret."

7. To tell you of gifts or money given to them.

8. Never to go into someone's home without your knowledge.

9. When away from home, scared, or uncomfortable, they have the right to use the telephone without anyone's permission.

10. To tell you of any situation where a statement or gesture is made about sex or love.

11. Never to answer the door when alone.

12. Never to admit to anyone over the telephone that they are home alone.

13. That you will always believe them about a molestation and will protect them from further harm. (Children do not lie about molestation.)

Parents Should Pay Attention to the Following:

1. Question any money or gifts your child brings home.

2. Ask your child who he or she is spending time with and of the activities they engage in.

3. Find out who their best friend is, and why.

4. Be watchful of any strong bond that seems to develop between your child and an adult figure in their life (including friends, teachers, coaches, clergymen, and so on).

5. Maintain constant and regular telephone contact with your child whenever one of you is away from home.

6. Never leave your child unattended, day or night.

7. Never leave your child alone in a car; molestation only takes a minute.

8. Be involved in any sports or activities your child has.

9. Listen when your child tells you he or she does not want to be with or go with someone. There may be a reason.

10. Never make your child submit to physical contact (that is, hugs and kisses, and so on) if he or she does not want to. Children have the right to say no.

11. No one should want to be with your child more than you. When someone is showing your child too much attention, ask yourself why.

12. Be sensitive to any changes in your child's behavior or attitudes. Encourage open communication with your child. Never belittle any fear or concern your child may express to you. Never compromise any private or confidential matter your child may share with you.

■ School Influences on the Developing Child

Early childhood education provides programs and constructive learning experiences to preschoolers. Today, approximately one-third of the nation's 3- and 4-year-olds are enrolled in some type of early childhood educational program. All indications are that enrollment figures will mushroom in years to come.

Generally speaking, early childhood education programs try to foster physical, linguistic, cognitive, personality, and social growth through a wide variety of learning experiences. Experts in the field of early childhood education stress the importance of promoting social, self-help, and self-image skills. Equally important is the role of nurturing cognitive and linguistic abilities and, in general, learning readiness skills. At the heart of many programs today is the desire to heighten levels of self-sufficiency and independence.

In striving to reach these goals, early childhood education programs seek to establish and maintain a healthy learning environment and provide positive guidance and discipline. The health, safety, and well-being of the preschooler are of obvious importance, as is the establishment of positive and productive relationships with parents.

The schedules and routines established by the preschool are the means through which goals and objectives are met. Although activities differ, the general thrust of programming is similar. Many schools offer a diverse mixture of free and structured play activities; creative play opportunities in art, music, and literature; and beginning subject-area exercises in cognitive skills, letter formation, language skills, and so forth. Other activities may focus on small and large muscle skills, listening abilities, recitation, or special programs, such as nutrition and safety awareness. The overall length of the preschool program (full- or half-day sessions) determines the extent of these activities.

How Early Childhood Education Programs Meet the Needs of Preschoolers

PHYSICAL

- Time, space, and equipment make it possible to develop motor skills using large and small muscles.

- Opportunities to develop eye-hand coordination.

- Safe indoor and outdoor activities.

- Balance between activity and rest.

- Balanced diet.

SOCIAL

- Play experiences with other children.

- Interaction with both men and women outside the family.

- Involvement with adults and children of different cultures and races.

- Opportunities to express both dependent and independent behaviors.

EMOTIONAL

- Development of a sense of security and a positive self-concept.

- Relationships with adults who respect and trust them.

- Adults who recognize each child as a unique human being.

- Contact with adults whose expectations are consistent and reasonable.

INTELLECTUAL

- A variety of experiences with concrete materials.

- Opportunities for creative expression.

- Opportunities to make discoveries and solve problems.

- Development of auditory and visual discrimination through the practice of communication skills.

(Lindberg and Swedlow, 1985)

■ Categories of Early Childhood Education

To better understand the nature and complexity of preschool educational programming, it is helpful to develop a classification system. Such a classification system can serve to separate the basic differences that exist in structure and operating procedure.

☐ Day Care

As the name implies, this program offers full-day coverage to parents of preschool children. Such an operation is especially appealing to dual-career families. Although they initially had no planned educational programs, most of them have since been reorganized to meet the child's social, emotional, physical, and intellectual needs. The cost of day care varies considerably, and in some instances the centers charge fees on a sliding scale based on the family's ability to pay.

☐ Home Day Care

Similar to the above, home day care is attractive to working parents. It offers care and attention during the hours of the working day, but within a caregiver's residence. Similar to all early childhood facilities, a home day care must be inspected and licensed by state officials and the operator must be certified.

☐ Compensatory Programs

Compensatory programs are subsidized by the federal government. The most well known of these is Project Head Start, which was introduced to help keep the blight of a deficient home environment from leaving a permanent impression on some of the country's children. Under the supervision of the Office of Economic Opportunity, federal grants were given to local community agencies capable of meeting basic outlined standards and implementing programs designed to improve the health of preschoolers and alleviate the prospect of school readiness deficiencies in disadvantaged children. Basically, Project Head Start consists of programs in education, medical and dental care, nutrition, social services, psychological services, parent education, and community volunteer programs.

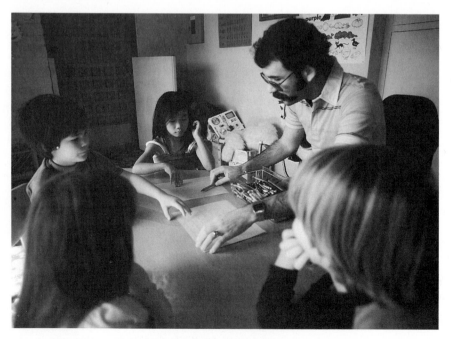

The early childhood education setting enhances many facets of growth and development.

☐ Private Nursery School

Although private nursery schools have experienced rapid growth in the recent past, their cost has restricted their services to wealthier families. Compared to day-care facilities, private nursery schools often offer half-day sessions. When staffed by competent professionals, private schools provide excellent care for their pupils; unfortunately, very few states set up adequate standards or provide educational supervision for the private nursery schools within their borders.

☐ Cooperative Nursery School

A cooperative nursery school is organized by parents who employ a trained teacher to carry out the program. While sometimes obliged to use churches, community centers, or other buildings (well-established schools frequently have their own buildings) for their sessions, these schools are able to provide sound programs at somewhat lower enrollment charges than a private school.

☐ Laboratory School

College or university laboratory schools were among the earliest types of nursery schools in the country. The laboratory school focuses its energies on preparental education, teacher learning, and research studies. Sometimes mobilizing the resources of an area to meet the needs of young children, the laboratory school is usually financed primarily by the academic institution.

☐ Special Needs Programs

Some nursery schools employ qualified staff members who are capable of working with physical, mental, and emotional handicaps, or other special needs. Often these experts consider it important to have the handicapped child placed in a regular nursery school group, as when a blind child is enrolled in a group of sighted children. With a trained person who understands the handicapped and can help the parents and the other children in the group deal constructively with the questions and anxieties a normal person inevitably feels, the experience may be a rewarding one for both the group and the handicapped child. In other situations, specially trained teachers work closely with psychiatrists to administer therapy to severely disturbed children, while some programs seek to fulfill the needs of the mentally retarded.

☐ Parent Education Programs

Some communities operate nursery schools under a parent education program, in which the parents actually participate and engage in "study discussion" sessions under the leadership of a professionally trained parent educator. The goals of such programs are to enhance the child-care skills and parenting abilities of those involved (Read and Patterson, 1980).

■ ATTENDING NURSERY SCHOOL IN CHINA

The scene is a nursery school located deep within the city of Peking, China. A middle-aged preschool teacher is reading to the 34 children in attendance, a mixture of 3- and 4-year-olds. The youngsters sit motionless and seemingly catch her every word. They do not talk, cry, or shove.

In an adjoining room, 18 toddlers receive a different set of activities. Some are playing with blocks while others climb through an assortment of large makeshift cubes. When success is achieved in one physical challenge, the toddlers are given new activities to develop their growing bodies.

For years, American educators have been attracted to the early childhood education strategies employed in China. Onlookers are invariably drawn to the almost universal good behavior of Chinese children. They are quiet, eager to follow their teacher's instructions, and seldom exhibit the aggressiveness demonstrated by American children. The established learning climate also encourages a cooperative spirit among the youngsters, which, in the process, downplays individuality.

Chinese parents may enroll children as young as 2 months of age, the time when the mother's maternity leave ends. Nurseries for the infants provide necessary custodial care as well as early stimulation to engage developing cognitive skills. When the children are age 1, attendants begin to toilet train them in a very structured fashion. Children are placed on enamel spittons and kept there until they defecate.

As time progresses, more highly structured situations await the children. Lesson plans are delivered in a crisp, methodical style, and most of the teachings involve rote memory and copying tasks modeled by the adult. Children also learn at an early age the premium placed on docility. Selfishness is not tolerated by the teachers, and sharing is encouraged whenever possible.

Although methodical and organized, the teachers are warm and kind in their dealings with the children. Good behavior seldom escapes notice and children receive a steady diet of praise and encouragement. When negative behavior occurs, firm disciplinary strategies are used rather than punitive approaches. Physical punishment does not have a place in Chinese preschools, nor does harsh verbal rebuke. The dignity of the child is always acknowledged. Experts maintain that such an approach fosters an early mutual respect between young and old.

■ The Peer Group

Moving from the family and being able to interact with others is an important criterion of social maturity. Peer group interaction provides opportunities for children to understand further their behavior and the effect it will have on others. Furthermore, early group relationships give youngsters the opportunity to increase their independence, competence, and emotional support. Peer relations may also provide more complex and arousing sensory stimulations than those available in the home, offer new models for identification, influence self-concept development, and alter the character of children's play (Howes, 1988; Berndt and Ladd, 1989; Walsh, 1980; Hartup, 1980; Fine, 1981). For example, the results of a recent investigation indicate that preschoolers who have higher levels of cooperative play at the beginning of the school year are more accepted by their peers throughout the school year. The study also found that arguing increased the likelihood of rejection by peers (Ladd, Price, and Hart, 1988).

Peer and family influences are not separate forces. Rather, they are additive and interactive in their influence. Sometimes peer group norms reflect the influence of adults, but at other times they reflect their own.

With age, peer group interaction increases.

Peer and adult influences on the child are also not always in harmony. Though there may be considerable consonance, sometimes peer and family influences produce cross pressures that can lead to conflict. How the youngster responds to such cross pressures varies. Willard Hartup (1980, 1983) maintains that sometimes the values and behaviors relative to the given situation are crucial. Other times, the attractiveness of the peer group, the extent of contact with friends, the degree to which the peer group functions as a reference, and the adequacy of family adjustment are important factors. The broader milieu of the peer group, the amount of time children spend with it, and the number of interactions they have with its members tend to intensify the group's influence.

Again, one must view development as an integrated whole rather than as a single facet of growth. For example, peer group development is affected by numerous forces, including cognitive, personality, family, and emotional influences. None of these areas of growth can be studied in a vacuum. Rather, the student of developmental psychology must decide how one affects the others.

Peer Group Interaction

Rarely do two children behave in the same way when placed in the company of others. Some may eagerly seek to join the company of others; others may scream to be taken away, and still others may become passive and watch the activity from a safe distance. When a certain degree of group comfort has been acquired, attempts at making further social contacts are often awkward. Having had limited peer group experiences, many simply do not know how to get along with their peers. As a result, children may resort to such immature social behaviors as hitting, kicking, or spitting to acquire the things they desire. Conflicts are common, but short-lived, and occur as frequently among friends as nonfriends, but among friends they are less intense, resolved more frequently with disengagement, and have a more satisfactory outcome (Hartup, Laursen, Stewart, and Eastenson, 1988).

Time and experience teach children that certain behaviors are socially acceptable and others are not. For example, hitting a playmate may release an inner impulse, but it may also cause friends and playmates to cry, strike back, or run away. Gradually, children realize that how they relate to their peers greatly influences the treatment that they in turn receive.

The peer group during early childhood is quite selective, usually consisting of individuals of approximately the same age. Group members tend to keep an air of exclusiveness about them, as they are bound by a common play interest. Children's ability to gain acceptance into an established group often depends not only on their ability to accept and comply with the members' ritual and routines but also on the degree of friendliness that they exhibit. As Zick Rubin (1980a) wrote, for children to be included and accepted, they must also include and accept.

Peer groups also discriminate on the basis of sex. Compared with the lack of sexual discrimination in play groups during toddlerhood, preschoolers prefer same-sex play-mates. This trend persists and even intensifies throughout middle childhood, although it is more pronounced in males than in females (Fu and Leach, 1980; Reis and Wright, 1982).

The peer group also contains dominance hierarchies. Shortly after the group forms, internal group processes select one or a few as its leaders. Others become followers. Often, the group leaders are above average in intelligence, assertive, and well liked by the others. Popular and unpopular group members also emerge over time. Popularity is usually linked to friendliness, extraversion, and the ability to cooperate (Hartup, 1983; Furman, 1982; Z. Rubin, 1980a).

The activity of the preschool peer group is interesting. A cooperative attitude is more evident than during toddlerhood, and more sharing takes place. The peer group is also capable of devising more activities for all members. Goal-directed behaviors are also present. However, this does not imply that all signs of emotional and social imma-turity have disappeared. On the contrary, selfishness, impatience, and disagreement punctuate many preschool peer groups (Asher, Renshaw, and Hymel, 1982; Bell, 1981).

Prosocial Development

An important facet of social development is being sensitive to the needs and feelings of others. Such peer sensitivity is called *prosocial behavior,* and it pertains to such areas as cooperation, altruism, sharing, and helping others. In a broad sense, it might be referred to as Good Samaritan behavior.

There has been considerable research on prosocial behavior, including the developmental trends in its expression. Surprisingly, it has been found that the ability to exhibit certain types of prosocial behavior begins early in life. Toddlers, for example, have been observed sharing with others and even demonstrating some insight into the emotional state and needs of others. By the same token, preschoolers may perform such prosocial acts as helping, cooperating with, and comforting others. However, it is important to stress that even though the ability to demonstrate prosocial behavior appears early in life, this does not mean that it is consistently expressed. Usually this does not transpire until later in childhood (Smith, 1982; Moore, 1982).

Several research reports support this latter contention. For example, a longitudinal study conducted by Nancy Eisenberg and her associates (1983) revealed that from early childhood to the elementary school years, empathic reasoning steadily increases. Another study (Burleson, 1982) focused on how children's empathy and comforting skills increased over time. In the research investigation, children from the first through the twelfth grades were placed in a hypothetical situation in which a same-sex friend was experiencing some form of emotional distress. For each situation, the subjects were asked to state everything they might say to make their distressed friend feel better.

The subjects' messages were coded for the number and variety of message strategies employed and for the extent to which these message strategies evidenced sensitivity to the feelings and perspective of the distressed other. An analysis of these messages revealed that the number, variety, and sensitivity of comfort-intended message strategies increased significantly with age. It was also found that females used a greater number, a greater variety, and qualitatively more sensitive comforting strategies than did males.

Early prosocial behavior seems to be greatly influenced by the child's exposure to positive adult role models and certain social situations. Children are apt to learn such behaviors as helping and cooperating by receiving adult guidance and positive reinforcement, by interacting with other children, and by observing adults and other children behaving in socially constructive ways. Youngsters exposed to altruistic adults are likely to imitate such behaviors, especially if the adult model is affectionate and nur-

Helping others is an important dimension of personality and social functioning.

turant. Other adult behaviors such as warmth of voice, gentleness in physical handling, and explaining to children the consequences of their actions with others have been shown to increase children's levels of prosocial behavior (Londerville and Main, 1981; Grusec and Arnason, 1982; Barnett et al., 1980).

How do American children compare with children in other countries in regard to prosocial behavior? This is difficult to assess, although cross-cultural child-rearing practices have been examined. The Soviet Union, Israel, and Mexico, for example, place a high premium on cooperation and the teaching of altruistic behavior. The same is true for Chinese children. Parents and educators alike stress the avoidance of interpersonal conflict and, instead, encourage cooperative interaction. The results of such training are evident in the high levels of prosocial behavior demonstrated by children in these countries.

This doesn't imply that American children are not taught the same lessons or lack prosocial sensitivity. What it does imply is that compared with youngsters from other nations, American children are not taught altruism as consistently (Whiting and Edwards, 1988). Rather than the other countries' everyday emphasis on helping others, American children often receive sporadic instruction in prosocial development and limited structured opportunities from adults to put this behavior into practice. But given such opportunities, prosocial behavior may develop more fully (Honig, 1982b; Bar-Tal and Raviv, 1982; Grusec, 1981; Rushton, 1980).

■ Socialization Through Play

Throughout all of childhood, play is an important social activity, through which youngsters can better understand themselves and how they relate to others. During early childhood, play groups enhance a sensitivity for the needs of others and foster a cooperative spirit. Play groups also help youngsters relinquish their singular, self-centered frame of reference. Overcoming egocentrism is one of the main tasks of the early childhood years, although as we learned earlier, preschoolers may not be as egocentric as we once thought (Black, 1981).

The play group during early childhood is usually small, restrictive, and short-lived. That is, many groups stop playing after 10 or 15 minutes. This is due to a number of factors, including limited attending skills and impulsive desires to end activities and start others (Cosaro, 1981).

The play group's temporary quality gives children the task of entering new social gatherings on a fairly regular basis. Some children are better at this than others, perhaps because they are more outgoing, gregarious, and secure in their relationships overall. The quiet, timid, or shy child may encounter more difficulty (Zimbardo and Radl, 1981).

The play group gradually teaches youngsters that certain behaviors are expected and certain rules must be followed. Furthermore, the play setting will show children the importance of sharing and working toward group goals. Children learn these social processes as they interact with one another and with adults in situations that require grown-up supervision and guidance (Z. Rubin, 1980a).

There has been some research on the extent to which adults should involve themselves in and structure children's playtime activities. Many maintain that adults should give children guidance, support, and a good environment for play. However, adults should not restrict the child's freedom. Frequently, adults with the best of intentions overinvolve themselves and overorganize play activities. The consequence of this is to restrict the child's spontaneity and free-play spirit. Adult intervention thus should be designed to minimize its obtrusive effects and not control all of the child's choices (Kleiber and Barnett, 1980). There is evidence that youngsters enjoy play involving more make-believe and games that have less structure than do older children (Baumeister and Senders, 1989).

☐ Varieties of Play

Almost all forms of play during this time give children the opportunity to develop muscular coordination, whether it be through climbing, balancing, or manipulating blocks or jigsaw puzzles. Motor skills are refined during this period, and self-confidence is increased as play materials are mastered. There is, however, considerable variation in children's performance. This is true for the physical aspects of play as well as for all motor skills. Furthermore, preschoolers often tend to perform well in one area and do poorly in others. As we mentioned earlier in this chapter, preschoolers generally have difficulty with those toys requiring fine muscle coordination (Malina, 1982; Wickstrom, 1983).

For these reasons, certain types of play remain difficult and elusive. It is interesting that children, even at this young age, can almost "sense" what types of activities are overpowering challenges to their developing physical capabilities. Of course, some activities are better suited to meet the needs of the children's developing motor abilities, so adults should learn to distinguish them (Gallahue, 1982; Foreman and Hill, 1980; Riggs, 1980).

One important type of play during the preschool years is imagination and make-believe. As we learned earlier, imagination is the result of developing cognitive, social, and emotional forces. Often it is a reflection of the child's inner needs and desires, which in turn may originate in real-life experiences. The transformation of these inner feelings, especially during this time, can help children better understand themselves, other people, and events. Because of this, many adults encourage imaginative play (Singer and Singer, 1985; Griffing, 1982; Singer and Switzer, 1980). There is also evidence of increased symbolic representation in imaginative play as children grow older. For example, children aged 4.5 were found to express more play symbols than were 3-year-olds (Göneü and Kessel, 1988).

Imagination is also a strong indication of originality and inventiveness. Toys, too, can provide an outlet for these traits. A youngster wanting to make a toy come alive with its own individual qualities (the Piagetian concept of animism) illustrates this. In this respect, a doll may "come alive" with its own thoughts and feelings; a chair may become a mysterious fort or castle; and a box may be turned into a car, complete with its own noisy engine. The child's play language, too, reflects the prevalence of animism during this stage of development. Children may refer to a "sleeping" tree, the "happy" sun, or "strong" mountains (Winner, McCarthy, and Gardner, 1980).

One other form of play worthy of our consideration is sociodramatic play. *Sociodramatic play* often is the imitation and identification of adult behavioral patterns. By becoming a doctor, parent, or law officer, children act out their desire to be like adults and may benefit from a valuable learning experience. Playing grown-up roles may prepare children for later life, as many of the grown-up situations acted out are characteristic of those of the adult years.

Sociodramatic play at this time has other dimensions as well. In addition to preschoolers' ability to plan and sequence make-believe activities, their sociodramatic play

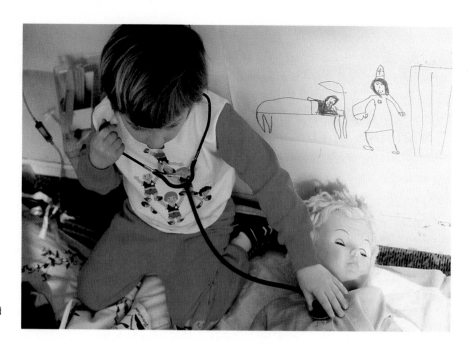

Play during early childhood is often sociodramatic.

separates the sexes. The themes used by both sexes are varied and elaborate, although boys' play often reflects the element of danger and is noisy, urgent, and intense. Girls, on the other hand, often pursue more nurturant or caretaking themes. These themes for boys and girls will persist throughout childhood. Both males and females are able to recognize the present element and use such phrases as "Let's make believe," "You be the nurse," and "This is not really real." Finally, the roles played require not only wearing the right costume but also assuming other characteristics and actions related to the role (Segal and Adcock, 1981).

Sociodramatic play has many benefits. It is creative, as it encourages children to use their past experiences in the sociodramatic framework. Adjusting to the ideas of others also motivates youngsters' creativity. Sociodramatic play is also mentally stimulating, as it encourages the use of cognitive powers, including linguistic ability, abstraction, concept formation, and new knowledge. Finally, children's social skills are sharpened through sociodramatic situations. Such play encourages positive give-and-take, tolerance, and consideration of others. Suffice it to say that sociodramatic play applies influences to many facets of growth and development (K. Rubin, 1980; Rubin and Everett, 1982).

The social benefits of pretend play were the focal point of research launched by Jennifer Connolly, Anna Doyle, and Erica Reznick (1988). The researchers observed the social interaction of preschoolers during social pretend play and nonpretend activities to determine whether positive and mature social behaviors were associated with the pretend context. Results showed that during pretend play, subjects' social interactions were more enjoyable, lasted longer, involved larger groups, and showed more play involvement and greater reciprocity. The researchers suggest that social pretend play provides a contextual framework within which mature social interaction can occur and social competencies may be acquired.

Researchers once felt that all children engaged in sociodramatic play and other varieties of pretending. There is evidence today, though, that when compared with middle-class youngsters, low-income and working-class children engage in *less* sociodramatic and pretend play. Numerous studies (see Sutton-Smith, 1983, for a review of the literature) point out that the play of working-class children is often characterized by sensory-motor and kinetic activity. Interestingly, this trend has been observed among low-income American children as well as such youngsters from Israel, Asia, and North Africa.

This developmental pattern may result from the fact that children from lower socioeconomic settings have work tasks or family responsibilities imposed on them, which in turn require a high level of physical activity. On the other hand, middle-class children usually have fewer demands placed on them in the form of household duties or work outside the home. Thus middle- and upper-class youngsters may have more opportunities to engage in sociodramatic play and the like, not to mention more adult encouragement. It is important to point out, though, that this topic has sparked debate among developmental psychologists and that not all (e.g., McLoyd, 1983) agree with these contentions.

■ Theories of Personality Development

☐ Sigmund Freud's Psychosexual Theory

THE ANAL STAGE OF DEVELOPMENT (AGES 2 TO 4) The preschool years are the period when children enter the *anal stage* of psychosexual development. This stage occurs when children become aware of their body's process of elimination. Pleasure is derived from both the elimination and retention of the feces. Youngsters are often fascinated by their excretions, even to the point of peering into the toilet bowl and observing or even handling the fecal matter. This also becomes a time for many children to engage in "toilet talk."

Adult reactions during this stage will determine the children's later behavior. Adults who express ideas of "dirty," "messy," or "bad" convey these feelings to the children, who may then feel that this "product of the body" is "bad." Children may reason that they, in turn, must also be bad. Also, parents who force early toilet training may produce children who are obsessively clean and neat, reflecting the adults' own rigid and somewhat Victorian outlook on the body's natural functions. On the other hand, parents who neglect toilet training may produce children who will later exhibit slovenliness, indifference, and other undesirable traits.

There are other interesting aspects of Freud's anal stage. Many children of this age (the terrible two's) resent adult authority and soon learn that although they can't yell or fight back at their parents, they do have two ways to retaliate—retention of feces and violent expulsion of them at inappropriate times. According to psychoanalytic interpretation, children who are slow to be toilet trained may actually not want to be trained, as this (untrained) behavior now becomes an outlet for pent-up frustrations and hostilities.

THE PHALLIC STAGE OF DEVELOPMENT (AGES 4 TO 6) The *phallic stage* is Freud's third stage of psychosexual development and covers the latter portion of the preschool years. During this stage, the child's desires for gratification shift from the anal to the genital area. Pleasure is derived from manipulating and fondling the genitals, which Freud termed childhood masturbation. Again, how parents handle children in this stage will in part determine their future psychosexual development. Maturation and phallic awareness occur simultaneously with children's social development in

The preschool years mark a time when new facets of the personality emerge.

terms of their imitation, identification, and sex-role typing. According to Freud, boys identify with their father and imitate paternal behavior because they have developed unconscious sexual feelings toward their mother. The threat of punishment for masturbating causes boys' sexual interest to shift from their penis to their mother. The result of this is jealousy of the father. Boys' sexual feelings do not include the desire for intercourse but, rather, for hugging and affection. Their feelings are romantic, not lustful. Boys become fearful when they realize that these urges place them in conflict with their father. This condition, the Oedipus complex, is further complicated when boys fear the reprisal of their father in the form of castration. (Boys believe that women, because they lack a penis, have already been castrated.) Castration anxiety can be resolved only by repressing these sexual desires and identifying with the father.

The less well known Electra complex is experienced by females during the phallic stage. Girls, according to Freud, are envious of the boy's penis (penis envy) and feel cheated. They blame this state of affairs on their mother, and their father becomes the object of their sexual attachment. Subsequently, the mother is placed in a competitive role for the father's attention.

For both the Electra and the Oedipus complexes to be resolved, the sexual attachment to the parent of the opposite sex must be discontinued. Freud considered it quite natural for a strong bond to remain between the daughter and father (he also believed that girls later seek a husband like their father). For boys, however, the Oedipus complex can become a more serious problem. A fixation at this stage can produce behaviors such as the boy's being "tied to his mother's apron strings" or being unable to reach the level of independence needed to function in society.

☐ Erik Erikson's Psychosocial Theory

INITIATIVE VERSUS GUILT (AGES 3 TO 6) *Initiative versus guilt* is the psychosocial crisis of early childhood proposed by Erik Erikson. Having established a sense of trust and autonomy during the first few years of life, children now set out to prove they have a will of their own. Youngsters actively explore their environment and try to satisfy their curiosity. Accompanying this high energy level are rapidly developing physical skills, an increased vocabulary, and the general ability to get around and do new and different things. All of this produces an active child in pursuit of a variety of goals:

> There is in every child at every stage a new miracle of vigorous unfolding, which constitutes a new hope and a new responsibility for all. Such is the sense and the pervading quality of initiative. The criteria for all these senses and qualities are the same: a crisis, more or less beset with fumbling and fear, is resolved, in that the child suddenly seems to "grow together" both in his person and in his body. He appears "more himself," more loving, more relaxed, and brighter in his judgment, more activated and activating. He is in free possession of a surplus of energy which permits him to approach what seems desirable (even if it also seems uncertain and even dangerous) with undiminished and more accurate direction. Initiative adds to autonomy the quality of undertaking, planning, and "attacking" a task for the sake of being active and on the move, where before self-will, more often than not, inspired acts of defiance or, at any rate, protested independence.

(Erikson, 1963, p. 255)

Whether or not children lean toward initiative or guilt depends largely, once again, on the quality of the children's interaction with their parents. If adults give youngsters an opportunity to exercise their physical skills, answer their questions, and encourage fantasy, initiative is likely to be the result. Conversely, if children feel that their questions are annoying or a nuisance and that indulgence in fantasy is a waste of time, guilt is likely to surface.

CHAPTER REVIEW

■ Unit One: Physical Development

Physical growth and development during the preschool years are quite rapid. By the fifth year, preschoolers have doubled their original birth length and increased their birth weight by five times. Because of rapid muscular growth and the development of coordination abilities, preschoolers show marked gains in small- and large-motor skills. This part of the chapter also discussed three phases of motor-skill development: the cognitive, associative, and autonomous stages.

■ Unit Two: Mental Development

Piaget's stage of preconceptual thought is characterized primarily by egocentrism, a self-centeredness that prevents children from understanding any point of view but their own. Egocentrism is evident not only in early socialization patterns, such as parallel play and collective monologues, but also in thought processes, mainly animism and artificialism.

The development of advanced cognition relies on the ability to acquire and categorize new concepts from the environment, including modifications and variations of shape, size, space, quantity, and time. Concept development is aided by perceptual advancements, although preschoolers are hindered by limited attention and attending skills.

Several factors contribute to preschoolers' overall language acquisition, including socioeconomic influences, intelligence, sex, whether they have a bilingual background, and whether they are a singleton or a twin. In contrast with their earlier telegraphic sentences, preschoolers are able to fabricate multiword sentences, complete with fairly complex syntactical constructions. They also advance in pragmatic skills during early childhood.

■ Unit Three: Personality and Social Development

This final part of the chapter was directed toward those factors affecting sex-role development, including parents, peers, play activity, and the media. Psychoanalytic, social learning, and cognitive-developmental theories were used to explain how sex roles develop. In regard to emotional development, preschoolers exhibit many new fears, owing to their emotional susceptibility and because they cannot understand many objects and events. Anger is not expressed physically as often as in the past and is replaced by verbal displays of resentment.

Interaction with the family has important influences on personality and social growth. We examined three types of parental control: authoritarian, authoritative, and permissive. Of the three methods, the authoritative style is regarded as the most effective. We also show how birth order and sibling relations shape the course of personality and social development. Attention was also focused on the dark side of family life, namely child abuse and sexual molestation.

Many preschoolers today are able to benefit from an early childhood education experience, and this unit explored the many varieties available.

Peers enable children to develop their independence and social skills. When they are with others, children can begin to work cooperatively and develop a sympathetic attitude toward one another. Peer groups may also breed a competitive spirit among the members and encourage conformity to the group's standards of behavior. The various forms of play discussed in this chapter contribute to children's social maturity.

Finally, this chapter explored the personality theories of Freud and Erikson. Freud theorized that children pass through two psychosexual stages at this time, the anal and the phallic stages. Erikson's psychosocial crisis for this period is initiative versus guilt.

KEY TERMS

anal stage	egocentrism
androgyny	Electra complex
animism	gender identity
artificialism	hostile aggression
authoritarian control	identification
authoritative control	immanent justice
battered child syndrome	incest
bilingualism	initiative versus guilt
collective monologue	instrumental aggression

Oedipus complex
parallel play
perception
permissive control
phallic stage
pragmatics
preconceptual thought
prosocial behavior

sex role
sexual identity
significates
signifiers
sociodramatic play
symbolic functioning
twin speech

RECOMMENDED READINGS

Bruner, J. and Hast, H. (Eds.). *Making Sense: The Child's Construction of the World.*
London: Methuen, 1987.
The dawning of cognitive functioning is approached from many angles by the contributors.

Daehler, M. W., and Bukatko, D. *Cognitive Development.* New York: Knopf, 1985.
This book discusses the basic processes in memory, attention, and its development, the
roots of cognitive development, and social cognition.

Dombro, A. L., and Wallach, L. *The Child Is Extraordinary: How Children Under Three
Learn.* New York: Simon & Schuster, 1988.
Students will especially enjoy the mental competencies of infants and toddlers as
explained by these two readable authors.

Pelligrini, A. D. (Ed.). *Psychological Bases for Early Education.* Chichester, England:
Wiley, 1988.
Those students wanting more depth on the topic of early education will find it in this
collection of readings.

Pitcher, E. G., and Schultz, L. H. *Boys and Girls at Play: The Development of Sex Roles.*
New York: Praeger, 1983.
The authors examine the interactions of 225 children in exploring sex-role develop-
ment. This book also contains an excellent review of the literature on sex roles.

Schaffer, H. R. *The Child's Entry into a Social World.* New York: Academic Press, 1984.
This text discusses children's acquisition of social competence and how social interactions shape its development.

Tobin, J. J., Wu, D. Y. H., and Davidson, D. H. *Preschool in Three Cultures.* New Haven,
Conn.: Yale University Press, 1989.
A fascinating cross-cultural examination of early childhood education.

Yawkey, T. D., and Pelligrini, A. D. (Eds.). *Child's Play: Developmental and Applied.* Hillsdale, N.J.: Erlbaum, 1984.
Students wanting more insight into play behavior will find a wide assortment of ideas
and perspectives in this reader.

Yawkey, T. D., and Johnson, J. E. *Integrative Processes and Socialization: Early to Middle
Childhood.* New York: Erlbaum, 1988.
A good assortment of readings that pay special attention to the child's social world
entry.

Yoder, J., and Proctor, W. *The Self-Confident Child.* New York: Facts on File, 1988.
Readers will enjoy how the seeds of autonomy promote confidence in children.

Middle Childhood

C H A P T E R   O U T L I N E

WHAT DO YOU THINK?

▪ Trevor was disappointed that he didn't make the local Little League team, but he rationalized later that he now had more time to devote to his homework. Kristen broke one of her mother's favorite pieces of china but tried to blame her younger brother, who happened to be standing nearby. Such patterns of behavior in both these cases are called defense mechanisms, and they are often used when mistakes, failures, or conflicts create inner anxiety. As we'll see, by middle childhood defense mechanisms are used with surprising frequency and become intertwined with the youngster's developing personality. When finished with this chapter, you'll better understand why many children cover up, cop out, and tattle.

▪ Nearly every home in the United States has a television; its presence has changed family life more than any other technological innovation of the twentieth century. Today, the average television set is turned on for about 7 hours each day. We'd like you to think carefully about that statistic, mainly because it's now possible to break the activities of the modern family into three fairly equal parts: 7 hours of television viewing; 9 hours of work or school, including transportation; and 8 hours of sleep. In this chapter we'll examine television as part of the American lifestyle and its impact on children.

▪ They are inseparable during the day, call each other on the phone, fill each other in on the latest news, share jokes and gossip, and swap possessions. Having a good friend is one of life's greatest treasures. By middle childhood, youngsters' friendships become more close-knit and mutual, a marked contrast with the frequent disharmony punctuating their earlier relationships. What factors account for such changes? Are there differences in the establishment and maintenance of friendships? Read on to find the answers.

■ The path to moral maturity continues throughout childhood and adolescence. The journey at best will lead to a personalized set of moral standards and a true conscience to guide behavior. But as many children will tell you, it's hard always to be good, or at least, it seems so. Indeed, life's daily testing ground for honesty and good behavior awaits the child and has the potential for triggering fibs, white lies, and crossed fingers when the truth is requested. How are such behaviors explained and overcome, if at all? How does childhood moral behavior pave the way for more advanced and sophisticated forms of expression? We'll spend some time in this chapter answering such questions and discuss the major theories explaining this developing morality.

■ Unit One:

PHYSICAL DEVELOPMENT

Middle childhood, also referred to as the school years, is a developmental stage embracing ages 6 through 12. On the whole, physical developments during middle childhood are slow but steady. As a result, year-to-year changes in size and proportion are less noticeable than the pronounced developments of the preschooler or toddler. This gradual physical change persists until the adolescent growth spurt.

Because bodily changes are less marked and physical size increases slowly, children gain control of and perfect motor skills they have been unable to master in the past. As a result, overall coordination, balance, and refinement in physical activities show an increase at this time. Such accomplishments affect children's physical and psychological self-concepts, not to mention their degree of acceptance into the peer culture.

■ Physical Changes During Middle Childhood

Boys are taller than girls between the ages of 6 and 8; by age 9, differences in height are negligible; and past age 9, the average girl is taller than the average boy. This trend will persist until the adolescent growth spurt, when males will catch up and then surpass females in height. On the average, children will add about 2½ inches to their height each year. By age 12, children have usually attained approximately 90 percent of their adult height.

Although girls weigh less than boys at birth, they are equal by age 8. By age 9, girls surpass boys in weight. As with height, however, males surpass females in weight during the adolescent growth spurt. During middle childhood, youngsters typically add approximately 5 pounds to their weight each year. By age 12, the average child weighs 80 pounds.

School-age children can demonstrate greater amounts of balance and agility.

Remember that wide variations exist in overall rates of physical growth and development. This becomes especially apparent when we look at the wide range of height and weight differences among elementary school children. Charts, tables, and other forms of normative data describing the growth of the "average" child must not be overused. While normative data are useful for comparisons, each child's growth pattern is unique. This is as true during middle childhood as it is during other stages of growth. Gains in height and weight can be affected by numerous variables, including nutrition, hereditary influences, endocrine balance, health care, exercise, and socioeconomic status. The progress of individuals should be charted in relation to their own rates of growth, not purely against the mass data available in the developmental tables.

☐ Changes in Proportion and Appearance

Despite the slow and gradual nature of physical change during middle childhood, it is a time when most youngsters lose the baby contours characterizing earlier years (see Figure 7-1). This change in physical appearance, you will recall, began during the preschool years. Generally speaking, rounded and chubby physiques give way to leaner appearances as fat layers decrease in thickness and change in overall distribution.

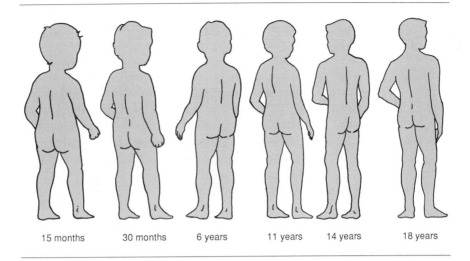

| 15 months | 30 months | 6 years | 11 years | 14 years | 18 years |

FIGURE 7-1 Changes in body proportions from infancy through adolescence. Note the changing physical appearance of the middle childhood youngster compared to other life stages.

By age 6, the trunk is almost twice as long and twice as wide as it was at birth. As the chest broadens and flattens, the ribs shift from a horizontal position to a more oblique one. Contributing to the leaner appearance is a rapid growth spurt of the arms and legs. Throughout middle childhood, there are no marked sex differences in body proportions.

The facial structure also undergoes change during middle childhood. For example, the forehead tends to flatten and the nose grows. As permanent teeth replace baby (deciduous) teeth, the jaw lengthens, becomes more prominent, and the face enlarges. The first tooth is usually lost sometime during the sixth year, giving rise to the characteristic toothless grin of middle childhood. Girls generally lose their baby teeth earlier than boys. By age 11 or 12, the permanent teeth of both boys and girls have rooted, with the exception of the second and third molars.

☐ Muscular, Skeletal, and Organ Development

MUSCLE GROWTH

Throughout middle childhood boys have considerably more muscle tissue than girls, and girls have more fat than boys. Muscle growth tends to be extremely rapid; the muscle changes not only in composition but also becomes more firmly attached to the bones. Despite these advances, the muscles remain immature in function at times, as reflected in children's frequent awkwardness and inefficiency in movement, erratic changes in tempo, inability to sit still for long, and fatigability. Developing muscles are also more susceptible to injury from overuse (consider the large numbers of young baseball players suffering from "Little League elbow"). The fitness and development of the muscles depends not only on good physical care, rest, and activity, but also on their structure and the use made of them. Proper muscle and nerve development provides increasing steadiness of movement, speed, strength, and endurance.

SKELETAL GROWTH

The skeleton continues to produce its centers of ossification (points at which ossification begins in a bone). Earlier, the child's bones were soft and spongy, consisting mostly of cartilage, but now minerals, particularly calcium and phosphorus, give hardness and rigidity to the bones. This process of bone development continues until the individual's twenties. The growth of the skeleton is frequently more rapid than the growth of muscles and ligaments. As a result, loose-jointed and gangling postures are not uncommon in middle childhood. Growth spurts are frequently accompanied by muscle pains. For many children, these "growing pains" are a very real phenomenon, caused by their developing muscles' attempts to catch up with their increased skeletal size.

Development of the Skeletal System

The skeletal system progresses through a series of changes as it approaches mature size and form (see Figure 7-2). Since the skeleton takes a long time to reach full maturity, it has characteristics that provide excellent examples of growth stages. At birth, for example, the skeleton lacks carpal, or wrist, bones and epiphyses, centers of ossification at the ends of the bones. Whereas the primary centers of ossification are located in the shafts of the bones, or diaphyses, the epiphyses will produce smaller bones at the ends of the long ones. This can be seen in the skeletal structure of the hand of the youngster during early childhood (A, B) and middle childhood (C). Growth of the long bones terminates when the epiphyses and diaphyses unite. This bone fusion occurs between early and late adolescence (D, E). When we speak of an individual's skeletal maturity, then, we are referring to the progress toward union of the epiphyses and the shaft of the bone.

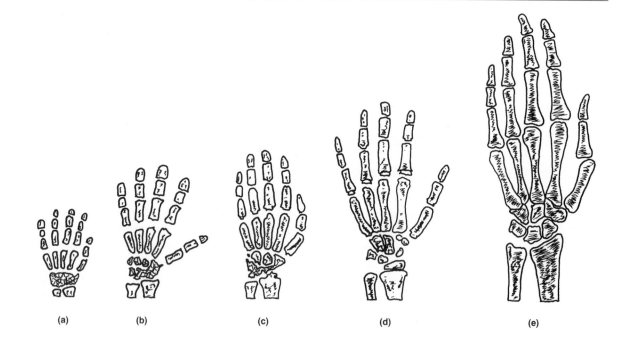

(a)   (b)   (c)   (d)   (e)

FIGURE 7-2

CIRCULATORY SYSTEM

The circulatory system grows at a slow pace, although by the school years, the weight of the heart has increased to approximately five times its birth weight. The heart is now smaller in proportion to body size than at any other point in the person's life. The heart rate, relatively high during the early years, declines gradually during the middle years, and the blood pressure rises. The average pulse rate is from 85 to 100 per minute, the blood pressure 95 to 108 systolic and 62 to 67 diastolic. The heart continues to grow until the end of the teenage years.

NERVOUS SYSTEM

The brain nears its mature size and weight during the years of middle childhood. Accompanying these increases in size and weight is an increase in head circumference. The average circumference grows from 20½ to 21 inches between the ages of 6 and 12. The spinal cord has quadrupled in weight by age 5 and will have increased eightfold by the end of the teenage years.

RESPIRATORY SYSTEM

The respiratory system also grows and changes. The weight of the lungs has doubled by 6 months, tripled by 1 year, and increased almost ten times by the end of middle childhood. Rates of respiration decrease, shifting from approximately 17 to 22 in middle childhood. In general, breathing becomes slower and deeper as the respiratory system works more economically and shows greater elasticity.

DIGESTIVE SYSTEM

The maturation of the digestive system is reflected in fewer upset stomachs at this age and the youngster's ability to digest a wider range of foods. In general, the body's activities of secretion, digestion, absorption, and excretion become more finely regulated. The school-age child can also retain foods for longer periods of time (which means that meals do not have to be served as often or as promptly), and calorie needs are not as great in relation to stomach size as they once were. Nutritional considerations are very important at this time since children need adequate protein and vitamins and not the "empty calories" offered in sweets, soft drinks, starches, and the like.

■ Motor-Skill Development

Driven by the Eriksonian desire to establish initiative and industry, the school-age child is eager to participate in a diversity of both gross- and fine-motor skills. The success that a child experiences in motor-skill activities depends on a number of factors, however, including rates of physical maturity, the cognitive skills needed to master the task, environmental opportunities to engage in physical activity, and degree of self-confidence. We must remember that children are still in the process of refining coordination abilities and mastering grace of movement. Improvement is gradual, and clumsiness and awkwardness can still be expected. The degree to which a motor skill is mastered may affect the child's sense of competence, achievement, and peer acceptance. Thus, beyond the physical dimensions of motor skills are implications for cognitive, personality, social, and emotional development.

The quest for motor-skill perfection continues throughout life.

Gross-motor-skill achievements are numerous during middle childhood. By age 6 most children can roller skate, skip rope, and begin to ride a bicycle. By age 7, most have perfected running and jumping skills as well as the basic movements necessary for catching, throwing, and hitting a baseball.

Fine-motor-skill coordination, while lagging behind gross-motor-skill development, matures at a gradual and steady pace. As children gain control of their arms, shoulders, wrists, and fingers, they become adept at a wide range of activities. For example, by the end of middle childhood, most youngsters are proficient in such fine-motor skills as building models. playing musical instruments, sewing, and creating detailed artwork. Advancements in fine-motor skills also have practical, everyday value. Children now have the physical ability to tie their shoelaces, fasten buttons, and dress themselves. They are more proficient in brushing their teeth, combing their hair, and bathing themselves. The simultaneous use of knife and fork at the dinner table is now possible. Advancements in fine-motor-skill development also enable elementary school children to refine their handwriting abilities (Kress, 1982; Williams and Stith, 1980).

The manner in which more advanced motor skills are mastered has received considerable research attention (Corbin, 1980; Williams, 1983; Schmidt, 1982; Ridenour, 1980). Most agree that motor-skill mastery entails the ability to refine coordination and develop overall accuracy of response toward the task at hand. This means the gradual elimination of unnecessary movements and expenditures of surplus energy to develop economy of performance. Other researchers, such as David Gallahue (1982), stress other factors behind motor-skill development, including agility, balance, speed, and power (see Table 7-1).

One experiment to study how the hand approaches and intercepts a moving target focused on children aged 5 to 11 years. Hand movement was analyzed in terms of speed and direction of the initial movement and speed and accuracy of the hand when near the target. It was found that the speed with which the hand initially moved was well planned based on the speed and trajectory of the moving target, but the direction in

TABLE 7-1 Components of Motor-Skill Fitness and Development Patterns

Motor Fitness Component	Common Tests	Specific Aspect Measured	Synthesis of Findings
Coordination	Cable jump	Gross body coordination	Year-by-year improvement with age in gross body coordination. Boys superior from age 6 on in eye-hand and eye-foot coordination.
	Hopping for accuracy	Gross body coordination	
	Skipping	Gross body coordination	
	Ball dribble	Eye-hand coordination	
	Foot dribble	Eye-hand coordination	
Balance	Beam walk	Dynamic balance	Year-by-year improvement with age. Girls often outperform boys, especially in dynamic balance activities until about age 8. Abilities similar thereafter.
	Stick balance	Static balance	
	One-foot stand	Static balance	
Speed	20-yd dash	Running speed	Year-by-year improvement with age. Boys and girls similar until age 6 or 7, at which time boys make more rapid improvements. Boys superior to girls at all ages.
	30-yd dash	Running speed	
Agility	Shuttle run	Running agility	Year-by-year improvement with age. Girls begin to level off after age 13. Boys continue to make improvements.
Power	Vertical jump	Leg strength and speed	Year-by-year improvement with age. Boys outperform girls at all age levels.
	Standing long jump	Leg strength and speed	
	Distance throw	Upper arm strength and speed	
	Velocity throw	Upper arm strength and speed	

From *Understanding Motor Development in Children* by David L. Gallahue. Copyright © 1982 by John Wiley & Sons, Inc. Reprinted by permission.

which the hand moved was not well planned. Eight-year-olds showed an increase in their ability to plan a movement, but 10-year-olds had developed the ability to control the ongoing movement (Bairstow, 1989).

As far as sex differences in motor-skill development are concerned, boys are usually ahead of girls in such areas as running, jumping, and throwing. However, such an edge, according to Corbin (1980), must be placed in proper perspective. The fact that, on the average, boys have more muscle tissue and greater levels of overall strength gives them an advantage in such comparisons. It must also be realized that in studies in which boys are compared with girls, the outcomes become factual data. The question that remains unanswered is whether these factual differences result from genetic variance or from practice, environmental opportunities, "sexism," or other social and cultural factors.

UNIT REVIEW

■ The child's physique becomes slimmer as fat decreases in thickness and changes in overall distribution.

■ The body's bones become hard and rigid; muscle growth is rapid; the circulatory system develops at a steady but slow pace; respiration becomes more economical; the brain reaches its mature size, but still is not fully functional; and the digestive system becomes more efficient.

- Both gross- and fine-motor skills advance during school years, although the latter proceed at slower rates.

- Numerous factors influence the course of motor-skill attainment. Although males typically surpass females in many motor-skill areas, such accomplishments must be placed into the proper perspective.

■ Unit Two:

MENTAL DEVELOPMENT

Advancing mental abilities coupled with school-learning experiences enable new cognitive accomplishments to take place. Words and symbols take on new meaning, and problem-solving abilities reflect greater levels of insight and deliberation. School-age children are also more adept at expressing themselves with more refined levels of linguistic proficiency.

Mental developments at this time are enhanced by the ability to deal systematically with many variables simultaneously. Speed and distance, for instance, can be successfully manipulated so that mathematical problems can be solved. Comprehending and manipulating multiple dimensions of the environment are regarded by many as critical to mental functioning (Case, 1980; Paris and Lindauer, 1982).

School-age children do have certain cognitive limitations, however. Although they are generally more systematic and objective than younger children are, they still cannot think abstractly. Abstract concepts remain completely outside the children's experience and cannot be grasped by analogy. Such cognitive accomplishments are only emerging and may not develop evenly in all content areas. Finally, there are significant differences in mental activity between younger and older school-age children (Feldman, 1980).

■ Piaget's Stages of Cognitive Development

□ Intuitive Thought

Between the ages of 4 and 7, children enter the stage of cognitive development known as *intuitive thought*. Intuitive thought, similar to preconceptual thought, is also a substage of the preoperational thought stage, which lasts from age 2 through age 7.

Children's thinking at this time is characterized by immediate perceptions and experiences rather than mental operations. Egocentrism still exists, but it often changes because of the children's cognitive advances. As a result, these new mental structures release children from a lower form of egocentrism but trap them in a higher form, namely, an egocentric orientation to symbols and the objects that they represent.

CENTERING Centering means concentrating on a single outstanding feature of an object and excluding its other characteristics. Centering is a distinct limitation of cognition, as the following examples demonstrate. Suppose a child is given two identical glasses filled with marbles. Undoubtedly, the youngster would acknowledge that each contained the same amount. However, if the marbles were presented in different-

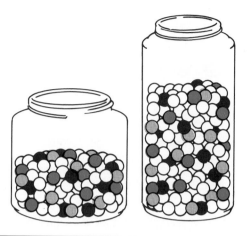

FIGURE 7-3 Centering means to focus on a single characteristic of an object while ignoring its other features. Although these two jars contain the same amount of beads, children in Piaget's intuitive thought stage will deny this fact. Rather than examining the size and shape of the containers, children are preoccupied with the different appearances of the beads.

sized containers, the typical child would deny that they held the same amount (Figure 7-3); centering has prevented the child from attending to all facets of the problem. In other words, attending to the problem's outstanding perceptual feature (level of marbles) caused other important features to be ignored (the different sizes of the two containers). At this stage of cognitive development, limited attending skills prevent the careful exploration of one's surroundings (Wadsworth, 1984; Furth, 1981).

TRANSDUCTIVE REASONING Children's thinking at this time is often *transductive,* that is, reasoning from particular to particular without seeking a generalization to connect them. Transductive reasoning is different from both *inductive* (particular to general) and *deductive* (general to particular) thought processes. Transductive reasoning may sometimes be correct, such as the statement "Mommy's got her hair up in curlers; she must be going out with Daddy tonight," but more often than not they are inaccurate.

Transductive reasoning is a good illustration of children's mental shortcomings during this time, particularly their tendency to perceive the world intuitively. In this, children look for some functional property to link objects or events and make statements of implication, even though there is no relationship between the events. Instead of seeking information systematically, children make inferences.

TRANSFORMATIONAL REASONING *Transformational reasoning* is often lacking during the intuitive thought phase. This type of reasoning means that when observing an event having a sequence of changes, a person can understand how one state is *transformed* into another. As an example, consider the following. You are asked to draw the sequential stages of a stick falling from a vertical, upright position to its final horizontal position. Depicting such a sequence of change is very easy for adults to do.

Children, however, have difficulty with this task. Instead of grasping the underlying concept of total change, they tend to restrict their attention to each successive state when it occurs. Such a cognitive strategy prevents them from understanding the con-

FIGURE 7-4 Younger children often have trouble understanding the principle of reversability. While they would agree that identical rows of checkers (a) contain the same amount, they are tricked by greater spacing (b) and contend that there must be more checkers in the longer arrangement.

cept of succession. Consequently, most children during this stage can depict only the initial and final positions of the stick. This also means that their reasoning is transductive. That is, their reasoning goes from particular to particular without seeking the generalization that connects the two.

REVERSIBILITY Another significant limitation in reasoning at this time is children's inability to reverse mental operations. *Reversibility* is defined as the ability to trace one's line of thinking back to where it originated. Piaget regarded reversibility as critical to advanced thinking.

The inability of children in middle childhood to reverse mental operations can be seen most clearly with numbers. More specifically, children have difficulty comprehending that for any unit, there is an opposite operation that can cancel it. For example, the number 2 can be added to the number 3 in order to arrive at 5. However, what isn't clearly understood is that 3 can be subtracted from 5 in order to return to the original 2.

Another example of the lack of reversibility is seen when presenting a child with two identical rows of checkers (Figure 7-4). When asked if both rows contain the same number of checkers, the child in the earlier stages usually agrees. However, the youngster gives a different response when the one row of checkers is spread out so that it occupies more space. Most children reason that because the row is now longer, it must contain more checkers. Such illogical thought is due to both centering and the inability to reverse mental operations. If the child could mentally return the row of checkers to its original length, the problem would have been solved.

☐ Concrete Operations

Concrete operations, occurring between the ages of 7 and 11, is Piaget's third stage of cognitive development. Children can think more logically about their environment and execute mental operations that they previously had to carry out physically. More importantly, concrete operations represents a stage when children reason consistently. To be sure, there are rules of logic that still remain elusive; however, children will no longer give the impression of comprehending something only to reveal moments later that they do not understand.

Elementary-school experiences will do much to activate cognitive abilities. For example, mathematical exercises, such as counting, manipulating, and sorting, will help develop the mental operations of reversibility, seriation, and conservation.

Projects in social studies, science, literature, and the like will teach procedures for systematically obtaining facts. Social cognition also increases as school-age children learn to appreciate the ideas, feelings, and opinions of others (Castaneda, Gibb, and McDermit, 1982; Jacobson and Bergman, 1980; Walsh, 1980).

Although children can understand concrete characteristics of objects, however, they still cannot understand abstractions. As the name of this stage suggests, children's thinking is restricted to the immediate and physical. One consequence of this is that youngsters cannot truly analyze their own thoughts or think about problems in the future. Although they can reason about what is, they cannot visualize what may be. In other words, their thinking is bound to the here and now.

CONSERVATION Children can now understand the concept of *conservation,* something that had created considerable confusion during earlier stages, and which means that the amount or quantity of matter remains the same, despite changes made in its outward, physical appearance. Thus, even though the distribution of matter changes, it nonetheless *conserves* its properties.

Before this stage, children had trouble understanding how the same matter could take on different appearances. Think back to the problems created by the same amount of marbles occupying different levels in different containers. The problem was caused

TABLE 7-2 Judging the Levels of the Child's Response on Piagetian Conservation Tasks

Conservation Tasks	Approximate Age Reached	Establish Equivalence	Transform or Rearrange	Conservation Question and Justification
Conservation of number: Number is not changed despite rearrangement of objects.	6–8			Will an ant have just as far to walk or...?
Conservation of length: The length of a string is unaffected by its shape or its displacement.	6–8			Are there the same number of red & green chips or...?
Conservation of liquid amount: The amount of liquid is not changed by the shape of the container.	6½–8½			Do the glasses have the same amount of water or...?
Conservation of substance (solid amount): The amount of substance does not change by changing its shape or by subdividing it.	7–9			Do you still have the same amount of clay?
Conservation of area: The area covered by a given number of two-dimensional objects is unaffected by their arrangements.	8–10	Grass / Garden	Is there still the same amount of "room" for planting or...? / Is there still the same amount of grass to eat or...?	
Conservation of weight: A clay ball weighs the same even when its shape is elongated or flattened.	9–11			Do the balls of clay still weigh the same or...?
Conservation of displacement of volume: The volume of water that is displaced by an object depends on the volume of the object and is independent of weight, shape, or position of the immersed object.	11–14			Will the water go up as high or...?

(Adapted from Labinowicz, 1980)

not only by centering but also because the youngster did not understand that matter could be altered in one outward dimension without changing the other dimensions. Likewise, children would agree that two balls of clay are equal when they have similar shapes. But if one ball were flattened, the child would reason that the flattened ball was larger because it was longer (or that the round ball had more clay because it was fatter). Although younger children can compare the like characteristics of two objects, they have difficulty accounting for physical changes.

In middle childhood, however, children can reason that matter remains the same despite changes in its outward appearance. They have thus learned to decenter as well as reverse their mental operations. That is, they understand that matter can still be restored to its original condition after changes have been made in its appearance. The ability to reverse mental operations enables youngsters to realize that the flattened ball of clay can be remolded into the original ball; a longer row of checkers can be restored to its original length; and marbles can be poured back into the first container to restore its original level. In such situations, children know that matter has been conserved despite the transformations. Moreover, children do not need to check this by repeating the operation.

The examples just described also demonstrate that there are different types of conservation, such as the conservation of mass or volume. Also, the different types of conservation are not mastered simultaneously. In this respect, the conservation of a particular property is not an all-or-nothing phenomenon, which means that children may have grasped conservation of number but not conservation of weight or volume. Table 7-2 displays the various types of conservation that exist and the approximate ages at which they are grasped by the child.

Demonstrating the Piagetian Principle of Conservation

Piaget's research studies investigating conservation abilities are relatively easy experiments to duplicate. To observe the developmental stages through which this principle is attained, children between approximately 6 to 10 years of age should be tested.

For conservation of substance, begin by showing the child two balls of clay, asking if the two contain identical amounts. The best way to ask this is "Does this one have more?", "Does this one have more?", or "Do they both have the same?" This is preferred over "Which one has more?" or "Are they the same?" If the child says they do contain the same amount, roll one of the balls into the shape of a sausage and then ask if they still contain the same amount. According to Piaget, children under 6 are most likely to respond that the amounts of clay now differ, reasoning that because the "sausage shape" occupies more space, it must therefore contain more clay. (You might employ younger subjects and record their reactions for comparison purposes.) Between ages 7 and 9, the typical response is that each still contains the same amount,

an indication that the law of conversation has been grasped.

Once you have tested for conservation of substance, consider examining for conservation of liquid. Start with two identical glasses and pour an equal amount of liquid into both. Do they appear the same to your subjects? If so, change the size or shape of one of the containers and fill them again. Are your subjects fooled by the appearance (level) of the liquid? Have they failed to decenter? Between ages 6½ and 8½, this facet of conservation should be mastered, although individual differences must be considered.

Do your subjects follow the prescribed sequence of conservation described in this chapter? If some of your subjects mastered liquid but not substance conservation, why do you think this is so? Does "coaching" your younger subjects affect the outcome of your experiment? Asking yourself questions like these illustrates some of the many dimensions that conservation has, not to mention why this facet of children's thinking has attracted the attention of child psychologists for years.

CLASSIFICATION Another cognitive advancement children make in middle childhood is in *classification.* You will recall that younger children had difficulty understanding the concepts of subclasses, classes, and class inclusion. In particular, children were confused when they were shown four red checkers and two black checkers and asked whether there were more red or more plastic checkers. Compared with their younger counterparts, school-age children do not perceive a class of objects as a location where all the elements must lie. Instead, they understand that the same element can exist in two classes at the same time. Children now know that all the checkers are plastic, and so there are more plastic checkers because there are six of them and only four red checkers. School-age youngsters thus come to recognize three classes of checkers: the red, black, and the inclusive class of plastic checkers. This type of reasoning is an important part of mental functioning, as it contributes to organization and classification abilities. In addition, it enables youngsters to move beyond a singular viewpoint and consider all features of objects and events (McCabe et al., 1982; Cameron and Goard, 1982; Winer, 1980). Furthermore, researchers have found that class inclusion is consistently easier for children to understand than are other concrete operational tasks (Chapman and Lindenberger, 1989).

SERIATION Ordering objects according to size is known as *seriation.* Seriation poses problems to children who are not yet in the concrete operations stage. Most children acquire the ability to seriate by age 7 or 8.

To test seriation, children are usually given sticks of varying lengths and asked to arrange them from the smallest to the biggest. Before they reach age 7 or 8, their confusion is obvious. Children between the ages of 5 and 6, for instance, align the tops of the sticks but pay little attention to the bottom of the sticks. Their ability to grasp more than one relationship is definitely limited. Younger children also try to solve this problem by using intuition and trial-and-error behavior. Older youngsters, however, order the sticks without using trial-and-error behavior. Most use methodical approaches, such as searching for the biggest stick, then the next biggest, and so on until the task is complete. Furthermore, they understand the task before they begin and have created a subjective ordering of the series so that it can be successfully constructed (Wadsworth, 1984; Gallagher and Reid, 1981).

■ Concept Development

It is during the school years that children refine and elaborate their concepts. They also learn to mentally connect objects or events having similar properties. Consequently, their environment becomes organized and meaningful rather than confusing. Many researchers believe that the organization that advanced concepts requires is a major feature of developing cognition (see Matlin, 1983; Wessells, 1982; Smith and Medin, 1981; Houston, 1981).

Developing perceptual abilities enable concepts to mature. And maturation is enabled by children's developing attention and attending skills. Unlike younger children, youngsters in middle childhood pay more attention to environmental events. Furthermore, they are better at examining the important features of a situation and ignoring what is irrelevant. Children of this age also know that their attention can be influenced by numerous variables, such as distractions and their motivation to learn (Miller and Weiss, 1981a; Miller and Zalenski, 1982).

Children's perception also has an economical quality. Youngsters learn to detect those features that distinguish one object from another and those characteristics of objects that remain constant. Similar to children performing conservation tasks, youngsters demonstrating economical perception know that clay rolled into different shapes still is the same amount or that the same quantity of liquid can reach different levels depending on the container's size.

☐ Size and Shape Concepts

School-age children show a greater awareness of size and shape concepts and how they relate to the environment. In particular, youngsters have a better understanding of size in relation to distance, and they can recognize forms in changed or strange surroundings. Research shows that children can now detect shapes having ambiguous contours (see Abravanel, 1982). These advancements show that children have become more selective and insightful in their overall environmental interpretations. Being able to maintain perceptual constancies also helps youngsters perceive shapes and sizes as constant (Goldstein, 1980).

☐ Spatial Concepts

Older children have a fairly good understanding of how objects can occupy different spatial positions and relationships with other objects. By roughly age 7, youngsters demonstrate an understanding of perspective and of how objects may look under different viewing conditions. Before this age, children do not consider such variables as the angle or distance from which they view objects. Rather, their spatial concepts are limited to an egocentric visual perspective.

Challenging classroom environments enhance learning skills including those related to concept formation.

☐ Relational Concepts

In middle childhood, children can correctly reason about relational concepts, such as left or right. Relational concepts created considerable confusion earlier, but now children can understand their own left and right perspective, as well as the perspective of those individuals opposite them. This is a noteworthy accomplishment, as it is maintained that the perception of left–right is harder to learn than are other relational orientations, such as front–back and up–down. Consider the difficulty of this concept the next time you are placed in a situation requiring a relational orientation. Teaching youngsters how to tie their shoes, for example, is difficult, especially when standing opposite the child.

☐ Quantity Concepts

Children's understanding of quantity concepts also advances in middle childhood. Numbers are gradually understood to the point that they can be manipulated and recognized as parts, wholes, and units. Most children of this age will be able to grasp the durability of numbers and not be restricted to a functional and nonverbal understanding of them (Kamii, 1981b, 1982; Ginsburg, 1982).

By age 8, most children can add, subtract, multiply, divide, and deal with simple fractions. These number concepts can also be applied to a wide range of measurements, such as weight, height, length, and volume. Money concepts also advance at this time. Before middle childhood, the identification of money was limited to pennies, nickels, and dimes. School-aged children, though, understand the value of coins and can manipulate fairly complex money combinations.

☐ Time Concepts

School-age children demonstrate an understanding of clock time as well as a knowledge of the days of the week, months, and seasons. Children can also reflect on what they did yesterday and anticipate what they're going to do tomorrow, another indication of developing time concepts. However, certain time concepts remain elusive, including clock time for younger children (Friedman and Laycock, 1989), and an appreciation of dates or historical chronology in general. These will not develop until the latter stages of middle childhood.

In a unique study of time orientations, 96 Canadian children between the ages of 4 and 12 were asked to speak for a doll in dialogues with an experimenter who spoke for another doll. The experimenter looked for speech acts in the dialogues that would commit the "dolls" to some *future* action. Each subject included at least one such speech act, but only the older subjects actually used the word *promise* to reassure the hearer of their commitment (Astington, 1988).

■ Development of Problem-Solving Abilities

The successful application of cognitive facilities to problems is one of the distinguishing features of the mature mind. With age, problem-solving abilities improve. In time, these abilities will become more systematic and reflect a distinct and orderly sequence.

Advanced thinking skills can be applied to many dimensions of life.

This methodical approach first entails the definition of the problem, particularly a clarification of its nature and the solution sought. Next a strategy, or set of strategies, must be developed in order to reach the solution. One, of course, must then implement the decided course of action and apply whatever internal and external resources are needed. Finally, effective problem solving requires monitoring and evaluating the progress made toward reaching the solution (Wessells, 1982; Hayes, 1981). A fairly recent investigation into children's ability to distinguish between *know-think* and *know-guess* in a problem-solving situation demonstrated that this ability also increases as children age (Moore, Bryant, and Farrow, 1989).

A number of reasons account for the child's overall improvement in problem-solving abilities. Among the obvious are the cognitive advancements described in this chapter in addition to the curriculum challenges of the elementary school. Problem-solving abilities are also enhanced by the child's work habits in general. As children grow older, most learn to not only develop persistence and concentration, but also independence when working on problems (Stipek, 1983; Fisher et al., 1980).

Advancements in problem-solving abilities are also a reflection of developing memory abilities and metacognition as a whole. As we discussed in Chapter 5, metacognition refers to the application of some cognitive process to a selected cognitive task. As far as memory is concerned, children become more adept at organizing, searching for, and retrieving the information that has been encoded or placed in memory storage (Horoben and Acredolo, 1989). Also developing are metacognitive skills designed to encourage remembering, called "metamemory" skills by some cognitive psychologists. Examples of these skills are rehearsal and **elaboration**, the latter being the technique of expanding verbal or visual material to increase the number of ways that it may be retrieved. Other noteworthy metacognitive advancements include the growing ability to recognize one's efforts as the primary cause of the problem's outcome and the ability to judge how accurately one is actually performing on a given problem (Kail and Hagen, 1982; Pressley, 1982; McGilly and Siegler, 1989). For example, to study metacognition, children in third and fifth grade classes were given an experimental curriculum designed to increase their awareness and use of effective reading strategies. Compared with children in the control group, who were not given the special curriculum, the experimental group made significant gains in metacognition (Cross and Paris, 1988).

Moreover, competency and proficiency in problem-solving situations are influenced by the youngster's intrinsic motivation. *Intrinsic motivation* means that the child undertakes an activity, such as problem solving, for the rewards or pleasures derived from that particular activity. While intrinsic motivation was limited earlier in childhood, it increases as youngsters grow older. Children learn to enjoy problems or situations that are challenging and responsive to their actions. In their quest for mastery of the environment, children develop an ever-increasing interest in that which can be explored or investigated (Gottfried, 1983; Deci and Ryan, 1980).

□ Cognitive Styles

There are significant differences and variations in how children evaluate problems. The characteristic ways in which information is organized and solutions to problems are found are referred to as *cognitive style.* Put another way, cognitive style represents the general pattern of behavior that an individual applies to cognitive tasks (Kogan, 1983).

Cognitive styles vary from child to child. Some children may examine the minute details of stimulus objects, establishing what is referred to as an analytic style. Others employ a superordinate style and look for shared attributes among objects. A functional-relational style means that a group of objects or events are linked because they have some sort of interactional value. Finally, functional-locational orientation represents a cognitive style in which classification is based on a shared location.

To examine these modes of cognitive style, children between the ages of 6 and 11 were presented with a series of pictures in a set (Figure 7-5) and were asked to determine which two figures were alike or in some way related. Older children were more likely to use superordinate or analytic styles. With the superordinate style, for example, the two shirts rather than the zebra would be paired in picture set *b*; the analytic style would mean pairing the watch and ruler in picture set *a* because both are used for measurement. Younger children, usually aged 4 to 6, have a tendency to classify the

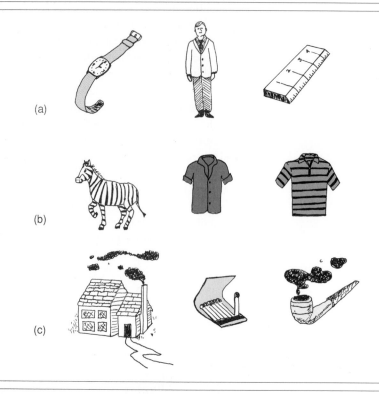

FIGURE 7-5 Picture sets designed to test children's cognitive styles. Subjects were asked to select two pictures in each group that are similar in some way.

(From Kagan et al., 1964)

pictures with a functional-relational style. For example, pairings are made because the match lights the pipe in picture set *c* or the man wears the watch in picture set *a* (Kagan et al., 1964).

☐ Conceptual Tempos: Impulsivity Versus Reflectivity

In addition to cognitive style, children differ in their conceptual tempos, the manner in which they evaluate and act upon a problem. *Impulsive* children usually accept and hurriedly report the first idea that they can generate, giving little consideration or thought to its accuracy. Others are *reflective* in their deliberations, devoting longer periods of time considering various aspects of a hypothesis. Related to the foregoing discussion, reflective, attentive children are more apt to be analytic in their cognitive style than impulsive youngsters.

Our knowledge of impulsivity and reflectivity has been greatly enhanced by Jerome Kagan and his colleagues (Kagan, 1965, 1966; Kagan et al., 1964). In a typical test designed to measure conceptual tempo, children are shown pictures from the *Matching Familiar Figures* test (Figure 7-6). In the test, children are asked to match a standard figure with one of six variants. The subjects' scores are based on the amount of time it takes them to select the appropriate figure and the number of errors they make in the process. Generally, the faster the children make their decisions, the more mistakes they are likely to make. Older children typically take longer to offer their first

FIGURE 7-6 Test items designed to measure impulsiveness-reflectivity. Subjects are asked to select from each group of six variants one that is identical to the uppermost standard figure.

(From Kagan, 1965)

answer and, as a result, tend to make fewer errors. Those children exhibiting reflective behavior in this test appear to be reflective in other situations. For example, they have a tendency to wait for longer periods of time in answering questions, make fewer incorrect guesses on reading tests, and make fewer errors in reading textual material.

Other studies have generally supported Kagan's research and found other interesting dimensions of conceptual tempo. One investigation (Toner, Holstein, and Hetherington, 1977) revealed that conceptual tempos may be measured to some degree in children as young as three years of age. Another (Cohen, Schleser, and Meyers, 1981) disclosed that among younger school-age children, those classified as reflective were more apt to understand the Piagetian principle of conservation. Impulsive children were more likely to react in a preoperational fashion.

One possible cause of a child's reflective attitude is anxiety over making a mistake, although research results conflict on this topic. Some feel that if children have a strong fear of error, they may foster reflective attitudes. These children usually want to be correct and will try to avoid whatever mistakes they can. Conversely, for reasons not clearly understood, impulsive children do not appear to become upset over their mistakes and therefore respond quickly. Research has revealed that American schoolchildren become more reflective with age than do children of other cultures. This may be true because the American value system encourages children to avoid mistakes and the humiliation of being wrong, which may explain why young children become excessively cautious and inhibited (Kagan, 1971; Duryea and Glover, 1982).

■ Language Development

Although rates of vocabulary acquisition begin to taper off after the preschool years, overall psycholinguistic development continues. By the time they are 6 years old, children know virtually all of the letters in the alphabet, recognize the printed form of a handful of words, and understand concrete terms. School-age children also increase

How to Help Children Become Better Thinkers

There is much that adults can do to foster the growth and development of the youngster's problem-solving skills and thinking abilities during middle childhood. Since intrinsic motivation is an important facet of mental development, children need mental challenges so that curiosity, mastery of the environment, and a sense of competency can be nurtured. When working on problems, children also need to learn the merits of a deliberate, methodical approach. Adults should encourage the youngster to reflect on the material at hand and think about the accuracy and quality of answers before they are given (Lepper, 1983; Stipek, 1983).

Adults should also encourage children to develop as much independence as possible in problem-solving situations. Patience needs to be generated on the adult's part to allow for trial-and-error learning. Jumping in and solving the problem for the child may produce the answer but frequently promotes dependency on the adult as well. Moreover, it robs the child of benefiting from a mistake or experimenting with multiple problem-solving approaches. Adult feedback, encouragement, and praise help to strengthen desired problem-solving strategies, not to mention the child's motivation to succeed (Deci and Ryan, 1982; Pittman, Boggiano, and Rubble, 1983).

Overall thinking abilities may be groomed so that school-age children more deeply question and analyze the learning material at hand. While children need to acquire the cognitive advancements described in this chapter, they also need to develop a capacity for genuine thought, not a mindless monologue of facts. In short, children need to learn how to think. According to James Alvino (1983) certain philosophical questions can be directed toward children to help them think and rethink ideas. When asked, these questions should convey honest interest in the child's reasoning powers, not adult smugness or arrogance. They should also serve to sow the seeds for later analytical reasoning skills. As "grown-up" as these questions sound, they have been implemented into the curriculum of thousands of elementary school systems. They emerged from the Institute of Philosophy for Children, a project founded by Matthew Lippman of Montclair State College. The questions and the explanation of what each query demands of the child's thought processes are:

1. *"Why?"* This requests an explanation of the basis for the youngster's response.

2. *"If that is so, what follows?"* Such a question requires that the child elaborate, extrapolate, and draw a valid inference, be it hypothetical or causal.

3. *"Aren't you assuming that . . . ?"* Here the adult is asking the child to explain the premises upon which the statement or argument may be based.

4. *"How do you know that?"* This calls for more information from the child, a source for the information given, or for the youngster's explanation of his or her line of reasoning.

5. *"Is the point you are making that . . . ?"* With this question, the youngster is asked to confirm the adult's comprehension of the main point.

6. *"Can I summarize your point as . . . ?"* This is similar to the previous question but requires the child to confirm the adult's restatement or condensation of the main point.

7. *"Is what you mean to say that . . . ?"* This rephrasing requires children to interpret their own statements and be certain of their meaning.

8. *"What is your reason for saying that?"* This is basically a request for the rationale behind making a judgment as well as the justification for it.

9. *"Doesn't what you say presuppose that . . . ?"* Here the adult is pointing out assumptions that may be hidden in the child's argument. Furthermore, this type of question requests that children explain the validity of their assumptions.

10. *"What do you mean when using that word?"* Such a question asks for the precise meanings and contextual usage of words.

11. *"Is it possible that . . . ?"* Here the adult is offering other possibilities and pointing out possible contradictions and inconsistencies in the child's argument.

12. *"Are there other ways of looking at it?"* This question calls for alternative perspectives and an examination of the child's objectivity and impartiality.

13. *"How else can we view this matter?"* Such a query places an emphasis on open-mindedness and mental flexibility. It also gives the child a chance to be creative.

their ability to use words as a vehicle of expression. Combined with cognitive skills, language is the means by which youngsters present evidence and support their perceptions of and ideas about the world.

Vocabulary and Semantic Development

School-age children's linguistic progress is remarkable. Consider their vocabulary acquisition. After their first year, children know only a few words. The number of words in youngsters' vocabulary by age 3, though, soars to approximately 900. About 2,600 words are known by age 6, and by the time children enter the sixth grade, they have a reading vocabulary of about 50,000 words. This large vocabulary is the result not only of growing linguistic competence, but also of cognitive growth, mainly the memory skills required to process and remember new words (Kail, 1984; Schank, 1982).

Although word acquisition rates are rapid, children's comprehension of word meaning and the relationships among words is slow to develop. The abstract qualities of many words lie beyond the cognitive capacities of school-age youngsters. Thus, the physical qualities of words are restricted in much the same way that the physical aspects of the environment are limited cognitively.

With age, children learn more about word definitions, and they become more aware of abstract relationships among words. In addition, they are able to name an agent of an action. For instance, if asked "What burns?" they can supply an appropriate answer. Word pairs, such as tall-short, before-after, and big-little, are also understood. Rather than just learning the part of the meaning that was common to both words, as they once did, youngsters now grasp the part of the meaning that distinguishes the two.

Syntactic Development

The use of incomplete syntactic structures declines during the school years, whereas the use of compound and complex sentences increases. At this time, the basic syntactic structure of children's sentences resembles adult grammar, as they have learned the

Linguistic ability rapidly improves during the middle years of childhood.

three basic rules of complex sentence formulation. First, they now recognize that a sentence has a noun phrase and a verb phrase. Second, they know that a noun phrase consists of an article and a noun. Finally, they know that a verb phrase includes a verb and a noun phrase. Although they have yet to learn other rules, they can use these three to fabricate sentences (G. Miller, 1981).

Children's syntax at this time also reveals a significant increase in the number of adjectives, adverbs, and conjunctions that are used. Their understanding of the use of proper names, pronouns, and prepositions also deepens. These advancements set the stage for the structural and functional changes in syntax that emerge during the school years. As they learn more about sentence structure, children find more ways to express different functions.

Understanding the concept of syntax is difficult, largely because of the complex language rules of English. In addition to comprehending the semantical features of words, children must understand sentence construction. This complex process, especially the relationship of language, memory, and thought, has always attracted considerable research attention (see Howard, 1983; Reed, 1982; G. Miller, 1981, and for a review of the literature on cognition, including syntactical and semantic models of thought, see Hunt, 1989).

☐ Pragmatics

In the last chapter we stated that children must learn the pragmatics of a language. Recall that pragmatics refers to how language is used in social contexts. As children overcome their egocentrism in solving problems, they also transcend egocentric forms of communication. When speaking, school-age children become increasingly more adept at taking their listeners into account.

Beyond the changes in pragmatics discussed earlier, such as the greater use of gestures, pauses, and facial expressions, children are now more skilled at taking turns during conversations. They also are better at adapting information to fit the listener's needs. Moreover, many can adopt the listener's point of view if the situation calls for it.

Other advances in pragmatics include a more meaningful exchange of questions and answers. Although younger children do ask questions, they often encounter problems in listening to the answers (see Patterson and Kister, 1981). School-age youngsters, on the other hand, use questions to acquire desired information. Fabricating a question, asking it, and listening for the answer all are an important social exchange that improves with age.

Children sometimes learn the pragmatic qualities of language through rote memory. This appears to be especially true for expressives and declaratives. Early in life, youngsters are taught that it is polite to say "Thank you," "Please," or "I'm sorry." Such expressives place no obligations on the speaker or listener, but they are usually regarded as important to harmonious social relations. While they may or may not reflect the speaker's feelings about someone or something, they display the feeling expected by a particular society in a particular situation. As a result, expressives are often difficult to explain or justify to young children (many parents do not even attempt to). Consequently, the parents' concern may often be purely social: "Tell Grandmother how much you missed her," or "Thank your brother for his gift." It isn't until the school years and even later that children understand why such expressions are used (Clark and Clark, 1977).

Language Dialects

Not everyone in our society speaks the same language or uses the same grammatical style or slang. Instead, there are variations in language, referred to as *dialects*. Dialects have at their roots the same general language but differ in their expressions and verbal details.

Dialectical differences are caused by several factors. Among them is the profession or occupation of the person speaking. Individuals in different careers not only converse about different topics, but they also use different words to represent the same thing. For instance, the words *forecast, prognosis,* and *prediction* all have similar meanings. However, depending on the speaker's occupation, one meaning is related to the weather, another to medicine, and the last one to science (Dale, 1976).

Another factor affecting dialectical differences is age. This is especially evident in the so-called generation gap. One age group may coin new words or phrases and contrive new meanings for existing words and phrases. Among parents, especially, the failure to understand such terminology (or, worse yet, to use outdated terminology) may create a distance between young and old. The tendency of speakers to continue using the language they learned when young preserves these age differences, even though the language in general may have changed since then.

Geography is another factor influencing dialects. Certain words may be difficult to understand when listening to geographical dialect differences. For instance, many of us had trouble getting used to the southern dialect used by President Jimmy Carter. Often, different words are used to refer to the same object in different geographical locations. For instance, the words *hotcake, pancake, flapjack,* and *griddle cake* each are used in different geographical regions. Likewise, *grinder* is the designation for a large sandwich in the Northeast, but elsewhere it is called a *hoagie, sub, wedge,* or *hero.*

Another factor influencing dialectical differences is social class. When a society is stratified, such as in the United States, social-class differences in language become more obvious. Often, the middle and upper classes use carefully organized and highly structured sentences, whereas the lower classes use syntactically simple and short sentences. Furthermore, although the middle and upper classes often elaborate on their meaning, the lower classes usually do not use such embellishment. Thus, the former may say "Please be quiet because your father is sleeping," while the latter might simply say "Be quiet."

There is considerable interest in whether lower-class language patterns are deficient in comparison with those of the middle and upper classes (see Feagans and Farran, 1982). Many researchers feel that persons living in lower-class environments merely have different linguistic patterns, rather than language skills deficiencies and that they use speech adapted to their respective social class. Their language is not only fluent and functional but also complete, with its own vocabulary and rules of grammar (Schacter and Strage, 1982; Hilliard and Vaughn-Scott, 1982).

Black English is a good illustration of the foregoing. Because not all black people speak in this language style, *black English* refers to a social dialect, not a racial one, and is used mostly by persons in the lower socioeconomic classes. Although black English differs from standard English, it is highly structured and meaningful. A misunderstanding of the grammatical patterns of the disadvantaged blacks' speech frequently leads many nonblacks to conclude that it has no true vocabulary or grammar, an erroneous belief (White, 1984; Hale, 1981; Folb, 1980).

Although black English is the speech for thousands of children and adults alike, it also, unfortunately, represents one of the nation's biggest educational headaches.

Black English is an example of a language style currently under the scrutiny of psycholinguists.

Youngsters speaking black English often have difficulty learning to read, as books are written in standard English. Teachers make matters worse if their attitude toward black English is negative. Such behaviors may lower the child's self-concept, as self-expectations are influenced strongly by the expectations of others. In addition, black children are tested for skills in cognitive development that often require forms of mental awareness derived from white middle-class experiences. When they fail, many conclude that they are inferior in overall cognitive development (Hale, 1981; Hilliard and Vaughn-Scott, 1982; Freeman, 1982).

In years to come, the status of black English in education will be a recurring theme in the literature. Obviously, educators must decide how best to structure the classroom for those children not speaking standard English. The public also needs to become aware of black English as a whole and to recognize that although black English differs from standard English in form, this does not mean that it is, therefore, deficient (Markham, 1984; Smitherman, 1981; Smith, 1980).

UNIT REVIEW

- Piaget's stages of intuitive thought and concrete operations span the school years. This unit explored the cognitive developments of centering, transductive reasoning, transformational reasoning, reversability, conservation, classification, and seriation.

- Children continue to refine their mental concepts. We studied growth in size and shape, spatial, relational, quantity, and time concepts.

- Problem-solving abilities rapidly improve at this time. The impact of cognitive styles, mainly impulsivity and reflectivity, was discussed.

■ Language growth is especially noticeable in vocabulary, semantic, syntax, and pragmatic development. This unit concluded with a discussion of language dialects and the variations of a spoken language.

■ Unit Three:

PERSONALITY AND SOCIAL DEVELOPMENT

Middle childhood is an active period for personality and social development. At this time, the interaction between the child and society expands and becomes more complex, whether it be in peer group relations, school activities, sports, or family activities. From these social relationships, youngsters learn that they must adjust their behavior to meet society's numerous expectations and demands.

Social relations enable children to gain more insight into themselves and their developing personalities. Through interactions with others and inferences from their personal experiences, they gain a sense of personal awareness. Some self-awareness was evident earlier, but it was often based on youngsters' physical qualities or possessions. Now, youngsters include other characteristics of themselves in their self-appraisals, such as how they are perceived by others and the abilities they possess (Perry and Bussey, 1984; Harter, 1983; Damon and Hart, 1982).

This suggests that mental development blends once again with personality and social functions. That is, their social cognition allows children to perceive themselves and others more accurately. Their developing social cognition thus paves the way for more skillful interpersonal relations. Among other social advancements, friendships acquire more depth and meaning, and youngsters come to appreciate the thoughts and sensitivities of others. Maturing social perceptions are apparent in other modes of expression, too. For example, children learn to distinguish situations requiring cooperation or competition. Youngsters also become able to detect people who are kind or unkind, selfish or unselfish, trusted or distrusted.

Developmental Tasks of Middle Childhood

1. Learning physical skills necessary for ordinary games.

2. Building wholesome attitudes toward oneself as a growing organism.

3. Learning to get along with age-mates.

4. Learning an appropriate masculine or feminine social role.

5. Developing fundamental skills in reading, writing, and calculating.

6. Developing concepts necessary for everyday living.

7. Developing conscience, morality, and a scale of values.

8. Achieving personal independence.

9. Developing attitudes toward social groups and institutions.

(Havighurst, 1972, 1980)

■ Emotional Development

Greater emotional maturity accompanies middle childhood. This means that there is a change from helplessness to independence and self-sufficiency. Emotional maturity also means the acquisition of emotional flexibility and greater emotional differentiation. Compared with infants and their limited forms of emotional expression, school-age children's range of emotions becomes more specific, diverse, and sophisticated.

Greater emotional differentiation allows children to express many feelings. An important task for children is learning the appropriate and inappropriate times for expressing emotions. Healthy emotional expression means not feeling guilty about what one feels but, rather, conveying it in a socially acceptable way. The acceptable degree of emotional control and channels for expressing emotion reflect children's developmental state and the emotional norms of their society (Williams and Stith, 1980).

Sex-role stereotyping also affects the nature and quality of emotional expression. Though all youngsters need emotional outlets, sex-role stereotyping often prevents this. In our society, boys are often taught not to cry or show fear, and girls are often criticized if they are physically aggressive. Boys who do cry are often labeled sissies, and aggressive girls are called tomboys. This type of sex-role stereotyping prevents youngsters from using their whole emotional repertoire.

☐ Fear and Anxiety

During middle childhood there is a decline in fears related to body safety (such as sickness and injury) and in the fear of dogs, noises, darkness, and storms. However, there is no significant decline in fears of supernatural forces, such as ghosts and witches. Most of the new fears emerging at this time are related to school and family, in accordance with children's expanding social boundaries. For example, test anxiety may develop in the school-aged child. Test anxious children also report more fears and general worries than children who do not experience test anxiety, and they also worry about negative evaluations (Beidel and Turner, 1988).

Fears of ridicule by parents, teachers, and friends also increases, as do fears of parental rejection and disapproval. Many school-age children also report fearing that their parents will die (Beale and Baskin, 1983). Some researchers believe that girls are more fearful than boys, that fourth and fifth graders are more fearful than sixth graders, and that rural children are more fearful than urban children (Davidson, White, Smith, and Poppen, 1989).

Living in a nuclear age has given rise to a new fear: that of thermonuclear war. Although more prevalent among adolescents and adults, children also fear nuclear war. Children as young as 5 or 6 know to some degree the consequences of such a disaster. Children of this age are frightened about what they hear on the news, even though they don't really understand it. By the school years, though, they are aware that a nuclear war could kill them and separate them from their families. By later childhood, many youngsters understand that people are trying to prevent nuclear wars. Many also start a denial process at this time; that is, they try not to think about it. Compounding this fear at all ages is that many adults do not mention—or want to discuss—nuclear war with children (Yudkin, 1984; Escalona, 1982).

Anger and Aggression

Anger and aggression continue to be expressed physically throughout middle childhood. Such outbursts as kicking, shoving, and hitting are common. But children also learn that anger can be channeled in other ways. For instance, they can verbally express it through insults, arguing, or swearing. Anger can also be buried and expressed through passive and sullen means, such as pouting or hateful stares.

Youngsters of this age tend to express greater amounts of *hostile aggression.* Recall that hostile aggression is intended to hurt another person. Hostile aggression often is used when persons feel intentionally hurt, threatened, or unjustly accused. There is an obvious parallel here with developing cognitive abilities. Before expressing hostile aggression, youngsters must think about the intentions or motives of another. This is something younger children have difficulty doing. Many researchers (e.g., Eron, 1980) regard aggressiveness as a learned form of behavior, and they have found that males are more aggressive than females (Maccoby and Jacklin, 1980), and expect both less guilt and less parental disapproval for aggression than do females (Perry, Perry, and Weiss, 1989). Also, aggressive boys tend to be persistent in direct confrontation and physical attacks through middle childhood and into early adolescence, while girls gradually show an increase in social aggression and ostracism in female-female conflicts (Cairns, Cairns, Neckerman, Ferguson et al., 1989).

Happiness and Humor

A wide variety of situations elicit happiness, including feelings of acceptance, the pleasures of accomplishment, the satisfaction of curiosity, or the development of new abilities. Curiosity about and mastery of the elementary school environment also creates pleasure (see Gottfried, 1983; Deci and Ryan, 1982). Being with friends and loved ones, surprises, treasured gifts and possessions, or the challenges of doing something new are other sources of joy and happiness.

Closely related to happiness is humor. Children especially enjoy jokes. Earlier, preschoolers enjoyed hearing jokes, but their understanding of them was limited. To understand jokes, youngsters need advanced cognitive facilities to appreciate such elements as subtleties, punch lines, and puns and incongruities. Only now are most of these elements appreciated. Because of their reliance on many cognitive ingredients, jokes and children's humor as a whole are regarded as an excellent reflection of their developing minds (McGhee, 1980; McGhee and Goldstein, 1983a, 1983b).

Love

Because love has many abstract qualities, children cannot fully understand it until their cognitive facilities are mature. However, youngsters learned about love early in life, particularly when they formed bonds of attachment with their parents. It is usually from these attachments that youngsters create early feelings of self-worth and acceptance. Those children who receive their parents' love usually come to accept themselves as important objects of affection to others. In addition, those who have received love and affection are capable of giving them in return (Orthner, 1981; Dinnage, 1980).

The expression of love changes during childhood. Preschoolers usually express love physically, such as through kissing and hugging. This is also true of school-age

Children learn to share love and affection in many different ways.

children, but they have also learned that love can be expressed through other channels, such as sharing and talking. Leaving behind an egocentric point of view and developing sensitivity toward others help their expression of love gradually to mature. Children love not only their family and friends but animals as well. Once again, masculine and feminine roles often dictate how this behavior is expressed. Should it be deemed unmasculine for a male to exhibit tenderness, then tenderness may not become part of a boy's expression of love. Thus, the sex roles that children acquire will be an important determinant of their definition and expression of love (F. Cox, 1984).

■ Moral Development

Morality is the conscious adoption of standards related to right and wrong. Although such codes of conduct differ from culture to culture, every society does adhere to certain behavioral standards. Early in childhood, these standards are established when youngsters learn that certain behaviors are labeled as good and others as bad. With age and experience, these standards of morality come to include empathy, as well as complex ideas, values, and beliefs (Hoffman, 1989; Carroll and Rest, 1982).

To appreciate the many dimensions of morality, including guilt, shame, lying, discipline, and religion, insight must be gained into how morality develops throughout childhood. Jean Piaget and Lawrence Kohlberg both attempted to explain the developmental aspects of morality.

□ Jean Piaget's Theory

Jean Piaget stated that morality is a system of rules transmitted by adults to children. Gradually, youngsters come to respect these standards of conduct. At the heart of Piaget's theory is the notion that children's understanding of right and wrong is molded by their cognitive awareness (Piaget, 1932).

To understand how morality is shaped by cognitive awareness, Piaget created pairs of stories and asked children to decide which of the two were "naughtier." In one set of stories, for example, a boy named John is called to dinner. As he opens the dining room door, it hits a tray holding 15 cups. All of the cups are broken from the door's impact. In the other story, a boy named Henry wants to get some jam from a cupboard while his mother is out of the house. He reaches for the jam while climbing on a chair, but in the process knocks over a cup and breaks it.

In the follow-up conversations, Piaget found that young children felt that the first story was "naughtier," simply because of the greater number of cups broken. The fact that the youngster unintentionally broke the cups did not influence the younger subjects. They were more concerned with the property value of the mistake. The older youngsters, though, regarded the second story as worse because they had begun to judge right and wrong behavior on the basis of the actors' motives.

Piaget's conversations with children led him to devise a three-stage theory of moral development. During the *premoral stage* (before age 5), children have a limited awareness of rules and the reasons for them. Some moral judgments begin in the stage called *moral realism* (generally from ages 5 to 10). In this stage, youngsters learn rules from parents but do not yet understand the reasons for them. Instead, the rules are regarded as sacred and untouchable. Children also feel that punishment compensates for their transgressions.

During the stage of *moral relativism* (beginning after age 10), children become aware of both the meanings of rules and the reasons for them. Now rules are coming to be regarded as a product of mutual consent and respect. Rules are also understood in relation to the principles they uphold. Moreover, youngsters come to realize the seriousness of a wrongdoing if the punishment fits the act. Justice is based on an "eye for an eye, and a tooth for a tooth," so that the pain felt by the transgressor must be proportional to the pain inflicted on others. Children in this stage believe that punishment should put things into perspective. Thus when they hear about the boy who breaks his little brother's toy, older children suggest that the boy give the brother one of his own toys (reciprocity) or pay to have it fixed (restitution). Conversely, younger children generally say that the boy should be deprived of his own toys for a week. Suffice it to say, children's moral reasoning, at this time, contains a social, cooperative, logical quality.

Piaget's research has stimulated the thinking of many researchers. Over the years, his notion that morality is closely linked to cognition has gained support (see Krebs and Gillmore, 1982). Researchers have also found that younger children do judge wrongdoings on the basis of the harm done rather than on the intent or motivations of the offender (see Surber, 1982). Yet to some, Piaget's research leaves many questions unanswered. Some maintain that Piaget overlooked the cultural and socioeconomic differences among children. Others criticize Piaget's notion that children's morality is formed by preadolescence. These critics argue that morality is a long and elaborate process and that it is not achieved until adulthood (Colby et al., 1983).

☐ Lawrence Kohlberg's Theory

Lawrence Kohlberg offered a more detailed explanation of the development of morality. Like Piaget, Kohlberg maintains that morality is achieved in a series of stages. Both acknowledge that children's successive stages of morality originate in the mental restructuring of their experiences. Kohlberg, however, suggests that moral development is a more complex and longer process than Piaget saw it as being. Kohlberg also sees the various stages as closely related. He believes that development is characterized by increasing differentiation and that each stage takes into account everything that transpired in the previous stages. Over time, the moral distinctions of which children had previously been only dimly aware are organized into a more comprehensive structure (Kohlberg, 1976, 1981a, 1981b, 1986).

Kohlberg's theory consists of six stages divided into three levels, the preconventional level (ages 0 to 9), the conventional level (ages 9 to 15), and the postconventional moral reasoning level (age 16 and onward). At the *preconventional level,* children have little awareness of socially acceptable moral behavior, but after two stages, they start to show signs of moral behavior. In stage 1, *obedience and punishment orientation,* youngsters start to follow rules in order to avoid punishment. True rule awareness has not yet been established; instead, their moral conduct is based largely on fear associated with rule violation. Kohlberg, like Piaget, also maintains that the seriousness of a violation at this time depends on the magnitude of the wrongdoing. Table 7-3 charts Kohlberg's stages of moral development.

During the *naively egoistic orientation,* stage 2, children reason that a tangible reward usually follows their doing something right. A type of reciprocity starts to surface here; that is, youngsters will do the right thing not only to satisfy their own needs but also to satisfy the needs of others. If the latter is the case, children reason that they will receive some sort of favor in return. ("You scratch my back and I'll scratch yours.")

As children approach adolescence, they reach the *conventional level.* At this level they learn the nature of authority, not only in the family, but also in society in general. During the third stage, called the *good boy–nice girl orientation,* there is a considerable degree of conformity. Children know that they must obey the rules in order to win praise or approval from others. During this phase, they also usually identify with emotionally important persons. Conforming behavior eventually leads to an internal awareness of rules and behavior, which in turn leads to a sense of respect. During the fourth stage, *authority-maintaining orientation,* children's identification shifts to institutions, such as church or school. Children seek to avoid the guilt and shame brought on by criticism from authoritarian figures.

TABLE 7-3 **Lawrence Kohlberg's Moral Development Stages**

Age	Stage	Example of Behavior
0–9	Preconventional level	
	1. Obedience and punishment orientation	Children follow rules so as to avoid punishment.
	2. Naively egoistic orientation	Children follow rules so as to earn rewards or favors.
10–15	Conventional level	
	3. Good boy–nice girl orientation	Children conform to rules so as to avoid social disapproval or rejection.
	4. Authority-maintaining orientation	Children want to avoid criticism from persons of authority.
16–	Postconventional Level	
	5. Contractual legalistic orientation	People select moral principles to live by.
	6. Universal ethical principle orientation	People behave in a way that respects the dignity of all.

The *postconventional level* is the last level of Kohlberg's theory. During this stage, individuals' morality reaches maturity. In the fifth stage, *contractual legalistic orientation,* individuals choose the moral principles to guide their behavior, being careful not to violate the rights and wills of others. In the sixth and final stage, *universal ethical principle orientation,* the emergence of a true conscience enables individuals to uphold behavior that respects the dignity of all humans. However, this last stage is difficult to distinguish from the preceding one. Even Kohlberg himself questioned whether stages 5 and 6 can be separated. And not everyone reaches the postconventional level of morality, just as not everyone attains Piaget's stage of formal operations (Colby et al., 1983).

A CRITIQUE OF KOHLBERG'S THEORY

Lawrence Kohlberg's theory of moral development has been influential among contemporary psychologists. It has attracted the attention of researchers and has stimulated much discussion of morality and how it is acquired. Most psychologists agree with Kohlberg's contention that cognitive developments underlie the progression of morality from level to level (Walker, 1982, 1989; Saltzstein, 1983; Fischer, 1983; Krebs and Gillmore, 1982; Page, 1981).

Some feel, however, that Kohlberg's sequence hypothesis is too restrictive. Others, such as Hoffman (1980) and Keller, Eckensberger, and von Rosen (1989), propose that morality may not necessarily progress in stages. There is also evidence that the stages represent alternative types of moral maturity rather than a progressive sequence. Related to this, it has been suggested that a careful examination must be made of moral judgment and moral behavior at all stages. More specifically, there may be a weak relationship between what one says and how one behaves (Kupfersmid and Wonderly, 1980; Maccoby, 1980; Blasi, 1980). Another criticism is that moral development is difficult to assess, particularly the moral dilemmas posed by Kohlberg (Rest, 1986).

Kohlberg's theory does appear to have cross-cultural applications. An examination of the moral responses of subjects from Taiwan and Mexico, for example, indicated that their overall development roughly parallels the maturation rate of American subjects (Kohlberg, 1969). Subjects from India and other nations also follow the chronology of Kohlberg's stages (Snarey, 1987; Parikh, 1980; Edwards, 1982).

In regard to Kohlberg's theory, one should recognize that morality is influenced by other factors, including the individual's uncertainty over how to resolve a moral conflict and his or her ego identity status. Exposure to moral arguments and involvement in role-playing exercises appear to advance the individual's level of moral reasoning. And on the whole, subjects tend to prefer moral reasoning that is more sophisticated than their own. Individuals' emotions also help determine their moral judgments, an area not examined by Kohlberg. Each of these factors appears to be important to the individual's overall level of moral reasoning (Krebs and Gilmore, 1982; Rest, 1981, 1983; Shweder, 1981).

Kohlberg's theory of moral development does not account for sex differences. Carol Gilligan (1982) maintains that females use different reasoning than males do when confronted with moral issues. More specifically, females tend to be concerned with relationships and responsibilities, whereas males typically center their responses on rights and rules. Because Kohlberg's stages of moral development are primarily structured on the basis of rules, females often fail to reach the zenith of moral functioning. Gilligan contends that the current sequence is therefore an inaccurate model by which to assess females' moral development.

☐ Alternative Perspectives on Morality

Our discussion has focused on the cognitive-developmental aspects of moral reasoning. Because conscience does not exist in a vacuum, there have been other attempts to define and explore morality. For example, Freudian theory regards moral standards as being the largely unconscious products of irrational motives and the need to keep antisocial impulses from consciousness. Because of this, Freudians focus on the guilt that results when these standards are transgressed.

Behaviorist theorists, on the other hand, emphasize the importance of the environment when examining morality. Behaviorists define morality on the basis of particular acts and avoidances that are learned through the use of rewards and punishments. Finally, the social learning school of thought also emphasizes the environment. However, rather than focusing on the role of rewards and punishments, social learning researchers stress the importance of imitating adults to children's developing morality. Children's moral behavior is thus regarded as an emulation of adults' behavior.

■ Family Influences on the Developing Child

The fact that children now attend school on a full-time basis, have greater interaction with their peers, and display heightened levels of independence places the family in a new perspective. Children still need and rely very much on their parents, but their boundaries with the outside world expand. As a result, their social relationships with other adults broaden considerably, including, for example, interactions with teachers, den mothers, Little League coaches, or summer camp leaders.

The negotiation of new social boundaries and the parents' reactions to the youngsters' strivings for independence earmark these years as especially challenging. Fired by the Eriksonian desire of industry, most children want to spend greater amounts of time away from the family, something that threatens many parents. Parents who feel threat-

A favorable home climate promotes a child's sense of trust and security.

ened need to be assured that this is a completely normal phase of child development and that they will remain special and unique in the wake of these social strivings. It is interesting to note that amidst these desires for social independence, many school-age children have a tendency to periodically slip back to dependency, although usually in private and on their own terms. This age also marks the time when many want to spend more time alone doing private things or being secretive about what they do, both within and away from the family.

Their greater interactions with others enables children to bring back to home an abundance of social experiences, whether it be tales about school, sports exploits, or news from the neighborhood. Their increasing powers of social cognition also enable them to compare and contrast their home environment with those around them. As a result, what they see is weighed against what they are allowed to do, a comparison likely to breed a fair amount of questions and possible disagreements with parents (how many parents have heard "Everyone else in the neighborhood does it, why can't I?"). Parental values and standards are also tested when children bring home ideas, language, and attitudes different from those taught at home.

☐ Experiencing a Favorable Home Environment

Youngsters need to experience a favorable home climate throughout all of childhood, but this is especially true during the school years. Children unquestionably need the support and guidance of parents as they seek to meet the challenges of this age. This is as true for achieving personal independence as it is for other facets of growth, such as developing a sense of morality, establishing healthy relations with siblings, learning appropriate sex roles, or building wholesome attitudes toward oneself.

Favorable home environments are those capable of providing warmth and acceptance to children. Positive home climates usually employ consistent measures of discipline, encourage competence, and are responsive to the child's growing needs. Healthy patterns of child development also hinge on the degree to which parents love, communicate, and seek to understand the needs of their offspring. Given these qualities, children are apt to become emotionally stable, cooperative, and happy. The unloved or rejected child, on the other hand, often becomes resentful, quarrelsome, lonely, and insecure (Evoy, 1982).

Charles Thomas and Virginia Rudolph (1983) stress the importance of nurturance and loving support in parent-child relations. They contend that among other outcomes, children from nurturing families are more likely to communicate more openly, be more honest with others, and adjust more readily to life's demands than children from non-nurturing homes. In addition, children from nurturing families know that they will be listened to by their parents when they talk and are regarded as special individuals. Furthermore, they know that their ideas will not be devalued.

A harmonious family life and a positive emotional climate are also evident in those homes sharing responsibility. Dolores Curran (1984) maintains that shared responsibility is a critical ingredient behind healthy family relations. By sharing responsibility, children learn to believe in their capacity to make a contribution. They also learn that each person counts in the family and makes a difference. Curran maintains that shared responsibility includes, but goes beyond, everyday chores and obligations. Responsibility also encompasses, for example, responsiveness to other family members' feelings or getting along with, and looking after, one another. Shared responsibility also has a tendency to breed other positive traits, such as affirmation, respect, and trust.

☐ The Family and Television

The contemporary child rarely escapes the clutches of television programming since a television is available in nearly every home in America. Television has changed family life more than any other technological innovation of the twentieth century. Remarkably, families often plan their schedules to accommodate television, sometimes even scheduling meals and social activities around or in front of the tube (Liebert, Sprafkin, and Davidson, 1982).

Perhaps a few statistics will illustrate how widespread television viewing was in the 1980s. For the family as a whole, the average television is turned on each day for a period of six to seven hours. For children under age 6, the average viewing time per day is about two and one-half hours. From age 8 until early adolescence, viewing time increases to almost four hours per day and then it begins to level off. By the end of high school, the average individual will have devoted about 12,000 hours to school but 15,000 hours to television. For the child born in the 1990s, more hours will be spent watching television than any other single activity besides sleep (Liebert, Sprafkin, and Davidson, 1982; Steinberg, 1980; Moody, 1980).

Think carefully about these statistics, particularly in relation to our analysis of the contemporary family. These figures mean that the general activity of the American household can now be divided each day into three fairly equal parts: six to seven hours of television viewing, nine hours of work or school, including transportation back and forth, and eight hours of sleep. To say that television has become part of the American lifestyle is an understatement.

TELEVISED VIOLENCE Few issues related to television have aroused more concern or sparked more debate than televised violence and its effects on children. Among psychologists and educators, the study of televised violence has been a hotbed of research activity for almost 20 years. Research activity among contemporary investigators indicates that this interest will persist for years to come.

Television programming for children contains a considerable amount of violence. Cartoons are invariably the guiltiest programming culprit (see Cramer and Mechem, 1982). Moreover, most research findings contend that televised violence has increased markedly in the last decade. For example, one investigation revealed that in the course of one program hour there is an average of nine acts of physical aggression and almost eight instances of verbal aggression (Williams, Zabrack, and Joy, 1982). It has been found that boys pay more visual attention to high action and high violence animated programs than do girls, who pay more attention to low action (Alvarez, Huston, Wright, and Kerkman, 1988).

What effect does viewing violence have on children's behavior? There are currently two major theories designed to answer this question. The *social learning theory of television viewing* maintains that children will imitate aggressive behavior when they are exposed to it on television. The *catharsis theory of television viewing* proposes that watching aggressive behavior on television provides a vicarious outlet for the viewer's own aggressiveness. Televised aggression thus enables viewers to drain off, or discharge, their aggressive tendencies.

Of the two theories, the social learning approach is the more popular. Support for it has been steadily increasing, and many today believe that there is a significant relationship between viewing televised violence and behaving aggressively. This was the main finding, for example, of a 10-year study conducted by the National Institute of Mental Health (1982).

Jerome Singer and his colleagues (Singer, Singer, and Rapaczynski, 1984) supplied us with some of the details of televised violence and how it affects children's aggressiveness. The team of researchers studied 63 children over a period of six years. The children were 4 when the television and family environment data were first obtained and 9 when the final data were collected.

The research revealed a link between 9-year-olds' suspicions or fearful view of the world and a history of watching the most violent television programs. The data also indicated that children's later aggression can be predicted by a combination of frequent viewing of violent television programs, preschool television viewing, and a family that emphasizes physical discipline and the assertion of power. Preschool children from homes with a high level of parental cultural involvement but with long exposure to violent television programs were more aggressive in their day-care centers or nursery schools.

Televised violence has other effects on the viewer. Seeing repeated acts of violence has a tendency to slowly desensitize the viewer to aggression. Over time, even one's level of physiological arousal toward violence declines. This indicates that individuals have become hardened to violence and aggression. Rather than emotionally sensitive to it, they are instead jaded (Thomas, 1982; Geen, 1981).

BENEFITS OF TELEVISION In spite of its potential harmful effects, television can pass along a wealth of information and positive experiences to viewers. Advancements made in educational television have proven to be beneficial. Television programming such as this can enhance a number of developmental areas, including language abilities, concept formation, reading skills, and prosocial development (see Singer, Singer, Desmond, and Hirsch, 1988; Tangney, 1988; Singer and Singer, 1983; Rice, 1983; Liebert, Sprafkin and Davidson, 1982). In other spheres, television is a visual masterpiece that, when not overused, can be a doorway to wholesome entertainment and a source of relaxation.

With such positive potential, television looms as a powerful teacher that has the capability of enhancing the quality of life for the individual as well as society. It is the most powerful communication tool that we have and without question it is here to stay. It becomes important, therefore, to continually examine the role that television has in our lives. As Alice Honig (1983a) aptly states, television can be used for violence, for crass commercialism, or for instruction and for enhancing and enriching lives. The imperatives are clear. We must take charge of television and harness its potential rather than have television control our lives. In so doing, television can become an ally for all concerned, not an adversary.

Children and Television: Promoting Healthy Viewing Habits

Adults can do much to help children develop healthy television viewing habits. Most experts maintain that controlling the amount of time children watch television and the kinds of programming they watch is a step in the right direction. More specific recommendations and suggestions include the following:

Familiarize yourself with children's television. To evaluate children's television programming and provide guidance to youngsters, become familiar with the range of shows available. Sample a cross-section of programs and critique each. A single Saturday morning should be an eye-opener.

Balance a child's television needs against other needs. A legitimate concern among adults is that television often detracts from other important facets of childhood. Balance television viewing against these other important activities, including play, reading, exploring, socializing, family interaction, and studying.

Decide on a schedule for television viewing. Monitor the amount of time children spend in front of the television set. Establish daily schedules specifying the hours of the morning, afternoon, or evening when television viewing is permissible. Many experts today feel that between 10 and 15 hours of television viewing per week is acceptable.

Select good television programs for children. Quality programming is available to children if one takes the time to look for it. Educational television, in particular, offers a multitude of programs for youngsters of different ages. Steer children toward suitable documentaries, music, and classic stories.

Help children distinguish between make-believe and real life. Young children, especially preschoolers, have difficulty understanding that the fantasy depicted on television cannot happen in real life. As a result, many are convinced of the extraordinary powers of their favorite superheroes, for example. Many also perceive the violence depicted in cartoons as acceptable and amusing since the victim always gets up and comes back for more. Try to help children differentiate between fantasy and fact and see the world as it really is.

Observe how children's behavior is affected by television. Too much television can overstimulate the child and cause mood shifts, including general irritability. Excessive amounts of television can also cause eyestrain and headaches. These negative reactions underscore the need to monitor television viewing time.

Express disapproval of television violence and other negative elements. Children need to know that im-portant adults in their lives do not like violence. They should learn that there are many ways to reach a desired goal in life other than through a path of senseless destruction. In addition, speak out against television programs that downgrade members of a societal group or depict unfair sexual stereotypes.

Seek to expose the deception in television advertisements. Products advertised on television are not always as glamorous or perfect as they appear to be. Children must learn that through advertising strategies they sometimes can be misled about toys or food, for instance. A farily recent study demonstrated that preventive intervention to improve children's discrimination of the persuasive tactics of television advertising was extremely effective (Peterson and Lewis, 1988).

Share television viewing time with children. More families need to share what television brings into their lives. Adults should arrange their time so that programs suitable for family viewing can be shared with the children. Moreover, adults can play instrumental roles in explaining sensitive programming topics. For example, children need understanding and support to deal with themes involving hatred, tragedy, loss, or sorrow.

Follow up on the positive qualities of television programming. Adults should seek to expand and integrate into children's lives those positive lessons reaped from television. This applies to educational instruction as well as to important life lessons portrayed in other programming endeavors.

(Adapted from Honig, 1983a; Kelley, 1983; Moody, 1980)

■ School Influences on the Developing Child

Entrance into school brings children into a new and complex social environment. Most children eagerly anticipate attending elementary school and each year look forward to the classroom's developmental challenges. Not only will the cognitive domains of the child be influenced, but numerous other parameters will be influenced as well. For example, youngsters will have to adjust to many new routines and demands, task-oriented behavior, conformity to authority, and impulse control, to name but a few areas. The adjustment from kindergarten to first grade even includes changes in physiological arousal, such as a rise in blood pressure and increased heart rate (Soussigan, Koch, and Montagner, 1988).

☐ The Influence of the Teacher

Because children are still very dependent on adults, many become attached to or are awed by their teacher. This is not only because the teacher acts in many respects as a substitute parent but because the teacher conveys to the child the assurance that adult authority is trustworthy and that the school environment is safe, stimulating, and satisfying. In fulfilling these and other needs, teachers begin to exert strong influences on the child's behavior. In the process of instruction and the manner in which it is delivered, teachers transmit their personal attitudes and beliefs to their pupils.

Teacher behaviors affect pupil performance. On the whole, teachers are effective when they demonstrate warmth, understanding, support, and compassion toward their students. Ineffective teachers frequently operate overly restrictive classrooms, are dependent, foster feelings of limited self-worth, and exhibit lack of self-control. Compared to effective teachers, ineffective instructors do not feel accepting of themselves and others.

Successful elementary school teachers have a tendency to exhibit generosity in their appraisals of behavior and are warm, empathetic, and friendly in their social relationships. Also, successful educators indicate a strong preference for nondirective classroom procedures. Conversely, unsuccessful teachers are less favorable in their expressed opinions of pupils, less satisfactory in emotional adjustment, and more critical and restrictive in their appraisals of the behavior and motives of others. Teachers who exhibit genuineness, warmth, and friendliness in their dealings with children, rather than punitive and authoritarian techniques, also encourage favorable behavior, particularly constructive attitudes, conscientious attitudes toward schoolwork, and less aggressive behavior.

Although the main task and responsibiliy is to teach academic subjects, the teacher is also responsible, to an extent, for the psychological well-being of pupils. And so it is that teacher behavior directly relates to the student's self-concept and peer acceptance. Teachers appear to be in a prime position to serve as a role model, as well as a reinforcer, of children's social interaction. The examples they set, the tone they establish for peer relations, and the feedback they give to children are important influences. However, children appear to be more reluctant about being told about matters of personal preference. In one study, children in first, third, and fifth grades were tested to determine if they distinguished among matters of fact versus matters of personal preference. They were all more likely to consider it legitimate for teachers to teach standard, "correct" answers in areas such as physical laws, but not in areas of personal preference (Nicholls and Thorkildsen, 1988).

☐ Methods of Classroom Control

Children are also exposed to different types of classroom control, from traditional types of leadership to more liberal approaches. In general, three types of classroom control have been identified: democratic, authoritarian, and laissez-faire. Numerous researchers have sought to focus on the effectiveness of each of these methods of classroom control. Let us try to uncover the major findings focusing on this topic.

Authoritarian leadership has a tendency to produce two major types of social atmospheres, aggressive or apathetic. Studies have shown that there are higher incidences of irritability and aggressiveness toward fellow group members in atmospheres created by authoritarian and laissez-faire leadership than in democratic climates. In addition, authoritarian teachers have a tendency to foster high interpersonal tension. Authoritarian classes are also often lower in task-related suggestions by the members; whenever authoritarian leaders are absent for short periods, work motivation among students has a tendency to decline.

Students taught by democratic and laissez-faire teachers often make more frequent requests for attention and approval than do students in authoritarian classrooms. Although interpersonal friendliness does not usually vary as a result of teaching

The classroom presents numerous developmental challenges.

styles, democratic and laissez-faire classes seem to have more of a "we" feeling than their authoritarian counterparts. Finally, the absence of democratic teachers for short periods of time does not appear to affect the task-oriented efforts of the class.

Deciding which particular type of classroom climate and control to establish may be one of the most difficult chores for the beginning teacher. Certainly one's formal education and one's likes and dislikes of various approaches, to some extent, will determine the emotional climate. So, too, will the relationship between the children's temperamental characteristics and the teacher's reactions to these behaviors.

Most experts agree that no general prescription can tell teachers what choices they should make in terms of classroom control. A teacher who has a strong personality can, to some degree, persuade students to subscribe to his or her values. But such a teacher may also arouse feelings of opposition in students whose values do not concur with the teacher's. Classroom harmony usually depends on the match between the values, temperaments, and the personalities of the children and those of the teacher.

■ Peer Group Influences on the Developing Child

Being a member of a peer group is important to school-age children. As they spend more time with their friends, children learn more about cooperation and getting along with others. The ability to consider others, especially their needs and sensitivities, enables friendships to flourish (Ladd, 1988; Berndt and Ladd, 1989).

Williard Hartup's (1984) analysis of peer relations during middle childhood suggests that interactions intensify at this time. Preschoolers establish the communication and coordination necessary for cooperation and competition with other children, and schoolchildren begin new interactions. New content (such as issues related to sex roles) begin to impinge on child-child interactions, but it is integrated into normative structures which may be traced back to early childhood.

Hartup also maintained that children must begin to construct equitable interactions with others and sustain them across situations and across time. Children must also learn a wider range of accommodations to their age-mates. Learning how to deal with their peers is itself one of the greatest challenges confronting children between their sixth and twelfth years.

Like those of early childhood, peer groups during the school years are very selective. Similar sex, age, social status, and race are often the criteria for acceptance. Some peer groups require physical attractiveness for membership (Schofield and Francis, 1982; Schofield and Whitley, 1983; Vaughn and Langlois, 1983; Schofield, 1981; Finkelstein and Haskins, 1983).

TABLE 7-4 Significant Social Developments during Middle Childhood

Age	Social Developments
6	Egocentrism, still present at this time, inhibits meaningful social relationships. Interactions with other children in the family are often competitive but vary according to the child's ordinal position in the family. Although friendships are sometimes erratic, 6-year-olds often establish a best friend, with whom they spend a good deal of time. Movement toward same-sex friends is most prevalent.
7	Increased sense of self and heightened sensitivity to others enhances social relationships. However, this heightened sensitivity makes the youngster acutely aware of shortcomings, failures, and criticisms. Consequently, brooding, feelings of shame, and negativism may be common. Advanced interpersonal skills allow the 7-year-old to become a better listener; growing evidence of empathy and understanding of the needs of others is present.
8	Noticeable separation between the sexes, even to the point where the opposite sex is excluded from group activities. However, the 8-year-old's attitude toward members of the opposite sex is a mixture of attraction and hostility, a pattern that will be seen again in early adolescence. At this age, most children are friendly and cooperative. Also there is social curiosity about other people, evidenced by the child's attentiveness to adult conversations and eagerness to observe at grown-up gatherings. Noticeable division of leaders and followers.
9	Heightened self-confidence and emotional security bolster social relationships. Close friendships started earlier are strengthened but a dichotomy of the sexes still exists. Much overt hostility between boys and girls. Organized games and other structured social activities begin to emerge.
10	Organized social activities continue to attract the attention of the child, and a diversity of interests emerge. Most 10-year-olds do not resent spending time with family rather than friends. A new admiration and respect for one's parents emerge. Interpersonal relationships and communication skills continue to increase.
11	A new level of maturity (the plateau between childhood and adolescence) frequently requires a redefinition of one's sense of self, as well as one's social relationships. Choices of friendships are now based on mutuality of interest and temperament rather than on proximity. Although friendships grow in number at this time, one or several intimate relationships are established. Interest in the opposite sex begins, although girls are likely to be more interested and vocal about their interest than boys.

(Adapted from Elkind, 1978)

Peer groups often meet certain needs at this time, such as a desire to be away from adults or to be in the company of like-minded individuals. Peer groups also select leaders and followers. Although such a division was apparent among groups of younger children, it is more consistently expressed by school-age children (see, for example, Stright and French, 1988; Berndt and Ladd, 1989). In comparing children 6 to 13 years of age, older children are more flexible in adopting social strategies (e.g., cooperation) than are younger ones (Schmidt, Ollendick, and Stanowicz, 1988). Table 7-4, on the preceding page, displays this facet of peer group interaction along with other significant social developments.

The peer group is composed of youngsters who are popular and unpopular. Popularity is not determined by the quantity of time youngsters spend together but can be traced to other sources. Popular children, for instance, are bright, friendly, and cooperative. On the other hand, unpopular children are often overly aggressive and display inappropriate behavior. Many unpopular children lack those social cognition skills necessary for harmonious social interaction, while popular children have good group-entry skills; in other words, popular children can enter groups without disturbing the activity at hand. They also possess more of the personality traits judged desirable by their friends (Berndt and Ladd, 1989; Shantz, 1988; Hartup, 1983; Dodge et al., 1983; Putallaz and Wasserman, 1989).

The consequences of peer rejection or unpopularity are worth noting. Children who are continually rejected or deemed unpopular often face negative consequences. For some, the loneliness accompanying rejection and unpopularity persists into later life, even adulthood. Others may have even more serious problems, such as neurosis or delinquent behavior (Hojat, 1982; Muehlbauer and Dodder, 1983; Rubenstein and Shaver, 1982).

☐ The Development of Children's Friendships

Finding a friend and sharing his or her experiences is indeed valuable. Although egocentrism hampered earlier friendships, those forming at this time are closer and more meaningful. It is from childhood friendships that individuals learn how to create and sustain friendships throughout life. As Sharon Brehm (1985) observes, a foundation of friendship behaviors and attitudes needs to be established so that one will always have friends, in good times as well as bad.

The fact that their egocentrism has weakened enables children to forgo some of their own personal desires and to adopt the viewpoints of others. Greater sensitivity to others, empathy, and cooperation permit close ties among friends. Better conflict-resolution skills, more meaningful exchanges of information, and a more systematic exploration of differences are regarded as necessary in order to establish meaningful friendships (Parker and Gottman, 1983; McGuire and Weisz, 1982; Furman and Bierman, 1983).

Robert Selman (1981) proposed four stages of friendship. The *playmateship stage* covers the preschool years, when friendships are greatly affected by the child's feelings at the moment, the physical presence of the other youngster, and the availability of toys or other resources. During the early school years, friendship are characterized by what Selman called the *one-way assistance stage.* At this time, a friend is someone who fills another person's need, such as providing toys or playtime companionship.

During the later school years, a stage known as *fair-weather cooperation* begins. Friendships now become more mutual and reciprocal. However, arguments and dis-

The influence of the peer group is unmistakable during the school years.

agreements still exist and can even disrupt the relationship. By late childhood or early adolescence, friendships contain more expressions of mutuality and supportive understanding. This final stage of friendships is called *intimate and mutually shared relationships* and is supported in the literature (Youniss, 1980; Newcomb and Brady, 1982; Howes, 1983; K. Rubin, 1980; Diaz and Berndt, 1982).

Youngsters usually form same-sex friendships, a pattern evident in early childhood as well. These same-sex friendships have several variations. Though both sexes focus their friendships on shared interests and activities, boys are typically more competitive and girls more cooperative. Boys tend to deemphasize the intimacy or closeness of their friendships. They are also more oriented to groups, whereas girls are drawn to one-to-one friendships. Moreover, girls are usually more expressive to one another than boys are (Wright, 1982; Reisman, 1981; Dickens and Perlman, 1981; K. Rubin, 1980). Girls' appreciation of the emotional bond that friendships offer spills over into the adolescent years (Wheeler, Reis, and Nezlek, 1983; Caldwell and Peplau, 1982; Richey and Richey, 1980; Coleman, 1980).

International Lifespan Development

■ CHILDREN'S FRIENDSHIPS IN SWEDEN AND ISRAEL

Are there differences in the friendships of children from other lands? Do they contain the same behavioral ingredients as American children's friendships do? Ann Tietjen's (1982) study of Swedish children contains some interesting parallels. She interviewed and observed 72 second and third graders and found that the males had contact with larger groups of friends than the females did. The

girls, though, spent more time in friendship dyads and with their families. As children grew older, they moved toward fewer and more intensive friendships with schoolmates, although this was more pronounced among females. This was accompanied by a gradual movement away from family members. Children from families without fathers had smaller peer networks than did youngsters from intact families. The former also spent less time with their families.

Ruth Sherabany and her associates (1981) studied Israeli children's friendships. Once again, there are parallels with American children. In this study, boys and girls from fifth, seventh, ninth, and eleventh grades were examined. The children were asked to rate their friendships with a same- or opposite-sex best friend.

The researchers found that there was a significant age difference in overall intimacy with same-sex friends. Frankness and spontaneity, knowing and sensitivity, attachment, exclusiveness, and giving and sharing were factors that changed with age. Opposite-sex friendships significantly increased with age. Boys and girls did not differ in reported opposite-sex friendship in the fifth and seventh grades, whereas girls in the ninth and eleventh grades reported greater intimacy than did boys. This sex-by-age pattern of interaction was particularly evident in attachment, trust, and loyalty. Like American girls, Israeli girls were higher in knowing and sensitivity and in giving and sharing.

■ Socialization Through Play

Although school-age children do play alone, the company of other youngsters is usually sought for playtime activities. Neighborhood and school interactions are the most popular play groups and encourage cooperative forms of play. Play-group experiences teach children how to share with and be responsible to one another, follow the directions of a leader, nurture self-confidence in a group setting, and cope with success and failure. In short, children learn what a group is, how it operates, and their role within it.

☐ Play and Sex Typing

Although sex-typed play activities begin in early childhood, they become quite widespread during the school years. School-age children identify with those sex-typed play activities that are characteristic of their own sex. Boys, more than girls, prefer physically oriented play. Boys' toys also require more physical expressions (Maccoby, 1980, 1988; Pitcher and Schultz, 1983).

Boys are also usually more aware of sex differences and avoid playing with objects that might be considered feminine. Girls are more willing to participate in male-oriented play activities. Though both sexes congregate into sex-typed play groups, boys hold more rigid, stereotyped attitudes and beliefs (DiPietro, 1981; Fagot and Kronsberg, 1982).

Sex-typed play occurs because of other reasons. Parents, for example, sometimes encourage their children to engage in sex-typed forms of play. This is more evident among fathers, who often insist on selecting sex-appropriate toys and play behaviors. Further pressure to engage in sex-typed play comes from the child's peer group, an increasingly important source of social approval and reinforcement (Langlois and Downs, 1980; Lamb, Easterbrooks, and Holden, 1980). Often, same-sex play groups openly torment one another, further solidifying gender boundaries. As Evelyn Pitcher and Lynn Schultz (1983) observed, when boys taunt and tease girls, the stage is usually set for the catcalls and whistles that will appear in the future.

But the traditional classification of "masculine" and "feminine" forms of play may well be eroding. The current emphasis on a more androgynous definition of the sexes may help reduce the separation between male and female play activities. Although girls still engage in "feminine" activities, today there are activities previously cast as "masculine" in which they enjoy competing, such as track and field events, basketball, golf, and softball.

☐ Team Sports

Team sports are popular during the school years. Being part of a team gives children an opportunity to develop their physical and mental prowess within the framework of competitive contests. Competing as a team member also helps develop children's characters. It gives them a common goal and allows them to contribute as members.

Team sports, however, can also bring frustration, especially if children are over-eager to prove themselves on the playing field. Having to sit on the bench, striking out with the bases loaded, or experiencing defeat are difficult for children, especially if they have never dealt with such situations before. Adults need to support children in such situations.

Team sports require considerable coordination, dexterity, cooperation, and concentration. In regard to the themes of this book, organized sports can thus be said to be a fusion of the major developmental processes. That is, team sports require the successful integration of physical, cognitive, social, and personal-emotional forces. Though these processes are required in virtually all forms of play, team sports appear to require a more rigorous application and successful integration of each.

Many youngsters fear failure in team sports. Sadly, many parents, coaches, and other adults dismiss these apprehensions and force children to continue playing despite these fears. Consequently, many children may become resentful, anxious, angry, or even lose their self-confidence.

Besides appreciating children's psychological needs, adults need to help children develop those skills needed for competitive play. Effective instruction usually includes

Team sports affect many facets of growth and development.

mastering a skill appropriate to a specific age, not forcing youngsters to work on skills for which they are not equipped. Adults should also realize that success in one phase of the game does not automatically mean success in all other phases. Adults must recognize that the basis of training is the development of such mental skills as concentration, determination, and dedication (Murphy, 1983).

Encouraging children to perform well is commendable, but children need to learn that winning is not the only goal. Winning all too often overshadows the enjoyment of just playing the game. Perhaps a solution is to emphasize developing skills, not finishing first (Smith et al., 1983).

■ Theories of Personality Development

☐ Sigmund Freud's Psychosexual Theory

The Latency Period (ages 6 to 11) During middle childhood, youngsters enter the latency period of psychosexual development. Following the oral, anal, and phallic stages, the *latency period* is marked by a diminishment of the biological and sexual drives. Compared with the turbulence of the other stages, it is a relatively quiet period of transition.

Although there are no prominent instinctive urges developing within the child, Freud acknowledges that new skills do emerge at this time. Paramount among them are skills promoting ego refinement, particularly those that strengthen and protect the ego from frustration and failure. Freud called such behaviors defense, or coping, mechanisms.

FREUDIAN COPING MECHANISMS

Coping mechanisms are patterns of behavior that function to relieve anxiety. We have all heard references to anxiety at one point or another: Mary has test anxiety, Stewart is anxiously awaiting the company's decision, or Phillip is always anxious and uptight. Anxiety, a most unpleasant emotion, is a reaction of inner apprehension often described as a response to a subjective, rather than an objective, danger. Put another way, it is psychological pain compared to physical pain. In many instances, anxiety originates from the conflicts in life that we face.

Coping mechanisms attempt to deal with the pain and turmoil of such threatening situations as failure, mistakes, and accidents and in some cases succeed in freeing the individual from some anxiety. By middle childhood, coping mechanisms are used with surprising frequency. With age, these mechanisms become more elaborate and intertwined with the child's overall personality. However, coping mechanisms are, at best, temporary and do not resolve underlying conflicts. In most cases, coping mechanisms produce automatic and rigid reactions that enable the individual to avoid, rather than deal with, struggles. Such patterns of behavior have a tendency to distort reality.

Although coping mechanisms are a normal behavioral expression and do have some beneficial value, they should not be used in excess. When they are used excessively, such as in the case of the perpetual excuse-maker or coverup artist, troubles begin. The very nature of their title—coping, or *defense*, mechanisms—indicates their temporary quality. As we are assaulted with the problems of daily life, defensive behavior yields few, if any, long-lasting solutions. Consequently, for the child or adult who persists in relying too frequently on coping mechanisms, life becomes a battle of offense versus defense, and although we hear that "the best offense is a good defense," defense alone may win a few battles, but never the war.

It has often been said that coping mechanisms deal with the symptoms rather than the causes of problems. Just as taking two aspirins for a headache or a sleeping pill for insomnia does not explain the root of the problem, continual use of a coping mechanism does not address the need or frustration that initially caused the anxiety. Thus, while coping mechanisms are considered useful, their adjustive or maladjustive quality depends on how often the child uses them.

TYPES OF COPING MECHANISMS Just as anxiety exists in all shapes and sizes, so too do coping mechanisms. It should be realized, however, that these behaviors are highly individualized and will differ from person to person and from situation to situation. In this sense, it is possible that no two people will use the same coping device in the same manner.

Rationalization is one of the most common coping mechanisms. It is the attempt to justify and provide logical reasons and explanations for one's failures or shortcomings. The youngster who is unable to make the local Little League team, for example, may attempt to rationalize this failure by claiming that the games are boring and uninteresting. Or to avoid a spanking after breaking some dishes, the rationalizing child may say it never would have happened if someone else had not stacked them so high. In its simplest form, rationalization is common excuse-making.

Projection is the placing of one's difficulties or failures on someone else. In order to guard against unfavorable self-evaluations, motives that are found personally unacceptable will be attributed to others. In this sense, a child who happens to be caught copying or cheating may attempt to defend the act by saying that everyone else in the class was guilty of the same misconduct or that the teacher is to blame for not taking adequate safeguards against cheating.

Displacement is the redirection of pent-up hostile feelings to people or objects less dangerous than those that initially aroused the emotion. Displacement is observable in the case of the young girl who has been spanked by her father for committing a misdeed. Obviously, she cannot return the blow to the parent, unless she wants to deepen her predicament. Instead, she may seek other channels through which to release her internal hostile feelings, such as kicking a ball or spanking a doll. Displacement may also explain why so many adolescent bedroom doors are slammed shut following family disagreements.

Denial of reality is a coping mechanism children frequently resort to. To protect the self, children may refuse to perceive the existence of hurtful situations. For this reason, youngsters may continually deny that a beloved relative has passed away. Older children may deny to their parents that they are doing poorly in school, despite knowing that they are failing four courses.

Compensation is used by many children when they seek to find a successful or rewarding activity that can be substituted for failure in another kind of activity. The unathletic boy who cannot successfully compete in sports may find satisfaction in developing a particular hobby. An unattractive girl may try to excel in all of her school subjects or seek to become the school's best dresser.

Interestingly, parents employ a type of compensation when they seek to satisfy their own ambitions through their children. A mother who experienced a deprived

Coping mechanisms are often used to relieve anxiety, including situations involving stealing and cheating.

childhood may go out of her way to give her children the best of everything. A father who always wanted to go to college but never had the chance may continually prod his son to pursue higher education. Although this type of compensation may satisfy the parent's needs it is questionable whether the child's needs are met.

Regression is a retreat to earlier developmental periods to escape the anxiety of a situation. This coping mechanism is quite apparent when a new baby arrives home from the hospital and an older child regresses to infantile behavior. In an effort to regain the parental attention that has been displaced because of the new arrival, a child may regress to behavior that characterized his or her experiences as a baby, such as bed-wetting, thumb-sucking, or crawling. It is conceivable that in the child's mind, earlier developmental stages represented security.

Reaction formation may be used by children to prevent unwanted and perhaps objectionable desires from being expressed. In this case, the child may learn to substitute an opposing one in its place. Growing children who are becoming anxious and concerned about their passivity and dependency, for example, may exhibit a type of reaction formation by behaving in an aggressive and assertive fashion when in the company of peers.

Escape and withdrawal are two interrelated coping mechanisms that children can use to avoid threatening or undesirable situations. When they are employed, attempts are made to procrastinate or put off doing an unpleasant task, such as presenting an oral report in class or having to do a disliked household chore.

Helping Children to Understand Coping Behaviors

Everyone needs feedback on their behavior, and children are no exception as far as coping behaviors are concerned. It is important for children to be aware of their actions, especially if defensiveness is a common occurrence. The importance of objective adult feedback and meaningful guidance cannot be overstressed here. Parents, teachers, guidance counselors, and other adults are in strategic positions to observe children and help them develop a sense of personal awareness. As an effort to help youngsters understand their coping behaviors, the following suggestions are offered:

Adults should examine their own coping mechanisms. Seeking to understand their own coping mechanisms and why we use them may provide adults with meaningful insight into children's defensive behavior. While adult coping mechanisms are more refined than children's, the fundamental design behind each is remarkably similar.

Respect the struggles, turmoils, and disappointments that are characteristic of childhood. An empathic adult is one who can appreciate the many anxious situations that confront the child throughout life. Because coping mechanisms are learned forms of behavior, children need models more than they need critics. Shaming the child or making fun of coping behavior accomplishes nothing and should be avoided.

Try to teach the child that success as well as failure is part of everyone's life. While everyone wants to succeed, only a handful are capable of succeeding on a continuous basis without failure. Accepting failure and disappointment are important dimensions of self-growth and should not be reasons for negative self-regard.

Seek to understand why coping mechanisms are used, especially those that are used excessively. This suggestion implies not only patience and gentle understanding on the adult's part but also careful observation of the events that triggered the coping device. Verbalization of the situation should be encouraged, but at a time when the anxiety of the event has diminished. It should be stated to the child that defending against and retreating from unpleasant situations are normal reactions; however, learning to deal with struggles head-on avoids reality distortion and nurtures a more accurate sense of self.

Avoid comparisons with other children. Children rarely employ coping mechanisms in exactly the same fashion nor do they accept the consequences of negative situations in similar manners. Therefore it is unfair to say such things as "You are always making excuses . . . Mary does not behave like you!" Such comparisons downplay the individuality of the child. Comparisons accomplish little, except possibly to produce further anxious feelings and inferior attitudes toward one's sense of self.

Try to understand coping mechanisms as part of the child's whole personality. Coping mechanisms do not exist separately as behavioral phenomenon; on the contrary, they frequently reflect significant aspects of the child's total personality. Thus, rather than attempting to understand coping behaviors and defensive episodes separately, adults might seek to explore their integration into the larger whole. This implies becoming aware of such areas as accuracy of the child's self-concept, levels of self-esteem, insecurities, and emotional sensitivities.

☐ Erik Erikson's Psychosocial Theory

Industry versus Inferiority (ages 6 to 11) The psychosocial crisis of *industry versus inferiority* occupies all of middle childhood and, as such, parallels Freud's latency period. During this crisis, children have reached the point in their cognitive development at which they can comprehend more about their surroundings. Youngsters seek to understand and build or make things that are practical to them. Play intermingles with work; play becomes productive, and the product is all-important to children's self-esteem. However, children who frequently fail to be productive may soon feel inferior and even worthless. In their search for positive self-regard and esteem, children need the support and guidance of adults. This is a point made by Erikson and a host of others (Leonetti, 1980; Clemes and Bean, 1981; Swayze, 1980).

Regardless of their culture, children need to be competent. In American society, they are expected to be competent in the classroom, whereas in simpler societies, children should be competent in the field, in tying fish nets, throwing spears, and the like. This is a time for schooling (in or out of the classroom) and continued socialization, particularly when it can lead to competence in adulthood.

Industrious youngsters take pleasure and pride in the accomplishment of new and different goals. For school-age children, these accomplishments may be winning a Monopoly game, becoming a member of a sports team, participating in a school play, or getting A's on a report card. The attainment of each goal motivates the achievement of new ones. However, Erikson warned that there is an obvious risk for children who lose their self-esteem because of failure:

> The child's danger, at this stage, lies in a sense of inadequacy and inferiority. If he despairs of his tools and skills or of his status among his tool partners, he may be discouraged from identification with them and with a section of the tool world. To lose the hope of such "industrial" association may pull him back to the more isolated, less tool-conscious familial rivalry of the oedipal time. The child despairs of his equipment in the tool world and in autonomy, and considers himself doomed to mediocrity or inadequacy. It is at this point that wider society becomes significant in its ways of admitting the child to an understanding of meaningful roles in its technology and economy. Many a child's development is disrupted when family life has failed to prepare him for school life, or when school life fails to sustain the promises of earlier stages.

(1963, p. 260)

CHAPTER REVIEW

■ Unit One: Physical Development

The rates of physical growth and development are rather slow during the middle years of childhood. By age 12, children have gained about 90 percent of their adult height, and they weigh approximately 80 pounds. Youngsters lose their babylike contours during the school years. This chapter examined the physiological changes that occur at this time. Children also develop their motor-skill abilities. By the age of 6, most children are able to participate in numerous activities that require large-muscle movement and refined coordination.

Children achieve a sense of physical self throughout childhood, through their growing awareness of bodily changes and through their improving motor skills. The degree of their achievement in motor-skill abilities depends on numerous factors, including rates of physical maturity, opportunities to engage in physical activities, and level of self-confidence.

■ Unit Two: Mental Development

During Piaget's stage of intuitive thought, children's thinking is based on immediate perceptions rather than on mental functions. Although symbolic functioning represents an important cognitive advancement, other modes of thought, particularly centering, transductive reasoning, transformational reasoning, and the inability to reverse mental operations, restrict intellectual advancement.

The stage of concrete operations is characterized primarily by the ability to comprehend conservation, a principle stating that object properties remain the same despite changes made in their shape or physical arrangement. Other advancements are made in classification and seriation. More efficient mental organization enables children to systemize and categorize concepts more finely, particularly those related to size and shape, spatial, relational, quantity, and time. Advancements in problem-solving abilities also refine intellectual operations at this time.

In regard to language developments, the average child has a reading vocabulary of nearly 50,000 words by the sixth grade. Understanding abstract word meanings and the relationships among certain words usually remains elusive. The use of compound and complex sentences increases during middle childhood, largely because youngsters have grasped three important rules: a sentence consists of a noun phrase and a verb phrase; a noun phrase consists of an article and a noun; and a verb phrase consists of a verb and a noun phrase. As their knowledge of sentence structure broadens, children learn more ways to convey different functions. This chapter also explored advancements in pragmatics, or how language is used in social settings, and how dialects create variations in language usage.

■ Unit Three: Personality and Social Development

Sex-role development becomes more deeply rooted during the school years, largely because of growing cognitive and social maturity. The school years also are when emotions become more specific and sophisticated. This is evident in such emotions as anger and aggression, fear, happiness and humor, and love.

Moral development also advances during the school years. Piaget emphasized the importance of cognitive development to morality and identified the premoral, moral realism, and moral relativism stages. Like Piaget, Kohlberg stressed the cognitive underpinnings of morality. He defined moral development as having preconventional, conventional, and postconventional levels.

The family and the peer group are important agents of socialization. In regard to the modern family, we explored the impact of television on children's behavior. Interactions with peer groups give youngsters the opportunity to share experiences, cooperate, and work toward group goals. Play continues to contribute to many facets of development. We concluded this chapter with an examination of Freud's latency period and Erikson's industry versus inferiority crisis.

KEY TERMS

authority-maintaining orientation
black English
catharsis theory of television viewing

centering
classification
cognitive style

compensation
concrete operations
conservation
contractual legalistic orientation
conventional level
coping mechanism
denial of reality
dialect
displacement
elaboration
escape
fair-weather cooperation stage
good boy–nice girl orientation
hostile aggression
impulsive
industry versus inferiority
intimate and mutually shared
   relationships
intrinsic motivation
intuitive thought
latency period
morality
moral realism

moral relativism
naively egoistic orientation
obedience and punishment
   orientation
one-way assistance stage
playmateship stage
postconventional level
preconventional level
premoral stage
projection
rationalization
reaction formation
reflective
regression
reversibility
seriation
social learning theory of television
   viewing
transductive reasoning
transformational reasoning
universal ethical principle orientation
withdrawal

RECOMMENDED READINGS

Belsky, J., Lerner, R. M., and Spanier, G. B. (1984). *The Child in the Family.* New York: Random House.
   This text examines the child-family relationship and how it contributes to overall development. The authors view both children and the adult members of the family as developing organisms.

Berndt, T. J., and Ladd, G. W. (1989). *Peer Relationships in Child Development.* New York: Wiley.
   An excellent collection of readings focusing on many diverse aspects of peer relationships.

Flavell, J. H. (1985). *Cognitive Development,* 2nd ed. Englewood Cliffs, N.J.: Prentice-Hall.
   A leading authority discusses a variety of topics, including perception, memory, language, and social cognition.

Hartup, W. W., and Rubin, Z. (Eds.) (1985). *Relationships and Development.* Hillsdale, N.J.: Erlbaum.
   A collection of essays exploring the nature and dynamics of children's social relationships and how these relationships affect child development.

Matlin, M. (1983). *Cognition.* New York: Holt.
   A very good overview of the study of cognition. Of special interest are discussions related to concept formation and problem solving.

Miller, G. A. (1981). *Language and Speech.* San Francisco: Freeman.
   This introduction to language covers many diverse topics in a very readable and enjoyable fashion.

Perry, D. B., and Bussey, K. (1984). *Social Development.* Englewood Cliffs, N.J.: Prentice-Hall.

A good exploration of many facets of social development. Separate chapters cover such topics as social cognition, morality, sex differences, and peer relations.

Rubin, K. H., and Ross, H. S. (Eds.) (1982). *Peer Relationships and Social Skills in Childhood.* New York: Springer-Verlag.

A total of 16 readings examine the nature of childhood socialization skills, including parent-child, sibling, and friendship relations.

Tavris, C., and Wade, C. (1984). *The Longest War: Sex Differences in Perspective,* 2nd ed. New York: Harcourt Brace Jovanovich.

Chapter 6 of this paperback explores how children learn sex-role differences.

Winn, M. (1985). *The Plug-in Drug: Television, Children, and the Family.* New York: Viking.

An up-to-date analysis of television and its effect on children's behavior.

Adolescence

CHAPTER OUTLINE

WHAT DO YOU THINK?

■ Few developmental processes over the course of the life cycle have more impact than puberty does. The physical changes associated with puberty affect nearly every tissue of the body and transform youngsters into sexually mature persons. Besides looking at puberty as a physiological event, this chapter will examine how it affects many other developmental spheres, including psychological, social, and emotional behavior. How do teenagers react to such physical change? Does being an early or late maturer have any bearing on the outcome of this developmental event? Read on and we'll give you some answers.

■ Who am I? Where have I been in life, and where do I want to go? It is during adolescence that questions such as these begin to be asked. Some authorities, such as Erik Erikson, have supplied us with considerable information regarding identity formation during the teenage years. We'd like to share his ideas with you, as well as those of others. In the process, perhaps you'll see your own strivings for identity in a new light.

■ Boy meets girl . . . and a new chapter of heterosexual development begins. For most, adolescence is the time that dating begins. As we explore trends in dating in this chapter, we'll also take a look at the historical changes in and functions of dating. We'll also examine the nature of teenage sexual relations. What have we learned about the sexual activity of today's teenagers? Are their sexual involvements as numerous and intimate as the media make them out to be? This chapter will answer these and other questions . . . perhaps those that you've always been afraid to ask.

■ Many teenagers are told by their elders that adolescence is the best years of their life, a time when they have everything to live for and enjoy. Yet despite such a positive portrayal, many adolescents display destructive behaviors unique to their subculture: suicide, drug abuse, delinquency, and anorexia nervosa. Where do these problems originate? Have they been increasing during the 1980s? What can be done to correct them? The final portion of this chapter will address these and other issues.

PHYSICAL DEVELOPMENT

Adolescence is the life stage between childhood and adulthood. Like the other phases of the life cycle, adolescence offers numerous developmental challenges. Adjustments and adaptations are needed in light of pronounced physical change, the psychological search for identity, and heightened levels of socialization, to name but a few areas.

Years ago, it was fashionable to refer to adolescence as a stormy and stressful life stage. Inner turmoil was an expected companion, and attention was usually directed toward teenagers' *problems.* In short, the literature portrayed adolescence as an unstable time that was likely to produce uncertainty, doubt, and apprehension.

Though adolescents may have problems, which we shall address in the latter portion of this chapter, most of today's researchers have altered their perspective of the teenage years. James Garbarino (1985), for example, saw the stormy and stressful analysis of adolescence as a professional stereotype. Indeed, the general conclusion that there is conflict and disruption throughout all of life's domains is not the typical pattern of development for adolescents. Morover, the exclusive focus on problem adolescents is misleading, because most teenagers successfully meet the challenges of this age (Petersen, 1988).

Adolescence is the bridge between childhood and adulthood.

M. Lee Manning (1983) concurred with this and added that we must also move away from always viewing adolescence as a time of rebellious, antisocial, and unacceptable behavior. Research does not support these and other contentions, such as the supposed generation gap between adolescents and their parents. Belief in such myths distorts our perceptions of persons in this life stage. We need to debunk these misconceptions so that we can maintain our objectivity and clearly distinguish fact and fiction.

With such present-day interpretations in mind, we can best understand adolescence as another transition in the life cycle. Barry Golinko (1984) referred to such a transition as one of four life pathways. The first occurs between the ages of 2 and 3 when children leave infancy and enter early childhood. The second pathway occurs when children enter adolescence. The third is when persons enter the vocational arena. The fourth transition takes place when people leave active adult life and become elder statespersons.

■ Puberty

□ Puberty and the Growth Spurt

Adolescence is a time of pronounced bodily development. *Puberty* is the technical name for the biological processes that transform children into adults. The key changes in puberty are the maturation of the reproductive system and the development of secondary sex characteristics. The changes manifested during puberty are so pervasive that virtually all tissues in the body are affected. However, to fully explore the impact of puberty, most researchers (Brooks-Gunn and Warren, 1989; Lerner, Lerner, and Tubman, 1989) emphasize the importance of examining it against the backdrop of cognitive, personality, emotional, and social developmental forces.

Teenagers experience a growth spurt that increases height and weight. For females the growth spurt begins, on the average, between ages 8½ and 10½, and for males it takes place between ages 10½ and 16. The peak of the growth spurt for females is between 12 and 13, and for males it is approximately at age 14. Because the rate of growth is greater in the legs than the trunk, many adolescents develop a leggy and gangling appearance. By age 17, most females have reached their adult height, and males reach this at age 21 (Tanner, 1981; Petersen and Taylor, 1980; Chumlea, 1982).

Both sexes show a noticeable increase in weight by the eleventh year, a gain averaging between 10 and 14 pounds during the peak years of development. Contributing to these weight gains are the increased size of the internal organs, skeleton, muscles, and body fat. A significant sex difference pertains to the distribution and amount of subcutaneous fat that affects the shape of body contours. Typically, females enter adulthood with more subcutaneous fat than do males, particularly in the pelvis, breasts, upper back, and the backs of the upper arms. Such distributions account for females' more rounded and softer bodily contours (Katchadourian, 1985).

Along with the gains in height and weight, there is an increase in both the number of muscle cells and their size. Between the ages of 5 and 16, males experience approximately a fourteenfold increase in the number of their muscle cells. Cell size continues to enlarge until the mid-thirties. For females, the number of muscle cells increases about ten times, with the maximum cell size occurring between ages 10 and 11 (Garbarino, 1985).

The skeletal structure also changes at this time. More specifically, it changes in composition, proportion, weight, and length. Females' skeletal development is more rapid than males', their bone structure reaching its mature size by the seventeenth year. Males attain this mature stage of development almost two years later. Skeletal weight for both males and females increases throughout puberty but appears to be more marked in males (Katchadourian, 1977).

 International Lifespan Development

■ INTERNATIONAL DIFFERENCES IN RATES OF TEENAGE PHYSICAL DEVELOPMENT

Teenagers from the United States are usually heavier and taller and have lower cholesterol levels than do teenagers from other nations. However, like teenagers from other lands, they appear to be just as prone to those health problems known to increase the risks of heart disease in adults.

These were some of the central findings of a study conducted by the Mahoney Institute of the American Health Foundation. The study examined 5,331, 13-year-olds in 15 countries. The researchers compared height, weight, blood pressure, cholesterol levels, and smokers and nonsmokers.

In regard to height, the teenagers from the Netherlands were the tallest, and those from Thailand were the shortest. Overall, the teenagers from the United States were ranked seventh. American boys, averaging 5 feet, 2 inches, ranked sixth, and American girls, also 5 feet, 2 inches, ranked seventh.

The heaviest teenagers were from Greece, followed by Yugoslavia. The lightest came from Thailand. American teenagers ranked third, with the average weight for boys being 110 pounds and that for girls being 108 pounds.

Cholesterol rates were highest among Finnish teenagers and lowest among Nigerian teenagers. American teenagers were ranked fifth from the bottom. The heaviest male smokers came from Kuwait. About 20 percent of the American boys smoked, ranking them sixth. The heaviest female smokers were from France. Approximately 25 percent of the American girls smoked, ranking them fourth.

Smoking, cholesterol, and obesity have been linked to heart disease. The prevalence of these factors at an early age are thus thought to increase the risk of cardiovascular illness later in life. The researchers pointed out that, in general, these international differences are not related to genetics but, rather, to a country's lifestyle. Furthermore, unhealthy lifestyles are not irreversible but can be changed so as to promote sound physical health and well-being.

(Mahoney Institute, 1981)

There is a temporary thickening and coarsening of the facial features. Among males especially, the mouth widens, the nose projects more, and the jaw becomes more prominent. This gives males a more muscular and angular face. Females, on the other hand, add a layer of fat which has a tendency to soften facial features.

Related to the physical changes associated with the adolescent growth spurt is the influence of what researchers call the secular trend. The *secular trend* means that children in more prosperous parts of the world are growing taller and heavier. The secular trend also means that adolescents are experiencing the growth spurt earlier than ever before and that the timetable for attaining physical and sexual maturation has accelerated. However, the secular trend ceases to have an impact when a nation's health and nutritional standards reach an optimum level (J. F. Adams, 1981; Garn, 1980; Tanner, 1981).

□ Puberty and Reproductive Maturity

As mentioned earlier, puberty is chiefly characterized by sexual development. Sexual development can be best understood by examining the maturation of primary and secondary sex characteristics.

Primary sex characteristics are the physiological features of the sex organs. For males, these organs are the penis and the testes, and for females they are the ovaries, uterus, clitoris, and vagina. *Secondary sex characteristics* are not directly related to the sexual organs but nevertheless distinguish a mature male from a mature female. Examples of secondary sex characteristics are the development of a beard in males and breasts in females. The gradial maturation of the primary and secondary sex characteristics signifies the end of childhood and the onset of reproductive maturity.

FEMALE SEXUAL DEVELOPMENT For both females and males, sexual development is fairly predictable. For females these changes include the development of the breasts and sexual organs, the appearance of pubic hair, the onset of *menarche,* or first menstrual period, and the characteristic widening of the hips, believed to be due to the influence of estrogen in the growth centers of the pelvic bones.

Most females' breasts will begin to develop between ages 10 and 11, although this can occur as late as ages 13 and 14. Over a span of about three years, the breasts develop from bud to mature size. At or about the same time that the breasts develop, the uterus and vagina also begin to mature. By the end of the adolescent years, the internal organs of reproduction have reached their adult status.

Females' pubic hair usually begins to appear after the breasts have begun to develop but before the beginning of menarche. Pubic hair appears initially on the outer lips of the vulva and takes on a horizontal distribution. By the end of the teenage years, pubic hair has become dark, curly, coarse, and has formed a triangular pattern (Morris and Udry, 1980).

Menarche, or the first menstrual period, is experienced by most North American girls between 12 and 13 years of age. The normal age range is from 10 to 15 years (Brooks-Gunn, 1988). Menarche is the most clearly defined sign of sexual maturity in females. It also appears to have other implications. Females who have reached menarche appear to have a clearer sexual identification than do same-aged females who have not (Rierdan and Koff, 1980).

The median age of menarche varies around the world, ranging from 9 to 18. Although menarche signifies a mature stage of uterine development, we must point out that it doesn't mean that the female has attained her total reproductive capacity. Early menstrual cycles often occur without an ovum being shed. Often there is a period of adolescent sterility, lasting for a year or 18 months after menarche (Tanner, 1981).

Other sexual developments transform the girl's indifferent body shape to the woman's distinguishing contours. For example, the pelvis widens, an important change when one considers that a baby's head must pass through this bony ring. At the same time, the increase of subcutaneous fat around the pelvic girdle exaggerates the breadth of the hips. Fat also is added to such areas of the body as the shoulder girdle, back, abdomen, and legs. As the breasts develop, the apparent depth of the chest is increased and further enhanced by growth changes in the bony and muscular structures beneath the breasts. Table 8-1 shows the average sequence of primary and secondary sex characteristics in females and males.

MALE SEXUAL DEVELOPMENT The testes begin to accelerate in growth by approximately age 12. Individual variations in development, however, account for the different rate of growth. By the end of adolescence, the penis has reached its adult length, width, and overall shape. The scrotum and testes have also reached their mature proportions and have dropped to their proper adult location (Morris and Udry, 1980).

The production of mature spermatozoa occurs by about age 15. As the reproductive system matures, males may experience *nocturnal emissions,* the ejaculation of

TABLE 8-1 Average Sequence of Primary and Secondary Sex Characteristics

Females	Age (Approximate)	Males
Onset of growth spurt	8–10	
Initial breast development	10–11	Onset of growth spurt
Development of pubic hair	12	Growth of testes
Onset of menarche (age range is 10 to 18)	13–14	Development of pubic hair
Development of underarm hair		Growth of penis and testes
Earliest normal pregnancy		
Completion of breast development (age range is 13 to 18)	15–16	Production of mature spermatozoa
		Nocturnal emissions
		Initial development of underarm and facial hair
		Deepening of the voice
Maturation of skeletal system	17–18	Development of chest hair
Increased activity of sweat glands		Maturation of skeletal system

semen during sleep. Nocturnal emissions are a normal phase of development and are frequently caused by sexual excitation in dreams or by some type of physical condition, such as a full bladder or pressure from pajamas.

Males' pubic hair begins to develop between approximately the ages of 12 and 14, usually starting at the base of the penis and extending outward. About two years after the pubic hair begins to grow, the axillary (underarm) and facial hair appear. Chest hair, which does not appear until late adolescence, continues growing throughout young adulthood. It is often considered by males to be the ultimate sign of virility, even more so than pubic hair.

There is a definite sequence in the development of the moustache and the beard. At first the downy hairs at the corners of the upper lip become more noticeable and begin to extend over the entire upper lip. This slowly forms a moustache of finer hair, which becomes, with age, coarser and darker. Later, hair begins to appear on the upper part of the cheeks and the midline below the lower lip. Finally, it develops on the sides and border of the chin and on the upper part of the face, just in front of the ears.

Other changes at this time include the increased activity of the sweat glands and marked voice changes. The sweat (apocrine) glands are similar to those located in the armpit and are found in other areas of the body, including the mammary, groin, genital, and anal regions. The apocrine glands differ, however, from the sweat glands distributed over the rest of the body, as the maturation of the apocrine glands is thought to be related to the development of the reproductive system. Voice changes, which are caused primarily by an increase in the length of the vocal cords, are greater in males than in females (Katchadourian, 1977; Petersen and Taylor, 1980).

☐ The Physiology of Puberty

It is fairly well understood that the bodily changes associated with puberty are the result of hormones. Before puberty, a part of the brain known as the hypothalamus stimulates the pituitary gland. The pituitary gland, often called the "master gland" because of its central role in the coordination of the endocrine system, then stimulates other glands. Figure 8-1 illustrates the glands of the endocrine system.

Puberty begins when the pituitary gland secretes increased amounts of the human growth hormone (somatotrophic hormone). This causes a rapid increase in body devel-

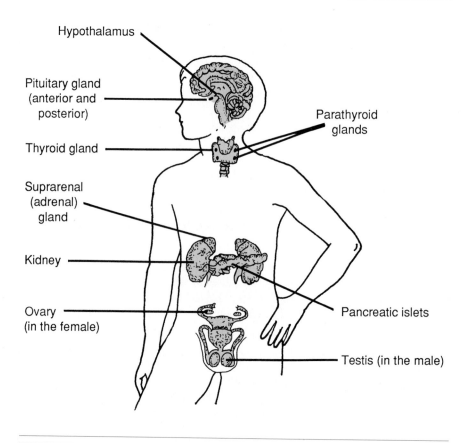

FIGURE 8-1 The glands of the endocrine system.

opment, thus signaling the onset of the adolescent growth spurt. Along with the growth spurt, increased amounts of thyroxin and adrenalin are produced that match the increase in cells, or total body weight.

Gonadotrophins are also released by the pituitary gland. These are hormones that stimulate the testes and ovaries (the parts of the endocrine system called the gonads). In turn, the testes and ovaries secrete their own sex hormones. The male sex hormone is called *testosterone,* and the female hormones are *estrogen* and *progesterone.*

Cells within the testes secrete testosterone, which directs the development of the genital organs, pubic hair, and other features of sexual development. Estrogen is secreted by the follicles of the ovary and controls the development of the uterus, vagina, and breasts. Progesterone aids in the development of the uterine wall, particularly its preparation for the implantation of a developing ovum and the placental development after implanation has taken place. Progesterone is also thought to be influential in breast development during pregnancy.

The high levels of sex hormones in the bloodstream are also largely responsible for terminating puberty. Once a particular phase of physical or sexual development is complete, these high levels of sex hormones signal the hypothalamus. The hypothalamus, in turn, ceases the further production of a given hormone (Doering, 1980; Higham, 1980).

☐ The Psychology of Puberty

Preoccupation with the changing physical self is common during adolescence. How teenagers react to such changes, including their perceived attractiveness or unattractiveness and their treatment by others, greatly affects how they evaluate themselves. It is in this way that physical and psychological development are related (Wright, 1989; Brooks-Gunn and Petersen, 1983; Petersen and Taylor 1980; G. Adams, 1980; Higham, 1980; Brooks-Gunn and Warner, 1988; Collins and Plahn, 1988).

The physical changes may cause psychological discomfort. For example, adolescents' leggy and gangling appearance and rapid hand and foot development may be a source of anxiety. Menarche also may produce emotional uneasiness. When these developments are coupled with such other physical adjustment problems as acne, awkwardness, and voice breaks, it is understandable that teenagers sometimes feel uncomfortable and, at times, insecure about their changing physical selves. In general, though, adolescents' preoccupation with physical traits declines with age (Brooks-Gunn and Petersen, 1983; Cramer, 1980; Fowler, 1989).

Strength and motor-skill coordination soar to new heights during adolescence.

Whether one is an *early* or *late maturer* may also produce self-consciousness. Because physical development varies from individual to individual, there are differences in overall rates of growth. Generally, adolescents report higher levels of personal satisfaction and more positive feelings about themselves when they mature before prescribed times. Furthermore, early maturation has been linked to success in other areas. Early maturers tend to be better socially adjusted overall. They seem to be more popular and have a greater capacity for leadership than do late maturers, who frequently encounter adjustment problems. Late maturers tend to generate poorer self-concepts and are overly concerned with matters related to social acceptance. They also frequently resort to attention-seeking behavior. In contrast, early maturers seem to be more independent, self-confident, and self-reliant (Petersen, 1987; Gross and Duke, 1980; Wilen and Petersen, 1980).

Even though their social adjustment may be smoother, early maturers may encounter problems in other areas. Compared with late maturers, who have a longer period of time to adjust to physical change, early maturers have a much shorter preparation time. This appears to be especially true for an early menarche. The shorter preparation time may produce more confusion and anxiety than among late maturers experiencing the same physiological event. Thus, the external harmony often exhibited by the early maturer may be accompanied by internal disharmony (Simmons and Blyth, 1988; Livson and Peskin, 1980).

☐ Puberty and Sexual Responsiveness

With the maturation of secondary sex characteristics, puberty increases the salience of specifically sexual meanings and behaviors for the individual. These changes make the teenager more aware of sexual activity, reproduction, and the processes of dating and mate selection that are socially defined as integral aspects of these physical, biological, processes. When individuals enter adolescence we expect them to begin the transition from childhood roles that emphasize submissiveness, nonresponsibility, and asexuality, to adult roles that emphasize dominance, responsibility, and sexuality. In this respect, there are both biological and social pressures toward sexual development (DeLamater, 1981).

Teenagers often become the recipients of inconsistent and mixed messages about sexuality. For example, the media promotes adolescent sexuality by using young actors, actresses, and models dressed in provocative fashions. On the other extreme, parents try to restrict activity or limit opportunities for sexual engagement by curfews and other limitations. Both messages convey the expectation of adolescent sexuality, but they differ in their approval. Teenagers need to evaluate these messages, but must do so against the background of the overall changing cultural context of sexuality (Garbarino, 1985).

In many other cultures, children and teenagers alike have virtually no guilt, shame, or inhibition to overcome. By contrast, American children and teenagers have a dozen or more years of learning, during which, typically, sex is shrouded in shameful mists. Outraged glares cause hands to be removed from genitals, and information is withheld or parceled out grudgingly. Perhaps a prolonged adolescent-youth phase in our culture is needed so that teenagers are allowed enough time to rid themselves of all the negative messages they have received over the years concerning sex (Sarrel and Sarrel, 1984).

This discussion implies that the sexual outcome of the teenage years is based on the physiological turbulence of the body and the psychological changes that accompany it. Again, as we have seen throughout this book, the interplay that exists between developmental forces cannot be overstated. Adolescents have to come to grips with the fact that they are now sexually mature. This implies an acceptance of one's physical changes—what a person looks like and what he or she is capable of. The teenager's new sexual capabilities of ejaculation or ovulation signal their untried fertility. These capabilities usually bring a heightened level of sexual responsivity. While adolescents are coming to terms with what they look like and what they can do, they also need to come to terms with their sexual identity.

■ Motor-Skill Development

One might expect adolescents' motor-skill development to be uneven and disruptive in light of so many bodily changes. However, most adolescents exhibit steady increases in strength, reaction, and coordination abilities. Males continue to surpass females in overall motor-skill development. This is largely because males have larger muscles and are able to develop more force per gram of muscle tissue (Tanner, 1981; Petersen and Taylor, 1980).

In regard to specific motor-skill activities, males are generally more proficient in such areas as accuracy in speed of response and overall body control. This proficiency may be demonstrated in running, throwing, and other motor-skill tasks requiring varying degrees of physical endurance. Strength and dexterity are also more pronounced for males during the adolescent years.

We remind you, though, that such findings must be placed into the proper perspective. Much of this research was conducted before the current increase in female adolescents' athletic activities. Moreover, even though males surpass females in their overall ability to perform certain athletic tasks, this may be because of the vast amounts of time and practice that they devote to developing these skills. Virtually all of the motor-skill research in the past studied the typical male rather than the typical female. Physical prowess depends considerably on exercises and training, which in turn depends on personal motivation, social expectations, and practical opportunities. Males have received more encouragement in this regard, which has contributed greatly to the gap in physical ability between the sexes (Petersen and Taylor, 1980; Katchadourian, 1977).

UNIT REVIEW

■ Puberty is a time of pronounced body development, including the maturation of the reproductive system and the development of secondary sex characteristics.

■ The body changes associated with puberty are caused by hormones. Overall, physical developments during adolescence follow a fairly predictable timetable for both males and females.

■ Whether one is an early or late maturer may influence one's psychological reactions to physical change. There are both biological and social pressures toward sexual development.

Unit Two:

MENTAL DEVELOPMENT

Piaget's Stages of Cognitive Development

Formal Operations

The ability to acquire and utilize knowledge reaches a peak during adolescence in the Piagetian stage of formal operations. *Formal operations* is the crystallization and integration of all the previous cognitive stages. Past developments combine during the formal operations stage to create a tightly organized and highly systematic mental whole. Thinking now becomes extremely rational and continues to develop throughout adulthood as these refined mental strategies are applied to greater numbers of problem-solving situations.

Like the other spheres of development, such as morality, age does not guarantee entry into a particular stage. Thus, not everyone reaches the stage of formal operations. One estimate is that only 40 to 60 percent of college students and adults reach this zenith of mental functioning (Keating, 1980; Super, 1980; Keating and Clark, 1980).

It is maintained that certain criteria can be used to see whether adolescents have reached the formal operations stage or are trapped in the concrete operations stage. For example, formal thinkers can perceive relationships between two ideas, can perform complex tasks by themselves, and can grasp information beyond the obvious so as to offer interpretation and application. Concrete thinkers have trouble seeing relationships between ideas, need to have things explained exactly, tend to interpret information literally, and cannot go from one task to another without explicit directions (Brazee and Brazee, 1980).

The attainment of the formal operations stage is not an all-or-nothing situation. In this respect, individuals may reach peak levels of mental functioning in certain areas but not in others. Also, some individuals, such as the very gifted, may demonstrate more precision and greater flexibility in certain skill areas or even in their overall cognitive operations (Keating and Clark, 1980; Hogan, 1980). Along these lines, one researcher (Carey, 1988) believes that formal thought is most likely applied to areas known best by the adolescent.

Likewise, the attainment of formal operations does not mean an increasing amount of creative behavior. On the contrary, research conducted by Fredric Wolf and Gerald Larson (1981) showed low and frequently negative correlations between measures of creativity and the attainment of the formal operations stage. Why is this so? The authors argued that children's apparently greater creativity, as compared with that of adolescents, may be more accidental than deliberate. This is because children's inability to incorporate all the facts and their inability to change in the light of new facts may generate responses that are viewed as creative by adults by virtue of what they omit. However, it is acknowledged that adolescents' greater cognitive capacity increases their potential for creative thinking. But this creative potential is often not realized because adolescents become increasingly aware of the heightened pressures for conformity, precisely because of their cognitive development.

There also may be sex differences in cognitive performances. Males tend to perform better on tests of mathematical reasoning and visual-spatial problems. Females, on the other hand, tend to excel in tasks involving verbal abilities (Demo, 1982; Springer and Deutsch, 1985). However, we need to point out that not all developmental psychologists agree with these contentions. For example, some researchers (Jacklin, 1989; Feingold, 1988) believe that sex differences are disappearing in cognitive skills, particularly verbal abilities.

CHARACTERISTICS OF FORMAL OPERATIONS

It is during the stage of formal operations that thinking becomes rather scientific. Individuals are now capable of thinking about the past, present, and future. They can also deal effectively with hypothetical problems. Moreover, when confronted with a problem, they can think of a number of possible solutions (Danner, 1989).

ABSTRACT THOUGHT During the earlier stages of cognition, there was a limited understanding of abstractions. *Abstractions* are subjective concepts or ideas outside ones' objective analysis of the tangible environment. Whereas objective reasoning skills are needed to solve concrete problems, such as those in science or math, abstract reasoning powers are needed to understand what cannot be seen.

Before the formal operations stage, youngsters are dependent on the physical or concrete properties of concepts. The ability to move beyond the mere physical properties of the environment and understand abstractions has enormous implications for cognitive development at this time. No longer are individuals anchored to current or

Formal operations brings heightened levels of thinking, including that which can be applied to identity formation.

recent concrete experiences. Whereas children can think about only what is, formal operators can imagine what might be (Keating, 1980).

Because of this, teenagers can now think more realistically about their identity and future, including their occupational and social roles. And they may experiment with these roles, just as they would experiment with hypotheses about physical events. Furthermore, adolescents are able to generate many new ideas about themselves and about life in general. Debates are now possible about a variety of moral and political issues, such as whether wars can ever be moral, whether abortions should be legal, whether there are basic inalienable human rights, and what an ideal community would be like. Teenagers can consider these issues from a variety of perspectives and see how the issues themselves are related to a larger set of social relationships. It is in this way that cognitive advancements fuse with numerous other aspects of development (Miller, 1983).

PROBLEM-SOLVING APPROACHES Formal thinkers can now approach problems and imagine all of the possible relationships that may be relevant. Propositions or data can be accepted as purely hypothetical and tentative and then be tested against whatever evidence is available. Earlier, children frequently accepted initial explanations of problem-solving situations as true. Now adolescents can analyze the full range of possibilities inherent in a problem before adopting one of them. James Byrnes (1988) refers to such sophisticated problem-solving strategies as "knowing how." That is, formal thinkers know the steps needed to successfully solve problems.

Such advancements mean that adolescents are capable of using *deductive reasoning*, that is, reasoning from a set of premises to reach a conclusion. Piaget called this type of thinking *hypothetico-deductive reasoning*. Teenagers are also able to use *inductive reasoning*, that is, starting with specific, individual experiences and proceeding to general principles. For a review of the literature on inductive and deductive reasoning skills, see Galotti (1989).

A good example of deductive logic is a syllogism. Suppose the following is given: (1) Socrates is a man, and (2) all men are mortal. Adolescents in the stage of formal operations are able to conclude that, therefore, (3) Socrates is a mortal. Such logic requires dealing with more than one aspect of a problem at a time. In our example, for instance, one must keep in mind that Socrates is a man and that all men are mortal.

LITERARY INSIGHT Mature cognition also allows teenagers to develop greater insight into literature. They are more receptive to facts and ideas and actively question what they are reading. Their advanced cognitive reasoning also enables them to learn a greater range of symbols, metaphors, word meanings, and characterizations. Historical chronology can now be grasped. Certain literary techniques that confused younger readers, such as irony and abstract concepts, now are better understood. Adolescents also can respond to a wider range of humor, including riddles, cartoons, and subtler expressions (Parr, 1982; Demorest, Silberstein, and Gardner, 1981; McGhee, 1980; Couturier, Mansfield, and Gallagher, 1981). Furthermore, the development of moral reasoning can be enhanced (Mills, 1988).

Much of this advancement in literary understanding is due to the fact that formal operations release readers from a singular, concrete interpretation of printed or spoken words. Furthermore, their ability to analyze facts and reason abstractly opens new horizons for thought. This is as true for adolescents' newly found interpretation of editorial cartoons as it is for their appreciation of the moral and social significance of such books as *Alice in Wonderland* or *Huckleberry Finn*. When such understanding emerges, adolescents' interest in such courses as English or literary appreciation also deepens. Such cognitive milestones in literary insight and other spheres of thinking thus have important curriculum implications (Danner, 1989; Burbules and Linn, 1988).

ADOLESCENT EGOCENTRISM One mental development that may distort cognitive functioning at this time is adolescent egocentrism. *Adolescent egocentrism* is a form of self-centeredness characterized by teenagers' concern about what people are thinking about them. Put another way, adolescents are now able to conceptualize their own thoughts while also being preoccupied with the thoughts of others. A major consequence of adolescent egocentrism is a heightened level of self-consciousness.

David Elkind (1967, 1980, 1981; Elkind and Bowen, 1979) sheds much light on the topic of adolescent egocentrism. Since his initial findings in the 1960s, researchers have generally acknowledged the existence of adolescent egocentrism. Furthermore, Elkind's ideas spurred other thoughts on the topic (Lechner and Rosenthal, 1984; Goossens, 1984; Adams and Jones, 1981; Enright, Shukla, and Lapsley, 1980).

As an example, Rolf Muuss (1982) studied how egocentrism changes as it passes through each of Piaget's cognitive stages. Adolescent egocentrism, then, is not a separate entity; rather, it is a transition from earlier expressions of egocentrism. The transition from one stage to another proceeds in a dialectic fashion: New and more sophisticated cognitive structures that release children from a lower level of egocentrism lead to a higher level of egocentrism. In this sense, egocentrism can be said to be a negative but necessary by-product of cognitive development, for it creates at each stage a new set of unrealistic, nonobjective representations of the world. The major mechanism contributing to the decline of egocentrism and to the movement from lower to higher levels of egocentrism is the developmental process of *decentering*. Decentering enables adolescents to shift the focus of their awareness from one limited aspect of reality or self to several different dimensions.

According to Elkind, adolescent egocentrism promotes two types of thinking. The first is the construction of an *imaginary audience.* That is, teenagers feel that they are always the focus of attention or on center stage. This perceived existence of an imaginary audience usually intensifies during potentially threatening social situations, such as having to speak in front of the class or walk alone into a crowded cafeteria.

The personal fable is the second consequence of adolescent egocentrism. *Personal fables* are stories that adolescents make up and tell about themselves. Personal fables reflect the adolescent's conviction of personal uniqueness and may contain such mistaken beliefs that one will not die or that one leads a charmed existence. Indeed, many teenaged girls become pregnant partly because their personal fable has convinced them that they cannot get pregnant, and therefore they take no precautions. The conviction that one leads a charmed life may also apply to reckless driving on the highway. These examples show how the imaginary audience and the personal fable can rationalize some types of adolescent behavior.

Adolescents abandon the imaginary audience and the personal fable when they are able to see themselves and others in a more realistic light. When this happens, individuals can establish true, rather than self-interested, interpersonal relationships. When confidences are shared and mutual relations are established, teenagers discover that others have similar feelings and have suffered and been enraptured in much the same fashion.

Although teenagers are often self-critical, they can also be self-admiring, and their imagined audience assumes the same affective coloration. Such egocentrism can be seen in behavior directed toward members of the opposite sex. Before going on a date, males may spend hours in front of a mirror combing their hair or flexing their muscles, whereas females may become engrossed in applying makeup or trying on outfits. Both are preoccupied with imagining what dramatic impressions they will make on the date. When the two adolescents eventually meet, each is more concerned with being observed than observing. Vanity and conceit, two traits frequently attributed to adolescents, may thus derive from lingering egocentrism (Elkind, 1980).

DO OTHER STAGES OF COGNITION EXIST?

Piaget maintains that formal operations is the final stage of cognitive development. Some researchers, though, feel that certain mental advancements transcend those acquired during the formal operations stage. This is the central theme of an impressive body of research by Michael Commons and his colleagues (Commons, Richards, and Armon, 1984; Commons and Richards, 1982; Commons, Richards, and Kuhn, 1982; Richards and Commons, 1982).

Commons proposed that a structural analytic stage follows formal operations. This stage includes certain qualities of cognition that are not covered by Piaget but that are characteristic of the intellectually mature person. More specifically, this stage includes systematic reasoning, the capacity to use the abstract thinking originating in the formal operations stage to create complex systems of mental operations. This structural analytic aspect comes into focus when people become able to compare relationships as well as entire representational systems and models. In addition, such individuals can use metasystematic reasoning, the ability to create new mental systems. An example is Albert Einstein's general theory of relativity.

The research by Commons and his colleagues offers an interesting extension of Piaget's work and adds an exciting dimension to the overall study of cognitive development.

UNIT REVIEW

■ Piaget's stage of formal operations encompasses the teenage years. Key cognitive advancements include the ability to think abstractly, the refinement of problem-solving abilities, and literary insight. Adolescent egocentrism, expressed in such behaviors as the imaginary audience and the personal fable, tends to distort cognitive functioning.

■ There may be other cognitive accomplishments beyond formal operations: Research by Michael Commons and associates suggests that a structural analytic stage may exist.

■ Unit Three:

PERSONALITY AND SOCIAL DEVELOPMENT

Social involvement during the teenage years acquires more meaning and significance than at any previous time. Careful observers of this age group discover that personal relationships among teenagers intensify not only because it is important for adolescents to be accepted by their peers, but also because they need to share their new feelings and experiences. At this time, peer groups offer support and security to adolescents who are attempting to break infantile ties to their families. In addition, peer groups provide models for teenagers seeking to establish an identity. Expressing concern over one's dress and appearance, doing extra chores around the house to earn dating money, explaining why an evening curfew was missed, bargaining for the family car, or carrying on frequent and lengthy telephone conversations are characteristic behavioral patterns that reflect adolescents' growing interest in social involvements.

One of the central processes of adolescence is *identity formation,* the procedure of clarifying and integrating oneself into a distinctive, whole person. This is a time when adolescents cognitively reexamine old values and attitudes as they experiment with new ones, a process that may be anxiety provoking for many young people. The ever-changing complexity of society and its many options do not make the quest for identity easy (Josselson, 1980).

Although anxiety is essential to growth, our society frequently regards this emotional reaction negatively. Consequently, members of the older generation may become poor guides for younger generations, being unable to teach them to tolerate growing pains. When most adolescents reach the questioning stage that characterizes this period, they may find the anxiety almost too great to bear, and so they may retreat to their former unquestioning acceptance of the status quo, or they may escape from their inner tension by means of drugs—or they may seek relief in both.

For many adolescents, this important stage may result in little, if any, psychological growth. Rather than discovering who they are, teenagers prematurely identify with their parents' values and goals without questioning whether or not they are right for them. Many abandon the painful task of self-growth for the easier alternative of letting themselves be socialized by others. Some adolescents become increasingly preoccupied with what others think but may be little concerned with what they themselves think. The price that they pay for social maturity thus may be lifelong psychological immaturity, which means that some may never outgrow adolescence.

Personality development takes place against the backdrop of family life.

All of this suggests that personality developments take place within the context of socialization. This means that the accuracy, stability, and acceptance of the self-concept affects the nature and degree of social relationships. Conversely, the feedback and reinforcement from others influence how adolescents perceive themselves. Other developmental forces, too, blend with personality and social growth. Heightened social-cognitive skills, for example, combine with other skills to enable teenagers to examine themselves and others around them with greater understanding and awareness. Adolescents' changing physical, mental, and emotional selves together influence their heterosexual interests, sexual behavior, and social development. Thus, it can be said that personality and social changes do not operate apart from other changes. Instead, they are only some of the developmental changes affecting the whole person (Rogoff, 1989; Wertsch, 1989).

Developmental Tasks of Adolescence

1. Achieving new and more mature relations with age-mates of both sexes.

2. Achieving a masculine or feminine social role.

3. Accepting one's physique and using the body effectively.

4. Achieving emotional independence of parents and other adults.

5. Preparing for marriage and family life.

6. Preparing for an economic career.

7. Acquiring a set of values and an ethical system as a guide to behavior—developing an ideology.

8. Desiring and achieving socially responsible behavior.

(Havighurst, 1972, 1980)

■ Family Influences on the Developing Adolescent

Family life is greatly affected by teenagers' desire for independence and autonomy. Parents at this time are often forced to redefine past child-parent relations and gradually increase the teenager's responsibilities. Parents may realize for the first time that their offspring will soon be moving on and establishing his or her own independent lifestyle and living arrangements. How these two forces blend, the adolescent's desire for greater autonomy and the parents' reaction to this desire, helps determine the emotional climate of the home during this time (Kamptner, 1988; Carter and McGoldrick, 1980).

Although many parents can meet the challenges of this stage, there are some who do not fare as well. Part of the problem is that they resist granting to their children even a little adult status. Rather than promoting responsible behavior, such parents instead overprotect their children and encourage their dependence. Some do not let go of their teenagers because they dread the thought of the next phase of family life, the empty-nest stage. Although the empty-nest stage has numerous positive consequences, some parents have difficulty imagining what life will be like without children in the home. This is especially true for traditional mothers. As Polly Greenberg (1985) observed, when the children leave home, a chapter of a traditional woman's life has ended.

Creating effective communication between parent and adolescent is an important task at this time. So, too, is the parents' need to establish management and control of their teenagers' behavior. This latter task may have caused earlier child-rearing problems, which may now become worse. Parents naturally want to enforce their own standards and values, but these may conflict with the most effective type of authority. Society's swiftly changing values and standards may further complicate this problem.

Evidence also indicates that parents perceive their relationship with their adolescent differently than do outsiders. To show this, two tasks were devised where mother, father, and their adolescent child had to interact. Afterward they viewed a videotape of their interaction and gave a self-rating. Self-ratings were more positive when compared with ratings with another mother-father-adolescent triad and also by a trained observer. Both sets of observers gave more negative ratings than the parents involved in the tasks (Noller and Callan, 1988).

David Knox (1985a) believes that some parents are uncertain whether they want to (or should) be a friend or authority to their offspring. Those wanting to be a friend sometimes report that their children take advantage of the friendship by trying to get out of work or to obtain extra privileges. Those parents that are authority figures sometimes feel like police officers and miss an emotional bond with their offspring. But it has been suggested that being a friend does not eliminate being an authority as well. Indeed, both roles are necessary for parents at various times. Children need parents who can be trusted, who will share their problems of growing up. They also need an authority who will teach them the social skills and work habits needed to survive in society. When successfully balanced, these two forces are likely to promote positive, close, and warm relations between young and old (Josselson, 1988; Baumrind, 1989).

In a study involving sixth, ninth, and twelfth graders, it was found that the older the child, the less cohesiveness they saw in family relationships with the exception of the mother-father dyad (Feldman and Gehring, 1988). However, when there is an intimate bond between parent and child, benefits accrue. One study found that mothers share greater degrees of intimacy with their children than fathers do. On the other hand, paternal intimacy was found to be a greater predictor of positive adolescent functioning than maternal intimacy was (LeCroy, 1988).

☐ Styles of Parental Control

The three major classifications of parental control, you will recall, are authoritarian (or autocratic), authoritative (or democratic), and permissive. In an authoritarian family setting, parents establish the standards of behavior to which the children must adhere. Frequently, respect for authority and work and the preservation of order and traditional structure are emphasized. Furthermore, disciplinary measures are predominantly harsh and forceful.

The authoritarian method of control often leads teenagers to rebel. Often there is a power struggle between parent and adolescent. If the parents are strict, with no room for give-and-take, this may also foster such behaviors as dependence, submissiveness, and conformity. For the parent who mixes authoritarian domination with physical punishment, other problems develop. The use of excessive physical punishment, as we earlier learned, tends to create maladjustment in many areas of personality and social development. In particular, it is likely to result in less self-reliance and confidence and more immaturity and aggressiveness (G. Collins, 1982; Reidy, 1980; Kinard, 1980).

The authoritative method of parental control, in which the adolescent is consulted on family matters, given a fair share of autonomy, and disciplined primarily verbally, tends to be the most effective and rewarding. Authoritative parents are more democratic, allow ample opportunity for adolescents to make their own decisions, but retain the final authority.

In permissive households, parents offer much emotional support to their offspring but exert little control. Adolescents from these homes are frequently allowed to come and go as they please. When permitted to behave as they wish, however, these adolescents may become selfish, insecure, and immature. Sometimes adolescents interpret their parents' lack of assertion as an uncaring attitude, even though the reverse might be true.

How do adolescents perceive these styles of parental control? Which style do they prefer? Such questions were at the heart of research by Cay Kelly and Gail Goodwin (1983). In their study, 100 adolescents were given a questionnaire that examined a number of areas, including the style of control that their parents used and their acceptance or rejection of such control.

Of the responses, 83 percent of the teenagers felt that they had democratic parents, 11 percent had authoritarian parents, and 6 percent had permissive parents. Subjects raised in democratic homes clearly favored this form of parental control. In support of this, they responded favorably to 68 percent of the items on the questionnaire reflecting democratic orientations. Those from autocratic and permissive homes, by comparison, responded positively to 50 percent and 32 percent of the questions, respectively. One important area of autonomy indicated by the adolescents was the right to choose their own friends and dates. As predicted, teenagers raised under democratic parental styles tended to react more positively to parental power than did those from permissive or autocratic homes. Interestingly, even among the teenagers raised in democratic homes, some covert rebellion against parental power was manifested in their assertion of the right to choose their dates and friends.

All of this discussion shows that adolescents prefer households regulated by honesty, fairness, and mutuality. Consultations between parents and teenagers on issues of

Toughlove as a Form of Parental Control

One of the more recent—and controversial—methods of parental control is called **toughlove.** Developed by David and Phyllis York (York and York, 1982; York, York, and Wachtel, 1982), toughlove is designed for parents who are having extreme problems with their teenaged children. Toughlove is a self-help organization that asks parents first to admit that they have a problem they can no longer handle on their own—that they cannot control their children's behavior. Parents turn to toughlove for a variety of teenage problems, including drug abuse and delinquency.

An important feature of toughlove is the view that parents often cannot be effective in a permissive, child-centered culture. Meeting regularly in parent-support groups and maintaining contact between sessions with other group members, toughlove parents are encouraged to take firmer positions with their children and to set a "bottom line" on acceptable behavior in their household. When this standard is violated, the parents, with the support of other group members, are expected to follow through with the consequences that they have established. Suppose that a teenager has a drinking problem and nothing that the family has done to help works. Should the teenager be arrested for drunk driving, a toughlove approach would be to let the adolescent stay in jail for three days. In other instances, the parents might withdraw material resources as the bottom line on unacceptable behavior.

The ultimate sanction is making the teenager move to some other living arrangement—often to the homes of other toughlove parents. These parents are called "advocates," and they help the teenager and his or her parents negotiate a contract setting out the conditions for returning home. Other concerned adults in the community, such as teachers, social workers, and therapists, may also serve as part of the toughlove network.

mutual concern and the provisions of opportunities to enhance the teenagers' autonomy appear to create the healthiest emotional climate. Not only are parent-adolescent relations likely to prosper with such operating principles, but the personal growth of each party is likely to flourish (Niemi, 1988; Larson, 1980). Moreover, a positive home climate may promote more harmonious peer relationships for the teenager (Parke, 1989).

☐ Family Disharmony

We have stressed the importance of a favorable home environment throughout this book. During adolescence, the home environment may be affected not only by the parents' method of discipline but also by how well parents and teenagers understand each other. A lack of understanding and empathy between parents and teenagers is likely to disrupt family harmony and lead to conflicts.

The disagreements and conflicts between parents and teenagers can be numerous and diverse. Some of the common reasons cited for parent-adolescent conflicts are sexual behavior, money, dress, drugs, school performance, friendships in general, and the use of the family car.

Psychological collisions between adolescents and parents also center on values. Mary Ann Lamanna and Agnes Riedmann (1985) wrote that because our society increasingly requires adults to possess their own set of values, teenagers may need to reject those of their parents, at least intellectually and for the time being. Value differences become difficult to negotiate when both teenagers and parents will not compromise. What is obviously needed is good communication between the two. Parents who are willing to listen, observed David Schulz and Stanley Rodgers (1985), will most likely have strong influences on their offspring, even though they may not always agree with them.

In regard to sex differences, males tend to disagree more with their parents. This may be, in part, because females are more susceptible to their parents' influences than males are. In general, females tend to view parental rules and expectations as fair and lenient (Kandel, 1980). Stephen Small, Gay Eastman, and Steven Cornelius (1988) believe that sex differences also exist in parents' reactions to domestic disharmony. Fathers tend to report higher levels of stress if their offspring do not follow prescribed advice or become involved in deviant activities. For mothers, greater levels of stress are often reported when children desire more autonomy and independence.

Often contributing to domestic disharmony is the teenagers' desire for adult status and the parents' resistance. Many teenagers want to establish independent lifestyles. One of the more difficult challenges of the teenage years thus becomes striving for individual autonomy while maintaining harmonious family relations (Smetana, 1988; Sullivan and Sullivan, 1980).

Many teenagers try to escape adult authority in their efforts to attain autonomy. However, whether teenagers actually obtain this latter goal is open to question, especially if they seek the exclusive shelter of their peer group. Sometimes the pressure to conform to group expectations is just as great, if not greater, than the pressure to conform at home. Adolescents may also find that their desire to be with others promotes a new type of dependence (Josselson, 1980).

Teenagers' very desire to be independent may produce its own conflict. Teenagers can no longer be treated as children; on the other hand, they are not yet considered adults. It is not clear when they pass from adolescent to adult status, as our culture has no rites of passage or formal initiation ceremonies that acknowledge an individual's entrance into adulthood. Complicating this issue is the fact that many adolescents have attained only token signs of independence. For example, adolescents may be given the privileges of dressing as they desire or going where they please, behaviors that on the surface seem to represent autonomy. Yet there is no guarantee that beneath the surface these same adolescents have attained psychological or emotional autonomy. Furthermore, some adolescents may have acquired privileges in exchange for their compliance with parental ideals and wishes. This type of trade-off causes many adolescents to settle for ritual signs of independence. Consequently, many forfeit true psychological growth.

Teenage Runaways: Flight from the Family

Family conflicts are not always resolved, and teenagers may thus decide to run away. Each year, about 750,000 choose this course of action, and most are between the ages of 15 and 17. There are slightly more male runaways than females (U.S. Bureau of the Census, 1988).

Most runaways are from white suburbs, although adolescent runaways come from all ethnic and social levels. Most leave home because of destructive family situations or because of a secret personal problem, such as breaking the law or pregnancy. Though some travel only a short distance from home and return in less than a week, three out of ten stay away for longer periods. And some never return home (Nye, 1980).

There are several explanations of why adolescents become runaways. Some leave home to escape pressure and conflict. Others run away because of the freedom that awaits them. In relation to this, some are drawn to drugs, sex, or an escape from routines in general. Finally, some runaways are throwaways. In the face of intolerable parent-adolescent relations, many teenagers are actually encouraged, and in some cases forced, to leave home (Ek and Steelman, 1988; Johnson and Carter, 1980; Turner, 1981).

In recent years, the care and treatment of runaways has increased significantly, although many runaways are never reported. Family therapy is frequently part of the overall treatment program. In cases of parental abuse or lack of parental cooperation, authorities may place the teenager in a foster home. An important step in combating this problem has been the establishment of toll-free hotlines that tell runaways the locations of temporary shelters and enable them to send messages to their parents if they desire. Two of the nationwide toll-free numbers are 800-621-4000 and 800-231-6946. These hotlines do not operate in Alaska or Hawaii (Turner, 1981; Wodarski and Ammons, 1981).

■ School Influences on the Developing Adolescent

Today's modern world is large and confusing, technically complex, and constantly changing. In order for adolescents to acquire that knowledge which will be of service to them in later life, the school remains more than ever a vital and essential institution. Through the efforts of educators, adolescents are prepared and equipped to function effectively in society (Bloome, 1989; Tharpe and Gallimore, 1989).

The school is important during adolescence not only because of the educational information that it transmits, but for other important reasons as well. For example, beyond the sheer amount of time spent in attendance, the school will come to represent the adolescent's society. It is a social setting where individuals from the same life stage can share common experiences and interests. The school also shapes the personality and social development of the adolescent. It offers a testing ground for ideas and discussions, along with an opportunity to engage in decision-making strategies. As such, the school tends to improve interpersonal relationships, including sensitivity to others and communication in general.

☐ Attitudes Toward School

Not all adolescents react to the secondary school setting in the same fashion. On the contrary, while some respond favorably, others react adversely and become quite critical of the institution that they attend. Several background factors, including one's social class, sex, and the effect of the peer group tend to influence the type of attitude exhibited by the adolescent.

Related to social class, attitudes toward high school are less favorable among lower-class adolescents than among those from higher socioeconomic classes. While there are exceptions, adolescents from wealthier families generally place a greater emphasis on the need for higher education and strive to attain good grades. Lower-class adolescents also tend to have lower levels of self-esteem than middle- and upper-class teenagers, a factor that has implications for school performances. A higher dropout rate is also more evident among minority groups and low-income students (Gibbs and Huang, 1989; LaFromboise and Low, 1989).

Sex differences are also apparent in school attitudes. Males seldom become deeply involved in educational endeavors that have low interest value or little significance to their later vocational aspirations. Females, conversely, appear to be equally concerned with all subjects and concentrate on obtaining good grades, a factor which is also linked to female peer acceptance. Females also tend to be more compliant toward the academic expectations and regulations of the school, such as the grading system, the number of absences allowed from class, or general attitudes expected. To adhere to these expectations may be difficult for traditional males because of the seemingly feminine quality that each bears.

The values and educational aspirations of adolescents are also closely associated with the peer groups with which they associate. For example, when the adolescent associates with a peer group that is college oriented, there is a tendency to become interested in educational pursuits appropriate to a college career. However, the closer adolescents are to each other, the greater agreement and similarity there are among such aspirations.

During the teenage years, individuals become increasingly preoccupied with educational and career aspirations.

☐ Student-Teacher Relationships

One of the most prominent factors affecting academic performance is the teacher-student relationship. Similar to earlier school experiences, students respond most favorably to those teachers who are self-controlled, warm, and friendly in their classroom interactions. Democratic and integrative systems of classroom control tend to encourage cooperation, sensitivity toward others, and task-oriented student behaviors.

Teachers are in a prime position to enhance the many challenges that accompany the secondary school experience. More specifically, teachers can help adolescents become academically successful, earn self-respect, and heighten individuality. Note the interplay here between developmental forces, notably adolescent cognitive functioning and the Eriksonian challenge of identity formation.

It is especially important for teachers to help teenagers achieve a sense of identity because the educational process tends to manufacture high levels of conformity. This may explain why so many adolescents are without any commitment to self, morally parochial, and compliant. It may also explain, in part, why identity foreclosure is so common at this age.

A possible solution to this may be the development of a curriculum that is suited to each individual's capacity to absorb, rather than following prearranged outlines. Treating the adolescent in a mature fashion and teaching the importance of responsibility are also important. The school needs to represent an environment where the adolescent can develop each day. All too often, teachers forget how many times the adolescent can be regarded as an adult, treating them instead with childish protectiveness and circumventing them with restrictions. Often, adolescents react to such measures with predictable behaviors: apathy, passive resignation, and rebellion.

The most favorable attitudes and greatest learning readiness evolve when students perceive that their teachers are interested in them as well as the subject material being taught. In an ideal setting, the two can discuss not only academics, but also the student's career ambitions, interests, and goals. Should this result, the teacher looms as an instrumental force in shaping the adolescent's mental awareness and nurturing the development of dignity and self-respect.

■ Peer Group Influences on the Developing Adolescent

As the need to be recognized and accepted magnifies during adolescence, the peer group becomes a critical agent of socialization. With the teenagers' dependence on the family lessened, replacement security is found among peers who share similar feelings and attitudes. As Sarah Cirese (1985) put it, adolescence becomes a critical time for belonging and fitting in. The companionship offered by the peer group or friendships in general is usually trusting, trustworthy, and steadfast. Not only do peers seek companionship from one another, but as they age, they are more apt to seek advice from each other, although adults remain important sources of support throughout adolescence (Wintre, Hicks, McVey, and Fox, 1988).

Teenagers' interactions with peers continue to be heavily influenced by their developing social cognition abilities. More specifically, their advanced mental abilities enhance their interpersonal awareness. For instance, adolescence is the time when individuals can empathize and understand the perspectives of others. As a result, teenagers become more sensitive to the needs of others. Adolescents are also able to make psychological inferences about people, a cognitive capacity that eluded them earlier (Clark and Ayers, 1988; Kelly and deArmas, 1989; McGuire and Weisz, 1982; Barenboim, 1981; Elkind, 1980).

Adolescents typically do not want to be perceived as being different from one another. As a result, they tend to conform closely to established peer group norms. Eager to attain social acceptance, adolescents pay close attention to current fads, such as length of hair, style of dress, and popular activities. They are also acutely aware of the types of behavior that will earn peer approval. Females, more than males, are concerned with popularity and group acceptance. The desire for social acceptance is also more pronounced among the middle and upper classes than among the lower socioeconomic classes (Sebald, 1981).

Susan O'Brien and Karen Bierman (1988) have supplied insight into how the peer group influences adolescent behavior. In their study, 72 fifth, eighth, and eleventh graders were interviewed to investigate developmental changes in perceptions of peer groups and group influence. Younger subjects defined groups on the basis of common activities and social behavior and considered group influence to be greatest in these domains. Older adolescents were more likely to describe peer-group influence as global and far-reaching, affecting one's appearance, attitudes, and values. Older adolescents, more so than the younger subjects, felt that peer group acceptance or rejection influenced self-evaluation.

☐ Patterns of Peer Group Interaction

Observe any adolescent social setting, whether it be a high school rock concert, a weekend sporting event, or any number of after-school activities, and you're likely to witness several socialization processes: the development of close-knit friendships, cliques, and crowds. Such gatherings represent elite and exclusive socialization processes. Membership is frequently determined on the basis of similarity in such areas as social class, interest areas (such as style of dress), use of slang, athletics, and intellectual abilities.

Relating with members of the opposite sex is an important part of adolescent socialization.

A *friendship* is the smallest type of peer group and is the pairing off of two individuals who are likely to have similar personalities and temperaments. Usually, early teenage friendships are based on shared interests and activities. This is also true of older adolescents' friendships, but they are also accompanied by a strong emotional bond and psychological commitment between the partners. Females are more drawn to emotional and intimate aspects of a friendship. For this reason, female friendships are said to be "face to face," and male friendships are "side to side" (Parker and Gottman, 1989; Wright, 1982; Coleman, 1980; Richey and Richey, 1980; Tesch, 1983; Berndt, 1982; Hunter and Youniss, 1982).

Similar to the friendship, but larger in size is the *clique*. Individuals in cliques have common interests and a strong emotional attachment to one another. The clique is highly exclusive, usually consisting of adolescents of the same socioeconomic background who hold similar interests, attitudes, and beliefs.

Finally, we come to the *crowd*. Although the crowd is more impersonal and lacks the strong bonds of attachment that cliques offer, it maintains rather rigid membership requirements. Being a member of a clique is often a prerequisite for crowd membership. The distinguishing features of crowds are heterosexual interaction and emphasis on social events, such as athletic contests and dances.

☐ Sex Differences in Adolescent Friendships

From the adolescent years on, the behavioral dimensions of female and male friendships acquire unique characteristics. Let us first examine the importance of intimacy, an ingredient of friendships that increases during this time (Berndt and Perry, 1990; Buhrmester, 1989).

Females tend to have more intimate and exclusive friendships than males do. Moreover, the closer the female's friendships are, the more revealing her self-disclosure will be. This is often true regardless of whether females are interacting with the same or the opposite sex. Males, on the other hand, tend to downplay intimate self-disclosure and the emotional closeness of a relationship. Their emphasis is, rather, on such things as interest in the same activities (Berndt, 1982; Dickens and Perlman, 1981; Wheeler, Reis, and Nezlek, 1983).

The notion that there are sex differences in the intimacy of self-disclosure has received considerable research attention. In one study (Grigsby and Weatherley, 1983), female and male adolescents were involved in a deception that led them to believe that they were sharing self-disclosures with a stranger of the same sex whom they would later meet. The recorded comments revealed clear-cut gender differences in the tendency to self-disclose. Clearly, females were more likely to disclose revealing information about themselves during the acquaintanceship process.

In regard to sex differences and amounts of self-disclosure, we should acknowledge the viewpoints of Sharon Brehm (1985). She found that both males and females need the same qualities in their interactions in order to avoid loneliness. Males usually desire emotional intimacy just as much as females do. But unfortunately, it is difficult for them to express this and to achieve interpersonal comfort and acceptance with their partners. However, this latter point may be changing, at least according to Letitia Peplau (1983). In reviewing the literature, she observed fewer sex differences in regard to self-disclosure, particularly among college students. It seems that younger, better-educated couples are moving away from the traditional pattern of silent men and talkative women.

There are other differences in regard to female and male friendships. For example, Thomas Berndt (1982) believes that females, more than males, expect to share thoughts and feelings with their partners. Females are also more sensitive to rejection from friends. Carol Gilligan (1982) added that females are also likely to be more selective and exclusive in their friendships. This may be because once they have found a friend, females are more apt to invest their resources emotionally and offer a strong psychological commitment to their partner. The commitment from males is often not as great and is more objective and rational.

Finally, there appear to be sex differences in regard to communication styles, particularly listening behavior. One study (Booth-Butterfield, 1984) focused on how the socialization process affects sex differences in listening. The authors contended that as boys and girls grow up, they are taught and reinforced in different styles of listening. The primary difference is in task versus interpersonal understanding; that is, males are taught to listen for facts, and females are taught to listen for the mood of the communication. Males thus often have trouble listening for nonverbal cues, whereas females, who are listening for the mood of the communication, pick them up much more readily.

■ Heterosexual Development

Dating typically begins during the adolescent years and is a process that will move the teenager from his or her single status to the married status of the adult. The dating process includes various relationships and experiences with members of the opposite sex, from casual encounters to deeper and more durable relationships with potential marriage partners (Dyer, 1983).

Dating has several important functions:

- ■ It serves as a form of recreation and a source of companionship.

- ■ It represents a social vehicle that enables teenagers to learn more about themselves and how they are perceived by others.

- ■ It teaches the importance of reciprocity, mutuality, and sensitivity.

- ■ It offers teenagers an opportunity to experience love and sexual relations within mutually acceptable limits.

- ■ It is a courtship process designed to facilitate mate selection.

Over the years, the character of dating has changed. Earlier in history, dating was formal and structured and reflected traditional sex-role stereotyping. The male usually asked the female out, provided transportation, and absorbed the expenses. Although traditional behaviors still exist, today dating is more likely to be casual and less sex-role stereotyped. Many couples now extend dating invitations to each other and share expenses and transportation (Bell and Coughey, 1980; Murstein, 1980).

Teenagers look for certain qualities in a date. Physical attractiveness, personality, and compatibility are equally important to both males and females. How prestigious their date is appears to be more important to females. This might be linked to the fact that females, more than males, view dating as a means to raise their popularity and status in the peer group. Finally, both males and females value honesty and their partner's contribution of companionship and enjoyment to a relationship (Duck, 1989; Lerner and Lerner, 1988; Hansen and Hicks, 1980; Rubin, 1980b).

A teenage couple may move from a casual relationship to a serious commitment. Depending on their social circle, this may be called "going steady" or "seeing someone." Although the meaning of this type of relationship varies from couple to couple, going steady generally implies a more serious relationship in which both parties refrain from dating others. J. Ross Eshleman (1985) saw it as a device for individuals to reduce the open competition and to provide anticipatory socialization for the marital role. This is not to say, however, that adolescents are faithful in their relationships. Dating infidelity is a frequent cause of frustration to adolescents (Roscoe, Cavanaugh, and Kennedy, 1988).

Adolescent Sexual Behavior

Research supports the fact that a greater percentage of today's teenagers and young adults are engaging in premarital intercourse than in the past. A comparison of Alfred Kinsey's classic studies of male and female sexual behavior (Kinsey, Pomeroy, and Martin, 1948; Kinsey, Pomeroy, Martin, and Gebhard, 1953) with more recent investigations will illustrate this point. When Kinsey conducted his research, he discovered that approximately 20 percent of all females and about 40 percent of all males queried had experienced sexual intercourse by the time they were 20. More contemporary research provides us with an interesting comparison. Many of these studies report significant increases in the percentages reported by Kinsey and his colleagues. In fact, a glance at the findings reveals that it is not uncommon to find approximately 50 percent of the females and about 70 percent of the males surveyed engaging in premarital intercourse before age 20 (Brooks-Gunn and Furstenberg, 1989; National Research Council, 1987; Kantner and Zelnik, 1980; Clayton and Bokemeier, 1980; Bell and Coughey, 1980; Robinson and Jedlicka, 1982).

In relation to the foregoing, consider the findings of a fairly extensive research study (Coles and Stokes, 1985). In this particular investigation, rates of premarital intercourse were about equal between the sexes: 53 percent of the females and 46 percent of the males reported having had intercourse by age 18. Interestingly, most of the teenagers had carefully planned this event. Well over half (57 percent) talked the

The dynamics of teenage sexual interactions have attracted considerable research attention.

matter over with their first partner before having intercourse. And, contrary to popular myth, females were more likely to have had such discussions—hence are less likely than males to have been "swept away"—by a margin of 64 percent to 52 percent.

Rarely did any of the respondents (less than 5 percent) have their first intercourse with a stranger. Statistics revealed that for approximately one-quarter (23 percent), the first partner was a friend; for more than two-thirds (68 percent), it was a boyfriend or girlfriend. Males seem to have been more casual than females, however; about one-third (32 percent) of them describe their first partner as a friend—more than half as many as the 61 percent whose partner was a girlfriend. By contrast, more than three-quarters of the females (76 percent) were with their boyfriends; only 13 percent were with friends. Females tend to be significantly older at the time of their first intercourse. In another study younger siblings were believed to have higher levels of sexual activity than their older siblings (Rogers and Rowe, 1988).

Coles and Stokes (1985) also found that more than half the teens (54 percent) first had intercourse at their own or their partners' houses, 15 percent were at a third party's house, only 2 percent were in a hotel or motel—not surprising given the ages at which first intercourse took place—and 15 percent were outdoors. The traditional trysting place, a parked car, was actually used by only 12 percent of teenagers.

Finally, it was discovered that, in general, no matter what the degree of planning or of logistic difficulty, most of the teens regarded their first experience positively. Only 5 percent said they were "sorry they had the experience;" the rest were pretty evenly divided between "glad" (43 percent) and "ambivalent" (46 percent). Females, however, were much more likely than males to express sadness or ambivalence.

It should be noted, though, that females were more likely than males to feel that their relationship with their first partner improved after intercourse. Their lingering regret, despite the improved relationship, suggests that females place a higher value on virginity. About half, for instance, want to be virgins when they marry, while only one-third of the boys want to marry a virgin. Fifteen percent of the females who had already had intercourse said they had wanted to be virgins when they married.

MOTIVES FOR PREMARITAL INTERCOURSE There are a variety of reasons for engaging in premarital intercourse, including desire for intimacy; feelings of trust, love, and caring; pressure to please one's partner; and an attempt to improve a couple's relationship. Other reasons include a physiological need for a sexual outlet or an experience to test the capacities, both sexual and physical, of marital compatibility.

Beyond these reasons, Roger Rubin (1985) adds that motivation often arises from loneliness; from a desire to release tension and frustration; from a need to control and dominate others; from a desire for revenge; from a desire to escape oneself; from a need to communicate; or to convey love and spiritual harmony. Sex is sometimes used to salvage a doomed relationship. It may also make a person feel wanted and loved, even without a deep commitment. It may serve as an outlet for aggression or an expression of gratitude. Sexual activity may be a way to bolster an ego because of an inadequate career or to flee the pressures of a family breakup. Finally, it may be a source of power, even for those who are often the weakest and most vulnerable.

A number of reasons are also given for *not* engaging in sexual intercourse. For females, two of the more common reasons are the fear of pregnancy and the guilt over loss of virginity. This is also a source of anxiety for males as far as responsibility is concerned. Some couples also fear public disapproval. For many, another important reason for refraining is the fear of contracting a sexually transmitted disease, a topic to be covered later in this chapter.

FACTORS AFFECTING PREMARITAL INTERCOURSE Certain factors affect the rates of premarital coitus. As the aforementioned statistics imply, rates will increase as adolescents get older. Actual frequency of premarital coitus is also greater among lower socioeconomic, noncollege adolescents than among higher socioeconomic youths who attend college. Rates are also greater for adolescents who do not attend church on a regular basis. Also, Protestant, college females have higher rates of premarital intercourse than either Catholic or Jewish females. Finally, blacks, more than whites, engage more frequently in premarital coitus (Laner and Housker, 1980; Clayton and Bokemeier, 1980; Bell and Coughey, 1980; Inazu and Fox, 1980).

As far as gender is concerned, rates of premarital intercourse are generally higher among males. However, research included in this discussion and other investigations (Sack et al., 1984) reveals that this is not always the case. However, it seems that males generally want sexual intercourse before females do during the dating relationship. Almost half the college-aged males surveyed in one study (Knox and Wilson, 1981) felt that intercourse was appropriate by the fifth date, in contrast to about 25 percent of females surveyed. Does this mean that individuals should circle their calendars and set their watches in anticipation of the fifth date? Hardly. This is strictly an average and should not be taken out of context.

Also related to gender, William Talmadge (1985) adds that males and females are becoming less different in relation to their sexual attitudes. The attitudes of both are becoming more permissive, and the degree of commitment in the relationship appears to be the key determining factor in sexual behavior. As we learned earlier, sexual intercourse with casual strangers is much less acceptable among young people. Should conservative sex attitudes prevail, they are likely to originate from such factors as guilt, inaccurate sex information, or fear of sexually transmitted diseases.

Finally, we need to acknowledge that sexual attitudes and behavior for both sexes are shaped by such factors as education or family influences. As far as the former is concerned, many sources (Tatum, 1989; Rosenberg, 1989; Hammes, 1989) believe that sexuality education helps teenagers to understand the place of sexuality in human life and loving. Some, such as Andrea Parrot (1984) feel that adolescents participating in

There are many motives for sexual intimacy.

sexuality education programs at home and school are more likely to postpone sexual experimentation longer than their peers. Furthermore, when they do become sexually active, they are more likely to use contraceptives to prevent pregnancy. In short, by providing adolescents with some information about their sexuality, they are apt to make decisions that are right for them based on fact, not peer pressure. Research has also shown (Davidson and Darling, 1988) that sexuality education enhances a person's knowledge of sexual practices, including more tolerant and accepting attitudes toward variations in sexual pleasuring.

Parents are quite influential in shaping teenagers' sexual attitudes and overall levels of sexual knowledge. Judith Alter (1989) writes that parents can exert positive influences by discussing sexuality with their offspring in supportive and nonthreatening ways. A study conducted by Gregory Sanders and Ronald Mullis (1988) illustrates the impact parents can have on adolescent sexual attitudes. The two researchers asked 65 female college students to complete a questionnaire assessing family strengths, premarital sexual permissiveness attitudes, sex-role behavior attitudes, and sexual knowledge. The gathered data showed that parents were rated highest in terms of influence on sexual opinions, beliefs, and attitudes. However, parents were rated lower than friends, schools, and books as sources of information. Specific family strengths as perceived by the subjects were related to amount of parental influence, parents' positive or negative reaction to sex education, and their sexual permissiveness.

ETHNIC DIFFERENCES IN PREMARITAL SEXUAL BEHAVIOR An interesting longitudinal study of teenagers' sexual behavior has revealed interesting ethnic differences. The two-year study, conducted by Edwin Smith and Richard Udry (1985), examined 492 white males and 516 white females, and 183 black males and 178 black females. When the subjects were first surveyed, they were between the ages of 12 and 15. At that time, 29.3 percent of the white males and 11.1 percent of the white females had already had intercourse. Among the adolescent black males, 75.8 percent had experienced intercourse and 40.5 percent of the black females were no longer virgins. Two years later, 67.9 percent of the 28 virgins among the black males had experienced intercourse, compared with 30.7 percent of the white males. Twenty-three percent of the white girls who were virgins at the beginning of the study had intercourse during the two-year period, compared with 41 percent of the virgin black girls. Similar studies substantiate these findings (e.g., Franklin, 1988).

Beyond the obvious differences between rates of premarital intercourse, unique ethnic and cultural patterns of sexual behavior appeared. In general, young white males and females followed a predictable sequence of precoital petting stages. They progressed from kissing and necking to light petting (above the waist and over the clothing) to heavy petting before reaching the point of first intercourse. The sequence tended to extend over a long period and allowed youngsters time between dates to think about where they were headed and consider the consequences. They could also date others without feeling they were reneging on a sexual commitment.

Black teens, on the other hand, were likely to follow a much less predictable pattern of precoital behavior. Progression to intercourse was more rapid, with teenagers often moving directly from light necking to intercourse with no stops between. In many instances, heavy petting was bypassed entirely.

The researchers felt that these different behavior patterns originate from different sets of cultural expectations. For example, white adolescents often grow up expecting to do a lot of necking and petting before eventually engaging in intercourse or rejecting it. This expectation allows a longer preparatory period before sexual commitment and can provide a rather long period of abstinence before "date" is ultimately transformed into "mate." The prolonged sequence also gives adolescents a chance to think about contraception and do something about it. Among black adolescents, however, the normative expectations often result in precipitous coitus.

It was also observed that the differences between black and white adolescents' approach to the physical aspects of dating obviously influenced the likelihood of contraceptive use. For white females, necking on one date was not likely to escalate into intercourse on the next. For black adolescents, however, necking might be one of the few behaviors engaged in before intercourse, the researchers felt. For white females, the "next move"—above the waist petting—was not affected by the lack of contraception. For black females, the next move might be unprotected intercourse and as a result, unwanted pregnancy.

These different patterns of expectations and subsequent behavior may be a partial explanation for the differing pregnancy rates in the two groups, the researchers suggest. They add that the need to obtain contraception when the most intimate experience a black youngster has had is necking probably may seem pointless from the youngster's perspective. However, if counselors and sex educators are more aware of cultural differences in sexual patterns, they may be able to reach black teens and help them adjust to their growing sexuality and its consequences.

☐ Premarital Pregnancy

Premarital pregnancies are rapidly increasing in the United States, most noticeably among teenagers. Approximately 1 million adolescent females become pregnant annually. Of this total, about 600,000 give birth to their babies. With birth rates for older women declining, statistics reveal that one out of every five new mothers today is a teenager. Perhaps the most shocking statistic is that approximately one out of every ten teenagers will become a mother by her eighteenth birthday (National Research Council, 1987; Nye and Lamberts, 1980). Figure 8-2 displays pregnancy rates of American teenage families with those from other nations.

These figures do not tell the whole story. Consider the following in relation to this social problem: Many adolescents become pregnant in their early or middle teens; about 30,000 of them each year are under age 15. Nearly half of all black females in the United States, whose pregnancy rate from the ages of 15 to 19 is almost twice that among white females, are pregnant by age 20. If the present trends continue, it is estimated that 40 percent of all of today's 14-year-old females will be pregnant at least once before the age of 20 (Wallis, 1985).

Many reasons can be cited to explain why these figures are so high. The liberal sexual attitudes and behavior of today's youth culture is often quoted, as is the earlier sexual maturity of teenagers. Some adolescents do not care about the consequences of their sexual behavior; others become pregnant because they want to have a baby. The misuse of contraceptives, or the absence of any birth control whatsoever, are other important contributing reasons (Kelley, 1981; Oskamp and Mindick, 1981; Strahle, 1983).

IMPLICATIONS OF UNWED PREGNANCY Teenage pregnancies introduce drastic disruptions into the lives of adolescents, their offspring, their parents, and the society as a whole. Lacking a supportive family and the requisite material and psychological resources for child rearing (see, for example, Culp and associates, 1988), the lives of the mother and of her child are disrupted from the start, and so are the lives of their families, parents, and grandparents. The problem is also passed on to the wider com-

Pregnancy rates per 1,000 teenage females
Each figure equals 10 pregnancies

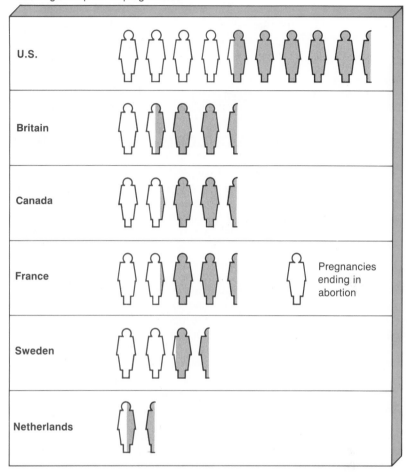

FIGURE 8-2 International comparison of teenage pregnancies (Source: Guttmacher Institute, 1985).

munity and to public institutions. Teenage mothers cost the taxpayers excessive sums of money each year and, in addition, they face social disapproval and financial hardships. Those who marry have an exceptionally high divorce rate. The sexually transmitted disease rate for these adolescents is also high, with gonorrhea rating in the adolescents second only to the common cold (Smith and Kolenda, 1984).

There are numerous health risks, too, for the children of teenage mothers. The younger the mother is, the greater the chances of infant death. Teenage mothers are more apt to have premature births than older mothers and are more likely to experience labor and delivery complications, including toxemia and anemia. The babies themselves frequently suffer from neurological problems and birth defects. Children of teenage mothers also tend to have lower IQs and perform more poorly in school than children of older mothers (Broman, 1981; Chilman, 1980). Studies also show (Davis, 1988) that many teenage mothers are from lower socioeconomic brackets. Babies born to poor teenage mothers tend to have lower birth weights and, during the first month of life, there is a greater risk for infant mortality.

This discussion highlights the magnitude of teenage pregnancies and their far-reaching implications. It represents a social problem needing the attention of everyone. Beyond the need for information on birth control, which we have already mentioned,

International Lifespan Development

■ CHILDREN HAVING CHILDREN: THE RISKS OF TEENAGE PREGNANCY

In cultures all around the world, the consequences of adolescent pregnancy and child rearing are dramatic. The most obvious set of risks are health related. Mothers under age 20, as a group, suffer more pregnancy and delivery complications than women who bear children at age 20 or later. Problems reported from diverse parts of the world include higher than average levels of toxemia, anemia, bleeding, cervical trauma, disproportion between the size of the infant's head and the mother's pelvis, prolonged and difficult labor, and death. The risk of a teenage mother developing such problems, though, are greater in developing than in developed nations, and greater among poorer compared to better-off adolescents within countries.

Worldwide, pregnancy-related deaths are the primary cause of death among females between the ages of 15 and 19. In Sierra Leone, Africa, the 15 to 28 age group accounts for almost 40 percent of pregancy-related complications. Poor living conditions in that country, as well as inadequate nutrition, prenatal care, and health education, aggravate the risks compared to developed nations. In most Latin American and Caribbean countries, childbearing and abortion are ranked in the top five causes of death for 15- to 19-year-old women, with the phenomenon most common in Jamaica. In Bangladesh, birth-related complications, including those developing from abortion, are the leading cause of death among teenage women.

Furthermore, pregnancy-related mortality rates are higher for teenagers than for older women in developed countries. In Canada, as an illustration, they are twice as high. Maternal mortality rates for females under 16 in England are four times the overall rate for older women. Additionally, many children born to teenage mothers suffer from reduced mental capability and psychological consequences. For example, many European babies born to teenage mothers suffer from slightly lower IQs, compared to children born to older mothers, and many are also at a greater risk for abuse and health hazards.

We must recognize, however, that many of the aforementioned consequences are not related directly with age but rather with inadequate prenatal care and nutrition. For example, European adolescents having first births and who participate in special prenatal programs tend to have no greater obstetrical risks than adult women. Among Swedish teenage mothers, complications are no more frequent than with older mothers if they experience proper prenatal attention. The same holds true for teenage mothers in Kenya.

However, one of the most dramatic and long-term consequences of teenage pregnancy is the curtailment of a woman's education and vocational aspirations. In some societies, pregnancy itself is a reason to expel a female from school. This is the case with 2 percent of all schoolgirls in Zambia. In Tanzania, 92 percent of female dropout students cite pregnancy as the primary reason. In the Caribbean, one-third of all pregnancies are to women under age 19. Consequently, a substantial number of females drop out of school and face little or no chance for readmission. In Costa Rica, 51 percent of pregnant females who attend school drop out because of the pregnancy, and 61 percent who work terminate their employment.

Finally, developing as well as developed nations report lowered occupational status and reduced income as a direct result of curtailed education. In the United States and many European nations, women who are teenage mothers earn about 50 percent of the income of those who first gave birth in their twenties. Moreover, the cycle of poverty is influenced by this fertility pattern. That is, the children of teenage parents are more likely to become teenage parents themselves than those who were born when their parents were older (Senderowitz and Paxman, 1985).

sex education as a whole needs to be stressed. This includes in the home, school, and within those institutional settings facing the problem. Making parents more aware of the problem and encouraging viable forms of communication with their teenage offspring is also being stressed. The emotional support that parents can offer is considered critical (Byrne, 1983; Fisher, 1983).

Finally, those teenagers who decide to keep their children need our help as well. Programs need to focus on the health-care needs of both mother and child. Attention also needs to be directed toward increasing the educational level of teenage parents, especially the mother, in addition to upgrading vocational skills (Wallace and Vienonen, 1989; Rickel, 1989; Edelman, 1987; Conger, 1988).

☐ Sexually Transmitted Diseases

Sexually active adolescents and adults must take special precautions to safeguard themselves against sexually transmitted diseases. A *sexually transmitted disease,* also called venereal disease, is a contagious infection passed on by intimate sexual contacts, including coitus, oral-genital sex, or anal intercourse. Five of the more common diseases are the acquired immune deficiency syndrome (AIDS), chlamydia, gonorrhea, syphilis, and genital herpes.

ACQUIRED IMMUNE DEFICIENCY SYNDROME (AIDS) The *acquired immune deficiency syndrome (AIDS)* is a fatal disease caused by a virus. It is characterized by a specific defect in the body's natural immunity against disease. People who suffer from AIDS become susceptible to a variety of rare illnesses. These illnesses remain dormant in or are fought off by people whose immune systems are normal.

To date, no one has ever been cured of AIDS. As of 1989, an estimated 1.5 million people were thought to be infected with the HIV virus. Over 100,000 individuals were diagnosed as having AIDS, and more than 55,000 had died from the disease. By the early 1990s, it is projected that more than 350,000 Americans will have AIDS and 190,000 will have died (Centers for Disease Control, 1989).

It should be pointed out that nobody actually dies of AIDS. Its victims are not claimed by a single mysterious disease. Rather, individuals with AIDS almost uniformly have reduced numbers of lymphocytes, specialized white blood cells that are critical in combating infectious diseases. AIDS patients thus die of infections and diseases that are able to thrive in a body with a hopelessly weakened immune system. Most of these diseases are treatable and, in fact, AIDS patients often are cured of them. But they either return or are followed by other diseases until the body simply can no longer resist.

AIDS is caused by a virus called the human immunodeficiency virus (HIV), formerly referred to as HTLV-III/LAV. Infection with the HIV virus does not always lead to AIDS and many infected persons may remain in good health. The virus is spread primarily through exchanging bodily fluids (blood, semen, urine, feces, saliva, and vaginal secretions) with an infected person. The virus cannot pass through unbroken skin; it must enter through an opening, such as a wound or other break in the skin. Anal intercourse, common in the hardest hit community of gay men, often damages the lining of the rectum, leaving an opening through which the virus can enter the body. AIDS can also be transmitted from men to women during anal sex or vaginal sex when penetration causes tiny abrasions in the vagina.

There are other ways to contract AIDS. Needles shared by intravenous drug addicts can carry the virus from one person to another. The HIV virus has also been found in blood donated to blood banks. Persons receiving a blood transfusion may have gotten the virus in this way, but since the development of a blood test for signs of infection by the virus, blood banks now throw away donated blood that is found to be contaminated. Women may be able to pass the disease to men, since the AIDS virus could be present in menstrual blood and vaginal secretions. The risk of AIDS is increased by having multiple sexual partners (Bingham, 1989; Hein, 1989).

The symptoms of AIDS include low-grade fever, swollen lymph glands, weight loss, fatigue, night sweats, long-standing diarrhea, and a generally sick feeling. Up to one-third of the victims develop a previously rare cancer known as Kaposi's sarcoma, which can appear as purplish bumps on the skin. Many develop a severe form of pneumonia. The main problem, however, is the inability of the body to fight many diseases that come along, including various cancers, skin infections, fungus growths, and tuberculosis.

As earlier indicated, there is no cure for AIDS to date. One of the drugs showing promise in the 1990's is *zidovudine* (ZDV), previously known as azidothymidine (AZT). ZDV is currently the only drug licensed as a treatment for AIDS. ZDV appears to delay the onset of AIDS in people who are HIV positive but have no symptoms. However, it remains unknown how long the use of the drug delays the development of such diseases as Kaposi's sarcoma or pneumocystis carinii. Because ZDV is highly toxic, about one-half of AIDS patients cannot tolerate its side effects, including various anemias. It is also an expensive medication. In 1990 dollars, ZDV cost approximately $7,500 per year.

Some AIDS patients with Kaposi's sarcoma are being treated experimentally with forms of interferon—a virus-fighting protein produced by the body. Although some success against Kaposi's sarcoma has been reported, interferon treatment does not

AIDS: How to Protect Yourself from Infection

Some personal measures are adequate to safely protect yourself and others from infection by the HIV virus and its complications. Among these are the following:

■ If you have been involved in any of the high-risk sexual activities just described or have injected illicit intravenous drugs into your body, you should have a blood test to see if you have been infected with the HIV virus.

■ If your test is positive or if you engage in high-risk activities and choose not to have a test, you should tell your sexual partner. If you jointly decide to have sex, you must protect your partner by always using a rubber (condom) during (start to finish) sexual intercourse (vagina or rectum).

■ If your partner has a positive blood test showing that he/she has been infected with the HIV virus or you suspect that he/she has been exposed by previous heterosexual or homosexual behavior or use of intravenous drugs with shared

needles and syringes, a rubber (condom) should always be used during (start to finish) sexual intercourse (vagina or rectum).

■ If you or your partner is at high risk, avoid mouth contact with the penis, vagina, or rectum.

■ Avoid all sexual activities which could cause cuts or tears in the linings of the rectum, vagina, or penis.

■ Do not have sex with prostitutes. Infected male and female prostitutes are frequently also intravenous drug abusers; therefore, they may infect clients by sexual intercourse and other intravenous drug abusers by sharing their intravenous drug equipment. Female prostitutes also can infect their unborn babies.

Source: Surgeon General's Report on ACQUIRED IMMUNE DEFICIENCY SYNDROME. *Washington, D.C.: U.S. Department of Health and Human Services, 1987.*

appear to restore immune function. There are other treatments, such as radiation, drugs, and surgery for many of the illnesses suffered by AIDS patients.

Limited trials of a substance called interleukin-2, which scientists believe may help fight the severe deficiencies seen in the immune system of AIDS patients, will begin soon. Preliminary laboratory results are promising, but much more work remains to be done. Also promising are vaccines designed to stimulate human antibody production. One of these, developed in 1987, consists of a purified protein substance from the outer coat of the AIDS virus. Theoretically, the protein will stimulate an immune response but will not cause the diseases, because other components that give the AIDS virus its virulence have been left out. Beyond these vaccines, there are the experimental drugs suramin, ribavirin, and foscarnet. All are believed to interfere with a key step in the AIDS virus's action. Others are placing their hopes on the natural properties of egg lecithin, first used in Israel.

CHLAMYDIA *Chlamydia* infections occur in the urethra, cervix, or rectum of sexually active adults. Such infections are caused by a parasite called chylamdia trachomatis, which has both viral and bacterial characteristics. In recent years, chlamydial infections have reached epidemic proportions, affecting over 3 million persons annually.

Chlamydia is an insidious disease; that is, signs and symptoms may not appear until complications set in. For women, these complications often include pelvic inflammatory disease (an infection of the female reproductive organs) and cervicitus (infection of the cervix). Pregnant women with chlamydial infection also risk spontaneous abortion, stillbirth, and postpartum fever. Infants can acquire this infection while passing through the birth canal, often developing an eye infection called chlamydial conjunctivitis and pneumonia. Chlamydial infections in men often lead to epididymitis (infection of the epididymis), nongonococcal urethritis (infection of the urethra), and proctitus (inflammation of the mucous membranes of the rectum).

Chlamydia is usually treated with tetracycline, erythromycin, or their derivatives. Because chlamydia commonly accompanies gonorrhea, treatment often includes tetracycline and penicillin to ensure eradication of both organisms. For neonates, an application of tetracycline or erythromycin ointment prevents chlamydial conjunctivitis.

GONORRHEA *Gonorrhea* is one of the most common of all sexually transmitted diseases, afflicting more than 1 million individuals each year. It is much more common in males and is highly contagious. Gonorrhea is caused by a bacterial infection and is spread by direct sexual contact with an infected person. It is a disease that usually affects the penis in men, the vagina in women, and the throat and anus in both sexes. Left untreated, it can lead to a generalized blood infection, sterility, arthritis, and heart trouble. Moreover, in men it can spread throughout the prostate gland and the male duct system, causing painful inflammation.

Also, gonorrhea can lead to infections if the eyes come in contact with the genital secretions. This can happen, for example, if the person rubs the eyes after handling the infected genital organs. Also, during the birth process, a baby can contract this disease when it passes through the mother's potentially infected birth canal. Today, most states require that a few drops of silver nitrate or penicillin be placed in the eyes of all newborns to prevent infection and possible blindness from this infectious disease.

For males, symptoms of gonorrhea include a yellow discharge from the penis, usually within two to ten days after the disease has been contracted. Painful and burning urination is also commonly reported. For females, gonorrhea may exist in the early stages without any observable symptoms. However, in time it is often marked by a discharge from the vagina and urethra; frequent, painful urination; cloudy urine; vomiting; and diarrhea. Gonorrhea can also lead to a pelvic inflammatory disease which, in turn, can cause sterility.

Gonorrhea can usually be controlled by antibiotics, with a single injection of penicillin effecting a cure. While under treatment, the patient should abstain from sexual activity until further tests have confirmed that gonorrhea is no longer present. This is usually done one week after treatment begins and sometimes again two weeks later. The treatment of gonorrhea, similar to all forms of sexually transmitted diseases, requires that every sexual partner of the infected person also be examined and treated if necessary.

SYPHILIS *Syphilis* claims an estimated 150,000 new victims each year. Syphilis is caused by spirochetes, thin corkscrewlike organisms that thrive in warm, moist environments. This highly infectious disease enters the body through any tiny break in the mucous membranes and then burrows itself into the bloodstream. Besides sexual contact through intercourse, syphilis can be contracted through the use of contaminated needles.

Left untreated, syphilis can affect all parts of the body: the brain, bones, spinal cord, and heart, as well as the reproductive organs. Blindness, brain damage, heart disease, and even death can result. Syphilis can also be transmitted from a mother to her unborn baby, causing congenital syphilis in the child. This may eventually result in blindness and deafness, among other serious consequences. Syphilis in a pregnant woman must be treated prior to the eighteenth week of the pregnancy in order to prevent passage of the disease to the fetus.

As a progressive disorder, syphilis passes through four stages: primary, secondary, latent, and late. Primary syphilis is marked by a painless, open sore called a chancre. This appears at the site where the spirochete entered the body and it is usually the size of a dime or smaller. The chancre typically appears between 10 and 90 days after exposure to the disease and, with or without treatment, disappears in three to six weeks. Although the chancre has disappeared, however, the disease is still active within the body and will enter the second stage if left unchecked.

Within six weeks to six months after contact with the disease, secondary syphilis appears. The symptoms of secondary syphilis include a skin rash, whitish patches on the mucous membranes of the mouth, temporary baldness, low-grade fever, headache, swollen glands, and large moist sores around the mouth or genitals. These symptoms typically last from three to six weeks without treatment; then the disease progresses to the third stage.

All symptoms usually disappear and the patient appears healthy during the latent stage of syphilis. However, the spirochetes are still in the bloodstream and at this point are burrowing themselves into the central nervous system and skeletal structure. This stage is a precursor to the highly destructive late stage.

During the late stage of syphilis, the symptoms are quite lethal and can appear up to 15 or 20 years after the initial exposure. Here, the entire body can come under siege of the disease, which may damage the brain, bones, spinal cord, and heart. Blindness, brain damage, heart disease, or even death can occur. Despite its damaging effects, syphilis is fairly easily treated. Similar to gonorrhea, syphilis can be controlled with antibiotics, usually penicillin.

GENITAL HERPES *Genital herpes* has created much public concern in recent years. An estimated 10 million Americans currently suffer from it and 500,000 new cases are reported each year. Because a cure for genital herpes remains to be found, the number of cases continues to spiral.

Genital herpes is caused by herpes simplex viruses. Herpes simplex comes in two varieties: herpes I, which causes cold sores and fever blisters above the waist, and herpes II, which causes lesions below the waist on the genitals, anus, buttocks, or thighs. However, the two forms often mix, and herpes II may appear both in the mouth and on the genitals.

Genital herpes is spread primarily through intimate sexual contact. The virus rests in the cell center of specific sensory nerves. These viruses become inactive, or latent, when they reach the nerve cell center. However, herpes will flare up in a recurrence and the virus will become reactivated. It is thought that the virus follows the same nerve and multiplies on the skin at, or near, the site of the original sore. Sexual contact is not necessary for a recurrence.

Approximately 2 to 20 days after the virus enters the system, the person experiences a primary, or first, outbreak. The infection typically begins as a rash of red patches with white blisterlike sores, usually in clusters. Genital herpes will usually make an appearance on or around the penis in men and the vagina in women. Internal sores can also occur in the mouth, vagina, cervix, anus, or anywhere on the body where the virus first entered the body. Beyond the rash, one or all of the following may be present: pain and discomfort in the area of the infection, fever, headache, and a general feeling of ill health. Also common is pain or burning when urinating. Glands in the groin area may become swollen. Women may notice a vaginal discharge.

Within a month's time, the sores usually heal. To all outward appearance, the infection seems to have left the body, but this is not the case. Even though the sores disappear, the virus remains in the nerve tissue in the body and possibly in the skin. The virus can multiply at a later date and cause sores and a recurrence. Generally, the symptoms of the first outbreak are the most serious.

As indicated, there is no cure for genital herpes. However, treatment for acute outbreaks is now available. It involves the use of either the antiviral drug cyclovir or laser therapy, both of which will heal blisters, reduce pain, and, most importantly, kill large numbers of the herpes virus. For many, cyclovir can reduce the reproduction of the virus in initial outbreaks, thus possibly lessening the number of subsequent outbreaks. However, laser therapy, in order to be effective, must be started immediately after the first sores appear.

■ Theories of Personality Development

☐ Sigmund Freud's Psychosexual Theory

THE GENITAL STAGE (PUBERTY ONWARD) The onset of the final psychosexual developmental stage, the *genital stage,* commences a turbulent time period for the adolescent male or female. The biochemical upheaval associated with the growth and development of primary and secondary sex characteristics makes youths acutely aware of the erotic zones of their bodies. Following the relatively calm and tranquil latent years, the sensual pleasures associated with the genital zone become apparent.

Unlike the early pregenital stages in which each period marked the onset of a new conflict, the genital stage revives old conflicts, particularly the Oedipus complex. Thus Freudians view adolescence as a recapitulation of infantile sexuality. Even though Freud saw adolescence as a distinct era in psychosexual growth, he continued to emphasize the all-important role of experiences during the first few years of life. The only new feature of the genital stage is the sublimation of oedipal feelings through the expression of libido, by falling in love with an opposite-sex person other than one's parent.

☐ Erik Erikson's Psychosocial Theory

IDENTITY VERSUS ROLE DIFFUSION Erik Erikson's fifth crisis, *identity versus role diffusion,* often referred to as the *search for identity,* is possibly the most famous of his eight crises of psychosocial development. Upon the onset of puberty and genital maturity, youths realize that their childhood has disappeared and adulthood is approaching. Because of this, their egos must reevaluate reality and, in so doing, teenagers become conscious of the ideas and opinions of others and pay particular attention to any discrepancies between their self-perception and the perception of others. Adolescents also become increasingly concerned with their skills and self-perceptions, especially when fitting these into society's occupational prototypes. During this stage all previous stages should blend into an integrated ego:

> The integration now taking place in the form of ego identity is, as pointed out, more than the sum of the childhood identifications. It is the accrued experience of the ego's ability to integrate all identifications with the vicissitudes of the libido, with the aptitudes developed out of endowment, and with the opportunities offered in social roles. The sense of ego identity, then, is the accrued confidence that the inner sameness and continuity prepared in the past are matched by the sameness and continuity of one's meaning for others, as evidenced in the tangible promise of a career.

(1963, p. 261)

Some form of role diffusion results when this integration fails to occur. The eternal adolescent questions of "Who am I?" and "What is my purpose in life?" indicates ego confusion, especially in attempts to integrate various roles and experiences. The

During the teen years, individuals become increasingly preoccupied with self-perceptions as well as life dreams.

teenager's dilemma is to choose a possible role with which to identify—to be rugged and masculine like a cousin, jolly and humorous like a sibling, warm and affectionate like a parent, perceptive and intellectual like a grandparent, or athletic and worldly like some other relative. Meanwhile, adolescents often develop subcultures with which they may also identity. Thus, they become clannish and accept very little deviance in dress, thought, or behavior. This intolerance of others is a temporary defense against role diffusion until the ego can develop a sense of identity. Ego identity is evidently enhanced when the adolescent is in a caring family; they are more likely to explore ego identity when there is a good parent-adolescent relationship (Papini, Sebby, and Clark, 1989).

James Marcia (1980, 1987) proposed that an individual possesses one of four identity statuses. These four statuses are determined by the extent of the teenager's commitment and crisis. According to Marcia, a commitment means the level of investment in life planning. A crisis is the period of choosing meaningful life alternatives. His theory has recently been challenged, however, because it lacks adequate integration of Erikson's theory (see Cote and Levine, 1988).

Identity achievement, the first identity status, means that a person has appraised his or her values and choices in life and has made a commitment to some goal or occupation. An *identity moratorium* is the time when an individual is rethinking his or her values and goals and is in the midst of an identity crisis. No commitment has yet been made to any goals or values. *Identity diffusion* occurs when the person has not even begun to examine his or her goals or values. Finally, *identity foreclosure* is said to result when an individual's goals have been established by others, usually the parents, and the individual chooses not to question or even examine them. These four identity possibilities add another dimension to Erikson's theory and show that the concept of identity is multifaceted, rather than being a singular psychological concept.

The growth in other developmental areas can also affect identity formation. For example, the attainment of Piaget's stage of formal thought facilitates identity formation during adolescence. However, this does not mean that an adolescent in the stage of formal thought automatically achieves identity status. That is, there is no guarantee that arrival in one stage ensures achievement in another. However, certain cognitive capacities in operation at this time, namely, the ability to think abstractly, enable teenagers to differentiate better among and integrate identities and new role behaviors into the self-system (Bernstein, 1980; Leadbeater and Dionne, 1981).

☐ Alternative Perspectives on Adolescence

Besides Erikson's and Freud's theories, there are other theories of adolescence.

KURT LEWIN'S THEORY   Kurt Lewin (1935) viewed adolescence as a turbulent time marked by pronounced growth and change. These changes affect teenagers' *life space,* that is, all of the personal and mental characteristics that affect their behavior. Lewin viewed the life space as a network of interrelated and interdependent characteristics. When one aspect of the life space is affected, all others are too. Thus, pronounced physical growth at this time affects all other domains: self-image, confidence, social comfort, and the like. Should adolescence produce negative reactions in one sphere, negative behaviors may result in other areas as well.

Lewin also emphasized that adolescence offers a marked contrast with earlier developmental stages. The childhood years brought stability to the individual's life space. Adolescence, though, often begins change, unreliability, and uncertainty. New and demanding social expectations, such as relinquishing childish behavior and acting in mature and responsible ways, require the negotiation and restructuring of new behaviors. Teenagers' expanding life space requires increasing refinement and differentiation.

G. STANLEY HALL'S THEORY We mentioned in Chapter 1 that G. Stanley Hall investigated many aspects of human development, including adolescence. Indeed, his book on adolescence (1904) was the first systematic attempt to explore this life stage. Like Lewin, Hall viewed adolescence as a disruptive life stage. He labeled the conflicts and uncertainties at this time *Stürm und drang,* or storm and stress.

Hall and Lewin differed, though, in regard to the origins of this turbulence. Whereas Lewin emphasized the concept of the life space, Hall focuses on evolutionary possibilities. More specifically, Hall viewed adolescence as an important transitional period, a time of awakened impulse and change. Adolescence is an evolutionary passage from earlier immature, childish behaviors to new levels of functioning. This is true for all developmental spheres, including a temporary dominance of sexual impulses. All of this, Hall maintained, brings the adolescent to higher levels of differentiation, but not without extremes in temperament, attitudes, and behavior.

ANNA FREUD'S THEORY Anna Freud (1958) emphasized that a "second awakening" of libidinal urges affects the teenager's personality functioning. You will recall that earlier in childhood, during the phallic stage, youngsters had romantic desires for the opposite-sex parent (the Oedipus or Electra complex). Anna Freud maintained that renewed—and more intense—desires now appear along with other forces, the result being inner turmoil and conflict. Should these feelings not be adequately resolved, maladaptive behavior at this time and even into adulthood could result.

How do adolescents confront these rekindled feelings? How do they cope with the disharmony among the id, ego, and superego? To resolve romantic attachments to their parents, adolescents typically engage in retreat behaviors, such as staying away from their parents or ignoring them. Being secretive and private and maintaining a distant psychological posture from the parents are examples. All of this represents the teenager's way of dealing with these uncomfortable sexual feelings.

Other ways of coping with these and other sexual feelings is to adopt new ego defense mechanisms. *Intellectualization,* for example—the use of elaborate logic and reason—and *asceticism*—the effort to avoid any type of physical pleasure or excitement—may be used to shroud inner sexual feelings. Adolescent asceticism may take the form of maintaining strict sexual rules of conduct on dates or dressing in a conservative fashion so as to downplay one's sexuality.

MARGARET MEAD'S THEORY Finally, let us acknowledge the contributions of Margaret Mead (1928). Mead was a cultural anthropologist who observed the adolescent experience in several non-Western societies, including those of Samoa and New Guinea. Unlike those theorists who painted a stormy and disruptive picture of adolescence, Mead observed that adolescence in these societies was a smooth and tranquil period. For most, it was a time for happiness, self-indulgence, and a relatively carefree—and conflict-free—lifestyle.

Such observations prompted Mead to discount the notion that a difficult adolescence was a universal experience, that it was always a period of conflict and turmoil. Rather, she maintained that the experience of adolescence varies according to cultural influences. Because of the role of culture, it is incorrect to assume that all adolescents share the same experiences.

■ The teenager's desire for independence affects numerous social spheres, including family life. We explored the importance of harmonious family relations and the authoritarian, authoritative, and permissive styles of parental control.

■ Family disharmony may originate from many sources, including the adolescent's strivings for autonomy, the parents' resistance to such strivings, and disagreements over values. In the wake of family discontent, some teenagers choose to run away from home.

■ Involvement in the peer group intensifies during adolescence, in friendships, cliques, and/or crowds. There are sex differences in male and female friendships, namely, girls tend to be more intimate and rank higher in self-disclosure.

■ Dating usually begins during the teenage years. In regard to sexual attitudes, both teenagers and adults are likely to adopt the permissiveness-with-affection standard. This unit also looked at premarital intercourse among adolescents and the problems posed by teenage pregnancies and sexually transmitted diseases.

■ Freud's genital stage encompasses the teenage years, as does Erikson's stage of identity versus role diffusion. Other theories, by Lewin, Hall, Anna Freud, and Mead, were also described briefly.

■ Unit Four:

THE TROUBLED ADOLESCENT

At the outset of this chapter, we noted that not all teenagers successfully accomplish the developmental tasks of adolescence. When faced with the complexities and pressures of modern society, some may exhibit a generalized feeling of futility or hopelessness. Many are simply not capable of dealing with life's demands and, as a result, react to this developmental stage with a mixture of self-defeating behaviors.

In recent years, a number of adolescent maladjustment problems have received attention from psychologists. All have grown alarmingly and have generated a great deal of public concern. These areas are teenage suicide, eating disorders, drug abuse, and juvenile delinquency.

■ Teenage Suicide

At an age when they should have everything to live for, about 5,000 teenagers and young adults, or about 13 a day, commit suicide each year. After accidents, the leading cause of death among young people is suicide. Perhaps the most shocking statistic is that since 1960, the suicide rate among adolescents has increased by *300 percent* (Colt, 1983). Overall, suicide accounts for about 12 percent of the mortality in the teenage and young adult age brackets (Brent, 1989).

Depression is often the cause of teenage suicide.

Suicide victims range from the happy-go-lucky types, who give no clear clues before acting, to the classic loners, who scream silently for help. Adolescent suicide attempts are often unplanned and impulsive, as many want to get help rather than die (Grueling and DeBlassie, 1980).

But the number of teenage suicides may be even greater than the statistics indicate, because many attempts fail and many medical examiners routinely list questionable deaths—especially for teenagers—as accidents. The actual suicide attempts may be as high as 200,000 to 400,000 each year. The use of firearms, shooting, and poison are the most common suicide methods (Maltsberger, 1988; Weiner, 1980).

Teenaged suicide victims come from many different backgrounds, but statistics reveal a significant increase of suicides among minority youths. Males outnumber females in the number of suicidal deaths reported each year. In regard to attempted suicides, females clearly outnumber males; however, there has been an increase of completed suicides among females in recent years (Brent, 1989; Neuringer and Lettieri, 1982; Weiner, 1980).

There are a number of reasons that adolescents commit suicide. One persistent theme is depression; many teens have a pervasive feeling of worthlessness, apprehension, and hopelessness. Other probable reasons are the loss of love objects and stress that sometimes occurs in family life. Many suicide victims are rejected youths who receive little affection or attention. Most are alienated persons who feel socially isolated from the rest of the world (Stork, 1989; Blumenthal and Kupfer, 1988; Neiger and

Hopkins, 1988; Colt, 1983; Grueling and DeBlassie, 1980; Konopka, 1983). Unfortunately, it is difficult to intervene and offer preventive measures to suicidal youths because of the difficulty of recognizing the symptoms. Few laypeople (parents, teachers, etc.) have the knowledge to recognize the symptoms. Guidance counselors, on the other hand, are best able to identity the characteristics of adolescent depression (Maag, Rutherford, and Parkes, 1988).

The increase of teenage suicide in recent years has prompted many segments of society to take preventive measures. The detection and identification of conflict and stress are vital and require the collaboration of parents, teachers, counselors, and other concerned adults. Crisis intervention programs are important to prevention and follow-up, the latter helping the victim cope with reality. Improving the conditions that may increase suicidal tendencies, such as human relations or educational and employment atmospheres, is important, too. The establishment of community resources, such as halfway houses, shelters, hotlines, and adolescent clinics, is a necessary step in prevention (Coleman, 1987; Davis, 1983).

■ Eating Disorders

A second problem related to adolescence falls under the category of eating disorders. *Anorexia nervosa* is a type of self-imposed starvation that affects growing numbers of teenagers each year. It is often referred to as a teenager's disorder because it affects adolescents, usually females, more than it does any other age group. Older teenagers rather than younger ones tend to be most affected by eating disorders. Each year about 1 out of every 200 female adolescents is diagnosed as having anorexia nervosa (Howatt and Saxton, 1988; Garfinkel and Garner, 1982; Crisp, 1980).

At the root of anorexia nervosa is a relentless desire to be thin. The desire to lose weight becomes an obsession, and the anorectic becomes terrified of becoming fat. As this drastic type of dieting continues, many anorectics fail to eat at all; some resort daily to laxatives; and virtually all deny their eventual emaciated appearances. Anorexia nervosa is a condition severe enough to cause serious dehydration, malnutrition, complications of metabolic and endocrine functions, and the cessation of menstruation in females. Deaths resulting from anorexia nervosa range from 5 to 20 percent of all patients (Brumberg, 1988; Schleimer, 1981; Maloney and Klykylo, 1983).

Anorexia nervosa usually is found among members of the upper and middle classes, perhaps because of these families' emphasis on fitness and leanness. It also afflicts individuals with above-average intelligence. It appears that the families of many anorectics are characterized by overprotectiveness, which can result in a poor sense of identity. These children, often compliant and dependent during childhood, misuse eating as an attempt to assert their independence (Brone and Fisher, 1988). Thus, anorectics tend to be perfectionists who feel that they are in complete control of themselves, even while they are starving. The typical patient has a distorted view of reality, a sense of inadequacy, sexual conflicts and, perhaps, severe depression bordering on the suicidal level (Stern, Dixon, Jones, Lake et al., 1989; Richardson, 1980; Hendren, 1983; Romeo, 1984).

As anorectics begin to starve themselves, they frequently induce vomiting and suffer from constipation. Their skin becomes dry, cracked, and rough. Their nails become brittle, and their hair thins. In addition to the cessation of menstruation, the development of secondary sex characteristics is curtailed in adolescent girls. In addition, there is usually no ovulation, and the vagina becomes vulnerable to infection.

Males' sexual interest diminishes, and in some cases, impotence ensues. Both sexes have extremely high activity levels (Landau, 1983; Gilbert and DeBlassie, 1984; Schleimer, 1981).

The treatment and cure of anorexia nervosa is usually a long and tedious process. Behavior modification has proved to be somewhat effective; other techniques are individual psychotherapy, nutritional counseling, and the use of insulin to induce weight gain. Sometimes intravenous or tube feeding is necessary when individuals are too weak to eat or refuse to eat. Anorectics treated in a psychiatric ward have the poorest prognosis for cure and the highest percentage of deaths (Richardson, 1980).

Treatment includes family therapy as well as helping anorectics to eat at regular intervals and to establish some self-sufficiency. Psychotherapy is often aimed at helping patients develop more effective problem-solving strategies, more self-esteem, and more accurate body images (Casper, 1989).

Anorexia nervosa is not the same as *bulimia,* another type of eating disorder. Bulimia is gorging oneself with excessive amounts of food and then inducing vomiting and/or using large amounts of laxatives. Bulimia (from the Greek word meaning "ox hunger") is often called the binge-purge disease (Hawkins, Fremouw, and Clement, 1983; Cauwels, 1983). In addition to these two serious disorders, there are adolescents who are compulsive overeaters. This latter group does not appear to have poorer health (mental or physical) than nonovereaters do, but they often perceive themselves and the quality of their relationships with others as less positive (Marston, Jacobs, Singer, Wideman et al., 1988).

Thanks to the efforts of concerned researchers and organizations such as the Anorexia Nervosa Aid Society and the American Anorexia/Bulimia Association, our understanding of these disorders has increased markedly over the past decade. Knowledge and treatment of anorexia nervosa and bulimia seem likely to increase in the future (Levenkron, 1982; Halmi, 1983; Anyan and Schowalter, 1983; Neuman and Halvorson, 1983).

■ Drug Abuse

Historically, drugs have been used to alter moods or produce intoxication. Today, drugs serve a wide range of purposes, both medical and recreational. Many drugs serve as protective armor—chemical shelters to combat and ward off the stresses and insecurities of modern life.

Although many teenagers drink alcohol, smoke marijuana, or take hallucinogens, equally as many adults take medicines that may be harmful, such as barbiturates, amphetamines, and painkillers. Many do not realize, do not care, or will not admit that they have become dependent on drugs.

ALCOHOL *Alcohol* consumption is widespread among both teenagers and adults. Overall, it is estimated that 75 percent of American males and 65 percent of American females drink. The consumption of alcohol is accepted in most societies and, as a result, it is often not regarded as a drug. However, it is a drug because it affects the central nervous system. Acting as a depressant, alcohol numbs the higher brain centers. As the concentration of blood alcohol increases, a progressive impairment of or a reduction in normal brain functions results. Gradually, the individual's awareness of and response to stimuli from the outside is diminished.

When alcohol is consumed in large quantities, behavior often becomes impulsive, unstable, and unpredictable (Meyer, 1988). Indeed, drunkenness is one of the most common reasons that juveniles break the law. Regular users of alcohol also run the risk of becoming alcoholics. In the United States, approximately 8 to 10 percent of males and 2 to 4 percent of females can be described as alcoholics at some point in their lives. Among teenage drinkers, heavy alcohol consumption is much more common among males (Johnston, O'Malley, and Bachman, 1988).

Adolescents are attracted to alcohol and other drugs for numerous reasons. Conformity to peer pressure and the desire to appear more grown-up are popular explanations. Because drinking is associated with adult role behavior, it may symbolize the attainment of adult status. It may also reduce anxiety or serve as a vehicle for socialization. It is known that adolescent drinking patterns are influenced by those of others in the community. Thus examples set by parents and other adults need to be examined when seeking to understand teenagers' drinking behavior (Carroll, 1989; Whiteman, and Gordon, 1983; Hawkins, 1982; E. Koop, 1983; Segal, Huba, and Singer, 1980). Along these same lines, the role alcohol plays in television needs examining. Two researchers recently evaluated television programs with an eye on appropriateness to youth. While some incidents were viewed as useful to alcohol education for young people, many shows had poor role models (deFoe and Breed, 1988).

Diane McDermott (1984) found that adolescents who used drugs were more likely to have one or both parents who did the same. Moreover, adolescents who perceived their parents as having permissive views regarding drug use were more likely to use drugs than were those who perceived their parents as holding nonpermissive views. Along similar lines, Glenn Johnson and his colleagues (1984) observed that relationships between the parents' use of drugs and teenagers' use of the same drugs were moderate and roughly equivalent across drugs.

MARIJUANA Next to alcohol, the most frequent and widely used nonmedical drug is *marijuana*. Marijuana is classified as a hallucinogen because it is capable of producing a hallucination. Although the results of surveys vary from region to region, it has been estimated that the number of Americans who have tried marijuana at least once in their lives may be as many as 43 million (Kaufman, 1982). Among adolescents, marijuana use is also extensive. One study found that about 50 percent of the respondents had tried it at some point in their lives, most during the previous year (Johnston, O'Malley, and Bachman, 1988).

The behavioral effect of marijuana is mostly determined by the dosage and the user's personality. The average person generally experiences a sense of relaxed well-being or exhilaration and an increased sensitivity to sounds and sights. Time, distance, vision, hearing, hand-leg reactions, and body balance may be slowed or distorted. Some people may feel drowsy and also have a feeling of greater physical and mental capacities than they actually possess. Marijuana also moderately increases the heart rate but does not seem to affect the respiratory rate, blood sugar, or pupil size. It also has a tendency to cause bloodshot and itchy eyes, a dry mouth, and increased appetite. When severely abused, marijuana produces lethargy and passivity, and excessive use may create high blood pressure and even lung cancer (Gieringer, 1988; Fligiel et al., 1988; National Academy of the Sciences, 1982).

LSD AND OTHER HALLUCINOGENS Marijuana is considered a mild hallucinogen. There are other drugs that are much stronger. For example, psychedelic drugs such as *LSD* and mescaline are capable of changing perceptions and the normal ways of looking

Drug abuse among the young is an acute social problem.

at the world and at oneself. Affecting cells, tissues, and organs and changing the transmission of neural impulses in the lower brain centers, LSD produces profound physiological and psychological reactions. Its effect, like those of other drugs, depend on its potency, the user's personality, and the social and psychological context in which it is taken.

LSD reached its peak of popularity during the mid-1960s. Since then, its use among adolescents and young adults has steadily declined, largely because of the increased awareness and apprehension of "bad trips," the recurrence of frightening "flashbacks," and the fear of brain damage or chromosomal defects.

AMPHETAMINES Adolescents may also turn to *amphetamines,* which act on the central nervous system. Examples of amphetamines are *cocaine,* benzedrine, and dexedrine. Amphetamines are known to produce many reactions, including constriction of peripheral blood vessels; increased blood pressure and heart rate; relaxation of the smooth muscles of the stomach, intestines, and bladder; and suppressed appetite.

Overdoses of amphetamines produce high blood pressure, enlarged pupils, unclear and rapid speech, and confusion. For some, the racing world created may be "out of control" and lead to temporary psychosis, characterized by panic, delusions, and hallucinations. When the drug wears off, individuals frequently "crash," by sleeping for long periods. Afterward, they are highly irritable, belligerent, and impulsive (Carroll, 1989).

Cocaine has increased in popularity in recent years; an estimated 15 percent of all adolescents have experimented to some degree with it. Cocaine is processed from the leaves of the coca bush. It produces effects similar to those of amphetamines and in mild doses creates heightened levels of energy and alertness. Cocaine initially produces a sense of euphoria and well-being. Users tend to feel smarter, more competent, and more masterful than others. However, these effects are temporary and tolerance sets in rapidly; and, as a result, increased dosages are needed to obtain the initial effect. Heavier doses and prolonged use, though, can induce hostility, withdrawal, and paranoid feelings. Collapse and death from cocaine are not uncommon (Goode, 1989).

There are a number of ways to self-administer cocaine. One way is to snort it, that is, taking the powder into the nose. Cocaine can also be injected and smoked. Freebasing is a preparation method that uses flammable chemicals to produce "base," the smokable cocaine product. A cheaper and easier method produces "crack," or "rock," another variation of smokable cocaine. Crack has opened whole new drug markets because of its low price, and many deaths from its use have been reported.

BARBITURATES Known by many as "downers," *barbiturates* were designed primarily to induce sleep and relaxation. Barbiturates exist in a variety of forms: nembutal, seconal, and librium are but a few. Barbiturates are physiologically addictive and are frequently used to commit suicide. Tolerance of the effects of barbiturates as well as withdrawal symptoms have been reported among heavy users.

Teenagers who are hard-core drug users often take barbiturates as supplements to other drugs. Barbiturates are addictive and are especially dangerous when taken in conjunction with alcohol. Barbiturates are also frequently used to moderate the stimulating actions of amphetamines or to accentuate the actions of heroin. Their habitual use produces drowsiness, mental confusion, and the loss of muscular coordination. In addition, the withdrawal symptoms of barbiturates may become particularly severe, often resulting in delusions, hallucinations, and even coma (Goode, 1989).

ADDICTING NARCOTICS Of all the *addicting narcotics,* heroin is the favorite drug of virtually all addicts because of its potency and ability to produce euphoric effects. Heroin is almost five times as powerful as morphine. After alcohol, heroin is the most physically addictive and accounts for the most drug-related deaths.

Heroin initially produces a feeling of relief and euphoria that lasts for a few minutes. The next several hours are characterized by a "high." The individual is usually in a state of well-being but is lethargic and withdrawn during this time. Following the euphoric and lethargic stages is a negative phase that produces a strong desire for more of the drug. When deprived of the drug, heavy users begin to experience withdrawal symptoms, the severity of which increase without the reintroduction of the drug. Restlessness, excessive sweating, nausea, severe abdominal cramps, vomiting, and delirium are a few of these withdrawal symptoms (Carroll, 1989).

■ Juvenile Delinquency

Juvenile delinquency is behavior by youths 18 years of age and younger that society deems unacceptable. The rates of juvenile delinquency have increased significantly in recent years. In support of this, consider the following: In the 1960s the majority of people arrested in this country were *over* 25 years of age. During the 1980s, over half of those arrested were 24 or *younger* (U.S. Bureau of Census, 1989).

Rates of delinquency are highest for teenagers between the ages of 15 and 16. By age 18, delinquent behavior is likely to decline. In many instances, it is the young adolescent who commits the less serious forms of delinquency, such as vandalism or running away from home, whereas the older adolescent is more likely to commit such offenses as drug abuse or truancy. More violent crimes, such as aggravated assault or forcible rape, are more apt to be committed by individuals between the ages of 18 and 24 or older (Federal Bureau of Investigation, 1989; U.S. Bureau of the Census, 1989).

It is also known that the percentages of juvenile offenses are greater among blacks than whites and among males than females. Males, at one time, heavily outnumbered females in the number of offenses, sometimes by as much as five to one. Today, it is closer to three to one. There is a difference, though, in the types of delinquency committed by males and females. Males are more likely to be reported for burglary and car theft. Females are more likely to be charged with running away from home, ungovernable behavior, and sex offenses (Gold, 1987; Gold and Petronio, 1980; Hindelang, 1981).

☐ Factors Affecting Juvenile Delinquency

Researchers have been able to uncover a number of factors related to delinquent behavior:

1. Broken homes. Homes divided by divorce, death, desertion, or a lack of affection and understanding can produce great stress in the child, not only before and during the time of separation but also during subsequent social development (Henggeler, 1989; Haskell and Yablonsky, 1982; Canter, 1982).

2. Lack of parental affection. In homes in which children are exposed to warm and affectionate relationships, delinquency is rare. Conversely, when parents, especially fathers, offer little affection to and reject their children, there is a strong likelihood that rebellious or delinquent behavior will be the result. Thus, the father's psychological absence from the home can contribute to delinquency just as much as his physical absence can (Gold and Petronio, 1980; Stott, 1982).

3. Abusive discipline. Rates of delinquency are higher when parents employ abusive and hostile measures of discipline. Adolescent attitudes of rebelliousness and defiance

Many juvenile offenders are defiant and impulsive in their behavior.

are likely to be created when whippings, beatings, and other types of physical punishment are used as methods of control. Hostile behavior by adolescents also may persist throughout adult life. This appears to be especially true when individuals start their own families. Those who were abused themselves have a strong tendency to employ similar violent techniques with their children (Gelles, 1980; Youngerman and Canino, 1983; Ulbrich and Huber, 1981; G. Collins, 1982).

4. Unstable parental behavior. Delinquent youths are more apt to be brought up by one or both parents exhibiting maladjustment problems. These problems include emotional disorders, alcoholism or other drug dependencies, antisocial attitudes, and sociopathic tendencies. When these problems are combined with patterns of rejection and hostility, delinquent behavior may be the result (Rosenbaum, 1989; Cavan and Ferdinand, 1981; Stott, 1982).

5. Economic deprivation. Economic deprivation is also related to juvenile delinquency. When economic deprivation is joined by such factors as low educational level, high unemployment, and overcrowding, rates of juvenile delinquency escalate. But although rates of delinquency are higher among lower, urban socioeconomic classes, it is incorrect to assume that the rural middle and upper socioeconomic classes are free of this problem. Especially the notion that juvenile crime is restricted to inner-city youth is erroneous. Delinquency is fairly commonplace in rural, affluent neighborhoods. In fact, some of the biggest annual crime increases among juveniles were in rural communities with populations of less than 25,000 (Henggeler, 1989; Simons and Gray, 1989; Chesney-Lind, 1989; Adler, Bazemore, and Polk, 1980).

☐ Characteristics of Delinquents

Certain patterns of behavior appear to be common among juvenile delinquents. For instance, many delinquents feel deprived, insecure, and defiant; that is, most juvenile delinquents deliberately set out to break the law (Gold and Petronio, 1980; Cavan and Gerdinand, 1981). Some researchers (Elliot, Huizinga, and Menard, 1989) believe that illicit drug use and dropping out of school increase the probability of juvenile delinquency.

Many juvenile delinquents are also excitable and impulsive. Many have low levels of moral development and deviant values. Consistent in the literature (Rosenbaum, 1989) is the finding that delinquents harbor poor self-concepts. Such feelings seem to originate from past failures in family, school, or other social situations. These inadequacies frequently produce behavior that is defensive, including ambivalence toward authority, hostility, and destructiveness (Gold and Petronio, 1980; Stott, 1982; Haskell and Yablonsky, 1982).

Research suggests that some delinquents have lower levels of intelligence than do nondelinquents, indicating that they may be unable to foresee the probable consequences of their actions or to understand their significance. This factor is seldom viewed as a determining one in predicting delinquency, however, as low intelligence appears to be significant in only 5 percent of incidents involving delinquent behavior (Coleman, Butcher, and Carson, 1984). School failure, whether because of low intelligence, learning disability, or a lack of motivation, also appears to be a contributor of delinquency (Grande, 1988). Also, in a study involving 150 eighteen-year-old delinquent and nondelinquent males, it was discovered that delinquents displayed significantly more immature modes of role-taking, logical thinking, and moral reasoning than did the nondelinquents (Lee and Prentice, 1988).

Finally, in an effort to identify differences in aggression, delinquents incarcerated for antisocial aggression were compared with high school students with high aggression, and another group with low aggression. The antisocial aggressive individuals were most likely to solve social problems by adopting hostile goals, seeking few additional facts, generating few alternative solutions to problems, and anticipating few consequences for their aggression. They were also more likely to have a belief system in support of aggression, including the idea that aggression is a legitimate response and that it increases self-esteem (Slaby and Guerra, 1988).

A recent investigation of public school vandalism involved 1,171 students in the seventh through twelfth grade. The highest rate of vandalism was found in seventh graders and decreased progressively with each increase in grade level. The strongest predictor of school vandalism was being from classes in the lowest academic track. High school vandals were generally those students who had a junior high school record of vandalism. Other factors included high rates of absenteeism and coming from higher status homes (Tygart, 1988).

Finally, delinquents may have more school problems, often as early as kindergarten. Lynn Meltzer (1984), for example, found that by the second grade, 45 percent of a group of delinquents were already delayed in reading and 36 percent in handwriting, compared with only 14 percent of a control group. Higher percentages in other skill areas were also found among delinquents. Thus, early learning difficulties may be an indication of risk for later delinquency.

CHAPTER REVIEW

■ Unit One: Physical Development

Pronounced bodily changes take place during the teenage years. Puberty, a time when sexual maturity is attained, is accompanied by a growth spurt. Height and weight gains are especially great during this time, as are skeletal changes and the further development of the internal organs. The maturation of the primary and secondary sex characteristics is also evident, triggered by the pituitary gland and directed by hormones of the endocrine system. The physical changes associated with puberty may produce psychological discomfort. We also explored the concepts of early and late maturation. Motor-skill development and coordination, in addition to strength and the speed of reaction time, steadily increase. Although males continue to surpass females in those motor skills that have been tested, it can be rightfully argued that this is because of the time and practice that they devote to developing these skills.

■ Unit Two: Mental Development

By the time Piaget's stage of formal operations is reached, individuals are able to deal with concrete as well as hypothetical and abstract problems. However, as we pointed out, not everyone reaches this stage. Formal operations is the last stage of the Piagetian design for intellectual growth, and it represents a period in which all past learning experiences are crystallized and contribute to higher-level thought processes. An outstanding feature of abstract thinking is the ability to use inductive and deductive logic.

Other key cognitive advancements that have been studied are refined problem-solving abilities and insight into literary materials. A limitation in reasoning at this time is adolescent egocentrism, best seen in the fabrication of the imaginary audience and the personal fable.

■ Unit Three: Personality and Social Development

Social involvement reaches new heights during adolescence. One of the more important developmental tasks associated with socialization is establishing harmonious family relationships. We identified three styles of parental control in this chapter: authoritarian, authoritative, and permissive. Of the three, adolescents tend to favor the authoritative, or democratic, style. We also discussed family disharmony and the problems of teenage runaways. Each year, an estimated 750,000 adolescents decide to flee from their homes.

Interactions with the school setting affect many areas of growth and development. This unit stressed the importance of healthy attitudes toward school and how teachers are instrumental in shaping such attitudes.

The peer group continues to be an important agent of socialization. During this time, adolescents may join a number of different social groups, ranging from friendships to cliques and crowds. There are sex differences in adolescent friendships, the main one being that females are more emotionally intimate with their partners. The adolescent's interest in heterosexual relationships is a distinguishing feature of social development. Dating typically begins at this time, and we explored teenagers' sexual interactions. Attitudes toward sex have become liberal in current society. Two areas of growing concern are teenage pregnancy and sexually transmitted diseases.

Freud and Erikson both proposed stages of adolescent personality functioning. For Freud, this is the genital stage, and for Erikson, it is the psychosocial stage known as identity versus role diffusion. We also examined other theories regarding the adolescent experience. In particular, we discussed the works of Kurt Lewin, G. Stanley Hall, Anna Freud, and Margaret Mead.

■ Unit Four: The Troubled Adolescent

This portion of the chapter dealt with four problems affecting the teenager: adolescent suicide, eating disorders, drug abuse, and juvenile delinquency. In the 1980s, adolescent suicide neared epidemic proportions. After accidents, suicide is the leading cause of death among young people. Anorexia nervosa is a type of self-imposed starvation that usually leads to physiological decline and psychological complications.

Drug abuse among teenagers was also explored in this chapter. Alcohol and marijuana tend to be the most popular drugs, but we also examined the use of other hallucinogens, amphetamines, barbiturates, and the addicting narcotics. Finally we discussed juvenile delinquency, defined as the behavior by youths ages 18 and younger that society deems unacceptable. Many factors contribute to delinquency, including broken homes, lack of parental affection, abusive discipline, unstable parental behavior, and economic deprivation. Many deliquents are insecure, defiant, and impulsive.

KEY TERMS

abstraction

acquired immune deficiency
    syndrome (AIDS)

addicting narcotic

adolescent egocentrism

alcohol

amphetamine

anorexia nervosa

asceticism

barbiturate

bulimia

chlamydia

clique

cocaine

crowd

deductive reasoning

early maturer

formal operations

friendship

genital herpes

genital stage

gonorrhea

hypothetico-deductive reasoning

identity achievement

identity diffusion

identity foreclosure

identity formation

identity moratorium

identity versus role diffusion

imaginary audience

inductive reasoning

intellectualization

juvenile delinquency

late maturer

LSD

marijuana

menarche

nocturnal emission

personal fable

primary sex characteristics

puberty

secondary sex characteristics

secular trend

sexually transmitted disease

syphilis

toughlove

RECOMMENDED READINGS

Allgeier, E., and McCormick, N. (Eds.) (1982). *Gender Roles and Sexual Behavior.* Palo Alto, Calif.: Mayfield.
This book of readings succeeds in providing a thorough analysis of how gender roles influence sexual behavior, including that of adolescents.

Brooks-Gunn, J., and Petersen, A. C. (Eds.) (1983). *Girls at Puberty.* New York: Plenum. Gender roles, eating disorders, menarche, nutrition, and early and late maturation are among the topics in this collection of readings.

Byrne, D., and Fisher, W. A. (Eds.) (1981). *Adolescents, Sex, and Contraception.* New York: McGraw-Hill.
A diverse collection of readings focusing on many aspects of teenage sexuality, including birth control, pregnancy, and the problems adolescent parents have in child rearing.

Csikszentmihaly, M., and Larson, R. (1985). *Being Adolescent.* New York: Basic Books. An interesting and frequently amusing look at what it's like to be a teenager in the 1980s. The authors recorded the thoughts and feelings of 75 adolescents.

Forisha-Kovach, B. (1983). *The Experience of Adolescent Development in Context.* Glenview, Ill.: Scott, Foresman.
The author takes a true lifespan approach to the subject. As a result, adolescence is treated as intregral to, rather than separate from, the overall developmental process.

Haskell, M. R., and Yablonsky, L. (1982). *Juvenile Delinquency,* 3rd ed. Boston: Houghton Mifflin.

A thorough and detailed account of virtually all aspects of juvenile delinquency.

Julien, R. M. (1986). *A Primer of Drug Action,* 4th ed. New York: Freeman.

An excellent overview of drugs and their effects on the body, mind, and behavior.

Leahy, R. J. (Ed.). (1983). *The Development of the Self.* New York: Academic Press.

This book of readings contains essays on psychological well-being in adolescence and the formation of the self-concept during the teenage years.

Montemayor, R. (Ed.) (1990). *Advances in Adolescent Research.* Greenwich, Conn.: JAI Press.

A good assortment of articles on many aspects of adolescent growth and development.

Muuss, R. E. (1989). *Theories of Adolescence,* 5th ed. New York: Random House.

This text discusses the psychology of adolescence from a number of different theoretical perspectives.

Phillips, J. L., Jr. (1981). *Piaget's Theory: A Primer.* San Francisco: Freeman.

Chapter 5 of this compact and well-written paperback focuses on the formal operations stage. Phillips includes a good assortment of Piagetian experiments.

Young Adulthood

What Do You Think?

■ Over 80 million Americans are overweight, and far too many don't bother to exercise. Leading sedentary lives, most people don't realize that they're programming themselves for cardiovascular illness and other assorted ailments at early ages. But it's never too late to launch a regular regimen of exercise and proper nutrition. This chapter will examine the benefits of such a healthful lifestyle, pointing out the merits of eating right and working up a sweat during adult life.

■ How do I love thee? Let me count the ways. Indeed you must, when seeking to understand this complex emotional state. We've all thought about love at one time or another, and we are constantly reminded of its presence—or lack of it—in adult relationships. It's difficult to escape the numerous portrayals of love in popular songs, soap operas, and pulp novels. But what exactly is love, and are there different ways to express it? We'll try to supply some answers.

■ "I do." The decision to marry is something that about 95 percent of us will do at some point in our lives. As we'll see, the motives for marriage are diverse, from love to tax breaks. We'll also focus on the alternatives to traditional marriage. What is it about a communal lifestyle or cohabitation, for example, that appeals to some adults?

■ Jim and Laura Travis have been married for almost nine years and want to have children . . . someday. At present, though, they each are busy with their careers and setting their immediate sights on vocational fulfillment. Jim and Laura's decision to delay parenthood is a contrast with those couples wanting children as soon as possible. A further contrast are those couples deliberately choosing to remain childless. In this chapter, we'll explore all of these trends as well as the impact that children have on couples.

Unit One:

PHYSICAL AND MENTAL DEVELOPMENT

Young adulthood begins a new stage of life. Young adults have survived adolescence and youth and now seek to attain the psychological maturity to face the challenges of adult life. These challenges are perhaps more complex and diverse than any that have yet been met.

Young adulthood is the time that individuals can embark on a chosen life course and find their niche in the outside world. Earlier, individuals could only chart their plans, only think about what they would like to do with their lives. But now, having broken away from their family and completed most of their formal schooling, young adults can put their plans into action. In the process, they will gain more confidence in their abilities, and their thinking will become more systematic and analytical. Adulthood has begun.

■ Physical Development

By late adolescence and early adulthood, almost all physical growth and maturation have been completed. Very young adults (20 to 30 years of age) generally give the appearance of youth and vitality, especially if they take care of themselves. Some, of course, gain too much weight or reveal some premature gray hairs, but most people in early adulthood have developed pleasant body proportions, having outgrown the gangly appearance of oversized limbs and adolescent facial characteristics that often marks the teenage years. Thus, for most, early adulthood is characterized by vim, vigor, freshness, and the general physical attractiveness of youth.

By age 17, muscle growth is complete, but the potential for increases in strength remains until about age 30. Even though peak strength has been reached, however (few actually realize their potential), it must be remembered that in any phase of life, the maximum is not maintained very long. Thus, for a few, gradual physical deterioration begins in young adulthood. For those who lead a sedentary life, it may begin as early as adolescence. For those who choose to pursue excellence in physical activities (professionals or serious amateurs), early adulthood represents less a time of preparing for the future than the peak of their careers. We tend blithely to assume that old age is a "relative" concept, but the ephemeral nature of the physical peak was brought to light when 14-year-old gymnast Nadia Comaneci, after winning seven gold medals at the 1978 Montreal Olympic Games, was asked whether this represented the pinnacle of her career. Or when Olga Korbut, who at 17 was the darling of the 1972 Olympics, was said to be looking "very old" at the age of 21 in the 1976 games.

The body reaches its maximum physical potential between the ages of 19 and 26, at least as far as the muscles and internal organs are concerned. In regard to the circulatory system, the heart and its network of blood vessels are fully mature. The average adult male's heart weighs about 10 ounces, the female's about 8 ounces. In its mature state, it is approximately the size of a closed fist and will beat about 72 times each

Young adulthood usually brings physical vitality and endurance.

minute of one's life. The average blood pressure is between 100 and 120 systolic and 60 to 80 diastolic. Systolic pressure is the greatest force caused by the heart's contractions, compared with the diastolic pressure, the relaxation phase between heartbeats.

The nervous system has been gradually developing and maturing since the organism was an embryo. Many people mistakenly believe that a young child is neurologically mature. But this is not so; the brain continues to grow into adolescence and young adulthood. Brain weight, for example, reaches its maximum during young adulthood. If we examined the electroencephalograph (EEG) waves of adults, we would not see mature patterns of brain wave activity until 19 or 20 years of age and, for some, the period of maturation continues to age 30. With advancing age, electroencephalograph evaluations, especially those indicating brain impairments, are considered significant predictors of longevity.

An examination of the respiratory system reveals that, compared with that of earlier years, breathing during adulthood has become slower and deeper. The average adult has a breathing rate of about 12 to 20 times a minute, which accelerates to about 40 breaths per minute during vigorous exercise. However, larger people usually have slower breathing rates, and smaller people have faster rates. Since birth, the lungs have increased in weight 20 times.

The sense organs exhibit little change in young adult life. There is a slight difference in hearing ability between the two sexes, in that men are less able than women to detect high tones. The lenses of the eyes lose some of their elasticity and they become less able to change shape and to focus on close objects. This represents a continuation of a hardening process that probably began at age 10 and is an example of aging beginning early in life. By age 30, however, the changes are seldom sufficient to affect significantly the eyes' function. Any slight loss of functional efficiency in the sensory organs of young adults is more than compensated for by the fact that they have learned to make fuller use of their senses than they did as children.

In regard to other changes in the body, the accordionlike vertebrae and spinal disks begin to settle, causing a slight decrease in height. This represents the start of a slow, imperceptible bodily change. For some, there is an increase in weight; even for those who maintain a consistent weight, there is an increase in fatty tissue with a corresponding decrease in muscle tissue. There is a slight loss in muscle strength between early and middle adulthood, with wide individual differences. Reaction times, which improve from childhood until age 19 or 20, remain fairly constant during young adulthood.

In sports such as boxing, baseball, and skiing, the speed, strength, and quick reactions of young adulthood are needed in order to be competitive. Sports such as golf or bowling or even tennis can be played fairly well by using concentration and planning and can, therefore, be played throughout the lifespan, especially by those who do not become obese, smoke heavily, or live a dissipated lifestyle. Given good health, a person can participate in skiing or tennis or bowling for decades.

☐ The Importance of Physical Well-Being

In countries all over the world today, there is an ever-increasing emphasis on physical fitness and well-being. More than ever before, adults are aware of the benefits of regular exercise and a healthful lifestyle. As a result, many adults of all ages pursue a diversity of physical activities. Jogging, working out, playing golf or tennis, or skiing on weekends has come to characterize the adult wishing to stay in shape.

A survey of adults of all ages reinforces the notion that more Americans are willing to work up a sweat in an effort to be physically fit. Sixty percent of the respondents exercised daily, compared with 47 percent in 1982. Jogging turned out to be the most popular regimen; 18 percent of those polled said they jogged daily (Gallup, 1984).

Regular exercise and proper nutrition undoubtedly help keep individuals healthy and fit, as there is a significant relationship between physical activity and the aging process. Indeed, physical activity and a healthy lifestyle greatly determine longevity (Fries and Crapo, 1981; Mann, 1980; Fredericks, 1983; Oberleder, 1982; Walford, 1983).

Regular exercise is extremely important at all ages. Among adults, though, regular exercise reduces the risk of an early death from a heart attack. People who exercise regularly can improve the strength and circulatory capacity of their cardiac muscles and reduce the severity of arteriosclerotic lesions. Exercise also keeps open the body's blood vessels (a process known as capillarization) and helps overall circulation. Also, exercise helps coordinate the heart's fibers.

Of course, there is no guarantee that exercise will prevent cardiac arrest. Genetic factors, one's total health, and lifestyle also need to be taken into account. This was especially apparent when in July 1984, running expert James Fixx collapsed and died from a heart attack while jogging. Nonetheless, exercise is more than a running step in the overall path to physical well-being. Consider the following in support of this: Placed on a regular treadmill exercise regimen, monkeys were able to withstand the effects of a diet designed to produce a coronary artery disease (Johnson, 1982).

In addition to its cardiac benefit, regular exercise increases muscle strength, joint flexibility, and lung efficiency. It is also recommended by many (see Sizer and Whitney, 1988; Shaffer, 1983; Tubesing, 1981; J. Adams, 1980; Davis, Eshelman, and McKay, 1981; Travis and Ryan, 1981) as a way to relieve the body and mind of stress and help combat stress-related illnesses. Regular exercise also helps fight fat buildup, perhaps the most visible result of physical inactivity. In short, regular exercise enables adults to feel better, look better, and live longer.

THE BUILDING BLOCKS OF PHYSICAL FITNESS If adults exercise, eat properly, and adopt a healthy lifestyle, they will become physically fit. But what is physical fitness? Many regard it as the capacity to carry out daily activities in work and play without excessive fatigue and with sufficient reserve energy for emergencies. Others look at it as being at an ideal weight. But physical fitness extends beyond these parameters. It is also the capability of the heart, blood vessels, lungs, and muscles to operate at optimal efficiency. More specifically, physical fitness embodies the following basic components:

Muscular Strength Muscular strength is a muscle's ability to exert proximal force against resistance. Muscular strength is a prerequisite to all other facets of physical fitness. It is developed by exercising specific muscles, such as those used in calisthenics or weight lifting.

Muscular Endurance Muscular endurance is a muscle's capacity to exert a force repeatedly over a given time span. Put another way, it is one's ability to apply and sustain strength. Muscular endurance can be developed by exercising muscles and gradually taxing them for extended periods of time.

Flexibility Flexibility means the optimal range of movement around body joints. This capacity is developed and maintained by regularly exercising all body parts. Especially productive flexibility exercises are those requiring the bending and stretching of muscles in the legs, arms, thighs, back, waist, and neck.

Balance Balance refers to the ability to maintain the body's equilibrium in some fixed position. Muscular strength and endurance, as well as practice, are needed to develop a good sense of balance.

Cardiovascular-Respiratory Fitness *Cardiovascular-respiratory fitness* is the most important fitness component. It is the ability of the heart, blood vessels, and lungs to deliver oxygen and nutrients to the tissues and to remove wastes as quickly and efficiently as possible. Cardiovascular-respiratory fitness is developed and maintained through whole-body movement over extended time periods, such as in jogging, bicycling, and swimming (Sorochan, 1981).

☐ The Influence of Nutrition on Physical Well-Being

Proper nutrition in the form of balanced diets is important throughout the entire life cycle. During the adult years, though, the temptation of a sedentary lifestyle and calorie-rich food overcomes many. Whether sitting behind a desk all day or living in the midst of countless energy-saving devices, it is relatively easy today to exercise less and eat more. Literally millions of people in this country do not know how to balance their food with energy needs. Consider the following:

- It is estimated that 80 million American adults (about half the adult population) are overweight.

- In any one year, 40 million Americans are dieting.

- Obesity and overweight persons are found at all ages, although the proportion of obese adults increases with age.

- American women tend to add extra pounds at two periods of adult life: when they are pregnant and at menopause.

- American men gain extra weight between the ages of 25 and 40. They gain weight faster after 40.

- Many of today's overweight adults were overweight children.

- More people are hospitalized, and more undergo surgery for digestive diseases than any other (Schwartz, 1982; Sorochan, 1981).

Phil Nuernberger (1981) went so far as to label dietary habits in the United States a natural disaster. People do not pay enough attention to the quality of food they eat, nor do they eat it properly. Many are not even aware that food without nutritional value is not healthful. People eat too fast and have lost the art of cooking and preparing food. They've also allowed junk food to dominate their diets.

Excess fat and cholesterol build up when people ingest more calories than they use. Thus, when individuals consume more calories than they expend throughout the day, they will gain weight. It is therefore important for adults to limit their daily calorie intake. An active 20- to 30-year-old usually needs 2,000 to 3,000 calories a day. From ages 30 to 40, few need more than 1,800 to 2,500, the amount depending on their activity level. Over age 40, few adults need more than 1,800 calories a day (Shaffer, 1983).

With excess weight usually come poor indigestion and susceptibility to stress-linked illnesses. If adults are 25 percent overweight, their chances of having a heart attack will be two and a half times greater than that of the person whose weight is normal. When the heart has to pump nourishment to the large quantity of tissue in the obese body, the risk of stroke, diabetes, hypertension, and heart disease escaiates. It is not difficult to see why the combination of poor nutrition and the lack of regular exercise should be avoided during the adult years (Travis and Ryan, 1981; Pelletier, 1981; Shaffer, 1983).

There is no such thing as an ideal diet, largely because a diet is a matter of individual requirement. We do know, though, what an adequate diet should provide. An adequate diet consists of the various nutrients that the body needs for maintenance and repair. It should be properly balanced, as the absence of a given nutrient, such as a vitamin, will create deficiencies in other areas. It has been established that the presence or absence of one essential nutrient may affect the availability, absorption, metabolism, or dietary need for others (Krause, 1984).

In order to reduce the risk of heart disease, hypertension, and other disorders linked to inadequate nutrition, adults are advised to pay attention to their calorie consumption each day and to their eating habits in general. Eating in moderation, taking vitamins, and avoiding between-meal snacks and large evening meals are advised. Furthermore, adults are urged to make five changes in their overall meal planning: first, reduce fat and cholesterol consumption, including animal and vegetable fats; second, reduce sugar consumption; third, reduce salt consumption; fourth, increase consumption of fruits, vegetables, and whole grains; and fifth, decrease consumption of meat, substituting poultry and fish (Schwartz, 1982).

As we said at the outset, a healthful lifestyle needs to be combined with proper nutrition and regular exercise. The healthiest adults are those who are able to handle life's many stresses and who get adequate sleep and rest. Healthy adults also do not abuse their bodies. Smoking and the abusive use of alcohol and other drugs are detrimental to the body and adversely affect well-being, often breeding illness and curtailing overall longevity (Hennekens, Mayrent, and Buring, 1984; Schlaadt and Shannon, 1982; Fries and Crapo, 1981).

Sophisticated thinking accompanies young adulthood.

■ Mental Development

By the time young adulthood is reached, the ability to acquire and utilize knowledge has neared its maximum capacity. This, therefore, is a time for systematic problem-solving abilities and new levels of creative thought. The mental advancements evident during young adulthood are both qualitative and quantitative. Qualitatively, we are able to see that over time, developing cognitive abilities brought mental flexibility and adaptation, as evidenced in our discussion of formal operations. Quantitatively, we discover that mental abilities have become greatly differentiated and reached new levels of proficiency. Thus, both the kinds and the amount of knowledge that young adults possess have changed from earlier years.

One of the ways to assess changes in mental abilities over time is through intelligence tests. Developmental psychologists have also found that these changes are best measured by means of longitudinal studies, which, as we learned earlier, collect data from the same individuals at different points in their lives. Longitudinal studies seem to produce more accurate intellectual data than do cross-sectional methods. You will recall that the cross-sectional technique is based on comparisons of groups who differ in age at a given time. This research technique was used in the early 1930s and 1940s and indicated that intelligence declines with age. However, it is maintained that the decline measured was due to differences among the age groups, such as educational background or socioeconomic standing, rather than age.

☐ Age and Intellectual Variations

Paul Baltes and K. Warner Schaie are among the growing number of researchers investigating how intelligence changes with age (Schaie, 1979, 1982, 1983, 1989; Baltes and Schaie, 1974; Willis and Baltes, 1980). In one longitudinal study (Baltes and Schaie, 1974), they were interested in discovering whether four types of intellectual functioning change with age. The first type of mental operation, called *crystallized intelligence,* includes those skills acquired through education and acculturation, such as verbal comprehension, numerical skills, and inductive reasoning. *Cognitive flexibility* refers to the individual's ability to shift from one way of thinking to another, within the context of familiar intellectual operations, as when one must provide either an antonym or a synonym of a word, depending on whether the word appears in capital or lowercase letters. *Visuomotor flexibility* is the capacity to shift from familiar to unfamiliar patterns in tasks requiring coordination between visual and motor abilities. Finally, *visualization* is the ability to organize and process visual materials, which involves tasks such as finding a simple figure contained in a complex one or identifying a picture that is incomplete.

The two researchers compared test performances on these four dimensions in 1956 and then again in 1963. Although there was no strong age-related change in cognitive flexibility, the crystallized intelligence and visualization test scores improved. For these two dimensions of intelligence, scores increased even into the retirement years. Only visuomotor flexibility showed a significant decrease with age.

Such findings apparently have helped dispel the myth of intellectual decline during the twilight years. In fact, such studies as this support the notion that adults with above average intelligence can improve, or at the very least maintain, their abilities until later adulthood, whereas those of average intelligence may experience a decline in some mental capacities. Whatever declines there are appear to be within the realm of visuomotor tasks. Because of the time limits imposed on them, the structure of standardized IQ tests, particularly those emphasizing visuomotor flexibility, therefore, favor the young (Birren, Woods, and Williams, 1980; Cunningham and Birren, 1980; Schaie, 1983, 1989; Siegler, 1980).

One other point regarding intelligence is worthy of our attention before we conclude this discussion. Observations and conclusions concerning intelligence are somewhat biased and based on inferences. Inferences, at best, are only guesses grounded in probability and, by definition, are subject to error. How one behaves or what a person does may in no way accurately reflect his or her mental abilities or intelligence. Consider, for example, the adult who enrolls in college and receives a mediocre or poor grade at the end of the semester. The inference might be made that the person is not very intelligent. However, the adult who receives this grade may have little or no motivation in regard to earning grades. Furthermore, this person may feel no need to demonstrate to others the subject matter that he or she has mastered. Thus, this grade fails to tell us anything about the person (McKenzie, 1980; Willis and Baltes, 1980).

☐ The Reliability of Assessment Instruments

Certain factors must be taken into account when evaluating adult learning performances on standardized tests. For example, the test taker may be anxious, tired, rigid, or bored. Younger and older persons also differ in their reactions to standardized testing situations. Older persons are more likely to be anxious, see less value in the

Adulthood is a rich terrain for the development of intellectual abilities.

testing, and are less prone to guess even when it would be a good strategy. Often, young subjects make many more errors of commission than omission, but the reverse is true for the elderly. The elderly may be more cautious because they have been discouraged more for doing the wrong thing. Although cautiousness may often be adaptive, in this instance it may make the elderly appear less competent than they actually are (Schaie, 1983, 1989; Kausler, 1982).

All of the foregoing suggests that maybe we need to rethink the nature of standardized tests. As we indicated, most are biased in favor of young persons and are dependent on education. The young have an advantage because they've received more formal education and have a greater range of test-taking abilities. For the elderly who have had little formal education, the standardized test cannot measure intellectual ability. It is also possible for both old and young to be able to deal with everyday sorts of problems but to score low on intelligence tests. The elderly, especially, have a reservoir of experience from which they can draw numerous solutions to problems. This reservoir often may be tapped only by problems or questions of living and not by a paper-and-pencil test of intelligence (Belsky, 1984; Cunningham and Birren, 1980).

From this discussion, it should be clear that adults do not experience a decline in all facets of intelligence as they grow older. As K. Warner Shaie (1983) stated, in abilities to which speed is not of prime importance, there is little change in intellectual functioning throughout adulthood. If there are decreases in intelligence test scores in later life, they are more likely attributable to the aforementioned reasons or to ill health (Cox, 1984).

Thus, adulthood marks a time when individuals can sustain or even increase their intellectual capacities. This is especially true for those living in varied rather than static environments. Adulthood is also when individuals can excel in a wide range of learning activities. Too, the efficiency of adults, especially those in the older generations, can be enhanced when their special interests are considered and their tasks are satisfying. Finally, with age, adults acquire perhaps the most sought-after qualities of mature thought, that is, wisdom, real-world learning, and practical insight (Knox, 1980; McKenzie, 1980).

■ Physical maturation has been completed by this life stage.

■ Regular exercise and proper nutrition are needed to maintain good health.

■ Mental development nears its maximum capacity during young adulthood.

■ Of the four main types of intellectual operations presented, only visuomotor flexibility decreases with age.

■ Observations and conclusions regarding adult intelligence are often based on inferences and are subject to error. The total person needs to be considered when evaluating adults' learning performances.

Developmental Tasks of Young Adulthood

1. Courting and selecting a mate for marriage.

2. Learning to adjust to, and living harmoniously with, a marriage partner.

3. Beginning a family and assimilating the new role of parent.

4. Rearing children and meeting their individual needs.

5. Learning to manage a home and assuming household responsibilities.

6. Embarking on a career and/or continuing one's education.

7. Assuming some type of civic responsibility.

8. Searching for a congenial social group.

(Havighurst, 1972, 1980)

Unit Two:

PERSONALITY AND SOCIAL DEVELOPMENT

Young adulthood is characterized by numerous developmental tasks. It is a time for further value clarification, important decision making, and careful life planning. It is also a period when young individuals attain greater insight into society's demands and expectations.

Young adulthood provides individuals with a rich terrain in which they can test ideas about themselves and the world in general. Whether it be launching a career, searching for a congenial social group, or courting and selecting a mate, these years are a time when individuals can experiment and explore against the general backdrop of society. In the process of experimentation and exploration, a foothold in the world of grownups can be established.

Self-growth soars to new heights at this time. As Gail Sheehy (1976, 1981) put it, the adolescent concerns of Who am I? or What is truth? shift to the young adult's emphasis on such questions as How do I put my aspirations into effect? What is the best way to start? or Where do I go? Although the tasks ahead are enormous, they can be exhilarating as well. To shape a dream and prepare for a life work is a project that will generate energy, vitality, and hope.

■ The Concept of Adult Maturity

Meeting the challenges of adulthood requires a considerable degree of maturity. Generally *maturity* refers to a state that promotes physical and psychological well-being. In most instances, the mature person possesses a well-developed value system, an accurate self-concept, stable emotional behavior, satisfying social relationships, and intellectual insight. To cope with the demands of adulthood, a mature individual realistically assesses future goals and ideals. Maturity implies the ability to deal with life's problems, increasing the effectiveness of planning strategies, deepening the appreciation of the surroundings, and expanding the resources for happiness.

Maturity is not a unitary concept or an all-or-nothing phenomenon. Rather, some people may have attained moral maturity but are not emotionally mature. Furthermore, age is no guarantee of maturity. The fact that one has reached adult status does

Successful adjustment throughout adult life relies on maturity and responsible behavior.

not mean that one is mature. As we shall see, maturity requires considerable conscious effort that depends on the individual and not on age.

Barbara Okun (1984) suggested that the concept of maturity has biological, psychological, and philosophical dimensions. She feels that the goals of maturity include the following, although adults often reach these goals at varying levels:

1. The capacity to be a self-differentiated person with meaning and purpose in life.

2. The capacity to maintain intimate relationships and to care for oneself. In other words, to be connected and integrated.

3. The capacity to assume responsibility for one's choices in life and their consequences. Also, one must be able to renounce unattainable choices and recognize that some variables influencing choices are out of one's control.

4. The capacity to handle frustrations and disappointments throughout adult life.

5. The capacity to balance individual, career, and family roles.

Certain measures can be taken to help individuals in their search for adult maturity. Being forced into maturity, for example, should be avoided; youths should be permitted some time to test the "ground rules" of their society. Clear-cut standards of responsibility are needed, so that individuals can define their own adult roles. In addition, youth cannot simply be given adult status as a gift; it must be earned, if mature roles are expected to be discharged adequately. Finally, it is felt that the adult world should be made attractive, so that youths are not hesitant or reluctant to join the adult population. Youths need to regard adults as worthy models and trust their leadership. It will be from worthy models that youths will develop their own unique sense of maturity and sound psychological growth (Rogers, 1982).

☐ Allport's Seven Dimensions of Maturity

Gordon Allport (1961) postulated that maturity is an ongoing process best characterized by a series of attainments by the individual. Each period of life has obstacles that must be overcome—roadblocks that require goal-formulating and decision-making abilities. Methods for dealing with life's failures and frustrations—as well as for accepting its triumphs and victories—have to be devised, if maturity is to be reached.

Allport identified seven criteria of maturity that are manifested during adulthood. These seven criteria are extension of the self, warm relationships with others, emotional security, realistic perception, possession of skills and competences, knowledge of the self, and a unifying philosophy of life.

EXTENSION OF THE SELF The first criterion of maturity, self-extension, requires that individuals gradually extend their comprehension to encompass multiple facets of their environment. The sphere of the young child is primarily limited to the family, but over time the child becomes involved in various peer groups, school activities, and clubs. Eventually, strong bonds develop with members of the opposite sex, and interest toward vocational, moral, and civic responsibilities is generated. Each outlet provides the young adult with the opportunity to become involved in more meaningful personal relationships and to fulfill the need to share new feelings and experiences with others.

A word or two of clarification about self-extension. Merely being involved in something does not necessarily imply satisfaction or happiness. Maturity is measured by one's active participation in an activity. It implies movement away from a state in which interests are casual, quickly dropped, and pursued only from motives that are not identified with the advancement of the interest or activity. True self-extension is a state in which a sense of reward comes from doing something for its own sake. In other words, maturity comes when the activity undertaken has true significance to the self.

RELATING WARMLY TO OTHERS Allport's second criterion of maturity is the ability to relate warmly to others. By this Allport means the capacity to be intimate with, as well as compassionate toward, others.

Intimacy is defined by Allport as understanding, acceptance, and empathy toward others. Despite the wide differences among people, intimacy implies the ability to overcome whatever interpersonal boundaries exist. The fully mature person places a high premium on love and a sense of oneness with others.

Intimacy also means a tolerance of the weaknesses and shortcomings of others. Mature individuals are capable of seeing beyond limitations in others, perhaps because they have seen and accepted similar weaknesses in themselves.

EMOTIONAL SECURITY Although numerous dimensions of maturity can be grouped under this third category, Allport maintained that four qualities in particular are important: self-acceptance, emotional acceptance, frustration tolerance, and confidence in self-expression.

Self-acceptance is the ability to acknowledge one's self fully, particularly in terms of one's imperfections. Mature people realize that they cannot be perfect in every respect; yet they nevertheless seek to fulfill their own potential. Total self-acceptance requires exploring and accepting one's weaknesses.

By means of *emotional acceptance,* people accept emotions as being part of the normal self. People acquiring this dimension of maturity do not allow emotions to rule their lives; yet at the same time they do not reject them.

Frustration tolerance is the capacity to continue functioning even during times of stress. To be able to handle life's frustrations and still manage to carry on is a formidable goal. For maturity to develop, one must learn how to best deal with life's frustrations and maintain a healthful lifestyle.

The final dimension of emotional maturity is *confidence in self-expression.* Maturity in this respect implies spontaneity; one is aware of one's own emotions, is not afraid of them, and has control over their expression. Immaturity, conversely, can manifest itself in a number of different ways, including timidity and shyness, emotional overreaction, or emotional underreaction.

REALISTIC PERCEPTION Allport's fourth criterion of maturity is *realistic perception.* Quite simply, maturity in this sense means being able to keep in touch with reality, without distorting the environment to meet individual needs and purposes. Sometimes the complexities of events and situations, combined with the individual's ego defenses, may produce an inaccurate interpretation of the environment. The mature mind is able to perceive the surroundings accurately.

Allport did not imply that the mature person does not use any type of defense or coping mechanism. On the contrary, defense mechanisms become quite automatic for many of us and tend to alleviate temporarily anxiety and frustration. Allport's point is that the overuse—or misuse—of such mechanisms usually distorts one's perception of the surroundings.

POSSESSION OF SKILLS AND COMPETENCES Possession of some type of skill or competence represents Allport's fifth dimension of maturity. Unless one possesses some basic skill, it is virtually impossible to nurture the kind of security necessary for maturity to develop. Though the immature adolescent may argue, "I'm no good at anything," mature adults strive to develop whatever skills they feel they possess.

Furthermore, skilled individuals are driven by a need to express their competence through some type of activity. They identify with their work and display pride in the skills needed to produce the finished product. In this sense, task absorption and ego-relevant activities are important to physical and psychological well-being.

KNOWLEDGE OF THE SELF Knowledge of the self, or self-objectification, is the sixth criterion. Most mature people possess a great deal of self-insight, of which many immature individuals have little. According to Allport, knowledge of the self involves three capacities: knowing what one *can* do, knowing what one *cannot* do, and knowing what one *ought* to do.

Knowledge and stabilization of the self is perhaps one of the most important growth trends of young adulthood. In general, the stabilization process owes much to those enduring roles that are characteristic of adult life. More specifically, as individuals modify their behavior in order to fulfill their roles as workers, marriage partners, and parents, their experience begins to accumulate more and more selectively. In this sense, the stored-up sources of stability and ego identity emerge from the behavior within roles.

ESTABLISHING A UNIFYING PHILOSOPHY OF LIFE The final criterion or dimension of maturity outlined by Allport is the development of a unifying philosophy of life that embodies the concepts of a guiding purpose, ideals, needs, goals, and values. Because the mature human being is a goal-seeking person, such a synthesis enables him or her to develop an intelligent theory of life and to work toward implementing it. Mature people tend to view goals from a balanced perspective and are able to cope with failure if these goals are not met.

Searching for suitable values in the midst of our complex contemporary society is a difficult and complex chore. Daniel Yankelovich (1981) cautioned that seekers of self-fulfillment must not destroy intimate relationships with others as they focus on their own personal search for meaning. Many people today, he feels, are striving to expand their lives by reaching beyond the self, but they are doing so with an ever-narrowing attitude of egocentrism that eventually constricts them.

Contributing to the problem is the fact that people sometimes unwittingly bring a set of flawed psychological premises to the quest for self-fulfillment, in particular, the premise that the human self is a hierarchy of *inner* needs and self-fulfillment is an *inner* journey to discover them. This premise is rarely questioned or examined, even though it frequently leads people to defeat their goals and become isolated and anxious instead of fulfilled. Looking *beyond* one's personal search for meaning in life in terms of maintaining meaningful relationships with others is an important part of the growth process.

To summarize, the seven dimensions proposed by Allport are important factors in the development of maturity. Because of Allport's emphasis on *individual uniqueness,* it should be mentioned that these dimensions can be expressed differently by different people. Unfavorable conditions may hinder personality growth and prevent the attainment of maturity. Some people may remain immature because they are trapped in a conflict between cultural expectations and personal requirements. Others may be prevented at the very beginning of life, by forces outside their control, from ever reaching personal fulfillment.

■ Theories of Personality Development

The developmental challenges of adult life, as we mentioned earlier, shape and mold the individual's personality. Three personality theorists have helped us understand the changes that take place at this time. These three are Erik Erikson (1963, 1982), Daniel Levinson (1978, 1980), and Roger Gould (1978, 1980).

☐ Erik Erikson's Theory

During early adulthood, mature psychosocial development is measured by the successful resolution of the stage known as *intimacy versus isolation.* Before early adulthood, the individual was in the midst of an identity crisis, a struggle that reached its peak during adolescence. Erikson stressed the idea that as a young adult, the individual is motivated to fuse this newly established identity with that of others. In short, the young adult is ready for intimacy, which means not only committing the self to personal relationships but also wanting to maintain them.

Although most young adults seek to gratify their need for intimacy through marriage, it is important to stress that intimate relationships other than sexual ones are possible. Individuals may develop strong bonds of intimacy in friendships that offer, among other features, mutuality, empathy, and reciprocity. Intimate relationships may easily develop out of a capacity to share with and understand others. The socially mature adult is capable of effectively communicating with others, being sensitive to another person's needs, and, in general, being tolerant of humankind. The growth of friendship, love, and devotion is much more prominent among highly mature people than among less mature people.

Yet not all relationships are characterized by intimacy. As Erikson explained, many of us are prepared to isolate and, if necessary, destroy those forces and people who seem dangerous to us, or whose "territory" appears to encroach upon our intimate relationships. The danger of this stage, Erikson warned, is that intimate, competitive, and combative relations are experienced with and against the same people. But as the areas of adult duty are delineated and as the competitive encounter and the sexual embrace are differentiated, they eventually become subject to the *ethical sense* that is the mark of the adult.

There may be other reasons for one's inability to develop intimacy with others. Maggie Scarf (1980) observed that women who suffer from depression during young adulthood often fail to establish a sense of intimacy. More specifically, many have difficulty severing ties with their family of origin and developing new bonds of intimacy with significant others.

☐ Daniel Levinson's Theory

Daniel Levinson traced the course of male adult development. Although he limited his study to 40 males, he succeeded in supplying unique insights into the nature of the adult personality. Women may pass through similar stages. Levinson refers to young adulthood, a preparatory phase of development, as the Novice Phase of adult life. He subdivided the Novice Phase into three periods: Early Adult Transition (17–22); Entering the Adult World (22–28); and Age Thirty Transition (on or about age 30). When the Age Thirty Transition ends (at approximately age 33), Levinson feels that the preparatory phase of adulthood has ended. Men are now full-fledged adults and, in most cases, have committed themselves to new life structures through which they will reach the culmination of early adulthood. These new life structures are labeled the Settling-Down Stage and are best interpreted as the outcome and chief end product of the Novice Phase.

The Early Adult Transition presents two major tasks. The first is to terminate the adolescent life structure and leave the preadult world. Separation from the preadult world means becoming less dependent on one's family of origin. Decreased dependency can be external, such as moving out of the familial home, becoming less financially dependent on one's parents, and entering new roles and living arrangements in which one is more autonomous and responsible. Separation can also be internal: increasing differentiation between self and parents, greater psychological distance from the family, and lessened emotional dependency on parental support.

The second task of the Early Adult Transition is to form a basis for living in the adult world before fully becoming a part of it. A young man's knowledge, aspirations, and values for a particular kind of adult life are frequently ambiguous and colored by parental fantasies. The task here is to obtain further training to learn more about oneself and the world in general. During this time, opinions for adult living must be more clearly defined, specific life goals must be planned, and self-definition as an adult must be measured. Thus, whereas the first task of this stage was one of termination, the second task can best be described as one of initiation.

The second stage Levinson proposed is Entering the Adult World. At this time young adults have to fashion and test out initial life structures that provide a viable link between their valued selves and the adult society. As Levinson observed, young men are at a point at which they should explore available options and possibilities in the world to arrive at a crystallized (though by no means final) definition of themselves as adults and to make and live with their initial choices regarding occupation, love relationships, lifestyle, and values. Shaping a dream of what they would like to do with their lives, as well as looking to others for guidance and direction, helps young adults in their efforts at self-definition.

The Age Thirty Transition is Levinson's third stage of young adulthood. This period gives the individual the opportunity to work on flaws in the life structure formed in the previous period and to create a basis for a more satisfactory structure that will typically be created in the ensuing period. At this time, the provisional, exploratory quality of the twenties is ending, and the individual experiences a sense of great urgency. Life is becoming more serious, more restrictive, and more realistic.

Levinson found two individual variations in the onset, course, and outcome of this stage. Some men experienced what Levinson labeled a "smooth process of change." Growth proceeded in a continuous fashion without overt disruption or any sense of crisis. Satisfactory relationships were maintained with family and friends, and occupational pursuits progressed smoothly. Others, though, experienced "the age thirty crisis," which manifested itself in a severe and stressful form. Those suffering from this crisis encountered great difficulty in working on the developmental tasks of this period and experienced considerable amounts of self-doubt and stress.

The Settling Down Stage represents the culmination of stages for the young adult years and consists of two substages: Early Settling Down and Becoming One's Own Man. Two tasks in particular need to be resolved during the Settling Down Stage. The first, characteristic of the substage Early Settling Down, is to establish one's niche in society or, as Levinson describes it, to dig in, build a nest, and pursue one's interest within a defined pattern. Successful resolution of such a task requires some type of deliberation, order, and stabilization.

The second task, more characteristic of the substage Becoming One's Own Man, is to work at advancement and strive to succeed onward and upward. Whereas the first task contributes to the stability of a defined structure, Levinson stressed that this task implies progression within the structure. Advancement in this sense may mean building a better life, improving and using one's skills, becoming more creative, or in general contributing to society. Becoming strongly connected to a segment of society, being responsive to its demands, and seeking the affirmation and rewards that it offers are the developmental tasks of Becoming One's Own Man.

☐ Roger Gould's Theory

The underpinnings of Roger Gould's theory of adult personality development rest on the notion that adults must strive to eliminate irrational childhood ideas that have a tendency to restrict their lives. These false assumptions frequently embody the concept of parental dependency, as Levinson proposed. Ideally, as life experience builds, adults must abandon these unwarranted expectations, rigid rules, and inflexible roles, which hinder individual autonomy. If this is accomplished, in time adults will come to be the true owners of their selves, with a more mature level of consciousness.

Gould maintained that young adulthood is a critical period of development, as it is at this point that individuals realize how they can begin to take control of their lives. In particular, four false assumptions acquired in childhood need to be questioned. These assumptions include the following: adults will always live with their parents; one's parents will always be there to help when things go wrong or not exactly as one wants; parents can always offer a simplified version (and solution) to complicated inner realities; and no evil or death exists in the world.

Gould maintained that by the time individuals reach young adulthood, they know intellectually that these assumptions are factually incorrect, but emotionally they retain hidden control of adult life until significant events unveil them as emotional as well as intellectual fantasies. The gradual shedding of these false assumptions, a process that lasts throughout adulthood, signifies an individual's shift from childhood consciousness to more mature levels of adult reasoning.

Although these are the major false assumptions intertwined throughout all of adulthood, Gould suggested that additional irrational ideas can be found in specific stages of adult life. Young adulthood contains three stages: Leaving Our Parents' World (ages 16–22), I'm Nobody's Baby Now (ages 22–28), and Opening Up to What's Inside (ages 28–34), each with accompanying false assumptions about adult life.

The main false assumption to be challenged in the stage called Leaving Our Parents' World is that individuals will always belong to their parents and believe in their world. The idea here is that parental influence is at times domineering, and young adults are in the midst of striving for independence and autonomy. Interwoven in this theme are other false assumptions, such as "If I get any more independent, it will be a disaster," "I can view the world only through my parents' eyes," "Only my parents can guarantee my safety," and "My parents are my only family." Notice that each embodies the concept of parental dependency and the lack of individual freedom. However, the young adult will soon learn that such life events like establishing independence away from the home, embarking on a career, expanding social horizons, or developing personal convictions about life in general will go a long way toward establishing adult independence.

The stage of I'm Nobody's Baby Now gives young adults the opportunity to challenge another false assumption. The illogical thought here is that adults feel that they

Adults must learn to take control of their lives and establish self-sufficiency.

have to do things their parents' way. Furthermore, if individuals become too frustrated, confused, or tired, their parents will step in and show them the right way.

This false assumption is similar to that of the previous stage; that is, young adults frequently adhere to the concept of absolute safety offered by omnipotent parents. However, Gould emphasized that as the architects of their own existence, young adults must learn to accept full responsibility for their life course and not depend on parental intervention. This means that certain life skills must be developed. Thinking and planning must become critical, analytical, sequential, and goal oriented. Young adults must also learn to value such attributes as perseverance, willpower, and common sense. Equally important is the ability to learn how to tolerate being wrong in order to learn how to be right.

In addition, young adults must learn to accept some of the consequences inherent in everyday life. For example, despite the feelings of many, one's efforts in the world will not always be the object of compensation. Young adults must also learn that there isn't always one correct way to do things, and loved ones can't always do what the individual can't.

Those willing to accept the challenges of this stage will build a solid base of confidence based on true competence. As young adults meet each novel experience or tackle each larger task, their sense of accomplishment grows. As Gould declared, fantasy powers are replaced by real powers. A feeling of movement or growth replaces the fear that one will always be small and an appendage of one's parents. As confidence, competence, and the sense of being adult increase, these mocking voices within will grow silent.

Opening Up to What's Inside is Gould's third stage of young adulthood. By this time in life, most adults have had eight to ten years of experience living outside their parents' home, or as Gould described it, outside the world of absolute safety. The basic ingredients of independent life have been established, and most adults have become self-reliant. However, now individuals have the opportunity to challenge the major false assumption that dominates this age period: Life is simple and controllable.

This age period allows adults to turn inward and reexamine themselves for something other than the narrow limits of independence and competence that were so important a few years earlier. Should they decide to turn their energies inward, they usually will discover coexisting contradictory forces and a new region of adult consciousness that is intensely private and personal. This region of consciousness may consist of desires, tendencies, wishes, talents, and strengths that adults have shut out of their lives during their early twenties because they didn't fit or caused too much conflict. These feelings now have a tendency to surface, and adults find themselves in a position to open up to what's experienced inside. The end result of this growth stage is that many adults discover a new way of perceiving the world.

With this new adult stage comes an attitudinal change as well. The adult realizes that dreams do not come true by wishing, but rather by a more direct route. If one wants to satisfy a wish, need, or desire, he or she must work on it directly.

The process of opening up in the thirties obviously requires an in-depth analysis of oneself. Consistent with Gould's overall theory, certain illogical ideas about life, especially its perceived simplicity and controllability, have to be examined. Close inspection will reveal that life is not as simple or as well ordered as one would like. Rather, it is frequently complicated and bewildering. The message is quite clear: Adults must learn to shape their future based on a realistic interpretation of what exists inside them as well as what surrounds them in their environment.

■ Development of Adult Sexual Relationships

Few adults can thrive on loneliness or isolation. On the contrary, most search for a partner so that meaningful human interaction can be experienced. The desired outcome of this quest is usually twofold: to know and better understand oneself and to construct a worthwhile and satisfying relationship with another person (Pocs and Walsh, 1985).

As we learned in the last chapter, dating begins at an early age in America. This is largely due to our encouragement of early heterosexual interactions in the school system, at social functions, or through the individual's contact with the mass media. This exposure and prompting, coupled with the perceived importance of dating, exert significant influences on the individual's personality and social development.

Dating becomes a conscious, deliberate process of mate selection by young adulthood. Because of heightened levels of maturity, dating now tends to be characterized by greater levels of mutuality and reciprocity. Young adults have typically declared their identity and have reached a point where they can share themselves intimately with others.

☐ Dating and Intimate Relationships

For some, dating will always be a casual and lighthearted form of interaction. For others, though, dating brings about the establishment of a serious, intimate relationship. Most adults will be involved in one or more of these relationships over the course of their lives, and we would like to explore some of the dynamics of such arrangements.

Some important terminology needs to be clarified before proceeding, particularly the word *intimacy*. Intimacy originates from the latin *intimus*, meaning "inner." In its broadest sense, intimacy means becoming close with another person. An *intimate relationship* represents a process in which we come to know the innermost, subjective aspects of another person, and we are known in a like manner. Put another way, an intimate relationship involves the mutual exchange of experiences in such a way that a further understanding of oneself and one's partner is achieved (Chelune, Robison, and Kommor, 1984).

True intimacy requires *self-disclosure,* the process by which individuals let themselves be known by others. Self-disclosure involves decisions about whether to reveal one's thoughts, feelings, or past experiences to another person, at what level of intimacy to reveal personal information, and the appropriate time, place, and target person for disclosure. As a relationship progresses to more intimate levels, partners generally disclose more information about themselves and at a more personal level (Derlega, 1984).

Individuals can disclose themselves through a number of different channels. Verbal self-disclosure is the use of words to let others know about you. Self-disclosure can also take place through body language or by one's tone of voice. The manner in which one gestures or chooses to emphasize words also says something about the person. Finally, persons disclose themselves through their actions (Corey, 1990).

☐ Components of Intimate Relationships

Certain qualities are necessary to the development and existence of intimate relationships. According to Gordon Chelune and associates (1984), these qualities include knowledge of the innermost being of one another, mutuality, interdependence, trust, commitment, and caring. These dimensions are interdependent, different from one another, but also overlapping. Chelune and colleagues offer the following details on each of these dimensions.

KNOWLEDGE An intimate relationship is a relational process in which the partners come to know the innermost, subjective aspects of one another. As intimate relationships develop, mutual self-disclosure of increasingly personal information coincides with reports of increased appraisals of intimacy. It appears to be of central importance to people to be able to share with others all aspects of themselves, and to feel understood and accepted as the people they are. Also, it is important to know, understand, and accept other people thoroughly at the same time. In an intimate relationship, these processes occur simultaneously and reciprocally. They appear to represent a single process characteristic of the relationship as a whole rather than descriptive of the needs and actions of two separate people.

MUTUALITY At the foundation of an intimate relationship is the assumption that both partners are engaged in a joint venture. With the passage of time, both come to know one another in greater depth. Intimate relationships have at their foundation a mutual process of sharing. When considering the quality of intimate self- and other-knowledge, it is clear that the mutual process of sharing this knowledge is as important as the knowledge itself.

It is important to mention that while mutuality embodies shared interaction, it does not require highly similar or identical interaction patterns. Intimate relationships seem to involve both *reciprocal* interactions, with the partners showing similar behavior either simultaneously or alternately, and *complementary* interactions, in which the behavior of each partner differs from, but complements, that of the other. Reciprocal interactions revealing similarity between partners seem to be associated with such areas as facilitation of communication and positively shared belief systems. Similarity in needs, skills, expectations, and worldview allow partners to interact as equals and to select life goals and directions satisfactory to both. Complementary interaction allows the partners to satisfy each other and provides opportunities for them to behave in a manner that they like to see in themselves.

Another feature of mutuality is the concept of "fairness" in rewards and costs resulting from interactions within the relationship. Intimate relationships are often characterized by a sense of fairness, shared by both partners, relating to their needs, input, and outcome. This concept of fairness is important to the mutuality of relationship definition and the mutuality of relationship control that characterize intimate relationships.

INTERDEPENDENCE Adults within intimate relationships learn in what ways they can depend upon one another for support, resources, understanding, and action. They also agree upon future dependency. Partners also share knowledge and goals, increase their interactions with one another while limiting others, pooling resources, and slowly intertwining their lives in a variety of ways. However, as intimate relationships escalate, there seems to be increasing room for interdependence with persons outside of the relationship also.

Elements of interpersonal attraction play a major role in finding a marriage partner.

Pathologically enmeshed marriages indicate extreme interdependence of the partners without the other qualities central to the existence of an intimate relationship. An interdependence structure that allows for the delicate intertwining of two lives for the greater satisfaction of each, but with limits and some flexibility, characterizes intimate relationships.

It should also be added that interdependence carries with it considerable mutual power. To the extent that interdependency is characteristic of a relationship, the partners will have mutual power to grant or withhold gratification of needs. We will see that one thing that makes this interdependency possible is the quality of trust.

TRUST As intimacy and increasing amounts of self-disclosure are shared, partners become psychologically vulnerable. The intimate relationship requires trust, a sense of confidence in the integrity, truthfulness, and fairness of the partner. In a general sense, trust ensures that no undue harm will be associated with the relationship. More specifically, partners trust one another to be accepting, to avoid purposefully hurting one another, to have the best interests of the partner and of the relationship in mind, to feel warm and caring toward the partner, to need the partner and respond to the needs of the partner, and to share and continue the relationship.

COMMITMENT Intimates continually assess their own desires for commitment and also those of the other. The other qualities of intimate relationships seem to be influenced by the extent of this mutual commitment. For example, it has been found that people will disclose easily and at great depth if the relationship is expected to be short-term. Conversely, commitment to the possibility of a long-term relationship instills caution, exemplified by gradual disclosures dependent upon reciprocal behavior in kind. Partners may also be committed to the relationship in varying ways; for example, a couple may realize that eventually circumstances will separate them geographically and in time, but they remain committed to the continuation of the relationship in an altered form. Or, couples may express their commitment to remain together emotionally and physically through a formal, announced engagement or a marriage ceremony. The variations in types of commitment are not as crucial as the mutuality of understanding and agreement to the terms of commitment.

CARING The last characteristic of intimate relationships outlined by Chelune and colleagues is caring. Relationships are formed for many reasons, including companionship, money, status, or power. Intimate relationships may develop from any or all of these reasons, but at least one reason will always be a strong sense of caring and affection between partners.

☐ Benefits of Intimate Relationships

Numerous benefits are attached to intimate relationships. An intimate relationship is a social vehicle that enables people to learn more about themselves and how they are perceived, including their strengths as well as weaknesses, by others. In this way, individuals gain self-awareness. An intimate relationship also teaches the importance of sensitivity, mutuality, and reciprocity and makes it possible to experience love as well as sexual relations within mutually acceptable limits. For unmarried persons, an intimate relationship also represents a process through which a marriage partner is selected.

There are other benefits, too. Intimate relationships provide partners with a sense of security and attachment. Partners typically provide one another with reassurance of worth and competency. Also, an intimate relationship provides a commitment and a common purpose. As David Burns (1985) sees it, the satisfaction that a couple feels when each partner has made a commitment to one another and struggled to resolve their differences can lead to feelings of tenderness and intimacy that are deeper and more gratifying than any feelings of romantic excitement.

It has also been found that a connection exists between intimacy and healthful adjustment (Cunningham and Strassberg, 1981; Waring et al., 1981; Waring and Russell, 1980). Some researchers (Berscheid and Peplau, 1983; Fisher and Striker, 1982) go so far as to say that intimate relationships represent one of life's most rewarding and important activities. A review of the literature by Sadell Sloan and Luciano L'Abate (1985) indicates other positive features as well. For example, intimacy serves as a major source of comfort and defense in the presence of crises throughout the life cycle. Indeed, the inability to be intimate with others triggers depression in many.

☐ Barriers to Intimate Relationships

Despite the numerous advantages that intimate relationships offer, many choose to avoid them. Why is this so? According to Valerian Derlega (1984), disclosing personal information while investing in an intimate relationship makes one psychologically vulnerable. He points to five potential risks that individuals incur when they self-disclose.

DISCOVERING THAT ONE'S PARTNER IS NOT INTERESTED IN HAVING AN INTIMATE RELATIONSHIP Here, a person may disclose intimate information with the notion of developing a serious relationship. But one's partner may not be interested in developing the relationship and becomes indifferent to this motive.

REJECTION OF ONE'S SELF-CONCEPT Individuals may find that others do not like them after they make a complete disclosure about certain matters. For example, disclosed information may be unacceptable or offensive to another, who in turn may terminate the relationship.

INFORMATION IS USED BY ONE'S PARTNER TO GAIN CONTROL OR POWER IN THE RELATIONSHIP The person listening to the disclosure may use the information to gain some advantage over the other. For example, sensitive and potentially embarrassing information may be disclosed by a partner but used against him or her when dominance in the relationship is sought.

BETRAYAL OF INFORMATION TO OTHERS AND BREAKING RELATIONSHIP BOUNDARIES Similar to the previous situation, disclosed information is used against the person. This time, though, personal and sensitive information goes outside of the relationship and is given to others. In other words, confidentiality is broken. The leakage of information to uninvited third parties erodes or totally breaks down the boundary that a couple established around itself.

INEQUITY ORIGINATING FROM A LACK OF EQUIVALENT INPUT INTO THE RELATIONSHIP Should individuals perceive that they are on the giving end of an inequitable relationship, they may become resentful and hurt. If one party always reveals something personal and the second person never does, the high discloser may see this arrangement as unfair as well as unrewarding.

Elaine Hatfield (1984) feels that risks such as these do exist in relationships, as does the potential for the psychological pain of disappointment and rejection. However, the avoidance of intimate involvements is not the answer to these problems. Rather, what is needed is a reappraisal of oneself and relationships in general. Perhaps the first step is encouraging people to establish independence and accept themselves as they are. Persons are entitled to be what they are—to have the ideas they have, the feelings they feel and to do the best that they can do. Establishing this in a relationship is important for both parties. Individuals also have to move away from the notion that they come into the world perfect.

Persons also need to recognize their intimates for what they are. Individuals are often hard on themselves, but they are generally harder on their partners. Is anyone entitled to a perfect partner? There are no guarantees that a different partner will be better than the one currently available. To enjoy an intimate relationship, persons must learn to enjoy others as they are, without hoping to "fix them up."

Lastly, individuals need to learn to be more comfortable about self-disclosure. To be intimate, partners have to push toward a more honest, trusting, complete, and patient communication process. Such qualities may reduce many, if not all, of the risks, just described, within intimate relationships. Partners must also understand that a person's ideas and feelings are necessarily complex, with many nuances, shadows, and inconsistencies. In love relationships, though, there is usually plenty of time to clear things up.

☐ Elements of Interpersonal Attraction

What attracts one person to another? Is it the way someone smiles, the quality of eye contact, or the intimate parts of the anatomy? How about hairstyle or the smell of one's perfume? While physical qualities do end up at the top of the list, they are not the only reason for such attraction. Rather, the roots of interpersonal attraction are far deeper. Researchers tell us that other important facets of interpersonal attraction are sensitivity, honesty, warmth, integrity, a sense of humor, and the ability to establish rapport (Simenauer and Carroll, 1982; Reiss, 1980).

There are other forces, too, behind interpersonal attraction and the formation of intimate relationships. More specifically, *filtering agents* will test the quality of "fit" between partners. As two individuals acquaint themselves with each other, they acquire information about one another through a series of these filters. Filtering agents, then, test the compatibility of partners and serve to narrow down the field of eligibles.

In order to more fully understand the nature of filtering agents, let us explore some of the more common ones. To begin with, interaction is enhanced when individuals reside near one another, be it at home or at work. This nearness in place is referred to as *propinquity.* In its broadest sense, propinquity means that individuals need to have continual contact if the relationship is to endure.

Another early filtering agent is physical attraction. In virtually all societies, physical appearance is important in attractiveness. However, there are wide variations in what is considered attractive. What physical traits are regarded as attractive in one culture may not be attractive in others.

Males, more so than females, are likely to be concerned about the physical appearance of their partners. Both males and females, though, respond more favorably to attractive dates than to unattractive ones. Interestingly, physically attractive persons tend to behave in more traditionally sex-typed ways. That is, physically attractive males tend to be assertive and socially active, and physically attractive females tend to be unassertive and socially passive (Brehm, 1985).

Usually, persons tend to associate with individuals having something in common with them. This is known as *homogamy.* More specifically, homogamy is the filtering agent based on such factors as similar education, age, and physical appearance. *Endogamous* pressures (such as social approval or disapproval) encourage persons to marry within their own social group. In other words, a Catholic marries a Catholic, or a black marries a black. To marry outside of one's particular social group would be an *exogamous* choice. As an illustration, a Catholic marries a Protestant, or a black marries a white.

The filtering agent of *complementary needs* assumes that individuals seek out mates to complement their own personalities. Thus, a mate is chosen to fill the void of one's own personality. Complementary needs also implies that individuals tend to complement personality traits that they lack, but still hold in high regard.

The *parental-image* filtering agent is Freudian in origin. It implies that during childhood, a person nurtured a deep affection for the parent of the opposite sex. When mate selection takes place, the individual sees the image of this childhood attachment. The popular clichés, "She's looking for someone with her father's qualities," or "He wants someone like his mother," are applicable in this case. This explanation places mate selection on a level below consciousness.

Exchange and role compatibility are two additional filtering agents. *Exchange* means that persons are attracted to those who provide the greatest relational rewards and the fewest number of trade-offs or sacrifices. *Role compatibility* embodies the notion that between two persons there is stability and harmony in role "fit." That is, the set of roles one brings into a relationship, as well as the role expectations one has for the partner, are mutually agreeable.

International Lifespan Development

■ INTERNATIONAL DIFFERENCES IN DATING AND MATE SELECTION

The manner in which Americans date and ultimately select a mate is a process unique to our culture, a system that reflects mutual choice. But according to Lloyd Saxton (1983), mutual choice is not the case in other countries. Some societies maintain that the parents, not the couple involved, should play the key role in the marital selection process. In Japan, for example, up to 50 percent of all marriages are arranged by the parents.

Other customs differ from the American system of mate selection. In contemporary Greece it is all but impossible for a female to marry without a sufficient dowry. (A dowry is money or property given by the bride's parents to her bridegroom.) In Africa and Taiwan the opposite exists in the form of a "bride price"; that is, the groom's family is asked to pay a sum of money because the woman is regarded as an economic asset.

Other nations strongly believe in supervising the couple and monitoring their activities. Countries such as Spain, Sicily, and parts of Mexico and Latin America insist that chaperones accompany dating couples. This is to ensure that the female is never left alone in the company of a young man.

☐ Love and Intimate Relationships

Love is perhaps the most complex and diverse of all human emotions and the pivotal feature of the intimate relationship. As such, it can be expressed and received in a number of different ways. Love and love relationships are often the central theme of movies, plays, and popular songs. Descriptions, accounts, and narratives of it can be found in virtually all forms of the media, from movies and television to paperback books and supermarket tabloids. The study of love has also produced a flurry of research activity (see, for example, Sarnoff and Sarnoff, 1989; Douglas and Atwell, 1988; Rubenstein, 1983; Loudin, 1981; Branden, 1981; Money, 1980).

Jim Henslin (1985) feels that from childhood onward we learn the romantic ideal attached to love. From many different agents of socialization, we are taught to expect to "fall" in love at some point in our lives. Moreover, we are taught that love is the eventual outcome of dating and the appropriate basis for establishing marriage and having children. Because of this programming, we come to expect the experience of love.

Taking a similar stance, Anne Kaza and Dicken Reppucci (1980) remark that we strive for love, revel in its pleasures, and often lose love. Romantic love is also different from other, more stable, forms of love, such as that between brothers and sisters or parents and offspring. The latter is more predictable, much like the climate in a particular area. Romantic love is different, more seasonal than climatic.

CHARACTERISTICS OF LOVE

The research of Robert Sternberg (1985) indicates that love may feel, subjectively, like a single emotion. However, *love* consists of a set of feelings, cognitions, and motivations that contribute to communication, sharing, and support. Broken down even further, love includes the following characteristics:

- Promoting the welfare of the loved one.

- Experiencing happiness with the loved one.

- Having high regard for the loved one.

- Being able to count on the loved one in times of need.

- Mutual understanding of the loved one.

- Sharing oneself and one's things with the loved one.

- Receiving emotional support from the loved one.

- Giving emotional support to the loved one.

- Intimate communication with the loved one.

- Valuing the loved one in one's own life.

Related to all of this, Clifford Swensen (1985) writes that the main content of a love relationship between two adults is communication, and the main method for mutual reward is verbal. For a couple who are in love and who plan to marry, the love is expressed through mutual statements of love and affection, self-disclosure, interest in each other's activities, encouragement and moral support, and toleration of the less desirable characteristics of each other. The amount of self-disclosure that furthers the relationship of a couple depends upon the degree to which each partner accepts both himself or herself and the other partner.

How Do You Love Me? Let Me Count the Ways

There are many different ways to experience and express love. For example, some people plunge into new relationships with emotional intensity. Others prefer to let love grow on a gradual basis, while some readily put their feelings into words. Still others prefer to demonstrate their affection in deeds (Atwater, 1986).

In an effort to distinguish its many forms, a number of love categories can be identified. These include ludus, pragma, mania, eros, storge, and agape.

LUDUS Derived from the word ludicrous, *ludus love* is playful and often self-centered and sexually permissive. Ludic lovers do not want long-range attachments from their partners. Most also do not want their partners to be dependent on them. Ludic love has often been described as playful love, a style that regards love as a game.

PRAGMA Pragma is from the Greek work *pragmatikos,* meaning practical and realistic. *Pragma love* is characterized by sensibleness and logic. Pragma lovers are realistic when they approach a potential partner and seek to match themselves with someone whose background is compatible with their own.

MANIA *Manic love* is intense and obsessive. Many manic lovers are overwhelmed by thoughts of their partners, so much so that they are always in a state of anxiety. They need continual affection and attention from their partners.

EROS *Eros love* is characterized by intense romance and idealization of one's partner. Often love is instant and partners are preoccupied with pleasing the other. Sexual intimacy is also strongly desired.

STORGE Storge (pronounced "stor-gay") is Greek in origin and means affectionate love. In its broadest sense, *storge love* embodies companionship and the enjoyment of doing things together. Intense emotional involvement is usually avoided.

AGAPE Agape is also Greek in origin and means altruistic love. *Agape lovers* care deeply about their partners and seek to satisfy their well-being in a warm and kind fashion. This gentle style of loving also asks nothing in return.

UNIT REVIEW

- Adult maturity promotes physical and psychological well-being. It has many biological, psychological, and philosophical dimensions.

- Adult personality theories were proposed by Erikson, Levinson, and Gould.

- Intimate relationships involve the mutual exchange of information, thus requiring considerable self-disclosure. Components of intimate relationships include knowledge of oneself and one's partner, mutuality, interdependence, trust, commitment, and sharing. Benefits and barriers to the formation of intimate relationships exist.

- Filtering agents include propinquity, physical attraction, homogamy, endogamy, exogamy, complementary needs, parental-image theory, exchange, and role compatibility.

- Love is a complex set of feelings, cognitions, and motivations. Types of love include ludus, pragma, mania, eros, storge, and agape.

MARRIAGE AND PARENTHOOD

■ Marriage

Perhaps no other culture in the world, past or present, has exhibited as great a social and personal concern with marriage as has the United States. Newspapers and magazines, television, radio, and movies devote vast amounts of time and energy to analyzing the subject. Much of this attention is focused on its problems: marital frustrations and unhappiness, sexual maladjustments, role confusion, and divorce. These areas, along with many others, have generated considerable interest among social scientists studying marriage in contemporary society (Bell, 1983).

Despite the fact that interest in alternative lifestyles is increasing, which we will discuss shortly, marriage in America is more popular than it was at the turn of the century. Marriage continues to be valued by a majority of Americans. Most expect to marry, and despite high divorce rates, most also expect their marriages to be lasting.

Statistics bear out the popularity of marriage. Approximately 95 percent of the population over age 46 has married. However, there have been some interesting shifts among young Americans. In 1970, about 45 percent of males and 64 percent of females in their twenties had already married. By 1988, corresponding figures had dropped to about 30 percent and 50 percent, respectively. Thus, while demographic trends indicate that most people marry, among modern Americans the decision is being postponed.

In 1988, the total number of marriages in the United States was just over 2,400,000. Such large numbers existed even in the presence of a declining *marriage rate,* the number of marriages each year per 1,000 members of the population. This is because the maturation of the large, post-World War II baby boom generation increased the number of people in the most common marriageable age bracket (National Center for Health Statistics, 1989; U.S. Bureau of the Census, 1989).

Marriage rates peaked in the United States in 1946 in the wave of marriages that occurred following World War II. During that time, the marriage rate was 16.4 per 1,000 people. Marriage rates remained relatively high throughout the 1950s and then started to show a decline in the 1960s and 1970s. The marriage rate today is about 10.5 (National Center for Health Statistics, 1989; U.S. Bureau of the Census, 1989).

☐ The Postponement of Marriage

We mentioned that the timing of marriage has changed over the years. Because of the growing numbers who are postponing marriage, the median age at first marriage has increased (median age means that one-half of the people marrying for the first time in a given year get married before the given age, and one-half marry after the given age). In support of this, consider how the median age for marriage has changed over the years. In 1890, the median age was 26.1 for males and 22 for women. In 1976, it was 23.8 and 21.3 for males and females, respectively. In 1983, it was 24.4 for grooms and 22.5 for brides. Statistics gathered for 1989 indicate that the median age has increased once more: 25.8 for men and 23.6 for women. This represents the highest median age ever recorded for American women and the highest for men since the median age of 25.9 in 1900 (U.S. Bureau of the Census, 1989; National Center for Health Statistics, 1989).

Numerous factors account for the postponement of marriage. A strictly demographic factor during the last two decades has been the "marriage squeeze." Given that women are usually two or three years younger than men at marriage, the marriage squeeze developed as a consequence of the upward trend of births during the baby boom. Because of this, a female born in 1947, when the birthrate had risen, was likely to marry a male born in 1944 or 1945, when the birthrate was still low. Consequently, about 20 years later, there was an excess of women in the primary ages for marriage, and this phenomenon continued for the length of time that the baby boom lasted. Therefore, by 1970, the number of men 20 to 26 years of age was only 93 percent of the

International Lifespan Development

■ MARRIAGE RATES AROUND THE GLOBE

As we have indicated, most Americans can expect to marry at some point in their adult lives. The United States remains near the top of the list in comparison with such industrialized nations as Japan, West Germany, Canada, Israel, and Australia. Moreover, many European nations such as France, Spain, and Ireland have over twice as many never-marrieds as the United States (Broderick, 1989).

Certain countries encourage early marriages, offering a unique contrast to the nuptial postponement patterns of the United States. Bangladesh, for example, has the highest known proportion of married 15- to 19-year-old women (70 percent) and the lowest mean age at marriage (11.6) in the world. Proportions of 15- to 19-year-old women are also high, and age at marriage low, in the populous countries of Indonesia (30 percent married, age at marriage 16.4), Nepal (59 percent and 16.0 years), and Pakistan (31 percent and 15.3 years). Collectively, the developed nations of Canada and the United States, Europe, Australia and New Zealand, and Japan have the lowest proportion of ever-married women aged 15 to 19. Virtually all are below 10 percent (Senderowitz and Paxman, 1985).

In parts of Northern and Western Europe, marriage rates have been declining since 1970. This is particularly evident in Sweden, Denmark, and Switzerland, nations where cohabitation and marriage postponement are widespread. Should these trends persist, it is predicted that only 60 percent of men and women in Northern and Western European countries will ever marry.

Cohabitation, especially, has become a way of life for many of Europe's young adults. Uncommon until the end of the 1960s, Sweden and Denmark were among the first countries to accept this lifestyle. Unlike the United States, cohabitation in these nations is not a prelude to marriage. Rather, it has become a lifestyle in and of itself. Instead of being a trial marriage, it is regarded by many as a distinct alternative to marriage.

Cohabitation thus affects the timing of marriage, should it occur at all. The mean age at first marriage for women in Sweden is 27.3, while in Denmark it is 26.1. In these two nations, as well as in Iceland where the proportion of out-of-wedlock births is also well above 40 percent, the mean age of women at first marriage is now higher than the mean age of women at first birth. Because of this, it is not uncommon for children to be present at their parents' first wedding ceremony.

In Northern and Western Europe, the decline in the propensity to marry has been paralleled by a general reluctance to remarry. While the number of second marriages has increased, many divorced or widowed men and women are now opting to remain single rather than entering a new legal bond. In many cases, this decision is influenced by financial concerns, such as the prospective loss of benefits or pensions derived from the former marriage. But a more basic reason may be the waning of marriage as an institution. With the dramatic improvement in living conditions, which has accompanied the advent of welfare states in Europe, and the widespread acceptance of cohabitation, marriage has fewer implications for one's young adult status. Consequently, not marrying or remarrying has become a legitimate option. For that matter, divorce is much easier to consider than it was generations ago.

(van de Kaa, 1987)

number of women aged 18 to 24. The corresponding figure for black males was 82 percent (Glick, 1984).

This meant that by 1970, there was a shortage of men in the primary marriageable ages for women. This was true for young adults regardless of race. By 1985, this percentage had escalated somewhat, to 98 percent for all races. By 1995, the figure is expected to reach 108 percent, as the declining birthrates of the 1960s and early 1970s create a reversal of the marriage squeeze phenomenon.

Besides demographic trends, there are other reasons for the postponement of marriage. More persons, especially women, are enrolling in college, graduate school, and professional schools. There are also expanding employment and career opportunities for women, and many men and women are placing their careers ahead of marriage plans. Finally, the high divorce rate in this country has prompted some to seriously question the traditional appeal of marriage and family life.

☐ The Motives for Marriage

The motives for marrying are multiple and diverse, but it is possible to identify some of the more popular reasons. Nick Stinnett and his colleagues (1984) isolated the following as the most common reasons to get married:

COMMITMENT Many people want to feel that someone is dedicated to them without reservation. Marriage is an expression of this type of dedication, and the marriage ceremony itself is an important symbol of this commitment.

ONE-TO-ONE RELATIONSHIP Many individuals desire an intimate, enduring, one-to-one relationship. Many want to be with someone who will provide emotional support through affection, respect, trust, and intimacy. Learning how to become intimate with another may, indeed, be the biggest task of young adulthood (Conger, 1981).

COMPANIONSHIP AND SHARING Marriage offers the opportunity to overcome loneliness and isolation, with its potential for companionship and chance to share activities. Research shows that sharing is an important facet of the overall relationship. When needs are mutually fulfilled and activities shared, relationships become more integrated and couples experience more satisfaction (Ammons and Stinnett, 1980).

LOVE The lives of many people are most satisfying when they mean a great deal to other people. Many people want to find a person from whom they will receive unqualified love and to whom they can return that love. Marriage offers the opportunity to fulfill the basic need for love.

HAPPINESS The pursuit of happiness is important to people in all facets of their lives. Many people expect that marriage will be a source of happiness. However, it must be understood that happiness does not lie in the institution of marriage. Rather, it lies in people and depends on the way that they interact in the relationship.

LEGITIMIZATION OF SEX AND CHILDREN Marriage provides social approval with respect to sexual behavior, although we noted in Chapter 8 that many men and women engage in nonmarital intercourse and that many of today's Americans have adopted a more tolerant view of nonmarital sexual relations. Legitimizing children is another reason for marriage.

Finally, we should note that there are "wrong" reasons for marriage. That is, some people may choose to marry for negative reasons, such as to acquire a sexual partner or to obtain economic or emotional security. Some marry to escape the loneliness of a solitary existence or because they want to get away from an unhappy home situation. Although these reasons may be important, they are not sound reasons when they are the principal motivation for marriage (Stinnett, Walters, and Kaye, 1984; Berkley, 1981).

☐ The Engagement and Wedding

The final stage of courtship has conventionally been the engagement. Well-established social customs surrounding the engagement appear to have remained durable and appealing despite our rapidly changing views. The engagement is typically a public announcement of a couple's intention to marry and serves as a preparatory period for marriage (F. Cox, 1984).

The engagement is a ritual symbolizing exclusive commitment to one's partner. As the final step before marriage, the engagement serves a number of functions that may overlap with, but differ somewhat from, those in the serious dating stage. Among the many functions of engagement Coleman (1984) lists the following:

1. The engagement provides a time for the couple to agree on and work out fundamental living arrangements. For example, where will the couple live? Will both work?

2. Engaged couples have an opportunity to reexamine and agree on both short-term and long-term goals. Furthermore, they can explore the methods they plan to use for reaching these goals.

3. The engagement period typically provides the opportunity to get acquainted with each other's families. The couple can also decide how they will relate to their in-laws and each other's friends.

4. The engagement is a time to make a final check of each other's interests, goals, values, and compatibility in general.

5. Engaged couples use this time to work out final details of the wedding.

Thus, the engagement is an important step on the path toward marriage. It is a time for serious life planning and an opportunity for partners to evaluate their expectations of each other. Such an intimate evaluation may reveal jagged edges in a relationship and cause the partners to go their separate ways. In this respect, the engagement does not bind a couple into an irrevocable commitment. Rather, it represents a final test period before a couple takes the big step (Broderick, 1989).

Before two people can marry, certain legal requirements must be met. First, both parties must be of a certain minimum age, which varies from state to state. In most states, the age of eligibility is 18 for the male and 16 for the female with parental consent, and 21 for the male and 18 for the female without parental consent. Marriages between close blood relatives are forbidden. Another requirement for marriage is that the couple obtain a marriage license. Most states also require a blood test to ensure that neither partner has a sexually transmitted disease. Most states also have a three-day delay between the time of the blood test and the actual issuance of the marriage license. Presumably, this delay represents a "cooling off" period, a period that gives couples one last chance to change their minds.

The actual wedding ceremony must be performed by someone legally licensed by the state. The wedding ceremony must be witnessed by two persons of legal age. Fol-

Marriage brings a new dimension to the life cycle.

lowing the ceremony, the couple, the two witnesses, and the official performing the ceremony must sign the marriage license. Finally, the completed license is sent to the state capitol where it is recorded and filed.

☐ Varieties of Marital Roles

There are several different types of marriages, each stressing different roles and responsibilities for the husband and wife. Although certain marital relationships can be identified, rarely does a pure strain exist. Rather, most marriages represent a blend of categories.

In the *patriarchal marriage,* the male is recognized as the undisputed head of the household. Although the wife has some authority in certain areas, such as child care, the husband dominates the relationship. It is maintained by some (e.g., Sennet, 1980) that absolute control by the husband has steadily declined since the turn of the century.

The *matriarchal marriage* is characterized by female domination. This power structure is more common in the lower classes, usually because the husband is often absent.

The *egalitarian* (also called equalitarian) *marriage* is popular among middle-class couples and emphasizes the sharing of authority, household chores, and responsibilities. Neither the husband nor the wife is regarded as the undisputed head of the household; rather, this marriage is characterized by mutuality and reciprocity.

The indications are that egalitarian marriages will increase in popularity in the future. The reasons for this include the greater number of women in the labor force, society's increasing deemphasis of sex-role differences and its emphasis on sex-role equality, and the fact that more women work before marrying. The greater rewards a couple might receive from such a marriage (greater satisfaction, happiness, and companionship) are another reason for the egalitarian marriage's popularity (Haas, 1982, 1985).

Although couples today may swap chores, research indicates that women still shoulder the majority of their traditional responsibilities. This was reinforced in a study

How Couples Stay Together in the Age of Divorce

We have only just begun. . . . For newly married couples, starting out in life together has enormous and exciting potential. But many couples find that the images they have attached to married life are filled with myths and misconceptions. For most, idealistic dreams are quickly replaced by the realities of day-to-day living.

What factors determine successful adjustment to married life? For that matter, what is the secret behind those marriages that endure over the years? Do couples need to nurture special relationship skills? These and other questions were at the foundation of research undertaken by Francine Klangsbrun (1985). Surveying 87 couples who had remained married for at least 15 years, she discovered that couples in strong relationships shared a number of abilities and outlooks:

An Ability to Change and Adapt Change is inevitable in marriages as time goes on, be it the children moving out of the home, career triumphs and failures, or caring for aging parents. Couples in enduring marriages are flexible in meeting change, in the process implementing positive adjustment and adaptive skills. Many also willingly choose to change themselves when necessary to keep their marriages vital and alive. This is especially apparent in everyday communication abilities.

Enjoyment of Each Other Couples in enduring and vital marriages honestly enjoy being in one another's company. They like talking with one another, communicate effectively, and share many common values. Moreover, their sex lives are active and considered by both partners to be vital to the overall relationship.

Trust for One Another While love may wax and wane within a relationship, trust in enduring marriages remains constant. Couples trusting one another report high levels of security and comfort as well as safety and nurturance. Partners maintain that trust rests at the foundation of their commitment to monogamy, since trust in marriage presupposes exclusivity.

An Ability to Live with the Unchangeable Couples in enduring relationships do not expect perfection from one another and accept their partners for whom and what they are. While differences do exist in the relationship, partners go on with their lives and focus on their marital strengths, rather than weaknesses.

An Assumption of Permanence Here, partners are committed to one another as well as to marriage as a whole. The concept of "forever" is not only a hope but an ongoing philosophy. The notion that marriage will be permanent has a tendency to temper the couple's approach to imperfections and conflicts.

A Balance of Dependencies In successful and enduring marriages, partners are mutually dependent. When they speak of needing each other, they are typically talking about strengths, not weaknesses. This in no way implies helpless and immature dependency when one's partner is absent; rather, partners turn to one another to fill in gaps and provide enrichment and enjoyment.

A Shared and Cherished History This implies that couples are attached to the significance of their past and of the time spent together. Couples in vital marriages have woven a history together and respect the chapters experienced: how they met, private jokes, rituals, and even shared sadnesses. This is not mere nostalgia but, instead, an appreciation of their shared attachment.

A Degree of Luck Successful relationships need a certain degree of luck to keep going. From the beginning, a person needs some luck in choosing a partner who has the capacity to trust, change, and grow in a relationship. A little luck with life is also needed. Extended illnesses, job losses, personal failures, or family feuds might push a marriage off course when it might otherwise have succeeded.

of women and household work by Catherine Berheide (1984). She studied time budgets, the division of labor, working conditions, and how women feel about their labor in the home.

She found that as more and more women enter the labor force, the number assuming a double load of work also rises, because the traditional patterns show few prospects for any change. With the exception of child care, the women studied had few strong positive or negative reactions to their daily tasks. Moreover, they did not feel particularly pressured, although they had little leisure time.

Although these women loved the people for whom they were doing household work, they also reported frustration when they constantly had to do the same jobs over and over. This feeling escalated when no one seemed to care. Because of its monotony and repetition, household work was not seen as offering any lasting rewards.

Another study (Zuckerman, 1983) showed that though working couples do share domestic responsibility, the women continue to bear the brunt of household chores. A majority of the female respondents, all partners in dual-career couples, prepared most of the meals, were responsible for paying the bills, and were the primary food shoppers. Research such as this suggests that household tasks are still not shared equally, despite the greater participation by husbands than ever before.

☐ Alternatives to Traditional Marriage

Although marriage is the chosen path for a clear-cut majority of the population, not everyone chooses to exchange traditional wedding vows. On the contrary, numerous alternatives to married life exist. In this facet of our discussion, we will explore some of the more popular alternatives: singlehood, cohabitation, open marriages, communal living, group marriage, swinging, and the gay lifestyle.

SINGLE ADULTHOOD

A growing number of adults in contemporary society simply prefer not to get married. There are currently over 20 million never-married, single adults 18 years of age and older. Moreover, this figure has been steadily rising. Since 1960, the number of singles living apart from relatives has increased over 100 percent (U.S. Bureau of the Census, 1989).

These figures do not take into account the numbers of divorced and widowed persons, populations that are also single and increasing in number. One out of every three married persons will be single within the next five years and the figure will increase to about one in every two by the end of the 1990s. They will join the ranks of the 67 million single adults in America, a group comprised of divorced and widowed individuals as well as those who have chosen to postpone marriage or never marry at all (U.S. Bureau of the Census, 1989; Simenauer and Carroll, 1982).

PUSHES AND PULLS TOWARD SINGLEHOOD *Singlehood* is a lifestyle marked by a person's desire not to get married. Numerous factors account for the increase in single adults. One important motive is the growing career and education opportunities available for women. Pursuing a career or a degree rather than marrying at an early age is attractive to many people today. Both single men and women are able to devote more time and energy to their careers.

Another reason for the increase in singlehood is that there are more women than men of marriageable age, thus creating a surplus of singles. Yet another reason is that more individuals desire freedom and autonomy. Many who choose this lifestyle are also aware of today's gloomy divorce statistics (Stein, 1981; 1989; Macklin, 1980).

Singlehood offers considerable potential for happiness, productivity, and self-actualization. Among the most fundamental benefits of single life are its unfettered opportunities for development and change. The years following high school and college are typically a time for men and women to clarify career goals, lifestyle preferences, and political and sexual identities; by remaining single, an individual enjoys that much more freedom to reflect, experiment, and make significant changes in beliefs and values should he or she so desire. The single person thus has an enormous opportunity to construct new identities—or, on the other hand, to be confused by finding too many new identities. Yet the friendships and support networks that singles can participate in may help to redress some of those conflicts (Stein, 1989; Stein and Fingrutd, 1985).

Thus, singlehood has become popular because of a new image attached to this lifestyle. In the past, however, singlehood was often viewed with suspicion. Singles were regarded by many as being different or lonely losers, the labels "old maid" or "spinster" capturing this image. Today, though, singlehood is recognized as a legitimate and fulfilling lifestyle. Most no longer regard getting married as necessarily better than remaining single and do not disapprove of those who eschew marriage (Lamanna and Riedmann, 1985; Cargan and Melko, 1985; Thornton and Freedman, 1982).

But while the societal image of singles has changed, we have to be careful of the perceptions we hold of this and other lifestyles, including marriage. There is a tendency among some to create the image of the swinging single: lounging at poolside, spending weekends at ski resorts, or dancing at discos, all in the process of encountering equally exciting singles. This lifestyle, in fact, is experienced by only a few. The truth of the matter is that many singles who begin an evening alone in a singles' bar or other social activity usually end up going home without a companion for the night (Saxton, 1990).

Choosing to marry or remain single has important implications for one's self-identity. Often the single finds the world of the married couple quite exclusive and can enter it only in a limited fashion. For the couple, the paired relationship fosters a strong sense of identity—not only as a couple but individually as well. Singles, on the other hand, construct their identity primarily on their own, unless, of course, they are involved in an intimate relationship (Bell, 1983).

Finally, the current literature indicates that singles are not as lonely as society paints them to be (Stein, 1989; Cargan, 1981; Cargan and Meiko, 1982, 1985). Research does suggest, however, that one of the more difficult chores in singlehood is developing and maintaining important friendships (Stein, 1981, 1985, 1989). The findings show that while singles do not report feelings of loneliness, they do struggle with sustaining a connection with those deemed significant in their lives.

COHABITATION

In addition to singlehood, many individuals choose cohabitation as a lifestyle in contemporary society. *Cohabitation* is defined as an unmarried man and an unmarried woman living together. While this form of alternative lifestyle did not gain prominence until the 1960s, today it is extremely popular.

Cohabitation became prominent in the 1960s because of a variety of social changes. On college campuses, administrators relaxed rules against opposite-sex visitors in response to student demands. Large numbers of students also took advantage of new options to rent off-campus apartments. At the same time, young adults began to liberalize their sexual attitudes and behaviors, making premarital sex more openly acceptable. These changes fell upon the fertile ground of a particularly large cohort of college students, products of the post-World War II baby boom years (Atwater, 1985).

The number of unmarried couples living together increased from nearly 1 million in 1977 to approximately 2.6 million in 1989. This is an increase of over 300 percent from the previous decade. Furthermore, it is projected that during the 1990s, about 7 percent of all U.S. households will consist of unmarried couples living together (National Center for Health Statistics, 1989; U.S. Bureau of the Census, 1989; Glick, 1988).

Many factors influence a couple's decision to cohabitate. For example, sexual values are changing and there is a growing acceptance of permissiveness. In addition, the availability of contraceptives and the relative ease of obtaining an abortion has reduced the risk of pregnancy among sexually active cohabitants. Peer support for such a lifestyle represents an additional reason, and many cohabitants are today less concerned about the status of marriage. Adults who have seen their parents' marriages break down may also have less faith in formal marriage as an institution that can provide security and happiness (Oliver, 1982).

Most cohabitants are under age 35, and this lifestyle continues to be popular among college students. The latter is due largely to the availability of off-campus housing, coed dormitories, and liberal student attitudes. In recent years, however, there has been an increase in the number of older cohabitants as well. It is estimated that there are approximately 350,000 persons over age 55 living together (U.S. Bureau of the Census, 1989; Glick, 1988; Glick and Spanier, 1980).

Just as there are many types of marriages and diverse motives for people joining together in marriage, so, too, there are many types of living-together arrangements. Some couples live together for purely economic reasons. Some cohabit without any desire to become involved in a personal, intimate relationship. For others, the opposite is true: Cohabitation offers the opportunity to establish a close relationship. The largest number of cohabitants, however, are those who believe marriage is on the horizon. In this sense, cohabitation is typically viewed as a precursor to marriage, not an alternative (Cherlin and Furstenberg, 1983).

OPEN MARRIAGE

In contrast with traditional marriages, an *open marriage* is usually one that is flexible and stresses the importance of continuing self-growth for both marriage partners. Although we would expect this in any marriage, the open marriage's underlying assumptions differ from those of the traditional marriage contract, which many couples still use to guide their individual marriages.

In general, open marriages do not place the partners in bondage to each other, diminish the individual identity of the partners, create a "couple-image," or enforce togetherness in the belief that only thus can the marriage be preserved. The open marriage does not substitute new regulations for old ones; rather, it suggests ways in which couples can learn to communicate openly with each other in order to arrive at a consensus for living (Wachowiak and Bragg, 1980).

COMMUNAL LIVING

The concept of the family *commune* has been around for a long time. Utopians from Plato to Thoreau suggested and often experimented with this type of family system. Today, there are approximately 3,000 rural and urban communes scattered throughout the United States and an estimated 1 million persons living in them. Communes were very popular during the 1970s but have declined in popularity since. Most communes last only one year (F. Cox, 1984; Stinnet, Walters, and Kaye, 1984).

Dennis Orthner (1981) identified four characteristics of communes. First, communes seek to become a community based on economic need. Members work together to meet one another's needs, with the rewards being distributed equally. Second, communes share a pioneer spirit. For many communes, this means going back to the land to derive some, if not all, of their subsistence. Third, many communes seek to resemble an extended family, with members sharing a common house and tending to one another's emotional needs. Fourth, communes usually share a common ideology. Some may share a political ideology, such as Gandhian nonviolence; others may be held together by a common spiritual bond.

Many people join communes to escape from an increasing sense of alienation and isolation. This alienation may prompt people to join rural communes in which they can see—and eat—the results of their labor. Communes often sanction behavior and ideas that differ from those of society as a whole (F. Cox, 1984).

Some communes, in an effort to instill intimacy among its members, minimize the importance of married couples. Married couples are asked to share allegiance to the group as a whole. Frequently, communes use only first names, encourage erotic and emotional relationships among other group members, and remove property belonging to the couple as a means of spreading the love bond between the husband and wife to the commune as a whole.

Many communes are characterized by equality, whether in the form of shared domestic tasks or in the provision of emotional support. Child rearing, for instance, is considered a community task. Work assignments are also equally dispersed. Men and women frequently work side by side and typically earn the same amount of money, which is channeled to the collective.

Although some communes succeed and meet their goals, many, as we mentioned at the outset, fail. Relinquishing all of one's resources to the group becomes a stumbling block for some. Others rebel at the loss of privacy. Many communes fail because the business enterprises undertaken, such as farming, are poorly planned and executed. Many communes also have a loose overall structure, which often leads to a general lack of leadership, authority, and needed direction (Golanty and Harris, 1982).

The communal lifestyle is but one alternative to traditional marriage.

SWINGING

Swinging, also referred to as "mate swapping," is a relationship involving two or more married couples who decide to switch sexual partners or to engage in group sex. Swingers are usually upper-middle-class individuals who are employed in professional and white-collar occupations. Similar to group marriage, swinging is rare for persons under 30, especially males.

Diane Levande and her colleagues (1983) reported that the actual participation in swinging may be the culmination of a gradual decision-making process. A couple often begins with a negative response to the idea, changes over time—usually under pressure from one spouse—to a partial acceptance of swinging on a limited, trial basis. If the first encounter is a traumatic one, further participation is unlikely. But if it is gratifying, the couple is apt to include swinging activities in their relationship more often.

Research indicates that many couples turn to swinging in the hope of strengthening an otherwise strained relationship. Some regard swinging as a sexual adventure, a way to act out their inner fantasies. For those who are very liberal minded, swinging is but one of many ways to gain sexual satisfaction.

Swinging appears to have many of the same problems associated with group marriages: guilt, jealousy, and too great an emotional price. Troubles also arise when the couple's interest in swinging is unequal. Negative reactions such as anger and jealousy are reported when one spouse (often the wife) feels pressured into the activity. When this happens, the couple must either mutually decide to drop out of the swinging scene, accept swinging as an activity not equally enjoyed, or separate (Macklin, 1980; Orthner, 1981).

THE GAY LIFESTYLE

Homosexuality is a broad term that refers to sexual attraction and emotional attachment to persons of the same gender. The word homosexual originates from the Greek word *homos,* which means "the same." Today, there is a movement away from using the term homosexual because of the tendency to think of it in sexually exclusive ways. While sexual interaction is shared by many partners, it is not the primary focus of all relationships. The terms **gay men** and **lesbian women,** or lesbians, are preferred because they seek to take into account nonsexual aspects of a person's life. The word *gay* is a general term that is often applied to both men and women.

Homosexuality has existed since the beginning of time and was practiced and tacitly approved in a number of societies. For example, it was practiced in ancient Greece, and by the Tanalans of Madagascar, the Siwamis of Africa, and the Keraki of New Guinea. Throughout history, homosexuality in the broad sense of our definition, was, to one degree or another, either the preferred or chosen sexual lifestyle of many eminent historical and literary figures, including Alexander the Great, Michelangelo, Francis Bacon, Lord Byron, Oscar Wilde, Somerset Maugham, Virginia Woolf, Tennessee Williams, Gertrude Stein, and James Baldwin.

Homosexuality is not a form of mental illness, although classification efforts have not always reflected this. Consider a brief history in the *Diagnostic and Statistical Manual,* an authoritative classification of mental disorders published by the American Psychiatric Association. In 1952, the first edition of the *Diagnostic and Statistical Manual* (DSM-I) classified homosexuality as a mental disorder. Sixteen years later, in its 1968 edition, DSM-II still classified homosexuality as psychopathological.

Professional attitudes toward homosexuality began to shift in 1973. Homosexuality per se as a mental disorder was eliminated and a new category called "sexual orientation disturbance" was substituted and placed in the seventh printing of DSM-II. With the publication of DSM-III in 1980, another diagnostic category was created: "ego-dystonic homosexuality." Individuals falling into this new classification experienced sustained and unwanted patterns of overt homosexual arousal along with persistent distress. The DSM-III-R, a revised edition published in 1987, does not include homosexuality in its list of disorders.

Thus, contrary to what was once thought, homosexuality is not a form of abnormal behavior or mental illness. Indeed, most homosexuals are well adjusted and emotionally stable. While some may exhibit anxiety or depression, so, too, do some heterosexuals. When maladaptive behavior does occur in homosexuals, some clinicians propose that it is often attributable to the social stigma attached to homosexuality instead of to something pathological in the nature of homosexuality itself (Sarason and Sarason, 1989; Ross, Paulsen, and Stalstrom, 1988; Stein, 1988).

Gay men and lesbian women are not confused about their gender identity. Lesbian women are not different from heterosexual women in their sureness of being female, nor do gay men differ from heterosexual men on this dimension. Related to behavior, most gay men are not effeminate in dress or manner, nor are lesbians usually masculine in their behavior. Even those individuals who sometimes act and dress like stereotypes of the other gender generally do so with a clear awareness of their own gender identity (Silberman and Hawkins, 1988; Peplau and Gordon, 1983).

Over the years, gay men and women have had to live with societal rejection and ridicule, not to mention discriminatory laws and practices. Andrea Parrot and Michael Ellis (1985) point out that this treatment of gay and lesbian Americans was still in evidence in the 1980s. For example, marriages between lesbian women and gay men are legally prohibited. Gay men and lesbian women are prevented from adopting. They are also barred from entrance to the armed services and various organizations and occupations. The educational system has frequently denied gay men and lesbian women teaching positions due to a fear that children will be corrupted and recruited to the so-called homosexual way of life. This is an unfounded fear since most people who sexually abuse and assault children are heterosexual men. The media also tends to depict homosexuality in an unfair and unrealistic light. There is also discrimination leveled against gay men and lesbian women in regard to family life:

- Gay men and lesbian women are often perceived as a threat to family life. The real threat, however, is the ignorance and prejudice that cause family members to turn their backs on a gay or lesbian family member, destroying the family unit. Lesbian and gay children are often rejected by their families because the family is embarrassed by them.

- Because gay marriages are not legal, certain inequalities exist. For example, some of the reasons often given for marriage of heterosexual couples include love, to have children, to support each other financially, to gain cultural recognition as a couple, and to file joint tax returns. Most of these reasons are also important to gay and lesbian couples but society discriminates against lesbian women and gay men by disallowing gay and lesbian marriages. Tax and insurance regulations also discriminate against homosexual couples. If one member of a married heterosexual couple is working and the other is not, their incomes are pooled and tax based on two deductions rather than one. The tax savings are significant.

- Although most gay men and lesbian women do not become parents through traditional means, those that do are often discriminated against in child custody cases. They are also often discriminated against when attempting to become parents through nontraditional means (Parrot and Ellis, 1985).

Aging experiences from a homosexual standpoint have only recently been explored. One source (Berger, 1982) maintains that although homosexuals adjust well to aging processes, they are often doubly constrained. That is, they are often shunned by a society that is predominantly heterosexual and that continues to put a premium on youth. Older homosexuals have also been neglected by younger gays and avoided by gerontologists as taboo subjects.

On the other hand, it might be argued (Almvig, 1982) that the battle gay men and lesbian women fight against alienation may have beneficial effects with age. That is, one's struggle for identity may result in an enhanced sense of self. One investigation (Harry, 1982) discovered that male homosexuals, over time, have devised various solutions to their problems of alienation. Some of these solutions turn out to be quite advantageous during adulthood for educational and career advancement. For example, through their alienation from conventional male-gender culture, they have been freed to originate modified gender roles, which draw on varying components of masculine and feminine culture that are closer to their individual needs.

RELATIONSHIPS OF GAY MEN AND LESBIAN WOMEN Gay men and lesbian women often want the type of relationship heterosexual couples have, and they hold many of the same values. They are likely, however, to reject traditional roles in favor of an egalitarian relationship. As far as sexual relationships are concerned, gay men and lesbian women, compared to heterosexuals, are more aware of their partners' sexual needs. This is probably because they possess more knowledge of their own sex (Peplau, 1981; Harmatz and Novak, 1983; Masters and Johnson, 1980).

A collection of research conducted by Letita Ann Peplau and associates (Peplau, 1981; Peplau and Gordon, 1983; Peplau and Cochran, 1981) has shed light on the intimate relationships of lesbian women and gay men. Among other findings, Peplau discovered that most gays want to have steady relationships, although this is somewhat more important to women than men. Both gay men and lesbian women, as well as heterosexual couples, desire certain elements in a close relationship: companionship, affection, and personal development. As far as qualities sought in partners, lesbian women, gay men, and heterosexuals all value such traits as honesty, affection, and warmth.

Another investigation (Peplau and Cochran, 1980) matched samples of lesbian women, gay men, and heterosexual women and men and rated the importance of various features of love relationships. These included such issues as revealing intimate feelings, spending time together, holding similar attitudes, having an equal-power relationship, and having sexual exclusivity. The gathered results showed that remarkably few overall group differences existed between heterosexuals and homosexuals. For example, on average, both groups gave the greatest importance to "being able to talk about my intimate feelings" with a partner.

One significant difference emerged between homosexuals and heterosexuals, however. Sexual exclusivity in relationships was much more important to heterosexuals than to homosexuals. Lesbian women and gay men gave sexual fidelity an average rating of somewhat more than 5, compared with a rating of just over 7 for the heterosexuals (the highest possible importance rating was 9). Homosexuals were less likely than heterosexuals to endorse monogamy as an ideal for relationships. Two interesting gender differences also became evident. Whatever their sexual orientation, women gave greater importance than men did to emotional expressiveness and the sharing of feelings. This finding is consistent with the emphasis in North American gender-role socialization that men should conceal their feelings and present a tougher exterior. Secondly, lesbian and heterosexual women cared more than men about having egalitarian relationships. The researchers feel that perhaps because of the women's movement, women showed greater sensitivity to equal power in love relationships.

All things considered, this study shows that gay men, lesbian women, and heterosexual couples are more alike than dissimilar in terms of relationship dynamics. This has prompted researchers such as Sharon Brehm (1985) to conclude that if we want to describe what goes on in a relationship between two gay men or lesbian women—what makes for the success of that relationship and what may lead to problems—we do not have to use a different language. We can use the same terms as we would in describing a relationship between two heterosexuals. In our intimate relationships, we are all much more similar than we are different.

■ Parenthood

One of the most important, most exciting developmental challenges that young married couples encounter is parenthood. The arrival of a newborn infant in the household is characteristically a joyous occasion, the culmination of many long months of anticipation and preparation. For those who have experienced this event, words cannot capture the feelings of pride, love, and warmth that family members can share.

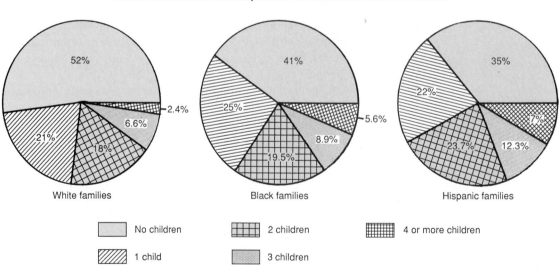

Percent Distribution of Families, by Number of Own Children Under 18 Years Old

White families

Black families

Hispanic families

No children
1 child
2 children
3 children
4 or more children

FIGURE 9-1 Percentage Distribution of Families by Number of Own Children Under 18 Years Old

(Adapted from U.S. Bureau of the Census, 1989)

Quite likely, the transition from a dyad to a triad relationship is one of the most complex and dramatic changes most people will ever make in their lives. Perhaps no other experience can cause as much personality growth as being a parent does. Furthermore, no single circumstance in the life of a child will be as influential as its relationship with its parents.

There are many reasons for wanting children. For many, children represent an extension of the self. Children are also a source of personal fulfillment and represent an enhancement of a couple's identity. Some adults want children because they look forward to the companionship that they'll bring. Others maintain that children will give security to them when they're old. Finally, many want children because of social expectation. In other words, it's the thing to do when you're an adult. Figure 9-1 shows the percentages of families in the United States who have children.

Of course, just as with marriage, there are many wrong reasons for having children. Having a baby because one's parents want grandchildren should not be the only motivation. As we shall later learn, a baby is not the cure for a marriage devoid of meaning. Some couples use the exclusive measure of a financial goal before they have children. Financial security by itself is not a sound motive for having children. Neither is the singular motive that a baby will give a totally bored couple something to do. Although a child will certainly be a source of activity, couples with this underlying motive often become just as bored with child-care chores.

☐ Voluntary Childlessness

Today, a growing number of couples are deciding not to have children. Not so long ago, most couples had little choice; if they were fertile and led active sex lives, a combination of unreliable contraceptives and social pressure almost guaranteed that they would become parents. Today, though, the situation has changed. Most *voluntarily childless* couples are very satisfied and content with their decision not to have children. They do not view parenthood as a requirement for happiness or fulfillment in adulthood (Orthner, 1981).

Demographers predict that 25 to 30 percent of young married women will elect not to have children (U.S. Bureau of the Census, 1980a, 1980b, 1989). This is an interesting trend when compared with the high premium placed on having children during earlier historical periods. Recall that in the Old Testament, God's directive to Noah was "Be fruitful and multiply." Often, parents faced certain consequences if they did not bear children and produce large families. In the classical age of Greece, barrenness was sufficient grounds for a man to divorce his wife. In colonial America, single men were viewed with suspicion and penalized with special taxes for not doing their share to increase the population. This is a far cry from the sentiment expressed today in certain countries, such as China, where parents are required to limit family size.

Childless couples tend to be well educated, financially secure, and from urban settings. In addition, they enjoy the company of each other and are very involved in their careers. Marian Faux (1984a) observed that many childless couples believed that their parents were very limited by the chores of parenting. Women, in particular, view their own mothers as never having had the careers they longed for or that they were cut off from once they became mothers.

The decision to remain childless is usually a difficult one. Recently, an organization called the National Alliance for Optional Parenthood was formed to help couples in their decision making. A central theme of this organization is that parenthood is an option for couples, not a duty. The organization tries to help couples recognize that it is perfectly acceptable not to have children.

Besides voluntary childlessness, some couples choose to postpone parenthood. Not only are the numbers of couples delaying parenthood increasing, they are also having fewer children. Delaying parenthood provides couples with the opportunity to develop their personal, career, and marital lives before they take on the responsibilities of parenthood (Ford, 1981; Wilkie, 1981; Knaub, Eversoll, and Voss, 1983).

Older women who have developed professional competence before bearing children often bring to the mothering experience strengths different from those of their younger counterparts. Older mothers with established careers are often more accepting and less conflicted in the parenting role than are younger professional women. They tend to reveal strengths concomitant with their level of maturity that are generally advantageous for their children's development. Research has indicated that levels of marital satisfaction are higher among women postponing parenthood and childless women than among mothers (Polonko, Scanzoni, and Teachman, 1982).

We must also acknowledge that there are forces that may work against the couple delaying parenthood. Perhaps the biggest risk is that a woman's fertility will decrease with age. The ideal childbearing years are between ages 20 and 35. Another problem is that older parents may not have the helping services of their aging parents. Also, couples delaying parenthood may find the tasks associated with child care physically exhausting, maybe even more so than younger parents do (Wilkie, 1981; Daniels and Weingarten, 1981).

International Lifespan Development

■ FAMILY PLANNING: FROM BABY BOUNTIES TO FERTILITY LAWS

The current emphasis placed on overpopulation and deliberate family planning has created a shrinkage of family size in many developed nations. In the United States, the average woman gives birth to two children, down from an average of 3.2 in 1960. Should present trends continue, the United States will reach zero population growth by the year 2020.

Other developed nations such as the Federal Republic of Germany, Austria, Denmark, and Hungary have already reached zero population growth. In fact, fertility levels (the number of live births occurring within a population) in these nations are dropping below the level of replacement, meaning that a population decrease is resulting. Nations such as Ireland, Poland, and the Soviet Union have fertility rates of above 2.10 lifetime births per woman. This is about the fertility level needed to balance a nation's births and deaths, thus maintaining a stable population.

In some parts of the world, government officials are so concerned about declining birthrates that "baby bounties" are offered. That is, couples are given cash incentives to drive the birthrate upward. In Quebec, for example, couples receive

$500 for a first or second child, and $3,000 for third and subsequent children. In the German Democratic Republic, priority in the allocation of housing is given to those couples having more than one child. Also, low-interest loans are available at the time of marriage and the birth of each child to subsidize buying a home or home furnishings.

In other parts of the world, birthrates are astronomically high and create different circumstances. For example, in Rwanda, East Africa, the fertility rate is 8.5 children per woman. The average Rwandan woman is married before the age of 20 and has her first child before her second wedding anniversary. Kenyan women average 8 children each, causing the population increase of this Texas-size country to be 4.2 percent a year. Kenya's population was estimated to be 21 million in 1986 and, if current fertility rates hold, it will quadruple to 83 million by 2025. Haitian women give birth to about six children, a total that parallels the fertility rate of Pakistani women. In Tunisia, women average about five children.

Knowledge of family planning is an obvious prerequisite to lowering the birthrate in overpopulated countries. However, we must not lose sight of the fact that the number of children brought into the world is influenced by many factors. One of the most important is the economic role of children, particularly in developing nations. Larger families can typically be found in those agricultural areas where intensive labor is needed, such as Latin America. In India and Bangladesh, large families result from the desire for healthy male children. Boys represent economic security for the mother, should she become widowed.

In some nations certain customs and practices contribute to high rates of fertility. For example, unlike some African countries, there is no taboo on postpartum intercourse in Rwanda (East Africa). This postpartum abstinence can reduce the fertility level since it can last for as long as two years, or until the child is weaned. As another illustration, Moslem culture encourages large families and has a strong bias against birth control of any kind.

No discussion of cross-cultural fertility rates is complete without some reference to the People's Republic of China. Here, family planning is not a voluntary decision made by couples. Rather, it is the government that dictates family planning. In an effort to reduce overpopulation, which rose above the 1 billion mark in 1984, couples in this nation are allowed to have only one child. China is thus the first nation to ever restrict a couple's right to procreate. It has also raised the minimum age for marriage to 20 for women and 22 for men. Even later marriages are encouraged to reduce the couple's risk of having more than one child.

The government imposes the one-child limit through incentives, peer pressure, and attempts to persuade newly married couples that their rational fertility decisions will mean a better future for their own families, their communities, and their nation. If the one-child limit is successful, it is estimated that the population will stabilize at 1.2 billion by the twenty-first century. If the plan is unsuccessful and the population continues to grow, China's ability to feed its people will be in jeopardy, among other consequences.

If Chinese couples follow government legislation, they are entitled to numerous benefits, including increased living space, pensions, free education, lower cost health care, and better medical intervention. Eventually, the only child receives preferential treatment in the school system as well as in the labor force. Should couples give birth to a second child, the family forfeits all of these benefits.

Complicating this fertility plan is the fact that Chinese families have traditionally preferred male children. Should a firstborn be female, couples may try to conceive again in an effort to bring a male into the world. This places couples at odds with the government and open to sanctions. Indeed, in one province of China, couples expecting a second child will have their wages docked if the woman decides not to have an abortion.

☐ Adjustments to Parenthood

Becoming a parent requires considerable adjustment and adaptation, to say the least. Some researchers (e.g., Miller and Sollie, 1980; Waldron and Routh, 1981) regard parenthood as a stressful period and have expounded on its disruptive effects. More specifically, research such as this views the married couple as an integrated social system, and so adding or removing members forces a major reorganization. With the baby's arrival, patterns of intimacy and affection are changed and must be redefined. Other lines of research suggest that the addition of children lowers the parents' overall marital happiness (see Campbell, 1981; Glenn and McLanahan, 1981).

We certainly don't want to give the impression that parenthood is a negative experience. Indeed, not all experts contend that it is a crisis period. Although it has its share of demands and strains, most parents are able to weather its difficulties. And even though the addition of children lowers marital happiness, most parents express overall satisfaction with their children and the parenting role in general (Chilman, 1980).

It is our contention that from the beginning, parents need to overcome the idealistic myth of having the perfect family. Just like marriage, parenthood has its share of triumphs, heartaches, and headaches. Too many new parents strive for perfection and in the process program themselves for failure.

Going a step further, the myth of the perfect family has greatly hindered human relations. As Morrison (1983) so aptly stated, to live in a family today is to be subjected to an ever-rising and broadening image of perfectionism. The family, however, is one of the contexts of modern life in which perfectionism stands the least chance of attainment, no matter what the standards may be. Perfectionist standards applied to the family prescribe inner states for people, rather than behavior. If a family is to be considered normal, healthy, and adjusted, regardless of the ideal image within which it is housed, it is supposed to experience emotions such as love, happiness, joy, and fun. This emphasis on inner experience intensifies the strains of family relationships. Probably as a result of this heightened strain, parents experience widespread guilt and anxiety over child rearing. The expectations for families must be reduced—their emotional lives depend on that. The family represents a perfectly imperfect world that is peaceful one moment and engaged in battle the next, simultaneously creative and stifling.

What are some of the adjustments required during parenthood? Mothers must learn to adjust to a loss of sleep and frequent physical fatigue. As the saying goes, people who say they've slept like a baby usually don't have one. Many worry about their personal appearance, changes in their figure, and the fact that they frequently feel edgy or emotionally upset. Fathers report such adjustments as additional domestic chores and, like mothers, sleepless nights. Many report increased worry over financial matters and irritation directed toward in-laws concerning proper child care (Roman and Raley, 1980; Sollie and Miller, 1980).

In time, though, these initial anxieties about child care usually subside. Many parents develop confidence in their abilities and take pride in their daily accomplishments. Their fears and anxieties also begin to disappear when parents learn that they don't have to do everything by the book, whether it be Spock or Brazelton. As a result of their experiences and lessons learned firsthand, parenthood begins to acquire a less tense and more relaxed quality.

☐ Stages of Parenthood

Becoming a parent is an important developmental challenge of adult life. From the moment the infant enters the world to the time when maturity is reached, parents and children alike experience significant aspects of growth and development. Moments of joy and happiness directed toward one's offspring are interwoven with such feelings as sadness and frustration. Parents and children become partners in myriad life experiences.

The dynamics that unfold between parent and child prompted psychologist Ellen Galinsky (1980) to suggest that parenthood unfolds in a seemingly predictable series of stages. She proposed six stages in all, based on interviews with over 200 parents from all parts of the country.

At the heart of her six-stage theory is the fact that parents experience a progressive transformation of their self-images. Parents mentally picture the way they think things should be, especially in terms of their own personal behavior and that of their children. If such images are successfully achieved, satisfaction and happiness will follow. But if they are not, parents will typically feel anger, resentment, and even depression. Consequently, parents' self-images—not to mention parents' development—are shaped by interactions with their children. Put another way, a child's development leads the parent from one stage to the next.

Children bring a multitude of experiences into the lives of adults.

The first stage, the *parental image phase,* occurs when the baby is born. During this time, parents treat their children as they would have liked their parents to treat them. Images of parenthood are constructed around a desire for perfection, even though most adults are fully aware that child-rearing perfection is nearly impossible.

The *nurturing stage* is the second phase of parental development and lasts approximately through the second year of the child's life. Forming bonds of attachment to the baby is the major chore at this point, in addition to learning how much and when to give, not only to oneself, but also to one's spouse, job, and friends.

The *authority stage,* between 2 and 4 years, is the phase in which adults question their effectiveness as parental figures. For the child, this is a time of newly discovered social independence, the testing of new powers, and saying no. Such developments may cause parents to discover flaws in their images of parental perfection. Parental growth at this time may be measured by accepting images that are untenable.

The *integrative stage,* encompassing the preschool years through middle childhood, is the fourth phase Galinsky proposed. Further childhood gains in autonomy and initiative, as well as expanding social horizons, force parents to reexamine and then test their own implicit theories about the way things should be ideally and how they are in fact. Discrepancies between these two polarities are difficult for adults groping for effective parenting skills to accept.

The fifth stage, the *independent teenage years,* is a time for adolescents to struggle for greater levels of freedom, responsibility, and, in some cases, emancipation from the home. In perhaps one of parenthood's most stressful stages, adults must learn to redefine authority regarding the teenager's growing independence while at the same time to lend support to the growing pains characteristic of the adolescent years.

The *departure stage,* approximately after age 18, occurs when adolescents leave home. For the parents, this final stage becomes a period of assessment and evaluation of their overall past performances. Taking stock of the entire experience of parenthood reveals positive as well as negative features: the loose or crumbling pieces, the cracks, in addition to the cohesiveness, of their whole lives. Such an overview at this time in the family cycle, coupled with the assessment inherent in each of the previous stages, provides adults with a thought-provoking analysis and narrative of their performance as parents.

☐ Parental Roles

THE ROLE OF THE MOTHER

Cross-cultural studies reveal that the mother-child relationship considered normal in the American middle class is quite different from that found in most other cultures. In most traditional societies, maternal and paternal roles are sharply defined, primarily because the father is cast in an authoritarian and exalted position in relation to his family. In contemporary middle-class American society, however, the distinction between the maternal and paternal roles, at least in influencing and controlling the children, has for the most part disappeared (Bell, 1983).

The myth of the perfect family paints a very unrealistic picture of motherhood. In many respects, motherhood has become idealized beyond recognition in our society. As Diane Levande and her colleagues (1983) noted, a classic illustration of the perfect mother can be seen in television advertisements for diapers. A baby wets its diaper, either in the crib or while being held in the arms of an embarrassed neighbor. A new more absorbent diaper makes its appearance, and in the next scene, we see a very happy mother and her equally happy and dry baby. Television never portrays infants having bowel movements or suffering from diarrhea. Never do we see a tired mother laboring to keep the infant clean and tending to all of the other household chores. Rather, we see an efficient, happy, and satisfied mother. People who buy such an idealistic image of motherhood are in for a rude awakening.

Often, the mother discovers that a child is more work than she ever imagined. Some women often feel overwhelmed by their physical role—not only providing and taking care of their infants but also tending to the father's needs. Obviously, a balance needs to be struck among everyone's needs, and in the process, mothers must develop feelings of competence and worth (Coleman, 1984).

Although the American woman of the 1990s frequently lives in a home filled with virtually every modern electronic convenience imaginable, she is still doing as much housework as her colonial counterpart did. In analyzing the technology of the home, Cowan (1983) feels that the workload has indeed increased for women, despite all the inventions intended to save time. When the cast-iron stove replaced the open hearth, for example, a variety of foods took the place of the one-pot dinner. Corn bread once was sufficient—but then milled flour came along, to make cakes and pastries. Whereas cooking, cleaning, and taking care of the needs of the family have become more complex and time-consuming, the alternatives—such as communes, hot-food delivery systems, and commercial vacuum cleaning—have never been accepted because they conflict with the family's desire for privacy and individuality.

It may well be that one of the problems facing the contemporary American mother is that she is overcommitted. She has more responsibilities than most can meet, and she is putting in more hours than her grandmother did running the household. E. E. LeMasters and John DeFrain (1983) point out that almost all of her role commitments have expanded to those of a wife, mother, home manager, community participant, breadwinner, and household decision maker. If a woman were paid wages for her work as a mother and housewife, according to the wage scale for babysitters, cooks, nurses and so on, in 1981 her services would have been worth over $40,000 a year (Strong et al., 1983).

But though the arrival of a child brings many changes and demands that mothers find difficult, a number are only temporary, and most mothers adjust. Most mothers—and fathers as well—report that having a child is worth the adjustments required. The key appears to be offsetting the hard work, constant demands, and emotional strain with love, caring, and warmth (Stinnet, Walters, and Kaye, 1984).

WORKING MOTHERS Not too long ago, mothers were expected to remain at home and care for their children, particularly during their offspring's early years of development. Many felt that this was the only way a mother could love and properly rear her children during this important life stage. To venture away from the family in search of a paycheck was viewed as uncaring and unwise.

Today, though, growing numbers of women are breaking this traditional stereotype of mothering and working outside the home. As Lois Hoffman (1989) notes, maternal employment outside the home has become a fact of modern life. Moreover, there is growing acceptance today that a woman can handle the multiple roles of breadwinner and mother. In the midst of busy work schedules, conscientious working mothers still manage to give their children love, care, and nurturance.

As testimony to the large number of mothers returning to the labor force, consider the following statistics:

- Unlike earlier times, when women took years away from the labor force for childbearing, the modern mother will return to work after not more than one year for each birth.

- It is estimated that within the next five years, 85 percent of American homes will consist of dual-career couples.

- Over 54 million women were in the labor force in 1989, representing 45 percent of the civilian work force. This figure tripled the number working just after World War II.

- About one out of every two married women with a child under six was working in 1989 (U.S. Bureau of the Census, 1989).

According to Martin O'Connell and David Bloom (1987), the most remarkable growth in the female labor force in the postwar period has been among females with very young children. Between 1976 and 1985, large increases were attributed to mothers who had newborns and who were (1) 30 to 44 years of age; (2) white; (3) divorced, separated, or widowed; and (4) who had completed a year or more of college. On the other hand, black women, high school dropouts, and young unwed mothers had modest gains in labor force participation.

Some of this shift can be summarized in the following four profiles of American mothers, which compare labor force participation rates in 1976 and 1985:

The Young Mother A young married white woman, whose first child was born before she was 24 years old. Her formal education stopped with high school graduation. The chance of her returning to work within a year of the birth of her child was 34 percent in 1976. In 1985, this figure rose to 54 percent.

The Delayed Childbearer A married white woman whose first child was born after age 24 and who completed some years of college. About 44 percent of the women in this category worked in 1976. This percentage jumped to 64 percent by 1985.

The Unmarried Mother A white woman, aged 25 to 44, from the growing ranks of the formerly married. A high school graduate with two or more children, her chances of working within a year of the birth of her last child doubled in the past decade from 27 to 54 percent.

The Young Single Mother A black woman, 18 to 24 years old, with two or more children. This woman has not married, nor has she completed high school. Her chances of working have actually decreased over the past decade, from 34 to 31 percent. In relative terms, she has lost ground to her contemporaries. Although less common than the other females profiled here, this female is not atypical of a growing percentage of women with out-of-wedlock births.

The typical profile of the mother most likely to return to work before her child's first birthday conforms to the human-resource theories of labor force behavior: the greater the investment of time and money in education, the more rapid the return to work after childbirth to minimize losses in earnings and depreciation of job skills. Beyond this, an investment in schooling may indicate a great personal commitment to a career. Any females who have spent many years in school may have delayed marriage and would, generally speaking, have fewer children than less educated women.

However, it is not only potential earning power which encourages females to seek employment, but potential wages in relation to the costs of working. For mothers of small children, as we discussed earlier, child care is typically the greatest expense. The primary reason for the leveling off of labor force activity among black females and high school dropouts, who earn lower average salaries than other women, may well be a lack of affordable child care (O'Connell and Bloom, 1987).

While the dual-career family reaps its share of benefits and personal satisfaction (see L. Hoffman, 1989; Gilbert, Holahan, and Manning, 1981; Voydanoff, 1984; Maracek and Ballou, 1981), certain sacrifices are common in homes with younger children. The responsibility of child rearing and tending to domestic chores appears to be the biggest obstacle for women to hurdle in pursuing careers. In many instances, the woman still carries the brunt of the household tasks. Consequently, the problem is that a two-career marriage is really a three-career marriage, with the woman typically holding down two careers.

John Scanzoni and Greer Fox's (1980) analysis of this lopsided arrangement reveals that the working mother still has the basic responsibility of organizing the family. Cleaning, cooking, and child care continue to be responsibilities of the female. Her employment status has minimal effect on what the husband does. This means that there is an increase in the length of the woman's day at the expense of her leisure time (Spitze, 1988).

Another study on this topic (Ferber, 1982) shows that while more men than ever before do help around the house, it is the wife who carries out most of the chores. Thus, despite gains in a more egalitarian work orientation, household chores still bear a sexist dimension. According to this particular study, men even acknowledge the fact that they could do more household chores.

The personal sacrifices of motherhood are numerous, but so too are the rewards.

There are other difficulties among working mothers. Many report some anxiety about their child's well-being and wonder if they've made the right choice. Many who are full-time mothers, however, often want to go back into the labor force. Thus, a type of "Catch-22" situation exists. In other instances, working mothers are happy and satisfied with their chosen profession, but feel inadequate in the mothering role. In this respect, many working mothers feel role conflict. Others report guilt and mixed feelings, if they happen to earn more money than their husbands (Rubenstein, 1982; Gilbert, Holahan, and Manning, 1981).

Studies also show that mothers, be they working outside the home or not, have less positive feelings about their husbands after giving birth than they had during pregnancy. They reported doing much more of the housework and child-care chores than they had expected. However, while these negative feelings affect some aspects of the marital relationship, they do not necessarily interfere with the core affection (Ruble, Fleming, Hackel, and Stanger, 1988).

THE DAY-CARE DILEMMA The issue of who is going to care for the children of working parents is an important one today. Whereas the Industrial Revolution virtually dictated that mothers would remain at home to care for their young, today's dual-career couples must turn to the outside for child-care assistance. The relinquishment of the youngster to child-care facilities offers a new twist to child-rearing practices and may place contemporary parents at odds with *their* parents. Many older generations cling to the notion that a woman's place is in the home. The modern woman's removal of these chains sometimes produces ambivalence on the older generation's part and, in some cases, hostility. There is, however, a growing acceptance of women entering the employment world, and we are certain to see increasing approval of child-care assistance.

Day-care facilities for the children of working parents are insufficient in number. The scarcity of child-care facilities is illustrated by the following statistics. Day-care centers, nursery schools, and the like, care for only 23 percent of working parents' children under the age of five. Thirty-seven percent are cared for at someone's home and about 31 percent are cared for by someone within the parents' home. About 9 percent watch their children while working (U.S. Department of Commerce, 1987).

It should be acknowledged, though, that finances have a great deal to do with the choice of child-care arrangements. Those able to take advantage of a day-care center or nursery school are usually well educated, work full time, and have a comfortable family income. Lower-income couples often find female relatives to care for their young, with grandparents an especially popular choice.

Among the child-care facilities that do exist, the day-care facility is the most convenient for working parents. It offers full day-care sessions, often beginning at 7 A.M. and lasting until 6 P.M. Some specialize in infant and toddler care and offer meals and learning sessions. For the children of working parents, day care represents a home away from home.

However, day-care centers have aroused considerable controversy among child psychologists, educators, and parents. Though such facilities offer protective care to children and enable mothers to work, concern is frequently voiced about the effects of day care on youngsters. Maternal separation and the disruption of attachment bonds to the caregiver are central issues for many. Some maintain that a full-time day-care center cannot provide this essential early social relationship, except under ideal conditions. Usually a child must share with other youngsters the attention of a day-care worker, and in the typical ten-hour center day, work shifts change at least once. Add to this vacations and job turnovers, and a child may well have no one special person to be close to. Sometimes the mother compounds the problem of an unhappy child by blaming the center and switching the child to another.

Not everyone agrees on the potential negative effects of day care. Many feel that children are capable of adjusting well to day-care situations at an early age, and many also believe that these institutions offer rewarding learning experiences. In a review of the literature, Susan Kontos and Robin Stevens (1985) found that quality day care can promote more sociable and considerate children and enhance their cognitive and linguistic competencies.

The positive impact of quality day care was the central finding of a study undertaken by Deborah Vandell and associates (1988). The researchers observed 20 four-year-olds during free play at good and poor quality day-care centers and again at 8 years as they participated in play activities. Maternal, peer, and observer ratings were also obtained. Compared with subjects from poorer quality day-care centers, subjects from better quality centers had more friendly interactions and fewer unfriendly interactions with peers, were rated as more socially competent and happier, and were less shy.

Obviously, then, it becomes a matter of searching for a quality day-care center and not settling for a mediocre one. This can be a tedious chore, but one well worth the effort. Parents need to look for centers with such positive features as low adult-to-child ratios, good nutrition programs, excellent sanitation conditions, and adequate staff training. A successful day-care experience goes beyond the center's qualifications, though. The parental warmth, acceptance, and care that the child receives in the home may greatly influence his or her response to the overall day-care experience.

As time evolves and public schooling begins, how do the children of working parents fare? Much of the current research points to the fact that children of working parents are no more problem-prone than others. Often they are better organized and more independent than those children with the mother or father at home. Many children of working parents also take on greater levels of household responsibilities (Petersen, 1982).

Interestingly, one study (Crouter, 1982) found that the child's sex and the socioeconomic status of the family are two important variables to study when evaluating the issue of working parents and children. Among girls, having a mother who works outside the home is especially beneficial. Girls are more likely to admire their mothers, to have a positive view of being female, and to be more independent than their peers whose mothers work at home (L. Hoffman, 1989). The pattern does not hold for boys, however. In middle-class families, sons of employed mothers perform less well in school than boys whose mothers work at home. Interestingly, this pattern does not hold for low-income families, perhaps because the income brought in by the mother is so important to the family economy that it offsets any negative consequences her working might have for her sons.

Joseph Pleck (1981) looks favorably on the dual-career household because of the role equality it brings. He feels that children experience the healthiest growth and development when both parents share in the upbringing. He also maintains that more balanced child rearing occurs when the parents' job lives are more equal. Thus, equal employment policies benefit not only women, but also children, to the degree that fathers, whose wives' earnings are important to the family, take more active roles with their children (Children's Defense Fund, 1982).

Overall, it is maintained that the critical variables in a child's happiness and adjustment are the parents' satisfaction with their activities and the quality, rather than quantity, of parent-child interactions. Moreover, parents need to keep work out of family life. Parents do not want to convey the impression that the child's daily concerns or domestic life in general are boring or trivial compared with the excitement and variety of the work world (Coleman, 1984; Petersen, 1982).

International Lifespan Development

■ WHO'S MINDING THE KIDS?

In the United States, day-care facilities for the children of working parents are scarce. This is in marked contrast to the federally sponsored day-care programs available in such nations as the Soviet Union, France, the German Democratic Republic, and Sweden. Some of these nations, experiencing a declining birthrate and labor shortages, have created national systems of day care as an incentive to women. The system encourages them to have babies and to also join the labor force. The United States, on the other hand, has no pressing needs for more babies or more people in the labor force (Nass and McDonald, 1982).

Although government-sponsored day care is available in over 100 developed nations, shortages in quality care are still reported. As women flood the marketplace all over the world, even countries with relatively comprehensive systems find that the demand is overwhelming. Still, the subsidized day-care programs offer marked contrast to the United States:

■ In France, almost 80,000 children are cared for in 1,500 centers, of which 167 are private. The state-run centers are open eleven hours a day and cost between $3 and $17 daily (1987 dollars). Because the centers are oversubscribed, the French government offers subsidies of as much as $340 a month to assist parents who hire child care at home.

- About 44 percent of Danish children 3 years of age and under and about 70 percent of those between 3 and 5 years are enrolled in public facilities. With fees as low as $115 a month (1987 dollars), though, the demand for such child care is high.

- In Israel, there are about 900 subsidized child-care centers, which charge between $27 and $90 a month, according to family income. Of 240,000 Jewish youngsters 4 years of age and under, nearly 26 percent are enrolled in day care.

- Child-care facilities in Japan vary between licensed and unlicensed, private and public. Most of the nearly 23,000 licensed centers do not accept newborns, and the better facilities have long waiting lists. This is attributable to the fact that the number of married Japanese women who have returned to work has quadrupled in the past 20 years (Wallis, 1987).

The United States also has no federal law giving working women a maternity leave of absence. On the other hand, most European nations have adopted extended maternity-leave policies in the last few decades. They vary from one to three years, with complete job security and some pay for the entire duration. In the United States, maternity leaves usually vary from company to company and are, for the most part, short compared to other nations. In many instances maternity-leave pay is nonexistent.

European maternity leaves do not exercise any negative impact on the situation of women in the labor market. Maternity leave in itself is not a threat to a woman's job identity: Hungarian women, for example, never doubt their work role as full workers; the vast majority of Swedish women reenter the labor market and hold their jobs. If anything, maternity leaves of greater length contribute to a stable work identity; women know when and where they are going back, if they choose to; whereas in the United States, women often quit or are forced to quit their jobs and, later, have a problem finding another job (Erler, 1982).

Many countries offer very attractive maternity-leave packages. For example, Hungary provides a child-care grant that equals about 40 percent of the mother's wages and lasts until the child is age 3. In Czechoslovakia and East Germany, supplemental leave is available after the birth of the second and subsequent children. Countries such as France, Norway, and Sweden permit either parent to take an unpaid, job-protected leave, ranging from one to two years, when the paid leave ends. In Austria, a one-year paid leave is available for single mothers; married mothers can take the same time off, but without pay. And in West Germany, Sweden, and Norway, the government also sponsors paid leave when care for a sick child is needed.

Such benefits to families are paid for in a unique fashion. These programs represent a type of "social insurance" and are similar in scope to Social Security and unemployment benefits in the United States. For example, in eight nations (Canada, France, Finland, East Germany, Hungary, Israel, Italy, and the United Kingdom), employers and employees each contribute a small percentage of their wages for such programs. In Sweden and Czechoslovakia, employers and the government finance the benefits. In Austria, West Germany, and Norway, financing originates from employer, employee, and government contributions, while in Denmark general tax revenues from national and local governments pay for it (Kamerman, 1985; Kamerman, Kahn, and Kingston, 1983).

THE ROLE OF THE FATHER

Until recently, the role and impact of the father in child care was overlooked. Although the importance of the father to the household has generally been recognized, part of the problem is that American society has been "mother centered" in its philosophy of child care. However, with more households being dual career and society's increasing deemphasis of sex-role differences, this focus may be changing. The father's influence on various aspects of the developing child is now being recognized. Many researchers are now examining the father's role and have given us a wealth of information (see Pruett, 1987; Lewis and Salt, 1986; Lewis and O'Brien, 1987; Pederson, 1980; Lamb, 1981; Parke, 1981).

Today's father offers a unique comparison with his historical counterpart. More men share a larger portion of the parenting role that had previously been limited to women. Such experiences as participation in childbirth, long closed to fathers, is now encouraged more and more. Also, in a growing number of cases, fathers are given custody of their children when there is a divorce. Such illustrations of the father's changing status in contemporary society is indicative of a trend that brings the father closer into the realm of parenthood and overall family development (Pruett, 1987; F. Cox, 1984; Beer, 1982; Keats, 1983).

The foregoing was the central finding uncovered in a research study examining the role of the father in 309 suburban families. In 71 of the families interviewed, fathers had the major responsibility for the day-to-day care of their children. Some had this responsibility because they were unemployed and their wives were working; others because they had deliberately chosen this lifestyle. Among the contentions of this study was that fathers and mothers are equally important to their children and are equally able to care for them, right from birth (Russell, 1983).

As we mentioned earlier, growing numbers of fathers are also participating in natural childbirth classes and assisting the mother during the delivery of the baby. Such involvement appears to have numerous positive consequences, in many instances extending beyond the delivery room. Fathers who have participated in the delivery

Over the years, the scope of fatherhood has changed considerably.

process tend to interact more with their newborn child and participate more in infant care than do uninvolved fathers (Miller and Bowen, 1982; Cordell, Parke, and Swain, 1980).

Fathers are able to establish strong bonds of attachment to their children and vice versa. Moreover, infants regularly turn to fathers in times of distress. What appears to be different in family relationships are the activities of the parents that foster attachment. The infant's stronger attachment to the mother may be attributable to her caretaking functions. Fathers, on the other hand, offer other types of stimulation, such as play activities and the exploration of the environment (Pruett, 1987; LaRossa and LaRossa, 1981; Fein, 1980).

Research has clearly indicated that the father has strong influences on the child's overall emotional, social, and intellectual development. His presence and his attention to his children have both short- and long-term benefits. The absence of his care also seems to affect the child's development. For example, children's academic achievement and IQ levels may be affected by the absence of a positive father-child relationship. The father can also affect how well their children progress in school, which subjects they prefer, and even the kinds of occupations they eventually choose. Fathers also influence social and sex-role development. Fathers influence children through their personalities, by serving as role models, and in their daily interactions (Parke, 1981; Radin, 1981).

Although the father's influence on the family cannot be overstressed, whether this influence is *positive* is another issue. This depends on a number of factors, including the father's involvement in child-care and family activities, his own upbringing, the quality of his other relationships, and the characteristics of his offspring (Lamb, 1982, 1983; Adams, 1984).

Although many fathers look forward to child care, there are some who resist the notion that they should be spending more time with their children. Many feel that they are poorly prepared already for the task of parenting, to say nothing of more child-care responsibilities. In this regard, many fathers report considerable anxiety, confusion, and uneasiness over the many needs of their children (Spieler, 1982; Nannarone, 1983).

Let it be said, though, anxiety and confusion over children's needs and parenting in general are normal for *both* fathers and mothers. Our society also does not adequately prepare adults for parenthood. The need for such preparation becomes especially obvious during infancy as many parents anxiously tend to the many urgent needs of their offspring (Waldron and Routh, 1981; Clark, 1981; Miller and Sollie, 1980).

UNIT REVIEW

- Most people in the United States will marry. The reasons for marriage are diverse, from companionship to legitimization of sex and children.

- Marital roles can be distinguished by patriarchal, matriarchal, and egalitarian styles.

- Of the other possible lifestyles (besides marriage), singlehood and cohabitation have been the most popular in recent years.

- Parenthood brings a wide assortment of adjustments and adaptations for the new mother and father.

- The parental roles of the mother and father have changed from those of earlier times. Mothers in the labor force and the increased participation of fathers in child-care duties are but two examples of these changing roles.

Unit Four:

CAREER DEVELOPMENT

All young adults, in some way, must establish themselves as worthwhile and significant individuals. Historically, this has usually been accomplished in the work world. Such recognition has typically been achieved by becoming a wage earner and serving some useful purpose in the labor force. Although this traditional emphasis is being challenged today, employment remains an important function of the individual for both the present and the near future.

Career development fuses with many other facets of an adult's life. Work is an important dimension of the adult's identity and fosters self-respect. It also is an activity through which people can express themselves. For some, work is status; for others, it is a source of pride. For many, work is a vehicle to strengthen capabilities and an opportunity to test values, beliefs, and ideas about the world (Crites, 1989; F. Brown, 1980; Cole, 1980).

Young adults discover that work and its consequent lifestyle are bound up tightly with their ego and self-image. They discover that "what they do" greatly affects their perceptions of people, sometimes at the expense of overlooking someone's entire identity. In the work world, young adults learn new skills and change some behaviors to fit new roles. Its implications extend far beyond the workplace, as individuals discover new involvements and new ways of perceiving themselves (Michelozzi, 1984).

Selecting a Career

Today, there are over 22,000 jobs from which to choose, compared with only several hundred at the turn of the century. Finding one's vocational niche in the face of such overwhelming numbers can be, to say the least, a bit unsettling. Questions about the work world also surface at this time: What is it that I really want to do? With whom do I want to work? Will I be good at what I do? Will I be happy? (London and Stumpf, 1982).

Young adults are often inefficient in planning their careers. This is because of five factors. First, many choose from among a very narrow group of occupations. Second, as many as 40 to 60 percent choose professional occupations, when in reality only 15 to 18 percent of the work force is engaged in professional work. Third, young adult males show a lack of interest in clerical, sales, and service occupations, although those fields have many job opportunities. Fourth, many hold romantic images of jobs that distort reality. And fifth, as many as a third of young adults are unable to choose any occupation (Shertzer, 1985).

Many students in the United States, as opposed to students in Japan and Europe, postpone or never really make a career decision. For better or worse, young adults

Leaving the educational arena and launching a career is an important development task during young adulthood.

enter the work world when their schooling is completed, and many act as though they were still college freshmen who have plenty of time to select a "major." Years may pass, and these young adults, unaware of the passing time and concluding only "I want to be a success," may still have not settled on a career direction (Blotnick, 1984).

Amidst the complexities and problems of choosing a career, though, are some very rewarding moments. A career search can be a time when people orient themselves to a new facet of their lives. It can be a time when individuals can examine themselves, look at where they've been in life, and where they're going. As Betty Michelozzi (1984) put it, choosing a career can lead you to question how you intend to spend your life for a time, or your time for the rest of your life.

Narrowing Down the Field of Career Possibilities

By the time a person reaches young adulthood, it is expected that some type of career commitment will have been made. To date, no one has been able to describe completely and precisely how to best select a line of work. What we do know is that individuals should concern themselves with a thorough examination of the vocational world, in addition to an in-depth analysis of themselves and what they want from a job. Vocational guidance expert Bruce Shertzer (1985) offers the following advice on narrowing down career possibilities:

1. *Explore occupations widely.* Young adults need to take the time to get to know occupations so that they can narrow down their choices. *The Dictionary of Occupational Titles* or the *Occupational Outlook Handbook,* published by the federal government, are excellent resources and are available in most school, college, or city libraries. By exploring occupations widely, individuals can learn of alternatives from which to choose and avoid making a premature choice.

2. *Explore interests and abilities.* Individuals should identify the abilities, interests, skills, and characteristics that they currently possess and want to more fully develop. As they explore occupations, individuals should seek to see if they possess compatible interests and abilities.

3. *Explore families of occupations.* By exploring occupational families, or related careers, individuals give themselves the flexibility needed to cope with occupational and labor-market fluctuations. It also shows people that they qualify for more jobs than they might have first thought.

4. *Select two or three occupations that are appealing and study them in depth.* This means a thorough examination of the vocations, including how these jobs fit one's abilities, needs, attitudes, and future life patterns. Other concerns might be the chances for advancement, the

job's social prestige, supply and demand of the work, or the security of the job.

5. *Talk to others about their careers.* By doing so, one can learn what others went through in the career-selection process. Sometimes one will uncover interesting things about abilities or interests or about an occupation in general.

6. *Explore the level of work.* Every occupation involves differing levels of responsibility or skill. Individuals need to realistically examine the level at which they want to work and assess their ability to attain this level. This means taking into account skills, competencies, and the time and energy required to get to this level.

7. *Study occupational changes and trends.* Individuals need to figure out what will be happening in a chosen occupation by the time they are ready to enter the labor market. Dead-end streets can be avoided if young adults carefully study the changes that are forecast by labor-market experts.

8. *Keep in mind that you will change, and the occupation will change.* In a way, choosing an occupation is done on the basis of incomplete information: People change and so do jobs. Individuals can be aware of their changing interests, though, and they can do the same with jobs. Going back to basic reference books and updated labor-market reports can keep one posted on the latest occupational changes and shifts.

9. *Remember that vocational development is really a stream of decisions.* Career development is a lifelong process that involves a number of decisions made over many years. The first job taken is not necessarily the only one for a whole working life. A career involves a continuing set of adjustments.

Stages of Career Selection

What steps are taken in selecting a career? Can any stages or sequences be predicted? Although there are individual variations in career development, seven stages are recognized.

Stage 1 is referred to as the *exploration phase.* This stage is characterized by generalized concern about the occupational world, but little or no progress toward the career choice. There is some knowledge of the self and the occupational world, but the person has little or no plan of action for satisfying the need for a career commitment.

The *crystallization stage* is second and is characterized by progress toward an occupational choice, but without its actual attainment. The individual recognizes alternatives and some of their consequences, particularly the conflict inherent in each. Career advantages and disadvantages are weighed at this point, and the bases for a decision are in the process of developing, at least implicitly. Career possibilities are being narrowed down through negative choices. Inappropriate earlier choices are recognized and frequently used as the basis for further decision making.

Stage 3 is the *choice phase*. At this time, a definite commitment to a particular goal is established, a goal that brings expressions of satisfaction and relief. Pessimism, characteristic of the exploration stage, gives way to a kind of naive optimism about the future. A singleness of purpose and a goal direction are typically expressed. Eagerness and impatience to reach the career goal are typical, although a focus on the consequences of the decision and further planning are not yet in evidence.

Career clarification is the fourth stage. Now the individual clarifies the consequences of the career commitment. Also, many elaborate and perfect their self-image in relation to the work at hand. Although planning to carry out the career commitment is characteristic of this stage, any actual action may be delayed until the environmental conditions are appropriate for action.

The fifth stage of career decision making is the *induction phase*, which is the implementation of a career decision. At this point, a person enters the new work environment. The process of accommodating a new group of people and a new situation represents a new developmental challenge. Many persons are hesitant about this new exposure and look for cues from others in the group to determine the group's values and goals. Furthermore, considerable attention is directed toward the group's expectations of the person, as the individual needs to receive some acceptance from the group. In time, the person begins to identify with the group by incorporating his or her own values and goals into the group's values, goals, and purposes. This stage terminates when the individual becomes aware of group acceptance.

The *reformation stage*, the sixth one, is the point at which the primary mode of individual interaction is assertiveness, and group involvement is prevalent. The person tries to conform to the group's values and goals. A strong sense of self abounds, although it is somewhat lacking in objectivity. At the same time, the self may be abandoned in favor of solutions and group purposes. A modification of the group's values, goals, and purposes is the end result of this stage.

The final phase is called the *integrative stage*. In this final period, older group members may react against the new worker's force for change, which in turn causes him or her to compromise or modify intentions. Thus, a greater objectivity toward the self and the group's purposes results. A synthesis is reached in which both the individual and the group strive to maintain consistency through collaborative activity. At this time, the individual is satisfied, at least temporarily; a successful self-image has been attained; and the worker is considered productive and successful by the group as a whole (Tiedeman and O'Hara, 1963).

☐ The Quest for Career Fulfillment

The quest for job fulfillment is common in contemporary society. Growing numbers of workers want work that is meaningful, rewarding, and challenging. The lack of it, on the other hand, produces frustration, boredom, and apathy.

Reflecting the desire among adults to find rewarding work are the large numbers of workers changing jobs. A surprisingly large number of workers are not at all satisfied with their vocation and, therefore, are faced with the choice of finding a different job or living with their unhappiness. On the average, adults change jobs three to five times over their lifetimes (Krannich, 1983).

In addition to meaningful and challenging work, what other factors constitute job satisfaction? If we had to rank the factors, the ability to make meaningful contributions, the ability to express oneself and have others listen, and pay would head the list. Other equally important factors, though, would be job security, the chances for advancement, quality of working conditions, and the status or prestige of the job (Schertzer, 1985; Yankelovich, 1981).

Career changes and the drive toward job satisfaction are more common among young adults than older adults and greater among those with a college education. Although high school graduates also desire meaningful and challenging work, they do not expect to acquire such jobs, because of their limited education. Young adults may have stronger desires for job satisfaction because they have just entered the work force and are at the bottom of their career ladder. The jobs they hold often offer limited satisfaction (Campbell, 1981).

We would like to interject that there is absolutely nothing wrong with wanting career satisfaction and fulfillment. In fact, it is an admirable goal, especially because occupational satisfaction contributes to mental and physical health as well as family stability (Hornung and McCullough, 1981). Marian Faux (1984b) put it this way: Personal satisfaction in a job is what compels someone to forge a career rather than just settle for a series of unrelated jobs. And satisfaction just doesn't come with a job; rather, it is something that one must seek. To obtain job satisfaction, an individual must know what he or she wants and how to go about getting it.

Because of the premium placed on job satisfaction, a new set of work values is emerging. Many question the traditional work ethic and feel there's more to a job than punching a time clock and receiving a paycheck. Although pay is important, meaningful work is becoming equally, if not more, significant.

Daniel Yankelovich (1981) believes that the quest for career satisfaction is an excellent reflection of a much larger theme: searching for personal fulfillment in a bustling society often turned upside down. He sees more young adults than ever before striving for personal satisfaction, the result being a new breed of young adults. For example, he found that today's young people are less fearful of economic insecurity than in the past. They want interesting and challenging work but often assume that their employers cannot—or will not—provide it. By their own admission they are inclined to take "less crap" than older workers are. They are not as automatically loyal to the organization as older generations are, and they are tuned in to their own needs and rights. Nor are they as awed by organizational and hierarchical authority. They are less fearful of "discipline" and the threat of losing their jobs. As a result, they feel free to express their discontent. Young people want more freedom and will bargain hard to keep their options open.

We might note that in the face of growing levels of career dissatisfaction, many industries and companies are designing more stimulating work environments. More flexible schedules, the encouragement of employee input, and the implementation of job incentives are but three examples of this trend. Results have shown that such changes enhance job satisfaction and open new doors for creativity and learning (Aslanian and Brickell, 1980; H. Greenberg, 1980).

☐ The Roots of Career Dissatisfaction

Job dissatisfaction comes in all shapes and sizes. Some maintain that their work is boring, and others regard their job as a rat race. Some complain that they're not getting paid enough for what they do. Other workers feel that their ideas are continually rejected. And there are those who say that they never receive feedback on their performances, let alone positive reinforcement. Still others complain that they're going nowhere with their present positions.

Many workers also become disillusioned about themselves and their jobs. One of the more interesting profiles of the triumphs and despairs of the working world was drawn by Srully Blotnick (1984). His research focused on the crises that adults face in the business world. Particularly relevant to our discussion is his analysis of three problems that young adults encounter during the early stages of their careers.

One of the problems arises from a sense of insecurity and, in some instances, a lack of preparation. A number of Blotnick's young adult subjects didn't feel that they had learned enough in school and were, therefore, thrilled to graduate with most of their shortcomings undetected. Once in the business world, their method for not being discovered was to move continuously and fast. They did not want cracks to show in the foundation of their new public facade. To shore up their sagging backgrounds, new lies were added to the old. When people began to see through the facade, new moves were needed. Gaps in knowledge and ability ultimately meant a transfer to another setting. As a result of such constant maneuvering and movement, these workers never realized that one area of work-related activity intrigued them more than another or that, overall, they could really get absorbed in their work. Rather, they spent much of their time waiting to be exposed publicly as being less than they had claimed to be.

Another problem arose when workers came to regard themselves as the company's divine saviors. Such workers develop a mental "monarchy" that causes them to view other employees as worthless and themselves as the company's most prized possession. Workers falling into this category typically proceed through five stages: First, they dismiss the competition; "The others all are careless and incompetent." Second, they praise themselves; "I'm the only capable and industrious person here." Third, they crown themselves; "I am *the* company, by default, because there are no other legitimate candidates for the title." Fourth, they luxuriate in the spoils of victory; "I deserve all the credit, not to mention the glory, for carrying the entire kingdom on my shoulders." And fifth, they suffer externally to hide their internal exultation; "Heavy is the head upon which sits the crown."

As long as workers fitting this description remained in their mental monarchies and out of contact with their coworkers for certain amounts of time, all went well. Problems arose, though, when other coworkers began doing the same thing. In short, two or more people had become rulers of the same mental kingdom. The result of this was a breakdown in teamwork and the creation of hostility, frustration, and dissension.

Another problem pertains to a discrepancy between the lifestyle that young adults wanted to have and the amount of money they earned. Within a few years, many felt that they needed more money in order to move into the right social circles and to buy the luxuries they wanted in life. When their paychecks could not provide these things, their frustration and negative attitudes needed a scapegoat. For many, the employer and the company as a whole became perfect targets. In fact, every negative feeling that they had toward both became magnified. Some, though, tried to get more money by "beating the system." That is, they tried to "look" busy or say the right things to the right people. When such empty efforts failed, they began cutting back on the work they did. As a result of all of this, there was a psychological gap between their career and their personal life. They viewed their work as an annoying waste of time, a job that didn't pay enough. Nonwork hours were viewed as the only potential source of pleasure or satisfaction.

CHAPTER REVIEW

■ Unit One: Physical and Mental Development

By young adulthood, physical growth and development are virtually complete. The body, at least the muscles and internal organs, reaches its maximum physical potential between the ages of 19 and 26. The sense organs change very little, although for many, the lenses of the eyes become less able to change and to focus on nearby objects. There is also a slight difference in hearing ability between the two sexes, in that men are less able than women to detect high tones.

Regular exercise, proper nutrition, and a healthful lifestyle are important throughout all of adulthood. Regular exercise has many benefits, the most important of which is reducing the risk of cardiac arrest. Regular exercise also increases muscle strength, joint flexibility, and lung efficiency; reduces fat; and helps rid the body of stress and stress-related illnesses.

Proper nutrition, like regular exercise, is important throughout all of adult life. Unfortunately, millions of people in the United States have poor dietary habits. One estimate puts the number of overweight people in this country at 80 million. Obesity increases the risk of poor digestion, stress-linked illnesses, strokes, diabetes, hypertension, and heart disease. This chapter stressed the importance of establishing a healthy diet so that the body will receive the nutrients it needs for maintenance and repair.

Quantitative dimensions of intelligence are best measured by longitudinal studies. Three aspects of intelligence remain constant over the adult years: crystallized intelligence, cognitive flexibility, and visualization. Visuomotor flexibility, on the other hand, does appear to decrease with age.

One must move beyond the realm of IQ test scores to evaluate adult learning performances. Many factors can influence a test score: anxiety, boredom, rigidity, fatigue, caution, or poor health. Often adults can excel in real-life problem solving, but not in standardized testing situations. Adults, especially older adults, also possess qualities that IQ tests seldom measure: wisdom, real-world learning, and practical insight.

■ Unit Two: Personality and Social Development

Young adulthood is a time for important decision making and careful life planning. Through experimentation and exploration, young adults can learn more about themselves and the world in general. Meeting the numerous developmental tasks of this time period requires considerable maturity, which we defined as a state that promotes physical and psychological well-being. We also explored the ideas that there are many sides to maturity and that age is no guarantee of maturity.

The concept of maturity as seen by Gordon Allport was examined. Allport's research is not new but is nonetheless still relevant today. Allport contended that maturity consists of seven important dimensions: (1) extension of the self, (2) relating warmly to others, (3) emotional security, (4) realistic perception, (5) possession of skills and competences, (6) knowledge of the self, and (7) establishing a unifying philosophy of life.

Three theories of personality development were discussed in this chapter. Erikson stated that young adulthood is the time for young adults to resolve the psychosocial crisis known as intimacy versus isolation. Levinson suggested that male development at this time begins with the stage of Early Adult Transition, followed by Entering the Adult World, the Age Thirty Transition, and the Settling Down Stage. Roger Gould, stressing that adults must learn to overcome irrational childhood notions and parental dependencies, proposed three stages: Leaving Our Parents' World; I'm Nobody's Baby Now; and Opening Up to What's Inside.

An intimate relationship involves the mutual exchange of experiences in such a way that a further understanding of oneself and one's partner is achieved. Intimacy embodies self-disclosure, the process by which individuals let themselves be known to others. Numerous forms of self-disclosure exist, such as through verbal means, body language, tone of voice, or by one's actions.

This chapter explored some of the components of intimate relationships: knowledge of oneself and one's partner, mutuality, interdependence, trust, commitment, and caring. We also examined barriers to intimate relationships. Such barriers included possible rejection of one's self-concept, discovering that one's partner is not interested in having an intimate relationship, finding that information is used by one's partner to gain power or control of the relationship, betrayal of information to others, and inequity originating from a lack of equivalent input into the realtionship. We also examined the filtering agents that serve to narrow the field of potential partners: propinquity, physical attraction, homogamy, endogamous and exogamous factors, complementary needs, parental image theory, exchange, and role compatibility.

Love consists of a set of feelings, cognitions, and motivations that contribute to communication, sharing, and support. Different styles of love can exist: ludus, pragma, mania, eros, storge, and agape.

■ Unit Three: Marriage and Parenthood

It has been estimated that approximately 95 percent of Americans will marry at some point in their lives. This statistic places the United States among the world's leaders for marriage rates. This unit explored how the engagement paves the way for marriage and also the major motives for marriage. These motives include the desire for commitment and a one-to-one relationship, companionship and sharing, love, happiness, and the legitimization of sex and children. We also explored the lifestyles available to those who decide not to marry: singlehood, cohabitation, communal living, swinging, and the gay lifestyle.

People decide to have children for many reasons. Among those cited were extension of the self, personal fulfillment, enhancement of a couple's identity, companionship, the security that children will bring when the parents are old, and social conformity.

The transition to parenthood is a difficult one. In the minds of many, there is an idealistic myth about parenthood, but striving to have the perfect family is an unattainable goal. In addition, the required adjustments to a baby are many, although we pointed out that domestic disruption and anxieties lessen over time. Ellen Galinsky's research enables us to better understand the stages of parenthood that exist. We also examined the roles of the mother and father and the changes that are taking place in the 1990s.

■ Unit Four: Career Development

By the young adulthood years, it is expected that most individuals will have arrived at a vocational choice. However, it is fairly well accepted that the pressures imposed by society and the complexity of today's vocational world make the career selection process a difficult one. With over 22,000 different jobs from which to choose, young adults need to plan their careers carefully. We cited seven stages in the career-development process: exploration, crystallization, choice, career clarification, induction, reformation, and integration.

Job satisfaction is the goal of many adults today. Employees appear to be happiest when they have challenging work, can make meaningful contributions, and can express themselves. The drive for job satisfaction is higher among young rather than older adults and more prevalent among those with a college education. Many employers have reacted to the need for job satisfaction by making work environments more stimulating.

KEY TERMS

agape love
cardiovascular-respiratory fitness
cognitive flexibility
cohabitation
commune
complementary needs
crystallized intelligence
egalitarian marriage
endogamy
eros love
exchange theory
exogamy
filtering agent
gay men
homogamy
homosexuality
intimacy
intimacy versus isolation
intimate relationship
lesbian women

love
ludus love
manic love
marriage rate
matriarchal marriage
maturity
open marriage
parental-image theory
patriarchal marriage
pragma love
propinquity
role compatibility
self-disclosure
singlehood
storge love
swinging
visualization
visuomotor flexibility
voluntary childlessness

RECOMMENDED READINGS

Allman, L. R., and Jaffe, D. T. (Eds.) (1982). *Readings in Adult Psychology,* 2nd ed. New York: Harper & Row.
This book of readings contains 47 articles on various dimensions of adult life as well as personal accounts of how people have faced crises during adulthood.

Bohannan, P. (1985). *All the Happy Families: Exploring the Varieties of Family Life.* New York: McGraw-Hill.

A good analysis of family life in the 1980s. Of particular interest is the material on single-parent families and stepfamilies.

Branden, N. (1981). *The Psychology of Romantic Love.* New York: Bantam Books.

A look at what love is, why it exists, why it sometimes grows, and why it sometimes dies.

Burns, D. D. (1985). *Intimate Connections.* New York: Signet.

A problem-solving approach to breaking out of loneliness and establishing intimate relations with others.

Cohen, R. S., Cohler, B. J., and Weissman, S. H. (Eds.) (1984). *Parenthood: A Psychodynamic Perspective.* New York: Guilford Press.

A wide assortment of readings focusing on parenthood in modern society. Among the topics are child care, divorce, child advocacy, and sociobiological perspectives on parenthood.

Duck, S. (1989). *Relating to Others.* Chicago: Dorsey Press.

An interesting look at the dynamics of interpersonal relationships.

Hanson, S. M., and Bozett, F. W. (Eds.) (1985). *Dimensions of Fatherhood.* Beverly Hills, Calif.: Sage.

An interdisciplinary approach to the study of fatherhood. Topics include grandfathers, househusbands, stepfathers, noncustodial fathers, and fathers in dual-career families.

Loudin, J. (1981). *The Hoax of Romance.* Ehglewood Cliffs, N.J.: Prentice-Hall.

An examination of the origins of romantic traditions and the manner in which ancient customs may adversely affect relationships today.

Murstein, B. (1986). *Paths to Marriage.* Beverly Hills, Calif.: Sage.

In this paperback, a noted scholar explores many facets of dating, from attraction and courtship to love and ultimate mate selection.

O'Donnell, L. N. (1985). *The Unheralded Majority: Contemporary Women as Mothers.* Lexington, Mass.: Heath.

An examination of the daily lives and values of contemporary mothers, including their attitudes toward employment and child rearing.

Shertzer, B. (1985). *Career Planning,* 3rd ed. Boston, Mass.: Houghton Mifflin.

Chapters 8 and 9 of this paperback explore the concept of career development, including how to find and keep a good job.

Middle Adulthood

CHAPTER OUTLINE

UNIT FOUR: CAREER DEVELOPMENT

Careers at Midlife

Changing Careers at Midlife

Women in the Labor Force

Persistent Vocational Inequalities

CHAPTER REVIEW

KEY TERMS

RECOMMENDED READINGS

WHAT DO YOU THINK?

■ Receding hairline . . . a bulging waistline . . . the need for reading glasses. Sooner or later, the various aging signs of middle adulthood are noticed. This may be a time when adults pause and reflect on their lives, taking a psychological inventory of their past and what lies ahead. For many, middle adulthood is a period to readjust and reassess, to take stock of triumphs and failures, and perhaps to reshape dreams. Does this happen to everyone at this time? Is it a negative event, as in the expression midlife *crisis*? Is it the same for men as well as women? We'll seek answers to these questions when we examine the psychological crossroads of midlife.

■ Stress. The mere mention of this word conjures up images of clenched fists, worry lines, sleepless nights, and the like. Stress comes in all shapes and sizes during adult life and can originate from a variety of sources, from economic worries and marital spats to employment blues. Stress is part of life, and learning to deal with it is of primary importance. What have we learned about stress, and does it always have to have a negative connotation? For that matter, why can one person's pleasure be another person's poison? Stress research in the 1990s has supplied us with some answers.

■ They were hailed as modern-day pioneers, not only because of their career triumphs but because no other women had ever accomplished such feats: Geraldine Ferraro's vice-presidential candidacy in 1984 and Sally Ride's outerspace exploits in 1983. However, even though women such as these continue to make inroads in the contemporary workplace, too many are still confined to low-status occupations. Their work is often tedious and unchallenging, and the pay is low. Why is this so? Why is there still job discrimination against women in these modern times, not to mention inequality?

■ And they lived happily ever after. For an astronomical number of married couples, young and old alike, this is hardly the case. Indeed, divorce rates are so high that about one-half of us will experience a divorce either as a child or as an adult, or both. Why are there so many divorces today, and what factors contribute to the collapse of a marriage? This chapter will address such issues, along with how divorce in the United States compares with that of other nations.

■ Unit One:

PHYSICAL AND MENTAL DEVELOPMENT

Middle age seems to be a paradox. It is a time of turbulence, a time of quiescence; a time of success, a time of failure; a time of joy, and a time of sadness. Yet youngsters, oldsters, and those in between seem to agree that the middle years represent the prime of life.

There are two almost diametrically opposed interpretations of middle age. To some it is a crisis, a period of self-evaluation (frequently with negative conclusions), unhappiness, and even depression. Evidently, to many, reaching 40 (or thereabouts), means "over the hill." Consequently, jokes about "middle-aged" people proliferate, for example, the running gag by the great comedian Jack Benny, who spent nearly half his life stating that he was "39."

The brighter side of middle age has been touted in books, such as *Life Begins at 40*, that stress "now you are free" and "do your own thing" themes. This viewpoint also emphasizes that middle age is a developmental period when individuals come into their own, become more accepting of themselves, mature, and achieve near perfect harmony

The middle years represent the prime of life.

with the universe as they develop a broader perspective. Thus, in many respects, middle age is what each person makes of it (Hale, 1984).

Following the years of early adulthood, middle age has a tendency to "creep up" on many people, seemingly without warning. Donald Donohugh (1981) suggested that people know they're middle aged when they notice the various aging cues. They may see a bulging waistline or a receding hairline. Or the death of a friend or a parent may shock them into realizing that they are not immortal but, rather, at the crossroads of their life.

Whatever the cues or clues, middle age is a point at which people often pause and ponder. They can look ahead and look back. From here on, they are changed, subtly but significantly. As we shall see, whether or not people understand life any better than they ever did or whether they ever will, many at least begin to try.

■ Physical Development

☐ External Aging

Aging is a process that is little understood. We do know, however, that part of the aging process is influenced by heredity and part by the environment. Because each of us is genetically different, we age at different rates. For some, the process is very gradual and barely noticeable on a year-to-year basis, whereas others appear to age before our very eyes.

We also know that no part of the body escapes the aging process. This is as true for those changes that are outwardly visible, known as *external aging*, as well as those occurring within the body, referred to as *internal aging*. As time goes on, both forms of aging will register their effects in both subtle and direct ways. Let us look first at changes in the skin and hair.

THE SKIN By middle adulthood, the skin is no longer able to stretch so tightly over the muscles. The sun's ultraviolet rays, as well as normal aging processes, are responsible for the change. The epidermal, or outer layer of the skin, thins with age and flattens. This is because the underlying ground substance in the dermis has become more fibrous, or stringy, and less gel-like. When the collagen and elastin fibers in the ground substance break down and lose their elasticity, the skin loses its firmness and begins to wrinkle and sag. The subcutaneous layer of fat beneath the skin also begins to decrease, also contributing to wrinkling.

Among middle-agers, the facial area exhibits the most change from the aforementioned processes. Wrinkles make their appearance at the corners of the eyes, referred to by many as crow's feet or laugh lines. Other wrinkles become evident around the mouth, forehead, and neck area. Sagging typically appears in the jowl area, and dark circles begin to make their way under the eyes.

Additionally, the sebaceous oil glands and sweat glands in the skin become less efficient with age. During earlier life stages, these glands were more active and served to lubricate the skin, keeping it smooth and supple. Less moisture is now produced, and, consequently, the skin dries out and begins to crack. The aging skin will also lose its water-holding capacity, further contributing to the skin's dryness.

Other skin changes may begin at this time and will become more pronounced with advancing age. Because the skin is thinner and less elastic, and because the circulation of the blood is becoming less efficient, the complexion becomes more sallow. It also may become splotchy and irregular in color, owing primarily to the fluctuating supply

External forms of aging become visible during middle age.

of pigmentation. Lentigines, or liver spots, caused primarily by exposure to the sun, may start to make their appearance on the face or backs of the hands.

The blood vessels close to the skin's surface can develop bulges due to vascular problems, which can cause blue discolorations called *venous lakes* on the lips and dilated red blood vessels on the face called *telangiectases*. Blue-red discolorations on the scrotum and cherry-red ones on the trunk are called *senile angiomas*. These skin conditions, as well as an itching disorder known as *pruritus*, typically afflict older adults but are not uncommon among middle-agers. Pruritus occurs because the thin, dried-out skin becomes sensitive to extremes of temperature, especially in dry winter air.

As indicated earlier, the sun accounts for many of the changes associated with aging skin, including skin cancer. *Basal cell carcinoma* is the most common form of cancer seen in the United States. It is a malignant, epithelial tumor that rarely metastasizes, and seldom occurs prior to middle adulthood. While it occurs in all races, it is uncommon in dark-skinned persons such as blacks or Asians. It is also more common in men than women.

Basal cell carcinomas usually occur on the head and neck and, contrary to popular thought, they can also appear on relatively sun-protected areas such as the scalp and behind the ears. The most common variety consists of a smooth-surfaced nodule whose border is often raised and pearly. If not removed, it will progressively enlarge and can result in considerable tissue destruction (Lin and Carter, 1986).

What can adults do to help protect and care for their aging skin? Avoiding excessive exposure to strong sunlight cannot be overemphasized. While a suntan may give the appearance of healthy skin, it increases the risk of skin cancer and, over time, creates leathery and prematurely aged skin. Should exposure to the sun be unavoidable, medical experts recommend that protective clothing be worn and a proper sunscreen applied on a regular basis.

Proper skin care always includes regular cleansing and, with the exception of those who have oily skin, the use of a moisturizer. Remember that the body is losing its ability to produce natural oils and water, therefore a moisturizer serves a practical replacement function. A moisturizer cannot prevent wrinkling, but it can make wrinkles less apparent. Also, middle-aged adults might want to avoid the use of excessive soaps and detergents because they tend to remove natural oil from the skin.

Finally, a word or two about exercise and skin tone. Exercise does tone the muscles and increase circulation. For these reasons, and a multitude of others, exercise is recommended for adults of all ages. However, exercise does not remove wrinkles, even though the skin typically flushes and seems healthier. The same holds true for facials, steam baths, and saunas. Whatever improvements observed are at best temporary.

Anatomy of a Wrinkle

Wrinkled skin is an inevitable part of aging processes. Wrinkles actually begin beneath the skin's outer layer in the dermis, the layer containing a rich supply of blood vessels, glands, and nerve endings. A gradual stiffening of connective tissue, called collagen, in this skin layer causes older skin to become less elastic (see Figure 10-1). Overall, this will cause the dermis to go through a shrinking process. The epidermis will therefore become too loose a covering, causing wrinkles to form. The decreased activity of the oil glands will also cause dryer, less supple skin.

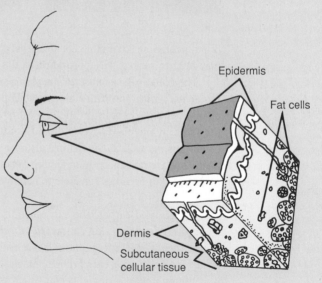

FIGURE 10-1 Anatomy of a Wrinkle (Source: Henig, 1985)

THE HAIR Most adults have gray hair by age 50. This color change is due to the progressive loss of melanin from the hair bulb. Scalp hair is believed to gray more rapidly than any other body hair because its ratio of growth phase to resting phase is considerably greater than that of other body hair.

For several reasons, the hair of both men and women begins to thin during middle adulthood. Hair growth slows and the hairs are therefore replaced more slowly. Also, the hair resting and growing cycle undergoes change. Earlier in life, each hair has a growing cycle of three to five years, during which time it grows about one-half inch per month. The hair then enters a resting cycle, at which it ceases growth for two to four months. Approximately 10 to 15 percent of one's hair is in this resting cycle at any time. During middle adulthood, however, the hair resting cycle becomes longer (Donohugh, 1981).

Hair loss, for both men and women, becomes a consequence of this longer resting cycle. However, among men it is much more pronounced. Interestingly, both sexes will lose about 50 to 100 hairs each day with normal brushing, but in earlier years, new hair had replaced approximately the same amount. Now, the longer resting cycle leads to an increased shedding of resting hairs. When this happens, the hair becomes thinner and miniaturized. Fine, nonpigmented hairs end up replacing coarse, pigmented ones, or in extreme cases, the replacement procedure does not happen at all.

For men, hair loss due to heredity is called *male pattern baldness.* Such hair loss is noticeable in approximately 37 percent of men aged 35, and 45 percent of those aged 45. It typically begins with a receding hairline, often as early as young adulthood. The next vulnerable portion of the scalp is the monk's spot, the circle on the back of the head. If a man experiences extensive baldness, the monk's spot will grow to a point where it meets the receding hairline. This will leave the top of the head nearly bare (Pesmen, 1984).

Women experience hair loss at much later ages, and the loss itself is less pronounced than it is in men. Thinning usually occurs at the vertex and frontal regions. The hair may also become finer and less dense over time. Some women also experience significant hair loss after menopause. However, most women who develop this condition are hereditarily predisposed to hair loss.

As women and men experience varying degrees of hair loss, they may be developing hair in unwanted areas. Coarse, pigmented hairs may develop on the chin and upper lip of women, while similar hair structures appear on the ears, nose, and eyebrows of men. Many men also experience hair growth on the back. For both sexes, axillary (underarm) and pubic hair usually becomes finer and not as thick as it once was.

Numerous suggestions exist on the topic of proper hair care and aging processes. To help slow down hair loss, persons should brush gently, avoid excessive heat from blow drying, and rinse with a conditioner after shampooing. Chemical treatments, such as permanents and bleachings, should be avoided. Hair breakage can be reduced by keeping the hair short. And, similar to skin care, excessive exposure to direct sunlight should be avoided.

Although a cure for baldness has yet to be found, a number of hair replacement options exist. While hairpieces offer the fewest complications, many persons today turn to other approaches to the problem. One such procedure is surgical hair transplantation. Small, cylindrical grafts of hair are taken from hair-bearing regions of the scalp (usually from the back of the head) and transplanted to the desired area. Sometimes, an entire strip of hair grafts is used to create a more natural hairline. Another approach is scalp reduction. Here, an incision is made and a small section of scalp is removed in order to reduce the area of baldness that needs to be filled in with transplanted grafts. Finally, a drug called minoxidil offers hope to those with bald heads. Minoxidil is an antihypertensive medication, but has the side effect of increasing hair growth. In research studies, minoxidil created new hair growth in 25 to 30 percent of the subjects receiving it. While its long-term effect remains to be seen, such early, partial success has been encouraging. This drug is available by prescription in the United States.

Aging processes are
unique to each
individual.

☐ **Internal Aging**

Unlike the visible signs of external aging, internal changes cannot be seen. We become aware of them only when we notice a difference in the way we feel or act. Some of the internal changes in aging that accompany middle adulthood can be summarized as follows.

THE CARDIOVASCULAR SYSTEM The amount of blood pumped by the heart decreases as one gets older. Assuming that a 30-year-old's heart functions at 100 percent capacity, its efficiency drops down to 80 percent by age 50. By age 80, it decreases to 70 percent.

Blood pressure tends to rise during the middle years, and the resting heart rate declines. The heart loses some muscle fibers, and blood vessels thicken and become less elastic. For many, arteriosclerosis, or hardening of the arteries, begins by middle adulthood.

THE RESPIRATORY SYSTEM By age 50, breathing capacity is down to 75 percent (compared with 100 percent at age 30). Structurally, the lungs lose some of their elasticity with age. In addition, the bony chest cage becomes stiffer, and the muscles that move the chest during inhalation and exhalation tend to become weaker. Consequently, the lungs cannot expand the way they once did. This means that a deep breath is not as deep as it once was. While a slight difference exists between the sexes, the following shows the maximum amount of air that can be generally taken into the lungs:

- Age 30: 6.0 quarts

- Age 40: 5.4 quarts

- Age 50: 4.5 quarts

- Age 60: 3.6 quarts

- Age 70: 3.0 quarts

THE NERVOUS SYSTEM The speed at which a nerve impulse travels from the brain to a muscle fiber in the body decreases by only approximately 10 percent throughout the life cycle. It has slowed to about half that figure by one's fifieth birthday. Structual changes in the brain at midlife are neglible.

Aging and Brain Changes

Certain changes in the brain are evident as aging occurs. For example, the brain at age 40 is smaller, lighter, wetter, and it gradually pulls away from its sheath, the cortical mantle (see Figure 10-2). The gyri, or valleys that separate the ridges of the brain matter, become wider and deeper. Throughout all of adult life, at an accelerated rate after age 20, brain cells will be lost. Such loss occurs in various regions of the brain including the cortex, the hippocampus (the region that affects learning, memory, and, perhaps, pleasure), and the locus ceruleus (the area that controls sleep, and, perhaps, intelligence). However, the physical changes that occur in the healthy, aging brain appear to have little effect on everyday cognitive functioning.

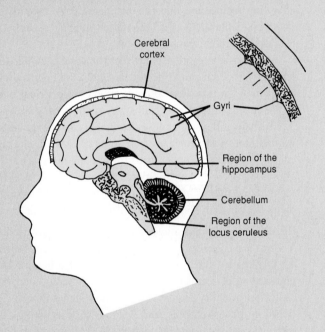

Cerebral cortex

Gyri

Region of the hippocampus

Cerebellum

Region of the locus ceruleus

FIGURE 10-2 Aging and Brain Changes (Source: Henig, 1985)

☐ Changes in Sensory Capacities

Although sensory changes were slight during the early adulthood years, there are more significant alterations in middle adulthood. Sensory contact with the physical environment is an extremely important aspect of the overall aging process. That is, what a person is capable of perceiving or sensing may well influence overall behavior and personality. The self-concept can easily be damaged when a sense defect prevents an individual from processing the numerous and diverse amounts of incoming perceptual information. Changes in sensory capacities are something that we'll all experience to a certain degree. But, provided there are no serious impairments, most adjust effectively to these changes (Botwinick, 1981, 1984).

VISION Vision, the sense we most depend on, changes noticeably during the middle years, especially after age 40. This is the age when many people begin holding newspapers and books farther in front of them, and bifocals make their appearance to compensate for *presbyopia,* or farsightedness. Presbyopia is the result of a change in the lens of the eye. The lens continues to grow throughout life, but because its cells are not shed, like those of the skin, it slowly compacts from childhood on. This ultimately affects accommodation, the manner in which the lens adapts to near and far vision.

Accommodation is achieved by the contraction and relaxation of the lens's muscles, flattening it or allowing it to become rounder by means of its own elasticity. By approximately age 55, this elasticity hardens, much as one's arteries harden with age. But sometime during the previous decade, individuals begin to realize that their vision at the usual reading distance of about 15 inches is becoming blurred. For a few years after this realization, one can compensate by holding objects further away or by increasing illumination. Ultimately, though, reading glasses become necessary (Donohugh, 1981).

Another change in vision is that the pupil becomes smaller with age. As a result, less light passes through it. Middle-aged adults generally need more illumination to compensate for this. They also may need longer periods of time to adapt to darkness or to glare. This latter fact explains why night driving becomes more difficult with age.

A change in visual abilities is often one of the earliest signs of middle age. Again, we find that most people are able to laugh and kid one another about their farsightedness and needing longer arms to read the newspaper; these people wear their new glasses and accept their condition. Others, however, try to hide their visual liabilities by memorizing menus at favorite eating places or by asking waiters what they recommend, rather than show the world they have to wear glasses.

HEARING Hearing is another sense that may start declining by age 40, and though Americans do not seem embarrassed to wear eyeglasses as their vision declines, they are apt to remain "tuned out" rather than wear a hearing aid. The ability to hear low-pitched sounds seems to remain constant in adulthood, but middle-agers, men especially, lose auditory acuity for the higher pitches (Marsh, 1980). This loss, as we mentioned in the last chapter, may begin as early as young adulthood. Hearing problems with age-related causes occur when the ear is unable to pick up and transmit sound to its inner parts. More specifically, the hair cells along the cochlea that send the auditory impulses begin to degenerate.

Auditory difference between the sexes may be caused, at least in part, by men's greater exposure to noise in certain traditionally male occupations: truck driving, mining, auto assembly-line work, and the like. But although people may know that their vision is worsening, they are generally not aware of the gradual loss of hearing. Thus, unless one is noticeably hard of hearing, this loss may have little psychological implication for one's development.

TASTE, TOUCH, AND SMELL The senses of taste, touch, and smell in adulthood have not been extensively investigated—in fact, relatively little empirical evidence is available. However, these senses seemingly decline at least somewhat over the years, but because we rely on taste and smell so little and because they are difficult to study, the evidence is, at best, general. The ability to distinguish tastes (sweet, sour, salt, bitter) remains reasonably constant; nevertheless, the taste threshold rises or the taste sensitivity declines, resulting in a slight difficulty in distinguishing among the four basic tastes (Donohugh, 1981).

Health Disorders of Middle Adulthood

We indicated earlier that middle adulthood usually represents the prime of one's life. This is as true for physical capacities as it is for other developmental spheres. However, similar to other life stages, middle age brings along its own unique set of health concerns, needed lifestyle adjustments, and dietary considerations.

Of all the preventable disorders in middle age, obesity looms as the most threatening. *Obesity* is defined as deposits of fat from 10 to 20 percent or more above normal range for age, sex, and height. *Overweight,* on the other hand, is commonly described as heaviness that is 10 percent or more above average weight, based on size. Thus, a person can be overweight—because of heavy muscle and bone—without being fat. The obese person is fat (Eisenberg and Eisenberg, 1980).

Middle-aged obesity originates from many different sources. Obesity may be the product of a glandular malfunction or other physiological problem. Or, it may develop because of a hereditary predisposition. Some people become obese because they do not exercise, or because they are under stress. Because of the latter, food looms as a way to relieve anxiety, or so it seems to the frustrated individual.

Others put on the pounds because they select foods of borderline nutritional value, consume them in unbalanced quantities, and eat them at the wrong time of the day. One source (Neurnberger, 1981) estimates that 60 to 70 percent of the average American diet is of suboptimal nutritional value. Consequently, fat molecules build up and the heart, lungs, and other organs must work harder.

Earlier in this book, we noted how adults of all ages need to be in or under desirable weight ranges. Any weight over the ideal range increases the risk of poor health. For example, disorders attributed wholly or partially to excess weight include hypertension, atherosclerosis, coronary artery disease, complications due to diabetes, and digestive disorders (gallstones and liver dysfunction).

The older an individual is, the greater his or her chance is of dying an obesity-related death. For example, Robert O'Connor (1980) points out that if you are 15 to 24 percent overweight, your chances of dying are increased 30 percent over the normal death rate for your age group. If you are 25 to 34 percent overweight, your chances of dying are increased 45 percent for your age group. If you are over 35 percent overweight, your chances of dying are increased 60 percent over your age-group norm.

Moreover, if your abdominal girth is two inches greater than your expanded chest expanded chest girth (for women, these measurements vary somewhat, of course), you have a "pot belly." If you have a pot belly, your chances of dying are increased an additional 50 percent. If this is not sobering enough, consider the following: If you are a man who is 40 percent overweight and you have a pot belly, your chances of dying are 110 percent higher than the normal death rate for your age group!

HYPERTENSION *Hypertension,* usually referred to as high blood pressure, is a common circulatory disorder. It is estimated that as many as 60 million Americans suffer from it, mostly middle-aged men and women. Among younger adults, more men than women have high blood pressure, but after age 55 the problem becomes more acute for females. Blacks and those from lower socioeconomic settings are also more vulnerable to hypertension.

Principles of Sensible Weight Reduction

- Be sure that you *really* want to lose weight. Make this decision out of self-love, not self-hate. Share your plan with those you can count on for support.

- Set yourself a realistic weight-loss target. Along the way, build up your confidence with small dieting victories.

- Be prepared for setbacks and do not feel guilty when you go off your diet. Take one day at a time.

- Concentrate on eating healthful foods.

- Eat three small meals a day rather than one or two large ones.

- Choose low-calorie snacks.

- Cut down on alcohol.

- Eat more slowly.

- Use a smaller plate—it will look full with less food on it.

- Do not feel as though you have to finish all the food on your plate.

- Avoid eating large meals at night when you cannot burn off calories with exercise.

- Do not binge and fast alternately.

- Remember that each of us is ultimately 100 percent responsible for our dieting success, or lack of it.

(Adapted from Bloomfield, 1986; Arnot, 1984)

Hypertension is often called the silent killer because it usually presents no observable symptoms. If left untreated, it can wear down vital organs and lead to heart disease, stroke, or kidney failure. About a million deaths each year are caused by hypertension (Lehmann, 1984).

To understand the danger that this disorder presents, one must first develop an appreciation of what blood pressure is. *Blood pressure* is the pressure exerted by the blood on the artery walls. A blood pressure reading, measured by a device called a sphygmomanometer, is expressed as a larger number (systolic) over a smaller number (diastolic). As an example, consider the blood pressure reading of 120 over 80. This means that when the heart contracts to pump out blood to the arteries (systole), the resulting reading on the pressure meter is 120 millimeters. When the heart relaxes between beats and is filling with blood (diastole), the blood pressure reading falls to 80 millimeters.

With age, blood pressure levels tend to increase, the result of the body's small arteries decreasing in diameter and elasticity. To illustrate the nature of age-related blood pressure changes, a reading of 120/80 is considered normal for persons under age 18. Between ages 18 and 50, however, a normal blood pressure reading extends to 140/85. Should the latter set of numbers continue to increase, though, a medical consultation is usually needed. As a footnote, there is no medical support that your blood pressure should be 100 plus your age.

Certain risk factors make persons more vulnerable to hypertension. For example, high blood pressure is thought to run in families, suggesting a genetic link to this disorder. Obesity, prolonged exposure to stress, and excessive amounts of alcohol tend to elevate blood pressure. Also, too much sodium (salt) in one's diet tends to create fluid retention, something which promotes hypertension.

While hypertension cannot be cured, a proper diet and a healthful lifestyle usually control it. To accomplish this, physicians often recommend a weight-loss program, regular exercise, relaxation techniques, restricted salt and cholesterol consumption, and moderate alcohol consumption. Some physicians also recommend that levels of potassium, magnesium, and calcium intake be increased.

Should medication be needed to control hypertension, *diuretics* are typically prescribed. Such drugs cause excess fluid and sodium to leave the body, which reduces the volume of blood and, in turn, lowers blood pressure. If the condition does not improve with diuretics, other drugs designed to relax and open up the body's blood vessels (called adrenergic-inhibiting agents), may be prescribed. Other drug possibilities include beta blockers, which block the action of epinephrine (adrenaline) and norepinephrine, thus decreasing the heartbeat rate and the vigor of each contraction. Finally, calcium channel blockers prevent calcium from entering the artery muscles and causing them to constrict, thus raising blood pressure.

ATHEROSCLEROSIS *Atherosclerosis* is the most common form of arteriosclerosis, or hardening of the arteries. It is a type of cardiovascular disease in which plaque (fatty materials) becomes attached to the inner walls of arteries. Beyond making the arteries thick and hard, plaque will also clog and even block the flow of blood.

Plaque consists of such fats as cholesterol. *Cholesterol* is a lipid (fat) that is produced naturally in the body. It is found in many locations, including in the blood, and is present in such foods as eggs, meat, and shellfish. Cholesterol is not soluble and consequently must attach itself to a soluble protein to move through the body. When this takes place and movement occurs, the excess cholesterol is deposited along artery walls and begins to create circulation problems.

It needs to be acknowledged that cholesterol in itself is not bad. On the contrary, the body needs cholesterol to assist in digestion and hormonal production, among other functions. It is excessive cholesterol intake that represents the problem. However, carefully monitoring cholesterol levels is a health guideline that too many adults choose to ignore. The American Heart Association (1987) recommends that the daily cholesterol intake should be between 150 to 240 milligrams per cubic centimeter of blood. Those with blood cholesterol levels of over 255 have five times the heart attack risk as those at 220.

Blockage due to fat buildups can lead to serious complications when the arteries involved lead to vital organs. For example, if blockage or clogging occurs in a vessel leading to the brain, a stroke can occur. Should a coronary artery be partially blocked, *angina* (chest pain) is usually experienced. Total coronary artery blockage leads to a heart attack. Atherosclerosis is thought to develop early in life, slowly blocking the body's network of arteries. Such changes usually go undetected for years since this disease presents no visible symptoms. Indeed, it is not usually until middle adulthood that any problems begin. By this time, artery walls may have become significantly reduced in size by fatty deposits, preventing blood from delivering life-sustaining oxygen to body parts. Figure 10-3 illustrates how atherosclerosis affects the lining of an artery.

Although the exact causes of atherosclerosis remain elusive, several factors that increase its progress have been identified. For example, the tendency to manufacture large amounts of cholesterol is thought to have a genetic basis. Hypertension, cigarette smoking, lack of exercise, and stress represent other risk factors. Diabetes has also been cited since blood sugar abnormalities appear to promote the production of cholesterol.

The treatment of atherosclerosis typically involves changes in lifestyle and eating habits. Among the recommendations are a reduction in cholesterol intake, including a low-fat diet (Table 10-1). Other suggestions include the elimination of cigarette smoking, and the implementation of sensible exercise and weight-loss programs. Should medication be needed, *anticoagulants* are often prescribed to thin the blood and prevent clotting. Surgical procedures to remove plaque from blocked arteries may also be necessary. However, such procedures are usually performed on relatively large vessels, such as those entering the heart, kidneys, or brain. Surgery typically cannot remove plaque deposits in the small blood vessels of these organs.

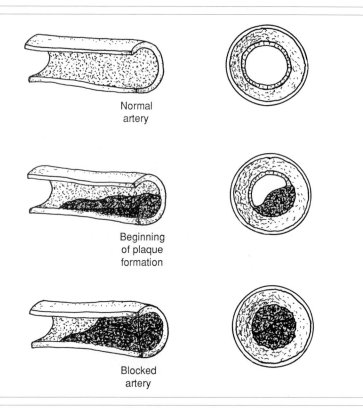

Normal
artery

Beginning
of plaque
formation

Blocked
artery

FIGURE 10-3 When atherosclerosis occurs, plaque begins to form on the lining of arteries. Eventually, blockage of the artery results.

TABLE 10-1 **Guidelines for Low-Fat Meals**

- Choose lean meat, fish, poultry, and dry beans and peas as protein sources
- Use skim or low-fat milk and milk products
- Moderate your use of egg yolks and organ meats
- Lift congealed fat off chilled soups, stews, and casseroles
- Limit your intake of fats and oils, especially those high in saturated fat, such as butter, cream, lard, heavily hydrogenated fats (some margarines), shortenings, and foods containing palm and coconut oils
- Trim excess fat off meats
- Broil, bake, or boil rather than fry
- Moderate your use of foods that contain fat, such as breaded and deep-fried foods
- Cook meats and poultry using fat-free methods—baking, broiling, roasting, and steaming—and cook on a rack. The rack ensures that fat drains down and out
- Read labels carefully to determine both amount and type of fat present in foods

(Adapted from U. S. Department of Agriculture, 1985)

CORONARY ARTERY DISEASE *Coronary artery disease* is the presence of athero-sclerosis in the coronary arteries. When this happens, the coronary arteries are nar-rowed so that less blood flows to the heart muscle. Coronary artery disease is serious and can cause heart attacks. Indeed, coronary artery disease (CAD) remains the most common cause of cardiac disease in adults and the leading cause of death in this country.

What specifically happens when a heart attack is experienced? While there are variations, most heart attacks occur when a poor blood supply causes a portion of the heart muscle (myocardium) to die (Figure 10-4). The destruction of myocardial tissue is known as a *myocardial infarction* and the infected tissue is called an *infarct*. Ath-erosclerosis can cause this to happen in one of three ways:

■ Atherosclerois can completely block a coronary artery.

■ The rough surface of the atherosclerosis can provide a location for a blood clot (*thrombus*) to form. If the clot gets big enough, it has the potential of closing off an artery. This kind of a heart attack is called a *coronary thrombosis*.

■ Coronary arteries narrowed by atherosclerosis, but not completely blocked, may be unable to give the heart muscle enough blood. This may occur when there is extreme physical exertion or emotional excitement. If there is not enough oxygen-rich blood, the heart may stop beating rhythmically.

If damage from the heart attack creates a small infarct, the heart will continue to function and scar tissue will form over the dead area. New blood vessels will develop to compensate for blocked or damaged ones. This is the heart's adaptive approach to the attack, a process known as *collateral circulation.* If damage to the heart tissue is massive and the coronary blood supply is not immediately restored, death results.

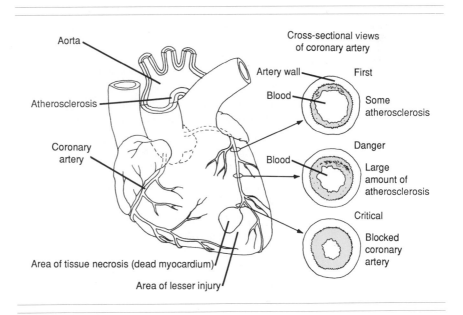

FIGURE 10-4 Illustration of how a heart attack occurs. Myocardial infarction results when the central area around the blocked artery actually dies (necrosis). Atherosclerotic depos-its have blocked the coronary arteries (see right side views), preventing the heart muscles from getting enough oxygen. The result is a heart attack (Sorochan, 1981, p. 311).

It is possible for someone to experience a heart attack without realizing it. Minor heart attacks are characterized by shortness of breath, sweating, blueness of fingertips and lips, fatigue, pale complexion, possible dizziness, and an irregular heartbeat. Often these symptoms subside and return. Usually, a minor heart attack is an indication that a major one is forthcoming.

The symptoms of a major heart attack are more obvious. They include the symptoms of a minor attack, but they are more intense. In addition, symptoms include intense pain in the middle of the chest, pain extending down one or both arms or in the neck and jaw area, profuse sweating, and nausea.

The chances of recovery from a heart attack today are better than ever before. A variety of medications are used to treat heart attack patients, such as anticoagulants, diuretics, beta blockers, digitalis (which establishes a steady heartbeat), antiarrhythmics (which inhibit irregularities in the heartbeat), and sedatives (which relax the body).

Treatment is also directed at changes in lifestyle and eating habits, including some of the earlier mentioned recommendations. For example, a healthier cardiovascular system can be promoted with the cessation of cigarette smoking, beginning a regular exercise program, reducing the amounts of stress in one's life, lowering fat intake, eating a diet high in fresh fruits and vegetables and low in refined sugar products, cutting salt intake, and reducing one's intake of alcholic beverages.

CANCER *Cancer* is a large group of diseases characterized by uncontrolled growth and the spread of abnormal cells. If the spread of cancer is not controlled or checked, it can result in death. However, many cancers can be cured if detected and treated promptly.

Cancer is the second most common cause of death in the United States, killing over 480,000 Americans annually. This breaks down to 1,323 people a day, about one every 65 seconds. Of every five deaths in the United States, one is from cancer. In 1989, about 965,000 people were diagnosed as having this disease. Going a step further, about 74 million Americans now living will eventually have cancer. Over the years, cancer will strike in approximately three out of four families (American Cancer Society, 1989).

The Nature of Cancer Throughout the body, cells normally reproduce themselves in an orderly manner so that worn-out tissues are replaced, injuries are repaired, and growth of the body proceeds. Occasionally, certain cells undergo an abnormal change and begin a process of uncontrolled growth and spread. These abnormal cells grow into masses of tissue called *tumors* (or neoplasms). Tumors can impinge on vital organs and block blood vessels, in the process robbing normal cells of needed nutrients.

Tumors can be either benign or malignant. A *benign tumor* is usually harmless and does not invade normal tissue. If it does, the invasion is limited. A *malignant tumor* is cancerous and invades surrounding tissues. It also can spread cancer throughout the body. The transfer of the malignancy from the original site to another site is known as *metastasis*. This can be accomplished by the direct extension of the original growth, or by it becoming detached and carried through the lymph or blood systems to other body parts.

Four types of cancer have been identified. *Carcinomas* arise from epithelial cells (skin, mucous membranes, etc.) and tend to be solid tumors. *Sarcomas* develop from muscle, bone, fat, and other connective tissues. *Lymphomas* originate in lymphoid tissues. Finally, *leukemias* are those cancers developing in the hematological system.

Cancer specialists have identified seven warning signs associated with cancer: (1) a sore that does not heal; (2) unusual bleeding or discharge; (3) a change in bowel or bladder habits; (4) nagging cough or hoarseness; (5) indigestion or difficulty in swal-

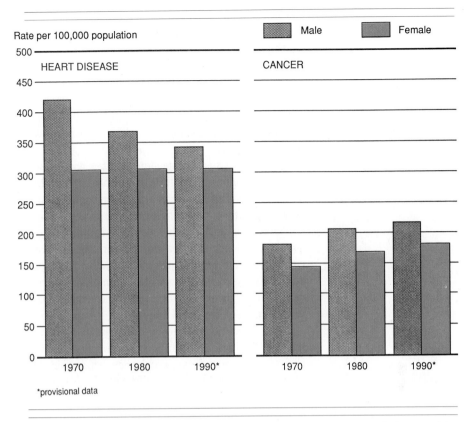

Rate per 100,000 population

□ Male   □ Female

HEART DISEASE   CANCER

*provisional data

FIGURE 10-5   Overall death rates by heart disease and cancer. (Source: U.S. Bureau of the Census, 1989)

lowing; (6) thickening or lump in breast or elsewhere; (7) and an obvious change in a mole or wart.

Cancer can occur at any point in the life cycle, although more than one-half of all cancer deaths occur in persons over age 65. From ages 20 through 40, cancer is more common in women than in men, but between ages 60 and 80 more cancers occur in men. Overall, more men than women die of cancer.

In women, the principal fatal cancers are in the lung, breast, colon and rectum, ovary, and uterus. Combined, these account for about 60 percent of all female cancer deaths. In men, the leading sites are lung, colon and rectum, and prostate. Figure 10-5 displays death rates by cancer and heart disease.

OSTEOPOROSIS *Osteoporosis* is a disorder characterized by a decrease in the calcium content of bone tissue. The word osteoporosis means, literally, "holes in the bones," and the condition has the potential of leading to fragility of bones and increased porosity. Also called brittle bone disease or "widow's hump," osteoporosis can cause bone deformity, crippling, and even a reduction in height.

An estimated 15 million Americans suffer from osteoporosis, but it is eight times more common in women. It afflicts one in four women over the age of 60, and fair-skinned white females are affected most often. Also, thin women with small frames are more susceptible to osteoporosis than larger, heavier females.

It is believed that osteoporosis is triggered by menopause and natural aging processes, although conclusive explanations remain elusive. Menopause is frequently cited because of the dramatic decrease in *estrogen* production, a hormone that affects the calcium content of bones. However, other reasons for its onset are also cited, including inactivity, inadequate exposure to sunlight (which helps the body manufacture vitamin D, which is essential for normal calcium absorption and use), and insufficient amounts of calcium and protein in the diet.

Certain conditions also seem to accentuate the possibility of contracting osteoporosis. Females with a family history of osteoporosis and those who have had their ovaries removed at an early age run a greater risk of developing this condition. Medical conditions such as chronic arthritis, alcoholism, thyroid problems, and liver disease also increase the likelihood of osteoporosis.

In its early stages, osteoporosis often goes unnoticed. For many, it presents no observable symptoms and little, if any, pain. Often, the only warning sign occurs when a minor fall or mishap results in a broken bone. Or, some may realize that the spine has become slightly curved. These are all indications that the disease has advanced.

Over time and left untreated, osteoporosis becomes a crippling disease. Simple exertion creates muscle spasms and pain, and the progressive loss of bone can lead to complicated fractures of the spine and limbs. The teeth can also fall out as the jawbone decays. Furthermore, the spinal column becomes progressively curved and the shoulders rounded. Victims can actually lose several inches in height because of a reduction in the length of the spinal column.

The prevention of osteoporosis is relatively simple. Women need to ensure that their bodies are receiving an adequate supply of calcium and vitamin D. This is true for all women, not just those nearing menopause or afflicted with osteoporosis. While the current recommended dietary allowance for calcium is 800 milligrams per day, most medical experts believe that women past the age of 40 need 1,000 to 1,500 milligrams daily. Keep in mind, too, that calcium supplements exceeding this daily requirement do not ensure added prevention. On the contrary, too much can create a toxic reaction; therefore, individuals should always check with a physician before increasing dosage levels. Along similar lines, excessive intakes of protein do not ensure the prevention of osteoporosis. Instead, this tends to create bone loss rather than strengthening of the skeletal framework.

Regular medical examinations are important for preventing osteoporosis. As we have indicated, feeling physically fit offers no guarantee whatsoever that osteoporosis is absent from the system. A number of methods are available for diagnosing osteoporosis, including X rays and devices designed to assess bone loss. Such diagnostic approaches are often part of annual checkups for any woman over the age of 25.

For patients afflicted with osteoporosis, doctors usually prescribe high dosages of calcium and vitamin D tablets. This usually retards the rate of bone loss but will not cause new bone to form. For females, estrogen slows the rate of bone loss and might be prescribed. However, similar to the cautions we gave earlier, estrogen may cause adverse side effects and each patient needs to be carefully evaluated and monitored. For men with osteoporosis, the male hormone testosterone might be administered, since it stimulates the growth of body tissues. For both females and males, physicians usually urge the adoption of a nutritious diet and an exercise program that will strengthen the muscles supporting the weakened bones.

☐ Lifestyle and Dietary Considerations

Middle age often requires greater adjustments in lifestyle and eating habits than in young adulthood. No longer can one stay up all night partying, for now the body demands more rest. The middle-aged person finds that the more hectic pace of youth

Exercise is an important part of a healthy lifestyle.

and early adulthood must be replaced by a more regulated lifestyle, including regular sleeping hours, although this does not necessarily mean more hours of sleep. Indeed, there is evidence that the older one gets, the less sleep one needs.

In our culture, middle age is generally associated with a higher income, a factor that affects one's physical lifestyle. Many can now afford more beer, wine, and snacks and more elaborate meals, but accompanying this richer diet is often a reduction of physical activity. Many, unfortunately, eat too much and exercise too little. A "middle-age paunch" may make its appearance, as muscle tone slowly deteriorates in people who do not exercise.

Middle-aged people select foods of borderline nutritional value and then consume them in unbalanced quantities and at the wrong time of day. One source (Nuernberger, 1981) estimated that 60 to 70 percent of the average American diet has suboptimal nutritional value. Triglycerides (fat molecules) and cholesterol build up as a result of the excessive intake of fatty foods, and so the heart, lungs, and other organs must work harder. Consequently, the middle-aged adult must begin to slow down and work for shorter periods when engaged in strenuous activities.

■ NORWEGIAN STUDY CONFIRMS BENEFITS OF LOW CHOLESTEROL DIET

In one of Norway's most extensive studies to date, researchers proved that changes in diet and smoking habits can reduce the risk of heart attacks and sudden deaths from heart disease by as much as 47 percent. The investigation was made by the Oslo Department of Health and Life Insurance Company's Institute for Medical Statistics.

The subjects were 1,232 men, ranging from 40 to 49 years of age. A profile of the men was taken before the experimental treatment began. Although they did not have high blood pressure, they did have high cholesterol levels. Their diets were high in saturated fats and cholesterol, including high levels of butter, cheese, eggs, and whole milk. About 80 percent of the men smoked.

The experimental group was advised to reduce or quit smoking and to follow certain dietary guidelines. Among other suggestions, they were to substitute skim milk for whole milk, eat only one egg a week, use polyunsaturated oil in cooking and baking, eat fruit for dessert, make sandwiches using high-fiber bread and fish, vegetables, or low-fat cheese as fillings, and serve dinners consisting of fish or low-fat meat with potatoes and vegetables.

The subjects followed these dietary considerations over a five-year period. At the end of this time span, it was found that there was a 60 percent difference in the incidence of heart disease; changes in smoking habits (mostly a reduction in smoking) accounted for about 25 percent of the difference. The subjects did not use drugs during the five-year period and made no significant changes in their exercise or weight-loss programs. Overall, cholesterol levels were 13 percent lower; triglyceride levels had diminished; and the ratio of protective HDL cholesterol had risen. The lower cholesterol levels among the experimental group did not lead to other illnesses, though, as has sometimes been speculated.

(Nusberg, 1982a)

Having to moderate work activities may not be particularly upsetting, as this is a very gradual process. Middle-aged construction workers, carpenters, and others who have physically demanding jobs recognize that they cannot keep pace with young adults who do the same type of work. They often bemoan the loss of energy needed to do "bullwork," as any job that requires relatively large amounts of strength is called. In order not to be unfavorably compared, some urge their younger coworkers to slow down and take it easy. However, most middle-aged people readily compensate by working at their own pace and being sensible about the activities they undertake.

It thus should be clear that middle-aged persons need to be especially cautious in regard to the health problems associated with this life stage. In particular, cardiovascular disease looms as more than just a remote possibility, and researchers (Holmes and Hearne, 1981) acknowledge that the incidence of cancer also rises with age.

In recognition of these risks, health expert Walter Sorochan (1981) suggested that adults take specific steps to safeguard their health and protect against cardiovascular disease and cancer. His suggestions for promoting a healthy cardiovascular system include stopping cigarette smoking, beginning a regular endurance exercise program, adjusting calorie intake and maintaining one's ideal weight, lowering fat intake, eating a diet high in fresh fruits and vegetables and low in refined sugar products, cutting salt intake, and reducing one's intake of alcoholic beverages. In addition, individuals should have regular medical checkups to detect hypertension and early signs of atherosclerosis. Finally, adults need to reduce the overall stress in their lives and learn how to relax.

In regard to cancer prevention, it should be pointed out that 75 percent of new cancer cases are related to eating, smoking, and drinking habits. It is important therefore that all of the aforementioned dietary and lifestyle recommendations be followed. In addition, individuals should avoid overexposure to the sun, carcinogenic chemicals (a *carcinogen* is an agent causing cancer), and fumes at work and in the home. Having a bowel movement each day and exercising regularly to help oxygenate all body cells are also recommended. So, too, is learning to cook meats in non-cancer-producing ways: instead of charcoal broiling, barbecuing, and pan frying, use an electric or gas broiler so the heat source is above the meat. Keeping the body clean and examining it regularly is also important, particularly checking those areas with sensitive tissues such as the mouth and genitals. Finally, adults should see a medical doctor on a regular basis. A comprehensive cancer checkup is important to ensure overall good health and to detect cancer early so that it can be treated properly.

☐ Menopause and the Climacteric

Menopause is a normal developmental event in a woman's life. The word *menopause* comes from two Greek words meaning "month" and "to cease." Today, *menopause* is simply defined as the cessation of menstruation. This is a straightforward medical definition, making no reference to the physiological changes that occur in all women or to the many psychological changes that occur in some women.

Menopause generally occurs during the late forties or early fifties, though some women have been known to experience it as early as the mid-thirties. The period from the beginning of irregular menses to their total cessation (menopause) is called the *climacteric*. The female climacteric may last only a few months or may extend over several years. During the climacteric stage, ovulation, menstruation, and reproductive capacity gradually cease.

The physiological changes that accompany menopause are as follows: After 30 to 40 years of menstrual cycles, a woman has released almost all her ova (eggs). Although the male continues to produce new sperm throughout adulthood, the human female is born with a fixed number of ovarian follicles (immature ova and their cases). The number of follicles present at birth is estimated to be 1 or 2 million. By the time puberty is reached, though, the number has diminished to about 300,000. Of this number, only 300 to 500 will mature. The rest will deteriorate. By age 45, a woman's supply of follicles is nearly depleted, and only a few remain (Tyler and Woodall, 1982). As the number of follicles decreases, there is an accompanying decline in the production of the female sex hormone estrogen. One result of this is that menstrual periods become irregular and often unpredictable. When estrogen production continues to lessen, the climacteric culminates in the complete cessation of cyclic ovarian activity—the menopause. Because of the rapid decrease in the secretion of the hormones estrogen and *progesterone* (a female sex hormone produced by the ovaries), the mammary glands atrophy, as do the uterus and vagina, in varying degrees.

In addition to these symptoms, menopausal women often have other worries caused by the normal stresses of middle adulthood. These may be anxieties about children as they enter into the adult world, financial worries, general concerns about growing old, and doubts regarding the attainment or nonattainment of life goals. Those women who do not have children or have chosen singlehood as a lifestyle may regard middle adulthood as the final chapter in their lives that, now, cannot be rewritten. This important physiological event contains many psychological elements (Millette and Hawkins, 1983).

The concept of hormones as being part of the cause-and-effect relationship is supported by some researchers, who state that menopausal symptoms can be reduced by taking estrogen. Some women use hormone replacement therapy to eliminate such physiological symptoms as hot flashes, hair loss, atrophy of the breasts and vagina, and loss of skin elasticity. However, while alleviating the symptoms, such treatment also prolongs their duration. Estrogen replacement therapy also has been known to produce undesirable side effects. For example, the long-term use of high doses of estrogen has been associated with uterine cancer. A recent study also indicates that the risk for breast cancer increases if either estrogen or estrogen-progestin-replacement therapy are used for six years, and the risk is greater if the two drugs are used in combination. After nine years the risk is still greater (Bergkvist et al., 1989). Other negative side effects sometimes associated with estrogen are high blood pressure, vaginal infections, and breast discomfort.

On the other hand, natural menopause has an unfavorable effect on lipid (fat) metabolism which may increase the risk of heart attack. Hormone replacement therapy may decrease this risk (Matthews et al., 1989). Because of such problems, many physicians are less than enthusiastic about prescribing it without careful consideration. Usually the decision to begin estrogen replacement therapy is based on the severity of the symptoms. Each woman needs to be evaluated individually, and even then, the lowest possible dose is usually given for the shortest period of time (Dan and Bernhard, 1989; Gastel and Hecht, 1980; Donohugh, 1981; Schultz, 1980).

Estrogen production does not stop after menopause, a commonly held misconception. Rather, it continues to be produced, but in areas other than the ovaries. The adrenal glands, the fatty tissue in the body, and the brain all begin to increase their levels of estrogen production. However, even though they produce some estrogen, it is not enough to continue the ovulatory cycle (Millette and Hawkins, 1983).

We indicated at the outset that women's reactions to menopause are multiple and diverse. However, it is possible to isolate two general periods when women experience the psychological effects of long-term hormonal changes. One occurs during the climacteric, and the other occurs upon reaching menopause.

During the climacteric, a woman must readjust her life from one that has been physiologically stimulated by the production of estrogen and progesterone to one that is devoid of these feminizing hormones. The loss of these hormones may cause such symptoms as hot flashes (moments of feeling warm and uncomfortable, often accompanied by perspiration); irritability, insomnia, frequent mood changes, and even depression; fatigue and anxiety; and, often, sensations of dyspnea (labored or difficult breathing). It has been estimated that between 50 and 85 percent of all women experience some of these symptoms. It is not known, however, whether these conditions result solely from hormonal changes or are, in part, a reflection of societal beliefs like those regarding menstrual mood swings (Dan and Bernhard, 1989; Millette, 1982; Uphold and Susman, 1981; Gray, 1981; Frey, 1981; Heilman, 1980; Guyton, 1981; Moore, 1984).

In addition to the physiological and psychological symptoms occurring during the climacteric, a woman's overall attitude toward what the climacteric and menopause mean to her must be considered. Many American women consider menopause to be a depressing and unpleasant experience, whereas others actually feel relief when menstruation is over. A meaningful support system that can offer understanding and sensitivity is considered helpful as such issues and others are raised. In addition, Brenda Millette and Joellen Hawkins (1983) feel that a woman's adjustment to menopause depends, in part, on the experiences of her mother, her peers, and other significant women in her life. Women also need factual data and not old wives' tales about menopause. Women should know what to expect regarding this important and normal developmental event, to realize that menopause is a milestone, not a millstone.

Misconceptions About Menopause

Menopause should be regarded as a normal developmental event in a woman's life. The notion that there is something "wrong" with menopause is the primary reason for the many myths and old wives' tales that surround it. Unfortunately, these myths are perpetuated by a lack of investigation and free discussion. As a result, they influence the thinking of both females and males and both young and old. The following are among the more popular myths.

Menopause is medically defined as a disease. Although this once was the case, it is no longer true. Doctors and the general public once regarded menopause as an illness and a condition requiring medical treatment. Today menopause is regarded as a deficiency syndrome, in that a woman's estrogen secretion has diminished. Some degenerative changes usually occur, which may or may not require medical attention.

After menopause women need full replacement of the hormone estrogen. As we've already indicated, even though the ovaries stop manufacturing estrogen, some is still produced in other body locations. There is still no clear-cut answer, however, as to whether a woman's estrogen deficiency needs to be corrected. We've covered some of the pros and cons associated with estrogen replacement therapy, and the pendulum swings back and forth regarding its use for everyone.

A natural part of menopause is depression and mental instability. There is little proof linking any psychiatric illness to menopause. At best, some of the symptoms attributed to menopause, such as anxiety, are in actuality spin-offs of other stresses that emerge during middle adulthood and may be only indirectly related to menopause.

All women suffer from severe and incapacitating hot flashes. There is a wide range in the percentages associated with the various symptoms of menopause. It is estimated by one source (Sarrel and Sarrel, 1984) that half to three-quarters of all menopausal women experience hot flashes or flushes. Other estimated percentages are lower. Most agree, though, that the percentage of those having severe and incapacitating flashes is small. Most are mild or moderate and do not disrupt normal activity.

A woman who has had a hysterectomy will not experience natural menopause during middle adulthood. This depends on the extent of the surgery. Should a partial hysterectomy be performed, only the uterus will be removed. A total **hysterectomy** means that the uterus and the cervix, and sometimes the ovaries, are removed. If a woman has either one or both ovaries remaining following the operation, she will experience a natural menopause as the ovarian cycle winds down.

Menopause signals the end of a woman's sexual desires. The reality is that many women find themselves enjoying sex more, particularly because they're no longer worried about birth control and pregnancy. A majority of women report that they feel no different about themselves sexually. Let us acknowledge, though, that there are some who do report a decrease in sexual desire. Whether or not this decrease is because of psychological or physiological (decrease in estrogen and androgen) factors is unknown.

One's activity level is lower after menopause. For most, the reverse is often the case. Postmenopausal women are usually peppier, healthier, and in better spirits than before the change of life. Many report being "freed" from the mood swings characterizing the menstrual cycle, as well as the previously mentioned worries concerning birth control and pregnancy.

Men are not affected by a woman's menopause. Men do care and are affected. A major problem is that there has been limited research on them and their feelings. What we do know is that many men know little about this developmental event and need to have the woman communicate her feelings and needs. This way, a more supportive and positive atmosphere can be created.

(Adapted from Skalka, 1984; Millette and Hawkins, 1983)

■ Mental Development

☐ Intellectual Variations at Midlife

In Chapter 9, we stated that, for the most part, intelligence remains fairly constant throughout adult life. Although tasks requiring visuomotor flexibility may pose some problems, few young adults are concerned with this issue. However, for many older adults, either approaching middle age or already there, it becomes something to think about. The fact that there might be a decline in memory with age may also arouse some anxiety.

Intelligence (whether in the middle-aged individual, the young adult, or the child) is difficult not only to measure but even to define. Historically, the IQ test was designed to predict academic achievement, which it does rather well—especially for those who are very like the white middle-class children on whom the test was standardized. Intelligence tests for adults, however, pose certain problems. If the principal purpose of the IQ test is to predict academic achievement, the test will lose value when applied to grown-ups, as it may not be a true indicator of adult intelligence. This fact should be kept in mind when declines in test scores appear. As Jack Botwinick (1984) asserted, there are just no data telling what test decline means in the daily routines of adult life.

What research has been conducted on the mental abilities of the middle-aged population? Some investigators have inferred that there are significant changes in the brain during the aging process. However, there is virtually no evidence that any physiological change occurs in the brain during middle adulthood. As already indicated,

Intelligence remains fairly constant throughout adult life.

electroencephalograms indicate that some people's brains may not even reach their full development until age 30.

However, it is known that reaction times decrease with age. This, of course, will affect intelligence test scores if the speed of responding is a factor in assessment. Younger subjects consistently score higher than older subjects do on tests requiring psychomotor dexterity. In most instances, though, the slowing of reaction time among middle-aged adults is slight. Donald Donohugh (1981) remarked that such slowing is significant only for athletes or others in highly competitive activities involving split-second decisions. But it doesn't affect the lives of most middle-aged adults.

The middle-aged person may also be slower to understand and solve a problem. This is not due to intellectual inferiority but, rather, to such variables as anxiety, caution, and deliberation. Having a wider range of life experiences, the older adult will also be more likely to recognize more variables in a given situation and thus take more time to decide on a solution (Labouvie-Vief and Hakin-Larson, 1989; Willis, 1989; Botwinick, 1984).

Drawing on life experiences and learned abilities is referred to as *crystallized intelligence.* Crystallized intelligence differs from *fluid intelligence,* which is defined as mental functioning based on the organization or reorganization of the information to be used to solve the problem. In general, it is maintained that although fluid intelligence decreases with age, crystallized intelligence increases over time. To problem-solving situations, such as those employed in standardized intelligence tests, young adults typically offer higher levels of fluid intelligence and confine themselves to the problem at hand. But for the same problems, older subjects employ higher degrees of crystallized intelligence and may deliberate longer before responding. Thus, in a psychometric sense, speeded tests are unfair and inappropriate when testing older subjects (McKenzie, 1980; Horn, 1982; Botwinick, 1984).

Consequently, although some decline in speed of response can be measured on standardized tests, this in no way implies that intellectual capacities have diminished. In fact, most researchers believe that people reach the height of their intellectual endowment during middle adulthood. Aside from psychomotor responses and the limitations imposed by timed tests, there is little or no decrement of intellectual performance requiring the use of information and the skills one has already achieved (Schaie, 1983; Siegler, 1980).

There are other variables in intellectual growth. On the average, higher IQ scores are achieved by those adults who are higher in social class, who have more education, who are healthy, and, of course, who had higher IQ scores as children. A stimulating environment is also important to maintaining intellectual functioning (Botwinick, 1984; Schaie, 1984).

In regard to sex differences, females tend to score higher than males do in such areas as word fluency, verbal meaning, and reasoning. Males, on the other hand, perform better in the areas of numbers and space. These are trends that began in childhood and will persist throughout adult life (Benbow and Stanley, 1980; Springer and Deutsch, 1985).

☐ Short-Term and Long-Term Memory

At one time, researchers believed that the aging process was accompanied by a deterioration of memory abilities. For people in midlife, it was proposed that the short-term memory bank was especially susceptible to decay. The *short-term memory* storage system is quite temporary and is affected considerably by distraction and interruption. The *long-term memory* bank, responsible for retaining information for relatively long periods of time, was believed to be more resistant to the aging process.

More recent research indicates that although changes are possible in memory abilities, notably short-term storage, such changes are simply not true for all. Generalizations fail to take into account individual cognitive capacities. Throughout this book we have tried to stress the uniqueness of each person's experience of aging. Although there are general developmental patterns, growing old follows no exact, predictable timetable. This holds true for intellectual functioning, physical aging, socialization, and personality development, to name but a few areas. Thus, though some middle-aged individuals *may* experience changes in the short-term memory bank, this does not hold true for all.

If there are short-term memory changes, consider some of the frustrations one is likely to encounter. Failing to remember an item on a shopping list or the name of a person just recently introduced, or not being able to remember where the car keys have

Strategies to Improve Memory Abilities

Memory loss situations come in all shapes and sizes: a forgotten item on a grocery list, a name that should go along with a face, or a misplaced set of car keys. But contrary to the thoughts of many, adults of all ages can improve their memory skills. What is needed is a commitment to sharpen this mental ability and perhaps a shift away from old habits. The following suggestions are often recommended to sharpen memory abilities.

Do Not Give Yourself the Chance to Forget. Do things as you think of them, rather than put off or procrastinate on the tasks at hand. You might also want to jot ideas down when you think of them. Along these lines, make use of such aids as calendars, appointment books, and notepads whenever possible.

Strive for Mental Organization. One prominent explanation of why adults have memory problems is that they do not organize the information they want to remember. For example, instead of trying to remember ten grocery items at random, place the list into a meaningful organization. Try grouping or clustering the vegetables and fruits together, then the paper products, followed by items from the dairy counter.

Use Practice and Reinforcement. Adults of all ages need to get into the practice of remembering. Memory is a mental skill that needs to be cultivated, and its repeated use can make all the difference. Look for activities to exercise memory skills and get into the habit of reinforcing yourself for information that can be successfully recalled.

Use Imagery. Imagery refers to the creation of mental images or pictures. The creation of such images often helps persons to remember the desired information

and, sometimes, the more bizarre the image, the better the recall. For instance, if you need to go to the grocery store for eggplant and ice cream and then need to stop at the shoe repair shop, you might create an image of a large purple eggplant bulging out of a sugar cone that is stuck in your shoe.

Devise Prompts to Help You Remember. Prompts are "hints" that can be either physical or mental. For instance, if you have trouble remembering someone's name, try to recall where you met the person. Did you meet him or her at a party, work, or in the neighborhood? Often, providing a context will trigger your memory for the name. A prompt can be more tangible, too. For instance, if you are going to a family reunion and have not seen relatives for years, do some homework before you go. Look at old photographs (perhaps with another family member) and familiarize yourself with names and faces.

Avoid Fatigue. Similar to other forms of learning, fatigue is an enemy of memory. Memory skills quickly evaporate when one is overworked and tired. Always begin memorization tasks when you are fully rested and at your best.

Exercise. Here is a good example of how the physical sphere affects the cognitive domain. Regular exercise can improve your memory, as well as other mental operations. Similar to good nutrition, exercise improves the functioning of the cardiovascular system, thus enabling more oxygen and blood to reach the brain. Additionally, exercise helps to alleviate depression, often a cause of memory difficulties.

(Averyt, 1987)

been left are examples of memory lapses associated with the short-term storage system.

Some adults may view such forgetfulness only with irritation, as events that happened long ago do not seem as susceptible to such erosion. Paradoxically, one might recall in greater detail an event that happened ten years ago than one that transpired only ten minutes ago. Even Plato, the Greek philosopher, noticed this: "I am not sure that I could remember all of the discourses of yesterday, but I would be very much surprised if I forgot any of the things which I learned long ago."

What causes memory changes to take place? Exact answers are somewhat elusive, although some explanations have been offered. Problems such as divided attention appear to contribute to difficulties. Attention is critical in order for correct information to be stored. Interference and distractions also account for the decline in short-term memory abilities. The strength of the original learning, the relevance of the material to be remembered, and the desire to retain incoming information are also important to overall retention abilities.

It is important to stress that even though some middle-aged people experience memory changes, measures can be taken to help individuals improve this mental capacity. Interestingly, such measures are applicable to young and old alike. For example, such techniques as giving adults instructions regarding organizational skills and attending skills and providing meaningful processing techniques have been shown to be helpful (Botwinick, 1984).

UNIT REVIEW

- Physical aging is both external and internal.

- Of the sensory changes at this time, vision and hearing are the most apparent.

- Cardiovascular disease and cancer are the leading causes of death during middle adulthood.

- Menopause, the cessation of menstruation, is a normal developmental event in a woman's life. Menopause has both physiological and psychological implications.

- Although reaction times lower at this time, the effect is negligible. Fluid intelligence decreases with age, whereas crystallized intelligence increases.

- Short-term memory may decrease, but individual variations must be taken into account.

■ Unit Two:

PERSONALITY AND SOCIAL DEVELOPMENT

Even though middle adulthood is the longest stage of the life cycle, it is not the most widely researched. In fact, it has only been in recent years that researchers have concentrated their efforts on and sought to understand better this life stage. The result of their labor is that we are dispelling many myths about middle adulthood, getting a clearer picture of the developmental forces in operation at midlife, and a clearer idea of how these forces interact and affect the whole person (see, for example, Haan, 1989; Maas, 1989; Chiriboga, 1989; Hunter and Sundel, 1989).

The study of personality during middle adulthood provides an excellent illustration of how developmental processes blend together (Wrightsman, 1988). For example, how people react to the physical changes at midlife, including the perceived attractions or unattractiveness of the aging process, as well as the treatment accorded by others, usually affects how middle-aged persons perceive themselves. Note the connection here among physical, personality, and social forces. Likewise, career triumphs and reactions to failures have important implications for personality stability, social relationships, and the body's stress levels. Clearly, developmental forces work together.

With this understanding in mind, how might we best describe personality development at midlife? Is the adult personality a continuation of that of previous stages, or is this a period of change? We think that it's a bit of both. This unit will show that some personality features continue and remain unaltered throughout adult life and that other facets of the personality change in accordance with new experiences and challenges at midlife. Many people report changes in their outlook on life after undergoing such events as the empty-nest syndrome, a midlife career switch, or grandparenthood.

Middle adulthood brings new developmental challenges, including those related to personality and social functioning.

Affecting whatever personality dynamics exist during middle adulthood is the realization that one has reached an in-between stage of life, the middle of one's existence. One can look back and ahead, perhaps more so than at any other age. For many, examining the past and anticipating the future often lead to an assessment of one's life: Where have I been, where am I now, and where do I want to go? Answering these questions, as we shall soon see, has important implications for personality growth.

■ The Midlife Transition

Some prefer to view the middle years as a chaotic and often crisis-oriented period filled with numerous conflicts. They emphasize the many changes that take place at this time, such as the permanent departure of children from the home, vocational adjustments, and necessity of coping with the physiological and psychological consequences of aging. To be sure, as in previous stages of life, there are certain developmental tasks (see box). Proponents of this interpretation of middle age, though, emphasize the disruption of such challenges.

Developmental Tasks of Middle Adulthood

1. Helping teenaged children to become responsible and happy adults.

2. Achieving adult social and civic responsibility.

3. Reaching and maintaining satisfactory performance in one's occupation.

4. Developing adult leisure-time activities.

5. Relating oneself to one's spouse as a person.

6. Accepting and adjusting to the physiological changes of middle age.

7. Adjusting to aging parents.

(Havighurst, 1972, 1980)

Others regard middle adulthood as just another stage of life, with its equal and expected share of developmental challenges and responsibilities. These tasks are no more complex or intense than are those at any other age. In fact, some go so far as to label middle adulthood a euphoric stage of life. The emphasis is on one's financial stability and one's freedom from the responsibilities of parenthood.

Thus, depending on the person consulted, one is likely to read about either the negative or the positive qualities of midlife. One is also likely to find some reference to the "inevitability" of a midlife "crisis" and the profound impact it has. According to some, heavy is the heart, and overworked is the mind that is struggling with the midlife crisis and the problems of this age.

Personally, we take exception to such portrayals of the midlife crisis. To begin with, it is not inevitable: There are many adults who go through life without any such experiences. Also, we think that the word *crisis* has a negative and disruptive ring to it. Our objection is that many midlife challenges and personal assessments are positive, productive, and rewarding. Although there are some serious moments, it is not a time characterized by continual conflict (Hunter and Sundel, 1989; Nicholson, 1980).

Because of this, we much prefer to label this time of life as *midlife transition,* not a crisis. It is a time when new dimensions are added to one's family life, career, intimate

There are many diverse reactions to the midlife transition.

relationships, community, and inner life. The midlife transition is characterized by a change in the way individuals see themselves and others around them. As persons move toward these new dimensions and perceptions, they may encounter uncertainty or strangeness. However, this is only natural as one moves from one stable state to another (Schlossberg, 1981, 1989; Golan, 1981).

During this transition, people often take stock of themselves, conducting a sort of psychological inventory of their abilities, accomplishments, and shortcomings. For some, this may be anxiety producing and even painful. There are some who just cannot bear to look at their inadequacies or shortcomings. As a result, they rob themselves of more growth and self-understanding. In its most productive form, the midlife transition enables individuals to examine their total selves, discovering strengths as well as weaknesses.

In so doing, many find that what they have yet to do in life is easier than what they have done so far. But they discover that instead of competing and clashing with the outside world, their tasks now lie *within.* The need to resolve these psychological tasks leads to intense introspection because midlife brings the realization that the future is not forever (Donohugh, 1981).

The midlife transition acquires negative dimensions when anxiety, depression, and a sense of futility enter into the picture. Some choose to become preoccupied with signs of aging and premature doom. (Incidentally, it is very normal at this age to read the obituary column with regularity.) Others dwell on the negative side of their lives and regard themselves as failures. Some report gloom and despair as they recall youthful dreams and current accomplishments and the gap between the two.

This last point is an important one, as the successful resolution of the issues raised depends on one's ability to reassess and readjust. The optimism and dreams of early adulthood need to be put into perspective by the realities of midlife. It is possible that certain goals in life will not be met, and this requires acceptance and adaptation. This may be a painful procedure for many, but it is important to renounce some dreams and to decide what is possible and available. This type of reassessment may well lead to greater self-fulfillment in later adult life (Levinson, 1980; Gould, 1980).

☐ Sex Differences in the Midlife Transition

Although the points made thus far can apply to both men and women, there are sex differences in the midlife transition. These differences are especially apparent in regard to family roles. Consider the situation of the male. Traditionally, his transition places more emphasis on career assessment than on family issues. But this does not mean that his family isn't important. It just means that in our competitive society, "making it" in the career world is a critical issue for males.

For many women, even among those working outside the home, the family is often the central issue. Therefore, a woman's midlife transition revolves around her husband, the growing independence of her children, and, ultimately, their departure from the home. When her children do leave, she may no longer feel needed. A part of her life may lose its meaning. Also, traditionally a woman spends years standing by her husband's side, offering support as he gropes for his occupational niche in the world. Of course, there are variations on these patterns, particularly if the mother works outside the home.

But if these traditional family patterns hold, women will define their life cycle in terms of their children's and husband's ages or, better yet, family stages. Whereas midlife for men may mean taking on new career challenges, such as becoming a mentor for younger workers, for women it may herald the empty-nest stage and a time to tend to personal needs. If women launch a new career or educational plans, they may encounter some of the tasks, challenges, and problems faced by their husbands when they were younger (Notman, 1980).

The female midlife transition is different, too, in regard to how a woman views the aging process. Accepting her changing physical self is an important part of her overall psychological adjustment. Often, though, there is a double standard attached to growing old that frequently places women on the losing end. For example, the same aging processes for men and women are often perceived differently: Older men get silver hair, women turn gray. Men grow more distinguished looking with age; women just grow old. Character lines crease men's faces; women have a collection of wrinkles. Unfortunately, many segments of society do not allow women to grow old gracefully.

Why is this so? Perhaps the biggest reason is that too much of what is valued about women is connected to their physical appearance. On the other hand, men at midlife appear to be perceived and measured more by what they've accomplished in life than by how they appear to others. Therefore, the physical signs of aging are often perceived as part of the male's achievement of success. We think that such perceptions will change, though, especially because of the greater sexual equality in the home, work force, and society in general. This will be as true for reactions to the aging process as it will be for women's role expectations in all facets of life.

Gail Sheehy (1976, 1981) suggested that women enter the midlife transition earlier than men do, approximately at age 35. Many women also experience a degree of urgency at this time, perhaps because this age brings with it the possibility of turmoil and instability. Some women experience a sense of "deadline" and urgency because of the life trends that are known to occur at age 35. Consider the following:

1. Thirty-five is when the average mother sends her last child off to school.

2. Thirty-five begins the dangerous age of infidelity.

3. Thirty-five is when the average married American woman reenters the working world.

4. Thirty-five is the average age at which the divorced woman remarries.

5. Thirty-five is the most common age for runaway wives.

6. Thirty-five brings closer the biological end of childbearing.

When these factors converge, many women begin to feel the need to change to a midlife perspective. However, whether the woman acts on her life assessment at this age and what part her husband plays in this psychological process are separate issues.

Interestingly, Sheehy found that once these issues were reckoned with, later middle life became more satisfying and rewarding. For both women and men in their fifties, their roles usually become more relaxed, and they have greater freedom to say what they think. In addition, there are greater opportunities for companionship with their spouse and more time and money for themselves. Sheehy also observed that with age, women often become more assertive and men more expressive (Sheehy, 1981).

■ Theories of Personality Development

As we've indicated thus far, middle adulthood is a time when new perceptions of the self and the environment emerge. For many, this becomes a time for reflective introspection, an age for turning inward and assessing the self. Helping us understand the changes at this time are four theories regarding the personality dynamics of midlife, developed by Erik Erikson (1963, 1982), Robert Peck (1968), Daniel Levinson (1978, 1980), and Roger Gould (1978, 1980).

☐ Erik Erikson's Theory

Erik Erikson considers the essence of personality development during middle adulthood to be the resolution of the psychosocial crisis known as *generativity versus stagnation.* For many, this is a time of productive work and caring. Much attention is directed toward one's children and their well-being and happiness. Children need and depend on their parents, but Erikson emphasized that this is a reciprocal arrangement. Parents, too, depend on their children. Children add a dimension to life that is beyond description. For many, it is hard to find the words to share the joy and happiness a parent feels as he or she watches a son or daughter grow from infancy to maturity.

By generativity, Erikson means that one seeks to attain a sense of sharing, giving, or productivity. Caring about the well-being of future generations and the world in which they will live embodies the concept of generativity. So, too, does using one's abilities, penchants, and talents. The fully functioning person seeks to channel his or her efforts into the most productive means possible to reap satisfaction. Life fulfillment may well be measured by knowing one has contributed to the growth and betterment of others through personal, social, and vocational commitments.

The force countering generativity is stagnation, which may take the form of self-absorption, egocentrism, or self-indulgence. Compared with the people-oriented quality of generativity, stagnation implies caring exclusively about oneself. Erikson labeled this type of attitude as personal impoverishment. A sense of emptiness characterizes the person's life, and abilities are not used to their fullest. The chronic complainer, critic, or grumbler may epitomize the life of stagnation. Life is dull and dreary, and many individuals feel trapped or confined in their life situations. Typically, whatever gains are made in life are measured in terms of personal relevancy, reinforcing the concept of egocentrism.

□ Robert Peck's Theory

Robert Peck added an interesting dimension to Erikson's work. Believing that Erikson placed too much emphasis on the psychosocial crises of childhood and adolescence and not enough on the last 40 or 50 years of life, Peck suggested that it might be useful to divide middle age into phases of psychological adjustment. Four such adjustments are *valuing wisdom versus valuing physical powers, socializing versus sexualizing in human relationships, cathectic flexibility versus cathectic impoverishment,* and *mental flexibility versus mental rigidity.*

VALUING WISDOM VERSUS VALUING PHYSICAL POWERS After the late twenties, one of the inescapable consequences of aging is a decrease in physical strength, stamina, and attractiveness (if "attractive" is defined as "young looking"). Yet, the experience acquired through living longer may enable the middle-aged adult to accomplish considerably more than a younger counterpart can. The term *wisdom* sums up this increment in judgmental powers that living longer brings. Wisdom is not the same as intellectual capacity. It is perhaps best defined as the ability to make the most effective choices among the alternatives that intellectual perception and imagination present for one's decision. Such choice making is affected by several factors, including emotional stability, unconflicted or conflicted motivation set, and mental ability. Individuals who age most successfully are those who "invert" their previous hierarchy of values, giving mental ability a higher position than physical prowess as their standard for self-evaluation and primary means of problem solving.

SOCIALIZING VERSUS SEXUALIZING IN HUMAN RELATIONSHIPS Sexual adjustment focuses on the sexual climacteric, which coincides with general physical decline but is partially separate from it. The climacteric may motivate men and women to value each other as individuals rather than primarily as sex objects. The sexual element may become less significant as interpersonal living takes on new dimensions of empathy, understanding, and emotional compassion.

CATHECTIC FLEXIBILITY VERSUS CATHECTIC IMPOVERISHMENT Psychological development in this sense means the ability to be emotionally flexible—to be able to shift emotional investments from one person or activity to another. Emotional flexibility is crucial in middle age because of psychologically critical developments such as the loss of parents, the departure of children from the home, and the death of friends and relatives of similar age. Unfortunately, some people experience an increasingly impoverished emotional life because, as their cathexis objects disappear, they are unable to reinvest their emotions in other people or pursuits. Adapting positively by finding new objects of emotional focus is required to overcome this crisis.

☐ Daniel Levinson's Theory

Daniel Levinson suggested that a period of time called the *Midlife Transition* provides a bridge from early to middle adulthood. This stage, occurring approximately between the ages of 40 and 45, brings a new set of developmental tasks. In particular, it is a time for a man to assess his success or failure in meeting the goals he established for himself in the previous stage, *Becoming One's Own Man*. Success is typically measured by whether a man feels as though he has been affirmed in his personal, social, and occupational world. Life satisfaction comes after assessing all aspects of one's life and feeling comfortable with what is found.

In his research, Levinson discovered that some individuals do very limited searching or questioning during the Midlife Transition. Apparently these individuals are untroubled by questions concerning the value, direction, and meaning of their lives. Others realize that the character of their lives is changing, but this recognition is not painful. The majority of men in Levinson's study, however, find this stage to be a period of significant struggle within the self and with the external world. As such, the Midlife Transition is a crisis period. Some men question nearly every aspect of their lives and feel as though they cannot proceed in life as they once had. They feel they need more time to form a new life path or to modify the existing one.

Three developmental tasks need to be dealt with during middle adulthood. The first is to reappraise the past. A review of the past goes on in the shadow of the future, but as Levinson noted, many individuals suffer from the doubt that they can be joined. The need to reconsider the past develops in part from a heightened awareness of one's own mortality and a desire to use the remaining time wisely. Assessing the past also helps reduce illusions, which are hopes, dreams, assumptions, and beliefs about the self and world that are not true. A process labeled by Levinson as *de-illusionment*, the end result of such an appraisal enables the person to attain a more realistic and practical sense of mortality.

The second task of middle adulthood is to take steps toward initiating this new period of life. Although the person is not yet ready to start constructing such a new life

Middle adulthood often heralds new perceptions of the self and one's surroundings.

structure, he must make choices that will modify the negative elements of his existing structure and provide the central elements for a new one. As a commitment to these choices is made and the individual embarks on a new plan of existence, the Midlife Transition draws to a close, and a new stage in adult life, *Entering Middle Adulthood,* begins. Entering Middle Adulthood occurs between the ages of 45 and 50.

Although the changes made at this time will be highly individualized, they can be characterized as *external* or *internal.* External changes may be drastic, such as a divorce or a major shift in occupation, or subtle, such as modification in the character of one's work. Internal changes may include changes in one's social outlook, personal values, or inner convictions. Inner changes may be highly conscious and openly expressed, or subtle and hidden.

The third task of middle adulthood is to experience what Levinson called *individuation.* Individuation refers to a person's relationship to himself and to the external world. Specifically, the goal of individuation at this time is to deal with the polarities that sometimes become sources of deep division in a person's life. Levinson suggested that adults must confront and integrate those tendencies or states that are usually experienced as opposites, almost as if the person must be one or the other and cannot be both. However, such paired tendencies are not mutually exclusive, and both sides coexist within virtually everyone. As time wanes during middle adulthood, such inner divisions ideally should be overcome, and these polarities should be integrated into one's life structure.

Let us consider some of the specific polarities that Levinson proposed. The *young/ old* polarity means that a person feels young in many respects yet also has a sense of growing old. Middle-aged men alternately feel young, and "in between." The developmental task is to come to grips with this condition of "in between" young and old.

Another polarity is that of *destruction/creation.* On the one hand, people experience more fully their own sense of mortality and the impending death of others. They also become more aware of the ways in which they have hurt parents, lovers, spouse, children, and friends. At the same time, they have a strong desire to be creative and to produce creations that are valuable to themselves and to others and to participate in collective enterprises that advance human welfare (a strong parallel to Erikson's concept of generativity). The task here is to come to know that powerful forces of destructiveness and creativity coexist in the human soul and one must integrate them in new ways.

A third polarity is that of *masculine/feminine.* This task requires the person to integrate qualitatively masculine and feminine roles rather than splitting the two. Extreme polarization, as taught by social upbringing, requires a man to devote himself to his occupation, frequently in a highly impersonal way. He is also taught to express a narrow range of feelings, usually those related to assertiveness, task attainment, and rivalry. His past gender orientation typically forbids him to experience feelings that involve dependency, intimacy, grief, sensitivity, and vulnerability. In middle adulthood, an important yardstick for growth is being more accepting of the so-called feminine qualities and allowing them to surface and become an integral part of the self. Put another way, the developmental task here is to come to terms in new ways with the basic meanings of masculinity and femininity.

The final polarity described by Levinson is *attachment/separateness.* The issue with this polarity is that if we become too attached to the environment, we will endanger our capacity for self-renewal, growth, and creative effort. If adults become too separate, their contact with the world will be lost and their capacity for survival will be jeopardized. A balance between attachment and separateness must be found, although it will likely change from one era of the life cycle to the next. The task thus becomes one of finding a balance between the needs of the self and the needs of society.

The process of individuation encompasses all developmental transitions, including what Levinson labeled the *Age 50 Transition*. Typically, adults can work further on the tasks described as well as the life structure formed in the mid-forties. Levinson reported that the Age 50 Transition may have its share of stresses and turmoils for those who changed too little in the Midlife Transition and hence constructed an unsatisfactory life structure.

Between 55 and 60, adults reach a stage referred to as Building a Second Middle Adult Structure. This stage provides a vehicle for completing middle adulthood. For those who were able to rejuvenate themselves and enrich their lives, the decade of the fifties can be a period of great fulfillment. In overall scope, this stage is analogous to the Settling Down Period of young adulthood. Progress in one's overall aspirations will bring its share of affirmation and rewards but also the responsibilities that accompany greater attainments in adult life.

☐ Roger Gould's Theory

Roger Gould designated ages 35 to 45 as the Midlife Decade of adult life. During one's early thirties, there is a tendency to act tentatively in regard to making life changes. Uncertainty is frequently expressed when inner dissatisfaction or restlessness surfaces. The Midlife Decade is when adults should act on their new visions of themselves and the world. The stability and continuity characterizing earlier years is now being replaced with a relentless inner demand for action. Quite simply, the sense of timelessness during the thirties gives way to an awareness of the pressure of time of the forties. Gould maintained that perceptions of life change and that the adult feels whatever is to be done must be done at this point.

Consistent with earlier discussions of Gould's theory, growth during adulthood is in part measured by one's ability to overcome irrational notions that restrict the emergence of mature, adult consciousness. Gould proposed five irrational assumptions characteristic of the Midlife Decade.

The first is the illusion that *safety can last forever.* In one way or another, middle-aged persons lose the vestiges of parental protection. As Gould noted, even if both parents are alive, vigorous, and independent, there will be a role reversal. Gradually, middle-aged adults end up standing in their parents' place. Many middle-aged adults now find themselves in commanding positions at work and feel powerful in the world, whereas their parents may have lost power through retirement or semiretirement.

Also at this time another role realignment takes place as one's children reach a new plateau in their lives. Children nearing adolescence demonstrate signs that they're competent and able to care for their own safety. Limitations of adult control over their safety become apparent. Consequently, parents are not only becoming more peripheral in the lives of middle-aged adults, but children are also becoming less involved in joint family life.

The second false assumption of middle age is that *death cannot happen to me or my loved ones.* The reality of middle age, though, is that the illness or death of a parent and a complex set of signals regarding one's own mortality are part of the life cycle.

Losing one's parents is the realization of a fear that most individuals have carried with them for most of their lives. Many adults have continually denied the possibility of such an event, but when it does happen, the limitation of one's own powers and the limited quantity of time left become a reality. During the period of mourning, which, in its various phases, lasts at least a year, sequences of denial alternate with periods of grief.

When one's parents die, the fear of one's own death often becomes exaggerated. Gould stated that sometimes an intense fear of death triggers an obsessional preoccupation with health. Many adults feel more vulnerable, almost as if their parents were a shield standing between them and death. When parents are gone, individuals may feel as though they are next and that death can strike at any time. Interestingly, if one parent is still alive, it may be reasoned that death is an orderly event and the individual can be protected through someone else. As Gould suggested, this is another invisible childhood protective device that individuals retain well into adulthood to preserve their illusion of safety.

The third false assumption is that *it is impossible to live without a partner in the world.* The fact that one's mortality is acknowledged under the previous assumption frequently traumatizes people for long periods of time. Women, though, realizing their own mortality, feel an increased mandate to act on their own behalf. Whatever fears have interfered with the female's achieving independence up to this point must now be confronted and mastered. Women, more than men, are especially vulnerable to the notion that life cannot go on without some type of protector:

> This assumption derives itself from the archaic version of femininity that has been socially reinforced for almost all women now in their mid-life decade. This outdated version of femininity says a woman can exercise power only indirectly, through a man. Feminism obviously has challenged this confining definition of a woman's options, and today women engaged in acute mid-life struggle enjoy enormous support as they strive to implement a modern definition of femininity: "I can engage my personal powers directly."
>
> (Gould, 1978, p. 246)

Once women shed this "protector myth," they are free to experience a broader range of social contact and expand their own personalities, whether through career, family, or leisure pursuits. In short, once women establish the independence needed at this age, they are free to become whole and authentic personalities.

The fourth false assumption that many adults subscribe to is that *no life or change exists beyond the family.* This notion means that one's family life is compartmentalized and paralyzed, especially if the husband and wife refuse to work on the continual growth and maturity of their lives. Working on improvement, though, is frequently avoided by couples because they fear that dialogue and conflict may endanger the stability of the old marriage structure.

■ The Self-Actualizing Personality

Throughout their adulthood, many people strive to reach a psychological ideal, a harmonious integration of their personality. Attaining self-actualization requires considerable ego strength and the ability to make use of all potentials and capabilities. As we discussed in Chapter 2, self-actualization is at the zenith of a person's striving for humanness and for achieving his or her full potential. Self-actualization is at the pinnacle of a hierarchy of basic needs. The other needs, from fundamental to more complex, are physiological, safety, belongingness, and esteem. In those who reach a self-actualizing state, we can expect to find a highly refined dimension of growth that is characterized by autonomy, individuation, and authenticity. Of course, not everyone reaches self-actualization, and the criteria for self-actualization may vary.

Self-actualization was described by Abraham Maslow, who defined the need for self-actualization as the desire to become more and more what one is, to become everything that one is capable of becoming. He argued that human behavior is motivated by far more than hedonistic pleasure seeking and pain avoidance or mere striving to reduce internal tension. Maslow did acknowledge that many motives are generated by tension in the organism and that higher forms of behavior are possible only after the tension level has been reduced (Maslow, 1954, 1968, 1970).

Maslow suggested that several preconditions must be satisfied before self-actualization can be attained. Individuals must be relatively free of mundane worries, especially those related to survival. They should be comfortable in their vocation and should feel accepted in their social contacts, whether these be family members or associates at work. Furthermore, individuals should genuinely respect themselves.

It may very well be that self-actualization is not attained until the middle years of adulthood. In the years before middle age, energy is frequently dissipated in diverse directions, including sexual relationships, educational advancement, career alignment, marriage, and parenthood. The need to achieve financial stability during those young adult years consumes considerable psychic energy. By middle age, however, many people have managed to fulfill most of these needs and can spare the energy to strive toward ego maturity.

It is important to realize that the examples used to illustrate self-actualizing persons are often unique and special. One need not be a great artist or scientist to be a self-actualizing person. Furthermore, all people have a variety of talents and penchants that can be deemed creative and special in their own way.

Individuals experiencing satisfaction and fulfillment in their daily lives may well be self-actualizing, provided that they are making full use of their abilities. Tinkering with a car, repairing an appliance, building furniture for the home, or simply helping other people are examples of self-actualizing skills as long as personal satisfaction is derived from undertaking such pursuits.

The issue here is that one need not be a Jonas Salk, Pablo Picasso, or Golda Meir to be in a state of self-actualizing. Ordinary people who enjoy their lives to the fullest and utilize the abilities that they were born with are equally likely candidates (McMahon and McMahon, 1982).

In order to study the self-actualizing personality, Maslow selected 48 individuals who appeared to be making full use of their talents and were at the height of humanness. Among his subjects were students and personal acquaintances as well as historical figures. In the final analysis, he described 12 probable, 10 partial, and 26 potential or possible self-actualizers. His analysis of these individuals revealed 15 traits that he felt were characteristic of the self-actualizing personality.

1. *More efficient perception of reality.* Many self-actualizing persons are able to perceive people and events realistically. That is, their own wishes, feelings, or desires do not distort reality. They are objective in their analysis of the environment and are able to detect what is dishonest or false.

2. *Acceptance of self and others.* People with self-actualizing personalities lack such negative characteristics as guilt, shame, doubt, and anxiety—characteristics that sometime interfere with the perception of reality. They are capable of accepting themselves for what they are and recognize their strengths and weaknesses without being guilty or defensive about them.

3. *Spontaneity.* Self-actualizing people are relatively spontaneous in their overt behavior as well as in their inner thoughts and impulses. Maslow discovered that some self-actualizing people develop their own values and do not accept everything just because others do. Though others may accept the status quo, self-actualizers perceive each person, event, or object as it really is and weigh it accordingly.

4. *Problem centering.* Unlike the ego-centered personality, who spends much time in such activities as introspection or self-evaluation, problem-centered individuals direct their energies toward tasks or problems.

5. *Detachment.* Maslow discovered that his subjects needed more solitude than the average person did. Self-actualizers enjoy privacy and do not mind being alone.

6. *Autonomy.* As can be inferred from nearly all the other characteristics of the self-actualizing personality, such people have a certain independence of spirit. Individuals are propelled by growth motivation more than by deficiency motivation and are self-contained personalities.

7. *Continued freshness of appreciation.* Self-actualizing people have the capacity to appreciate continually all of nature and life. There is a naiveté, a pleasure, even an ecstasy in experiences that have become stale in others. Regardless of the source, these occasional ecstatic feelings are very much a part of the self-actualizing personality.

8. *The mystic experience.* Self-actualizers are not religious in the sense of attendance at formal worship, but they do have periodic peaks of experience that Maslow described as limitless horizons opening up to the vision, the feeling of being simultaneously more powerful and also more helpless than one ever was before, the feeling of great ecstasy and wonder and awe, the loss of placing in time and space with, finally, the conviction that something extremely important and valuable has happened, so that the subject is to some extent transformed and strengthened even in daily life by such experiences.

9. *Gemeinschaftsgefühl.* This German word, first coined by Alfred Adler, was used by Maslow to describe the feelings toward humankind that self-actualizing persons experience. This emotion, which might be loosely described as "the love of an older brother," is an expression of affection, sympathy, and identification.

10. *Unique interpersonal relations.* Self-actualizers have fewer "friends" than others do, but they have close relationships with those friends they do have. Outside these friendships, they tend to be kind to and patient with all whom they meet. An exception is the harsh way in which they sometimes speak to hypocritical, pretentious, or pompous people. However, for the most part, what little hostility they exhibit is based not on character but on the situation.

11. *Democratic character structure.* Maslow found that without exception, the self-actualizing people he studied were democratic, being tolerant of others with suitable character, regardless of their social class, race, education, religion, or political beliefs.

12. *Discrimination between means and ends.* Unlike the average person, who may make decisions on expedient grounds, self-actualizing people have a

highly developed ethical sense. Even though they cannot always verbalize their moral positions, their actions frequently take the "higher road." Self-actualizers distinguish means from ends and will not pursue even a highly desirable end by means that are not morally correct.

13. *Philosophical, unhostile sense of humor.* The humor of self-actualizers is not of the ordinary type. As Maslow (1970) described it:

> They do not consider funny what the average man considers to be funny. Thus they do not laugh at hostile humor (making people laugh by hurting someone) or superiority humor (laughing at someone else's inferiority) or authority-rebellion humor (the unfunny, Oedipal, or smutty joke). Characteristically what they consider humor is more closely allied to philosophy than to anything else. It may also be called the humor of the real because it consists in large part in poking fun at human beings in general when they are foolish, or forget their place in the universe, or try to be big when they are actually small. This can take the form of poking fun at themselves, but this is not done in any masochistic or clownlike way. Lincoln's humor can serve as a suitable example. Probably Lincoln never made a joke that hurt anybody else; it is also likely that many or even most of his jokes had something to say, had a function beyond just producing a laugh. They often seemed to be education in a more palatable form, akin to parables or fables. (pp. 169–170)

14. *Creativeness.* Without exception, every self-actualizing person that Maslow studied was creative in some way. This creativity is not to be equated with the genius of a Mozart or an Einstein, as the dynamics of that type of creativity are still not understood. Rather it is what Maslow called "the naive and universal creativeness of unspoiled children." He believes that creativity in this sense is possibly a fundamental characteristic that we all are born with but lose as we become encultured. It is linked to being spontaneous and less inhibited than others, and it expresses itself in everyday activities. Described quite simply, it is a freshness of thought, ideas, and actions.

15. *Resistance to enculturation.* Self-actualizers accept their culture in most ways, but they still, in a profound sense, resist becoming encultured. Many desire social change but are not rebellious in the adolescent sense. Rather, they are generally independent of their culture and manage to tolerate the behavior expected by their society. This, however, must not be construed as a lack of interest in making the changes they believe in. If they feel an important change is possible, their resolution and courage will put them at the forefront of the battle. Maslow believes that the self-actualizers he described are not revolutionaries, but that they very easily could be. He further stated that they are not against fighting for social change; rather, they are against ineffective fighting.

The subjects Maslow studied were, for the most part, highly intelligent and possessed several or even many of the characteristics so far presented. However, this does not mean they were perfect. In fact, Maslow noted a number of human failings associated with self-actualized people. Some can be boring, stubborn, or vain, have thoughtless habits, be wasteful or falsely proud. They may have emotions of guilt, anxiety, or strife and may experience inner conflicts. They are also "occasionally capable of an extraordinary and unexpected ruthlessness." This ruthlessness may be seen when they feel they have been deceived by a friend or if someone has been dishonest with them. They might, with a surgical coldness, cut the person verbally or abruptly sever the relationship.

■ Stress During Adulthood

Developmental theories of personality tend to center on the idea that successful adjustment means mastering tasks, challenges, and stresses that confront individuals at various points in their lives. For example, during young adulthood, the developmental tasks include establishing an intimate relationship with a mate, rearing children, and finding a suitable career.

For many, the stresses and strains of adult life persist into middle and late adulthood. Coping with the departure of children during the empty-nest stage, caring for one's aging parents, or adjusting to the aging experience are but a few of the many potentially stressful life situations. Job-related stress is especially prominent among adults today (French, Caplan, and Van Harrison, 1982; Phillips, 1982; Veninga and Spradley, 1981; Cooper and Marshall, 1980).

Stress is a topic that is actively researched by today's psychologists. A look at the literature reveals a wide assortment of attempts to explore the many stresses of adult life and how individuals are affected by them (Spielberger, Sarason, and Strelau, 1989; Hobfoll, 1988; B. Brown, 1984; Hamberger and Lohr, 1984; Lazarus and Folkman, 1984; Cooper, 1983; Greenberg, 1983; Meichenbaum and Jarembko, 1983).

At the heart of this research is the notion that changes in life are part of everyone's existence and that adjustments have to be made both physically and psychologically. Although certain stresses accompanying life changes are minimal and can be easily handled, others are not so easily managed and could create a crisis. Learning how to avoid crisis situations and taking charge of one's life are important features of the well-adjusted and smoothly functioning personality.

□ What Is Stress?

Stress can be defined as the common, nonspecific response of the body to any demand made upon it, be it psychological or physiological. *Stressors* are external events or conditions that affect the organism's equilibrium. Put another way, stressors are those situations placing the person in a stressful state. Some common stressors include fatigue, fear, disease, physical injury, and emotional conflict. Emotional stress is tension, frustration, conflict, and sometimes anxiety. Day-to-day stressors include domestic tensions, personal tensions, noise, indecision of college and/or career choices, fear of crime, and so forth. Obviously, stressors vary. What is one person's stressor may be viewed with indifference by someone else (Breznitz and Goldberger, 1982; Coyne and Lazarus, 1980; Endler and Edwards, 1982; Pearlin, 1982).

Several stressors may work together at the same time. Some may be big, small, nagging, or acute, and some stressors may remain unidentified. In all, there are five categories of stressors. First, there are *social stressors* such as noise or crowding. Second are *psychological stressors,* including such mental elements as worry and anxiety. *Psychosocial stressors,* such as the loss of a job or the death of a friend, are a third variety. Fourth, *biochemical stressors* include heat, cold, injury, pollutants, toxicants, or poor nutrition. Finally, *philosophical stressors* often create value-system conflicts, lack of purpose, or lack of direction (Curtis and Detert, 1981).

Mark Fried (1982) believes that another type of stressor can be added that reflects life in contemporary society: the *endemic* stressor. *Endemic stressors* are long term and have become so prevalent or so much a part of our lives that we have learned to live with them. Instead of trying to deal with them head on, most of us passively integrate them into our lives. Often, we have a sense of hopelessness toward them. Examples of endemic stressors are inflation or the fear of nuclear war.

Stressors should thus be viewed as conditions producing physical turbulence or some type of reactive change that triggers physical reactions. But both good and bad stressors can interfere with the body's equilibrium. As Jackie Schwartz (1982) pointed out, whether you're fired or promoted, hit with a brick or caressed by a lover, you experience a state of stress. One's body has a similar reaction every time.

Stress, therefore, can have positive and negative dimensions. *Eustress,* or positive stress, occurs when the body's reactive change is put to productive use. For example, athletes often use the anxiety and tension in their bodies before a game as a method of "psyching" themselves for the competition. Some researchers, such as Spencer Rathus and Jeffrey Nevid (1983), suggested that humans function best at moderate levels of stress, or as they labeled it, "healthy" tension. The lack of stress often produces a reaction known as "cabin fever syndrome." Here, there is too little stimulation, variety, and challenge, and people begin to question their value.

Distress, however, is harmful and unpleasant stress. Distress occurs when the body and mind are worn down from repeated exposure to an unpleasant situation. In this respect, stress can affect the body's overall immunity, nervous systm, hormone levels, and metabolic rates. When one's emotional state leads to real physical illnesses, the disease is called *psychosomatic* (*psycho* means "mind," *somatic* means "body"). Such disorders include hypertension, headache, arthritis, rheumatism, peptic ulcers, obesity, backache, skin disorders, impotence, menstrual irregularities, and possibly even some types of heart ailments.

☐ Stress and the General Adaptation Syndrome

Hans Selye (1976, 1980a, 1980b, 1982), a Canadian scientist, coined the phrase *general adaptation syndrome* (GAS) to help explain the physiological changes that occur when a person remains under prolonged physical or emotional stress. There are three stages in the general adaptation syndrome: (1) the alarm reaction, (2) resistance, and (3) exhaustion.

During the first stage, *alarm reaction,* the body's defenses prepare for the stressful situation. Hormones that arouse—for example, epinephrine (adrenaline)—are produced, and the person switches from the parasympathetic nervous system (the system that usually controls the internal organs) to the sympathetic nervous system (the "backup" or "reserve" and emergency system). For short spurts of energy, the backup nervous and hormonal (endocrine) systems are quite efficient.

If, however, one continues to remain under stress, the stage of *resistance* is reached. In this stage, the body continues to produce huge amounts of energy. People may remain in the second stage for hours, days, months, or years. However, while the body is in high metabolic gear during this stage, the wear and tear on the organism can be phenomenal. Selye observed, though, that each of us goes through these two stages regularly with no significant impact on our health and well-being. This is because most stressors are alternately introduced and removed.

The final stage of the general adaptation syndrome is *exhaustion.* Exhaustion occurs as a counterreaction of the nervous system, when the body's functions slow down to abnormal levels. Continued stress during this stage may lead to depression or even death. Whether or not one reaches the stage of exhaustion depends on a number of factors, including the intensity of the stressor and the amount of time spent in

Distress often brings psychological turbulence.

resistance. The exhaustion stage often produces stress-related diseases, the most common being peptic ulcers in the stomach and upper intestine, high blood pressure, heart attacks, and nervous disturbances.

These three stages must be regarded as a cycle of adaptation. If they are repeated too many times, Selye (1982) also cautioned that the human machine runs the risk of wear and tear. Our reserves of adaptation energy can be compared to a bank account from which we can make withdrawals but cannot make deposits. Following exhaustion from stressful activity, sleep can restore resistance and overall adaptation very close to previous levels, but total restoration is probably impossible. Every biological activity produces wear and tear. The activity will leave some irreversible chemical scar, which accumulates to constitute the aging process. In this sense, adaptability should be used wisely and sparingly rather than squandered.

☐ Stress and the Type A Personality

Some individuals are more susceptible to stress than others are. Indeed, there is growing evidence that one person's pleasure is another person's poison. Evidence indicates that some people can be classified as "hot reactors." Their psychological and physical makeup is such that stress disrupts their physical well-being. Other people may react to the same stipulation without physical or psychological harm or with only a brief disruption in their well-being (Wilding, 1984).

Research conducted by Meyer Friedman, Ray Rosenman, and Margaret Chesney (Friedman and Rosenman, 1974; Rosenman and Chesney, 1980, 1982; Chesney and Rosenman, 1980a, 1980b) showed that a stressful personality type known as the *Type A personality* is prone to cardiovascular disease. Individuals with Type A personalities are extremely competitive and impatient and always seem to strive toward accomplishing more than what is feasible. Type A behavior also includes difficulty in controlling anger and aggression, which usually is expressed in the form of fist clenching, facial grimaces and nervous tics, and tensing of the muscles. Type A traits also include hurried speech, no compassion for other Type A persons, and feelings of guilt during periods of relaxation.

Type A behavior is a contrast with that of the *Type B personality,* which is characterized by a generally relaxed attitude toward life, no hostility, and competitiveness only when the situation demands it. Type B personalities have no sense of urgency and do not have free-floating hostility. Unlike Type A personalities, Type B personalities can relax without feeling guilty.

As indicated, there is a significant relationship between Type A behavior and heart disease. Not only are Type A personalities more likely than Type B's are to suffer coronary heart disease, but they also have fatal heart attacks almost twice as frequently. The relationship between Type A behavior and heart disease is reported to be especially significant (Hymes and Nuernberger, 1980). This research illustrates that although cardiovascular disease is caused by many factors, such as obesity and smoking, the role of the stressful personality cannot be overlooked. Type A personalities are found in both males and females. Among women, the most prominent group of Type A personalities are those who have changed their lifestyle to fit executive careers.

The notion that Type A personalities demonstrate more stress and anxiety than do Type B personalities has been an active topic for researchers. Three representative investigations may help show how the behaviors of these two personality types differ. In one, a research team headed by David Holmes (1984) sought to determine whether different levels of challenge had different effects on arousal levels. To test this hypothesis, 30 Type A and 30 Type B male undergraduates worked on an intelligence test task (digits backwards recall) that was classified as easy, moderately difficult, or extremely difficult. Arousal was measured in terms of systolic blood pressure, diastolic blood pressure, pulse rate, pulse volume, skin resistance, and subjective arousal. Results showed that while working on the extremely difficult task, the Type A's showed reliably higher systolic blood pressure than did the Type B's. However, there were no reliable differences between the two groups in systolic blood pressure at other levels of challenge or on other measures of arousal.

In another study, Deens Ortega and Janet Pipal (1984) observed Type A and Type B persons as they engaged in tasks requiring various activities. Then, in another part of the experiment, they assessed the subjects' challenge-seeking tendencies. It was found that Type A's sought greater degrees of challenge than did Type B's. Also, the more active the Type A subjects had been immediately before the challenge-seeking opportunity, the greater was the degree of challenge they sought. On the other hand, earlier activities did not significantly influence challenge seeking in the Type B's. The Type A's also had significantly faster heart rates during their performance of a challenging task. The researchers concluded that Type A behavior may be translated into heart disease through the cumulative deleterious effects of chronic and excessive challenge-induced cardiovascular excitation.

Finally, Michael Strube and his colleagues (1985) investigated psychological well-being among Type A and Type B individuals across the life cycle. They hypothesized that the hard-driving, achievement-oriented lifestyle exhibited by Type A's would be adaptive in younger age groups but would lead to lower well-being in later life because of increased limitations on the range and level of activities. By contrast, the more relaxed, easygoing style of the Type B's would match better the slower pace of old age but would not be as conducive to success in younger age groups. Their subjects, 319 adults (aged 18 to 89) completed a battery of tests, including those that surveyed activity levels and types of life changes. The results confirmed the researcher's hypothesis, but they noted that the psychological differences might have been mediated in part by differences in physical well-being. Experience with life events and the structure and function of social networks might have also contributed to the differences in well-being.

We might add that another personality type has recently been recognized: the Type C personality. *Type C personalities* are individuals who sustain considerable stress but have learned to cope with it. Whether or not they are bothered by cardiovascular illness depends on how effectively they have learned to cope. Many of us are in this category, as nearly all of us have, to a certain degree, some characteristics of the Type A and the Type B personalities (Nuernberger, 1981).

The study of personality types and its relationship to cardiovascular disease adds an interesting dimension to the study of stress. It certainly gives us something to think about in regard to our day-to-day living patterns. Such research has demonstrated the risks associated with Type A behaviors, in addition to acting as a springboard for other researchers to develop their own ideas on the subject (Friedman and Booth-Kewley, 1988; Matthews, 1988; Heft et al., 1988; Kobasa, Maddi, and Zola, 1983).

☐ Handling the Stresses of Adult Life

We established at the outset that the key to harmonious living is the ability to handle, both physically and psychologically, the stresses of everyday life. Specifically, the fundamental issue is coping with stress *without* inducing distress.

The ways to achieve this goal have been an active field of research recently. In particular, a number of self-help and do-it-yourself manuals have appeared to help persons take everyday stress in stride and not to succumb to distress. Stress management, as it is called, offers a panorama of techniques, skills, exercises, and coping strategies, all designed to heighten well-being and prevent stress-related diseases (Charlesworth and Nathan, 1982; Greenberg, 1983; Shaffer, 1982; Curtis and Detert, 1981; Stroebel, 1982; McGuigan, 1981; Nuernberger, 1981).

What does this material advise? Essentially, the general suggestion each makes, although disguised in various approaches, is to deal directly with stress and not to let it control us. When we rationalize our situation and claim that nothing can be done, we become defensive participants in battles that cannot ever be won.

Taking control of stress embodies the notion of strengthening the body's overall reserves. As the general adaptation syndrome (GAS) is activated to meet daily challenges, precious energy sources are depleted. This means that individuals must restore the body's reserves or run the risk of reaching a state of exhaustion. Consequently, sufficient sleep, proper nutrition, and regular exercise are needed (Shaffer, 1982; Sorochan, 1981; Everly and Rosenfeld, 1981; J. Adams, 1980).

Other coping strategies designed to combat distress are self-relaxation techniques, including deep breathing exercises, muscle relaxation exercises, and meditation exercises. Deep breathing exercises help individuals restore their breathing to normal if it becomes too fast or shallow during stressful times. Progressive muscle relaxation in which persons tense and then relax their muscles is particularly effective in discharging stress from the body. Despite the many meditation techniques, the principle of most is to relieve stress by emptying the mind of anxious thoughts (Wilding, 1984; Williams and Long, 1983; Stoyva and Anderson, 1982).

Time management skills are also helpful. All too often, time can be a curse in our lives, a devastating stressor in three areas of adult life: the time devoted to oneself, to one's family, and to one's vocation. Should individuals use time differently from the way they would like to be using it, conflict and stress will often result. Time management skills, then, are instrumental in structuring one's daily life so as to avoid as much stress as possible (Curtis and Detert, 1981; Shaffer, 1982).

The use of biofeedback is a relatively recent innovation in stress management. With biofeedback, a person's skin temperature, muscle contractions, and electrical conductance are monitored by sensors attached to the body. If a person is in a stressful state, he or she can recognize this condition through feedback, and, with guidance, learn to control it. Though the effectiveness of biofeedback varies, particular success has been reported among sufferers of migraine headaches, a condition often associated with stress and tension (Blanchard and Andrasik, 1982; Rice and Blanchard, 1982; Martin and Poland, 1980).

Finally, having a meaningful support system when going through stressful times is important. Talking out one's problems with sympathetic friends or family members is an important prescription for stress. Not having the emotional support of others often intensifies the stressor's effects. In support of this, loners are at a greater risk of contracting a mental or physical disease than are individuals having the support of others (Wilding, 1984; Leavy, 1983).

Relaxation Techniques: How to Reduce Your Body's Distress

Relaxation helps to reduce distress by both distracting your mind away from anxiety-provoking thoughts and countering the body turbulence that often accompanies stress reactions. Relaxation is a skill well worth learning, although it takes considerable practice. Robert Arnot (1984) suggests the following relaxation hints.

LEARNING RELAXATION

1. Do not try to learn relaxation when you are feeling tired. You will learn more effectively when fresh and alert.

2. Seek to minimize background sources of stress, such as the presence of other people or noise.

3. Do not watch the clock or rush through relaxation exercises. If you are worried about the time, set an alarm clock or timer to ring after 20 minutes or so.

4. If you are not succeeding at relaxation, do not try harder. This typically makes persons more tense. Instead, give yourself a rest for a couple of days and try again, giving an emphasis to the parts of relaxation that you found most effective.

BEFORE YOU BEGIN

1. Select a comfortable, quiet location.

2. Loosen any tight clothing and remove your shoes.

3. Sit or lie down in a comfortable position.

4. Close your eyes, uncross your legs and hold your hands flat, one on each knee or thigh area.

RELAXING EACH BODY PART

1. Tense each part of the body as described below for a count of 10. Take a deep breath in, feel the tension, then let the tension go as you breathe out, quietly saying the word "relax" to yourself as you do so to reinforce the message of relaxation.

Toes Curl your toes toward you or down to the floor.

Calves Point your toes toward your face.

Buttocks Push your buttocks hard against your chair or mat, at the same time trying to make your body feel as heavy as possible.

Abdomen Tense your abdomen, as if preparing to receive a punch in the stomach.

Shoulders Shrug your shoulders as high as they can possibly go.

Throat Use your chin to press your throat hard.

Neck and Head Press your neck and head against the backs of your shoulders.

Face Tighten as many facial muscles as possible, including your forehead, jaw, chin, and nose.

UNIT REVIEW

■ The midlife transition is a time of reassessment, a psychological inventory of one's life. It can have negative as well as positive dimensions, which depend on the person consulted. There appear to be sex differences in the midlife transition.

■ The midlife personality theories of Erikson, Peck, Levinson, and Gould were discussed.

■ Maslow proposed the concept of a self-actualizing state and identified the characteristics of self-actualizers.

■ Stress is a normal part of adult life, and learning to deal with it is an important task. Research into the many sides of stress, such as the general adaptation syndrome and the Type A personality, has given us much insight and understanding.

■ Unit Three:

THE FAMILY

Many marriages begin in early adulthood, and children are added to the primary family unit shortly thereafter. By the time many of these parents reach middle age, their children are teenagers or young adults, and their families are probably stable with respect to the number of children.

During this time, middle-aged parents find that they must face a number of developmental tasks. For example, many middle-aged parents discover that they represent the "squeeze," or "sandwich" generation. That is, they have their children on one end of the generational cycle, their aging parents on the other, and themselves in the middle. As a result of this squeeze, middle-aged persons frequently face growing pressures, and they cope with the needs of their offspring and parents simultaneously.

Another important chore is adjusting to the adolescent's desire to be independent. Parents at this time are confronted with the task of redefining past child-parent relations and gradually increasing the teenager's responsibility. It is also a time when many parents realize for the first time that their offspring will soon be moving on and establishing their own independent lifestyle and living arrangements. This latter point, adjusting to the empty-nest stage of life, is a developmental challenge in itself. As we will see, how all of these forces blend will greatly determine the emotional climate of the home during this time.

■ Parent-Adolescent Interaction

The creation of effective communication patterns between parent and adolescent is an especially important task. Parent-adolescent communication must, of course, work two ways.

Teenagers, as well as parents, are responsible for developing meaningful interaction skills, and this can be the most difficult of all the developmental challenges that face both parties. Success in parent-adolescent communication may well depend on the degree of successful parenting exhibited when the children were younger. Indeed, experience seems to support the conjecture that success at parenting depends on how successful one's own parents were.

In recent years, attention has focused on whether a *generation gap* exists between parents and teenagers. A generation gap refers to differences in values, attitudes, and behavior between two generational groups. For example, teenagers often have a knack of telling parents about the distance that separates the two age groups. Some may remark that their parents are "over the hill" and that their ideas are "outdated" or "out of step" with the times. Language use, especially slang and catch phrases, has a tendency to differ between young and old. Adults are often told that certain words and expressions just are not used anymore and are a sure giveaway to a person's age. The same may hold true for everything from hairstyles and clothing to preferences in music.

Does a generation gap always exist between young and old? Is it an inevitable part of family life or is it more of a myth? To answer these questions, we must realize that the values, attitudes and beliefs of today's teenagers are different from those of adolescents 10 or 20 years ago. As they seek to nurture accurate self-concepts, teenagers have to discover the things they believe in, which may include perceptions of what is right or wrong, moral or immoral, and important or unimportant to them. To do this, they must look around and examine the views of their own generation and compare their beliefs with numerous societal agents. As young adults, they will learn that numerous environmental factors, including parents, peers, schools, and the communication media can influence their value system.

Since childhood, youths have incorporated their parents' values into many of their own, but teenagers are quick to realize that times have changed since their parents' youth. While there are those who adopt parental viewpoints without question, there are many who do not. The teenager's desire to be independent, in combination with newly discovered cognitive skills that enable the adolescent to analyze the world more fully, may promote a more questioning attitude than ever before.

Do age differences contribute to the creation of contrasting points of view? Is a generation gap almost certain to develop between young and old? Not necessarily. In fact, most researchers today regard the generation gap as largely a myth. More often

Living harmoniously with growing children is a challenge for middle-aged parents.

than not, differences that exist between parent and adolescent are ideological, not generational. That is, conflict results between new and old, not young and old. Moreover, adolescents and parents are likely to agree on more issues than one might expect. While teenagers may overtly differ from parents in such areas as dress or mannerisms, both groups are surprisingly similar in such areas as attitudes and fundamental values (Hamid and Wyllie, 1980; Coleman, 1980).

■ Postparental Adjustments

□ The Empty Nest

Postparental life is characterized by the *empty-nest* stage, that point in the family cycle where children have grown and departed from the home. For the middle-aged couple, this means a time when they are alone and living in a house that is filled with memories of their children. For some parents, this becomes a time of reflection, restlessness, and even dissatisfaction. For others, the empty-nest stage brings new levels of marital satisfaction and fulfillment (Greenberg, 1985).

Let's examine why the empty-nest stage might be viewed as a crisis period. Many parents, more often the mother, have focused all or too much of their time and attention on the children. Those mothers who totally wrap themselves up in their children discover that when they reach the empty-nest stage, they have little left to live for. The adjustment difficulties frequently encountered by the mother can be a soul-rending experience. This generally occurs in the late thirties or early forties, when a mother has acquired considerable free time. After what seems like a lifetime of caring for others, she may long to feel that she is still needed and serves some practical function. Her identity crisis becomes a time of self-evaluation and assessment (Radloff, 1980).

Perhaps the biggest problem facing both mothers and fathers is letting go of their offspring. In the past, this wasn't a problem, because the task of socialization was to prepare the child to remain *with* the family, rather than depart from it for an independent existence. Letting go is especially hard for many today, since this must occur after many years of interacting with a dependent child. It becomes complicated when some young adults do not want or are not ready for independence when their parents want them to have it. For it to be successful, both the parents and the offspring must be willing and able to let go (Bell, 1983).

The opposing view of the empty-nest stage maintains that it is a positive stage of growth. Recent research indicates that although a period of adjustment is typical for parents, once children have left the home, positive feelings accompany the postparental phase of life. High degrees of marital happiness, shared activities, and open communication have been reported more by postparental adults than those with children still at home. Furthermore, postparental adults look back at their child-rearing years and report a high degree of pleasure, reward, and inner satisfaction in their roles as parents. Although some sadness is experienced, this emotion is outweighed by the joys and pleasures of past parenting.

In reviewing the literature, Everett Dyer (1983) concurs with the foregoing and adds that this is apt to be a time of freedom: freedom from financial worries, freedom from so much housework, freedom to travel, and freedom to be oneself for the first time since the children came along. He adds that in analyzing these two opposing stances on the empty-nest stage, more parents today regard it with relief than with gloom.

It appears that the parents who best weather the empty-nest stage are those who do not try to foster dependency on the part of their children, but rather encourage autonomy and independence. Parents who believe that their children are mature enough for the work world, college, or marriage are more apt to let go than parents who still perceive their young adults as immature. Ideally, parents recognize their children as separate individuals in their own right and strive to show genuine care and concern, but not to the extent of overinvolvement. It seems likely that the fewer long-range goals parents (especially the mother) have developed for their children, the sooner the parental phase of life will be successfully completed.

The empty-nest stage brings new meaning to middle-aged marriages.

Some parents may be fortunate in being able to adjust to the empty-nest stage on a gradual basis. For instance, college, military service, or extended trips away from home may separate young adults from their parents for relatively short periods of time. This allows the parents to experience a household with one less child—or no children—without the anguish of fearing they will never see the child again. Thus, even though the "nest" is "semi-empty," the experience is at least softened by the expectation that the child will return. Gradual adjustments to the empty-nest stage also give parents time to evaluate themselves and their goals.

Once children have left the home, the husband and wife may discover that they have drifted apart over the years. With time together now, they may even be surprised at changes in one another that had gone unnoticed for some time. A popular anecdote involving a middle-aged couple says it all. The two are sitting at the breakfast table, sipping coffee and earnestly reading the morning newspaper. The husband, out of the blue, lowers his paper and with a puzzled expression on his face says, "When did you get reading glasses?" The wife looks at him and replies, "About five years ago. By the way," she adds, "when did you go bald?"

If couples find themselves dissatisfied with their marriage and discover they no longer really "know" each other, it is difficult for them to offer mutual support and understanding during the critical middle years. Some couples, assuming a pessimistic attitude, believe their functions and responsibilities as parents are finished and thus view their lives as practically over. Some feel there is little left to do with a life that has become devoid of meaning.

As a result of these feelings, many couples must work hard to revitalize their marriages at midlife (Rollins, 1989). The successful reconstruction of sagging marriages often hinges on the notion of dealing with the here and now, not with what has been or might have been. Partners must also acknowledge the fact that no matter how a marriage was begun, it *has* succeeded in surviving to middle age. This usually implies that each partner has done much to match the other and each has helped to develop enough common areas of interest to often neutralize trouble spots. While they cannot go back to the beginning and start over, couples do have something to build upon. Unless a reconstruction is started, for many only a miserable marriage or the single world is waiting (Donohugh, 1981).

For many couples, the postparental stage is the most rewarding and happiest period of their life. When the children are gone from the home, mothers as well as fathers report an improvement in marital relations. Some feel that these years rival the happiness and satisfaction felt when the couple first met. Some even go so far as to label these years as a second honeymoon.

Couples feeling this way usually have experienced much mutual understanding and support over the years. They are also likely to be optimistic about the future and have confidence in themselves and their abilities as a couple. They are also likely to have good communication skills, a strong sense of intimacy, and feelings of mutuality and reciprocity (Rollins, 1989; Mudd and Taubin, 1982; Sheehy, 1981; Ammons and Stinnett, 1980).

☐ The Full Nest

By middle age, most parents will experience the empty-nest stage of family life. Their offspring will have grown up, set their sights on the future, and physically left the home. However, this might not always be the case. Indeed, growing numbers of American families are part of a new trend in household living: the *full nest*. Today, an unprecedented number of grown-up children are not moving out of the home but, instead, continue to live with their parents. In 1989, an estimated 20 million adults between the ages of 18 and 34 chose such living arrangements and all indications are that this number will swell in years to come (U.S. Bureau of the Census, 1989).

The full nest represents an interesting demographic trend, and some of the reasons given for remaining at home reflect modern times. Financial explanations invariably find their way to the top of the list: Young people often have trouble affording an independent lifestyle. Some remain in the roost to combat loneliness, while others want to perpetuate a close-knit family bond. There are also those who are still going to school and those who are postponing marriage. Also, grown children may be using the home as a haven or retreat during times of unemployment or career changes.

The full nest often brings its share of domestic happiness and satisfaction. However, it can also herald pressures and problems. For example, there is an attitude among some outsiders that effective parenthood includes launching children out of the home and into the mainstream of society. Other internal problems include conflicts over possessions and noise as well as disagreements about household space or territory. Finally, "nesters" may be disruptive to everyday household activity and thus create stress on the parental marriage bond (O'Kane, 1981).

☐ Caring for Aging Parents

Today, growing numbers of middle-aged children provide care for their elderly parents. About 1 million adults provide direct physical care to their parents every day and many more tend to daily living needs, including financial support, household chores, shopping, and transportation. All indications are that these figures will mushroom in years to come.

As we pointed out at the beginning of this text, most of today's elderly are not feeble, weak, and sickly. Indeed, they are living longer than ever before and most are enjoying healthy and rewarding lives. Moreover, the majority of aged persons are capable of carrying out daily routines and activities on their own. However, advancing age often brings the need for assistance in such areas as personal care and home management. Moreover, incidences of chronic illness and disability steadily increase with age, further necessitating the need for intervention.

But this does not mean that the elderly needing care and attention are nursing home candidates or residents. This is a myth that needs to be debunked. The fact of the matter is that only about 5 percent of the *entire* elderly population 65 years of age or older can be found within institutional settings. Most of today's aged reside, instead, in family settings: About 75 percent of men and 38 percent of women live with a spouse; 7 percent of men and 18 percent of women live with relatives. The remaining numbers live alone or with nonrelatives (U.S. Bureau of the Census, 1989).

Thus, when care is needed, it is more likely to come from within the family, not from outside sources (Troll, 1989). It is also more likely to originate from adult offspring, since four out of five elderly persons have children. Many sons and daughters tend to live within close proximity of their parents, a factor making them more available for assistance when it is needed.

PATTERNS OF CARE AND ASSISTANCE

The majority of today's grown-up offspring appear more than willing to help their aging parents, shattering the myth that the elderly are alienated from their families. Ethel Shanas (1982) contends that the aged in contemporary society are not apart or rejected by their kin network, especially children. Nor does the existence of today's widespread health care organizations remove the input of families. The modern-day family continues to loom as an extremely important source of care and support.

The notion that most younger generations want to help was recently borne out in a study by Elaine Brody (1985). Exploring generational attitudes about familial closeness and care, she found that young women in particular were just as committed to caring for aged relatives as were their middle-aged mothers and their grandparents. Most of the women also reported that they sincerely wanted to care for aging family members, not because they were obliged to do so or because it was their "duty." In addition, aging parents reported that they wanted to be cared for by their offspring if it was at all possible.

Adult children who want to offer caregiving assistance to their parents cite various reasons for pitching in, but one desire looms dominant: to return the kind of support and security that was once received. Most feel it is the right and proper thing for a child to do, an unwritten expectation that is an integral part of the life cycle.

 International Lifespan Development

■ HOW OTHER NATIONS LEND A HELPING HAND

The manner in which younger generations provide assistance to aging parents has unique international variations. For example, consider the situation in some parts of Hungary. This nation *requires* families to take care of their older family members! Those that do not can have the cost for services which then must be provided by the state withheld from their wages, or they may forfeit their right to inherit their parents' home. In instances in which the younger generations have relinquished all responsibility and the old person must enter a nursing home, the family is assessed for the cost of the state's care. Also, the government of Hungary imposes penalties on persons who, through neglect, endanger the life or health of an older individual who is unable to take care of himself or herself.

In Flemish-speaking parts of Belgium, close ties exist between old and young family members, even when the two maintain separate residences. Most elderly parents are visited weekly by at least one of their children, with many reporting daily visits. Daughters and daughters-in-law provide most of the daily assistance, including shopping, tending to personal hygiene needs, and housekeeping chores. For elderly parents in Belgium, similar to their counterparts throughout the world, the emotional support given by grown children is of far greater importance than material assistance.

The Turkish family network is also a tightly interwoven one. Family members exchange material support, live in close proximity to one another, and seek to maintain generational solidarity. As old age nears, living with one's son is the ideal norm, but widespread migration by the young to the cities has loosened this family tie. However, sons typically find a way to supply economic support to their parents, while daughters tend to emotional and social needs. Such forms of family assistance reflect the imprint of rigid sex-role expectations, variations of which are often unacceptable. For example, it is considered disgraceful in some parts of Turkey for parents to receive material support from their daughters, such as sharing a residence.

In China, elderly parents are regularly cared for by their families, a responsibility supported by tradition as well as legislation. Many aged parents share a household with an adult child, and even the childless have options in later life. While childless Chinese males often rely upon their traditional authority or economic prowess to ensure care and well-being during their later years, childless females often turn to rather ingenious retirement planning. As early as age 40, these women often develop "pseudo-kin" relationships with younger villagers, helping them with child care and an assortment of domestic chores. These contributions are taken very seriously by the younger generations, who reciprocate by caring for the woman during her later years.

(Adapted from Nusberg, 1982, 1983)

But while many share these and similar sentiments, not all have the flexibility to provide extensive care. For example, many adult children have to settle for less intensive involvement because of vocational and other family commitments. There are some, though, who balk at the prospects of extensive caregiving for other reasons. Some regard it as an imposition and prefer that it be done by others, perhaps those deemed more competent.

Let us acknowledge, too, that while most children say that they will care for aging parents, this may not always happen or it may not be to the extent that one envisioned. Rather, a gap may exist between inner desire and realistic follow-through. As we will presently see, wanting to be a good caregiver and then setting out to handle the day-to-day realities that go along with the job may emerge as two separate entities.

THE COMPLEXITIES AND COSTS OF CAREGIVING

The care of aging parents brings many changes, including ones affecting the underlying family structure. Often, the assistance received prompts parents to reflect on the past while looking ahead to the future. Barbara Okun (1984) feels that when aging parents do this, they often find themselves redefining generational roles. At one point in their lives, she observes, parents gave the assistance. Now they are receiving it. Consequently, they must pass the "baton of power" on to the middle generation, in the process attempting to retain as much independence and involvement as the family system allows. The process of realigning power can be distressing for some elderly parents, particularly if adult children are not aware of the changes brought about.

All of this may prompt both old and young to rethink earlier relationships. As Robert Bell (1983) sees it, most family relations prior to this point are characterized by regular contact, affection, and a desire to help in time of need. But when the obligation and/or need to help becomes the dominant element in the family relationship, trouble often brews. Problems may even begin when actual aid enters into the relationship because it has the potential for weakening the enjoyable aspects of it. Thus, realignment of care from the parent to the offspring may create problems because it represents something that neither party is used to.

According to Frank Pittman (1987), friction may also develop as the child grapples with the task of becoming parent to the parent. Either party can become offended. Either may also overplay the role—the child may be autocratic or the aged parent may collapse, dependently and demandingly. Compounding the problem is that children may have to coax the parent to draft a will, or they may have to make decisions about funeral arrangements and division of property. Such dreaded subjects may detonate psychological explosions and, consequently, may have to be negotiated by an outside, objective professional.

Caregiving brings other adjustment challenges and demands. Today, the typical caregiver is middle-aged and often caught in the earlier mentioned "squeeze" generation. Couples at midlife are also typically confronted with competing role responsibilities and time demands. The rigors of providing regular care while maintaining one's own household is physically and psychologically exhausting. The loss of personal freedom, the lack of time for social and recreational activities, and other restrictions are often part of the sacrifices that must be made. In a survey of 181 women who were raising a family and caring for an older, demented relative, it was found that employed women, who were also at-home caregivers, used more negative coping strategies when under the strain of caregiving than did unemployed women (Pett, Caserta, Hutton, and Lund, 1988).

The pressures of caregiving are especially evident among daughters, who traditionally shoulder most of the work. While men do provide assistance, it is women who handle the personal care and housekeeping chores. This means that most of today's mothers are handling caregiving responsibilities in addition to balancing careers and tending to the needs of their own family.

CAREGIVING IN MULTIGENERATIONAL HOUSEHOLDS

Many adult children are providing around-the-clock care to parents within their own home, which is an arrangement more common for unmarried offspring. However, recently there have been more married couples opening their doors to aging parents. For those caregivers sharing a residence, there is security knowing that a loved one is just a room away and not being neglected. It also may be a deliberate attempt by a grown child to postpone the nursing home decision.

However, additional stresses have been known to surface in such living arrangements: isolation and loneliness, increased financial expenses, loss of privacy, or lack of sleep. Many caregivers also react negatively to an increased reduction in personal time, not to mention having to witness a loved one's health decline. The maintenance of harmonious and strife-free intergenerational relationships may also become a chore, especially if children are present.

Unrelenting friction and turbulence between adult child and dependent parent has been known to produce a dark side to caregiving patterns: abuse of the elderly. Abusers of the aged are not maladaptive personality types, such as those portrayed in the media. Rather, the abuser is more likely to be a parent's middle-aged caregiver, often the daughter (Steinmetz, 1988). Richard Gelles and Claire Cornell (1985) write that abusers are typically normal persons who are encountering escalating stress levels. For middle-aged female caregivers, such stress may accompany their traditional nurturing role. They most likely start caring for an elderly parent at the time when their own children are beginning to leave home. Being placed back into a nurturing role, just when it is expected that this responsibility is finished, may prove overwhelming.

Donna Ambrogi and Cecilia London (1985) add that pressured caregivers often face a workload without relief. They point out that a dependent, frail elder often requires constant demanding care, both physical and emotional. Caregivers may have to get up several times during the night to toilet the elder to manage incontinence, thus interrupting their own needed sleep. And, if the elder has had a stroke and is severely disabled, the caregiver may have to bathe, dress, and feed the elder. All of this drains precious coping resources (Steinmetz, 1988).

In recent years, a number of support groups have been established to help adult children better handle the pressures, including abusive tendencies, of caring for aging parents. One such group is Children of Aging Parents, based in Pennsylvania but branching out recently to other states. Other organizations, recognizing the need for providing support services, offer a wide range of guidance and assistance.

Finally, whether sharing a residence or tending to the needs of the elderly on a visitation basis, caregivers must reckon with the financial burden. The material support of an aging parent is an expensive venture, be it the amount of time given or actual dollars expended. According to the Population Reference Bureau (1985), the cash value of services performed by families far exceeds the combined cost of government and professional services to both elderly living in the community and those living in institutions. It is estimated that the support provided to a disabled elderly family member accounted for the equivalent of full-time work in between 30 and 40 percent of households providing care.

Tish Sommers (1985) adds that most people are not aware of how expensive caregiving is or how little coverage exists until the crisis hits. Medical costs at hospitals and nursing homes have increased dramatically, resulting in depletion of Medicare and Medicaid funds. If there is no one at home to care for the elderly parent, services must be paid for from someone's pocket. Obviously, the continuing care for a loved one represents a most expensive venture.

All of this means that adult children need to seriously address the issue of who is going to care for aging parents. Obviously, planning in advance is the key. When an aged parent is stricken with an illness or faces acute financial hardship, it is often too late to do the most effective planning. The time to work out financial and legal considerations that may be lurking ahead is *before* they occur, when parents are optimally healthy and content with their lives.

Anne Averyt (1987) concurs with this and adds that family discussions should take place repeatedly over the years. Nothing has to be decided definitively after the first conversation since most strategies and decisions need to evolve. Family members usually need time to think about matters and refine their own particular ideas.

Family discussions and advance planning need not be restricted to finances, either. Frank, open discussions are needed about all aspects of family life. When this is done in productive and healthy ways, an assortment of parents' plans and wishes usually unfolds. Better yet, difficult situations in later years can be eased, since a well-informed adult offspring is in the best position to ensure that parents' best interests are protected (Bayless, 1985).

■ Divorce and Separation

The dissolution of a family by divorce or separation can occur at any stage of adulthood and can be a major crisis for all its members. Although death is the leading cause of a family breakup in the United States, divorce rates are at an astronomically high level. In support of this, consider the following. In 1989, 1,158,000 divorces were granted in this country. Such a total involves nearly 2.5 million adults and over 1 million children (National Center for Health Statistics, 1989).

One method of computing the frequency of divorce is to examine the crude divorce rate. The crude divorce rate indicates the number of divorces per 1,000 members of the population in a given year. In the United States in 1989, there were 4.8 divorces per 1,000 population. This is considered to be a high rate of divorce. Compare this to Poland, for example, where the divorce rate is 1.3, while in El Salvador it is only 0.3. The U.S. crude divorce rate of 4.8 in 1989 was almost double the rate recorded in 1965 (National Center for Health Statistics, 1989; U.S. Bureau of the Census, 1989).

However, there are indications that couples are working harder today to keep their marriages intact. Since 1985, a decrease in divorce rates has been apparent. For example, the 1989 divorce rate was the lowest rate since 1974. While it is too early to predict that the age of disposable marriages is over, it does appear that America's high divorce rates, for the time being, are leveling off (National Center for Health Statistics, 1989).

It is often reported that almost 50 percent of all marriages end in divorce. This is a very misleading statement to make, and such a statistical analysis must be placed into a proper perspective. This percentage was arrived at by comparing all divorces granted in one year with the marriages performed in that same year. In 1989, for example, there were about 50.5 divorces for all new marriages (National Center for Health Statistics, 1989). This is quite different from the crude divorce rate and tends to be somewhat misleading. This is because divorces granted in any year are the result of marriages performed in earlier years: That is, marriages contracted either one year or 50 years previously are compared to the number of current year weddings (Crosby, 1980).

Divorce does not affect all social groups equally. For example, divorce rates are higher for blacks than for whites. Also, the higher the educational level, the lower the divorce rate will generally be. However, one interesting exception to this latter trend are women with graduate degrees. They have disproportionately high divorce rates, due perhaps to increased social independence and economic security. Another variation to consider is the timing of divorce in the marriage cycle. Those who divorce tend to do so relatively early in their marriage. Divorce rates are at their highest two to five years

International Lifespan Development

■ FAMILY BREAKUPS: DIVORCE RATES IN TURBULENT TIMES

The United States has the highest divorce rate among all Western nations. However, a few nations have had higher divorce rates but at different times in history, such as Japan between 1887 and 1919, Algeria between 1887 and 1940, and Egypt between 1935 and 1954 (Eshleman, 1988).

Statistics on divorce in European nations show a substantial increase since 1965. In the nations where divorce is most common—Austria, Denmark, England and Wales, the German Democratic Republic, Hungary, and Sweden—the annual rate is about 10 to 12 divorces per 1,000 existing marriages. When the total divorce rate is compared to the total first marriage rate, the proportions of marriages likely to end in divorce can also be statistically analyzed. Currently leading the list are Sweden (45.4 percent), Denmark (45 percent), England and Wales (40 percent), and Hungary (32 percent).

In Poland, where the influence of the Roman Catholic Church remains strong, the increase has been negligible: 14.6 percent in 1970 to 15.5 percent in 1983. Divorce also tends to be infrequent in Southern Europe; in some nations, it is still prohibited, and in others, the law has been relaxed only recently. The increase in the number of divorces in Northern and Western Europe is related to legislative enactments of the early 1970s that permitted divorce by "mutual consent," which, since, has replaced "matrimonial offense" as the most common grounds for divorce (van de Kaa, 1987).

Northern Ireland is an example of a nation that legally prohibits divorce. Its 1937 constitution clearly states that no law shall be enacted providing for the dissolution of marriage, nor will it recognize divorces granted abroad to Irish citizens. In 1987, a pro-divorce campaign was launched, but citizens soundly defeated it in a referendum and upheld the nation's constitutional ban. The referendum proposed amending the constitution so that couples could obtain a divorce if their marriage had been in a failed state for a period of five years "with no reasonable possibility of reconciliation." Rejecting the proposal by a 3 to 2 voter margin, Northern Ireland reaffirmed itself as Western Europe's staunchest bastion of Roman Catholicism (about 97 percent of Ireland's 3.5 million people are Catholic).

If Australia's divorce rate continues to spiral, 40 percent of all marriages will end in dissolution. The rates of divorce there are about the same for people marrying for the first time as for those remarrying following a divorce. Divorced persons remarrying have slightly higher rates of divorce for the first ten years of marriage, but lower rates in the following 15 years. This comparison must take into account that couples marrying for the first time include a subgroup who would not obtain a divorce in any circumstances. But there are few such couples among those remarrying following divorce (McDonald, 1983).

after marriage, a statistic that has changed little over the years (Spanier and Thompson, 1984).

Also, divorce statistics only tell us one thing: how many marriages were legally dissolved in a given period of time. Conclusions drawn from present-day statistics are invalid unless they are contrasted with a referent period of time with due consideration given to the social-cultural milieu of the referent period (Crosby, 1980).

☐ Life After Divorce

In the aftermath of divorce, individuals need to critically examine themselves and their plans for the future. The time immediately following divorce proceedings, however, may be a difficult time to think clearly enough to employ good, logical judgment. The legal battle may have been long, tiring, and drawn out. Following a divorce, it is not uncommon to experience many psychological states, including a sense of failure, loneliness, sadness, and fear. Of course, amidst the disruption that often characterizes the rebuilding process, many people feel relieved and glad to be starting over.

As divorced individuals move from mutual identity toward autonomy, a redefinition of the self often evolves. The uncoupling process is a status transformation which is complete when the individual defines his/her salient status as "single" rather than "divorced." When one's newly constructed, separate subworld attains a sort of order and life begins to make sense, the uncoupling process is completed. But, the completion of uncoupling does not occur at the same moment for each participant. For either or both of the participants, it may not happen until after the other has created a coupled identity with another person. With that step, the tentativeness is usually gone. Finally, the uncoupling process for some may never be completed. One or both of the participants may never be able to construct a new and separate subworld that becomes self-validating (Vaughan, 1983).

Men, more so than women, deny that they need help or support after the divorce. Such sentiments may reflect the image of independence that traditional men have been programmed to display. There is no discounting the fact that the man, though, faces considerable changes in his lifestyle. In addition to alimony and other court-related expenses, he is usually faced with the economic burden of finding a new place to live and is separated from his children. Chores he might not have previously concerned himself with now become everyday realities: cooking, laundering, cleaning, and other domestic tasks (Price and McKenry, 1988; Price-Bonham and Balswick, 1980; Rosenthal and Keshet, 1980; Oakland, 1984).

Adjustments and adaptations await women, too. This is particularly true if children are involved. Women must deal with new financial challenges and they usually carry the brunt of child-care responsibilities. Rebuilding a social life is especially hard when a woman has children needing continual care and attention. A divorced woman also often encounters difficulty establishing credit, a factor hampering her financial independence. Frequently banks, oil companies, and stores treat her differently than her male counterpart in similar economic situations.

One research investigation (Albrecht, 1980) shows that women, compared to men, regard the divorce experience as more stressful and traumatic. Surveying 500 ever-divorced persons, it was found that 27 percent of the female respondents attributed a very high degree of stress to the experience, while only 16 percent of the males felt this way. Conversely, 20 percent of the males, compared to 13 percent of the females, described the divorce experience as relatively painless.

Postdivorce adjustment often entails a new orientation to daily chores and responsibility.

In spite of the hurdles for both women and men, Elizabeth Cauhape (1983) sees most as successful in making adjustments to new routines. Of course, a new lifestyle brings costs, trade-offs, and sacrifices along the way. Success and happiness depend on a person's ability to turn problems into opportunities for new self-definitions, something most individuals are equipped to do.

Thus, divorce can be an opportunity for growth. In the process of adapting and adjusting, many people discover strengths and emotional resources they never knew they possessed. They find they can survive loneliness and loss. They use the new freedom to learn about themselves, seek new interests, change lifestyles, pursue other careers, and find more fulfilling relationships (McKay et al., 1984).

☐ Children and Divorce

Each year, nearly 1 million children will see their parents' marriage collapse. Should current rates hold, one of every three white children and two of every three black children born after marriage will experience a parental marital dissolution by the time they are 16. Most children of divorced parents live with their mother, and the majority will experience living in a fatherless home for at least five years. Moreover, the divorce experience is not necessarily over when the mother remarries. About one-third of white and one-half of black children whose mothers remarry will experience a second parental marital dissolution before they reach adulthood (U.S. Bureau of the Census, 1989; National Center for Health Statistics, 1989; Thornton and Freedman, 1983).

Divorce has the potential of creating numerous problems for children and its effects vary (Hetherington, Stanley-Hagan, and Anderson, 1989). Some children feel personally responsible for the divorce. Many are persuaded to take sides by their parents. Others may bear the brunt of displaced parental aggression. Coping with the divorce may also spill over to other aspects of the child's life and create additional problems, such as in schoolwork (Wallerstein and Blakeslee, 1989; Wallerstein and Kelley, 1980; Hetherington, 1981; Berger, 1983). It is often believed that older children, such as adolescents, are better at coping with a divorce than younger children. However, one study showed that adolescents also suffer. In comparing adolescents of intact families with adolescents from a divorced family, the latter frequently used less mature defensive coping strategies (Irion, Coon, and Blanchard-Fields, 1988).

In the minds of some, a divorce should never occur while dependent children are at home. Advocates of this position realize that the stresses of marital discord may force children into roles that can exact a tremendous emotional toll. However, this course of action has exceptions. Family violence and sexual abuse, in which the abuser is unwilling to seek help or is unresponsive to it, are examples where it is unhealthy for families to remain together (Van Meter, 1985).

There are others, though, who feel that under no circumstances should embittered parents stay together just for the sake of the children. Unhappy parents should get a divorce, thus disrupting the marital war and removing the children from the crossfire. Proponents of this position feel that couples have a right to their own happiness, even when they have children (Gershenfeld, 1985).

However, either of the courses of action just described may pose problems to the children. They may be subjected to continual quarreling and tension if the parents stay together, or they may be brought up by a single parent who is frequently beset by numerous adjustment problems. The following are critical in the overall transition: psychologically healthy parents with empathic attitudes, cooperation, and open lines of communication between parents and children (Kurdek, 1981; Ahrons, 1984; Goldstein and Solnit, 1984).

Helping Children to Cope With Divorce

No matter how hard it is to face children and talk about an impending divorce, it is a job that must be done. It also is a chore that cannot be done in the form of a simple announcement. The dialogue between parent and child is the beginning of a process where youngsters can express feelings, get reassurance, and gradually integrate this important change into their lives. The following suggestions may prove helpful.

■ Your most important task is telling children clearly and directly what divorce means. Explain to them in an understandable way what problems and issues have led you to the decision. Be prepared to repeat this information several times before the younger children really acknowledge what has happened.

■ Encourage children to ask questions. Do not let their thoughts and feelings about the divorce get psychologically buried. This includes not just at the beginning, but throughout the long process of adjustment. Let them know you are listening by repeating back in your own words the concerns they express to you.

■ Do not assess blame. State that each parent has been hurt in his or her own way and that each has felt pain. If you are angry, acknowl-

edge it, but do not express your rage and blame to the kids.

■ Emphasize that the children in no way caused the divorce and are not responsible for the problems between their parents. Explain that you are divorcing each other, not your kids. It is equally important to let children know that nothing they can do can bring about a reconciliation. Little children often harbor fantasies of mending your broken marriage.

■ Try to explain that your decision comes from much careful thought about the marriage and not from impulse.

■ If possible, describe any changes the children can expect in their day-to-day experiences.

■ Make sure that you stress that both parents will continue to love and care for the children. Be specific. Share your tentative decisions about visitation or shared custody.

■ Assure children that they will always remain free to love both parents. No pressure will be brought to reject one parent in order to continue getting nurtured by the other.

(Adapted from McKay et al., 1984)

☐ Single-Parent Households

The single-parent family is the fastest growing family form in the United States today. Approximately 12 million children live in single-parent families. This means that almost one out of every five families is of the single-parent variety. This represents about a 50 percent increase since 1970 (Furstenberg and Nord, 1982; Grossman, 1981).

Women head about 85 percent of all single-parent families. But while the single-parent family often consists of a divorced mother and her children, divorce does not represent the only reason for family dissolution. Rather, single parents may also be widowed, separated, or never-married men or women. Others may have had their children naturally, through adoption, or through artificial means.

Black children are more likely than white children to live with their mother alone because of blacks' higher rates of marital dissolution, out-of-wedlock childbearing, and lower rates of marriage and remarriage. Fifty-seven percent of black children who were age 6 and under in 1970 experienced family life without a father for a period of time in the 1970s, compared to 20 percent of white children. Nearly 20 percent of black children spent the entire decade in a family headed by the mother, and only one-third lived continuously in a two-parent home (Thornton and Freedman, 1983).

Single parents face numerous problems; paramount among these is financial hardship. Many single-parent families are poor, especially if a female is head of the household. Social scientists inform us that almost 40 percent of female-headed, single-parent homes are living in poverty. Conversely, only 16 percent of male-headed families are in the same category (Payton 1982; B. Johnson, 1980).

Such economic difficulty reflects the problems associated with job discrimination against women, conflicts between employment and home responsibilities, and a reluctance by both ex-husbands and community agencies to help the female head of household. Because of the generally low incomes of single-parent families, a small cash flow imposes a serious economic constraint on the management ability of the single mother. Reduced income may mean a change in buying patterns, increased debt, and a change in housing to a less expensive neighborhood (Hogan et al., 1983).

Single mothers face other economic hardships. Court-ordered child support is not large and is frequently not paid. In 1986, only 75 percent of the divorced and separated women legally due child support payments received any money from the children's father, and only one-half of those got the full amount. It is expensive, time consuming, and stressful for mothers to collect unpaid child support from their former husbands, and few are successful (Thornton and Freedman, 1983).

The supervision and care of the children becomes an additional financial problem, not to mention the quest itself for reliable day care. This is difficult for couples and magnified even more for single parents, particularly if one considers the absorption costs, transportation, teacher conferences, and the like. Role realignment, loneliness, and stigmatization are other commonly reported adjustment problems. Furthermore, both parent and child have to adapt to a changed family structure.

A number of publications have recently focused on the needs of single parents (see, for example, Grief, 1985; Renvoize, 1985; Bustanoby, 1985; Murdock, 1980). Most of them stress the importance of minimizing guilt and ambivalence toward single parenthood and generating positive acceptance about this new social role. Many, such as Knight (1986), emphasize the positive features of rearing children this way, from the establishment of a single and consistent standard of discipline within the home to the encouragement of more self-reliance within one's offspring. While single parenting is a draining and often thankless task, it is not without its rewards.

☐ Remarriage

Most divorced persons tend to remarry instead of living alone. More specifically, statistics tell us that five-sixths of divorced men and three-fourths of divorced women remarry. Also, those who choose to remarry do so within relatively short periods of time. The average interval between divorce and remarriage is approximately three years (Glick, 1984, 1988; Furstenberg, 1987; Sager, 1983).

Divorce rates among the remarried are quite high. One source (Bumpass and Martin, 1989) indicates that the divorce rate for remarriages is about 25 percent higher than it is for first marriages. Why is this so? Shouldn't there be a lower divorce rate based on what was learned the first time around? While these may be valid questions to ask, most experts point to a new set of problems confronting remarrieds. For example, frequently cited difficulties include the economic drain of providing for two families, stepchildren, and lingering emotional problems (anger and guilt, for example) related to ex-spouses.

The remarried family system, like all forms of family organization, is not a static structure but one that is continually evolving. As the literature on the separation-divorce-remarriage process shows (see Pasley and Ihinger-Tallman, 1989; Bray, 1988; Furstenberg, 1988; Zill, 1988; Cherlin, 1985; Goetting, 1985; Furstenberg and Spanier, 1984; Sager, 1983; Wald, 1981), we can see a number of processes or sequences that many go through as they go from the family of first marriage to the family of established remarriage.

For example, one source (Whiteside, 1982) views the remarriage developmental sequence in the following stages. First, the married family (usually with children) dissolves. This is a period of parting, which includes marital separation, divorce, and the establishment of two separate households; a courting period with plans for remarriage; early remarriage; and established remarriage. The three major family groupings—first marriage, one-parent (or joint custody), and remarried family—entail different forms of family organization in terms of family boundaries, the roles in the family, legal ties, and the emotional relationships. Although there is continuity as a family moves from one phase to the next, each transition means significant disruption and change.

UNIT REVIEW

- Living harmoniously with teenagers is an important developmental task of family life.

- Middle-aged parents are part of the squeeze generation, caught on one side by the needs of their offspring and on the other side by the needs of their parents.

- Whereas the empty nest was once viewed as a crisis event, it is often viewed today as a time of happiness and freedom for parents.

- Divorce is extremely widespread, and there are numerous adjustments and difficulties both during and after divorce. Those who remarry do so rather quickly, many within three years of the divorce.

Unit Four:

CAREER DEVELOPMENT

Traditionally, our society has encouraged persons to adhere to the "work ethic," which emphasizes hard work and dedication to one's chosen profession. It is expected that persons will climb the socioeconomic work ladder. Moreover, they will realize in the process that work represents its own reward, that is, that one's job is itself a source of satisfaction, fulfillment, and incentive.

For many middle-aged workers, work is characterized by stability and maintenance. Careers at midlife represent a plateau in the overall scheme of vocational development. Many middle-aged adults report that they enjoy their work and are happy with their chosen professions (Jahoda, 1981; Zunker, 1981).

For others, the middle-life experience today is one of reestablishment rather than of maintenance. The processes of change in our culture contribute to a search by many for a new sense of establishment in life and work. People feel disestablished and look for certainty and confirmation, for ways to realign themselves comfortably and meaningfully in the same occupational milieu, if not the same job.

☐ Careers at Midlife

As we have learned, midlife often brings a reassessment of goals, aspirations, and life ambitions. For some, it heralds a full-scale reorientation of major values, including those associated with one's work. The person who has spent a major portion of his or her life searching for power or responsibility may now want inner meaning. Such an inner quest, according to Daniel Levinson (1980), may produce tranquility or, in some cases, turbulence. An internal reassessment may raise havoc not only with one's work but also with one's lifestyle, interpersonal relationships, and family life.

Careers at midlife provide an interesting comparison with those launched during the young adult years. For those assessing their lives, it is likely that they will gauge the amount of time they have left. Many perceive that time is short in relation to their work. Unlike young adulthood, during which idealistic assumptions are often made about career goals, many middle-aged persons assume that it's too late to begin new careers or try another kind of work. Moreover, many adults at midlife feel that life is not as flexible as it once was. However, as we shall soon see, middle adulthood *is* a stage of life filled with numerous options and possibilities, especially in regard to careers (Gilbert and Davidson, 1989; Bolles, 1981; Isaacson, 1981).

Douglas Kimmel (1980) suggested that the issue of time and the midlife career assessment embodies a concept known as the *career clock*. The career clock is similar to the social-age clock discussed in Chapter 1; it represents a person's subjective sense of being "on time" or "behind time" in career development. Middle-aged individuals are often acutely aware of the number of years left before they will retire and of the speed with which they are reaching their goals. If individuals are "behind time" or if their goals are unrealistic, reassessment and readjustment will be necessary.

If this concept of the career clock holds true, then we would expect the young adult years to be a time for the development, implementation, and refinement of a career. Should this not have been done, it usually becomes evident by middle adulthood and

An assessment of one's career is usually part of the midlife transition.

may even aggravate the stresses of midlife. Of course, careers can still be planned at midlife, but the realization that this wasn't accomplished earlier is often painful.

The career process is intertwined with other developmental forces. Likewise, career reassessment at midlife occurs within the contexts of personal and family reassessment. At midlife, there needs to be a balance of individual, family, and career roles and responsibilities. One needs to weigh the satisfactions and dissatisfactions of all of these roles, discover which impinge on others too much, and decide what priorities in life need to be established. Men, for example, may discover that their occupational roles have dominated their lives, but having proved that they can be successful, they can change their priorities. Women may discover that they have put their occupational roles on the back burner for too long and that now is the time to turn to these needs. Of course, any change in role priorities for both men and women will affect other life roles. In this respect, an important task is to determine the allocation and balance of one's resources and energies (Okun, 1984).

☐ Changing Careers at Midlife

It should be evident that many middle-aged adults evaluate their past career accomplishments as well as their hopes and aspirations for the future. In a growing number of cases, especially among white-collar professionals, such an assessment may trigger a midlife career change. Such changes are not restricted to males. Both males and females are part of a host of workers switching careers in an effort to find new horizons and greater levels of personal fulfillment (Klein and Feinstein, 1982; Thain, 1982).

The quest for fulfillment in the workplace represents a motive virtually unheard of among our forebearers. For that matter, the entire notion of changing careers at any point in the life cycle was practically nonexistent among our grandparents and previous generations. People were expected to stay at one job for the entire course of their work lives and not ask whether they were happy, let alone change jobs. Job satisfaction was secondary to job subservience. In modern times, though, a new value has permeated many facets of society, including the workplace: the need to be satisfied and fulfilled with one's life. This value has prompted both young and old alike to question themselves and the work they do each day. Taking into account this value may help explain why so many workers today are vocationally packing it in and embarking on new and different career paths.

Career changes can be minor or major. Some people may choose to shift their emphasis within the same general career path, such as a public health nurse who decides to switch to pediatric nursing. This is known technically as movement within a career cluster. Other career changes are more dramatic and involve a complete vocational switch, such as an accountant becoming a sociologist. Such changes are more disruptive and require more adaptation than do those within a career cluster.

The motives for changing a career vary widely. However, we do know that many individuals change because they feel stale or fed up with a dull or grinding routine. For some, a career change is the result of the realization that what they want out of life is not what they're doing (Shertzer, 1985).

Dissatisfied employees contemplating a career change often have failed to achieve a sense of accomplishment from their work contributions. Also, many recognize that there is a gap between their perceived abilities and the utilization of these abilities on the job. Many also report a lack of conformity between their own personal goals and the company's goals and policies (Zunker, 1981).

We might add, too, that career success does not guarantee vocational satisfaction. Many men and women achieve long-sought career goals only to ask, "Was it worth it?" Some may have moved up into administration and now find themselves in prestigious positions that they do not enjoy. Sometimes such jobs involve long hours, frequent moving, and trips away from home. Often, the result of this is alienation from the family, a loss of nurturing that can be critical, especially during the midlife transition (Michelozzi, 1984).

Marilyn Kennedy (1980) wrote that changing careers is a worker's reaction to what she called the "killer B's": blockage, boredom, and burnout. She maintains that these "killer B's" will ultimately find those workers who are trapped in mundane, unchallenging, or stressful positions.

The topic of career burnout is a relatively recent area of investigation. It is an extension of the general research area of stress, a topic we explored in Unit 2. *Burnout* implies that individuals have worn themselves out at work by depleting their physical and mental resources. Although burnout can happen at earlier ages, growing numbers of middle-aged workers are reporting this condition. Stress is said to be the primary underlying cause of burnout, but another cause may be unrealistic personal expectations for on-the-job success (Pines and Aronson, 1989; Freudenberger and Richelson, 1980).

It has been proposed that burnout may strike individuals through a series of stages, although it is difficult to attach a timetable to any given period. Following a period of enthusiasm about a given job, disenchanted workers move through stages of stagnation, frustration, and apathy. Many burnout victims blame themselves for their predicament, but in a significant number of cases the blame is rightfully placed on the job (Pines and Aronson, 1980; Edelwich and Brodsky, 1980).

Burnout also strikes a fairly predictable segment of the population. Those most susceptible are dynamic, goal-oriented men and women who are determined idealists. They want their career accomplishments to sparkle, their marriages to be the best, and their children to shine. Although these are commendable life goals, burnout victims make the mistake of striving for perfection. They are also *over*committed and *over*dedicated to their life ambitions (Freudenberger and Richelson, 1980).

We mentioned in our earlier discussion of stress that numerous resources are available for the person wanting to explore this topic. The same holds true for stress in the workplace. Numerous researchers have studied its many sides and the ways that workers can lead more productive and satisfying lives (see Pines and Aronson, 1989; Maslach, 1982; H. Greenberg, 1980; Machlowitz, 1980; Welch, Mederos, and Tate, 1982; Cooper, 1980).

There are other motives or reasons for switching careers. Some workers do so for family-related reasons, such as a divorce or the death of one's spouse. The departure of the last child from the home often prompts middle-aged women to consider a career change, many times to a position that can reaffirm their sense of self-worth and usefulness. For many women at midlife, a career change means moving from part-time to full-time employment (Gilbert and Davidson, 1989).

Some workers change careers involuntarily. For instance, unemployment forces many into entire new lines of work. Or the threat of unemployment may do the same thing. That is, employees change vocations because they know that their company is failing and that being laid off lies on the not-too-distant horizon. Others switch career fields because they know that their jobs are soon going to be replaced by automation. In regard to working-class differences and career changes, L. Eugene Thomas (1980) found that blue-collar workers more often change jobs involuntarily, whereas white-collar workers usually change jobs voluntarily.

☐ Women in the Labor Force

The history of women's participation in the work force has been characterized by considerable resistance, expressed by many segments of society, including women themselves. Women who worked were often regarded as unfeminine, immoral, or negligent in their mothering duties. Employers and society in general often did not take working women seriously. No doubt, the increased number of women joining the labor force has helped remove these attitudes and, in turn, has encouraged more women to seek employment (Anderson, 1988; Nieva and Gutek, 1981).

According to statistics, women account for 43.5 percent of the total labor force. One source (Fuchs, 1988) reveals that women are increasing the labor force at a rate of almost 2 million every year. Between 1982 and 1989, women accounted for 64 percent of all new workers. Currently, approximately 63 percent of all women over the age of 16 work, and this figure is expected to climb to 75 percent during the 1990s (U.S. Bureau of Labor Statistics, 1989).

"Rosie the Riveter" of World War II days would have been hard pressed to find many females working outside the factories or secretarial world. Today, growing numbers of women are occupying positions once exclusively held by men. For example,

Today's female workers have entered new positions of employment, but still face career discrimination and financial inequality.

Geraldine Ferraro was the Democratic candidate for vice president of the United States in 1984, and astronaut Sally Ride was part of a space shuttle team in 1983.

Indeed, today's female worker represents an interesting comparison with her historical counterpart. The total number of years that the average female spends in the labor force has increased from 6 at the turn of the century to about 23 years today. The total number of years for men is about 40. Also, about one-half of all middle-aged women now work, compared with only one out of every five women in 1920 (Bell, 1983; Campbell, 1981).

PERSISTENT VOCATIONAL INEQUALITIES

Despite the fact that growing numbers of women are entering the labor force and launching themselves in new directions, many are frequently confined to low-status occupations. Women continue to be a minority in professional and skilled careers, especially managerial positions. The majority of women today work in office settings, handling clerical chores, while the more prestigious vocations are dominated by men. Compared to the white-collar, executive world of males, females are often relegated to the pink-collar world of the office secretary (Diamond, 1988; Gutek, 1988; Tittle, 1988; Rothenberg, 1988; Miller and Garrison, 1984).

The uneven distribution of men and women in various careers can be seen by examining occupational groupings. Most physicians, dentists, and lawyers are male, while most secretaries, nurses, schoolteachers, and librarians are female. Few women work in such occupations as construction or engineering, although their representation in nontraditional jobs is increasing. If the political arena is examined, the number of women holding office has increased over the years, but remains disappointingly small. For example, women make up only about 5 percent of Congress and 16 percent of state legislators (U.S. Bureau of the Census, 1989).

Worse, even when they occupy the same jobs as men, women receive substantially lower salaries. On the average, women earn less than 70 cents for every dollar that a man is paid. The clustering of women in low-paying jobs is the largest factor accounting for such a discrepancy. Even women with college degrees tend to earn less than men without any higher education. Retirement benefits are also far lower for females. In 1989, the average retirement benefit for a woman was barely half that for a retiring male (U.S. Bureau of the Census, 1989; Anderson, 1988).

Career stagnation and financial instability start almost immediately in the female career cycle (Helson, Elliot, and Leigh, 1989). A survey of over 3,000 tenth and eleventh graders starting their first job bears this out. Adolescents' first jobs were already significantly segregated by sex. On the average, females worked fewer hours per week than males and earned lower hourly wages. Furthermore, hourly wages were higher in job types that were dominated by males. In general, these differences were maintained over young people's early job histories (Greenberg and Steinberg, 1983).

International Lifespan Development

■ WOMEN, WORK, AND VOCATIONAL DISCRIMINATION

Around the world, women comprise more than one-third of the total paid labor force, with 47 percent of all women aged 15 to 64 working. However, this percentage varies depending on the nation being studied. For instance, while about 60 percent of all U.S. women are in the labor force, Russia tops the list with 71 percent of its women being employed. In Latin America, only 30 percent of females are in the paid labor force.

There is no mistaking the fact that women all around the globe earn less than men. In support of this, females working in the manufacturing industry in 1985 earned an average of 70 cents for every dollar earned by their male counterparts (a figure consistent with the earlier mentioned situation of American women). In some nations, the situation is better, such as in Sweden where women earn over 81 cents to the male dollar. In Italy and Denmark, it is 86 cents, and in France, 78 cents. Unequal pay is also usually accompanied by other negative employment conditions. Compared to men, women are trapped in lower paying, unskilled types of occupations. Additionally, their chances for advancements all around the world in all vocational areas are fewer. Thus, inequality and discrimination are problems that plague most female workers, not just those from the United States.

Let us take this a step further and examine women's total work involvement, including inside the household. While female labor force participation rates are available, the housework and child care carried out by women around the world is largely invisible (which can rightfully be argued about American women, too). It is not included in a nation's labor or economic statistics. But, if the value of the cleaning, cooking, and child-care activities that make up this work were calculated, it would equal half the gross national product in many nations. As an example, consider that a woman in rural Pakistan spends 63 hours a week on domestic work, and in the developed world, women spend about 56 hours per week on household chores.

All of this means that on a worldwide basis, females spend more hours working and have less free time than working men. Illustrative of this are women in rural Rwanda, who do three times the amount of work men do. In Europe, a working woman has less than half the free time that her husband has, and in Java, women work over 20 percent more than men (Cancellier and Crews, 1986; Hewlett, 1986).

There is added discrimination beyond job segregation and financial inequality. Much of this is less apparent than the aforementioned but is no less real. Paramount is the fact that the workplace operates on the assumption that all families are traditional. Companies and firms operate as if every employee were a male who had a wife at home to care for his and his children's needs. But women do not have wives at home. That is, allowances are not made in the workplace for the special needs of working mothers, for example, schedule flexibility, emergency time off to care for sick children, day-care needs, and so on (Strong et al., 1983).

Robert Bell (1983) added that often women are also discriminated against because of whatever marital choice they make. Often, employers discriminate against unmarried women because they believe that they will get married and so become less productive workers. Single men who get married, on the other hand, are viewed as becoming more productive. Also, many men react to career women with confusion. If the woman is attractive, they often can't cope with her as a nonsexual being. And because many men are conditioned to view women primarily as sexual objects, they find it difficult to perceive them as something more.

All of the foregoing suggests that as a nation, we need to reexamine the structure of the labor force and remove the segregation, inequality, and discrimination that have persisted over the years. As it now stands, the labor force often exploits women. Females are frequently trapped in work that is tedious, low-paying, unchallenging, and sometimes even degrading. This is as true for single women as it is for married women, young and old (Rose and Larwood, 1988; Gutek, Stromberg, and Larwood, 1988; Dixon, 1983; Roos, 1983).

CHAPTER REVIEW

■ Unit One: Physical and Mental Development

Aging during middle adulthood is both external and internal. Externally, the hair thins, turns gray, and loses some of its luster. Many men's hairlines recede, and some become bald. The skin loses some of its elasticity and is no longer able to stretch quite so tightly over the muscles. Because of this, facial wrinkles appear. Over time, the body produces less oil, a precious source of skin lubrication.

Internally, the amount of blood pumped by the heart decreases, and the blood pressure tends to rise. Blood vessels also thicken and become less elastic. Arteriosclerosis—hardening of the arteries—and atherosclerosis—narrowing of the arteries owing to fatty deposits—may also occur at this time. The brain's structural function does not change, and overall breathing capacity falls to 75 percent.

Many middle-aged adults have the visual condition known as presbyopia, or farsightedness. Simply stated, this means that the lens of the eye is unable to focus on near objects, and so reading glasses are usually needed. Middle-aged adults may also experience a decline in hearing efficiency. Men, especially, lose their auditory acuity for higher pitches. The senses of taste, touch, and smell show a slight decline.

Of the health problems associated with middle age, obesity is the most threatening. Excessive weight often contributes to hypertension, complications of diabetes, and digestive disorders. Hypertension, known as the silent killer because it usually has no symptoms, afflicts nearly 35 million Americans and contributes to about 1 million deaths each year. The leading causes of death during middle age are cardiovascular disease, cancer, and stroke. With such health problems abounding, individuals need to maintain balanced diets, engage in regular exercise, and adopt a lifestyle supportive of good health and personal care.

Menopause, generally occurring during the late forties or early fifties, is defined as the cessation of menstruation. The period from the onset of irregularity of the menses to total cessation, or menopause itself, is called the climacteric. During these months or even years, the rapid decline in estrogen and progesterone levels may be accompanied by hot flashes, irritability, anxiety, and other symptoms. As the amount of estrogen diminishes, the mammary glands atrophy, as do the uterus and vagina, in varying degrees. Some women experience a loss of bone density. Estrogen replacement therapy is often used to combat the symptoms of menopause, but the pendulum sways back and forth in regard to its total safety and effectiveness. This unit explored some of the negative side effects of estrogen replacement therapy, including uterine cancer and hypertension.

Intelligence does not decline with age, with the possible exception of two areas, visuomotor flexibility and fluid intelligence. Reaction times decrease somewhat, but we emphasized that the amount of decline does not affect the lives of most middle-aged adults. In a practical sense, the older one gets, the better one can draw on previous experience—a perspective that can be termed wisdom. Changes in short-term memory abilities, if they occur at all at this age, may be due to divided attention, interference, distractions, and numerous other variables. Research indicates that memory can be enhanced through techniques aimed at improving organizational, attending, and processing skills.

■ Unit Two: Personality and Social Development

Personality growth during middle adulthood is a fairly recent research pursuit. This unit showed that personality growth at this time is marked by continuity as well as change and that personality blends with other developmental forces and affects the whole person. One can find either positive or negative qualities in this stage of growth.

One of the primary goals of this unit was to dispel some of the myths surrounding the midlife crisis. We emphasized, among other points, that it is not as disruptive as some believe it to be, nor does everyone experience it. There can be many positive outcomes to what Levinson called the Midlife Transition, including a reassessment of the self and a realignment of life goals, if needed. This period of reflective introspection also enables middle-aged adults to take a psychological inventory of their abilities, accomplishments, and shortcomings.

Several theories of adult personality development were examined. Erikson emphasized the psychosocial stage known as generativity versus stagnation, a period when harmonious living is characterized by a concern for future generations. Peck added to Erikson's work by suggesting that four kinds of psychological adjustments have to be made by middle-aged persons: valuing wisdom versus valuing physical powers, socializing versus sexualizing in human relationships, cathectic flexibility versus cathectic impoverishment, and mental flexibility versus mental rigidity.

Daniel Levinson suggested that the middle years unfold via four main stages: the Midlife Transition (ages 40 to 45), Entering Middle Adulthood (ages 45 to 50), Age 50 Transition (ages 50 to 55), and Building a Second Middle Adult Structure (ages 55 to 60). Roger Gould believes that middle adulthood is a time to shed irrational notions about life, five of which we discussed: that the illusion of safety can last forever, death cannot happen to me or my loved ones, it is impossible to live without a partner in the world, no change or life exists beyond the family, and I am an innocent being.

Adulthood is a time when many individuals strive for self-actualization, a highly refined dimension of growth characterized by autonomy, individuation, and authenticity. Characteristics of self-actualizing individuals are (1) a more efficient perception of reality; (2) acceptance of self and others; (3) spontaneity; (4) problem centering; (5)

detachment; (6) autonomy; (7) continued freshness of appreciation; (8) mystic experiences, or an oceanic feeling; (9) *Gemeinschaftsgefühl,* or social interest; (10) unique interpersonal relations; (11) democratic character structure; (12) discrimination between means and ends; (13) philosophical sense of humor; (14) creativeness; and (15) resistance to enculturation.

Stress is defined as the body's common, nonspecific response to any demand made on it, be it psychological or physiological. Stress can be either positive (eustress) or negative (distress). Stress is a response to stimuli called stressors, which range from fear and fatigue to physical injury and emotional conflict. There can be a variety of stressors working together at any one time. Stressors can be social, psychological, psychosocial, biochemical, philosophical, and endemic in scope. Research has revealed that having Type A behavior, or a stressful personality, can lead to cardiovascular disorders, especially during middle adulthood. Hans Selye devised the general adaptation syndrome, a sequence of physiological events that occur when one is under stress. The three stages are alarm, resistance, and exhaustion.

We concluded this unit by recommending techniques for coping with stress. The key to harmonious living is handling stress in day-to-day living without being in distress. Sufficient sleep, proper nutrition, and regular exercise are needed to replenish the body's reserves and adaptive abilities. Coping strategies include deep breathing exercises, muscle relaxation exercises, meditation, biofeedback, and time management skills. A meaningful support system of family and friends is also beneficial during stressful times.

■ Unit Three: The Family

The middle-aged couple is faced with several family tasks. One of the more important is adjusting to their adolescent children's striving for independence. Other tasks include creating effective communication with teenagers, supporting them in their search for identity, and assisting them in becoming responsible, independent, and well-adjusted young adults.

The empty-nest syndrome occurs when grown children physically leave the home. While the full nest is growing in popularity, the empty nest is the norm rather than the exception and thus becomes an important challenge.

Divorce is a crisis that affects the whole family. The poor and the poorly educated, members of the working class, and those who marry young have higher divorce rates than do better-educated and middle-class professionals. Most divorced persons remarry, many within three years of their divorce. Remarried families constitute about one-fifth of the American population. As we pointed out, remarriages require adjustment and adaptation by the couple.

■ Unit Four: Career Development

Reassessing one's career life is often an important part of the midlife transition. For many, it is likely that a career reappraisal will gauge the amount of time left. Douglas Kimmel's concept of the "career clock" found that persons can be behind time, on time, or ahead of time in regard to their career accomplishments.

In their quest for career satisfaction, middle-aged adults may change their careers. Vocational changes may be relatively minor, such as changing jobs within a career cluster, or they may mean looking for work in a totally new profession. There are many reasons for making a career change: lack of fulfillment at one's present job, a sense of limited accomplishment, boredom, involuntary reasons such as unemployment, and burnout. Burnout results when individuals wear themselves out at work and deplete their physical and mental resources. Burnout is most likely to strike dynamic, goal-oriented workers who are determined idealists.

Women are joining the labor force in increasing numbers. The total number of years that a woman will spend in the labor force is approximately 23, compared with about 40 for men. But certain vocational inequalities regarding women have persisted even to the present decade, principally job segregation and salary discrimination.

KEY TERMS

angina
anticoagulant
atherosclerosis
basal cell carcinoma
benign tumor
biochemical stressor
blood pressure
burnout
cancer
carcinogen
carcinoma
cathectic flexibility versus cathectic
   impoverishment
cholesterol
collateral circulation
coronary artery disease
coronary thrombosis
climacteric
crystallized intelligence
distress
diuretic
empty nest
endemic stressor
estrogen
eustress
external aging
fluid intelligence
full nest
general adaptation syndrome
generation gap
generativity versus stagnation
hypertension
hysterectomy
infarct
internal aging
leukemia

long-term memory
lymphoma
male pattern baldness
malignant tumor
menopause
mental flexibility versus mental rigidity
metastasis
midlife transition
myocardial infarction
obesity
osteoporosis
overweight
philosophical stressor
presbyopia
progesterone
pruritus
psychological stressor
psychosocial stressor
sarcoma
senile angiomas
short-term memory
socializing versus sexualizing in human
   relationships
social stressor
stress
stressor
telangiectases
thrombus
tumor
Type A personality
Type B personality
Type C personality
valuing wisdom versus valuing physical
   powers
venous lakes

RECOMMENDED READINGS

Askham, J. *Identity and Stability in Marriage.* New York: Cambridge University Press, 1984.
This text describes the various goals that couples work toward throughout marriage, emphasizing how couples seek personal identity, stability, and security.

Baruch, G. K., and Brooks-Gunn, J. *Women in Midlife.* New York: Plenum, 1984.
Topics include the psychological well-being of women at midlife, sexuality and the middle-aged woman, and life events for women in midlife.

Botwinick, J. *Aging and Behavior,* 3rd ed. New York: Springer, 1984.
A well-known researcher explores a variety of intellectual capacities, from problem-solving abilities to memory.

Elias, J. W., and Marshall, P. H. *Cardiovascular Disease and Behavior.* New York: Hemisphere, 1987.
In light of material covered in this chapter, readers may want to explore this book for the many implications of cardiovascular disease.

Field, T. M., McCabe, P., and Schneiderman, N. (Eds.). *Stress and Coping.* Hillsdale, N.J.: Erlbaum, 1985.
Among the topics are the effects of stress on the immune response, stress and depression, and models of coping.

Hunter, S., and Sundell, M. (Eds.). *Midlife Myths: Issues, Findings, and Practical Implications.* Beverly Hills, Calif.: Sage, 1989.
Students wanting more information on middle adulthood will find it in this collection of diverse readings.

Landy, F. J. *Psychology of Work Behavior,* 3rd ed. Homewood, Ill.: Dorsey Press, 1985.
The importance of job satisfaction is discussed in Chapter 11 of this book.

Messinger, L. *Remarriage: A Family Affair.* New York: Plenum Press, 1984.
Messinger examines a number of issues, including the ingredients needed to produce harmony and stability in remarried families, divorce, custody of the children, and meeting new mates.

Millette, B., and Hawkins, J. *The Passage Through Menopause: Women's Lives in Transition.* Reston, Va.: Reston, 1983.
This book does much to expose the myths surrounding menopause. It is beautifully written, loaded with information, and frank in its appraisal of this developmental event.

Perlman, D., and Duck, S. *Intimate Relationships: Development, Dynamics, and Deterioration.* Beverly Hills, Calif.: Sage, 1987.
Part three of this paperback deals with the deterioration and reorganization of relationships.

Roskies, E. *Stress Management for the Healthy Type A: Theory and Practice.* New York: Guilford Press, 1986.
A thorough look at the Type A personality and innovative clinical intervention strategies.

Wallerstein, J., and Blakeslee, S. *Second Chances: Men, Women, and Children a Decade After Divorce.* New York: Ticknor and Fields, 1989.
A probing look at the impact of divorce on marriage partners and children.

CHAPTER ELEVEN

Late Adulthood

CHAPTER OUTLINE

WHAT DO YOU THINK?

■ The notion that America is predominantly a youthful society is pushed at us from all angles, from fashions and food to lifestyles in general. But do we actually live in the land of the young, as we're led to believe? Not really. Indeed, those under 25 years of age constitute less than 40 percent of the population. We need to examine those segments of the population that are growing faster than any other: those 65 years of age and older. This chapter will study this shift in demographics, known as the graying of America, and its implications.

■ They're often seen as being lonely, sick, frail, grouchy, and a burden to all. These negative stereotypes regarding the elderly have existed for years and are scarcely representative of the truth. Also bothersome is the gloomy and depressing connotations given to the retirement years in general. Where do such attitudes originate, and why do some people choose to cling to them? What have researchers discovered about this final stage of the life cycle?

■ It has been labeled by medical experts as one of the most puzzling diseases of the 1990s. Alzheimer's disease claims over 100,000 new victims each year and carries a prognosis of 50 percent reduction in remaining life expectancy. It is characterized by progressive neurological degeneration that reduces patients to an immobile, speechless, and vegetative state. To date, there is no known cure.

Unit One:

PHYSICAL AND MENTAL DEVELOPMENT

Old age, or the retirement years, is the last stage of the lifespan. The study of the aged and the aging process is known as *gerontology*. The term *gerontology* comes from the Greek work *geras*, meaning "old age," and *logos*, the study of something. Gerontology, although a fairly recent discipline, is nonetheless one of the most active subfields of developmental psychology.

Gerontology is a very broad investigatory discipline. Closely allied with it is the subfield known as social gerontology. *Social gerontologists* seek to meet the needs of the aged population by providing them with special services, programs, and policies. They are most concerned with the quality of life for the elderly. *Geriatrics* is that branch of medicine concerned with the elderly.

Each of these related fields gives the public increasing amounts of information each year concerning the aged population. Researchers studying the psychological aspects of old age may discover intellectual changes, patterns of adjustment, motivation, emotions, and attitudes. Those studying social issues may concentrate on subjects such as family relations, retirement, political and religious activities, and social norms and expectations. Researchers focusing on the biology of aging may examine the phys-

For most people, the retirement years are satisfying and rewarding.

iological and anatomical changes that accompany the aging process. Developing preventive measures to combat the diseases and illnesses that afflict the aged and seeking ways to prolong life are also active fields of investigation. Researchers frequently cross the boundaries of these subfields and concurrently probe the psychological, social, and biological aspects of a particular concern related to old age (McKenzie, 1980).

Gerontologist Robert Butler (1983) regards research on the elderly as both derivative and interdisciplinary, as it straddles the area between unexplored, healthy aging and uncertain knowledge about pathological aging. There are very few service-related research activities to enhance the efficiency, cost, and quality of the health and social services. In light of the enormous health costs, this is a glaring omission, and there is much to be done in developing assessment and methodology for appropriate placement and understanding health predictors and risk factors. Research on aging will have to be unusually inventive, taking advantage of a broad range of collaborations to telescope its natural development. Both the government and the private sector must contribute to this endeavor.

■ Aging and Ageism

Stereotypes aimed at the elderly are what gerontologists call ageist attitudes. *Ageism*, in its broadest sense, refers to discrimination and prejudice against individuals on the basis of their age. The elderly are especially vulnerable to ageist attitudes because they are frequently seen as being sick, senile, or useless.

Yet, although the elderly are usually the victims of ageist attitudes, it is possible that some ageism is leveled at all life stages. Consider some of the unfair, yet common generalities about certain age groups: Children don't respect their elders and are spoiled; teenagers are lazy and flighty; college students are irresponsible and liberal; young adults have too many idealistic plans; and the middle aged are too busy to do anything except work on their midlife crises. Humorous as these sound, it's surprising how many people have come to accept them. A person who has reached a certain age is assumed to have acquired generalized qualities. In other words, it's guilt by age association.

Where do such ageist attitudes originate? Apparently many have deep historical roots, at least in this country. Starting with the colonial period, a proportion of the elderly were categorized as superannuated, unnecessary, and a burden to others. With the growth of cities and the Industrial Revolution of the nineteenth century, these attitudes became applicable to greater numbers of the aged. By the early twentieth century, the aged were already recognized as a wide-ranging social problem. Old age had become characterized as a time of dependence and disease (Haber, 1983).

Ageist attitudes, like other attitudes, are a product of the socialization process. As such, they can be transmitted by a number of social agents: parents, siblings, schools, peers, books, and other forms of the media. In many instances the elderly are portrayed by the media in a way that reinforces these stereotypes. At other times, they are practically invisible to the general public; that is, the media prefer to describe the image of the younger adult.

Several studies have verified this last point. One (Kuansnicka, Beymer, and Perloff, 1982) found that only 8 percent of the people portrayed in the advertisements of general-interest magazines were elderly. In television commercials the situation is just as bad. One investigation (Hiemstra, 1983) discovered that among 358 human characters appearing on commercials, only 11 were judged to be age 60 or older. Only 41 appeared to be 50 or older. Of the 130 human characters considered central figures in the commercials, only 6 were thought to have been 60 or older.

More exposure to and the younger public's greater knowledge of the elderly are needed to break ageist stereotyping. Too many young people regard aging as a remote event, something that can't happen to them. It may also help remove the overall negative quality of the aging process itself, another attribution held by many young people (Shulman, Agostino, and Krugel, 1982; Cartensen, Mason, and Caldwell, 1982).

We need to move away from the negative picture we often paint of old age. Indeed, for most people, these years are healthy, satisfying, and productive. We also must reconceptualize the roles of older persons; the majority can no longer be viewed as nothing more than dependents. Instead, they must be appreciated as individuals, who, for the most part, still have much to contribute to society (Eisdorfer, 1983).

Perhaps we need to follow the lead taken by other nations in regard to their perceptions and treatment of the elderly. Nations such as Japan and China, for example, respect and revere old age, particularly the wisdom that comes with it. In France, the later years of life are called *le troisième âge*, meaning the 'third age." Following childhood and adulthood, the third age reaches a new plateau in life, an age of discovery and a time when contributions can be made to oneself and to others. Although there is death, illness, and pain during the retirement years, the French acknowledge that there is also beauty and novelty to be discovered and shared with others (Orthner, 1981; Maeda, 1980).

■ When Does One Become Elderly?

One of the most perplexing problems facing gerontologists is deciding when old age begins or, for that matter, defining exactly what old age is. Because of the ambiguity and uncertainty surrounding these questions, formulating precise answers is nearly impossible.

How would you designate the onset of old age? Perhaps the most obvious way would be to use chronological or calendar age. Ages 65 to 70 seem logical as a life-stage division, as the Social Security Administration, various retirement regulatory agencies, and the Internal Revenue Service use one or another of these ages. But "old" can be defined in other ways, such as physical appearance, cognitive competence, social role, health, certain physiological changes, and attitude (Kalish, 1982a).

Compounding the problem is the fact that individuals do not age at the same rate. Though the metabolic processes are slower in older people, and the cells, tissues, and organs function at lower rates, there are also obvious differences in the aging process. For example, crippling and degenerative illness and disorders may affect a man of 60, but an 85-year-old may experience no such problems. Vigor, vitality, and stamina may also vary in similar ways. This leads us to believe that people may have the characteristics of old age at a number of chronological ages (Atchley, 1988).

Is there, then, an answer to the question, When is a person old? This discussion probably reveals that satisfactory answers to the question are elusive. The definition of old age depends on whom you ask, how you personally perceive old age, the standards of comparison being used, and other variables. To label an individual "old," on the basis of relative age differences, physical appearance, or absolute number of years accumulated since birth has often proved to be unsatisfactory. Old age is obviously a subjective concept. Perhaps it is fitting to say that relative age is in the eye of the beholder (McKenzie, 1980).

■ The Demographics of Aging

Never in the history of Western civilization have so many lived for so long. Regardless of whether we use age 65 or 75 as the beginning period of old age, American society has more older people now, both absolutely and proportionately, than ever before. Furthermore, experts predict that these numbers will continue to grow, at least for the short-term future into the early decades of the twenty-first century. Perhaps a few statistics will illustrate what is now referred to as the elderly population explosion:

■ Each day, 5,000 persons in the United States reach the age of 65.

■ Among America's ethnic groups, the Japanese have the highest proportion of aged persons in their population. The lowest percentage is found among those of Spanish and Indian heritage.

■ Those 75 years and older represent the fastest-growing population segment in the nation.

■ There are seven times as many elderly people in society today than there were at the turn of the century.

■ Many individuals turning 65 today can expect to live an average of 15 more years and will be in good health for 10 of those years.

■ The white population in the United States has a greater proportion of aged persons than does the black population.

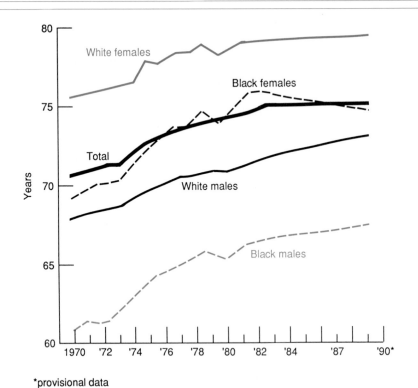

FIGURE 11-1
Life expectancy at birth, United States. (Source: U.S. Bureau of the Census, 1989)

*provisional data

Statistics show that the average life expectancy varies according to race and sex (Figure 11-1). Whereas female life expectancy was 48.3 years in 1900, today it is about 78.2 years. Males lived an average of 46.3 years at the turn of the century but can expect to live about 72 years today (U.S. Bureau of the Census, 1989).

Some other interesting trends in life expectancy and sex differences can be noted. Between 1950 and 1975, life expectancy among females increased by 5.5 years compared with 3.2 years for males. However, since 1975 average life expectancy has increased by 2.2 years for males and 1.7 years for females. Because of these trends, the difference in life expectancy between males and females increased between 1950 and 1975 from 5.5 to 7.8 years and subsequently has declined to about 7.3 years (National Center for Health Statistics, 1989).

Today, 65-year-old males can expect to live about another 14.5 years compared with 18.8 years for females. Between 1950 and 1970, life expectancy at 65 years of age among males increased by 0.3 years compared with 1.4 years between 1970 and 1988.

International Lifespan Development

■ GROWING OLDER, LIVING LONGER

The United States is not alone in its elderly population explosion. The aging of populations is a universal phenomenon, although the rate of increase is considerably greater in the developing nations. For example, by the year 2000, there will be a 130 percent increase in the population 60 years of age and older in the developing nations, compared with 52 percent in the developed nations. Such differences exist because developing nations are only now improving their health-care systems and achieving other advancements. As they do, significant numbers of the population will live longer, resulting in a higher percentage increase. Among the developed nations, such advancements have long been established, and, as a result, their most significant extensions of the life cycle came earlier. Thus, their percentage increases are not as great. Some other worldwide trends include the following:

- By the year 2000, the developing nations will hold 360 million persons 60 years of age and older, compared with 230 million for the developed nations.

- In the year 2025, Asia alone will account for 57 percent of the world's elderly population.

- By the year 2000, the developing nations will have added an average of 9.4 years to the life cycle, compared with 6.8 for the developed nations.

- By the year 2025, the number of persons 80 years of age and older should have increased by 415 percent in the developing world and 132 percent in the developed nations (Soldo and Agree, 1988; Nusberg, 1982). Table 11-1 shows life expectancy at birth, for selected nations.

TABLE 11-1   Life Expectancy at Birth, for Selected Nations

| | Life Expectancy | | |
Nation	Both Sexes	Male	Female
Australia	75	71	78
Canada	74	70	77
Egypt	54	53	55
France	74	70	78
India	50	51	50
Italy	73	70	76
Japan	76	73	79
Mexico	61	59	63
Netherlands	76	72	79
Pakistan	48	49	47
Poland	71	67	75
Spain	73	70	76
Uganda	46	46	47
United States	74	72	78

(Source: Adapted from U.S. Bureau of the Census, 1989)

Female life expectancy after age 65 increased 2.0 years between 1950 and 1970 and about 1.8 years since 1970 (National Center for Health Statistics, 1989).

By the year 2000, it is expected that about 50 million persons in the United States, about 20 percent of the total population, will be over age 65. This surge is owing to numerous reasons, such as new medical discoveries, an improved health-care system, and better nutrition. Furthermore, advances in the control of cancer and heart and vascular diseases could increase the average life expectancy by over 10 or 15 years. More profound repercussions will be created with the discovery of deterrents to the basic causes of aging (C. Koop, 1983; Crimmins, 1983).

■ Physical Development

The aging process is lifelong. We readily accept this process through young adulthood because it signals our physical readiness to enter the adult world (something most of us have dreamed of doing since early childhood). We soon discover, however, that being a "grown-up" entails a bit more responsibility than we were initially prepared to assume. By the time reality catches up with our earlier fantasies about what it means to be an adult, most of us are rapidly approaching middle age. Suddenly, we become acutely, if not painfully, aware of our own aging process. Many individuals caught up in the later stages of this process may begin to have a good deal of anxiety over their physical changes. This is perhaps out of fear of losing their membership in one of the most exclusive clubs in the world: "youth."

During late adulthood, persons experience the highest incidence of physical disorders and are the largest users of medication. Why aging leaves people more susceptible to physical illness is not completely understood; what must be accepted is that certain biological changes take place in the course of "normal" aging. These changes mean an inevitable decline in the function of specific organs and in the body as a whole and are comparatively independent of other factors such as stress, trauma, and disease. In addition to the many normal biological and physiological changes, there is also a progressive rise in the incidence of chronic diseases (Teusink and Shamoian, 1983).

☐ Theories of Physical Aging

Physical aging is a complex, degenerative, physiological process. Although it is not totally understood, there are theories that explain the degenerative changes that accompany aging. These are the wear-and-tear, cellular, collagen, and immunity theories.

The *wear-and-tear theory* of physical aging asserts that the organism simply wears out, much like a machine, over the course of the life cycle. Over time, the body has sustained damages caused by external sources. These sources may be direct (lethal agents) or indirect (the organism is weakened and is consequently more susceptible to such influences as malnutrition, addictions, and stress). By the time old age is reached, the body is exhausted and susceptible to some extraneous factor that eventually destroys it (Bowles, 1981).

The *cellular theory* pays close attention to the role of errors in cell division in the aging process. As cells divide in the body, there may be errors. An error may produce two faulty cells that then divide, creating four faulty cells, divide again, producing eight, and so on. Whatever function that particular group of cells has is thus impaired.

Cellular theory also emphasizes free radicals and the concept of *cross linkage*. A *free radical* is a highly reactive molecule that has become separated during a chemical reaction. Free radicals try to unite with almost any other molecule with which they come in contact, particularly those of fibrous protein. When this happens, they become "cross linked," or bound at the middle. Should this cross linkage become extensive, the normal functions of these proteins will be affected, and they will become tougher and less resilient.

These latter changes associated with the body's fibrous protein represent the focal point of the closely allied *collagen theory*. Collagen is the basic structural component of connective tissue. It consists of large, fibrous, elastic molecules and is found in all body organs. For example, it is found in its pure form in tendons; it is also found in bones, between cells, in muscle fibers, and in the walls of blood vessels. Collagen is flexible, and it also offers great resistance to pulling forces. In its flexibility and strength, collagen is analogous to a cable that ties a ship to a wharf. Although it is sufficiently pliable to be coiled when not in use, the cable will not allow movement of the ship while at anchor. In much the same manner, fibrous collagen allows skin, tendons, or blood vessels to transmit tension and compression without becoming deformed. These fibers are exceedingly strong, capable of being stretched and then returning to their natural length. However, if they are stretched for a long enough period of time, their stretched length gradually becomes their unstretched length, a process known as "creeping" (Guyton, 1981; Eyre, 1980).

As collagen loses its elastic properties because of the cross-linkage process, organs become less resilient. For example, the bones of the elderly are fragile because of a change in bone mineralization, which makes them more porous and brittle. A decrease in the quality of collagen also allows calcium salts to be deposited in this now-degenerating tissue. Calcium salts, which are normally prevented from accumulating in tissue other than bone, are deposited in arterial walls, causing arteries to become bonelike tubes, known technically as arteriosclerosis (Eyre, 1980; Krane, 1980).

A simple test enables persons to observe the effects of collagen change and cross linkage in their skins. Place your wrist and hand palm down on a flat surface with the fingers stretched as widely as possible (see Figure 11-2). Take a pinch of skin on the back of the hand between the thumb and forefinger and pull it up as far as you comfortably can. Hold this pinched skin for five seconds, then release it. Count the seconds it takes for the skin to smooth itself.

The skin usually snaps back very rapidly in healthy teenagers. Between the teenage years and age 45, two or three seconds are usually required. After this, though, the time increases rapidly. For a 65-year-old, about 20 seconds are required. And in an 80-

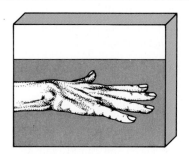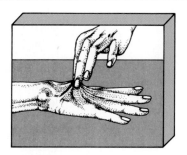

FIGURE 11-2
A test for skin elasticity.

year-old, the pinched skin may still form a visible ridge 5 minutes later. This is because of the cross-linkage damage to collagen that accompanies the aging process. This skin becomes far less resilient and flexible over time (Walford, 1983; Pearson and Shaw, 1982).

Finally, the *immunity theory* proposes that changes in the body's immune system result in physical degeneration. More specifically, as the body ages, its immune system becomes less efficient, and so harmful cells are allowed to survive. Thus, the body loses its ability to protect itself from disease and malfunctioning cells. Related to the immunity theory is the *autoimmunity theory*. This theory suggests that with age there are more mutations and changes in the body's cell division. However, the body itself reacts differently to these changes. These cell mutations or other changes may lead to protein that the body does not recognize as part of its system. The body perceives these changes as foreign matter and responds by producing antibodies, or an autoimmune response. The end result is that the body attacks itself.

☐ External Aging

As we established in Chapter 10, external aging refers to the superficial symptoms of growing old. The more observable changes are those associated with the skin, hair, teeth, and general posture.

THE SKIN The most pronounced change is wrinkling, a process begun during the middle years. Wrinkling is influenced by consistency of expression, loss of subcutaneous fat tissue, and loss of skin elasticity. Subcutaneous fat insulates the body, and therefore less tissue means the loss of body heat. The loss of subcutaneous fat also accounts for the characteristically emaciated look of old age (Kart, 1990).

Normal skin cells in an average 70-year-old live only 46 days, compared with about 100 days for a 30-year-old. In the aged, skin cells are also replaced more slowly. The number of nerve cells enervating the skin also declines, the result being that the sense of touch is less sensitive. The skin also loses its ability to retain fluids, and consequently it becomes dry and less flexible. Spots of darker pigmentation also accompany the physical aging process, and wounds tend to heal less quickly than before (Kermis, 1984).

Of all the changes in the skin, the most serious is its gradual inability to aid in the complex homeostatic regulation of body temperature. With age, persons become more susceptible to pathological conditions because, physiologically, they no longer can respond easily to changes in the external temperature. A significant reduction in the number of the body's sweat glands and the accompanying inability to sweat freely can lead to heat exhaustion. Furthermore, the loss of the insulating layer of subcutaneous fat, coupled with the diminished capacity of the circulation system, can make the elderly susceptible to the cold. The latter fact helps explain why the elderly often report feeling chilly (Crandall, 1980).

THE HAIR With advancing age, the hair continues to turn white and lose its luster. For most, the hair continues to thin, and about 65 percent of all men become bald. Hair loss on the arms and legs may also be extensive, and men's beards usually become more sparse. Men usually grow coarse hair in their ears, eyebrows, and nostrils. For women, the change in the androgen-estrogen ratio may produce undesirable facial hair, particularly on the upper lip and chin (Crandall, 1980; Pesman, 1984).

THE TEETH Coping with the loss of teeth is an adjustment faced by many during the retirement years. It is estimated that at age 65, 50 percent of the population have lost all of their teeth. For many, dentures become a way of life during the retirement years, at least for those who can afford them (Kermis, 1984).

Tooth degeneration over time may be caused by poor dental hygiene or age-related changes. For example, over time, the production of saliva is diminished, which increases the risk of tooth decay. Periodontal disease often afflicts the elderly and makes extractions necessary. Years of using toothbrushes with bristles that are too hard may wear down tooth enamel and create yellow teeth with dark spots. Years of chewing food and grinding the teeth also produce a worn, flattened tooth surface (Crandall, 1980).

GENERAL POSTURE Among the elderly, the shrinkage of the disks in the spinal column leads to a slight loss of physical stature. This process, you may recall, begins during young adulthood but only now becomes evident. The loss of collagen between the spinal vertebrae also causes the spine to bow. This, coupled with the tendency of the elderly to stoop, often makes them look even shorter. Postural changes may be especially evident in older women, who often develop a widow's, or dowager's, "hump" at the back of the neck. This is the result of *osteoporosis*, a disorder common among older women, which results in a gradual loss of bone mass (Belsky, 1990; Aiken, 1982).

Posture and steadiness are often affected by physical aging processes.

☐ Internal Aging

Internal aging refers to the symptoms of growing old that cannot be seen, that is, the degenerative changes that occur inside the body. We shall examine some of the changes in the nervous, cardiovascular, respiratory, gastrointestinal, muscular-skeletal, urinary, and immune systems.

THE NERVOUS SYSTEM There are several changes that take place in the brain with age. Beginning approximately at age 60, there is a reduction of cerebral blood flow as well as a decline in oxygen and glucose consumption. There are also signs of cerebral atrophy and a loss of brain weight. We should emphasize, however, that age-related cerebral atrophy is by no means uniform. For example, the cerebral cortex atrophies more than the brain stem does. Also, certain neurons demonstrate greater age-dependent changes than do others (Carlsson, 1983).

THE CARDIOVASCULAR SYSTEM The heart usually maintains its size with age, although heart tissue may atrophy. The aorta, the larger artery that receives the blood pumped from the heart and whose branches carry blood to all body parts, loses its elasticity. Also, the hardening and skrinking of the arteries make it hard for blood to flow freely in the body. As a result, the heart has to work harder to accomplish less. In addition, there is a loss of cardiac muscle strength, reduced cardiac-muscle cell size, and reduced cardiac output. Indeed, the cardiac output, at best, of an average 75-year-old is about 70 percent of that of an average 30-year-old (Kart, 1990).

THE RESPIRATORY SYSTEM With age, there is a measurable reduction in the efficiency of the respiratory system. There are decreases in the maximum breathing capacity, residual lung volume, total capacity, and basal oxygen consumption. All of these lower the metabolic rate. There is also decreased flexibility and elasticity of the lungs, the result of collagen changes in the lung tissue and walls of blood vessels (Weg, 1983). These changes in the respiratory system have important health implications for the aging person. Marguerite Kermis (1984) reminds us that certain amounts of oxygen are essential to the synthesis of body building blocks such as amino acids, glucose, and fatty acids and the production of energy. Thus, an individual who is not getting enough oxygen will be less aware, less active, and less strong than one who is getting sufficient amounts.

THE GASTROINTESTINAL SYSTEM The gastrointestinal system changes with age, decreasing its production of digestive juices and reducing its peristalsis. Peristaltic action, waves of contractions that push the contents of the digestive system downward, is required to metabolize and excrete food. It therefore is very important to overall health. Constipation, which occurs frequently among the aged, is indicative of how the digestive system changes (Kermis, 1984; Kart, 1990).

THE MUSCULOSKELETAL SYSTEM Muscle strength and power and muscle mass and elasticity decline during the retirement years. Some of the loss of muscle mass and function results from atrophy due to nonuse. Thus, those who exercise regularly show less of a decline in muscle mass and function than do those who lead sedentary lives (Crandall, 1980).

In regard to the skeletal system, the bones become less firm and their density begins gradually to decrease. As we mentioned earlier, the gradual loss of bone density is called osteoporosis, and it is more common among older women. Deposits of mineral salts in the bones also increase, and so stiffness and pain in the joints of the lower spine, hips, and knees become common. Synovial fluid, which lubricates the joints, is less abundant and may create arthritis pain. In general, the bones become more brittle in later life. All of this implies that falling has significant consequences for the elderly, as bones are more apt to break and take longer to heal (Aiken, 1982).

The Shrinking Spine

Adults are able to withstand gravity only so long. Over time, the spine and its support system begin to weaken and the back will begin to slump. The discs between the bones in the spine will also start to deteriorate, causing the vertebrae to move closer together (see Figure 11-3). These processes will be evident for both males and females, even if the latter are free from osteoporosis. The result will be barely visible during young adulthood but by the retirement years, an inch or two of height will be lost.

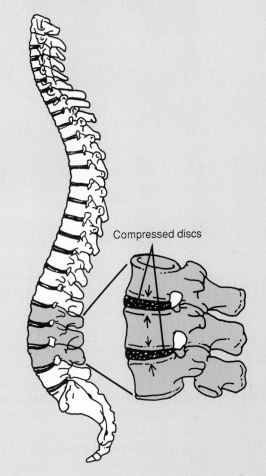

Compressed discs

FIGURE 11-3 Compression of the spine. (Source: Adapted from Pesman, 1984)

THE URINARY SYSTEM The kidneys, bladder, and ureters constitute the urinary system. In general, the urinary system's efficiency decreases with age. The desire to urinate is often delayed among the elderly. The number of cells in the kidney drops, causing less efficient excretion of toxins and wastes from the body. In addition, the

Although there is systematic decrement in bodily functions, most of the elderly can meet the challenges of everyday life.

bladder becomes less elastic with age. The bladder of an aged person has a capacity of less than one-half that of a young adult. A common urinary problem of older males is frequent urination, caused by the enlargement of the prostate gland (Kermis, 1984; Kart, 1990).

THE IMMUNE SYSTEM The immune capacity appears to be less responsive with age. The body is just not as effective in eliminating foreign substances from its system as it once was. The immune system loses its efficiency partially because of a breakdown in the body's feedback system. As we learned earlier, the immune system tends to turn against the body in an autoimmune response, as increasing numbers of cells become faulty. The body's failing immune system is most evident in health statistics for the elderly. For example, the mortality rate among the aged for pneumonia is six to seven times the rate for young adults, and the elderly also have higher incidence rates of cancer and tuberculosis (Nandy, 1983; Weg, 1983; Kermis, 1984).

Because of these system changes, many people feel that old age is nothing more than a downward slide, a series of degenerative body changes that leave the elderly in physical disrepair. But Ruth Weg (1983) feels that an examination of physical, systematic aging does not support the image of the elderly as invalid and relegated to mindless senility and death. Though there is a systematic decrement, loss of reserve, and a decrease of homeostatic control, these do not necessarily create physical or psychological incompetence and invalidism. Most of the aged population have more than enough systematic capacities to meet the demands of everyday life. Furthermore, each person has the opportunity and responsibility to nurture and extend his or her remaining capacities.

☐ Changes in Sensory Capacities

Advancing age brings a gradual diminishment of the sensory abilities. Individuals usually do not react as quickly to sensory stimuli, and they often no longer receive adequate perceptive information about their environment. These physiological changes have psychological consequences for the elderly. As Cary Kart (1990) put it, it is the senses of vision, hearing, taste, touch, and smell that link a person to the outside world. The senses orient a person to the world and interpret it. Also, the world's perception of the elderly may be influenced by the sensory changes a particular person has experienced. For example, the older person with impaired vision or hearing may be viewed as being stubborn, senile, or eccentric.

VISION Poor eyesight is not inevitable with age. Many elderly persons maintain good eyesight throughout this stage of life. For others, though, physical changes that occur as one grows older require that adjustments be made. Illustrative of this are degenerative changes in the retina, the lens of the eye, and the optic nerve. More specifically, the lens continues to lose elasticity, the pupils become smaller and irregular in shape, and the eye does not admit as much light. The eyelids also have a tendency to sag, often acutely enough to interfere with vision. Color vision may also become less efficient with age. This is because the lens usually yellows over time and, consequently, filters out violet, blue, and green (Crandall, 1980).

The visual changes accompanying aging processes have practical, everyday implications. The elderly generally need brighter light for such tasks as reading or cooking. The decreasing ability to adapt to glare makes night driving especially difficult. Eye strain may also reduce the amount of time a person can spend reading or being active in hobbies or other activities. However, eyeglasses can correct many of these visual difficulties. For those with more severe impairments, large-print versions of books and other reading material may have to be relied upon, or one may have to resort to the use of a magnifying glass.

EYE DISEASES AMONG THE ELDERLY Beyond the changes in the eye that often accompany normal aging processes is the risk of eye disease. Eye disease can occur at any point in the life cycle, but two conditions are more common among older adults. These are cataracts and glaucoma.

Cataracts are an opaqueness of the lens that interferes with the passage of light to the retina, producing blurred vision. *Cataracts* usually develop gradually and without pain, redness, or tearing. Cataracts also usually develop in both eyes. Some will remain small and do not affect vision. If they become larger or denser, though, visual problems usually result.

Besides blurred vision, persons with cataracts often experience glare in bright light. This is because the clouded lens scatters rather than focuses incoming light. This visual limitation is especially pronounced when the lens focuses on distant objects. As the condition progresses, the lens becomes milky white, causing further visual degeneration.

Left untreated, cataracts can cause blindness. However, cataracts can be surgically removed in a relatively safe and highly successful operating procedure. Once this occurs, vision is restored by using special eyeglasses or contact lenses or by having an intraocular lens implant (a plastic lens that is surgically implanted in the eye).

Glaucoma is pressure within the eyeball that is caused by a buildup of aqueous humor, a fluid that circulates in the eye's anterior chamber. This buildup of fluid disturbs the normal drainage ability of the eye, creating internal pressure as well as damage to the eye's structure and nerve endings. Similar to cataracts, *glaucoma* can cause blindness if left untreated.

Glaucoma often begins without any noticeable symptoms. In this respect, visual deterioration is gradual and painless. However, its progression usually brings impairment of peripheral vision, blurring, difficulty in adjusting to brightness and darkness, and pain in or around the eye. In most instances, glaucoma also causes individuals to perceive halos or faint white circles surrounding lights.

The effective treatment of glaucoma relies on its early detection. Among the measures taken are special eyedrops (to promote fluid drainage) and oral medications (to decrease production of eye fluid). Should either approach prove unsuccessful, surgery may be needed to restore the eye's draining ability.

How to Safeguard Yourself Against Eye Diseases

All adults need to take steps to prevent eye diseases. This is especially true for cataracts and glaucoma, two diseases which are more common among older adults and usually begin without any warning symptoms. To protect the eyes, the following tips are suggested:

■ Have a complete eye examination every two to three years. Examinations should include a vision (and eyeglasses) evaluation, eye muscle check, glaucoma test, and internal and external eye check. Should individuals have a family history of eye disease, more frequent examinations are recommended.

■ Have regular health examinations to detect such treatable diseases as diabetes and high blood pressure. Both of these and numerous other conditions can cause eye problems.

■ Do not hesitate to contact a doctor if you experience such problems as loss of vision, blurring, double vision, eye pain, sudden appearance of moving or floating dark spots (called floaters), excessive discharge from the eye, or redness or swelling of the eye or eyelid.

HEARING Hearing impairments are much more common in the elderly than in middle-aged adults. It has been estimated that approximately 30 percent of adults age 65 through 74 and about 50 percent of those age 75 through 79 suffer some degree of hearing loss. In the United States, more than 10 million older adults are hearing impaired.

Presbycusis is the most common hearing impairment among the elderly and is a hearing loss associated with aging processes. Changes in the workings of the inner ear lead to difficulties in understanding speech, sometimes an intolerance for loud sounds, but rarely total deafness. This hearing loss, you will recall, begins first in the higher sound frequencies. Remember, too, that men have more trouble hearing higher sound frequencies than women.

Conductive deafness is another form of hearing loss sometimes experienced by the elderly. This type of deafness typically involves blockage or impairment of the outer or middle ear so that sound waves are not able to travel properly. Such a condition can be caused by packed ear wax, excessive fluid, abnormal bone growth in the ear, or infection. Individuals suffering from conductive deafness usually find that sounds have a muffled quality, but their own voices sound louder than normal. Consequently, they often speak softly.

Sensorineural deafness is another form of hearing loss among the elderly, although it is less common than those mentioned. *Sensorineural deafness* is a hearing loss caused by damage to the inner ear, to the auditory nerve carrying sound messages to the brain, or to the hearing center of the brain itself. This type of deafness has many possible causes, including extended bacterial and viral infections, head injuries, and prolonged exposure to loud noises.

The nature of the hearing loss, as well as its extent, will determine the treatment. In some instances, surgery or flushing the ear canal to remove packed ear wax may restore some or all of hearing ability. A hearing aid may also restore hearing. It is estimated that more than three-quarters of older people with permanent hearing loss can benefit from the use of a hearing aid. However, only one in five hearing-impaired older adults use them. Why is this so? Anxiety, vanity, and a lack of understanding about them are the major reasons. Of course, there are those who cannot be helped by hearing aids, as well as those who totally refuse help.

We might add, too, that a hearing impairment can lead to a diminished social life, leaving a person lonely and sometimes even with a paranoid sense of abandonment. Richard Crandall (1980) observes that many aged people avoid social interaction because they are afraid that their verbal responses or behavior will be inappropriate. To avoid such feelings and to maximize communication with a hearing-impaired person, the following is recommended:

- Speak to the person at a distance of three to six feet. Make sure that you position yourself near adequate lighting so that your lip movements, facial expressions, and gestures may be seen clearly.

- Do not begin speaking until you are visible to the person. Do not cover your mouth when speaking, and avoid chewing and eating.

- Speak slightly louder than normal. Realize, though, that shouting will not make the message any clearer. In fact, it might distort it.

- Speak at your normal rate, but not too rapidly. Also, do not overarticulate since this distorts the sounds of speech and makes the use of visual clues more difficult.

- If what you say is not understood, rephrase the idea in short, simple sentences.

- Never speak directly into the person's ear. This prevents the listener from making use of visual clues.

- Arrange rooms so that everyone will be clearly visible and not more than six feet apart.

- Always treat the hearing-impaired person with respect. Include the person in all discussions about him or her. This will help to reduce the feelings of isolation that many hearing-impaired people experience.

TASTE AND SMELL The senses of taste and smell decline with age. Such declines have important implications, as they affect appetite and nutritional requirements. The four basic tastes, sweet, bitter, sour, and salty, all generally diminish in sensitivity. As a result, the elderly may prefer food that is overly sweet or spicy, or more heavily seasoned than what a younger person might enjoy (Kermis, 1984; Weg, 1983).

One's taste of food is affected by the sense of smell. The elderly thus may prefer stronger flavors and may not be bothered by odors that younger adults find offensive or unbearable. Certain factors affect both smell and taste. For example, serious respiratory illness affects one's sense of smell and consequently one's sense of taste. Dentures may block gustatory nerve endings, and smoking may have a negative influence on taste sensitivity (Aiken, 1982; Marsh, 1980).

Aging and Tasting Ability

With advancing age, adults taste less. At age 30, each papilla has about 245 tastebuds (Figure 11-4). The tastebuds are embedded in the papillae beneath the surface of the tongue. By age 80, each papilla has only about 88 left. This deterioration and atrophy is a normal and inevitable consequence of the aging processes. However, it is believed that good oral hygiene can help prevent some of the deterioration and thus preserve an older adult's ability to taste.

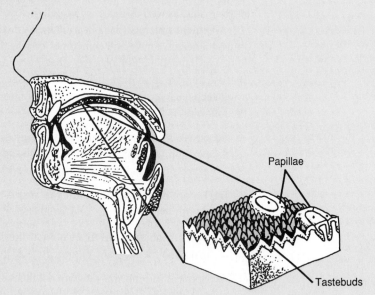

FIGURE 11-4 Close-up of papillae and tastebuds. (Source: Adapted from Pesman, 1984)

TOUCH Beginning at about age 55, the ability to feel sensations on the skin begins to diminish. The elderly generally also become less sensitive to temperature changes, touch, and pain. The loss of this sense usually starts in the lower half of the body and extends upward. It is usually most pronounced in the lower extremities. There are several important implications of this sensory loss. For instance, persons may not be aware of cuts and bruises. As a result, a relatively mild condition can become serious if a person is not aware of its existence. The diminishment of this sense, though, may have some redeeming features; for example, a person may be partially released from the pain of a chronic condition such as arthritis (Crandall, 1980).

☐ Health Disorders

Contrary to popular and unfair stereotypes, the elderly are not always sick or unhealthy. Although some need care, most do not. Old age is not synonymous with poor health. This was borne out in a study focusing on the health status of persons

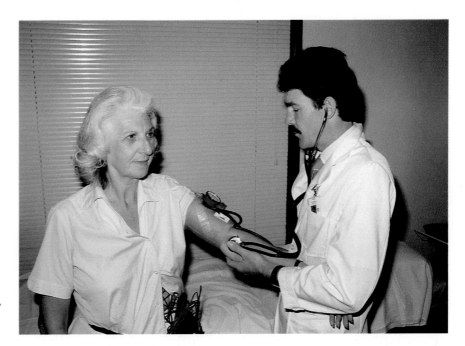

Proper health care is important during adulthood, especially in the retirement years.

between the ages of 60 and 90. Over 70 percent described their health as "excellent" or "good," 25 percent regarded their health as "fair," and only 3 percent reported their health as being "poor" (Starr and Weiner, 1981).

The health status of the elderly need not be viewed apart from younger adults, either. In preventative medicine, the surgical procedures and drugs used on the elderly are the same as those used on the young. For example, pneumonia is treated with antibiotics, whether the person is 18 or 88 years old. The difference is that while the young have a natural tendency to rebound from illness, the rate of recovery is slower for the aged, or the condition will deteriorate even further.

The aged population is vulnerable to certain disorders and diseases, though. Among the more prevalent are arthritis, hypertension, heart disease, cerebrovascular accident, and cancer. Let's examine the nature of each of these more fully.

ARTHRITIS *Arthritis* is an inflammation of a joint and is a disorder common among older adults. Few cures exist for this condition, which can last for years and intensify with the aging process. Of the nearly 100 types of arthritis that exist, two are most common: osteoarthritis and rheumatoid arthritis.

Osteoarthritis *Osteoarthritis* is also called degenerative arthritis and is the most common form of arthritis. It affects over 40 million persons living in the United States and is characterized by the gradual wearing away of cartilage in the joints. In its most common form, osteoarthritis involves large weight-bearing joints such as the knees and hip area. Usually, pain and swelling result from the cartilage degeneration, and joints stiffen. Joint stiffness can be brief, is often relieved by activity, but can recur upon rest.

Rheumatoid Arthritis *Rheumatoid arthritis* affects all of the connective tissues in the body. It typically develops slowly and most often has its onset before later adulthood. Rheumatoid arthritis is much more common in women than men. In its most severe form, this arthritic condition inflames the membranes lining and lubricating the joints. Pain and swelling are common reactions to this inflammation, as well as fatigue and fever. Eventually, the cartilage will be destroyed. As scar tissue gradually replaces the damaged cartilage, the joint becomes rigid and misshapen.

Treatment for both forms of arthritis are geared to relieving stiffness and pain, halting joint degeneration, and maintaining mobility. Aspirin and anti-inflammatory drugs, as well as carefully designed fitness programs, are typically prescribed to treat arthritis. Contrary to popular thought, rest is not always the best medicine for arthritis. While rest can reduce joint inflammation, too much of it tends to create stiffness. Therefore, physicians are likely to recommend daily exercise programs such as walking or swimming. Finally, for those with severely damaged joints, surgery often helps to relieve pain and restore mobility.

HYPERTENSION Recall from earlier discussions that *hypertension* refers to high blood pressure. It is a disorder characterized by persistently elevated pressure of blood within and against the walls of the arteries, which carry blood from the heart through the body. This excessive force being exerted on the artery walls often causes damage to the arteries themselves and thereby to such body organs as the heart, brain, and kidneys.

While many middle-aged persons have hypertension, the chances of contracting this disorder steadily increase with age. In support of this, about 40 percent of whites and over 50 percent of blacks 65 years of age and older have significant elevations of blood pressure. Such elevations are thought to be part of aging processes since there is a gradual loss of elasticity and decreasing diameter of the small arteries throughout the body.

Similar to earlier stages of adulthood, hypertension presents few, if any, reliable symptoms during the retirement years. While palpitations, excessive headaches, and anxiety are thought to be cues, high blood pressure may exist for years without being detected. For this reason, the elderly need to have their blood pressure taken at least once a year. Left untreated, hypertension can lead to heart and brain disease, among other complications. It is also a condition that can be aggravated by such factors as smoking, poor dietary habits, and lack of exercise.

Although high blood pressure can usually be controlled by drugs and changes in daily habits, misconceptions about prescribed medicines exist. For example, some feel that once blood pressure is brought down to acceptable levels, medication is no longer needed. Antihypertensive drugs are typically prescribed with long-term use in mind, although reductions in amount are possible over time.

HEART DISEASE As we learned in Chapter 10, a heart attack is a life-threatening disease. Indeed, it is the largest single cause of death in the United States, accounting for 36 percent of all deaths among males aged 35 to 64. Approximately one-sixth of white men and women and over one-third of black men and women between the ages of 45 and 64 are afflicted with heart disease. Heart disease also accounts for more visits to the doctor, more required hospitalization, and more days of bed recuperation than any other disease; according to the National Center for Health Statistics (1982), it accounts for 10 percent of all doctor visits, 18 percent of all hospital stays, and 18 percent of all bed-confined recuperative time.

CEREBROVASCULAR ACCIDENT A *cerebrovascular accident,* or *stroke,* is any interruption of the brain's arterial flow which results in a loss of body functions. When such an interruption occurs, the brain is deprived of its supply of oxygen and nutrients. Strokes have the potential to create numerous impairments, including loss of vision, paralysis, speech difficulties, memory loss, and coma. The specific nature and extent of the impairment depend upon which side of the brain is damaged by the stroke (damage to the right side of the brain, for example, will impair the function of the left side of the body). Death may result if the brain's vital centers, such as those controlling circulation or breathing, are destroyed.

About 80 percent of stroke victims are 65 years of age and older. Each year, about 400,000 Americans suffer from stroke and approximately 160,000 die immediately or shortly after the stroke's onset. Of every 100 who survive the accident, about 10 will be able to return to work virtually without impairment, 40 will be slightly disabled, 40 will be more seriously disabled and require special services, and 10 will need institutional care. Only about 16 percent of the 1.8 million Americans today who have survived a stroke are completely independent (Zamula, 1986).

Cerebrovascular accidents can be caused by several factors. Most are caused by the narrowing of a brain artery and/or by a blood clot. Another possibility is that a blood clot formed in another part of the body finds its way to an artery leading to or within the brain. Strokes may also result from hemorrhage, or bleeding, into the brain after damage to a blood vessel.

Certain conditions increase the risk of a cerebrovascular accident. Unchecked hypertension is an especially dangerous risk because this disease promotes weakened and damaged arteries, not to mention hemorrhage. A personal history of heart attack or other forms of heart disease also increases the risk of cerebrovascular accident. Also at risk are those with a family history of strokes. Smoking, heavy alcohol consumption, high cholesterol intake, and diabetes also increase the risk of contracting this disease. As far as sex differences are concerned, strokes are more frequent in males until the age of 75. After this point, the incidence is about the same for both males and females. Finally, black persons are more vulnerable to cerebrovascular accidents because hypertension is much more common in blacks than it is among whites.

Some of the more common symptoms of a stroke include sudden weakness or numbness in the leg, arm, or face on one side of the body; slurring of speech; difficulty in understanding others speak; and physical unsteadiness. In some instances, a minor stroke may be experienced, called a *transient ischemic attack (TIA)*. While such strokes cause an abrupt loss of body function, the symptoms usually clear up within 24 hours. However, a TIA often precedes the appearance of a larger and much more serious cerebrovascular accident.

The prevention of strokes rests heavily on the control of high blood pressure and the careful monitoring of the aforementioned risk conditions. For persons experiencing stroke warning signs or a TIA, an arteriography is usually performed so that obstructions of the arteries can be located. If needed, arteries can then be surgically cleaned out or treated with anticoagulants (agents that inhibit the normal clotting of the blood). For those suffering from severe strokes, blood pressure must be normalized and drug therapy administered so that further damage to the brain is halted. Once the crisis period is over, physical, speech, and occupational therapy are aimed at restoring as much of the patient's lost functions as possible.

CANCER While cancers can occur at any point in the life cycle, the risk of contracting this disorder steadily increases with age. As we learned earlier, skin, lung, and female breast cancer are some of the more common varieties of this disease, should it be contracted during middle adulthood. These same cancers are also prevalent among the elderly, along with cancers of the colon and rectum, pancreas, urinary tract, and genital organs.

Cancer Prevention Checkups for Older Adults

Adults age 40 and over should have a cancer-related checkup every year. This examination should include the procedures listed here plus health counseling (such as tips on quitting cigarettes) and examinations for cancers of the thyroid, testes, prostate, mouth, ovaries, skin, and lymph nodes. It is important to add that some people are at a higher risk for certain cancers and may need to be tested more frequently. Also, these guidelines are not rules and only apply to people without symptoms. If you have any of the seven warning signs of cancer, a doctor should be seen immediately. The following are the key detection procedures and high-risk factors for specific types of cancers:

BREAST

- An examination by a doctor every year.
- A self-examination every month.
- A breast X ray every year after age 50 (between ages 40 to 50, ask your doctor).
- Higher risk for breast cancer: personal or family history of breast cancer, never had children, first child after age 30.

UTERUS

- A pelvic examination every year.

CERVIX

- A Pap test (after two initial negative tests one year apart) *at least* every three years.
- Higher risk for cervical cancer: early age at first intercourse, multiple sex partners.

ENDOMETRIUM

- Endometrial tissue sample tested at menopause, if at risk.
- Higher risk for endometrial cancer: infertility, obesity, failure of ovulation, abnormal uterine bleeding, estrogen replacement therapy.

COLON AND RECTUM

- A digital rectal examination every year.
- A Guaiac slide (stool) test every year after age 50.
- A Procto examination (after two initial negative tests one year apart) every three to five years after age 50.
- Higher risk for colorectal cancer: personal or family history of colon or rectal cancer, personal or family history of polyps in the colon or rectum, ulcerative colitis.

(Adapted from the American Cancer Society, 1989)

■ Mental Development

☐ Intellectual Variations During Later Life

Many of us regard the elderly as forgetful, unable to think clearly, repetitive, and even senile. As we explained earlier, many of our impressions of old age originate from inaccurate knowledge or social stereotypes. Although it is true that sensory and motor abilities decline with age, judgment and accumulated knowledge can compensate for these losses. A majority of older people are capable of functioning satisfactorily, the most practical criterion of adaptive ability. Thus, it is unfair to say that all elderly persons experience a decline in all phases of mental ability (Aiken, 1982).

How do the elderly perform on IQ tests? For this information to be at all meaningful, we must first understand what the standard intelligence test is measuring. Research findings indicate that there is a general decline in the elderly's ability to complete tasks requiring physical performance (e.g., the subject is asked to arrange blocks) and speed (for certain tasks, the quicker a task is accomplished, the higher the score will be). Thus, lower scores on IQ tests may be due not to a decline in intellectual functions but, in part, to slower reaction times. Indeed, as we have repeatedly emphasized, many individuals can improve, or at the very least maintain, certain intellectual abilities well into old age (Baltes et al., 1988; Botwinick, 1984; Schaie, 1980, 1989).

The elderly can maintain and even improve certain types of intellectual functioning.

Some decline might be evident on tests requiring a response within a fixed interval of time (Cunningham, 1989). General knowledge does not appear to decline with age. Also, scores on verbal subtests (e.g., vocabulary) occasionally decline slightly with age but more often remain constant. For more intelligent individuals, it is not uncommon to find an increase in certain verbal abilities. Thus, among the elderly, we often find reduced abilities for complex decision making, diminished speed of performance, and a decline in some forms of perception. We find few or no losses in verbal comprehension, social awareness, and the application of experience (Kalish, 1982b).

The foregoing means that we need to look carefully at tests and other forms of assessment and decide what they're trying to measure. One cannot generalize about mental abilities; each facet of intelligence must be scrutinized. Moreover, when we give elderly persons everyday learning tasks, we should consider what has been revealed in clinical settings. The elderly work best when they are away from pressure and can set their own pace. Allowing them to proceed at their own speed thus enhances their learning performances (Pezdek and Miceli, 1982).

Another factor to consider regarding intellectual functioning and old age is the general state of health. Healthy aged people generally show little or no loss of intellectual abilities, whereas those approaching death or combating disease may exhibit a marked decline in intellectual function. Such deterioration of intellectual functioning before death is referred to by psychologists as the *terminal drop*. In addition to the terminal drop, thinking processes may be altered by a decrease in the blood supply to the brain, extensive hardening of the arteries, significantly high blood pressure, and other cardiovascular problems.

☐ Changes in Memory

In Chapter 10 we discussed the importance of individual variations in mental processes. Although the aging process may diminish some people's memory abilities, this in no way implies that similar changes will occur for all. However, it is felt that if there are changes, the short-term rather than the long-term memory storage system is more likely to be affected. Short-term storage is remembering recent events or new information that is to be used for only a brief period of time. Among older people, the inefficiency of the short-term memory store may not only lead to frustration and irritation but may also interfere with any type of learning that must pass from short-term to long-term storage (Hultsch and Pentz, 1980).

Long-term memory contains the accumulated experiences and knowledge of a lifetime and does not appear to change greatly with age. In fact, one study (Fozard, 1980) shows that older persons are extremely efficient in retrieving information from long-term storage, particularly when they're not anxious. However, the character of long-term memory needs to be examined before any definitive conclusions can be made. It may well be that only practical long-term memories, for example, those that are frequently recalled, can be readily remembered. Do unrehearsed memories also resist dissolution? The answer to this question has practical significance for all levels of mental functioning. In virtually every instance, well-educated and mentally active people do not exhibit the same memory decline as do their age peers who do not have similar opportunities to use their minds. Nevertheless, with few exceptions, the time

Aging, Creativity, and Life Accomplishments

When Michelangelo began work on St. Peter's Basilica at age 70, he was known to scoff at critics who said he was too old and feeble to undertake such a task. Undaunted by these remarks, he succeeded in creating perhaps the world's most critically acclaimed religious edifice.

Benjamin Franklin fell victim to similar cynicism when he reached his twilight years. The crafty and cunning Franklin, however, proved to his younger counterparts that he was more than equal to the tasks required by a young and fledgling United States of America. At age 70 he helped to write the Declaration of Independence and at 79 was named chief executive of the state of Pennsylvania.

These are but two examples that discount the myth of mental decline during the retirement years. Older persons have succeeded in proving that later adulthood can be a productive period of growth and development in intellectual and creative output. Consider just the following:

■ Johann von Goethe finished the masterpiece *Faust* at age 82.

■ Sophocles wrote *Oedipus Rex* when he was 70 and *Electra* when he was 90.

■ St. Augustine continued to pen theological doctrines well beyond his 70th birthday.

■ Giuseppe Verdi composed the operas *Otello* when he was 72 and *Falstaff* at 77.

■ Laura Ingalls Wilder wrote some of her best children's stories when she was in her seventies. In fact, her very first book was not published until she was 65.

■ Mohandas (Mahatma) Gandhi led India's moral opposition to British rule when he was 77.

■ Albert Schweitzer was awarded the Nobel Peace Prize in recognition of his efforts toward world peace when he was 77.

■ At 72, Konrad Adenauer became chancellor of West Germany and served in that capacity for 14 years.

■ Jomo Kenyatta became Kenya's first president when he was 70.

■ Douglas MacArthur was appointed commander of the U.N. forces in Korea when he was 70.

■ Cecil B. DeMille made the movie *The Ten Commandments* when he was 75.

■ Ronald Reagan celebrated his 75th birthday during his sixth year in office as president of the United States.

Such examples of intellectual and creative ability have undoubtedly etched themselves forever in the annals of time. However, one need not soar to such lofty heights to disprove the myth of mental decline during the retirement years. Intellectual and creative mastery of the world exists in many shapes and forms and may manifest itself in the everyday exploits of older individuals. Thus, though earlier periods of adulthood are years in which to accumulate life experiences and accomplishments, many are now realizing that the retirement years offer an equally fruitful and productive span of the life cycle.

required for memory scanning for both recent and remote recall is longer among the elderly and is more likely the result of social and health factors than of any irreversible effects of age (Hendricks and Hendricks, 1981).

Two other dimensions of memory deserve our attention, namely, recall versus recognition memory. *Recall memory*, which seems to decrease with age, is searching for and retrieving information in storage. Studies indicate that older adults may encounter less difficulty remembering structured events than remembering other types of material (Rattner, Padgett, and Bushey, 1988). Another experiment demonstrated that older adults could significantly raise serial word recall (Kliegl, Smith, and Baltes, 1989). *Recognition memory*, which does not appear to decline with age, does not involve retrieval but, rather, the selection of a correct response from incoming information. For example, a test designed to test recall memory might ask, "Who was the third president of the United States?" The correct answer requires a search of one's memory storage system and retrieval of the answer: Thomas Jefferson. To test recognition memory, the subject might be asked, "Among these five names, which one is the third president of the United States?" Here, a match is required. Retrieval is not thought of as part of the mental process (Botwinick, 1984; Birren, Woods, and Williams, 1980; Smith, 1980).

UNIT REVIEW

- Gerontology and its allied disciplines are today extremely active fields of study.

- The elderly population explosion is becoming a worldwide phenomenon.

- The wear-and-tear, cellular, collagen, and immunity theories were devised to explain physical aging processes.

- Physical aging is both external and internal. There is also a gradual decrease in sensory capacities, mainly hearing and vision.

- Major causes of death among the elderly, in order, are diseases of the heart, cancer, and strokes.

- Although the elderly may exhibit declines in certain mental functions, such as reaction times, intelligence remains fairly constant. If memory storage systems are affected by aging processes, it is more likely to be the short-term bank.

Unit Two:

PERSONALITY AND SOCIAL DEVELOPMENT

The retirement years, similar to early and middle adulthood, have their share of developmental work. In many respects, these complex life tasks may pose more of a challenge than do those faced during any other stage of the life cycle. Financial adjustments are especially difficult to make, particularly for those who have only a Social Security check or a modest pension to depend on. These adjustments may be hard for a retired couple who are accustomed to a higher standard of living. Financial difficulties may disrupt not only the older couple's retirement lifestyle but also their marital harmony. Old age is also a period of self-assessment, a time to reevaluate one's successes and failures. And while evaluating the past and attempting to deal with the present, older persons must prepare for the future. In addition, the retirement years are a time to find new horizons for vocational interests and to experience new status, wisdom, and creativity.

Maintaining their self-acceptance and self-esteem is also important for the aged. Evaluations from significant people and successes and failures in dealing with the environment will help determine how individuals view themselves. Their resulting self-concept encompasses not only their evaluations of their body and behavior but also the overall value that they place on themselves. Biological factors such as physical appearance, health, and certain aspects of temperament help determine the frequency and kinds of one's social experiences and the degree of one's social acceptance. These biological factors interact in complex ways, though, and they always operate within a social context. Therefore, the social evaluations of the physical and behavioral characteristics of individuals who have a particular biological makeup—and consequently their evaluation of themselves—depend on the specific sociocultural group to which the person belongs (Aiken, 1982).

Investigators do not agree as to what effect the aging process in general and retirement in particular have on self-esteem. Some indicate that self-esteem reaches its peak during the middle years and then begins to taper off. Another view is that self-esteem increases with age, provided that the individual does not encounter disruptive life experiences such as a death in the family; that standards of living are not below the individual's level of aspiration; and that the individual is not faced with the fear of being alone or isolated. Fluctuations in self-esteem may reflect the individual's awareness of new life tasks that challenge his or her abilities. In the later years of life, a person's capacity to maintain a feeling of worth depends on the existence of a supportive social environment and the ability to integrate past life events. It seems likely that self-esteem does not change simply as a function of aging but, rather, continues to fluctuate in accordance with the individual's personality and any crises that may occur (Newman and Newman, 1980).

■ Theories of Personality Development

There are several theories explaining personality growth in later life. Two of these, the theories of Erik Erikson (1963, 1982) and Daniel Levinson (1978, 1980), apply to all of adulthood. Robert Peck's (1968) theory also represents a continuation from the middle years of adulthood. Gerontologist Robert Butler (1968; Butler and Lewis, 1981) has also commented on personality dynamics during old age.

☐ Erik Erikson's Theory

Erik Erikson suggested that the key to harmonious personality development in the later years of life is the ability to resolve the psychosocial crisis known as *integrity versus despair*. Ego integrity implies a full unification of the personality, and the manner in which this crisis is met depends on a number of other factors, including social roles, lifestyles, and physical health.

Developmental Tasks of Late Adulthood

1. Adjusting to declining physical strength and health.

2. Adjusting to retirement and reduced income.

3. Adjusting to death of spouse.

4. Establishing an explicit affiliation with one's age group.

5. Adopting and adapting social roles in a flexible way.

6. Establishing satisfactory physical living arrangements.

(Havighurst, 1972, 1980)

Ego integration enables individuals to view their lives with satisfaction and contentment. Having had satisfying social relationships and a productive life promotes a feeling of well-being. Integrity also implies a sense of purpose:

> Although aware of the relativity of all the various lifestyles which have given meaning to human striving, the possessor of integrity is ready to defend the dignity of his own lifestyle against all physical and economic threats. For he knows that an individual life is the accidental coincidence of but one life cycle with but one segment of history; and that for him all human integrity stands or falls with the one style of integrity which he partakes. The style of integrity developed by his culture or civilization thus becomes the . . . seal of his moral paternity of himself . . . In such final consolidation, death loses its sting.
>
> (1963, p. 268)

The lack of this accrued ego integration is frequently signaled by a fear of death and the feeling that life is too short. Individuals experiencing despair feel that time is running out and that it is too late to start another life or try out alternative roads to integrity. Consequently, they view their lives with regret and disappointment. Many wish that they had made fuller use of their potential to attain goals established earlier in life. Thus, the stage of integrity versus despair has psychological as well as social relevance to development in the retirement years.

Robert Peck's Theory

Robert Peck maintains that psychological growth during the retirement years is characterized by three psychological adjustments: *ego differentiation versus work-role preoccupation, body transcendence versus body preoccupation,* and *ego transcendence versus ego preoccupation.*

EGO DIFFERENTIATION VERSUS WORK-ROLE PREOCCUPATION Vocational retirement represents a crucial shift in individual value systems. Personal worth must be reappraised and redefined so that the retiree can take satisfaction in activities that extend beyond his or her long-time specific work role. The salient adjustment issue is related to the question, "Am I a worthwhile person only insofar as I can do a full-time job; or can I be worthwhile in other, different ways—as a performer of several other roles, and also because of the kind of person I am?" Peck believes that ego differentiation is a central issue at the time of retirement. A sense of self-worth derived from activities beyond one's career is apparently crucial to establishing a continued, vital interest in living instead of a despairing loss of meaning in life. Consequently, establishing a variety of valued self-attributes so that any one of several alternatives can be pursued with satisfaction may be a prerequisite for successful aging.

BODY TRANSCENDENCE VERSUS BODY PREOCCUPATION The retirement years bring most people a marked decline in resistance to illness, a decline in recuperative powers, and an increase in bodily aches and pains. For those who equate comfort and pleasure with physical well-being, this decline in health may represent the gravest of insults. Many retired people's lives seem to move in a decreasing spiral because of their growing concern with the state of their bodies. Many experience a state referred to as inner preoccupation. Other older people, however, experience declining health yet enjoy life greatly. This has led some researchers to believe that the elderly person's bodily concerns are not related to age per se but, rather, reflect special life circumstances. Peck suggested that some people may have learned to define "happiness" and "comfort" in terms of satisfying human relationships or creative mental activities, with which only physical destruction could seriously interfere. In their value system, social and mental pleasures and self-respect may go beyond physical comfort alone. This kind of value system may well have to be developed by early adulthood, if it is to be achieved at all, and the retirement years may bring the most critical test of whether or not such a value system has indeed been internalized.

EGO TRANSCENDENCE VERSUS EGO PREOCCUPATION One of the principal tasks of elderly people is realizing that they will die. In earlier years, death often comes unexpectedly, but in old age its inevitability is recognized. As Henry Wadsworth Longfellow wrote, "The young may die, but the old must." Buddhist, Confucian, and Hindu philosophers, as well as Western thinkers, have suggested that a positive adaptation even to this most unwelcome of prospects is possible. The constructive lifestyle might be defined accordingly:

> To live so generously and unselfishly that the prospect of personal death—the night of the ego, it might be called—looks and feels less important than the secure knowledge that one has built for a broader, longer future than any one ego

Personality and social dynamics continue along the entire life course.

ever could encompass. Through children, through contributions to the culture, through friendships—these are ways in which human beings can achieve enduring significance for their actions which goes beyond the limit of their own skins and their own lives. It may, indeed, be the only *knowable* kind of self-perpetuation after death. (1968, p. 91)

Such an adaptation is not a stage of passive resignation or ego denial. To the contrary, it requires an active effort to make life more secure and meaningful, or happier, for those who will go on living after one dies. Adaptation to the prospect of death may well be the crucial achievement of later life. The "successful aged" is the person who is purposefully active as an ego-transcending perpetuation of the culture that, more than anything else, differentiates human life from animal life. Such people are interested in the future and do all they can to make it a good world for their familial or cultural descendants. This might be interpreted as vicarious satisfaction, but it actually represents an active involvement with daily life as long as one lives. It might also be viewed as the most complete kind of ego realization, even as it is focused on people and issues beyond immediate self-gratification in the narrow sense.

☐ Daniel Levinson's Theory

Daniel Levinson theorized that old age, similar to early and middle adulthood, is initially characterized by a transition period. The *Late Adult Transition* occurs between the ages of 60 and 65. Levinson stressed that a person may not suddenly become "old" at this time but that changing mental and physical capacities intensify one's own aging and sense of mortality.

Like Robert Peck, Levinson emphasized the relationship between physical changes of the body and one's personality. He suggested that at this time, there is an increasing frequency of death and serious illness among a person's loved ones and friends. There may also be reminders of decreasing capacities, such as aches and pains. Though there are always individual variations in health, there is a strong likelihood that a person will experience at least one major illness or impairment—whether it be heart disease, cancer, defective vision or hearing, or depression. Such physical changes may be hard to accept, especially for the person who is accustomed to good health. Sometimes medical advice necessitates an accommodation or major change in one's mode of living.

The Late Adult Transition is also marked by the individual's awareness that there is a culturally defined change of generation for those in their sixties. If the person found the term *middle-age* vague and frightening, society's terminology and imagery for the subsequent years of life may be even more difficult to accept. Such terms as *elderly, golden age,* and *senior citizen* tend to acquire negative connotations reflecting personal and cultural anxiety about aging. As Levinson asserted, to a person in his twenties, it appears as though passing 30 is getting "over the hill." When 30, turning 40 is a powerful threat. At each point in life, it seems that the passing of the next age threshold is anticipated as a total loss of youth, vitality, and life itself. What, then, does it mean to approach 60 and feel that all forms of youth, those seemingly last vestiges remaining in middle age, are about to disappear? Levinson answered this:

The developmental task is to overcome the splitting of youth and age, and find in each season an appropriate balance of the two. In late adulthood the archetypal figure of age dominates, but it can take various forms of the creative, wise elder as long as the man retains his connection to youthful vitality, to the forces of growth in the self and in the world. During the Late Adult Transition, a man fears that the youth within him is dying and that only the old man—an empty, dry structure devoid of energy, interests or inner resources—will survive for a brief and foolish old age. His task is to sustain his youthfulness in a new form appropriate to late adulthood. He must terminate and modify the earlier life structure. (1978, p. 35)

In late adulthood, persons realize that they can no longer occupy the center stage of their world. They are called upon, and increasingly call upon themselves, to reduce middle adulthood's heavy responsibilities and to live in a changed relationship with society and themselves. Moving out of center stage can be a traumatic affair, as people receive less recognition and have less power and authority. Their generation is no longer the dominant one. As part of the "grandparent" generation in the family, individuals still can be helpful to their grown offspring and serve as a source of wisdom, guidance, and support. However, a major shift has taken place. As Levinson pointed out, it is time for a person's offspring, as they approach and enter middle adulthood, to assimilate the major responsibility and authority in the family. If authority is not relinquished, aging individuals may become tyrannical rulers—despotic, unwise, unloved, and unloving—and their adult offspring may become puerile adults unable to love their parents or themselves.

Retiring with dignity and security is another important developmental challenge. Whatever the age of retirement, this event should reflect a person's needs, capabilities, and life circumstances. If this is the case, then after retirement the individual can engage in valued work. Now, however, it should stem from creative energies rather than from external pressure and financial need. Having paid one's dues to society, an individual has earned the right to be and do what is personally rewarding and pleasing.

At the end of the life cycle, people face the process of dying and must prepare for their own death. Whereas at the end of the previous stages they looked forward to the start of a new era and a new basis for living, now they know that death is imminent. Even though death may come in a few months or 20 years, individuals live in its shadow and at its call. They must be prepared for some kind of afterlife if they believe in the immortality of the soul. If not, persons may yet be concerned with the fate of humanity and their own mortality as part of human evolution. They are developing, in that they are giving new meaning to life and death in general, and to their own life and death in particular. If individuals maintain vitality, engagement in social life may be continued. They may also serve as examples of wisdom and integrity to others around them.

At this time, persons are above all else reaching their ultimate involvement with themselves. What matters most now is their final sense of what life is about, what Levinson described as "one's view from the bridge" at the end of the life cycle. Such an analysis offers a unique parallel to the Eriksonian sense of integrity described earlier. The task is finally coming to terms with the self, particularly knowing it and loving it reasonably well, and being ready to give it up.

☐ Robert Butler's Life Review

Many older people reminisce about the past as death draws nearer. Gerontologist Robert Butler referred to this process as the *life review* and described it as a looking-back process set in motion by the prospects of one's death. This process allows the individual to relive past experiences and deal with persisting conflicts. The concept of a period of life review is strikingly similar to Erikson's psychosocial stage of integrity versus despair. It may culminate in wisdom, serenity, and peace, or it may produce depression, guilt, and anger.

Reviewing one's past life is especially important to the aged. Faced with isolation, the loss of loved ones, and the nearness of death, the elderly frequently escape into the past. Some memories will produce nostalgia, others mild regret, and still others despair. In extreme cases, an older person's preoccupation with the past may cause panic, terror, or even suicide.

The life review may first consist of stray and seemingly insignificant thoughts about oneself and one's life history. These thoughts may persist in brief intermittent spurts or may become continuous. Some thought patterns may be continually reorganized and reintegrated at various levels of awareness.

The existence of a life review is also evident in dreams and thoughts. The elderly frequently report dreams and nightmares that focus on the past and death. Furthermore, images of past events and symbols of death often appear in waking life as well, indicating that the life review is a highly visual process. Those who can think clearly and have good memory skills can bring accurate episodes of their past to a conscious level (Butler and Lewis, 1981).

The life review is a major step in overall personality development. Butler contends that memory serves our sense of identity and provides continuity and wisdom. The act of recall renews our awareness of the present and restores our sense of wonder. By making a life review, individuals can survey and reflect upon the past and thus achieve new insight into their life experience.

■ Patterns of Successful Aging

Successful aging is difficult to define, and frequently the description merely reflects the values of the person doing the defining. But in any case, successful aging has two important aspects. One is older persons' satisfaction with their life. Are they content with their lives? Do they have a positive self-regard? (Of course, an individual's belief that he or she is growing old gracefully may not be shared by friends or relatives.) The second aspect of successful aging pertains to social roles or interpersonal obligations and responsibilities. That is, successful aging may have an inner, or psychological, criterion and an outer, or social, one. These two aspects of the personality will be somewhat consistent, but there is not necessarily a one-to-one relationship between the psychological and the social aspect of aging (Kalish, 1982b).

Currently there are two theories of successful aging: the disengagement theory and the activity theory. Although some support can be found for both positions, most experts agree that neither theory fully explains the phenomenon of successful adjustment.

☐ The Disengagement Theory

The *disengagement theory* views aging as a mutual withdrawal process between aging persons and the social system to which they belong. Contrary to popular impression, such a gradual withdrawal from society is not a negative experience for the elderly. Rather, the aged frequently view disengagement positively, as this is an age of increased reflection, preoccupation with the self, and decreased emotional investment in people and events. Because of this, disengagement is viewed as a natural rather than an imposed process.

The disengagement theory was the result of a five-year investigation of a sample of 275 elderly persons between the ages of 50 and 90 years. The study was conducted in

Many factors contribute to successful aging.

Kansas City and headed by Elaine Cumming and William Henry (1961). The researchers noted that disengagement was generally initiated by the individuals themselves or by the social system. Retirement, for example, is an event that releases older people from specific social roles and enables them to become disengaged to some extent. Loss of a spouse is another example. In time, when the disengagement is complete, the balance that existed between the person and society in the middle years has shifted to an equilibrium characterized by greater psychological distance, altered relationships, and less social interaction.

Seven years after this study, a follow-up study was made by Robert Havighurst, Bernice Neugarten, and Sheldon Tobin (1968). Because of such factors as deaths and geographical moves, the follow-up sample contained only 55 percent of the people in the original study. This second study showed that although increasing age is accompanied by increasing disengagement from common social roles, some elderly people who had remained active reported relatively high degrees of contentment. On the whole, those who were the most active were the happiest.

This latter point represents the bigger criticism of the disengagement theory, which in general has aroused considerable controversy among gerontologists. That is, many feel that adults who remain socially active are happier than those who have chosen to withdraw. Furthermore, many of the past societal conditions forcing adults into restricted environments have changed. Improved health care, early retirement, increased Social Security benefits, and higher education levels have created new pursuits for the elderly. Because of these social factors, disengagement may be discouraged, and more active lifestyles encouraged. The current view among gerontologists is that disengagement is only one of many possible patterns of aging (Kermis, 1984).

☐ The Activity Theory

The *activity theory* of aging was devised by George Maddox (1964) and his colleagues at Duke University. The activity theory of successful aging suggests that retired individuals prefer to remain productive and active. In contrast with the disengagement theory, this viewpoint suggests that the aged resist preoccupation with the self and psychological distance from society. Happiness and satisfaction originate from involvement and the older person's ability to adjust to changing life events.

How valid is the activity theory of aging? Once again, this theory is only one possible aging pattern. It cannot be applied to all, as not all activities influence people's self-concept and life satisfaction in general. As Russel Ward (1984) pointed out, one's activity can decline without affecting one's morale. Indeed, a more leisurely lifestyle is often regarded as one of the rewards of old age.

The activity theory has received little empirical support. Some research, such as that conducted by Charles Longino and Cary Kart (1982), actually revealed a negative association between formal and social activities and overall life satisfaction. This led many to believe that the activity theory is oversimplified. It may not be appropriate to substitute pastimes, geared to what is believed to be older persons' interests and abilities, for those roles they relinquished as they moved beyond middle age. Occupying oneself with enterprises meaningless in accord with dominant cultural values, presumably still held by older people, may not in itself contribute to adjustment. Nevertheless, there may be an association among morale, personality adjustment, and activity levels (Hendricks and Hendricks, 1981).

☐ Personality Makeup and Successful Aging

Because some individuals are satisfied with disengagement and others prefer to maintain a high level of social engagement, there must be a broader perspective. Many agree that a theory regarding the relationship of personality to successful aging is needed.

One such theory was developed by Suzanne Reichard, Florine Livson, and Paul Peterson (1962). In an analysis of 87 men ranging in age from 55 to 84, these researchers identified five personality types: mature (constructive), rocking-chair type (dependent), armored (defensive), angry (hostile), and self-haters. Mature people seem to be ideally adjusted. They accept themselves (their strengths as well as their weaknesses) and their past lives. Most are relatively free of neurotic conflicts and maintain close personal relationships. The rocking-chair type also has a high level of self-acceptance, although this acceptance is frequently passive. Individuals in this category are dependent on others and perceive old age as freedom from responsibility. The armored rely considerably on defense mechanisms to cope with any negative emotions. Typically well adjusted, the armored are fairly rigid individuals who maintain active lifestyles, presumably as a means of demonstrating their independence. The angry are not well adjusted and make a habit of expressing their bitterness, often in an aggressive manner. They openly blame others for their troubles and are easily frustrated. The self-haters are similar to the angry but blame themselves for their difficulties and failures. They are characteristically depressed and view old age as a demoralizing stage of life. The mature, the rocking-chair type, and the armored were successful at aging. The angry and the self-haters were less adaptive.

A similar classification of personality types and their implication for successful aging was made in another study (Neugarten, Havighurst, and Tobin, 1968). Investigating elderly subjects between the ages of 70 and 79, these researchers viewed personality and role activity as critical determinants of life satisfaction. They identified personality types similar to those devised by Reichard and her associates (1962), namely, integrated, armored-defended, passive-dependent, and unintegrated. However, unlike the Reichard group, the Neugarten group categorized specific types of role activities within these major types.

The integrated type of personality includes the reorganizers, the focused, and the successfully disengaged. The reorganizers are involved in a wide range of activities. The focused engage in moderate levels of activity. They are more selective in their activities than the reorganizers are, and they tend to devote their energy to one or two roles. The disengaged have low activity levels and high life satisfaction (thus supporting the disengagement theory of successful aging). With age, they voluntarily move away from role commitments.

The armored-defended category includes holding-on and constricted personality patterns. Holding-on individuals attempt to cling as long as possible to the activities of middle age. As long as they can do this, they attain high levels of life satisfaction. The constricted reduce their role activities and involvements with other people, presumably as a defense against aging. They differ from the focused group in that they have less integrated personalities.

The passive-dependent personality category consists of two types, succorance-seeking and apathetic. The succor seekers are dependent on others and frequently seek emotional support. They maintain a medium level of role activity and life satisfaction. Apathetic individuals are characteristically passive and have little or no interest in their surroundings.

Growing Old Gracefully: Ingredients to Success

The retirement years can be just as positive, satisfying, and rewarding as any other period in the life cycle. Testimony to this are the millions of older adults in the United States who are leading active, happy, and useful lives. What is it about their lifestyle or personality dynamics that promote stability? Can any factors be identified that promote successful aging? Although answers to such questions are complex, certain factors associated with successful aging have nonetheless been identified.

Life satisfaction Satisfaction with one's life is essential to successful aging. Those who feel that their life has been rewarding typically face their later years with few regrets and considerable personal satisfaction. Persons with life satisfaction also have a positive attitude about the past and the future. Consequently, life remains stimulating and interesting. Moreover, those who have met most of their personal, career, and financial goals will be able to relax during retirement and even go on to set new goals.

Social support system We are all social creatures, and the need for human contact is lifelong. All adults need a stimulating, caring network of family and friends to keep involved and interested in life. One's social network fills the need for affection, attachment, belonging, and a positive sense of well-being. All of these needs are psychological vitamins that better prepare individuals for the retirement experience.

Good physical and mental health The status of body and mind is critical to one's overall sense of well-being. Proper nutrition, exercise, and preventative health care are the ingredients to good health and to feeling good about oneself. Developing good health habits will keep the body fit, improve mental attitudes, help to relieve anxiety and depression, and stimulate mental functioning.

Financial security Not having enough money to meet the demands of day-to-day living can cause concerns throughout all of adulthood, not just the retirement years. However, the lack of it at this time can intensify many of the problems associated with growing old. This underscores the need for careful financial planning, including investment protection and adequate health-care coverage. Also, older adults need to familiarize themselves with community programs, such as senior discounts, prescription subsidies, and fuel or telephone assistance. Steps taken to safeguard financial stability will help promote inner security and well-being.

Personal control over one's life Everyone needs to feel independent and autonomous, but especially so during late adulthood. Personal control plays an important role in successful aging since adults need to be in charge of their personal fate. Even the well-intentioned intervention of family and friends can rob an older adult not only of control, but sometimes of the will to continue living. Independence is vital to the maintenance of a positive self-concept, sense of dignity, and self-worth.

(Adapted from Averyt, 1987)

The last category consists of disorganized persons. Many have poor control over their emotions and have deteriorated thought processes. They barely maintain themselves in the community and have low, or at best, medium levels of life satisfaction.

These two studies indicate that personality is the pivotal factor in determining whether an individual will age successfully and that the activity and disengagement theories alone are inadequate to explain successful aging. Successful aging is greatly influenced by many factors, including health, socioeconomic status, self-esteem, and self-concept. The relationships between levels of activities and life satisfaction are influenced by all facets of one's personality makeup and particularly by the extent to which the individual remains able to integrate the emotional and rational elements of his or her personality (Sherman, 1981).

It is also apparent that no one pattern of aging guarantees satisfaction in one's later years. Satisfaction, morale, and adaptation in later life generally appear to be closely related to a person's lifelong personality style and general way of dealing with stress and change. In this sense, the past is prologue to the future. Though the personality changes somewhat in response to various life events and changes, it generally remains stable throughout all of adult life (Reedy, 1983).

■ Psychological Maladjustment

Late adulthood, or for that matter any stage of the life cycle, is not always characterized by mental stability and successful adjustment. On the contrary, the stresses associated with aging may cause some individuals to become maladjusted. Such maladjustment may be principally psychological, in which case we say the individual has a *functional disorder*. Examples of functional disorders are anxiety disorders, psychoses, depression, suicide, and personality disturbances. Other aged persons may become maladjusted owing to actual brain damage arising from physical deterioration caused by stress or disease. Individuals in this latter category may suffer from any one of a number of disorders called *organic disorders*. Examples of organic disorders are organic brain syndromes, including senile dementia and cerebral arteriosclerosis.

Margaret Reedy's (1983) review of the literature indicated that about 15 percent of the elderly in the United States suffer from at least moderate psychopathology. The incidence rate is higher for those who are in poor physical health, who are advanced in age, or who are unmarried as a result of divorce, separation, or widowhood. About 2 to 3 percent of the aged have been institutionalized because of psychiatric illness, usually in nursing homes rather than in private or public mental institutions. They also tend to receive social and custodial, rather than psychiatric, care.

The statistics also show that the elderly seldom use mental health services. Only about 2 percent of patients seen at public mental hospitals are elderly. There are several reasons for this. First, older persons are often reluctant to seek help. Second, a certain amount of mental illness may be expected and tolerated in the aged. Third, some therapists may be reluctant to treat the elderly because they mistakenly think the aged cannot benefit from counseling. Finally, therapists may not have the training or background to deal with the psychological problems of the elderly. Thus, though this age group's need for mental health services is as great, if not greater, than that of any other adult age group, only a few receive such services (Reedy, 1983; Knight, 1983; Patterson, 1982).

The financial problems often besetting the elderly affect the nature and quality of the mental health care they do receive. Many simply cannot afford care. Those who can

It is estimated that about 15 percent of the elderly population suffers from psychological maladjustment.

may receive less-than-adequate treatment. Furthermore, the medical profession is sometimes guilty of misdiagnosing symptoms or misprescribing medication for the aged. Some may prescribe medication when it's not needed or prescribe excessive amounts.

Part of the problem appears to be the negative attitudes of some physicians and their inadequate professional training in geriatrics. Negative attitudes toward aging and the aged have been largely responsible for the therapeutic nihilism in regard to the treatment of the elderly. The proponents of this nihilism often reflect the view that because old age is irreversible, illness (particularly mental illness) occurring in later life must likewise be beyond significant assistance. As a consequence, palliation and "straitjacketing" accompanied by psychotropic medications often become the treatments of choice, with scarcely any concern for finding reversible causes, effecting a remission, or bringing about optimal rehabilitation. The goal of optimal psychopharmacologic technique in the treatment of the elderly should be to produce remission in the shortest time possible, while avoiding as many side effects as possible (Levenson and Beller, 1983).

☐ Functional Disorders

Functional disorders in old age are related to psychological causes and interpersonal factors that may persist from youth into the later years or may appear for the first time in the aged person. The following is a brief overview of some of the more common functional disorders of old age.

ANXIETY DISORDERS People suffering from *anxiety disorders* do not grossly distort reality or exhibit profound personality disorganization. Anxiety may take the form of tension, trembling, rapid heartbeat, or accelerated breathing. Anxiety disorders are less common among the aged than among younger adults. Among the more common sources of anxiety during old age are perceived helplessness or loss (Simon, 1980).

PSYCHOTIC DISORDERS In *psychotic disorders,* the disorganization of the personality is extensive, and there is failure to evaluate reality correctly. Severe mood swings, memory distortion, and deficits in language and perception are characteristic symptoms. Paranoid disorders have a tendency to increase among the aged, including feelings of persecution and suspicion. However, whereas in young people paranoia often reflects severe psychiatric disturbance, among the elderly it has fewer psychiatric implications. Likewise, there are degrees of paranoia and suspiciousness among the elderly who have sensory deficits, particularly hearing deficiencies (Reedy, 1983).

DEPRESSION *Depression* is regarded as the most common functional disorder of old age. The elderly are vulnerable because they usually experience multiple losses during these years. Severe depression is characterized by intense sadness, hopelessness, pessimism, and low self-regard. Some depressed elderly may also abuse prescription medication, although for many, this is totally unintentional (Simon, 1980).

☐ Organic Disorders

Individuals with *organic brain syndromes* constitute the largest group of institutionalized elderly mental patients. These disorders afflict 5 to 10 percent of people between the ages of 65 and 75 and a steadily rising proportion in older age groups. Among individuals between the ages of 90 and 100, the number with organic disorders climbs to 20 percent. Organic brain syndromes are primarily the result of a massive loss of brain cells in the cerebral cortex. They produce such symptoms as disorientation, loss of memory for both recent and distant events, and the inability to perform routine tasks (Reedy, 1983; Teusink and Shamoian, 1983).

THE DEMENTIAS The irreversible disorders caused by brain impairment are known technically as the dementias. *Dementia* refers to generalized cognitive and intellectual deterioration caused by brain dysfunction. *Senile dementia* refers to the dementia syndrome beginning later in life, usually after age 65. *Presenile dementia* also refers to the dementia syndrome, but beginning before age 65. *Arteriosclerotic dementia* is another part of the dementia group, but this dysfunction is the result of cerebral arteriosclerosis (Reisberg, 1983a).

Let us examine three examples of dementia: arteriosclerotic dementia, Pick's disease, and Alzheimer's disease. Arteriosclerotic dementia is the hardening of brain arteries. This interferes with the exchange of essential substances between the bloodstream and the brain tissue. When arteries become blocked because of the hardening process, the brain is deprived of oxygen and nutrients. Arteriosclerotic dementia typically afflicts persons 60 years of age and older but accounts for only about 20 percent of all cases of dementia. The rupture of a small blood vessel may result in a variety of psychological and physical problems, including mental confusion, dizziness, headaches, and unsteady gait. A succession of small strokes is also possible, resulting in cumulative brain damage. The rupture of a large vessel causes a major stroke, and the person may go into a coma and sustain residual brain damage. Major strokes, known as cerebrovascular accidents, kill more than 200,000 persons in the United States each year and handicap at least 3 million more (Coleman, Butcher, and Carson, 1984).

Pick's disease can strike as early as age 40 or 50. More common in women than men, persons afflicted with *Pick's disease* experience disorientation, impaired judgment, fatigue, and impaired physical and intellectual functions. Atrophy of the frontal and prefrontal lobes of the brain is common. The prognosis of this disorder is unfavorable; most deaths occur within five years after the disease first occurs.

Alzheimer's disease has been labeled the disease of the 1990s, largely because of the number of victims it claims and the mysteries surrounding it. *Alzheimer's disease* has claimed the lives of over 2.5 million persons in the United States and is the fourth leading cause of death after heart disease, cancer, and strokes. It carries a prognosis of a 50 percent reduction in remaining life expectancy and claims 100,000 to 120,000 lives each year (Branconnier and Devitt, 1983; McHugh, 1982; Thomas, 1981).

Because Alzheimer's disease has reached such epidemic proportions, we shall present more than just a brief summary of it. Alzheimer's disease usually afflicts persons over the age of 65, but it can also occur during middle adulthood. Like Pick's disease, it is marked by a progressive, irreversible, neurological degeneration. Some individuals decline rapidly, others more slowly. Some cope successfully with their disabilities and progressive losses, whereas others do not (Jarvik and Winograd, 1988; Cohen, Coppel, and Eisdorfer, 1983; Eisdorfer and Cohen, 1981).

The earliest symptom of Alzheimer's disease is forgetfulness. Later, individuals no longer function as well in demanding employment or social situations. A sense of confusion and helplessness often sets in. Deficits develop in all cognitive and functional areas. Victims become unsteady in their movements and ultimately lose their psychomotor abilities to the extent that they can no longer ambulate. Many become overtly agitated, talk to themselves, cry, and eventually become very passive. In the latter stages of the disease, all ability to speak is lost. Most can only blankly stare and make grunting, guttural sounds (Reisberg, 1981, 1983a, 1983b; Powell and Courtice, 1983).

The exact cause of Alzheimer's disease is not known, but at least six possible explanations exist. One explanation suggests that in Alzheimer's disease there is a deficiency or imbalance of neurochemicals, particularly the enzyme choline acetyltransferase, which is a catalyst responsible for the synthesis of acetylcholine, an essential neurotransmitter. A second explanation suggests that excessive accumulations of toxins in the brain may trigger this disease. Recent research has focused on the effects of repeated exposure to such elements as aluminum and certain salt compounds, although a definite association for any of these elements has yet to be made. Third, it is possible that the brain has somehow lost its capacity for synthesizing proteins. A fourth theory proposes that there might be a genetic connection to Alzheimer's disease. Proponents of this theory speculate that children of Alzheimer's victims have as much as a 50 percent chance of developing the disease. To date, though, researchers have yet to discover the gene or combination of genes responsible for the disease. A fifth theory suggests that Alzheimer's disease might be the result of a unique viral infection, one that does not feature the standard symptoms of infection, such as a fever or an elevated white blood-cell count. A final explanation is the blood-flow theory. This theory suggests that Alzheimer's disease is caused by a marked decrease in blood flow to the brain, as well as a reduction in the amount of oxygen and glucose present in the blood (Cohen, 1983; Sims and Bowen, 1983; Carlsson, 1983; Mann, 1983).

While conclusive answers about the origins of this disease remain elusive, we do know about the brain damage it creates. Early on, the cortical cells of the brain begin a thinning process. As the disease progresses, this thinning becomes more widespread. This will be most evident in the dendritic areas, particularly in horizontally oriented

International Lifespan Development

■ TREATING THE PUZZLE OF DEMENTIA

The widespread nature of dementia and how to best treat it are not issues restricting themselves to the United States. Around the world, it is estimated that 5 to 8 percent of persons aged 65 and over suffer from some type of severe dementia. About half of the dementias occurring in the older population have Alzheimer's disease and another 20 to 30 percent suffer from arteriosclerotic dementia. It is projected that we will see a 100 percent or more increase in dementia in less developed nations before the year 2000 and a 50 percent increase in developed countries.

Even though most dementia patients live in the community, those suffering from this illness constitute the majority of the elderly found in long-term care facilities. In Japan, for instance, about 52 percent of the elderly in psychiatric hospitals suffer from dementia, as do 27 percent of those in special nursing homes. In Israel, 50 percent of the aged who are institutionalized in psychiatric institutions have this condition. Almost 50 percent of all of the institutionalized psychiatric elderly patients in France and the United States are also dementia patients. In relation to all of these statistics, it must be pointed out that family members usually seek institutional care as a last resort. Therefore, many institutionalized dementia victims are in the latter stages of the disease.

Despite gloomy incidence rates, learning how to provide optimal care to dementia patients is an active pursuit in many nations. Many countries are experimenting with variations of day care and day hospitals, other forms of respite care, home health services, and family support groups. In Stockholm, Sweden, special day-care programs affiliated with nursing homes tend to delay institutionalization for many dementia patients. In Great Britain, doctors often alternate periods of in-patient care with periods of care at home in an effort to buttress families who are caring for loved ones with dementia. Respite care such as this is also growing in Japan. Medical programs have been established to provide accommodations for dementia patients whose families face emergency situations. In Israel, respite care services are available to families caring for relatives with dementia and to other chronically ill older persons under the state's "Nursing Services Law."

The care and treatment of dementia patients within the institutional framework presents special problems and concerns. Increasing numbers of dementia victims are being cared for in nursing homes and other long-term care facilities that are poorly equipped and insufficiently funded to meet the special needs of this population. As an illustration, many nursing homes do not have the staff-to-patient ratios or specially trained staff needed to meet the special needs of dementia patients.

To overcome these problems, many nations are implementing model institutional care programs. In Japan, the Ministry of Health designated an existing nursing home in each of its prefectures as a specialized facility for treating dementia victims. In Australia, an innovative program focuses on those who are ambulant but suffering from dementia. The program includes thorough assessment, special environmental design features, recreational and other forms of therapy, and research. And in Spain, the first home for dementia victims was built in 1985 in Orense, an area with a high proportion of elderly persons (Gibson, 1984).

branches. Also becoming evident is the accumulation of degenerated brain tissue (called "plaques") in the hippocampus and temporal lobe of the brain and, later, in the frontal and parietal lobes (Scheibel, 1983).

Gertrude Steinberg (1983) writes that families of an Alzheimer's disease patient endure years of emotional and physical distress. In addition, they frequently bear the frustration that results from knowing that no matter how much effort goes into caring for the patient, there is no hope for recovery. As a result, the family faces a harrowing future, caring for someone with whom communication eventually becomes impossible, whose personality changes, and one who will, if he/she lives long enough, become a human vegetable.

Because of such a tremendous psychological burden, family members need formalized clinical and community services to help guide them. They must also learn to cope with their own feelings and maintain their health throughout this ordeal. An important task for the family is to try to restore dignity to the patient in the wake of progressive deterioration (Barnes, Raskin, and Scott, 1981; Cohen, Coppel, and Eisdorfer, 1983; Reifler and Eisdorfer, 1980).

Especially hard for families is placing an Alzheimer's disease patient in a nursing home, which usually happens when home care is no longer possible. Of course, the decision ought to be based on what is best, both for the patient and for the family. If the patient is disabled, needs continual assistance at night, wanders and gets lost, makes dangerous mistakes in judgment and behavior, or no longer recognizes others as individuals, then institutionalized care is probably best (Haycox, 1980, 1983).

In summary, researchers are trying to fit together the pieces of this disorder. In 1981, $15 million was spent on research designed to uncover answers. We need to fully identify the causes and mechanisms of its development, determine who is at risk and why, devise methods of early and accurate diagnosis, and apply the knowledge through well-trained and organized caregivers (Jarvik and Winograd, 1988; Butler and Emr, 1983; Heston and White, 1983; Powell and Courtice, 1983; Filinson, 1984; Schneck, Reisberg, and Ferris, 1982).

UNIT REVIEW

- Personality theories focusing on the retirement years were developed by Erikson, Peck, Levinson, and Butler.

- The disengagement and activity theories are two attempts to explain the concept of successful aging. Certain personality elments are thought to be connected to successful aging.

- Maladaptive behavior can be either functional or organic. About 15 percent of the elderly suffer from at least moderate psychopathology.

- Of all the forms of maladaptive behavior among the elderly, Alzheimer's disease is receiving the most attention in the 1990s. It has claimed the lives of over 2.5 million persons since it was first discovered and, to date, there is no cure.

Unit Three:

THE FAMILY

By the time most married couples reach retirement, their children have already matured, married, and established independent households. As a result, the typical older family in society today is composed of simply the husband and wife. About two-thirds of all elderly persons are husband-wife couples living alone, most of whom maintain their own households (H. Cox, 1984; U.S. Bureau of the Census, 1989).

The shift of focus away from children and the incorporation of the husband into the home give married life among the elderly a special character. Physical, economic, social, and emotional factors all affect marital relations at this time. However, how well the husband adapts to retirement seems to be especially important. The working woman's adjustment to retirement also needs to be explored. With more women now having full-time jobs, we need to know more about their adjustment and adaptation to this life event (Gratton and Haug, 1983).

Generally, most marriages are characterized by satisfaction and not disenchantment during the retirement years. Elderly couples tend to be happier, less lonely, and financially more stable than aged single persons. Together, the couple is apt to live out their remaining years comfortably. Moreover, if their social ties have loosened because of retirement or disability, the role of the spouse acquires even greater importance. For many, this relationship often becomes the focus of everyday life (Barrow and Smith, 1983; Cohen, 1980).

Diana Harris and William Cole (1980) acknowledged that the event of retirement is responsible for bringing couples closer together. Before retirement, a couple's interests are centered on child rearing and earning a living, but now their interests are directed toward each other. Robert Atchley (1988) added that over time these shared interests are likely to create even more closeness. Furthermore, these happily married couples often have a high degree of interdependence, particularly in caring for each other in times of illness. After retirement, the relative power of some husbands and wives may change. That is, the husband's power may decline when he loses the "leverage" provided by his breadwinner role. The same probably holds true of those women who are the family's principal wage earner.

The sharing of certain domestic chores and tasks is evident among many retired couples. Thus, many marriages become egalitarian when they were not before. Successful marriages tend to be those that have moved away from the instrumental functions of marriage, such as providing money and status, to a relationship based on a common identity of sharing and cooperating. Marital harmony at this and all family stages also is based on the regard and esteem that the partners have for each other (Atchley, 1988; Crandall, 1980).

■ Living Arrangements

One of the more difficult decisions confronting the elderly couple is whether to remain in the home in which they reared their children or to move. Suitable living arrangements, whether they be existing residences or new locations, are quite important to the elderly because they spend so much time at home. Furthermore, suitable living arrangements and neighborhood belongingness greatly influence their morale and sense of well-being (Bohland and Herbert, 1983).

According to the statistics, retired couples prefer to remain in the same geographical location. The U.S. Bureau of the Census tells us that compared with all other segments of the population, the elderly change residency the least. Moving is disruptive at any age, but apparently more so for the elderly. Frequently, the actual problems of moving are compounded by social isolation, intergenerational conflict, or the feeling of imposing upon someone or being imposed upon. A major illness, financial difficulties, or perceptual-motor impairments may interfere even more. These problems are usually interdependent, and the move is part of the overall complex process (U.S. Bureau of the Census, 1989; Lieberman and Tobin, 1983).

Today, approximately a quarter of the elderly live in rural areas, a third live in inner cities, and another 40 percent reside in older working-class neighborhoods on the fringes of central cities. Recently, there has been an increase in the numbers of elderly residing in rural areas. Almost 70 percent of all heads of households over age 65 own their own homes (U.S. Bureau of the Census, 1989; Lichter, 1981).

Yet, although most of the elderly in society today own their own home, this does not always imply a positive situation. The assets we attach to home ownership, such as equity and capital assets, may be nonexistent. Many elderly own their own home but are cash poor. Many of the residences for the aged are also old and shabby. Running such a home is a costly venture, particularly when income from Social Security and pensions depreciates, and health problems curtail a home's maintenance (Howell, 1982; Firman, 1983; Nachison and Leeds, 1983).

☐ Institutional Care

When older people are disabled or can no longer take care of themselves, institutional care may be required. Although only about 5 percent of the elderly are institutionalized, the population of nursing homes is disproportionately old, in many cases over age 80. Most of the residents of nursing homes will die there (U.S. Bureau of the Census, 1989; Atchley, 1988; Kart, 1990).

TYPES OF INSTITUTIONAL CARE

Nursing homes offer different categories of care, depending on the individual's personal needs. Georgia Barrow and Patricia Smith (1983) identified four types of nursing home facilities:

SKILLED NURSING FACILITY *Skilled nursing facilities* provide full-time nursing care for persons with chronic illnesses or convalescing from illness. Typically, such homes have registered nurses who carry out orders from physicians and supervise the patients' care. Licensed practical nurses usually provide the direct care. Typical patients are those requiring daily medications, injections, catheterizations, or cardiac or orthopedic care.

INTERMEDIATE CARE FACILITY *Intermediate care facilities* place less of an emphasis on intensive care nursing and more on personal care service. The patient is usually not in medical distress but, rather, needs help in daily routines, such as eating, bathing, dressing, or walking. Though a registered nurse may serve as a consultant, the patients are often supervised by licensed practical nurses and cared for by aides.

RESIDENTIAL CARE FACILITY *Residential care facilities* are for persons who are functionally independent but who desire a safe, clean, and sheltered environment in which to live. Social and recreational needs are emphasized more than medical needs. Residential care facilities usually provide personal services such as housekeeping, laundering, and meals.

ADULT DAY-CARE FACILITY In *adult day-care facilities,* persons maintain their own residence but go daily to a specially designated center to receive daily nursing, nutritional, and medical monitoring. The adult day-care facility is a fairly recent innovation and is increasing in popularity. Some of these centers offer day-care supervision to children as well, creating a unique blend of young and old. Many spokespersons, such as Toni Liebman (1984), feel that such a mixture of ages is a positive arrangement and enables the young to understand better the old, and vice versa.

GEOGRAPHICAL DISTRIBUTION OF NURSING HOME RESIDENTS

In the United States, there is a variation in the proportion of the elderly who are institutionalized (see Figure 11-5). The northern states have the highest rate of nursing home use: 7 of the 10 North Central states have 12.5 percent or more of their elderly in nursing homes. Four of these states, Minnesota (16.1), North Dakota (16.0), South Dakota (15.3), and Iowa (15.1) had the largest percentages of elderly persons in institutions. States with high rates of nursing home use tend to have extremely cold winters, which may be hard on the health of the elderly and thereby increase their need

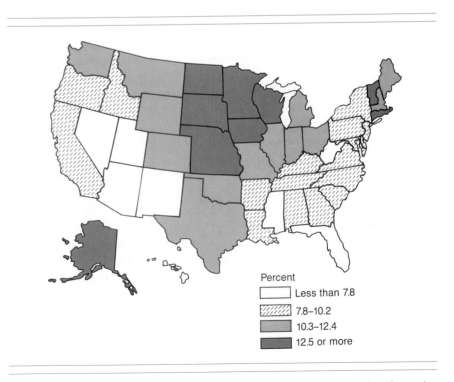

Percent

☐ Less than 7.8
▨ 7.8–10.2
▨ 10.3–12.4
▨ 12.5 or more

FIGURE 11-5 Percentage of persons 75 years of age and over institutionalized in nursing homes. (Source: National Center for Health Statistics, 1984, p. 301)

for nursing home care. Also, these states may have high rates of use because they have small black populations, and overall the white population has a higher proportion institutionalized than the black population.

Conversely, the lowest percentages of the elderly in nursing homes are located predominantly in the southern and western states. In four of these states, less than 6 percent of the population 75 years of age and over live in nursing homes: Florida (4.2), New Mexico (4.7), West Virginia (4.9), and Arizona (5.4). The low rate for Florida can be attributed to the immigration of many retired persons whose health is generally superior to that of the overall elderly population. The reasons for the low rates of nursing home institutionalization in New Mexico and West Virginia are not as clear, though it is possible that the larger Latin population in New Mexico may use nursing homes less than the white population does (National Center for Health Statistics, 1984).

ADJUSTMENT TO INSTITUTIONALIZATION

In the traditional nursing home, the aged are patients as well as residents. Typically, they share rooms, preventing much privacy or much personal decorating. Many nursing homes have a recreation room for those not confined to their beds, and some offer social activities, but most residents spend their time watching television or reading. The majority of residents in nursing homes are single, their spouses having died before them (Leslie and Leslie, 1980).

Adjusting to institutional care may be difficult. Let us make it clear at the outset that there are many who adjust well to institutionalized care. However, many do not. For example, many view nursing homes very negatively because they want to remain in familiar surroundings and near relatives and friends. Most of the aged, though, have negative feelings toward institutionalization because of their loss of independence and because they believe that their placement in a nursing home represents formal proof that death is near. Many also have a fear that once placed in a nursing home, they will be rejected and forgotten by their children (Atchley, 1988; Howsden, 1982). Financial adjustments also deserve recognition. On the average, nursing homes cost about $22,000 a year. One source (Ruffenach, 1988) estimates that many elderly residents without family go broke within six months.

Many react negatively to the impersonalization of nursing homes, which often includes feeding and bathing in an assembly line and treating all of the residents alike, with little or no regard for individual differences. Sometimes, residents are spoken to only when orders are given. Dress, manners, and conversations are under constant scrutiny. The result is the total visibility of the resident and a complete lack of privacy (H. Cox, 1984).

Therefore, nursing home residents often develop what Robert Butler and Myrna Lewis (1981) call *institutionalism,* a psychological state brought about by a depersonalized environment. Persons afflicted with institutionalism often develop automatic behaviors, expressionless faces, and general apathy. They become uninterested in their personal appearance, and their morale deteriorates. For many, social relationships become a thing of the past. In those nursing homes in which the resident's identity, interests, and strengths are not respected, institutionalism is likely to surface.

CRITICISMS OF INSTITUTIONAL CARE

In the past, nursing homes have received a fair amount of criticism, much of it focusing on the depersonalized treatment of the residents and administrative inefficiency. Some criticize the programming in general, citing the limited intellectual stimulation of the residents. In short, the elderly simply have nothing to do in many institutions. Many nursing homes in the nation also are substandard, in some instances failing to provide even minimally acceptable conditions (Kalish, 1982b; Vladeck, 1980).

There have been numerous recommendations to upgrade insitutional care facilities, particularly their psychological and social climate. Attempts must be made to promote new relationships to take the place of those lost in the process of growing old or sick. The social integration of long-term-care residents is very important, particularly if social isolation and detachment are to be avoided. Residents should participate as much as possible in establishing the ground rules for their living situations. Some choice is important to preserving their self-concept and identity. The physical structuring of space should offer freedom and safety as well as privacy. Finally, regular interpersonal contacts with the residents will help the transition to the nursing home. This also will convey to the residents that they are not alone, isolated, and discarded, and that they are still valued (Kermis, 1984; Jones, 1982).

Other recommendations are aimed at improving the staffing and professionalism of the institution's personnel, including its doctors. In both the past and the present, doctors have had little contact with nursing home patients. There are several reasons, including the low reimbursement from medicaid and medicare and the feeling of many physicians that the elderly, institutionalized patients are depressing. Improving all aspects of treatment, including psychiatric and dental care, is a consistent theme in the

CHOOSING A NURSING HOME

Selecting a good institutional care facility for the elderly is not easy. They differ in methods of care and treatment, programming designs are not universal, and neither are costs. In an effort to narrow down the choices and find the best possible facility, Barbara Deane (1985) suggests the following:

1. Try to determine, with the aid of physicians or social workers if necessary, which type of facility your parent will need. Examine your parent's financial resources. Does he or she have private means? Does he or she qualify for government-funded nursing home care? Some nursing homes will not accept nonprivate patients or those who will become so in the near future.

2. Try to make several visits—some unannounced—on weekends and late at night to each facility. Does the home seem clean and comfortable? Are the meeting rooms cheerful?

3. Find out if the staff/patient ratio is adequate. How many staff members are licensed professionals (RNs and LPNs)? Does the facility have a licensed physical therapist or a registered dietician on staff?

4. Make sure the staff is warm, sincere, and friendly and that they are willing to answer questions fully.

5. Look to see if most patients are clean and neat. Are those patients who are able to sit up dressed in street clothes by 10 A.M.?

6. Check the bulletin boards, dayrooms, and other areas for evidence of programs and activities. Is there an activities director?

7. Make sure the food is of good quality and that daily nutritional needs are met. If possible, order a tray while visiting and try it yourself.

8. Ask if aides receive training from the professional staff. (Aides have the most direct contact with patients.)

9. What do others say about the facility? Do doctors, nurses, and the families of patients recommend it? Nursing homes often are required to show the results of licensing inspections. Ask for them, but be aware that many inspections concentrate only on small violations.

10. See if the facility works with the families of its patients. Does it provide educational programs or support groups for patient's families?

literature. So, too, is more in-service training on all levels of geriatric health care (J. Mitchell, 1982; Bennett, 1980).

Stricter accreditation and certification requirements have upgraded many institutions and closed down those deemed inadequate. Continued investigation and reform are needed to ensure that the best possible care and treatment are available in these facilities. At the very least, institutional care needs to be made more accountable (Spilerman and Litwak, 1982; Vladeck, 1980; Jones, 1982).

■ The Economics of Family Life

Financial security largely determines the alternatives in adjusting to all stages of adulthood. Old age is no exception. Those persons with sufficient financial resources can, for example, afford to travel, entertain friends, or seek the best of health care. Older individuals with little money can afford to do none of these things. Many will never have any of these luxuries and, even worse, some cannot even afford the basic necessities of life (Atchley, 1988). However, many of the elderly poor were poor before retirement and have adjusted to living simply.

Of those elderly persons 65 years of age and older, about 12 percent live below the poverty level in the United States. Many of the nation's elderly have annual incomes below $6,000. The financial status of black elderly persons, however, is worse: Approximately 38 percent live below the poverty level (U.S. Bureau of the Census, 1989; Schultz, 1982).

Older persons are not only poorer than other families are, but their chances of improving their economic status through personal initiative are extremely limited. Though not all of the nation's elderly are classified as poor, most are dependent on economic resources that lie outside their control. In most instances, the economic status of the elderly is determined by a fixed income, such as Social Security, pensions, or retirement payments. A *fixed income* is defined as those financial benefits that do not vary. Although some receive private income from employment investments and property, such revenue sources are typically supplemental and fail to meet day-to-day living expenses. Living on a fixed income also makes the elderly more vulnerable to the effects of inflation (McKenzie, 1980).

The cost of benefits to the elderly (i.e., Social Security) has increased dramatically during the last two decades and now accounts for about one-third of the federal budget (excluding the billions of dollars in tax subsidies and nonpublic spending). However, these programs are not helping the elderly who really need them—the poor, sick, and incapacitated. On the contrary, the gap between the best off and the worst off among the elderly is widening, creating a crisis for those Americans who today depend on these programs for their survival. Many of America's aged have low or poverty-level incomes, suffer escalating medical costs, live in inadequate housing, and do not have enough supportive social services (Crystal, 1982; Olson, 1982).

More women than men are below the level of poverty. Like men, women need to realize that the "golden retirement years" are largely mythical. The general public and policymakers must also help dispel such myths. An entire generation of women, currently middle aged, will probably follow in the footsteps of their mothers and grandmothers who, when widowed, found themselves at or below the poverty line. Those in their middle years may also become the victims of changing family structures and the life expectancy gap between men and women. Educational materials and personal retirement counseling can help demonstrate to these middle-aged women the need to plan more carefully for old-age income (Nickols and Wanzer, 1983).

The elderly are often beset with financial burdens.

Economic status affects individuals in other ways. Those with low incomes are more vulnerable to crime, poor health, inadequate clothing, and poor housing than are those elderly persons with higher incomes. Low incomes, then, can be said to aggravate many of the problems associated with growing old (Neuman, 1988; Crandall, 1980).

SOCIAL SECURITY, MEDICARE, AND MEDICAID

Before concluding our discussion of the elderly's economic status, let us examine the nature of Social Security, medicare, and medicaid assistance.

Social Security is the nation's basic method of assuring a continuing income to individuals and their families when earnings stop or are reduced because of retirement, disability, or death. Social Security payments are not intended to replace all lost earnings. Rather, the system was designed to be supplemented by savings, pensions, investments, or other forms of insurance.

Initiated in 1935, Social Security at first extended its coverage only to retired workers. Since that time, though, it has extended benefits to disabled workers. Workers who become severely disabled before age 65 can obtain disability checks. (Under Social Security, you are considered disabled if you have a severe physical or mental condition which prevents you from working, is expected to last at least 12 months, or is expected to result in death.)

Social Security also includes medicare. *Medicare* is a health insurance program for people 65 years of age or older, people of any age with permanent kidney failure, and

How to Beat the High Cost of Living at Any Age

The economics of day-to-day living is more than a passing thought for most elderly. More than ever before, older adults need to carefully examine their financial status, and they need to spend their money wisely. Taking the time to make decisions about spending priorities will help ensure that individuals and couples alike get more for their money. Cynthia Page (1984) observes that there are many ways to go about spending money in the wisest possible fashion. She recommends the following:

- Decide how much will be spent each month for various items and stick to this amount.

- Investigate methods for cutting back on utility costs. Turn off the electricity that is not in use and check home weatherization to maximize heating dollars.

- Try to plan ahead for large expenditures such as mortgages, roofing, siding, major appliances, and automobiles. Also, consult consumer buying guides at the local library to check the quality of a product before making major purchases.

- Eliminate paying interest by purchasing items with cash or a check.

- Rent, do not buy, those items rarely used.

- Plan purchases to coincide with seasonal sales. Also, do not overlook factory outlets, discount stores, garage sales, or even auctions for reduced bargains.

- When planning to travel, investigate package deals and tours, unlimited mileage offers in buses and trains, off-season and off-hour discounts, and the like. These typically offer substantial savings. Careful planning while "on the road" can also save significant amounts of money.

- When grocery shopping, always use a list and never shop when hungry. Carefully examine the cost per unit price and become familiar with grading regulations. A higher grade may refer to the appearance of meat or eggs, rather than to nutritional value.

- Avoid impulse buying. Also, carefully study supermarket advertisements. When an exceptional sale on nonperishable items comes along, buy in quantity. Even though your household may be small, you will eventually use the item.

- Try cooking "from scratch" more often. When convenience foods are purchased, consumers usually pay dearly for the time that is saved.

- Be a comparison shopper. Shop two or three different supermarkets for competitive prices and keep a list of the prices charged for similar items.

---

certain disabled persons. Medicare has two parts—hospital insurance and medical insurance. Hospital insurance helps pay for inpatient hospital care and certain follow-up care. Other benefits extend to skilled nursing care, home health, and hospice care. Medical insurance helps pay for physical care as well as other medical services. Medicare does not cover, however, the following:

- Private-duty nursing care.

- Skilled-nursing home care costs (beyond what is covered by medicare).

- Custodial-nursing home care costs.

- Intermediate-nursing home care costs.

- Physician charges above medicare's approved amounts.

- Drugs (other than prescription drugs furnished during a hospital or skilled-nursing-facility stay or outpatient drugs for symptom management or pain relief provided by a hospice).

■ Care received outside the United States, except under certain conditions in Canada and Mexico.

Beyond the assistance provided by Social Security and medicare is medicaid. *Medicaid* is a program of medical assistance to those in need of services which they cannot afford. Unlike medicare, which is insurance provided by the premiums paid by recipients (past, present, and future), medicaid is provided entirely by grants from federal, state, and, sometimes, county governments. Medicaid was established in 1966 to help the elderly absorb the medical expenses not covered by medicare, as well as to provide medical assistance to other needy groups.

■ Kin Relations

The elderly usually keep in touch with whatever kin they have. For some, this means contact with aging brothers and sisters, but for most, the focus of kin relations is on children and grandchildren. More than 80 percent of the aged have living children and often interact with them (Lee, 1980; Streib and Beck, 1980).

Aging parents need to establish generational roles as they become the family system's elderly members. Now they pass the "baton of power" on to the middle generation, in the process attempting to retain as much independence and involvement as the family system will allow. Through much of the life cycle, help flowed mainly from parents to children. This flow is gradually reversed as the parents grow old and need help from their offspring. As a result, the adult offspring become the caregivers, and the elderly parents become the care receivers. For some elderly couples, this can be distressing, particularly if they do not perceive this need and want to lead more independent lives. Consequently, it is important to assess each person's perceptions of need (Okun, 1984).

Ethel Shanas (1982) wrote that many feel that old people are alienated from their families. This is largely a myth. Most of the aged in contemporary society are neither rejected by their families nor alienated from their children. However, most research (e.g., Francis, 1984) points out that the elderly often *worry* about their families no longer wanting or needing them. Further, when old people have no children, a principle of family substitution seems to operate, and brothers, sisters, nephews, and nieces often fulfill the roles and assume the obligations of children. The truly isolated old person, despite his or her prominence in the media, is a rarity in the United States. Another mistaken myth is that because of the existence of large human service bureaucracies, families are no longer important as a source of care for the elderly. But the family of the 1990s is an extremely important source of care and support, more now than perhaps ever before. Moreover, research reveals (see Weiner, Teresi, and Streich, 1983) that individuals are seriously concerned about their elderly parents and want to be an integral part of their care and support.

Retired persons tend to live near their children, although this is more true in urban environments than in rural settings. Females maintain closer relationships with other family members than males do. Couples tend to live nearer to the wife's parents and are likely to visit them more often. Also, working-class families are likely to have close family ties, which are maintained by living near relatives. Middle- and upper-class families also have strong ties, but members are often geographically scattered because of career obligations (U.S. Bureau of the Census, 1989; Barrow and Smith, 1983; Kauffman and Ames, 1983).

The emotional support given to aged parents is more important to their psychological well-being than financial support. Furthermore, a large percentage of retired persons refuses to accept financial assistance from their children, largely because they want to be financially independent. This notion of independence extends beyond financial matters and, for many aged persons, means a certain degree of ambivalence. The aged generally do not wish to impose or to be dependent, but neither do they wish to be neglected or ignored (Ward, 1984).

■ Community Resources for the Elderly

Beyond the help and assistance provided by relatives, most surrounding communities offer services to elderly persons. Such services range from counseling and employment opportunities to transportation and financial assistance. But while communities offer a wide range of programs, Eugene Nelson and colleagues (1986) point out that the programs are often not fully utilized by the elderly. This is often due to a lack of knowledge of their existence, misinterpretation of the eligibility requirements, pride or desire to resolve problems on one's own, or misconceptions that resources available to older persons are restricted to the underpriviliged or indigent.

Knowledge of community resources can help retired persons to maintain their functional health and contribute to a containment of health-care costs. It can also promote independent living and a sense of security and general well-being. This is especially true if future needs are prepared for before a problem develops. With this in mind, Nelson and his associates offer the following description of community programs and services most widely available to the elderly.

AREA AGENCY ON AGING OR COUNCIL ON AGING These organizations represent the local units designated by the State Office on Aging. They are supported by federal funds provided by the Older American Act and are in existence to redistribute these federal funds. Typically, they provide no direct service but subcontract for many services, such as legal aid and transportation. They are also required to maintain a referral and information service.

COOPERATIVE EXTENSION SERVICES County extension services are typically located at state universities and have county-level units with statewide staff supports. Programs that emerge are developed in cooperation with the U.S. Department of Agriculture. Cooperative Extension Services provide a wide variety of programs, including topics on nutrition, health, and economics. Information on community resources is also available.

SENIOR CENTERS These centers offer a multitude of services to the elderly in the surrounding neighborhood. Programs include meals, transportation, recreational activities, and education, to name but a few areas.

CITY OR COUNTY PUBLIC HEALTH DEPARTMENT The health-care needs of community residents are targeted by these and similar agencies. Information on the nature of health-care services in the area is usually available.

AMERICAN ASSOCIATION OF RETIRED PERSONS Local chapters of this organization maintain information about community programs and provide a wide range of publications of concern to older adults. A variety of services and educational programs are also available, including Widowed Persons Service, Tax Aide, Health Advocacy, and Citizen Representation. Adults 50 years of age and older are eligible for membership.

AMERICAN RED CROSS Local chapters of this organization, listed in the telephone directory, provide such services as friendly visiting and transportation. Some chapters may also offer courses to older adults on such topics as family health, nutrition, high blood pressure, and home care. First aid and cardiopulmonary resuscitation are also among the topics taught.

VOLUNTARY HEALTH ORGANIZATIONS These organizations are also easily found in the telephone directory. Organizations such as the American Heart Association, American Cancer Society, and the American Lung Association have local chapters with educational materials and programs directed toward the health concerns of the elderly.

SELF-HELP GROUPS These organizations share successful ways of coping with problems, in the process providing support to members. Among the nearly 150 major self-help organizations throughout the country are Alcoholics Anonymous, the American Diabetes Association, and Alzheimer's Disease and Related Disorders Association. Organizations previously mentioned, such as the Area Agency on Aging, should have directories listing self-help groups in one's neighborhood.

MEALS ON WHEELS Free delivery of hot meals (usually one per day, along with a cold meal) to the homebound is sponsored by this organization. Some Meals on Wheels programs have age or income guidelines for eligibility; others do not.

HOME HEALTH AGENCIES These organizations typically include the professional skills of visiting nurses, physical therapists, medical social workers, occupational therapists, and speech therapists. Homemakers and home health aides are also often part of these agencies. Homemakers usually provide personal and homemaking services, such as meal preparation, laundry, and transportation. Home health aides typically assist in personal care activities of the elderly, such as dressing and eating. Typically, care from all facets of home health agencies are available at least eight hours a day, five days a week, and should be available on a need basis 24 hours a day, seven days a week.

■ Grandparenthood

Because men and women are living longer today, more children than ever before will get to know their grandparents. Over three-fourths of persons age 65 and older have grandchildren, and three-quarters of these see their grandchildren every week or so. For many, grandparenthood begins during middle adulthood, giving adults the opportunity to make a lasting contribution to their grandchildren, if they desire. Grandparents can serve as sources of knowledge, wisdom, love, and understanding and can greatly affect the lives of their grandchildren (Orthner, 1981; Wood, 1982).

The grandchild typically establishes a bond of a common interest between the grandparents and the younger couple. Becoming a grandparent also adds a new dimension to the lives of retirees, and, in most instances, this dimension is a positive one. Many feel that the connection between the grandparents and the grandchild is an important one, an experience that gratifies both old and young (Kornhaber and Woodward, 1981). Helen Kivnick (1982) found that many grandparents idealize the role and importance of grandparenthood.

But becoming a grandparent is not always a positive experience. For some, it represents a visible sign of aging. And there may be disagreements between grandparents and adult offspring regarding child rearing. Many resist the stereotyped qualities and expectations attached to grandparenthood, such as the time, care, and services that

Grandparenthood offers a unique bond to both young and old.

grandparents are supposed to give to their grandchildren. Likewise, some feel exploited for babysitting services. One study (Cohler and Grunebaum, 1980) found that not all grandparents are willing to carry out the perceived expectations of grandparenthood, mainly child care.

The role of grandparent seems to have special significance for the grandmother. Grandparenthood may even be viewed as a maternal experience, largely because of the woman's dominant role in child rearing. Although most men enjoy being a grandfather, grandmothers assume a more active role right from the beginning. Grandmothers frequently care for the new mother, her baby, and her family during the immediate postnatal period. She therefore often becomes the person who first diapers, bathes, and otherwise cares for the baby outside the brief intervals when the mother does so. After she returns to her own home, she is usually expected to continue a grandmotherly concern for the mother's well-being and the grandchild's care. The adjustments made by many grandmothers do not change appreciably as they age, as many do not have to cope with retirement. They continue essentially the same roles right into old age. Their care of grandchildren thus usually is welcomed, and they can gradually slow the pace as their physical and emotional needs dictate (Leslie, 1982).

Grandfathers appear to become more involved with their grandchildren after retirement. Without jobs to claim most of their energy, many want to spend more time with their grandchildren. They begin to visit with them more, take them for walks, buy them gifts, and participate in their overall care (Leslie, 1982).

We might point out, though, that the roles of grandparents have changed over the years. For example, the grandmother today is apt to be a working woman. Also, the fact that now many grandparents are middle aged means that the rocking-chair image of the grandparents must be changed. This latter point has important implications for adult socialization, role modeling, and family interaction (Bell, 1983).

In the minds of many, grandparenthood is a generational relationship primarily between very young grandchildren and their grandparents. Unfortunately, there has been very little research on the relationship between adolescent grandchildren and their grandparents. But often there is a closeness or affinity between the two, and common circumstances may promote such an affinity. First, both are age groups adjacent to the age group that dominates society; yet often neither has much power over or influence on the decision makers. Second, both tend to be aware of their nonproductive roles (at least the retired elderly and the adolescents who are not yet employed), and both may perceive themselves as "taking from society without putting anything back in" (although the adolescent's potential to be productive in the future is denied to the elderly). Third, both are viewed as having a leisurely life: Education and retirement are seen as pleasure, not as work or boredom. Fourth, both live with their time quite unstructured. The time structure that does exist for the two is seldom perceived by middle-aged parents. Fifth, both are frequently viewed as being inadequately educated, the adolescents not yet educated by experience and the elderly often lacking more formal education. Finally, both are seen as relatively poor and consequently as vulnerable and weak. Yet, despite these similarities, there are tensions between the young and the old, largely based on their differing needs and values (Kalish, 1982b).

UNIT REVIEW

- Most marriages during the retirement years are characterized by happiness and satisfaction, not disenchantment.

- About 10 percent of the aged require institutional care. Types of institutions include skilled nursing, intermediate care, residential care, and adult day-care facilities. Institutionalization requires numerous adjustments.

- Many of the elderly have financial problems. In particular, the poor, sick, and incapacitated need greater federal benefits.

- Satisfying kin relations are important to the aged. The notion that the elderly are alienated from their families is a myth.

- Grandparenthood adds a unique dimension to the lives of retirees, which differ somewhat for grandmothers and grandfathers.

■ Unit Four:

RETIREMENT

Retirement from the world of work is a developmental task that can be viewed in a variety of ways—as a social process or as a phase of life. *Retirement* means the end of formal work and the beginning of a new role in life, one that involves behavioral expectations and a redefinition of self. Regardless of the perspective from which it is viewed, however, one thing is certain—retirement is a complex social phenomenon that touches the life of almost everyone (Atchley, 1988; Schuller, 1989; Laczko, 1989).

Underlying any attitudes toward retirement is the predominant role of work in our society. Coupled with the high premium placed on youth, the work ethic places most older persons in double jeopardy. The youth orientation discourages people from acknowledging their aging: The highest compliment in the minds of many is "You don't look your age." The work orientation in our society discourages people from identifying themselves as retired; some are embarrassed or uneasy socially when asked, "What do you do?" (Sinick, 1980).

For many, retirement serves as a reminder of advancing age. Some regard it is an outright insult and demotion to second-class citizenship. Let us not forget those, though, who look forward to retirement. Many do so eagerly, having waited years to be free to do the things they have always wanted to do, without having to go to work each day. These individuals would be most upset if the option of retirement were removed (Kalish, 1982a).

Daniel Sinick (1980) proposes that satisfaction with work usually has something to do with why some dread retirement and others look forward to it. The opportunity to take early retirement is often a touchstone of job satisfaction. People who like their work, including job duties, coworkers, and work situation, stay on despite retirement income inducements. Dissatisfaction with one's work is a common reason for looking forward to retirement.

Retirement is a phenomenon of modern industrial society. In the United States, there are more than 27 million persons over the age of 65 who are classified as retired. Furthermore, the proportion of retirees in the general population will steadily increase. If present trends continue, it is estimated that there will be 33 million retirees in the year 2000 (U.S. Bureau of the Census, 1989).

The retirement period for most people is also growing longer. On the average, the man who retires at age 65 will live for another 14 years. A woman who retires at 65 will live for another 18 years. By the turn of the century, it is expected that, on the average, a person will live another 25 years after retirement (U.S. Bureau of the Census, 1989; National Center for Health Statistics, 1989).

Retirement is a process that affects both husband and wife.

Dimensions of Retirement

Retirement has numerous dimensions and consequently can be defined in several ways. The most inclusive definition of a retired person is an individual who is not employed full time throughout the year and who receives some kind of retirement pension from previous years of employment. However, some individuals—such as career military personnel—finish their terms of employment only to begin another full-time job. Thus, even though such individuals draw pensions and are likely to receive other retirement benefits, they cannot be classified as retired. Similarly, numerous older workers lose their jobs and cannot find another. Until they reach the minimum age, they are unable to draw retirement pensions and consequently are classified as unemployed rather than retired (Atchley, 1988; Parker, 1982).

Retirement is viewed as the concluding stage of the occupational cycle. It is a transition from an economically productive role, which is clearly defined, to an economically unproductive role, which is often vague and ambiguous. This ambiguity in the retirement role is because of its relatively new and different social position, for which there is no precedent. In the past, people worked for nearly their entire lives. But today, people retire and live out their remaining years doing other things (Laczko, 1989; Harris and Cole, 1980).

Though there has been much research on male retirement, more research is needed on female retirement. More women than ever before are retiring from the labor force, and we need to understand what prompts them to leave as well as how they adapt to retirement. In addition, retirement programs may need to be adjusted for the many women in the labor force. These programs probably should be realigned to serve the divergent needs of male and female retirees (Rosenthal, 1990; Grace, 1989; Gutek, Stromberg, and Larwood, 1988; Henretta and O'Rand, 1983; Gratton and Haug, 1983; Szinovacz, 1982; Johnson and Price-Bonham, 1980).

MYTHS ABOUT OLDER WORKERS The impressions we have about older workers may have a bearing on our attitudes toward retirement. Unfortunately, a number of myths and misconceptions about aged employees exist, and need to be debunked. Among these are the following:

- *Older workers are slow. They cannot meet the production requirements of the company.* This is a widespread myth that is basically unfounded in fact. There is no significant decline in performance and productivity in older workers. On the contrary, many older employees exceed the average output of younger workers.

- *Older workers are absent from work too often.* If anything, it is the younger worker who is guilty of missing work too often. The attendance record of workers over the age of 65 compares favorably with that of any other age group.

- *Older employees can't meet the physical demands of the job.* Today, only about 14 percent of jobs require great strength and heavy lifting. Labor-saving machinery makes it possible for older workers to handle 86 percent of modern jobs without difficulty.

- *Older employees are inflexible. They're difficult to train because they can't accept change.* Adaptability depends on the person, rather than on his or her age. Most elderly demonstrate flexibility in accepting changes in occupational demands.

> ■ *Hiring older workers will increase company pensions and insurance costs.* Today, most pension plans provide for benefits related to length of service, or earnings, or both. When incurred, small additional pension costs are usually offset by the older employee's quality of work, experience, and low turnover. Moreover, costs of group life, accident, health insurance, and workers' compensation are materially increased by hiring older employees (adapted from Arnold et al., 1982).

■ Early Retirement

We mentioned earlier that not all workers are angered or saddened by retirement. On the contrary, many look forward to the time when they won't have to work. Statistics also show that workers are retiring earlier than ever before; the average retirement age in the United States is edging closer to age 60. Many of these early retirees are military personnel and civil servants, but this vocational trend is spreading among workers in a diversity of employment settings (Allan and Brotman, 1981; Prentice, 1980; Foner and Schwab, 1981).

There are many reasons why workers decide on early retirement. Early retirement is often associated with a favorable financial outlook and a suitable standard of living for the retiree. Likewise, many retire early because pension plans are financially attractive. Some early retirees want a lighter workload; others may be in declining health. Some opt for early retirement because they are having difficulty keeping up with their work. Some are drawn to the status and positive image that early retirement often generates. Finally, we can add to this list that many retire early because of the support they receive from others. Family and friends, as well as fellow workers, may endorse early retirement.

Many experts predict that the trend toward early retirement will continue. A number of industries and businesses have made early retirement attractive to their employees by offering larger pension benefits, pension supplements, and lump-sum payments. Lowering the age of eligibility for Social Security benefits to age 62 has also fueled this trend, as have rising Social Security benefits in general. The result of all this is that more workers, blue collar as well as white collar, are choosing early retirement (Harris and Cole, 1980).

International Lifespan Development

■ PASSAGES TO RETIREMENT: OPTIONS AND OPPORTUNITIES

Numerous firms overseas offer phased, gradual, or gliding retirement programs. This way, older workers are allowed to reduce their working time in stages—daily, weekly, monthly, or annually—in the months and, in some instances, years preceding full retirement. This is usually accomplished with little or no reduction in net compensation and benefits.

Most of these programs abroad appear to have been instituted by employees, but a number of them have been implemented through collective bargaining within firms or across industries—in both cases, often out of a sense of social responsibility for employees who have provided long service. Two countries, Sweden and Norway, provide the opportunity for older workers to ease into retirement through nationally legislated policies affecting all firms in these nations. And France has recently enacted legislation which permits firms that enter into "solidarity contracts" with the government to allow their older employees, starting at age 55, to reduce their work time by half, provided employers replace the lost hours with new personnel (Swank, 1982).

Interesting cross-cultural variations exist in regard to early retirement, too. Because of high unemployment, a number of European nations have liberalized eligibility requirements permitting older workers who are either unemployed or who voluntarily surrender their jobs and agree not to seek other employment to take an early retirement. Such early retirement programs start at about age 60 with little loss in income or benefits. Additionally, individuals remain eligible for full pension benefits at the normal retirement age.

In France, for example, early retirement is regarded as a desirable goal among the work force. Unemployed older workers who are laid off at age 60 or older (sometimes even at age 55), or who resign and agree not to take another job, can draw a pension roughly equivalent to 70 percent of their last salary. This "guarantee of resources" is even adjusted twice a year for inflation. When early retirees reach age 65, they become eligible for full pension benefits.

In the Netherlands, workers in trade and industry may opt for an early retirement at age 62 or 63 (if they have worked for the same employer over the preceding ten years) at approximately 85 percent of their full-time wages. They also preserve the right to claim a full pension at the national retirement age of 65. However, the number of persons electing to do this is relatively small, and only about 25 percent of jobs opened by such early retirements are being filled by persons who are unemployed. Many of the vacant positions are simply abolished.

Finally, let us acknowledge that even on a cross-cultural basis, there are many workers who resist the very notion of retirement. Consider the employment picture of Japan, which has the highest proportion of men (from any nation) aged 60 and over participating in the labor force. About 74 percent of Japanese men between the ages of 60 and 64 are working, in contrast to about 67 percent in Great Britain, 57 percent in the United States, 44 percent in West Germany, and 40 percent in France. In Japan, employment is enhanced by a perception of work being rewarding and good for health; the prevalence of family business units; widespread practices of rehiring and continuation of services following official retirement; and management's willingness to compensate for older workers' changing physical and mental status (Osako, 1986).

Realizing the value of older employees, some countries offer strong incentives for older workers to remain in the labor force. In the Soviet Union, labor shortages and a healthier and more long-lived older population has prompted the government to promote the employment of retirees. Statistics support how successful these efforts have been: The Soviet Union has a national average of about 8 million active retirees out of a total retired population of about 32 million. To assist older workers, special committees at the regional, city, and district levels locate appropriate employment vacancies and oversee working conditions. Additionally, vocational orientation programs have been established and lists of suitable professions and trades are regularly published. Beyond such programming, government policy provides workers with powerful financial incentives to remain in the labor force. Many retirees can receive both a full pension and a full salary, increasing their income substantially. Moreover, retirees postponing their retirement for five years beyond the normal pensionable age (60 for men, 55 for women) are eligible for a 20 to 30 percent higher pension (Nusberg, 1986).

■ Adjusting to Retirement

Today's retired persons, particularly those who decide to retire early, are healthier than were the retirees of past generations. Because retirement as a period of life is such a new developmental phenomenon, however, our culture has yet to decide on the suitable behavior for this time. Consequently, each of us may react differently.

□ Psychological Adjustments

Leaving the world of work and relinquishing a significant part of one's identity is a difficult psychological adjustment. For many, such a transition brings a major loss of self-esteem. The ability to deal with this stage of life depends to a considerable extent on past adjustment patterns. Those who adjust well to retirement are typically able to develop a lifestyle that continues their past one and meets their long-term needs. Successful adjustment is also characterized by the harmonious resolution of demands and tasks throughout the course of one's life.

In general, most are able to adjust to the retirement role. Should the experience be negative, it is usually because the retirement event is perceived as being stressful or because of health and/or financial trouble (see Rikers and Myers, 1989; Foner and Schwab, 1981; George, 1980). According to Paula Morrow (1980), some are unhappy because of inappropriate expectations for retirement or because they were overcommitted to their work role. Interestingly, though some retirees report missing a feeling of being useful, most do not miss the work itself (National Council on the Aging, 1981).

Retirement for many brings about considerable satisfaction. Herbert Parnes (1981) found that about 80 percent of retirees felt that retirement fulfilled or exceeded their expectations. Furthermore, about 75 percent reported that they would retire at about the same time or earlier if they had it to do over. However, there is evidence (Foner and Schwab, 1981; George, 1980) that white-collar workers are generally more satisfied with retirement than blue-collar workers.

☐ Financial Adjustments

For many persons, the biggest adjustment to retirement is financial. A dramatic drop in income almost always accompanies retirement. Statistics show that in 1989, about 12 percent of persons age 65 years and older were below the poverty level in the United States. The figure jumps to 38 percent for black persons 65 years of age and older (U.S. Bureau of the Census, 1989). Figure 11-6 displays sources of income for members of the retired population.

For most retired persons, Social Security is their main source of income. When this is the case and there are no job-related benefits, economic hardship may be the

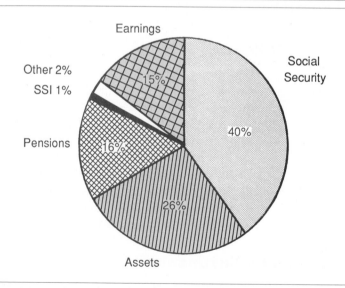

FIGURE 11-6 Sources of income of older U.S. population. (Source: Adapted from the U.S. Bureau of the Census, 1988)

result. Obviously, the retired worker needs far more than Social Security benefits to live comfortably. Job-related pensions are critical, especially for women, who often face yet another instance of vocational inequality. On the average, retirement benefits are far lower for women than they are for men. In 1989, for example, the average retirement benefit for a retiring woman was about one-half that for a retiring man (U.S. Bureau of the Census, 1989; Porter, 1980; Soldo, 1980; Marsh, 1981; Soldo and Agree, 1988).

Russell Ward (1984) found that many elderly become "poor" for the first time in their lives during retirement. Though some are financially stable, most are not. Moreover, there is no evidence that a reduced income reduces the need or desire for consumer goods and services. Compared with younger families, older families often spend a greater share of their income on food, housing, and health care.

☐ Social Adjustments

Retirement signifies the loss of job-related social contacts, although many compensate for this by establishing new friendships. The retiree must also adjust to the fact that his or her work-related reference group is now gone. The absence of feedback from employer and coworkers has important implications for the retiree's sense of identity. For many, this becomes a time to search elsewhere for a meaningful reference group and realign and reassess their self-image. More specifically, individuals need to establish who they are beyond the work they performed each day. This is another good example of how development in one area affects development in other areas. In this case, social development (the loss of a work-related reference group) affects psychological development (the need to reassess one's identity). Truly, developmental forces are joined throughout the entire life cycle.

It appears that those who make the best adjustments are the ones who develop new interests quickly. Healthy adjustment is characterized by managing to resist the shrinkage of one's social world. Finding substitutes for work and maintaining a support network of friends are characteristic of those who adjust well to retirement (H. Cox, 1984; Rikers and Myers, 1989).

Retirement can be both positive and negative for husband-wife relations. On the positive side, a couple can now spend more time together and pursue mutual interests. Retirement can mean years of relaxation and enjoyment of one another's company. On the negative side, the increased time together may strain the marriage. The couple may get on each other's nerves, and household chores may increase.

Elizabeth Hill and Lorraine Dorfman (1982) explored the reactions of women to their husband's retirements and found that a majority appreciated the companionship and time availability that this life stage can bring. However, these researchers also found that there are negative dimensions to retirement. Among the more common complaints were financial difficulties and the husbands' lack of things to do. Twenty-two percent of the respondents felt that retirement brought too much time together.

How do retirees spend all of their free time? For many, there is an alternation between busy periods devoted to commitments and relatively unstructured periods devoted to recreation. In addition, those people who learned to structure their time when they were younger continue to do so when they are retired. Leisure activities are probably the pivot of the temporal order of the elderly, and the fulfillment of commitments is undoubtedly carried out as a function of this pivot. It also appears that the interaction of economic status and personal characteristics is the determining factor in how time is managed (Delisle, 1982).

Increasing numbers of retirees are going back to school. The Elderhostel, first begun in 1975, has become especially attractive. The Elderhostel invites the elderly to reside on college campuses at low costs and attend a wide variety of classes, seminars, and workshops.

■ Stages of Retirement

To understand the adjustments required of elderly persons, it is helpful to know the various processes and phases of retirement. Our understanding of these areas has been enhanced by Robert Atchley (1982a, 1982b; 1988; Atchley and Robinson, 1982). Atchley views retirement not only as a process but also as a social role with six phases that require different adjustments. Because the retirement period is an individual phenomenon that varies in duration, relating these six phases to chronological ages is impossible. And, individuals may not go through all the phases or encounter them in the order proposed.

Before we examine these six phases, we need to understand the significance and ramifications of retirement. Atchley (1982b) maintained that the process of retirement begins with attitudes toward retirement, retirement policies, and factors in the decision to retire. The retirement transition has varying effects, depending on how persons arrive at retirement. Those who retire voluntarily usually have little or no difficulty adjusting. Those who are forced out by mandatory retirement policies tend to be dissatisfied at first, but eventually they adjust. Those who retire because of poor health are understandably the most dissatisfied, although retirement improves the health of many of them. Retirement itself has no predictable negative effect on physical health, self-esteem, or life satisfaction. But it does tend to reduce activity levels. A good adjustment in the retirement years depends on having a secure income, good health, meaningful activities, and a happy marriage.

□ The Preretirement Phase

The preretirement phase can be further divided into two substages, remote and near. In the remote phase, retirement is perceived as an event that is reasonably far in the future. This phase can begin before a person takes his or her first job, and it ends when retirement nears. Anticipatory socialization and adjustment for retirement at this point are usually informal and unsystematic. The individual may also become exposed to negative stereotypes of retirement. Of course, an individual's positive or negative reaction depends in part on the prevailing view of retirement of relatives, friends, and co-workers.

The near phase begins when workers become aware that they will retire very soon and that adjustments are necessary for a successful transition. This phase may be initiated by a company's preretirement program or by the retirement of slightly older friends. Some workers may develop negative attitudes at this time because the realities of retirement are much clearer, and financial prerequisites for retirement may not have been met. Many workers also fantasize about retirement and imagine what their life-styles might be after they stop working. Preretirement programs appear to be successful in reducing anxious feelings about the subject.

One study (Atchley and Robinson, 1982) examined the relationship between distance from the retirement event, both before and after, and attitudes toward retirement. The study found that attitudes often become more negative just before retirement and that people who have been retired longer often have more negative attitudes than do those who recently retired. These ideas were taken as hypotheses and tested with data from 173 people in the preretirement stage and 176 people who had retired. In both samples, attitudes toward retirement were generally positive and were unrelated to distance from retirement. Health and income adequacy were the main predictors of attitude toward retirement. The postretirement sample was slightly less optimistic about retirement than was the preretirement sample. The researchers attributed this to the higher incidence of disability in the postretirement sample.

☐ The Honeymoon Phase

The honeymoon phase, immediately following the actual retirement event, is frequently characterized by a sense of euphoria that is partly the result of one's newfound freedom. It is a busy period for many people, filled with such activities as fishing, sewing, visiting family members, and traveling, although these activities are influenced by numerous factors including finances, lifestyle, health, and family situation. The honeymoon period may be short or long, depending on the resources available and how they are used.

☐ The Disenchantment Phase

After the honeymoon phase is over and life begins to slow down, some retirees become disenchanted and feel letdown or even depressed. The depth of this emotional letdown is related to factors such as declining health, limited finances, or unfamiliarity with such an independent lifestyle. In some cases, eagerly anticipated postretirement activities (e.g., extensive traveling) may have lost their original appeal. As one retiree recently confessed to us, there are only so many times you can repaint the house and trim the shrubs. Unrealistic preretirement fantasies as well as inadequate anticipatory socialization for retirement may also promote disenchantment. One retired teacher seemed to say it all: "I miss my students and the activities attached to the school day. I miss being a part of students' lives."

☐ The Reorientation Phase

For those whose retirements either never got off the ground or landed with a loud crash, a reorientation phase of adjustment is necessary. At this time, one's experience as a retired person is used to develop a more realistic view of life alternatives. Reorientation may also be exploring new avenues of involvement, sometimes with the assistance of groups in the community. Many become actively involved in jobs especially designed for retirees, either on a volunteer basis or for pay (Sheppard, 1981).

Retirees often offer their services to others, either informally or formally, through such organizations as the Retired Seniors Volunteer Program. Whether formal or informal, volunteer work has become a desirable and widely recommended pursuit for retired and older Americans. Its benefits include a decreased role loss that frequently comes with advancing age, a means of self-actualization, and a vehicle through which the elderly can voice their political concerns. To society's advantage, older volunteers usually are an experienced and reliable source of unpaid labor (Chambre and Low, 1983).

☐ The Stability Phase

Stability does not refer to the absence of change but, rather, to the routinization of criteria for dealing with change. People who reach this stage have established a set of criteria for making choices, which allow them to deal with life in a fairly comfortable and orderly fashion. They know what is expected of them and know what they have to work with, strengths as well as weaknesses. In the stability phase, the individual has mastered the retirement role.

☐ The Termination Phase

Although death may end retirement in any phase, the termination phase of retirement is usually caused by the illness and disability that sometimes accompany old age. When people are no longer capable of doing housework or caring for themselves, they are transferred from the retirement role to the sick and disabled role. The role transfer is based on the loss of able-bodied status and autonomy, both of which are instrumental in carrying out the retirement role. The retired status is also lost, of course, if a full-time job had been taken.

CHAPTER REVIEW

■ Unit One: Physical and Mental Development

The technical name for the study of aging and the aged population is gerontology. Social gerontologists seek to meet the needs of the elderly population by providing them with special services, programs, and policies. Geriatrics is the branch of medicine concerned with the health care of aged persons. The United States is currently experiencing a population explosion of its elderly, and all indications are that this demographic trend will continue. It is estimated that by the year 2000, 20 percent of the population will be 65 years of age or older.

Physical aging is a complex, degenerative physiological process. Though it is not fully understood, we examined four theories in this unit that have tried to supply answers: the wear-and-tear, cellular, collagen, and immunity theories. There are many external signs of the physical aging process. The skin, for example, wrinkles and loses its elasticity. The hair grays and loses its luster, and many elderly lose their teeth. Because the disks in the spinal column shrink, the aged often experience a slight loss of physical stature.

Internal aging includes degenerative changes that cannot be seen. The heart and lungs no longer operate at full capacity during old age, and there is a reduction of cerebral blood flow in the brain, as well as a decline in oxygen and glucose consumption. The gastrointestinal system produces less digestive juices, and peristalsis is reduced. Muscle strength generally declines, and the bones become less firm and their density decreases. The efficiency of the urinary system also drops and, in general, the body is not as effective in eliminating foreign substances from its system.

Of the sensory changes that accompany the aging process, vision has a tendency to degenerate, and many elderly need eyeglasses in order to see properly. Cataracts and glaucoma are two visual conditions often afflicting the elderly. Hearing impairments due to the aging process, known technically as prebycusis, are also widely reported, particularly among men. Taste sensitivity deteriorates over time, evident at times in the elderly's preference for overly sweet or heavily seasoned foods. The ability to feel sensations on the skin also declines with age.

Elderly people suffer from the same diseases as younger people do, but younger persons have a natural tendency to recover, whereas the elderly have a tendency to deteriorate further. Three leading causes of death among the elderly are heart disease, cancer, and cerebrovascular accidents. Together, these three account for 75 percent of all deaths among the elderly. Of the three, cancer is the only major cause of death to have increased over the years. To safeguard their health, the elderly need to take special care of themselves. Physical activity and balanced diets are considered essential to good health.

Intellectual functions change in old age, but not to the extent that our cultural myths would have us believe. Very few actually lose their intellectual abilities. Although many aged individuals have slower reaction times, their general knowledge and vocabulary usually remain constant over time, and the verbal abilities of superior people may even increase. Some, however, may experience what is known as a terminal drop, the deterioration of intellectual functioning before death.

We concluded this unit with an examination of memory abilities. Although there are individual differences, it is believed that long-term memory remains fairly constant at this time, though there may be a decline in short-term memory. The elderly may also demonstrate losses in recall memory, but little or no change in recognition memory.

■ Unit Two: Personality and Social Development

Like the other stages of the life cycle, the retirement years are characterized by numerous developmental tasks. Particularly significant are coping with declining physical health, establishing satisfactory financial and living arrangements, adjusting to the death of a spouse, maintaining self-esteem, and living on a reduced income. Most experts agree that old age is also a time to reevaluate past successes and failures.

Personality theories concerning the retirement years were developed by Erik Erikson, Robert Peck, Daniel Levinson, and Robert Butler. Erikson believes the key to harmonious personality growth is the successful resolution of the psychosocial crisis known as integrity versus despair. Peck provided a detailed account of three adjustments required by individuals in their retirement years, referred to as ego differentiation versus work-role preoccupation, body transcendence versus body preoccupation, and ego transcendence versus ego preoccupation. Levinson maintains that old age, like other stages of adulthood, is initiated by a transitional period. The aged person must define the self in terms of retirement, decreasing physical capacities, and impending death. Robert Butler's concept of the life review proposed that the elderly reminisce about the past as death draws near.

Successful aging is difficult to define, although it appears that satisfactory adjustment has an inner, psychological aspect and an outer, social aspect. Two theories of successful aging were studied, but neither fully explains successful adjustment. The disengagement theory, which views aging as a mutual withdrawal process between aging persons and society, is by far the more controversial. The activity theory directly contradicts the disengagement theory, maintaining that retired people adjust successfully when they remain productive and active.

Because some retired people are satisfied with disengagement, and others prefer to remain active, it is evident that the dynamics of successful aging involve an additional factor, namely, personality. Three personality types ideal for successful adjustment were identified: mature (constructive), rocking-chair type (dependent), and armored (defensive). Unsuccessful personality types are the angry (hostile) and the self-haters. A study by Bernice Neugarten and her associates found similar personality types but concentrated more on role activities and the resulting life satisfaction within each type. These studies indicate that personality may well be the pivotal factor in determining patterns of aging and in predicting relationships between activity levels and life satisfaction.

Not all retired persons age successfully. Some may react negatively to the pressures of later life. The rates of psychiatric disturbances are higher for those who are in poor health, advanced in age, or unmarried because of divorce, separation, or widowhood. Maladaptive behavior can be principally psychological or functional. Examples of functional disorders are anxiety disorders, psychotic disorders, and depression.

Other types of maladaptive behavior are organic. This means that maladjustment is the result of brain damage caused by physical deterioration. The largest group of institutionalized, elderly mental patients are those with organic brain syndromes, known as the dementias. Generally, dementia produces such symptoms as disorientation, loss of memory for both recent and distant events, and an inability to perform routine tasks.

In this unit we considered three types of dementia. Arteriosclerotic dementia is caused by the hardening of the brain's arteries. This eventually causes blockage, and so the brain is deprived of oxygen and nutrients. Pick's disease is a type of presenile dementia and can afflict persons as young as age 40 or 50. It is more common among women and usually kills its victims within five years of its discovery.

We also discussed Alzheimer's disease, a type of dementia that has claimed over 2.5 million victims. Some label it the disease of the 1990s; each year it claims between 100,000 to 120,000 lives. We explored its progressive, irreversible, neurological degeneration, including deficits developing in all cognitive and functional areas. To date, the exact cause of Alzheimer's disease is not known and, like Pick's disease, there is no cure. Families of patients need special care and support as they try to help their loved ones through the physical and psychological struggles of Alzheimer's disease. Finding a cure and answers to the many questions posed by this disorder is a high priority.

■ Unit Three: The Family

Most retired couples report considerable satisfaction with their marriages. Retirement is responsible for bringing couples closer together. After retirement, the husband frequently assumes new domestic responsibilities, and his involvement in household chores changes his and his wife's domestic orientation and self-image. Because they now share certain household chores and tasks, many marriages become egalitarian.

Most retired couples do not want to change their residence, primarily because they do not wish to face the adjustment difficulties associated with moving. Declining health and limited income are other anchoring variables. Alternative living arrangements for the elderly include mobile homes, senior citizen hotels, and retirement communities.

When the elderly are afflicted with a disability or can no longer care for themselves, institutional care may be required. Though problems of adjustment are centered on the deterioration of morale, social relationships, and the ability to care for oneself, smooth transitions to institutional care are made when the resident's strengths, interests, and skills are assessed, respected, and developed. Four types of institutions for the elderly were discussed in this unit: skilled nursing facilities, intermediate care facilities, residential care facilities, and adult day-care facilities. Recently, all types of institutional care facilities have fallen under the scrutiny of concerned officials, and efforts have been made to improve their quality and standards.

The financial situation of most aged persons in the United States is not good. About 13 percent of those 65 years of age and older live below the poverty line. Unfortunately, most of the nation's elderly rely on fixed incomes and have virtually no way of improving their economic status. Experts feel that a more adequate Social Security system may be the answer.

Kin relations for most retired couples focus on children and grandchildren. Many aged people live near their children and interact rather frequently, although this is more true in urban environments than in rural settings. The emotional support given to aged parents is especially important. At this point in the family life cycle, grown children become the caregivers and the elderly parents become the care receivers.

Grandchildren add a new dimension to the lives of middle-aged and retired couples, although grandparenthood is frequently seen as a maternal experience. After they retire, grandfathers typically become more involved with their grandchildren. Grandparenthood can have both positive and negative dimensions.

■ Unit Four: Retirement

A retired person is someone who is not employed for the entire year and who receives some kind of retirement pension from previous years of employment. We stated that this often entails a transition from an economically productive role, which is clearly defined, to an economically unproductive role, which is often ambiguous. This ambiguity stems from the relative newness of the retirement role in history. This unit stressed the importance of more fully defining the retirement role, for men as well as women.

Even though most do not want to lose the right to continue working, many employees are retiring early. The average age of retirement in the United States is now nearly age 60, and other nations are also experiencing similar trends. A number of reasons prompt workers to retire early: a favorable financial outlook, a desire for a lighter workload, poor health, difficulty in keeping up with the workload, the perceived attractiveness of the early retirement role, and the meaningful support of others who endorse the idea.

Adjusting to retirement has psychological, financial, and social dimensions. Psychologically, retirees must relinquish a significant part of their lives and reassess their identities. Too often, people base their total identity on what they do. Financial adjustments usually are the biggest task for retirees. For many, Social Security benefits are the only source of income, which may bring economic hardship. Retirement usually means the loss of work-related social contacts and an important reference group.

The retirement transition has varying effects on the person. Robert Atchley views retirement not only as a process but also as a social role with six phases: (1) the preretirement phase, (2) the honeymoon phase, (3) the disenchantment phase, (4) the reorientation phase, (5) the stability phase, and (6) the termination phase.

KEY TERMS

activity theory

adult day-care facility

ageism

Alzheimer's disease

anxiety disorder

arteriosclerotic dementia

arthritis

autoimmunity theory

body transcendence versus body
preoccupation

cataract

cellular theory

cerebrovascular accident

collagen theory

conductive deafness

cross linkage

dementia

depression

disengagement theory

ego differentiation versus work-role
preoccupation

ego transcendence versus ego
preoccupation

fixed income

free radical

functional disorder

geriatrics

gerontology

glaucoma

hypertension

immunity theory

institutionalism

integrity versus despair

intermediate care facility

medicaid

medicare

organic brain syndrome

organic disorder

osteoarthritis

osteoporosis

Pick's disease

presbycusis

presenile dementia

psychotic disorders

recall memory

recognition memory

residential care facility

retirement

rheumatoid arthritis

senile dementia

sensorineural deafness

skilled nursing facility

social gerontologist

Social Security

stroke

terminal drop

transient ischemic attack (TIA)

wear-and-tear theory

RECOMMENDED READINGS

Atchley R. C. (1988). *Social Forces and Aging: An Introduction to Social Gerontology*, 5th
ed. Belmont, Calif.: Wadsworth.
An important contributor to the field explores many facets of gerontology and human
aging.

Bengston, V. L., and Schaie, K. W. (Eds.) (1989). *The Course of Later Life: Research and
Reflections.* New York: Springer.
A good collection of readings focusing on late adulthood.

Birren, J. E., and Bengtson, V. L. (Eds.) (1988). *Emergent Theories of Aging.* New York:
Springer.
A detailed discussion of the major theories of aging, including biological, psycholog-
ical, and social perspectives.

Gearing, B., Johnson, M., and Heller, T. (Eds.) (1988). *Mental Health Problems in Old Age:
A Reader.* Chichester: Wiley.

An assortment of readings that cover a wide range of topics, including the implications of mental health and well-being for the aged.

Lesnoff-Caravaglia, J. (Ed.) (1984). *The World of the Older Woman: Conflicts and Resolutions* , vol. 3. New York: Human Sciences Press.
An important contribution to the field of aging, which examines the elderly widow, role adaptations in later life, and social relationships.

McGaugh, J. L., and Kiesler, S. B. (Eds.) (1981). *Aging: Biology and Behavior*. New York: Academic Press.
Topics in this reader include lifespan extension, aging and the brain, diseases in the elderly population, and mental disorders among the aged.

McNeely, R. L., and Cohen, J. N. (Eds.) (1983). *Aging in Groups*. Beverly Hills, Calif.: Sage.
An exploration of the aging experience among blacks, Hispanics, American Indians, and Asian Americans.

Powell, L. S., and Courtice, K. (1983). *Alzheimer's Disease*. Reading, Mass.: Addison-Wesley.
An excellent overview of this tragic illness with special emphasis on helping families cope. Easy to read and filled with many helpful suggestions.

Smyer, M. A., and Gatz, M. (Eds.) (1983). *Mental Health and Aging*. Beverly Hills, Calif.: Sage.
This book contains a wide assortment of mental health interventions aimed at the aged who are acutely distressed or chronically ill. Case studies of different programs demonstrate how each type of intervention works.

Volicer, L., et al. (Eds.) (1988). *Clinical Management of Alzheimer's Disease*. Rockville, Md.: Aspen.
Topics include the epidemiology and prevention of Alzheimer's disease, respite care, and drug treatment.

Death and Bereavement

CHAPTER OUTLINE

WHAT DO YOU THINK?

■ Eastern cultures regard death as part of life. Life and death are said to complement each other. Hinduism, for example, teaches that the body passes through the life stages and that at death, the soul assumes another body. Western culture, though, views death apart from life, a dreaded stranger to be feared rather than accepted. Why is this so? What makes us uneasy and anxious about death? Why is death a taboo subject of conversation?

■ As a teenager, she was exposed to human suffering and dying as she traveled throughout Europe at the end of World War II. At Majdanek, one of Hitler's worst death camps, where 960,000 children were killed, she vividly recalls the odor of the crematoriums and seeing the barracks with inscriptions made by the children before they died. It was at Majdanek, as well as in other parts of war-devastated Europe, that Elisabeth Kübler-Ross vowed to study medicine and make a meaningful contribution to humanity. Her theory of the psychological stages of dying made her a pioneer in the field of death education.

■ For travelers in the Middle Ages, the hospice was a welcome sight because it meant hospitality and a place to rest before continuing their journey. Today, the hospice has a new meaning. The hospice offers humane care to terminally ill patients in a homelike environment and freedom from physical and psychological suffering. In so doing, many feel that the indignities often associated with dying in conventional medical settings are removed. We'll discuss the hospice concept in this chapter, including its program design and goals.

■ Never has the issue of euthanasia received more publicity and attention than in the celebrated Karen Ann Quinlan case. Karen Ann Quinlan was a teenager in 1975 when she lapsed into a severe coma, the exact reasons for which are uncertain. A year later, in a monumental decision by the New Jersey Supreme Court, Quinlan's parents were given permission to remove all life-supporting equipment. Unexpectedly, Quinlan continued to live on her own until her death in 1985. As we'll see in this chapter, the Quinlan ruling sparked a flurry of medical, legal, and moral questions that remain controversial even today. How do you feel about euthanasia? Do you think most people are in favor of it? Has the Quinlan ruling established any sort of precedent?

■ Death and Dying in Modern Society

To live means eventually to die. This inevitable consequence of life is a person's final developmental task. It is formidable in scope, and few persons react to death in the same way. Emotional reactions range from fear and sorrow to resignation or defiance (Kalish, 1981; Rowe, 1982).

In Western cultures, the subject of death seems to be taboo. It is, for most, a sensitive topic, one that is avoided and frequently repressed. Some people try to deny it; others live in fear of it. Even medical specialists are often uncomfortable talking about death and do not like to be present when their parents die (Vianello and Lucamante, 1988; Rhodes and Vedder, 1983; Aiken, 1982).

To many, death is not a real part of the human experience. Yet paradoxically, the thoughts of death that are denied by the culture reemerge in perverse forms, as is seen in the large segments of the population who are preoccupied with violence, killing, and war. John Stephenson (1985) went so far as to say that death is obscene and pornographic. Multitudes are drawn to newspaper and television accounts of death and react with a mixture of fascination, curiosity, and excitement. Others are attracted to violent movies and paperback novels that depict death in countless ways. We deny death, but we are also obsessed by it (Ariés, 1981).

In many instances, the dying are kept hidden or isolated from all but close relatives, doctors, and nurses. We frequently give hospitals the responsibility of caring for the dying; yet many are ill equipped to deal with such a task. It goes without saying that death is disturbing to virtually everyone, but the facility with which it can be hidden makes it possible to deny its presence. Often it is treated as a closely guarded secret, even when it is obvious and everyone talks about it (Leming and Dickinson, 1990; Charmaz, 1980).

Partly because of this isolation and denial, death, like other disturbing events, arouses awe and dread. Death has been made more difficult to comprehend and accept.

For all humanity, to live means to eventually die.

Younger people frequently have little direct experience with death and the humility that it can bring. This removal of death from the living offers a striking contrast with past societal customs. Death before the turn of the century usually meant that people died in their own homes, with the remaining family present. Dealing with the dead body was an ordinary part of domestic life. Today, people die away from the home, and the task of preparing the dead for burial is handled by others who are paid to perform this service. Our participation today in the rituals surrounding the dead is minimal (DeSpelder and Strickland, 1990).

As a result, death has become bureaucratized and anonymous in today's society. The dying are kept away from the mainstream of the living, and as a result, death becomes a hidden affair. Many don't understand death because they're not given the chance to confront it (Nisbet, 1984).

Most authorities agree that the denial or repression of death results in limited self-growth. To comprehend it, on the other hand, may add a new and healthy dimension to our existence. Death always has been and always will be with us. Because it is an integral part of human existence, it will always be a subject of deep concern. It is our task to learn to view death not as a dreaded stranger but rather as an expected companion to life. If we can do this, we can also learn to live our lives with more meaning—with full appreciation of our finiteness, our limited time here (Shneidman, 1984; Kübler-Ross, 1981; Leming and Dickinson, 1990).

In recent years, more people have demonstrated an interest in better understanding death and dying. *Thanatologists,* those researchers investigating death and dying, have educated increasingly larger segments of the population. Books, journals, classes, and research centers devoted to this topic have emerged. Articles in popular magazines, television talk shows, and documentaries attest to the fact that the shroud once covering this topic is now being lifted (Horan and Mall, 1980; Rhodes and Vedder, 1983; Kalish, 1985; Kastenbaum, 1981).

■ Dimensions of Death

Understanding death becomes especially difficult when people think about their own death. This is especially true among younger people who tend to cling to the idea of personal immortality. We often avoid the mention of death when it has a personal connotation. It is impossible for us to picture an ending to our own life, and such an end is usually attributed to a malicious intervention from the outside. To put it another way, in our unconscious, we can only be killed; we cannot die of old age or a natural cause. Death in itself, therefore, is associated with a bad act or a frightening happening, something that calls for retribution and punishment (Kübler-Ross, 1981; Shneidman, 1984; Marshall, 1980; Neimeyer, 1988).

Dorothy Rowe (1982) emphasized that it is difficult to think about one's own death. But thinking about it or not, we all know that death lies in wait for us. Not knowing when our death will arrive gives urgency to the question of what we should do with our lives. To answer this question, though, means to consider another; we have to decide whether death is the end or whether it is a doorway to another life. The meaning we attach to death, our personal death, can fill us with either satisfaction or pain and fear.

Though death can—and does—occur at any age, elderly people are more aware of its imminence. And even though death preoccupies them more than it does younger people, the elderly seem less afraid of it. Indeed, the elderly often fear loneliness and

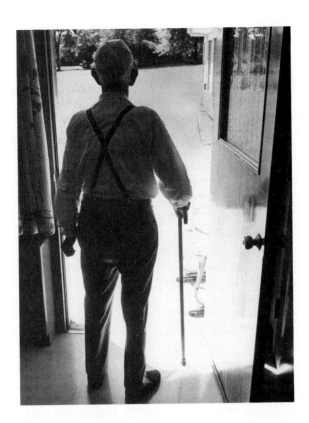

Accepting the reality of death looms as life's final developmental task.

pain more than death. Some older people may even perceive death as an acceptable alternative to a life that has become devoid of meaning (Marshall, 1980; Kalish, 1981).

Unfortunately, the dying person is sometimes trapped in a conspiracy of silence by relatives or medical staff members. The situation may be discussed, but not with the patient. Some relatives and friends may avoid any discussion whatsoever because they are too uncomfortable with the topic. Should dying people ask questions about their fate, their inquiries are often avoided. Usually, their questions are turned aside, and the central issues are denied (Morgan, 1988; Weisman, 1984).

David Hendin (1984) referred to this as the "say nothing" philosophy, indicating that it is just as common among family members as it is among physicians. Studies have repeatedly shown that a majority of physicians favor a conspiracy of silence regarding their fatally ill patients. There are at least three reasons for this. First, there is a real fear among physicians that patients, when given such information, may give up or attempt to commit suicide. Second, a physician simply may have no way of determining how long a person has to live. Furthermore, the possibility of a disease's spontaneous remission always exists. Third, there is always the chance that a cure will be found.

When told about their impending death, most dying people are thankful to be told the truth and to be able to discuss it. Being honest with patients about their fate is believed to help them accept their impending death. However, we must keep in mind the previously mentioned variations among people regarding the topic of death. *When* and *how* such news should be shared is difficult to decide, and the patient's best interests must always be considered. The individual's personality, emotional constitution, and ability to function under stress must be taken into account (DeSpelder and Strickland, 1990; Kalish, 1985; Veatch and Tai, 1980).

■ ACCEPTANCE OF DEATH FACILITATED BY SUPPORTIVE DUTCH PHYSICIANS

It is generally recognized among contemporary experts (e.g., Leming and Dickinson, 1990; Kalish, 1985; Stephenson, 1985) that dying persons want to discuss their fate openly and not be trapped in a conspiracy of silence. Research conducted in the Netherlands (Nusberg, 1984) also indicated that a patient's acceptance of death can be facilitated by psychologically supportive medical care. Should this be the case, it is maintained that terminally ill patients are less likely to request any form of euthanasia, or a deliberate measure taken to hasten death.

Paramount in patient care is the establishment of empathy rather than paternalism between the doctor and patient. How the doctor informs the patient and his or her family about the course of the illness also affects how the information will be accepted. Dutch doctors feel that if patients are informed gradually, according to their own needs and initiative, they will be in a better position to accept death.

It is also felt that telling family members about a terminal illness before telling the patient can do much harm. Often, this leads to disturbances in the relationships between the patient and the family. Finally, it has been observed that Dutch patients who learn of their condition as soon as they are capable of processing the information are more likely to die at home rather than in a hospital or nursing home.

■ The Dying Process: Theoretical Perspectives

☐ Elisabeth Kübler-Ross's Theory

Few researchers have contributed more toward understanding the dying process than Elisabeth Kübler-Ross. Describing herself as a "country doctor," Kübler-Ross is a psychiatrist who joined the faculty at the University of Chicago in 1965. Shortly afterward, she served as an adviser to a group of theological graduate students who were investigating various aspects of death. To gather more complete information and to increase her own knowledge of death, Kübler-Ross began interviewing dying patients. It was from these hundreds of interviews and her seminars, workshops, and lectures, that her thoughts on the topic of death emerged (Kübler-Ross, 1969, 1974, 1975, 1981, 1982, 1983).

At the heart of Kübler-Ross's research is the concept that the dying process consists of five stages. Individuals pass through these five stages as death draws nearer, although in different ways: They may skip some stages, return to others, or go through the stages in a different order. The following discussion is based on her research.

DENIAL The first stage of the dying process is called *denial*. When informed of impending death, most people react with shock and the general feeling of "No, not me, it cannot be true." Because in our unconscious minds we all are immortal, we have difficulty acknowledging that we will die. When first told that they are going to die, some patients may demand more tests or change doctors in the hope of receiving a more favorable prognosis. In essence, the reality of the situation is denied.

One terminally ill patient described by Kübler-Ross was convinced that her X rays had been mixed up by the hospital and could not possibly be back so soon. When none of this could be confirmed, she asked to leave the hospital and began to seek other physicians to get a more satisfactory explanation for her symptoms. Whether or not these doctors confirmed the original diagnosis, she reacted in a similar fashion each time; she requested examination and reexamination, partially aware that the original diagnosis was accurate but also wanting additional opinions in the hope that the first conclusion was an error. At the same time, she wanted to stay in contact with these doctors so that she could have their help "at all times."

Denial, or at least partial denial, is employed by virtually all patients and is believed to be a relatively healthy way of initially dealing with this uncomfortable news. Denial can serve as a "buffer" after unexpected shocking news. It enables patients to collect their thoughts and, with time, utilize other, less radical defenses. The use of these other defenses, however, will depend on several factors, including how patients are told the news and how much time they have to acknowledge the inevitable event gradually.

David Carroll (1985) found three forms of denial. *Absolute denial* is a flat refusal to believe what one has been told. According to his research, some patients refuse to accept the diagnosis and others block it out. Thus, people who otherwise seem stable can exhibit sudden pathological responses to news of terminal illness. Such people can, for instance, wipe out the memory of weeks, even months spent in the hospital staring blankly at anyone who mentions the event. At times it may even seem that the person is losing his or her mind, but the truth is that each person has his or her own tolerance for bad news and his or her own method of digesting it.

Fluctuating denial is another form. Individuals under a sentence of death often change their capacity to deal with the truth. Sometimes this capacity may be puzzlingly inconstant, emerging and vanishing from hour to hour like the sun through the clouds. A dying patient may carry on long discussions with the night nurse or even the janitor, making it quite clear that he or she is aware of the seriousness of the disease. Then, in front of family members or friends, the patient does a complete about-face, chatting away, quite sincerely, about personal plans that extend far into the future.

Carroll stated that the ego is in many ways a wise and kindly governor. It knows its own limitations; it knows when to shut down. If a moment arrives when it can no longer endure bad news, it mercifully sets up a dividing wall between itself and the world and protects its integrity. The amount of avoidance a dying person employs is exactly the amount that he or she needs in order to function.

Finally, there is a *modified denial*, in which a person may acknowledge part of the truth, but a truth tailored to suit his or her particular needs. A patient may, for instance, admit to being very sick but not to being terminally sick. The patient may twist medical opinion, considering a physician's statement that "We'll do everything we possibly can" as a promise of cure. The patient may inform friends, "They're not giving me radiation treatment. I think that must mean I don't have cancer." This type of avoidance behavior allows a person to acknowledge that something is wrong, perhaps seriously amiss, but not amiss enough to constitute a crisis.

ANGER The second stage of the dying process is *anger*. When denial is no longer successful, the patient typically experiences feelings of anger, rage, envy, and resentment. Whereas the patient's reaction to catastrophic news in stage 1 is "No, it's not true, there must be some mistake," the patient may say in stage 2, "Why me? Why not someone else?"

Compared with the period of denial, this stage is difficult for the family and medical staff, largely because the patient's anger is projected and displaced at random. Kübler-Ross illustrated how patients may displace anger. They may complain that

> . . . the doctors are just no good, they don't know what tests to require and what diet to prescribe. They keep the patients too long in the hospital or don't respect their wishes in regard to special privileges. They allow a miserably sick roommate

to be brought into their room when they pay so much money for some privacy and rest, etc. The nurses are even more often a target of their anger. Whatever they touch is not right. The moment they have left the room, the bell rings. The light is on the very minute they start their report for the next shift of nurses. When they do shake the pillows and straighten out the bed, they are blamed for never leaving the patients alone. When they do leave the patients alone, the light goes on with the request to have the bed arranged more comfortably. The visiting family is received with little cheerfulness and anticipation, which makes the encounter a painful event. They then either respond with grief and tears, guilt or shame, or avoid future visits, which only increases the patient's discomfort and anger. (1969, pp. 50–51)

It is important for family members and hospital personnel to empathize with the dying patient and realize why and how anger originates. But patients who are understood and given some time and attention will soon lower their voices and reduce their angry demands. In time, they will come to realize that they are valuable human beings who are cared for and permitted to function at the highest possible level as long as they can.

BARGAINING The third stage of the dying process is termed *bargaining*. Whereas patients were unable to face the truth in the first stage and were generally angry in the second, they now hope that death can be postponed or delayed in some way. Some may entertain thoughts of entering into some type of agreement with their creator: "If God has decided to take us from this earth and he did not respond to my angry pleas, he may be more favorable if I ask nicely."

The terminally ill patient may know from past experience (usually from childhood) that good behavior may result in a reward, sometimes the granting of a wish for special privileges. Now the patient usually wishes for an extension of life or for a few days without pain or physical discomfort. An example of bargaining is provided by the patient who was

> . . . in utmost pain and discomfort, unable to go home because of her dependence on injections for pain relief. She had a son who proceeded with his plans to get married, as the patient had wished. She was very sad to think that she would be unable to attend this big day, for he was her oldest and favorite child. With combined efforts, we were able to teach her self-hypnosis which enabled her to be quite comfortable for several hours. She had made all sorts of promises if she could only live long enough to attend the marriage. The day preceding the wedding she left the hospital as an elegant lady. Nobody would have believed her real condition. She was "the happiest person in the whole world" and looked radiant. I wondered what her reaction would be when the time was up for which she had bargained.
>
> I will never forget the moment when she returned to the hospital. She looked tired and somewhat exhausted and—before I could say hello—said, "Now don't forget I have another son!" (Kübler-Ross, 1969, p. 83)

Thus, in essence, the bargain is an attempt to postpone. Among its most important features, bargaining includes a prize offered "for good behavior," a self-imposed "deadline" (e.g., the son's wedding), and an implicit promise that the patient will not request more if this one delay is granted. (In regard to the last, however, few, if any, patients keep their promises.) Interestingly, Kübler-Ross reported that a large number of patients promise "a life dedicated to God" or "a life in the service of the church" in exchange for some additional time. Many also promised to donate parts of their body to science, if, in return, the doctors would use their knowledge of science to extend their lives.

DEPRESSION *Depression* is the fourth stage of the dying process. When the terminally ill cannot deny their illnesses any longer, when additional surgery or hospitalization is required, and when more symptoms develop, they become engulfed with a sense of great loss. To be sure, the terminally ill patient must endure numerous hardships in addition to physical problems, including financial burdens and the loss of employment because of many absences or an inability to function. Instead of reacting with anger or rage at this point, as they might have earlier, patients are likely to experience depression.

There are two kinds of depression. The first, called *reactive depression*, results from a loss that has already occurred. The cause of the depression can usually be elicited by an understanding person, and some of the unrealistic guilt or shame that often accompanies this depression can be alleviated. The woman who has had breast surgery and is worried about no longer being a woman can be complimented for some other especially feminine feature. In this way she can be reassured that she is still as much a woman as she was before the operation.

The second type of depression, called *preparatory depression*, occurs in response to the impending loss. Whereas encouragement and reassurance are useful in helping people suffering from reactive depression, they are not effective in helping those experiencing preparatory depression. Here, depression is a preparation for the impending loss of love objects, a means by which to reach a state of acceptance. For this reason, it would be contradictory for us to tell the patient to look at the sunny side of things and not to be sad, especially as everyone else is terribly sad.

A better approach is to allow depressed patients who are terminally ill to express their sorrow so that a final acceptance of their condition will be easier. Such patients frequently express gratitude toward those who can sit nearby during this period of depression and not constantly remind the patient that sadness is to be avoided.

Unlike reactive depression, preparatory depression is frequently a silent response. Many times there is no or little need for words:

> It is much more a feeling that can be mutually expressed and is often done better with a touch of a hand, a stroking of the hair, or just a silent sitting together. This is the time when the patient may just ask for a prayer, when he begins to occupy himself with things ahead rather than behind. It is a time when too much interference from visitors who try to cheer him up hinders his emotional preparation rather than enhances it. (Kübler-Ross, 1969, pp. 87–88)

ACCEPTANCE The fifth and final stage of the dying process is called *acceptance*. If patients have had enough time, that is, if the death is not sudden or unexpected and if they have been given some assistance in working through the four previous stages, they will reach a stage in which they are neither depressed nor angry about their "fate."

In most instances patients in the acceptance stage have had the opportunity to express their previous feelings: their envy for the healthy and living and their anger and resentment toward those who do not have to face death so soon. The need to mourn the impending loss of meaningful people and places has usually been met, and patients typically contemplate their approaching death with a certain degree of quiet expectation. Acceptance is a period almost devoid of feeling. For this reason, the families usually need more help and support during this time than do the patients themselves.

Patients in this stage prefer to be left alone much of the time, and their interests generally diminish. They also need frequent brief intervals of sleep. Because patients in the acceptance stage are seldom talkative, communication is generally more nonverbal than verbal. It is as if the pain has disappeared and the struggle is over. It becomes a time for "the final rest before the long journey."

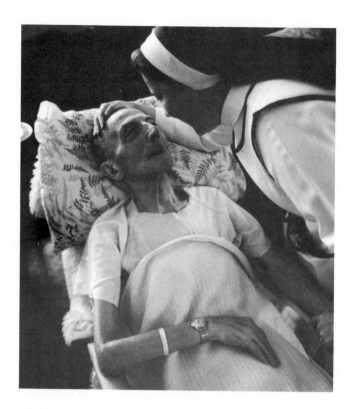

The dying have many psychological needs.

A few patients may struggle right to the very end, fighting to keep alive whatever hopes they can. These individuals cannot reach this stage of acceptance. In other words, the harder one fights to avoid the inevitable death and the more one denies it, the more difficult it will be to die with peace and dignity.

☐ Edwin Shneidman's Theory

Edwin Shneidman (1978, 1980, 1984), although acknowledging the presence of such feelings as denial, anger, bargaining, depression, and acceptance, does not believe that these states represent stages in the dying process. Rather, he suggests that persons undergo a cluster of intellectual and affective stages. Such states may be fleeting, lasting for a day or a week, and are set, not unexpectedly, against the backdrop of one's personality and philosophy of life.

Rather than progressing through a series of five stages, terminally ill patients experience a variety of emotional states that constantly alternate between disbelief and hope. Against these as a backdrop, there is a waxing and waning of anguish, terror, acquiescence and surrender, rage and envy, disinterest and boredom, pretense, taunting and daring, and even yearning for death. All of these emotions occur in the context of bewilderment and pain.

☐ E. Mansell Pattison's Theory

E. Mansell Pattison (1977), like Shneidman, believes that because each patient is an individual, he or she will react differently to the experience of dying. Pattison proposed a model of the dying process that contains three *phases*, rather than stages. Pattison emphasized that individual differences and a wide range of emotional responses can be expected. The three processes, or phases, are the *acute phase*, the *chronic living-dying interval*, and the *terminal phase*.

THE ACUTE PHASE The *acute phase* begins when an individual realizes that death due to a terminal illness is imminent. The knowledge of impending death produces a crisis and creates considerable anxiety. This anxiety may be accompanied by other emotions, such as anger, fear, or resentment.

THE CHRONIC LIVING-DYING INTERVAL The *chronic living-dying interval* is characterized initially by a reduction in anxiety but is soon replaced by numerous and diverse emotional states not previously experienced. The following are some of the more common feelings of the dying patients.

Fear of the Unknown As death draws nearer, dying patients may be afraid because they do not know what lies ahead. They wonder: What is my fate in the hereafter? What will happen to my body after I die? How will my family and friends respond to my death? What will happen to my survivors? Some of these questions can be answered rather quickly; others will take longer; and some will remain unanswered.

Loneliness When one is sick, one feels a sense of isolation from oneself and from others. For the dying person, this feeling becomes even more pronounced and produces a fear of loneliness—in many cases right from the very beginning. Withdrawal from work or recreational activities, increasing physical debilitation and bed confinement, and perhaps not knowing what to say when friends do visit may contribute to this fear.

Sorrow The dying face many losses, including those of loved ones, their jobs, and future plans, to mention but a few. Accepting these losses and learning to tolerate the sorrow that accompanies each may produce a state of fear or anxiety.

Loss of Body Because our bodies form part of our self-concept, illnesses affect us both physically and psychologically. Patients may thus react to debilitating conditions with shame and feelings of disgrace, inadequacy, and lowered self-esteem.

Loss of Self-Control As the debilitating disease progresses, the patients become less capable of self-control. Generally, they become less energetic, less lively, and less responsive. Most people think less quickly and accurately and may fear this loss of mental function.

Suffering and Pain The fear of suffering and pain is not just a physical one but also a fear of the unknown and the unmanageable. Although senseless pain is intolerable to most people, unavoidable pain may be accepted and dealt with if it does not involve punishment, being ignored, or not being cared for.

Loss of Identity The loss of human contact, family and friends, body structure and function, self-control, and total consciousness all threaten one's sense of identity. Human contacts affirm who we are; family contacts affirm what we have shared; and contact with our body and mind affirms our own self-being. The dying process therefore threatens many facets of one's self-identity.

THE TERMINAL PHASE The *terminal phase* is the third process of dying. This is a time when the patient begins to withdraw from people and events. The emotional states described in the previous phase may still be evident, but withdrawal seems to dominate.

To appreciate these three phases of dying, one must understand what is referred to as a dying trajectory. A ***dying trajectory*** is the duration and form of the dying process.

There are four possible trajectories. First, a person may be told that the end of life is near (one is given six months to live). Second, death may also be imminent, but the exact time is unknown (one is told that death can strike anytime between six months and a year). Third, the possibility of death means that it is unclear whether a patient will die, though this question will be answered in time (if surgery is successful, a person may recover). Fourth, death may also be uncertain if it is not known whether a person will die, and the question remains unanswered (the patient may have a chronic heart problem). These four dying trajectories have obvious implications for the three phases of dying just described (Glasser and Strauss, 1968; Strauss and Glasser, 1970).

In helping the patient through these three phases of dying, Pattison recommends the following guidelines:

1. Share the responsibility for the crisis of dying with the patient so that he or she has help in dealing with the first impact of anxiety and bewilderment.

2. Clarify and define the realities of the day-to-day existence with which the patient can deal.

3. Make continued human contact available and rewarding.

4. Assist in the separation from and grief over the realistic losses of family, body image, and self-control, while retaining communication and meaningful relationships.

5. Assume necessary body and ego functions for the person without incurring shame or depreciation and while maintaining respect for the patient and helping him or her keep his or her self-respect.

6. Encourage the patient to accept his or her life situation with dignity and integrity so that the patient may gradually regress without conflict or guilt.

For those working with a terminal patient, the patient's death is not the principal problem but, rather, how the person faces death and goes about the process of dying. Although the ultimate problem of death cannot be resolved, considerable help and support can be given to the dying person.

■ Dying with Dignity

Whatever the specific illness or situation, the quality of life before death should be peaceful. Psychologically, this means that dying patients need to maintain their security, self-confidence, and dignity. Efforts should be made to help relieve loneliness, depression, and fears (Gray, 1984; Gonda and Ruark, 1984).

The patient also should be physically comfortable. Though most of the unpleasant symptoms accompanying terminal illness can be controlled by skilled medical care, many medical personnel have never learned how to do so. Physical symptoms accompanying terminal illness are sometimes inadequately treated. However, surgical procedures and the wise use of drugs can control many of them. Drugs are most commonly used to control pain, although some medical practitioners are afraid that patients will become addicted to powerful painkillers. However, craving a drug to relieve the pain instigated by a terminal illness is not considered addiction (Simpson, 1979; Gray, 1984).

Drugs such as morphine and diamorphine are commonly used to control pain. In administering these drugs, the physician usually determines the dosage of the drug the patient is to receive. However, it can be argued that the patient's opinions should also be taken into consideration. After all, patients are the most aware of their own pain tolerance as well as the fluctuations of their internal states. Ideally, the medical staff and the patient should be able to anticipate and prevent pain rather than alleviate it once it is present (Schulz, 1978; Gray, 1984).

There are other ways to reduce pain besides using morphine and diamorphine. Alcohol and marijuana also are occasionally prescribed as antidotes for pain and nausea. LSD has also been administered to terminal patients suffering from the painful effects of cancer. In some instances, LSD has proved effective in alleviating pain, and its effects last longer than the usual opiates do. Exactly how LSD blocks out pain is not known. Even after the LSD trip terminates, the relief from pain continues. When the pain does return, many patients retain their equanimity and no longer consider the pain important. However, more research is needed to evaluate this alternative to pain (Schulz, 1978; Grof and Grof, 1980).

There also are other ways to reduce pain besides using drugs. In some instances, patients can be taught self-hypnosis to block out pain. Other techniques that have proved to be of some value are relaxation therapy and desensitization.

Although modern medicine has done a great deal to overcome physical pain, it has not made equal gains in easing the final burden of loneliness. As David Hendin (1984) observed, the dying must face emotional pain, grief, and indignity—and they often must face them alone. Today's society has failed to provide a model, an ideal to be striven for in dying. The ultimate sting of death is solitude.

Of particular importance to the dying is the need to share emotional pain. Emotional pain can be just as overwhelming as physical pain is, and much sympathy and understanding are needed from health-care professionals in dealing with it. Emotional pain is often expressed in body language and physical symptoms because it is too agonizing and difficult to express in words, but it can be eased if the underlying fear and anxiety are elicited and shared. In terminal illness, the slow, relentless destruction of the body seems to threaten the destruction of the social and emotional life of the

How to enhance the quality of life before death is a concern of many people.

individual and his or her family, but when the deteriorating body is loved and cared for, the emotional pain is often relieved, and the family is reintegrated and enabled to support one another. In a similar way, the pain of the bereaved relatives can be expressed in acute physical pain that mirrors the pain suffered by the loved one who has died. The genuine care and concern for such pain in the bereaved can enable them to talk about it. Emotional pain is subjective in its quality, intensity, and outward manifestation (Earnshaw-Smith, 1982).

Often hindering the efforts to assist the dying is the hospital's bureaucratic organization. Many patients experience loneliness and often a loss of identity when they become part of the hospital's impersonal routines and daily rituals. Many are hooked up to mechanical life-sustaining equipment that transforms them into a set of repetitious life signs to be measured and monitored. The constantly changing shifts of hospital personnel, coupled with their heavy workloads, often precludes the patient from creating any close relationship in which sensitivities and fears can be discussed.

In such an impersonal atmosphere, it is no wonder that many terminally ill patients rebel at the thought of having to spend their final days in a hospital. If given a choice, most would rather die at home. In one study of terminally ill patients, 76 percent preferred to die at home if they could be cared for there (Burger, 1980).

☐ The Hospice Movement

Hospice programs seek to give terminally ill patients humane, individual care. The word *hospice* extends back to the Middle Ages and at that time referred to a place where travelers could rest and receive hospitality before they continued their journey. It has since come to mean care for the terminally ill in a homelike environment and freedom from physical or psychological pain.

The hospice program is a flexible one. Its major theme is moving away from the indignities of dying often associated with conventional medical settings. The hospice program may include a separate facility, a hospice ward in a general hospital with special routines and staff, or hospice care in the home of a dying patient. There are about 400 hospice programs throughout the United States (Holden, 1980).

There are no restrictions on visiting hours at a hospice facility. In fact, the family of the terminal patient is encouraged to visit as often as possible as well as participate in the treatment program. By participating, relatives and loved ones outside the family have the opportunity not only to work through their relationship with the patient but also to perform practical services for the dying, such as preparing special meals. This type of interaction also enables the family to get to know the hospice staff. It is thought that this type of participation also minimizes feelings of guilt during bereavement. Furthermore, the staff's involvement with relatives and friends does not end with the patient's death. Relatives and friends are encouraged to consult with the hospital staff should support be needed during bereavement (Saunders, 1984; Hamilton and Reid, 1980; Kübler-Ross and Magno, 1983).

Life in the hospice program is flexible enough to accommodate the patients' wishes. Patients are encouraged to do what they want to do and are able to do. Patients make the decisions concerning themselves as long as they can and it is in their best interests. They are the key members of a treatment team composed of doctors, nurses, clergy, and, as already mentioned, the patient's family (Hendin, 1984).

The hospice program also has a unique pain-control program. In severe cases, this involves regular oral doses of what is called the Brompton mix, dubbed a "cocktail." It consists of diamorphine (heroin), cocaine, gin, sugar syrup, and chlorpromazine syrup.

Hospice programs offer innovative care to terminally ill patients.

The diamorphine dose usually starts at 5 to 10 milligrams, and patients rarely need more than 30 milligrams at a time. When a patient's fears and anxieties are relieved, the dosage can usually be lowered. This is possible because much of the subjective sensation of pain is caused by emotional distress. The medication thus removes patients from pain but keeps them alert (Holden, 1982).

☐ Euthanasia: The Right to Die

Euthanasia is extremely controversial. Essentially, the issue is whether we should prolong useless life or painful dying by means of modern medical technology. This is an issue that affects the conscience not only of the dying and their relatives but also that of the physician. The moral balance between preserving life and preventing suffering must be determined. Large numbers of people today are concerned about the *quality* of lives being saved by modern technology (Zucker, 1988; DeSpelder and Strickland, 1990).

The term *euthanasia* is derived from the Greek *eu,* meaning "well," and *thanatos,* meaning "death." Combined, it meant "a good or peaceful death." Its original meaning, however, has both expanded and become somewhat obscured. Known popularly as "mercy killing," it has come to mean assisting the dying in hastening their death. There are two types of euthanasia. *Positive,* or **active euthanasia,** implies that definite steps are taken to cause death. *Negative,* or **passive euthanasia,** means that death is not actively prevented through any type of intervention (Charmaz, 1980).

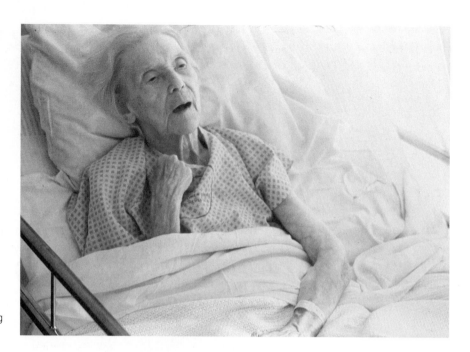

Dying patients need to maintain their dignity during life's final passages.

As we said at the outset, the concept of euthanasia is a controversial one. Many are opposed to the very thought of taking another's life, regardless of the circumstances. Others, though, view it more sympathetically. However, of the two types of euthanasia, many people appear to favor negative euthanasia. This is probably because they see negative euthanasia as letting the body take its own course of action and not as actually taking another's life (Hendin, 1984).

There are differences among those who accept the general concept of euthanasia and those who reject it. For example, fewer older adults than younger adults accept euthanasia. Also, women and nonwhites are generally less apt to accept euthanasia than men are, probably because of their greater religiosity (Ward, 1980).

The euthanasia movement first started in England in 1935 in an effort to advance legislation to "make the act of dying more gentle." In the United States, the euthanasia movement was begun in 1938 to educate the medical profession and public alike on the realities of death. The movement emphasized examining medical procedures and attitudes toward terminal illness and seeking ways to humanize death. Today, the Euthanasia Society and the Euthanasia Educational Council promote the concept of death with dignity.

The "living will," developed by the Euthanasia Educational Council, supports the individual's "right to die." The living will seeks to give dying individuals some choice or control over their fate. It is estimated that more than 200,000 Americans have signed living wills.

Arguments against euthanasia typically center on four points. The first rests on religious grounds. As we mentioned earlier, although some clergy may support negative euthanasia, opponents cite the immorality of killing oneself or others. A second, related argument is based on the sanctity of human life. Euthanasia means taking a life and thus is viewed by some as tantamount to murder. Furthermore, even if death is voluntary—either self-imposed or assisted—there may be abuses. Third, there is concern over the possibility of error by the physician concerning the patient's health. And, new medical breakthroughs may radically alter the patient's prognosis. Fourth, many feel that there is no way of knowing what patients would want if they were able to communicate. Although the patient may have signed a living will at some point, he or she may no longer desire such action (Charmaz, 1980).

Before the widely publicized Karen Ann Quinlan case of 1976, there were no legally sanctioned procedures for stopping treatment of any kind. Karen Ann Quinlan lapsed into a coma in 1975 after attending a party with friends. Four things may have caused the coma: a blood sugar problem, a fall on concrete about two weeks before the party, exposure to lead poisoning in the factory where she worked, or a combination of alcohol and Valium. Quinlan had been in a coma for over a year before the New Jersey Supreme Court gave her parents permission to have her life-supporting respirator removed. However, the unexpected happened. Despite the removal of the respirator, which doctors felt would cause her death, Quinlan lived until 1985.

If the Quinlan ruling becomes widely established by subsequent court rulings, then a relatively clear procedure can be outlined to obtain consent for stopping medical treatment without criminal liability. According to this ruling, the consent of four parties is necessary to stop treatment:

1. The patient's implied consent to the termination of life support, to which the other parties can only consent if it is in the patient's best interests.

2. The consent of the family, guardian, or immediate next of kin.

3. The agreement and consent of the attending doctors that "there is no reasonable possibility of return to cognitive and sapient life" or that "there is irrefutable evidence that biological death is imminent."

4. The consent of the hospital ethics committee. This committee is composed of physicians, social workers, attorneys, and theologians and serves to protect the patients and their caregivers by exploring all of the options for a particular patient, discussing the individual's situation, and allowing the responsibility of these judgments to be shared (Simpson, 1979).

■ At the Moment of Death

Typically, dying persons become more isolated as death draws near. This isolation is caused by the consuming nature of the patient's condition, the patient's withdrawal, and others' avoidance of the patient. In the face of their growing isolation, some patients seek attention from anyone who will give it. Others may give up. Increasingly, more dying patients are receptive to volunteers who seek to help them in their final days. However, this latter alternative is not available to many (Charmaz, 1980).

As death approaches, the patient typically experiences a sequence of physiological and psychological events. Ruth Gray (1984) described the events as follows:

■ *The patient's sensation and power of motion as well as reflexes are lost in the legs first and then gradually in the arms.* Pressure on the extremities seems to bother the patient, such as when bedsheets are too tight. Careful positioning and turning of the body seem to help reduce the discomfort.

■ *As peripheral circulation fails, there is frequently a "drenching sweat," and then the body surface cools, regardless of room temperature.* Sweating tends to be most profuse on the upper parts of the body and on the extensor surfaces rather than on the flexor surfaces. Many dying patients are never conscious of

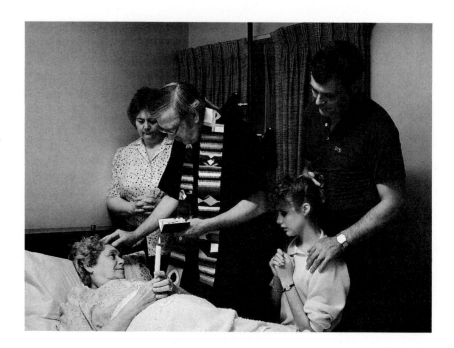

The life cycle culminates at the moment of death.

being cold, though, regardless of how cold their body surface becomes. Their restlessness is often caused by the sensation of heat.

- *Dying persons characteristically turn their heads toward the light.* As sight and hearing fail, the patient can see only what is near and hear what is distinctly spoken. Because of this, adequate lighting should be provided, visitors should sit at the head of the patient's bedside, and whispering should be avoided.

- *The dying patient's touch sensation is diminished; yet his or her sense of pressure remains.* When touch sensation fails, patients may not realize, for example, that their hand is being held. Slight pressure may increase the person's awareness of a visitor's intention to initiate physical contact.

- *Dying patients may seem to be in less pain as death nears.* Though there may have been pain in earlier stages, a patient nearing death may be in less pain than onlookers think, provided, of course, that all the patient's needs have been met. Patients also frequently reach a point at which they feel as though they've said all that needs to be said, a state of mind that brings internal serenity to many. Frequently, only minimal pain medication is needed as death nears.

- *The dying patient is often conscious to the very end.* Contrary to the thoughts of many, a comatose state or period of unconsciousness does not always precede death. The fact that many patients remain conscious until death emphasizes the need for total care to the very end.

- *Spiritual needs often arise strongly at night.* If dying patients have led a strong spiritual life, they're apt to want to talk about their experiences with those near them. Many want to talk specifically with their minister, rabbi, or priest. This need has been known to intensify during the night.

- *There seems to be an interval of peace before death.* Those patients who are conscious to the very last minute state, almost invariably, that they are not suffering. In fact, many report a feeling of tranquility and peace, as if a long journey is finally over. As William Hunter, the noted anatomist, whispered just before he died, "If I had the strength to hold a pen, I would write how easy and pleasant a thing it is to die."

■ Death from a Physiological Perspective

Death is a process as well as an event, and though there are numerous signs that signal the termination of life, each in itself does not prove that irreversible extinction has taken place. Research on the nature of death (the study of death is known technically as thanatology) reveals that even after *clinical death* has occurred, the body is not *biologically* dead. The hair, for example, continues to grow for several hours; the liver converts glycogen to glucose, and the muscles contract (this is referred to as rigor mortis). Rigor mortis generally begins 2 hours after death, the muscles remaining contracted for approximately 30 hours.

The criteria for death are not fixed, and only recently has the medical profession attempted to establish guidelines for evaluating this condition. It goes without saying that the heart, lungs, and brain form the trinity on which the standards for irreversible death are established. More specific criteria include (1) an absence of respiration, (2) the absence of a heartbeat, and (3) a flat electroencephalogram. The flat electroencephalogram means that *brain death* has occurred. This definition of death is perhaps the most widely accepted today, as the brain is the only system that cannot be directly supported by machines. When all of these signs are coupled with such obvious alterations as the absence of pupillary reflexes, the clouding of the cornea, and an absence of body movement, it can quite certainly be said that death has occurred.

Despite these criteria, not everyone agrees on a legal definition of death (Veatch, 1988). Many times, the definition of death is determined by hospital policy. This becomes a delicate and frequently controversial issue; if one hospital defines death as the cessation of heartbeat and respiration and another uses brain death as the defining criterion, it may be possible, then, that the same person could be pronounced dead in one hospital and alive in another.

The Near-Death Experience: Is There One Step Beyond?

I had heart failure and clinically died. . . . I remember everything perfectly vividly. Suddenly I felt numb. Sounds began sounding a little distant. . . . All this time I was perfectly conscious of everything that was going on. I heard the heart monitor go off. I saw the nurse come into the room and dial the telephone, and the doctors, nurses, and attendants came in.

As things began to fade there was a sound I can't describe; it was like the beat of a snare drum, very rapid, a rushing sound, like a stream rushing through a gorge. And I rose up and I was a few feet up looking down on my body. There I was, with people

working on me. I had no fear. No pain. Just peace. After just probably a second or two, I seemed to turn over and go up. It was dark—you could call it a hole or a tunnel—and there was the bright light. It got brighter and brighter. And I seemed to go *through* it.

All of a sudden I was just somewhere else. There was a gold-looking light, everywhere. Beautiful. I couldn't find a source anywhere. It was just all around, coming from everywhere. There was music. And I seemed to be in a countryside with streams, grass, and trees, mountains. But when I looked around—if you want to put it that way—there were not trees and things like we know them to be. The strangest thing to me about it was that there were people there. Not in any kind of form or body as we know it; they were just there.

There was a sense of perfect peace and contentment; love. It was like I was part of it. That experience could have lasted the whole night or just a second. . . . I don't know.

(Moody, 1977, pp. 138–139)

This dialogue is from a middle-aged woman who suffered severe cardiac arrest. Although pronounced clinically dead, she was resuscitated and brought back to life. The fact that she was able to relate such a unique series of events is remarkable in itself. What is even more fascinating, however, is that hundreds of other persons who have had near-death experiences report similar experiences and events.

Raymond Moody (1975, 1977) along with numerous others (see Ring, 1980, 1984; Siegel, 1980; Vicchio, 1981a, 1981b; Sabom, 1982) investigated what is now called the **near-death experience.** Many have collected scores of interviews with persons pronounced clinically dead, and although there are individual differences, the stories bear a striking resemblance to one another. The following are some of the more common features of the near-death experience:

1. Awareness of loud noises (some people report buzzing, vibrations, or loud clicking sounds).

2. A feeling of being drawn through a dark tunnel, funnel, or cave. At the end of the passage is a bright light.

3. Recognizing the presence of dead relatives who were reportedly there to help the person make the transition from life to death.

4. Being asked by a distant voice in the presence of a brilliant light to provide a review of one's life. The light is described by many as "a being of love." Questions ranged from "Are you satisfied with your life?" to "What do you want to share with me?"

5. Seeing a panoramic view of one's life. Many report watching their entire lives pass before them in color, in three dimensions, and in the third person.

6. Being given full acceptance by the "being of love," even though some persons felt that their past actions and behaviors were cause for rejection or embarrassment.

7. Being told that their time for death would be at another time. Many were instructed to return to complete their lives, care for loved ones, and tell others what it was like on the "other side."

Also, many persons reporting such experiences were not afraid of death anymore and had a more positive attitude toward life. However, though the data gathered are certainly thought provoking, one should not automatically assume that an afterlife exists. It must be remembered that this research was conducted with persons experiencing clinical death, which is not the same as brain death. Whether or not one experiences such events after brain death has occurred is a question defying a scientific answer.

■ Bereavement and Grief

No one is ever fully prepared for death. Rather, it invariably has a sudden impact, even in those cases where it is anticipated. The reality of the death of a loved one is very hard for most to accept. Our own feeling of immortality is rudely shattered when someone close to us dies. Few of us expect it to happen—at least not to us or our loved ones (Loewinsohn, 1984). But death is a fact of life and as we earlier learned, accepting its inevitability is everyone's chore. The psychological pain that survivors face, including such feelings as loneliness, despair, and fear, are normal reactions in the face of loss. Learning how to free oneself emotionally from the deceased, readjusting to a life in which the dead person is missing, and forming new relationships with other individuals are important tasks for the mourner (Hiltz, 1989).

Before we proceed, we need to first clarify some terminology. *Bereavement* is defined as the loss of a loved one by death. It is a statement of fact and does not embody one's reactions to a loss. *Grief* refers to the deep and poignant distress caused by such a loss. It represents one's emotional reaction to another's death.

☐ Coping with Loss

There are many stress points across the life cycle, but few (if any) parallel the loss of a loved one. Indeed, some contemporary researchers feel that the death of a loved one looms as the most stressful event ever to be encountered (Brown, 1984; Curtis and Detert, 1981; Schwartz, 1982; Nuernberger, 1981; Shaffer, 1983).

Consider, for example, the loss of a spouse. The very nature of widowhood itself usually creates significant turmoil. Survivors must adjust to new role realignments and the establishment of new patterns of authority and decision making. Survivors also typically face loss of economic (financial) security, establishing a new social support network, and concern for children's and other family members' grief. And perhaps most stressful, survivors must face the loss of emotional support.

The loss of a parent is also stressful, an emotional experience that enables the concept of death to edge in. Many individuals perceive one's parent as a buffer between themselves and death. With the loss of a parent, the force of finality of death becomes apparent in a way that the loss of, say, a grandparent cannot compare. And the realization that "I, too, am mortal" is now apparent. Sibling rivalries often resurface. A different view of life and death may affect interpersonal relationships, as well as interactions with one's spouse during the grieving period. And when the ultimate point is reached that both parents have passed on, the realization occurs that one is an orphan for life.

Consider, also, the impact of losing a child. The usual expectation is that the offspring will outlive the parent. Lynne DeSpelder and Albert Strickland (1990) write that it is almost expected that the child will carry something of the parent into the future, even after the parent's death. In this sense, the child's very existence grants a kind of immortality to the parent, and this is taken away if the child dies before the parent's own life has ended. The parent's plans for the child are suddenly of no consequence.

But while the death of any loved one has the potential of emerging as a catastrophic event, John Crosby and Nancy Jose (1983) feel that the *degree* of stress and grief experienced is dependent on several interacting variables. The first variable is how death occurs. Unexpected death often creates extreme stress because survivors are totally unprepared for it. Other forms of death produce different levels of stress, such as the emotional depletion that often accompanies anticipated but prolonged death. All forms of death require their share of *grief work*, that is, coming to terms with the physical and emotional demands brought on by another's death. However, it may occur at different times in the overall process of dying and create different stress levels.

Whether the survivor is encountering other stressful crises is another variable to consider. The death of a loved one usually increases the level of stress to an almost intolerable level. That is, personal and interpersonal resources may be depleted by the other stressors, leaving little in reserve to cope with the death. The accumulation of many stressors acting upon the survivor may lead to or compound the crisis, taxing the person's resources and coping ability to such a point that coping becomes increasingly dysfunctional.

Another important variable contributing to the survivor's stress are the numerous "arrangements" that require attention following the death. Consider this in relation to surviving spouses. Initially, the spouse must deal with the funeral and burial. This includes contacts with morticians, cemeteries, and well-meaning sympathizers. Moreover, the survivor is inundated by a myriad of professionals involved in settling the estate (lawyers, employers, insurance companies, and government employees).

Combined, each of these factors will affect the stress level of loss. Moreover, they will interact and influence the nature and duration of grieving.

☐ Expressions of Grief

Grief is a complex and multifaceted form of expression. Richard Kalish (1987) believes, though, that grief can be categorized physically, cognitively, affectively, and behaviorally. He also maintains that certain distinctions can be made concerning how older and younger persons express grief.

PHYSICAL EXPRESSIONS Grieving persons report many different physical symptoms, including a tight feeling in the throat and chest, hollow feeling in the stomach, oversensitivity to noise, sense of numbness and depersonalization (nothing seems physically real), dry mouth, breathlessness, muscular weakness, and a lack of energy. While it is unlikely that the first four symptoms are age-related, the last four are typically reported more by elderly persons.

COGNITIVE EXPRESSIONS Among the cognitive reactions to loss are confusion, disbelief, preoccupation with thoughts of the deceased, and attempting to make sense of the event. Attempting to relate cognitive expressions to age is problematic. However, we do know that when the age of the mourner is concerned, people react differently to cognitive expressions of grief. For example, when the grieving person is not elderly, expressions of confusion, disbelief, and preoccupation are likely to be attributed to the loss and are usually assumed to be temporary. Among aged persons, though, especially those who have already displayed some forgetfulness, these same cognitive expressions might be interpreted as deterioration rather than the reversible results of situational stress and loss.

AFFECTIVE EXPRESSIONS The affective expressions that typically accompany loss are well known. Among the more common are sorrow, sadness, guilt, anger, relief, denial, and depression. While depression tends to be the most familiar expression,

There are numerous facets to grief and bereavement.

particularly among the aged, it must be understood that these affective states usually mix together. Consequently, for both young and old, affective expressions often create a snowball effect. For example, consider the loss of a spouse. The survivor has experienced the severance of an important attachment, with all of its emotional implications, as well as an alteration of many life circumstances. These developments, in turn, may create a multitude of additional affective expressions, such as fear, anxiety, or withdrawal.

BEHAVIORAL EXPRESSION Invariably, grief leads to changes in behavior. However, each variety of behavior can also be viewed as the outcome of a physical, cognitive, or affective change as well. For instance, the affective responses of sadness coupled with the physical symptoms of lack of energy may lead to slow movement or longer reaction time. Research also suggests that a few of these behavioral expressions are unique to young and old. For example, bereaved elderly persons tend to cry more often and to experience insomnia more than do younger bereaved individuals.

☐ Stages of Grief

With the loss of a loved one, individuals react in different ways. The more common emotional reactions include a mixture of sorrow, misery, emptiness, and loneliness. Some report a general feeling of "numbness" and only vague awareness of the events taking place around them. For others, life may not seem worth living anymore, and some may even look forward to their own early death. Individuals will also differ widely in their appraisal of the death event itself. It may be perceived as a tragedy, a blessing, a mystery, a transition, or a release (Vail, 1982).

According to Phyllis Silverman (1986), the process of grieving and the psychological healing process follow a chronology of three stages: impact, recoil, and accommodation. She developed these stages while observing the behaviors of 233 widows over a six-year period. While Silverman's research was confined to females, it is conceivable that males pass through similar stages. It is also likely that her research can be applied to the loss of any loved one. The following discussion is based on Silverman's research.

THE IMPACT STAGE

Initially, widows report that numbness envelops them when they are told of their husband's death. Many experience a sense of disbelief and their behavior becomes still and robotlike. The woman's new legal status as a widow has no social and emotional meaning to her. Automatically, she thinks and acts as her husband's wife, still tailoring her behavior as she probably did while he was alive and doing those things that would please him. Continuing to play the role of wife, she knows how to behave and what is expected of her. Her numbness helps her to perform her role reflexively.

The intensity and duration of a widow's numbness will vary depending on whether her husband died suddenly or after a long illness. When death follows a long illness, the widow inevitably has a certain sense of relief, and the shock is not as profound as when death comes as a surprise. This observation by Silverman is compatible with our earlier discussion of stress and the variations that can exist at the moment of death.

Silverman found that psychological numbness often becomes a valuable asset in averting a state of collapse. In this sense, it may help the survivor to handle emotionally taxing chores, such as arranging the funeral. However, this protection against acute anguish is only temporary, and widows need the support and assistance of loved ones.

Along these lines, most widows are grateful that someone else is willing to help, and even think for them at this time. Relatives and friends usually help to arrange the funeral, help with shopping and housekeeping chores, or chauffeur the children to visit friends. At a time when she is least able, the widow must begin dealing with a complex set of financial issues, and others may be able to help with these matters as well. Among other tasks, the widow has to find out about her insurance, collect back pay, determine what money she has for current expenses, apply for Social Security and veterans' benefits, and, if there is an estate, deal with the lawyer. Some things only she can handle. Eventually she will have to go to bed in the empty bedroom, see her husband's belongings around her, eat alone, and deal, by herself, with household routines.

It is important to emphasize that the impact stage has no predictable duration. Nor is it a purely numb period without any breakthrough of feelings. The widow does have many concrete chores that involve her in necessary and important activities, and these keep her engaged in the real world. However, the meaning of what has happened also begins to enter her consciousness. The people who are available to help at this time may be deceived by her outward reactions. They may think that she is doing well, and they are pleased about how well she is holding up. They are unaware, and she also may not recognize, that this is but the first stage in a long and painful process.

THE RECOIL STAGE

At this time numbness will begin to lessen, but most widows will fight its departure. This is because the return of feelings brings the full realization of the loss. Many have avoided the meaning of the loss, and may continue to do so as their new reality intermittently breaks through. As we'll discover, dysfunctional and functional methods of coping emerge during this stage.

Many widows report that a part of them is missing during this time. Also common is a loss of appetite, sleeplessness, or, conversely, a desire to eat or sleep all the time. A widow may find herself impatient and restless, not wanting to be with people but not wanting to be alone either. She may begin to feel increasingly misunderstood, that friends and relatives are becoming impatient and uncomfortable with her continuing grief. Some women feel that if they can simply keep themselves so busy that they grow too tired to do anything except fall into bed, they will be able to keep their feelings at bay. This way, they can avoid thinking about either the past or the future.

Many widows want to review the circumstances of the spouse's deaths over and over again, wondering whether anything could have been done. Feelings of anger and remorse are not unusual. The widow may feel angry that her husband did not take better care of himself. She may also feel remorseful that she did not do enough.

Ann Stearns (1984) points out, however, that while survivors may genuinely *feel* blameworthy, usually their self-blaming thoughts are unrealistic; in other words, they are overly harsh with themselves. They stretch their imaginations to believe that they are responsible for anticipating or preventing events which ordinary mortals could not possibly have prevented. Or twisting human size mistakes into criminal proportions, they feel guilty as if they had intentionally brought harm to themselves or to another person, which is rarely the case. The following are examples of unrealistic guilt:

> "Maybe if I were not so selfish and caught up in my work, our marriage could have lasted. . . ."

> "If I had stayed home that night, the accident would never have happened."

> "I never had the chance to tell her how much she really meant to me."

It is normal to feel that one could have better loved a departed spouse. However, Stearns emphasizes that we all feel guilty during a time of loss. What survivors need is a support system to help them sort out these feelings, one that can minimize unrealistic guilt. For example, a comforting friend can help to separate realistic from unrealistic guilt by asking questions: "Why are you the only one to blame?" "How could you have known that?" "Are you expecting yourself to have known things that could not have been known with certainty?" "Are you tormenting yourself with thoughts of self-blame, as if no other reason or explanation could account for the events that happened?"

As time goes on, survivors typically learn from the kindness of others to ask themselves questions that are similarly kind, but objective. Gradually their feelings of unrealistic guilt begin to diminish as the situation gains a more accurate perspective.

During the Recoil Stage, many widows are not prepared for the negative feelings they experience. They have to discover that there is no easy way around their misery, given the nature and meaning of their loss. If they know that their suffering is normal and inevitable, they may find it easier to endure. Of course, this underscores the need for a reassuring and trusting support network.

DYSFUNCTIONAL AND FUNCTIONAL METHODS OF COPING Sorting through these negative feelings and confronting the other demands of bereavement can produce a wide range of behaviors. As we indicated earlier, some of these will be healthy and productive, others will not. John Crosby and Nancy Jose (1983) expound upon the diversity of behaviors by referring to dysfunctional and functional modes of coping. The following represents some examples of dysfunctional coping observed by these researchers.

Avoidance This is known as the "keep busy" strategy and many feel that it is therapeutic and functional. However, when used over an extended period of time, it more often than not is a dysfunctional ploy which may encourage the denial of a loved one's death. By keeping busy we defend ourselves against the anxiety that arises when we "are doing nothing." Keeping busy enables survivors to apply their mental-emotional energy to the task at hand, thus diverting thoughts and feelings away from death. Keeping busy is, in itself, not wrong. It turns into a dysfunctional strategy, though, when it becomes the primary method of coping.

Some survivors employ a variation of this by the "getting away" or "taking a trip" strategy. Grief resolution requires coming to grips with loss, loneliness, personal effects, routines, and all manner of behaviors of the deceased. When the bereaved takes a trip (visits relatives, vacations, tours, etc.) soon after the death of a loved one, the grief work is *partially* postponed. The portion that is postponed is precisely that which needs to be confronted first. A person only needs to fantasize coming back home after such a trip (i.e., walking into the empty house, the empty bedroom, etc.), in order to appreciate that the first level of grief work needs to be dealt with in the context of the deceased person's position, role, and immediate family environment prior to death.

Obliteration This represents an effort by survivors to erase the former existence of the deceased. Obliteration goes beyond denial and avoidance. Obliteration involves the attempt of total erasure of the deceased person's prior existence. This may involve disposal of all personal effects, belongings, collections, hobbies, pictures, and other possessions. In short, obliteration means wiping away all memories of the deceased.

Idolization Idolization is just the opposite of obliteration. Here, the survivor makes the deceased greater in death than he/she was in life. The deceased is endowed with a quality of perfection that is suprahuman. It is to restore life by holding fast to the belief

The loss of a loved one produces many emotional reactions.

that the deceased is really present. Personal effects are left intact. Possessions, mementos, pictures, and hobbies are endowed with an importance they previously lacked. No survivor can ever hope to measure up, and shame, self-doubt, guilt, and inferiority are prescribed feelings for those who must live in the wake of such splendor.

Our discussion thus far has stressed the difficult and demanding adjustments posed by widowhood. Betty Wylie's research (1982) echos our discussion, and she adds that no part of coming to terms with the loss of a spouse can be shirked or avoided, for it will have to be faced and gone through sometime, whether now or later, including the complications that often result from denial or repression.

Some widows will use some or all of the dysfunctional methods of coping we have described and adjust poorly. Other researchers, such as Mary Vachon (1982) have uncovered other factors related to poor coping behavior. She found that the following groups of widows encountered the most difficulty:

- those with poor social support

- those under 45 whose husbands died suddenly; or, conversely, those over 65, whose husbands suffered a lingering death

- those with an ambivalent relationship to the deceased (those who have the most difficulty recovering are those who had the worst marriages)

- those who were denied the grief experience because of minimal funeral ceremonies

■ those with previous psychiatric difficulties (If they were suicidal before, their chances of death by suicide are greatly increased; suicide is a high risk for the first five years following a spouse's death.)

Compared to other widows, the groups just described were more likely to experience higher levels of stress and anxiety. In addition to psychological maladjustment, there were physical consequences. For example, health-related disorders and hospital admission rates were higher for these women.

PATTERNS OF FUNCTIONAL COPING Constructive grief work relies on the support network being permissive of feelings. Additionally, the network needs to be positively accepting and supportive. Crosby and Jose feel that this implies the ability of the individuals to engage in honest and frank types of communication and direct their energies toward the actual loss as experienced collectively and individually. In order to accomplish this freedom of mutual acceptance, there needs to be an absence of scapegoating, blaming, excessive caretaking, and computerlike rationale, which substitutes reason and logic for feelings and emotion. Commitment to the process of communication between the support network and the survivor creates an atmosphere in which the survivors may feel secure in their grief. With this, they are free to self-disclose. They are free to feel whatever they feel, but they are also free to challenge their own beliefs and the beliefs of others, knowing that feelings are often the result of internalized beliefs which are irrational or illogical.

Unlimited possibilities for grief reduction are created when open communication is established. If feelings are shared (even if not in identical ways), an open stage for talk and reliving past episodes is created. At this time, beliefs and values may need to be questioned openly, that is, challenged and confronted. Moreover, the open confrontation of beliefs may help survivors to see the irrationality of some of the assumptions they may be making regarding their personal role and responsibility in events that, in actuality, are far beyond their control. As we have learned, those who are in mourning and grief sometimes have a gigantic overestimation of their own power: They reason that if they had done something differently, the death would never have happened. Thus, the stage is set for prolonged grieving because the person takes upon himself or herself the responsibility for things far beyond his or her control. This accounts for much of the "guilt" that becomes mixed up with "grief."

Toward the end of the recoil stage, Silverman writes that loved ones may be misled by how well the widow is doing. Many may assume that the worst of grief and mourning is over. Friends and relatives also have their own lives to lead and they may become impatient with any continuing need the widow may express. When family and friends do remain available and supportive, therefore, their attention may not be helpful. They will often try to help by distracting the widow from her grief, but the grief is what she needs to experience at this stage. Only when the widow can at last acknowledge her pain, doubts, and fears can she begin to make the necessary changes toward the last stage of grief.

■ Coping with the Pain of Loss ■

Losing a loved one is devastating at any point in the life cycle and poses an assortment of adjustments for survivors. While no perfect answers exist as to how one should adapt and rebound from loss, numerous suggestions have been proposed. The following are among the major recommendations.

Be patient with yourself. There is no predictable

timetable that indicates how long or short grieving processes should be. Each particular case is unique and the overall duration of recovery knows wide variations.

Do not be afraid or ashamed to express your emotions. Grieving processes include a wide range of affective states, including sadness, remorse, anger, depression, and anxiety. Releasing these emotions, rather than suppressing them, is both normal and healthy.

Realize that emotional reactions to loss vary widely. There will be days when the sorrow of loss will be more evident than others. Sensitivity usually heightens for example, around holiday times, birthdays, or other special days shared with the deceased. Be prepared for good and bad days as you reorganize your life, especially during the early stages of recovery.

Seek to accentuate the positive memories you have of the deceased. Survivors tend to dwell on the things they did not do for the deceased, or think of the parts of a relationship that could have been improved.

While it is normal to feel guilty, remember that guilt is self-imposed and needs to be put into a proper perspective. This means not ignoring the positive dimensions of your relationship with the deceased.

Share your feelings with others. It is important to talk about your loss, be it with friends, relatives, or skilled helpers. Along these lines, a support group may be an excellent source of guidance, security, and trust. Working through your grief with others also helps to combat the loneliness that is prevalent following the loss of a loved one.

Take steps to maintain your physical and psychological well-being. Losing a loved one is a stressful life event that has the potential of creating inner turmoil and disruption. It is important to safeguard your health by getting adequate rest, nutrition, and exercise. Your susceptibility to illness may also not be as great as it was before the loss, and many bereaved persons suffer from insomnia, loss of appetite, migraine headaches, and excessive anxiety. Should any of these conditions persist, do not hesitate to see a physician.

THE ACCOMMODATION STAGE

During this final stage, the survivor discovers new ways of looking at the world. Entering this stage does not mean the end of depressed feelings or an end to the pain of her loss. These feelings do become less intense and pervasive, however, and, as they decrease, she will have a different perspective on her experience.

She may learn, for instance, that she can laugh and that she has things worth living for; she can enjoy people and look forward to getting up in the morning. She can look upon her husband and her past without despairing of her present or her future. Remembering that past, she can cry without becoming frightened or uncomfortable about it, without worrying about other people's reactions. Survivors within this stage accept the fact that part of them will always be sad when they think about the past and most consider this natural and right.

It is important for the widow to *remember* during this stage. Her ways of remembering are her ways of honoring her dead husband and of building continuity between her past and her future. Some widows set up memorial funds, some donate flowers annually on their husbands' birthdays, some become active in a project or area that was important to him. Others make scrapbooks, or carefully store those personal possessions that their children may use when they are older.

Becoming involved in work and leisure, as well as discovering new friends, are ways of building new roles for herself. She may also begin to change the old habits of daily living that framed her life and develop new ones appropriate to her current situation. She finds ways to take charge of her own life, in the process achieving a new sense of competence.

■ Endings and New Beginnings

Before drawing this chapter to a close, we would like to comment on the ongoing nature of grief and bereavement. Following the death of a loved one, family and friends typically rally around the survivor. However, as time progresses, the social network decreases its support of the survivor. Neighbors and friends may look after the survivor or help with such domestic chores as meal preparation, but there is an expectation that the survivor is responsible for day-to-day activities. Children and siblings may continue their support; however, it decreases a few weeks after the funeral. Generally, the social network is on alert but not on active duty several weeks after the death (Brubaker, 1985).

It is our contention that the later periods of bereavement, when ritualized support for the survivor is lessened or removed, may represent the most difficult period of adjustment. Carolyn Balkwell (1985) reinforces this by saying that pressures typically mount as survivors have to independently carve out new identities and lifestyles.

Overcoming loneliness is typically the biggest emotional hurdle that survivors must face. As we stated earlier, during the first few months after the funeral, loneliness is often masked by busywork. However, loneliness usually lingers and will surface in a number of different ways. Research undertaken by Helena Lopata (1973, 1979, 1981) describes some of the ways in which loneliness may be expressed:

- a desire to be with the person who is no longer available

- feelings that one is no longer an object of love

- homesickness for a past lifestyle

- a desire for a deep companionate relationship

- feelings that one no longer has anyone to love

- a desire for the presence of another person in the home

- unhappiness over the absence of anyone to share the workload

- alienation owing to a drop in status

- anger at past friends because of less frequent interaction with them. Such anger may originate from (a) differing definitions of the appropriate time and form for expressing grief, (b) a gradual withering away of associates if a long illness preceded the husband's death, (c) awkwardness in interactions when grief is expressed, (d) a friend's desire not to associate with people who have been close to death particularly if the friend fears his or her own death, (e) the complications involved in including an extra single woman in mixed-sex activities, (f) the wife having relied on the husband to make social contacts in the past, or (g) financial considerations that may make past activities unavailable

- a composite of the preceding, which may be compounded by the inability to make new friends

Most researchers (Lund, 1989; Taves, 1981; Vail, 1982; Burnham, 1982) stress the importance of reorganizing day-to-day living to effectively combat loneliness. Tasks such as cooking and cleaning, financial concerns, and the expenditure of free time need to be deliberately restructured. Learning to live alone and accepting the isolation that often goes with it needs to be addressed. Moreover, everything a survivor has been accustomed to doing now bears scrutiny and reevaluation. A new life script has been written and old habits and routines may no longer fit.

Developing new social relationships is another way to overcome loneliness. Four kinds of relationships, in particular, mitigate against loneliness. The first three are family relationships, friendships, and sexual relationships. The fourth is a personal commitment to a cause, such as a course of action, a community, a productive type of work, or a social network of some kind. It is significant that each of these relationships is other-directed and can be used to combat loneliness (Wylie, 1982).

Survivors might also consider turning to support groups and other service programs for assistance. Perhaps the most widely known is the *Widow-to-Widow Program*. Volunteers who have been widowed maintain phone hotlines and make home visits to newly widowed persons. The phone hotlines serve to provide listeners to the lonely, to help widowed persons make new friends, and to provide specific information. The primary aim of the program is to help the widowed person progress through the developmental stages involved in the transition from married life to widowed life. Aides provide support and serve as role models of what it is to be widowed. Another program, which, in additon to the hotline and home visits, provides social gatherings and community seminars, has also been developed (Balkwell, 1985).

In a review of the literature, Timothy Brubaker (1985) observes that, over time, adjusted survivors have developed ways to cope with the day-to-day problems of living and receive emotional support from various persons. While there are still feelings of loneliness and a sense of loss, successfully adjusted survivors have developed ways to cope with these problems. These survivors have established a new identity with the help of their support network.

Those who have successfully adjusted to loss also continue to find new outlets for their energies. Amidst such change, though, the deceased is never forgotten. Rather, survivors can cling to memories forever. It may well be that experiencing the pain of loss promotes stronger faith and more compassionate care and appreciation of the living. Those who have felt such pain often learn to live their lives with more meaning—with appreciation of their finiteness and of the limits of their time here (Schuster and Butler, 1989; Lund, 1989; Schneider, 1984; Weizman and Kamm, 1985; Miles and Crandall, 1983).

CHAPTER REVIEW

One of life's most formidable tasks is learning to understand and accept death. For many people, death is a sensitive topic that is avoided in conversations and often repressed. Our reactions to the subject are varied.

Elderly people appear to be more aware of death's imminence than younger individuals are. Research also indicates that older people are seemingly less afraid of death and may even perceive it as an acceptable alternative to a life that has become devoid of meaning.

Contrary to the popular tradition, dying patients usually want to talk openly about their impending death. Unfortunately, well-meaning family members or medical personnel may cover the terminally ill in a shroud of silence and avoid discussing the topic. Most experts agree that dying patients need to verbalize their feelings.

The dying process has attracted the attention of numerous researchers, most notably Elisabeth Kübler-Ross. At the heart of her research is a five-stage theory of the dying process. These stages include denial, anger, bargaining, depression, and acceptance. Though Kübler-Ross attained wide acclaim for her work, some researchers feel that the process of dying does not flow in one steady stream toward acceptance. Rather, Edwin Shneidman feels, the terminal patient experiences a variety of different emotions against a constant interplay of disbelief and hope. E. Mansell Pattison proposed that death is approached through three phases: the acute phase, the chronic living-dying interval, and the terminal phase. The quality of life before death, including psychological and physical needs, deserves careful examination. Drugs are commonly used to control pain, one of the most unpleasant symptoms accompanying terminal illness. Although drugs such as morphine and diamorphine are commonly used, experiments with other drugs, including marijuana and LSD, have been conducted. The hospice approach seeks to improve every aspect of the quality of life for the terminally ill. Hospice institutions provide humane and individualized care and are being established in many areas of the United States.

Euthanasia, known as mercy killing, is a controversial issue. Passive euthanasia means that death is not actively prevented through any type of intervention, and active euthanasia implies that steps are taken to cause death. It is likely that this topic will grow in importance as medical technology improves and attitudes toward life and death change.

The experience of dying usually consists of a sequence of physiological events. Death is said to occur when there is an absence of respiration, heartbeat, and a flat electroencephalogram. The latter means that brain death has occurred, and this is the most widely accepted criterion of death.

This chapter also focused on the nature of bereavement and grief. Bereavement is the loss of a loved one by death; grief refers to the deep distress caused by such a loss. We explored the fact that the loss of a loved one is stressful at any time in the life cycle, and survivors face many adjustment tasks.

Phyllis Silverman has proposed three fairly distinct periods of grief: the impact, recoil, and accommodation stages. Within these stages are functional and dysfunctional coping strategies. During the later periods of bereavement, social support for the survivor has usually lessened. Overcoming loneliness and reorganizing day-to-day living seems to be the biggest psychological hurdles that survivors must overcome.

Grief does not end when the funeral is over. Rather, feelings of emptiness and loneliness continue for extended periods. However, if satisfactory adjustment has been made during the mourning process, the bereaved, in time, will find new outlets for their energies. When this is the case, the deceased will have gained a certain immortality in the memory of survivors.

KEY TERMS

acceptance stage
active euthanasia
acute phase
anger stage
bargaining stage
bereavement
chronic living-dying interval
denial stage
depression stage
dying trajectory

euthanasia
grief
hospice
near-death experience
passive euthanasia
preparatory depression
reactive depression
terminal phase
thanatologist

RECOMMENDED READINGS

Kalish, R. A. (1985). *Death, Grief, and Caring Relationships,* 2nd ed. Monterey, Calif.: Brooks/Cole.
Among the topics covered are the meaning of death, the process of dying, and the grieving process.

Kurtz, E. (1982). *What a Widow Needs to Know: A Guide for Widows and Helpers.* Palo Alto, Calif.: R & E Research Associates.
A good resource book for those wanting more information on death, grief, and bereavement.

Kushner, H. S. (1981). *When Bad Things Happen to Good People.* New York: Schocken.
A thought-provoking look at the concept of loss and the adjustments needed to regain stability.

Leming, M. R., and Dickinson, G. E. (1990). *Understanding Death, Dying, and Bereavement,* 2nd ed. Ft. Worth, Tex.: Holt.
The authors provide very readable coverage concerning all aspects of dying and grieving experiences.

Lukeman, B. (1982). *Embarkations: A Guide to Dealing with Death and Parting.* Englewood Cliffs, N.J.: Prentice-Hall.
One of the better practical books on death and how to handle its many sides, including bereavement.

Monley, A. (1985). *The Hospice Alternative.* New York: Basic Books.
An excellent presentation of what the hospice represents, why it is growing in popularity, and why it is changing health care in this country.

Raphael, B. (1985). *The Anatomy of Bereavement.* New York: Basic Books.
An examination of all the stages of mourning and how the effects of loss differ at each stage of life.

Rosenberg, J. F. (1983). *Thinking Clearly About Death.* Englewood Cliffs, N.J.: Prentice-Hall.
Rosenberg's objective reporting of this sensitive topic makes this worthwhile reading.

Seskin, J. (1985). *Alone But Not Lonely.* Glenview, Ill.: Scott, Foresman.
Widowed persons will benefit from the topics in this paperback, including tips on independent living and self-fulfillment activities.

Silverman, P. R. (1986). *Widow to Widow.* New York: Springer.
Part one of this text offers comprehensive detail to the three stages of grief and mourning described in this chapter.

Weizman, S. G., and Kamm, P. (1985). *About Mourning: Support and Guidance for the Bereaved.* New York: Human Sciences Press.
Much guidance and advice for those assisting the bereaved is made available by the authors.

Glossary

abstinence standard A moral standard asserting that it is wrong for both unmarried males and females to engage in sexual intercourse.

abstraction A subjective concept or idea apart from one's objective analysis of the tangible environment.

acceptance stage According to Kübler-Ross, the fifth psychological stage of dying. The person is no longer angry or depressed but desires to be left alone or with just a few loved ones.

accommodation According to Piaget, the restructuring of mental organizations so that new information or previously rejected information may be processed.

acquired immune deficiency syndrome (AIDS) Disorder characterized by a specific defect in the body's natural immunity against disease.

active euthanasia Deliberate steps taken to cause death. Also called positive euthanasia.

active theory A theory of development stating that individuals are capable of actively governing and regulating their own development. An example is cognitive-developmental theory.

activity theory The theory that active and productive people are happiest, even in old age.

acute phase According to Pattison, the first of three phases of dying.

adaptation According to Piaget, a mental process that will provide a meaningful understanding of the environment. It hinges on the mental properties of assimilation and accommodation.

addicting narcotic A narcotic such as opium and heroin that produces pronounced physical and psychological addiction.

adolescence The life stage that begins with puberty and encompasses the teenage years.

adolescent egocentrism The ability to conceptualize one's own thoughts in addition to being preoccupied with the thoughts of those in one's surroundings. Two types of adolescent egocentrism are the imaginary audience and the personal fable.

adrenal gland A gland of the endocrine system located near the kidneys.

adult day-care facility A facility that offers daily nursing, nutritional, and medical monitoring to the elderly, who, however, maintain their own residences.

adult psychology The systematic field of study that examines the physical, intellectual, personal, and social characteristics of humans during the adult years.

agape love Type of love characterized by caring and altruistic behavior.

ageism Discrimination against or unkind stereotyping of a person on the basis of his or her age. Ageism is most prevalent against the elderly.

agenesis A lack of failure of development.

alcohol A liquid that is the intoxicating agent in fermented and distilled liquors.

allele Any of several alternative genes at a given chromosomal locus.

Alzheimer's disease A category of dementia characterized by progressive mental deterioration.

amino acid The basic unit of structure for protein.

amniocentesis The removal of fluid from the amniotic sac so that chromosomes of the fetus may be analyzed.

amniotic fluid A liquid that holds the embryo or fetus in suspension and protects it against jarring and from any pressure exerted by the mother's internal organs.

amniotic sac A transparent membrane completely enveloping the embryo or fetus, except where the umbilical cord passes through the placenta.

amphetamine A drug that serves as a stimulant and acts on the central nervous system. Examples of amphetamines are cocaine, benzedrine, dexedrine, and methedrine.

anal stage Freud's second stage of psychosexual development. During this period, children's erotic feelings center on the anus and on elimination.

analytic style A type of cognitive style in which objects are categorized according to their similar components or properties.

anatomy The branch of biology that studies the structure, position, location, and shape of some biological object.

androgen The sex hormone that regulates the male secondary sex characteristics. Androgen is also found in lesser amounts in females.

androgyny Having both masculine and feminine personality traits.

anger stage According to Kübler-Ross, the second psychological stage of dying. The person accepts the fact of his or her impending death but is angry about its seeming unfairness: "Why does it have to be me?"

angina A cardiac condition that occurs when the supply of blood to a part of the heart muscle is not enough to meet its needs, such as during exercise.

animism According to Piaget, the tendency of children to give life to inanimate objects. Animism is most prevalent between the ages of 2 and 7.

anorectic A person suffering from anorexia nervosa.

anorexia nervosa A severe diminishment of appetite, particularly among teenagers. This disorder is more common in females than in males and is believed to have psychogenic origins.

anticoagulant A drug that thins the blood and prevents clotting.

anxiety A state of inner apprehension most frequently characterized as a generalized fear of a subjective danger.

anxious-avoidant attached According to Ainsworth, infants who are distressed when caregivers are away but are ambivalent when they return.

anxious-resistant attached According to Ainsworth, infants who avoid contact with their mothers after brief separation.

Apgar test An evaluation of the newborn's basic life processes, administered approximately one minute after birth and again five minutes later. The life signs tested are heart rate, respiratory regularity, muscle tone, reflex irritability, and coloration.

arcuate fascicular An area of the brain that plays a significant role in producing meaningful speech.

arteriosclerotic dementia Part of the dementia syndrome grouping, but this dysfunction is caused by cerebral arteriosclerosis.

arthritis Inflammation, pain, and swelling of the joints.

artificialism The childhood notion that everything in the world, including natural objects and events, is designed by human beings.

asceticism An ego defense mechanism characterized by the avoidance of any type of physical pleasure or excitement.

assimilation Perceiving and interpreting new information in terms of existing knowledge and understanding.

atherosclerosis A condition that results when fatty deposits narrow the arteries and reduce or block the flow of blood through them.

atrophy The degeneration of body tissues or organs.

attachment An affectionate bond between infant and caregiver.

authoritarian control An attempt to control behavior by enforcing a set standard of conduct. Emphasis is placed on obedience and punitive discipline.

authoritative control An attempt to control behavior by establishing democratic, meaningful, and realistic expectations.

authority-maintaining orientation Kohlberg's fourth stage of moral development.

autoimmunity theory A theory of physical aging suggesting that with age there are more mutations and changes in the body's cell division.

autonomy versus shame and doubt The second of Erikson's eight psychosocial crises.

autosome Any chromosome other than a sex chromosome.

axon The long and slender portion of a neuron that extends outward from the cell body. The axon carries the electrochemical impulse from the dendrite to the end plates.

babbling A stage of early language development, beginning by approximately the sixth month. Babbling first emerges a syllable at a time and includes both vowels and consonants.

Babinski reflex A major reflex present in the newborn. When the sole of the foot is stimulated, the toes fan outward.

baby biography A day-to-day account of the development of an infant or child.

barbiturate A depressant drug that induces sleep and provides relaxation. Examples are Nembutal, Seconal, and Librium.

bargaining stage According to Kübler-Ross, the third psychological stage of dying. The dying person bargains with God, doctors, or anyone else he or she believes can stave off death.

basal-cell carcinoma A form of skin cancer that usually appears on the head and neck. It is a malignant tumor that rarely metastasizes.

basic trust versus mistrust The first of Erikson's eight psychosocial crises.

battered child syndrome The technical name given to child abuse.

behavioral genetics The study of inherited behavior.

behavioral predisposition A term implying that one has a tendency toward certain behavioral characteristics, given certain environmental conditions.

behaviorism A school of thought emphasizing that an organism's behavior is a product of conditioning and learning experiences. Emphasis is on the organism's observable behaviors.

benign tumor A tumor that is typically harmless and does not invade normal tissue.

bereavement The loss of a loved one through death.

bilingualism The ability to speak more than one language.

biochemical stressor A stressor having a biochemical origin, such as a pollutant or poor nutrition.

biological aging One of the three main types of aging processes. Biological aging refers to physiological functioning over time.

birthing room For the parents of newborns, a room offering a homelike and relaxed atmosphere within the hospital's general delivery unit.

black English A social dialect used mostly by black people at lower socioeconomic levels.

blended family A family form in which one or both of the partners have been married before. The new union may also include children from the previous marriage.

blending action A type of biochemical activity in which no one gene dominates the other; rather, the two proteins manufactured by the ribosome mix together.

blood pressure The pressure exerted by the blood on the artery walls.

body transcendence versus body preoccupation According to Peck, a psychological adjustment to be made during the later years of adulthood.

breech delivery Delivery of a baby's buttocks or feet first.

Broca's area The portion of the brain that is located adjacent to the motor cortex and controls the muscles involved in speech. Damage to this area produces motor aphasia and causes speech to be slow and labored.

bulimia An eating disorder characterized by gorging oneself with excessive amounts of food and then inducing vomiting and/or using large amounts of laxatives.

burnout The depleting of physical and mental resources because of stress.

cancer A large group of diseases characterized by uncontrolled growth and the spread of abnormal cells.

carcinogen An agent causing cancer.

carcinoma A type of cancer originating from epithelial cells.

cardiovascular-respiratory fitness The ability of the heart, blood vessels, and lungs to deliver oxygen and nutrients to the tissues and to remove wastes as quickly and efficiently as possible.

career clock According to Kimmel, a person's subjective sense of being on time or behind time in regard to career development.

cataract A visual problem characterized by opacity in the lens of the eye.

catharsis theory of television viewing A theory proposing that watching aggressive behavior on television provides a vicarious outlet for the viewer's own aggressiveness.

cathectic flexibility versus cathectic impoverishment According to Peck, a psychological adjustment to be made during middle adulthood.

cell A living unit of organized material that contains a nucleus and is enclosed in a membrane.

cellular theory A theory of physical aging that emphasizes the role that errors in cell division play in the aging process.

centering The tendency to concentrate on the outstanding characteristics of an object while excluding its other features.

central nervous system Part of the nervous system that consists of the brain and the spinal cord.

cephalocaudal development Physical growth that takes place from the head downward.

cerebellum A part of the hindbrain controlling body balance and coordination.

cerebral arteriosclerosis Severe hardening of the arteries of the brain, often leading to vascular and cognitive disturbances.

cerebral cortex The surface layer of the cerebrum.

cerebrovascular accident (CVA) The rupture or blockage of a large cerebral blood vessel, usually leading to a stroke.

cerebrum The largest portion of the forebrain. The cerebrum consists of a left and a right hemisphere, connected by the corpus callosum.

cervix The lowest part of the uterus.

cesarean delivery The delivery of the baby through a surgical incision made in the mother's abdominal and uterine walls.

chaining See serialization.

chlamydia A sexually transmitted disease that creates infections in the urethra, cervix, and rectum.

cholesterol A lipid (fat) produced naturally in the body.

chromosomal abnormalities Occurrences that affect the number of genes and/or chromosomes for a given species.

chromosomes Thin rodlike structures in a cell that contain the essential mechanisms for directions of the cell's activity.

chronic living–dying interval According to Pattison, the second of three phases of dying.

circumcision A surgical procedure in which all or part of the foreskin of the penis is removed.

classical conditioning A fundamental type of learning theory originated by Pavlov, also referred to as respondent conditioning. In this form of conditioning, a subject responds to a previously neutral stimulus after it has been effectively paired with the unconditioned stimulus that originally produced the response.

classification In Piagetian logic, the ability to understand the concepts of subclasses, classes, and class inclusion.

climacteric The period of life from the onset of irregularity of the menses to total cessation.

clique A small peer group characterized by social exclusiveness and a strong emotional bond among its members.

closure The fact that any two mental structures can combine to form a third structure.

cocaine An amphetamine that exists as a bitter crystalline alkaloid.

coding A process of compacting information so that it may be placed into long-term memory.

cognition An individual's intellectual activity. The mental process involving all aspects of thought and perception.

cognitive-developmental theory A theory of development that proposes specific stages leading to mature thinking.

cognitive dissonance An inconsistency or conflict in one's thoughts, beliefs, attitudes, or behavior, resulting in a tension state that the individual is motivated to reduce.

cognitive flexibility The ability to shift from one way of thinking to another.

cognitive social learning theory A theory that integrates what is known about learning processes to explain social behavior.

cognitive style The manner in which an individual organizes information and discovers solutions to problems.

cohabitation A man and woman living together who are not married.

cohort A group of persons born approximately at the same time.

cohort analysis An analysis of the experiences common to a particular age group.

collagen The fibrous elastic muscles found in all body organs.

collagen theory A theory of physical aging that examines changes associated with the body's fibrous protein.

collateral circulation The heart's adaptive approach to damage. If a small infarct is created by a heart attack, new blood vessels will develop to compensate for damaged ones.

collective monologue A type of egocentric communication characterized by inability to listen effectively to what others are saying.

commune A group of people who live together because of common interests or needs.

companionate love Love characterized by sharing and doing things together. Also called *storge* love.

compensation Finding a successful or rewarding activity that can be substituted for failure in another kind of activity.

complementary needs A theory of mate selection proposing that individuals seek partners who complement their own personalities.

concept A mental image formed to represent an object or event.

conception The union of the male sperm with the female ovum, creating a zygote.

concrete operations The fourth stage of Piaget's theory of cognitive development, occurring approximately from ages 7 to 11. The stage marks a time when cognition is used consistently and the child can reason logically in new and challenging situations.

conductive deafness Deafness involving blockage or impairment of the outer or middle ear so that sound waves are not able to travel properly.

confounded data Data (such as age and cohort) in a research study that cannot be assessed separately.

conservation The recognition that the amount or quantity of matter remains the same despite changes in its outward physical appearance.

consonant A speech sound characterized by constriction or closure at one or more points in the breath channel.

constitution A term referring to an individual's physical and mental makeup.

contact comfort motive According to Harlow, an infant's desire to seek objects offering softness and warmth. Contact and comfort from such objects are said to strengthen attachment behaviors.

continuous development theory A theory of development not adhering to age-prescribed stages. Rather, it sees change as gradual and continuous.

contractual legalistic orientation Kohlberg's fifth of six moral development stages. This stage is grouped under the major division or level known as postconventional morality.

control group A group of subjects in a research study who receive the same treatment as does the group being experimented upon, except that they do not receive the stimulus (independent variable) under observation.

controlled experiments An experimental situation in which the subject is placed in a structured and perhaps unnatural environment that can be manipulated by the experimenter.

conventional level Kohlberg's second of six moral development stages, covering ages 9 through 15.

cooing A type of vocalization taking place during the second month of infancy.

coronary artery disease A disease characterized by the presence of atherosclerosis in the coronary arteries.

coronary thrombosis A type of coronary artery disease in which a blood clot closes off an artery and causes a heart attack.

corpus callosum A bundle of nerve fibers connecting the left and right cerebral hemispheres.

correlation The relationship between any two events, frequently expressed as a number between +1.00 and −1.00. Different statistical procedures are used to discover degrees of relationship.

correlational method Method of observing and comparing naturally occurring events to discover any relationships that may exist.

cri-du-chat syndrome A genetic disorder caused by a partial loss of a chromosome on the fifth position. Characteristics include severe mental retardation, microcephaly, growth retardation, low birth weight, limited eye control, and a peculiar, catlike cry.

critical (or sensitive) period The point in an organism's early life stages at which strong bonds of attachment are established with the mother or other caregiver.

crossing over The tendency of chromosomes to exchange genes before cell division.

cross linkage The union of free radicals with other molecules, particularly fibrous molecules.

cross-sectional method A method of comparing developmental trends among groups who differ in age at a given time.

crowd A group of people larger than a clique but more impersonal and lacking strong bonds of attachment but having rather rigid membership requirements.

crystallized intelligence The dimension of intelligence

that includes verbal comprehension, numerical skills, and inductive reasoning.

cytoplasm Protoplasm found inside the cell but outside the nucleus.

daughter cell A new cell created in cell division.

deductive reasoning Reasoning from a set of premises to a conclusion. Piaget called this hypothetico-deductive reasoning.

deep structure The conceptual framework or meaning of a particular sentence.

defense mechanism A behavioral response enabling one to escape from anxiety.

dementia The irreversible cognitive and intellectual deterioration caused by brain dysfunction.

denial of reality A defense mechanism characterized by the individual's refusal to perceive the existence of hurtful situations.

denial stage According to Kübler-Ross, the first psychological stage of dying. During this stage, the person is unable to accept the fact that he or she is going to die.

deoxyribonucleic acid (DNA) The chemical substance constituting chromosomes and genes.

dependent variable The change, if any, brought about by the independent variables in experimental studies. Changes appear in the experimental group, especially when contrasted with the control group.

depression An emotional state characterized by feelings of dejection and worthlessness.

depression stage According to Kübler-Ross, the fourth stage of dying. When the patient can no longer deny the illness, he or she becomes engulfed with a sense of great loss.

depth perception A visual ability enabling persons to judge distance and descent.

destructive play A type of play characterized by creation (blocks, artwork) and then destruction.

developmental psychology A general term encompassing the psychology of childhood, adolescence, and all the remaining years of the human life span.

dialect A regional variation of a language.

diploid state A cell that has its full quota of chromosomes.

discontinuous development theory A theory of development emphasizing distinct spurts in growth and development. Also called an age-stage theory.

disengagement theory The theory that it is natural and indeed desirable to withdraw gradually from society as one grows old.

displacement The releasing of pent-up hostile feelings onto objects less dangerous than those that initially aroused the emotion.

distress Harmful and unpleasant stress. Distress occurs when the body and mind are worn down from repeated exposure to an unpleasant situation.

diuretic A drug that causes excess fluid and sodium to leave the body.

DNA See deoxyribonucleic acid.

dominant gene A gene that always expresses its hereditary characteristic.

double standard A moral standard asserting that males can have sexual relations before marriage but that females are expected to abstain.

Down syndrome Referred to as trisomy 21, a chromosomal abnormality in which there is an extra chromosome on the twenty-first position. Children afflicted with this disorder have, among other characteristics, epicanthic eye folds, round heads, and mental retardation.

dying trajectory The duration and form of the dying process.

early maturer A person who matures physically before the prescribed timetables.

early retirement Departure from the work world before the time mandated by age or tenure.

egalitarian marriage A marriage that emphasizes sharing authority, household chores, and responsibilities.

egg The female ovum.

ego In psychoanalytic theory, the part of the personality that serves as a rational agent and the mediator between the id and the superego.

egocentrism A style of thinking that causes children difficulty in seeing any point of view other than their own; self-centeredness.

ego differentiation versus work-role preoccupation According to Peck, a psychological adjustment to be made during the later years of adulthood.

ego ideal The part of the superego that results from rewarding experiences.

ego transcendence versus ego preoccupation According to Peck, a psychological adjustment to be made during the later years of adulthood.

elaboration The technique of expanding verbal or visual material to increase the number of ways that it can be retrieved.

Electra complex According to Freud, a girl's romantic feelings for her father and aggressive feelings for her mother. The Electra complex is prevalent during the phallic stage of psychosexual development.

embryo An organism between the second and eighth weeks of prenatal development.

embryonic period The period of prenatal development beginning when the ovum is implanted in the uterine wall and the cells begin to exhibit marked differentiation.

emotion A variation or change in one's arousal level that may either interfere with or facilitate motivated behavior.

empathy The ability to sympathize with or share the emotions of others.

empty nest The period of life when the children have left home and the couple is now alone.

endemic stressor A stressor that is long term and often cannot be eliminated.

endocrine gland A ductless gland that secretes hormones into the bloodstream.

endocrine system A system of glands that secrete hormones into the bloodstream and affect other body organs.

endogamy Pressure to marry from within one's own social group.

environmentalist A person who asserts that the environment is the major contributor to an individual's behavior and development.

epigenetic principle A theory stating that all development is genetically programmed.

equilibration According to Piaget, the balance between assimilation and accommodation.

eros love Love characterized by intense romance and idealization of one's partner.

erythroblastosis A condition in which maternal antibodies attack and destroy fetal blood cells.

escape A defense mechanism characterized by retreat or withdrawal behaviors.

estrogen A female sex hormone.

ethology The study of human and animal behavior in natural settings, including the role of instincts and biologically inherited responses on growth and development.

eustress A type of positive stress that occurs when the body's reactive change is put to productive use.

euthanasia The act of ending a life to alleviate suffering.

exchange filtering agent A filtering agent proposing that persons are attracted to those who provide the greatest relational rewards and the fewest number of sacrifices.

exogamy Pressure to marry from outside of one's social group.

experimental group A group of subjects in an experimental study that receives a special stimulus or treatment, the effect of which is under observation.

experimental method A series of steps by which the researcher tries to determine relationships among differing phenomena either to discover principles underlying behavior or to find cause-and-effect relationships. The method is characterized by control and repetition.

extended family A household containing three or more generations.

external aging Physical aspects of aging that are visible to the eye.

external validity The degree to which conclusions drawn from one set of observations can be generalized to other sets of observations.

fact A statement of an observation.

fair-weather cooperation stage According to Selman, friendships made during the later school years.

fallopian tube Either of two tubes that extend from the ovary region to the uterus. Also called the uterine tube.

fertilization The union of the egg and the sperm.

fetal period The period between eight weeks of prenatal development and birth.

fetoscopy A technique that photographs the fetus and samples fetal tissue and blood.

fetus The human organism in the womb from approximately the third prenatal month until birth.

filtering agent Sequence of decisions made by the couple about the quality of "fit" between their individual attributes. Filtering agents will test the compatibility of partners and serve to narrow down the field of eligibles.

fine-motor skills Motor skills requiring the use of small body parts, particularly the hands. Examples are writing and sewing.

fixation A preoccupation with one particular aspect of psychosexual development (e.g., thumbsucking) that may interfere with or be manifested in subsequent psychosexual stages.

fixed income Financial benefits that do not vary.

fluid intelligence A general cognitive ability that reflects relational thinking and the capability of thinking independently of culturally based content. Fluid intelligence is believed to peak during young adulthood.

forebrain The frontal and upper portion of the brain. The forebrain consists of the cerebrum, cerebral cortex, corpus callosum, thalamus, and hypothalamus.

formal operations The final stage of Piaget's theory of cognitive development, occurring between the ages of 11 and 15. The stage is characterized by systematic reasoning abilities and the successful integration of all past cognitive operations.

fraternal twins Twins conceived when two ova are released simultaneously by the female and both are penetrated by male sperm cells. Also referred to as dizygotic twins.

free association A cathartic process used in psychoanalysis. When patients use free association, they verbalize whatever comes into their minds.

free radical A highly reactive molecule that has become separated during a chemical reaction.

friendship The pairing off of, usually, two individuals who are likely to be similar in temperament and personality and share common interests.

frontal lobe An area of the cortex that controls the sense of smell as well as body movement and control.

full nest Reference to the period of life when a couple's children have reached adult status, but residency within the home continues.

functional disorder A disorder caused by psychological and interpersonal factors.

gamete A reproductive cell, either the female ovum or the male sperm.

gay men Males whose sexual orientation and affectional attraction are to other males.

gender identity The psychological awareness of being either a male or a female.

general adaptation syndrome Selye's model of stress reaction. The three stages are alarm, resistance, and exhaustion.

generation gap A term applied to the differences in values, attitudes, and behavior between two generational groups.

generativity versus stagnation According to Erikson, the psychosocial crisis that typically takes place during middle adulthood.

genes Biological units contained in the chromosomes, the transmitters of hereditary characteristics.

genetic epistemology The study of the origin of knowledge.

genetics The science of heredity.

genital herpes Sexually transmitted disease caused by herpes simplex viruses. The virus itself rests in the cell center of specific sensory nerves.

genital stage According to Freud, the stage of psychosexual development at which normal and mature sexual behavior is attained.

geriatrics The branch of medicine that pertains to the health problems of the elderly.

germ cells The cells frequently referred to as sex cells, or gametes.

gerontology The branch of developmental psychology that investigates the aged and aging processes.

gestation period The duration of pregnancy.

glaucoma An eye disease that results from increased pressure within the eyeball. Glaucoma causes a gradual loss of vision and damage to the optic disk.

gonads The reproductive organs: the ovaries in the female and the testes in the male.

gonorrhea Sexually transmitted disease caused by a bacterial infection and spread by sexual contact with an infected person. Gonorrhea is much more common in males than in females and is highly contagious.

good boy–nice girl orientation Kohlberg's third of six stages of moral development. This stage is grouped under the major division or level known as conventional morality.

grief Deep distress caused by the loss of a loved one.

gross-motor skills Motor skills requiring the coordination of large body parts. Examples are running, tumbling, and climbing a ladder.

growth Physical changes in the body or any of its parts because of an increase in cell number.

hallucinogen A drug capable of producing illusions, delusions, or hallucinations.

handedness An individual's hand preference.

haploid state A genetic condition in which a cell contains only half the number of chromosomes that are natural for its species.

hedonistic principle The motivation to seek out what is pleasurable and to avoid what creates discomfort.

hereditarians Persons who believe that most behavior is dependent on one's genetic endowment.

heredity Characteristics genetically transmitted to offspring by their parents.

heterozygous A genetic condition in which both gene pairs in an organism differ for a given trait (one dominant, one recessive).

hindbrain The lower portion of the brain responsible for those bodily functions necessary for survival. The hindbrain consists of the medulla, cerebellum, pons, and part of the reticular activating system.

holophrase The one-word stage of language development that occurs between 12 and 18 months.

home birth The delivery of a baby in the parents' home rather than in a hospital. The delivery is often conducted by a licensed nurse-midwife.

homogamy A mate-choice theory that states that mates are chosen on the basis of similar characteristics.

homosexual An individual who is attracted to members of the same sex.

homosexuality Sexual attraction and emotional attachment to persons of the same gender.

homozygous A genetic condition in which both genes are identical for a given trait (two dominant or two recessive).

hormone A product of the endocrine glands secreted into the bloodstream.

hospice A facility for terminally ill patients that focuses not only on providing humane medical care but also on fulfilling the patients' emotional needs.

hostile aggression A type of aggression directed at another person with the intention of hurting that person.

humanistic theory One of child psychology's major schools of thought. Humanists such as Maslow and Rogers stress the importance of helping children to maximize their uniqueness and potential in life.

hypertension High blood pressure.

hypothalamus Part of the forebrain that regulates hunger, thirst, sex, and body temperature. The hypothalamus is also a control center for pleasure and pain.

hypothesis A predicted solution of a problem.

hypothetico-deductive reasoning See deductive reasoning.

hysterectomy The surgical removal of all or part of the uterus.

id According to psychoanalytic theory, the instinctual part of the personality, which is concerned with the immediate gratification of motives.

identical twins Twins that occur as the result of the zygote splitting into two separate but genetically identical cells. Also referred to as monozygotic twins.

identification The process in which individuals perceive themselves as being alike or similar to other people and behave accordingly. During childhood, parents are the first models for identification.

identity According to Piaget, an awareness that certain mental actions may leave other mental structures unchanged.

identity achievement According to Marcia, an appraisal of values and choices in life and a commitment to some goal.

identity diffusion According to Marcia, the failure to examine any goals or values.

identity foreclosure According to Marcia, the idea of having life goals established by others.

identity formation The establishment of an integrated ego, usually during adolescence.

identity moratorium According to Marcia, the notion of rethinking values and goals, which often leads to an identity crisis.

identity versus role diffusion The fifth of Erikson's eight psychosocial crises. Identity versus role diffusion occupies the teenage years.

imaginary audience A consequence of adolescent egocentrism. Teenagers imagine that they are always the focus of attention.

immanent justice The childhood assumption that the world has a built-in system of law and order.

immunity theory A theory of physical aging suggesting that the body's immune system degenerates with age.

imprinting An organism's rapid attachment to an object (generally its caregiver), usually shortly after birth.

impulsive A conceptual tempo characterized by a hurried response and little, if any, consideration of the response's accuracy.

incest Sexual intercourse or sexual relations between persons so closely related that they are forbidden by law to marry.

independent variable A stimulus administered to the experimental group of subjects but not to the control group.

inductive reasoning Reasoning from specific, individual experiences and proceeding to general principles.

industry versus inferiority The fourth of Erikson's eight psychosocial crises. Industry versus inferiority occupies all of middle childhood.

infarct The infected tissue of a myocardial infarction.

initiative versus guilt The third of Erikson's eight psychosocial crises. Initiative versus guilt occurs between the ages of 3 and 6.

institutionalism A psychological state of apathy and deterioration, brought about by a depersonalized, institutionalized environment.

instrumental aggression A type of aggression aimed at acquiring objects, territory, or privileges.

integrity versus despair The eighth psychosocial crisis proposed by Erikson. At this time (late adulthood), individuals seek to nurture a sense of accomplishment about one's life rather than negative attitudes.

intellectualization An ego defense mechanism characterized by the use of elaborate logic and reason to hide inner sexual feelings.

interactionists Individuals who believe that development is shaped by the interaction of heredity and environment.

intermediate care facility A nursing facility that places less emphasis on intensive care nursing and more on personal care service.

internal aging Physical aspects of aging that cannot be seen.

internal validity A term used to indicate that research observations are logically interrelated and fit the theoretical structure of which they are a part.

intimacy Becoming close with another person through the process of self-disclosure.

intimacy versus isolation The sixth of eight psychosocial crises postulated by Erik Erikson. It occurs during young adulthood.

intimate and mutually shared relationships According to Selman, friendships during late childhood and early adolescence.

intimate relationship Process in which a person comes to know the innermost, subjective aspects of another individual.

intrinsic motivation The undertaking of an activity for the reward or pleasure derived from it.

introjection The process of assimilating the attributes of others or incorporating external values and attitudes into one's own ego structure.

intuitive thought The third stage of Piaget's cognitive development theory, occurring approximately between ages 4 and 7. The child's thought patterns are bound by immediate perceptions and experiences rather than by flexible mental functions.

invention of new means through mental combinations The last of Piaget's six substages of sensorimotor development. This substage occurs between 18 and 24 months.

juvenile delinquency Behavior by youths 18 and under that society deems unacceptable.

karyotype A special treatment of cells during their division that allows researchers to observe, measure, and compare the treated chromosomes with normal chromosomes to check for suspected imperfections.

kernel words Words that can be strung together to make a statement that is usually declarative.

kibbutz A collective farm settlement where children are raised communally and apart from their parents.

Klinefelter's syndrome A chromosomal abnormality in which males have two normal X chromosomes plus the Y (XXY). Those afflicted have small external male sex organs but the general contour of a female and are sterile.

lactation The secretion of milk by the female breast.

Lamaze method A natural childbirth approach emphasizing a conditioned learning technique in which the mother replaces one set of learned responses (fear, pain) with another (relaxation, muscle control).

language The system of grammatical rules and semantics that makes speech meaningful.

language acquisition device According to Chomsky, a system of linguistic programming dependent on mature cells in the cerebral cortex.

lanugo A fine downy growth of hair appearing on the entire body of the fetus and newborn.

late maturer A person who matures physically after the prescribed timetables.

latency period The fourth stage of Freud's psychosexual theory in which the individual's sexual feelings are submerged.

lateralization Specialization of the left and right cerebral hemispheres.

learning A relatively permanent change in behavior as the result of experience.

Leboyer method Proposed by French obstetrician Frederic Leboyer, this technique emphasizes a gentle delivery of the baby as well as the establishment of a peaceful and soothing delivery room environment.

lesbian women Females whose sexual orientation and affectional attraction are to other women.

leukemia A type of cancer that develops in the hematological system.

lexicon One's vocabulary.

libido According to Freud, energy, which is basically sexual, that serves the basic human instincts.

locomotion An organism's ability to move from place to place; to walk.

logic The use of formal rules applied to reasoning.

longitudinal method A method in which the researcher repeatedly collects data on the same group of individuals over a long period of time.

long-term memory A storage system that enables individuals to retain information for relatively long periods.

love A set of feelings, cognitions, and motivations that contribute to communication, sharing, and support.

love withdrawal A disciplinary style in which parents emotionally remove themselves from their offspring.

LSD Lysergic acid diethylamide, a hallucinogenic compound produced from ergot.

ludus love Playful, self-centered, and sexually permissive love.

lymphoma A type of cancer originating in lymphoid tissues.

male pattern baldness Male hair loss due to heredity.

malignant tumor A tumor that is cancerous and invades surrounding tissues.

manic love Love that is intense and obsessive.

marijuana A hallucinogenic drug obtained from a mixture of the tops, leaves, seeds, and stems of female hemp or cannabis plants. The strongest grade of marijuana is known as hashish.

marriage rate Number of marriages each year per 1,000 members of a population.

masturbation The stimulation of the genital organs to climax by self-manipulation rather than sexual intercourse.

matriarchal marriage A household characterized by female domination.

maturation The development of body cells to full maturity, at which time they are fully utilized by the organism.

maturity A state that promotes physical and psychological well-being.

Medicaid A government-sponsored, medical care plan for welfare clients, regardless of age.

Medicare A government-sponsored insurance program that partially finances the health-care costs of persons 65 years and older.

medulla oblongata A part of the hindbrain that connects the brain and spinal cord and regulates heartbeat, respiration, digestion, and blood pressure.

meiosis The process of germ cell division.

memory span The number of items that can be held in one's short-term memory bank.

menarche The first menstrual period.

menopause The cessation of menstruation, generally in the mid-to-late forties or early fifties.

mental flexibility verus mental rigidity According to Peck, a psychological adjustment to be made during middle adulthood.

messenger RNA A type of RNA that carries the DNA message to the ribosomes so that protein can be synthesized.

metacognition A person's awareness of how a cognitive process can be applied to a selected mental task.

metamemory A person's awareness of how a memory strategy can be employed to prevent forgetting the material at hand.

metastasis The spread of cancer throughout the body.

midbrain The connecting link between the forebrain and the hindbrain.

midlife transition The life stage marked by one's entry into middle adulthood.

midwife A person who usually holds a bachelor's degree in nursing and a master's degree in nurse-midwifery and works on a medical team consisting of a gynecologist and an obstetrician. Midwives often deliver babies in the mother's home.

mitosis The process of somatic cell division.

moral development The process by which individuals learn the standards of right and wrong established by the culture in which they live.

morality The conscious adoption of standards related to right and wrong.

moral realism According to Piaget, a stage of morality during which children between the ages of 5 and 10 perceive rules but do not understand why they exist.

moral relativism According to Piaget, a stage of morality in which children 10 years of age and older view rules in relation to the principles they uphold.

Moro reflex A major reflex present in the newborn. Any loud noise or loss of support will cause newborns to draw the legs up, arch the back, and fling the arms. Also called the startle reflex.

morpheme The smallest unit of a language that has recognizable meaning. The word *boys,* for example, has two morphemes, *boy* and *s.*

motherese A language style employed by adults, most often the mother, when speaking to young children. Motherese consists of shortened sentences, easy words, the duplication of syllables, and an increase of voice frequency.

motor skill The ability to coordinate the bodily movements that enable an individual to execute a particular physical task.

mutagens Agents such as X-rays or radiation that are capable of producing mutations in the DNA molecule.

mutation A gene error or dysfunction that produces a change in the characteristic that the gene determines. Mutations may be positive, negative, or neutral.

mutual respect stage In Piaget's theory of moral development, the point at which children become aware of the meanings of rules and the reason for their formation.

myelin A white fatty substance that covers many nerve

fibers of the body. Nerves that are covered with myelin transmit their electrochemical messages at a more rapid rate than do nonmyelinated nerves.

myelination The process by which the neuron develops an outer sheath.

myocardial infarction The destruction of myocardial tissue.

naively egoistic orientation Kohlberg's second of six moral development stages. This stage is grouped under the major division or level known as preconventional morality.

natural childbirth A method of childbirth avoiding the use of anesthesia and allowing both husband and wife to play an active role in the baby's delivery.

nature-nurture controversy A controversy that focuses on the relative importance of the genetic endowment and the nurturing environment.

near-death experiences Experiences of persons who are pronounced clinically dead but who are later resuscitated.

negative reinforcement In instrumental conditioning, an unpleasant stimulus is taken away from a subject following a desired response. This is done in order to strengthen that particular response.

neonate A term for the newborn infant during the first few weeks of life.

nervous system All the neurons in the body that carry electrochemical signals either to the central nervous system (CNS—brain and spinal cord) or from the CNS to the body (autonomic nervous system—ANS—or peripheral nervous system—PNS).

neuron A cell of the nervous system that transmits information in the form of electrochemical impulses.

neuroses Emotional disturbances characterized by the presence of anxious behavior and the individual's desire to avoid it.

nocturnal emission The ejaculation of semen during sleep.

nucleic acid A substance found in the chromosomes, mitochondria, and cytoplasm of all cells.

nucleoplasm Protoplasm found inside the nuclear membrane.

nucleus The control center for the cell's activity, located in or near the center of the cell.

obedience and punishment orientation Kohlberg's first of six stages of moral development. This stage is grouped under the major division or level known as preconventional morality.

obesity Deposits of fat from 10 to 20 percent or more above the normal range for age, sex, and height.

object permanence The mental ability that enables one to realize that objects exist even if they are out of one's field of vision.

observational learning Learning by watching others and observing the consequences of their actions.

occipital lobe An area of the cortex enabling the brain to interpret the sensory information transmitted by the eyes.

Oedipus complex According to Freud, the romantic

feelings a boy has for his mother and the fear of the father's retaliation. The Oedipus complex is prevalent during the phallic stage of psychosexual development.

one-way assistance stage According to Selman, friendships made during the early school years.

open class word A word in early sentence structure that is connected to pivot words. Pivot words rarely exist as single-word utterances and are usually in the first position of early two-word sentences.

open marriage A marriage that is flexible and stresses the importance of continual self-growth for both marriage partners.

operant conditioning See instrumental conditioning.

operants According to Skinner, instrumentally conditioned responses.

opium An addicting narcotic obtained from the flower pods of a particular poppy species. Its derivatives include morphine and heroin.

oral stage According to Freud, the initial phase of psychosexual development. During this period infants seek gratification from stimulation of the mouth.

ordinal position A child's place in the family, such as being the first-born or second-born.

organic brain syndrome A disorder characterized by a massive loss of brain cells in the cerebral cortex.

organization According to Piaget, the mental ability to order and classify new schemata.

organogenesis The period marking the beginning of organ development, from the third week of pregnancy through the second or third month.

osteoarthritis Inflammation of the joints, usually caused by changes in bone and cartilage.

osteoporosis The gradual loss of bone density.

ova Female eggs or germ cells (singular ovum).

overregularization The extension of a grammatical rule to situations to which it does not apply—for example, *goed* instead of *went*.

overweight Heaviness above average body weight for size of 10 percent or more.

ovulation The release of the egg from the ovary.

parallel play A variation of egocentrism expressed in young children's playtime activities. Because children between 2 and 4 are fundamentally self-centered and unable to separate themselves from their thoughts, playmate interaction is restricted.

parental-image theory A Freudian theory of mate selection. Because of close attachment to the parent of the opposite sex, individuals seek partners possessing characteristics similar to those of that parent.

parent cell The original cell in cell division.

parietal lobe An area of the cortex controlling the sense of touch and the transmission of essential spatial information.

passive euthanasia No deliberate steps taken to prevent death. Also called negative euthanasia.

passive theory A theory of development stating that individuals passively learn behavior from others. An example is behaviorism.

patriarchal marriage A household characterized by male domination.

perception The process of being aware of and interpreting stimuli in the environment.

perceptual constancy The tendency of an object to remain the same under different viewing conditions.

perfection principle The operating principle of the superego.

period of the ovum In early prenatal development, the process of cell division that continues for approximately two weeks after fertilization of the ovum.

peripheral nervous system A network of neural tissue that connects the brain and the spinal cord with other parts of the body.

permissive control A style of parental control characterized by a nonpunitive orientation and relaxed rules and regulations.

permissiveness with affection A moral standard asserting that sexual relations between unmarried persons are acceptable if accompanied by emotional attachment between partners.

permissiveness without affection A moral standard asserting that sex between unmarried persons without emotional attachments is acceptable; also called recreational sex.

personal fable A consequence of adolescent egocentrism. Teenagers are convinced of their personal uniqueness and construct stories about themselves that are not true.

phallic stage According to Freud, the period characterized by genital manipulation and attraction for the parent of the other sex.

phenotype The visible or easily measurable appearance of an organism.

philosophical stressor A stressor that has a philosophical basis, such as a value-system conflict.

phoneme The most fundamental element of a language. The sound of *b* in *big* or *th* in *thick* is a phoneme.

phonology The study of phonemes and other sounds made in speech.

physiology The science concerned with the functions of living matter.

Pick's disease A presenile, degenerative brain disorder.

pilot study An experiment with a very small sample in order to ascertain, among other things, that the equipment is operable, that the researcher feels confident with the experimental procedures, or that the subjects understand the directions.

pivot word A word that is usually small in size and connected to open class words. Pivot words are usually used in the second position or early two-word sentences.

placenta The organ that allows nourishment to pass from the mother to the embryo and fetus and waste products to be channeled from the embryo and fetus to the mother.

playmateship stage According to Selman, friendships made during the preschool years.

polygenes A number of genes that work together with additive and/or complementary effects.

pons A part of the hindbrain bridging the two lobes of the cerebellum.

positive reinforcement In instrumental conditioning, a pleasant stimulus given to a subject following a desired response, so as to strengthen that response.

postconventional level Kohlberg's third major division or level of moral development, occurring from age 16 onward. Stages within this level include the contractual legalistic orientation and the universal ethical principle orientation.

pragma love Love that is practical and sensible.

pragmatics The manner in which language is used in a social context.

preconceptual thought The second of Piaget's five cognitive development stages. Preconceptual thought occurs between the ages of 2 and 4.

preconventional level According to Kohlberg, the initial phase of moral development occurring during the early childhood years. Substages within this period include obedience and punishment orientation and naively egoistic orientation.

prehension The ability to grasp objects between the fingers and opposable thumb.

prematurity A term applying to infants weighing less than 2500 grams and who have spent less than 36 weeks in utero.

premoral stage According to Piaget, a stage of morality in which children 5 and under have little, if any, awareness of rules.

prenatal period The time between conception and birth.

preparatory depression According to Kübler-Ross, an emotional reaction to an expected loss in the future.

presbycusis Impaired hearing caused by the aging process.

presbyopia A farsighted condition that occurs in the elderly when the lens of the eye loses its elasticity.

presenile dementia A dementia syndrome that begins before age 65.

primary circular reactions The second of six substages comprising Piaget's sensorimotor stage of cognitive development. This substage occurs between 1 and 4 months of age.

primary reinforcers Satisfying stimuli related to primary, unlearned drives. Food and drink are primary reinforcers related to the hunger and thirst drives.

primary sex characteristics Sex characteristics that relate directly to the sex organs—the penis and testes in the male, and the ovaries, clitoris, and vagina in the female.

projection The defense mechanism of blaming one's difficulties or failures on someone else.

progesterone A female sex hormone produced by the ovaries.

propinquity A mate-choice theory that states that individuals living in close geographical proximity will marry.

prosocial behavior Being sensitive to the needs and feelings of others.

protoplasm The entire living substance that constitutes a cell.

proximo-distal development Growth from the center of the body outward.

pruritus An itching disorder caused by thin and dry skin.

psychoanalytic theory The school of thought proposed by Sigmund Freud.

psycholinguistics The study of the child's developing communication processes from early stages of crying and babbling to spoken words and meaningful sentences. Psycholinguistics include the closely related areas of language, mental imagery, cognitive development, and symbolization.

psychological aging One of the three main types of aging processes. Psychological aging refers to one's self-awareness and ability to adapt to progressive aging.

psychological stressor A stressor such as worry or anxiety.

psychosexual stage A stage in Freud's developmental theory.

psychotic disorders Mental disorders marked primarily by a loss of contact with reality.

psychosocial stage A stage in Erikson's developmental theory.

psychosocial stressor A stressor caused by such psychosocial events as the loss of a job or the death of a friend.

puberty The point in the life span when sexual maturity is attained.

Punnett square A diagrammatical means of computing the possible genotypes and phenotypes for any given characteristic.

rationalization The attempt to justify and provide logical reasons and explanations for particular patterns of behavior.

reaction formation The defense mechanism of substituting an opposing attitude for an unwanted and perhaps objectionable desire.

reactive depression According to Kübler-Ross, an emotional reaction to a loss that has already occurred.

readiness A state of maturation that enables a child to perform a task.

reality principle The ego's selection of attainable goals before discharging tension or energy.

recall memory The search for and retrieval of information in storage.

recessive gene A gene whose hereditary characteristics are present only when paired with another recessive gene.

recognition memory The selection of a correct response from incoming information.

reconstituted family See blended family.

reflective A conceptual tempo characterized by a careful and deliberate approach to problem solving.

reflex The automatic elicitation of a specific response without the involvement of higher brain functions.

reflex activities The first of six substages constituting Piaget's sensorimotor stage of cognitive development. This substage occurs during approximately the first month of life.

reflex smile The earliest type of smile, occurring during the first few weeks of life. This smile is primarily physiological and is usually the infant's response to a number of different stimuli, including internal stimulation (a bubble of gas in the stomach), being fed, or being stroked on the cheek.

regression A defense mechanism characterized by the individual's reverting to behavioral responses characteristic of earlier developmental levels.

reinforcement The process of strengthening an organism's response. In classical conditioning, the unconditioned stimulus serves as the reinforcement, and in instrumental conditioning, the use of a reward.

reinforcer Anything that strengthens the probability of a response.

residential care facility A home for aged persons who are functionally independent but who desire a safe, hygienic, and sheltered environment in which to live.

reticular activating system A part of the hindbrain controlling arousal, attention, and the sleep cycle.

retirement Withdrawal from one's professional occupation or from an active working life.

reversibility The ability to trace one's line of reasoning back to where it originated.

rheumatoid arthritis A type of arthritis that inflames the membranes lining and lubricating the joints.

Rh factor A substance found in red blood cells. An Rh incompatibility between mother and father can create serious difficulties in their newborn baby.

ribonucleic acid (RNA) A substance formed by DNA that carries genetic messages to the ribosomes for the manufacturing of specific proteins.

ribosomes Small particles in the cytoplasm that manufacture proteins under the direction of DNA.

RNA See ribonucleic acid.

role compatibility Filtering agent stressing the importance of role stability and harmony between two persons.

rooming-in facility A facility allowing the parents to care for their baby in the mother's hospital room.

rooting reflex An early reflex response of babies that includes head turning and sucking attempts when the cheek is touched.

sarcoma An often malignant tumor of connective tissue, striated muscle, bone, or cartilage.

schemata Organized patterns of thought. Sensory stimuli, objects, and events are examples of schematic organizations.

scientific method The testing of hypotheses concerning natural events and relationships.

secondary circular reactions The third of six substages constituting Piaget's sensorimotor stage of cognitive development. This substage occurs between 4 and 8 months.

secondary reinforcer A stimulus that was previously neutral but when paired frequently over successive trials with a primary reinforcer gains reinforcing qualities.

secondary sex characteristics Sex characteristics that are not related directly to the sex organs but distinguish a mature male from a mature female.

secular trend A pattern of physical growth and development whereby children in more prosperous parts of the world are taller and heavier and enter puberty earlier than do youngsters from less prosperous nations. This is due primarily to improved nutrition and better health care.

securely attached A type of attachment described by Ainsworth. Securely attached infants explore the environment and show little anxiety when the mother is away for short periods of time. Upon the mother's return, securely attached infants are happy and desire close contact with her.

selective social smile A type of smile appearing approximately between 5 and 6 months of age. The selective social smile is directed only to familiar figures, such as the mother or other caregivers.

self-actualization According to Maslow, the fullest development of one's potentials, capacities, and talents.

self-disclosure Process by which individuals let themselves be known by others.

semantics The study of meaning in a language.

senile angiomas Skin discolorations on the scrotum and trunk due to damaged blood vessels.

senile dementia An organic disorder with the dementias. Its onset is in later life, usually after age 65.

sensorineural deafness Hearing loss caused by damage to the inner ear, to the auditory nerve carrying sound messages to the brain, or to the hearing center of the brain itself.

sensorimotor stage Piaget's first stage of cognitive development (0 through 2 years). Learning activities at this point are directed toward the coordination of simple sensorimotor skills.

sensory memory The part of the memory system that receives and holds all incoming sensory stimuli for a fraction of a second. They then decay or are transferred to short-term memory.

separation anxiety A distress reaction expressed by infants upon separation from the caregiver. Separation anxiety occurs approximately by 1 year.

serialization Ordering subjects on a perceptual basis.

seriation Ordering objects according to size.

sex-limited genes Genes that are normally expressed in only one sex, although they are carried by both sexes.

sex-linked characteristics Inherited characteristics carried by the genes of the X and Y chromosomes.

sex role Those attitudes and behaviors felt to be appropriate to males and females.

sex-role development The process of socialization in which appropriate male and female roles are learned.

sexual identity The physiological differences between males and females.

sexual love Love characterized by physical intimacy.

sexually transmitted disease A contagious infection passed on by intimate sexual contacts with others.

shaping In operant conditioning, a procedure in which part of a behavior is reinforced, ultimately leading to the whole behavior that is desired.

short-term longitudinal method A research design in which data are gathered over a short period of time and fewer behavioral phenomena are studied.

short-term memory The temporary retention of information (usually 30 to 60 seconds). Unlike the long-term memory store, short-term memory is affected considerably by interference and interruption.

sickle-cell anemia A disease of the red blood cells, common among blacks of African background.

significates The objects or events that signifiers are used to represent.

signifiers Words or images.

singlehood A life-style marked by a person's desire not to get married.

skilled nursing facility A nursing facility that provides full-time nursing for persons with a chronic illness or who are convalescing.

social-age clock According to Neugarten, societal expectations of how people should behave at given ages.

social aging One of the three main types of aging processes. Social aging refers to one's perceptions of the aging process as it relates to a given society.

social cognition The awareness of how individuals perceive themselves and others, including other person's thoughts and feelings.

social gerontologist A person working in the field of social gerontology, which seeks to meet the needs of the aged population by providing them with special services, programs, and policies.

socializing versus sexualizing in human relationships According to Peck, a psychological adjustment to be made during middle adulthood.

social learning theory One of psychology's major schools of thought. This view proposes that behavior is influenced by observing and copying others.

social learning theory of television viewing A theory proposing that persons will imitate aggressive behavior when they are exposed to it on television.

social security Government-sponsored income to individuals and their families when earnings stop or are reduced because of retirement, disability, or death.

social smile A type of smile emerging by the second or third month of life. The social smile may be evoked by the appearance or voice of a caregiver, movement, or certain noises.

social stressor A stressor created by social situations such as crowding.

sociodramatic play Imaginative or make-believe play shared with a partner.

somatic cells Cells in the human body, with the exception of the sex cells.

speech A concrete, physical act that consists of forming and sequencing the sounds of oral language.

sperm Male germ cell, or gamete.

storge love Type of love characterized by affection and companionship.

stranger anxiety A distress reaction expressed by infants when unfamiliar people are introduced. Infants show stranger anxiety after the sixth month of life.

stream of consciousness According to Freud, one's fleeting immediate awareness.

stress The body's common, nonspecific response to any demand made upon it, be it psychological or physiological.

stressors External events or conditions that affect an organism's equilibrium.

structured observation An extension of naturalistic observation that enables the researchers to administer simple tests.

sudden infant death syndrome (SIDS) A disorder that affects infants usually between the ages of one and six months of life. The fatal disorder kills more than 5,000 infants each year in the United States for unexplained reasons.

superego According to Freud, the part of one's personality that represents societal expectations and demands.

surface structure Sentence structure that is dictated by the rules of grammar.

swinging The exchange of sex partners by married couples; mate swapping.

symbolic functioning An act of reference in which a mental image is created to stand for something that is not present.

syntax The rules for combining words into sentences.

syphilis Highly infectious, sexually transmitted disease. Syphilis enters the body through any break in the mucous membrane, burrowing into the bloodstream.

telangiectases Dilated blood vessels on the facial area.

telegraphic sentences A type of sentence used by children at approximately 2 years. Telegraphic sentences include only the words necessary to give meaning. Connecting words are usually omitted.

temporal lobe An area of the cortex responsible for hearing as well as the storage of permanent memories.

teratogenic agent Any substance that causes a change in the genetic code, which in turn may produce an abnormality, anomaly, or malformation.

terminal drop A drop in intelligence and personality functioning in the months preceding death.

terminal phase According to Pattison, the third of three dying processes.

tertiary circular reactions The fifth of six substages constituting Piaget's sensorimotor stage of cognitive development. This substage occurs between 12 and 18 months.

testis-determining factor A gene responsible for the sequence of events that leads to male sexual development.

thalamus Part of the forebrain that relays nerve impulses from sensory pathways to the cerebral cortex.

thanatologist A person working in the field of thanatology, the study of dying and death.

theory A formulation of apparent relationships that have some degree of verification and supportive evidence.

thrombus A blood clot.

time-lag design A research methodology whereby researchers can compare people of the same age at different times.

toughlove A style of discipline used by parents to control teenagers' extreme, problematical behaviors.

transductive reasoning Reasoning from particular to particular without generalization.

transformation Understanding the relationship between the deep and surface structures of a sentence.

transformational reasoning The ability to appreciate how one state transforms itself into another when an event has a sequence of change.

transient ischemic attack A minor stroke causing an abrupt loss of body function but usually subsiding within 24 hours. Often, this type of stroke precedes a larger and more serious cerebrovascular accident.

trimester One of the three, three-month segments of pregnancy.

triple X syndrome A female chromosomal abnormality that produces mental retardation, menstrual irregularity, and premature menopause.

trisomy 21 See Down syndrome.

tumor A mass of tissues created by the uncontrolled growth and spread of cells. Also called neoplasms, tumors can be either benign or malignant.

Turner's syndrome A female chromosomal abnormality (only one sex chromosome) distinguished by a webbed neck, short fingers, and short stature. No secondary sex characteristics appear at the time of puberty (XO).

twin speech A style of language used by twins, usually consisting of private and unique forms of communication.

Type A personality A type of personality characterized by stress. Type A personality has been related to cardiovascular disorders.

Type B personality A type of personality characterized by an easy-going personality and no hostility. Type B personalities are less likely to suffer coronary heart diseases than are Type A personalities.

Type C personality A type of personality characterized by the presence of considerable stress, but coping strategies have been developed.

ultrasonography The use of sound waves to examine internal body structures. Often used to determine a fetus's size and position.

umbilical cord A "body stalk" containing three blood vessels: a vein carrying oxygenated blood from the placenta to the infant and two arteries carrying blood and waste products from the infant to the placenta.

universal ethical principle orientation Kohlberg's sixth stage of moral development. This stage is grouped under the major division or level known as postconventional morality.

uterus A thick-walled, hollow, muscular organ in which the fertilized egg develops into an infant.

vagina A short, muscular tube in females that extends from the uterus to an exterior opening, also called the birth canal.

valuing wisdom versus valuing physical powers According to Peck, a psychological adjustment to be made during middle adulthood.

variations A term used in genetics when offspring, whether plant or animal, show differences from their parents.

venous lakes Blue discolorations on the lips or other facial areas caused by damaged blood vessels.

vernix caseosa A waxy substance covering the fetus during prenatal development.

visual cliff A testing apparatus designed to measure depth perception in infants and animals.

visualization A mental operation requiring the ability to organize and process visual materials.

visuomotor flexibility The capacity to shift from familiar to unfamiliar patterns in tasks dictating coordination between visual and motor abilities.

voluntary childlessness A couple's voluntary decision not to have children.

vowel The most prominent sound in a syllable.

wear-and-tear theory A theory of physical aging that asserts that organisms wear out, much like machines, over their life cycle.

Wernicke's area A portion of the brain, located in the temporal lobe; it is responsible for the comprehension of speech.

withdrawal An ego defense mechanism characterized by the avoidance of, or movement away from, undesirable or hurtful situations.

withdrawal symptoms Unpleasant side effects, such as nausea and cramping, that are caused by the absence of an addicting drug.

X chromosome A sex-determining chromosome. Females have two X chromosomes, whereas males have one X chromosome and one Y chromosome.

XYY syndrome Also called the aggressive syndrome, this chromosomal abnormality is characterized by violent and antisocial behavior.

Y chromosome A sex-determining chromosome. When paired with the X chromosome, a male offspring is produced.

zygote A cell formed by the union of the male sperm and the female ovum; the fertilized egg.

Bibliography

Abbe, K. M., and Gill, F. M. *Twins on Twins*. New York: Crown, 1981.

Abravanel, E. Perceiving subjective contours during early childhood. *J. of Exper. Child Psychol.* 1982, 33, 280–287.

Ackerman, B. P. Young children's understanding of a speaker's intentional use of a false utterance. *Devel. Psychol.* 1981, 17(4), 472–480.

Acredolo, L. P., and Hake, J. L. Infant perception. In B. B. Wolman (Ed.), *Handbook of Developmental Psychology*. Englewood Cliffs, N.J.: Prentice-Hall, 1982.

Adams, G. R. The effects of physical attractiveness on the socialization process. In G. W. Lucker, K. A. Ribbens, and J. A. McNamara (Eds.), *Psychological Aspects of Facial Form* (Monograph No. 11, Craniofacial Growth Series). Ann Arbor, Mich.: Center for Human Growth and Development, 1980.

Adams G. R., and Jones, R. M. Imaginary audience behavior: A validation study. *J. of Early Adol.* 1981, 1, 1–16.

Adams, G. R., and Schvaneveldt, J. D. *Understanding Research Methods*. New York: Longman, 1985.

Adams, J. *Understanding and Managing Stress*. San Diego: University Associates, 1980.

Adams, J. F. Earlier menarche, greater height and weight: A stimulation-stress factor hypothesis. *Genet. Psychol. Monogr.* 1981, 104(1), 3–22.

Adams, P. L. Fathers absent and present. *Canadian J. Psychiat.* 1984, 29(3), 228–233.

Adams, R. J. Newborns' discrimination among mid- and long-wavelength stimuli. *J. of Exper. Child Psychol.* 1989, 47(1), 130–141.

Adams, R., Maurer, D., and Davis, M. Newborns' discrimination of chromatic from achromatic stimuli. *J. of Exper. Child Psychol.* 1986, 41, 267–281.

Adams, R. L., and Phillips, B. N. Motivation and achievement differences among children of various ordinal birth positions. *Child Devel.* 1972, 43, 155–164.

Adams, V. The sibling bond: A lifelong love/hate dialectic. *Psychol. Today* June 1981.

Adler, C., Bazemore, G., and Polk, K. Delinquency in non-metropolitan areas. In D. Sichor and D. H. Kelley (Eds.), *Critical Issues in Juvenile Delinquency*. Lexington, Mass.: Lexington Books, 1980.

Ahrons, C. R. The continuing coparental relationship between divorced spouses. In D. H. Olson and B. C. Miller (Eds.), *Family Studies Review Yearbook* (Vol. 2). Beverly Hills, Calif.: Sage Publications, 1984.

Aiken, L. R. *Later Life* (2nd ed.). New York: Holt, Rinehart and Winston, 1982.

Ainsworth, M. D. S. *Infancy in Uganda*. Baltimore: Johns Hopkins University Press, 1967.

Ainsworth, M. D. S. Infant-mother attachment. *Amer. Psychologist* 1979, 34, 932–937.

Aizenberg, R., and Harris, R. Family demographic changes: The middle generation squeeze. *Generations* 1982, 7(2), 6–7.

Albanese, A. A., and Wein, E. H.: Nutritional problems of the elderly. *Aging* Sept.–Oct. 1980, nos. 311–312, U.S. Dept. of Health and Human Services, Office of Human Developmental Services, Administration on Aging, DHHS Pub. No. (OHD/AoA) 79-20949. Washington, D.C.: U.S. Government Printing Office, Division of Public Documents.

Alberts, J. R. Ontogeny of olfaction: Reciprocal roles of sensation and behavior in the development of perception. In R. N. Aslin, J. R. Alberts, and M. R. Petersen (Eds.), *Development of Perception* (Vol. 1). New York: Academic Press, 1981.

Albrecht, S. L. Reactions and adjustments to divorce: Differences in the experience of males and females. *Family Relations* 1980, 29(1), 59–68.

Albrecht, S. L., Bahr, H. M., and Goodman, K. L. *Divorce and Remarriage: Problems, Adaptations, and Adjustments*. Westport, Conn.: Greenwood Press, 1983.

Allan, L., and Brotman, H. *Chartbook on Aging in America*. Washington, D.C.: White House Conference on Aging, 1981.

Allgeier, E. R., and Allgeier, A. P. *Sexual Interactions*. Lexington, Mass.: Heath, 1981.

Allport, G. W. *Pattern and Growth in Personality*. New York: Holt, Rinehart and Winston, 1961.

Almvig, C. *The Invisible Minority: Aging and Lesbianism*. Syracuse, N.Y.: Utica College, 1982.

Alter, J. Sexuality education for parents. In C. Cassell and P. M. Wilson (Eds.), *Sexuality Education*. New York: Garland Publishing, 1989.

Alvarez, M. M., Huston, A. C., Wright, J. C., and Kerkman, D. D. Gender differences in visual attention to television form and content. *J. Applied Devel. Psychol.* 1988, 9, 459–475.

Alvino, J. Philosophical questions help children think and rethink ideas. *Gifted Children Newsletter*. December, 1983.

Ambrogi, D. and London, C. Elder abuse laws: Their implications for caregivers. *Generations* 1985 10(1), 37–39.

American Cancer Society. *Cancer Facts and Figures, 1989*. New York, 1989.

American Heart Association. *Reducing the Risk of Heart Attack*. Dallas, Tex., 1987.

American Psychological Association. Ethical principles of psychologists. *American Psychological Association,* 1990, 1981, 1973.

Ames, L. B., Ilg, F. L., and Haber, C. C. *Your One Year Old*. New York: Delacorte, 1982.

Ammons, P., and Stinnett, N. The vital marriage: A closer look. *Family Relations* 1980, 29, 37–42.

Anderson, M. *Thinking about Women: Sociological Perspectives on Sex and Gender*. New York: Macmillan, 1988.

Anderson, T. B. Widowhood as a life transition: Its impact on kinship ties. *J. Marriage and the Family* 1984, 10(1), 1–10.

Anyan, W. R., and Schowalter, J. E. A comprehensive approach to anorexia nervosa. *J. Amer. Acad. Child Psychiat.* 1983, 22, 59–62.

Archer, C. J. Children's attitudes toward sex-role division in adult occupational roles. *Sex Roles* 1984, 10(1), 1–10.

Argyle, M. Why do marriages break down? *New Society* 1983, 64, 259–260.

Aries, P. *Centuries of Childhood* (Trans. R. Baldick). New York: Knopf, 1962.

Aries, P. *The Hour of Death*. New York: Knopf, 1981.

Armstrong, J. C. Decision behavior and outcome of mid-life career changers. *Vocational Guidance Q.* 1981, 29, 205–213.

Arnold, S., Brock, J., Ledford, L., and Richards, H. *Ready or Not: A Handbook for Retirement* (9th ed.). New York: Manpower Education Institute, 1982.

Arnot, R. *The Complete Manual to Fitness and Well-Being*. New York: Viking, 1984.

Aronson, E. *The Social Animal* (4th ed.). New York: W. H. Freeman, 1984.

Asher, S. R., and Hymel, S. Children's social competence in peer relations: Sociometric and behavior assessment. In J. D. Wine and M. D. Smye (Eds.), *Social Competence*. New York: Guilford Press, 1981.

Asher, S. R., Renshaw, P. D., and Hymel, S. Peer relations and the development of social skills. In S. G. Moore and C. R. Cooper (Eds.). *The Young Child: Reviews of Research* (Vol. 3). Washington, D.C.: National Association for the Education of Young Children, 1982.

Aslanian, C. B., and Brickell, H. M. *Americans in Transition: Life Changes as Reasons for Adult Learning*. New York: College Entrance Examination Board, 1980.

Astington, J. W. Children's production of commissive speech acts. *J. Child Language* 1988, 15, 411–423.

Aston, A. *Toys that Teach Your Child: From Birth to Two*. Charlotte, N.C.: East Woods Press, 1984.

Atchley, R. C. *The Social Forces in Later Life* (3rd. ed.). Belmont, Calif.: Wadsworth, 1980.

Atchley, R. C. Retirement as a social institution. In R. Turner and J. Short (Eds.), *Annual Review of Sociology*. Palo Alto, Calif.: Annual Reviews, 1982. (a)

Atchley, R. C. Retirement: Leaving the world of work. *Ann. Amer. Acad. Polit. and Soc. Sci.* 1982, 464, 120–131.(b)

Atchley, R. C. *Social Forces and Aging: An Introduction to Social Gerontology* (3rd ed.). Belmont, Calif.: Wadsworth, 1988.

Atchley, R. C., and Robinson, J. L. Attitudes toward retirement and distance from the event. *Research on Aging* 1982, 4(3), 288–313.

Atwater, L. Long-term cohabitation without a legal ceremony is equally valid and desirable. In H. Feldman and M. Feldman (Eds.), *Current Controversies in Marriage and Family*. Beverly Hills, Calif.: Sage Publications, 1985.

Auerbach, S. *Choosing Child Care: A Guide for Parents*. New York: Dutton, 1981.

Ault, R. *Children's Cognitive Development*. New York: Oxford University Press, 1983.

Ault, R. L., and Vinsel, A. Piaget's theory of cognitive development. In R. L. Ault (Ed.), *Developmental Perspectives*. Santa Monica, Calif.: Goodyear, 1980.

Ausberger, C., Martin, M. J., and Creighton, J. *Learning to Talk Is Child's Play: Helping Preschoolers Develop Language*. Tuscon, Ariz.: Communication Skill Builders, 1982.

Averyt, A. C. *Successful Aging*. New York: Ballantine, 1987.

Baillargeon, R., and Graber, M. Evidence of location memory in 8-month-old infants in a nonsearch AB task. *Devel. Psychol.* 1988, 24, 502–511.

Bairstow, P. J. Development of planning and control of hand movement to moving targets. *J. Devel. Psychol.* 1989, 7, 29–42.

Balkwell, C. Transition to widowhood: A review of the literature. In L. Cargan (Ed.), *Marriage and Family: Coping with Change*. Belmont, Calif.: Wadsworth, 1985.

Baltes, P. B. Prototypical paradigms and questions in life-span research on development and aging. *Gerontologist* 1973, 113, 458–467.

Baltes, P. B., and Schaie, K. W. Aging and the IQ: The myth of the twilight years. *Psychol. Today* 1974, 7, 35–40.

Baltes, P. B., Smith, J., Staudinger, V. W., and Sowarka, D. Wisdom: One facet of successful aging? In M. Perlmutter (Ed.), *Late-life Potential*. Washington, D.C.: Gerontological Association of America, 1988.

Bandura, A. Social learning through imitation. *Nebraska Symposium on Motivation*. Lincoln: University of Nebraska Press, 1962, 211–269.

Bandura, A. Social cognitive theory. In R. Vasta (Ed.), *Six Theories of Child Development: Revised Formulations and Current Issues*. Greenwich, Conn.: JAI Press, 1989.

Bandura, A., and Huston, A. Identification as a process of incidental learning. *J. Abnorm. Soc. Psychol.* 1961, 63, 311–318.

Bandura, A., Ross, D., and Ross, S. Transmission of aggression through imitation of aggressive models. *J. Abnorm. Soc. Psychol.* 1961, 63, 575–582.

Bandura, A., and Walters, R. *Social Learning and Personality Development*. New York: Holt, Rinehart and Winston, 1963.

Bank, S. P., and Kahn, M. D. *The Sibling Bond*. New York: Basic Books, 1982.

Bankoft, E. A. Social support and adaptation to widowhood. *J. Marriage and the Family* 1983, 45(4), 827–840.

Barenboim, C. The development of person perception in childhood and adolescence: From behavioral comparisons to psychological constructs to psychological comparisons. *Child Devel.* 1981, 52, 129–144.

Barnes, R. F., Raskin, M. A., and Scott, M. Problems of family caring for Alzheimer patients: Use of a support group. *J. Amer. Geriatric Society* 1981, 29, 80–85.

Barnes, S., Gutfreund, M., Satterly, D., and Wells, G. Characteristics of adult speech which predict children's language development. *J. Child Language* 1983, 10(1), 65–84.

Barnett, M. A., King, L. M., Howard, J. A., and Dino, G. A. Empathy in young children: Relation to parents' empathy, affection, and emphasis on the feelings of others. *Devel. Psychol.* 1980, 16, 243–244.

Barrow, G. M., and Smith, P. A. *Aging, the Individual, and Society* (2nd ed.). St. Paul: West Publishing, 1983.

Bar-Tal, D., and Raviv, A. A cognitive-learning model of helping behavior development: Possible implications and applications. In N. Eisenberg (Ed.), *The Development of Prosocial Behavior*. New York: Academic Press, 1982.

Bar-Tal, D., Raviv, A., and Shavit, N. Motives for helping behavior: Kibbutz and city children in kindergarten and school. *Devel. Psychol.* 1981, 17(6) 766–772.

Bartlett, J. Selecting an early childhood language curriculum. In C. B. Cazden (Ed.), *Language in Early Childhood Education*. Washington, D.C.: National Association for the Education of Young Children, 1981.

Baruch, G., Barnett, R., and Rivers, C. *Lifeprints*. New York: McGraw-Hill, 1983.

Baruch, G., and Brooks-Gunn, J. *Women in Midlife*. New York: Plenum, 1984.

Basow, S. S. *Sex Role Stereotypes: Traditions and Alternatives*. Monterey, Calif.: Brooks/Cole, 1980.

Bass, D. M., Pestello, F. P., and Garland, T. N. Experiences with home hospice care: Determinants of place of death. *Death Education* 1984, 8(4), 199–222.

Baumeister, R. F., and Senders, P. S. Identity development and the role structure of children's games. *J. Genet. Psychol.* 1989, 150, 19–37.

Baumrind, D., Current patterns of parental authority. *Dev. Psychol. Monogr.* 1971, 1, 1–103.

Baumrind, D. New directions in socialization research. *Amer. Psychol.* 1980, 35, 639–652.

Baumrind, D. Are androgynous individuals more effective persons and parents? *Child Devel.* 1982, 53(1), 44–75.

Baumrind, D. Parenting styles and adolescent development. In J. Brooks-Gunn, R. Lerner, and A. C. Petersen (Eds.), *The Encyclopedia of Adolescence*. New York: Garland, 1989.

Bayless, P. J. *Caring for Dependent Parents*. New York: Research Institute of America, 1985.

Bayley, N. Comparison of mental and motor test scores for ages 1–15 months by sex, birth order, race, geographical location and education of parents. *Child Devel.* 1965, 36, 379–411.

Beale, C. J., and Baskin, D. Children's fears: Who's afraid of the big bad wolf? *Child Psychiat. Q.* 1983, 16(2), 68–75.

Beebe, B., and Stern, D. Engagement-disengagement and early object experience. In M. Freedman and S. Grenel (Eds.), *Communicative Structures and Psychic Structures*. New York: Plenum Press, 1977, 33–35.

Beer, W. R. *Househusbands: Men and Housework in American Families*. New York: Praeger, 1982.

Beidel, D. C., and Turner, S. M. Comorbidity of test anxiety and other anxiety disorders in children. *J. Abnorm. Child Devel.* 1988, 16, 275–287.

Beilan, H. Piagetian theory. In R. Vasta (Ed.), *Six Theories of Child Development: Revised Formulations and Current Issues*. Greenwich, Conn.: JAI Press, 1989.

Beaty, J. J. *Observing Development of Children*. Columbus, Ohio: Charles E. Merrill, 1986.

Bell, R. R. *Worlds of Friendship*. Beverly Hills, Calif.: Sage Publications, 1981.

Bell, R. R. *Marriage and Family Interaction* (6th ed.). Homewood, Ill.: Dorsey Press, 1983.

Bell, R. R., and Coughey, K. Premarital sexual experience among college females, 1958, 1968, and 1978. *Family Relations* July 1980, 353–357.

Bellinger, D. C., and Gleason, J. B. Sex differences in parental directives to young children. *Sex Roles* 1982, 8(11), 1123–1139.

Belmont, L., and Marolla, F. A. Birth order, family size, and intelligence. *Science* 1973, 182, 1096–1101.

Belsky, J. *The Psychology of Aging* (2nd ed.). Monterey, Calif.: Brooks/Cole, 1990.

Benbow, C. P., and Stanley, J. C. Sex differences in mathematical ability: Fact or artifact? *Science* 1980, 210, 1262–1264.

Bennett, C. *Nursing Home Life: What It Is and What It Could Be*. New York: Tiresias Press, 1980.

Berger, R. M. *Gay and Gray: The Older Homosexual Man*. Champaign: University of Illinois Press, 1982.

Berger, S. *Divorce Without Victims: Helping Children Through Divorce with a Minimum of Pain and Trauma.* Boston: Houghton Mifflin, 1983.

Bergkvist, L., Hans-Olov, A., Hoover, R., and Schairer, C. The risk of breast cancer after estrogen and estrogen-progestin replacement, *The New England J. Medicine* 1989, 321, pp. 293–297.

Berheide, C. W. Women's work in the home: Seems like old times. *Marriage and Family Review* 1984, 7(3), 37–55.

Berkley, B. R. People who marry without love. *Medical Aspects of Human Sexuality* 1981, 15 (8), 23, 30–34.

Berndt, T. J. The features and effects of friendship in early adolescence. *Child Devel.* 1982, 53(6), 1447–1460.

Berndt, T. J., and Ladd, G. W. *Peer Relationships in Child Development.* New York: Wiley, 1989.

Berndt, T. J., and Perry, T. B. Distinctive features and effects of early adolescent friendships. In R. Montemayor (Ed.), *Advances in Adolescent Research.* Greenwich, Conn.: JAI Press, 1990.

Bernstein, R. M. The development of the self-system during adolescence. *J. Genet. Psychol.* 1980, 136(2), 231–245.

Berscheid, E., and Peplau, L. A. The emerging science of relationships. In H. H. Kelly (Ed.), *Close Relationships.* New York: Freeman, 1983.

Bettes, B. A. Maternal depression and motherese: Temporal and intonational features. *Child Devel.* 1988, 59, 1089–1096.

Bialystok, E. Levels of bilingualism and levels of linguistic awareness. *Devel. Psychol.* 1988, 24, 560–567.

Bijou, S. W. Behavior analysis. In R. Vasta (Ed.), *Six Theories of Child Development: Revised Formulations and Current Issues.* Greenwich, Conn.: JAI Press, 1989.

Bingham, C. R. AIDS and adolescents: Threat of infection and approaches to prevention. *J. Early Adolescence* 1989, 9, 50–66.

Birren, J. E., Woods, A. M., and Williams, M. V. Behavioral slowing with age: Causes, organization, and consequences. In L. W. Poon (Ed.), *Aging in the 1980's.* Washington, D.C.: American Psychological Association, 1980.

Bjorklund, D. F., and Hock, H. S. Age differences in the temporal locus of memory organization in children's recall. *J. Exper. Child Psychol.* 1982, 33, 347–362.

Black, J. K. Are young children really egocentric? *Young Children* 1981, 36(6).

Black, R. B., and Weiss, J. D. Genetic support groups in the delivery of comprehensive genetic services. *Amer. J. Hum. Genet.* 1989, 45:647–654.

Blanchard, E. B., and Andrasik, F. Psychological assessment and treatment of headaches: Recent developments and emerging issues. *J. Consulting and Clinical Psychol.* 1982, 50, 859–879.

Blasi, A. Bridging moral cognition and moral action: A critical review of the literature. *Psychol. Bull.* 1980, 88, 1–45.

Blatchford, P., Battle, S., and Mays, J. *The First Transition: Home to Preschool.* Atlantic Highlands, N.J.: Humanities Press, 1983.

Blitchington, W. P. Traditional sex roles result in healthier sexual relationships and healthier, more stable family life. In H. Feldman and A. Parrot (Eds.), *Human Sexuality: Contemporary Controversies.* Beverly Hills, Calif.: Sage Publications, 1984.

Block, M. R., Davidson, J. L., and Grambs, J. D. *Women over Forty.* New York: Springer, 1981.

Bloom, L., Beckwith, R., and Capatides, J. B. Developments in the expression of affect. *Infant Behavior and Development* 1988, 11(2), 169–186.

Bloomberg, S. Influence of maternal distress during pregnancy on complications in labor and delivery. *Acta Psychiat. Scand.* 1980, 62(5), 339–404.

Bloome, D. *Classrooms and Literacy.* Norwood, N.J.: Ablex, 1989.

Bloomfield, H. *The Achilles Syndrome.* Englewood Cliffs, N.J.: Prentice-Hall, 1986.

Blotnick, S. *The Corporate Steeplechase.* New York: Facts on File, 1984.

Blumenthal, S. J., and Kupfer, D. J. Overview of early detection and treatment strategies for suicidal behavior in young people. *J. Youth and Adolescence* 1988, 17, 1–14.

Bohannon, J. N., and Stanowicz, L. B. The issue of negative evidence: Adult responses to children's language errors. *Devel. Psychol.* 1988, 24, 684–689.

Bohannon, P. *Divorce and After.* New York: Doubleday, 1970.

Bohannon, P. The six stations of divorce. In L. Cargan (Ed.), *Marriage and Family: Coping with Change.* Belmont, Calif.: Wadsworth, 1985.

Bohland, J. R., and Herbert, D. T. Neighborhood and health effects of elderly morale. *Environment and Planning* 1983, 15(7), 929–944.

Bolles, R. N. The "warp" in the way we perceive our life in the world of work. *Training and Development J.* 1981, 11, 20–27.

Booth-Butterfield, M. She hears . . . he hears: What they hear and why. *Personnel J.* 1984, 63, 36–41.

Borland, D. A cohort analysis approach to the empty-nest syndrome among three ethnic groups of women: A theoretical position. *J. Marriage and the Family* 1982, 44(2), 117–129.

Bornstein, M. H. Human infant color vision and color perception, reviewed and reassessed: A critique of Warner and Wooten. *Infant Behavior and Development* 1981, 4, 119–150.

Botwinick, J. *We Are Aging.* New York: Springer, 1981.

Botwinick, J. *Aging and Behavior* (3rd ed.). New York: Springer, 1984.

Bouchard, T. J., Jr. Familial studies of intelligence: A review. *Science* 1981, 212(4498), 1055–1059.

Bower, T. G. R. *Development in Infancy* (2nd ed.). San Francisco: W. H. Freeman, 1981.

Bowlby, J. *Attachment and Loss* (Vol. 1). *Attachment* (2nd ed.). New York: Basic Books, 1982.

Bowlby, J. *Attachment and Loss* (Vol. 3). New York: Basic Books, 1980.

Bowlby, J. *Secure Base: Parent-Child Attachment and Healthy Human Development.* New York: Basic Books, 1988.

Bowles, L. T. Wear and tear: Common biological changes of aging. *Geriatrics* 1981, 32(4), 77–86.

Bowling, A., and Cartwright, A. *Life after Death: A Study of the Elderly Widowed.* London: Tavistock, 1982.

Bradbard, M. R., and Endsley, R. C. How can teachers develop young children's curiosity? In J. F. Brown (Ed.), *Curriculum Planning for Young Children.* Washington, D.C.: National Association for the Education of Young Children, 1982.

Bradley, R. H., Caldwell, B. M., Rock, S. L., Ramey, C. T. et al. Home environment and cognitive development in the first 3 years of life: A collaborative study involving six sites and three ethnic groups in North America. *Devel. Psychol.* 1989, 25, 217–235.

Branconnier, R. J., and Devitt, D. R. Early detection of incipient Alzheimer's disease: Some methodological considerations on computerized diagnosis. In B. Reisberg (Ed.), *Alzheimer's Disease: The Standard Reference.* New York: Free Press, 1983.

Branden, N. *The Psychology of Romantic Love.* Los Angeles: J. P. Tarcher, 1981.

Bratic, E. B. Healthy mothers, healthy babies coalition. *Prevention* 1982, 97, 503–509.

Bray, J. H. The effects of early remarriage on children's development: Preliminary analyses of the developmental issues in stepfamily research project. In E. M. Hetherington and J. D. Arasteh (Eds.), *Impact of Divorce, Single-Parenting, and Stepparenting on Children.* Hillsdale, N.J.: Erlbaum, 1988.

Brazee, E. N., and Brazee, P. E. Cognitive development in the middle school. *Colorado Educational Research* 1980, 19, 6–8.

Brazelton, T. B. Effects of prenatal drugs on the behavior of the neonate. *Amer. J. Psychiat.* 1970, 126, 1261–1266.

Brehm, S. S. *Intimate Relationships.* New York: Random House, 1985.

Brent, D. A. Suicide and suicidal behavior in children and adolescents. *Pediatrics in Review* 1989, 10, 269–275.

Breznitz, S., and Goldberger, L. Stress research at the crossroads. In L. Goldberger and S. Breznitz (Eds.), *Handbook of Stress.* New York: Free Press, 1982.

Brier, J., and Runtz, M. Post-sexual abuse trauma. In G. E. Wyatt and G. J. Powell (Eds.), *Lasting Effects of Child Sexual Abuse.* Beverly Hills, Calif.: Sage Publications, 1988.

Bright, M., and Stockdale, D. F. Mothers', fathers', and preschool children's interactive behaviors in a play setting. *J. Genet. Psychol.* 1984, 144(2), 219–232.

Broderick, C. B. *Marriage and the Family* (3rd ed.). Englewood Cliffs, N.J.: Prentice-Hall, 1989.

Broderick, C. B. *Marriage and the Family* (2nd ed.). Englewood Cliffs, N.J.: Prentice-Hall, 1984.

Brody, E. M. Parent care as a normative family stress. *Gerontologist* 1985, 25(1), 19–29.

Broman, S. H. Long-term development of children born to teenagers. In H. G. Scott, T. Field, and E. Robertson (Eds.), *Teenage Parents and Their Offspring.* New York: Grune and Stratton, 1981.

Brone, R. J., and Fisher, C. B. Determinants of adolescent obesity: A comparison with anorexia nervosa. *Adolescence* 1988, 23, 155–169.

Bronson, G. W. *The Scanning Pattern of Human Infants: Implications for Visual Learning.* Norwood, N.J.: Ablex, 1982.

Brook, J., Whiteman, M., and Gordon, A. S. Stages of drug abuse in adolescence: Personality, peer, and family correlates. *Devel. Psychol.* 1983, 19(2), 269–277.

Brooks-Gunn, J. Antecedents and consequences of variations in girls' maturational timing. In M. D. Levine and E. R. McAnarney (Eds.), *Early Adolescent Transitions.* Lexington, Mass.: Lexington Books, 1988.

Brooks-Gunn, J., and Furstenberg, F. F., Jr. Adolescent sexual behavior. *Amer. Psychol.* 1989, 44, 249–257.

Brooks-Gunn, J., and Petersen, A. (Eds.). *Girls at Puberty.* New York: Plenum, 1983.

Brooks-Gunn, J., and Warren, M. P. The psychological effects of secondary sexual characteristics in nine-to-eleven-year-old girls. *Child Devel.* 1988, 59, 1061–1069.

Brooks-Gunn, J., and Warner, M. P. How important are pubertal and social events for different problem behaviors and contexts. Paper presented at the biennial meeting of the Society for Research in Child Development, April 1989.

Brown, B. B. *Between Health and Illness: New Notions on Stress and the Nature of Well-being.* Boston: Houghton Mifflin, 1984.

Brown, F. *Transition of Youth to Adulthood: A Bridge too Far.* Boulder, Colo.: Westview Press, 1980.

Brown, R. The development of the first language in the human species. *Amer. Psychologist* 1973, 28, 97–106. (a)

Brown, R. *First Language: The Early Stages.* Cambridge, Mass.: Harvard University Press, 1973. (b)

Brown, S. V. Early childbearing and poverty: Implications for social services. *Adolescence* 1982, 17(66), 397–408.

Brown, T. S., and Wallace, P. M. *Physiological Psychology.* New York: Academic Press, 1980.

Brubaker, T. *Later-Life Families.* Beverly Hills, Calif.: Sage Publications, 1985.

Brumberg, J. J. *Fasting Girls.* Cambridge, Mass.: Harvard University Press, 1988.

Bruner, J. S. The social context of language acquisition. Paper presented at the Witkin Memorial Lecture, Educational Testing Service, Princeton, N.J., May 1980.

Brunson, B. L., and Matthews, K. A. The Type A coronary-prone behavior pattern and reactions to uncontrollable stress: An analysis of performance strategies, affect, and attributions during failure. *J. Personality and Social Psychol.* 1981, 40, 906–918.

Buhrmester, D. *Changes in friendship, interpersonal competence, and social adaptation during early adoles-*

cence. Unpublished manuscript, Department of Psychology, University of California, Los Angeles, 1989.

Bumpass, L. L., and Martin, T. C. Recent trends in marital disruption. *Demography* 1989, 2, 26–41.

Burbules, N. C., and Linn, M. C. Response to contradiction: Scientific reasoning during adolescence. *J. Educ. Psychol.* 1988, 80, 67–75.

Burchinal, M., Lee, M., and Ramey, C. T. Type of day-care and preschool intellectual development in disadvantaged children. *Child Devel.* 1989, 60, 128–137.

Burger, S. Three approaches to patient care. In M. P. Hamilton and H. F. Reid (Eds.), *A Hospice Handbook.* Grand Rapid, Mich.: Eardmans, 1980.

Burleson, B. R. The development of comforting communication skills in childhood and adolescence. *Child Devel.* 1982, 53(6), 1578–1588.

Burnham, B. *When Your Friend Is Dying.* Grand Rapids, Mich.: Zondervan, 1982.

Burnham, S. The heroin babies are going cold turkey. *N.Y. Times Mag.* Jan. 9, 1972.

Burns, D. B. *Intimate Connections.* New York: Signet, 1985.

Bushnell, I. W. Discrimination of faces by young infants. *J. Exper. Child Psychol.* 1982, 33(2), 298–308.

Bushnell, I. W., Sai, F., and Mullin, J. T. Neonatal recognition of the mother's face. *British J. Devel. Psychol.* 1989, 7, 3–15.

Bustanoby, A. *Single Parent.* Grand Rapids, Mich.: Zondervan, 1985.

Butler, R. N. The life review: An interpretation of reminiscence in the aged. In B. Neugarten (Ed.), *Middle Age and Aging.* Chicago: University of Chicago Press, 1968.

Butler, R. N. An overview of research on aging and the status of gerontology today. *Milbank Memorial Fund Q.: Health and Society* 1983, 61(3), 351–361.

Butler, R. N., and Emr, M. An American perspective on Alzheimer's disease. In B. Reisberg (Ed.), *Alzheimer's Disease: The Standard Reference.* New York: Free Press, 1983.

Butler, R., and Lewis, M. *Aging and Mental Health.* St. Louis: C. V. Mosby, 1981.

Butterworth, G., and Hopkins, B. Hand-mouth coordination in the newborn baby. *British J. Devel. Psychol.* 1988, 6(4), 303–314.

Byrne, D. Sex without contraception. In D. Byrne and W. A. Fisher (Eds.), *Adolescents, Sex, and Contraception.* Hillsdale, N.J.: Erlbaum, 1983.

Byrnes, J. P. Formal operations: A systematic reformulation. *Devel. Review* 1988, 8, 66–87.

Cairns, R. B., Cairns, B. D., Neckerman, H. J., Ferguson, L. L. et al. Growth and aggression: I. Childhood to early adolescence. *Devel. Psychol.* 1989, 25, 320–330.

Caldera, Y. M., Huston, A. C., and O'Brien, M. Social interactions and play patterns of parents and toddlers with feminine, masculine, and neutral toys. *Child Devel.* 1989, 60, 70–76.

Caldwell, M. A., and Peplau, L. A. Sex differences in same-sex friendship. *Sex Roles* 1982, 8, 721–732.

Cameron, C. A., and Goard, C. Procedural factors in children's class inclusion. *J. Genet. Psychol.* 1982, 140(2), 313–314.

Campbell, A. *The Sense of Well-being in America.* New York: McGraw-Hill, 1981.

Campos, J. J., Bertenthal, B. I., and Caplovitz, K. The interrelationship of affect and cognition in the visual cliff situation. In C. Izard, J. Kagan, and R. Zajone (Eds.), *Emotion and Cognition,* New York: Plenum, 1982.

Campos, J. J., Haitt, S., Rampsay, D., Henderson, C., and Svejda, M. The emergence of fear on the visual cliff. In M. Lewis and L. Rosenblum (Eds.), *The Origins of Affect.* New York: John Wiley, 1978.

Campos, J. J., and Sternberg, C. R. Perception, appraisal, and emotion: The onset of social referencing. In M. Lamb and L. Sherrod (Eds.), *Infant Social Cognition.* Hillsdale, N.J.: Erlbaum, 1981.

Cancellier, P. H., and Crews, K. A. *Women in the World: The Women's Decade and Beyond.* Washington, D.C.: Population Reference Bureau, 1986.

Canter, R. J. Family correlates of male and female delinquency. *Criminology* 1982, 20(2), 149–167.

Cantor, J., and Sparks, G. G. Children's fear responses to mass media: Testing some Piagetian predictions. *J. Communication* 1984, 34(2) 90–103.

Carbonara, N. T. *Techniques for Observing Normal Child Behavior.* Pittsburgh: University of Pittsburgh Press, 1961.

Carey, S. Are children fundamentally different kinds of thinkers and learners than adults? In K. Richardson and S. Sheldon (Eds.), *Cognitive Development to Adolescence.* Hillsdale, N.J.: Erlbaum, 1988.

Cargan, L. Singles: An examination of two stereotypes. *Family Relations* 1981, 30, 377–385.

Cargan, L., and Melko, M. Being single on Noah's ark. In L. Cargan (Ed.), *Marriage and Family: Coping with Change.* Belmont, Calif.: 1985.

Carlsson, A. Changes in neurotransmitter systems in the aging brain. In B. Reisberg (Ed.), *Alzheimer's Disease: The Standard Reference.* New York: Free Press, 1983.

Carrol, C. R. *Drugs in Modern Society* (2nd ed.). Dubuque, Ia.: Wm. C. Brown, 1989.

Carroll, D. *Living with Dying.* New York: McGraw-Hill, 1985.

Carroll, J. L., and Rest, J. R. Moral development. In B. B. Wolman (Ed.), *Handbook of Developmental Psychology.* Englewood Cliffs, N.J.: Prentice-Hall, 1982.

Carroll, J. J., and Steward, M. S. The role of cognitive development in children's understanding of their own feelings. *Child Devel.* 1984, 55(4), 1486–1492.

Cartensen, L., Mason, S. E., and Caldwell, E. C. Children's attitudes toward the elderly: An intergenerational technique for change. *Educational Gerontology* 1982, 8(3), 291–301.

Carter, D. B. and Levy, G. D. Cognitive aspects of early sex-role development: The influence of gender schemas on preschoolers' memories and preferences for sex-typed toys and activities. *Child Devel.* 1988, 59, 782–792.

Carter, E. A., and McGoldrick, M. (Eds.). *The Family Life Cycle: A Framework for Family Therapy.* New York: Gardner, 1980.

Cartwright, C. A., and Cartwright, G. P., *Developing Observation Skills.* New York: McGraw-Hill, 1984.

Case, R. The underlying mechanism of intellectual development. In J. R. Kirby and J. B. Biggs (Eds.), *Cognition, Development, and Instruction.* New York: Academic Press, 1980.

Case, R., and Khanna, F. The missing links: Stages in children's progression from sensorimotor to logical thought. In K. W. Fischer (Ed.), *Cognitive Development* (New Directions for Child Development, no. 12). San Francisco: Jossey-Bass, 1981.

Case, R., Kurland, D. M., and Goldberg, J. Operational efficiency and the growth of short-term memory span. *J. Exper. Child Psychol.* 1982, 33, 386–404.

Casper, R. C. Psychodynamic psychotherapy in acute anorexia nervosa and acute bulimic nervosa. In A. H. Esman (Ed.), *International Annals of Adolescent Psychiatry.* Chicago: University of Chicago Press, 1989.

Cassata, M., Anderson, P. A., and Skill, T. Images of old age on day-time television. In M. Cassata and T. Skill (Eds.), *Life on Daytime Television.* Norwood, N.J.: Ablex, 1983.

Castaneda, A. M., Gibb, E. G., and McDermit, S. A. Young children and mathematical problem-solving. *School Science and Math* 1982, 82(1), 22–28.

Cataldo, C. Z. Infant-toddler education. *Young Children* 1984, 39(2), 25–32.

Cauhape, E. *Fresh Starts: Men and Women after Divorce.* New York: Basic Books, 1983.

Cauwels, J. *Bulimia: The Binge/Purge Compulsion.* New York: Doubleday, 1983.

Cavan, R. S., and Ferdinand, T. N., *Juvenile Delinquency* (4th ed.). New York: Harper & Row, 1981.

Cazden, C. B. *Language in Early Childhood Education.* (rev. ed.). Washington, D.C.: National Association for the Education of Young Children, 1981.

Centers for Disease Control. *AIDS Weekly Surveillance Report.* February 10, 1989.

Chalmers, B. Psychological aspects of pregnancy: Some thoughts for the 80's. *Social Science and Medicine* 1982, 16(3) 323–331.

Chambre, S. M., and Low, I. B. Volunteering and the aged: A bibliography for researchers and practitioners. *J. Volunteer Administration* 1983, 2(2), 35–44.

Chandler, L. A. *Children under Stress: Understanding Emotional Adjustment Reactions.* Springfield, Ill.: Chas. C. Thomas, 1982.

Chapman, M., and Lindenberger, U. Concrete operations and attentional capacity. *J. Exper. Child Psychol.* 1989, 47, 236–258.

Charlesworth, E. A., and Nathan, R. G. *Stress Management: A Comprehensive Guide to Wellness.* Houston: Biobehavioral Press, 1982.

Charmaz, K. *The Social Reality of Death.* Reading, Mass.: Addison-Wesley, 1980.

Chelune, G. J., Robison, J. T., and Kommor, M. J. A cognitive interactional model of intimate relationships. In V. J. Derlega (Ed.), *Communication, Intimacy, and Close Relationships.* New York: Academic, 1984.

Cherlin, A. Remarriage as an incomplete institution. In L. Cargan (Ed.), *Marriage and Family: Coping with Change.* Belmont, Calif.: Wadsworth, 1985.

Cherlin, A., and Furstenberg, F. The American family in the year 2000. *The Futurist* 1983, 17, 7–14.

Chesney, M. A., and Rosenman, R. H. Strategies for modifying Type A behavior. *Consultant* 1980, 20, 216–222.(a)

Chesney, M. A., and Rosenman, R. H. Type A behavior in the work setting. In C. Copper and R. Payne (Eds.), *Current Issues in Occupational Stress.* New York: John Wiley, 1980. (b)

Chesney-Lind, M. Girl's crime and woman's place: Toward a feminist model of female delinquency. *Crime and Delinquency* 1989, 35, 5–30.

Chess, S., and Thomas, A. Infant bonding: Mystique and reality. *Amer. J. Orthopsychiat.* 1982, 52(2), 213–222.

Children's Defense Fund. *Employed Parents and Their Children: A Data Book.* Washington, D.C.: Children's Defense Fund, 1982.

Children's Protective Society. (OHDS) 81-30203. Washington, D.C.: U.S. Government Printing Office, 1981.

Chilman, C. S. Parent satisfactions, concerns, and goals for their children. *Family Relations* 1980, 29(3), 339–346.(a)

Chilman, C. S. Social and psychological research concerning adolescent child-bearing: 1970–1980. *J. Marriage and the Family* 1980, 42, 793–806.(b)

Chiriboga, D. A. Mental health at midpoint: Crisis, challenge, or relief. In S. Hunter and M. Sundell (Eds.), *Midlife Myths: Issues, Findings, and Practical Implications.* Beverly Hills, Calif.: Sage Publications, 1989.

Chomsky, N. *Language and Mind.* New York: Harcourt Brace Jovanovich, 1968.

Chomsky, N. *Rules and Representation.* New York: Columbia University Press, 1980.

Chukovsky, K. *From Two to Five.* Berkeley and Los Angeles: University of California Press, 1966.

Chumlea, W. C. Physical growth in adolescence. In B. B. Wolman (Ed.), *Handbook of Developmental Psychology.* Englewood Cliffs, N.J.: Prentice-Hall, 1982.

Cicirelli, V. G. *Helping Elderly Parents: The Role of Adult Children.* Boston: Auburn House, 1981.

Cirese, S. *Quest: A Search for Self* (2nd ed.). New York: Holt, Rinehart and Winston, 1985.

Clark, A. (Ed.). *Culture and Childrearing.* Philadelphia: F. A. Davis, 1981.

Clark, E. V. and Hecht, B. F. Comprehension, production,

and language acquisition. *Ann. Review of Psychol.* 1983, 34, 325–349.

Clark, H. H., and Clark, E. V. *Psychology and Language: An Introduction to Psycholinguistics.* New York: Harcourt Brace Jovanovich, 1977.

Clark, M. L., and Ayers, M. The role of reciprocity and proximity in junior high school friendships. *J. Youth and Adolescence* 1988, 17(5), 403–407.

Clayton, R. R., and Bokemeier, J. L. Premarital sex in the seventies. *J. Marriage and the Family* 1980, 42, 759–775.

Clemes, H., and Bean, R. *Self-esteem.* New York: Putnam, 1981.

Cohen, D., Coppel, D., and Eisdorfer, C. Management of the family. In B. Reisberg (Ed.), *Alzheimer's Disease: The Standard Reference.* New York: Free Press, 1983.

Cohen, G. D. Prospects for mental health and aging. In J. E. Birren and R. B. Sloane (Eds.), *Handbook of Mental Health and Aging.* Englewood Cliffs, N.J.: Prentice-Hall, 1980.

Cohen, G. D. Historical views and evolution of concepts. In B. Reisberg (Ed.), *Alzheimer's Disease: The Standard Reference.* New York: Free Press, 1983.

Cohen, R., Schleser, R., and Meyers, A. Self-instructions: Effect of cognitive level and active rehearsal. *J. Exper. Child Psychol.* 1981, 32, 65–76.

Cohler, B. J., and Grunebaum, H. V. *Mothers, Grandmothers, and Daughters.* New York: John Wiley, 1980.

Coker, D. R. The relationship among gender concepts and cognitive maturity in preschool children. *Sex Roles* 1984, 10(1), 19–31.

Colby, A., Kohlberg, L., Gibbs, J., and Lieberman, M. A longitudinal study of moral judgment. *Monographs of the Society for Research in Child Development* 1983, 48 (1, serial no. 200).

Cole, S. Send our children to work? *Psychol. Today* 1980, 14(2), 44–68.

Coleman, J. (Ed.). *Working with Troubled Adolescents.* Orlando, Fla.: Academic Press, 1987.

Coleman, J. C. Friendship and the peer group in adolescence. In J. Adelson (Ed.), *Handbook of Adolescent Psychology.* New York: John Wiley, 1980.

Coleman, J. C. *Intimate Relationships, Marriage, and the Family.* Indianapolis: Bobbs-Merrill, 1984.

Coleman, J. C., Butcher, J. N., and Carson, R. C. *Abnormal Psychology and Modern Life* (7th ed.). Glenview, Ill.: Scott, Foresman, 1984.

Coleman, J. C., and Cressey, D. R. *Social Problems.* New York: Harper & Row, 1984.

Coles, R., and Stokes, G. *Sex and the American Teenager.* New York: Harper & Row, 1985.

Coley, J. D., and Gelman, S. A. The effects of object orientation and object type on children's interpretation of the word *big. Child Devel.* 1989, 60, 372–380.

Collins, G. Research links violent juvenile behavior to abuse. *Justice Assistance News* 1982, 3(9), 3–4.

Collins, J. K., and Plahn, M. R. Recognition accuracy, stereotypic preference, aversion, and subjective judgment of body appearance in adolescents and young adults. *J. Youth and Adolescence* 1988, 17, 317–334.

Collins, R. C. The impact of Head Start on children's cognitive development. *Administration for Children, Youth and Families.* Washington, D.C.: Offices of Human Development Services, May 1982.

Colt, C. H. Suicide in America. *Harvard Magazine,* Sept./Oct., 1983.

Commons, M. L., and Richards, F. A. A general model of stage theory. In M. L. Commons, F. A. Richards, and S. Armon (Eds.), *Beyond Formal Operations: Late Adolescent and Adult Cognitive Development.* New York: Praeger, 1982.

Commons, M. L., Richards, F. A., and Armon, C. *Beyond Formal Operations: Late Adolescent and Adult Cognitive Development.* New York: Praeger, 1984.

Commons, M. L., Richards, F. A., and Kuhn, D. Systematic and metasystematic reasoning: A case for levels of reasoning beyond Piaget's stage of formal operations. *Child Devel.* 1982, 53, 1058–1069.

Conger, J. J. A fascination with youth and with writing about it. *APA Monitor* 1981, 12, 1ff.

Conger, J. J. Hostages to the future: Youth, values, and the public interest. *Amer. Psychologist* 1988, 43, 291–300.

Connolly, J. A., Doyle, A. B., and Reznick, E. Social pretend play and social interaction in preschoolers. *J. Applied Devel. Psychol.* 1988, 9(3), 301–313.

Cooper, C. L. *The Stress Check: Coping with the Stresses of Life and Work.* Englewood Cliffs, N.J.: Prentice-Hall, 1980.

Cooper, C. L. (Ed.). *Stress Research: Issues for the Eighties.* Chichester, England: Wiley, 1983.

Cooper, C., Detre, T., Weiss, S. M., Bristow, J. D., and Carleton, R. Coronary-prone behavior and coronary heart disease: A critical review. *Circulation* 1981, 63, 1200–1215.

Cooper, C. L., and Marshall, J. (Eds.). *White Collar and Professional Stress.* Chichester, England: Wiley, 1980.

Corbin, C. B. *A Textbook of Motor Development* (2nd ed.). Dubuque, Iowa: Wm. C. Brown, 1980.

Cordell, A. S., Parke, R. D., and Swain, D. B. Father's views on fatherhood with special reference to infancy. *Family Relations* 1980, 29, 331–338.

Coren, S., Porac, C., and Duncan, P. Lateral preference behaviors in preschool children and young adults. *Child Devel.* 1981, 52, 443–450.

Corey, G. *I Never Knew I Had a Choice* (4th ed.). Monterey, Calif.: Brooks/Cole, 1990.

Corrigan, R. The effects of task and practice on search for invisibly displaced objects. *Devel. Review* 1981, 1, 1–17.

Corrigan, R. The development of representational skills. In *Levels and Transactions in Children's Development.* (New Directions for Child Development, no. 21.) San Francisco: Jossey-Bass, 1983.

Corsaro, W. A. Friendships in the nursery school: Social organization in a peer environment. In S. R. Asher and J. M. Gotlman (Eds.), *The Development of Children's Friendships*. New York: Cambridge University Press, 1981.

Coté, J. E. and Levine, C. A critical examination of the ego identity status paradigm. *Devel. Review* 1988, 8, 147–184.

Courtney, A. E., and Whipple, T. W. *Sex Stereotyping in Advertising*. Lexington, Mass.: Heath, 1983.

Couturier, L. C., Mansfield, R. S., and Gallagher, J. M. Relationships between humor, formal operational ability, and creativity in eighth graders. *J. Genet. Psychol.* 1981, 139(2), 221–226.

Cowan, R. S. *More Work for Mother: The Ironies of Household Technology from the Open Hearth to the Microwave*. New York: Basic Books, 1983.

Cox, F. D. *Human Intimacy: Marriage, the Family, and Its Meaning*. St. Paul: West Publishing, 1984.

Cox, H. *Later Life: The Realities of Aging*. Englewood Cliffs, N.J.: Prentice-Hall, 1984.

Coyne, J. C., and Lazarus, R. S. Cognitive style, stress perception, and coping. In I. L. Kutash and L. B. Schlesinger (Eds.), *Handbook on Stress and Anxiety*. San Francisco: Jossey-Bass, 1980.

Crain, W. C. *Theories of Development: Concepts and Applications*. Englewood Cliffs, N.J.: Prentice-Hall, 1985.

Cramer, P. The development of sexual identity. *J. Personality Assessment* 1980, 44(6), 601–612.

Cramer, P., and Mechem, M. B. Violence in children's animated television. *Devel. Psychol.* 1982, 3(1), 23–29.

Crandall, R. C. *Gerontology: A Behavioral Science Approach*. Reading, Mass.: Addison-Wesley, 1980.

Cribier, F. Changing retirement patterns: The experience of a cohort of Parisian salaried workers. *Aging and Society* 1981, 1(3), 12–18.

Crimmins, E. M. Implications of recent mortality trends for the size and composition of the population over 65. *Review of Public Data Use* 1983, 11(1), 37–48.

Crisp, A. H. *Anorexia Nervosa*. New York: Academic Press, 1980.

Crites, J. O. Career differentiation in adolescence. In D. Stern and D. Eichorn (Eds.), *Adolescence and Work*. Hillsdale, N.J.: Erlbaum, 1989.

Crnic, K. A. Social interaction and developmental competence of preterm and full-term infants during the first year of life. *Child Devel.* 1983, 54(5), 1199–1210.

Crosby, J. F. A critique of divorce statistics and their interpretation. *Family Relations,* January, 1980, 51–56.

Crosby, J. F., and Jose, N. L. Death: Family adjustment to loss. In C. R. Figley and H. I. McCubbin (Eds.), *Stress and the Family*. New York: Brunner/Mazel, 1983.

Cross, D. R. and Paris, S. G. Development and instructional analyses of children's metacognition and reading comprehension. *J. Educ. Psychol.* 1988, 80, 131–142.

Cross, H. J., and Kleinhesselink, R. R. Psychological perspectives on drugs and youth. In J. F. Adams (Ed.), *Understanding Adolescence* (4th ed.). Boston: Allyn & Bacon, 1980.

Crouter, A. C. The children of working parents. *Children Today* 1982, 11(4), 25–28.

Crystal, S. *America's Old Age Crisis*. New York: Basic Books, 1982.

Cullingford, C. *Children and Television*. New York: St. Martin's Press, 1984.

Culp, R. E., Appelbaum, M. I., Osofsky, J. D., and Levy, J. A. Adolescent and older mothers: Comparison between prenatal maternal variables and newborn interaction measures. *Infant Behavior and Development* 1988, 11(3), 353–362.

Cumming, E., and Henry, W. E. *Growing Old*. New York: Basic Books, 1961.

Cunningham, J., and Strassberg, D. Neuroticism and disclosure reciprocity. *J. Counseling Psychol.* 1981, 28, 455–458.

Cunningham, W., and Birren, J. Age changes in the factor structure of intellectual abilities in adulthood and old age. *Educational and Psychological Measurement* 1980, 40, 271–290.

Cunningham, W. R. Intellectual abilities, speed of response, and aging. In V. L. Bengston and K. Warner Schaie (Eds.), *The Course of Later Life: Research and Reflections*. New York: Springer, 1989.

Curran, D. *Traits of a Healthy Family*. Minneapolis: Winston Press, 1984.

Curtis, J. D., and Detert, R. A. *How to Relax: A Holistic Approach to Stress Management,* Palo Alto, Calif.: Mayfield, 1981.

Daehler, M. W., and Bukatko, D. *Cognitive Development,* New York: Random House, 1985.

Dale, P. *Language Development: Structure and Function* (2nd ed.). New York: Holt, Rinehart and Winston, 1976.

Dale, P. Is early pragmatic development measurable? *J. Child Language* 1980, 1, 1–12.

Damon, W., and Hart, D. The development of self-understanding from infancy through adolescence. *Child. Devel.* 1982, 53, 341–864.

Dan, I. J., and Bernhard, L. A. Menopause and other health issues for midlife women. In S. Hunter and M. Sundell (Eds.), *Midlife Myths: Issues, Findings, and Practical Implications*. Beverly Hills, Calif.: Sage Publications, 1989.

Daniels, P., and Weingarten, K. *Sooner or Later: The Timing of Parenthood in Adult Lives*. New York: W. W. Norton, 1981.

Danner, F. Cognitive development in adolescence. In J. Worrell and F. Danner (Eds.), *The Adolescent as Decision Maker*. New York: Academic Press, 1989.

Darnell, J. E. RNA, *Scientific American* 1985, 253(4), 69–88.

David, H. P. China's population policy: Glimpses and a "minisurvey." *Intercom* 1982, 10(1), 3–4.

Davidson, J. K., Darling, C. A. Changing autoerotic attitudes and practices among college females: A two-year follow-up study. *Adolescence* 1988, 23(92), 773–792.

Davidson, P. M., White, P. N., Smith, D. J., and Poppen, W. A. Content and intensity of fears in middle childhood among rural and urban boys and girls. *J. Gene. Psychol.* 1989, 150, 51–58.

Davis, M., Eshelman, E., and McKay, M. *The Relaxation and Stress-Reduction Workbook.* Richmond, Calif.: New Harbinger, 1981.

Davis, P. A. Suicidal Adolescents. Springfield, Ill.: Chas. C Thomas, 1983.

Davis, R. A. Adolescent pregnancy and infant mortality: Isolating the effects of race. *Adolescence* 1988, 23(92), 899–908.

Davis, S. M., and Harris, M. B. Sexual knowledge, sexual interests, and sources of sexual information of rural and urban adolescents from three cultures. *Adolescence* 1982, 17, 471–492.

Day, R. H., and McKenzie, B. H. Infant perception of the invariant size of approaching and receding objects. *Devel. Psychol.* 1981, 17, 670–677.

Deane, B. When your parents need help. *Ladies Home Journal* April 1985, 74–82.

DeCasper, A. J., and Fifer, W. P. Of human bonding; Newborns prefer their mother's voices. *Science* 1980, 208, 1174–1176.

DeChesnay, M. Incest: A family triangle. *Nursing Times* 1983, 79(8), 64–65.

Deci, E. L., and Ryan, R. M. The empirical exploration of intrinsic motivational processes. In L. Berkowitz (Ed.), *Advances in Experimental Social Psychology* (Vol. 13). New York: Academic Press, 1980.

Deci, E. L., and Ryan, R. M. Curiosity and self-directed learning: The role of motivation in education. In L. G. Katz (Ed.), *Current Topics in Early Childhood Education* (Vol. 4). Norwood, N.J.: Ablex, 1982.

deFoe, J. R. and Breed, W. Youth and alcohol in television stories, with suggestions to the industry for alternative approaches. *Adolescence* 1988, 23, 533–550.

DeFord, D. Young children and their writing. *Theory into Practice* 1980, 19, 157–162.

Delamater, J. The social control of sexuality. *Annual Review of Sociology* 1981, 7, 76–89.

Delisle, M. Elderly people's management of time and leisure. *Canada's Mental Health* 1982, 30(3), 30–32.

DeMaris, A., and Leslie, G. R. Cohabitation with the future spouse: Its influence upon marital satisfaction and communication. *J. Marriage and the Family* 1984, 46(1), 77–84.

Demo, D. Sex differences in cognition: A review and critique of the longitudinal evidence. *Adolescence* 1982, 17(68), 779–788.

Demorest, A. Words speak louder than actions: Understanding deliberately false remarks. *Child Devel.* 1984, 55(4), 1527–1534.

Demorest, A., Silberstein, L., and Gardner, H. From understatement to hyperbole: Recognizing non-literal language and its intent. Paper presented at the Society for Research in Child Development, Boston, 1981.

Denkle, R. E. The effect of elders' household contributions on their depression. *J. Gerontol.* 1983, 38(6), 732–737.

Denny, D., Denny, L., and Rust, J. D. Preschool children's performance on two measures of emotional expressiveness compared to teacher's ratings. *J. Genet. Psychol.* 1982 140(1), 149–150.

Derlega, V. J. Self-disclosure and intimate relationships. In V. J. Derlega (Ed.), *Community, Intimacy, and Close Relationships.* New York: Academic Press, 1984.

DeSpelder, L. A., and Strickland, A. L. *The Last Dance: Encountering Death and Dying.* Palo Alto, Calif.: Mayfield, 1983.

Devi, D. R., and Ravindran, M. Women's work in India, *Int. Social Science J.* 1983, 35(4), 683–701.

Dewsbury, D. A. Comparative psychology, ethology, and animal behavior. *Ann. Review of Psychol.* 1989, 40, 581–602.

D'Hondt, W., and Vandewiele, M. Perception of authority and liberty by Senegalese secondary school students. *Adolescence* 1984, 19(73), 213–219.

Diamond, E. E. Women's occupational plans and decisions: An introduction. In B. A. Gutek (Ed.), *Applied Psychology: An International Review.* Beverly Hills, Calif.: Sage, 1988.

Diaz, R. M., and Berndt, T. J. Children's knowledge of a best friend: Fact or fancy? *Devel. Psychol.* 1982, 18(6), 787–794.

Dickens, W. J., and Perlman, D. Friendship over the life-cycle. *Personal Relationships.* New York: Academic Press, 1981.

Dickson, P. D. *Children's Oral Communication Skills.* New York: Academic Press, 1981.

Dileo, J. H. Graphic activity of young children: Development and creativity. In L. Lasky and R. Mukerji (Eds.), *Art: Basic for Young Children.* Washington, D.C.: National Association for the Education of Young Children, 1980.

Dileo, J. H. *Interpreting Children's Drawings.* New York: Brunner/Mazel, 1983.

Dinnage, R. Understanding Loss: The Bowlby canon. *Psychol. Today* 1980, 13, 56–60.

DiPietro, J. Rough and tumble play: A function of gender. *Devel. Psychol.* 1981, 17, 50–58.

Dixon, M. *The Future of Women.* San Francisco: Synthesis Publications, 1983.

Dixon, S. D. Mother–child interaction around a teaching task: An African-American comparison. *Child Devel.* 1984, 55(4), 1252–1264.

Dodd, D. H., and White, R. M., Jr. *Cognition: Mental Structures and Processes.* Boston: Allyn & Bacon, 1980.

Dodge, K. A., Schlundt, D. C., Schocken, I., and Delugach, J. D. Social competence and children's sociometric status: The role of peer group entry strategies. *Merrill-Palmer Q.* 1983, 29(3), 309–336.

Doering, C. H. The endocrine system. In O. G. Brim, Jr., and J. Kagan (Eds.), *Constancy and Change in Human Development.* Cambridge, Mass.: Harvard University Press, 1980.

Donohugh, D. *The Middle Years.* Philadelphia: Saunders, 1981.

Doolittle, R. F. Proteins. *Scientific American* 1985, 253(4), 89–100.

Douglas, J. D., and Atwell, F. C. *Love, Intimacy, and Sex*. Beverly Hills, Calif.: Sage, 1988.

Downs, A. C. Sex-role stereotyping on prime-time television. *J. Genet. Psychol.* 1981, 138, 253–258.

Dreyer, P. H. Sexuality during adolescence. In B. B. Wolman (Ed.), *Handbook of Developmental Psychology*. Englewood Cliffs, N.J.: Prentice-Hall, 1982.

Duck, S. *Relating to Others*. Chicago: Dorsey Press, 1989.

Dunn, J. Sibling relationships in early childhood. *Child Devel.* 1983, 54(4), 787–811.

Dunn, J., and Kendrick, C. *Siblings: Love, Envy and Understanding*. Cambridge, Mass.: Harvard University Press, 1982.

Dunn, J., and Shatz, M. Becoming a conversationalist despite (or because of) having an older sibling. *Child Devel.* 1989, 60, 399–410.

Durkin, K. Children's account of sex-role stereotypes in television. *Communication Research* 1984, 11(3), 341–362.

Durrett, M. E., Otaki, M., and Richards, P. Attachment and the mother's perception of help from the father. *Int. Behav. Devel.* 1984, 7(2), 167–176.

Duryea, E. J., and Glover, J. A. A review of the research on reflection and impulsivity in children. *Gen. Psychol. Monog.* 1982, 106(2), 217–237.

Dyer, E. D. *Courtship, Marriage, and Family: American Style*. Homewood, Ill.: Dorsey Press, 1983.

Earnshaw-Smith, E. Emotional pain in dying patients and their families. *Nursing Times* 1982, 78(44), 1865–1867.

Ebeling, K. S. and Gelman, S. A. Coordination of size standards by young children. *Child Devel.* 1988, 59, 888–896.

Edelman, M. W. *Families in Peril: An Agenda for Social Change*. New York: Alan Gutmacher Institute, 1987.

Edelwich, J., and Brodsky, A. *Burnout: Stages of Disillusionment in the Helping Professions*. New York: Human Sciences Press, 1980.

Edwards, C. P. Moral development in comparative cultural perspective. In D. A. Wagner and H. W. Stevenson (Eds.), *Cultural Perspectives on Child Development*. San Francisco: W. H. Freeman, 1982.

Egeland, B., and Farber, E. A. Infant-mother attachment: Factors related to its development and changes over time. *Child Devel.* 1984, 55(3) 753–771.

Egeland, B., Jacobvitz, D., and Stroufe, L. A. Breaking the cycle of abuse. *Child Devel.* 1988, 59, 1080–1088.

Einstein, E. *The Stepfamily: Living, Loving, and Learning*. New York: Macmillan, 1982.

Eisdorfer, C. Conceptual models of aging: The challenge of a new frontier. *Amer. Psychologist* 1983, 38(2), 197–202.

Eisdorfer, C., and Cohen, D. Management of the family and patient coping with dementing illness. *J. Fam. Practice* 1981, 12, 831–837.

Eisenberg, A., and Eisenberg, H. *Alive and Well: Decisions in Health*. New York: McGraw-Hill, 1980.

Eisenberg, A., Murkoff, H. E., and Hatheway, S. E. *What to Expect When You're Expecting*. New York: Workman, 1984.

Eisenberg, N. Social development. In C. B. Kopp and J. B. Krakow (Eds.), *The Child: Development in a Social Context*. Reading, Mass.: Addison-Wesley, 1982.

Eisenberg, N., Lennon, R., and Roth, K. Prosocial development: A longitudinal study. *Devel. Psychol.* 1983, 19(6), 846–855.

Eisner, E. W. *Cognition and the Curriculum*. New York: Longman, 1982.

Ek, C. A., and Steelman, L. C. Becoming a runaway. *Youth and Society* 1988, 19, 334–358.

Elkind, D. Egocentrism in adolescence. *Child Devel.* 1967, 38, 1025–1034.

Elkind, D. *A Sympathetic Understanding of the Child: Six to Sixteen*. Boston: Allyn & Bacon, 1971.

Elkind, D. Strategic interactions in early adolescence. In J. Adelson (Ed.), *Handbook of Adolescent Psychology*. New York: John Wlley, 1980.

Elkind, D. *Children and Adolescents: Interpretive Essays on Jean Piaget* (3rd ed.). New York: Oxford University Press, 1981.

Elkind, D., and Brown, R. Imaginary audience behavior in children and adolescents. *Devel. Psychol.* 1979, 15, 38–44.

Elliot, D. S., Huizinga, D., and Menard, S. *Multiple Problem Youth: Delinquency, Substance Abuse, and Mental Health Problems*. New York: Springer-Verlag, 1989.

Emde, R. N., and Harmon, R. J. (Eds.), *The Development of Attachment and Affiliative Systems*. New York: Plenum, 1981.

Endler, N. S., and Edwards, J. Stress and personality. In L. Goldberger and S. Breznitz (Eds.), *Handbook of Stress*. New York: Free Press, 1982.

Endres, J. B., and Rockwell, R. E. *Food, Nutrition, and the Young Child*. St. Louis: Times Mirror/Mosby, 1985.

Enright, R. D., Shukla, D. G., and Lapsley, D. K. Adolescent egocentrism-sociocentrism and self-consciousness. *J. Youth and Adolescence* 1980, 9, 101–116.

Erikson, E. H. *Childhood and Society* (2nd ed.). New York: W. W. Norton, 1963.

Erikson, E. H. *Identity and the Life Cycle*. New York: W. W. Norton, 1980.

Erikson, E. H. *The Life Cycle Completed: A Review*. New York: W. W. Norton, 1982.

Erier, G. Maternity and parental leaves in Europe. *Work Times* 1982, 1(1), 1–5.

Eron, L. D. Prescription for reduction of aggression. *Amer. Psychologist* 1980, 35, 244–252.

Escalona, S. The effects of the nuclear threat on childhood development. In *Preparing for Nuclear War: The Psychological Effects*. New York: Physicians for Social Responsibility, 1982.

Eshelman, J. R. *The Family: An Introduction* (5th ed.). Boston: Allyn & Bacon, 1988.

Eshelman, J. R. *The Family* (4th ed.). Boston: Allyn & Bacon, 1985.

Estioko-Griffin, A., and Griffin, P. B. Woman the hunter: The Agta. In F. Dahlberg (Ed.), *Woman the Gatherer*. New Haven, Conn.: Yale University Press.

Etaugh, C. Effects of nonmaternal care on chldren: Research evidence and popular reviews. *Amer. Psychologist* 1980, 35, 309–319.

Everly, G. S., and Rosenfeld, R. *The Nature and Treatment of the Stress Response*. New York: Plenum, 1981.

Evoy, J. J. *The Rejected: Psychological Consequences of Parental Rejection*. University Park: Pennsylvania State University Press, 1982.

Eyre, D. R.: Collagen: Molecular diversity in the body's protein scaffold. *Science* 1980, 207, 1315–1322.

Faber, A., and Mazlish, E. *How to Talk so Kids Will Listen and Listen so Kids Will Talk*. New York: Avon Books, 1980.

Fagot, B. I., and Kronsberg, S. J. Sex differences: Biological and social factors influencing the behavior of young boys and girls. In S. G. Moore and S. G. Cooper (Eds.), *The Young Child: Reviews of Research* (Vol. 3). Washington, D.C.: National Association for the Education of Young Children, 1982.

Faux, M. Childless by Choice. New York: Doubleday, 1984. (a)

Faux, M. *Entering the Job Market*. New York: Monarch Press, 1984. (b)

Feagans, L., and Farran, D. C. (Eds.). *The Language of Children Reared in Poverty: Implications for Evaluation and Intervention. Papers from a Conference, Chapel Hill, N.C., May 1980*. New York: Academic Press, 1982.

Federal Bureau of Investigation. Uniform crime reports for the United States. *Statistical Abstract of the United States*. Washington, D.C.: U.S. Government Printing Office, 1980.

Federal Bureau of Investigation. *Uniform crime reports for the United States, 1989*. Washington, D.C.: U.S. Government Printing Office, 1989.

Fein, R. Research on fathering. In A. Skolnick and J. Skolnick (Eds.), *The Family Transition*. Boston: Little, Brown, 1980.

Feingold, A. Cognitive gender differences are disappearing. *Amer. Psychologist* 1988, 43, 95–103.

Feinstein, L. Type A behavior and women: A measure of sexual equality? *Health and Medical Care Services Review* 1981, 3(1), 3–12.

Feldman, D. H. *Beyond Universals in Cognitive Development*. Norwood, N.J.: Ablex, 1980.

Feldman, S. S. and Gehring, T. M. Changing perceptions of family cohesion and power across adolescence. *Child Devel.* 1988, 59, 1034–1045.

Feldstein, J. H., and Feldstein, S. Sex differences on televised toy commercials. *Sex Roles* 1982, 8, 581–593.

Felsenfeld, G. DNA. *Scientific American* 1985, 253(4), 58–68.

Fernald, A., and Simon, T. Expanded intonation contours in mothers' speech to newborns. *Devel. Psychol.* 1984, 20, 104–113.

Field, T. M., Cohen, D., Garcia, R., and Greenberg, R. Mother-stranger face discrimination by the newborn. *Infant Behavior and Development* 1984, 7(1), 19–25.

Field, T. M., Sostek, A. M., Vietze, P., and Leiderman, P. H. (Eds.). *Culture and Early Interactions*. Hillsdale, N.J.: Erlbaum, 1981.

Filinson, R. Diagnosis of senile dementia Alzheimer's type: The state of the art. *Clinical Gerontologist* 1984, 2(4), 3–23.

Fine, G. A. Friends, impression management, and preadolescent behavior. In S. R. Asher and J. M. Gottman (Eds.), *The Development of Children's Friendships*. New York: Cambridge University Press, 1981.

Finkelhor, D. How widespread is child sexual abuse? *Children Today* 1984, 13(4), 18–20.

Finkelhor, D. Sexual abuse of boys. In A. W. Burgess (Ed.), *Rape and Sexual Assault: A Research Handbook*. New York: Garland Publishing, 1985.

Finkelhor, D. The trauma of child sexual abuse: Two models. In G. E. Wyatt and G. J. Powell (Eds.), *Lasting Effects of Child Sexual Abuse*. Beverly Hills, Calif.: Sage Publications, 1988.

Finkelstein, N. Aggression: Is it stimulated by day care? *Young Children* 1982, 37(6), 6–13.

Finkelstein, N., and Haskins, R. Kindergarten children prefer same-color peers. *Child Devel.* 1983, 54(2), 502–508.

Firman, J. Reforming community care for the elderly and disabled. *Health Affairs* 1983, 2(1), 66–82.

Fischer, K. W. Illuminating the processes of moral development. *Monographs of the Society for Research in Child Development* 1983, 48 (1–2, serial no. 200), 97–107.

Fischer, K. W., and Jennings, S. The emergence of representation in search: Understanding the hider as an independent agent. *Q. Review of Devel.* 1981, 1, 18–30.

Fisher, C., Berlinger, D., Filby, N., Mariave, R., Cahen, D., and Dishaw, M. Teaching behaviors, academic learning time, and student achievement: An overview. In C. Denham and A. Lieberman (Eds.), *National Institute of Education*, Washington, D.C.: 1980.

Fisher, E. Television and language development. *J. Educational Television* 1984, 10(2), 85–90.

Fisher, M., and Striker, G. (Eds.). *Intimacy*. New York: Plenum, 1982.

Fisher, W. A. Adolescent contraception: Summary and recommendations. In D. Byrne and W. A. Fisher (Eds.), *Adolescents, Sex, and Contraception*. Hillsdale, N.J.: Erlbaum, 1983.

Flavell, J. Cognitive monitoring. In W. P. Dickson (Ed.), *Children's Oral Communication Skills*. New York: Academic Press, 1981.

Flavell, J. *Cognitive Development* (2nd ed.). Englewood Cliffs, N.J.: Prentice-Hall, 1985.

Flavell, J., and Ross, L. (Eds.). *Social Cognitive Development*. New York: Cambridge University Press, 1981.

Flexer, B. K., and Roberge, J. J. Control of variables and propositional reasoning in early adolescence. *J. Gen. Psychol.* 1980, 103, 3–12. (a)

Fligiel, S. E., Venkat, H., Gong, H., and Tashkin, D. P. Bronchial pathology in chronic marijuana smokers: A light and electron microscopy study. *J. Psychoactive Drugs* 1988, 20, 33–42.

Folb, E. A. *Runnin' Down Some Lines: The Language and Culture of Black Teenagers*. Cambridge, Mass.: Harvard University Press, 1980.

Foner, A., and Schwab, K. *Aging and Retirement*. Monterey, Calif.: Brooks/Cole, 1981.

Ford, K. Socioeconomic differentials and trends in the timing of births. Washington, D.C.: U.S. Department of Health Services, *Vital and Health Statistics* 6, 1981.

Foreman, G. E., and Hill, F. *Constructive Play*. Monterey, Calif.: Brooks/Cole, 1980.

Formanek, R., and Gurian, A. *Why? Children's Questions*. Boston: Houghton Mifflin, 1980.

Fosarelli, P. D. Television and children: A review. *Devel. and Behav. Ped.* 1984, 5(1) 30–37

Fowler, B. A. The relationship of body image perception and weight status to recent change in weight status of the adolescent female. *Adolescence* 1989, 95, 557–567.

Fowler, W. *Infant and Child Care: A Guide to Education in Group Settings*. Boston: Allyn & Bacon, 1980.

Fozard, J. L. The time for remembering. In L. W. Poon (Eds.), *Aging in the 1980's: Psychological Issues*. Washington, D.C.: American Psychological Asociation, 1980.

Francis, D. *Will You Still Need Me, Will You Still Feed Me, When I'm 84?* Bloomington: Indiana University Press, 1984.

Francks, O. R. Scribbles? Yes, they are art. In J. F. Brown (Ed.), *Curriculum Planning for Young Children*. Washington, D.C.: National Association for the Education of Young Children, 1982.

Franklin, D. L. Race, class, and adolescent pregnancy: An ecological analysis. *Adolescence* 1988, 58, 339–354.

Fredericks, C. *Programs for Living Longer*. New York: Simon & Schuster, 1983.

Freeman, E. B. The Ann Arbor decision: The importance of teacher's attitudes toward language. *Elementary School J.* 1982, 83, 41–47.

French, J. R., Caplan, R. D., and Van Harrison, R. *The Mechanisms of Job Stress and Strain*. Chichester, England: Wiley, 1982.

French, P., and McClure, M. Teacher's questions, pupils' answers: An investigation of questions and answers in the infant classroom. *First Language* 1981, 2, 31–47.

Freud, A. Adolescence. *Psychoanal. Study of the Child* 1958, 13, 255–278.

Freudenberger, H. J., and Richelson, G. *Burnout: The High Cost of High Achievement*. New York: Bantam, 1980.

Frey, K. A. Middle-aged women's experience and perceptions of menopause. *Women and Health* 1981, 6, 25–36.

Fribourg, S. Cigarette smoking and sudden infant death syndrome. *J. Obstet. and Gynecol.* 1982, 142(7), 934–941.

Fried, M. Endemic stress: The psychology of resignation and the politics of scarcity. *Amer. J. Orthopsychiat.* 1982, 52(1), 4–19.

Fried, P. A., and Oxorn, H. *Smoking for Two: Cigarettes and Pregnancy*. New York: Free Press, 1980.

Friedman, H. S., and Booth-Kewley, S. Validity of the Type A construct: A reprise. *Psychol. Bull.* 1988, 104(3), 381–384.

Friedman, M., and Rosenman, R. H. *Type A Behavior and Your Heart*. New York: Knopf, 1974.

Friedman, W. J., and Laycock, F. Children's analog and digital clock knowledge. *Child Devel.* 1989, 60, 340–356.

Fries, J. F., and Crapo, L. M. *Vitality and Aging*. San Francisco: W. H. Freeman, 1981.

Frodi, A. M. Father–mother–infant interaction in traditional and nontraditional Swedish families: A longitudinal study. *Alternative Lifestyles* 1983, 5(3), 142–163.

Fu, V., and Leach, D. J. Sex-role preferences among elementary school children in rural America. *Psychol. Reports* 1980, 46, 555–560.

Fuchs, V. R. *Women's Quest for Economic Equality*. Cambridge, Mass.: Harvard University Press, 1988.

Furman, W. Children's friendships. In T. M. Field, A. Huston, H. C. Quay, L. Troll, and G. E. Finley (Eds.), *Review of Human Development*. New York: John Wiley, 1982.

Furman, W., and Bierman, K. L. Developmental changes in young children's conceptions of friendship. *Child Devel.* 1983, 54(3), 549–556.

Furstenberg, F. F., Jr. Reflections on remarriage. *J. Family Issues* 1980, 1(4), 443–453.

Furstenberg, F. F., Jr. *Recycling the Family: Remarriage after Divorce* (rev. ed.). Beverly Hills, Calif.: Sage Publications, 1987.

Furstenberg, F. F., Jr. Child care after divorce and remarriage. In E. M. Hetherington and J. D. Arasteh (Eds.), *Impact of Divorce, Single-Parenting, and Stepparenting on Children*. Hillsdale, N.J.: Erlbaum, 1988.

Furstenberg, F. K., Jr., and Nord, C. W. The life course of children of divorce: Marital disruption and parental contact. *Family Planning Perspectives* 1982, 14, 211–221.

Furstenberg, F. K., and Spanier, G. G. *Recycling the Family: Remarriage after Divorce*. Beverly Hills, Calif.: Sage Publications, 1984.

Furth, H. *Piaget and Knowledge: Theoretical Foundations*. Chicago: University of Chicago Press, 1981.

Galinsky, E. *Between Generations: The Six Stages of Parenthood*. New York: Times Books, 1980.

Gallagher, J., and Reid, D. *The Learning Theory of Piaget and Inhelder*. Monterey Calif.: Brooks/Cole, 1981.

Gallahue, D. L. *Understanding Motor Development in Children*. New York: John Wiley, 1982.

Gallup, G. *Gallup Poll*. Princeton, N.J.: George Gallup, 1981.

Gallup, G. Gallup poll on daily exercise. *InfoGraphics,* August 2, 1984.

Galotti, K. M. Approaches to studying formal and everyday reasoning. *Psychol. Bull.* 1989, 105, 331–351.

Garbarino, J. *Adolescent Development: An Ecological Perspective.* Columbus, Ohio: Chas. E. Merrill, 1985.

Garcia, E. E. Bilingualism in early childhood. *Young Children* 1980, 35 (4), 4–11.

Gardner, H. *Artful Scribbles.* New York: Basic Books, 1980.

Garfinkel, P., and Garner, O. *Anorexia Nervosa: A Multidimensional Perspective.* New York: Brunner/Mazel, 1982.

Garn, S. M. Continuities and change in maturational timing. In O. G. Brim, Jr., and J. Kagan (Eds.), *Constancy and Change in Human Development.* Cambridge, Mass.: Harvard University Press, 1980.

Garner, J. D., and Mercer, S. O. (Eds.). *Women as They Age.* New York: Harrington Park Press, 1989.

Garrett, W. *Seasons of Marriage and Family Life.* New York: Holt, Rinehart and Winston, 1982.

Garton, A. F., and Renshaw, P. D. Linguistic processes in disagreements occurring in young children's dyadic problem solving. *British J. Devel. Psychol.* 1988, 6, 275–284.

Gastel, B., and Hecht, A. Estrogens: Another riddle for middle age. *FDA Consumer* 1980, 14, 14–15.

Geen, R. G. Behavioral and physiological reactions to observed violence: Effects of prior exposure to aggressive stimuli. *J. Personality and Social Psychol.* 1981, 40, 868–875.

Geiser, R. L. Incest and psychological violence. *Int. J. Family Psychiat.* 1982, 2(3), 291–300.

Geist, H. *The Psychological Aspects of the Aging Process: With Sociological Implications* (2nd ed.). Huntington, N.Y.: Krieger, 1980.

Gelles, R. J. Violence in the Family: A review of research in the seventies. *J. Marriage and the Family* 1980, 42, 873–885.

Gelles, R. J., and Cornell, C. P. *Intimate Violence in Families.* Beverly Hills, Calif.: Sage Publications, 1985.

Gelman, S. A. and O'Reilly, A. W. Children's inductive influences within superordinate categories: The role of language and category structure. *Child Devel.* 1988, 59, 876–887.

George, L. K. *Role Transitions in Later Life.* Monterey, Calif.: Brooks/Cole, 1980.

Gershenfeld, M. K. Couples have the right to divorce even if they have children. In H. Feldman and M. Feldman (Eds.), *Current Controversies in Marriage and Family.* Beverly Hills, Calif.: Sage Publications, 1985.

Gettys, L. D., and Cann, A. Children's perceptions of occupation sex stereotypes. *Sex Roles* 1981, 7, 301–308.

Gianino, A., and Tronick, E. Z. The mutual regulation model: The infant's self and interactive regulation coping and defense. In T. Field, P. McCabe, and N. Schneiderman (Eds.), *Stress and Coping.* Hillsdale, N.J.: Erlbaum, 1988, 47–68.

Gibbs, J. T., and Huang, L. N. A conceptual framework for assessing and treating minority youth. In J. T. Gibbs and L. N. Huang (Eds.), *Children of Color.* San Francisco, Calif.: Jossey-Bass, 1989.

Gibson, M. J. Early retirement: A widespread phenomenon in Western countries. *Ageing International* 1982, 9(2), 15–17.

Gibson, M. J. Early intervention following admission may be critical to life expectancy. *Ageing International* 1983, 9(4), 8–9.

Gibson, M. J. Some societal responses to dementia in developed countries. *Ageing International* 1984, 11 (5), 11–16.

Giele, J. Z. *Women in the Middle Years: Current Knowledge and Directions for Research and Policy.* New York: John Wiley, 1982.

Gieringer, D. H. Marijuana, driving, and accident safety. *J. Psychoactive Drugs,* 1988, 20, 93–102.

Gilbert, A. L., and Davidson, S. Dual-career families at midlife. In S. Hunter and M. Sundell (Eds.), *Midlife Myths: Issues, Findings, and Practical Implications.* Beverly Hills, Calif.: Sage Publications, 1989.

Gilbert, E. H., and DeBlassie, R. R. Anorexia nervosa: Adolescent starvation by choice. *Adolescence* 1984, 19(76), 839–846.

Gilbert, L. A., Holahan, C. K., and Manning, L. Coping with conflict between professional and maternal roles. *Family Relations* 1981, 6, 420–431.

Gillies, J. *A Guide to Caring for and Coping with Aging Parents.* Nashville, Tenn.: Thomas Nelson, 1981.

Gilligan, C. *In a Different Voice.* Cambridge, Mass.: Harvard University Press, 1982.

Gilstrap, R. (Ed.). *Toward Self-Discipline: A Guide for Parents and Educators.* Washington, D.C.: Association for Childhood Education International, 1981.

Ginsburg, H. P. *Children's Arithmetic: How They Learn It and How You Teach It.* Austin, Tex.: PRO-ED Publishing, 1982.

Ginzberg, E. The elderly: An international policy perspective. *Milbank Memorial Fund Quarterly: Health and Society* 1983, 61(3), 473–488.

Glasser, B. G., and Strauss, A. *Time for Dying.* New York: Macmillan, 1968.

Gleitman, L. R. Maturational determinants of language growth. *Cognition* 1981, 10, 103–114.

Glenn, N. D. The well-being of persons remarried after divorce. *J. Fam. Issues* 1981, 2, 61–75.

Glenn, N. D., and McLanahan, S. The effects of offspring on the psychological well-being of older adults. *J. Marriage and the Family* 1981, 43(5), 409–421.

Glick, P. C. Marriage experiences of family life specialists. *Family Relations* 1980, 29(1), 16–24. (a)

Glick, P. C. Remarriage: Some recent changes and variations. *J. Fam. Issues* 1980, 1(12), 455–478. (b)

Glick, P. C. Marriage, divorce, and living arrangements. *J. Fam. Issues* 1984, 5, 7–26.

Glick, P. C. Fifty years of family demography: A record of social change. *J. Marriage and the Family* 1988, 861–873.

Glick, P. C., and Spanier, G. Married and unmarried cohabitation in the United States. *J. Marriage and the Family* 1980, 42, 19–30.

Goetting, A. The six stations of remarriage: Developmental tasks of remarriage and divorce. In L. Cargan (Ed.), *Marriage and Family: Coping with Change.* Belmont, Calif.: Wadsworth, 1985.

Goffin, S. G., and Tull, C. Q. Problem solving: Encouraging active learning. *Young Children* 1985, 40(3), 28–32.

Golan, N. *Passing through Transitions.* New York: Free Press, 1981.

Golanty, E., and Harris, B. B. *Marriage and Family Life.* Boston: Houghton Mifflin, 1982.

Gold, M. Social ecology. In H. C. Quay (Ed.), *Handbook of Juvenile Delinquency.* New York: Wiley, 1987.

Gold, M., and Petronio, R. J. Delinquent behavior in adolescence. In J. Adelson (Ed.), *Handbook of Adolescent Psychology.* New York: John Wiley, 1980.

Goldstein, E. B. *Sensation and Perception.* Belmont, Calif.: Wadsworth, 1980.

Goldstein, S., and Solnit, A. J. *Divorce and Your Child: Practical Suggestions for Parents.* New Haven, Conn.: Yale University Press, 1984.

Golinko, B. E. Adolescences: Common pathways through life. *Adolescence* 1984, 19(75), 749–751.

Gonda, T. A., and Ruark, J. E. *Dying Dignified: The Health Professional's Guide to Care.* Menlo Park, Calif.: Addison-Wesley, 1984.

Göneö, A., and Kessel, F. Preschoolers' collaborative construction in planning and maintaining imaginative play. *Int. J. Behav. Devel.* 1988, 11, 327–344.

Goode, E. *Drugs in American Society* (3rd ed.). New York: Alfred Knopf, 1989.

Goossens, L. Imaginary audience behavior as a function of age, sex, and formal operational thinking. *Int. J. Behav. Devel.* 1984, 7(1), 77–93.

Gordon, S. Sexuality education in the late 1980's: No more retreats. *J. Sex Education and Therapy* 1982, 8(2), 6–8.

Gottesman, I. I., and Shields, J. *The Schizophrenic Puzzle.* New York: Cambridge University Press, 1982.

Gottfried, A. E. Intrinsic motivation in young children. *Young Children* 1983, 39(1), 64–73.

Gottman, J. M. How children become friends. *Monographs of the Society for Research in Child Development* 1983, 48 (3, serial no. 201).

Gould, R. L. *Transformations: Growth and Change in Adult Life.* New York: Simon & Schuster, 1978.

Gould, R. L. Transformations during early and middle adult years. In N. Smelser and E. Erikson (Eds.), *Themes of Work and Love in Adulthood.* Cambridge, Mass.: Harvard University Press, 1980.

Gove, W. R., Hughes, M., and Style, C. B. Does marriage have positive effects on the psychological well-being of the individual? *J. Health and Social Behav.* 1983, 24(2), 122–131.

Grace, L. (Ed.). *Women in Their Later Years.* New York: Harrington Park Press, 1989.

Grambs, J. D. *Women over 40: Visions and Realities* (rev. ed.). New York: Springer, 1989.

Grande, C. G. Delinquency: The learning disabled student's reaction to academic school failure. *Adolescence* 1988, 23, 209–219.

Gratton, B., and Haug, M. R. Decision and adaptation: Research on female retirement. *Research on Aging* 1983, 5(1), 59–76.

Gray, M. *The Changing Years: The Menopause without Fear* (3rd ed.). New York: Signet Books, 1981.

Gray, V. R. The psychological response of the dying patient. In P. S. Chaney (Ed.), *Dealing with Death and Dying* (2nd ed.). Springhouse, Penn.: International Communications/Nursing Skillbooks, 1984.

Greenberg, E., and Steinberg, L. D. Sex differences in early labor force experience: Harbinger of things to come. *Social Forces* 1983, 62(2), 467–486.

Greenberg, H. M. *Coping with Job Stress: A Guide for All Employers and Employees.* Englewood Cliffs, N.J.: Prentice-Hall, 1980.

Greenberg, J. Inheriting mental illness: Nature and nurture. *Science News,* Jan. 1980, 25–29.

Greenberg, J. S. *Comprehensive Stress Management.* Dubuque, Iowa: Wm. C. Brown, 1983.

Greenberg, P. The empty-nest syndrome. In L. Cargan (Ed.), *Marriage and Family: Coping with Change.* Belmont, Calif.: Wadsworth, 1985.

Greenfield, P. M., and Tronick, A. *Infant Curriculum.* Santa Monica, Calif.: Goodyear, 1980.

Greive, R., and Dow, L. Bases of young children's judgment about more. *J. Exper. Child Psychol.* 1981, 32(1), 36–37.

Grief, G. L. *Single Fathers.* Lexington, Mass.: D. C. Heath, 1985.

Griffing, P. Encouraging dramatic play in early childhood. In J. F. Brown (Ed.), *Curriculum Planning for Young Children.* Washington, D.C.: National Association for the Education of Young Children, 1982.

Griffitt, W., and Hatfield, E. *Human Sexual Behavior.* Glenview, Ill.: Scott, Foresman, 1985.

Grigsby, J. P., and Weatherley, D. Gender and sex role differences in intimacy of self-disclosure. *Psychol. Reports* 1983, 53(1), 891–897.

Grof, S., and Grof, C. *Beyond Death: The Gates of Consciousness.* New York: Thames and Hudson, 1980.

Gross, R. T., and Duke, P. M. The effect of early vs. late maturation on adolescent behavior. *Ped. Clinics of North Amer.* 1980, 27, 71–77.

Grossman, A. Working mothers and their children. *Monthly Labor Review* 1981, 104, 49–54.

Grossman, A. More than half of all children have working mothers. *Monthly Labor Review* 1982, 105(2), 41–43.

Grossman, M. Children with AIDS. In I. C. Corless and M. Pittman-Lindeman (Eds.), *AIDS: Principles, Practices, and Politics.* New York: Hemisphere, 1988.

Grueling, J. W., and DeBlassie, R. R. Adolescent suicide. *Adolescence* 1980, 15, 589–601.

Grusec, J. E. Socialization processes in the development of altruism. In J. P. Rushton and R. M. Sorrentino

(Eds.), *Altruism and Helping Behavior*. Hillsdale, N.J.: Erlbaum, 1981.

Grusec, J. E., and Arnason, L. Consideration for others: Approaches to enhancing altruism. In S. G. Moore and C. R. Cooper (Eds.), *The Young Child: Reviews of Research* (Vol. 3). Washington, D.C.: National Association for the Education of Young Children, 1982.

Gunderson, M. P., and McCary, J. L. Effects of sex education on sex information and sexual guilt, attitudes, and behaviors. *Family Relations* 1980, 29, 375–379.

Gusella, J. L., Muir, D. and Tronick, E. A. The effect of manipulating maternal behavior during an interaction on three- and six-month-olds' affect and attention. *Child Devel.* 1988, 59, 1111–1124.

Gutek, B. A. Sex segregation and women at work: A selective review. In B. A. Gutek (Ed.), *Applied Psychology: An International Review*. Beverly Hills, Calif.: Sage Publications, 1988.

Gutek, B. A., Stromberg, A. H., and Larwood, L. (Eds.). *Women and Work*. Beverly Hills, Calif.: Sage Publications, 1988.

Guttmacher Institute. *Teenage Pregnancy*. New York: Alan Guttmacher Institute, 1985.

Guyton, A. C. *Textbook of Medical Physiology* (6th ed.). Philadelphia: Saunders, 1981.

Haan, N. Personality at midlife. In S. Hunter and M. Sundell (Eds.), *Midlife Myths: Issues, Findings, and Practical Implications*. Beverly Hills, Calif.: Sage Publications, 1989.

Haas, L. Determinants of role-sharing behavior: A study of egalitarian couples. *Sex Roles* 1982, 8(7), 747–760.

Haas, L. Role-sharing couples. In L. Cargan (Ed.), *Marriage and Family: Coping with Change*. Belmont, Calif.: Wadsworth, 1985.

Haber, C. *Beyond Sixty-Five: The Dilemma of Old Age in America's Past*. Cambridge, England: Cambridge University Press, 1983.

Hafer, W. K. *Coping with Bereavement*. Englewood Cliffs, N. J.: Prentice-Hall, 1981.

Hale, C. *The Super Years*. Fleming H. Revell, 1984.

Hale, J. Black children: Their roots, culture, and learning styles. *Young Children* 1981, 36(2), 37–50.

Hales, D., and Creasy, R. K. *New Hope for Problem Pregnancies*. New York: Harper & Row, 1982.

Hallberg, E. *The Gray Itch: The Male Metapause Syndrome*. New York: Warner Books, 1980.

Halmi, K. A. Psychosomatic illness review: Anorexia nervosa and bulimia. *Psychosomatics* 1983, 24, 111–132.

Hamberger, L., and Lohr, J. (Eds.). *Stress and Stress Management*. New York: Springer, 1984.

Hamid, P. N., and Wyllie, A. J. What generation gap? *Adolescence* 1980, 15, 385–391.

Hamilton, E. N., and Whitney, E. N. *Nutrition: Concepts and Controversies*. St. Paul: West Publishing, 1982.

Hamilton, M. P., and Reid, H. F. *A Hospice Handbook*. Grand Rapids, Mich.: Eerdmans, 1980.

Hammes, M. Human sexuality in higher education. In C. Cassell and P. M. Wilson (Eds.), *Sexuality Education*. New York: Garland Publishing, 1989.

Hansen, S. L., and Hicks, M. W. Sex role attitudes and perceived dating-mating choices of youth. *Adolescence* 1980, 15, 83–90.

Hardyck, C., and Petrinovich, L. F. Lefthandedness. *Psychol. Bull.* 1977, 84, 385–404.

Hardyck, C., Petrinovich, L. F., and Goldman, R. D. Lefthandedness and cognitive deficit. *Cortex* 1976, 12(3), 266–279.

Harlow, H. The nature of love. *Amer. Psychologist* 1958, 13, 637–685.

Harlow, H. The heterosexual affectional system in monkeys. *Amer. Psychologist* 1962, 16, 1–9.

Harlow, H., and Zimmerman, R. R. Affectual responses in the infant monkey. *Science* 1959, 130, 421–432.

Harlow, H. F. *Learning to Love*. San Francisco: Albion, 1971.

Harman, G., (Ed.). *On Noam Chomsky: Critical Essays* (2nd ed.). Amherst, Mass.: University of Massachusetts Press, 1982.

Harmatz, M. G., and Novak, M. A. *Human Sexuality*. New York: Harper & Row, 1983.

Harner, L. Immediacy and certainty: Factors in understanding future reference. *J. Child Language* 1982, 9(1), 115–124.

Harris, D. K., and Cole, W. E. *Sociology of Aging*. Boston: Houghton Mifflin, 1980.

Harris, M. B., and Satter, B. J. Sex-role stereotypes of kindergarten children. *J. Genet. Psychol.* 1981, 138(1), 49–61.

Harris, P. L., Olthof, T., Terwogt, M., and Terwogt, M. M. Children's knowledge of emotion. *J. Child Psych. Psychiat. and Allied Disciplines* 1981, 22(3), 247–261.

Harry, J. *Gay Children Grow Up: Gender Culture and Gender Deviance*. New York: Praeger, 1982.

Harry, J. *Gay Couples*. New York: Praeger, 1984.

Harter, S. Developmental perspectives on the self-system. In P. H. Mussen (Ed.), *Handbook of Child Psychology* (4th ed.), Vol. 4: E. M. Hetherington (Ed.). *Socialization, Personality, and Social Development*. New York: John Wiley, 1983.

Hartup, W. W. Peer relations and family relations: Two social worlds. In M. Rutter (Ed.), *Scientific Foundations of Developmental Psychiatry*. London: Heinemann Medical Books, 1980.

Hartup, W. W. Peer relations. In P. H. Mussen (Ed.), *Handbook of Child Psychology* (4th ed.), Vol. 4: E. M. Hetherington (Ed.). *Socialization, Personality, and Social Development*. New York: John Wiley, 1983.

Hartup, W. W. The peer context in middle childhood. In W. A. Collins (Ed.), *Development During Middle Childhood: The Years from Six to Twelve*. Washington, D.C.: National Academy Press, 1984.

Hartup, W. W., Laursen, B., Stewart, M. I., and Eastenson, A. Conflict and the friendship relations of young children. *Child Devel.* 1988, 59, 1590–1603.

Haskell, M. R., and Yablonsky, L. *Juvenile Delinquency* (3rd ed.). Boston: Houghton Mifflin, 1982.

Haswell, K. L., Hock, E., and Wenar, C. Techniques for dealing with oppositional behavior in preschool children. *Young Children* 1982, 37(3), 13–17.

Hatfield, E. The dangers of intimacy. In V. J. Derlega (Ed.). *Communication, Intimacy, and Close Relationships.* New York: Academic Press, 1984.

Haug, M. R., Ford, A. B., and Seafor, M. (Eds.). *The Physical and Mental Health of Aged Women.* New York: Springer, 1985.

Havighurst, R. J. *Developmental Tasks and Education* (3rd ed.). New York: D. McKay, 1972.

Havighurst, R. J. More thoughts on developmental tasks. *Personal and Guidance J.* 1980, 58, 330–335.

Havighurst, R. J., Neugarten, B. L., and Tobin, S. S. Disengagement and patterns of aging. In B. L. Neugarten (Ed.), *Middle Age and Aging.* Chicago: University of Chicago Press, 1968.

Hawkins, R. D. Adolescent alcohol abuse: A review. *J. Devel. and Behav. Ped.* 1982, 3(2), 83–87.

Hawkins, R., Fremouw, W., and Clement, P. *The Binge-Purge Syndrome.* New York: Springer, 1983.

Haycox, J. A. Late care of the demented patient: The question of nursing home placement. *New England J. Med.* 1980, 303, 165–166.

Haycox, J. A. Social management. In B. Reisberg (Ed.). *Alzheimer's Disease: The Standard Reference.* New York: Free Press, 1983.

Hayes, J. R. *The Complete Problem-Solver.* Philadelphia: Franklin Institute, 1981.

Hayflick, L. The cell biology of human aging. *Scientific American* 1980, 242, 58–65.

Hays, K. (Ed.). *TV, Science, and Kids: Teaching Our Children to Question.* Reading, Mass.: Addison-Wesley, 1984.

Heft, L., Thoresen, C. E., Kirmil-Gray, K., and Widenfeld, S. A. Emotional and temperamental correlates of Type A in children and adolescents. *J. Youth and Adolescence* 1988, 17(6), 461–475.

Heilman, J. R. Menopause: Myths are yielding to new scientific research. *Science Digest* 1980, 87, 66–68.

Hein, K. AIDS in adolescence. *J. Adolescent Health Care* 1989, 10, 105–135.

Helson, R., Elliot, T., and Leigh, J. Adolescent antecedents of women's work patterns. In D. Stern and D. Eichorn (Eds.), *Adolescence and Work.* Hillsdale, N.J.: Erlbaum, 1989.

Hendin, D. *Death as a Fact of Life.* New York: W. W. Norton, 1984.

Hendren, R. L. Depression in anorexia nervosa. *J. Amer. Acad. Child Psychiat.* 1983, 22, 59–62.

Hendricks, G., and Hendricks, K. *The Moving Center: Exploring Movement Activities for the Classroom.* Englewood Cliffs, N.J.: Prentice-Hall, 1983.

Hendricks, J., and Hendricks, C. D. *Aging in Mass Society: Myths and Realities* (2nd ed.). Cambridge, Mass.: Winthrop, 1981.

Henggeler, S. W. *Delinquency in Adolescence.* Beverly Hills, Calif.: Sage, 1989.

Henig, R. M. *How a Woman Ages.* New York: Ballantine Books, 1985.

Hennekens, C. H., Mayrent, S. L., and Buring, J. E. Epidemiological aspects of aging, mortality, and smoking. In R. Bosse and C. L. Rose (Eds.), *Smoking and Aging.* Lexington, Mass.: Heath, 1984.

Henretta, J. C., and O'Rand, A. M. Joint retirement in the dual worker family. *Social Forces* 1983, 62(2), 504–520.

Henslin, J. M. (Ed.). *Marriage and Family in a Changing Society* (2nd ed.). New York: The Free Press, 1985.

Hess, D. J., and Grant, G. W. Prime-time television and gender role behavior. *Teaching Sociol.* 1983, 10(3), 371–388.

Hess, R. D., and Shipman, V. C. Early experiences and the socialization of cognitive modes in children. In M. Kaplan-Sanoff and R. Yablans-Magid (Eds.), *Exploring Early Childhood.* New York: Macmillan, 1982.

Heston, L. L., and White, J. A. *Dementia: A Practical Guide to Alzheimer's Disease and Related Illnesses.* New York: W. H. Freeman, 1983.

Hetherington, E. M. Tracing children through the changing family. *APA Monitor* 1981, 12, 14–22.

Hetherington, E. M., Stanley-Hagan, M., and Anderson, E. R. Marital transitions: A child's perspective. *Amer. Psychologist* 1989, 44, 303–312.

Hewlett, S. *A Lesser Life: The Myth of Women's Liberation in America.* New York: William Morrow, 1986.

Hicks, R. E., and Kinsbourne, M. Human handedness: A partial cross-fostering study. *Science* 1976, 192, 908–910.

Higham, E. Variations in adolescent psychohormonal development. In J. Adelson (Ed.), *Handbook of Adolescent Psychology.* New York: John Wiley, 1980.

Hill, E. A., and Dorfman, L. T. Reaction of housewives to the retirement of their husbands. *Family Relations* 1982, 4, 195–200.

Hillard, P. A., and Panter, G. G. *Pregnancy and Childbirth.* New York: Ballantine, 1985.

Hilliard, A. G., and Vaughn-Scott, M. The quest for the "minority" child. In S. G. Moore and C. R. Cooper (Eds.), *The Young Child: Reviews of Research* (Vol. 3). Washington D.C.: National Association for the Education of Young Children, 1982.

Hiltz, S. R. Widowhood. In J. M. Henslin (Ed.), *Marriage and Family in a Changing Society* (3rd ed.). New York: The Free Press, 1989.

Hindelang, M. J. Variations in sex-race-age-specific incidence rates of offending. *Amer. Sociol. Review* 1981, 46, 461–474.

Hindley, C. B., Filliozat, A. M., Klakenberg, G., Nocolet-Meister, D., and Sand, E. A. Differences in age of walking in five European longitudinal samples. *Hum. Biol.* 1966, 38, 364–379.

Hobfoll, S. E. *The Ecology of Stress.* New York: Hemisphere, 1988.

Hobson, R. P. The question of egocentrism: The young child's competence in the coordination of perspectives. *J. Child Psychol. and Psychiat.* 1980, 21, 325–331.

Hoffman, L. W. Effects of maternal employment in the two-parent family. *Amer. Psychologist* 1989, 44, 283–292.

Hoffman, M. L. Moral development in adolescence. In J. Adelson (Ed.), *Handbook of Adolescent Psychology*. New York: John Wiley, 1980.

Hoffman, M. L. Empathy, social cognition, and moral action. In W. Kurtines and J. Gewirtz (Eds.), *Moral Behavior and Development: Advances in Theory, Research, and Application*. Hillsdale, N.J.: Erlbaum, 1989.

Hogan, M. J., Buehler, C., and Robinson, B. Single parenting: Transitioning alone. In H. I. McCubbin and C. R. Figley (Eds.), *Stress and the Family*. New York: Brunner/Mazel, 1983.

Hogan, R. The gifted adolescent. In J. Adelson (Ed.), *Handbook of Adolescent Psychology*. New York: John Wiley, 1980.

Hojat, M. Loneliness as a function of parent-child and peer relations. *J. Psychol.* 1982, 112, 129–133.

Holden, C. The hospice movement and its implications. In R. Fox (Ed.), *The Social Meaning of Death: Annals of the American Academy of Political and Social Science* 1980, 447, 59–63.

Holden, C. Hospices: For the dying, relief from pain and fear. In S. H. Zarit (Ed.), *Readings in Aging and Death* (2nd ed.). New York: Harper & Row, 1982.

Holmes, D. S., McGilly, G. M., and Houston, B. K. Task-related arousal of Type A and Type B persons: Level of challenge and response specificity. *J. Personality and Social Psychol.* 1984, 46(6), 1322–1327.

Holmes, F. F., and Hearne, E. Cancer state to age relationship: Implications for cancer screening in the elderly. *J. Amer. Geriat. Society* 1981 (2), 55–57.

Holt, K. S. Diets and development. *Child Care, Health and Development* 1982, 8(4), 183–201.

Hom, H. L., Jr., and Hom, S. L. Research and the child: The use of modeling, reinforcement/incentives, and punishment. In D. G. Range, J. R. Layton, and D. L. Roubinek (Eds.), *Aspects of Early Childhood Education: Theory to Research to Practice*. New York: Academic Press, 1980.

Honig, A. What are the needs of infants? *Young Children* 1981, 37(1), 3–10.

Honig, A. Research in review: Prosocial development in children. *Young Children* 1982, 37(5), 51–62. (a)

Honig, A. Language environments for young children. *Young Children* 1982, 38(1), 56–67. (b)

Honig, A. Research in review: Television and young children. *Young Children* 1983, 38(4), 63–76. (a)

Honig, A. Research in review: Sex role socialization in early childhood. *Young Children* 1983, 38(6), 57–70. (b)

Honig, A., and Laly, R. *Infant Caregiving: A Design for Training* (2nd ed.). New York: Syracuse University Press, 1981.

Hook, E. Rates of chromosome abnormalities at different maternal ages. *Obstetrics and Gynecology* 1981, 282–284.

Hooper, J. D., and Traupmann, J. A. Older women, the student role, and mental health. *Educational Gerontol.* 1983, 9, 233–242.

Horan, D. J., and Mall, D. (Eds.). *Death, Dying, and Euthanasia*. Frederick, Md.: University Publications of America, 1980.

Horn, J. L. The aging of human abilities. In B. B. Wolman (Ed.), *Handbook of Developmental Psychology*. Englewood Cliffs, N.J.: Prentice-Hall, 1982.

Hornung, C. A., and McCullough, B. C. Status relationships in dual-employment marriages: Consequences for psychological well-being. *J. Marriage and the Family* 1981, 43(1), 125–141.

Horobin, K., and Acredolo, C. The impact of probability judgments on reasoning about multiple possibilities. *Child Devel.* 1989, 60, 183–200.

Horowitz, G. P., and Dudek, B. C. Behavioral pharmacogenetics. In J. L. Fuller and E. C. Simmel (Eds.), *Behavior Genetics*. Hillsdale, N.J.: Erlbaum, 1983.

Hotcher, T. *Pregnancy and Childbirth*. New York: Avon Books, 1984.

Houston, J. P. *Fundamentals of Learning and Motivation* (2nd ed.). New York: Academic Press, 1981.

Howard, D. V. *Cognitive Psychology: Memory, Language, and Thought*. New York: Macmillan, 1983.

Howatt, P. M., and Saxton, A. M. The incidence of bulimic behavior in a secondary and university school population. *J. Youth and Adolescence* 1988, 17, 221–231.

Howell, S. Crisis for elders: House, home or shelter. *Generations* 1982, 6(3), 43–44.

Howes, C. Patterns of friendship. *Child Devel.* 1983, 54, 1041–1053.

Howes, C. Peer interaction of young children. *Monographs of the Society for Research in Child Development* 1988, 53(1), 94–104.

Howes, C., Unger, D., and Seidner, L. B. Social pretend play in toddlers: Parallels with social play and with solitary pretend. *Child Devel.* 1989, 60, 77–84.

Howsden, J. L. *Work and the Helpless Self: The Social Organization of a Nursing Home*. Lanham, Md: University Press of America, 1982.

Hubert, H. B., Fabsitz, R. R., Feinleib, M., and Brown, K. S. Olfactory sensitivity in humans: Genetic versus environmental control. *Science* 1980, 208, 607–609.

Hudspeth, W. Paper presented at the Western Psychological Association Annual Meeting. Long Beach, Calif., April 15–17, 1987.

Hultsch, D. F., and Pentz, C. A. Research on adult learning and memory: Retrospect and Prospect. *Contemporary Educational Psychol.* 1980, 5, 298–320.

Hunt, E. Cognitive science: Definition, status, and questions. *Ann. Review of Psychol.* 1989, 40, 603–629.

Hunter, F., and Youniss, J. Changes in functions of three relations during adolescence. *Devel. Psychol.* 1982, 18(6), 806–811.

Hunter, S., and Sundel, M. An examination of key issues concerning midlife. In S. Hunter and M. Sundel (Eds.), *Midlife Myths: Issues, Findings, and Practical Implications*. Beverly Hills, Calif.: Sage, 1989.

Hyde, J. S. *Understanding Human Sexuality* (2nd ed.). New York: McGraw-Hill, 1982.

Hyde, J. S., and Linn, M. C. Gender differences in verbal ability: A meta-analysis. *Psychol. Bull.* 1988, 104, 53–69.

Hymes, A., and Nuernberger, P. Breathing patterns found in heart attack patients. *Research Bulletin of the Himalayan International Institute* 1980, 2(2), 10–12.

Ilg, F. L., Ames, L. B., and Baker, S. M. *Child Behavior: Specific Advice on Problems of Child Behavior.* (rev. ed.). New York: Harper & Row, 1981.

Inazu, J. K., and Fox, G. L. Maternal influence on the sexual behavior of teenage daughters. *J. Fam. Issues* March 1980, 81–102.

Irion, J. C., Coon, R. C., and Blanchard-Fields, F. The influence of divorce on coping in adolescence. *J. Youth and Adolescence* 1988, 17, 135–145.

Irwin, D. M., and Bushnell, M. M. *Observational Strategies for Child Study.* New York: Holt, Rinehart and Winston, 1980.

Isaacson, L. Counseling male midlife career changers. *Vocational Guidance Q.* 1981, 29, 324–331.

Ives, W., Wolf, D., Furigna, G., and Smith, N. The earliest two-dimensional symbols: Properties, media, and strategies. Paper presented at the American Psychological Association, Los Angeles, Sept. 1981.

Izard, C. E. The young infant's ability to produce discrete emotional expressions. *Devel. Psychol.* 1980, 16, 132–140.

Izard, C. E. (Ed.). *Measuring Emotions in Infants and Children.* Cambridge, England: Cambridge University Press, 1982.

Jacklin, C. N. Female and male: Issues of gender. *Amer. Psychologist* 1989, 44, 127–133.

Jackson, N. E., Robinson, H. B., and Dale, P. S. *Cognitive Development in Young Children.* Monterey, Calif.: Brooks/Cole, 1977.

Jacobson, D. S. Stepfamilies. *Children Today* 1980, 9, 2–6.

Jacobson, D. S. Neonatal correlates of prenatal exposure to smoking, caffeine, and alcohol. *Infant Behav. and Devel.* 1984, 7(3), 253–265.

Jacobson, W. J., and Bergman, A. B. *Science for Children: A Book for Teachers.* Englewood Cliffs, N.J.: Prentice-Hall, 1980.

Jahoda, M. Work, employment, and unemployment: Values, theories, and approaches in social research. *Amer. Psychologist* 1981, 36, 184–191.

Jarvik, L. F., and Winograd, C. H. (Eds.). *Treatments for the Alzheimer Patient.* New York: Springer, 1988.

Jessor, R., Casta, F., Jessor, L., and Donovan, J. E. Time of first intercourse: A prospective study. *J. Personality and Social Psychol.* 1983, 44, 608–626.

Johnson, B. Single-parent families. *Family Economics Review,* Summer-Fall 1980, 22–27.

Johnson, C. J., Pick, H. L., Jr., Siegel, G. M., Cicciarelli, A. W., and Garber, S. R. Effects of interpersonal distance on children's vocal intensity. *Child Devel.* 1981, 52, 721–723.

Johnson, C. K., and Price-Bonham, S. Woman and retirement: A study and implications. *Family Relations* 1980, 7, 381–385.

Johnson, G. M., Shontz, F. C., and Locke, T. P. Relationship between adolescent drug use and parental drug behaviors. *Adolescence* 1984, 19(74), 295–299.

Johnson, G. T. (Ed.). An update on exercise in monkeys. *Harvard Medical School Newsletter* 1982(5), 5.

Johnson, H. C. Working with stepfamilies: Principles of practice. *Social Work* 1980, 25, 304–308.

Johnson, R., and Carter, M. M. Flight of the young: Why children run away from their homes. *Adolescence* 1980, 15, 483–489.

Johnston, L. D., Bachman, J. G., and O'Malley, P. M. Highlights from student drug use in America 1975–1980. Rockville, Md.: *National Institute on Drug Abuse, Division of Research,* 1980.

Johnston, L. D., O'Malley, P. M., and Bachman, J. G. *Illicit Drug Use, Smoking, and Drinking by America's High School Students, College Students, and Young Adults, 1975–1987.* Washington, D.C.: National Institute of Drug Abuse, 1988.

Jones, C. C. *Caring for the Aged: An Appraisal of Nursing Homes and Alternatives.* Chicago: Nelson-Hall, 1982.

Jones, K. L., Shainberg, L. W., and Byer, C. O. *Dimensions of Human Sexuality.* Dubuque, Iowa: Wm. C. Brown, 1985.

Jones, S. *Good Things for Babies* (2nd ed.). Boston: Houghton Mifflin, 1980.

Josselson, R. Ego development in adolescence. In J. Adelson (Ed.), *Handbook of Adolescent Psychology.* New York: John Wiley, 1980.

Josselson, R. The embedded self: I and thou revisited. In D. K. Lapsley and F. C. Powers (Eds.), *Self, Ego, and Identity: Integrative Approaches.* New York: Springer-Verlag, 1988.

Julien, R. M. *A Primer of Drug Action* (3rd ed.). San Francisco: W. H. Freeman, 1981.

Kagan, J. Personality, behavior and temperament. In F. Falkner (Ed.), *Human Development.* Philadelphia: W. B. Saunders Company, 1966.

Kagan, J. Impulsive and reflective children: Significance of conceptual tempo. In J. Krumboltz (Ed.), *Learning and the Educational Process.* Chicago: Rand McNally, 1965.

Kagan, J. Reflection-impulsivity: The generality and dynamics of conceptual tempo. *Journal of Abnorm. Psychology* 1966, 71, 17–24.

Kagan, J. *The Second Year: The Emergence of Self-awareness.* Cambridge, Mass.: Harvard University Press, 1981.

Kagan, J., Reznick, J. S., Snidman, N., Gibbons, J. et al. Childhood derivatives of inhibition and lack of inhibition to the unfamiliar. *Child Devel.* 1988, 59, 1580–1589.

Kagan, J., Rosman, B., Day, D., Albert, J., and Phillips, W. Information processing in the child. *Psychology Monograph* 1964, 78(1, whole no. 578).

Kail, R. *The Development of Memory in Children* (2nd ed.). New York: W. H. Freeman, 1984.

Kail, R., and Hagen, J. W. Memory in childhood. In B. B. Wolman (Ed.), *Handbook of Developmental Psychology*. Englewood Cliffs, N.J.: Prentice-Hall, 1982.

Kalat, J. W. *Biological Psychology*. Belmont, Calif.: Wadsworth, 1980.

Kalish, R. A. *Death, Grief, and Caring Relationships* (2nd ed.). Monterey, CA: Brooks/Cole, 1985.

Kalish, R. A. *Death, Grief, and Caring Relationships*. Monterey, Calif.: Brooks/Cole, 1981.

Kalish, R. A. Death and survivorship: The final transition. *Amer. Acad. Polit. and Soc. Sci.* 1982, 464, 163–173. (a)

Kalish, R. A. *Late Adulthood: Perspectives on Human Development* (2nd ed.). Monterey, Calif.: Brooks/Cole, 1982. (b)

Kalish, R. A. Older people and grief. *Generations* 1987, 21 (3), 33–38.

Kamerman, S. B. Time out for babies. *Working Mother* 1985, 4(9), 80–82.

Kamerman, S. B., Kahn, A. J., and Kingston, P. W. *Maternity Policies and Working Women*. New York: Columbia University Press, 1983.

Kamii, C. Application of Piaget's theory to education: The preoperational level. In I. E. Siegel, D. M. Brodzinsky, and R. M. Golinkoff (Eds.), *New Directions in Piagetian Theory and Practice*. Hillsdale, N.J.: Erlbaum, 1981. (a)

Kamii, C. Piaget, children and number. In M. Kaplan-Sanott and R. Yablans-Magid (Eds), *Exploring Early Childhood: Readings in Theory and Practice*. New York: Macmillan, 1981. (b)

Kamii, C. *Number in the Preschool and Kindergarten*. Washington, D.C.: National Association for the Education of Young Children, 1982.

Kamptner, N. L. Identity development in late adolescence: Causal modeling of social and familial influences. *J. Youth and Adolescence* 1988, 17(6), 493–514.

Kandel, D. B. Peer Influence in Adolescence. Paper presented at the Society for Research in Child Development, Boston, April 1980.

Kantner, J. F., and Zelnik, M. Sexual and contraceptive experience of young unmarried women, 1979. *Family Planning Perspectives* 1980, 16, 17–24.

Kaplan, P. S., Scheuneman, D., Jenkins, L., and Hilliard, S. Sensitization of infant visual attention: Role of pattern contrast. *Infant Behavior and Development* 1988, 11(3), 265–276.

Kaplan-Sanoff, M. Motor Development: A broader context. In M. Kaplan-Sanoff and R. Yablams-Magid (Eds.), *Exploring Early Childhood Readings in Theory and Practice*. New York: Macmillan, 1981.

Kart, C. S. *The Realities of Aging*. Boston: Allyn & Bacon, 1981.

Kastenbaum, R. J. *Death, Society, and Human Experience* (2nd ed.). St. Louis: C. V. Mosby, 1981.

Katchadourian, H. *The Biology of Adolescence*. San Francisco: W. H. Freeman, 1977.

Katchadourian, H. A. *Fundamentals of Human Sexuality* (4th ed.). New York: Holt, Rinehart and Winston, 1985.

Kauffman, J. R., and Ames, B. D. Care of aging family members. *J. Home Economics* 1983, 75(1), 45–46.

Kaufman, E. Marital problems caused by marijuana use. *Medical Aspects of Human Sexuality* 1982, 6(12), 17–81.

Kausler, D. H. *Experimental Psychology and Human Aging*. New York: John Wiley, 1982

Kavanaugh, R. D., and Jirkovsky, A. M. Parental speech to young children: A longitudinal analysis. *Merrill-Palmer Q.* 1982, 28(2) 297–311.

Kay, D., and Anglin, J. M. Overextension and underextension in the child's expressive and receptive speech. *J. Child Language* 1982, 9(1), 83–98.

Kaye, C. Genetic counseling. *Medical Aspects of Human Sexuality* 1981, 15(3), 164–180.

Kaye, K. Why we don't talk "baby talk" to babies. *J. Child Language* 1980, 7, 489–507.

Kaye, K. *The Mental and Social Life of Babies*. Chicago: University of Chicago Press, 1982.

Kaye, K., and Fogel, A. The temporal structure of face-to-face communication between mothers and infants. *Devel. Psychol.* 1980, 16(5), 454–464.

Kaza, A. E., and Reppucci, D. *On Love and Loving*. San Francisco, Calif.: Jossey-Bass, 1980.

Keating, D. P. Thinking processes in adolescence. In J. Adelson (Ed.), *Handbook of Adolescent Psychology*. New York: John Wiley, 1980.

Keating, D. P., and Clark, L. V. Development of physical and social reasoning in adolescence. *Devel. Psychol.* 1980, 16, 23–30.

Keats, Co-parenting. *Issues in Health Care of Women* 1983, 3(5), 371–374.

Keete, S. E. Real and ideal extended familism among Mexican Americans and Anglo Americans: On the meaning of "close" family ties. *Human Organization* 1984, 43(1), 65–70.

Keller, M., Eckensberger, L. H., and von Rosen, K. A critical note on the conception of preconventional morality: The case of stage 2 in Kohlberg's Theory. *Int. J. Behav. Devel.* 1989, 12, 57–69.

Kelley, K. Adolescent sexuality: The first lessons. In O. Byrne and W. A. Fisher (Eds.), *Adolescents, Sex, and Contraception*. New York: McGraw-Hill, 1981.

Kelley, M. R. *A Parent's Guide to Television: Making the Most of It*. New York: John Wiley, 1983.

Kellogg, R. Understanding children's art. In J. P. DeCecco (Ed.), *Readings in Educational Psychology Today*. Del Mar, Calif.: CRM Books, 1970.

Kelly, C., and Goodwin, G. C. Adolescents' perception of three styles of parental control. *Adolescence* 1983, 18(71), 567–571.

Kelly, J. A., and de Armas, A. Social relationships in adolescence: Skill development and training. In J. Worell and F. Danner (Eds.). *The Adolescent as Decision-maker*. San Diego: Academic Press, 1989.

Kempe, R. S., and Kempe, C. H. *The Common Secret:*

Sexual Abuse of Children and Adolescents. New York: W. H. Freeman, 1984.

Kendig, H. L. and Rowland, D. T. Family support of the Australian aged: A comparison with the United States. *Gerontologist* 1983, 23(6), 643–649.

Kendrick, C., and Dunn, J. Caring for a second baby: Effects on interaction between mother and firstborn. *Devel. Psychol.* 1980, 16, 303–311.

Kennedy, M. *Career Knockouts.* Chicago: Follett, 1980.

Kephart, W. M. *The Family, Society, and the Individual* (5th ed.). Boston: Houghton Mifflin, 1982.

Kermis, M. D. *The Psychology of Aging: Theory, Research, and Practice.* Boston: Allyn & Bacon, 1984.

Kessen, W. *The Child.* New York: John Wiley, 1965.

Kessner, D. M. Infant death: An analysis by maternal risk and health care. Washington, D.C.: National Academy of Sciences, 1973.

Khoury, M. J., Gomez-Farias, M., and Mulinare, J. Does maternal cigarette smoking during pregnancy cause cleft lip and palate in offspring? *Amer. J. Diseases of Children* 1989, 143, 333–338.

Kidwell, J. S. Number of siblings, sibling spacing, sex, and birth order: Their effects on perceived parent-adolescent relationships. *J. Marriage and Family,* May 1981, 330–335.

Kimmel, D. C. *Adulthood and Aging: An Interdisciplinary View* (2nd ed.). New York: John Wiley, 1980.

Kinard, E. M. Emotional development in physically abused children. *Amer. J. Orthopsychiatr.* 1980, 50, 686–696.

Kivnick, H. *The Meaning of Grandparenthood: Research in Clinical Psychology* (No. 3). Ann Arbor, Mich.: JMI Research Press, 1982.

Klatzky, R. L. *Human Memory* (2nd ed.). New York: W. H. Freeman, 1980.

Kleiber, D. A., and Barnett, L. A. Leisure in childhood. *Young Children* 1980, 35(5), 47–53.

Klein, L., and Feinstein, L. L. *Career Changing.* Boston: Little, Brown, 1982.

Kliegl, R., Smith, J., and Baltes, P. Testing-the-limits and the study of adult age differences in cognitive plasticity of a mnemonic skill. *Devel. Psychol.* 1989, 25, 247–256.

Klingman, A. Biblioguidance with kindergartners: Evaluation of a primary prevention program to reduce fear of the dark. *Clinical Child Psychology* 1988, 17, 237–241.

Knaub, P. K., Eversoll, D. B., and Voss, J. H. Is parenthood a desirable adult role? An assessment of attitudes held by contemporary women. *Sex Roles* 1983, 9(3), 355–362.

Knaub, P. K., and Hanna, S. L. Children of remarriage: Perceptions of family strengths. *J. Divorce* 1984, 7(4), 73–90.

Knight, B. Assessing a mobile outreach team. In M. A. Smyer and M. Gatz (Eds.), *Mental Health and Aging: Programs and Evaluations.* Beverly Hills, Calif.: Sage Publications, 1983.

Knight, B. M. *Enjoying Single Parenthood.* New York: Van Nostrand Reinhold, 1986.

Knox, A. Proficiency theory of adult learning. *Contemporary Educational Psychol.* 1980, 5, 378–404.

Knox, D. *Choices in Relationships.* St. Paul: West Publishing, 1985. (a)

Knox, D. *Human Sexuality.* St. Paul: West Publishing, 1985. (b)

Knox, D., and Wilson, K. Dating behaviors of university students. *Family Relations,* April, 1981 255–258.

Kobasa, S. C., Maddi, S. R., and Zola, M. A. Type A and hardiness. *J. Behav. Med.* 1983, 6, 41–51.

Kochanska, G., Kuczynski, L., and Radke-Yarrow, M. Correspondence between mother's self-reported and observed child-rearing practices. *Child Devel.* 1989, 60, 56–63.

Kogan, N. Stylistic variation in childhood and adolescence: Creativity, metaphor, and cognitive style. In P. H. Mussen (Ed.), *Handbook of Child Psychology,* Vol. 3: J. H. Flavell and E. M. Markman (Eds.), *Cognitive Development.* New York: John Wiley, 1983.

Kohlberg, L. *Stages in the Development of Moral Thought and Action.* New York: Holt, Rinehart and Winston, 1969.

Kohlberg, L. Moral stages and moralization. In T. Lickona (Ed.), *Moral Development and Behavior.* New York: Holt, Rinehart and Winston, 1976.

Kohlberg, L. Moral education in the schools: A developmental view. In M. Kaplan-Sanoff and R. Yablans-Magid (Eds.), *Exploring Early Childhood: Readings in Theory and Practice.* New York: Macmillan, 1981. (a)

Kohlberg, L. *Philosophy of Moral Development.* New York: Harper & Row, 1981. (b)

Kohlberg, L. A current statement on some theoretical issues. In S. Modgil and C. Modgil (Eds.). *Lawrence Kohlberg.* Philadelphia: Farmer Press, 1986.

Kohlberg, L., and Turiel, E. Continuities in childhood and adult moral development revisited. In P. B. Baites and K. W. Schaie (Eds.), *Life Span Developmental Psychology: Personality and Socialization.* New York: Academic Press, 1973.

Kolb, B., and Whishaw, I. *Fundamentals of Human Neuropsychology.* New York: Freeman, 1988.

Kompara, D. R. Difficulties in the socialization process of stepparenting. *Family Relations* 1980, 29, 69–73.

Konopka, G. Adolescent suicide. *Exceptional Children* 1983, 49(5), 390–394.

Kontos, S., and Stevens, R. High quality child care: Does your center measure up? *Young Children* 1985, 40(2), 5–9.

Koop, C. E. Toward a philosophy of aging for the public health professions. *Public Health Reports* 1983, 98(3), 203–206.

Koop, E. Teenagers and alcohol. *Public Health Reports* 1983, 98(1), 1.

Kornhaber, A., and Woodward, K. L., *Grandparents/Grandchildren: The Vital Connection.* New York: Doubleday, 1981.

Kotkin, M. Sex roles among married and unmarried couples. *Sex Roles* 1983, 9(9), 975–985.

Krane, S. M. Understanding genetic disorders of collagen. *New England J. Med.* 1980, 303(2), 19–36.

Krannich, R. L. *Re-Careering in Turbulent Times.* Manassas, Va.: Impact Publications, 1983.

Krause, M. V. *Food, Nutrition and Diet Therapy* (7th ed.) Philadelphia: Saunders, 1984.

Krebs, D., and Gillmore, J. The relationships among the first stages of cognitive development, role-taking abilities, and moral development. *Child Devel.* 1982, 53, 877–886.

Kress, G. *Learning to Write.* Boston: Routledge and Kegan Paul, 1982.

Krishef, C. H. *An Introduction to Mental Retardation.* Springfield, Ill.: Chas. C. Thomas, 1983.

Kuansnicka, E., Beymer, B., and Perloff, R. M. Portrayals of the elderly in magazine advertisements, *Journalism Q.* 1982, 59(4), 656–658.

Kübler-Ross, E. *On Death and Dying.* New York: Macmillan, 1969.

Kübler-Ross, E. *Questions and Answers on Death and Dying.* New York: Macmillan, 1974.

Kübler-Ross, E. *Death: The Final Stage of Growth.* Englewood Cliffs, N.J.: Prentice-Hall, 1975.

Kübler-Ross, E. *Living with Death and Dying.* New York: Macmillan, 1981.

Kübler-Ross, E. *Working It Through.* New York: Macmillan, 1982.

Kübler-Ross, E., and Magno, J. B. *Hospice: A Handbook for Families and Others: Facing Terminal Illness.* Santa Fe, N. M.: Bear, 1983.

Kuhn, D. The role of self-directed activity in cognitive development. In I. E. Siegel, D. M. Brodzinsky, and R. M. Golinkoff (Eds.), *New Directions in Piagetian Theory and Practice.* Hillsdale, N. J.: Erlbaum, 1981.

Kuhn, D. Cognitive development. In M. H. Bornstein, and M. E. Lamb (Eds.), *Developmental Psychology: An Advanced Textbook* (2nd ed.). Hillsdale, N. J.: Erlbaum, 1988.

Kupfersmid, J. H., and Wonderly, D. M. Moral maturity and behavior: Failure to find a link. *J. Youth and Adolescence* 1980, 9, 249–262.

Kupke, K. G., and Müller, U. Parental origin of the extra chromosome in trisomy 18. *Amer. J. Hum. Genet.* 1989, 45, 599–605.

Kurdek, L. A. An integrative perspective on children's divorce adjustment. *Am. Psychol.* 1981, 36, 856–866.

Labouvie-Vief, G., and Hakin-Larson, J. Developmental shifts in adult thought. In S. Hunter, and M. Sundell (Eds.), *Midlife Myths: Issues, Findings, and Practical Implications.* Beverly Hills, Calif.: Sage Publications, 1989.

Laczko, F. Between work and retirement: Becoming old in the 1980s. In B. Bytheway, T. Keil, P. Allat, and A. Bryan (Eds.). *Becoming and Being Old: Social Approaches to Later Life.* Beverly Hills, Calif.: Sage Publications, 1989.

Ladd, G. W. Friendship patterns and peer status during early and middle childhood. *J. Devel. and Behav. Ped.* 1988, 9, 229–238.

Ladd, G. W., Price, J. M., and Hart, C. H. Predicting preschoolers' peer status from their playground behaviors. *Child Devel.* 1988, 59, 986–992.

LaFromboise, T. D., and Low, K. G. American Indian children and adolescents. In J. T. Gibbs, and L. N. Huang (Eds.), *Children of Color.* San Francisco, Calif.: Jossey-Bass, 1989.

Lamanna, M. A., and Riedmann, A. *Marriages and Families: Making Choices throughout the Life Cycle* (2nd ed.). Belmont, Calif.: Wadsworth, 1985.

Lamb, M. E. (Ed.). *The Role of the Father in Child Development* (2nd ed.). New York: John Wiley, 1981

Lamb, M. E. Paternal influences on early socio-emotional development. *J. Child Psychol. and Psychiat. and Allied Disciplines* 1982, 23(2), 185–190.

Lamb, M. E. The changing role of the father. Paper presented at the Greater New York Area Fatherhood Forum. Bank Street College of Education, June 17, 1983.

Lamb, M. E., Easterbrooks, M. A., and Holden, G. W. Reinforcement and punishment among preschoolers: Characteristics, effects, and correlates. *Child Devel.* 1980, 51, 1230–1236.

Lamb, M. E., Garn, S., and Keating, M. T. Correlates between sociability and motor performance scores in 8-month olds. *Infant Behavior and Development* 1982, 5(1), 97–101.

Lamb, M. E., Hwang, C. P., Prodi, A. M., and Prodi, M. Security of mother-and-father-infant attachment and its relation to sociability with strangers in traditional and nontraditional Swedish families. *Milbank Memorial Fund Q. Health and Society* 1983, 61(3), 430–440.

Lamb, M. E., Prodi, A. M., and Hwang, C. Characteristics of maternal and paternal behavior in traditional and nontraditional Swedish families. *Int. Behavioral Devel.* 1982, 5(1), 131–141.

Lamb, M. E., and Sherrod, L. R. (Eds.). *Infant Social Cognition: Empirical and Theoretical Considerations.* Hillsdale, N. J.: Erlbaum, 1981.

Lamb, M. E., and Sutton-Smith, B. *Sibling Relationships: Their Nature and Significance across the Lifespan.* Hillsdale, N. J.: Erlbaum, 1982.

Lambert, W. E. *Faces and Facets of Bilingualism.* Washington, D.C.: Center for Applied Linguistics, 1981.

Lamer, M. R., and Housker, S. L. Sexual permissiveness in younger and older adults. *J. Fam. Issues* 1980, 1, 103–124.

Landau, E. *Why Are They Starving Themselves? Understanding Anorexia Nervosa and Bulimia.* New York: Julian Messner, 1983.

Landreth, C. *Preschool Learning and Teaching.* New York: Harper & Row, 1972.

Langlois, J. H., and Downs, A. C. Mothers, fathers, and peers as socialization agents of sex-typed play behaviors in young children. *Child Devel.* 1980, 51, 1217–1247.

Langton, P. Vulnerable breadwinners; Larim women in East Africa. *IDRC Reports* 1984, 13(2), 8–9.

Lapsley, D. K. Continuity and discontinuity in adolescent social cognitive development. In R. Montemayor, G. Adams, and T. Gullota (Eds.), *Advances in Adolescent Research* (Vol. 2). Orlando, Fla.: Academic Press, 1989.

LaRossa, R., and LaRossa, M. M. *Transition to Parenthood: How Infants Change Families*. Beverly Hills, Calif.: Sage Publications, 1981.

Larson, L. E. The influence of parents and peers during adolescence: The situation hypothesis. In R. E. Muuss (Ed.), *Adolescent Behavior and Society* (3rd ed.). New York: Random House, 1980.

Lasky, R. E. The effect of visual feedback of the hand on the reaching and retrieval behavior of young infants. *Child Devel*. 1977, 48, 112–117.

Lasky, R. E. Social interactions of Guatemalan infants: The importance of different caregivers. *J. Cross-Cultural Psychol*. 1981, 14(1), 17–28.

Lasky, R. E., and Klein, R. E. Fixation of the standard and novelty preference in six-month-old well and malnourished infants. *Merrill-Palmer Q*. 1980, 26, 171–178.

Lauersen, N. H. *Childbirth with Love*. N.Y.: Berkley Publishing Co., 1983.

Lazarus, R., and Folkman, S. *Stress, Appraisal, and Coping*. New York: Springer, 1984.

Leadbeater, B. J., and Dionne, J. P. The adolescent's use of formal operational thinking in resolving problems related to identity resolution. *Adolescence* 1981, 16(61), 111–121.

Leavy, R. L. Social support and psychological disorder: A review. *J. Community Psychol*. 1983, 11, 3–21.

Leboyer, F. *Birth without Violence*. New York: Knopf, 1975.

Lechner, C. R., and Rosenthal, D. A. Adolescent self-consciousness and the imaginary audience. *Genetic Psychol. Monogr*. 1984, 110(2), 289–305.

Le Croy, C. W. Parent-adolescent intimacy: Impact on adolescent functioning. *Adolescence* 1988, 23, 137–147.

Lee, G. Kinship in the seventies: A decade review of research and theory. *J. Marriage in the Family* 1980, 42, 923–934.

Lee, M., and Prentice, N. M. Interrelations of empathy, cognition and moral reasoning with dimensions of juvenile delinquency. *J. Abnorm. Child Psychol*. 1988, 16, 127–139.

Lehmann, P. Living longer with hypertension. *America's Health* 1984, 6(1), 14–19.

LeMasters, E. E., and DeFrain, J. *Parents in Contemporary America* (4th ed.). Homewood, Il: Dorsey Press, 1983.

Leming, M. R., and Dickinson, G. E. *Understanding Dying, Death, and Bereavement* (2nd ed.). Ft Worth, Tex.: Holt, Rinehart and Winston, 1990.

Leming, M. R., and Dickinson, G. E. *Understanding Dying, Death, and Bereavement*. New York: Holt, Rinehart and Winston, 1985.

Lenneberg, E. H. Understanding language without the ability to speak. *J. Abnorm. Soc. Psychol*. 1962, 65, 419–425.

Lenneberg, E. H. *Biological Foundations of Language*. New York: John Wiley, 1967.

Leonetti, R. *Children's Conceptions of Death*. New York: Springer, 1980.

Lepper, M. R. Extrinsic reward and intrinsic motivation: Implications for the classroom. In J. M. Levine and M. C. Wand (Eds.), *Teacher and Student Perceptions: Implications for Learning*. Hillsdale, N.J.: Erlbaum, 1983.

Lerner, R. M. and Lerner, J. V. Effects of physical attractiveness. *William T. Grant Foundation Annual Report*. New York: William T. Grant Foundation, 1988.

Lerner, R. M., Lerner, J. V., and Tubman, J. Organismic and contextual bases of development in adolescence: A developmental contextual view. In G. R. Adams, R. Montemayor, and T. P. Gullota (Eds.), *Biology of Adolescent Behavior and Development*. Beverly Hills, Calif.: Sage Publications, 1989.

Leslie, G. R., and Leslie, E. M. *Marriage in a Changing World* (2nd ed.). New York: John Wiley, 1980.

Leslie, G. R. *The Family in Social Context* (5th ed.). New York: Oxford University Press, 1982.

Levande, D. I., Koch, J. B., and Koch, L. Z. *Marriage and the Family*. Boston: Houghton Mifflin, 1983.

Levenkron, S. *Treating and Overcoming Anorexia Nervosa*. New York: Scribner's 1982.

Levenson, A. J., and Beller, S. A. Psychotropic drug use in the elderly: Optimal technique. *Urban Health* 1983, 12(2) 32–35.

Levine, S., and Carey, S. Up front: The acquisition of a concept and a word. *J. Child Language* 1982, 9(3), 645–657.

Levinson, D. *The Seasons of a Man's Life*. New York: Ballantine, 1978.

Levinson, D. Conceptions of the adult life course. In N. Smelser and E. Erikson (Eds.), *Themes of Work and Love in Adulthood*. Cambridge, Mass.: Harvard University Press, 1980.

Levinthal, C. F. *Introduction to Physiological Psychology* (3rd ed.). Englewood Cliffs, N.J.: Prentice-Hall, 1990.

Levy-Shiff, R. Adaptation and competence in early childhood: Communally raised kibbutz children versus family raised children in the city. *Child Devel*. 1983, 54(6), 1606–1614.

Lewin, K. *Dynamic Theory of Personality*. New York: McGraw-Hill, 1935.

Lewis, C., and O'Brien, M. (Eds.). *Reassessing Fatherhood*. Beverly Hills, Calif.: Sage, 1987.

Lewis, M., and Coates, D. L. Mother-infant interaction and cognitive development in twelve-week-old infants. *Infant Behavior and Development* 1980, 3, 95–105.

Lewis, M., and Michaelson, L. *Children's Emotions and Moods: Developmental Theory and Measurement*. New York: Plenum, 1983.

Lewis, R. A. and Salt, R. E. (Eds.). *Men in Families*. Beverly Hills, Calif. Sage, 1986.

Lichter, D. T. Components of change in the residential concentration of the elderly population. *J. Gerontol*. 1981, 36(4), 480–489.

Lickona, T. Research on Piaget's theory of moral development. In T. Lickona (Ed.), *Moral Development and Behavior*. New York: Holt, Rinehart and Winston, 1976.

Lieberman, M. A., and Tobin, S. S. *The Experience of Old Age: Stress, Coping, and Survival*. New York: Basic Books, 1983.

Liebert, R. M., Sprafkin, J. N., and Davidson, E. S. *The Early Window: Effects of Television on Children and Youth* (2nd ed.). New York: Pergamon Press, 1982.

Liebman, T. H. When will you be back? We bring generations together. *Young Children* 1984, 39(6), 70–75.

Lin, A. N., and Carter, D. M. Skin cancer in the elderly. In B. A. Gilchrest (Ed.), *The Aging Skin*. Philadelphia: W. B. Saunders, 1986

Lindberg, L., and Swedlow, R. *Young Children: Exploring and Learning*. Boston, Mass: Allyn and Bacon, 1985.

Lipscomb, T. J., and Coon, R. C. Parental speech modification to young children. *J. Genet. Psychology* 1983, 143(2), 181–187.

Lipson, A. Contamination of the fetal environment—A form of prenatal abuse. In K. Oates (Ed.), *Child Abuse: A Community Concern*. New York: Brunner/Mazel, 1984.

Livson, N., and Peskin, H. Perspectives on adolescence from longitudinal research. In J. Adelson (Ed.), *Handbook of Adolescent Psychology*. New York: John Wiley, 1980.

Loewinsohn, R. J. *Survival Handbook for Widows*. Glenview, Ill.: Scott, Foresman, 1984.

Londerville, S., and Main, M. Security of attachment, compliance, and maternal training methods in the second year of life. *Devel. Psychol.* 1981, 17, 289–299.

London, M., and Stumpf, S. A. *Managing Careers*. Reading, Mass.: Addison-Wesley, 1982.

Longino, C., and Kart, C. Explicating activity theory: A formal replication. *J. Gerontol.* 1982, 36, 713–722.

Longstreth, L. E. Human handedness: More evidence for genetic involvement. *J. Genet. Psychol.* 1980, 137, 275–283.

Lopata, H. Z. *Widowhood in an American city*. Cambridge, Mass.: Schneckman, 1973.

Lopata, H. Z. *Women as Widows*. New York: Elseview, 1979.

Lopata, H. Z. Widowhood and husband sanctification. *Marriage and the Family* 1981, 83, 439–450.

Loudin, J. *The Hoax of Romance*. Englewood Cliffs, N.J.: Prentice-Hall, 1981.

Lovallo, W. R., and Pishkin, V. A. A psychophysiological comparison of Type A and B men exposed to failure and uncontrollable noise. *Psychophysiol.* 1980, 17, 29–36.

Lund, D. A. (Ed.). *Older Bereaved Spouses: Research with Practical Applications*. New York: Hemisphere, 1989.

Maag, J. W., Rutherford, R. B., and Parkes, B. T. Secondary school professionals' ability to identify depression in adolescents. *Adolescence* 1988, 23, 73–82.

Maas, H. S. Social responsibility in middle age. In S. Hunter and M. Sundell (Eds.), *Midlife Myths: Issues,* *Findings, and Practical Implications*. Beverly Hills, Calif.: Sage Publications, 1989.

Maccoby, E. E. *Social Development*. New York: Harcourt Brace Jovanovich, 1980.

Maccoby, E. E. Gender as a social category. *Devel. Psychol.* 1988, 24, 755–765.

Maccoby, E. E., and Jacklin, C. N. Sex differences in aggression: A rejoinder and reprise. *Child Devel.* 1980, 51, 964–980.

Machlowitz, N. M. *Workaholics: Living with Them, Working with Them*. Reading, Mass.: Addison-Wesley, 1980.

Mack, S. A. and Berman, L. C. A group for parents of children with fatal genetic illnesses. *Amer. J. Orthopsychiat.* 1988, 58, 397–404.

Macklin, E. D. Nontraditional family forms: A decade of research. *J. Marriage and the Family* 1980, 42, 4, 905–922.

Maddox, G. L. Disengagement theory: A critical evaluation. *The Gerontologist* 1964, 4, 80–82.

Maeda, D. Japan. In E. Palmore (Ed.), *International Handbook on Aging: Contemporary Development and Research*. Westport, Conn.: Greenwood Press, 1980.

Magg, P. B., and Ornstein, M. R. *Come with Us to the Playgroup: A Handbook for Parents and Teachers of Young Children*. Englewood Cliffs, N.J.: Prentice-Hall, 1981.

Mahoney Institute of the American Health Foundation. *1981 Survey*. New York: Mahoney Institute.

Mahoney, E. R. *Human Sexuality*. New York: McGraw-Hill, 1983.

Malina, R. M. Motor development in the early years. In S. G. Moore and C. R. Cooper (Eds.), *The Young Child: Reviews of Research* (Vol. 3). Washington, D.C.: National Association for the Education of Young Children, 1982.

Maloney, M. J., and Klykylo, W. M. An overview of anorexia nervosa, bulimia, and obesity in children and adolescents. *J. Amer. Acad. Child Psychiat.* 1983, 22, 99–107.

Maltsberger, J. T. *Suicide Risk*. New York: Human Sciences Press, 1988.

Mann, D. M. Changes in protein synthesis. In B. Reisberg (Ed.), *Alzheimer's Disease: The Standard Reference*. New York: Free Press, 1983.

Mann, J. A. *Secrets of Life Extension*. New York: Bantam, 1980.

Manning, M. L. Three myths concerning adolescence. *Adolescence* 1983, 18(72), 823–829.

Manuel, R. C. (Ed.). *Minority Aging: Sociological and Social Psychological Issues*. Westport, Conn.: Greenwood Press, 1982.

Maracek, J., and Ballou, D. J. Family roles and women's mental health. *Profess. Psychol.* 1981, 12, 39–46.

Marcia, J. The identity status approach to the study of ego identity development. In T. Honess and K. Yardley (Eds.), *Self and Identity: Perspectives across the Lifespan*. London: Routledge and Kegan Paul, 1987.

Marcia, J. E. Identity in adolescence. In J. A. Adelson (Ed.), *Handbook of Adolescent Psychology*. New York: John Wiley, 1980.

Markham, L. R. Assisting speakers of black English as they begin to write. *Young Children* 1984, 39(4), 15–24.

Markus, H. Sibling personalities: The luck of the draw. *Psychol. Today* 1981, 15(6), 36–37.

Marsh, G. A. Perceptual changes with aging. In E. W. Busse and D. G. Blazer (Eds.), *Handbook of Geriatric Psychiatry.* New York: Van Nostrand Reinhold, 1980.

Marsh, R. The income and resources of the elderly in 1978. *Social Security Bull.* 1981, 44(12), 3–11.

Marshall, V. W. *Last Chapters: A Sociology of Aging and Death.* Belmont, Calif.: Wadsworth, 1980.

Marston, A. R., Jacobs, D. F., Singer, R. D., Wideman, K. F. et al. Characteristics of adolescents at risk for compulsive overeating on a brief screening test. *Adolescence* 1988, 23, 59–65.

Martin, B. *Abnormal Psychology: Clinical and Scientific Perspectives.* New York: Holt, Rinehart and Winston, 1977.

Martin, G. B., and Clark, R. D. Distress crying in neonates: Species and peer specificity. *Devel. Psychol.* 1982, 18, 3–9.

Martin, M. J., and Walters, J. Familial correlates of selected types of child abuse and neglect. *J. Marriage and the Family* 1982, 44, 267–276.

Martin, R. A., and Poland, E. Y. *Learning to Change: A Self-Management Approach to Adjustment.* New York: McGraw-Hill, 1980.

Masamba ma Mpolo. Older persons and their families in a changing village society: A perspective from Zaire. Washington, D.C.: International Federation on Ageing, 1984.

Maslach, C. *Burnout: The Cost of Caring.* Englewood Cliffs, N.J.: Prentice-Hall, 1982.

Maslow, A. H. *Motivation and Personality.* New York: Harper and Brothers, 1954.

Maslow, A. H. *Toward a Psychology of Being* (2nd ed.). Princeton, N.J.: Van Nostrand Reinhold, 1968.

Maslow, A. H. *Motivation and Personality* (2nd ed.). New York: Harper & Row, 1970.

Maslow, A. H. *The Farther Reaches of Human Nature.* New York: Viking, 1971.

Masnick, G., and Bane, M. J. *The Nation's Families: 1960–1990.* Cambridge, Mass.: Joint Center for Urban Studies of MIT and Harvard University, 1980.

Masters, W. H., and Johnson, V. E. *Homosexuality in Perspective.* Boston: Little, Brown, 1980.

Masters, W. H., Johnson, V. E., and Kolodny, R. C. *Human Sexuality* (2nd ed.). Boston: Little, Brown, 1985.

Masur, E. F. Mother's responses to infant's object-related gestures: Influences on lexical development. *J. Child Language* 1982, 9(1), 23–30.

Matlin, M. *Human Experimental Psychology.* Monterey, Calif.: Brooks/Cole, 1980.

Matlin, M. *Cognition.* New York: Holt, Rinehart and Winston, 1983.

Matthews, K. A. Coronary heart disease and Type A behaviors. *Psychol. Bull.* 1988, 104(3), 373–380.

Matthews, K. A., Meilahn, E., Kuller, L. H., Kelsey, S. F., Cagguila, A. W., Wing, R. D. Menopause and risk factors for coronary heart disease, *New England J. Medicine* 1989, 321, 641–646.

Mazer, B., Piper, M. C., and Ramsay, M. Developmental outcome in very low birth weight infants six months to 36 months old. *J. Devel. and Behav. Pediatrics* 1988, 9(5), 293–297.

McCabe, A., and Lipscomb, T. J. Sex differences in children's verbal aggression. *Merrill-Palmer Q.* 1988, 34, 389–401.

McCabe, A. E., Siegel, L., Spence, I., and Wilkinson, A. Class inclusion reasoning: Patterns of performance from three to eight years. *Child Devel.* 1982, 53(3), 780–785.

McCubbin, H., and Dahl, B. B. *Marriage and Family.* New York: John Wiley, 1985.

McDermott, D. The relationship of parental drug use and parents' attitude concerning adolescent drug use. *Adolescence* 1984, 19(73), 89–97.

McDonald, P. What percentage of Australian marriages end in divorce? *Institute of Family Studies Newsletter* 1983, 8, 4–8.

McGhee, P. E. Development of the sense of humour in childhood: A longitudinal study. In P. E. McGhee and A. J. Chapman (Eds.), *Children's Humour.* New York: John Wiley, 1980.

McGhee, P. E., and Goldstein, J. H. (Eds.). *Handbook of Humor Research, Vol. I: Basic Issues.* New York: Springer-Verlag, 1983. (a)

McGhee, P. E., and Goldstein, J. H. (Eds.). *Handbook of Humor Research, Vol. 2: Applied Studies.* New York: Springer-Verlag, 1983. (b)

McGilly, K. and Siegler, R. S. How children choose among serial recall strategies. *Child Devel.* 1989, 60, 172–182.

McGuigan, F. J. *Calm Down: A Guide to Stress and Tension Control.* Englewood Cliffs, N.J.: Prentice-Hall, 1981.

McGuire, K. D., and Weisz, J. R. Social cognition and behavior correlates of preadolescent chumship. *Child Devel.* 1982, 53(6), 1478–1484.

McHugh, P. R. Alzheimer's disease. In J. B. Wyngaarden and L. H. Smith (Eds.), *Cecil's Textbook of Medicine* (16th ed.). Philadelphia: Saunders, 1982.

McKay, M., Rogers, P. D., Blades, J., and Goose, R. *The divorce book.* Oakland, Calif.: New Harbinger Publications, 1984.

McKenzie, S. C. *Aging and Old Age.* Glenview, Ill.: Scott, Foresman, 1980.

McKinney, J. D., and Feagans, L. (Eds.). *Current Topics in Learning Disabilities.* Norwood, N.J.: Ablex, 1983.

McLaughlin, B., White, D., McDevitt, T., and Raskin, R. Mothers' and fathers' speech to their young children: Similar or different? *J. Child Language* 1983, 10(1), 245–252.

McLoyd, V. C. Class, culture, and pretend play: A reply to Sutton-Smith and Smith. *Devel. Review* 1983, 3(1), 11–17.

McMahon, F. B., and McMahon, J. W. *Psychology: The Hybrid Science.* Homewood, Ill.: Dorsey Press, 1982.

McManus, I. C., Sik, G., Cole, D. R., Mellan, A. F. et al. The development of handedness in children. *British J. Devel. Psych.* 1988, 6, 257–273.

McPherson, B. D. *Aging as a Social Process: An Introduction to Individual and Population Aging.* Toronto: Butterworths, 1983.

McShane, J. *Learning to Talk.* Cambridge, England: Cambridge University Press, 1980.

Mead, M. *Coming of Age in Samoa.* New York: Mentor Books, 1928.

Meichenbaum, D., and Jarembko, M. E. (Eds.). *Stress Reduction and Prevention.* New York: Plenum, 1983.

Meltzer, L. An analysis of the learning styles of adolescent delinquents. *J. Learning Disabilities* 1984, 17(10), 600–608.

Mercer, R. T., Nichols, E. G., and Doyle, G. C. *Transitions in a Woman's Life: Major Events in a Developmental Context.* New York: Springer, 1989.

Mervis, C. B., and Mervis, C. A. Role of adult input in young children's category evolution: I. An observational study. *J. Child Language* 1988, 15, 257–272.

Messinger, L. *Remarriage: A Family Affair.* New York: Plenum, 1984.

Meyer, J. E. The personality characteristics of adolescents who use and misuse alcohol. *Adolescence* 1988, 23, 385–404.

Michel, G. Right-handed: A consequence of infant supine head orientation preference? *Science* 1981, 212, 685–687.

Michelozzi, B. N. *Coming Alive from Nine to Five* (2nd ed.). Palo Alto, Calif.: Mayfield, 1984.

Miles, M. S., and Crandall, E. K. The search for meaning and its potential for affecting growth in bereaved parents. *Health Values: Achieving High Level Wellness* 1983, 7(1), 19–23.

Miller, B. C., and Bowen, S. L. Father-to-newborn attachment behavior in relation to prenatal classes and presence at delivery. *Family Relations* 1982, 31, 71–78.

Miller, B. C., and Sollie, D. L. Normal stress during the transition to parenthood. *Family Relations* 1980, 29, 459–465.

Miller, G. A. *Language and Speech.* San Francisco: W. H. Freeman, 1981.

Miller, J., and Garrison, H. H. Sex roles: The division of labor at home and in the workplace. In D. H. Olson and B. C. Miller (Eds.), *Family Studies Review Yearbook* (Vol. 2). Beverly Hills, Calif.: Sage Publications, 1984.

Miller, J. B. Psychological recovery in low-income single parents. *Amer. J. Orthopsychiat.* 1982, 52(2), 346–352.

Miller, N. E., and Dollard, J. *Social Learning and Imitation.* New Haven, Conn.: Yale University Press, 1941.

Miller, P. H. *Theories of Developmental Psychology* (2nd ed.). San Francisco: W. H. Freeman, 1989.

Miller, P. H., and Weiss, M. G. Children's and adults' knowledge about what variables affect selective attention. *Child Devel.* 1981, 53, 543–549. (a)

Miller, P. H., and Weiss, M. G. Children's attention location, understanding attention, and performance on the incidental learning task. *Child Devel.* 1981, 52, 1183–1190 (b)

Miller, P. H., and Zalenski, R. Preschoolers' knowledge about attention. *Devel. Psychol.* 1982, 18(6), 871–875.

Miller, S. H. Childbearing and childrearing among the very young. *Children Today* 1984, 13(3), 26–29.

Millette, B. Menopause: A survey of attitudes and knowledge. *Issues of Health Care in Women* 1982, 3, 263–276.

Millette, B., and Hawkins, J. *The Passage through Menopause: Women's Lives in Transition.* Reston, Va: Reston Publishing, 1983.

Mills, R. K. Using Tom and Huck to develop moral reasoning in adolescents: A strategy for the classroom. *Adolescence* 1988, 23, 325–329.

Mischel, W. *Personality* (4th ed.). New York: Holt, Rinehart and Winston, 1987.

Mischel, W., and Mischel, H. N. *Essentials of Psychology.* New York: Random House, 1977.

Mitchell, G. A. *A Very Practical Guide to Discipline with Young Children.* Mt. Ranier, Md.: Gryphon House, 1982.

Mitchell, J. B. Physician visits to nursing homes. *Gerontologist* 1982, 22(1), 45–48.

Mitchell, K. The price tag of responsibility: A comparison of divorced and remarried mothers. *J. Divorce* 1983, 6(3), 33–42.

Moerk, E. L. A behavioral analysis of controversial topics in first language acquisition: Reinforcements, corrections, modeling, input frequencies, and the three-term contingency pattern. *J. Psycholing Research* 1983, 12, 129–156.

Money, J. *Love and Love Sickness.* Baltimore: Johns Hopkins University Press, 1980.

Montgomery, T. A., and Leashore, B. R. Teenage parenthood. *Urban Research Review* 1982, 8(3), 1–13.

Moody, K. *Growing Up on Television.* New York: Times Books, 1980.

Moody, R. A. *Life after Life.* New York: Bantam, 1975.

Moody, R. A. Cities of light. In R. Fulton, et al. (Eds.), *Death and Dying: Challenge and Change.* Reading, Mass.: Addison-Wesley, 1977.

Moore, C., Bryant, D., and Furrow, D. Mental terms and the development of certainty. *Child Devel.* 1989, 60, 167–171.

Moore, K. L. *The Developing Human* (2nd ed.). Philadelphia: Saunders, 1977.

Moore, P. G. Assessment of the effects of menopause on individual women: A review of the literature. *Issues in Health Care of Women* 1984, 4(6), 341–350.

Moore, S. G. Prosocial behavior in the early years: Parent and peer influences. In B. Spodek (Ed.), *Handbook of Research in Early Childhood Education.* New York: Free Press, 1982.

Morell, P., and Norton, W. T. Myelin. *Scientific American* 1980, 242(5), 89–119.

Morgan, J. D. Living our dying: Social and cultural considerations. In H. Wass, M. Berardo, and R. A. Neimeyer (Eds.), *Dying: Facing the Facts*. New York: Hemisphere, 1988.

Morris, N. M., and Udry, J. R. Validation of a self-administered instrument to assess stages of adolescent development. *J. Youth and Adolescence* 1980, 9, 271–280.

Morris, R. J., and Kratochwill, T. R. Childhood fears and phobias. In R. J. Morris and T. R. Kratochwill (Eds.), *The Practice of Child Therapy*. New York: Pergamon Press, 1983.

Morrison, G. S. *Early Childhood Education Today*. (3rd ed.). Columbus, Ohio: Charles E. Merrill, 1984.

Morrison, T. The perfect family. *Transition* 1983, 13(4), 11–13.

Morrow, P. C. Retirement preparation: A preventative approach to counseling the elderly. *Counseling and Values* 1980, 24(4), 236–246.

Mudd, E. H., and Taubin, S. Success in family living: Does it last? A twenty-year follow-up. *J. Family Therapy* 1982, 10, 59–67.

Muehlbauer, G., and Dodder, L. *The Losers: Gang Delinquency in an American Suburb*. New York: Praeger, 1983.

Mukerjee, N., and Ganguli, H. Maternal behavior of Hindu and Sikh mothers. *J. Soc. Psychol.* 1984, 124(1), 7–13.

Muller, R., and Goldberg, S. Why William doesn't want a doll: Preschoolers' expectations of adult behavior toward boys and girls. *Merrill-Palmer Q.* 1980, 26, 259–269.

Munley, A. *The Hospice Alternative: A New Context for Death and Dying*. New York: Basic Books, 1983.

Murdock, C. V. *Single Parents Are People, Too!* New York: Butterick, 1980.

Murphy, C. *Teaching Kids to Play*. New York: Leisure Press, 1983.

Murray, P. L., and Mayer, R. E. Preschool children's judgements of number magnitude. *J. Educ. Psychol.* 1988, 80, 206–209.

Murstein, B. I. Mate selection in the 1970's. *J. Marriage and the Family* 1980, 42, 777–792.

Muuss, R. E. *Theories of Adolescence* (5th ed.). New York: Random House, 1989.

Muuss, R. E. Social cognition: David Elkind's theory of adolescent egocentrism. *Adolescence* 1982, 17(66), 249–265.

Myers-Walls, J. A., and Fry-Miller, K. M. Nuclear War: Helping children overcome fears. *Young Children* 1984, 39(4), 27–32.

Nachison, J. S., and Leeds, M. H. Housing policy for older Americans in the 1980's: An overview. *J. Housing for the Elderly* 1983, 1(1), 3–13.

Naeye, R. L. Influence of maternal cigarette smoking during pregnancy on fetal and childhood growth. *J. Obstet. and Gynecol.* 1981, 57(1), 18–21.

Nandy, K. Immunologic factors. In B. Reisberg (Ed.), *Alzheimer's Disease: The Standard Reference*. New York: Free Press, 1983.

Nannarone, N. Career father. *Marriage and Family Living* 1983, 65, 8–11.

Nass, G. D., and McDonald, G. W. *Marriage and the Family* (2nd ed.). Reading, Mass.: Addison-Wesley, 1982.

National Academy of the Sciences, *Marijuana and Health*. Washington, D.C.: National Academy of the Sciences, 1982.

National Center for Health Statistics. Reported in *Marriage and Divorce Today* 1981, 7, 3–4.

National Center for Health Statistics. *Health, United States, 1982*. Public Health Service. Washington, D.C.: U.S. Government Printing Office, 1982.

National Center for Health Statistics. *Health, United States, 1984*. Public Health Service. Washington, D.C.: U.S. Government Printing Office, 1984.

National Center for Health Statistics. *Health, United States, 1986*. Public Health Service. Washington, D.C.: U.S. Government Printing Office, 1986.

National Center for Health Statistics. *Monthly Vital Statistics Report*, November, 1987, 54(4). Washington, D.C.: U.S. Government Printing Office, 1987.

National Center for Health Statistics, 1989. *Monthly Vital Statistics Report*, December 1, 1–3. Washington, D.C.: U.S. Government Printing Office, 1989.

National Council on the Aging. *Aging in the Eighties: America in Transition*. Washington, D.C.: Louis Harris, 1981.

National Institute of Health. *Cesarean Childbirth*. Consensus Development Conference Summary, Vol. 3, no. 6. Washington, D.C.: U.S. Government Printing Office, 1982.

National Institute of Mental Health. *Television and Behavior: Ten Years of Scientific Progress and Implications for the Eighties*. Washington, D.C.: U.S. Government Printing Office, 1982.

National Institute on Drug Abuse (special report on cocaine, March 9, 1981). Reported by Lang, J. S., Cocaine spreads its deadly net. *U.S. News and World Report*, March 22, 1982, 27–29.

National Research Council. Equal Employment Opportunity Commission Report. *San Francisco Chronicle* September 2, 1981.

National Research Council. *Risking the Future: Adolescent Sexuality, Pregnancy, and Childbearing*. Washington, D.C.: National Academy Press, 1987.

Neiga, B. L., and Hopkins, R. W. Adolescent suicide: Character traits of high-risk teenagers. *Adolescence* 1988, 23, 467–475.

Neimeyer, R. A. Death anxiety. In H. Wass, M. Berardo, and R. A. Neimeyer (Eds.), *Dying: Facing the Facts*. New York: Hemisphere, 1988.

Nelson, K. Individual differences in language development: Implications for development and language. *Devel. Psychol.* 1981, 17, 170–187.

Neugarten, B. L. Adult personality: Toward a psychology of life cycle. In B. L. Neugarten (Ed.), *Middle Age and Aging*. Chicago: University of Chicago Press, 1968.

Neugarten, B. L. Acting one's age: New rules for old. *Psychol. Today* April 1980, 66–80.

Neugarten, B. L., Havighurst, R. J., and Tobin, S. S. Personality and patterns of aging. In B. L. Neugarten (Ed.), *Middle Age and Aging*. Chicago: University of Chicago Press, 1968.

Neugarten, B. L., and Weinstein, K. K. The changing American grandparent. In B. L. Neugarten (Ed.), *Middle Age and Aging*. Chicago: University of Chicago Press, 1968.

Neuman, K. *Falling from Grace: The Experience of Downward Mobility in the American Middle Class*. New York: Basic Books, 1988.

Neuman, P. A., and Halvorson, P. A. *Anorexia Nervosa and Bulimia: A Handbook for Counselors and Therapists*. New York: Van Nostrand Rheinhold, 1983.

Neuringer, C., and Lettieri, D. J. *Suicidal Women: Their Thinking and Feeling Patterns*. New York: Gardner Press, 1982.

Newcomb, A. F., and Brady, J. E. Mutuality in boys' friendship relations. *Child Devel.* 1982, 53, 392–395.

Newman, B. M., and Newman, P. R. *Personality Development through the Lifespan*. Monterey, Calif.: Brooks/Cole, 1980.

Ney, P. G. Transgenerational child abuse. *Child Psychiatr. and Human Devel.* 1988, 18, 151–168.

NIAID Study Group. *Sexually Transmitted Diseases: 1980 States Report*. Washington, D.C.: U.S. Government Printing Office (NIH Publications no. 81-2213), 1981.

Nicholls, J. G. and Thorkildsen, T. A. Children's distinctions among matters of intellectual convention, logic, fact, and personal preference. *Child Devel.* 1988, 59, 939–949.

Nicholson, J. Three seasons of life. *New Society* 1980, 53, 926–928.

Nickols, S. Y., and Wanzer, L. Economic security for older women. *J. Home Economics* 1983, 75(1), 22–25.

Nicolich, L. M. Toward symbolic functioning: Structure of early pretend games and potential parallels with language. *Child Devel.* 1981, 52, 785–797.

Nielsen, T. Sexual abuse of boys: Current perspectives. *Personnel and Guidance J.* 1983, 62(3), 139–142.

Niemi, P. M. Family interaction patterns and the development of social conceptions in the adolescent. *J. Youth and Adolescence* 1988, 17(5), 429–444.

Nieva, V. F., and Gutek, B. A. *Women and Work: A Psychological Perspective*. New York: Praeger, 1981.

Nisan, M. Distributive justice and social norms. *Child Devel.* 1984, 55(3), 1020–1029.

Nisbet, R. Death. In E. S. Shneidman (Ed.), *Death: Current Perspectives* (3rd ed.). Palo Alto, Calif.: Mayfield, 1984.

Noble, E. *Having Twins: A Parent's Guide to Pregnancy, Birth and Early Childhood*. Boston: Houghton Mifflin, 1980.

Noller, P., and Callan, V. J. Understanding parent-adolescent interactions: Perceptions of family members and outsiders. *Devel. Psychol.* 1988, 24, 707–714.

Norman, D. A. *Learning and Memory*. New York: W. H. Freeman, 1982.

Norman, W. H., and Scaramella, T. J. *Mid-life: Developmental and Clinical Issues*. New York: Brunner/Mazel, 1980.

Notman, M. T. Changing roles for women in mid-life. In W. H. Norman and T. J. Scaramella (Eds.), *Mid-life: Developmental and Clinical Issues*. New York: Brunner/Mazel, 1980.

Nuernberger, P. *Freedom from Stress*. Honesdale, Pa.: Himalayan International Institute of Yoga, Science, and Philosophy Publishers, 1981.

Nunner-Winkler, G., and Sodian, B. Children's understanding of moral emotions. *Child Devel.* 1988, 59(5), 1323–1328.

Nusberg, C. Norwegian study confirms benefits of low-cholesterol diet. *Ageing International* 1982, 9(2), 18–19. (a)

Nusberg, C. World assembly seeks to alert developing countries about their aging populations. *Ageing International* 1982, 9(2), 7–9. (b)

Nusberg, C. Filial responsibility still required in Hungary. *Ageing International* 1983, 9(4), 8–9.

Nusberg, C. Acceptance of death facilitated by supportive Dutch physicians. *Ageing International* 1984, 11(2), 2–3.

Nusberg, C. Pensioners urged to work in the Soviet Union. *Ageing International* 1986, Winter, 4–5.

Nye, I. F. *Runaways: A Report for Parents* (Extension Bulletin no. 0743). Pullman: Washington State University, 1980.

Nye, I. F., and Lamberts, M. B. *School-Age Parenthood*. Pullman: Washington State University Cooperative Extension, 1980.

Oakland, T. *Divorced Fathers: Reconstructing a Quality Life*. New York: Human Sciences Press, 1984.

Oberleder, M. *Live Longer, Live Better: Avoid the Aging Trap and Feel Good at Any Age*. Washington, D.C.: Acropolis Books, 1982.

O'Brien, S. *Child Abuse and Neglect: Everyone's Problem*. Wheaton, Md.: Association for Childhood Education International, 1984.

O'Brien, S. F., and Bierman, K. L. Conceptions and perceived influence of peer groups: Interviews with preadolescents and adolescents. *Child Devel.* 1988, 59(5), 1360–1365.

Occupational Outlook Handbook. Bureau of Labor Statistics. Division of Occupational Outlook. Washington, D.C.: U.S. Department of Labor, 1982.

O'Connell, M., and Bloom, D. E. *Juggling Jobs and Babies: America's Child Care Challenge*. Washington, D.C.: Population Reference Bureau, 1987.

O'Connor, N. *Letting Go with Love: The Grieving Process*. Apache Junction, Ariz.: La Mariposa Press, 1984.

O'Connor, R. *Choosing for Health*. New York: Holt, Rinehart and Winston, 1980.

O'Kane, M. L. *Living with Adult Children*. St. Paul, Minn.: Diction Books, 1981.

Okun, B. F. *Working with Adults: Individual, Family and Career Development*. Monterey, Calif.: Brooks/Cole, 1984.

Oliver, D. Why do people live together? *J. Soc. Welfare* 1982, 7, 209–222.

Oller, D. K., and Eilers, R. E. Similarity of babbling in Spanish- and English-learning babies. *J. Child Language* 1982, 9(3), 565–577.

Olsho, L. Auditory frequency discrimination in infancy. *Devel. Psychol.* 1982, 18(5), 721–726.

Olson, L. K. *The Political Economy of Aging: The State, Private Power, and Social Welfare.* New York: Columbia University Press, 1982.

O'Neill, C. Families threaten, hit, hurt one another. *Family Therapy News* 1983, 14(4), 1–2.

Onyehalv, A. S. Inadequacy of sex knowledge of adolescents: Implications for counseling and sex education. *Adolescence* 1983, 18(71), 627–630.

Orr, M. T. Sex education and contraceptive education in U.S. public schools. *Family Planning Perspectives* 1982, 14, 304–313.

Ortega, D. F., and Pipal, J. E. Challenge seeking and the Type A coronary-prone behavior pattern. *J. Personality and Soc. Psychol.* 1984, 46(6), 1328–1334.

Orthner, D. K. *Intimate Relationships.* Reading, Mass.: Addison-Wesley, 1981.

Osako, M. Japanese workers resist early retirement. *Ageing International* 1986, Winter, 33–34.

OsKamp, S., and Mindick, B. Personality and attitudinal barriers to contraception. In D. Byrne and W. A. Fisher (Eds.), *Adolescents, Sex, and Contraception.* New York: McGraw-Hill, 1981.

Overton, W. Cognitive development. In R. Montemayor, G. Adams, and T. Gullota (Eds.), *Advances in Adolescent Research* (Vol. 2). Orlando, Fla.: Academic Press, 1989.

Owvamanam, D. O. Providing for job tenure, job satisfaction and productivity in teachers. *Adolescence* 1984, 19(7), 221–224.

Page, C. *Your Retirement: How to Plan for a Secure Future.* New York: Arco Publishing, 1984.

Page, D. C., Mosher, R., Simpson, E. M., Fisher, E. M. C., Mardon, G., Pollack, J., and Brown, L. G. The sex-determining region of the human Y chromosome encodes a finger protein. *Cell* 1987, 51, 1091–1104.

Page, R. A. Longitudinal evidence for the sequentiality of Kohlberg's stages of moral judgment in adolescent males. *J. Genet. Psychol.* 1981, 139(1), 3–9.

Palmore, E. *Social Patterns in Normal Aging.* Durham, N.C.: Duke University Press, 1981.

Papini, D. R., Sebby, R. A., and Clark, S. Affective quality of family relations and adolescent identity exploration. *Adolescence* 1989, 24, 457–466.

Parikh, B. Development of moral judgment and its relation to family environmental factors in Indian and American families. *Child Devel.* 1980, 51, 1030–1039.

Paris, S. G., and Lindauer, B. K. The development of cognitive skills during childhood. In B. Wolman (Ed.), *Handbook of Developmental Psychology.* Englewood Cliffs, N.J.: Prentice-Hall, 1982.

Parke, R. D. *Fathers.* Cambridge, Mass.: Harvard University Press, 1981.

Parke, R. D. The role of the family in the development of peer relations. In K. Kreppner and R. M. Lerner (Eds.), *Family Systems and Lifespan Development.* Hillsdale, N.J.: Erlbaum, 1989.

Parke, R. D., and Slaby, R. G. The development of aggression. In P. H. Mussen (Ed.), *Handbook of Child Psychology* (4th ed.), Vol. 4: E. M. Hetherington (Ed.), *Socialization, Personality, and Social Development.* New York: John Wiley, 1983.

Parker, J. G., and Gottwan, J. M. Social and emotional development in a relational context: Friendship interaction from early childhood to adolescence. In T. J. Berndt and G. W. Ladd (Eds.), *Peer Relationships in Child Development.* New York: Wiley, 1989.

Parker, S. *Work and Retirement.* Winchester, Mass.: Allen and Unwin, 1982.

Parkes, C. M., and Weiss, R. S. *Recovery from Bereavement.* New York: Basic Books, 1983.

Parnes, H. *Work and Retirement: A Longitudinal Study of Men.* Cambridge, Mass.: MIT Press, 1981.

Parr, S. R. *The Moral of the Story: Literature, Values and American Education.* New York: Columbia Teacher's College Press, 1982.

Parrot, A. Sex education. In H. Feldman and A. Parrot (Eds.), *Human Sexuality: Contemporary Perspectives.* Beverly Hills, Calif.: Sage Publications, 1984.

Parrot, A. and Ellis, M. J. Homosexuals should be allowed to marry and adopt and rear children. In H. Feldman and M. Feldman (Eds.), *Current Controversies in Marriage and Family.* Beverly Hills, Calif.: Sage Publications, 1985.

Pasley, K., and Ihinger-Tallman, M. *Remarriage and Stepparenting: Current Research and Theory.* New York: Guilford, 1989.

Patterson, C. J., and Kister, M. C. The development of listener skills for referential communication. In W. P. Dickson (Ed.), *Children's Oral Communication Skills.* New York: Academic Press, 1981.

Patterson, R. L. *Overcoming Deficits of Aging: A Behavioral Approach.* New York: Plenum, 1982.

Pattison, E. M. The experience of dying. In E. M. Pattison (Ed.), *The Experience of Dying.* Englewood Cliffs, N.J.: Prentice-Hall, 1977.

Paul, W. (Ed.). *Homosexuality: Social, Psychological, and Biological Issues.* Beverly Hills, Calif.: Sage Publications, 1982.

Payton, I. Single-parent households: An alternative approach. *Family Economics Review*, Winter 1982, 11–16.

Pearlin, L. I. The social context of stress. In L. Goldberger and S. Breznitz (Eds.), *Handbook of Stress.* New York: Free Press, 1982.

Pearson, D., and Shaw, S. *Life Extension: A Practical Scientific Approach.* New York: Warner Books, 1982.

Peck, R. C. Psychological developments in the second half of life. In B. L. Neugarten (Ed.), *Middle Age and Aging.* Chicago: University of Chicago Press, 1968.

Pederson, F. A. (Ed.). *The Father–Infant Relationship: Observational Studies in the Family Setting.* New York: Praeger, 1980.

Pellegrini, A. D. Elementary-school children's rough and tumble play and social competence. *Develop. Psychol.* 1988, 24, 802–806.

Pelletier, K. R. *Longevity: Fulfilling Our Biological Potential.* New York: Delacorte Press, 1981.

Peplau, L. A. What homosexuals want. *Psychol. Today* March, 1981, 28–38.

Peplau, L. A. Roles and gender. In H. H. Kelley, (Ed.), *Close Relationships.* New York: W. H. Freeman, 1983.

Peplau, L. A., and Cochran, S. D. Sex differences in values concerning love relationships. Paper presented at the annual meeting of the American Psychological Association, Montreal, 1980.

Peplau, L. A., and Cochran, S. D. Value orientations in the intimate relationships of gay men. *Journal of Homosexuality,* 1981, 6, 1–19.

Peplau, L. A., and Gordon, S. L. The intimate relationships of lesbians and gay men. In E. R. Allgeier and N. B. McCormick (Eds.), *Changing boundaries: Gender roles and sexual behavior.* Palo Alto, Calif.: Mayfield, 1983.

Perry, D. G., and Bussey, K. *Social Development.* Englewood Cliffs, N.J.: Prentice-Hall, 1984.

Perry, D. G., Perry, L. C., and Weiss, R. J. Sex differences in the consequences that children anticipate for aggression. *Develop. Psychol.* 1989, 25, 312–319.

Pesmen, C. *How a Man Ages.* New York: Ballantine, 1984.

Peters, A. M. *The Units of Language Acquisition.* New York: Cambridge University Press, 1982.

Peters, D. L., Hodges, W. L., and Nolan, M. E. Statewide evaluation of child care: Problems and benefits. *Young Children* 1980, 35(3), 3–14.

Peters, S. O. Child sexual abuse and later psychological problems. In G. E. Wyatt and G. J. Powell (Eds.), *Lasting Effects of Child Sexual Abuse.* Beverly Hills, Calif.: Sage Publications, 1988.

Petersen, A. C. Those gangly years. *Psychol. Today* June, 1987, 28–34.

Petersen, A. C. Pubertal change and psychosocial development. In D. L. Baltes, R. M. Featherman, and R. M. Lerner (Eds.), *Lifespan Development and Behavior* (Vol. 9). New York: Academic Press, 1988.

Petersen, A., and Taylor, B. The biological approach to adolescence: Biological change and psychological adaptation. In J. Adelson (Ed.), *Handbook of Adolescent Psychology.* New York: John Wiley, 1980.

Peterson, L. and Lewis, K. E. Preventive intervention to improve children's discrimination of the persuasive tactics in televised advertising. *J. Pediatric Psychol.* 1988, 13, 163–170.

Peterson, L. S. Keeping work out of family life. *Family Therapy News* 1982, 13(6), 1–3.

Pett, M. A., Caserta, M. S., Hutton, A. P. and Lund, D. A. Intergenerational conflict: Middle-aged women caring for demented older relatives. *Amer. J. Orthopsychiat.* 1988, 58, 405–417.

Pezdek, K., and Miceli, L. Life-span differences in memory integration as a function of processing time. *Devel. Psychol.* 1982, 18(3), 485–490.

Pfouts, J. Birth order, age spacing, I. Q. differences, and family relations. *J. Marriage and Family,* August, 1980, 519–525.

Phillips, E. L. *Stress, Health, and Psychological Problems in the Major Professions.* Washington, D.C.: University Press of America, 1982.

Piaget, J. *The Moral Judgment of the Child* (Trans. M. Gabain). New York: Harcourt, 1932.

Piaget, J. *Play, Dreams and Imitation in Children.* New York: W. W. Norton, 1951.

Piaget, J. Piaget's theory. In P. H. Mussen (Ed.), *Handbook of Child Psychology* (4th ed.), Vol. 1: W. Kessen (Ed.), *History, Theory, and Methods.* New York: John Wiley, 1983.

Piaget, J., and Inhelder, B. *The Child's Conception of Space.* London: Routledge, 1956.

Piers, M. W., and Landau, G. M. *The Gift of Play: And Why Young Children Can't Live Without It.* New York: Walker, 1980.

Pinard, A. *The Concept of Conservation.* Chicago: University of Chicago Press, 1981.

Pines, A., and Aronson, E. *Burnout: From Tedium to Personal Growth.* New York: Free Press, 1980.

Pines, A., and Aronson, E. *Career Burnout: Causes and Cures.* New York: The Free Press, 1988.

Pipes, P. L. *Nutrition in Infancy and Childhood.* St. Louis: C. V. Mosby, 1981.

Pitcher, E. G., and Schultz, L. H. *Boys and Girls at Play: The Development of Sex Roles.* New York: Praeger, 1983.

Pitcher, E. G., Feinberg, S. G., and Alexander, D. *Helping young children learn* (4th ed.). Columbus, Ohio: Charles E. Merrill, 1984.

Pittman, F. S. *Turning Points: Treating Families in Transition and Crisis.* New York: Norton, 1987.

Pittman, T. S., Boggiano, A. K., and Rubble, D. N. Intrinsic and extrinsic motivational orientations: Limiting conditions on the undermining and enhancing effects of reward on intrinsic motivation. In J. M. Levine and M. C. Wang (Eds.), *Teacher and Student Perceptions: Implications for Learning.* Hillsdale, N.J.: Erlbaum, 1983.

Platt, C. B., and MacWhinney, B. Error assimilation as a mechanism in language learning. *J. Child Language* 1983, 10, 401–414.

Pleck, J. H. Changing patterns of work and family roles. Paper presented at the American Psychological Association's annual meeting, Los Angeles, August 24–25, 1981.

Plomin, R. Environment and genes: Determinants of behavior. *Amer. Psychol.* 1989, 44, 105–111.

Plomin, R., and Foch, T. T. Sex differences and individual differences. *Child Devel.* 1981, 52, 383–385.

Plomin, R., McClearn, G. E., Pederson, N. L., Nesselroade, J. R., et al. Genetic influence on childhood family environment perceived retrospectively from the last half of the life span. *Devel. Psychol.* 1988, 24, 738–745.

Pocs, O., and Walsh, R. (Eds.). *Marriage and Family 85/86.* Guilford, Conn.: Dushkin, 1985.

Polonko, K. A., Scanzoni, J., and Teachman, J. D. Child-lessness and marital satisfaction. *J. Family Issues* 1982, 3(4), 545–573.

Population Reference Bureau. *U.S. Population: Where We Are, Where We're Going.* Washington, D.C.: Population Bureau, 1982.

Population Reference Bureau. *Population Handbook* (2nd ed.). Washington, D.C.: Population Bureau, 1985.

Porter, S. Your money. *San Francisco Chronicle* April 1, 1980.

Postman, N. *The Disappearance of Childhood.* New York: Delacorte Press, 1982.

Powell, L. S., and Courtice, K. *Alzheimer's Disease.* Reading, Mass.: Addison-Wesley, 1983.

Prentice, R. S. White collar working women's perception of retirement. *Gerontologist* 1980, 20, 90–95.

Pressley, M. Elaboration and memory development. *Child Devel.* 1982, 53, 296–309.

Pribram, K. H. The biology of emotions and other feelings. In R. Plutchik and H. Kellerman (Eds.), *Emotion: Theory, Research, and Experience* (Vol. 1). New York: Academic Press, 1980.

Price, J. Who waits to have children? In J. Rosenfeld (Ed.), *The Marriage and Family Reader.* Glenview, Ill.: Scott, Foresman, 1982.

Price, S. J., and McKenry, P. C. *Divorce.* Beverly Hills, Calif.: Sage Publications, 1988.

Price-Bonham, S., and Balswick, J. O. The noninstitutions: Divorce, desertion, and remarriage. *J. Marriage and the Family* 1980, 42, 959–972.

Pruett, K. D. *The Nurturing Father.* New York: Warner, 1987.

Putallaz, M., and Gottman, J. M. Social skills and group acceptance. In S. R. Asher and J. M. Gottman (Eds.), *The Development of Children's Friendships.* Cambridge, England: Cambridge University Press, 1981.

Putallaz, M., and Wasserman, A. Children's naturalistic entry behavior and sociometric status: A developmental perspective. *Devel. Psychol.* 1989, 25, 297–305.

Rabin, A. I., and Beit-Hallahmi, B. *Twenty Years Later: Kibbutz Children Grown Up.* New York: Springer, 1982.

Radin, N. Childrearing fathers in intact families: Some antecedents and consequences. *Merrill-Palmer Q.* 1981, 27(4), 489–514.

Radloff, L. S. Depression and the empty nest. *Sex Roles A Journal of Research* 1980, 6, 6.

Raether, H. C., and Slater, R. C. Immediate postdeath activities in the United States. H. Feifel (Ed.), *New Meanings of Death.* New York: McGraw-Hill, 1977.

Raphael, B. *The Anatomy of Bereavement.* New York: Basic Books, 1983.

Rathus, S. A., and Nevid, J. S. *Adjustment and Growth: The Challenges of Life* (2nd ed.). New York: Holt, Rinehart and Winston, 1983.

Rattner, H. H., Padgett, R. J., and Bushey, N. Old and young adults' recall of events. *Devel. Psychol.* 1988, 24, 664–671.

Read, K., and Patterson, J. *Nursery School and Kindergarten: Human Relations and Learning* (7th ed.). New York: Holt, Rinehart and Winston, 1980.

Reardon, P., and Bushnell, E. M. Infants' sensitivity to arbitrary pairings of color and taste. *Infant Behavior and Development* 1988, 11(2), 245–250.

Reed, S. K. *Cognition: Theory and Application.* Monterey, Calif.: Brooks/Cole, 1982.

Reedy, M. N. Personality and aging. In D. S. Woodruff and J. E. Birren (Eds.), *Aging: Scientific Perspectives and Social Issues* (2nd ed.). Monterey, Calif: Brooks/Cole, 1983.

Reichard, S., Livson, F., and Peterson, P. C. *Aging and Personality.* New York: John Wiley, 1962.

Reichenbach, L., and Masters, J. C. Children's use of expressive and contextural cues in judgments of emotion. *Child Devel.* 1983, 54(4), 993–1004.

Reidy, T. J. The aggressive characteristics of abused and neglected children. In G. J. Williams and J. Money (Eds.), *Traumatic Abuse and Neglect of Children at Home.* Baltimore: Johns Hopkins University Press, 1980.

Reifler, B. V., and Eisdorfer, C. A clinic for the impaired elderly and their families. *Amer. J. Psychiat.* 1980, 137, 1399–1403.

Reis, H. T., and Wright, S. Knowledge of sex-role stereotypes in children aged 3–5. *Sex Roles* 1982, 8, 10–49.

Reisberg, B. *Brain Failure: An Introduction to Current Concepts of Senility,* New York: Free Press, 1981.

Reisberg, B. (Ed.). *Alzheimer's Disease: The Standard Reference.* New York: Free Press, 1983. (a)

Reisberg, B. An overview of current concepts of Alzheimer's disease, senile dementia, and age-associated cognitive decline. In B. Reisberg (Ed.), *Alzheimer's Disease: The Standard Reference.* New York: Free Press, 1983. (b).

Reisman, J. E. Touch, motion, and proprioception. In P. Salapatek and L. Cohen (Eds.), *Handbook of Infant Perception: Vol. 1. From Sensation to Perception.* Orlando, Fla.: Harcourt Brace Jovanovich, 1987.

Reisman, J. M. Adult friendships. In S. Duck and R. Gilmour (Eds.), *Personal Relationships.* New York: Academic Press, 1981.

Reiss, I. L. *Premarital Sexual Standards in America.* New York: Free Press, 1960.

Reiss, I. L. *Family Systems in America* (3rd ed.). New York: Holt, Rinehart and Winston, 1980.

Reiss, I. L. Some observations on ideology and sexuality in America. *J. Marriage and the Family* 1981, 43, 271–283.

Reite, M., Kaemingk, K., and Boccia, M. L. Maternal separation in bonnet monkey infants: Altered attachment and social support. *Child Devel.* 1989, 60, 473–480.

Renvoize, J. *Going solo: Single mothers by choice.* London: Routledge and Kegan Paul, 1985.

Renvoize, J. *Incest: A Family Pattern.* London: Routledge and Kegan Paul, 1982.

Rest, J. R. The impact of higher education on moral judgment development. Paper presented at the convention of the American Educational Research Association, Los Angeles, April 1981.

Rest, J. R. Morality. In P. H. Mussen (Ed.), *Handbook of Child Psychology* (4th ed.), Vol. 3: J. H. Flavell and E. M. Markman (Eds.), *Cognitive Development*. New York: John Wiley, 1983.

Rest, J. R. *Moral Development: Advances in Theory and Research*. New York: Praeger, 1986.

Rheingold, H. L., and Adams, J. L. The significance of speech to newborns. *Devel. Psychol.* 1980, 16(5), 397–403.

Rhodes, C., and Vedder, C. B. *An Introduction to Thanatology: Death and Dying in American Society*. Springfield, Ill.: Chas. C. Thomas, 1983.

Ribordy, S. C., Camras, L. A., Stefani, R., and Spaccarelli, S. Vignettes for emotional recognition research and affective therapy with children. *J. Clin. Child Psychol.* 1988, 17(4), 322–325.

Rice, K. M., and Blanchard, E. B. Biofeedback in the treatment of anxiety disorders. *Clin. Psychol. Review* 1982, 2, 557–577.

Rice, M. The role of television in language acquisition. *Devel. Review* 1983, 3(2), 211–224.

Rice, M. L. Children's language acquisition. *Amer. Psychologist* 1989, 44, 149–156.

Richards, F. A., and Commons, M. L. Systematic, metasystematic, and cross-paradigmatic reasoning: A case for stages of reasoning beyond formal operations. In M. L. Commons, F. A. Richards, and S. Armon (Eds.), *Beyond Formal Operations: Late Adolescent and Adult Cognitive Development*. New York: Praeger, 1982.

Richards, R. A. A comparison of selected Guilford and Wallach-Kogan creative thinking tests in conjunction with measures of intelligence. *J. Creative Behav.* 1976, 10, 151–164.

Richardson, G. A., Day, N. L., and Taylor, P. M. The effect of prenatal alcohol, marijuana, and tobacco exposure on neonatal behavior. *Infant Behavior and Development* 1989, 12, 199–209.

Richardson, T. F. Anorexia nervosa: An overview. *Amer. J. Nursing* 1980, 80, 1470–1471.

Richarz, A. S. *Understanding Children Through Observation*. St. Paul: West Publishing, 1980.

Richey, M. H., and Richey, H. W. The significance of best-friend relationships in adolescence. *Psychol. in the Schools* 1980, 17, 536–540.

Rickel, A. U. *Teen Pregnancy and Parenting*. New York: Hemisphere, 1989.

Ridenour, M. V. (Ed.). *Motor Development: Issues and Applications*. Princeton, N.J.: Princeton Book Company, 1980.

Rierdan, J., and Koff, E. The psychological impact of menarche: Integrative versus disruptive changes. *J. Youth and Adolescence* 1980, 9, 49–58.

Riggs, M. L. *Jump for Joy: Helping Children Grow Through Active Play*. Englewood Cliffs, N.J.: Prentice-Hall, 1980.

Rikers, H. C., and Myers, J. E. *Retirement Counseling*. New York: Hemisphere, 1989.

Ring, K. *Life At Death: A Scientific Investigation of the Near Death Experience*. New York: Coward, McCann and Geoghegan, 1980.

Ring, K. *Heading Toward Omega: In Search of the Meaning of the Near-Death Experience*. New York: Morrow, 1984.

Ringler, N. M. The development of language and how adults talk to children. *Infant Mental Health Journal*, 1981, 2, 71–83.

Roberts, R. J., Jr., and Patterson, C. Perspective taking and referential communication: The question of correspondence reconsidered. *Child Devel.* 1983, 54, 1005–1014.

Robinson, I. E., and Jedlicka, D. Change in sexual attitudes and behavior of college students from 1965 to 1980: A research note. *J. Marriage and the Family*, February 1982, 237–240.

Rogers, C. R. *On Becoming a Person*. Boston: Houghton Mifflin, 1961.

Rogers, D. *The Adult Years: An Introduction* (2nd ed.). Englewood Cliffs, N.J.: Prentice-Hall, 1982.

Rogers, J. L., and Rowe, D. C. Influence of siblings on adolescent sexual behavior. *Devel. Psychol.* 1988, 24, 722–728.

Rogoff, B. *Apprenticeship in Thinking: Cognitive Development in a Social Context*. New York: Oxford University Press, 1989.

Rollins, B. C. Marital quality at midlife. In S. Hunter and M. Sundell (Eds.), *Midlife Myths: Issues, Findings, and Practical Implications*. Beverly Hills, Calif.: Sage Publications, 1989.

Roman, M., and Raley, P. E. *The Indelible Family*. New York: Rawson, Wade, 1980.

Romeo, F. F. Adolescence, sexual conflict and anorexia nervosa. *Adolescence* 1984, 19(75), 551–555.

Roos, P. A. Marriage and women's occupational attainment in cross-cultural perspective. *Amer. Sociol. Review* 1983, 48(6), 852–864.

Roscoe, B., Cavanaugh, L. E., and Kennedy, D. R. Dating infidelity: Behaviors, reasons and consequences. *Adolescence*, 23, 35–43.

Rose, S., and Larwood, L. (Eds.), *Women's Careers: Pathways and Pitfalls*. Westport, Conn.: Greenwood Press, 1988.

Rose, S. A. Differential rates of visual information processing in full-term and preterm infants. *Child Devel.* 1983, 54(5), 1189–1198.

Rose, S. A. Shape recognition in infancy: Visual integration of sequential information. *Child Devel.* 1988, 59(5), 1161–1176.

Rose, S. A., Feldman, J. F., McCarton, C. M., and Wolfson, J. Information processing in seven-month-old infants as a function of risk status. *Child Devel.* 1988, 59, 589–603.

Rosenbaum, J. L. Family dysfunction and female delinquency. *Crime and Delinquency* 1989, 35, 31–44.

Rosenberg, E. Beyond the facts: Sexuality education in junior high/middle school. In C. Cassell and P. M.

Wilson (Eds.), *Sexuality Education*. New York: Garland Publishing, 1989.

Rosenman, R. H., and Chesney, M. A. The relationship of type A behavior pattern to coronary heart disease. *Activitas Nervosa Superior* 1980, 22, 1–45.

Rosenman, R. H., and Chesney, M. A. Stress, type A behavior, and coronary disease. In L. Goldberger and S. Breznitz (Eds.), *Handbook of Stress*. New York: Free Press, 1982.

Rosenstein, D., and Oster, H. Differential facial response to four basic tastes in newborns. *Child Devel.* 1988, 59, 1555–1568.

Rosenthal, E. (Ed.). *Women, Aging, and Ageism*. New York: Harrington Park Press, 1990.

Rosenthal, E., and Keshet, H. F. *Fathers Without Partners*. New York: Rowman and Littlefield, 1980.

Roskies, E. Considerations in developing a treatment program for the coronary-prone type A behavior pattern. In P. O. Davidson and S. M. Davidson (Eds.), *Behavioral Medicine: Changing Health Life Styles*. New York: Brunner/Mazel, 1980.

Ross, M. W., Paulsen, J. A., and Stalstrom, O. W. Homosexuality and mental health: A cross-cultural review. In M. W. Ross (Ed.), *The Treatment of Homosexuals with Mental Health Disorders*. New York: Harrington Park Press, 1988.

Rothenberg, P. S. *Racism and Sexism: An Integrated Study*. New York: St. Martin's Press, 1988.

Rothstein-Fisch, C., and Howes, C. Toddler peer interaction in mixed-age groups. *J. Applied Devel. Psychol.* 1988, 9, 211–218.

Roug, L., Landberg, I., and Lundberg, L. J. Phonetic development in early infancy: A study of four Swedish children during the first eighteen months of life. *J. Child Language* 1989, 16, 19–40.

Rovet, J., and Netley, C. The triple X chromosome syndrome in childhood: Recent empirical findings. *Child Devel.* 1983, 54, 831–845.

Rowe, D. *The Construction of Life and Death*. New York: John Wiley, 1982.

Rubenstein, C. Real men don't earn less than their wives. *Psychol. Today* 1982, 5, 36–41.

Rubenstein, C. The modern art of courtly love. *Psychol. Today* 1983, 17, 40–49.

Rubenstein, C., and Shaver, P. *In Search of Intimacy*. New York: Delacorte Press, 1982.

Rubin, K. H. Fantasy play: Its role in the development of social skills and social cognition. In K. H. Rubin (Ed.), *Children's Play: New Directions for Child Development*. San Francisco: Jossey-Bass, 1980.

Rubin, K. H., and Everett, B. Social perspective-taking in young children. In S. G. Moore and C. R. Cooper (Eds.), *The Young Child: Reviews of Research* (Vol. 3). Washington, D.C.: National Association for the Education of Young Children, 1982.

Rubin, R. H. It is important that both men and women have premarital sex, especially with the person they are considering for marriage. In I. H. Feldman and M. Feldman (Eds.), *Current controversies in marriage and family*. Beverly Hills, Calif.: Sage Publications, 1985.

Rubin, Z. *Children's Friendships*. Cambridge, Mass.: Harvard University Press, 1980. (a)

Rubin, Z. Self disclosure in dating couples: Sex roles and the ethic of openness. *J. Marriage and the Family* 1980, 42, 305–317. (b)

Ruble, D. N., Fleming, A. S., Hackel, L. S., and Stangor, C. Changes in the marital relationship during the transition to firsttime motherhood: Effects of violated expectations concerning division of household labor. *J. Personality and Social Psychol.* 1988, 55, 78–87.

Ruffenach, G. Nursing home care as a work benefit. *Wall Street Journal* June 30, 1988, 23–25.

Rushton, J. P. *Altruism, Socialization, and Society*. Englewood Cliffs, N.J.: Prentice-Hall, 1980.

Russell, G. Highly participant Australian fathers: Some preliminary findings. *Merrill-Palmer Q.* 1982, 28(1), 137–156.

Russell, G. *The Changing Role of Fathers?* Lawrence, Mass.: Queensland University Press, 1983.

Russo, N. F., and Cassidy, M. M. Women in science and technology. In I. Tinker (Ed.), *Women in Washington: Advocates for Public Policy*. Sage Yearbooks in Women's Policy Studies (Vol. 7). Beverly Hills, Calif.: Sage Publications, 1983.

Ryan, K., and Cooper, J. M. *Those who can, teach* (3rd ed.). Boston: Houghton Mifflin, 1980.

Sabom, M. B. *Recollections of death: A medical investigation*. New York: Harper & Row, 1982.

Sack, A. R., Keller, J. F., and Kinkle, D. E. Premarital sexual intercourse: A test of the effects of peer group, religiosity, and sexual guilt. *J. Sex Research* 1984, 20, 168–185.

Sager, C. J. *Treating the Remarried Family*. New York: Brunner/Mazel, 1983.

Sagi, A. Mothers' and non-mothers' identification of infant cries. *Infant Behav. and Devel.* 1981, 4(1), 37–40.

Sahler, O. J. Z. Adolescent parenting: Potential for child abuse and neglect. *Ped. Ann.* 1980, 9(3), 67–75.

Saltzstein, H. D. Critical issues in Kohlberg's theory of moral reasoning. *Monographs of the Society for Research in Child Development* 1983, 48(1–2, serial no. 200), 108–119.

Sanders, G. F., and Mullis, R. L. Family influences on sexual attitudes and knowledge as reported by college students. *Adolescence* 1988, 23(92), 837–846.

Sanoff, H. *Planning Outdoor Play: A Manual Organized to Provide Design Assistance to Community Groups*. Atlanta, Ga.: Humanics Limited, 1982.

Santrock, J., Warshak, R., Lindbergh, C., and Meadows, L. Children's and parents' observed social behavior in stepfather families. *Child Devel.* 1982, 53, 472–480.

Sarason, I. G., and Sarason, B. R. *Abnormal Psychology* (6th ed.). Englewood Cliffs, N.J.: Prentice-Hall, 1989.

Sarnoff, I., and Sarnoff, S. *Love-centered Marriage in a Self-centered World*. New York: Hemisphere Publishers, 1989.

Sarrel, L. J., and Sarrel, P. M. *Sexual Turning Points: The Seven Stages of Adult Sexuality.* New York: Macmillan, 1984.

Saul, S. C., and Scherman, A. Divorce grief and personal adjustment in divorced persons who remarry or remain single. *J. Divorce* 1984, 7(3), 75–85.

Saunders, C. St. Christopher's Hospice. In E. S. Schneidman (Ed.), *Death: Current Perspectives* (3rd ed.). Palo Alto, Calif.: Mayfield, 1984.

Sax, G. *Principles of Educational and Psychological Measurement.* Belmont, Calif.: Wadsworth, 1989.

Saxe, G. B., and Sicilian, G. Children's interpretation of their counting accuracy: A developmental analysis. *Child Devel.* 1981, 52, 1330–1332.

Saxton, L. *The Individual, Marriage, and the Family* (7th ed.). Belmont, Calif.: Wadsworth, 1990.

Saxton, L. *The Individual, Marriage, and the Family* (5th ed.). Belmont, Calif.: Wadsworth, 1983.

Scanzoni, J., and Fox, G. L. Sex roles, family, and society: The seventies and beyond. *J. Marriage and the Family* 1980, 11, 34–39.

Scarf, M. *Unfinished Business.* Garden City, N.Y.: Doubleday, 1980.

Schacter, F. F., and Strage, A. A. Adult's talk and children's language development. In S. G. Moore and C. R. Cooper (Eds.), *The Young Child: Reviews of Research* (Vol. 3). Washington, D.C.: National Association for the Education of Young Children, 1982.

Schaie, K. W. A general model for the study of developmental problems. *Psychol. Bull.* 1965, 64, 92–107.

Schaie, K. W. The primary mental abilities in adulthood: An exploration of psychometric intelligence. In P. B. Baltes and O. G. Brim, Jr. (Eds.), *Life-span Development and Behavior* (Vol. 2). New York: Academic Press, 1979.

Schaie, K. W. Intelligence and problem-solving. In J. Birren and R. B. Sloane (Eds.), *Handbook of Mental Health and Aging.* Englewood Cliffs, N.J.: Prentice-Hall, 1980.

Schaie, K. W. The Seattle longitudinal study: A twenty-one year exploration of psychometric intelligence in adulthood. In K. W. Schaie (Ed.), *Longitudinal Studies of Adult Psychological Development.* New York: Guilford Press, 1982.

Schaie, K. W. Age changes in adult intelligence. In D. S. Woodruff and J. E. Birren (Eds.), *Aging: Scientific Perspectives and Social Issues* (2nd ed.). Monterey, Calif.: Brooks/Cole, 1983.

Schaie, K. W. Midlife influences upon intellectual functioning in old age. *Int. J. Behav. Devel.* 1984, 7(4), 463–478.

Schaie, K. W. Individual differences in rate of cognitive change in adulthood. In V. L. Bengston and K. Warner Schaie (Eds.), *The Course of Later Life: Research and Reflections.* New York: Springer, 1989.

Schaefer, C. E., and Millman, H. L. *How to Help Children with Common Problems.* New York: Van Nostrand Rheinhold, 1981.

Schank, R. C. *Dynamic Memory.* New York: Cambridge University Press, 1982.

Scheibel, A. B. Dendritic changes with Alzheimer's disease. In B. Reisberg (Ed.), *Alzheimer's Disease: The Standard Reference.* New York: Free Press, 1983.

Scheinfeld, A. *The New You and Heredity.* Philadelphia: Lippincott, 1950.

Schiller, P. New advances in sex education. In P. Forleo and W. Pasini (Eds.), *Medical Sexology.* Littleton, Mass.: PSG Publishing, 1980.

Schinzel, A. (1984). *Catalogue of Unbalanced Chromosome Aberrations in Men.* Berlin: Walter de Gruyter, 1984.

Schlaadt, R. G., and Shannon, P. T. *Drugs of Choice.* Englewood Cliffs, N.J.: Prentice-Hall, 1982.

Schleimer, K. Anorexia nervosa. *Nutrition Review* 1981, 38, 99–103.

Schlossberg, N. K. A model for analyzing human adaptation to transition. *The Counseling Psychologist* 1981, 9, 2–18.

Schlossberg, N. K. *Overwhelmed: Coping with Life's Ups and Downs.* Lexington, Mass.: Lexington Books, 1989.

Schmidt, C. R., Ollendick, T. H., and Stanowicz, L. B. Developmental changes in the influence of assigned goals on cooperation and competition. *Devel. Psychol.* 1988, 24, 574–579.

Schmidt, C. R., and Paris, S. G. The development of children's communication skills. In H. Reese and L. Lipsitt (Eds.), *Advances in Child Development and Behavior.* New York: Academic Press, 1983.

Schmidt, R. *Motor Skills.* New York: Harper & Row, 1975.

Schmidt, R. *Motor Control and Learning: A Behavioral Emphasis.* Champaign, Ill.: Human Kinetics, 1982.

Schneck, M., Reisberg, B., and Ferris, S. An overview of current concepts of Alzheimer's disease. *Amer. J. Psychiat.* 1982, 139, 165–173.

Schneider, J. *Stress, Loss, and Grief: Understanding Their Origins and Growth Potential.* Frederick, Md.: University Park Press, 1984.

Schneider, S. Helping adolescents to deal with pregnancy: A psychiatric approach. *Adolescence* 1982, 17(66), 285–292.

Schofield, J. W. Complementary and conflicting identities: Images and interaction in an interracial school. In S. R. Asher and J. M. Gottman (Eds.), *The Development of Children's Friendships.* Cambridge, England: Cambridge University Press, 1981.

Schofield, J. W., and Francis, W. D. An observational study of peer interaction in racially mixed "accelerated classrooms." *J. Educ. Psychol.* 1982, 74, 722–732.

Schofield, J. W., and Whitley, B. E., Jr. Peer nomination vs. rating scale measurement of children's peer preferences. *Soc. Psychol.* 1983, 46, 242–251.

Schuller, T. Workending, employment, and ambiguity in later life. In B. Bytheway, T. Keil, P. Allat, and A. Bryan (Eds.), *Becoming and Being Old: Social Approaches to Later Life.* Beverly Hills, Calif.: Sage Publications, 1989.

Schultz, D. Estrogen replacement: A qualified okay. *Science Digest* 1980, 87(3), 56–58.

Schultz, J. H. Pension policy at the crossroads: What should be the pension mix? *Gerontologist* 1981, 21(1), 46–53.

Schultz, J. H. Inflation's challenge to aged income security. *Gerontologist* 1982, 22(2), 115–116.

Schulz, D. A., and Rogers, S. F. *Marriage and the Family and Personal Relationships* (3rd ed.). Englewood Cliffs, N.J.: Prentice-Hall, 1985.

Schulz, R. *The Psychology of Death, Dying and Bereavement*. Reading, Mass.: Addison-Wesley, 1978.

Schuster, T. L., and Butler, E. W. Bereavement, social networks, social support, and mental health. In D. A. Lund (Ed.), *Older Bereaved Spouses: Research with Practical Applications*. New York: Hemisphere, 1989.

Schwartz, J. *Letting Go of Stress*. New York: Pinnacle Books, 1982.

Schwartz, J. I. Children's experiments with language. *Young Children* 1981, 36(5), 16–23.

Sebald, H. Adolescent's concept of popularity and unpopularity, comparing 1960 with 1976. *Adolescence* 1981, 16(61), 187–193.

Segal, B., Huba, G. J., and Singer, J. L. Reasons for drug and alcohol use by college students. *Int. J. Addictions* 1980, 15, 489–498.

Segal, M., and Adcock, D. *Just Pretending: Ways to Help Children Grow Through Imaginative Play*. Englewood Cliffs, N.J.: Prentice-Hall, 1981.

Selman, R. The child as friendship philosopher. In J. M. Gottman (Ed.), *The Development of Children's Friendships*. Cambridge, England: Cambridge University Press, 1981.

Selye, H. Stress. *The Rotarian* October 1976, 12–18.

Selye, H. (Ed.). *Selye's Guide to Stress Research*. New York, Van Nostrand, 1980. (a)

Selye, H. The stress concept today. In I. L. Kutash and L. B. Schlesinger (Eds.), *Handbook of Stress and Anxiety*. San Francisco: Jossey-Bass, 1980. (b)

Selye, H. History and present status of the stress concept. In L. Goldberger and S. Breznitz (Eds.), *Handbook of Stress*. New York: Free Press, 1982.

Senderowitz, J., and Paxman, J. M. *Adolescent Fertility: Worldwide Concerns*. Population Reference Bureau, 40(2), 1985.

Sennett, R. *Authority*. New York: Knopf, 1980.

Sera, M. D., Troyer, D., and Smith, L. B. What do two-year-olds know about the sizes of things? *Child Devel.* 1989, 59, 1497–1503.

Shaffer, M. *Life After Stress*. New York: Plenum, 1983.

Shanas, E. The family relations of old people. *National Forum* 1982, 62(4), 9–11.

Shantz, C. O. Conflicts between children. *Child Devel.* 1988, 59, 283–305.

Shapiro, A. H. Test anxiety: Urban/kibbutz differences. *J. Genet. Psychol.* 1982, 141(2), 287–288.

Sheehy, G. *Passages: Predictable Crises of Adult Life*. New York: Dutton, 1976.

Sheehy, G. *Pathfinders*. New York: Morrow, 1981.

Shepard-Look, D. L. Sex differentiation and the development of sex roles. In B. B. Wolman (Ed.), *Handbook of Developmental Psychology*. Englewood Cliffs, N.J.: Prentice-Hall, 1982.

Sheppard, H. L. National council on the aging survey shows pronounced preferences for part-time work. *Aging and Work* 1981, 4(4), 221–223.

Sherabany, R., Gershoni, R., and Hofman, J. E. Girlfriend, boyfriend: Age and sex differences in intimate friendship. *Devel. Psychol.* 1981, 17(6), 800–808.

Sheridan, M. K., and Radlinski, S. Brief report: A case study of an adolescent male with XXXXY Klinefelter's Syndrome. *J. Autism and Developmental Disorders* 1988, 18, 449–456.

Sherman, E. *Counseling the Aged: An Integrative Approach*. New York: Free Press, 1981.

Shertzer, B. *Career Planning* (3rd ed.). Boston: Houghton Mifflin, 1985.

Shneidman, E. S. Death work and the stages of dying. In R. Fulton et al. (Eds.), *Death and Dying*. Reading, Mass.: Addison-Wesley, 1978.

Shneidman, E. S. *Voices of Death*. New York: Harper & Row, 1980.

Shneidman, E. S. (Ed.). *Death: Current Perspectives* (3rd ed.). Palo Alto, Calif.: Mayfield, 1984.

Shulman, G. M., Agostino, S., and Krugel, M. The effects of aging, attitude and communication behavior: A life span perspective. *Communication: Journal of the Communication Association of the Pacific* 1982, 11(3), 6–22.

Shweder, R. A. What's there to negotiate? Some questions for Youniss. *Merrill-Palmer Q.* 1981, 27, 405–412.

Sideroff, S. I., and Jarvik, M. E. Conditional responses to a videotape showing of a heroin-related stimuli. *Int. J. Addictions* 1980, 15, 529–536.

Siegel, R. K. The psychology of life after death. *Amer. Psychologist* 1980, 35, 911–931.

Siegler, I. C. The psychology of adult development and aging. In E. W. Busse and D. Blazer (Eds.), *Handbook of Geriatric Psychiatry*. New York: Van Nostrand Rheinhold, 1980.

Siegler, R. S. *Developmental Sequences Within and Between Concepts*. Chicago: University of Chicago Press, 1981.

Sigman, M., Neumann, C., Carter, E., and Cattle, D. Home interactions and the development of Embu toddlers in Kenya. *Child Devel.* 1988, 59(5), 1251–1261.

Silberman, B. O., and Hawkins, R. O. Lesbian women and gay men: Issues for counseling. In E. Weinstein and E. Rosen (Eds.), *Sexuality Counseling: Issues and Implications*. Monterey Calif.: Brooks/Cole, 1988.

Silk, A. M., and Thomas, G. V. The development of size scaling in children's figure drawings. *British J. Devel. Psychol.* 1988, 6, 285–299.

Silverman, P. R. *Widow to Widow*. New York: Springer, 1986.

Silverman, P. R., and Couperband, A. Widow-to-widow: The elderly widow and mutual help. In G. Lesnoff-Caravaglia (Ed.), *The World of the Older Woman: Conflicts and Resolutions*. New York: Human Sciences Press, 1984.

Simenauer, J., and Carroll, D. *Singles: The New Americans*. New York: Simon & Schuster, 1982.

Simkins, L. Consequences of teenage pregnancy and motherhood. *Adolescence* 1984, 19(73), 39–54.

Simmons, R. G., and Blyth, D. A. *Moving into Adolescence: The Impact of Pubertal Change and School Context*. New York: Aldine, 1988.

Simon, A. The neuroses, personality disorders, alcoholism, drug use and misuse, and crime in the aged. The J. E. Birren and R. B. Sloane (Eds.), *Handbook of Mental Health and Aging*. Englewood Cliffs, N.J.: Prentice-Hall, 1980.

Simona, J. A., and Martens, R. Youth sports: A challenge to parents. *PTA Today* 1983, 8(5), 14–17.

Simons, R. L., and Gray, P. A. Perceived blocked opportunity as an explanation of delinquency among lower-class black males: A research note. *J. Research in Crime and Delinquency* 1989, 26, 90–101.

Simpson, M. A., *The Facts of Death*. Englewood Cliffs, N.J.: Prentice-Hall, 1979.

Sims, N. R., and Bowen, D. M. Changes in choline acetyltransferase and in acetylcholine synthesis. In B. Reisberg (Ed.), *Alzheimer's Disease: The Standard Reference*. New York: Free Press, 1983.

Singer, D. G., and Singer, J. L. Television viewing and aggressive behavior in preschool children: A field study. *Forensic Psychol. and Psychiat.* 1980, 347, 289–303.

Singer, D. G., and Singer, J. L. *Make Believe: Games and Activities to Foster Imaginative Play in Young Children*. Oakland, N.J.: Scott, Foresman, 1985.

Singer, J. L., and Singer, D. G. Psychologists look at television: Cognitive, developmental, personality, and social policy implications. *Amer. Psychologist* 1983, 38, 826–834.

Singer, J. L., Singer, D. G., and Rapaczynski, W. Family patterns and television viewing as predictions of children's belief and aggression. *J. Communication* 1984, 34(2), 73–89.

Singer, J. L., Singer, D. G., Desmond, R., and Hirsch, B. Family mediation and children's cognition, aggression, and comprehension of television: A longitudinal study. *J. Applied Devel. Psychol.* 1988, 9(3), 329–347.

Singer, J. L., and Switzer, E. *Mind Play: The Creative Uses of Fantasy*. Englewood Cliffs, N.J.: Prentice-Hall, 1980.

Singh, B. K. Trends in attitudes toward premarital sexual relations. *J. Marriage and the Family* 1980, 42, 387–393.

Sinick, D. Attitudes and values in aging. *Counseling and Values* 1980, 24(3), 148–154.

Siv-Kai, L. Perception of authority by Chinese adolescents: The case of Hong Kong. *Youth and Society* 1984, 15(3), 259–284.

Sizer, F. S., and Whitney, E. N. *Life Choices: Health Concepts and Strategies*. St. Paul: West, 1988.

Skalka, P. *The American Medical Association Guide to Health and Well-Being After Fifty*. New York: Random House, 1984.

Skeen, P., Robinson, B. E., and Flake-Hobson, C. Blended families: Overcoming the Cinderella myth. *Young Children* 1984, 3(2), 25–36.

Skinner, B. F. How to teach animals. *Scientific American* 1951, 185, 26–29.

Skinner, B. F. *Science and Human Behavior*. New York: Macmillan, 1953.

Skinner, B. F. *Verbal Behavior*. New York: Appleton, 1957.

Skinner, B. F. *Cumulative Record*. New York: Appleton, 1961.

Slaby, R. G., and Guerra, N. G. Cognitive mediators of aggression in adolescent offenders: I. Assessment. *Devel. Psychol.* 1988, 24, 580–588.

Sloan, S. Z., and L'Abate, L. Intimacy. In L. L'Abate (Ed.), *The handbook of family psychology and therapy*. Homewood, Ill.: The Free Press, 1985.

Slobin, D. Universals of grammatical development in children. In G. B. Flores d'Arcais and W. J. M. Levelt (Eds.), *Advancements in Psycholinguistics*. Amsterdam: North Holland, 1970.

Slobin, D. (Ed.). *The Cross-Cultural Study of Language Acquisition*. Hillsdale, N.J.: Erlbaum, 1982.

Sluckin, A. *Growing Up in the Playground: The Social Development of Children*. London: Routledge and Kegan Paul, 1981.

Sluckin, W., Herbert, M., and Sluckin, A. *Maternal Bonding*. Oxford, England: Basil Blackwell, 1983.

Small, S., Eastman, G., and Cornelius, S. Adolescent autonomy and parental stress. *J. Youth and Adolescence* 1988, 17(5), 377–391.

Smetana, J. G. Concepts of self and social convention: Adolescents' and parents' reasoning about hypothetical and actual family conflicts. In M. R. Gunnar and W. A. Collins (Eds.), *The Minnesota Symposia* (Vol. 21). Hillsdale, N.J.: Erlbaum, 1988.

Smith, A. D. Age differences in encoding, storage and retrieval. In L. W. Poon, J. L. Fozard, L. S. Cermak, D. Arenberg, and L. Thompson (Eds.), *New Directions in Memory and Aging*. Hillsdale, N.J.: Erlbaum, 1980.

Smith, B. K. *Looking Forward: New Options for Your Later Years*. Boston: Beacon Press, 1983.

Smith, C. H. *Promoting the Social Development of Young Children: Strategies and Activities*. Palo Alto, Calif.: Mayfield, 1982.

Smith, E. A., and Udry, J. R. Coital and non-coital sexual behavior of white and black adolescents. *Amer. J. Public Health* 1985, Oct., 1200–1218.

Smith, E. E., and Medin, D. L. *Categories and Concepts*. Cambridge, Mass.: Harvard University Press, 1981.

Smith, P. B., and Kolenda, K. The male role in teenage pregnancy. In O. Pocs (Ed.), *Human Sexuality 84/85*. Guilford, Conn.: Dushkin, 1984.

Smith, P. B., and Pederson, D. R. Maternal sensitivity and patterns of infant-mother attachment. *Child Devel.* 1988, 59, 1097–1101.

Smith, P. K., Eaton, L., and Hindmarch, A. How one-year-olds respond to strangers: A two-person situation. *J. Genet. Psychol.* 1982, 140(1), 147–148.

Smith, R. E., Zane, N. W., Smoll, F. L., and Coppel, D. B. Behavioral assessment in youth sports: Coaching behaviors and children's attitudes. *Med. Sci. Sports Exerc.* 1983, 15, 208–214.

Smitherman, G. (Ed.). *Black English and the Education of Black Children and Youth.* Detroit: Wayne State University Center for Black Studies, 1981.

Snarey, J. A question of morality. *Psychol. Today* 1987, June, 6–8.

Soldo, B. America's elderly in the 1980's. *Population Bull.* 1980, 35(4), 1–47.

Soldo, B. J., and Agree, E. M. *America's Elderly.* Washington, D.C.: Population Reference Bureau, 1988.

Sollie, D. L., and Miller, B. C. The transition to parenthood as a critical time for building family strengths. In N. Stinnett, B. Chesser, J. DeFrain, and P. Knaub (Eds.), *Family Strengths: Positive Models for Family Life.* Lincoln: University of Nebraska Press, 1980.

Somers, T. Caregiving: A woman's issue. *Generations* 1985, 10(1), 9–15.

Sorce, J. F., Emde, R. N., Campos, J. J., and Klinnert, M. D. Maternal emotional signaling: Its effect on the visual cliff behavior of one-year-olds. *Devel. Psychol.* 1985, 21(1), 195–200.

Sorochan, W. D. *Promoting Your Health.* New York: John Wiley, 1981.

Soussignan, R., Koch, P., and Montagner, H. Behavioral and cardiovascular changes in children moving from kindergarten to primary school. *J. Child Psychol. & Psychiat. & Allied Disciplines* 1988, 29, 321–333.

Spanier, G. B., and Furstenberg, F. F., Jr. Remarriage after divorce: A longitudinal analysis of well-being. *J. Marriage and the Family* 1982, 44(3), 709–720.

Spanier, G. B., and Glick, P. C. Marital instability in the United States: Some correlates and recent changes. *Family Relations* 1981, 31, 329–338.

Spanier, G. B., and Thompson, L. *Parting: The Aftermath of Separation and Divorce.* Beverly Hills, Calif.: Sage Publications, 1984.

Speer, J. R., and McCoy, J. S. Causes of young children's confusion of "same" and "different." *J. Exper. Child Psychol.* 1982, 34(2), 291–300.

Spickard, A., and Thompson, B. R. *Dying for a Drink.* Waco, Tex.: World Books, 1985.

Spielberger, C. C., Sarason, I. G., and Strelau, J. (Eds.). *Stress and Anxiety.* New York: Hemisphere, 1989.

Spieler, S. Can fathers be nurturers? *Marriage and Divorce Today* 1982, 7, 1.

Spilerman, S., and Litwak, E. Reward structures and organizational design: An analysis of institutions for the elderly. *Research on Aging* 1982, 4, 43–70.

Spitze, G. Work and family. *J. Marriage and the Family* 1988, 50, 37–48.

Springer, S. P., and Deutsch, G. *Left Brain, Right Brain,* (rev. ed.). San Francisco: W. H. Freeman, 1985.

Stark, E. The unspeakable family secret. *Psychol. Today* May 1984, 38–46.

Starr, B. D., and Weiner, M. B. *Sex and Sexuality in the Mature Years.* Briarcliff Manor, N.Y.: Stein & Day, 1981.

Stearns, A. K. *Living through crises.* New York: Ballantine, 1984.

Steele, B. F. Psychodynamic factors in child abuse. In C. H. Kempe and R. Helfer (Eds.), *The Battered Child.* Chicago: University of Chicago Press, 1980.

Stein, P. J. (Ed.). *Single Life: Unmarried Adults in Social Context.* New York: St. Martin's Press, 1981.

Stein, P. J. Major tasks faced by single adults. In L. Cargan (Ed.), *Marriage and Family: Coping with Change.* Belmont, Calif.: Wadsworth, 1985.

Stein, P. J. The diverse world of the single adults. In J. M. Henslin (Ed.), *Marriage and Family in a Changing Society* (3rd ed.). New York: Free Press, 1989.

Stein, P. J., and Fingrutd, M. The single life has more potential for happiness than marriage and parenthood for both men and women. In H. Feldman and M. Feldman (Eds.), *Current controversies in marriage and family.* Beverly Hills, Calif.: Sage Publications, 1985.

Stein, T. S. Theoretical considerations in psychotherapy with gay men and lesbian women. In M. W. Ross (Ed.), *The Treatment of Homosexuals with Mental Health Disorders.* New York: Harrington Park Press, 1988.

Steinberg, C. S. *TV Facts.* New York: Facts on File, 1980.

Steinberg, G. Long-term continuous support for family members of Alzheimer patients. In B. Reisberg (Ed.), *Alzheimer's Disease: The Standard Reference.* New York: Free Press, 1983.

Steinmetz, S. K. *Duty Bound: Elder Abuse and Family Care.* Beverly Hills, Calif.: Sage Publications, 1988.

Stephenson, J. S. *Death, Grief, and Mourning.* New York: Free Press, 1985.

Stern, S. L., Dixon, K. N., Jones, D., Lake, M., Nemzer, E., and Sansone, R. Family environment in anorexia nervosa and bulimia. *Int. J. Eating Disorders* 1989, 8, 25–31.

Sternberg, R. J. The measure of love. *Science Digest* 1985, 60, 78–79.

Stevens, J. H., Jr. Everyday experience and intellectual development. *Young Children.* November 1981, 66–71.

Stinnett, N., Walters, J., and Kaye, E. *Relationships in Marriage and the Family* (2nd ed.). New York: Macmillan, 1984.

Stipek, D. Work habits begin in preschool. *Young Children* 1983, 38(4), 25–32.

Stipek, D., and Weisz, J. Perceived personal control and academic achievement. *Review of Educ. Research* 1981, 41, 101–137.

Stockard, J., and Johnson, M. The social origin of male dominance. *Sex Roles* 1980, 5(2), 1106–1121.

Stork, J. Suicide and adolescence. In A. H. Esman (Ed.), *International Annals of Adolescent Psychiatry.* Chicago: University of Chicago Press, 1989.

Stott, D. *Delinquents, Parents, and Maladjustment.* New York: SP Medical and Scientific Books, 1982.

Stoyva, J., and Anderson, C. A coping-rest model of relaxation and stress management. In L. Goldberger and S. Breznitz (Eds.). *Handbook of Stress.* New York: Free Press, 1982.

Strack, J. *Drugs and Drinking.* New York: Thomas Nelson, 1985.

Strahle, W. M. A model of premarital coitus and contraceptive behavior among female adolescents. *Arch. Sex. Behav.* 1983, 12, 67–94.

Straker, G., and Jacobson, R. S. Aggression, emotional maladjustment and empathy in the abused child. *Devel. Psychol.* 1981, 17(6), 762–765.

Straus, M. A., and Gelles, R. J. Violence in American families: How much is there and why does it occur? In E. W. Nunnally, C. S. Chilman, and F. M. Cox (Eds.), *Troubled Relationships.* Beverly Hills, Calif.: Sage Publications, 1988.

Strauss, A., and Glasser, B. G. *Anguish: A Case Study of a Dying Trajectory.* Mill Valley, Calif.: Sociology Press, 1970.

Strauss, M. A., Gelles, R. J., and Steinmetz, S. K. *Behind Closed Doors: Violence in the American Family.* Garden City, N.Y.: Doubleday, 1980.

Streib, G., and Beck, R. Older families: A decade of review. *J. Marriage and the Family* 1980, 42, 923–934.

Streissguth, A. P. Intrauterine alcohol and nicotine exposure: Attention and reaction time in four-year-old children. *Devel. Psychol.* 1984, 20(4), 533–541.

Streissguth, A. P., Barr, H. M., and Martin, D. C. Maternal alcohol use and neonatal habituation assessed with the Brazelton Scale. *Child Devel.* 1983, 54(5), 1109–1118.

Streissguth, A. P., Barr, H. M., Sampson, P. D., and Darby, B. IQ at age 4 in relation to maternal alcohol use and smoking during pregnancy. *Devel. Psychol.* 1989, 25(1), 3–11.

Stright, A., and French, D. C. Leadership in mixed-age children's groups. *Int. J. Behav. Devel.* 1988, 11(4), 507–516.

Stroebel, C. F. *QR: The Quieting Reflex.* New York: Putnam's, 1982.

Strong, B., Devault, C., Suid, M., and Reynolds, R. *The Marriage and Family Experience* (2nd ed.). St. Paul: West Publishing, 1983.

Strong, B., Wilson, S., Robbins, M., and Johns, T. *Human Sexuality: Essentials.* St. Paul: West Publishing, 1981.

Strube, M. J., Berry, J. M., Goza, B. K., and Fennimore, D. Type A behavior, age, and psychological well-being. *J. Personality and Soc. Psychol.* 1985, 49(1), 203–218.

Sullivan, K., and Sullivan, A. Adolescent-parent separation. *Devel. Psychol.* 1980, 16, 93–99.

Sullivan, W. Reverence of elderly: A factor of longevity in Caucasus. *New York Times News Service* December 1, 1982.

Summit, R. C. Hidden victims, hidden pain: Societal avoidance of child sexual abuse. In G. E. Wyatt and G. J. Powell (Eds.), *Lasting Effects of Child Sexual Abuse.* Beverly Hills, Calif.: Sage Publications, 1988.

Suomi, S. J., and Harlow, H. F. Abnormal social behavior in young monkeys. In J. Helmuth (Ed.), *Exceptional Infant: Studies in Abnormalities* (Vol. 2). New York: Brunner/Mazel, 1971.

Super, C. M. Cognitive development: Looking across at growing up. In C. M. Super and S. Harkness (Ed.), *New Directions for Child Development* (No. 8). *Anthropological Perspectives on Child Development.* San Francisco: Jossey-Bass, 1980.

Surber, C. F. Separable effects of motives, consequences, and presentation order on children's moral judgments. *Devel. Psychol.* 1982, 18, 257–266.

Sutton, H. E. *An Introduction to Human Genetics* (3rd ed.). Philadelphia: Saunders, 1980.

Sutton-Smith, B. Commentary on social class differences in sociodramatic play in historical context: A reply to McLoyd, *Devel. Review* 1983, 3(1), 1–5.

Sutton-Smith, B., and Roberts, J. M. Play, toys, games, and sports. In H. C. Triandis and A. Heron (Eds.), *Handbook of Developmental Cross-Cultural Psychology.* Boston: Allyn & Bacon, 1981.

Swank, C. Phased retirement: The European corporate experience. *Ageing International* 1982, 9(2), 10–15.

Swayze, M. C. Self-concept development in young children. In T. D. Yawkey (Ed.), *The Self-concept of the Young Child.* Provo, Utah: Brigham Young University Press, 1980.

Sylvester, R. A. A child's brain. *The Instructor Magazine,* September, 1982, 12–18.

Sylvester, R. The neurosciences and the education profession. In M. Frank (Ed.), *A Child's Brain.* New York: The Haworth Press, 1983.

Szinovacz, M. (Ed.). *Women's Retirement: Policy Implications of Recent Research.* Sage Yearbooks in Women's Policy Studies (Vol. 6). Beverly Hills, Calif.: Sage Publications, 1982.

Talmadge, W. C. Premarital sexuality. In L. L'Abate (Ed.), *The Handbook of Family Psychology and Therapy.* Homewood, Ill.: Dorsey, 1985.

Tangney, J. P. Aspects of the family and children's viewing content preferences. *Child Devel.* 1988, 59, 166–182.

Tanner, J. M. Growth and maturation during adolescence. *Nutrition Review* 1981, 39, 43–55.

Tatum, M. L. A perspective on school sex education programs. In C. Cassell and P. M. Wilson (Eds.), *Sexuality Education.* New York: Garland Publishing, 1989.

Tavecchio, L. W. The division of labor in Dutch families with preschool children. *J. Marriage and the Family* 1984, 46(1), 231–242.

Taves, I. *The Widow's Guide.* New York: Schocken Books, 1981.

Tavris, C., and Wade, C. *The Longest War: Sex Differences in Perspective* (2nd ed.). New York: Harcourt Brace Jovanovich, 1984.

Taylor, M., and Bacharach, V. R. The development of drawing rules: Metaknowledge about drawing influences performance on nondrawing tasks. *Child Devel.* 1981, 52, 373–375.

Tellegen, A., Lykken, D. T., Bouchard, T. J., Wilcox, K. J. et al. Personality similarity in twins reared apart and together. *J. Personality and Social Psychol.* 1988, 54, 1031–1039.

Tesch, S. A. Review of friendship development across the life span. *Hum. Devel.* 1983, 26(5), 266–276.

Teusink, J. P., and Shamoian, C. A. Understanding the body: Aging, illness, and medications. *Generations* 1983, 8(2), 6–9.

Teyler, T. J. *A Primer of Psychobiology* (2nd ed.). New York: W. H. Freeman, 1984.

Teyler, T. J., and Chiaia, N. Brain structure and development. *J. Children in Contemp. Society.* 1983, 16(2), 23–43.

Thain, R. J. *The Mid-Career Manual.* Englewood Cliffs, N.J.: Prentice-Hall, 1982.

Tharpe, R. G., and Gallimore, R. G. *Rousing Minds to Life.* New York: Cambridge University Press, 1989.

Thatcher, R., Walker, R. A., and Guidance, S. Paper presented at the Western Psychological Association Annual Meeting. Long Beach, Calif., April 15–17, 1987.

Thomas, G. V., and Tsalimi, A. Effects of order of drawing head and trunk on their relative sizes in children's human figure drawings. *British J. Devel. Psychol.* 1988, 6, 191–203.

Thomas, L. On the problem of dementia. *Discover* 1981, 2, 34.

Thomas, L. E. A typology of mid-life career changes. *J. Vocational Behav.* 1980, 16, 173–182.

Thomas, M. H. Physiological arousal, exposure to a relatively lengthy aggressive film, and aggressive behavior. *J. Research in Personality* 1982, 16, 72–81.

Thomas, R. M. *Comparing Theories of Child Development* (2nd ed.). Belmont, Calif.: Wadsworth, 1984.

Thompson, C., and Rudolph, V. *Counseling Children.* Monterey, Calif.: Brooks/Cole, 1983.

Thompson, R. A., Connell, J. P., and Bridges, L. J. Temperament, emotion, and social interactive behavior in the Strange Situation: A component process analysis of attachment system functioning. *Child Devel.* 1988, 59, 1102–1110.

Thornton, A., and Freedman, D. Changing attitudes toward marriage and single life. *Family Planning Perspectives* 1982, 14(6), 297–303.

Thornton, A., and Freedman, D. *The changing American family.* Washington, D.C.: Population Reference Bureau, 1983.

Tiedeman, D. V., and O'Hara, R. P. *Career development: Choice and Adjustment.* New York: College Entrance Examination Board, 1963.

Tietjen, A. M. The social networks of preadolescent children in Sweden. *Int. J. Behav. Devel.* 1982, 5(1), 111–130.

Tittle, C. K. Validity, gender research, and studies of the effects of career development interventions. In B. A. Gutek (Ed.), *Applied Psychology: An International Review.* Beverly Hills, Calif.: Sage Publications, 1988.

Tomaszewski, R. J., Strickler, D. P., and Maxwell, W. A. Influence of social setting and social drinking stimuli on drinking behavior. *Addictive Behav.* 1980, 5, 235–240.

Tomikawa, S. A., and Dodd, D. H. Early word meaning: Perceptually or functionally based? *Child Devel.* 1980, 51, 1103–1109.

Toner, I. J., Holstein, R. B., and Hetherington, E. M. Reflection-impulsivity and self control in preschool children. *Child Devel.* 1977, 48(1), 239–245.

Travis, J. W., and Ryan, S. *The Wellness Workbook.* Berkeley, Calif.: Ten Speed Press, 1981.

Troll, L. E. Myths of midlife intergenerational relationships. In S. Hunter and M. Sundell (Eds.), *Midlife Myths: Issues, Findings, and Practical Implications.* Beverly Hills, Calif.: Sage Publications, 1989.

Tronick, E. Z. Emotions and emotional communication in infants, *Amer. Psychologist* 1989, 44, 112–119.

Trosberg, A. Children's comprehension of "before" and "after" reinvestigated. *J. Child Language* 1982, 9(2), 381–402.

Tubesing, P. *Kicking Your Stress Habits.* Duluth, Minn.: Whole Person Associates, 1981.

Turner, J. S. Our battered American families. *Marriage and Family Living* 1980, 62(7), 24–29.

Turner, J. S. My teenager is missing: The trauma of adolescent runaways. *Marriage and Family Living* 1981, 63(8), 9–15.

Tygart, C. Public school vandalism: Toward a synthesis of theories and transition to paradigm analysis. *Adolescence* 1988, 23, 171–185.

Tyler, S., and Woodall, G. *Female Health and Gynecology Across the Life Span.* Bowie, Md.: Robert J. Brady, 1982.

Tzuriel, D. Sex role typing and ego identity in Israeli, Oriental, and Western adolescents. *J. Personality and Social Psychol.* 1984, 46(2), 440–457.

Ulbrich, P., and Huber, J. Observing parental violence: Distribution and effects. *J. Marriage and the Family* 1981, 43, 623–631.

Ullian, D. Z. Why boys will be boys: A structural perspective. *Amer. J. Orthopsychiatr.* 1981, 51(3), 493–501.

Ungerer, J. A., and Sigman, M. Developmental lags in preterm infants from one to three years of age. *Child Devel.* 1983, 54(5), 1217–1228.

Uphold, C., and Susman, E. Self-reported climacteric symptoms. *Nursing Research* 1981, 30(2), 84–88.

Upp, M. Relative importance of various income sources of the aged, 1980. *Social Security Bull.* 1983, 46(1), 3–10.

U.S. Bureau of the Census. *Annual Summary for the United States, 1979,* and DHHS Publication no. (PHS) 81-1120. Washington D.C.: U.S. Government Printing Office, November 1980. (a)

U.S. Bureau of the Census. *Current Population Reports.* Series P-20, nos. 326, 340, and 352. Washington, D.C.: U.S. Government Printing Office, December 1980. (b)

U.S. Bureau of the Census. *Statistical Abstract of the United States: 1980* (100th ed.). Washington, D.C.: U.S. Government Printing Office, 1980. (c)

U.S. Bureau of the Census. *Current Population Reports,* Series P-20, no. 365. Washington D.C.: U.S. Government Printing Office, 1981.

U.S. Bureau of the Census. *Current Population Reports,* Series P-20, no. 371. Washington, D.C.: U.S. Government Printing Office, May 1982. (a)

U.S. Bureau of the Census. Marital status and living arrangements. *Current Population Reports*. Washington D.C.: U.S. Government Printing Office, December 1982. (b)

U.S. Bureau of the Census. *Statistical Abstract of the United States, 1982* (102nd ed.). Washington, D.C.: U.S. Government Printing Office, 1982. (c)

U.S. Bureau of the Census. Marital status and living arrangements. *Current Population Reports,* Series P-20, no. 389. Washington, D.C.: U.S. Government Printing Office, March 1983.

U.S. Bureau of the Census. *Statistical Abstract of the United States, 1984* (104th ed.). Washington, D.C.: U.S. Government Printing Office, 1984.

U.S. Bureau of the Census. *Statistical Abstract of the United States,* 1985 (105th ed.). Washington, D.C.: U.S. Government Printing Office, 1985.

U.S. Bureau of the Census. *Statistical Abstract of the United States,* 1987 (107th ed.). Washington, D.C.: U.S. Government Printing Office, 1987.

U.S. Bureau of the Census. *Statistical Abstract of the United States,* 1988 (108th ed.). Washington, D.C.: U.S. Government Printing Office, 1988.

U.S. Bureau of the Census. *Statistical Abstract of the United States,* 1989 (109th ed.). Washington, D.C.: U.S. Government Printing Office, 1989.

U.S. Bureau of Labor Statistics. *Monthly Labor Review.* July 1984.

U.S. Department of Agriculture. *Dietary Guidelines for Americans.* Washington, D.C.: U.S. Government Printing Office, 1985.

U.S. Department of Commerce. Bureau of the Census. Daytime care of children. *Current Population Reports,* Series P-20. Washington D.C.: U.S. Government Printing Office, June 1982.

U.S. Department of Commerce. *Who's Minding the Children?* Washington, D.C.: U.S. Government Printing Office, 1987.

U.S. National Center for Health Statistics. *Monthly Vital Statistics Report,* March 1981.

Uttal, D. H., and Wellman, H. M. Young children's representation of spatial information acquired from maps. *Devel. Psychol.* 1989, 25(1), 128–138.

Vachon, M. L. S. Grief and bereavement: The family's experience before and after death. In I. Gentles (Ed.). *Care for the dying and the bereaved.* Toronto: Anglican Books, 1982.

Vail, E. *A Personal Guide to Living with Loss.* New York: John Wiley, 1982.

Van de Kaa, D. Europe's second demographic transition. *Population Bulletin* 1987, 42(1).

Vandell, D. L., Henderson, V. K., and Wilson, K. S. A longitudinal study of children with daycare experiences of varying quality. *Child Devel.* 1988, 59(5), 1286–1292.

Van Dyke, C. V., and Byck, R. Cocaine. *Scientific American,* March 1982, 128–141.

Van Meter, M. J. Couples who have children should stay together even if they are unhappy with each other. In H. Feldman and M. Feldman (Eds.), *Current Controversies in Marriage and Family*. Beverly Hills, Calif.: Sage Publications, 1985.

Vaughn, B. E., and Langlois, J. H. Physical attractiveness as a correlate of peer status and social competence in preschool children. *Devel. Psychol.* 1983, 19, 561–567.

Vaughan, D. Uncoupling: The social construction of divorce. In H. Robby and C. Clark (Eds.), *Social Interaction: Readings in Sociology.* New York: St. Martin's Press, 1983.

Veatch, R., and Tai, E. Talking about death: Patterns of lay and professional change. In R. Fox (Ed.), *The Social Meaning of Death: Ann. Amer. Acad. Polit. and Soc. Sci.* 1980, 447, 29–45.

Veatch, R. M. The definition of death: Problems for public policy. In H. Wass, M. Berardo, and R. A. Neimeyer (Eds.), *Dying: Facing the Facts.* New York: Hemisphere, 1988.

Veninga, R. L., and Spradley, J. P. *The Work/Stress Connection: How to Cope with Job Burnout.* Boston: Little, Brown, 1981.

Vianello, R., and Lucamante, M. Children's understanding of death according to parents and pediatricians. *J. Genet. Psychol.* 1988, 149(3), 305–316.

Vicchio, S. J. Near death experiences: Some logical problems and questions for further study. *Anabiosis: J. International Association for Near Death Studies* 1981, 1, 66–87. (a)

Vicchio, S. J. Near death experiences: A critical review of the literature and some questions for further study. *Essence: Issues in the Study of Aging, Death, and Dying* 1981, 5 (1), 77–89. (b)

Visher, E. B., and Visher, J. S. *How to Win As a Stepfamily.* New York: Dembner Books, 1982.

Vladeck, B. C. *Unloving Care: The Nursing Home Tragedy.* New York: Basic Books, 1980.

Voydanoff, P. (Ed.). *Work and Family: Changing Roles of Men and Women.* Palo Alto, Calif.: Mayfield, 1984.

Vukelich, C., and Golden, J. Early writing: Development and teaching strategies. *Young Children* 1984, 39(2), 12–18.

Wachowiak, D., and Bragg, H. Open marriage and marital adjustment. *J. Marriage and the Family* 1980, 42, 57–62.

Wadsworth, B. J. *Piaget's Theory of Cognitive and Affective Development* (3rd ed.). New York: Longman, 1984.

Waggoner, J. E., and Palermo, D.S. Betty is a bouncing bubble: Children's comprehension of emotion-descriptive metaphors. *Devel. Psychol.* 1989, 25(1), 152–163.

Wald, E. *The Remarried Family: Challenge and Promise.* New York: Family Service Association of America, 1981.

Waldron, H., and Routh, D. K. The effect of the first child on the marital relationship. *J. Marriage and the Family* 1981, 43, 785–788.

Walford, R. L. *Maximum Lifespan.* New York: Avon Books, 1983.

Walker, L. J. The sequentiality of Kohlberg's stages of moral development. *Child Devel.* 1982, 53(5),1330–1336.

Walker, L. J. A longitudinal study of moral reasoning. *Child Devel.* 1989, 60, 157–166.

Wallace, H. M., and Vienonen, M. Teenage pregnancy in Sweden and Finland: Implications for the United States. *J. Adolescent Health Care* 1989, 10, 231–236.

Wallach, H. Perceiving a stable environment. *Scientific American* 1985, 252(5), 118–124

Wallerstein, J., and Blakeslee, S. *Second Chances: Men, Women, and Children a Decade After Divorce.* New York: Ticknor and Fields, 1989.

Wallerstein, J. S. Children of divorce: Preliminary report of a ten-year follow-up of young children. *Amer. J. Orthopsychiatr.* 1984, 54(3), 444–458.

Wallerstein, J. S., and Kelley, J. B. *Surviving the Breakup: How Children Actually Cope with Divorce.* New York: Basic Books, 1980.

Wallis, C. Children having children. *Time* December 9, 1985, 76–90.

Wallis, C. The child-care dilemma. *Time* June 22, 1987, 54–63.

Walsh, H. M. *Introducing the Young Child to the Social World.* New York: Macmillan, 1980.

Walters, J., and Walters, C. H. Trends affecting adolescent views of sexuality, employment, marriage, and child-rearing. *Family Relations* 1980, 29, 191–198.

Ward, R. A. Age and acceptance of euthanasia. *Journal of Gerontology* 1980, 35(3), 421–431

Ward, R. A. *The Aging Experience: An Introduction to Social Gerontology* (2nd ed.). New York: Harper & Row, 1984.

Waring, E. M., and Russell, L. Cognitive family therapy. *Journal of Sex and Marital Therapy* 1980, 6, 258–273.

Waring, E. M., Tillman, M. P., Frelick, L., Russell, L., and Weisz, G. Concepts of intimacy in the general population. *Journal of Nervous and Mental Disease* 1981, 168, 471–474.

Watson, J. B. *Psychological Care of Infant and Child.* New York: W. W. Norton, 1928.

Watson, J. B., and Crick, F. H. C. Molecular structure of nucleic acids: a structure for deoxyribose nucleic acid. *Nature* 1958, 171, 737–738.

Watson, J. B., and Rayner, R. Conditioned emotional reactions. *J. Exper. Psychol.* 1920, 3, 1–14.

Weg, R. B. Changing physiology of aging: Normal and pathological. In D. S. Woodruft and J. E. Birren (Eds.), *Aging: Scientific Perspectives and Social Issues.* Monterey, Calif.: Brooks/Cole, 1983.

Wehren, A., and DeLisi, R. The development of gender understanding: Judgments and explanations. *Child Devel.* 1983, 54, 1568–1578.

Weinberg, R. A. The molecules of life. *Scientific American* 1985, 253(4), 48–58.

Weiner, I. B. Psychopathology in adolescence. In J. Adelson (Ed.), *Handbook of Adolescent Psychology.* New York: John Wiley, 1980.

Weiner, M. B., Teresi, J., and Streich, C. *Old People Are a Burden, But Not My Parents.* Englewood Cliffs, N.J.: Prentice-Hall, 1983.

Weingarten, H. Remarriage and well-being: National survey evidence of social and psychological effects. *J. Fam. Issues* 1980, 1(4), 533–559

Weisman, A. Common fallacies about dying patients. In E. S. Shneidman (Ed.), *Death: Current Perspectives.* Palo Alto, Calif.: Mayfield, 1984.

Weizman, S. G., and Kamm, P. *About Mourning: Support and Guidance for the Bereaved.* New York: Human Sciences Press, 1985.

Welch, I. D., Mederos, D. C., and Tate, G. A. *Beyond Burnout: How to Prevent and Reverse the Effects of Stress on the Job.* Englewood Cliffs, N.J.: Prentice-Hall, 1982.

Wellman, H. M. The foundation of knowledge: Concept development in the young child. In S. G. Moore and C. R. Cooper (Eds.), *The Young Child: Reviews of Research* (Vol. 3). Washington, D.C.: National Association for the Education of Young Children, 1982.

Wenar, C. On negativism. *Human Development* 1982, 25(1), 1–23.

Werner, P. D., and Larussa, G. W. Persistence and change in sex-role stereotypes. *Sex Roles* 1985, 12(9/10), 1089–1100.

Wertsch, J. V. A sociocultural approach to the mind. In W. Damon (Ed.), *Child Development Today and Tomorrow.* San Francisco: Jossey-Bass, 1989.

Wessells, M. G. *Cognitive Psychology.* New York: Harper & Row, 1982.

Westlake, H. G. *Parenting and Children.* Lexington, Mass.: Ginn, 1981.

Whaley, L., and Wong, D. L. *Essentials of Pediatric Nursing* (3rd ed.). St. Louis: C. V. Mosby, 1989.

Wheeler, L., Reis, H., and Nezlek, J. Loneliness, social interaction, and sex roles. *J. Personality and Social Psychol.* 1983, 45, 943–953.

White, B. Should you stay home with your baby? *Young Children* 1981, 37(1), 9–14.

White, J. *The Psychology of Blacks: An Afro-American Perspective.* Englewood Cliffs, N.J.: Prentice-Hall, 1984.

Whiteside, M. F. Remarriage: A family developmental process. *J. Marital and Family Therapy* 1982, 8(2), 59–68.

Whiting, B. B., and Edwards, C. P. *Children of Different Worlds: The Formation of Social Behavior.* Cambridge, Mass.: Harvard University Press, 1988.

Wickstrom, R. L. *Fundamental Motor Patterns.* Philadelphia: Lea and Febiger, 1983.

Wiggins, J. S., and Holzmuller, A. Further evidence on androgyny and interpersonal flexibility. *J. Research in Personality* 1981, 15, 67–80.

Wilding, T. Is stress making you sick? *America's Health* 1984, 6(1), 2–7.

Wilen, J. B., and Petersen, A. C. Young adolescents' responses to the timing of pubertal changes. Paper presented at the Psychology of Adolescence conference, Michael Reese Hospital, Chicago, June 1980.

Wilkie, J. R. The trend toward delayed parenthood. *J. Marriage and the Family* 1981, 43, 583–591.

Wilkinson, A. C. Growth functions for rapid remembering. *J. Exper. Child Psychol.* 1981, 32, 354–371.

Williams, F., LaRose, R., and Frost, F. *Children, Television, and Sex-Role Stereotyping.* New York: Praeger, 1981.

Williams, G. J. Management and treatment of parental abuse and neglect of children: An overview. In G. J. Williams and J. Money (Eds.), *Traumatic Abuse and Neglect of Children at Home.* Baltimore: Johns Hopkins University Press, 1983.

Williams, H. G. *Perceptual and Motor Development.* Englewood Cliffs, N.J.: Prentice-Hall, 1983.

Williams, J., and Stith, M. *Middle Childhood* (2nd ed.). New York: Macmillan, 1980.

Williams, R. B., Thomas, T. L., Lee, K. L., Kong, Y., Blumenthal, J. A., and Whalen, R. E. Type A behavior, hostility, and coronary atherosclerosis. *Psychosomat. Med.* 1980, 42, 539–549.

Williams, R. L., and Long, J. D. *Toward a Self-managed Lifestyle* (3rd ed.). Boston: Houghton Mifflin, 1983.

Williams, T. M., Zabrack, M. L., and Joy, L. A. The portrayal of aggression on North American television. *J. App. Soc. Psychol.* 1982, 12, 360–380.

Willis, S. L. Adult intelligence. In S. Hunter and M. Sundell (Eds.), *Midlife Myths: Issues, Findings, and Practical Implications.* Beverly Hills, Calif.: Sage Publications, 1989.

Willis, S. L., and Baltes, P. B. Intelligence in adulthood and aging: Contemporary issues. In L. W. Poon (Ed.), *Aging in the 1980's.* Washington, D.C.: American Psychological Association, 1980.

Winchester, A. M. *Human Genetics* (2nd ed.). Columbus, Ohio: Chas. E. Merrill, 1975.

Winer, G. A. Class-inclusion reasoning in children: A review of the empirical literature. *Child Devel.* 1980, 51, 309–328.

Winick, M. Food and the fetus. *Natural History,* January 1981, 88, 38–44.

Winn, M. *The Plug-in Drug: Television, Children, and the Family.* New York: Viking, 1985.

Winner, E., McCarthy, M., and Gardner, H. The ontogenesis of metaphor. In A. P. Honeck and R. R. Hoffman (Eds.). *Cognitive and Figurative Language.* Hillsdale, N.J.: Erlbaum, 1980.

Wintre, M. G., Hicks, R., McVey, G., and Fox, J. Age and sex differences in choice of consultant for various types of problems. *Child Devel.* 1988, 59, 1046–1055.

Wishart, J. G., and Bower, T. G. The development of spatial understanding in infancy. *J. Exper. Child Psychol.* 1982, 33(3), 363–385.

Wodarski, J. S., and Ammons, P. W. Comprehensive treatment of runaway children and their parents. *Family Therapy* 1981, 8(3), 229–240.

Wolf, F. M., and Larson, G. L. On why adolescent formal operations may not be creative thinkers. *Adolescence* 1981, 16(62), 345–348.

Wood, V. Grandparenthood: An ambiguous role. *Generations* 1982, 7(2), 22–23.

Worden, J. W. *Grief Counseling and Grief Therapy.* New York: Springer, 1982.

Wright, M. R. Body image satisfaction in adolescent girls and boys. *J. Youth and Adolescence* 1989, 18, 71–84.

Wright, P. H. Men's friendships, women's friendships, and the alleged inferiority of the latter. *Sex Roles* 1982, 8, 1–20.

Wrightsman, L. S. *Personality Development in Adulthood.* Beverly Hills, Calif.: Sage Publications, 1988.

Wyckoff, J., and Unell, B. C. *Discipline Without Shouting or Spanking.* New York: Meadowbrook Books, 1984.

Wylie, B. J. *The Survival Book for Widows.* New York: Ballantine, 1982.

Yankelovich, D. *New Rules in American Life: Searching for Self-fulfillment in a World Turned Upside Down.* New York: Random House, 1981.

Yoder, J. D., and Nichols, R. C. A life perspective comparison of married and divorced persons. *J. Marriage and the Family* 1980, 43, 413–419.

York, P., and York, D. Toughlove. *Family Therapy Networker* 1982, 6(5), 35–37.

York, P., York, D., and Wachtel, T. *Toughlove.* New York: Bantam, 1982.

Youngerman, J. K., and Canino, I. A. Violent kids, violent parents: Family pharmacotherapy. *Amer. J. Orthopsychiat.* 1983, 53(1), 152–156.

Youniss, J. *Parents and Peers in Social Development.* Chicago: University of Chicago Press, 1980.

Yudkin, M. When kids think the unthinkable. *Psychol. Today* 1984, 18(4), 18–25.

Zajonc, R. B. Family configurations and intelligence. *Science* 1976, 192, 227–236.

Zamula, E. Stroke: Fighting back against America's number three killer. *The Consumer.* HHS Publication No. 86-1131. Washington, D.C.: U.S. Government Printing Office, 1986.

Zigler, E. F., and Turner, P. Parents and day care workers: A failed partnership? In E. F. Zigler and E. W. Gordon (Eds.), *Day Care: Scientific and Social Policy Issues.* Boston: Auburn House, 1982.

Zill, N. Behavior, achievement, and health problems among children in stepfamilies: Findings from a national survey of child health. In E. M. Hetherington and J. D. Arasteh (Eds.), *Impact of Divorce, Single-Parenting, and Stepparenting on Children.* Hillsdale, N.J.: Erlbaum, 1988.

Zimbardo, P. G., and Radl, S. L. *The Shy Child.* Garden City, N.Y.: Doubleday, 1981.

Zion, L. I. Body concept as it relates to self concept. *Res. Quart. Am. Assoc. Hlth. Phys. Educ. Recreat.* 1965, 36, 490–495.

Ziporyn, T. Taste and smell: The neglected senses. *J. Amer. Med. Assn.* 1982, 247, 277–285.

Zucker, A. The right to die: Ethical and medical issues. In H. Wass, M. Berardo, and R. A. Neimeyer (Eds.), *Dying: Facing the Facts.* New York: Hemisphere, 1988.

Zuckerman, D. M., and Sayre, D. H. Cultural role expectations and children's sex role concepts. *Sex Roles* 1982, 8, 453.

Zuckerman, M. J. Working couples: They're swapping family chores. *Family Therapy News* 1983, 14(4), 5–7.

Zunker, V. G. *Career Counseling*. Monterey, Calif: Brooks/Cole, 1981.

Chapter 1. *Chapter opening*, Universal Media Inc.; *page 4*, Suzanne Szasz/Photo Researchers, Inc.; *page 9* (top), Stock Boston; (bottom), Kent Reno/Jeroboam; *page 12*, Cary Wolinsky/Stock Boston; *page 13*, Holt, Rinehart and Winston Library; *page 14*, Lason Laure/Woodfin Camp; *page 18*, Photo/Edit; *page 23*, G. Menzie/Photophile; *page 25*, Larry Racioppo.

Chapter 2. *Chapter opening*, David Schaefer, 1991/Jeroboam; *page 33*, Carol Palmer/The Picture Cube; *page 34*, Frank Siteman/Taurus Photos; *page 37*, HRW Photo; *page 41*, the Harvard University Archives; *page 44*, Wide World Photos; *page 51*, Courtesy B.F. Skinner; *page 55*, Courtesy Albert Bandura.

Chapter 3. *Chapter opening*, Arnold J. Kaplan/The Picture Cube; *page 71*, Joseph NeHis/Photo Researchers; *page 72*, Joyce Photographics/Photo Researchers; *page 83*, Michael Weisbrot; Doris Pinney/Photo Researchers; *page 92*, Greg Kopacka/Photophile; *page 94*, Susan Johns/Photo Researchers; *page 96*, Tony Mendoza/Picture Cube; *page 97*, Martin H. Rotker/Taurus Photos.

Chapter 4. *Chapter opening*, PhotoMedia LTD; *page 114*, Landrun B. Shettles, M.D.; *page 118*, Alan Oddie/Photo Edit; *page 126*, Photophile; *page 127*, David Austen/Stock Boston; *page 130*, Jerry Woke/Photo Researchers.

Chapter 5. *Chapter opening*, Robert Brenner/Photo Edit; *page 141*, Suzanne Szasz/Photo Researchers; *page 144*, Alan Carey/The Image Works; *page 149*, Paula M. Lerner/The Picture Cube; *page 156*, C. Vergara/Photo Researchers; *page 162*, Suzanne Arms Wimberly/Jeroboam, Inc.; *page 164*, Superstock; *page 170*, Superstock; *page 172*, Universal Media, Inc.; *page 174*, Janet S. Mendes/The Picture Cube; *page 180*, Ray Ellis/Photo Researchers; *page 183*, Superstock.

Chapter 6. *Chapter opening*, Photo Media LTD; *page 194*, Photo Media LTD; *page 197*, Tony Freeman/Photo Edit; *page 201*, Frank J. Staub/The Picture Cube; *page 203*, Ann Chwatsky/Jeroboam; *page 206*, Robert Brenner/Photo Edit; *page 210*, Alan Oddie/Photo Edit; *page 217*, EKM Nepenthe; *page 219*, Mary Kate Denny/Photo Edit; *page 223*, Chester Wiggins/Rapho/Photo Researchers; *page 227*, Susan Johns/Photo Researchers; *page 229*, UPI-Bettmann; *page 234*, Robert V. Eckert, Jr./EKM Nepenthe; *page 237*, Superstock; *page 239*, Tony Freeman/Photo Edit; *page 242*, Superstock; *page 244*, Superstock.

Chapter 7. *Chapter opening*, Bonnie Rauch/Photo Researchers; *page 252*, B. Kliewe/Jeroboam; *page 256*, Tony Freeman/Photo Edit; *page 264*, Milton Feinberg/Picture Cube; *page 266*, Blair Seitz/Photo Researchers; *page 271*, Bob Smith/Photo Researchers; *page 274*, Tom Ticcy/Photophile; *page 278*, Suzanne Szasz/Photo Researchers; *page 282*, Mark Walker/Photophile; *page 288*, Michael Siluk/EKM Nepenthe; *page 291*, Richard Hutchings/Photo Edit; *page 293*, Richard Hutchings/Photo Edit; *page 296*, Mark Walker/Photophile.

Chapter 8. *Chapter opening*, 1988 Myrleen Ferguson/Photo Edit; *page 305*, Day Williams/Photo Researchers; *page 311*, Superstock; *page 315*, Tony Freeman/Photo Edit; *page 319*, Blair Seitz/Photo Researchers; *page 325*, Robert Brenner/Photo Edit; *page 327*, Superstock; *page 330*, Superstock; *page 332*, Lisl/Photo Researchers; *page 342*, Richard Hutchings/Photo Researchers; *page 346*, Superstock; *page 350*, Mark Walker/Photophile; *page 352*, Barbara Burnes/Photo Researchers.

Chapter 9. *Chapter opening*, Photo Media; *page 362*, Tony Freeman/Photo Edit; *page 366*, Richard Hutchings/Photo Edit; *page 368*, Robert Brenner/Photo Edit; *page 370*, Spencer Grant/Photo Researchers; *page 377*, Gregg Mancuso/Jeroboam; *page 380*, Superstock; *page 391*, Photo Media; *page 396*, Eric Kroll/Taurus Photos; *page 405*, Tim Davis/Photo Researchers; *page 409*, Doug Wilson/Photophile; *page 413*, Superstock; *page 416*, Wesley Bocte/Photo Researchers.

Chapter 10. *Chapter opening*, 1988 Myrleen Ferguson/Photo Edit; *page 429*, Margot Granitsas/The Image Works; *page 431*, Superstock; *page 434*, Superstock; *page 445*, Richard Hutchings/Photo Researchers; *page 450*, Photomedia; *page 454*, Superstock; *page 456*, Alex von Koschembahr/Photo Researchers; *page 460*, Superstock; *page 469*, Robert Brenner/Photo Edit; *page 475*, Richard Hutchings/Photo Researchers; *page 476*, Ellis Herwig/Stock Boston; *page 485*, Diane Enkelis/Stock Boston; *page 490*, Superstock; *page 493*, Gregg Mancuso/Jeroboam.

Chapter 11. *Chapter opening*, Photo Media LTD; *page 503*, Photophile; *page 511*, Robert Brenner/Photo Edit; *page 514*, Mark Walker/The Picture Cube; *page 519*, L.L.T. Rhodes/Photophile; *page 523*, Doug Wilson/Photophile; *page 528*, Robert Brenner/Photo Edit; *page 532*, Photo Media; *page 536*, Superstock; *page 547*, Robert Brenner/Photo Edit; *page 552*, Photophile; *page 554*, Frank Keillor/Jeroboam.

Chapter 12. *Chapter opening*, Mark M. Walker/Photophile; *page 571*, Alan Oddie/Photo Edit; *page 573*, Bruce Roberts/Rapho/Photo Researchers; *page 578*, Abraham Menashe/Photo Researchers; *page 581*, Alan Oddie/Photo Edit; *page 583*, Superstock; *page 584*, Alan Oddie/Photo Edit; *page 586*, Dennis MacDonald/The Picture Cube; *page 590*, Michael Weisbrot; *page 594*, Michael Weisbrot.

Name Index

Landberg, I., 164
Landreth, C., 213
Langlois, J. H., 216, 289, 292
Lapsley, D. K., 48, 317
LaRose, R., 218
LaRossa, M. M., 414
LaRossa, R., 414
Larson, G., 314
Larson, L. E., 322
LaRussa, G. W., 220
Larwood, L., 495, 555
Lasky, R. E., 143, 153, 170
Lauersen, N. H., 98
Laursen, B., 238
Laycock, F., 265
Lazarus, R. S., 467
Leach, D. J., 217, 219, 238
Leadbeater, B. J., 343
Leavy, R. L., 472
Leboyer, F., 126–127
Lechner, C. R., 317
LeCroy, C. W., 321
Lee, G., 549
Lee, M., 353
Leeds, M. H., 542
Lehmann, P., 438
Leigh, J., 494
LeMasters, E. E., 407
Leming, M. R., 571, 572, 574
Lenneberg, E. H., 161, 163
Leonetti, R., 298
Lepper, M. R., 270
Lerner, J. V., 306, 329
Lerner, R. M., 306, 329
Leslie, E. M., 544
Leslie, G. R., 544, 552
Lettieri, D. J., 346
Levande, D., 397, 406
Levenkron, S., 348
Levenson, A. J., 536
Levine, C., 343
Levine, S., 212
Levinson, D., 62–63, 65, 374–376,
    457, 458, 460–462, 489, 526,
    529–530
Levinthal, C. F., 137
Levy, G. D., 216
Levy-Shiff, R., 176
Lewin, K., 343–344
Lewis, C., 412
Lewis, M., 165, 171, 177, 526, 531,
    544
Lewis, R. A., 412
Lichter, D. T., 542
Lieberman, M. A., 542
Liebert, R. M., 284, 285

Lin, A. N., 431
Lindauer, B. K., 258
Lindberg, L., 218, 233
Lindenberger, U., 263
Linn, M. C., 210, 317
Lippman, M., 270
Lipscomb, T. J., 223
Lipson, A., 122
Litwak, E., 545
Livson, F., 533
Livson, N., 312
Loewinsohn, R. J., 588
Lohr, J., 467
Londerville, S., 169, 184, 240
London, C., 481
London, M., 415
Long, J. D., 471
Longino, C., 533
Longstreth, L. E., 144
Lopata, H., 597
Lorenz, K., 16, 58–59, 65
Loudin, J., 385
Low, I. B., 561
Low, K. G., 325
Lucamante, M., 571
Lund, D. A., 480, 598
Lundberg, L. J., 164
Lykken, D. T., 93

Maag, J. W., 347
Maas, H. S., 454
MacArthur, D., 525
Maccoby, E. E., 168, 216, 223, 277,
    281, 292
Machlowitz, M. M., 492
Mack, S. A., 98
Macklin, E. D., 394, 397
MacWhinney, B., 167
Maddi, S. R., 471
Maddox, G., 532–533
Maeda, D., 505
Magg, P. B., 199
Magno, J. B., 582
Mahoney Institute of the American
    Health Foundation, 307
Main, M., 169, 184, 240
Malina, R. M., 193, 196, 226, 241
Mall, D., 572
Maloney, M. J., 347
Maltsberger, J. T., 346
Mann, D. M., 539
Mann, J. A., 7, 363
Manning, L., 408, 409
Manning, M. L., 306
Mansfield, R. S., 316
Manuel, R. C., 24

Maracek, J., 408
Marcia, J., 343
Markham, L. R., 274
Marsh, G. A., 436, 518
Marsh, R., 559
Marshall, J., 467
Marshall, V. W., 572, 573
Martin, 330
Martin, B., 94
Martin, D. C., 121
Martin, G. B., 159
Martin, M. J., 165
Martin, R. A., 472
Martin, T. C., 488
Maslach, C., 492
Maslow, A., 60, 61–62, 65,
    464–466
Mason, S. E., 505
Masters, J. C., 221
Masters, W. H., 96, 399
Masur, E. F., 165
Matlin, M., 16, 263
Matthews, K. A., 448, 471
Maugham, S., 397
Maurer, D., 157
Mayer, R. E., 207
Mayrent, S. L., 365
Mays, J., 214
Mazer, B., 116
Mazlish, E., 165
McCabe, A., 223, 263
McCarthy, M., 241
McClearn, G. E., 81, 93
McClure, M., 205
McCoy, J. S., 212
McCubbin, H., 224
McCullough, B. C., 419
McDermit, S. A., 261
McDermott, D., 349
McDonald, G. W., 411
McDonald, P., 484
McGhee, P. E., 178, 277, 316
McGilly, K., 267
McGoldrick, M., 320
McGuigan, F. J., 471
McGuire, K. D., 290, 327
McHugh, P. R., 538
McKay, M., 363, 485, 486
McKenry, P. C., 484
McKenzie, B. H., 153
McKenzie, S. C., 6, 367, 368, 451,
    504, 505, 546
McLanahan, S., 403
McLaughlin, B., 165
McLoyd, V. C., 243
McMahon, F. B., 464

Subject Index

Absolute denial, 575
Abstract thought, 315–316
Acceptance stage, of dying, 577–578
Accommodation, 45–46
Acquired immune deficiency syndrome (AIDS), 123–124, 337–339
Active euthanasia, 583
Active gene, 83
Active theory, of development, 36
Activity theory, 532–533
Acute phase, of dying, 579
Adaptation, 45
Addicting narcotics, 351
Adolescence
    Anna Freud's theory of, 344
    cognitive development during, 314–318
    drug abuse during, 348–351
    eating disorders, 347–348
    Erikson's psychosocial theory of, 342–343
    family influences during, 320–324
    Freud's psychosexual theory of, 341–342
    Hall's theory of, 344
    heterosexual development during, 329–341
    international perspectives on, 307, 336–337
    juvenile delinquency and, 351–354
    Lewin's theory of, 343–344
    Mead's theory of, 344
    mental development during, 314–318
    motor-skill development during, 313
    parent-adolescent interaction, 474–475
    peer group influences during, 326–329
    personality and social development during, 318–344

physical development during, 305–313
premarital intercourse during, 330–334
premarital pregnancy during, 334–337
puberty and, 306–313
school influences during, 324–326
sexual development during, 307–309
sexuality during, 312–313
sexually transmitted diseases and, 337–341
styles of parent contol during, 321–322
suicide and, 345–347
Adult day-care facilities, 543
Adult maturity, 370–373
Adulthood. See also Late adulthood; Middle adulthood; Young adulthood
    adult-stage theories of, 62–63
    historical perspectives on, 9–10
Afterbirth, 111
Agape, 386
Age differences, 21
Age-stage theories, 35
Aged. See Late adulthood
Ageism, 504–505
Agenesis, 122
Aggression
    in early childhood, 223–224
    genetic factors and, 97–98
    in infancy and toddlerhood, 178–179
    instrumental versus hostile, 223
    juvenile delinquency and, 354
    in middle childhood, 277
    social learning theory and, 56
    televised violence and, 284–285
Aggressive syndrome, 97–98
Aging
    ageism and, 504–505
    aging processes in perspective, 6–10

biological aging, 6–7
brain changes and, 435
changes during, 21
creativity and, 524–525
cross-cultural life expectancies, 8
definition of old age, 505
demographics of, 506–507
external aging, 430–433, 510–511
internal aging, 434–435, 512–514
patterns of successful aging, 531–535
psychological aging, 7
sensory capacities and, 435–437
sociological aging, 7
theories of physical aging, 508–509
AHG. See Antihemophilic globulin (AHG)
AIDS. See Acquired immune deficiency syndrome (AIDS)
Albinos, 84
Alcohol use/abuse
    in adolescence, 348–349
    during pregnancy, 121–122, 123
Alleles, 80
Alzheimer's disease, 538–539
Amino acids, 80
Amniocentesis, 99–100
Amniotic fluid, 111
Amniotic sac, 111
Amphetamines, 350–351
Anal stage, of psychosexual development, 40, 243
Androgyny, 220
Anger
    in early childhood, 223–224
    in infancy and toddlerhood, 178–179
    in middle childhood, 277
Anger stage, of dying, 575–576
Angina, 439
Animism, 46–47, 203–204, 241
Anorexia nervosa, 347–348
Anticoagulants, 439–440

Antihemophilic globulin (AHG), 78
Anxiety
    definition of, 178
    in infancy and toddlerhood, 178
    in middle childhood, 276
Anxiety disorders, 537
Anxious-avoidant children, 172–173
Anxious-resistant children, 172–173
Apgar test, 130
Aphasia, 160
Arcuate fasciculus, 160
Art, 146–147, 198–199
Arthritis, 519–520
Artificialism, 204
Assimilation, 45
Atherosclerosis, 439–440
Attachment
    contact/comfort and, 174–175
    definition of, 168–169
    indicators of, 171–172
    individual variations on, 172–173
    international perspectives on,
        169–170, 175–176
    theoretical perspectives on, 170–
        171
Attachment/separateness polarity,
    461–462
Attraction, interpersonal, 383–384
Authoritarian (autocratic) control,
    224, 287, 321
Authoritative (democratic) control,
    224–225, 287–288, 321–322
Authority stage, of parenthood, 405
Authority-maintaining orientation,
    of moral development (Kohl-
    berg), 280
Autonomy versus shame and doubt,
    42, 182, 184

Babbling, 164–166
Baby biographies, 13–14
Baldness, 79, 433, 510
Barbiturates, 351
Bargaining stage, of dying, 576
Basal-cell carcinomas, 431
Basic trust versus basic mistrust,
    42, 182–184
Battered child syndrome, 228–230
Behavioral genetics
    definition of, 89
    intelligence and behavior, 91–93
    musical ability and, 88–89
    polygenes and behavior, 89–91
Behavioral predisposition, 89
Behaviorism, 36, 48–54, 161, 282
Benign tumors, 442

Bereavement, definition of, 588.
    See also Grief
Bilingualism, 210–211
Biochemical genetics
    basic cell structure, 73–75
    determination of gender, 76
    DNA, 79–81
    dominant and recessive charac-
        teristics, 82
    genetic individuality, 81–82
    sex- or X-linked inheritance, 77–
        79
    simple types of gene action, 83–
        88
Biochemical stressors, 467
Biochemically active genes, 83
Biochemically passive genes, 83
Biofeedback, 472
Biological aging, 6–7
Birth order, 226–228
Birth process
    cesarean delivery, 128–129
    home births, 127, 128
    Lamaze method, 126
    Leboyer method, 126–127
    natural childbirth, 126
    neonatal reactions following,
        129–130
    nontraditional delivery tech-
        niques, 126–127
    rooming-in and birthing room
        hospital facilities, 127
    stages of labor and delivery, 124–
        125
Birthing rooms, 127
Black English, 273–274
Blending action, 87
Blood pressure, 434, 438–439, 520
Blood typing, 85, 86
Body transcendence versus body
    preoccupation, 528
Brain
    aging and, 435
    in early childhood, 193
    during infancy and toddlerhood,
        138–140
    language development and, 160
    lateralization of, 138–139, 152
    myelination and brain matura-
        tion, 139–140
    structure of, 138–139
Breech delivery, 124
Broca's area, 160
Brompton mix, 582–583
Bulimia, 348
Burnout, 491–492

Caffeine use, during pregnancy,
    121–122
Cancer, 431–432, 442–443, 446–
    447, 521–522
Carcinomas, 442
Cardiovascular system
    in late adulthood, 512
    in middle adulthood, 434
    in middle childhood, 255
Cardiovascular-respiratory fitness,
    364
Career change at midlife, 490–492
Career clock, 489
Career development
    in middle adulthood, 489–495
    older workers, 555–556
    quest for career fulfillment, 418–
        419
    roots of career dissatisfaction,
        420–421
    selection of career, 415–417
    stages of career selection, 417–
        418
Career dissatisfaction, 420–421
Caring, in intimate relationships,
    381. *See also* Intimate rela-
    tionships; Love
Case study, 16
Castration anxiety, 244
Cataracts, 515
Catharsis theory of television view-
    ing, 284
Cathectic flexibility versus cathectic
    impoverishment, 459
Cells
    aging and, 508–509
    basic structure of, 73–75
    definition of, 73
    division of, 74, 75
    germ cells, 74, 75
    somatic cells, 74
Centering, 258–259
Central nervous system, 137
Cephalocaudal development, 114
Cerebellum, 139
Cerebral cortex, 139
Cerebrovascular accidents, 520–
    521, 538
Cerebrum, 138
Cesarean delivery, 128–129
Chaining, 154
Child abuse, 228–230
Child care, 411–412
Child sexual abuse, 230–232
Child-parent relations. *See* Parent-
    child relations

Fathers. *See also* Parenthood; Parents
   role of, 412–414
   sex-role development and, 216
Fear
   in early childhood, 221–222
   in infancy and toddlerhood, 178
   in middle childhood, 276
Females. *See* Mothers; Sex differences; Women
Fertility laws, 402–403
Fetoscopy, 101–102
Fetus, 113–115. *See also* Prenatal development
Filtering agents, 383–384
Fixation, 40, 181
Fluctuating denial, 575
Fluid intelligence, 451
Forebrain, 138
Formal operations (Piaget), 47, 314–318
Formal thought, 47
Fraternal twins, 110
Free association, 37
Friendships. *See also* Peers
   in adolescence, 327–328
   international perspectives on, 291–292
   in middle childhood, 290–292
   same-sex friendships, 291
   sex differences in adolescent friendships, 328–329
Frontal lobe of brain, 139
Frustration tolerance, 372
Full nest, 477–478
Functional disorders, of aging, 537

Gametes, 75
GAS. *See* General adaptation syndrome (GAS)
Gastrointestinal system, in late adulthood, 512
Gay life-style, 397–400
Gender, determination of, 76
Gender identity, 215
General adaptation syndrome (GAS), 468–469, 471
Generation gap, 474–475
Generativity versus stagnation, 43, 458–459
Genes, 79, 80, 83–88
Genetic counseling, 98–102
Genetic epistemology, 44
Genetics
   aberrations and mutations, 95–98

behavioral, 88–95
biochemical, 73–88
compared with heredity, 71–72
definition of, 72
dominant and recessive characteristics, 82
genetic counseling, 98–102
terminology of, 80
twin studies, 91–95
Genital herpes, 340–341
Genital stage, of psychosexual development, 40, 41, 341–342
Genotypes, 77, 80
Geriatrics, 503
Germ cells, 74, 75
Gerontology, 503–504
Gestation period, 108
Glaucoma, 515–516
Gonads, 75
Gonorrhea, 339–340
Good boy-nice girl orientation, of moral development (Kohlberg), 280
Grandparenthood, 551–553
Grief
   coping with loss, 589–590, 593–596
   definition of, 588
   dysfunctional methods of coping, 593–595
   endings and new beginnings, 597–598
   expressions of, 590–591
   stages of, 591–596
Growing pains, 254
Growth, 34

Hair
   in late adulthood, 510
   in middle adulthood, 432–433
Hair color, 83–84, 86
Hairy pinna, 79
Hallucinogens, 349–350
Handedness, 144
Haploid state, 75
Happiness, in middle childhood, 277
Head Start, 234
Hearing
   in infancy and toddlerhood, 159
   in late adulthood, 516–517
   in middle adulthood, 436
Heart attacks, 439, 441–442
Heart disease, 520
Hedonistic principle, 38
Hemispheres of brain. *See* Laterali-

zation of brain
Hemophilia, 78–79, 100
Hereditarians, 33
Heredity, 71–72
Heroin, 351
Herpes, genital, 340–341
Heterozygous, 80
Hierarchy of needs, 61
Hindbrain, 139
HIV virus, 123–124, 337
Holophrase, 166
Home births, 127, 128
Home environment. *See* Families; Fathers; Mothers; Parent-child relations
Homogamy, 384
Homosexuality, 397–400
Homozygous, 80
Hospice movement, 582–583
Hostile aggression, 223, 277
Human development. *See* Development
Humanistic theory, 60–62
Humor, 178, 277, 316
Hypertension, 438–439, 520
Hypothalamus, 139, 309
Hypothesis, 19
Hypothetico-deductive reasoning, 316

Id, 36, 38
Identical twins, 110
Identification, 215
Identity achievement, 343
Identity diffusion, 343
Identity foreclosure, 343
Identity formation, 319, 343
Identity moratorium, 343
Identity, search for, 342
Identity versus role diffusion, 43, 342–343
Imaginary audience, 317
Imitation, 56
Immanent justice, 204
Immune system, in late adulthood, 514
Immunity theory, of aging, 510
Imprinting, 58–59
Impulsivity, 268–269
Incest, 231
Incomplete development, of fetus, 122
Independent teenage years, as stage of parenthood, 405–406
Independent variable, 19–20
Individuation, 461

Inductive reasoning, 259, 316
Industry versus inferiority, 43, 297–298
Infancy and toddlerhood. *See also* Birth process
AIDS and, 123–124
cognition and memory, 155–157
concept development during, 152–155
early attachment behavior, 168–176
emotional development during, 177–179
Erikson's psychosocial theory of, 182–184
Freud's psychosexual theory of, 181–182
international perspectives on, 169–170, 175–176
language development during, 159–167
locomotion during, 141–143, 145
mental development during, 148–167
neonatal adjustments and adaptations, 129–132
nervous system development during, 137–139
personality and social development during, 168–176
physical development during, 137–147
prehension during, 143–147
premature infants, 116
scribbling and, 146–147
sense-organ development during, 157–159
sensorimotor stage, 148–152
socialization through play, 179–181
Infarct, 441
Initiative versus guilt, 42–43
Institutionalism, 544
Instrumental aggression, 223
Instrumental learning, 51–54
Integrative stage, of parenthood, 405
Integrity versus despair, 43, 526–527
Intelligence. *See also* Mental development
age and, 367
genetic factors of, 91–93
in late adulthood, 522–523
in middle adulthood, 450–451

reliability of assessment instruments, 367–368
Interactionists, 33
Intercourse. *See* Sexuality
Interdependence, in intimate relationships, 380–381
Intermediate care facilities, 542
Internal aging, 434–435, 512–514
International perspectives
adolescence, 307, 336–337
adult children caring for aging parents, 479–480
attachment, 169–170, 175–176
child care, 411–412
death and dying, 574
divorce, 483–484
family planning, 402–403
friendships, 291–292
home births, 128
intimate relationships, 384
Israeli kibbutz, 175–176
late adulthood, 10, 507–508
life expectancies, 8
marriage, 388–389
middle childhood, 291–292
motor-skill development of toddlers, 142–143
nursery schools in China, 236
nutrition, 446
retirement, 556–557
Sweden's ban on spanking, 230
treatment of dementia, 539–540
women's employment, 444
young adulthood, 384
Interpersonal attraction, 383–384
Interviews, 17
Intimacy, definition of, 378–379
Intimacy versus isolation, 43, 374
Intimate and mutually shared relationships, 291
Intimate relationships. *See also* Love; Marriage
barriers to, 382–383
benefits of, 381–382
components of, 379–381
dating and, 378–379
definition of, 378–379
elements of interpersonal attraction, 383–384
international perspectives on, 384
love and, 384–386
Intrinsic motivation, 267
Intuitive thought (Piaget), 258–260
Invention of new means through mental combinations, 150

Israeli kibbutz, 175–176

Jobs. *See* headings beginning with Career
Juvenile delinquency, 351–354

Kernel words, 163
Kibbutz, 175–176
Kin relations during late adulthood, 549–550
Klinefelter's syndrome, 96–97
Knowledge, in intimate relationships, 379

Labor and delivery, 124–125
LAD. *See* Language acquisition device (LAD)
Lamaze method, 126
Language acquisition, 200–201, 210
Language acquisition device (LAD), 161–162
Language, definition of, 160
Language development
brain and, 160
Chomsky's theory of, 161–163
definition of speech compared with language, 160
dialects and, 273–274
in early childhood, 200–201, 209–213
guidelines for improvement in preschoolers, 213
in infancy and toddlerhood, 159–167
in middle childhood, 270–274
reinforcement theory of, 161
social learning theory of, 161
stages of, 163–167
theoretical interpretations of, 161–163
Language dialects, 273–274
Lanugo, 114
Late adulthood
activity theory of, 532–533
adult children caring for aging parents, 478–482
aging and ageism, 504–505
Butler's theory of, 530–531
community resources for, 550–551
definition of old age, 505
demographics of, 506–507
disengagement theory of, 531–532
economics of family life, 546–549

Erikson's psychosocial theory of, 526–527
family and, 541–553
gerontology as study of, 503–504
grandparenthood, 551–553
health disorders during, 515–517, 518–522
institutional care for, 542–546
international perspectives on, 10, 507–508
kin relations during, 549–550
Levinson's theory of, 529–530
living arrangements during, 541–546
mental development during, 522–524
nursing homes for, 543–546
patterns of successful aging, 531–535
Peck's theory of, 527–529
personality development during, 525–540
personality makeup and, 533–534
physical development during, 508–522
population statistics on, 4–5
psychological maladjustment during, 535–540
research problems in studying, 23–24
retirement and, 553–562
Late maturer, 312
Latency period, of psychosexual development, 40–41, 294–297
Lateralization of brain, 138–139, 152
Laughter, 178
Learning, 34
Leboyer method, 126–127
Lesbians, 397–400
Lesch-Nyhan syndrome, 100
Leukemias, 442
Libidinal energy, 38
Libido, 38
Life expectancies, 8, 507
Life review, 530–531
Life space, 343
Life structure, 62–63
Literary insight, 316–317
Locomotion, 141–143, 145
Long-term memory, 156, 451–452, 523–524
Longitudinal design, 20–21
Love. *See also* Intimate relationships

characteristics of, 385
intimate relationships and, 384–386
in middle childhood, 277–278
romantic ideal of, 385
types of, 385–386
LSD, 349–350
Ludus, 386
Lymphomas, 442

Makeup, 89
Male pattern baldness, 79, 433
Males. *See* Fathers; Men; Sex differences
Malignant tumors, 442
Mania, 386
Manipulative play, 180
Marijuana, 349
Marriage. *See also* Divorce
alternatives to traditional marriage, 393–400
engagement and wedding, 390–391
factors in successful adjustment to, 392–393
international perspectives on, 388–389
motives for, 389–390
open marriage, 395
postponement of, 387–388
remarriage, 488
statistics on, 387
swinging, 397
varieties of marital roles, 391–392
Masculine/feminine polarity, 461
Matriarchal marriage, 391
Maturation, 34
Maturity, 370–373
Medicaid, 549
Medical technology, and genetic counseling, 99–102
Medicare, 548–549
Medulla oblongata, 139
Meiosis, 75, 81
Melanin, 83–84
Memory
improvement strategies for, 452–453
in infancy and toddlerhood, 155–157
in late adulthood, 523–524
in middle adulthood, 451–452
Memory span, 156
Men
adjustments after divorce, 484

adult-stage development theories concerning, 62–63
cancer and, 443
life expectancy of, 507
male sexual development, 308–309
Menarche, 308
Menopause and the climacteric, 447–449
Mental development
in adolescence, 314–318
in early childhood, 200–213
during infancy and toddlerhood, 148–167
in late adulthood, 522–524
in middle adulthood, 450–453
in middle childhood, 258–274
reliability of assessment instruments, 367–368
in young adulthood, 366–368
Mercy killing. *See* Euthanasia
Messenger RNA, 79–80
Metacognition, 156–157, 267
Metamemory skills, 156, 267
Midbrain, 139
Middle adulthood
career development in, 489–495
caring for aging parents, 478–482
divorce and separation during, 482–486
Erikson's psychosocial theory of, 458–459
family and, 473–488
Gould's theory of, 462–463
health disorders of, 437–444
international perspectives on, 479–480
Levinson's theory of, 460–462
life-style and dietary considerations, 444–447
menopause and the climacteric, 447–449
mental development during, 450–453
midlife transition, 455–458
parent-adolescent interaction, 474–475
Peck's theory of, 459
personality development during, 453–473
physical development during, 429–449
post-parental adjustments, 475–482

Overregularization, 167
Overweight. *See* Obesity
Ovum, 75, 109

Parallel play, 202
Parent cell, 74
Parent education programs, 235
Parent-child relations
  in adolescence, 320–324
  discipline and, 224–226
  early attachment behavior, 168–176
  impact on teen sexuality, 333
  international perspectives on, 169–170, 175–176
  juvenile delinquency and, 352–353
  and language development of infants and toddlers, 165–166
  in middle childhood, 282–285
  parent-adolescent interaction, 474–475
  sex-role development and, 216
  toughlove, 322–323
Parental image phase, of parenthood, 405
Parental-image theory, 384
Parenthood. *See also* Fathers; Mothers; Parent-child relations
  adjustments to, 403–404
  international perspectives on, 411–412
  motives for, 401
  post-parental adjustments, 475–482
  role of father, 412–414
  role of mother, 406–412
  single-parent households, 487
  stages of, 404–406
  voluntary childlessness, 401–402
Parietal lobe of brain, 139
Participant observation, 12
Passive euthanasia, 583
Passive gene, 83
Patriarchal marriage, 391
Peers. *See also* Friendships
  in adolescence, 326–329
  in early childhood, 236–240
  influences during middle childhood, 288–292
  sex-role development and, 217
Perceptual constancy, 153
Perfection principle, 39
Peripheral nervous system, 137
Permissive control, 225, 287–288

Permissive (laissez-faire) control, 321, 322
Personal fables, 317
Personality development
  in adolescence, 318–344
  Anna Freud's theory of, 344
  Butler's theory of, 530–531
  in early childhood, 214–245, 243–245
  Erikson's psychosocial theory of, 41–43, 182–184, 245, 297–298, 342–343, 374, 458–459, 526–527
  Freud's psychosexual theory of, 37–40, 181–182, 243–244, 294–297, 341–342
  Gould's theory of, 376–378, 462–463
  Hall's theory of, 344
  in infancy and toddlerhood, 168–176, 181–184
  in late adulthood, 525–540
  Levinson's theory of, 374–376, 460–462, 529–530
  Lewin's theory of, 343–344
  Mead's theory of, 344
  in middle adulthood, 453–473
  in middle childhood, 275–298
  Peck's theory of, 459, 527–529
  in young adulthood, 369–386
Phallic stage, of psychosexual development, 40–41, 243–244
Phenotypes, 77, 80
Philosophical stressors, 467
Philosophy of life, 373
Phonemes, 163
Phonology, 163
Physical aging, 508–509
Physical attraction, 383
Physical development
  in adolescence, 305–313
  in early childhood, 193–200
  during infancy and toddlerhood, 137–147
  in late adulthood, 508–522
  in middle adulthood, 429–449
  in middle childhood, 251–257
  in young adulthood, 361–365
Physical well-being, 363–365
Pick's disease, 538
Pilot study, 19
Pituitary gland, 309
Pivot words, 166–167
Placenta, 111
Placenta previa, 101
Placental abruption, 101

Play
  destructive play, 181
  in early childhood, 240–243
  exploratory and manipulative play, 180
  in infancy and toddlerhood, 179–181
  parallel play, 202
  sex-role development and, 216
  socialization through, 240–243
  sociodramatic play, 241–242
Playmate-stage of friendship, 290
Pleasure principle, 38
Polygenes, 89–91
Pons, 139
Positive reinforcement, 52
Postconventional level, of moral development (Kohlberg), 281
Posture, in late adulthood, 511
Pragma, 386
Pragmatics, 212, 272
Preconceptual thought, 201–204
Preconscious, 37–38
Preconventional level, of moral development (Kohlberg), 280
Pregnancy. *See also* Birth process
  AIDS infection and, 123–124
  alcohol and drug use during, 121–122, 123
  danger signs of, 128
  first trimester of, 109–112
  length of, 108–109
  maternal emotion during, 122
  nicotine use during, 119–120
  nutrition during, 117, 118–119
  premarital pregnancy, 334–337
  prenatal environment, 117–124
  Rh factor and, 119–120
  second trimester, 113–115
  suggestions for healthy pregnancy, 120
  teratogenic agents and, 122–123
  third trimester, 115–116
Prehension, 143–147, 199
Premarital intercourse, 330–334
Premarital pregnancy, 334–337
Prematurity, 116
Premoral stage (Piaget), 279
Prenatal development. *See also* Birth process
  AIDS infection and, 123–124
  danger signs of pregnancy, 128
  first trimester of, 109–112
  length of pregnancy, 108–109
  maternal emotion and, 122

maternal nutrition and, 117,
118–119
medical technology and, 99–102
nicotine and, 119–120
premarital pregnancy and, 334–
337
prematurity and, 116
prenatal environment and, 117–
124
Rh factor and, 119–120
second trimester, 113–115
teratogenic agents and, 122–123
third trimester, 115–116
Preoperational thought, 46–47, 201
Preparatory depression, 577
Presbycusis, 516
Presbyopia, 436
Preschool children. *See* Early child-
hood
Primary circular reactions, 149
Primary reinforcer, 52
Primary sex characteristics, 308,
309
Prime of life, 10
Problem-solving abilities
in adolescence, 316
in middle childhood, 265–270
Progesterone, 310, 447
Projection, 295
Propinquity, 383
Prosocial behavior, 238–240
Protector myth, 463
Protoplasm, 73
Proximo-distal development, 114
Pruritus, 431
Psychoanalytic theory
attachment and, 171
critique of, 43–44
Erikson's psychosocial theory,
41–43, 182–184, 245, 297–
298, 342–343, 374, 458–459,
526–527
Freud's psychosexual theory, 40–
41, 181–182, 243–244, 294–
297, 341–342
Freud's theory of the personality,
37–40
moral development and, 282
sex-role development and, 215
Psycholinguistics, 159
Psychological aging, 7
Psychological stressors, 467
Psychosexual stages (Freud), 37,
40–41, 47, 181–182, 243–244,
294–297, 341–342
Psychosocial stages (Erikson), 42–

43, 47, 182–184, 245, 297–
298, 342–343, 374, 458–459,
526–527
Psychosocial stressors, 467
Psychosomatic illness, 468
Psychotic disorders, 537
Puberty
growth spurt and, 306–307
physiology of, 309–310
psychology of, 311–312
reproductive maturity and, 307–
309
sexual responsiveness and, 312–
313
Punishment, 52, 53–54, 352–353
Punnett square, 77

Quantity concepts, 207–208, 265
Quesionnaires, 16–17
Questioning behavior, 204–205

Rationalization, 295
Reaction formation, 296
Reactive depression, 577
Reactive theory, of development, 36
Readiness principle, 140–141
Realistic perception, 372
Reality principle, 38
Reasoning. *See* Cognitive develop-
ment
Recall memory, 524
Recessive characteristics, 82, 83
Recessive genes, 80, 83
Reciprocal interactions, in intimate
relationships, 379–380
Recognition memory, 524
Reflectivity, 268–269
Reflex activities, 148
Reflex smile, 171
Regression, 296
Reinforcement, 52–54
Relational concepts, 265
Relaxation, 471, 472–473
Remarriage, 488
Repression, 40
Reproductive maturity. *See* Sexual
development
Residential care facilities, 543
Respiratory system
in late adulthood, 512
in middle adulthood, 434
in middle childhood, 255
Reticular activating system, 139
Retirement
adjustments to, 557–560
attitudes toward, 553–554

dimensions of, 555–556
early retirement, 556
financial adjustments to, 558–
559
international perspectives on,
556–557
psychological adjustments to,
557–558
social adjustments to, 559–560
stages of, 560–562
Reversibility, 260
Rh factor, 119–120
Rheumatoid arthritis, 519–520
Ribonucleic acid (RNA), 79
Ribosomes, 74
RNA. *See* Ribonucleic acid (RNA)
Role compatibility, 384
Romantic ideal of love, 385
Rooming-in, 127
Runaways, 324

Sarcomas, 442
Schemata, 45
Schizophrenia, 94–95
School-age children. *See* Middle
childhood
Schools
adolescents' attitudes toward,
325
adolescents' relationships with
teachers, 326
early childhood education, 232–
236
influences during adolescence,
324–326
influences during middle childhood, 286–288
juvenile delinquency and, 354
preschools, 217–218, 232–236
sex-role development and, 217–
218
vandalism in, 354
Science, definition of, 11
Scientific methods
age and cohort factors, 21–22
case study, 16
correlational method, 18
ethics and, 24–25
experimental method, 18–19
longitudinal and cross-sectional
designs, 20–21
observation, 11–16
research problems and, 22–24
survey method, 16–17
time-lag design, 22
Scribbling, 146–147

Secondary circular reactions, 149–150

Secondary reinforcer, 53

Secondary sex characteristics, 308, 309

Securely attached children, 172–173

Selective social smile, 171

Self-acceptance, 372

Self-actualization, 61, 463–466

Self-directed regulatory behaviors, 177

Self-disclosure, 379, 385

Self-esteem, 526

Self-expression, 372

Self-extension, 371–372

Self-fulfillment, 373

Self-objectification, 373

Self-regulation, 57

Semantic development
 in early childhood, 211–212
 in middle childhood, 271

Semantics, 167

Senile Angiomas, 431

Sensorimotor development, 46

Sensorimotor stage (Piaget), 148–152

Sensorineural deafness, 517

Sensory aphasia, 160

Sensory capacities
 in infancy and toddlerhood, 157–159
 in late adulthood, 515–518
 in middle adulthood, 435–437

Sensory memory, 155

Separation anxiety, 172

Sequential designs, 20

Serialization, 154

Seriation, 263

Sex differences
 in adolescent friendships, 328–329
 in adolescents' attitudes toward school, 325
 in family disharmony during adolescence, 323
 in friendships, 291
 in intelligence, 451
 in language development, 210
 in midlife transition, 457–458
 in motor-skills development, 257
 in premarital intercourse, 332

Sex- or X-linked inheritance, 77–79

Sex-limited genes, 79

Sex-role development
 in early childhood, 214–220

influences on, 215–220
 in middle childhood, 292–293
 play and, 292–293
 stereotyping and, 276
 stereotyping in, 218–219
 theories of, 215

Sexual abuse of children, 230–232

Sexual development
 in adolescence, 307–309
 female, 308, 309
 male 308–309

Sexual identity, 215

Sexuality
 in adolescence, 312–313, 329–341
 development of adult sexual relationships, 378–386
 international perspectives on, 384
 premarital intercourse, 330–334

Sexuality education programs, 332–333

Sexually transmitted diseases, 337–341

Shape concepts, 153–154, 205–206, 264

Shaping behavior, 53

Short-term memory, 156, 451–452, 523–524

Short-term method, 20

Siamese twins, 110

Sibling relations, 226–228

Sibling rivalry, 227

Sickle-cell anemia, 90

SIDS. *See* Sudden infant death syndrome (SIDS)

Significates, 202

Signifiers, 202

Single adulthood, 393–394

Single-parent households, 487

Size concepts, 153–154, 205–206, 264

Skeletal system. *See* Musculo-skeletal system

Skilled nursing facilities, 542

Skin
 in late adulthood, 510
 in middle adulthood, 430–432

Skinner boxes, 51

Skinnerian conditioning, 51–54

Smell
 in infancy and toddlerhood, 159
 in late adulthood, 517–518
 in middle adulthood, 436

Smiling, 171, 178

Smoking. *See* Nicotine

Social cognition, 168

Social gerontology, 503

Social learning theory, 55–58, 161, 170, 215, 284

Social Security, 548

Social smile, 171

Social stressors, 467

Social-age clock, 7

Socialization
 in infancy and toddlerhood, 179–181
 in middle childhood, 292–294
 through play, 179–181, 292–294

Socializing versus sexualizing in human relationships, 459

Sociodramatic play, 241–243

Sociological aging, 7

Soma, 74

Somatic cells, 74

Spatial concepts, 154, 206–207, 264

Speech, definition of, 160

Spontaneous recovery, 50

Sports, in middle childhood, 293–294

Standardized tests, 367–368

Stimulus discrimination, 46, 50

Stimulus generalization, 45, 50

Storge, 386

Stranger anxiety, 171–172

Stress
 definition of, 467
 description of, 467–468
 general adaptation syndrome and, 468–469, 471
 handling stresses of adult life, 471–473
 Type A personality and, 469–471

Stressors, 467

Strokes, 520–521, 538

Structured observation, 12

Successive approximations, 53

Sudden infant death syndrome (SIDS), 131

Suicide, adolescent, 345–347

Superego, 36, 40

Surface structure of language, 162–163

Survey, 16–17

Swinging, 397

Symbolic functioning, 202

Syntactic development
 in early childhood, 212
 in middle childhood, 271–272

Syntax, 167

Syphilis, 340

Systematic reasoning, 318